CHINA'S ECONOMIC REFORMS

SUCCESSES AND CHALLENGES

CHINA'S ECONOMIC REFORMS

SUCCESSES AND CHALLENGES

Peter Koveos

Syracuse Univerisity, USA

Yimin Zhang

University of Shanghai for Science and Technology, China

World Scientific

NEW JERSEY · LONDON · SINGAPORE · BEIJING · SHANGHAI · HONG KONG · TAIPEI · CHENNAI · TOKYO

Published by

World Scientific Publishing Co. Pte. Ltd.
5 Toh Tuck Link, Singapore 596224
USA office: 27 Warren Street, Suite 401-402, Hackensack, NJ 07601
UK office: 57 Shelton Street, Covent Garden, London WC2H 9HE

Library of Congress Cataloging-in-Publication Data
Names: Koveos, P. (Peter) author. | Zhang, Yimin, 1932–   author.
Title: China's economic reforms : successes and challenges /
    Peter Koveos, Syracuse Univerisity, USA,
    Yimin Zhang, University of Shanghai for Science and Technology, China.
Description: Hackensack, NJ : World Scientific, [2022] |
    Includes bibliographical references and index.
Identifiers: LCCN 2022008149 | ISBN 9789811256516 (hardcover) |
    ISBN 9789811256523 (ebook) | ISBN 9789811256530 (ebook other)
Subjects: LCSH: China--Economic policy--2000– | China--Economic conditions--2000– |
    Economic development--China. | Investments, Chinese. | China--Foreign economic relations.
Classification: LCC HC427.95 .K68 2022 | DDC 330.951--dc23/eng/2022-0216
LC record available at https://lccn.loc.gov/2022008149

British Library Cataloguing-in-Publication Data
A catalogue record for this book is available from the British Library.

For any available supplementary material, please visit
https://www.worldscientific.com/worldscibooks/10.1142/12841#t=suppl

Desk Editors: Soundararajan Raghuraman/Daniele Lee

Typeset by Stallion Press
Email: enquiries@stallionpress.com

Foreword

In the 40 years since China's economic reforms began, the country has made unprecedented progress in its economic development and its position in the global stage. As a result, interest in China has motivated numerous books focusing on the world's second largest economy. However, a single volume cannot possibly explain the complex nature of China's economic system and its relationship with the rest of the world. Therefore, demand for additional analysis of China's economy and the country's unique reform experience remains high. Our book contributes to the understanding of China's reforms by offering a detailed analysis of critical components of the country's economic architecture. We contrast China's performance before and after reforms and examine the challenges China still faces. We accomplish our objective by exploring the results of China's reforms at both the national economy and individual sector levels.

Most of the books about China's economy offer conclusions based primarily on qualitative analysis of China's reforms. Our book incorporates both qualitative and quantitative analysis in a balanced manner. We reinforce our arguments by offering detailed data and statistical analysis on each topic, while providing the reader with careful explanations for our findings. We begin by presenting the background of the nature of reforms in general and the Chinese reform strategy. We point to the importance of China's past for its present and its future. We proceed by examining the general performance of China's economy and comparing it with aspects of performance of other economies. Following that, we present the changes in China's industrial structure associated with China's transition into a market-based socialist economy. We also discuss urban–rural disparities and the existence and implications of inter-provincial disparities.

We then analyze changes pertaining to the internal and industrial structures of the economy. State-owned enterprises (SOEs) have been one of the most important and challenging components of China's transition. Therefore, we explore the performance of the SOE sector and its contribution to the overall economy in Chapter 6. Our next two chapters deal with China's external sector: its foreign trade system (see Chapter 7) and its inward and outward foreign direct investment (FDI) (see Chapter 8). We conclude by analyzing China's reforms associated with the finance sector. In Chapter 9, we review China's financial institutions, while in Chapter 10, we discuss China's financial markets, including the foreign exchange market.

We hope our work contributes to the reader's appreciation of both the accomplishments and the challenges of China's reforms. Of course, China's story has not been concluded. By all accounts, China's future is both exciting and of significance to the global economy. Hence, we encourage all serious students of economic developments to continue learning about China and its relationships with the rest of the world after reading our book.

About the Authors

Peter Koveos (PhD, Pennsylvania State University) is Professor of Finance, Kiebach Chair in International Business Studies, and Director of the Kiebach Center for International Business at Syracuse University. He has previously served as Interim Dean, Associate Dean, and Senior Director for International Programs. His research interests include the areas of international finance and China's economic reforms. His research has been published in the *Journal of Monetary Economics, Journal of International Business Studies,* and other journals. He was also the Editor of the *Journal of Developmental Entrepreneurship* during 2004–2021. He has served as President or Executive Director of the Eastern Finance Association, the North American Economics and Finance Association, the Africa Business and Entrepreneurship Research Society, and the New England Business and Economic Association.

Professor Koveos visited China in 1990, at the invitation of the Shanghai Branch of the Industrial and Commercial Bank of China. He established partnerships with universities in Shanghai, Jinan, and Beijing, as well as in Taipei and Seoul. In 1998, he was recognized as Outstanding Foreign Expert and awarded the Magnolia Award by the Municipality of Shanghai. He also served as Associate Dean for the Shanghai-Syracuse International School of Business.

Yimin Zhang received his undergraduate and graduate diplomas in Power Engineering from the Harbin Institute of Technology. He subsequently served as the Leader of the engine combustion liquid rocket chamber group at the Shanghai Mechanical and Electrical Design Institute of the Chinese Academy of Sciences. As Chief of Information Section of the Shanghai Aero Engine Factory, he wrote his first book on *Aviation Turbofan Engines*, a pioneering publication on the topic.

In 1960, Dean Zhang joined the Harbin Institute of Science and Technology as Director of the Missile Department and Liquid Rocket Engine Department. He served as the Senior Engineer, Chief of Information Section, at the Shanghai Aero Engine Factory during 1971–1985. He subsequently joined the School of Business, University of Shanghai for Science and Technology (1985). He co-founded the Shanghai-Syracuse International School of Business, where he served as Professor and Dean. He retired in 2000.

Contents

Chapter 1

Introduction to Transition and Reform

1. Introduction

To most of the world, China's departure from Mao's regime in 1978 and the collapse of the Berlin Wall in 1989 represent the beginning of the economic transition of the last quarter of the 20th century. Although these two events presented a strong visual representation of the convergence of two distinct economic and political systems, transition in effect started at different times for the various countries involved. Furthermore, the process has proven to be much more complicated than the well-defined activity of bringing down a wall. Transition has been complex, dynamic, controversial, rewarding, as well as frustrating.

Transition's key elements are "the replacement of physical allocation of a nation's resources by allocation in response to price signals, which requires both price liberalization and enterprise reform."[1] For the country to make the transition from one economic system to another, it must make appropriate changes to its economy. Hence, transition and reform are related concepts. Transition indicates what the country wants to accomplish; it defines the destination of the economic system. On the other hand, reform is the process; it reveals how the country changes its economy to reach its destination. It is the strategy the country pursues to transform its economy.

---

[1] Sharma, A. (ed.) (1992). *Perestroika: A Comparative Perspective*. Westport, CT: Praeger/ Greenwood Publishing Co.

The reforms experience since the late 1970s is practically the reverse image of the process that surfaced at the end of WWI and the establishment of the Soviet Union. The Soviet central planning system started taking effect in the 1920s. The geopolitical situation that resulted from WWII allowed the Soviet Union to expand its territory of influence. As the Baltic States and countries of Central, Eastern, and Southeastern Europe were falling under Moscow's political and military control, they were becoming components of a single economic central plan that extended beyond previously sovereign national boundaries. Without reliance on economic principles, countries were quickly going through every stage of integration leading to economic and political union. Other countries in Asia and the Americas aligned themselves politically, militarily, and economically with the Soviets: Mongolian People's Republic, Democratic People's Republic of Korea, North Vietnam, Cuba and, most importantly, the People's Republic of China. The Soviet centrally planned economies (CPEs) grew at a 4.5% annual rate in the 1950s, compared to 3.5% for the Western market economies. However, the adoption of political and military priorities led to the creation of a rigid system, in which the efficient allocation of resources was sacrificed for political objectives. Thus, while market economies were growing at 4.5%, 2.8%, and 2% in the ensuing decades, the Soviet economic machine had slowed down to 3.6%, 2.8%, and 0.8% in the 1960s, 1970s, and 1980s.[2]

The USSR abandoned central planning in 1987 through the abolishment of output targets.[3] Following the demise of the USSR in 1991, Russia took a big step in its transition by liberalizing prices (January 1992). As satellite countries were breaking away from Moscow's grip, they were also abandoning central planning.[4]

In the book's first chapter, we examine the concept of economic reform in general, and the Chinese experience in particular. We discuss the two opposing approaches to reform, the role of institutions in the success of reforms, and the overall versus local approaches. We then present

---

[2] Svejnar, J. (2002). Transition economies: Performance and challenges. *Journal of Economic Perspectives*. 16(1) Winter.

[3] Pomphret, R. (2002). *Constructing a Market Economy: Diverse Paths from Central Planning in Asia and Europe.* Cheltenham, UK: Edward Elgar.

[4] For timing and other economic data on transition for various countries, see: International Monetary Fund (2000). *World Economic Outlook: Focus on Transition Economies.* October. See also: Fischer, S. and R. Sahay (2000). *Economies in Transition: taking Stock.* Finance & Development, International Monetary Fund, September, 37(3).

selected aspects of China's reforms and the nature and importance of China's Five-Year Plans (FYPs). We point to the changes in the nature and objectives of these FYPs as the country went through the various stages of economic development. We conclude by discussing the resolution passed at the Sixth Plenum of the 19th Central Committee and explaining the concept of common prosperity.

2. Reform Approaches and Elements

The transformation from CPE to market is a very complex systematic engineering project. It involves all aspects of the economic system — i.e., ownership, decision-making, production and distribution, business organizations, government regulations, and foreign economic relations. Obviously, such an enormous, complex transformation cannot be accomplished in a short period. Nevertheless, from the 1950s to the 1970s, many CPEs adopted various comprehensive and piecemeal economic reforms with poor results. Those who oppose reforms find support in three widely shared sociopolitical concerns: the conflict between income inequality and the precepts of a socialist society; unemployment and the reduction or elimination of price subsidies because of profit maximization, and the resulting inflation.[5] The unsuccessful history of a gradualism approach in the 1950s to the 1970s led some Western advisors to propose the shock therapy approach,[6] which Poland, the Czech Republic, the former Soviet Union, and other Eastern bloc countries chose to pursue.

The question, of course, is what is the best approach to reform? Up to the current period, the quest for the optimum approach to reform has been expressed in terms of two major ideologies that have been pitted against each other: the "Washington Consensus" and the "evolutionary-institutionalist perspective."[7] The former reflects the views of the major

---

[5] United Nations (1988). *World Economic Survey 1988, Current Trends and Policies in the World Economy*. United Nations Publication.

[6] Sachs, J. (1991). Helping Russia: Good will is not enough, *Economist*, December 21.

[7] Roland, G. (2001). *Ten Years After Transition and Economics*. IMF Staff Papers, Vol. 48. Special Issue. See also: Kolodko, G. W. (2001). *Post-Communist Transition and Post-Washington Consensus: The Lessons for Policy Reforms*. In Bleijer, M. and M. Skreb (eds.). *Transition: The First Decade*. Boston: MIT Press. For a criticism of the Washington Consensus, see: Stiglitz, J. E. (2002). *Globalization and its Discontents*. New York, NY: W.W. Norton and Co.

Washington-based international institutions, the IMF and the World Bank. It is also referred to as the Big Bang or shock therapy approach, depicting the high-speed component of this particular view. The evolutionary perspective is also referred to as the gradualist or incrementalism view.

The term "Washington Consensus" was coined by J. Williamson, but has had many connotations since its introduction.[8] Williamson offered a list of 10 policy reforms Washington pursued in refocusing the economies of most Latin American countries in the late 1980s. These policy reforms were[9]:

1. Fiscal Discipline
2. Reorientation of Public Expenditures
3. Tax Reform
4. Financial Liberalization
5. Unified and Competitive Exchange Rates
6. Trade Liberalization
7. Openness to FDI
8. Privatization
9. Deregulation
10. Securing of Property Rights

The differences between these two approaches extend beyond considerations of mere speed. There are many additional differences between the macro- and micro-effects of transition and reform and the general assumptions made about the way the world and economic systems work. Proponents of the Washington Consensus favor a "build it and they will come" assumption about the effectiveness of reform strategies. Relying on neoclassical price theory and standard macro-economic analysis, they maintain that comprehensive reforms focusing on liberalization, stabilization, and privatization will be certain to generate efficiency gains for the rebuilt economic system. Conducting all necessary reforms at once puts the economy along an irreversible path featuring strong market influence and weak government intervention. Once the old structures disappear,

---

[8] Williamson, J. (ed.) (1990). What Washington means by reform. In *Latin American Adjustment: How Much Has Happened?* Washington, D.C.: Institute for International Economics.

[9] Rodrick, D. (2002). After Neoliberalism, what? Remarks at the BNDES seminar on "New Paths to Development." Rio de Janeiro, September 1–3.

new laws and mass privatization enable the economy to take full advantage of the new environment.[10]

Proponents of the evolutionist perspective view the outcome of reforms as uncertain. To be successful, reforms must be managed, with minimum disruption to the country's economic and social fabric. Building the institutional infrastructure is an integral component of reforms and enhances the probability of a successful transition, but it needs to be done gradually and in the appropriate sequence. Government plays an important role by securing property rights and providing law enforcement services.[11]

The Washington Consensus and evolutionist perspectives have each received their share of criticism. Opponents of the Big Bang point to the large adjustment costs and the resulting discontent that could lead to a reversal of the entire process. Evolutionists, on the other hand, have been criticized for their perceived reluctance to bring meaningful change. Neither approach is considered by some observers as being, by itself, capable of offering a recipe for formulating appropriate reform policies.

This imposing list presented by Williamson reveals the immense challenges faced by countries and underscores the observation that these reforms cannot be achieved at once, nor can they always follow the same sequence of implementation in every country. Therefore, dimensions, such as sequencing and speed, may be pursued as a matter of practical consideration rather than reliance on a proven theoretical framework. The most important aspect of putting together a reform program is for policy makers to understand what works best for the country and for each individual sector of the economy.

3. Economic Performance and the Role of Institutions

The performance of economies in transition has been uneven. One explanation for the performance differential is often offered in terms of each country's initial conditions.[29] These conditions include the structure of the economy, initial distortions, and the quality of the country's institutions.

---

[10]Roland, G. (2001). *op. cit.*

[11]*Ibid.*

Indeed, Clement and Murrell[12] stated that the transition from planned economy to market is actually a transition from "Plan and Planned Institutions to Market and Market Institutions."

Building the institutional framework necessary to promote the "rule of law," then, can be an important factor for the success of the transition. However, the exact degree of its importance has been widely debated.[13] After a seemingly slow start, countries are now realizing the importance of effective legal institutions and are making efforts to make up for lost time.[14] The task has been difficult. Changes in the laws on the books have not guaranteed effectiveness of these new laws. The use of these laws in practice depends on both the voluntary compliance rate and the effectiveness of institutions enforcing them.[15]

4. Overall "Blueprint" versus "Local Experiment"

Reforming the economy encompasses various challenges to policy makers. Among them are the coverage and sequencing of the reform. Policy makers must decide whether to put together an "overall blueprint" or engage in a series of "local experiments." Because of the extreme complexity of economic reforms and lack of the clear objective in the 1950s, 1960s, and 1970s, some advisors suggested that designing an overall blueprint for economic reforms is necessary at the beginning of the reforms. Because no CPEs had ever made the transition successfully before, and because the path was poorly marked, reformers proceeded by trying a certain approach for a while; if it did not produce the desirable results quickly, they would move on to another or even reverse themselves, only to end up at another dead end. In fact, because of the reluctant and half-hearted nature of many of these economic efforts, many economies suffered significant declines. The effect was to discredit such efforts

---

[12]Clement, C. and P. Murrell (2003). Assessing the value of law in transition economies: An introduction. In P. Murrell (ed.). *Assessment of Law in Transition Economies*. Ann Arbor: The University of Michigan Press.

[13]Pistor, K., M. Raiser, and S. Gelfer (2002). Law and finance in transition economies. *Economics of Transition*, 8 (2), 325–368.

[14]Clement, C. and P. Murrell (2003). *op. cit.*

[15]Pistor, K., M. Raiser, and S. Gelfer (2002). *op. cit.*

altogether and complicate subsequent economic reform initiatives other reformers might attempt.[16]

Reformers must also answer the sequencing question. Assuming policy makers decide to follow the gradualist approach, which sector do they reform first? Do they start with agriculture, manufacturing, or services? Do they reform a particular sector in its entirety, or do they experiment with a specific component? For example, do they liberalize the market for all agricultural products, or a selected few? Do they change the structure of the banking system for the country as a whole, or experiment with changes in a particular geographic or economic region?

5. China's Reforms

Any discussion about reform experiences must include those of the world's most populous country, China. The essence of China's transition is to gradually shift from a centrally planned system to a market-oriented one. A main feature of China's reforms has been the country's attempt to accommodate people's increasing demand for a greater variety of consumer goods. Annual growth rate of per capita consumption increased from 2.26% (1952–1978) to 7.93% (1978–2016).[17] Shortage of supply, an integral feature of the CPE economy, was transformed into a buyer's market (relative surplus) in the mid-1990s. China's reform process had a key philosophy: "Try to bring the immediate benefits to the people, because one could not promote the reforms while making people suffer. Otherwise, they may not support the reforms. That is, more benefits to the people mean more momentum for them to support the reforms."[18]

China's experience is unique because of the gradual and experimental nature of the reforms undertaken, as well as the special relationship

---

[16]Shama, A. (1992, edited). *Perestroika, A Comparative Perspective*. Westport, CT: Praeger Publishers.

[17]Calculated using data from All China Data Center, China Yearly Macro-Economic Statistics (National): Household Consumption 1952–2016; National Bureau of Statistics Household Survey Organization Complied: China Yearbook of Household Survey 2013 (in Chinese), Table 2.1–2.3; China National Bureau of Statistics: China Statistical Yearbook 1991, China Statistics Press, Table 8.2, Table 8.3.

[18]Zhou, X. (2004). How China became an economic tiger, May 6. http://web.worldbank. org/WBSITE/EXTERNAL/NEWS/0,contentMDK:20200140~menuPK:34457~pagePK: 34370~piPK:34424~theSitePK:4607,00.html.

between China's economic and political systems. Indeed, China's transition objective, appropriately called "market socialism," depicts a symbiotic co-existence between the market-based economic system and the old party-controlled political architecture.

China's transition began in 1978. By that time, the country had withstood two major shocks within its planned economy experience: the Great-Leap-Forward period (1958–1961) and the Cultural Revolution (1966–1976). In the period between these two shocks (1964), Premier Zhou Enlai identified the four cornerstones or modernizations of China's development: modernizations of agriculture, industry, science and technology, and national defense. The period between 1976 and 1978 is considered as the adjustment period leading to the post-Mao era.

By 1978, China's senior leader Deng Xiaoping had reached the conclusion that, to foster rapid growth and development, the economy needed to be restructured to enhance productivity and accomplish efficient use of resources. To achieve this objective, market-oriented reforms and opening to the outside world had to be adopted. However, a single blueprint for the architecture of the economic system on which the reform process should converge was not established. Instead, the Chinese authorities adopted a cautious, pragmatic, and experimental approach. They followed a process of learning by doing, or as Deng put it, of "crossing the river while feeling the rocks" to avoid wide-scale difficulties that were sure to arise given the enormity of the restructuring task. Reforming China's economy has proceeded in an incremental fashion. Indeed, experiments with different types of reforms were implemented on a small scale, and only applied to a wider basis if they were proven successful.[19] As a result, the pace and degree of the reforms varied greatly across economic sectors and regions of the country.

5.1. *Reform periods*

To better understand China's post-1978 transition path, we may identify five sub-periods, each featuring a variety of reforms in carefully selected sectors and regions:

---

[19]Szapary, G., S. Dunaway, D. Burton, and M. Bléijer (1991). *China; Economic Reform and Macroeconomic Management*. Washington, DC: International Monetary Fund. (Occasional paper; no. 76).

1. The first sub-period, 1978–1984, featured a larger role for the market and the introduction of incentives. For political and economic reasons, agriculture was the sector of emphasis.
2. The second sub-period, 1984–1988, included reform of a number of additional sectors, including finance and foreign exchange. To attract foreign investment, 14 coastal cities were designated as the principal entry points.
3. As inflation and other obstacles surfaced, the third sub-period became one of retrenchment from reforms (1988–1991).
4. Reforms were again intensified during the 1992–2001 period.
5. Further opening to the outside world was achieved, including China's accession to the WTO in 2001.

Since 2013 and in the period to come, high-quality development is the fundamental requirement for determining the development path, making economic policies, and conducting macro-economic regulation. The overall blueprint for reform became necessary. "We have pursued reform in a more systematic, holistic, and coordinated way, increasing its coverage and depth. Thanks to the launch of over 1,500 reform measures, breakthroughs have been made in key areas, and general frameworks for reform have been established in major fields."[20]

5.2. *Sequence of China's reform: Selecting the first task as a breakthrough*

The long record of unsuccessful economic reforms in CPEs discredited the very instruments — cooperatives, joint ventures, family farming, management, adopting advanced technology, enterprises autonomy, and price flexibility — that must ultimately be well established for reform to succeed. Private ownership is the foundation of a market economy and genuine market competition requires private enterprises.[21] Therefore, the

---

[20] Xi, J. (2017). Secure a decisive victory in building a moderately prosperous society in all respects and strive for the great success of socialism with Chinese characteristics for a new era delivered at the 19th National Congress of the Communist Party of China, October 18.

[21] Sachs, J. D. and D. Lipton (1990). Poland's economic reform. *Foreign Affairs* 69(3), Summer.

former Soviet Union and Central and Eastern Europe's reformers paid great attention to ownership transfers, making privatization of state ownership the precondition for other important reforms. In the early days of the reform, however, the state's productive assets are valued at a sum far in excess of the savings available to the private sector (see Chapter 6). In other words, the immediate situation pits too many firms against too few buyers. Ownership might become concentrated in the hands of a relatively few individuals with money or connections. In practice, selling state-owned firms has proven time-consuming, frustrating, and expensive. Setting such ambitious targets is a difficult task, especially in the short run.

China's approach involved identifying aspects of reforms that were the easiest and most pressing to reform, and it implemented reforms in these first. Successes in these areas helped build public support for the reform process. China's reforms began with the agricultural sector because of a pressing need to expand food production. This element of the reform is known as the "household responsibility system." Farmers could at last sell part of their output in the open market. There was a definite need to reform this sector first. Grain output in 1936 (the peak year prior to 1949) was 150 million tons, increasing to 304.8 million tons by 1978. At the same time, however, the country's population increased from 479.08 million to 962.06 million. Therefore, grain per capita was only 317 kg. in 1978, about the same as the 1936 record of 313 kg (see Figure 1.1). To maintain a reasonable balance between supply and demand, China implemented grain-rationing coupons for urban citizens and imported grains.

In addition to satisfying a pressing need, reform in agriculture presented the advantage of being relatively straightforward because rural households had considerable experience in responding to market signals within the system of individual farm plots. To facilitate reform further, the government raised prices for farm products. Increases averaged 20.1% in 1978, 8.1% in 1980, and about 3% annually thereafter. The average annual growth rate of income per capita for rural households increased by 7.4% during 1978–2016, as opposed to only 2.75% during 1952–1978.[22]

---

[22]Calculated using data from All China Data Center, China Yearly Macro-Economic Statistics (National): Per Capita Annual Income and Expenditure Urban and Rural

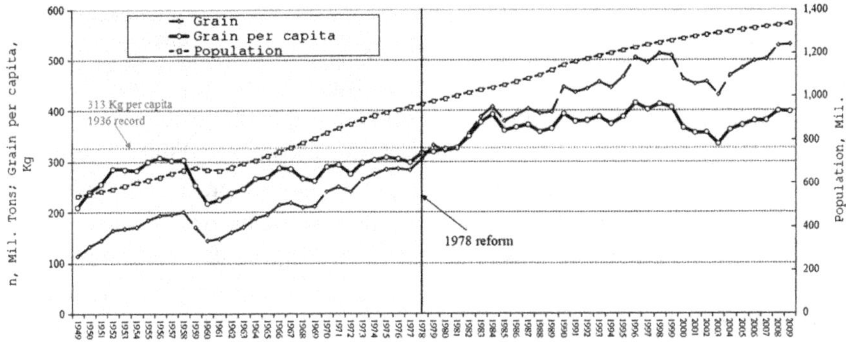

Figure 1.1.   Grain per capita in China, 1949–2016.

Notes: Calculated using data from All China Data Center, China Yearly Macro-Economic Statistics (National): Output of Major Farm Crops of China 1949–2016, Total Permanent Population 1949–2016; China National Bureau of Statistics: China Statistical Yearbook 2010, China Statistics Press, Table 3.1, Table 13.2; 2009, Table 1.7, Table 3.1, Table 12.15, Table 12.24; Statistical Yearbook of China 1981 (English Edition), Compiled by the State Statistical Bureau, PRC. Published by Economic Information & Agency, Hong Kong, October 1982; Directorate General of Budget, Accounting and Statistics, Executive Yuan, R.O.C.: "China Population Statistical Analysis" (in Chinese), 1946.

5.3. *The Township and Village Enterprise (TVE) phenomenon*

Agricultural reforms greatly increased agricultural productivity, increased farm incomes, and released workers from farm production. In 1979, restrictions on non-agricultural activities in the rural areas were relaxed, and enterprises in these areas were allowed to sell their products at market prices. As a result, a large number of individually or collectively owned TVEs were established or expanded, thus absorbing significant amount of surplus labor and capital. TVEs received no budgetary allocation or subsidies from the government. By the end of 2008, the value added of TVEs had risen to some 28.0% of the national GDP, to CNY8.14 trillion (USD1.19 trillion) employing 154.51 million workers, or 29.3% of the rural labor force. TVEs exported CNY3,509.2 billion (USD513.8 billion)

Households, 1957–2016; China National Bureau of Statistics: China Statistical Yearbook 2013, China Statistics Press, Table 9.2; 1991, Tables 7.2 and 8.1.

worth of their production, accounting for 19.5% of national exports in 2008.[23] By the end of 2011, TVE revenues had risen to CNY53.1 trillion (USD8.21 trillion) with 161.86 million workers employed, amounting to 40% of the rural labor force that now received payments of CNY2.63 trillion (USD407.2 billion). TVEs paid CNY1.34 trillion (USD207.4 billion) in taxes, or 22.7% of total enterprises tax.[24] Moreover, TVEs made an important contribution to China's economic reforms by providing competition for state enterprises and creating an environment for the development of entrepreneurial skills. Therefore, China's successful agricultural reforms had a significant effect on other sectors as well. In addition, early successes enhanced the credibility of Chinese leaders and made it easier for them to move forward with their reforms.

However, TVEs were burdened with many problems, including over-employment and heavy social welfare obligations. Many of their managers were also accused of corrupt practices. In addition, TVE debt was skyrocketing, reaching 65% and even 75% of total outstanding loans in Jiangsu, Zhejiang province from the Agricultural Bank of China and Rural Credit Cooperatives (RCC). TVEs' limited access to financing was another factor that made them lose ground to the SOEs. Much of the financing for TVEs came from local RCC. Local villagers deposited their savings in cooperatives, which then made loans to local governments, who used the money to establish TVEs, which in turn created jobs for local people. The RCCs had a close relationship with local governments and trusted them to make assessments as to the potential profitability of various TVE projects. Unfortunately, rural financial systems were not very developed and RCCs had low loan-to-deposit ratios. After 1998, TVEs had difficulty competing with the SOEs for financing and the dual-track price system diminished. The Statistics and Analysis of Township Enterprises Section in the Ministry of Agriculture was also eliminated

---

[23]Calculated using data from the Survey of China's Township Village Enterprises at China's 60th anniversary (in Chinese), http://nc.people.com.cn/GB/61154/9804661.html; China National Bureau of Statistics: China Statistical Yearbook 2009, Table 17.3; China Statistical Yearbook 2006, Tables 3.1, 5.3, and 18.3.

[24]Calculated using data from China's Township Village Enterprises and Processing of Agricultural Products Yearbook (in Chinese) 2012, pp. 95–96; China National Bureau of Statistics: China Statistical Yearbook 2013, Table 13.4; China Statistical Yearbook 2012, Table 8.4.

after 2012.[25] As a result, their contribution to China's growth declined significantly.

5.4. *SOE reform*

One of the weaknesses of a CPE lies in the inefficiency of its SOEs. One prominent explanation for the poor performance of these enterprises lies in the lack of incentives for managers and workers. The term used to describe this phenomenon is "soft budget" constraint.[26] According to Maskin,[27] the soft-budget constraint syndrome pertains "whenever a funding source — e.g., a bank or government — finds it impossible to keep an enterprise to a fixed budget, i.e., whenever the enterprise can extract ex-post a bigger subsidy or loan than would have been considered efficient ex-ante."

To eliminate the soft budget constraint, China gradually provided management, production, and financing independence to a small number of its SOEs in 1978. In 1984, the "managerial responsibility system" was implemented. This initiative was similar to the household responsibility system implemented in agriculture; it allowed enterprises to sell part of their output for their own profit after forwarding their assigned quota to the government. The managerial responsibility system was succeeded by the "contract responsibility system" of 1987, which allowed enterprises to keep a profit after paying a tax to the government. Enterprises could use their profit share to pay their workers and managers or expand their operations. However, SOE reform did not enjoy the same success as agricultural reform. The incentives provided to enterprise managers failed to motivate managers sufficiently.[28] Reform of SOEs, and the related issue of private sector activity, remains a challenge for China. Further

---

[25]Cheng, J. (2017). *An Economic Analysis of the Rise and Decline of Chinese TVE*. Palgrave Studies in Economic History Series; K. Deng, editor; Kung, J. K. Y. (2007). The decline of township-and-village enterprises in China's economic transition. *World Development*, 35(4), April, 569–584; Graceffo, A. (2010). The decline of China's TVE; Financial reform and transition in China. *Agricultural Finance Review*, 70(3), 305.

[26]Kornai, J. (1979). *Economics of Shortage*. Amsterdam: North-Holland.

[27]Maskin, E. S. (1996). Theories of the soft-budget constraint. *Japan and the World Economy*, 8, 125–131.

[28]Chow, G. C. (2004). Economic reform and growth in China. *Annals of Economics and Finance*, 5, 127–152.

discussion of this challenging aspect of China's transition is presented in Chapter 6.

5.5. *Price reform and the dual-track system*

CPEs traditionally use administratively set prices to promote their political objectives. These prices have no economic meaning. In its efforts to make a successful transition to a market-based economy, China has been gradually reforming its own price-system from centrally administered to one in which prices play an important role in the efficient allocation of resources by providing the signals that guide economic decision-making.

China's price system reform entailed the design of a dual-track or two-tier system. As the name implies, under this system, there exist two distinct prices for a product sold in two different markets. In one of these markets, products are sold at a predetermined price in a manner prescribed by the planned economy. In the other market, prices are determined through interaction between supply and demand and serve as signals that help direct consumption and production activities.

China's price reforms began with agricultural products and spread to consumer and intermediate goods. Between 1979 and 1987, the dual-track system was applied to about 40% of all prices. The reform process was halted in 1988 as inflation set in, but it started again in 1989.[29]

The dual-track price system epitomizes China's approach to reform. In addition to its implementation in establishing prices, the system provided the blueprint for reform in just about every sector in the economy. The system also reflected the co-existence between the planned and market components of China's transition.

6. Reform Linked With Opening to the Outside World: Mutual Motivation

The success of the domestic component of reforms can be reinforced by opening to the rest of the world. Participation in the global economy forces the country to comply with global standards. Unlike domestic reforms, whose directions can be uncertain at times, growing participation

---

[29] World Bank (1992). Price reform in China, Report No. 10410-CHA, May 28.

in the world economy entails competition in world markets. Therefore, domestic economic policies become increasingly more compatible with international standards.

Opening to the outside world is a vital part of the new development strategy of intensive growth — growth through adoption and diffusion of technology, especially foreign technology. Broadly interpreted, foreign technologies include not only technologies embodied in plant and equipment, but also knowledge, including management skills and even the practices and ideas of an advanced economy. Prior to the reforms, China also imported foreign technologies, including capitalist technologies, but its technological gap with the rest of the world continued to widen. Systematic Western involvement in the application and use of these technologies enhanced the effect of reforms on economic development. Opening to the outside world policy in early 1979 became one of the earliest and most encompassing elements of the reform package, coming at a time when the only reforms taking place were in rural areas. The policy of opening to the outside world was also a major departure from the preceding decades of self-reliance and autarkic quasi-economic and technological development.

The strategy was successful in generating dramatic increases in international trade and FDI, thereby contributing to higher efficiency and higher growth of the Chinese economy. Following economic reforms, the foreign trade participation ratio (TPR, total volume of foreign trade/GDP) increased. With a TPR of 32.7% in 2017[30] (9.7% in 1978), China could afford to import high-quality equipment not available domestically and to overcome bottlenecks in other areas. Moreover, the high value of TPR signifies the country's full participation in the world economy, which came with heavy competitive pressure from abroad. China became a member of many international organizations and joined the WTO in 2001. Therefore, Chinese enterprises had to learn how to compete in a global marketplace. These developments became the foundation of the country's drive toward a market economy.

Milestones of China's reforms are included in Appendix 1.A.

---

[30] Calculated using data from All China Data Center, China Yearly Macro-Economic Statistics (National): Total Imports and Exports 1950–2016, Gross Domestic Product of China 1952–2016; China National Bureau of Statistics: China Statistical Yearbook 2013, China Statistics Press, Tables 2.1 and 16.3.

7. China's Development: The Role of Five-Year Plans (FYPs)

To gain a better understanding of China's formulation of its reform strategy, we discuss the country's FYPs. China's FYPs for National Economic and Social Development have been the vehicle through which the country has mapped out its development strategy. These Plans are blueprints, providing overall objectives and goals related to social and economic growth and industrial planning in key sectors and regions. Policy makers at all levels of government use these Plans as guidelines that set economic targets to strive toward over the ensuing five-year period. Each FYP builds on previously implemented regional and long-term development plans and contains hundreds of policy initiatives. Progress toward goals and objectives of the plan is constantly assessed and the necessary revisions are made. In recent years, not only has the methodology of China's plan formulation changed, but the key elements of these plans have been enriched to accommodate the on-going social and economic changes. For example, since the sixth plan period (1980–1985), the FYP for Economic Development was renamed as the FYP for Economic and Social Development. Since the 11th plan period (2006–2010), the word "plan" [计划 JiHua] was replaced by "program" [规划 GuiHua]. Meanwhile, the planning process is becoming increasingly open and standardized.

7.1. *The first ten FYPs*

China has just concluded its pursuit of the objectives of the 13th FYP, while finalizing the details of its 14th FYP. As we will see, however, not all Plans are the same. In this section, we briefly discuss China's first to tenth FYP. The details of these plans are shown in Appendix 1.B.[31] Of these ten plans, the first four were concluded under central planning and emphasized economic self-reliance. The plans emphasized centralization of decision-making and relied on politically motivated targets. They offered no incentives for productivity gains, and ultimately led to poor allocation of resources.

---

[31] Xinhua (1976). The outline of FYP for National Economic and Social Development (in Chinese). 1st to 10th FYP; Chinese Primer: Report on the Work of the Government, Delivered at the National People's Congress (various years); China National Bureau of Statistics: China Statistical Yearbook, Various years, China Statistics Press.

The first FYP (1953–1957) allocated national resources to industrial construction with particular focus on heavy industry and ownership reform. The industrial restructuring component of the plan was successfully carried out, but ownership reform was pushed forward too quickly and failed.

The indicators used to formulate the second FYP (1958–1962) were shaped by the promises of the Great Leap Forward. Unfortunately, they were set at an unrealistic level, resulting in economic disaster. The misalignment of the economy was accompanied by a terrible drought and a loss of millions of lives during the ensuing famine.

The third FYP (1966–1970) favored resource allocation designed to prepare the country for war. This resulted in production inefficiencies and, ultimately, economic decline. Fulfillment of the objectives of the fourth (1971–1975) and fifth (1976–1980) FYPs was adversely affected by the Cultural Revolution. When the reform period started in 1978, policies were adopted toward "readjustment, reform, rectification, and improvement." However, the original targets were not met.

In December 1978, the government began focusing on modernization, so plans from the 6th to 10th FYP were formulated and implemented under the gradual transformation of the CPE economy to a market-oriented economy opening to the outside world. The dramatic decline of political instability served as facilitating factor in the eventual fulfillment of the targets set by the sixth FYP to the tenth FYP.

The sixth FYP focused on "adjust, reform, rectify, and improve" to further resolve various economic development issues left unsolved from past years. Reform was initiated in rural areas; therefore, the agricultural sector experienced its fastest growth since the establishment of the new China.

The seventh FYP put reform at the top of the agenda and coordinated economic development with reform. The path of transition toward a market economy had now become irreversible. However, emphasis on further growth caused overheating of the economy and inflation.

The objectives of the eighth FYP Plan included the balance between social demand and supply and further restructuring of the economy. Economic reform was moving forward, but challenges arose in the form of rapid inflation, large regional disparity, and agricultural sector weakness.

The ninth FYP aimed at developing a social market economy and changing the nature of economic growth mode from extensive to intensive. Per capita GDP grew by 409% compared to its 1980 level, fulfilling the stated target four years ahead of time. The market started to play a more significant role in resource allocation. However, inflation remained a threat, with the retail sales price index average rising by 11.4% per year.

The tenth FYP emphasized continuation of economic restructuring and pointed to technological progress as the driving force. GDP was to grow at a high rate, while keeping inflation low. However, transformation of the economic growth mode proved to be slow; energy consumption per unit GDP increased 2% during the period of the plan; environmental pollution worsened; city and countryside, regional disparity and income gap continued to expand.

7.2. *The 11th FYP*

The 11th FYP ushered a new era of qualitative growth. China's experience has been so far viewed as a successful experiment in transition. It has not been without its challenges, however. The promises of the 11th FYP included higher income, affordable housing, better education, and less pollution. It is the first FYP that sought all-round social and economic benefits for citizens, instead of just for economic expansion. Its objective was to strengthen the construction of a harmonious society and promote economic development with a people-centered approach.

The major indicators of economic and social development in the 11th FYP period are listed in Table 1.1. The 22 major indicators identified in the Plan are divided into "obligatory" and "anticipated," and into five major categories: Economic Growth; Economic Structure; Population, Resources, and Environment; Public Services; and Life Quality. Among the 8 obligatory indicators, 5 are in the Population, Resources, and Environment category, pointing to the importance the Chinese authorities have placed on such issues. Energy and water conservation are now policy priorities. Among the 8 obligatory major indicators, 7 exceeded the stated targets. The 8th indicator, energy consumption per unit of GDP, dropped to 19.06%, close to the goal of a 20% decrease.

Among the 14 anticipated indicators of the 11th FYP, only 3 failed to achieve their target, as shown in Table 1.2 in Italian font. The Plan also placed emphasis on the development of the country's tertiary sector. The goal was to increase the share that the service sector contributes to GDP to 43.5% by

Table 1.1. Major indicators of economic and social development in the 11th FYP period and their implementation.

		Main indicators (target in 11th five year plan)				Implemented	
Category	Indicators	Yr. 2005	Yr. 2010	Annual growth rate (%)	Attribute	Yr. 2010	Annual growth rate (%)
Economic growth	GDP (trillion CNY)	18.2	26.1	7.5	Anticipated	39.8	11.2
	Per capita GDP (CNY)	13985	19270	6.5	Anticipated	29748	10.6
Economic Structure	Ratio of added value of service industry (%)	40.5	43.5	[3]	Anticipated	43	[2.5]
	Employment ratio of service industry (%)	31.3	35.3	[4]	Anticipated	34.8	[3.5]
	Ratio of expenditure on R&D to GDP (%)	1.3	2	[0.7]	Anticipated	1.75	[0.45]
	Urbanization rate (%)	43	47	[4]	Anticipated	47.5	[4.5]
Population, resources, and environment	Total population (10,000 people)	130756	136000	<[0.8]	Obligatory	134100	[5.1]
	Reduction of energy consumption per unit GDP (%)			−[20]	Obligatory		−[19.1]
	Reduction of Water Consumption per Unit Industrial added value (%)			−[30]	Obligatory		−[36.7]
	Efficient utilization Coefficient of agricultural irrigation water	0.45	0.5	[0.05]	Anticipated	0.5	[0.05]
	Comprehensive utilization rate of Industrial solid wastes (%)	55.8	60	[4.2]	Anticipated	69	[13.2]
	Total cultivated land (100 mil. Ha.)	1.22	1.2	−0.3	Obligatory	1.212	−0.13
	Reduction of total major pollutants emission volume (%) SO$_2$			[10]	Obligatory		[14.29]
	chemical oxygen demand			[10]			[12.45]
	Forest coverage (%)	18.2	20	[1.8]	Obligatory	20.36	[2.16]

(Continued)

Table 1.1.   *(Continued)*

Category	Indicators	Main indicators (target in 11th five year plan)				Implemented	
		Yr. 2005	Yr. 2010	Annual growth rate (%)	Attribute	Yr.2010	Annual growth rate (%)
Public services and life quality	Average schooling years of citizens (Yr.)	8.5	9	[0.5]	Anticipated	9	[0.5]
	Population covered by basic pension in urban areas (billion people)	1.74	2.23	5.1	Obligatory	2.57	8.1
	Coverage of new rural cooperative healthcare system (%)	23.5	>80	>[56.5]	Obligatory	96.3	[72.8]
	New increased urban employment (10,000 people)			[4500]	Anticipated		[5771]
	Rural labor force transferred (10,000 people)			[4500]	Anticipated		[4500]
	Registered urban unemployment rate (%)	4.2	5		Anticipated	4.1	
	Per capita disposal income of urban households (CNY)	10493	13390	5	Anticipated	19109	9.7
	Per capita net income of rural households (CNY)	3255	4150	5	Anticipated	5919	8.9

Sources: National Development and Reform Commission (NDRC): The outline of 11th FYP, May 29, 2006; Wen Jiabao, Premier of the State Council: The Report on the Work of the Government, Delivered at the Fourth Session of the 11th National People's Congress on March 5, 2011; China National Bureau of Statistics: China Statistical Yearbook 2010, China Statistics Press.

Table 1.2.   Major indicators of economic and social development in the 12th FYP period and their implementation.

| Category | Indicators | Main indicators (target in 12th five year plan) | | | | Implement |
		Yr. 2010	Yr. 2015	Value or growth rate (%)	Attribute	Yr. 2012
Economic development	GDP (trillion CNY)[a]	39.8	55.8	7	Anticipated	8.5%
	Ratio of added value of service industry (%)	43	47	{4}	Anticipated	1.4
	Increase the value-added of strategic emerging industries in GDP (%)	3	8	{5}	Anticipated	−3.00
	Urbanization rate (%)	50.0	54	{4}	Anticipated	2.62
Science, education	Nine year compulsory education consolidated rate (%)	89.7	93	{3.3}	Obligatory	0
	High school stage education gross enrollment rate (%)	82.5	87	{4.5}	Anticipated	0
	Ratio of expenditure on R&D to GDP (%)	1.75	2.2	{0.45}	Anticipated	0.22
	Innovation patent per 10,000 people (piece)	1.0	3.3	{2.3}	Anticipated	0.6
Resources, environment	Total cultivated land (100 mil.mu.)	18.18	18.18	{0}	Obligatory	0.08
	Reduction of water consumption per unit industrial added value (%)			−{30}	Obligatory	−17.2
	Efficient utilization coefficient of agricultural irrigation water		0.53		Anticipated	
	The proportion of non-fossil fuels in primary energy consumption (%)[d]	8.6	11.4	[2.8]	Obligatory	0.8
	Reduction of energy consumption per unit GDP (%)			−[16]	Obligatory	−100.0

(*Continued*)

Table 1.2.   (*Continued*)

Category	Indicators		Yr. 2010	Yr. 2015	Value or growth rate (%)	Attribute	Implement Yr. 2012
	Reduction of CO_2 emissions per unit GDP (%)[d]				–[17]	Obligatory	0.00
	Reduction of total major pollutants emission volume (%)[e]	Chemical oxygen demand (COD)	2551.7	2347.6	–[8]	Obligatory	–100.0
		Sulfur dioxide (SO_2)	2185.2	2086.4	–[8]		–3.1
		Ammonia Nitrogen	264.4	238	–[10]		–100.0
		Nitrogen oxides	2273.6	2046.2	–[10]		–100.0
	Increment of forests[e]	Forest Coverage (%)	20.36	21.66	{1.3}	Obligatory	
		Woodstorage increment (100 Mil. M^3)	137	143	{6}		
People's living conditions	Per capita disposal income of urban households (CNY)[c]		19109	>26510	>[7]	Anticipated	9.0%
	Per capita net income of rural households (CNY)[c]		5919	>8310	>[7]	Anticipated	11.0%
	Registered urban unemployment rate (%)		4.1	<5		Anticipated	4.05
	New increased urban employment (10,000 people)				{4500}	Anticipated	2415
	Population covered by basic pension in urban areas (billion people)		2.57	3.57	{1}	Obligatory	0.65
	Increment of participation rate in the basic health care system for working and non-working urban residents %[e]				{3}	Obligatory	

The new rural cooperative medical care system for rural residents (%)[e]	96	100	{4}	Obligatory	2.26
The total number of new government-subsidized housing for low income households in urban and town (10000 units)[d]			{3600}	Obligatory	0
Total population (10,000 people)	134100	<139000	<0.72%	Obligatory	0.49
Life expectancy (year old)	73.5A	74.5	{1}	Anticipated	

Notes: [a]Data of GDP are calculated at 2010 prices, the growth rate is calculated at constant prices.

[b]Data in bracket{}is cumulative value in five years; in bracket [] is growth rate in five years.

[c]The growth rate of per capita income of urban and rural households should be not lower than the growth rate of GDP.

[d]New added four obligatory Indicators in 12th FYP.

[e]Comparing with 11th FYP three obligatory Indicators extended their contents.

A Data from "China Statistical Yearbook-2013" Table 3.6 this value would be 74.8.

Sources: Xinhua (2011). The outline of 12th FYP for National Economic and Social Development (in Chinese), March 16, http://www.gov.cn/2011lh/content_1825838.htm; China National Bureau of Statistics (2013). China Statistical Yearbook 2013, China Statistics Press, Tables 2.1, 2.2, 2.5, 2.8, 3.1, 3.7, 7.1, 7.15; 2011, Table 12.24; Compiled by National Bureau of Statistics, Ministry of Environment Protection, China Statistical Yearbook on Environment 2013, Table 4.2, Appendix II; Tables 1.5, 7.5, 8.2; Compiled By Department of Energy Statistics, National Bureau of Statistics China Energy Statistical Yearbook 2013, Table 4.4; British Petroleum: BP Statistical Review of World Energy 2014, June 2014; Compiled by National Bureau of Statistical and Ministry of Human Resources and Social Security: China Labor Statistical Yearbook 2013, Table 1.5; Compiled by National Health And Family Planning Commission of PRC: China Statistical Yearbook of Health and Family Planning, Table 13.1.1; Report on the Implementation of The 2012 Plan For National Economic and Social Development and on the 2013 Draft Plan for National Economic and Social Development on First Session of the 12th National People's Congress; Report on the Implementation of The 2011 Plan For National Economic and Social Development and on the 2012 Draft Plan for National Economic and Social Development on Fifth Session of the Eleventh National People's Congress; Report on the Implementation of The 2010 Plan For National Economic and Social Development and on the 2011 Draft Plan for National Economic and Social Development on 4th Session of the Eleventh National People's Congress.

2010, with the final figure being 43%, and to increase the employment ratio of the service sector to 35.3% by 2010, with the final figure being 34.8%. All these failed anticipated indicators belong to the Economic Structure category, revealing the slow progress toward the transformation of the economic growth pattern and promotion of innovation during the 2006–2010 period. All 8 obligatory indicators for the 11th FYP have been completed.

7.3. *The 12th FYP (2011–2015)*

The 12th FYP picked up where the 11th FYP left off in terms of broad policy direction. However, the development of the 12th FYP took place in a markedly different internal and external environment. The aftereffects of the global financial crisis, rising property prices, and increasing risk of social instability represented serious challenges for China that were prominently addressed by this program. The 12th FYP focused on China's GDP and income growth, economic transformation and reform, development of new industries and services, trade and investment, regional development, urbanization, rural modernization, environmental protection, and improvement of social welfare to make China a moderately prosperous society by 2020. The major indicators of economic and social development in the 12th FYP period are listed in Table 1.2. The targets of the new model included economic growth, science and education, structural adjustment, social services development, carbon mitigation and environmental protection, and transparency and governance reforms. Calls for the transformation of China's economic development model are not new. In the past, calls for development were for marginal improvement of the development model. This time, in addition to the efficiency improvement, it is to avoid potential economic crisis.

Behind China's average 9.8% GDP growth over the preceding three decades lie a number of issues that have the potential to lead to serious problems in the future. Trade surpluses have resulted in huge foreign exchange reserves, excess liquidity, high inflation pressure, and bubbles in the capital and property markets. High GDP growth has failed to generate a proportionate increase in people's well-being, while public services developed supply bottlenecks. Manufacturing had excess capacity, shortages developed in service sector providers, particularly in medicine, education, finance, and banking. Substantial and growing risks appeared from the massive local government debt.

Rapid growth was also associated with rapid environmental degradation, a fact that made China's shift to a low carbon economy increasingly imperative.[32] Therefore, the country's development model needed to transition from the current low-efficiency, high-growth model to a more balanced model. The 12th FYP contributed to that transition.

As China continued to grow, it became evident to policy makers that two transformations had to be achieved. First, the country must establish an economically and socially "balanced" model, with the high-income Western societies serving as a benchmark. Second, China had to initiate low-carbon growth policies to lower emissions and deal with fossil fuel depletion. In the past, calls to transform China's development model were not heeded. However, the potential crises hidden in the existing development model were being more widely recognized. An impetus for meaningful change was created. The financial crisis of 2007–2008, in particular, made Chinese officials aware of the importance of creating a growth model that moves away from the country's over reliance on investments and exports and toward consumption-led growth. Increasing consumption would also help meet the government's goal of raising income and social-benefit levels for all of China's citizens.

The 12th FYP's guiding principles promoted the government's focus on "inclusive growth," which means ensuring the benefits of economic growth are spread to a greater proportion of Chinese citizens. The program's key themes were rebalancing the economy, ameliorating social inequality, and protecting the environment. All these themes focused on improving people's livelihood, resources, and the environment, thus reflecting the strengthening of the government's public service functions and responsibilities. The environmental-protection quota required that government, business, and the public all had to play a role in promoting the construction of a resource saving and environmentally friendly society.

There are another 27 indicators listed in the outline of the 12th FYP whose attributes are neither obligatory nor anticipated; we label them reference indicators (see Table 1.3).[33] Among these 27 reference

---

[32] Zhang, Y. (2011). The impact of China's 12th Five Year Plan, East Asia Forum, April 24.

[33] Xinhua (2011). The outline of 12th Five-Year Plan for National Economic and Social Development (in Chinese), March 16, http://www.gov.cn/2011lh/content_1825838.htm; China Statistical Yearbook of Health and Family Planning, Tables 2.3.4, 13.1.1, and 13.2; Report on the Implementation of the 2012 Plan For National Economic and Social Development and on the 2013 Draft Plan for National Economic and Social Development on First Session of the 12th National People's Congress; Report on the Implementation of the 2010 Plan for National Economic and Social Development and on the 2011 Draft Plan for National Economic and Social Development on 4th Session of the 11th National People's Congress.

Table 1.3.   Major indicators of economic and social development in the 13th FYP period and their implementation in 2017.

Indicator		Yr. 2015	Yr. 2020	5-year average [5-year cumulative total]	Type of indicator	Implement Yr. 2017
• Economic development						
1. GDP (trillions of yuan)[a]		67.7	>92.7	>6.5%	Anticipatory	82.7
2. Overall labor productivity (10,000 yuan per employed person)[a]		8.7	>12	>6.6%	Anticipatory	10.1
3. Urbanization	Permanent urban residents (%)	56.1	60	[3.9]	Anticipatory	58.5
	Registered urban residents (%)	39.9	45	[5.1]	Anticipatory	42.4
4. Value-added of the service sector (% of GDP)		50.5	56	[5.5]	Anticipatory	51.6
• Innovation-driven development						
5. Research and development expenditure (% of GDP)		2.1	2.5	[0.4]	Anticipatory	2.12
6. Patents per 10,000 people		6.3	12	[5.7]	Anticipatory	9.8
7. Contribution of scientific and technological advances to economic growth (%)		55.3	60	[4.7]	Anticipatory	57.5
					—	
					—	
					—	
					—	
8. Internet access	Households with fixed broadband (%)	40	70	[30]	Anticipatory	[23]
	Mobile broadband users (%)	57	85	[28]	Anticipatory	[18]

• Well-being of the people

10. Average year of education received by the working-age population (years)	10.23	10.8	[0.57]	Obligatory	10.5
11. New urban employment (10000 people)	n/a	n/a	[>5000]	Anticipatory	2665
12. Rural population lifted out of poverty (10000 people)	n/a	n/a	[55.75]	Obligatory	25.29
13. Basic old-age insurance coverage (%)	82	90	[8]	Anticipatory	88
14. Rebuilt housing in rundown urban areas (millions of units)	n/a	n/a	[20]	Obligatory	[1215]
15. Average life expectancy (years)	n/a	n/a	[1]	Anticipatory	[0.36]

• Resources and the environment

16. Arable land (millions of hectares)	124.3	124.3	[0]	Obligatory	2015 at 124.3
17. Increase in land newly designated for construction (millions of hectares)	n/a	n/a	[<2.17]	Obligatory	[<0.095]
18. Water use reduction per 10,000 yuan of GDP (%)	n/a	n/a	[−23]	Obligatory	[−11.5]
19. Energy consumption reduction per unit of GDP (%)	n/a	n/a	[−15]	Obligatory	[−8.1]
20. Non-fossil energy (% of primary energy consumption)	12	15	[3]	Obligatory	[−2.7]
21. CO_2 emissions reduction per unit of GDP (%)	n/a	n/a	[−18]	Obligatory	[−5.1]
22. Forest growth — Forest coverage (%)	21.66	23.04	[1.38]	Obligatory	21.6
Forest growing stock (billions of m³)	15.1	16.5	[1.4]	Obligatory	15.1

(Continued)

Table 1.3. (*Continued*)

Indicator		Yr. 2015	Yr. 2020	5-year average [5-year cumulative total]	Type of Indicator	Implement Yr. 2017
			Main Indicators in 13th Five-Year Plan			
23. Air quality	Days of good or excellent air quality in cities at and above the prefectural level (% of the year)	76.7	>80	n/a	Obligatory	78
					—	
					—	
					—	
					—	
					—	
	Reduction in $PM_{2.5}$ intensity in cities at and above the prefectural level missing the target (%)[c]	n/a	n/a	[−18]	Obligatory	[−7.8]
24. Surface water quality	Grade III or better (%)	66	>70	n/a	Obligatory	67.8
	Worse than Grade V (%)	9.7	<5	n/a	Obligatory	

25. Aggregate major pollutant emissions reduction (%)	Chemical oxygen demand (COD)	n/a	n/a	[−10]	Obligatory	[−5.1]
	Sulfur dioxide (SO_2)	n/a	n/a	[−10]	Obligatory	[−5.6]
	Ammonia nitrogen	n/a	n/a	[−15]	Obligatory	
	Nitrogen oxide	n/a	n/a	[−15]	Obligatory	[−4.0]

Notes: [a]GDP and overall labor productivity are computed using comparable prices, while absolute figures are computed using 2015 constant prices.

[b]Figures in square brackets are five-year cumulative totals.

[c]Missing the target for PM2.5 means the annual average figure exceeds 35μg per cubic meter.

[d]New added four Obligatory indicators in 13th FYP and marked with single underscores.

Sources: The outline of the Thirteenth Five-Year Plan for National Economic and Social Development (in Chinese), March 16, http://www.guancha.cn/society/2016_03_17_354244_6.shtml; Highlights of Government Work Report. Delivered by Premier Li Keqiang, March 5, 2018. http://www.chinadaily.com.cn/a/201803/05/WS5a9cb2daa3106e7dcc13f93f_1.html; Report on the Work of the Government. Delivered by Premier Li Keqiang, March 15, 2017. http://www.fmprc.gov.cn/ce/cebn/eng/zgxw/t1446895.htm. Statistical Communiqué of the People's Republic of China on the 2017 National Economic and Social Development, National Bureau of Statistics of China, 2018; Statistical Communiqué of the People's Republic of China on the 2016 National Economic and Social Development, National Bureau of Statistics of China, 2017.

Xinhua (2011). The outline of the 13th FYP for National Economic and Social Development (in Chinese), March 16, http://www.guancha.cn/society/2016_03_17_354244_6.shtml; Highlights of Government Work Report Delivered by Premier Li Keqiang, March 5, 2018, http://www.chinadaily.com.cn/a/201803/05/WS5a9cb2daa3106e7dcc13f93f_1.html; Report on the Work of the Government Delivered by Premier Li Keqiang, March 15, 2017, http://www.fmprc.gov.cn/ce/cebn/eng/zgxw/t1446895.htm; Statistical Communiqué of the People's Republic of China on the 2017 National Economic and Social Development, National Bureau of Statistics of China, 2018-02-28 10:18; Statistical Communiqué of the People's Republic of China on the 2016 National Economic and Social Development, National Bureau of Statistics of China 2017-02-28 09:30.

indicators, 12 indicators relate to "people's living conditions" and 7 to resources, environment, once again emphasizing the strengthening of the government's public service functions and responsibilities. Among the achievements of the 12th FYP are the growth rate of the minimum wage standard beyond the average growth rate and the greater attention paid by the social security system to the needs of lower income citizenry. These sections of the FYP potentially speak to future efforts to adjust the income distribution and gradually narrow the income gap.

The 12th FYP included four more obligatory indicators than did the 11th FYP (see Table 1.2 marked with double underscores), while three additional obligatory indicators expanded their contents (see Table 1.1 marked with single underscores). Of the new increased four obligatory indicators, two are in the resources and environment group, one in people's living conditions and one in science and education; among the three expanded obligatory indicators in the 12th FYP, two are part of the resources and environment and one is part of the people's living conditions group. All these focused on improving people's livelihood, resources, and the environment, further confirming the government's social and environmental responsibilities.

The 12th FYP's key themes are rebalancing the economy, ameliorating social inequality, and protecting the environment. The evaluation of implementation of 2011–2015 shows that of the 28 indicators that can be counted and evaluated, only 1 lags behind, the target ratio of Expenditure on R&D to GDP is 2.2% and the actual value in 2015 is 2.1. The evaluation of implementation of the 12th FYP from 2011 to 2014 by Hu Angang (one of the 13 FYP members of the "National Expert Committee on Development Planning) found only 2 indicators of lagging progress (R&D expenditure as a proportion of GDP, total number of new government-subsidized housing for low-income households in urban and town), accounting for 7.1% of all indicators. The conclusion is that the score of the mid-term evaluation of the implementation of the "12th FYP" is 93.1 points, which is a marked improvement over the five-year score (87 points) of the "11th FYP," thereby reflecting the satisfactory outcome of China's national governance.

According to the World Development Index (WDI) data, China's CO_2 emissions (kg per 2010 USD of GDP) in 2010 was 1.442, which fell to 1.237 in 2014, a growth rate of −14.7%. Therefore, in Table 1.2, a value for this indicator −17% is acceptable. However, the resources and environment indicators do not generate optimism. According to the China Statistical

Yearbook data, China's CO_2 emissions (million tons) in 2010 was 12.38, which rose to 22.95 in 2014, a growth rate of 179.6%. According to the U.S. Environmental Protection Agency, in 2014, the top 3 emissions by country were China (30%), the United States (15%), and EU-28(9%) accounting for 54% of world emissions. A key reason for China's emissions growth is the heavy reliance on coal-fired power generation. Demand for oil and gas continues to rise because of increased car ownership and electricity demand. Nitrogen oxides emissions increased to 2.39 million tons in 2014 from 1.20 million tons in 2010, a positive increase of 98.3%.

7.4. *The 13th FYP (2016–2020)*

From the beginning of the reform, China has made remarkable progress to date. It became the world's second largest economy in 2010, the largest trading nation of goods since 2013, the second largest destination for FDI and the third largest global investor in 2017; it is also the largest holder of foreign exchange reserves since 2006. It achieved average GDP growth of 7.8% from 2010 to 2015, 48.1% of which was contributed by the services sector, thereby exceeding contributions by manufacturing and construction. It reached an urbanization rate of 58.5%, while lifting over 100 million people out of poverty.

The architects of the 13th FYP recognized that China faced several major structural challenges. Among them, over-reliance on exports and fiscal investment for GDP growth, industrial over-capacity and declining profits, widening gap of economic development between regions and social groups, severe environmental pollution and rising constraints of natural resources, rising cost of labor, education, housing and healthcare for an aging population, government over-regulation, and poor quality of services. In the words of CPC leadership, China's economic growth model is "unbalanced, uncoordinated, and unsustainable," and in need of change.

The 13th FYP is the first FYP formulated under President Xi Jinping's leadership. It is considered strategically important, as 2020 was the centennial anniversary of the founding of the CPC and the deadline for realizing China's goal of becoming "a moderately prosperous society in all respects." In concrete terms, China had to double its 2010 GDP and per capita income of both urban and rural residents by 2020 — an enormous task given the uncertainties prevalent in any transition economy. To achieve the goal, the party emphasized five guiding principles:

Table 1.4.   Comparing the number and attribute of major indicators of economic and social development: 11th, 12th, and 13th FYP periods.

Attribute	Category	11 FYP	12 FYP	13 FYP
Obligatory	Economic development	0	0	0
	Science, education	0	2	0
	Resources and the environment	6	11	16
	People's living conditions	3	4	3
	Subtotal	9	17	19
Anticipated	Economic development	2	3	5
	Science, education	4	2	5
	Resources and the environment	2	1	0
	People's living conditions	6	5	4
	Subtotal	14	11	14
Total		23	28	33

1. Innovation.
2. Coordination.
3. Green development.
4. Opening up.
5. Sharing.[34]

As shown in the last column of Table 1.4, the targets of the 13th FYP were well implemented as of 2016 and 2017.

The Chinese government recognizes that heavy industry and low-end manufacturing are creating neither sustainable engines of growth nor the jobs matching China's increasingly educated and skilled workforce. The 13th FYP reiterates support for the "Made in China 2025" and "Internet Plus" initiatives as key policies to move up the value-added chain. These initiatives seek to accelerate China's transition to higher-value-added,

---

[34]Xinhua (2011). The outline of the 13th Five-Year Plan for National Economic and Social Development (in Chinese), March 16. http://www.guancha.cn/society/2016_03_17_354244_6.shtml; Suggestions of the CPC Central Committee on the 13th Five-Year Plan for National Economic and Social Development, http://mn.china-embassy.org/eng/xw/t1322243.htm.

intelligent manufacturing by focusing on innovation and upgrading emerging industries, such as high-end equipment, integrated circuits, bio-medicines, cloud computing, mobile Internet, and e-commerce. In support of these sectors, the Chinese government cultivates local and national champions, negotiates for technology transfers as the price of market access, regulates foreign investment, and technology imports through government catalogs, promotes Chinese technology standards domestically and internationally, and supports greater Chinese exports through its "Going Out" strategy.

However, without meaningful reform, the 13th FYP's policies to move up the value-added chain through indigenous innovation and other state-directed policies risk recreating the overproduction and distorted market conditions that occurred under the 12th FYP with strategic emerging industries for a list of strategic emerging industries.

Table 1.4 shows that four innovation-driven indicators have been introduced in the 13th FYP. Comparing with the 12th FYP shows that 4 new anticipated indicators: marked with single underscores: expressed as "Overall labor productivity," "Registered urban residents" and two "Internet access," and 1 Obligatory "the education for the working-age population." China's economy has seemingly made the transition from a period of rapid growth to a period of high-quality development. This is a crucial stage in transforming the country's growth model, improving the economic structure and driving new growth forces. The 13th FYP introduced 16 indicators in the "resources and environment" category, all of them described as obligatory. Five indicators are new, "air quality 2," "surface water quality 2," and "land newly designated for construction."

In March 2018, the concept of "ecological civilization" was added to the Chinese constitution, and sweeping ministerial reforms soon followed, with the Ministry of Ecology and Environment of PRC and the Ministry of Natural Resources of PRC formed to manage and protect China's environment. Zhao Yingmin, Deputy Minister of the Ministry of Ecology and Environment of PRC, said "efforts to mitigate climate change have been comprehensively advanced." The carbon intensity reduction target of the "13th FYP" was continuously implemented. According to preliminary calculations, the national carbon emission intensity decreased by 45.8% in 2018 compared to 2005 and continued to decline. Moreover, this number has reached the 40% reduction in carbon emission intensity in 2020. The commitment of –45% basically reversed the situation of rapid growth of greenhouse gas emissions, and the proportion of non-fossil energy in energy consumption reached 14.3%.[35]

This shows that China intends to speed up the establishment of a legal and policy framework to promote green production and consumption, a healthy economic structure, and green, low-carbon and recycling development.

8. Transformation of China's Economic Development Model

Although economic rebalancing has been a government priority for many years, the sharp decrease in Chinese exports during the 2007–2008 financial crisis, which led to the layoff of millions of factory workers, underscored the importance to Chinese decision-makers of moving to a more balanced growth structure. It brought about an urgency in the creation of a growth model that moves away from the country's over reliance on investments and exports and toward consumption– and innovation-led growth. Increasing consumption would also help meet the government's goal of raising income and social-benefit levels for all citizens. Economic rebalancing became a consistent policy priority for several important reasons. These include: (1) the perceived un-sustainability of an exceptionally high growth rate and large global trade and foreign exchange imbalances that led to tensions between China and its major trading partners; (2) the desire to spread the fruits of decades of growth to a wider proportion of the population; and (3) the inefficient use of resources that accompanies high levels of public Fixed Asset Investment (FAI) to avoid overcapacity. China is marking a path where the quality of growth in terms of composition, efficiency, and environmental effect now commands more attention at the margin than sheer quantity. This includes efforts to rebalance aggregate demand toward domestic consumption and service-sector activity and away from export manufacturing and investment.

---

[35] China News Office held a press conference on the "2019 Annual Report on China's Policies and Actions against Climate Change," and invited Zhao Yingmin, Deputy Minister of the Ministry of Ecology and Environment of PRC, to introduce the relevant information on the China Annual Report on Policies and Actions on Climate Change 2019. 2019-11-27. *Source*: China Government Website.

The 13th FYP includes policies that support a lower GDP growth rate, consumption-driven growth, upgraded industries, strengthened "national champions", and more backing for the government's indigenous innovation drive. A lower growth rate will also allow officials to reduce their focus on FAI and give them breathing space to set in place policies that will slowly increase consumption without having to focus unduly on ambitious growth targets. As the 11th FYP period experienced a GDP growth rate of 11.2%, most analysts agree that the government will try harder to enforce a lower rate this time around. The 13th FYP strongly emphasized the importance of shifting to consumption-driven growth to achieve several outcomes, such as reducing income disparity, moving away from FAI because of overcapacity concerns, reducing China's dependency on exports and thus, reducing its current account surplus. Figure 1.2 shows that in the 11th FYP, household consumption declined from 53.0% in 1981 to 35.6% of GDP by 2010, although the 11th FYP was considered a major policy shift from a focus on "growth at any cost" toward a more balanced and sustainable growth pattern. The economic

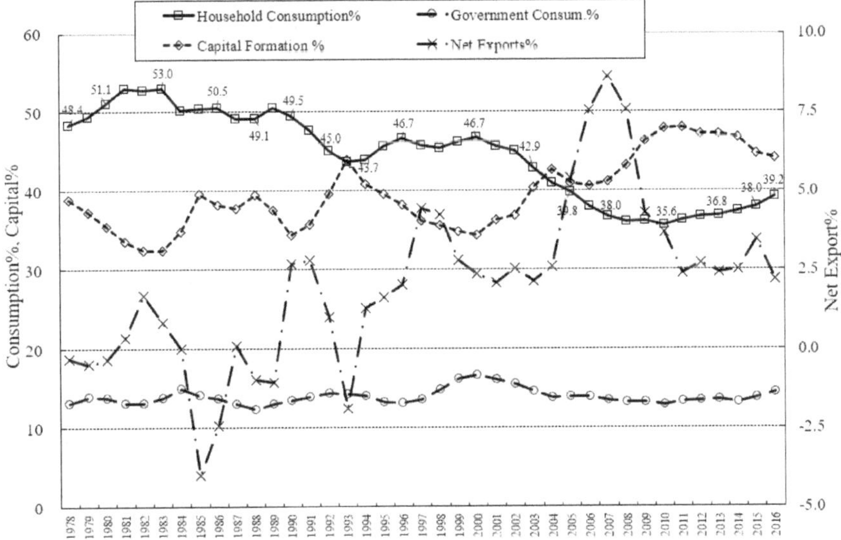

Figure 1.2.　Composition of China's GDP 1978–2016.

Sources: Calculated using data from all China data center, China yearly Macro-Economic statistics (National): Gross domestic product by expenditure approach of China, 1952–2016; China Statistical Yearbook 2010, China Statistics Press, Table 2.18.

rebalancing initiatives were laid out in the 11th FYP (2006–2010) — a policy bias already well known.

Expanding domestic consumption has proven to be a challenging task. A State Council official predicted it would increase from the 2010 level of 35.6–40% by 2015 (actual implemented 38%). This is still too low compared with other countries: India 56.2%, US 68.7%, Japan 56.5%, and World 56.8% in 2015 (see Figure 1.3). To enable consumption to grow quickly, the government instituted programs aimed at increasing household disposable income, particularly through higher minimum wages and increased social safety net, such as health care and social welfare payments. Decisive progress has already been made in the fight against poverty.

If China's efforts to rebalance aggregate demand toward domestic consumption and service-sector activity away from export manufacturing and investment succeed, the country will also succeed in reducing material-intensity and energy-intensity versus the levels achieved in recent years.

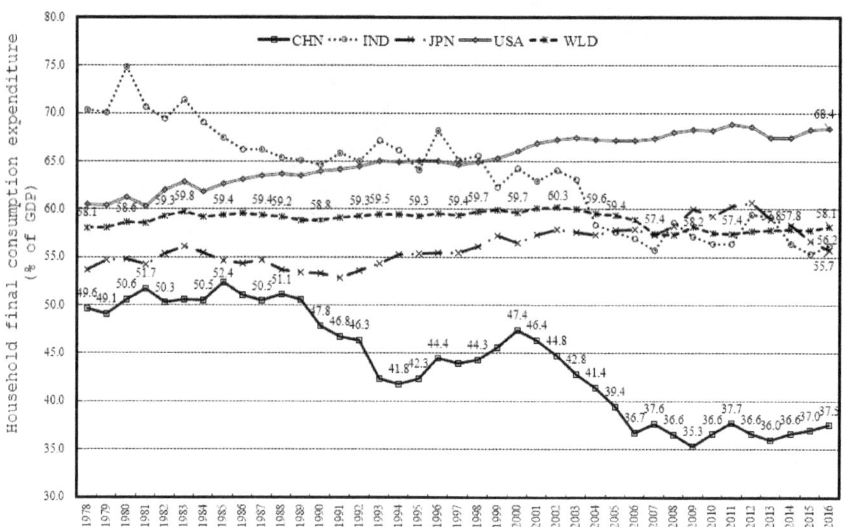

Figure 1.3.   Household final consumption expenditure (percent of GDP) for selected countries during 1978–2016.

Sources: Calculated using data from World Bank: World Development Indicators 2017 online released 2017.

However, rising input costs (including labor, energy, environmental compliance, and possibly capital costs) represent a challenge to the sustainability of profit margins of the manufacturing enterprises. These initiatives could lead to a decline in China's overall profits-to-GDP and in the remarkable rise in China's industrial enterprise profits as a percentage of GDP. On the other hand, we would expect these pressures to increase relative premiums on those Chinese firms capable of instituting new cost-efficiencies or those with sufficient pricing power to pass rising costs on to final users. Although these initiatives will generate relative winners, they may also imply downward pressure on margins generally. The rise in industrial enterprise profits as a percent of GDP appears to have peaked in 2010 (13.21%, as shown in Figure 1.4). It then declined to 9.64% in 2015; and increased to 9.71% in 2016. This may be because of the new emphasis on economic restructuring, scientific innovation, opening-up, and more effective governance practices.

Figure 1.4.   China's industrial enterprise profits as a percent of GDP, 1990–2016.

Sources: Calculated Using Data From China National Bureau of Statistics: National Data, Database: Annual, Main Indicators of Industrial Enterprises Above Designated Size and Gross Domestic Product, 2012–2016, Gross Domestic Product 1997–2016; China Statistical Yearbook 2010, China Statistics Press, 2013, Table 2.1; Compiled by Department of Industry and Transport Statistics, National Bureau of Statistics: China Industry Economy Statistical Yearbook 2013, China Statistics Press, Table 1.11; 2012, Table 3.1.

Therefore, the 12th FYP included policies that promote investments in new manufacturing equipment and technology, which in turn should assist China in meeting its energy efficiency goals. Specific policies targeted at forcing sector consolidation were also adopted in several industries — the auto sector is a good example where the government wants to see the current 80 or so manufacturers reduced to only a few dozen tier-one and tier-two producers within a decade.

Chinese planners have included several preferential taxes, fiscal, and procurement policies designed to develop 7 "Strategic Emerging Industries" (SEIs). Planners hope these industries will become the backbone of China's economy in the decades ahead, and represent sectors in which Chinese corporations are expected to succeed on a global scale. The State Council decided to proceed with Accelerating the Fostering and Development of New Strategic Industries.

1. Energy conservation and environment-friendly industry, including key generic technology for recycling of resources, recycling of discarded commodities, clean use of coal, and comprehensive utilization of sea water.
2. Next-generation information technology industry, including next-generation mobile communications, and core equipment and intelligent terminals for the next-generation Internet.
3. Biological industry, including biotechnological pharmaceuticals, new vaccines and diagnostic reagents, chemical pharmaceuticals, and modern Chinese medicines.
4. High-end equipment manufacturing industry, including aviation equipment, rail transport equipment, and marine engineering equipment.
5. Alternative energy industry, including nuclear energy, solar thermal technology, wind power, and biomass energy.
6. New materials industry, including rare earth functional materials, high performance film materials, special types of glass, functional ceramics, semi-conductor lighting materials, high-quality special steel, new alloys, engineering plastics, carbon fibers, aramid fibers, ultrahigh molecular weight polyethylene, materials that are nanometer in size, super-conducting, and intelligent.
7. Alternative energy automotive industry, such as plug-in hybrid automobiles, electric automobiles, and fuel cell automobiles.

The government was reportedly prepared to spend more than CNY4 trillion on these 7 SEIs during the 12th FYP period, with the aim of increasing SEI's contribution from today's approximately 5% of GDP to 8% by 2015 and 15% by 2020.[36] Even more important than the numerical targets, however, is the role of the 12th FYP in transforming the economy "from an investment-led powerhouse focused exclusively on GDP growth to a sustainable model that balances growth with social harmony, and innovation with environmental protection."[37]

8.1. *Promoting social equality*

The 12th FYP continued the focus on the rubric of "inclusive growth." Interestingly, the 12th FYP guidelines changed the previous creed of "Strong State, Wealthy People" into "Wealthy People, Strong State," implying that "Wealthy People" is now the greater priority.

Urban/Rural Divide: The divide in quality-of-life indicators between China's urban and rural residents is especially large, even for a developing country, and contributes to a range of problems for the government, including mounting social unrest in rural areas. The urban consumption and rural consumption are shown in Figure 1.5. It shows that the consumption in rural areas declined from 48.8% in 1978 to 16.2% of Final Consumption Expenditures in 2012; in the urban areas, it increased from 29.8% in 1978 to 56.6% in 2012. The population in urban areas increased from 17.9% of the total in 1978 to 52.57% in 2012 due to urbanization. Per capita consumption accounted for 138 and 387 current CNY in rural and urban areas, respectively, by 1978 and increased to CNY6,588 and CNY20,808 (current CNY) by 2012. Figure 1.5 shows that the ratio of per capita consumption in urban areas to per capita consumption in rural areas declined from 2.80 in 1978 to 2.07 in 1984, then increased to the peak 3.7571 in 2004, and further slightly declined to 3.16 in 2012. As we noted earlier in this chapter, China's reforms began with agriculture, so in the earlier period of reform the per capita income of farmers increased faster than that of urban dwellers. Therefore, the ratio of per capita consumption in urban to per capita consumption in rural areas declined during the 1978 to 1984 period. In 1984, it reached a peak of 37.5% because of the

---

[36] Xinhua (2011). The outline of 12th Five-Year Plan for National Economic and Social Development (in Chinese), March 16, http://www.gov.cn/2011lh/content_1825838.htm.

[37] Li, G. and J. Woetzel. (2011). What China's five-year plan means for business. *McKinsey Quarterly*, July.

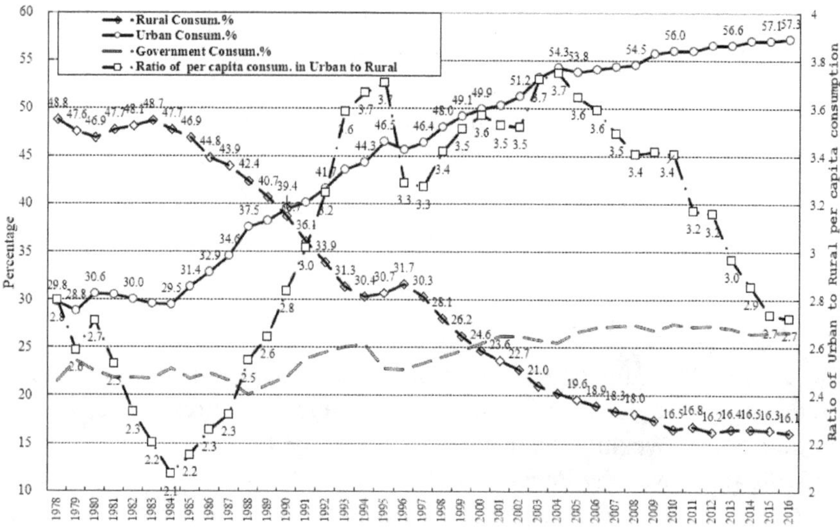

Figure 1.5.   Composition of China's consumption 1978–2016.

Sources: Calculated Using Data From China National Bureau of Statistics: National Data, Database: Gross Domestic Product by Expenditure Approach 1997–2016; All China Data Center, China Yearly Macro-Economic Statistics (National): Population of China 1949–2016; China National Bureau of Statistics: China Statistical Yearbook 2013, China Statistics Press, Table 3.1; 2010, Table 2.18.

contribution of township enterprises. However, China's agricultural sector remains weak because of its small scale and backward technology. When reform reached the urban areas, the disparity between urban and rural areas was magnified. From 2015 to 2016, however, the ratio of per capita consumption in urban areas to per capita consumption in rural areas dropped by 2.74% and 2.72%, respectively, most likely because of increasing emphasis on stable development of the agricultural sector and farm incomes.

Government policy up to that time had favored the development of a modern agricultural sector, but its implementation had not been effective. Therefore, the urban–rural divide still loomed large. The 12th FYP was expected to reduce this gap by focusing on increasing urbanization, partially by reforming the rigid and outmoded household registration system. The 12th FYP also provided an improved social safety net for China's rural population, including basic health care coverage and improved rural land distribution. China needs to double its GDP and per capita income of both urban and rural residents by 2020 (compared to 2010). China's economy has been transitioning from a phase of rapid growth to a stage of high-quality development. This is a pivotal stage for transforming the growth model, improving economic structure, and fostering new drivers of growth. To achieve high-quality growth under the new development concept, China must promote economic growth through innovation, prevent and resolve major risks, carry out targeted poverty alleviation programs, and prevent and control pollution. Issues relating to agriculture and the rural areas and their residents are fundamental to China because they directly concern the country's stability and people's well-being.

8.2. *Regional development*

As labor costs rise in China's eastern coast (see Table 1.5), the western region is expected to be more attractive to manufacturers. Long a government priority to drive development in that relatively less affluent region, the government will continue to grow the west through preferential policies such as land credit, lower taxes, and subsidies for manufacturers looking to locate inland. Although a small proportion of individuals has become extremely wealthy, income of many citizens has not kept pace with economic growth over the past decade. Therefore, income disparity needs to decline. The 12th FYP aimed at increasing income through raising minimum wage (the government announced its plan to increase minimum wages by 40% by 2015 as shown in Table 1.2). Other policy tools include the expansion of the government-funded social welfare and health care system and promoting labor-intensive service industries. Improved livelihoods are in turn expected to boost consumption as a percent of GDP growth, a key goal of the 12th FYP.

Official data from the National Bureau of Statistics (NBS) and the Ministry of Human Resource and Social Security showed that only nine regions increased their minimum wage in 2016. However, by the end of December 2017, 20 regions had adjusted their minimum wage with an average increase rate of 9.69%, which was higher than the previous year. This further illustrates the emphasis placed by the 13th FYP on people's well-being. As show in Table 1.6, the monthly minimum wage standards in various regions of the country by China Ministry of Human Resources

Table 1.5.   Monthly minimum wage by region 2010 and 2012 (Figure 1.6).

Eastern			Middle			Western		
	2012	2010		2012	2010		2012	2010
Shanghai	1450	1120	Shanxi	1125	850	Xinjiang	1160	960
Tianjin	1310	920	Hubei	1100	900	Ningxia	1100	710
Zhejiang	1310	1100	Henan	1080	800	Inner Mongolia	1050	900
Guangdong	1300	1030	Hunan	1020	850	Sichuan	1050	850
Beijing	1260	960	Anhui	1010	720	Shaanxi	1000	760
Shandong	1240	920	Jilin	1000	820	Guangxi	1000	820
Jiangsu	1140	960	Heilongjiang	880	880	Gansu	980	760
Liaoning	1100	900	Jiangxi	870	720	Tibet	950	950
Fujian	1100	900				Yunnan	950	830
Hebei	1100	900				Guizhou	930	650
Hainan	830	830				Qinghai	920	600
						Chongqing	870	680
Average	1195	958	Average	1011	818	Average	997	789
Growth rate yoy	11.7%		Growth rate yoy	11.2%		Growth rate yoy	12.4%	

Sources: Calculated Using Data From Li, J. (2013). 32 Provinces and Municipalities 2012 Minimum Wage Standard, (in Chinese), China News Network (Financial Channel) on April 27; China National Bureau of Statistics: China Statistical Yearbook 2013, China Statistics Press, Table 4.15.

and Social Security[38] in June 2019 has only four regions (Shanghai, Beijing, Chongqing, and Shanxi) implement the monthly minimum wage standards; Hebei still adopts the standard as of July 1, 2016. Therefore, in Figure 1.7, the monthly minimum wage comparisons for the 3 regions still use 2014–2016. In 2019, the monthly minimum wages in 27 provinces (excluding four major municipalities) accounted for 17.1–36.1% of the average monthly salary. The top 2 are Henan and Heilongjiang, accounted

---

[38] Calculated Using Data from Monthly Minimum Wage Standards in Various Regions of the Country (as of June 2019) Release Date: 2019-07-24. *Source*: Ministry of Human Resources and Social Security of the People's Republic of China.

Figure 1.6.   Monthly minimum wage by region 2010.

Source: Compiled government date.

for 36.1% and 33.2%, respectively; the bottom 2 are Tibet and Qinghai with 17.1% and 22.1%, respectively.

8.3. *Protecting the environment*

China's rapid industrialization, reliance on coal as the principal energy source, relatively large and energy-intensive manufacturing industry, and lax environmental protection and enforcement have caused severe environmental degradation. The 12th FYP addressed reducing pollution, increasing energy efficiency and ensuring a stable, reliable, and clean energy supply, as shown in Table 1.2. China's environmental goals have a far-reaching effect as they affect and shape a range of other industrial policies in a multitude of sectors. The 12th FYP contains preferential measures for developing energy-efficiency technology, as well as an expected mandatory energy emissions target of approximately 17% (down from the

Table 1.6.   Monthly minimum wages by region 2014–2016 and 2019.

Eastern	2017	2016	Middle	2017	2016	Western	2017	2016
Shanghai	2300	2190	Jilin	1780	1480	Xinjiang	1820	
Shenzhen	2130		Hubei	1750	1550	Inner Mongolia	1760	1640(15)
Zhejiang	2010	1860	Henan	1720	1600	Guizhou	1680	1600(15)
Tianjin	2050	1950	Shanxi	1680	1620	Yunnan	1670	
Beijing	2000	1890	Heilongjiang	1680	1480	Ningxia	1660	1480(15)
Guangdong	1895	1895	Jiangxi	1680		Shannxi	1680	1480(15)
Jiangsu	1890	1770	Hunan	1580	1390	Guangxi	1680	
Shandong	1810	1710	Anhui	1520		Tibet	1650	
Fujian	1700	1500				Gansu	1620	1470(15)
Hebei	1650	1650				Qinghai	1500	1600(15)
Liaoning	1620	1530				Sichuan	1500	
Hainan	1430	1430				Chongqing	1500	
0	1874	1761	Average	1674	1520	Average	1643	
0	6.4%		Growth rate yoy	10.1%		Growth rate yoy	11.1%	

Eastern	2019	Implement date	Middle	2019	Implement date	Western	2019	Implement date
Shanghai	2480	4/1/2019	Hunan	1900	10/1/2018	Xinjiang	1820	1/1/2018

Province	Wage	Date	Province	Wage	Date	Province	Wage	Date
Beijing	2200	7/1/2019	Henan	1900	10/1/2018	Inner Mongolia	1760	8/1/2017
Guangdong	2100	7/1/2018	Jilin	1780	10/1/2017	Guizhou	1680	7/1/2017
Tianjin	2050	7/1/2017	Hubei	1750	7/1/2016	Yunnan	1670	5/1/2018
Jiangsu	2020	8/1/2018	Shanxi	1700	10/1/2017	Ningxia	1660	10/1/2017
Zhejiang	2010	12/1/2017	Heilongjiang	1680	10/1/2017	Shannxi	1800	5/1/2019
Shandong	1910	6/1/2018	Jiangxi	1680	1/1/2018	Guangxi	1680	2/1/2018
Fujian	1700	7/1/2017	Anhui	1550	11/1/2018	Tibet	1650	1/1/2018
Hainan	1670	12/1/2018				Gansu	1620	6/1/2017
Hebei	1650	7/1/2016				Qinghai	1500	5/1/2017
Liaoning	1620	1/1/2018				Sichuan	1780	7/1/2018
						Chongqing	1800	1/1/2019
Average	2093		Average	1750		Average	1760	
Growth rate 17–19	5.7%		Growth rate 17–19	2.3%		Growth rate 17–19	3.5%	

Sources: Calculated Using Data from Yin, Z. and N. Marro. (2017). Minimum wage rises in the cities, stalls in the provinces, USCBC on January 24. https://www.chinabusinessreview.com/minimum-wage-rises-in-the-cities-stalls-in-the-provinces/; China Minimum Wage Updates 2017, SGS SAS, January 19, 2018, http://www.sgs.com/en/news/2018/01/safeguards-00518-china-minimum-wage-updates-2017.

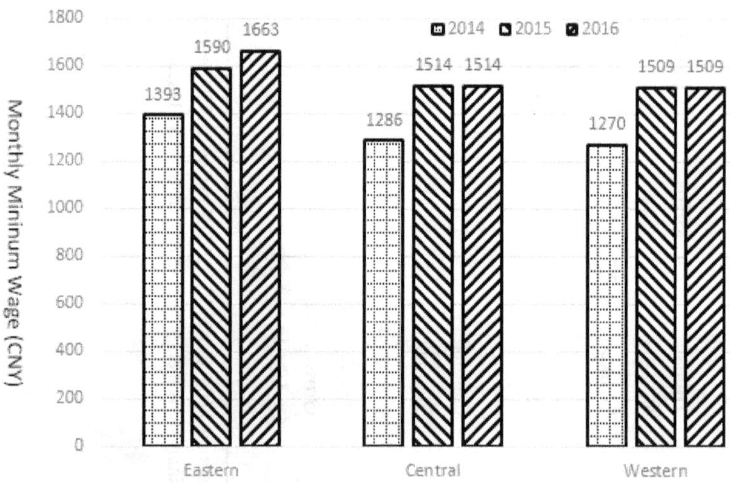

Figure 1.7. Comparison between geographic regions' monthly minimum wages from 2014 to 2016 (excluding four major municipalities).

11th FYP's 20%). This program contains green indicators that will hold local government officials accountable for promoting green development, such as water consumption per unit of GDP, and proportion of GDP that is invested in environmental protection. The 12th FYP set a target for reduction in carbon intensity by 17%, and an increase in the share in consumption of renewable energy options. This is in the broader context of China's 2020 goal of reducing carbon emissions by 40–45% per unit of GDP (that China pledged to the international society), especially for high-polluting and high-energy usage sectors. To meet that commitment, government officials have been debating the implementation of a carbon tax as well as some type of carbon trading system. The 12th FYP also contains measures for ensuring better environmental quality for cities and towns, including a "blue sky day" target and other mandatory emissions targets.

The 12th FYP reflects China's pledge to the international society to have 15% of its energy come from non-fossil fuels by 2020, from 8.1% in 2010 to approximately 11.4% by 2015 (see Figure 1.8). The Program includes a cap on domestic coal production, China's largest energy source and a major contributor to the country's environmental problems. The Program also contains significant support for nuclear and hydropower development with wind power seeing a threefold expansion in capacity.

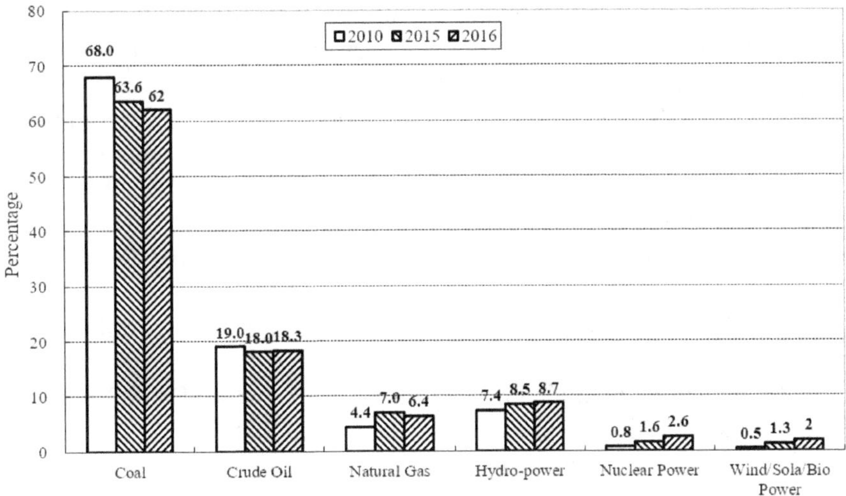

Figure 1.8. The composition of China's total energy consumption in the 12th FYP and in 2016.

Sources: Calculated Using Data From China National Bureau of Statistics: National Data, Database: Total Energy Consumption 2000–2016; China National Bureau of Statistics: China Statistical Yearbook 2012, China Statistics Press, Table 7.6; 2011, Table 7.2; Xinhua: The outline of the 12th FYP for National Economic and Social Development (in Chinese), March 16, 2011, http://www.gov.cn/2011lh/content_1825838.htm; Circular of the State Council issued on the "12th FYP" energy-saving emission reduction plan, August 22, 2012, on Gov.cn net.

Domestic natural gas consumption was set to increase during the 12th FYP period. In the first year of 13th FYP, green energy consumption (nuclear power, hydropower, and wind/Solar/Bio power) increased by 16.6%; during the five years of the 12th FYP, it only increased 32.6%.

9. Implications for Foreign Business

As China continues to stimulate demand and consumption at home, it is well on the way to becoming the world's largest consumer market. China has attracted over USD633 billion of foreign investment during the 12th FYP and USD270 billion in the first 2 years of the 13th FYP. This has enabled foreign businesses to be an important part of China's development and to share in the growing boom of the Chinese market. In 2010,

China invested nearly USD60 billion overseas, ranking first among developing countries. In 2009, overseas branches and subsidiaries of Chinese companies paid a total of USD10.9 billion in local taxes and hired a local work force of 438,000. In the 2009–2010 period, China gave a record loan amount of USD110 billion to other developing countries, higher than the World Bank.[39] In 2013, China's FDI inflows reached USD123.9 billion, ranking second in the world only after the United States (USD187.5 billion); invested FDI reached USD101 billion, after United States and Japan.[40]

In 2016 and 2017, China's FDI inflows reached USD133.7 billion and USD134.1 billion ranking third in the world after the United States and United Kingdom; China also invested USD196.1 and USD158.3 billion, ranking second in the world only after the United States.[41]

Changes to the business environment: If the objectives of the 12th FYP are ultimately achieved, foreign business can expect costs to both rise and fall. Increased costs could result from proposed minimum wage hikes, value-added tax hikes, raw materials resource price reforms, as well as the implementation of potential environmental insurance plans, carbon markets, and other environment-related taxes. However, there are benefits to foreign business embedded is this plan as well. Foreign companies can expect the government to continue its focus on opening-up China's service sectors, further developing its recruitment of talent through education reform and through strengthening the country's intellectual property regime. The government's plan to increase SEI's share of GDP through government investment should also yield significant opportunities for foreign companies because of the creation of incentives available to private investment. Foreign business should monitor China's SEI policy closely and look for opportunities to inject comment and input into its development. Foreign firms may also consider the use of partnerships with local companies to better access the significant funding opportunities available. Three sectors that will particularly stand to benefit as a result of the 12th FYP are energy/environment, technology, and health care. Not only have certain segments of these sectors been identified as SEIs, but

---

[39]Keynote Speech by H. E. Ambassador Liu Xiaoming at the Lunch Hosted by the Cardiff Business Club, March 7, 2011, Hilton Cardiff Hotel.

[40]United Nations Conference on Trade and Development (UNCTAD, 2014). World Investment Report 2014, Annex Tables 1 and 2.

[41]*Ibid.*

they also dovetail with the emphasis of the 12th FYP on "inclusive growth," another reason why they can expect to receive special policy backing and funding from the government. In conjunction with heavy government investment and preferential tax, fiscal, and procurement policies, government officials have emphasized the important role foreign investment will play in the development of the energy/environment, technology, and health care. Foreign business has been encouraged to establish R&D bases in China and will be allowed to apply with Chinese firms for government-funded R&D projects.

Energy and the Environment: Meeting China's increasing energy demand, while simultaneously reducing pollution, has been a long-term priority of the government. During the 11th FYP, for example, the government's allocation of CNY200 billion for energy efficiency and environmental protection measures allegedly created a large knock-off effect, generating an additional CNY2 trillion in economic activity. The government has stated that China's investment in the environmental protection industry during the 12th FYP period will exceed CNY3 trillion, with the industry growing by 15–20% annually, with a huge potential for international cooperation.

Technology: A key priority of the 12th FYP is for China to transition from "Made in China" to "Created in China." To achieve this goal, the government plans to heavily invest in science and technology education and R&D, further develop China's intellectual property rights system and support "Next-Generation IT" as an SEI. China's indigenous innovation drive will also continue to play a central role in this sector throughout the 12th FYP period.

Health Care: The 12th FYP focuses on creating a modern health care industry through continued health care reform, consolidating the pharmaceutical distribution sector, and encouraging significant investments in biotechnology. In 2009, China released an aggressive health care reform plan that included short-term objectives such as greatly expanding access to basic medical coverage for citizens, modernizing the country's health care infrastructure, and improving grassroots health care delivery. The 12th FYP supported these health care system reforms with specific policies and funding, including broader basic health care coverage, expanded infrastructure for grassroots medical networks, public awareness in disease prevention, improved health care administration, creation of national health care benchmarks and standards, and heavy investments in health care IT. There is also a need to restructure the Pharmaceutical Sector. The current structure of many of the 13,000 small distribution enterprises operating largely within the informal economy is a contributing factor to the high markup of drugs and risks for consumers buying fake or shoddy products. The government plans to consolidate the industry around one or two national-level companies, with revenues reaching CNY100 billion. At the regional level, the government plans to create 20 major companies, with sales of nearly CNY10 billion each. Biotechnology is recognized as an SEI because of the sector's potential for large productivity gains and its ability to solve health problems associated with China's rapidly aging society. The plan will support the development of innovative biotech products, high-end medical devices, and patented medicines. The government will reportedly put forth a spending package of more than CNY12 billion for R&D of new drugs from 2011 to 2015.

In the 13th FYP, China does not close its door to the world and will only "become more and more open." China commits to adopting policies to promote high-standard liberalization and facilitation of trade and investment, significantly "ease market access," and "protect the legitimate rights and interests" of foreign investors. "All businesses registered in China will be treated equally." The government also plans to build 11 high-standard pilot free trade zones and adopt practices that will ensure success of these zones.

10. The 14th FYP (2021–2025)

In December 2018, the National Development and Reform Commission met to evaluate the implementation of the 13th FYP and start the process for the formulation of the 14th FYP. The Plan is expected to continue the tradition established by Plans 11–13 with respect to addressing multiple welfare fronts: economic, social, and environmental. Almost two years later, from October 26 to 29, 2020 the 5th Plenum of the 19th Central Committee of the Chinese Communist Party was held. The event included an assessment of the 13th FYP and the formulation of Proposals for the articulation of the objectives and content of the 14th FYP (2021–2025) and an analysis of the country's goal to become a "modern socialist country" by 2035, the so-termed "Vision 2035." The final version of the Plan is expected to be ratified in March 2021, during the legislature's annual meeting.

10.1. *Assessment of the 13th FYP, the 2021 government work report and the 14th FYP*

The 13th FYP included 33 quantitative targets. By the end of 2019, China had met 24 of the 33 targets, and was on track to meet seven others. Two of the 33 will not be met: Services as a percent of GDP and R&D spending as a percent of GDP. The Plan, however, did succeed in lifting 56 million people from rural poverty, creating 60 million new jobs in urban areas, and providing medical insurance and pension benefits to 1 billion citizens.[42]

In March 2021, Premier Li Keqiang delivered the Government Work Report at the National People's Congress Annual Meeting. As part of the Report, Premier Li touted the country's accomplishments and its success-ful re-emergence following the 2020 global slowdown associated with the pandemic. The 14th FYP amplifies the innovation-driven development strategy proposed in previous Plans, especially the 13th FYP. The empha-sis is on technology-based innovation and self-reliance on developing and using innovation. In addition, the 14th FYP the following[43]:

1. **Dual circulation strategy (DCS):** DCS is viewed as the single most significant and over-reaching component of the Proposals. DCS refers to expansion of domestic demand, which will be the foundation of China's development strategy, while expanding the country's pres-ence abroad. To succeed in this strategy, the plan also emphasizes the need for reforming the supply-chain. China, then, will be able to meet the challenges of a changing environment.
2. **Deepening economic reform:** China Will Maintain and Further Improve the Basic Socialist Economic System, Continue to Allow the Market to Play a Decisive Role in Resource allocation, and integrate the operation of the market with that of a well-functioning govern-ment. While SOE reform and mixed-ownership reform will continue,

---

[42]European Institute for Asian Studies (2020). The 14th five-year plan: A high-speed road-map for China. https://www.eias.org/news/the-14th-five-year-plan-a-high-speed-roadmap-for-china/.

[43]PWC (2020). Interpretations on the 14th five-year plan and the long-range objectives through the year 2035. December. https://www.pwccn.com/en/research-and-insights/14th-five-year-plan-2035-goals-dec2020.html. Also, see Sutter, K. M. and M. D. Suthoerland. (2021). China's 14th five-year plan; A First Look. January 5. Congressional Research Service. https://crsreports.congress.gov.

the proper environment will be created for the private sector to flourish.

3. **Promotion of technological innovation:** The Plan emphasizes the importance of indigenous innovation and technology independence, while still in a position to access foreign technology. The southern city of Shenzhen will serve as the home of the pilot for the innovation activities.

4. **Environmental technologies and the environment:** The Plan includes policies that will improve China's environment, such as the proportion of vehicles to be environmentally friendly (electric or hybrid) by 2035. The advancement of environmental technologies builds on overall technological advancement. China will accelerate green and low-carbon development, and continuously improve over-all environmental quality.

5. **Manufacturing:** Technological advancements will also be applied to the manufacturing sector. The sector will use 5G, Big Data, digital technologies, and other advanced and green technologies to enhance China's degree of self-reliance.

6. **Food security and agriculture:** A new food security plan is being designed. Provincial governors will bear the responsibility for imple-menting appropriate security measures, increasing the province's capability, and diversifying sources for agricultural imports.

7. **Finance:** China is undertaking steps to move away from its depen-dence on the US dollar. The People's Bank of China (PBOC) is devel-oping a digital currency to be used in trade and finance.

8. **Standards, antitrust, and IP:** China's newly (2018) established mar-ket regulator, the State Administration for Market Regulation (SAMR), and the Academy of Engineering are teaming up to produce *China Standards 2035*. The document sets standards for the advancement of China's industrial objectives, including civilian and military stan-dards. The enforcement of antitrust and IPR will also be emphasized.

9. **Healthcare and human services:** The 14th FYP places an increased emphasis on public health services provided to the citizens. Also emphasized is the need to improve the education system and pensions and other services for the aged.

10. **Addressing inequalities:** Urban–rural and other types of inequa-lities will be addressed through employment, wage, and income

enhancements. Rural revitalization will remain an important focus of the Plan.

11. **Culture and "soft power":** The cultural sector will be continuously strengthened. China will also deliver its "soft power" to promote its socialist ideology.

12. **High-level opening-up and mutually beneficial cooperation:** Opening-up will be carried out in a deeper and more comprehensive manner to help China's economic development and strengthen its relations with the rest of the world pursuant to the spirit of economic globalization. Trade and investment barriers will fall further, and the rights of foreign partners will be respected as dictated by national treatment and adherence to the negative list. Internally, China will extend the use of free zones. Finally, RMB internationalization will remain an objective to be achieved in conjunction with capital account RMB convertibility.

As part of his report to the Congress, Premier Li reviewed the country's accomplishments and strategic success in responding to COVID-19. He also acknowledged the many development risks and challenges yet to be faced, but confirmed that China's economic fundamentals have remained unchanged, even through the setbacks caused by the pandemic. He also presented the projected targets for development in 2021. They are[44]:

- GDP growth rate of over 6%.
- Over 11 million new urban jobs.
- An urban unemployment rate of around 5.5%.
- CPI increase of around 3%.
- Continuous increase in imports and exports.
- Equilibrium Balance of Payments.
- Steady growth in personal income.
- Further improvement in the quality of the environment.
- A decrease of about 3% in energy consumption per unit of GDP.
- A continued decrease in major pollutant discharge.
- Grain output of over 650 million metric tons.

---

[44]Li, K. (2021). Report on the Work of the Government. Delivered at the 4th Session of the 13th National People's Congress of the People's Republic of China on March 5, 2021. http://www.xinhuanet.com/english/download/2021-3-12/report2021.pdf.

Table 1.7.   Comparing the 14th FYP with the 13th FYP.

2016 13th FYP	2021 14th FYP (*Predicted*)
Part I Guiding Thinking and Development Philosophy	Part I Guiding Ideology and Development Philosophy
Part II Innovation-Driven Development	Part II Innovation and Domestic R&D
Part III New Systems Development	Part III Modern Industrial System and Manufacturing Power
Part IV Agricultural Modernization	Part IV Dual Circulation Economy and Domestic Demand
Part V Optimized Modern Industrial System	Part V
Part VI The Cyber Economy	Part VI Rural Revitalization
Part VII Modern Infrastructure Networks	Part VII New Urbanization
Part VIII New Urbanization	Part VIII Regional Coordination and Spatial Planning
Part IX Development Coordinated Between Regions	Part IX Cultural Industries Development and Soft Power
Part X Ecosystems and the Environment	Part X Ecosystems and the Environment
Part XI All-Around Opening Up	Part XI New Style International Cooperation
Part XII Deeper Cooperation Mainland, Hong Kong and Macao	Part XII
Part XIII The Fight Against Poverty	Part XIII
Part XIV Better Education and Health for All Citizens	Part XIV Human Services in Education and Health
Part XV Support Public Wellbeing	Part XV Human Services in Employment, Ageing and Pensions
Part XVI Socialist Cultural and Ethical Progress	Part XVI
Part XVII Better and More Innovative Social Governance	Part XVII
Part XVIII Socialist Democracy and Rule of Law	Part XVIII
Part XIX Coordinated Economic and Defense Development	Part XIX New Style National Security
	Part XX Defense Forces Modernization

Source: Kenerdine, T. (2020). China's Fifth Communique, Especially When Compared to the 2015 Outcomes. *The Diplomat*, November 4. https://thediplomat.com/2020/11/chinas-fifth-plenum-old-goals-and-shifting-priorities/.

Table 1.7 contrasts the various aspects of the 14th FYP with those of the 13th FYP. The differences may be attributed to internal as well as external factors that China needs to address. Internally, despite the progress made under the 13th FYP, China still faces such challenges as income and wealth inequality, poverty, the environment, demographics, and the pandemic. Externally, China continues to deal with its soured relations with the US and a military threat from India. The 14th FYP, then, includes components that address these challenges beyond the extent to which they were dealt with in the 13th FYP. On the other hand, other issues, including financial reform, SOE reform, and quantitative GDP targets were either omitted or not as heavily emphasized as they were in previous FYPs.

11. Made in China (MIC) 2025

In May 2015, China's State Council introduced the MIC 2025 initiative. One of China's principal motivations behind the initiative was to avoid the so-called "middle-income gap." The middle-income gap phenomenon refers to the inability of rapidly developing economies to discover new sources of growth after exploiting the benefits of initial reforms. The solution: find new sources of growth. Therefore, instead of being the "factory of the world," China should be the birthplace of innovation. Furthermore, Chinese companies, while becoming self-sufficient, should move up the global supply chain.

MIC 2025 identifies nine priority tasks[45]:

1. Improving Manufacturing Innovation.
2. Technology/Industry Integration.
3. Strengthening the Industrial Base.
4. Fostering Chinese Brands.
5. Enforcing Green Manufacturing.
6. Promoting Breakthroughs in ten Key Sectors.
7. Advancing Restructuring of the Manufacturing Sector.
8. Promoting Service-oriented Manufacturing and Manufacturing-related Service Industries; and
9. Internationalizing Manufacturing.

---

[45]Morrison, W. (2019). The made in China 2025 initiative: economic implications for the United States. Congressional Research Service. Version 4, April 12. www.crs.gov.

MIC 2025 represents the first of three steps (the second being in 2035) culminating with China becoming the manufacturing innovation and technology global leader by 2049 (the 100th year anniversary of the PRC).

The initiative generated a sea of controversy from China's critics. It has been seen as a way for the State to further direct the allocation of resources and subsidize its domestic industry. Furthermore, the domestic content goals included in MIC 2025 are criticized as an expression of protectionism by the Chinese government. Reaction has been especially strong by the Trump Administration, which launched a Section 301 (national security grounds) investigation and responded by raising tariffs for Chinese imports to the United States. We further examine the US–China "trade-war" in the last chapter of this book.

MIC 2025 is a strategic plan, the guiding ideology of adhering to the decisive role of the market in resource allocation was established; adhere to innovation, intelligence, green, and sustainable concept of development; adhere to the idea of open cooperation, mutual benefit, and win–win. The Chinese government has always emphasized that MIC 2025 treats Chinese and foreign companies equally, and welcomes foreign companies to participate in the development of China's manufacturing industry. Since 2012, China's industry value added (constant 2010 USD) was USD3,666.2 billion exceeding the U.S. industrial value-added of USD3,034.5 billion. According to WDI data, in 2017, China's Industry value added accounted for 21.0% of the World, the United States and Japan were 14.3% and 8.5%, respectively. However, China's per capita industry value added is much lower than other countries, as shown in Table 1.8, where it is only 6.9%, 15.3%, 20.9%, and 72.3% of Norway, Japan, the United States, and the World, respectively.

At present, in the MIC 2025 smart manufacturing, green manufacturing, and other engineering construction, there are companies from many countries and regions such as the United States, Germany, and the United Kingdom that participate and cooperate. For example, from June 12th to 14th, 2016, German Chancellor Angela Merkel visited China for the 9th time, co-chaired the 4th round of Sino-German government consultations with Li Keqiang, and promoted the in-depth docking of MIC 2025 with Germany's "Industry 4.0" as a highlight. Among them, cars are the highlight. After channel integration, Mercedes-Benz's sales in China have grown rapidly. The latest data show that in May 2016, Mercedes-Benz global sales were 183,400 units, a 13% increase yoy; that month,

Table 1.8. Industry value added per worker (constant 2010 USD); China compared with selected other countries.

Country	Industry value-added per worker 2010 (USD)	Rank
Norway	310,612	1
Singapore	143,827	8
Japan	117,562	18
United States	103,366	22
South Korea	70,137	36
World	29,847	71
Russian Federation	25,977	82
China	21,567	102

Sources: Calculated using data from World Development Indicators (2019); Last updated 12/20/2019.

Mercedes-Benz sold 38,000 units in China, a surge of 38.9% yoy, setting a new sales record for the same period. Another example is the US Tesla Shanghai Gigafactory groundbreaking ceremony in Shanghai, January 7, 2019. The 50 billion CNY (USD7.3 billion) plant is the company's first factory outside the United States and the first automobile production project wholly owned by foreign capital in China. The first automobile production project wholly owned by foreign capital in China. The first Chinese-made Tesla (TSLA) Model 3 cars started arriving November 22, 2019. The cars have a starting price of 355,800 yuan (USD50,623), making them about 2% cheaper than an imported model. Shanghai Tesla is targeting annual production of 150,000 units of the Model 3. U.S. electric vehicle maker Tesla and a group of China banks have agreed on a new 10 billion yuan (USD1.4 billion), five-year loan facility for the automaker's Shanghai car plant. China Construction Bank (CCB), Agricultural Bank of China (ABC), Industrial and Commercial Bank of China (ICBC), and Shanghai Pudong Development Bank (SPDB) are among the banks that have agreed to give Tesla the financial support.[46]

---

[46]Misinterpreting "Made in China 2025"-Interview with Zhao, C. (Minister of Industrial Economics Research, Development Research Center of the State Council) (in Chinese); Wang, R. "Made in China 2025" docked with "Industry 4.0" in Germany, 2016-06-24. (in

After initiating the reforms, China's economy has shown a sustained and rapid growth, various social initiatives were undertaken, the overall strength of the country was intensified, and the standard of living improved notably. China has smoothly transited from CPE to a basically market-oriented economy. Of course, China is still facing serious problems and difficulties. Only by sustaining economic growth based on better performance can the country mitigate the operational problems facing enterprises, alleviate unemployment pressure, make structural adjustments possible, balance regional disparity, further improve living standards, and deepen reforms. This is also essential to increase the state revenue, prevent financial risks, and maintain social stability. However, recent insufficient domestic consumption demand is a reflection of inadequate purchasing power and the lagging nature of supply structure compared to demand structure. To meet domestic demand and further stimulate growth, China must accelerate its strategic restructuring of the economy. Adjustment and optimization of the economic structure should be market-oriented, rely on scientific and technological advances, and adopt new systems and methods compatible with the development of a resource saving, and environment-friendly "green economy." Developing western China, revitalizing the northeast and other traditional industrial bases, and energizing the central region will receive strategic priority as the government channels more funds, technologies, and talents to these regions. Development of China's western regions will focus on infrastructure facilities, ecological, and environmental protection.

12. Setting a Future Direction for China: Building a Modern Economic System[47]

The year 2019 marked the 70th anniversary of the People's Republic of China. It also marked the completion of almost 40 years since the first

---

Chinese); Shanghai Plant Shows Tesla's Ambition, *China Daily* 2019-01-08; The First Shanghai-Made Teslas are now Rolling out Across China, by He, L. (2019). *CNN Business,* November 22. Tesla to Take New $1.4 billion Loan from Chinese Banks for Shanghai factory, Reuters, December 23, 2019.

[47]Xi, J. (2017). Secure a Decisive Victory in Building a Moderately Prosperous Society in All Respects and Strive for the Great Success of Socialism with Chinese Characteristics for a New Era Delivered at the 19th National Congress of the Communist Party of China:

FYP under the post-Mao regime was adopted (the 6th FYP overall). The question, of course, is "where to now, China?"

Chairman Xi provided a partial answer to this question in his speech delivered at the 19th National Congress of the Communist Party on October 18, 2017. In his speech, Xi emphasized some important ideas: remaining true to our original aspiration … holding high the banner of socialism with Chinese characteristics … building a moderately prosperous society in all respects … and working tirelessly to realize the Chinese Dream of national rejuvenation. Of course, Xi's speeches contain important messages for the country. According to the traditional sense of the relationship between the political systems, a one-Party system is associated with a CPE. However, China aimed at building an economic system that defies conventional wisdom, market socialism. The divergence between political and economic ideology does not imply that the political system has no influence on the economy. We have indeed learned about the relationship between the State and the economy by our journey through China's FYPs. Therefore, Xi's statements carry implications for China's political landscape as well as its economic future.

Xi emphasized the two centenary goals: realizing the dream of national rejuvenation and steadily improving people's lives. To accomplish these goals, Xi put forth the following components of the national strategy:

1. **Furthering supply-side structural reform:** Focus will be on the real economy by improving the quality of the supply system and enhancing the economy's strength in terms of quality.
2. **Making China a country of innovators:** China will strive to be at the frontiers of science and technology, strengthen basic research, and make major breakthroughs in basic research and original innovations.
3. **Pursuing a rural vitalization strategy:** Systems, mechanisms, and policies will be put together to promote the development of agriculture and rural areas.
4. **Implementing the coordinated regional development strategy:** More effort will be directed to the development of the western, central, and northeast regions.

Part V. Applying a New Vision of Development and Developing a Modernized Economy, October 18.

5. **Accelerating efforts to improve the socialist market economy:** China will improve its property rights system to ensure market-based resource allocation, improve management of state assets.
6. **Making new ground in pursuing opening up on all fronts:** China will become more and more open. It will pursue the Belt and Road Initiative as a priority and give equal attention to "bringing in" and "going global."

Xi's statements loom big in determining where China is going in the future. The strategy components are not associated with specific timelines, but they warrant our attention in enabling us to understand China's future development.

13. The Sixth Plenum of the 19th Central Committee

The importance of Xi's statements became even more evident in the early part of November 2021. On November 8–12, the Chinese leadership gathered for the sixth plenary session of the 19th Party Congress. Commonly known as the Sixth Plenum, the four-day meetings saw the Central Committee, comprising more than 300 top party members, adopt a rare resolution on the "major achievements and historical experience" of the Communist Party of China (CPC) in the 100 years since its founding as well as its "future directions." In the "new era," Chinese authorities can be expected to further intensify efforts to build a more self-reliant, sustainable, and inclusive economy at home, while pursuing an increasingly assertive foreign policy abroad.

Over the course of its five-year terms, the Central Committee holds seven plenary sessions, meeting at least annually to assess China's political and socio-economic development. The Sixth Plenums are often notable for unveiling significant planned changes in China's future course of development — closing the page on one chapter and opening another. They usually focus on ideology and CPC affairs (see Appendix 1.C. for the characteristics and important resolutions of each Sixth Plenum since reform and opening-up). However, this year's conclave was even more important than usual, as it took place at a critical historic juncture in the CPC's plans to achieve "national rejuvenation" through two centennial goals. After President Xi announced in July that the first goal of building a "moderately prosperous society" had been completed, China embarked on its official journey toward realizing the second goal of becoming a "great modern socialist country" by 2049, the 100th anniversary of the founding of the PRC.

The Central Committee also passed a resolution to hold the 20th Party Congress in the second half of 2022, as China's latest political cycle ends. This will see a significant shakeup in the Chinese leadership, as some senior officials retire, and others move up in the hierarchy. At the previous Sixth Plenary Sessions of the Central Committee, at least one important resolution was passed, and the guiding ideology and tasks with the characteristics of the times were clarified (see Table C1).

The Sixth Plenary Session of the 19th Central Committee of the Party was a meeting of great historical significance held at an important historical juncture. The most important outcome of the plenary session was the deliberation and approval of the "Resolution of the Central Committee of the Communist Party of China on the Party's Major Achievements and Historical Experience in a Century of Struggle" (hereinafter referred to as the "Resolution").

Throughout the "Resolution," a fusion is presented of the struggle, sacrifice, and creation of the Communist Party of China in fulfilling the original mission of seeking happiness for the Chinese people and for the rejuvenation of the Chinese nation. "Can continue to succeed" is a Marxist programmatic document, a political manifesto for Chinese Communists in the new era to keep in mind their original mission, adhere to and develop socialism with Chinese characteristics, and use history as a mirror to create the future and realize the great rejuvenation of the Chinese nation.

Four characteristics of the content of the "Resolution" are worth noting here[48]:

1. The first feature is that it mainly summarizes the major achievements and historical experience of the party's centuries of struggle.
2. The second feature is to highlight the focus of the new era of socialism with Chinese characteristics and use a larger space to summarize the original ideas, transformative practices, breakthrough progress,

---

[48] Communiqué of the Sixth Plenary Session of the 19th Central Committee of the Communist Party of China, http://en.qstheory.cn/2021-11/12/c_680818.htm.

and landmark achievements since the 18th National Congress of the Communist Party of China.

3. It was stressed at the session that Chinese communists, with Comrade Xi Jinping as their chief representative, have established Xi Jinping Thought on Socialism with Chinese Characteristics for a New Era on the basis of adapting the basic tenets of Marxism to China's specific realities and its fine traditional culture, upholding Mao Zedong Thought, Deng Xiaoping Theory. He is thus the principal founder of Xi Jinping Thought on Socialism with Chinese Characteristics for a New Era. This is the Marxism of contemporary China and of the 21st century. It embodies the best of the Chinese culture and ethos in our times and represents a new breakthrough in adapting Marxism to the Chinese context.

4. The Party has established Comrade Xi Jinping's core position. It was stated at the session that the Central Committee, with Comrade Xi Jinping at its core, has demonstrated great historical initiative, tremendous political courage, and a powerful sense of mission. Keeping in mind both domestic and international imperatives, the Central Committee has implemented the Party's basic theory, line, and policy and provided unified leadership for advancing our great struggle, great project, great cause, and great dream.

As only the third such document enacted by the CPC, the world's largest political organization, the new resolution elevated President Xi's status in the CPC's history and laid the groundwork for him to secure a landmark third term in office next year. The first two proclamations were passed in 1945 and 1981 under Mao Zedong and Deng Xiaoping. President Xi is now enshrined as a crucial historical figure on par with the two former paramount leaders, providing an important boost to his legacy. Notably, the communique adopted at the Sixth Plenum credited President Xi for the first time in an official document as the "principal founder" of Xi Jinping Thought on Socialism with Chinese Characteristics for a New Era.

The communique underscored how China has "achieved the tremendous transformation from standing up and growing prosperous to becoming strong." Looking ahead, the country will forge ahead on the "new journey that lies before us in the new era" and fulfill the second centenary goal by 2049, according to the document. This new era has been highlighted by the

Chinese leadership for years, but the resolution appears to mark its official commencement.

14. Common Prosperity

Observing China and its economy is not a task for the fainthearted. The reforms made during the post-1978 period brought about changes that are unprecedented in the annals of global economic history. China's economy has grown in terms of both size and quality. However, there are plenty of challenges ahead. One of the most daunting such challenges facing China's policymakers is the persistent and multi-faceted economic inequality. We will be further discussing the issue of economic inequality in Chapter 5. For discussion purposes, however, we present Table 1.9. The table shows the extent to which the per-capita income (in terms of current USD) of various

Table 1.9. Four provinces and three cities raise the country, and 22 provinces are grateful.

	Regional per capita income: departure from national average, 2019				
Guangdong	8,307	Hainan	−332	Inner Mongolia	−1418
Shanghai	8,202	Shanxi	−563	Guangxi	−1642
Beijing	7,310	Ningxia	−586	Hunan	−1662
Jiangsu	4,091	Chongqing	−594	Yunnan	−1723
Zhejiang	3,274	Shaanxi	−796	Guizhou	−1739
Shandong	2,152	Hubei	−849	Tibet	−1739
Tianjin	2,136	Hebei	−990	Gansu	−1924
Fujian	427	Qinghai	−1140	Xinjiang	−2085
Liaoning	67	Jiangxi	−1171	Henan	−2138
		Anhui	−1188	Heilongjiang	−2255
		Jilin	−1315	Sichuan	−2381

Sources: China Financial Yearbook (2019); China Tax Yearbook (2029); Yuekai Securities Research Institute book (2019); Yuekai Securities Research Institute (2019, in Chinese).

provinces and cities/municipalities deviates from the national average. So, Guangdong's per capita income in 2019 was USD8,307 higher than the average; Sichuan Province's was USD2,381 below the national average. Indeed, a few regions are above average, while most are below average.

At the conclusion of the first centennial, China has become a moderately prosperous society. Building the country into a great modern socialist nation has now become the goal for the second centennial. In October 2020, the Fifth Plenum of the 19th Central Committee approved the proposals included in the 14th Five-Year Plan and The Long-Range Objectives Through the Year 2035. One of the proposals brought forward included the goal of Common Prosperity. Common Prosperity refers to "shared influence, both in material and cultural terms."[1] Another way of expressing the meaning of the concept is "to get rich (prosperity) together (common)." The concept of Common Prosperity is not new. It first appeared in the *People's Daily* on December 12, 1953, as a way of illustrating the benefits of socialism.[49] Deng Xiaoping presented another perspective of socialism by positing that some sectors of the economy could prosper before others, while common prosperity would follow at a later stage of the country's development. The conclusion of the CPC's first centennial was the appropriate time to place common prosperity on the forefront of its priorities. In an article published in *Qiushi*, Xi Jinping wrote "Common prosperity is an essential requirement of socialism and an important feature of Chinese-style modernization. The common prosperity we are talking about is the common prosperity of all people. It is the prosperity of all people in their material and spiritual (and moral) lives. Common prosperity does not mean prosperity for a (selected) few, nor is it neat and tidy egalitarianism."[50] According to Xi, common prosperity will be accomplished in stages. Thus, by 2025 (end of 14th Five-Year Plan), the country will have taken a solid step toward common prosperity and the income and consumption gap will have been reduced. Common prosperity will become more visible for all Chinese by 2035. Finally, by 1949 (coinciding with the centennial of the PRC), common

---

[49]Hass, R. (2021). Assessing China's "common prosperity" campaign. Brookings, September 9; https://www.brookings.edu/blog/order-from-chaos/2021/09/09/assessing-chinas-common-prosperity-campaign/.

[50]Xi, J. (2021). To firmly drive common prosperity. *Quishi*, October 18. As translated by Adam Ni. https://www.neican.org/to-firmly-drive-common-prosperity/.

prosperity will be achieved for all citizens and the income-consumption gap will be within a reasonable range.[51]

The pursuit of common prosperity has been characterized as both a challenge and a contribution. It is a challenge because it is a cause that, according to its proponents, is unparalleled and unequaled. It is also a contribution to the world by presenting an entirely new concept.[52] Common prosperity must provide equal opportunities for development and help those left behind in society. And it takes government and market cooperation to provide for an efficient approach to common prosperity.[53]

To accomplish common prosperity, China must create the appropriate economic and social environment. The institutional infrastructure must be conducive to income and wealth distribution; the middle-income group must increase; incomes of the low-income groups must rise; excessive incomes must be reined in through means such as taxation and transfer payments; and illicit incomes prohibited.[54]

Zhenjiang Province provided the appropriate environment for a pilot program leading to common prosperity for the entire country. The province set up targets for addressing urban–rural inequalities, strengthening the training of its workforce, and involving the private sector in the process. As the Province is also the headquarters of many successful private companies, these companies were called upon to contribute to the province's efforts by sharing their success. Indeed, Alibaba pledged CNY100 billion (about USD15.5 billion) by 2025. Other companies followed. Tencent pledged to donate CNY50 billion to low-income groups, healthcare, and education. Wang Xing, founder of Meituan, donated 10% of his equity in the company to his philanthropic foundation.[55]

---

[51] *Ibid.*

[52] Lu, X. (2021). Common prosperity: A challenge and a contribution. Xinhua, September 13. https://news.cgtn.com/news/2021-09-14/Common-prosperity-A-challenge-and-a-contribution-13ytz1UWcZW/index.html (in Chinese).

[53] Li, D. and K. Li. (2021). The path to common prosperity with Chinese characteristics. December 20. http://www.china.org.cn/china/2021-12/20/content_77941955.htm (in Chinese).

[54] *Global Times* (2021). China's common prosperity in numbers, September 1. https://www.globaltimes.cn/page/202109/1233098.shtml (in Chinese).

[55] Taplin, N. and J. Wong. (2021). Common prosperity: Decoding China's new populism. *Wall Street Journal*, August 21. https://www.wsj.com/articles/common-prosperity-decoding-chinas-new-populism-11630159381).

China's common prosperity goal has important implications for the rest of the world. If the initiatives undertaken turn the policymakers' attention toward the domestic economy, then dealing with a more isolated and self-sufficient China may be more challenging. On the other hand, the rest of the world will benefit by a significant increase in the size of the country's middle class.

Discussing "common prosperity" at a concluding press conference on the Sixth Plenum's guiding principles, a senior official stressed that, "enterprises must operate legally and honestly, treat employees kindly and create wealth, which is the right way for business." It will be critical for companies to demonstrate their support for the national movement toward "common prosperity" and not be perceived as a hindrance to it. Otherwise, they could face serious risks to their future business prospects in China.

15. Chapter Summary and Concluding Comments

Forty plus years of reform and opening up have brought about historic changes in China's development — the planned economic system has been smashed gradually and a market economic system has basically shaped up, creating a rocketing economy that is now the second largest in the world. While boosting the economy, China has tried to maintain a balanced development, including social security, health, and education. China's booming economy is providing residents with ever-rising living standards and a better quality of life.

In addition to enabling the Chinese to lead better lives, China's gain in prosperity benefits the rest of the world. In 1978, China's GDP accounted for only 1.1% of the world economy, whereas its share rose to 12.6% in 2017.[56] In 1978, China's share of global trade was 9.65%. In 2017, its share jumped to about 38.14%.[57] China's development has opened a huge market for international capital, attracting USD2,149.2 billion of realized foreign investment value during 1979–2017, accounting for 17.3% GDP (2017).[58]

---

[56] Calculated Using Data from World Bank: World Development Indicators 2014 Online, Released 2019.

[57] *Ibid.*, Released 2020.

[58] Statistical Bulletin of FDI in China 2019, Ministry of Commerce of the People' Republic of China; China National Bureau of Statistics: China Statistical Yearbook 2018, China Statistics Press, Table 3.3.

Direct overseas investment by Chinese companies had also grown substantially to USD129.8 billion in 2018, accounted for 12.8% of the World, only after Japan (14.1%).[59] China now contributes to 27.9% of global economic growth in 2017[60] and 13.7% of global trade expansion in 2017.[61]

Despite the new-found wealth, prosperity has come at a price. One negative effect is serious environmental damage. Exploitation of natural resources, ecological degradation, and environmental pollution has outweighed China's economic benefits in recent years. Another problem is the uneven distribution of wealth. Official data from 2007 showed the country's Gini Coefficient, which measures the inequality of income distribution, has surpassed the warning mark of 0.4. Regional disparity remains big. Meanwhile, economic operations in China now face a series of challenges and uncertainties.

Let us now provide highlights of the changes in the formulation of China's FYPs.[62]

1. The FYP was renamed as the Five-Year Program during the 11th FYP period.
2. The center of plan formulation shifted from setting growth targets to putting forward development strategies. In line with these strategies, policies are formulated to meet the needs of governance reform and public goods provision. For environmental protection purposes, binding targets are introduced to save energy and reduce greenhouse gas emission.
3. A simple general plan is expanded to a comprehensive plan set, with special long-term plans and spatial plans playing an increasingly important role. Efforts are made to keep plans of various kinds internally consistent and mutually reinforcing.
4. De-centralized decision-making is promoted to give local governments more autonomy in the formulation of local plans.

---

[59] Calculated Using Data From UNCTAD: World Investment Report 2019, Annex Table 2. FDI Outflows, by Region and Economy, 1990–2018.

[60] Calculated Using Data From World Bank: World Development Indicators 2020 Online, Released 2020.

[61] *Ibid.*

[62] World Wide Fund for Nature (WWF, 2010). The Formulation of China's Major Plans and Programs 2008–2010 and Onwards, October 12.

5. The planning process is changed from a closed one to an open one, with a high degree of transparency and public participation. For example, as many as 160 pre-study projects of the 11th Plan were contracted out to institutes at home and abroad. An agency was set up at NDRC to collect suggestions and opinions from the public.
6. The planning process and procedures become increasingly standardized.

Therefore, the 13th FYP aimed at achieving more balanced, inclusive, and sustainable development by coordinating a range of economic indicators; promoting advanced manufacturing and agricultural modernization; becoming an innovation-driven nation; further increasing consumption's contribution to economic growth; narrowing the income gap, eliminating poverty and improving people's livelihood through expanding public services on employment, education, culture, social security, and health care; further opening up its economy; strenuously promoting environmental protection and low carbon growth.

The 14th FYP, MiC 2025, and Vision 2035 are building the foundations for a new China, one that emphasizes its internal strengths while competing globally with the world's most advanced economies. Technological innovation, advanced manufacturing, rural revitalization, health care, and pensions, "soft power," and other concepts will be emphasized in the years ahead, while there is a promise for reform deepening.

Our discussion about China's economic reforms and its FYPs raises an interesting question: What kind of economic system does China have now, and what is its system of the future?

Economists and other scholars have for centuries felt compelled to classify economic systems under a particular "ism." Following that practice, China's current system has been widely branded as "market socialism." The characterization is probably accurate, but perhaps too simplistic. Thus, in our review of China's FYPs, we saw that China marked a unique path is in its departure from pure Soviet-style planning. As Hu (2013) states, China did not merely replace the Plan for the Market, like other former socialist economies attempted to do. Instead, it replaced the Plan with the Plan and the Market. The Market is still functioning in allocating resources. In addition, the State uses the Plan to achieve its social development objectives. The two elements have a symbiotic relationship, with each reinforcing the other's existence and success.

As we go through this book, then, we should keep in mind that we are exploring an economic system that is unlike anything the world has seen before. Indeed, we are witness to one of the most disruptive developments in the history of the world economy. The bad news, of course, is that the system is also much more complicated than the traditional market-based or plan-based alternatives.

Selected Bibliography

Baum, R. (1980). *China's Four Modernizations: The New Technological Revolution*. Boulder, Colorado: Westview Press.

Chi, F. (Ed.) (2016). *Breakthroughs in Transformation: The 13th Five Year Plan Period: Historical Challenges for Structural Reform*. Beijing: China Intercontinental Press.

Hu, A. (2013). The Distinctive Transition of China's Five-Year Plans. Modern China, 39(6), November, 629–639.

Kornai, J. (1979). *Economics of Shortage*. Amsterdam: North-Holland.

Li, K. (2021). Report on the work of the government. Delivered at the fourth session of the 13th National People's Congress of the People's Republic of China on March 5, 2021. http://www.xinhuanet.com/english/download/2021-3-12/report2021.pdf.

Morrison, W. (2019). The made in China 2025 initiative: Economic implications for the United States. Congressional Research Service. Version 4, April 12. www.crs.gov.

Williamson, J. (1990). What Washington means by reform. In Williamson, J (ed.). *Latin American Adjustment: How much has Happened?* Washington, D.C., April 5–20.

World Bank (1992). Price reform in China. Report No. 10414-CHA, May 28.

Xi, J. (2017). Secure a decisive victory in building a moderately prosperous society in all respects and strive for the great success of socialism with Chinese characteristics for a new era delivered at the 19th National Congress of the Communist Party of China: Part V. Applying a New Vision of Development and Developing a Modernized Economy, October 18.

Appendix 1.A.   Highlights of China's reforms.

Year	Events
1978	Third Plenary Session declares reform and opening-up as approach to build a modern socialist China.
1979	Establishment of Special Economic Zones (Shenzhen, Shantou Xiamen, Zhuhai).
1982	Household Responsibility System Established.
1984	14 Coastal cities designated Economic and Technical Development Zones.
1986	Management Responsibility System Established.
1990	Shanghai Stock Exchange opens.
	Pudong New Area of Shanghai established.
1992	Deng Tours southern China.
	Ten cities are designated for preferential policies.
	Six Development Zones are established along the Yantzhe River Valley.
1996	Currency becomes convertible on Current Account.
2001	China joins the WTO.
2005	China becomes world's fourth largest economy.
	RMB is freed from dollar peg.
2013	China proposes the Belt and Road Initiative.
	The Asian Infrastructure Investment Bank (AIIB) is launched.
	First Pilot Free-Trade Zone established in Shanghai (Pudong).
2015	Renminbi joins Special Drawing Rights (SDR).
2016	We have been vigorously advancing supply-side structural reform.
	and taking the initiative to adjust the relationship between supply and demand.
	Pursue an innovation-driven development strategy to create stronger growth drivers.
2017	Secure a Decisive Victory in Building a Moderately Prosperous Society in All Respects.
	18th CPC Central Committee called for "innovative, green, balanced, open and shared" development.
2018	The National Development and Reform Commission and the Ministry of Commerce released the shortened negative list for FTZs on Saturday, The new list reduces the number of sectors restricted for foreign investors to 45 in all free trade zones, from 95 last year. It is effective after July 30.
	We must uphold the basic economic system and give full play to micro, small, and medium-sized enterprises and the private sector in economic and social development.

Appendix 1.A.   (*Continued*)

Year	Events
	To further open the Chinese market and expand imports, China is holding the China International Import Expo (CIIE), the world's first import-themed national-level exhibition. The Expo is conducive to achieving better development, promoting economic globalization, liberalizing trade, and creating a "beautiful opportunity" for global development.
	Plans for expansion of the Shanghai Pilot Free Trade Zone to include a new section Stock Exchange and experiment with a registration system for listed companies.
	Support for integrated development of the Yangtze River Delta region. The region will develop in tandem with the Belt and Road Initiative (BRI), the Beijing-Tianjin-Hebei coordinated development area, the Yangtze River Economic.
	Best, and the Guangdong–Hong Kong–Macao Greater Bay Area.
	Boao Forum for Asia to highlight rereform, opening-up, innovation.
2019	Premier Li Keqiang said on March 5, when delivering government work report at the opening of the session of the second session of the 13th National People's Congress, that China will step up reform and opening-up to improve market mechanisms and foster new strengths in international economic cooperation and competition.
	China will work to diversify export markets. The Ministry of Commerce has already unveiled a list of 30 key markets for foreign trade expansion, which will see China actively tap into the potential of emerging and developing economies under the Belt and Road Initiative while continuing to explore the traditional markets in the developed world.
	China will improve import mix while actively expanding import volume. China is committed to building an open world economy. China will hold the second import expo this year, which will attract more participants and further boost imports and consumption.
	The country will take more effective measures to attract foreign investment in 2019. It will further relax controls over market access, shorten the negative list for foreign investment, and permit foreign-funded enterprises to operate in more sectors, according to the government work report.
	Xi Jinping presided over the 11th meeting of the Central Committee for deepening overall reform on November 26.

(*Continued*)

Appendix 1.A.   (*Continued*)

Year	Events
	The meeting reviewed and approved a series of documents concerning market-based allocation of factors of production, systems for supporting and protecting agriculture, medical insurance system reform, labor education in primary and secondary schools and colleges, modernization of the environmental governance system, education supervision system reform, and agricultural technology services.
2020	Xi specified the requirements in a speech on June 30 at the 14th meeting of the Central Committee for deepening overall reform. The breakthrough and leading role of reforms must be given full play for the country to achieve the goals and tasks outlined in the 13th Five-Year Plan, win the battle against poverty, complete the building of a moderately prosperous society in all respects, and embark on a new journey toward building a modern socialist country, said Xi, who heads the committee. The meeting reviewed and approved a series of reform plans and guidelines on State-Owned Enterprises (SOEs), the integrated development of new generation information technology and the manufacturing industry, the rural homestead system, the integrated development of media, the education evaluation system, and the State-Owned art troupes.
	With China's social and economic development stepping into a new stage, the country's leadership has decided to follow the "dual circulation" development pattern, which is centered on the domestic economy ("internal circulation") and aims to integrate the domestic economy with the global economy ("external circulation") to achieve overall healthy economic development. To achieve this goal, China needs to improve the domestic supply chains, so as to fully meet domestic demand and strike a dynamic balance between domestic supply and demand during the 14th Five-Year Plan (2021–25).
	President Xi Jinping on November 12 called for new roles and new missions for Shanghai's Pudong as the country celebrates the 30th anniversary of the area's development and opening-up. Xi urged the achievement of major innovations in basic science and technology and major breakthroughs in key and core technologies, and called for accelerated creation of world class industrial clusters in sectors including integrated circuits, bio-medicine, and artificial intelligence in Pudong. Xi made the remarks while presiding over the 17th meeting of the Central Committee for deepening overall reform. The meeting also reviewed and approved a series of guidelines and plans on integrating the Party's leadership into corporate governance of centrally administered State-Owned Enterprises (SOEs), developing an economic system.

Appendix 1.A.   (*Continued*)

Year	Events
	for green and low-carbon circular development, law-based environmental information disclosure, administrative data-sharing, deepening reforms on budget management, enhancing ideological and political work, improving tax law enforcement, and establishing a financial court in Beijing.
2021	President Xi stressed full, accurate, and comprehensive implementation of the new development philosophy, as well as the crucial role of reform in establishing a new development paradigm. He made the remarks while presiding over the 18th meeting of the Central Committee for deepening overall reform.
	The meeting also reviewed and approved a series of guidelines including those on improving the price control mechanism of important livelihood commodities, promoting high-quality development of public hospitals, enhancing regulatory capacity-building for pharmaceuticals, and establishing and improving the value realization mechanism of ecological products. Significant progress has been made in deepening economic reforms over the past year, the meeting concluded.
	The meeting stressed the essential role of reforms in establishing the new development paradigm, while calling for efforts to remove institutional barriers that restrict the improvement of core competitiveness of science and technology. The meeting urged efforts to expand domestic demand in deepening reform, improve systems and mechanisms for coordinated regional development and integrated urban–rural development, as well as accelerate the development of a new type of urbanization that puts people at the core. China should push forward high-level opening-up, fostering a market-oriented, law-based, and internationalized business.
	To foster the development of Small- and Medium-Enterprises, the Beijing Stock Exchange opened on November 15.

Source: Author calculation and Reuters Staff (2008). TIMELINE: China's Milestones Since 1978, September 8. https://www.reuters.com/article/us-china-reforms-chronology-sb/timeline-china-milestones-since-1978-idUKTRE4B711V20081208.

Appendix 1.B.   Details of the first ten five-year plans.

Plan/ Program	Years	Plan objectives	Result
First	1953–1957	To concentrate efforts on the construction of 694 large and medium-sized industrial projects, including 156 with the aid of the Soviet Union, so as to lay down the primary foundations for China's socialist industrialization; to develop agricultural producers' cooperatives to help in the socialist transformation of the agriculture and handicraft industries; to put capitalist industry and commerce on the track of state capitalism so as to facilitate the socialist transformation of private industry and commerce.	These tasks were successfully carried out during this time. Industrial production increased at an average annual rate of 25%; national income grew at a rate of 9% a year. The combined output of the state-run, cooperative, and joint state-private ownership economies boosted national income from 21.3% in 1952 to 92.9% in 1957. The major problems that arose during this period were: agricultural production couldn't keep pace with industrial production. Socialist transformation was pushed forward too quickly, which left long-lasting after-effects.
Second	1958–1962	To continue industrial construction with a focus on heavy industry. To continue socialist transformation, consolidate and enlarge the shares of collective ownership and ownership by the people. However, many planning targets were modified and raised continuously during this time. In August 1958, China would have a strong, independent, and complete industrial system, surpassing the United Kingdom, and catching up with the United States in terms of the quality of key products. The grain production in 1962 would reach 750 million tons, steel 80 million tons.	The Great Leap Forward and Anti-Rightist movements that emerged in 1958 caused imbalances in the national economy, fiscal deficits over consecutive years, great hardship for the people. However, the Great Leap Forward, which diverted millions of agricultural workers into industry, and the great sparrow campaign, which led to an infestation of locusts, caused a huge decrease in food production. Simultaneously, rural officials, under huge pressure to meet their quotas, vastly overstated how much grain was available. As a result, most of it was allocated to

			urban areas, while many peasants starved to death. Grain production in 1962 only reach 154 million tons (20.5% of target), steel 6.7 mil. Tons (8.4% of target). Grain production decreased 58.5 million tons in 1961 from 1957. The annual growth rate of grain was minus 8.5%. The annual growth rate of GDP accounted for minus 7% during 1958–1962.
Third	1966–1970	To spare no efforts to develop agriculture, solve problems concerning people's food, clothing and other basic needs; To strengthen national defense, and endeavor to make breakthroughs in technology. The Plan also called for the prioritization of national defense in the light of a possible big war, actively preparing for conflicts and speeding up construction in three key areas; national defense, science and technology, and industry and transport infrastructure.	All major economic indicators were fulfilled in accordance with the plan. The grain output increased 45.5 million tons with annual growth rate 4.3% during 1966 to 1970. The annual growth rate reached 6.9% during the third FYP period. However, as with the earlier two Plans, the blind pursuit of rapid development and accumulation actually created a barrier for future development of the national economy.
Fourth	1971–1975	To ensure that average annual growth rate of gross output value of industry and agriculture reaches 12.5%; 130 billion Yuan would be budgeted for infrastructure construction within five years; grain output should reach between 300 and 325 million tons, steel output between 35 and 40 million tons.	The average annual growth rate of gross output value of industry and agriculture reached 8.6% and 4%, respectively. The annual growth rate of GDP accounted for 5.9% during fourth FYP period. Grain output reached between 240 million tons, steel output 17.8 million tons.

(Continued)

Appendix 1.B.   *(Continued)*

Plan/ Program	Years	Plan objectives	Result
Fifth	1976–1980	The central government stipulated the 1976–1985 10 Year Plan Outline of Developing National Economy (Draft) in 1975, which included the 5th FYP (the Plan). In March 1978, the 10 Year Development Outline was amended because the original version stipulated that by 1985, steel and petroleum outputs should reach 60 and 250 million tons, respectively, and 120 large projects. These were impossible targets and ran counter to economic development rules. In December 1978, the third Plenary Session of the 11th Communist Party Central Committee shifted the work focus of the Communist Party to modernization. In April 1979, the central government formally put forward new principles of readjustment, reform, rectification, and improvement.	Steel and petroleum outputs should reach 38 and 106 million tons, respectively, by 1980. The annual growth rate of GDP accounted for 6.9% during 5th FYP period.
Sixth	1981–1985	General objectives of the Plan were to keep pursuing the principle of "adjust, reform, rectify, and improve" Specific objectives included: To achieve an average annual growth rate of 5% for industrial and agricultural products. To keep the supply and quality of consumer products in line with the growth of social purchasing power and changes in consumption structure, and to keep market prices stable.	The Plan achieved great achievements. First, the overall national economy kept a stable growth. The average annual growth rate of GDP was 10.8%. Steel and petroleum outputs should reach 46.8 and 106 million tons, respectively, by 1985. The average annual growth rate of steel and grain accounted for 4.7% and 3.4%, respectively. The problems included a disproportionately high fixed asset ratio. Further,

good air quality and excellent days has increased. In 2017, among the 338 prefecture-level and above cities, the cities meeting air quality standards accounted for 29.3%, and the cities that did not meet the standards accounted for 70.7%; the average number of excellent days was 78.0%. The living environment of urban and rural residents continues to improve.

Tables 2.7–2.9 show that China's economic development level was approximately 98, 91, and 55 years behind the USA's in 1978, 2000, and 2015, respectively. From 1978–2015, China's economy developed significantly, but the gap between China and the US in per capita indicators has been narrowed only by 43 years. But, productivity and technology from 1978–2015 were much more advanced than those from 1880–1960. In addition, during the 22 years between 1978 and 2000, the gap had been narrowed by 7 years only. However, during the 15 years of 2000–2015, the gap was narrowed by 36 years. This shows that China has made breakthroughs in deepening its reform so that its economy has been transitioning from a phase of rapid growth to a stage of high-quality development. When then will China be able to catch up with the United States in terms of GDP per capita? The GDPs per capita of United States and China in 2015 were USD56,207 and USD8,069 (current USD),[18] respectively. Let us assume that both China's GDP and the United States' GDP grow at rates of GDP per capita of 6% and 2%, respectively. It is easy to calculate that it will take 50.5 years for China to exceed the United States in GDP per capita. Even based on Purchasing Power Parity Exchange Rate (PPP), the GDP per capita of the United States and that of China were USD56,207 and USD12,196 (constant 2005 PPP),[19] respectively, in 2015; it also will still take 39.7 years for China to catch up to the United States.

When will China be able to catch up to the United States in terms of absolute GDP? John Rohwer, author of Asian Rising, and John Naisbitt, of Mega Trends Asia, forecast that in 50 years or so China's economy will be larger than the U.S., the European Union, and Japan together by a sizeable margin.[20] This forecast, however, may be optimistic. The United States' and China' GDPs were USD16.60 trillion and USD8.91

---

[18] Calculated using data from World Bank (2017): World Development Indicators online, released 2017.

[19] *Ibid.*

[20] Copper, J. F. (2002). Economic future in the West: Continued economic boom in China or a bust about to happen? Vital Speeches of the Day; New York; October 1.

Table 2.7.   China's economic development level in 1978 versus that of the USA.

	China		USA
	1978		
Persons supplied, per farmworker	3.4	1789	3.7
Illiteracy rate, %	37	1842	22
Per capita output, of steel, Kg	33.0	1890	33.6
Per capita electricity, KWh	230.9	1910	250
Railway operation mileage, KM	48,600	1860	49,288
Highway mileage, KM	8,90,200	1920	8,96,062
Telephones per 1,000 people	2	1883	2.3
Proportion of labor, 1st:2nd:3rd sectors	70.5:17.3:12.2	1835	66.8:23.1:10.1
% GDP of 1st:2nd:3rd sectors	28.1:48.2:23.7	1869	23.7:20.3:56
Population ratio, urban and rural areas	18.2:81.8	1860	17.5:82.5
Per capita GNP (1995USD)	USD147	1869	170
Per capita GNP (PPPUSD)	USD337	1906	336
Life expectancy	66	1944	65.4
Mortality rate (per 1000 live births)	41	1942	40.4
School enrollment, middle school (gross)	45.9(80)	1850	47.2
Average		1878	

Source: Calculated using data from World Bank: WDI 2017 online; U.S. Census Bureau: Statistical Abstract of the United States 2011, Table 819, 1067; China National Bureau of Statistics: China Statistical Yearbook 1981, 2001, 2013, China Statistics Press, Tables 1.7, 2.2, 3.1, 3.7, 3.16, 4.3, 16.3; U.S. Department of Commerce: Business Statistics; US Department of Commerce, U.S. Census Bureau: Historical Statistics of the United States, Colonial time to 1970, Part I, pp. 8, 12, 55, 57, 139, 224, 240, 370, 382, Part II pp. 693, 694, 710, 731, 783, 828; Central Intelligence Agency: The World Fact book; Worldsteel Association: Steel Statistical Yearbook 2013; Table 1, Worldsteel Committee on Economic Studies — Brussels; BP Statistical Review of World Energy June 2014.

trillion (constant 2010), respectively, in 2015.[21] Assuming again that both China and the United States will maintain respective growth rates

---

[21]Calculated using data from World Bank (2017). World Development Indicators. online, released 2017.

		consumption volumes grew too fast, and there was a fiscal over-supply. These factors were to have a negative impact on the country's stable growth.
Seventh 1986–1990	To put reform at the top of the agenda and coordinate economic development with reform. To maintain a basic balance between the national budget, credit, and materials. To improve economic efficiency. GDP increase by an average annual rate of 7.5%. Production goals for grain were between 425 and 450 million tons for grain, and between 55 and 58 million tons for steel.	The average annual growth rate of GDP was 7.9%. The grain and steel production in 1990 reached 446 million tons and 67 million tons with average annual growth rate 4.3% and 7.2%, respectively. However, economic development and reform have emphasized growth rate, which caused overheating of the economy and inflation, and fragmentation of some aspects of the national economy, weakening the national macro-control capability.
Eighth 1991–1995	Maintains the total social demand and the total social supply in balance, it controls the inflation under the premise, raises the economic efficiency as the center, promotion of the economy, suitable for growth. Pays special attention to the readjustment of the economic structure prominently. GDP increase by an average annual rate of 6 %. Production goals were 475 million tons for grain, and 72 million tons for steel. Reduction of Energy Consumption per Unit GDP 11% in five years.	The average annual growth rate of GDP was 11.6 %. The grain and steel production in 1995 reached 467 million tons and 95 million tons with average annual growth rate 0.9%and 7.5%, respectively. Reduction of Energy Consumption per Unit GDP 25% in five years. The economic restructuring makes the breakthrough progress, the national economy marketability and socialized degree significantly improved. However, there was serious inflation, retail sales price index average rises 11.4% per year. Difficulties occurred in production and operation of SOEs. Agriculture is still the weak link in the national economy.

(*Continued*)

Appendix 1.B.   (*Continued*)

Plan/ Program	Years	Plan objectives	Result
Ninth	1996–2000	To complete the second phase in the modernization drive; To control population less than 1.3 billion by 2000; To quadruple per capita GNP as compared to 1980; and to speed up the establishment of a modern enterprise system. GDP increase by an average annual rate of 8.1%. Production goals for grain were between 490 and 500 million tons for grain, and 105 million tons for steel. Reduction of Energy Consumption per Unit GDP 23% in five years.	Population reached 1.27 billion by 2000. The per capita GDP accounted for 509% as compared to 1980. The average annual growth rate of GDP was 8.3%. The grain and steel production in 2000 reached 462 million tons and 129 million tons with average annual growth rate minus 0.2% and 6.1%, respectively. Reduction of Energy Consumption per Unit GDP was 27% in five years. The total volume of China's imports and exports reached USD474.3 billion in 2000, with exports accounting for USD249.2 billion, a rise of 69% and 67%, respectively, over the 1995 figures. Economic restructuring was extensively carried forward, and a socialist market economy was preliminarily established. The principal problems are as follows: inappropriate industrial structure and non-coordinated development of local economies; low overall quality of the national economy and low competitiveness in the international market; a shortage of important resources such as water and petroleum and the deterioration of the ecological environment in some regions.

Tenth	2001–2005	Stress a balance between high growth rate and good economic returns and attaining fairly rapid growth by improving economic returns; Concentrating on economic restructuring; Making reform and opening-up and technological progress the driving force. Making improvement of the people's living standards the basic starting point. Achieve an average annual economic growth rate of about 7%. Increase the number of urban employees and the number of surplus rural laborers transferred to the cities to 40 million each, thereby controlling registered urban unemployment rates at about 5%. Ratio of added value of the primary, secondary, and service Industry 13%, 51%, and 36%, respectively, with those employed by these industries accounting for 44%, 23%, and 33%. Capping population at no more than 1.33 billion by 2005. The growth rates of disposable income of urban residents and the net income of rural residents to 5% each.	Population reached 1.31 billion by 2005. The average annual growth rate of GDP was 9.5%. Increase the number of urban employees and the number of surplus rural laborers transferred to the cities to 42 million each, thereby controlling registered urban unemployment rates at about 5%. Ratio of added value of the primary, secondary, and service Industry 12.1%, 47.4%, and 40.5 %, respectively, with those employed by these industries accounting for 44.8%, 23.8%, and 31.4%. The growth rates of disposable income of urban residents and the net income of rural residents accounted for 9.2% and 5.3%, respectively. However, the economic structure is unreasonable, independent innovation ability is not strong, transforming economic growth mode is slow, energy consumption per unit GDP increased 2% during 10th FYP period; environmental pollution has aggravated. The city and countryside, regional disparity and income gap continues to expand.

Compiled by the authors.

Appendix 1.C.   Characteristics and resolution of each sixth plenum since reform and opening-up.

Year	Central committee	Characteristics	Important resolution
1981	11th Central Committee	Reform and opening	Deliberated and passed "Resolution on Certain Historical Issues of the Party since the Founding of The People's Republic".
1986	12th Central Committee	Strengthen the construction of spiritual civilization	Passed the "Resolution of the Central Committee of the Communist Party of China on the Guidelines for the Construction of Socialist Spiritual Civilization".
1990	13th Central Committee	Keep the Party in close contact with the masses	Deliberated and approved the "Decision of the Central Committee of the Communist Party of China on Strengthening the Contact between the Party and the People".
1996	14th Central Committee	Strengthen the construction of spiritual civilization	Deliberated and approved the "Decision of the Communist Party of China on Several Important Issues Concerning Strengthening the Construction of Socialist Spiritual Civilization".
2001	15th Central Committee	Strengthen and improve the Party's work style	Deliberated and approved the "Decision of the Central Committee of the Communist Party of China on Strengthening and Improving the Party's work style".
2006	16th Central Committee	Building a harmonious society	Deliberated and approved the "Decision of the Central Committee of the Communist Party of China on Major Issues Concerning the Construction of a Harmonious Socialist Society".
2011	17th Central Committee	Deepen cultural system reform and development	Deliberated and approved the "Decision of the Central Committee of the Communist Party of China on Several Major Issues Concerning Deepening of the Cultural Reform and Promoting the Great Development and Prosperity of Socialist Culture".

(Continued)

Appendix 1.C.   (*Continued*)

Year	Central committee	Characteristics	Important resolution
2016	18th Central Committee	Governing the Party strictly and Promoting the Process of Alleviating Poverty	Deliberated and passed the "Several Guidelines on Political Life within the Party under the New Situation" and the "Regulations on Inner-Party Supervision of the Communist Party of China," as well as deliberated and passed the "Resolution on Convening the Nineteenth National Congress of the Party".
2021	19th Central Committee	Summarize the major achievements and historical experience of the Party's centuries of struggle	Deliberated and passed the "Resolution of the Central Committee of the Communist Party of of China on the Party's Major Achievements and Historical Experience in a Century of Struggle," and passed the "Resolution on Convening the Twentieth National Congress of the Party".

Source: What has been the concerns of the Sixth Plenary Sessions of the Central Committee since the reform and opening-up, and how important are they? (2021). https://www.sohu.com/a/499951760_16179, November 9.

Chapter 2

Overview of the Economic Development and Reform in China

1. Introduction

Poor allocation of resources, lack of adequate incentives for productivity gains, and subjugation of economic decision-making by political authorities have been the main weaknesses of CPEs. To address these weaknesses, CPEs began reforming their economies in the 1950s, with the major reforms appearing in the 1970s and 1980s. Of course, the reform experience has not been the same for all CPEs. Factors such as institutional infrastructure, the state of the economy at the beginning of reforms, and the approach to reforms have affected the effectiveness of reforms for each country. For example, China's economic performance resulting from economic reforms has been quite different from that of Central and Eastern Europe countries (CEEs).

In view of the length and scope of economic reform experience, an analysis of its achievements and the problems encountered could certainly provide helpful insights for further reforms. The goal of economic reforms should be balanced growth and improved efficiency with the intention of raising living standards.[1] Up to this point, at least, the

---

[1]Kemme, D. M. and C. E. Gorden. (1990, Editors). *The End of Central Planning? Socialist Economy in Transition: The Cases of Czechoslovakia, Hungary, China, and the Soviet Union.* Boulder: Westview Press. Institute for East-West Security Studies, Hellenic Foundation for Defense and Foreign Policy, p. 57.

gradualist and pragmatic approaches have proved more suitable for a successful reform than the "shock therapy" or "big bang" approach. Reforms must begin with a pressing need and a relatively straightforward task. Quick successes in the early stages will enhance the credibility of the leaders, convince the citizens of their legitimacy, and make it easier to move ahead with further reforms.[2] Opening to the outside world results in a growing participation in the world economy, which pushes the economy toward marketization.[3]

In Chapter 2, we first take a brief look at China's place in the world economy through the years. China's economy flourished prior to the invasions by and wars with major western powers and Japan. Almost 30 years after Mao's victory over the Nationalists, the country embarked on the long road to recovery and reinstitution of the "Chinese Dream." The first years of the transition to a market economy required heavy dependence on China's natural resources. The development mode, however, has been changing emphasis from high speed to high quality. We proceed by examining selected aspects of China's economy and their contribution to economic development. Since commencing on its reform efforts, China has become a global power in foreign trade and FDI flows. We, therefore, conduct a preliminary assessment of these two topics. Subsequent chapters (see Chapters 7 and 8) will cover foreign trade and investment in greater detail.

2. China in the World

Today, China's economy is one of the two largest in the world. This is not the first time, however, that the country has had this distinction. As shown in Table 2.1, China was the world's largest economy in 1820, accounting for 32.9% of the World GDP. Yet, by 1890, China's share of World GDP had dropped to 13.2%, further falling to 8.8% by 1913. By the time reforms began (1978), the country's GDP was 1.12% of the World GDP (0.70% in 1962). In 1978, the GDP per capita (constant 2010 USD) was

[2]Goodman, M. I. (1991). *What Went Wrong With Perestroika*. New York, London: W. W. Norton & Company.

[3]*The Economist*. (1991). The South China miracle — a great leap forward. *The Economist*, October 5, p. 19; Brabant, J. M. V. (1990, Editor). *Economic Reforms in Centrally Planned Economies and their Impact on the Global Economy*. New York: United Nations. Series, Journal of development planning.

Table 2.1.   China's geopolitical standing, 1820–1952.

	1820	1890	1913	1952
Share of World GDP	32.9	13.2	8.8	4.6
Share of World population	36.6	26.2	24.4	22.5
Per capita GDP as a % of World average	90	50.3	41.7	23.8
GDP ranking	1	2	3	3
Share of World exports	n.a.	1.7	1.6	1

Note: Maddison, A. (1998). *Chinese Economic Performance in the Long Run*. Paris: Development Centre of the Organisation for Economic Co-Operation and Development, p. 56.

USD307.1, ranking 161 among 164 countries and regions; it was even lower than Heavily Indebted Poor Countries (HIPC) at USD731.4, ranking at 139.[4] So, a natural question arises: What transpired between 1820 and 1978? The answer lies in the number of conflicts in which China engaged with the European military giants and Japan, and the steep price China paid because of these conflicts.

2.1. *The century of national humiliation (1839–1949): the Opium wars*

In the country's long and glorious history, there was a long period of self-sufficiency and isolation from the rest of the world. The wall behind which China was hiding from the rest of the world started showing cracks in 1793. That was when the first British envoy to China, George Macartney, arrived in 1793 and presented himself to the Qualong Emperor bearing gifts from King George III. Both Macartney and his gifts, however, were quickly rebuffed by the Emperor. The two countries represented two different worlds. The Chinese were proud of their cultural achievements and looked down on the barbarians from the west. The British, on the other hand, viewed China as a backward country, but a

---

[4]Calculated using data from World Bank World Development Indicators online 2019, Last Updated: 12/20/2019.

valuable source of tea. The demand for imported tea was strong in Britain, but the Brits were running large trade deficits, creating severe budget problems for the British Treasury.

Macartney's objective was to establish a free trade agreement with the Chinese, thus lowering the cost of bringing tea to Britain. To pay for that tea, the British envisioned using opium produced in other Colonies, especially India. Unfortunately for the Brits, Emperor Kia Kang declared the opium trade illegal. Despite the Emperor's order, foreign traders smuggled large quantities of opium through the port of Canton. To address the situation, Commissioner Lin ordered all foreign traders to surrender their opium. The British responded by sending their military, thus initiating the First Opium War.

The 1840 conflict was just the beginning of a tumultuous and long period for China, appropriately termed the "National Humiliation Period". In addition to their human and social costs, these wars had devastating effects on China's national pride and economy. Hostilities were customarily concluded through the signing of Treaties between China and the conquering foreign powers. These Treaties have been termed Unequal Treaties for the simple reason that they contained terms unfavorable to the defeated party, China. As a result of these Treaties, China had to part with territory, pay indemnities, surrender its revenue sources, or transfer other privileges to the winners. For example, the First Opium War (1840–1842) ended with the Treaty of Nanjing in August 1842. In conjunction with the Treaty, China ceded Hong Kong, paid indemnity to the British, lowered tariffs, and allowed British traders to trade at five Chinese ports. 1 year later, the Treaty of the Boquet amplified the concessions made by the Chinese by granting British citizens extraterritorial rights, that is, putting them under British law and exempting them from Chinese law. In addition, China granted Britain a Most-Favored-Nation (MFN) status, ensuring that any trade agreements with other countries signed by China would also be available to Britain (Encyclopaedia Britannica). These developments show how China's status in the global stage changed since the Opium Wars.

In the decades ahead, China was invaded by and engaged in many more military conflicts with foreign powers, especially Britain, France, Japan, the United States, Germany, and Russia. These conflicts brought more defeats for China and more unequal treaties. The Second Opium War (1856–1860) ended with the Treaty of Peking and saw the Summer Palace and the Old Summer Palace being looted and burned down by the British and French armies. In 1894, the first Sino-Japanese War broke out over control of Korea. It ended a year later with China's defeat and the signing of the Treaty of Shimonoseki (1895). China recognized Korea's independence, ceded Taiwan and additional territory to Japan, and paid indemnity to Japan. The scenario was always the same. Each such treaty was associated with more concessions and incurred more damage to the Chinese economy. China signed Treaties with 19 countries. These Treaties transferred revenues of the Treaty ports (49 of them) to foreigners, gave foreign citizens immunity from Chinese law and freedom to move around the country, allowed the maintenance of foreign troops in China, permitted foreign vessels to navigate in Chinese waterways, and awarded foreign countries MFN status. China's public finances were depleted as a result of the huge indemnities the country had to pay to the conquerors. To pay off its obligations, the country had to enter the international financial system to borrow. In addition, the country was robbed of any prospect of collecting revenues from its most lucrative sources, port fees, and railroad charges. Table 2.2 illustrates China's entrance into the international capital market to raise funds to meet some of its obligations.

Conflicts were also initiated inside China. The Taiping Rebellion broke out in 1850, and was squashed in 1864 with British and French help. In 1890, the Boxer Rebellion represented a nationalist uprising

Table 2.2.   Selected Chinese foreign debt issues, 1861–1898.

Date	Type	Currency	Purpose	Security or collateral (if known)
1861	Loan	Tael	War	Shanghai custom voucher
1866	Loan	Tael		Maritime customs/provincial
1878	Loan	Tael	War	
1885	Bond	Sterling	War	Maritime customs
1894	Bond	Tael	War (1st JP)	Maritime customs
1895	Bond	Sterling	Indemnity	Maritime customs
1895	Bond	Sterling	Indemnity	Maritime customs
1896	Bond	Gold	Indemnity	Maritime customs
1897	Bond	Sterling	Rail	Lung-Tsing-U-Hai-Railway
1898	Bond	Franc	Rail	Cheng-Tai railway

Source: Goetzmann, W.N., A.D. Ukhov, and N. Zhu (2007). China and the world financial markets 1870–1939: Modern lessons from historical globalization. *Economic History Review*, 60(2), 267–312. https://doi.org/10.1111/j.1468-0289.2007.00376.x.

against foreign military and religious intervention. The foreign troops, however, triumphed and reaped the rewards of their victory in the form of capturing and even destroying many Chinese cities. The Boxer Protocol (1901) concluded the Rebellion and awarded foreigners with additional indemnities.

2.2. *The Republican era, U.S., and silver*

A revolt by the military dethroned the last Imperial Dynasty, the Qing, in 1911. Imperial China was replaced by the Republic of China (1912–1949), with Sun Yat-Sen as its natural leader. In many parts of China, however, the various warlords fought each other for territorial control. Sun Yat-Sen, founder of the Kuomintang party, envisioned a China built on his three principles: nationalism, democracy, and the welfare of the people. Sun, however, was not able to witness the operation of his principles since he died in 1925, aged 59. His successor, Chiang Kai-Shek, was able to reunite China in 1927 by defeating the warlords. The political developments, obviously, had an adverse effect on China's economy.

The Chinese economy suffered another blow in the 1930s because of U.S. policy. In 1933, the US passed the Farm Relief Bill (1933). Under the Thomas Amendment of the Farm Bill, the US began purchasing silver; the demand for silver and the metal's price both skyrocketed. At the time, China was one of the few countries on the Silver Standard. As the global price of silver increased, China's reserves decreased significantly, leading to deflation in China during the 1934–1936 period. Faced with strong popular protests, the Nationalist government had to go off Silver and adopt a fiat paper standard. The shift to the fiat standard plus the war with Japan (1937–1945) and the conflict with Mao's Communists forced Chiang Kai-Shek's government to increase the money supply significantly. The resulting hyperinflation of 1948–1949 represented another huge blow to the Chinese economy.[5] By the end of the period, of course, China's political power had changed hands, and its economy began the transition to a centrally planned system.

---

[5]Friedman, M. (1992). Franklin D. Roosevelt, Silver, and China. *Journal of Political Economy*, 100(1), February, 62–83.

3. China's Performance Pre- and Post-Reform

We will, first, take a quick look at what China has accomplished since the First FYP was implemented (1952). The numbers shown in Table 2.3 are indeed impressive. Naturally, there are many more aspects indicating China's growth than what is shown in Table 2.3. China has improved the people's standard of living significantly. It has made great progress in eliminating poverty, in educational opportunities for its citizens, and in technology, to note just a few areas of significant progress achieved since 1952 and, especially, since 1978.

Let us look closer at some of the contributors to China's growth and their behavior since the reforms began. We will also examine the performance of China's economy in relation to the performance of other economies.

As shown in Table 2.3, China has become the world's second largest economy, the largest manufacturer, the largest trader in goods, the second largest consumer of commodities, and the second largest recipient of FDI. However, the per capita GDP (constant USD in 2010) in 2018 was USD 7752.6, ranking 105th among 237 countries and regions: lower than the

Table 2.3.   China's performance; selected indicators, 1952 and 2020.

Category	1952	2020	Growth
GDP	¥67.9 billion	¥101.6 trillion	196 times
Fiscal revenue	¥6.2 billion (in 1950)	¥24.56 trillion	16.8% annually
Industrial added value	¥12 billion	¥31.3 trillion	995 times
Per capita GDP	¥119	¥72,447	78 times
Final consumption rate	78.90%	57.30%	—
Non-financial FDI	USD920 mil. (in 1983)	USD144 billion	156 times
Trade in goods	USD1.9 billion	USD5.0 trillion	2,587 times

Source: State Council Information Office of the People's Republic of China (2019). China and the World in the New Era. September. http://english.www.gov.cn/archive/whitepaper/201909/27/content_WS5d8d80f9c6d0bcf8c4c142ef.html., Statistical. Communiqué of the People's Republic of China on the 2020 National Economic and Social Development, www.stats.gov.cn/tjsj/zxfb/202102/t20210227_1814154.html.

Upper Middle Income (UMC) of USD8434.0, ranking 99th. Therefore, China is still a developing country.[6]

4. China's Resources and China's Economic Development

First, we examine a basic ingredient of economic growth and development: natural resources.

Almost 30 years after the 1949 overthrow of the Nationalists by Mao's troops, in 1978, China's economy began its long road to another transition, this time to a market system, albeit with Chinese characteristics. To develop its economy, the country had to, first, rely on its own resources. Resources, especially natural resources, denote such things that under certain time and place can increase economic value, which can subsequently improve current and future welfare (Definition from United Nations Environmental Program) and are related with specific technical and economic conditions. Natural resources include two categories: natural materials and energy. China has been endowed with a large quantity and variety of natural resources. Although the amount of China's resources is large in absolute terms, the country's per capita resources are far below the world average. Furthermore, the distribution of natural resources varies from region to region. In general, however, the country's degree of exploitation and efficient utilization of its natural resources have been quite low and have resulted in serious waste.

Figure 2.1 illustrates the country's per capita natural resources compared to the world average and those of selected countries. It shows that China's per capita natural resources amount to approximately 30% of the world average, whereas the US' resources are two times the world average. China's economic structure is still quite unbalanced, with too much of its growth based on extensive production because of excess energy consumption, serious waste of resources, and environmental pollution. China's economic growth reached as high as 10 % in 2003, but was also associated with resource overuse and ecological deterioration. Table 2.4 shows that the year-on-year (yoy) growth rate of coal, steel, petroleum, cement, and electricity was much higher than the year-on-year growth rate of GDP. In 2003,

---

[6]Calculated using data from World Bank World Development Indicators online 2019, Last Updated: 12/20/2019.

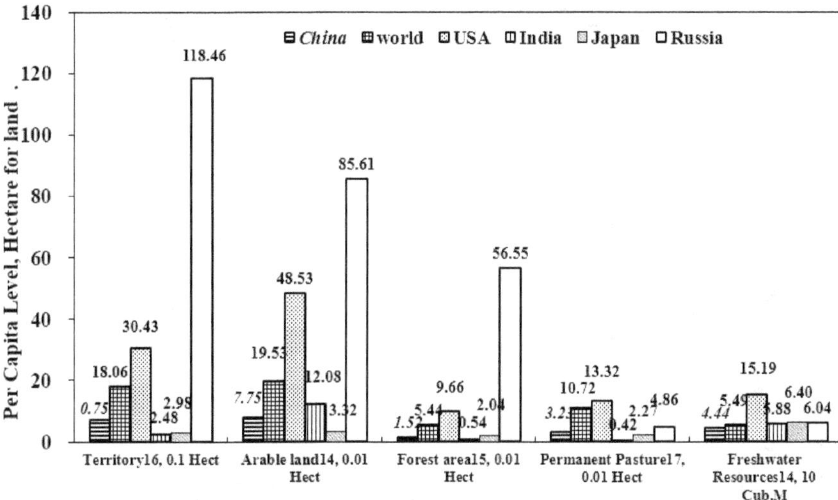

Figure 2.1.   Comparison of natural resources.

Note: Calculated using data from World Bank World Development Indicators online 2017; Food and Agriculture Organization (United Nations) database, 2017; Compiled by China National Bureau of Statistics: International Statistical Yearbook 2013, Tables 2.1, 2.3, 2.4.

China's GDP accounted for 5.4 % in constant 2000 USD of the world's total, but China consumed coal, steel, petroleum, cement, electricity, and water at a much higher percentage of the world total consumption. In 2003, China consumed steel more than twice as much as the United States. China also ranked first in coal, copper, and cement consumption in the world. Petroleum and electricity consumption in China was 490 million tons and 4.99 trillion Kwh in 2012, respectively, making China the second largest petroleum consumer in the world, second only to the United States, and the first electricity consumer, as China consumed 17.4% more electricity than the United States did. In 2012, the petroleum and electricity consumption in China was 125% and 350.1% more than that of Japan, respectively, while Japan's GDP was 3.9% (based on constant USD 2005) higher than China's GDP. These data indicate that China's high economic growth rate is based on extensive production, with much higher consumption and lower efficiency than the world average. However, China is poor in terms of per capita natural resources, containing roughly only 20 % of the world average (see Figure 2.1). Calculated from Table 2.4, coal consumption, petroleum

Table 2.4.   China's GDP growth and resource overuse in 2003, 2004, 2006, 2012, and 2017.

Item	GDP	GDP increment	Coal consump.	Petro. consump.	Electricity consump.	Apparent steel use	Cement production	Water use
Unit	Billion constant 2010 USD	Billion constant 2100 USD	Million T. oil equivalent	Million T.	Trillion wh	Crude steel equivalent, million T.	Million T.	Billion Cub. M
2003 value	2904.0	293.6	853.1	271.7	1910.6	258.6	862.1	532.0
2003 yoy (%)	10.0	19.9	19.5	9.8	15.5	25.7	18.9	−3.2
Share of World total (%)	5.4	17.5	32.8	7.4	11.4	26.6	42.7	16.0
2004 value	3197.6	157.3	983.0	318.9	2203.3	296.6	970.0	554.8
2004 yoy (%)	10.1	10.9	15.2	17.4	14.8	14.7	12.5	4.3
2004 Share of World (%)	5.7	12.5	35.5	8.4	#DIV/0!	27.7	44.3	15.0
2006 value	2113.0	219.6	1215.0	346.1	2865.7	393.4	1236.8	579.5
2006 yoy (%)	11.6	24.3	10.4	5.6	14.6	8.7	15.7	2.9
2006 Share of World (%)	6.6	18.0	39.9	8.9	15.1	31.7	47.6	
2008 value	2602.6	214.9	1406.3	375.7	3433.4	465.5	1400.0	581.9
2008 yoy (%)	9.0	−22.5	7.1	3.6	4.6	9.1	38.8	1.6
2008 share of World (%)	7.8	37.8	42.6	9.6	17.0	34.7	47.4	

2012 value	7192.7	524.1	1873.5	495.3	4976.3	687.6	2416.1	613.1
2012 yoy (%)	7.9	−9.8	1.2	4.8	5.9	2.9	7.4	0.4
2012 Share of World (%)	10.3	30.6	47.9	11.5	23.0	44.2	59.2	66.1
2017 value	10131.9	641.3	1746.6	610.7	6129.7	767.5	2330.8	604.3
2017 yoy (%)	6.8	7.1	3.3	4.0	5.6	8.2	−3.3	0.1
2017 Share of World (%)	12.6	26.1	46.5	13.3	25.7	44.7	57.6	43.4

Source: World Bank (2014). World Development Indicators (online). British Petroleum (2014, 2019): BP Statistical Review of World Energy, June 2014; 2019, 68th edition, June 2019; Worldsteel Association (2008). Steel Statistical Yearbook 2008, Worldsteel Committee on Economic Studies — Brussels, 2009, Table 37; 2018; U.S. Geological Survey (2004). Minerals Yearbook–2004, Table T.22; 2007, USGS Minerals Yearbook 2012, volume III, The Mineral Industry of China in 2012, Table 1; China National Bureau of Statistics (2013): China Statistical Yearbook 2013, China Statistics Press, Table 7.12, 2014, Table 8.12; 2018, Tables 8.7, 9.6, 13.12, PBOC: Monetary Policy Report 4th Quarter, 2003 (in Chinese), February 26, 2004, p. 14; U.S. Geological Survey, Mineral Commodity Summaries, February 2014, pp. 38–39; U.S. Geological Survey, Mineral Commodity, v. I, Metals and Minerals, chapter for Cement. (preliminary release), Table 22.

consumption, electricity consumption, apparent steel use, and cement production, divided by GDP in 2003, were 0.328, 0.074, 0.114, 0.266, and 0.427, respectively. In 2008, they were 0.426, 0.096, 0.146, 0.317, and 0.474, respectively. The consumption measures have risen. Except for a slight increase in cement production divided by GDP, the rest have risen significantly. We can, therefore, surmise that rapid economic growth has utilized relatively more natural resources from 2002–2008. From 2008–2017, China's economy has been transformed from high-speed growth to high-quality growth, and the consumption of natural resources increased slightly. On the other hand, in 2016, the annual water consumption per capita of China and the United States was 443 cubic meters and 1583 cubic meters, respectively.

To contribute to its development, China imported USD63.3 billion in mineral fuels and non-edible raw materials in 2003, the yoy growth rate being 50.7%; that value increased to USD82.74 billion in 2012 with a yoy growth rate of 24.9%.[7] 91.12 million tons of crude oil and 28.24 million tons of refined oil were imported, up by 31.3% and 38.9% yoy, respectively, in 2003.[8] In 2012, China imported 271.03 million tons of crude oil and 39.82 million tons of refined oil, up by 11.5% and 3.5% average yoy, respectively.[9] In 2018, China imported 2605.2 billion USD in crude oil and refined petroleum products, accounting for 10.6% of total imports.

According to China's General Administration of Customs, the quantity of iron ore and aluminum oxide imported in 2003 rose by 75.4% and 82.7%, respectively, compared with the year-earlier period. China has become such a large importer of some raw materials that the country's purchases have affected global prices.[10] In 2003, half of the consumed aluminum oxide in China was imported. Its C.I.F. (cost, insurance, and freight) in October 2003 increased more than twice the C.I.F. of the earlier year.[11] According to government statistics, China produced 10.3% of the world GDP by consuming 47.9% of the world coal, 44.2% of the world

---

[7]China National Bureau of Statistics: China Statistical Yearbook 2013, China Statistics Press, Table 6.5.

[8]China National Bureau of Statistics: China Statistical Yearbook 2004, China Statistics Press, Tables 18.5, 18.9.

[9]*Ibid.*, 2013, Tables 6.5, 6.9.

[10]The Economist Intelligence Unit: Country Report, March 2004, p. 23.

[11]The resources constrain contradiction become more prominent in China's economic development, XINHUA, December 1, 2003.

steel, 11.5% of the world crude oil, and 59.2% of the world cement in 2012 (see Table 2.4). The situation was even worse than that of 2003.

The above data reinforce the argument that, despite the absolute size of its natural resource base, China's per capita resources remain inadequate to satisfy the needs of its immense population. China is still a developing country and imports a great deal of its resources from its trading partners.

5.　China's Dependence on Imports

We can further illustrate China's dependence on resources from abroad by calculating its Import Dependence Rate (IDR). The IDR shows the degree to which a country's consumption is satisfied by foreign output. It is defined as follows:

$$IDR = \frac{IMP}{GO - EXP + IMP} \qquad (2.1)$$

where *IDR* – import dependence rate, *MP* – import; *EXP* – Export, *GO* – domestic output.

China's IDRs for several years for crude oil, iron ore, copper, nickel, and rubber are shown in Table 2.5. In 2003, the IDR for major raw materials increased sharply, as seen in Table 2.5. This implies that, if crude oil price increases by USD1 per barrel, Sinopec will pay an extra USD6.6 billion for crude oil. Furthermore, an unreliable energy supply could seriously jeopardize China's ability to maintain its high growth. In 2019, China had net imports of crude oil of 506.79 million tons, and the

IDR increased to 77.9%. China net imported 1063.5 million tons of iron ore in 2019, which accounted for 88.8% of world total imports. China is also the largest importer of copper and manganese. As a result, China saw a trade deficit in crude materials, inedible, and mineral fuels of USD2.9 billion in 1995, which increased to USD38.0 billion in 2003, increased to USD415.6 billion in 2012, and further increased to USD556.8 billion in 2018.[12] In 2004, GDP increased 10.1% yoy, but

---

[12]Calculated using data from China National Bureau of Statistics (2013, 2019). China Statistical Yearbook 2019, Table 11.3; 2013, Table 6.6.

Table 2.5. The IDR of primary goods of China, 1995–2019.

IDR%	Crude oil	Iron ore	Copper	Nickel	Natural rubber
1995	68.2	0.0	0.0		1995.0
2003	7.8	37.8	42.6	9.6	17.0
2007	10.3	30.6	47.9	11.5	23.0
2017 value	10131.9	641.3	1746.6	0.0	6129.7
2019	77.9	88.8	63.9	79.5	94.3

Source: China National Bureau of Statistics (2019): China Statistical Yearbook. Tables 11.6, 11.7, 13.12; 2014, Tables 11.6, 13.12; 2008, Tables 13.22, 17.9, 17.10; 2004, Tables 14.21, 18.8, 18.9; 2004, Tables 12.21, 16.8, 16.9; The nickel's apparent consumption of China in 2007–2008 (in Chinese), May 11, 2009; Wang, 2009). China Rubber resource status and development trend of supply and demand (in Chinese), November 30. China's import and export customs statistics of nickel 1 on December 2012 (in Chinese), China Industry Economy Statistical Yearbook 2013, China Statistics Press, p. 36; USGS Minerals Yearbook 2014; USGS Minerals Yearbook 2014; USGS: myb1-: 2012-nicke.xls; Overview of China's nickel industry development in 2019, import and export trade and Landscape Scene Analysis, China Industry Information Network, September 11, 2020 (in Chinese), https://www.chyxx.com/industry/202009/894608.html; Pinizzotto, S. (2020). International Rubber Study Group (IRSG) The Condition and Outlook of World Natural Rubber Supply and Demand, www.rubberstudy.com; BP Statistical Review of World Energy June. http://www.bp.com/statisticalreview; Daniel Workman: Iron Ore Imports by Country 2019, www.worldstopexports.com/iron-ore-imports-by-country/; Copper 2019 review and 2020 outlook: the weak economic cycle remains unchanged, the price is high before and low after, finance.sina.com.cn/money/future/fmnews/2019-12-19/doc-iihnzahi8565698.shtml; Basson: 2020 World Steel in figures.

energy consumption per 10,000 CNY GDP reached 1.58 ton Standard Coal Equivalent (SCE), a yoy rise of 5.3%; and, the consumption of coal, steel, aluminum oxide, and cement rose by 14.4%, 15.1%, 9.7%, and 12.4% year-on-year, respectively.[13] Table 2.6 shows China's consumption rankings of primary goods and their shares of the world total consumption in 2004 and 2012. Table 2.6 shows that the consumption of primary good in 2012 increased sharply since 2004. The dependence on imports of primary goods, then, has increased through the years as China's appetite for these resources has grown through the years. This points to the necessity for China to eventually develop a new sustainable economic growth model.

---

[13] Mei, Y. and S. Chao. (2004). The international response on China's economic operation to give rise more concern. *China Economic Times*, June 25.

Table 2.6. China's consumption rankings of primary goods in 2004 and 2019.

Year	2004		2012		2019	
	World rank	World (%)	World rank	World (%)	World rank	World (%)
Crude oil	2	7	2	11.8	2	14.6
Iron ore	1	32	1	40.2	1	87.8
Aluminum	2	20	1	45.0	1	33.0
Nickel	2	11	1	19.0	1	54.0
Copper	1	22	1	32.4	1	50.0
Steel	1	28	1	45.7	1	51.3
Thermal coal	1	31	1	49.9	1	52.4

Notes: CLSA (Credit Lyonnais Securities Asia; 2005). *Asia–Pacific Markets*; calculated using data from China Industry Economy Statistical Yearbook 2013, p. 36; China Statistical Yearbook 2013, Tables 6.8, 6.9, 14.12; World Steel Association: Steel Statistical Yearbook 2012, 2020 World Steel in Figures; China Industry Economy Statistical Yearbook 2013; USGS Minerals Yearbook 2014; BP Statistical Review of World Energy June 2014; The Highest Iron Ore Producing Countries In The World Worldsteel Association: BP Statistical Review of World Energy June 2020, www.bp.com/statisticalreview.

Figure 2.2[14] shows China's iron ore demand and its IDR. The import of iron ores increased from 14.9 million tons in 1985 to 618.6 million tons in 2010 and to 1064.6 million tons in 2019. China's imports of iron ore accounted for 4.4% of world total trade in 1985 and increased to 57.7% in 2010 and to 87.8% in 2019 (see Figure 2.2). Its IDR of iron ore quickly increased from 9.7% in 1985 to 36.4% in 2010, and then slightly declined to 31.2% in 2014 and to 88.8% in 2019. Figure 2.3[15] illustrates China's Net Imports of crude oil, copper, and soybeans as a % of the world trade in commodities. It shows China's net imports of crude oil volume as a % of the world trade in commodities. It also shows China's net imports of crude oil volume as a % of World total import volume from 1987–2014. It indicates that China was a net export country in crude oil and soybeans in 1987, but, since 1995, China became a net import country with imports increasing sharply. Oil (Standard Coal Equivalent) was 4.9%, then

---

[14] Worldsteel Association (2020). World Steel in Figures.

[15] Lum, T. and D. K. Nanto. (2005). China's trade with the United States and the World, CRS (Congressional Research Service) Report RL31403, Updated April 29. Washington, DC: The Library of Congress, p. 15.

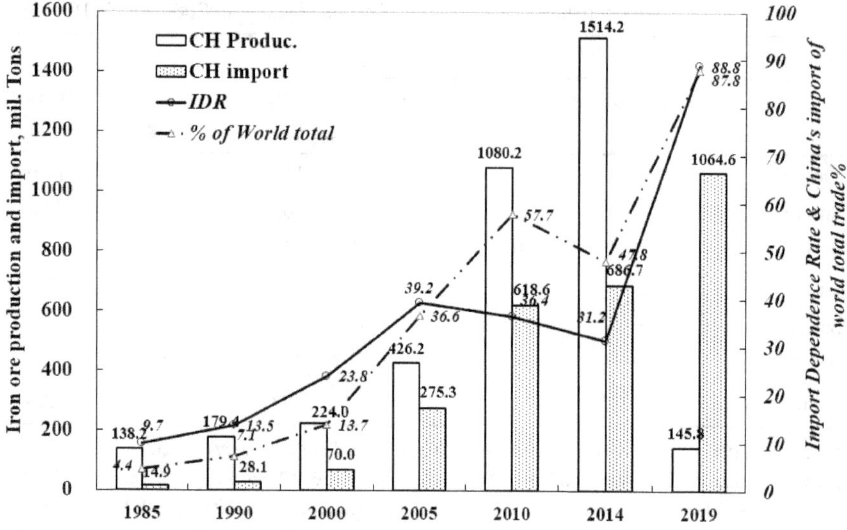

Figure 2.2.   China's iron ore demands and its IDR 1985–2019.

Source: China National Bureau of Statistics (2019): China Statistical Yearbook. Tables 11.6, 11.7, 13.12; 2014, Tables 11.6, 13.12; 2008, Tables 13.22, 17.9,17.10; 2004, Tables 14.21, 18.8, 18.9; 2004, Tables 12.21, 16.8,16.9; The nickel's apparent consumption of China in 2007–2008 (in Chinese), May 11, 2009; Wang, 2009). China Rubber resource status and development trend of supply and demand (in Chinese), November 30. China's import and export customs statistics of nickel 1 on December 2012 (in Chinese), China Industry Economy Statistical Yearbook 2013, China Statistics Press, p. 36; USGS Minerals Yearbook 2014; USGS Minerals Yearbook 2014; USGS: myb1-: 2012-nicke.xls; Overview of China's nickel industry development in 2019, import and export trade and Landscape Scene Analysis, China Industry Information Network, September 11, 2020 (in Chinese), https://www.chyxx.com/industry/202009/894608.html; Pinizzotto, S. (2020). International Rubber Study Group (IRSG). The Condition and Outlook of World Natural Rubber Supply and Demand, www.rubberstudy.com; BP Statistical Review of World Energy June. http://www.bp.com/statisticalreview; Daniel Workman: Iron Ore Imports by Country 2019, www.worldstopexports.com/iron-ore-imports-by-country/; Copper 2019 review and 2020 outlook: the weak economic cycle remains unchanged, the price is high before and low after, finance.sina.com.cn/money/future/fmnews/2019-12-19/doc-iihnzahi8565698.shtml; Basson: 2020 World Steel in Figures.

increased to 6.2% from 1996 to 2013 and decreased to minus 0.5% from 2013–2016.

The composition of coal in total energy consumption reached 76.2% (maximum) in 1990 and declined to 69.6% in 2016 to decrease the pollution created by coal. China has plans to diversify to hydropower, gas,

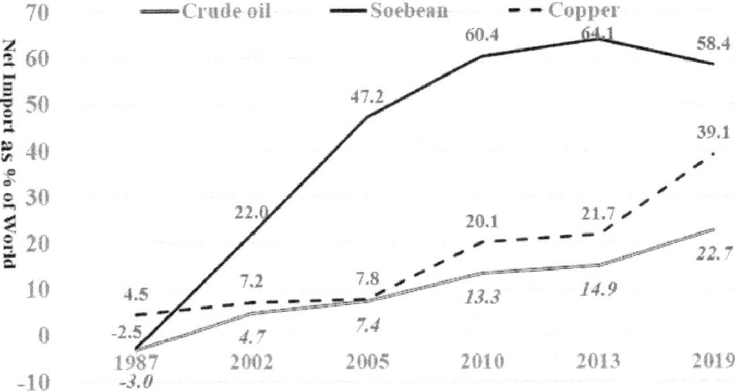

Figure 2.3.   China's net imports of crude oil, copper, and soybeans as % of the world trade during 1987–2019.

Notes: Calculated using data from China National Bureau of Statistics: National Data, Database: Annual, Main Imported Goods in Volume and Value by Category of Commodities, 2020; BP Statistical Review of World Energy June 2020; UNCTAD Data Center, Merchandise: Trade matrix by products, imports, annual, 2019, 1995–2014; The Department of Economic and Social Affairs of the United Nations: The 2013 International Trade Statistics Yearbook (2013 ITSY) Volume II, Trade by Product, UNITED NATIONS PUBLICATION, 2014; FAO Agricultural market information system (AMIS) Market Database 2015; Global and China soybean industry output distribution, consumption structure, import and export volume and inventory analysis in 2019, China Industry Information Network, April 29, 2020 (in Chinese) www.chyxx.com/industry/202004/857598.html; Thomas Lum and Dick K. Nanto: China's Trade with the United States and the World, CRS (Congressional Research Service) Report RL31403, Updated April 29, 2005, The Library of Congress, p. 15.

and nuclear energy. Hydropower use increased from 3.4% in 1978 to 16.9% in 2016. Figure 2.5 shows China's total consumption of energy and oil, and their corresponding ICR (net Import Consumption Ratio, see Eq. (2.2)). It is seen that in 1990, the ICRs for China's total consumption of

$$ICR_{total} = 1 - \frac{\text{Energy Available for Consum}_{total}}{\text{Total Consumption}_{total}}$$

$$ICR_{oil} = 1 - \frac{\text{Net import}_{oil}}{\text{Total Consumption}_{oil}} \tag{2.2}$$

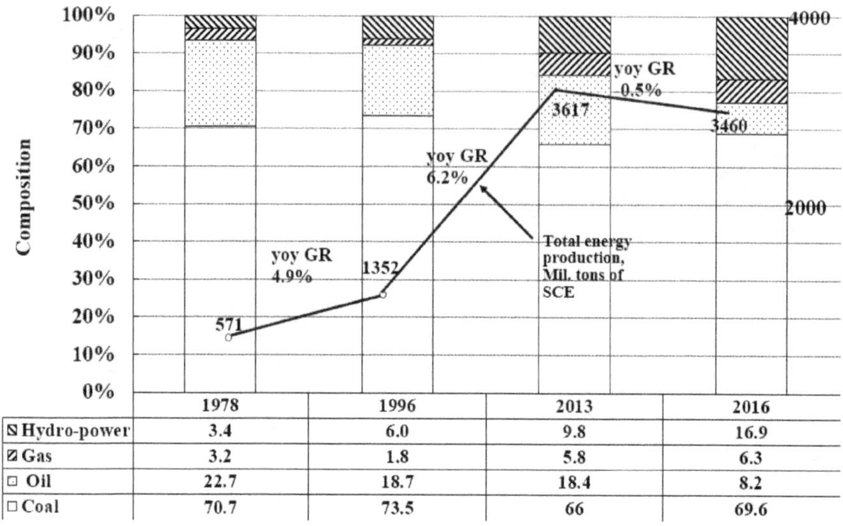

	1978	1996	2013	2016
▨ Hydro-power	3.4	6.0	9.8	16.9
▨ Gas	3.2	1.8	5.8	6.3
▢ Oil	22.7	18.7	18.4	8.2
▢ Coal	70.7	73.5	66	69.6

Figure 2.4.   China's total production of energy and its composition during 1978–2016.

Note: China National Bureau of Statistics: China Statistical Yearbook 2013, China Statistics Press, Tables 8.1 and 8.2; 2014, Tables 9.1, 9.2; Database of China National Bureau of Statistics, Annual Data, Total Production of Energy annual growth rate of SCE (Standard Coal Equivalent) was 4.9%.

energy and oil were negative, which means that China had net exports of energy and oil. In 2016, the ICR_{total} for China's total consumption of energy was 15.9%, which means that 84.1% consumption of energy will be satisfied by the domestic supply. In terms of energy consumption, China does not depend heavily on the international market, so it is unnecessary to overreact to the increases in China's energy consumption. The ICR_{oil} for China's oil increased from −35.2% in 1990 to 9.3% in 2013, which means China was a net exporter of crude oil from 1978 to 1995. In 1990, China's net exports of crude oil amounted to 13.2 million tons (SCE), but, in 2016, China's net imports of crude oil reached 522.5 million tons (SCE). In 2013, China imported 286.2 million tons of oil, which is 74.36% of the oil imports of the United States, or 15.0% of world total imports. In 2018, China's per capita primary energy consumption accounted for 96.9 Gigajoule, which is only 32.86% of the United States' and 64.79% of Japan's (see Figure 2.6). China's growth model, then, is still in extensive mode as China moves on to a higher stage of

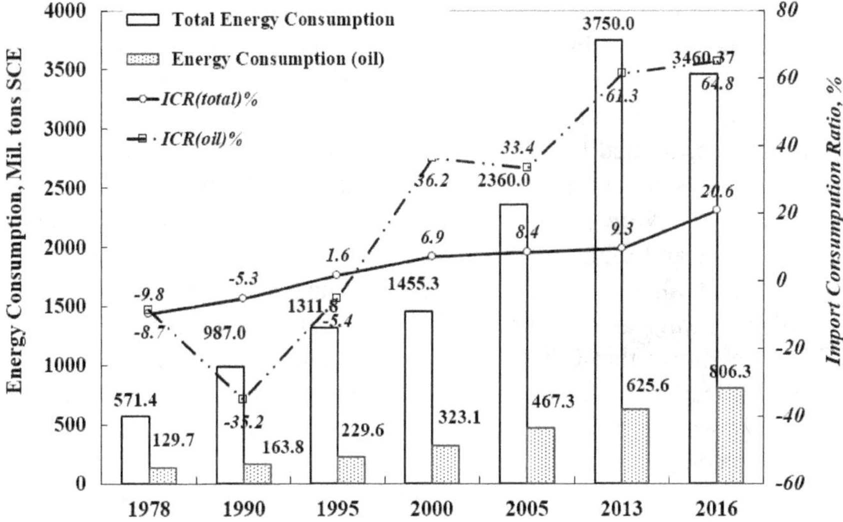

Figure 2.5. China's total consumption of energy and oil, and the corresponding ICR, 1978–2016.

Note: Calculated using data from China Energy Statistical Yearbook 2018, Table 9.2.

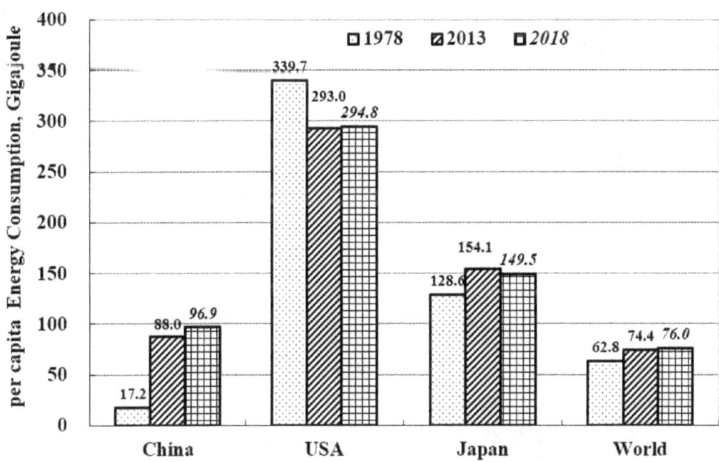

Figure 2.6. China's Per capita total consumption of energy compared with other countries during 1978–2018.

Note: Calculated using data from BP Statistical Review of World Energy 2020, Primary energy: Consumption per capita.

industrialization, it is facing resource constraints. It, therefore, needs to pursue a "resource-saving" approach to keeping its economy steaming. According to the data in Figure 2.6, from 1978–2013, China's per capita primary energy consumption grew at an average annual rate of 6.7%, while the growth rated for the United States and Japan were minus 0.6% and 0.7%, respectively. From 2013 to 2018, China's per capita energy consumption grew by 1.9%, while those of the United States and Japan grew by 0.1% and minus 0.6%, respectively. Figure 2.6 also shows that from 1978–2013, the world's per capita primary energy consumption grew at an average annual rate of 0.7%; from 2013–2018, it increased by 0.4%. This shows that China's per capita primary energy consumption growth rate is higher than the growth rates of the United States, Japan, and the average for the world. This is another indication that China is still a developing country in 2018.

Unfortunately, China's rapid economic development has also caused major ecological damage, seemingly contributing to frequent natural disasters. For example, in 2003, China's cultivated land decreased by 2.537 million hectares and the per capita water resource availability was 2,076 cubic meters, a decrease of 5.6% yoy. Throughout 2003, the crop areas covered and affected by natural disasters totaled 54.383 million hectares, representing an increase of 15.4% yoy.

Losses caused by marine disasters in 2003 increased by 22% compared to the previous year.[16] The country is now changing its development priority from rapid growth to the promotion of all-round, balanced, and sustainable development.[17] Since the "13th FYP" (2015–2020), the party central committee and the state council have jointly promoted the overall layout of the "five in one" and the "four comprehensive" strategic layout, and proposed a new development concept of "innovation, coordination, green, openness, sharing," with the construction of "beautiful China" being the grand goal. In 2015, national chemical oxygen demand emissions were at 22.24 million tons, down 8.3% from 2012; ammonia nitrogen emissions were 2.3 million tons, down 9.3%; sulfur dioxide emissions were 18.59 million tons, down 12.2%; and nitrogen oxide emissions were 18.51 million tons, down 20.8%. The four major pollutants have achieved the 12th FYP total emission control targets. The number of cities with

---

[16]Tung, C.-Y. (2004). Current Chinese economic situation. *China Economic Analysis Monthly* (Cross-Strait Interflow Prospect Foundation), No.10, March.

[17]Wang, M. (2004). Balanced growth a priority. *China Daily*, March 31.

Table 2.8.   China's economic development level in 2000 versus that of the USA.

	USA	China	USA
	2000	2000	
Persons supplied, per farmworker	73.99	3.80	1811
Illiteracy rate (%)	0.6(94)	15.9	1887
Per capita output, of steel, Kg	386.01	101.51	1897
Per capita electricity, KWh	11832.00	1064.34	1933
Railway operation length, KM	5858012.16	68700	1868
Length of highways, KM	6304194	1402698	1921
Telephones per 1,000 people	700	112	1917
Proportion of labor, 1st:2nd:3rd sectors	2.6:22.9:74.5	50:22.5:27.5	1870
Population ratio, urban and rural areas	77.2:22.8	35.7:64.3	1896
Per capita GNP, 1998	34100	840	1926
PPP	34100	3920	1967
Life expectancy	77	70.3	1968
Mortality rate (per 1000 live births)	7.1	32	1949
School enrollment, middle school (gross)	94.6	62.7(99)	1917
Average			1909

Source: Calculated using data from World Bank: WDI 2017 online; U.S. Census Bureau: Statistical Abstract of the United States 2011, Table 819, 1067; China National Bureau of Statistics: China Statistical Yearbook 1981, 2001, 2013, China Statistics Press, Tables 1.7, 2.2, 3.1, 3.7, 3.16, 4.3, 16.3; U.S. Department of Commerce: Business Statistics; US Department of Commerce, U.S. Census Bureau: Historical Statistics of the United States, Colonial time to 1970, Part I, pp. 8, 12, 55, 57, 139, 224, 240, 370, 382, Part II pp. 693, 694, 710, 731, 783, 828; Central Intelligence Agency: The World Fact book; Worldsteel Association: Steel Statistical Yearbook 2013; Table 1, Worldsteel Committee on Economic Studies – Brussels; BP Statistical Review of World Energy June 2014.

of 6.2% and 2.6%, we calculate that it will take 18.0 years for China to overtake the United States in terms of absolute GDP. But, there is one point we may have to keep in mind. It is as difficult for China to maintain a growth rate of 6.2% for another twenty years as it is for the U.S. economy to grow at a rate of 2.6% annually. Obviously, even a theoretical assumption does not support the prediction that China is to overtake

Table 2.9.   China's economic development level in 2015 versus that of the USA.

	USA	China	Eq_USA
Year	2015	2015	
Persons supplied, per farmworker	142.67	6.27	1,865
Illiteracy rate (%)	1	3.6	1,940
Per capita output, of steel, Kg	278.59	584.76	2,025
Per capita electricity, KWh	13,458.06	4,240.0	1,960.63
Railway operation length, KM	228,218	121,000	1,885
Length of highways, 1000 KM	6,518.97	4,994.9	1,976.75
Telephones per 100 people	155.20	109.30	2,007
Proportion of labor, 1st:2nd:3rd sectors	1.6:18.5:19.9	28.3:29.9:42.4	1,940
Proportion of GDP, 1st:2nd:3rd sectors	1.1:20.0:78.9	8.8:40.9:50.2	1,929
Rural population (% of total population)	18.383	44.386	1,925.95
Per capita GDP (current USD)	56,207.04	8,069.21	1,975
Per capita GDP (constant current International USD)	56,207.04	12,196.07	1,984
Life expectancy at birth, total (years)	78.74	76.12	1,998
Mortality rate, infant (per 1,000 live births)	5.7	8.6	1,993
School enrollment, Middle school (% gross)	97.56	94.30	2,000
Matching			1,960

Source: Calculated using data from World Bank: WDI 2017 online; U.S. Census Bureau: Statistical Abstract of the United States 2011, Table 819, 1067; China National Bureau of Statistics: China Statistical Yearbook 1981, 2001, 2013, China Statistics Press, Tables 1.7, 2.2, 3.1, 3.7, 3.16, 4.3, 16.3; U.S. Department of Commerce: Business Statistics; US Department of Commerce, U.S. Census Bureau: Historical Statistics of the United States, Colonial time to 1970, Part I, pp. 8, 12, 55, 57, 139, 224, 240, 370, 382, Part II pp. 693, 694, 710, 731, 783, 828; Central Intelligence Agency: The World Fact book; Worldsteel Association: Steel Statistical Yearbook 2013; Table 1, Worldsteel Committee on Economic Studies – Brussels; BP Statistical Review of World Energy June 2014.

the United States soon. China is still a developing country and developing the economy is its pressing need. During the 19th Century and the first 50 years of the 20th Century, per capita GDP in China was stagnant and even declined because of social instability (including war and civil wars). So, a peaceful environment has proven very favorable to China's economic development.

The International Comparison of Prices (ICP) project recently released revised estimates of different countries' GDP and per capita GDP calculated on purchasing power parity (PPP) basis. The purpose of PPP exercises is to correct for differences in prices. The ICP exercise involves collecting data on prices of more than 1000 different goods and services. For the current ICP effort, 146 countries participated. China participated in the survey conducted by the Asian Development Bank for the first time, and India participated for the first time since 1985.[22] Previous PPP estimates for China were academic guestimates in the 1980s and were clearly imperfect. For this round of the ICP, price data were collected in 11 Chinese cities. In each city, some rural districts were included, but there is a question as to whether these nearby rural areas really represent rural Chinese prices. If they do not, then there would be some upward bias in the estimated average price levels. Since only a small amount of GDP is produced in rural areas, this would probably not create a big error for the overall GDP estimate. The ICP project found that prices in China — for the GDP basket — were around 42% of those in the US. Table 2.10 shows shares of the world economy in 2005 according to the real market exchange rate and PPP (old and revised) for the United States, China, and India.

In Figure 2.7, the label "Electricity17, 10KwH" means that the Electricity production per capita in 2017 for the world averaged 3280 KwH. Figure 2.7 shows the per capita output of primary industrial goods where China is higher than the world average (except for vehicles in use

Table 2.10.   GDP as share of the world % in 2005 for USA, China, and India.

	Market exchange rate	PPP Old	PPP Revised
US	28	20.5	22.5
China	5	14.2	9.7
India	1.8	6.2	4.3

Source: International Comparison of Prices (ICP), World Bank, Office, Beijing: China Quarterly Update — February 2008, Table 1.

---

[22]Keidel, A. (2007). China: Now with 40 percent less GDP! — the limits of a smaller, poorer China. *Financial Times*, November 13.

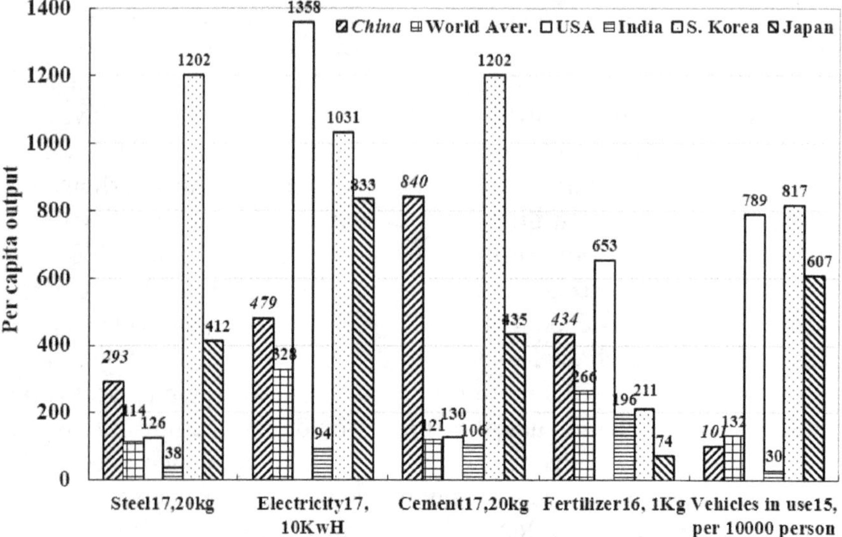

Figure 2.7.   China's per capita outputs of principle industry products versus foreign countries in 2017.

Source: Calculated using data from World Bank: World Development Indicators 2019, Published 2019 by World Bank; British Petroleum: BP Statistical Review of World Energy 2019; World Steel Association: Steel Statistical Yearbook 2018, Tables 1, 1, 2; International Statistical Yearbook 2018, China Statistical Press, Chapters 11 and 12; U.S. Geological Survey, Mineral Commodity Summaries, Cement, p. 39, January 2015.

per capita). It is surprising that per capita consumption of fertilizers in 2106 in the United States is the highest among listed countries. China ranks second at 66.5% of the United States, and Japan is the lowest with only 11.5% of the United States. From Figure 2.8, the label "Meat16,100g" means that the Meat production per capita for world average equaled 44.4 Kg in 2016. From Figure 2.8, we see that per capita output of principal agriculture goods is slightly higher than the world average, except for milk per capita. From Figures 2.7 and 2.8, we see that the United States ranked first in per capita outputs of principal industrial and agricultural products, significantly higher than other countries. The above also indicates that China was still a developing country in 2017.

Figures 2.9 and 2.10 show per capita output of main agricultural and industrial goods in China before and after economic reforms. The growth rate of per capita output for main agricultural and industrial goods in

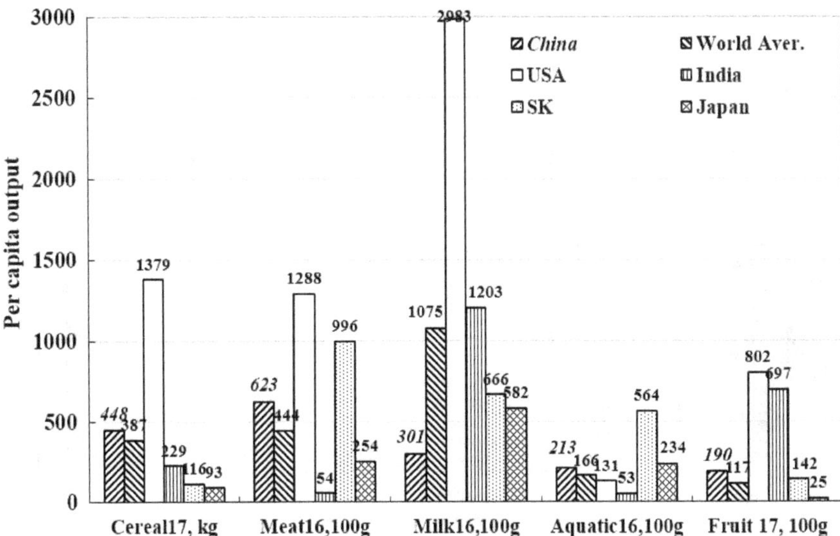

Figure 2.8. China's per capita outputs of principle agriculture products versus foreign countries in 2017.

Source: Calculated using data from World Bank: World Development Indicators 2019, by World Bank; FAO Yearbook: Fishery and Aquaculture Statistics, 2012, Table A4, p. 28; FAO Statistical Yearbook 2013, World Food and Agriculture, Table 34; International Statistical Yearbook 2018, China Statistical Press, Tables 11.3, 11.6 and 11.7.

China before and after economic reforms is shown in Figure 2.11. The annual growth of agricultural goods closely traces the market demand for improving the livelihood of the people. "We must ensure China's food security so that we always have control over our own food supply."[23] Figure 2.10 indicates that the per capita output of main industrial products also increased significantly.

For example, per capita electricity increased from 268 KwH in 1978 to 5359 KWh in 2019, and per capita output of paper increased from 4.6 kg in 1978 to 83.3 kg in 2019. Figure 2.11 shows that the average annual growth rate of per capita output for main agricultural products after

---

[23] Xi, J. (2017) Secure a Decisive Victory in Building a Moderately Prosperous Society in All Respects and Strive for the Great Success of Socialism with Chinese Characteristics for a New Era Delivered at the 19th National Congress of the Communist Party of China, October 18, 2017.

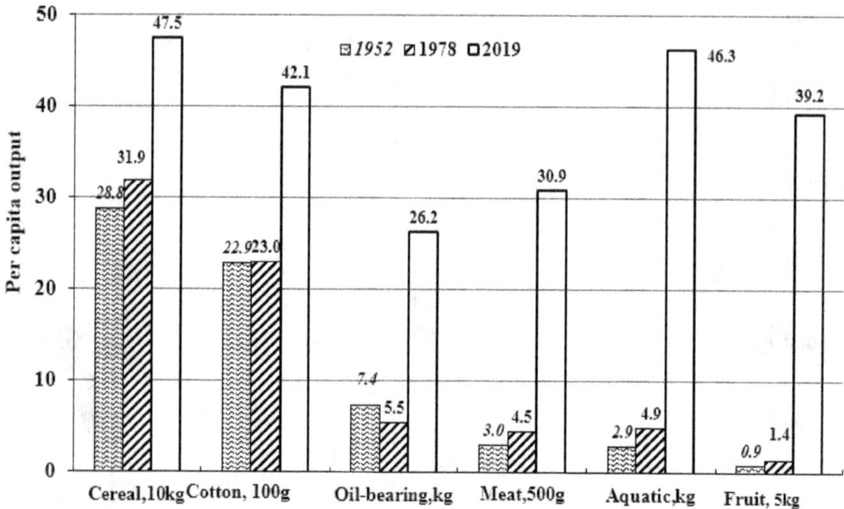

Figure 2.9. Per capita outputs of major agriculture products in China during 1952–2019.
Source: Calculated using data China National Bureau of Statistics, Database; Annual, per capita output of farm products, 2001–2019; Total output of aquatic products, 2001–2019.

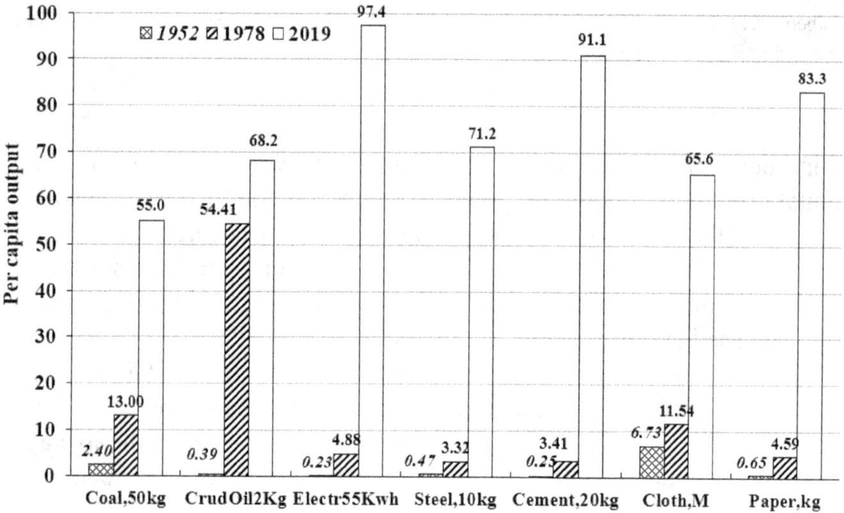

Figure 2.10. Per capita outputs of major Industrial products in China during 1952–2016.
Source: Statistical Communiqué of the People's Republic of China on the National Economic and Social Development, National Bureau of Statistics of China, February 28, 2020; China Statistical Yearbook 2018, China Statistics Press, Table 13.12; 1996, Table 12.20.

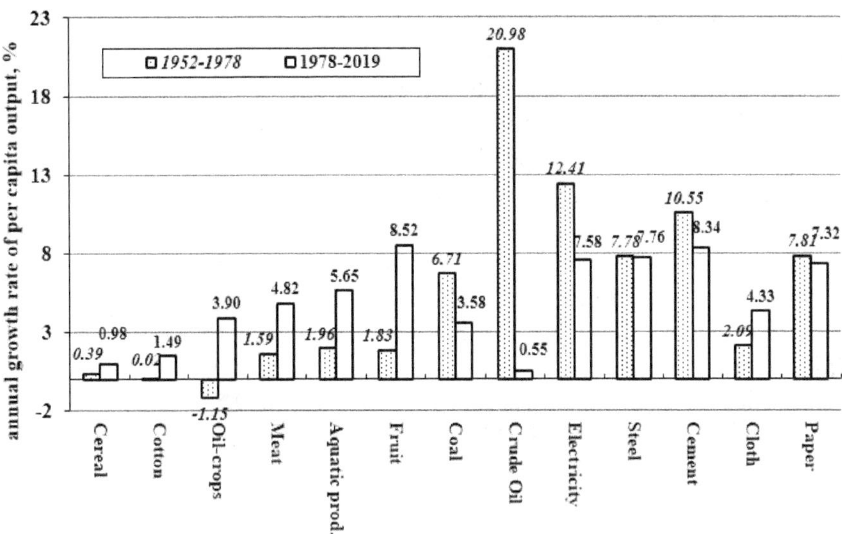

Figure 2.11.   Growth rate of per capita outputs of major products in China before and after reform.

Source: Statistical Communiqué of the People's Republic of China on the National Economic and Social Development, National Bureau of Statistics of China, February 28, 2020; China Statistical Yearbook 2018, China Statistics Press, Table 13.12; 1996, Table 12.20.

economic reforms was significantly higher than that before the reforms. But, it may be surprising to see that the average annual growth rates of per capita output for main industrial goods (except for cloth and paper) after the reforms are lower than those before the reforms. The per capita output for main industrial goods in 1952 was very low (see Figure 2.10), so their average annual growth rate seemed high before the reform. The annual growth rate of per capita output for crude oil declined from 21% to 0.55% due to the lack of new oil fields after the reform; per capita output of crude oil in 1952 was only 0.8 Kg, increasing to 108.8 Kg per capita by 1978. The average annual growth rate in per capita output for coal declined from 6.7% to 3.6% because China decreased the share of coal in total energy resources to accommodate environmental protection. For example, the coal share of total energy consumption declined from 76.2% in 1990 to 59.0% in 2018.[24] The average annual growth rate in per capita output for

---

[24]China National Bureau of Statistics (2019). China Statistical Yearbook, China Statistics Press, Table 9.2.

electricity and steel declined from 12.4% and 7.8% to 7.6%, and 7.8%, respectively, due to industrial structure changes and developing energy and raw material saving products, as well as the fact that the electricity and steel in 1952 were at the very low level of 12.7 KWH per capita and 4.7 kg per capita output, respectively.

Figures 2.12 and 2.13 show that following economic reforms (1978–2019), the annual growth rate of GDP in China (8.8%) is obviously higher than that before the reforms (6.1%, 1952–1978). 1952 is the beginning of the first FYP in China. Because the absolute value of these main indicators increased dramatically, the logarithm scale is adopted for vertical *Y*-axis. China's foreign trade performance has also been notable. Between 1978 and 2019, China's total exports rose from USD21.1 to USD9,519 billion, with an average annual growth rate of 12.8%. Of the USD2,486.7 and 2,125.8 billion

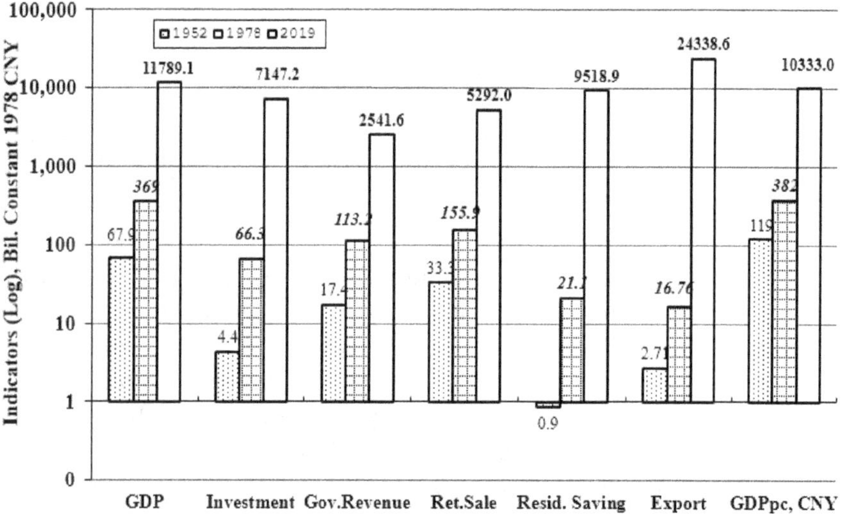

Figure 2.12.   Major economic indicators in China during 1952–2019.

Note: Calculated using data from China National Bureau of Statistics: China National Bureau of Statistics: National Data, Database: Annual, Indices of National Accounts, Investment in Fixed Assets, Price index at Fixed Base, Government revenue, Retail Trade, and Export; Compiled by Department of Comprehensive Statistics: China Compendium of Statistics 1949–2004, China Statistics Press, 2005, Tables 1.6, 1.12, 1.57, 1.58; Statistical Yearbook of China 1981 (English Edition), Published by Economic Information & Agency, Hong Kong, October 1982, p. 299; RMB credit income and expenditure of financial institutions (balance at the end of the year) 2018–2020, https://data.stats.gov.cn/tablequery.htm?code=AD0E.

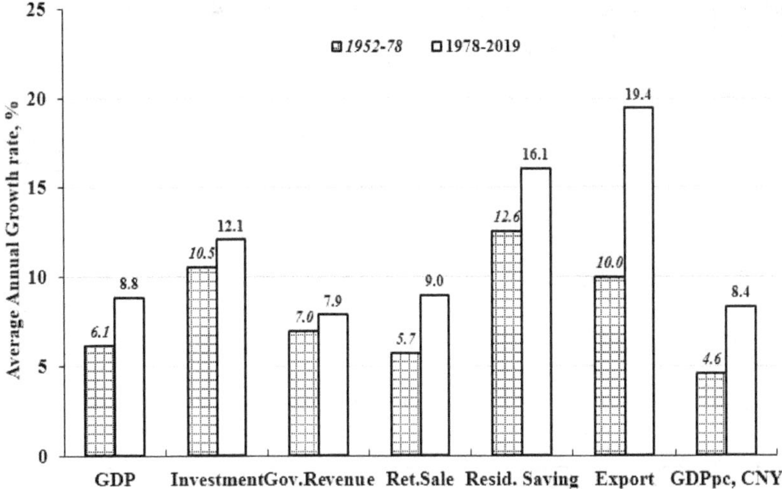

Figure 2.13.   Average annual growth rate of major economic indicators in China.

increments in exports between 2000 and 2019, 95.2% of the total export was contributed by manufactured goods exports.[25]

Such foreign trade performance can be compared to that of Asian Newly Industrializing Economies (NIEs) during their "miracle experiences," and is well above the average for developing countries. Following reform, the high annual growth rate of savings deposits (12.6%, per Figure 2.14) and retail sales (9.0%) reflects substantial improvement of people's living standards. The annual growth rate of total investment in fixed assets has increased from 10.5% prior to reforms to 12.1% after reforms.[26] The high annual growth rate of exports and investments culminated in high annual growth rate of GDP. But, the ratio of investment to GDP increased from 18.5% in 1978 to 60.6% in 2019, 18.5% in 1978 to 60.6% in 2019, which is considered too high. The economy is still driven by investment and exports, which is not sustainable. The annual growth rate of government revenue was 7.0% before economic reforms and 7.9%

---

[25]All China Data Center, China Yearly Macro-Economic Statistics (National): Value of Exports by Category of Commodities by STIC.

[26]Calculated using data from China Statistical Yearbook 2013, China Statistics Press, Table 5.1; 1993, Table 5.5; All China Data Center, China Yearly Macro-Economic Statistics (National): Overall Price Indices of China.

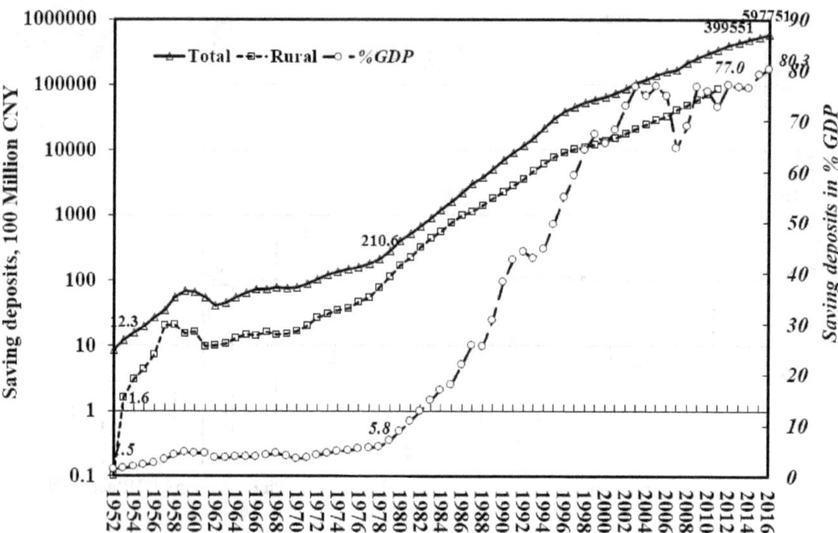

Figure 2.14.   Savings from urban and rural areas in China: 1952–2016.

Source: Calculated using data from National Bureau of Statistics of China: China Statistical Yearbook 2013, Tables 2.1, 9.1; Compiled by the State Statistical Bureau, PRC: Statistical Yearbook of China 1981 (English Edition). Published by Economic Information & Agency, Hong Kong, October 1982, p. 403; All China Data Center, China Yearly Macro-Economic Statistics (National): total government revenue and expenditures and their increase rate, overall price indices of China, 1952–2016.

after reforms. The share of government revenue to GDP accounted for 25.6%, 31.0%, and 21.6% of the total in 1952, 1978, and 2019, respectively. One principal reason for the decline was the transfer of many of the government's commitments to enterprises and/or residents after the 1990s' reform of the social welfare system. For example, price subsidies for daily necessities, free housing distribution, and low housing rent systems were abolished. Students now had to pay tuition fees for higher education. Therefore, items in the government expenditure account declined. As Figure 2.12 shows, however, the absolute amount of government revenue still increased dramatically.

Chinese citizens had practically no savings deposits in 1949. The residents' savings deposits only reached CNY860 million (USD260.2 million) in 1952. By the end of 2012, these deposits had increased to CNY39.96 trillion (USD6.33 trillion) and further increased to

CNY59.78 trillion (USD9.00 trillion) in 2016,[27] as shown in Figure 2.14. Before economic reform, the ratio of rural deposits to total deposits increased from 0.81% in 1953 to 36.4% in 1958, as land reform ignited farmers' enthusiasm for production. But, this value declined to 18.8% in 1971 as a result of the events of the Great Leap Forward and Cultural Revolution. After the early stage of economic reform, the ratio increased from 26.4% to 36.1% from 1978–1984, since economic reform was initiated in rural area. When economic reforms were implemented in urban areas in 1984, the ratio declined again to 17.4% in 2005 and increased to 21.4% in 2012. Per capita savings deposits were CNY12,997 (USD2,105) in the rural areas and CNY45,487 (USD7,206) in the urban areas. Total per capita savings deposits were CNY39,955 (USD6,330) in 2012 and increased to CNY59,775 (USD9,002) in 2016. Of course, many urban area residents possess other kinds of financial assets, including savings deposits, treasury bonds, stocks, pensions, and medical care insurance. The total accounted for 1.5%, 5.8%, and 80.3% of GDP in 1953, 1978, and 2016, respectively. Figure 2.15 shows the per capita savings deposits in the urban and rural areas from 1952–2012. It shows that a large gap of per capita savings deposits between urban and rural areas does exist, and that the gap narrowed during the late 1980s. The ratio of per capita savings deposits in China's rural areas to urban areas reached its peak value of 857.03 in 1953 and declined dramatically to 9.6 in 1958. Following economic reforms, the ratio declined from 13.1 in 1978 to 6.43 in 1984, but then increased again to 9.50 in 1995, then fluctuated to 3.50 in 2012, which means the gap between the urban and rural areas was narrowed significantly during the early periods of reform. After 2012, the PBOC has not separately listed urban and rural savings deposits.

Figures 2.16 and 2.17 show a comparison of China's GDP (based on constant 2000, constant 2005, and constant 2010 USD) growth against

---

[27]Calculated using data from National Bureau of Statistics of China: China Statistical Yearbook 2013, China Statistics Press, Table 2.1, Table 11.3; 2010, Table 2.1, 10.3; 2004, Table 10.3; 1996, Table 9.3; 1991, Table 8.8, Calculated using data from Statistical Yearbook of China 1981 (English Edition), Compiled by the State Statistical Bureau, PRC. Published by Economic Information & Agency, Hong Kong, October 1982, p. 410; Almanac of China's Financial Banking, Compiled by Editorial Board of Almanac of China's Finance and Banking, 2007, p. 361; 2013 p. 360, 362; China National Bureau of Statistics: National Data, Database: Residential Buildings And Amount of Savings Deposit in Urban and Rural Areas, 2016; China Yearly Macro-Economic Statistics (National) Gross Domestic Product Of China, 2016.

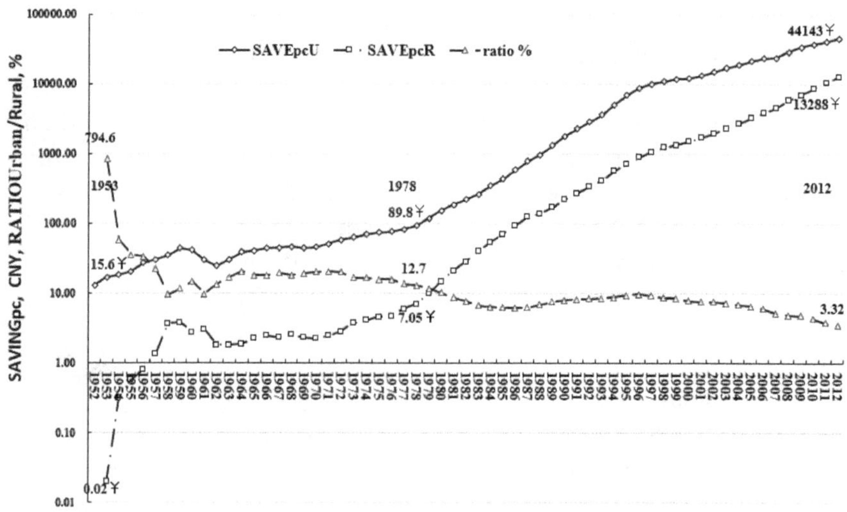

Figure 2.15. Per capita savings deposits in China's urban and rural areas from 1952–2012.

Source: Calculated using data from National Bureau of Statistics of China: China Statistical Yearbook 2013, Tables 2.1, 9.1; Compiled by the State Statistical Bureau, PRC: Statistical Yearbook of China 1981 (English Edition). Published by Economic Information & Agency, Hong Kong, October 1982, p. 403; All China Data Center, China Yearly Macro-Economic Statistics (National): total government revenue and expenditures and their increase rate, overall price indices of China, 1952–2016.

that of the United States, Japan, India, South Korea, and the World during 1960–1978 and 1978–2016. They indicate that before economic reforms (1978), China's GDP growth (an average annual growth rate of 4.59% during 1960–1978) was below the world average (4.74%). GDP decline was especially noteworthy from 1961–1964 due to the Great Leap Forward. The other East Asian countries, South Korea and Japan, had an average annual growth rate of 8.31% and 7.79%, respectively. China lost a good opportunity to develop its economy due to the Great Leap Forward and the Cultural Revolution in the 1960s and 1970s. However, after economic reform (1978), China's GDP growth began to grow dramatically faster (the average annual growth rate from 1978–2016 was 9.52%), much higher than the world average growth rate of 2.87%. Even during the 1997–1998 South East Asia financial crisis, China's GDP continued to grow steadily. The average annual growth rates of South Korea and India are 5.66% and 6.29%, respectively, which are higher than the world

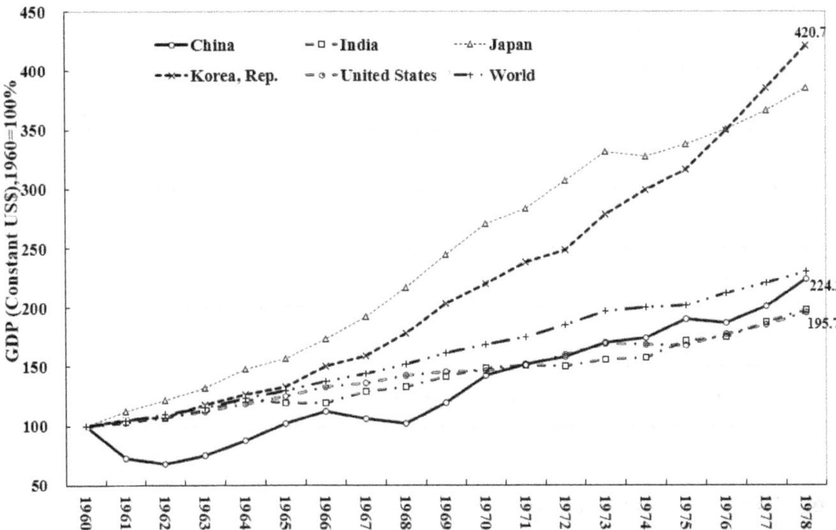

Figure 2.16.   The growth of China GDP versus the world and other countries during 1960–1978.

Source: World Bank: World Development Indicators online, released by World Bank 2009, 2015, and 2017.

average. The United States and Japan had average annual GDP growth rates of 2.67% and 1.97%, respectively, which are lower than the world average growth rate (2.87%). From 1960 to 2016, the average annual growth rate of China and Korea Republic reached 7.53% and 5.38%, respectively, which is higher than the world average growth rate of 3.37%. India and Japan ranked third and fourth with an average annual GDP growth rate of 5.38% and 3.07%, respectively.

Contribution to the world GDP increment (in constant 2000, 2005, 2010 USD) by China, United States, Japan, South Korea, and India is shown in Figure 2.18. China's contribution to the world GDP increment increased from negative 5.7% in 1961 to 32.4% in 2016. This is higher than the United States' 14.6% and India's 8.9%. Since 1998, China's contribution to the world GDP increment was higher than Japan's, except for the year 2000. Contributions by the United Kingdom, Germany, France, Canada, and Italy to world GDP increment were 2.64%, 3.79%, 1.79%, 1.43%, and 1.06%, respectively, with the total achieved by these countries amounting to 8.28% in 2016. Since 2013, then, China has been the real

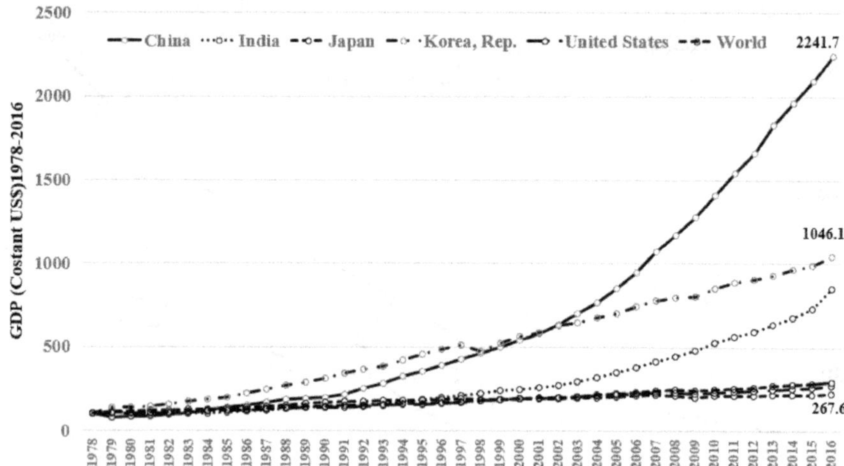

Figure 2.17.   The growth of China GDP versus the world and other countries during 1978–2016.

Source: World Bank: World Development Indicators online, released by World Bank 2009, 2015, and 2017.

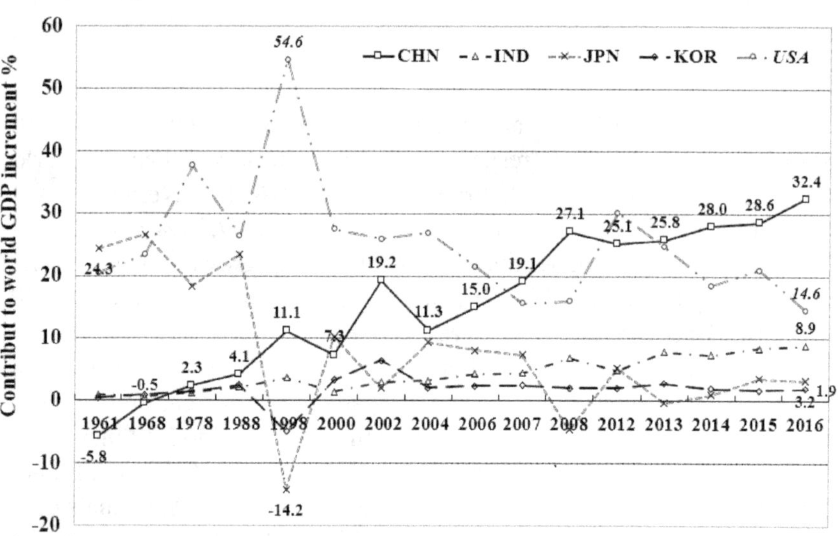

Figure 2.18.   The world GDP increments (constant USD) of China, the USA, and others in % from 1961–2016.

Source: World Bank: World Development Indicators online, released by World Bank 2009, 2015, and 2017.

engine in the world's economic growth. Its contribution to world GDP increment increased to 27.1% in 2008, while that of the United States and Japan declined to 15.9% and negative 4.60%, respectively, due to the global financial crisis. The contribution increments of the other five countries to the world GDP increment amounted to only 4.62% in 2008. This indicates that the global financial crisis affected the economy of developed countries more seriously than it did the economies of developing countries. Figure 2.18 shows that from 2012 to 2016, China's contribution to the world GDP increment increased from 25.1% to 32.4%, while the United States' contribution declined from 30.1% to 14.6%. Since 2013, China has become the main contributor to the world GDP increment. The five countries listed in Figure 2.18 contributed an average of 60.5%% to the world GDP increment during 2013–2016.

Figures 2.19 and 2.20 compare China's GDP per capita (based on constant 2000 USD for Figure 19 and constant 2005, constant 2010, and constant 2015 USD for Figure 20) growth to that of the United States, Japan, India, South Korea, and the World during 1960–1978 and 1978–2016. Prior to economic reform (1978), the growth of China's GDP per capita (average annual growth rate of 1.89% during 1960–1972) was even lower than the world average (3.50%). China's GDP per capita further declined from 1961–1968 due to the Great Leap Forward and the Cultural Revolution. Other East Asian countries, such as Japan and South Korea, had an average annual growth rate of GDP per capita of 9.42% and 5.82%, respectively, during 1960 to 1972. After economic reform (1978), China's GDP per capita began to grow dramatically faster (an average annual growth rate of 8.58% from 1978–2016), much higher than the world average growth rate (1.30%). South Korea and India grew at average annual growth rate of 5.15% and 4.12%, respectively, faster than the world average growth rate. The United States and Japan had an average annual growth rate of GDP per capita at 1.63% and 1.80%, respectively, also faster than the world average growth rate. From 1960–2016, the average annual GDP per capita growth rate of China reached 5.8% and South Korea ranked second with 5.40%. These are far beyond the growth of the world average (1.65%). India and Japan ranked third and fourth with an average annual GDP per capita growth rate of 2.98 and 2.73%, respectively.

Asia has been a remarkably dynamic region over the past four decades. Following Japan's economic rejuvenation between the 1950s and

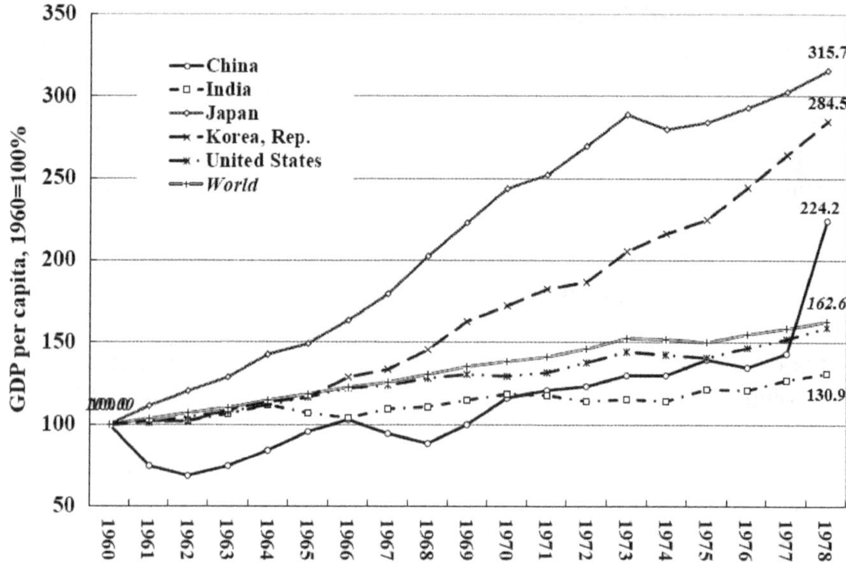

Figure 2.19.   The growth of China's GDP per capita versus the world's and other countries' 1960–1978.

Source: World Bank: World Development Indicators online, released by World Bank 2009, 2015, and 2017.

the 1980s, the fast pace of economic growth of Asian Newly Industrializing Economies (NIEs) since the 1960s constituted the now well-known "East Asian Miracle." China and India entered this process after the 1980s. Despite their rapid growth over several years, both China and India still have relatively low levels of per capita income (see Table 2.11). However, due to the countries' sizes and the fact that they are home to about two-fifths of the world population, their economic performances have already had a significant impact on international trade patterns, global output growth, and the economic prospects of other developing countries.

Table 2.11 shows that in the first 20 years of the GDP's rapid growth period, China's average annual growth rate was comparable to that of Japan's and South Korea's. India's annual real GDP growth rate reached 7.9% in 2005.[28]

---

[28] The Economist Intelligence Unit: Country Report, India, March 2006.

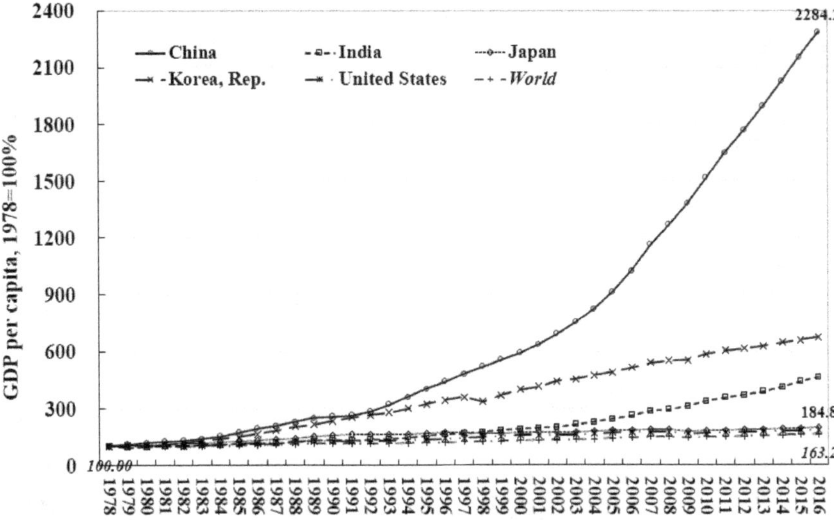

Figure 2.20. The growth of China's GDP per capita versus the world's and other countries' 1978–2016.

Source: World Bank: World Development Indicators online, released by World Bank 2009, 2015, and 2017.

6. The Role of Exports

China's GDP annual growth rate after economic reform is much higher than that before economic reform. Some argue that China's growth was principally attributed to the country's net exports. Mr. Yukon Huang, the World Bank's China Program Director, said, "7 years ago, trade balance accounted for 25% of China's growth rate. Today it accounts for nothing. This is unique, only "China and the US have this characteristic." "China is the only other so-called continental economy, like the US, where the source of growth is increasingly domestically determined by its own investment, its own consumption." [29]

To calculate the contribution of exports to GDP annual growth rate, we use the net export method and the value-added export method. In the net export method, the annual growth rate of GDP is contributed by domestic consumption and net exports as shown in Eq. (2.3).

---

[29] www.worldbank.org.cn/English/Content/885u62823843.shtml.

Table 2.11. Real GDP per capita and GDP growth in China, India, Japan, and South Korea during rapid growth periods.

	Consumption		Gross fixed	Trade		Average
	Private consump.	Public expend.	Capital formation	Exp.	Imp.	GDP growth[a]
1st decade						
China (79–88)	4.88	1.39	3.05	0.61	−1.06	10.1
India (80–89)	3.25	0.75	1.33	0.32	−0.57	5.89
Japan (57–66)	4.89	0.58	4.4	1.34	−1.27	9.41
Korea R. (65–74)	6.08	0.65	4.27	3.8	−5.25	9.01
2nd decade						
China (89–98)	3.88	1.1	3.62	2.03	−1.96	9.41
India (90–99)	3.11	0.7	1.51	1.16	−1.38	5.7
Japan (67–76)	3.45	0.64	3.1	1.38	−0.97	7.41
Korea R. (75–84)	3.96	0.43	3.43	4.33	−3.67	7.35

Note: [a] Differences between the sum of the contributions and GDP growth are due to variations in stocks and/or statistical discrepancies.

Source: World Bank: World Development Indicators 2005, 2009, 2012, and 2017 online, released by World Bank; United Nations Conference on Trade and Development (2005). Trade and Development Report, p. 29.

$$Contr_C = \frac{C_{t+1} - C_t}{GDP_{t+1} - GDP_t}, Contr_I = \frac{I_{t+1} - I_t}{GDP_{t+1} - GDP_t},$$

$$Contr_{NE} = \frac{NE_{t+1} - NE_t}{GDP_{t+1} - GDP_t}$$

$$(2.3)$$

where $Contr_C$, $Contr_I$, and $Contr_{NE}$ are the share of the contribution of domestic consumption, investment, and net exports to the annual growth rate of GDP, respectively.

C_{t+1}, C_t –domestic consumption at year $t + 1$ and t;

I_{t+1}, I_t –domestic investment at year $t + 1$ and t;

NE_{t+1}, NE_t – net export at year $t + 1$ and t.

Using Eq. (2.3), the results of our calculations reveal how much of the GDP's annual growth rate was attributed to domestic consumption, domestic investment, and net exports. The results are listed in Table 2.12, which shows that during 2000–2004, the contribution of net exports to the annual growth rate of GDP is small. The average contribution of net exports to the annual growth rate of GDP equals 7.06% during 1979–2008, but its standard deviation is 23.3%. The large fluctuation reflects the effect of macro-controls by China's central government. When China's economy is overheating, investment's contribution reaches its peak, and the contribution of net exports becomes negative. For example, the contribution by investment reached 85.5% in 1993, 72.0% in 2003, and 86.5% in 2009. Because of the huge investment increments that occurred in 1993, 2003, and 2009, more raw materials and advanced equipment were imported. Net exports declined, their contribution to economic growth amounting to –3.5% in 1993 and –13% in 2001. In 2009, net exports declined quickly due to the global financial crisis, so the contribution of net exports became –42.6% in 2009. In 2016, the contribution of consumption reached 66.5%, the highest since 2001. We can, therefore, attest to the need for improvement of China's systems and mechanisms for stimulating consumer spending, and for leveraging the fundamental role of consumption in promoting economic growth.

Table 2.13 presents the contribution of different components of the GDP growth in Asia, which suggests that an effective policy should not only focus on exports and imports but also on balancing foreign and domestic stimuli. We use Eq. (2.3) to calculate the contribution of different components of GDP growth to China's economy (see Table 2.12). These results are then compared with Table 2.13.

Notice that there is little difference between the results calculated using Eq. (2.3) and the values from the countries considered. Domestic demand, comprising investment and consumption, plays a much more important role in quantitative terms. While India lags in its investment dynamics, China and the other Asian drivers have used an approach where both external and domestic demand have had a significant impact on the sustainability of GDP growth. Obviously, large and populous countries, such as China and India, cannot rely on exports as the only engine for growth; (point to make is that domestic demand (investment and consumption is as important as exports are. But, using Eq. (2.3) to calculate the contribution of the foreign trade to GDP growth seems to contradict certain economic development concepts. In the net export method, imports are considered a negative factor in GDP growth (see Table 2.12); however, its dynamic effect on economic development is

Table 2.12. The contribution of domestic consumption, investment, and net exports to the annual growth rate of the GDP, 1978–2019.

Year	GDP yoy grow.	Contribu. by consump.	Contribu. by invest.	Contribu. by net export	Year	GDP yoy grow.	Contribu. by consump.	Contribu. by invest.	Contribu. by net export
1978	11.7	39.3	65.8	−5.1	1999	7.7	88.1	21.7	−9.8
1979	7.6	49.8	24.5	24.9	2000	8.5	78.1	22.4	−0.5
1980	7.9	57.2	38.5	4.5	2001	8.3	49.0	64.0	−13.0
1981	5.1	70.2	23.8	5.8	2002	9.1	55.6	39.8	4.6
1982	9	56.8	14.1	29.9	2003	10	35.4	70.0	−5.4
1983	10.8	67.3	29.8	2.2	2004	10.1	42.6	61.6	−4.2
1984	15.2	80.8	36.2	−15.8	2005	11.4	54.4	33.1	12.5
1985	13.5	76.6	24.6	−1.9	2006	12.7	42.0	42.9	15.1
1986	8.9	50.6	51.0	−1.3	2007	14.2	45.3	44.1	10.6
1987	11.7	39.8	53.3	7.4	2008	9.7	44.2	53.2	2.6
1988	11.3	28.8	72.0	−1.6	2009	9.4	56.1	86.5	−42.6
1989	4.2	29.5	65.0	6.1	2010	10.6	44.9	66.3	−11.2
1990	3.9	27.3	37.8	33.6	2011	9.5	61.9	46.2	−8.1
1991	9.3	33.5	41.7	25.6	2012	7.9	54.9	43.4	1.7
1992	14.3	42.1	39.1	19.4	2013	7.8	47.0	55.3	−2.3
1993	13.9	44.2	57.9	−3.5	2014	7.3	48.8	46.9	4.3
1994	13.1	34.4	36.6	29.0	2015	6.9	59.7	41.6	−1.3
1995	11	46.4	46.4	7.3	2016	6.7	66.5	43.1	−9.6
1996	9.9	62.6	34.3	3.0	2017	6.9	55.9	39.5	4.7
1997	9.2	43.5	14.1	42.4	2018	6.7	64.0	43.2	−7.2
1998	7.8	64.6	28.8	6.6	2019	6	58.6	28.9	12.6

Source: Calculated using data from China National Bureau of Statistics: National Data, Database: Annual, Contribution Share and Contribution of Three components to the Growth of GDP, 2020; Indices of GDP (preceding year = 100).

ignored. Since this is counterintuitive, Eq. (2.12) was mainly used to explain the contribution of investment and consumption.

To identify the contribution of exports to China's high average annual growth rate of GDP, we use the value-added export method.

$$GDP_t = NEP_t + EXP_t \tag{2.4}$$

Table 2.13.   Results of different components of the GDP growth in China compared with the value from the TDR 2005.

Year	Data source	Contribu. by consump.	Contribu. by invest.	Contribu. by net exp.
1979–1988	Calculate by Eq. (2.3)	6.57	3.89	−0.14
	From TDR 2005	6.27	3.05	−0.45
1989–1998	Calculate by Eq. (2.3)	5.59	3.36	0.47
	From TDR 2005	4.98	3.62	0.07
1978–1908	Calculate by Eq. (2.3)	4.67	4.29	0.82
	Share of contribu. to Gr.	47.73	43.84	8.39

Source: United Nations Conference on Trade and Development (2005). Trade and Development Report, p. 29.

NEP_t — value-added of non-export domestic output at year t; EXP_t — value-added of exports at year t.

$$Contr_{EXP} - \frac{EXP_{t+1} - EXP_t}{GDP_{t+1} - GDP_t}, Contr_{NEP} = \frac{NEP_{t+1} - NEP_t}{GDP_{t+1} - GDP_t} \qquad (2.5)$$

where $Contr_{EXP}$ and $Contr_{NEP}$ are the share of contribution of export (value-added) and domestic output to the annual growth rate of GDP, respectively.

$$GR_{GDP} = GR_{EXP} \times \frac{EXP_t}{GDP_t} + GR_{NEP} \times \frac{NEP_t}{GDP_t} \qquad (2.6)$$

where GR_{GDP}, GR_{EXP}, GR_{NEP} are annual growth rate of *GDP*, *EXP*, and *NEP*, respectively. The calculated result is shown in Table 2.14. It should be noted that *EXP* is the value-added of export gross value since *GDP* is also value-added of its gross output. They would not otherwise be comparable. The first term in Eq. (2.6) represents the contribution to the annual growth rate of the *GDP* by the annual growth rate of exports; the second term in Eq. (2.6) denotes the contribution to the annual growth rate of *GDP* by the annual growth rate Output table 1980, 1987, 1992, 1995,

Table 2.14. The contribution of exports (value-added) and domestic outputs to the annual growth rate of the GDP 1979–2016.

Year	GRGDP	GREXP	GRNEP	Contribu. by exp.	GDP GR by exp.	GDP GR by dom.	Year	GRGDP	GREXP	GRNEP	Contribu. by exp.	GDP GR by exp.	GDP GR by dom.
1979	7.57	21.21	7.33	4.94	0.37	7.20	2000	8.55	25.29	7.32	20.30	1.74	6.82
1980	7.84	23.47	7.52	5.94	0.47	7.38	2001	8.06	4.35	8.37	4.28	0.34	7.71
1981	5.20	32.51	4.56	14.22	0.74	4.46	2002	9.55	22.14	8.50	17.75	1.69	7.85
1982	9.25	13.00	9.14	4.03	0.37	8.88	2003	10.64	31.99	8.64	25.67	2.73	7.91
1983	11.13	5.09	11.31	1.35	0.15	10.98	2004	10.41	26.92	8.54	26.33	2.74	7.67
1984	15.30	10.66	15.44	1.95	0.30	15.01	2005	11.16	23.76	9.49	24.92	2.78	8.38
1985	13.22	43.98	12.37	8.95	1.18	12.03	2006	11.80	19.72	10.61	21.77	2.57	9.23
1986	8.54	27.41	7.87	10.97	0.94	7.60	2007	13.30	12.39	13.45	13.00	1.73	11.57
1987	11.52	29.09	10.78	10.13	1.17	10.35	2008	8.90	0.11	10.31	0.18	0.02	8.88
1988	11.31	7.24	11.51	2.97	0.34	10.97	2009	8.34	−21.92	12.76	−33.44	−2.79	11.13
1989	4.16	2.09	4.25	2.25	0.09	4.06	2010	10.15	22.02	8.96	19.89	2.02	8.13
1990	4.07	44.59	2.21	48.09	1.96	2.11	2011	8.73	−2.43	9.99	−2.83	−0.25	8.97
1991	9.11	19.86	8.41	13.29	1.21	7.90	2012	8.14	12.70	7.68	14.22	1.16	6.98
1992	14.07	12.76	14.16	6.07	0.85	13.21	2013	7.10	1.03	7.74	1.37	0.10	7.00
1993	13.67	−2.12	14.79	−1.03	−0.14	13.81	2014	7.80	4.04	8.17	4.64	0.36	7.44
1994	13.11	63.52	10.06	27.62	3.62	9.49	2015	6.90	−3.49	7.88	−4.38	−0.30	7.20

1995	9.33	3.56	9.85	3.15	0.29	9.04	2016	6.69	−3.06	7.51	−3.57	−0.24	6.93
1996	10.19	−4.94	11.47	−3.78	−0.39	10.58	2017	7.30	10.76	7.04	10.45	0.76	6.54
1997	9.63	19.11	8.94	13.36	1.29	8.34	2018	6.30	7.06	6.24	8.20	0.52	5.78
1998	7.31	0.83	7.82	0.83	0.06	7.25	2019	6.30	5.02	6.40	5.88	0.37	5.93
1999	7.94	7.84	7.95	6.79	0.54	7.41							

Source: Calculated using data from China National Bureau of Statistics (2009). China Statistical Yearbook, China Statistics Press, Table 2.26; 2003, Table 3.19; 2000, Table 3.17; 1998, Table 3.17; 1996, Table 2.1 1981 (English Edition), Published by Economic Information & Agency, Hong Kong, October 1982, p. 357; and China Input-output Table 1980, 1987. China National Bureau of Statistics: Data Database Input-Output Table, Intermediate use part, Intermediate use 2016; Contribution share of the three components to the increase of GDP, 2001–2020.

1997, 2000, 2005, and 2007, 2010, and 2012.[30] The value of this ratio is relatively stable with a standardized error of less than 2%. Therefore, we take their average value with the results shown in Table 2.14. The average contribution of exports (value-added) to the annual growth rate of GDP equals 8.7% during 1979–2019, with a standard deviation of 12.64. The large fluctuation reflects the overheating and soft landing of China's economy. For example, the contribution of exports (value-added) became −2.12% in 1993 and 44.6% in 1990. In 1993, exports increased by 13.0%, but China's imports of machinery equipment increased by 34.7%, so net exports declined to CNY70.1 billion. So, using the net export method, we find the contribution of foreign trade to GDP growth rate to be negative at 3.5% (see Table 2.12). However, it becomes a negative 1.03% when using the export (value-added) method (see Table 2.14). In 1990, exports rose to 52.6%, imports only increased to 17.0%, and net exports increased to CNY41.2 billion. Using the net export method, the contribution of foreign trade to GDP growth rate becomes 3.61% (see Table 2.12). When using the export (value-added) method, it became 5.79% (see Table 2.14). From these examples, it seems that the export (value-added) method reflecting the contribution of foreign trade to GDP growth generated relatively reasonable results. To compare the contribution of foreign trade to GDP growth before and after economic reforms, we consider the 1952–1978 and 1978–2016 periods, and use Eq. (2.5) to calculate the contribution of the exports (value-added) to GDP growth, as shown in Table 2.15.

The table shows that the difference in China's GDP annual growth rate before and after economic reforms was 5. 20%, of which the contribution of the change in export growth was 3.58%. The share of contribution of exports (value-added) to the annual growth rate of GDP accounted for 5.46% and 1.87% after reforms and before reforms, respectively. This model quantitatively demonstrates the role of the booming export sector in China's GDP annual growth rate after the reforms and reflects the effect of the policy of "opening to the outside world." Using the net export method (Eq. (2.3)), we find that the contribution of the net export growth to GDP average annual growth rate was 8.39% during 1978–2016 (see Table 2.12) and became 9.62% using the export value-added methods (see Table 2.14). So, using the net export method and export (value-added) method to calculate the contribution to the average annual growth rate of GDP, Comparing Table 2.12 and Table 2.14, we see that the growth rate

---

[30] See Table 2.14 for source.

Table 2.15. Decomposition of the annual growth rate % of the GDP into the growth rate % of the EXP and the growth rate % of the NEP in China before and after the economic reforms.

Bil. 1978 constant CNY	GDP	EXP value-added	NEP value-added
2019	13512.0	984.5	12527.5
1978	362.4	6.4	356.0
1952	129.6	1.0	128.6
1978–2019 growth rate	9.23%	13.07%	9.07%
Contribut to annual Gr.		0.50%	8.72%
Share of contribut Gr.		5.46%	94.54%
1952–1978 growth rate	4.03%	4.62%	4.02%
Contribut to annual Gr.		0.08%	3.96%
Share of contribut Gr.		1.87%	98.13%

Source: Calculated using data from China National Bureau of Statistics (2009). China Statistical Yearbook, China Statistics Press, Table 2.26; 2003, Table 3.19; 2000, Table 3.17; 1998, Table 3.17; 1996, Table 2.1 1981 (English Edition), Published by Economic Information & Agency, Hong Kong, October 1982, p. 357; and China Input-output Table 1980, 1987. China National Bureau of Statistics: Data Database Input-Output Table, Intermediate use part, Intermediate use 2016; Contribution share of the three components to the increase of GDP, 2001–2020.

during 1978– 2016 was 9.45% and 9.23%, respectively. The contribution of Value-added Export in Table 14 is shown as 5.46%, and in Table 12 the contribution of net export is 3.41%. So, using the export (value-added) method to calculate the contribution to the average annual growth rate of GDP generates relatively more reasonable results.

7. Opening to Outside World

While reforms in the urban industrial and commercial sectors proceeded at a slower pace in the 1980s, the introduction of the policy of "opening to the outside world" in early 1979 was one of the earliest and most widely ranging elements of the reform package, and a major departure from the two preceding decades (1949–1972) of self-seclusion and autarkic economic and technological development. The policy of "opening to the outside world" has been very successful, yielding dramatic increases in international trade and transactions, and contributing to higher efficiency and higher growth of the Chinese economy. China's export achievements were notable, as shown in Figures 2.21 and 2.22, and the foreign trade balance has been positive after economic reform. Figure 2.22 shows that before 1993, the balance was negative and reached minimum USD14.9 billion. It then increased to USD298.1 billion in 2008 and declined to USD154.9 billion in 2011. It further increased to USD593.9 billion in 2015 (peak) and declined to 421.1 billion in 2019.

To obtain a more precise comparison of the average growth before and after 1978, we consider the following empirical model:

$$Ln(FT_t) = \beta_0 + \beta_1 t + \beta_2 I_t(1978) + \beta_3 t I_t(1978) \tag{2.7}$$

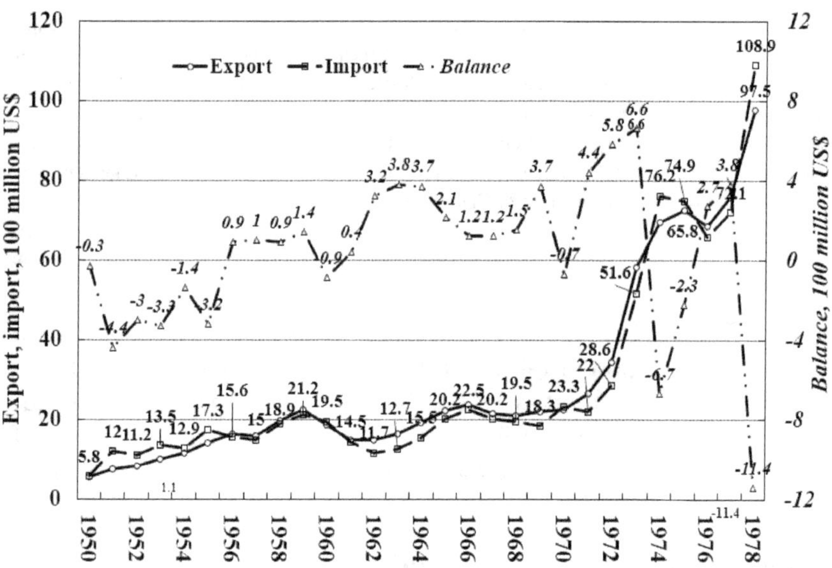

Figure 2.21.   The Exports, imports, and trade balances prior to the reforms in China.

Source: Calculated using data from China National Bureau of Statistics: China Statistical Yearbook 2013, Tables 6.2, 6.3; Compiled by Department of Comprehensive Statistics: China Compendium of Statistics 1949–2004, 2005 (in Chinese), Tables 1.58, 1.59; SAFE: Exchange Rate of Renminbi (in Chinese); All China Data Center, China Yearly Macro-Economic Statistics (National): Total Imports and Exports, 1950–2016; The General Administration of Customs of the PRC (GACC): China's Total Value of Imports and Exports, 2017 (USD) [in Chinese].

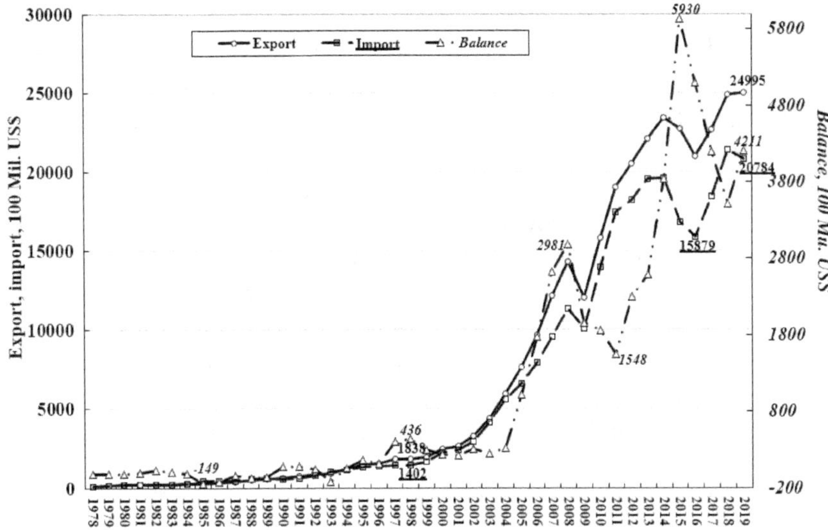

Figure 2.22. The exports, imports, and trade balances after the reforms in China, 1978–2019.

Source: Calculated using data from China National Bureau of Statistics: China Statistical Yearbook 2013, Tables 6.2, 6.3; Compiled by Department of Comprehensive Statistics: China Compendium of Statistics 1949–2004, 2005 (in Chinese), Tables 1.58, 1.59; SAFE: Exchange Rate of Renminbi (in Chinese); All China Data Center, China Yearly Macro-Economic Statistics (National): Total Imports and Exports, 1950–2016; The General Administration of Customs of the PRC (GACC): China's Total Value of Imports and Exports, 2017 (USD) [in Chinese].

where FT_t – Total volume of foreign trade in year t, in constant 2000 USD.

t = Current Year–1952, Year $\in$ (1952, 2016);

$$I_t \text{ — Dummy,} \quad I_t = \begin{cases} 0, t \in (a, 1978) \\ 1, t \in (1979, b) \end{cases} \tag{2.8}$$

a = 1950 for China; 1960 for U.S.A., Japan, South Korea, and India
b = 2016 for China, India, and South Korea; 2015 for United States and Japan

In Eq. (2.7), the estimate of β_1 can be interpreted as the average growth of the total trade before 1978, and the estimate of β_3 provides the difference in the average growth before and after the year 1978. In other words, $\beta_1 + \beta_3$ denotes the average growth after the year 1978, as shown in Table 2.16.[31] b0 gives the magnitude of the total trade that cannot be described by the model Eq. (2.7), or it is interpreted as a measurement of the uncertainty after adjusting for the yearly growth. The R-squared ranges from 0.9766 to 0.9783 for the five countries considered. Based on the parameter estimates, we can conclude that South Korea has the highest growth in absolute value in the first period, while China has the highest growth in absolute value in the second period. China and India are basically in the same category $((\beta_1+\beta_3)/\beta_1 > 1)$, with a higher growth rate in the second period than in the first period; United States, South Korea, and Japan are in another category, with a lower growth rate in the second period than in the first period). The empirical analysis shows that economic reforms in conjunction with the policy of "opening to the outside world" have significantly improved China's

Table 2.16. Summary of the fitting models using Eq. (2.7).

	R^2	β_0	β_1	β_3	$\beta_1 + \beta_3$	$(\beta_1 + \beta_3)/\beta_1$	df
China	0.9956	2.68	0.0745	0.0711	0.1456	1.95	63
t-ratio			13.54	10.74			
India	0.9918	22.99	0.0373	0.0788	0.1161	3.11	53
t-ratio			4.40	8.75			
USA	0.9766	25.88	0.0711	−0.0259	0.0453	0.64	52
t-ratio			8.48	−2.89			
KOR	0.9983	20.68	0.1978	−0.0936	0.1041	0.53	53
t-ratio			37.93	−16.93			
Japan	0.9970	24.43	0.1220	−0.0735	0.0485	0.40	52
t-ratio			35.02	−19.80			

Source: Calculated using data from China National Bureau of Statistics: China Statistical Yearbook 2013, China Statistics Press, Tables 2.1, 2.4, 2.5, 2.19, 6.2, 6.3; 2009, Tables 2.3, 2.17; World Bank: World Development Indicators 2014 online, released 2014 by World Bank; United Nations Conference On Trade And Development: Trade And Development Report 2005, United Nations, New York and Geneva, 2005, p. 34.

---

[31]Calculated using data from World Development Indicators online, Released 2017 by World Bank; China National Bureau of Statistics: China Statistical Yearbook 2014, China Statistics Press, Tables 6.2, 6.3; 1991, Table 15.1; All China Data Center, China Yearly Macro-Economic Statistics (National): TOTAL IMPORTS AND EXPORTS, 1950–2016; The General Administration of Customs of the People's Republic of China (GACC): China's Total Value of Imports and Exports, 2017 (USD) [in Chinese].

foreign trade profile. China has the highest $(\beta_1 + \beta_3)$ value among the five countries, which points to the effectiveness of the policy of "opening to the outside world."

Figures 2.23 and 2.24 indicate that, before 1978, China's foreign trade growth (average annual growth rate of 1.49%) was much lower than the world average (6.86%). This was especially true for the period 1960–1972 due to the Great Leap Forward and Cultural Revolution. The other East Asian countries, such as South Korea and Japan, had an average annual growth rate of 20.40% and 11.77%, respectively, which coincides with the conclusions from the empirical model from Eq. (2.7); South Korea and Japan had the highest β_1. After economic reforms (1978–2019), China's foreign trade growth began to increase much faster (an average annual growth rate of 11.45%) than the world average of 5.68%. India's and South Korea's trade grew at an average annual growth rate of 9.26% and 9.08%, respectively, which was also faster than the world average. From 1978–2019, China and India grew at a much higher rate than that of the 1960–1978 period;

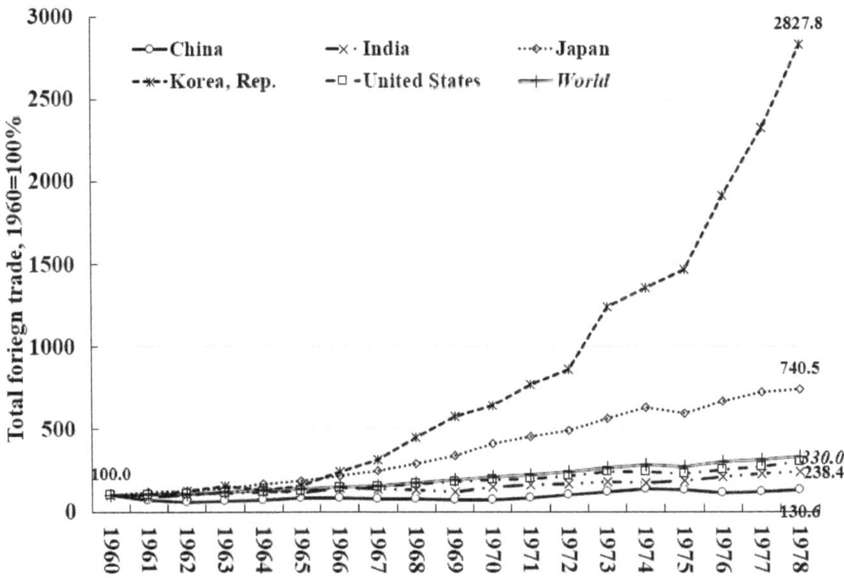

Figure 2.23.   China's foreign trade growth versus the world and other countries during 1960–1978.

Source: Calculated using data from World Development Indicators online 2017, Released 2017 by World Bank; World Development Indicators 2000 CD, Published 2000 by World Bank.

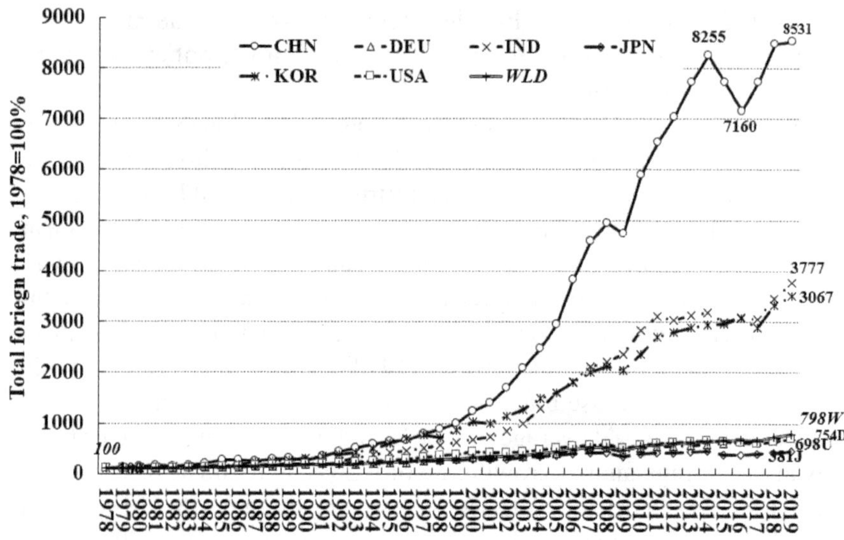

Figure 2.24. China's foreign trade growth versus the world and other countries during 1978–2016.

Source: Calculated using data from World Development Indicators online 2017, Released 2017 by World Bank; World Development Indicators 2000 CD, Published 2000 by World Bank.

South Korea and Japan exhibited a lower growth rate than that of the 1960–1978 period. These also coincide with the conclusions from the empirical model in Eq. (2.7), since $(\beta_1+\beta_3)/\beta_1$ for China and India exceeds 1, and $(\beta_1+\beta_3)/\beta_1$ for South Korea and Japan is below 1. From 1960 to 2019, foreign trade growth rate for South Korea and India reached 11.62% and 7.65%, respectively. China ranked third with 6.15%. These three rates were faster than the world average of 5.66% for 1960–2019. United States and Japan had an average annual growth rate of 5.24 and 5.30%, respectively, from 1960–2019. By 2012, China had become the second biggest foreign trade country in the world, with an overall foreign trade volume of 3,197.7 billion constant 2005 USD, only after the US (4081.9 billion constant 2005 USD).[32] China rose from the 34th place in the world in

---

[32]Calculated using data from World Development Indicators online 2017, Released 2017 by World Bank.

1978 to the second place in 2012. China replaced United States and Germany as the top exporter based on strong China trade data in 2013, but exports fell and thus it became the second highest exporter during 2014–2015.[33]

In the regression analysis for the export data during the period 1952–2016, we use the GDP, imports, foreign exchange rate, dummy policy variable, and the time lag as independent variables. The result is shown in Eq. (2.9):

$$Ln(Export) = -3.013 + 0.778Ln(GDP) + 0.502I_t(1978) + 0.0325t$$
$$(-7.60) \qquad (11.23) \qquad\qquad (4.56) \qquad\quad (3.61)$$
$$R = 0.9965,\ df = 64,\ F = 3019,\ s = 0.2287 \tag{2.9}$$

where export (the dependent variable) — exports during 1952–2019, in USD100 million;

GDP – Gross Domestic Product, in billion CNY.

I_t (1978) – Dummy policy variable as in Eq. (2.8)

t = Current Year –1952, Year $\in$(1952, 2019) as in Eq. (2.8)

Numbers in parentheses are t-ratios.

According to Eq. (2.9), the dominant source of export growth during 1979–2016 was the policy of opening to the outside world, which is explained by the positive coefficient, +0.455. It means that export growth rate increased by 0.455% per year after 1978. Eq. (2.9) also reveals that, when GDP grows by 100%, exports increase by 0.780*Ln (2) = 0.5408%. Foreign trade liberalization was implemented after 1979.

In the regression analysis for import data during period 1952–2019, we use GDP, Exports, Foreign exchange rate, foreign trade balance, and the time lag as independent variables. We get Eq. (2.10). The regression analysis result for imports is shown in Eq. (2.10)[34]:

---

[33] *Ibid.*

[34] Calculated using data from China National Bureau of Statistics (2013). China Statistical Yearbook, China Statistics Press, Tables 6.2, 6.3; 2009 Table 17.3, 2005, Table 18.3; 2004, Table 3.1; Table 18.3; 1996, Table 16.3; 1991, Table 15.1; Compiled by Department of Comprehensive Statistics: China Compendium of Statistics 1949–2004, China Statistics Press, 2005 (in Chinese), Tables 1.58 and 1.59; SAFE: Exchange Rate of Renminbi (in Chinese); All China Data Center, China Yearly Macro-Economic Statistics (National): Total Imports and Exports, 1950–2016.

$$Ln(\text{Import}) = -2.51 + 0.711 Ln(GDP) + 0.772 I_t(1978) + 0.0297t$$
$$\quad\quad (-4.53) \quad\quad (7.66) \quad\quad\quad (5.086) \quad\quad (2.67)$$
$$R = 0.9934, \ df = 64, \ F = 1416, \ s = 0.2822 \tag{2.10}$$

where *IMPORT* (the dependent variable) – imports during 1952–2019, in USD100 million.

GDP – Gross Domestic Product, in CNY billion.

I_t (1978) – Dummy policy variable as shown in Eq. (2.8) t = Current Year –1952, Year$\in$(1952, 2016) as in Eq. (2.8).

Numbers in parentheses are t-ratios.

The independent variable ln (*GDP*) in (2.11) represents the GDP growth rate. If the economy is overheated, imports will increase dramatically; if the economy cools down, imports will increase at a slow rate, or even decrease. Part of the explanation here lies in the composition of China's imports during the period. Machinery and equipment occupy a large fraction of China's imports; they are used for capital construction and are, therefore, most sensitive to GDP swings. Eq. (2.10) reveals that when GDP grows by 100%, imports will increase by 0.711*Ln (2) = 0.493%. The positive sign coefficient of +0.7716 for the dummy policy variable I_t indicates a strong positive effect of the policy of "opening to the outside world" on imports. It means that the import growth rate increased by 0. 7716% per year after 1978. Thus, the regression analyses used above indicate a strong positive impact of the policy of "opening to the outside world" on imports. We can, therefore, conclude that there is a strong positive effect of this policy on China's foreign trade performance.

Figures 2.25 and 2.26 show the % of China's foreign trade to total world trade from 1960–1978 and from 1978–2019, respectively. We observe a dramatic increase from 0.83% in 1978 to 11.4% in 2019. China was still behind the United States (12.6%) in 2019. Since 2009, the total amount of China's foreign trade (8.18%) in world trade has surpassed that of Germany (7.78%).

7.1. *Foreign investment*

Prior to the reforms and opening to the outside world, China had hardly any foreign investment influx. However, since 1978, the inflow and

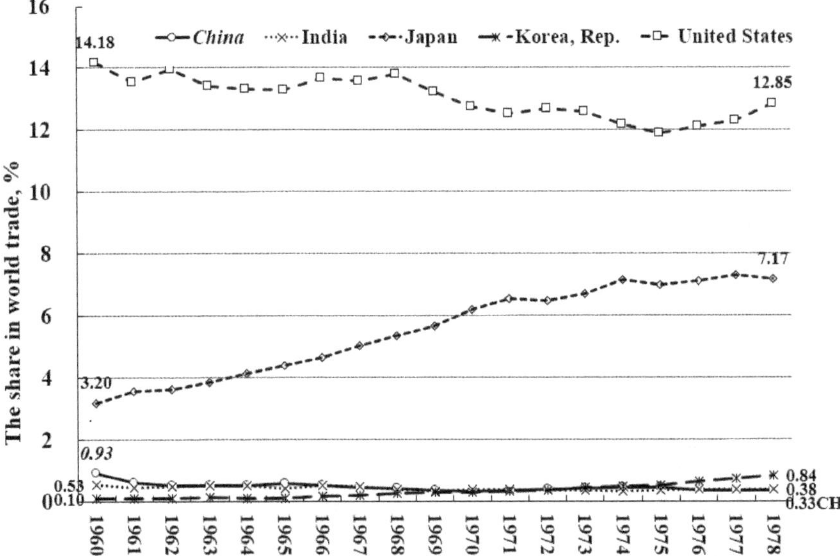

Figure 2.25. China's share of the world trade versus other countries during 1960–1978.

Source: Calculated using data from World Development Indicators online 2017, Released 2017 by World Bank; World Development Indicators 2000 CD, Published 2000 by World Bank.

utilization of foreign capital underwent a rapid transformation. By the end of 2012, China had established 446,487 foreign-invested enterprises (FIEs) with total investment of USD2.993 trillion, registered capital of USD1.729 trillion, and 33.55 million employed persons.[35] Figure 2.27 shows China's influx of foreign capital actually used after the economic reforms, although the initial response by foreign investors to the opening policy was much less than enthusiastic.[36] Total foreign capital used from 1979–1990 was only USD68.7 billion, but since increased to USD2,223.5 billion from 1991–2018. From 1979–1990, foreign loans accounted for 66.7% of all foreign capital inflows, but they declined to 4.56% between 1991 and 2018. No foreign loans entered China after 2001.

---

[35] Data from China National Bureau of Statistics: China Statistical Yearbook 2013, China Statistics Press, Table 6.16.

[36] Zhang, Y., L. Chang, and C. Chen. (1995). The role of foreign direct investment in China's post-1978 economic development. *World Development*, 23(4), 691–703.

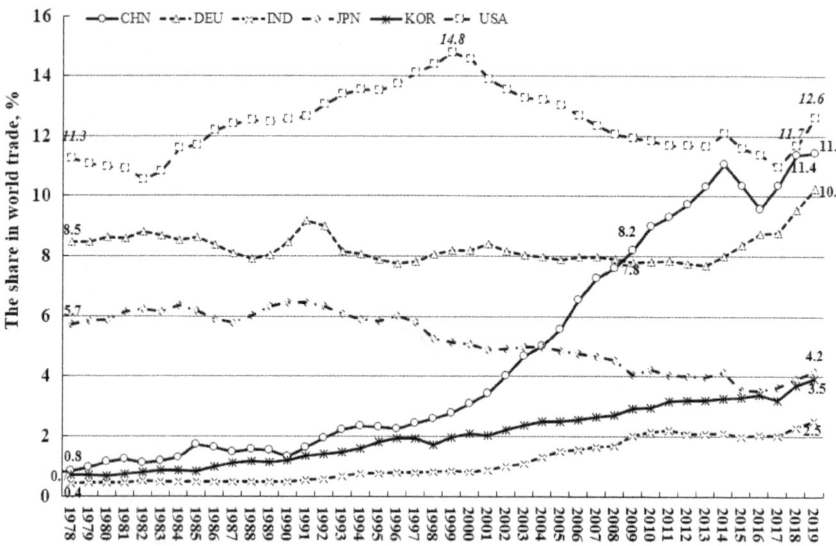

Figure 2.26. China's share of the world trade versus other countries during 1978–2019.

Source: Calculated using data from World Development Indicators online 2017, Released 2017 by World Bank; World Development Indicators 2000 CD, Published 2000 by World Bank.

One of the reasons for such abrupt increases in the FDI could lie in the more positive attitude toward FDI by the Chinese authorities. Various legislative investment incentives were offered during this period, and the joint venture approval process was gradually simplified as more local governments were allowed to approve such deals. In particular, the Chinese government promulgated various investment and ownership laws and increased the protection of private property rights and contracts, thus creating greater confidence among foreign investors and leading to increases in FDI. At the same time, China also attracted foreign capital through such channels as investment in securities, sale share, international leases, compensation trade, and processing and assembly. The total amount of foreign capital to China increased from USD0.34 billion in 1979 to USD138 billion in 2019.[37] The right *Y*-axis in Figure 2.27

---

[37] Data from China National Bureau of Statistics: National Data Database Annual, Foreign Investment Actually Utilized Value by Form, 2020; China Statistical Yearbook 2019, China Statistics Press, Table 11.14; 2009, Table 5.4, Table 17.14; 1991, Table 15.10; 1986; Compiled by the State Statistical Bureau.

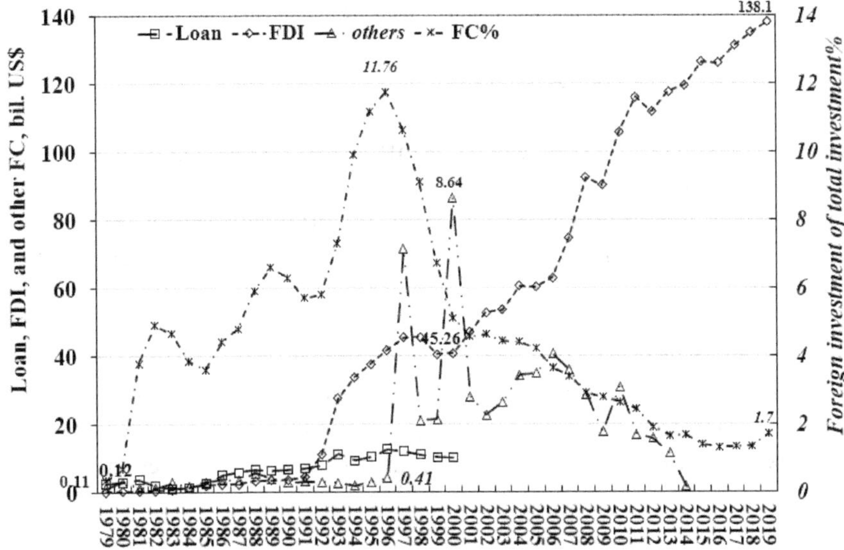

Figure 2.27.   China's influx of foreign capital actually used (1979–2019).

Note: Calculated using data from China National Bureau of Statistics: National Database: Annual, Foreign Investment Actually Utilized Value by Form, Reference Exchange Rate of RMB (Period average), Total Investment in Fixed Assets in the Whole Country, 2020; China Statistical Yearbook 2014, Tables 5.1, 11.13, 11.6; 2013, Tables 5.1, 5.2, 6.2, 6.12; 2010, Table 6.12; 2009, Tables 5.4, 17.14; 1991, Table 15.10; 1986; New China 65-year data sheet.
Source: National Bureau of Statistics' Release time: 2015-02-12. www.stats.gov.cn/ztjc/ztsj/201502/ t20150212_682681.html; Zhang, Y., L. Chang, and C. Chen. (1995). The role of direct foreign investment in China's post-1978 economic development. *World Development*, 23(4), 691–703.

represents the % of foreign capital to total investment, which increased from 0.34% in 1979 to a peak value of 11.8% in 1996. It then declined to 1.7% in 2019 due to the growth rate of total investment being higher than that of foreign investment.

Asia continued to register growth in FDI inflows in 2017 (with annual growth 4.1%), to reach a new high of USD645.7 billion. FDI inflows to the Association of Southeast Asian Nations (ASEAN) reached a new high of USD268 billion, 27% higher than in 2012. Inflows into the major economies in the region also varied: they surged in the Republic of Korea, India, Malaysia, and Thailand; continued to grow in Singapore, China, and Hong Kong (China); and dropped slightly in Indonesia. Outward FDI from Asia rose to USD492.7 billion, due mainly to large outflows from Hong Kong (China), Japan, and China. The FDI inflows continued to be concentrated in China, Hong Kong (China), and Singapore. The top five host economies took 81.9% and 79.4% of the region's total inflows in 2016 and 2017, respectively (see Figure 2.28), ranked by the magnitude of 2016 FDI inflows and outflows, respectively. FDI inflows to China rose by 0.3% yoy in 2017, to USD134.1 billion (18.2% of the FDI to all Developing and Transition economies), reinforcing China's position as the largest recipient of FDI inflows in the developing world.

China's large domestic market, strong economic growth, and increased export competitiveness have played a positive role in attracting foreign investors to have operations in China. Given its location advantages, it is attractive to resource-seeking, efficiency-seeking, and market-seeking FDIs. A large proportion of the FDI influx in China comes from the

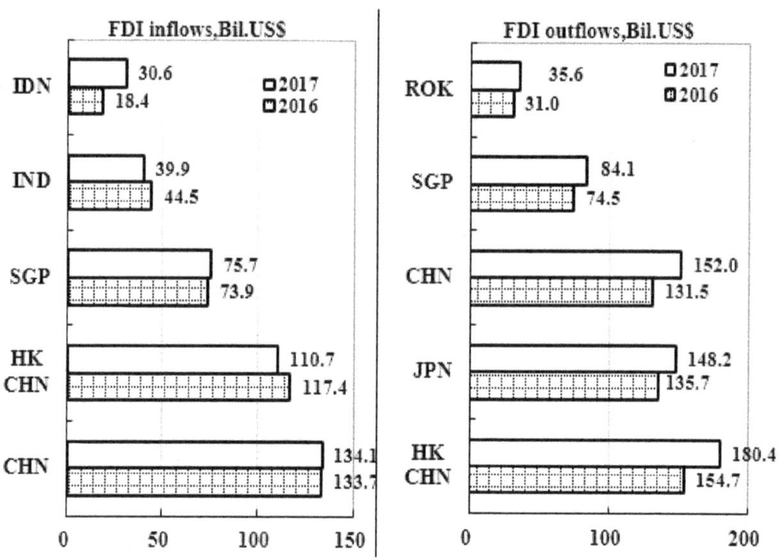

Figure 2.28. The FDI inflows: top five economies in Asia on 2016, 2017 (in billions USD).

Source: Calculating using data from United Nations Conference on Trade and Development (UNCTAD): The World Investment Report 2019, Special Economic Zones, Annex Table 1. Annex Table 4, United Nations Publication, 2019; World Development Indicators online 2019, Released 7/10/2019 by World Bank.

overseas Chinese networks and other TNCs, which are less affected by the global economic slowdown and have contributed to the increase in the FDI inflows to China. The four overseas Chinese foreign investment partners (Hong Kong, Macao, Taiwan, and Singapore) accounted for 41.9% of the total foreign capital inflows in 2004, 48.4% in 2012, and 70.7% in 2018.[38] During the early period of economic reforms, this share was even larger. Hong Kong and Macao alone accounted for 58.6% of total FDI in China during 1979–1991. As shown in Figure 2.29, FDI outflows from developing Asia rose to USD326 billion. Investment from Chinese TNCs climbed by 15% to USD101 billion owing to a surge in cross-border M&As (examples include the USD19 billion CNOOC–Nexen deal in Canada and the USD5 billion Shuanghui–Smithfield Foods deal in the United States). In the meantime, investments from Hong Kong (China) grew by 5% to USD92 billion. FDI outflows from the Republic of Korea declined by 4.6% to USD29.2 billion. As shown in Figure 2.29, FDI outflows from developing Asia rose to USD1,161 billion, accounting for 57.6% of total world FDI outflows. More than 75 of the UNCTAD top 100 MNEs from developing and transition economies today are from developing Asia, and most of these ranked companies are headquartered in China.

Amid a sharpening financial and economic crisis, global FDI inflows fell from a historic high of USD 1,979 billion in 2007 to USD1,697 billion in 2008, a decline of 14%. The slide continued into 2009. After the 2012 slump, global FDI returned to a growth mode, with inflows rising 9% in 2013, to USD1.45 trillion. It grew to USD1.75 trillion in 2016. The crisis has also changed the investment landscape, with developing and transition economies' share in global FDI flows surging to 43% in 2008. In 2013, developing economies maintained their lead. FDI flows to developed countries increased by 2.7% to USD 687 billion, leaving them at 47.5% of global flows, while those to developing economies reached a new high of USD771 billion, or 53.5% of the total. Developing and transition economies in 2013 constituted half of the top 20 countries ranked by

---

[38] Data from China National Bureau of Statistics: China Statistical Yearbook 2013, China Statistics Press, Table 6.13; 2006, Table 18.16; United Nations Conference on Trade and Development (2017). 2017 Handbook of Statistics. Chapter 3. World Bank (2017). World Development Indicators online 2017, Released 2017. Ministry of Commerce of the People's Republic of China (2019). Statistical Bulletin of FDI in China 2019, Table 1.

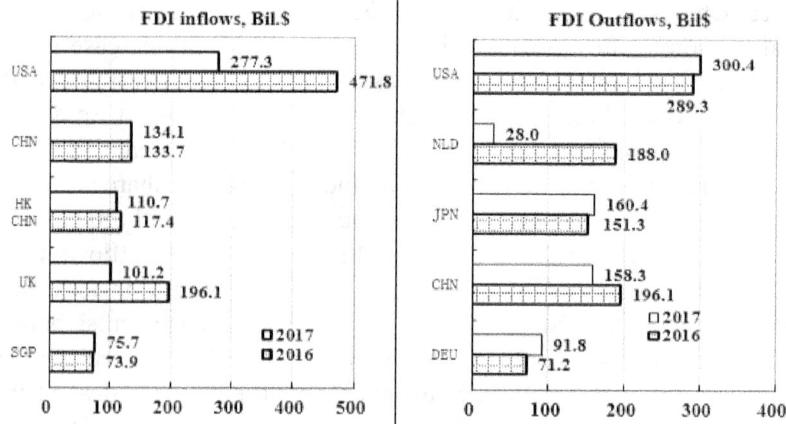

Figure 2.29.   The Global FDI inflows and outflows: top five economies in 2016 and 2017 (In billions USD).

Note: Calculating using data from United Nations Conference on Trade and Development (UNCTAD): World Investment Report 2015 — The World Investment Report 2015, Reforming International Investment Governance, United Nations Publication, Annex Table.1, Figures 1.3 and 1.8; United Nations Conference on Trade and Development, 2017 Handbook of Statistics, Chapter 3 Economic trends, United Nations Conference on Trade and Development, 2016 Handbook of Statistics, Chapter 6 International Finance; World Development Indicators online 2017, Released 2017 by World Bank.

FDI inflows. FDI outflows from developing countries also reached a record level, but declined to 37% in 2016. Transnational corporations (TNCs) from developing economies are increasingly acquiring foreign affiliates from developed countries located in their regions. Developing and transition economies together invested USD553 billion, or 39% of global FDI outflows, compared with only 12% at the beginning of the 2000s.

Dramatic changes in FDI patterns over the past decade have caused changes in the overall rankings of the largest host and home countries for FDI flows. While the United States maintained its position as the largest host and home country in 2013, many developing and transition economies emerged as large recipients and investors: they accounted for 61% and 39% of global FDI inflows and outflows, respectively, in 2013. Several European countries saw their rankings slide in terms of both FDI inflows and outflows. The top five host economies took 36.6% and 54.1%

of global total inflows and outflows, respectively, in 2013. Developing Asia remains the world's largest recipient region of FDI flows at USD426.4 billion. Asia–Pacific Economic Cooperation (APEC) countries and the BRICS (Brazil, Russian Federation, India, China, and South Africa) countries saw a dramatic increase in their share of global FDI inflows from the pre-crisis period. APEC now accounts for more than half of global FDI flows, like the G-20, while the BRICS jumped to more than one-fifth. The United States maintained its position as the recipient of the largest FDI inflows in 2013. In 2016, the United States still maintained its position as the recipient of the largest FDI inflows, followed by United Kingdom and China, as shown in Figure 2.29. In 2016, the developed economies group accounted for 59.1% of global FDI flows, while developing economies occupied 37%. East Asia declined to 14.9%. This shows that the economic recovery of developed economies has been quite smooth.

In 2013, outward FDI from developed countries rose to USD326 billion. Outflows exceeded inflows by USD292.4 billion, so developed countries retained their position as the largest net outward investor group. Investments from the largest investor — the United States — increased to USD337 billion in 2014. Among the top five FDI source countries, China is the only developing country. In 2016, FDI outflows from developed economies declined to USD875 billion, while still accounting for 52.2% of global FDI outflows. Investments by North American multinational enterprises (MNEs) held steady at USD365 billion. The United States still the origin of the largest amount of outward FDI in 2016, as shown in Figure 2.29. Overall outflows from developing economies were almost flat at USD383 billion, while accounting for 26.4% of global FDI outflows. Developing Asia saw its outward investments recover by 7% to USD363 billion, thanks to record outflows from China, while accounting for 20.1% of global FDI outflows. As shown in Figure 2.29, in 2017, FDI inflows into the United States declined by 41%, to USD277 billion, mainly due to a fall by one-third of cross-border M&A sales; FDI flows to the United Kingdom also declined, by 48% to USD101 billion, as new equity investments were cut in half. Therefore, in 2017, FDI into the top five host economies in the world declined by 30%, to USD694 billion. Despite the FDI decline, the United States remained the largest recipient of FDI, followed by China and Hong Kong (China). FDI outflows from top five home economies declined by 6.5%, to USD1,161 billion. The

United Kingdom was replaced by the Netherlands among the top five investment economies. There are three developing economies among the top FDI recipients, but only one developing country in investment of FDI. This shows that the developed economies invested in developing economies. Only the United States and China are listed as top five FDI inflow as well as FDI outflow countries. Therefore, cooperation between the two countries is of great benefit to them as well as to the world economic environment.

Outward FDI flows from East Asia decreased for the second consecutive year to USD271 billion in 2018. This was largely due to investment from China, which declined by 18% to an estimated USD130 billion. Government policy to curb overseas investment in industries such as real estate, entertainment, and sports clubs continued in 2018 with tightened foreign exchange controls. Investment policy uncertainties and tightened investment screening regulations also weighed on Chinese outward FDI to the United States and the EU, which declined significantly. Outward flows nonetheless included new strategic stakes in manufacturing companies and acquisitions in technology-intensive sectors. For example, Chinese automotive manufacturer Geely acquired stakes in Daimler (Germany) and Volvo (Sweden) for USD9 billion and USD4 billion, respectively. An investor group composed of China Grand Pharmaceutical and Healthcare Holdings acquired Sirtex Medical, a Sydney-based manufacturer of medical equipment, for USD1.4 billion (see Table 2.17).

To investigate the contribution of foreign capital to China's rapid economic growth, we analyze the behavior and the relationship between the GDP, foreign capital, and domestic savings by conducting multiple regression analysis on annual data for the period 1979–2016.[39] To examine the impact of foreign capital on GDP, we let GDP of the current year be the dependent variable and foreign capital of the previous year be the

---

[39]Calculated using data from China National Bureau of Statistics: National Database: Amount of Foreign Investment by Forms 1998–2016, Gross Domestic Product by Expenditure Approach 1997–2016; All China Data Center, China Yearly Macro-Economic Statistics (National): Residential Buildings and Amount of Savings Deposit in Urban and Rural Areas 1952–2016; China Statistical Yearbook 2013, Tables, 2.16.12, 11.3; 2009, Tables 2.1, 17.14; 1991, Table 15.10; 1986, p. 499; Zhang, Y., C. Chen, and L. Chang. The role of direct foreign investment in China's post-1978 economic development. World Development, 23(4), 691–703; China National Bureau of Statistics: China revises its GDP growth rate in 1993–2004 period (in Chinese), *People's Daily*, January 09, 2006.

Table 2.17.   Cross-border M&As by region/economy, 2017–2018 (millions of dollars).

Region/economy	Sales		Purchases	
	2017	2018	2017	2018
World	2,07,730	4,17,874	1,80,665	3,15,901
Developed economies	1,12,195	2,00,540	54,209	56,891
European Union	49,305	88,023	12,455	20,706
United States	31,205	59,080	32,463	24,398
Japan	22,988	37,568	2,158	3,511
Developing economies	88273	20507	112492	241365
China	17,035	51,458	23,777	40,137
Indonesia	86	4,327	7,733	31,597
Singapore	10,528	18,677	5,212	5,386
India	2,403	7,353	6,295	26,575
Turkey	1,037	705	1,417	6,035
United Arab Emirates	6,185	22,185	2,581	5,085

Note: United Nations Conference on Trade and Development (UNCTAD): World Investment Report 2019 — SPECIAL ECONOMIC ZONES Chapter II Regional Trends, Table B, p. 41.

independent variables. The regression result shows that if the t-ratio of foreign capital (FC_{t-1}) is 3.82, we get

$$Ln(GDP_t) = 0.9004 + 2.3305 Ln(FC_{t-1})$$
$$(-11.29) \qquad (3.82) \qquad\qquad (2.11)$$
$$R = 0.8858,\ df = 35,\ F = 127,\ s = 0.9306$$

where $Ln(GDP_t)$ — the current year GDP after natural logarithm transformation.

$Ln(FC_{t-1})$ — the previous year utilized foreign capital after natural logarithm transformation

Eq. (2.11) suggests the presence of a positive relationship between realized foreign capital of the previous year and the current economic growth (GDP). That is, if realized foreign capital of the previous year increased 10%, the current GDP will increase by 2.3305* Ln (1.1) = 22.2%. An empirical model with domestic savings as dependent variable and (FC_{t-1}) and t (year) as independent variables is analyzed for the period

1979–2016,[40] where the variable year (time) is employed to reduce the potential impact of multicollinearity. The resulting regression analysis is shown below:

$$Ln(SAV_t) = 1.5852 + 0.5990 Ln(FC_{t-1}) + 0.0982(t)$$

$$(8.51) \quad (13.71) \quad\quad\quad (12.50) \quad\quad (2.12)$$

$$R = 0.9970,\ df = 34,\ F = 2844,\ s = 0.1745$$

where t = current year–1979

Other variables are the same as defined in (2.11).

This model is reasonably good as indicated by the large R = 0.9970. With adjustment of the linear trend, the effect of the previous year FC on the current domestic savings is statistically significant, indicating a positive relationship between current domestic savings and the previous year's realized foreign capital. In other words, for the period 1979–2016, there is no statistically significant evidence that foreign capital influx has a negative effect on domestic savings. Specifically, for every 1% increase in the realized previous year's foreign capital, current domestic savings will increase by 0.5990%, instead of decreasing. Thus, as FFEs created opportunities for employees with higher salaries, individual savings will increase. Foreign capital influx, then, indirectly has a positive effect on GDP. Therefore, China and foreign-funded enterprises can achieve mutual benefits.

7.2. *Foreign debt*

In 2016, the balance of China's foreign debt reached USD1,415.8 billion. Figures 2.30 and 2.31 show three risk indicators, foreign debt ratio, debt service ratio, and liability ratio, which are defined as follows:

$$DSR = \frac{PPI}{FER},\ FDR = \frac{BFD}{FER},\ LR = \frac{BFD}{GDP} \qquad (2.13)$$

---

[40]Calculated using data from China National Bureau of Statistics: National Database Annual, Amount of Foreign Investment by Forms 1998–2016; All China Data Center, China Yearly Macro-Economic Statistics (National): Residential Buildings and Amount of Savings Deposits in Urban and Rural Areas 1952–2016; China Statistical Yearbook 2013, China Statistics Press, Tables 2.1, 6.12, 11.3; 2009, Tables 10.3, 18.13.

where: *PPI* — Payment of principal and interest of foreign debts of the current year.

FER — Foreign exchange receipts from foreign trade and non-trade services of the current year.

BFD — Balance of foreign debts of the current year.

GDP — Gross domestic product of the current year.

All three indicators are in a safe area, except for the debt service ratio in 1982 and 1986 (see Figures 2.30 and 2.31). According to the SAFE, China's foreign debt stood at USD198.3 billion at the end of 2018, up by 37.7% yoy. Short-term debt was up by 15.6% yoy, and long-term foreign debt was up by 40.2% yoy.[41] The liability ratio in 2018 was 14.4%, –0.69% lower than in 2017; debt service ratio was at 5.5%, same

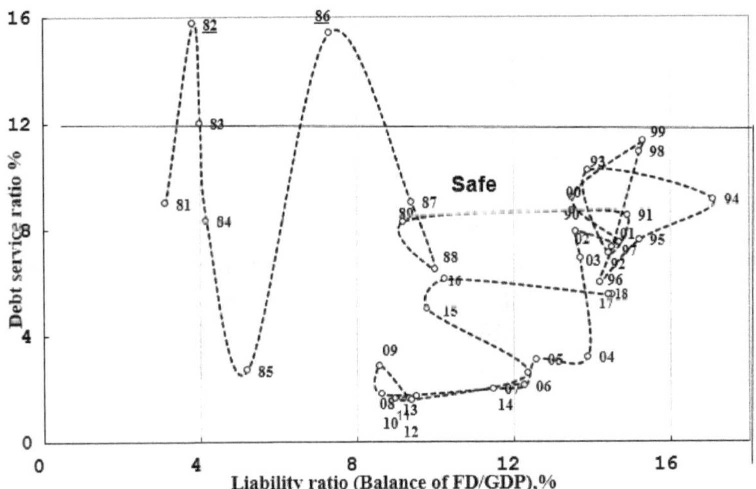

Figure 2.30.   Foreign debt risk I in China (1981–2018).

Source: Calculated using data from China National Bureau of Statistics: National Database: Annual, Outstanding of External Debts 1997–2016; China Statistical Yearbook 2014, China Statistics Press, Table 7.9; 2013, Table 9.13; 2010, Table 8.14; 2004, Table 8.13; 2002, Table 8.21; 1996, Table 7.21; 1991, Table 15.10; China SAFE: Overall situation of External debt (2001–2014) (in Chinese); The time-series data of China's Gross External Debt Position by Sector, since 2014Q4, Dispatch date: 2021-03-26; The SAFEwww.safe.gov.cn/en/2018/0329/1412.html.

---

[41] Data from Administrator of the SAFE: Data and Statistics, China's Gross External Debt Position by Sector since 2014Q4; China National Bureau of Statistics: National Data, Database: Annual, Outstanding of External Debts 1997–2016; The time-series data of

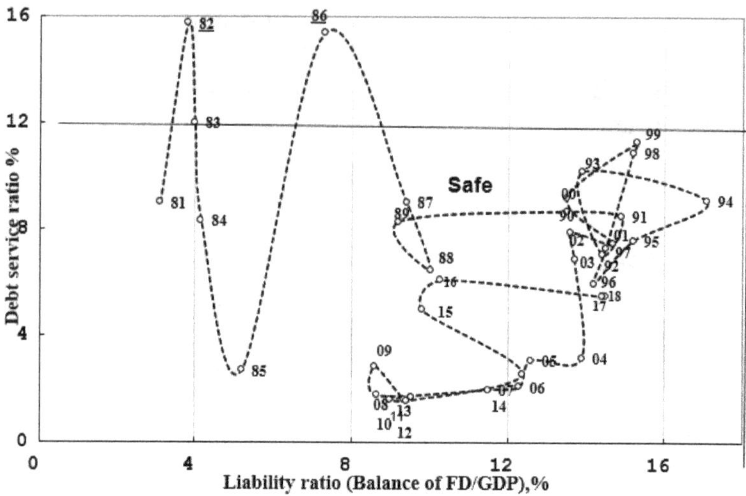

Figure 2.31.　Foreign debt risk II in China (1981–2018).

Source: Same as Figure 2.30.

as in 2017; and foreign debt ratio was at 74.1%, up 1.5% compared to 2017. All these indicators are within international safety levels. China's foreign exchange receipts increased rapidly from 1998–2012, so the foreign debt ratio declined significantly in that period; however, foreign debt ratio increased from 2013–2018 (see Figure 2.30). We will further discuss China's foreign trade and foreign investment performance and the policy of opening to the outside world in more detail in Chapter 7.

8. Ownership Structure Changes

Another important issue on reforms is ownership structure changes. China has adjusted its structure of ownership by developing multi-ownership systems. This issue will be discussed in Chapter 6.

China's Gross External Debt Position by Sector, since 2014Q4, Dispatch date: 2021-03-26; Source: The SAFE.

9. Summary and Concluding Remarks

China's economic history is very long and complicated. Until the outbreak of the First Opium War in the middle of the 19th century, the country remained isolated from the rest of the world. Its economy, however, was one of the largest in the world. All that changed with the conflicts and instability that plagued the country through the greater part of the 20th century.[42] The reforms that were initiated in 1978 helped the country regain its global economic status. Chapter 2 showed evidence of China's growth and covered some of the factors behind that growth.

China's size has been both a blessing and a curse. The country has been endowed with an abundance of natural resources and human capital. At the same time, it is a poor country in terms of per capita natural resources. In comparing China's economic development level with that of the US, we can state that China is still a developing country.

China's implementation of its policy of "opening to the outside world" after 1978 has been a success. Since 2004, the country has been one of the three largest traders in the world, improving its rank from 34th in 1978. In 2017, the total import and export volume of goods reached USD4.1 trillion, an increase of 197.9 times over 1978, with an average annual growth rate of 14.5%, ranking first in the world. China surpassed the United States as a recipient of the FDI in 2003, although it did not receive any FDI prior to 1978. In 2017, China's actual use of FDI was USD131 billion, an increase of 91.3 times over 1984, with an average annual growth rate of 14.7%.

The features of China's economic reforms since 2015 are depicted in Figure 2.32. They include the extensive growth mode, backward agriculture and poor farmers, income disparity, regional gap, low efficiency and severe industrial pollution, large number of non-performing loans with state-owned banks, and insufficient social security systems. In 2017, significant changes in economic structure markedly improved coordination and sustainability of development. The modern agricultural transformation from a single-crop-based traditional agriculture to agriculture, forestry, animal husbandry, and fishery has been realized. The industrial

---

[42]Maddison, A. (2007). *Contours of the World Economy, 1-2030 AD: Essays in Macro-Economic History*. Oxford: Oxford University Press. Friedman, M. (1992). Franklin D. Roosevelt, Silver, and China. *Journal of Political Economy*, 100(1), February, 62–83.

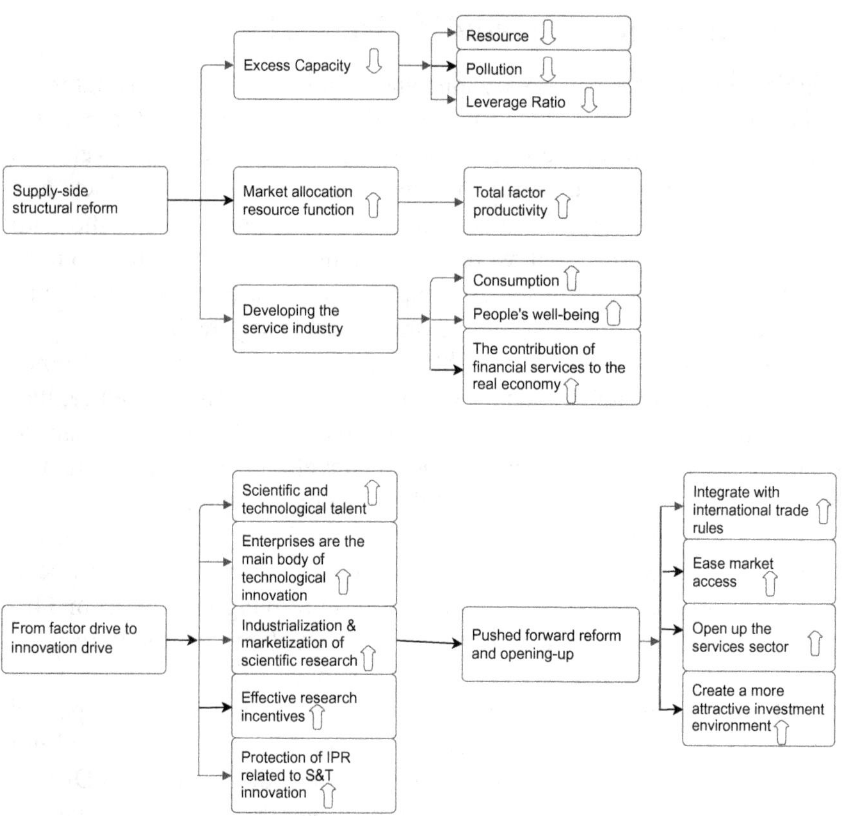

Figure 2.32.   China: from a high-speed growth stage to a high-quality development stage (since 2015).

Note: At the 11th Lujiazui Forum, Vice Premier Liu He of the State Council: China's economy has shifted from a high-speed growth stage to a high-quality development stage, June 13, 2019, (in Chinese).
Source: Finance Union, www.cls.cn/roll/355743.

structure is constantly moving toward the mid- to high-end level. In 2017, the GDP proportion of the service industry increased to 51.6%, an increase of 27% over 1978. China is now on track to pursuing "a scientific approach to development," one that makes economic and social development more people-oriented, comprehensive, balanced, and sustainable. In its development approach, it needs to consider its people's welfare, resources, environmental sustainability, and a more harmonious society with a people-centered approach. Since 2015, China's economy has steadily moved from a high-speed growth stage to a high-quality development stage, and total factor productivity has continued to rise. The promotion of the supply-side structural reform has achieved remarkable results in terms of capacity, leverage, debt control, real estate control, and environmental protection. A new round of technological revolution and industrial transformation is fundamentally reshaping the production process and economic and technological paradigm, which is both an opportunity and a challenge for China on its course to participate in the global division of labor and long-term development. It must implement an innovation-driven development strategy and build an innovative country. For a long time, lack of innovation has been the "Achilles' heel" of China's economy. But, with years of relentless investments and policy support, the country is now catching up fast in making its economy both big and smart. On the Global Innovation Index rankings, China climbed 15 positions, rising from 29th in 2015 to 14th in 2020. Eco-friendly ways of work and life will be advanced to cover all areas of society, and there will be a fundamental improvement in the environment with the goal of building a Beautiful China. Opening the domestic market and contributing to the global economy have been China's commitment for a long time. China aims to turn its market into a market for the world, a market shared by all, and a market accessible to all. Deeper involvement in the international market was also in line with China's new development pattern of "dual circulation," where the domestic and foreign markets can boost each other, with the domestic market as the mainstay.[43]

Selected Bibliography

Goodman, M. I. (1991). *What Went Wrong With Perestroika*. New York, London: W. W. Norton & Company.

Kemme, D. M., and C. E. Gorden. (1990, Editors). *The End of Central Planning? Socialist Economy in Transition: The Cases of Czechoslovakia, Hungary, China, and the Soviet Union.* Boulder: Westview Press. Institute for East–West Security Studies, Hellenic Foundation for Defense and Foreign Policy.

---

[43]Xinhua Headlines (2020). To the next march, what to expect from China's development strategies through 2035? November 16. www.xinhuanet.com/english/2020-11/06/c_139496617.htm.

Lum, T. and D. K. Nanto. (2005). China's trade with the United States and the world, CRS (Congressional Research Service) Report RL31403, Updated April 29. Washington, DC: The Library of Congress.

Maddison, A. (1998). *Chinese Economic Performance in the Long Run.* Paris: Development Centre of the Organisation for Economic Co-Operation and Development.

Chapter 3

Structural Changes in Chinese Economy After Reform

1. Introduction

On November 6, 2019, China's National Development and Reform Commission (NDRC) issued the Catalog for Guiding Industry Restructuring. The 2019 Catalog, revising and updating the 2011 version, aims at upgrading China's industrial structure and promoting high quality development. The Catalog addresses changes affecting 48 industries and identifies three industry categories: an "encouraged" category, a "restricted" category, and an "obsolete" category. The "encouraged" category includes advanced technologies and industries that are integral to high-quality development. Backward technologies products that are in need of reform were included in the "restricted" category Finally, the "obsolete" category includes products that are not associated with safe production, that waste resources or pollute the environment. The last category of projects will eventually be phased out.[1] In the 2019 Catalog, artificial intelligence, human resources and human capital services, elderly care and household services have been added to the new category, while mining services has been added

---

[1]Zhang, Z. (2019). China's 2019 catalogue for guiding industry restructuring. *China Briefing*. November. Downloaded from www.china-briefing.com/news/chinas-2019-catalogue-guiding-industry-restructuring/?shared=email&msg=fail.

to the obsolete category.[2] The Catalog offers valuable inputs for future investment decisions and reveals the emphasis that the Chinese government places on industrial structure as a tool for economic development. The Catalog became effective on January 1, 2020. It represents a clear indication that China views its industrial structure as a valuable component to the country's development. Indeed, China's industrialization, urbanization, marketization, and globalization have been pressing ahead swiftly since the reform started, giving rise to the adjustment of its industrial structure.

In our discussion, we will consider Industrial Structure (IS) as comprising three sectors: Primary (such as Agriculture and Mining), Secondary (Manufacturing), and Tertiary (Services). The change in the industrial structure is mainly dependent on various economic and noneconomic factors. Economic factors include the country's demand structure, its supply structure, the relationship between demand and supply structures, and the relationship between each of these structures and the growth patterns of industry. Non-economic factors include the different policies implemented by the government. In China's case, of course, IS was determined by the government during its Central Planning period (1949–1978).

In this chapter, we cover some of the changes in China's industrial structure that have taken place in conjunction with the reforms. The nature of a country's industrial structure is affected by a complicated set of economic and non-economic factors. In turn, as industrial structure takes its shape, it impacts the country's economic and social development. In this chapter, we will discuss various characteristics of China's IS We provide a description of changes associated with China's IS before and after economic reforms. In addition, we analyze China's IS in relation to that of other selected countries.

We first examine the change in industry employment. Specifically, we find the change of employment share and GDP share by industrial sector and the importance of the sector to the country's output.

Since 1978, China has also witnessed changes in both demand and supply structures. These changes have also impacted China's IS. To understand these changes, we examine consumption propensities for urban and rural areas since the reforms. They confirm the increasing emphasis on consumption. We also show income disparities between

---

[2] Shijia, O. (2020). NDRC issues new guidance catalogue to boost high-level development. *China Daily, Global Edition*. June 17. Accessed at https://www.chinadaily.com. cn/a/201911/06/WS5dc2869aa310cf3e35575cbb.html.

China and other countries during different periods. We proceed with a discussion on urbanization. China's low level of urbanization has resulted in its underdeveloped tertiary industry and the world's largest dual economic entity. We conclude by exploring the dilemmas associated with China's industrial structure adjustments.

2. The Nature and Measurement Direction and Size of Industrial Structure Change

IS denotes the link among various industrial sectors. From a quantitative perspective, it denotes the shares of output, employment, and investment among different industry sectors, thus revealing the extent of structural balance. From a qualitative viewpoint, the nature of IS in the economy indicates the level and performance of IS. A changing IS results in different allocation of resources, changing economic output, and affects the country's long-term economic development. As a country moves through the different stages of economic development, some industrial sectors will potentially account for a larger share of output, while the share of yet others may shrink. This is called IS change. The IS, then, will be optimized during the economic development process. Since we usually represent the level of economic development by per capita GDP, therefore optimization of the IS is related to per capita GDP. Optimization of the IS is not only the result of past economic development, but also the condition for further economic development. Final demand is directly connected to per capita income; increase in final demand will stimulate investment. Therefore, intermediate demand is also indirectly related to per capita income, i.e., when per capita income increases, the Engel coefficient and the Hoffman coefficient will decline, increasing the share of tertiary industry. We can therefore represent different stages of economic development through per capita GDP and the accompanying IS change. The importance of IS and its change to the economic development process, then, should not be underestimated. Furthermore, industrial structure is dynamic within a country and across countries. Global economic powerhouses come and go as their industrial structures change.

2.1. *Measuring IS*

To quantitatively study the nature and change of IS, we use two measures: the IS change coefficient K and the IS similarity coefficient $R1$:

$$K = \frac{\sum_{i=1}^{n} Abs\left[s_i(e) - s_i(0)\right]}{n} \qquad\qquad K_{ann} = \frac{K}{Yr} \qquad (3.1)$$

$$R1 = \left[\frac{\sum_{i=1}^{n} s_i(e) * s_i(0)}{\sqrt{\left\{\sum_{i=1}^{n} s_i^2(e)\right\} * \left\{\sum_{i=1}^{n} s_i^2(0)\right\}}}\right] \qquad (3.2)$$

$s_i(e)$ — share of sector i to total value at the end of the period.
$si(0)$ — share of sector i to total value at beginning of period.
n — number of industrial sectors.
K — IS change coefficient. ?$(0, 2/n)$.
Yr — number of years during the changing period.
K_{ann} — Annual IS change coefficient.

$R1$ – IS similarity coefficient $[0, 1]$; if there is no change in IS, then s_i $(t) = s_i(t + m)$, therefore, $R1 = 1$; if at t, all gross output produced by sector i alone and at $t+m$ by sector j alone, then $R1 = 0$. Therefore, a larger $R1$ indicates greater similarity in IS through time.

3. The Change of Employment Share by Industrial Sectors

From Figure 3.1, we observe that the percentage share of first Industry in China is relatively high; it declines slowly but is still 44.8% in 2005; it further falls to 25.1% in 2019. Table 3.1 shows that, after economic reform (1978–2019), the annual IS change coefficient $K_{ann} = 0.74$ is larger than $K_{ann} = 0.33$, the change coefficient before economic reform (1952–1978). We can therefore conclude that the industrial structure change taking place after economic reform is larger than the change before economic reform. Meanwhile, the IS similarity coefficient during 1978–2019 $R1 = 0.6364$, is smaller than $R1 = 0.9868$, the coefficient associated with the prior to economic reform (1952–1978). Also, we can see that $K_{ann}=$

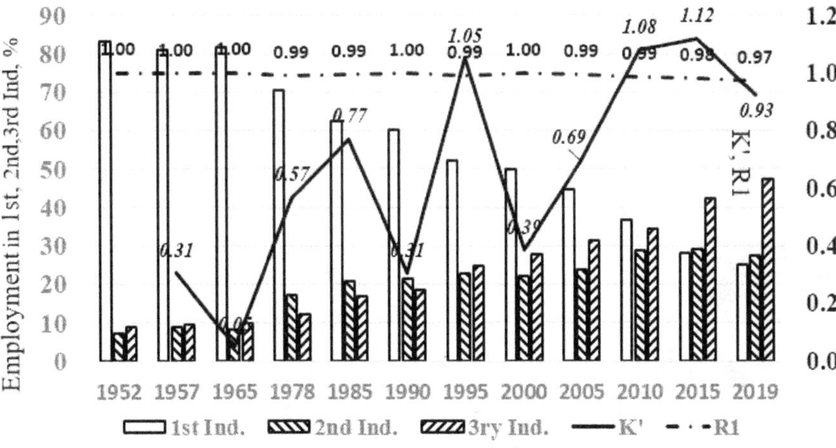

Figure 3.1.   Percentage share of employment by sector, 1952–2019.

Source: Calculated using data from China National Bureau of Statistics: China Statistical Yearbook, China Statistical Press, 2006, Table 5.2: China National Bureau of Statistics, Database; Employed Persons by 1st, 2nd, 3rd Industry, 2001 and 2019.

0.74 during the full post reform period considered here (1978–2019), but $K_{ann} = 1.1$ during the last 14 years of the post reform era (2005–2019). This implies that the pace of industrial structure change accelerated during the recent period. We can, therefore, conclude that China's industrial structure entered a more dynamic phase under reform. China's industrialization has entered a new stage.

3.1. *China's IS versus that of other countries*

We now compare each sector's employment share in China with that of other countries. In Figure 3.2, coefficient K and $R1$ are calculated using China as reference. From Table 3.2, we find out that compared with developed country $K > 30\%$ in 2002, China from 1952–2005 K equals 25.8%, which takes 53 years. Even after economic reform K reaches 17.13% for 27 years. If China's IS changes at such a higher rate (after economic reform), it will take another 47 years for K to achieve 30% change, which indicates that China's IS needs a long time to catch up with the IS of a developed country. The world average value of labor force in agriculture is 28.4% in 2017; for middle-income group, it is 33.9%, and it is 26.9%

Table 3.1.   Percentage Share of employments by sector, China 1952–2019.

	1952	1957	1965	1978	1985	1990	1995	2000	2005	2010	2015	2019	52–78	78-19	52-19	05-19
1st Ind.	83.5	81.2	81.6	70.5	62.4	60.1	52.2	50.0	44.8	36.7	28.3	25.1				
2nd Ind.	7.4	9	8.4	17.3	20.8	21.4	23.0	22.3	23.8	28.7	29.3	27.5				
3rd Ind.	9.1	9.8	10	12.2	16.8	18.5	24.8	27.7	31.4	34.6	42.4	47.4				
K'		0.31	0.05	0.57	0.77	0.31	1.05	0.39	0.69	1.08	1.12	1.22	0.33	0.74	0.65	1.10
$R1$	1.0000	0.9997	1.0000	0.9897	0.9934	0.9993	0.9895	0.9983	0.9945	0.9860	0.9808	0.9579	0.9868	0.6364	0.5982	0.9397

Source: Calculated using data from China National Bureau of Statistics: China Statistical Yearbook, China Statistical Press, 2006, Table 5.2: China National Bureau of Statistics, Database; Employed Persons by 1st, 2nd, 3rd Industry, 2001 and 2019.

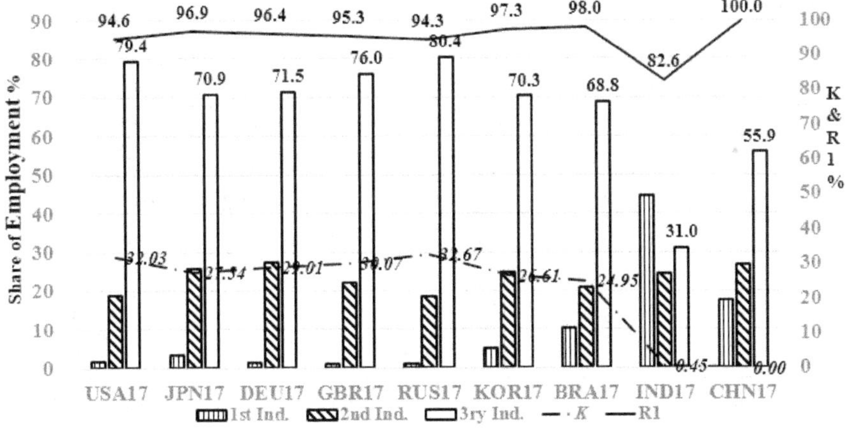

Figure 3.2.   Comparing % of employment by sector, China with other countries, 2017.

Source: Calculated using data from World Bank (2019). World Development Indicators online 2019, Released July 10.

for upper middle-income groups.[3] China's value lies between middle-income groups and upper middle-income group.

In Table 3.2, we compare China's shares of sector employment with those of the United States during the past decades. We find that, during the 1952–2017 period, the share of employment by industries in China was similar with the United States during the 1810–1908 period, which is confirmed by the IS resemblance coefficient $R1 > 0.9592$ (see Table 3.3). Before reform, the change in China's IS is equivalent to 20 years of IS change in the United States; after reform, however, China's IS changes in 39 years are equivalent to 78 years of change in the United States. The fast pace of China's IS changes following the reforms also reflects China's overall improved economic performance.

In Table 3.3, we compare the share of sector employment between China and Japan during the same time. The results show that, from 1957–1980, the difference in employment industry structure between China and Japan increased, as confirmed by the decrease in R1 from 0.749 to 0.4206. The two economies followed different paths during the period; Japan's

---

[3]Calculated using data from World Bank (2019). World Development Indicators online 2019. Released July 10.

Table 3.2. Comparing percent points of employment between China and the United States with similar industrial structure of employment.

	CH	USA	CH	USA	CH	USA	CH	USA
CHUS empl%	1952	1810	1978	1830	2005	1888	2017	1908
1st Ind.	83.5	83.9	70.5	70.7	44.8	44.7	28.3	19.2
2nd Ind.	7.4	10.0	17.4	23.1	23.8	31.2	29.3	22.90
3rd Ind.	9.1	6.1	12.1	6.2	31.4	24.2	42.4	57.2
Sum	100	100	100	100	100	100	100.0	100
K		2.00		3.94		4.90		10.10
$R1$		0.9989		0.9939		0.9850		0.9592

Source: Calculated using data from World Bank (2019). World Development Indicators online 2019. Released July 10.

economy grew rapidly, while China's economy stagnated because of the great leap forward and the cultural revolution. However, from 1980–2004, R1 increased from 0.4206 to 0.6838, signifying a narrowing of the IS difference between the two countries. From 2004–2017, R1 further rose to 0.9592. This shows that, after economic reform and especially during the recent 12 years included in the table, China's IS with respect to employment caught up with Japan's.

3.2. *GDP and the service industry*

Figures 3.3 and 3.4 show that the relationship between the share of employment and value added in tertiary industry relative to per capita GDP is different before and after economic reform (1978). Before economic reform, the share of employment and value added in tertiary industry seems to have no relation with per capita GDP (see Figure 3.3). After economic reform, when per capita GDP increases, the percentage share by employment and by value added in tertiary industry also rises (see Figure 3.4).

We further examine the role per capita GDP played in determination of the percentage share of employment in tertiary industry. Using the data listed in Table 3.5, we can establish the relationship between percentage share of service sector in GDP and per capita GDP before and after economic reform. Using 1978 constant GDP, the estimated relationship before economic reform (1952–1978) is depicted in Eq. (3.4).

Table 3.3. Comparing the percentage share of sector employment between China and Japan (concurrent).

	CHN	JPN	CHN	JPN	CHN	JPN	CHN	JPN	CHN	JPN	CHN	JPN
CHJPempl%	1957	1957	1970	1970	1980	1980	1990	1990	2004	2004	2017	2017
1st Ind.	81.2	37	80.7	17.4	68.7	10.4	60.1	7.2	46.9	4.6	27.0	3.4
2nd Ind.	9	26	10.1	35.2	18.2	34.8	21.4	33.6	24.7	28.7	29.0	24.6
3rd Ind.	9.8	37	9	47.3	11.7	54.6	18.5	58.7	28.4	66.7	44.0	71.9
K		29.47		42.23		39.27		35.10		28.22		18.59
$R1$		0.7490		0.4345		0.4206		0.4953		0.6440		0.8818

Source: Calculated using data from China National Bureau of Statistics: China Statistical Yearbook, China Statistical Press, Table 5.2; Statistics Bureau, Ministry of Internal Affairs and Communications: Japan Statistical Yearbook 2006.

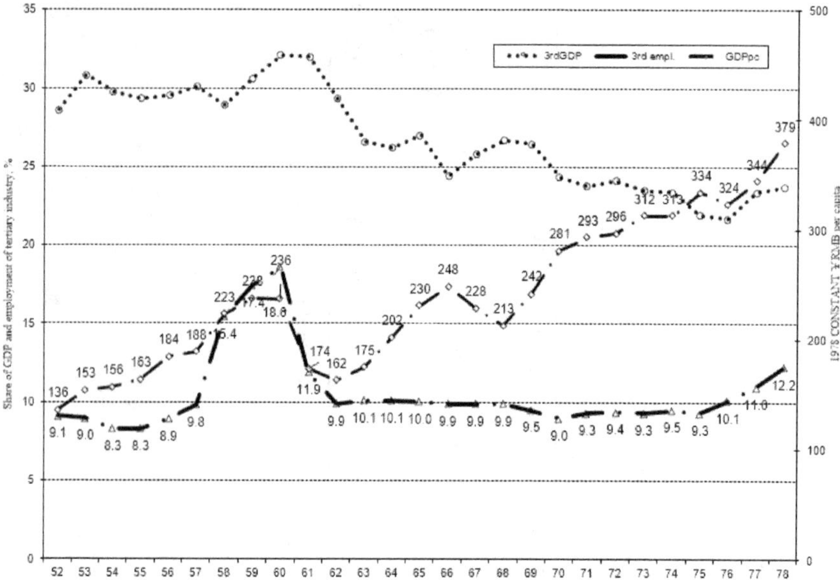

Figure 3.3.   GDPpc and %EMP of service industry in China, 1952–1978.

Source: Calculated using data from China National Bureau of Statistics: China Statistical Yearbook, China Statistical Press, 2005, Table 5.2; 1991, Table 4.6; China National Bureau of Statistics, Data base; Composition of GDP by the three strata of industry, GDP(%), 1997 to 2016; Employed Persons by the three strata of industry, 1997– 2016 (http://data.stats.gov.cn/english/asyquery.htm?cn=C01).

$$sere \% = 3.9353 + 1.2191 \, Ln \, (GDP_{pe\,78})$$

$$(0.14) \qquad (0.41)$$

$$R = 0.1361, F = 25, df = 0.47, s = 2.59$$

Eq. (3.4) shows the relationship after economic reform (1978–2019):

$$sere \% = -46.5641 + 9.6365 \, Ln \, (GDP_{pe\,78})$$

$$(-39.25) \qquad (24.65) \tag{3.4}$$

$$R = 0.9873, F = 1541, df = 40, s = 1.6680$$

The value in the bracket is *t*-ratio, R is the coefficient of determination; F represents the F-ratio, and s is the standard error of the estimate. The estimated values indicate that there is no statistically significant

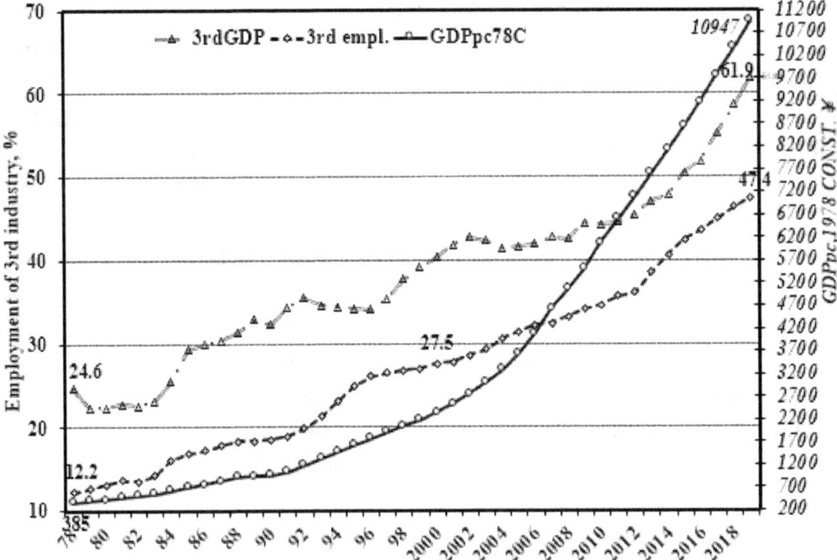

Figure 3.4.   GDPpc and %EMP of service industry in China, 1978–2019.

Source: Calculated using data from China National Bureau of Statistics: China Statistical Yearbook, China Statistical Press, 2006, Tables 3.2, 3.3, 5.2; 2002, Tables 3.3, 5.2; China National Bureau of Statistics, Database; Composition of GDP by the three strata of industry, GDP(%), 1997–2016.

relationship between employment in the service sector and per capita GDP, In the regression Eq. (3.3), R is only 0.1361 and t-ratio are less than 0.5. It is statistical unacceptable. According to China's data from 1952–1978, per capita GDP grew by 179%, the percentage share of employment in tertiary industry rose by 34.1%. Since there is no capital market under the planned economy, there is no need for the development of tertiary industry.

After the reform, it can be seen from equation (3.4) that the per capita GDP increased by 100%, and the employment of the tertiary industry increased by 41.60%. We know that it will take a long time for per capita GDP to increase by 100%. If the annual growth rate of per capita GDP reached 6% — this is a high value — it will take 12 years to grow by 100%. Using data from Table 3.5 and Eq. (3.4), we calculated that the employment in service industry was 10.7% in 1978 and 41.4% in 2019; that is, it took 41 years for the change to take place.

From Table 3.4, we observe that the percentage share of employment in service sector increased dramatically from 1957 (9.1%) to 1960 (18.6%), then declined in 1962 (to 9.9%). The great leap forward resulted in serious decrement of the percentage share of employment in agriculture from 81.2% in 1957 to 58.2% in 1958. On the other hand, the percentage share of employment in industry and service sectors increased dramatically. The development of the economy was not sustained, though, so GDP per capita and the percentage share of employment in service sector declined in the following years. After economic reform, we observe that the trend of the percentage share of employment in service sector and GDP per capita increase continuously with time, which coincides with the global trend. From the above static and dynamic relationships of the percentage share of employment in China, we draw the conclusion that the country's IS was equivalent to the IS of developed countries in the 1950s.

4. The Change of GDP Share by Industrial Sectors

Table 3.5 shows that the percentage share of GDP in tertiary industry is low in 1952, increases slowly; up to the 1990s, it is still near 30%. From 1957–1976, the GDP composition of tertiary industry declines, and there is a unilateral increase in the percentage share of GDP of the second industry, as shown by Figure 3.5. As shown in, the change coefficient for the percentage share of GDP by sector (K_{ann} = 0.47) from 1978–2015 is less than from 1952–1978 (K_{ann} = 0.69). Figure 3.5 reveals that, before economic reform, the GDP composition of the first industry declined and the GDP composition of the third industry also slightly declined, so the GDP share of second industry increased significantly. This was the result of a heavy industry-oriented development strategy, which was commonly adopted by CPEs (Central Planned Economies). By its nature, heavy industry is capital-intensive, but China was a least developed country with a capital-scarce agrarian economy in the 1950s. Like other CPEs, China adopted low wage rates with low price levels for necessities, so the purchasing price of agricultural products was very low. The original capital used to develop its heavy industry was taken from workers and farmers. To develop its heavy industry, the government created an environment of artificially depressed interest rate, over-valued exchange rate, low price for raw materials, planned allocation of credits, foreign exchange, and raw materials. To implement these policies, SOEs and collective agricultural

Table 3.4.   GDP$_{pc78}$ and employment of service sector in China, 1952–2019.

Year	3rd GDP	GDPpc*	3rd empl.	Year	3rd GDP	GDPpc*	3rd GDP	Year	3rd GDP	GDPpc*	3rd empl.
1952	28.6	136	9.1	1979	24.8	408	9.1	2006	41.9	4080	32.2
1953	30.8	153	9	1980	22.3	428	13.1	2007	42.8	4635	32.4
1954	29.7	156	8.3	1981	22.3	445	13.6	2008	42.6	5057	33.2
1955	29.3	163	8.3	1982	22.1	478	13.5	2009	44.4	5507	34.1
1956	29.5	184	8.9	1983	22.7	523	14.2	2010	44.3	6063	34.6
1957	30.1	188	9.8	1984	25.1	594	16.1	2011	44.6	6609	35.7
1958	28.9	223	15.4	1985	28.9	665	16.8	2012	45.4	7091	36.1
1959	30.6	238	17.4	1986	29.4	713	17.2	2013	47.1	7602	38.5
1960	32.1	236	18.6	1987	29.9	783	17.8	2014	47.8	8119	40.6
1961	32	174	11.9	1988	30.7	857	18.3	2015	50.4	8638	42.4
1962	29.3	162	9.9	1989	32.2	879	18.3	2016	51.8	9165	43.5
1963	26.6	175	10.1	1990	31.8	899	18.5	2017	52.7	9752	44.9
1964	26.2	202	10.1	1991	33.9	968	18.9	2018	53.3	10366	46.3
1965	27	230	10	1992	35.0	1092	19.8	2019	54.3	10947	47.4
1966	24.4	248	9.9	1993	33.9	1231	21.2				
1967	25.8	228	9.9	1994	33.8	1376	23				
1968	26.7	213	9.9	1995	33.0	1510	24.8				
1969	26.5	242	9.5	1996	33.0	1644	26				
1970	24.3	281	9	1997	34.4	1779	26.4				

(*Continued*)

Table 3.4.   (*Continued*)

Year	3rd GDP	GDPpc*	3rd empl.	Year	3rd GDP	GDPpc*	3rd GDP	Year	3rd GDP	GDPpc*	3rd empl.
1971	23.8	293	9.3	1998	36.5	1900	26.7				
1972	24.1	296	9.4	1999	38.0	2027	26.9				
1973	23.5	312	9.3	2000	39.3	2181	27.5				
1974	23.4	313	9.5	2001	40.7	2345	27.7				
1975	21.9	334	9.3	2002	41.7	2541	28.6				
1976	21.7	324	10.1	2003	41.4	2778	29.3				
1977	23.4	344	11	2004	40.7	3039	30.6				
1978	24.18559332	379	12.2	2005	39.9	3331	31.4				

Note: *1978 constant CNY.

Source: Calculated using data from China National Bureau of Statistics: China Statistical Yearbook, China Statistical Press, 2006, Tables 3.2, 3.3, 5.2; 2002, Tables 3.3, 5.2; All China Data online: China Yearly Macro-Economic Statistics (National) GDP, 1952–2016; China National Bureau of Statistics, Data base; Annual, Composition of GDP by the three strata of industry, GDP(%), 2001–2020; Indices of Gross National Income 2001–2020.

Table 3.5.   Composition of GDP, China, 1952–2015.

CHgdp%	1952	1957	1965	1978	1990	2000	2005	2010	2015	2019	c78/19	c05/19	c52/78
1st Ind.	50.5	40.3	37.9	27.9	26.9	14.8	12.6	9.5	8.8	7.1	27.9	12.6	27.9
2nd Ind.	20.9	29.7	35.1	47.9	41.3	45.9	47.5	46.4	40.9	38.6	47.9	47.5	47.9
3rd Ind.	28.6	30.1	27	24.2	31.8	39.3	39.9	44.1	50.2	54.3	24.2	39.9	24.2
Sum	100	100.1	100	100	100	100	100	100	99.9	100	100	100	100
K		6.83	3.63	8.52	5.07	8.03	1.49	2.80	4.10	2.70	20.08	9.60	17.98
K_{ann}		1.37	0.45	0.66	0.42	0.80	0.30	0.56	0.82	0.67	0.49	0.69	0.69
$R1$		0.9760	0.9935	0.9623	0.9861	0.9713	0.9991	0.9968	0.9920	0.9975	0.8291	0.9643	0.8318

Source: Calculated using data from China National Bureau of Statistics: China Statistical yearbook, China Statistical Press, 2006, Table 3.2; 2002, Table 3.2; China National Bureau of Statistics, Data base; Composition of GDP by the three strata of industry, GDP(%), 1997–2016.

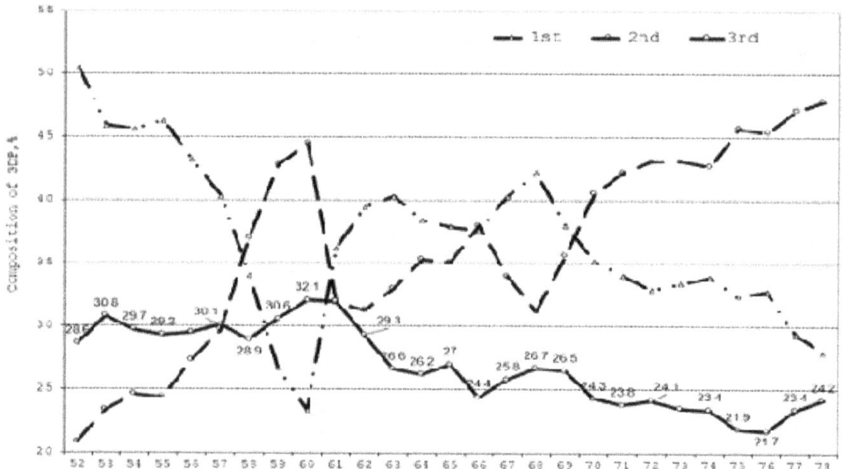

Figure 3.5. Composition of GDP, China (1952–1978).

Source: Calculated using data from China National Bureau of Statistics: China Statistical Yearbook, China Statistical Press, 2002, Table 3.2; China National Bureau of Statistics, Data base; Composition of GDP by the three strata of industry, GDP(%), 1997–2016.

organizations were widely promoted. Heavy industry developed quickly before economic reform at the cost of structural imbalance, low efficiency, low incentive, and low growth rate. China's economy became an economy characterized by shortages. Under such policy, the GDP share of secondary industry increased dramatically between 1952 and 1959. From 1959–1962, the GDP share of secondary industry declined significantly because of serious shortages of agricultural products. When the food supply was improved slightly in 1962, the GDP share of secondary industry increased again until 1966. During the next two years (1966–1968), the GDP share of secondary industry declined due to the Cultural Revolution, as shown in Figure 3.5. From 1969–1978, the GDP share of secondary industry again increased.

After economic reform, China pursued a market-oriented development strategy, so the GDP composition of the primary sector declined, and was offset by an increase in the GDP composition of the tertiary industry (see Figure 3.6). Improved people's living standard and increased job opportunities coincided with the global trend of industrial structure changes.

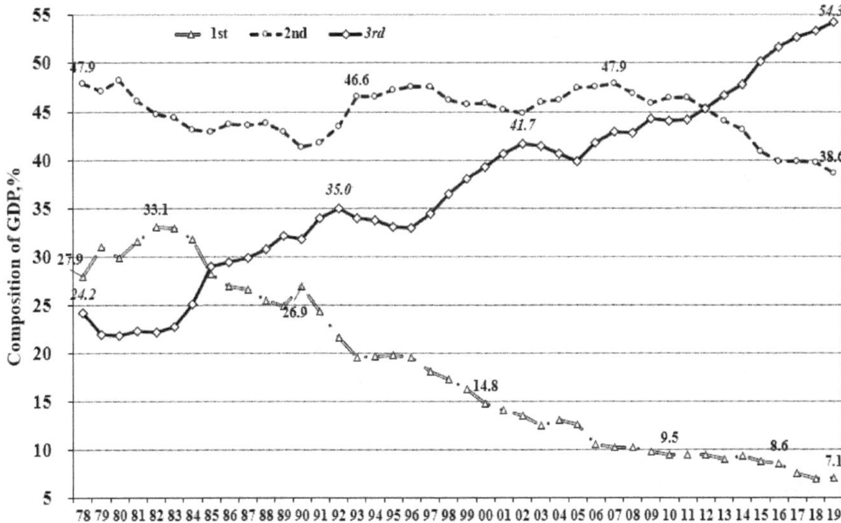

Figure 3.6.   Composition of GDP, China (1978–2019).

Source: Calculated using data from China National Bureau of Statistics: China Statistical Yearbook China Statistical Press, 2006, Table 3.2; China National Bureau of Statistics, Data base; Composition of GDP by the three strata of industry, GDP(%), 2001–2020.

4.1. *GDP composition: China and other countries*

We now compare the composition of GDP in China with that of other countries. Figure 3.7 shows the calculated K and $R1$ coefficients using China as reference. As shown in Table 3.6, in 2004, China is most similar with Brazil with respect to the IS composition of GDP. However, China's GDP composition of second industry (46.2%) is higher than Brazil's (40%), and its GDP composition of tertiary industry (40.7%) is lower than Brazil's (46.4%). Comparing China with India, we find that China's GDP composition of second industry (46.2%) is much higher than India's (27.1%), and its GDP composition of tertiary industry (40.7%) is much lower than India's (51.7%). From Table 3.6, we observe that, compared with developed countries, the IS change coefficient K is on average greater by more than 20 % points. From Table 3.5, we find that the change coefficient K for GDP composition in China is only 25.3% points for the 53-year period spanning from 1952–2015. If China's composition of GDP changes at the same rate, it will take another 50 years to get the change coefficient K for composition of GDP to reach 23.9% which

Table 3.6. Comparison of GDP composition, China and selected countries, 2004.

	CH	JP	CH	France	CH	DEU	CH	US	CH	DEU
Year	1952	1895	1978	1896	1990	1935	2005	1889	2017	1991
1st Ind.	50.5	42.7	27.9	25.0	14.8	16.2	12.6	16.4	7.9	1.2
2nd Ind.	20.9	18.2	47.9	46.2	45.9	50.3	47.5	24.8	40.5	33.6
3rd Ind.	28.6	39.1	24.2	28.8	39.3	31.5	39.9	58.8	51.6	56.3
K		7.00		3.08		4.50		15.13		6.09
$R1$		0.9763		0.9955		0.9895		0.8945		0.9291

Source: Calculated using data from World Bank (2006). World Development Indicators online 2006, released April. China National Bureau of Statistics (2006). China Statistical Yearbook, China Statistics Press, Table 3.2.

indicates that China needs another half century for the composition of its GDP to catch up with the developed countries' current GDP composition. As shown in Table 3.6, when comparing the GDP composition of China with that of lower middle-income groups, we find that the change coefficient K is 3.8 and the similarity coefficient $R1$ equals 0.9928. This means that China's composition of GDP is quite similar with the average value of lower middle-income groups in 2004. From Table 3.6, we also found that China's GDP composition of second industry (46.2%) is higher than the average value of lower middle-income groups (41.2%), but its GDP composition of tertiary industry (40.7%) is lower than the average value of lower middle-income groups (46.4%). These numbers indicate that China's GDP composition of second industry is high, while its GDP composition of tertiary industry is low. Further, the high value-added service industry in China's tertiary industry accounts for a lower portion of GDP. This fact is explained by China's heavy industry-oriented development strategy before 1978. Lower GDP composition of the tertiary industry not only effected economic development and people's living standard, but also provided fewer job opportunities. Therefore, the urbanization rate was low (we will further discuss this topic in Chapter 4). As shown in Figure 3.7, in 2017, China is most similar with South Korea with respect to the IS of GDP ($R1$ = 0.9944). But China's GDP composition of second industry (40.5%) is higher than South Korea's (30.5%), and its GDP composition of tertiary industry (51.9%) is slightly lower than South Korea's (52.8%). Comparing China's GDP composition with that of middle-income groups, we find the change coefficient K for composition of GDP to be 3.84 and the similarity

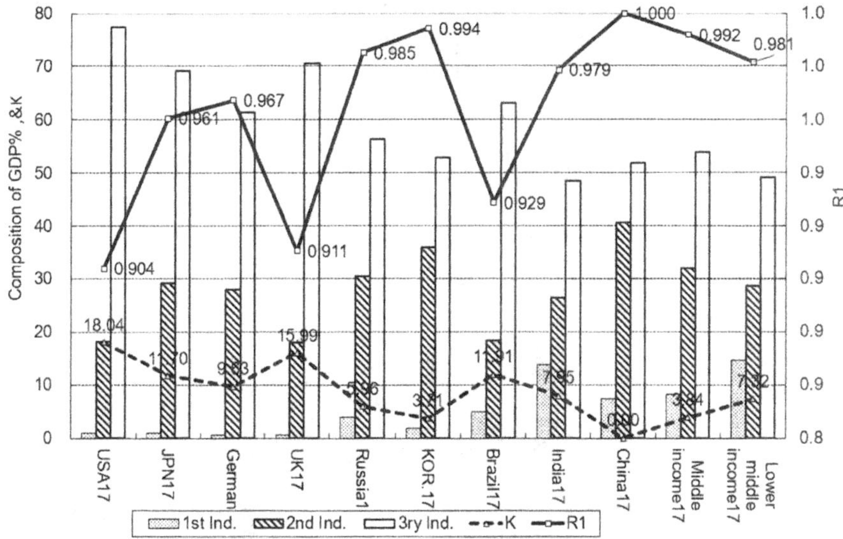

Figure 3.7.   World comparison for composition of GDP, 2017.

Source: Calculated using data from World Bank (2018). World Development Indicators online 2018. Released in September.

coefficient $R1$ to equal 0.9928. This means that China's composition of GDP is quite similar with the average value of middle-income groups. From Figure 3.7, we observe that China's GDP composition of second industry (40.5%) is higher than the average value of middle-income groups (32%), but its GDP composition of tertiary industry (51.9%) is lower (54%). These results indicate that China's GDP composition of second industry is high, while its GDP composition of tertiary industry is low.

We can see from Tables 3.6 and 3.7 that the GDP composition structure in China from 1952–2017 is equivalent to that of developed countries from 1895–1991, as is confirmed by the similarity coefficient *R1* (see Table 3.7). China's composition of GDP in 2005 is similar to that of the Unites States in 1889, as by *R1* = 0.8945 (see Table 3.7). China's GDP composition in 2017 is similar to that of Germany in 1991, which is shown by *R1* = 0.9291. The main difference is that the composition of the second industry in China's GDP is lower than that of the tertiary industry. From the viewpoint of GDP's composition in 2005, China lags behind the United States by more than 100 years. In 2017, China was only 26 years

Table 3.7.   Comparison of the similar structure of GDP composition, China with selected countries.

	CH	JP	CH	JP	CH	JP	CH	JP	CH	JP	CH	JP
Year	1957	1960	1970	1970	1978	1978	1988	1988	2002	2002	2017	2017
1st Ind.	40.3	13.1	35.2	5.9	28.1	4.6	25.7	2.6	15.4	1.3	7.3	0.9
2nd Ind.	29.7	44.2	40.5	45.2	48.2	40.7	44.1	39.0	51.1	30.	40.5	29.1
3rd Ind.	30.1	42.7	24.3	48.9	23.7	54.7	30.2	58.4	33.5	69.	51.9	69.1
$R1$		0.8518		0.8194		0.8179		0.8524		0.8970		0.9606
K		18.09		19.53		20.65		18.77		18.03		11.70

Source: Calculated using data from International Statistical Yearbook, China Statistical Press; China National Bureau of Statistics: China Statistical Yearbook, China Statistics Press, 2006, Table 3.2; 2002, Table 3.2; US Department of Commerce, U.S. Census Bureau: Historical Statistics of the United States, Colonial time to 1970, Part I, p. 240; World Bank, World Development Indicators online 2018, released September 2018.

behind Germany. Between 2005 and 2017, then, China GDP composition improved significantly.

Table 3.8 shows that, from the 1950s to the 1970s, the similarity coefficient *R1* declines, implying that the difference in GDP composition structure between China and Japan increased. Between 1978 and 1988, the difference in GDP composition structure between China and Japan decreased, as shown by the increased value of the *R*1 coefficient. From 1988–2003, the similarity coefficient *R1* declined due to the increase of the difference in GDP composition of second industry between China and Japan from 5.1% to 20.7%, while the difference in GDP composition of the third industry between China and Japan declined from 28.1% to 27.0%. This shows that China developed its heavy industry, allowing its third industry to further decline. From 2003–2017, the third industry developed vigorously, so the similarity coefficient reached its highest level, 0.9611. This means that the difference in GDP composition structure between China and Japan was narrowed after China's economic reform.

As can be seen from Figure 3.8, before economic reform, enterprises were unwilling to provide service to their customers, so the number of customers served by enterprise workers increased dramatically. For example, one worker in social service sector served 587 customers in 1952 and 1719 customers in 1978. After reform, the numbers fell to 86 customers in 2003 and 50 in 2016. People's daily lives became much more comfortable after 1978. The number of persons served by workers within enterprises dropped significantly. The key issue under a planned economic system, of course, is the lack of an incentive mechanism. Herein lies a big difference between a heavy industry oriented and market-oriented economy.

5. Comparative Productivity of Industrial Structure

The economic benefit of a country's industrial structure can be represented by the increase of value added to GDP in response to the change in IS. We begin our analysis by defining each sector's productivity as PS, or:

$$PS_t = \frac{(\% GDP)_t}{(\% Empl)_t} \qquad (3.11)$$

Table 3.8.   Comparison of GDP composition between China and Japan (concurrent).

	CH	JP	CH	JP	CH	JP	CH	JP	CH	JP	CH	JP
Year	1957	1960	1970	1970	1978	1978	1988	1988	2003	2003	2016	2016
1st Ind.	40.3	13.1	35.2	5.9	28.1	4.6	25.7	2.6	12.6	1.3	8.6	1.2
2nd Ind.	29.7	44.2	40.5	45.2	48.2	40.7	44.1	39.0	51.1	30.4	39.9	29.3
3rd Ind.	30.1	42.7	24.3	48.9	23.7	54.7	30.2	58.4	41.4	68.4	51.6	68.8
K		18.09		19.53		20.65		18.77		23.19		11.74
$R1$		0.8518		0.8194		0.8179		0.8524		0.8199		0.9611

Source: Calculated using data from World Bank: World Development Indicators online 2006, Released April 2006 by World Bank; China National Bureau of Statistics: China Statistical Yearbook, China Statistical Press 2006, Table 3.2; China National Bureau of Statistics: International Statistical Yearbook, China Statistical Press 2005, The Economist Intelligence Unit: Country Profile 2006, Japan; Ministry of Internal Affairs and Communications: Historical Statistics of Japan, Japan Statistical Association, 1987–1988.

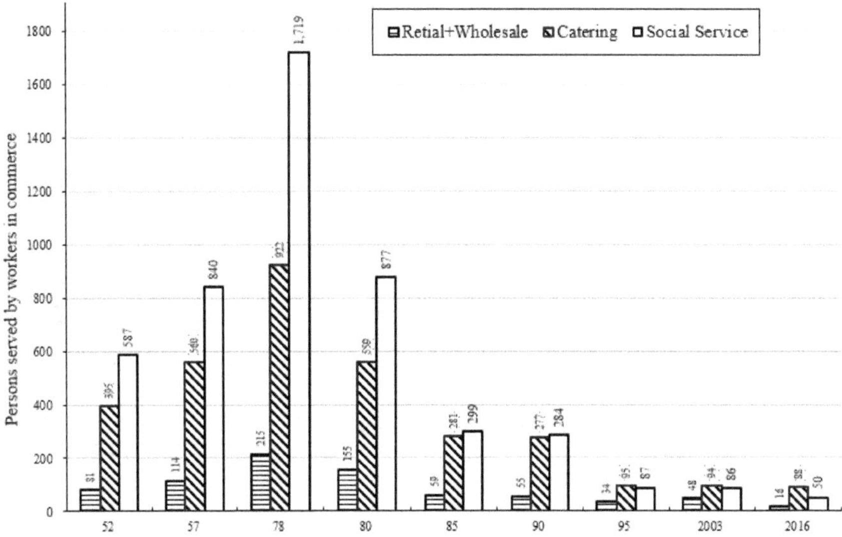

Figure 3.8.   Persons served by workers in commerce, China 1952–2016.

Source: Calculated using data from China National Bureau of Statistics: China Statistical Yearbook, China Statistical Press 2004, Tables 5.7, 5.8, 5.16; 1991, Table 14.13; 2016 Tables 4.5, 4.6; China National Bureau of Statistics, Data base; Composition of GDP by the three strata of industry, GDP(%), 1997–2016; Basic Statistics on Population, 1982–2016; All China Data online: China Yearly Macro-Economic Statistics (National)_Gross Domestic Product of China, 1952–2016.

where PS_i – is the productivity of sector i, and $(\%GDP)_i/(\%Empl)_i$ — is the percentage change in GDP of sector i in conjunction with the change in employment in the same sector.

Comparative productivity is the ratio of the primary sector's comparative productivity to the second and tertiary sectors' comparative productivity, which is expressed as

$$CPS_{\frac{1}{2+3}} = \frac{(CPS)_1}{(CPS)_{2+3}} \tag{3.12}$$

From Figure 3.9, we see that $CPS_{1/(2+3)}$ is low in China, and increases slowly from 1952–1978, declining from 0.202 to 0.138 (1965), and then recovering to 0.162(1978). From 1978–1985, it increased to 0.239 (1985)

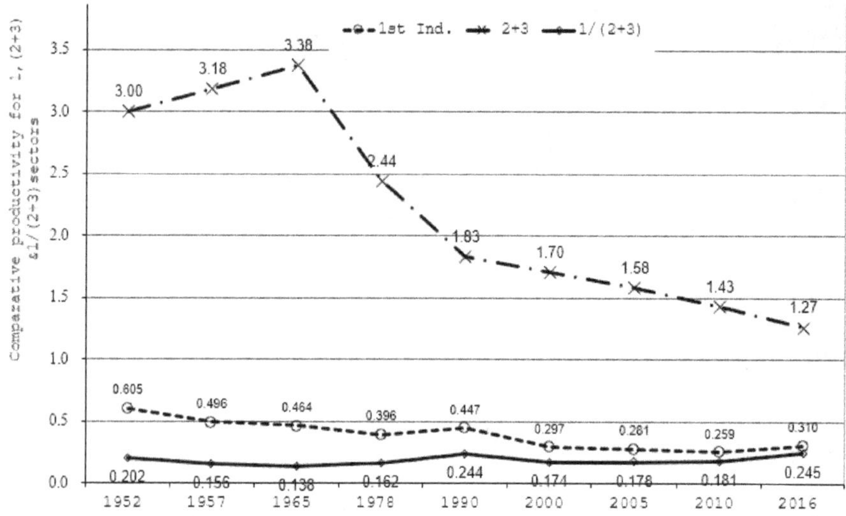

Figure 3.9. Comparative productivity by sector in China, 1952–2016.

Source: Calculated using data from China National Bureau of Statistics: China Statistical Yearbook, China Statistical Press, 2006, Tables 3.2, 5.2; China National Bureau of Statistics, Data base; Composition of GDP by the three strata of industry, GDP (%), 1997–2016; Employed Persons in Primary, Secondary, and Tertiary Industry.

and remained about 0.24 until 1995; it then declined to 0.174 in 2000 due to lagged agriculture modernization, then rose to 0.181 in 2010 and 0.245 in 2016. We can conclude that the primary sector's performance has been poor and characterized by fluctuations. We can also conclude that improving $CPS_{1/(2+3)}$ is very challenging. Allocating a high portion of the country's labor force to primary industry, a low productivity sector, leads to low productivity of China's IS.

Before economic reform, the low value of $CPS_{1/(2+3)}$ appeared in 1962 due to "Great Leap Forward" and the "three years natural disaster" and the accompanying poor agricultural output. After economic reform, beginning with agricultural reform, the household responsibility system was implemented and the status of agriculture was improved, thus increasing the value of $CPS_{1/(2+3)}$. However, after 1990, there were a lot of problems in agriculture (low price of agricultural products, delayed impact of agricultural modernization); agricultural production grew slowly, so $CPS_{1/(2+3)}$ declined again. For reference, Figure 3.10 shows the $CPS_{1/(2+3)}$ of other countries. It is obvious that

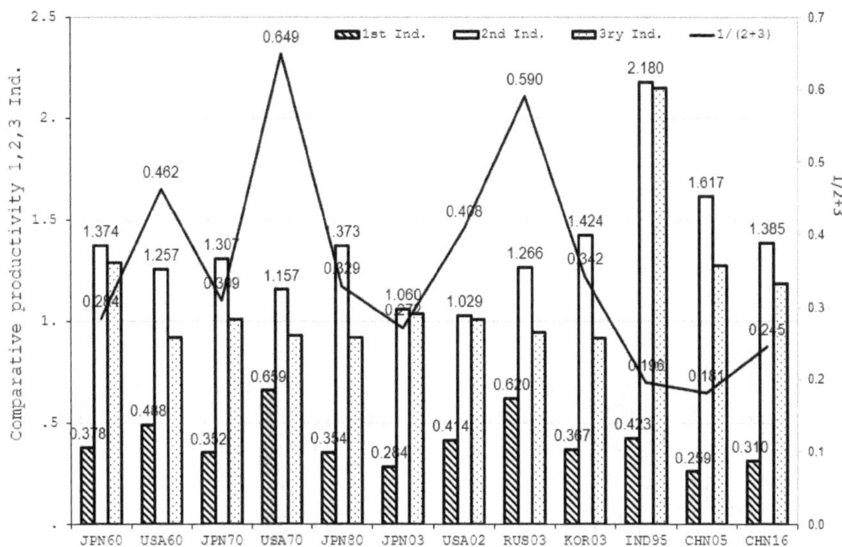

Figure 3.10.　Comparative productivity: China versus other countries.

Source: Calculated using data from World Bank: World Development Indicators online 2006, Released April 2004 by World Bank; World Bank: World Development Indicators online 2018, released September 2018.

China's $CPS_{1/(2+3)}$ is equivalent to India's (see Figure 3.10). Japan's $CPS_{1/(2+3)}$ increased from 0.28 (1960s) to 0.33 (1980s) then declined to 0.27 (2001). That of the United States increased from 0.46 (1960s) to 0.65 (1970s), then declined to 0.41 (2002). For the United States and Japan, the decline of $CPS_{1/(2+3)}$ after 1970s is mainly due to the use of high technology and the significant increase in the productivity of the service sector.

Figure 3.11 shows that $CPS_{1/(2+3)}$ increased from low-income groups to lower middle-income groups and higher middle-income groups and surged significantly upward to high-income groups. But, in recent years, $CPS_{1/(2+3)}$ for high-income groups declined from 0.5878 in 1990 to 0.4447 and 0.4494 in 2000 and 2016, respectively. As shown in Figures 3.11 and 3.10, according to the comparative productivity of the primary sector in relation to secondary and tertiary sectors, $CPS_{1/(2+3)}$, from 1981–2000 places China in the low-income groups; in 2016, it joined the middle- income groups.

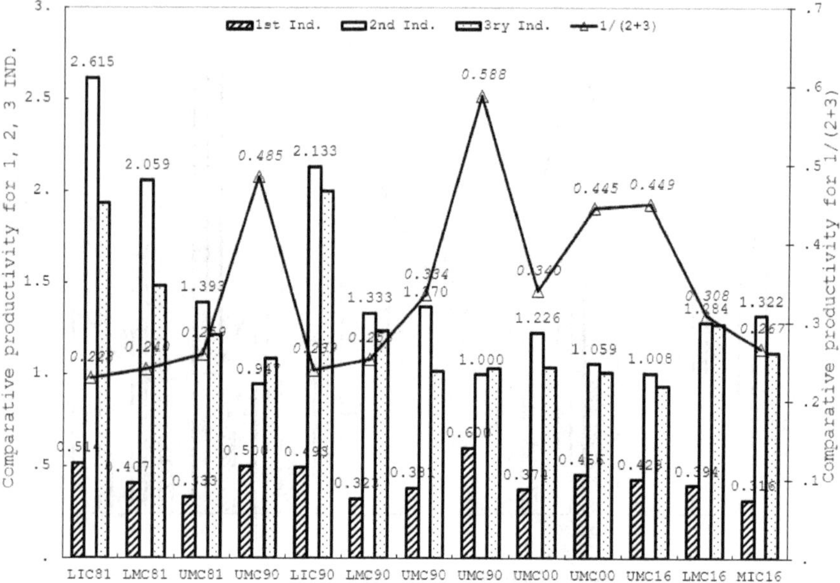

Figure 3.11. Comparative productivity for different income groups 1981–2016.

Source: Calculated using data from World Bank: World Development Indicators 2003, CD-ROM, Published July 2003 by World Bank, WDI 2002; WDI 2000; World Bank: World Development Indicators online 2018, released September 2018.

6. Changes in the Industrial Structure

A country's IS may change over the years depending on several factors, economic as well as non-economic. In a planned economy, the central planner determines the allocation of resources, and thereby the industrial sectors to which these resources will be directed. The Soviet model and China's Maoist economies favored heavy industrialization. Consequently, the defense industry (especially in the case of the Soviet Union) and industries such as steel grew at the expense of agriculture and services. In a market economy, changes in industrial structure occur in resources, demand structure, supply and demand response, technology, and international economic relations. Countries that characterize their economic system as market-based may also pursue policies in accordance with their

Industrial Policy, therefore influencing there IS, as a result of many other factors.[4] These factors include the country's human and natural resources.

In this chapter, we will address some of these factors influencing China's IS. Specifically, we will examine the impact of changes in demand, Income Disparity, Consumption patterns, and real estate and urbanization on the country's IS before and after reforms. Additional factors, such as foreign trade and investment, will be examined in later chapters.

7. Changes in Demand

A main feature of China's reform has been the country's attempt to accommodate people's increasing demand for a greater variety of consumer goods. After reform, per capita GDP increased rapidly, so per capita income of urban and rural residents also increased significantly. Per capita income in urban and rural areas (values obtained from the sample survey by the China National Bureau of Statistics) and their annual growth rates are shown in Figures 3.12 and 3.13, respectively. It is obvious from these two figures that the per capita income (all in 1978 constant CNY) increased much faster after economic reform than before reform. The per capita income in rural areas increased from CNY84.8 in 1952 to CNY133.6 in 1978, with the annual growth rate of only 1.76%.[5] After economic reform, it rose from CNY133.6 in 1978 to CNY834.3 in 2005, an average annual growth rate of 7.02%, or three times larger than before economic reform; from 2005–2015, it rose to 9.23%.[6] The per capita income in urban area followed a similar pattern, increasing from CNY148.2 in 1952 to CNY316 in 1978. After economic reform, it rose dramatically to CNY1,919.4 in 2005. The annual growth rate was 2.94%[7] before economic reform, and 7.38% after economic reform.

---

[4] Dang, Y., S. Liu, and Y. Wang (2011). *Optimization of Regional Industrial Structures and Applications*. Boca Raton, FL: Taylor & Francis Group.

[5] Calculated using data from China National Bureau of Statistics (1991). China Statistical Yearbook, China Statistical Press, 1991, Table 8.3.

[6] Calculated using data from China National Bureau of Statistics (2014). China Statistical Yearbook, China Statistical Press, 2014, Table 6.4.

[7] Calculated using data from China National Bureau of Statistics (1991). China Statistical Yearbook, China Statistical Press, 1991, Table 8.3.

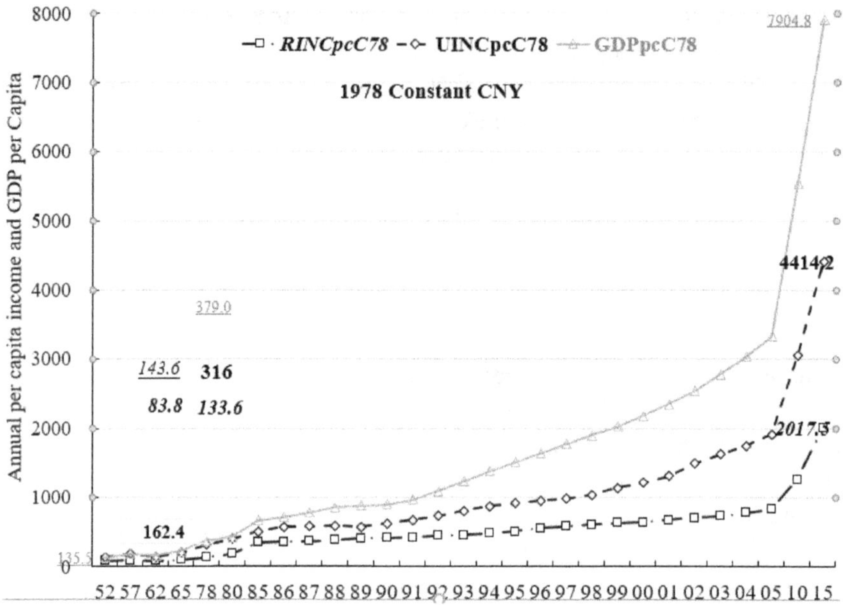

Figure 3.12.   Annual per capita income in urban and rural areas and per capita GDP 1952–2015.

Source: Calculated using data from China National Bureau of Statistics: China Statistical Yearbook, China Statistical Press, 2006 Tables 3.3, 3.18, 4.1, 10.2; 1996, Table 9.4; 1991, Table 8.3; China National Bureau of Statistics, Data base; Annual, Per capita income &, Growth%, 2013–2019; Per capita income of urban households, 2000–2012; Per capita income of rural households 2000–2012.

After economic reform, the average annual growth rate of per capita income in rural and urban areas was less than the average annual growth rate of per capita GDP (8.56%). The annual growth rate of per capita income was even higher than the annual growth rate of GDP in the early stage of reform, and then again in recent years. As shown in Annual growth rate in Figure 3.13, during 1957–1962, 1978–1980, 1980–1985, 1987, 1988, 1989, 1995, 1996, 1997, and from 2010 to 2015, the average annual growth rate of per capita income in rural areas is higher than annual growth rate of per capita income in urban areas. As shown in Figure 3.13, from 1957 to 1962, the annual growth rates of per capita income for both the rural and urban areas are negative (−5.51% and −8.55%, respectively) due to the great leap forward. From 1980–1985, the

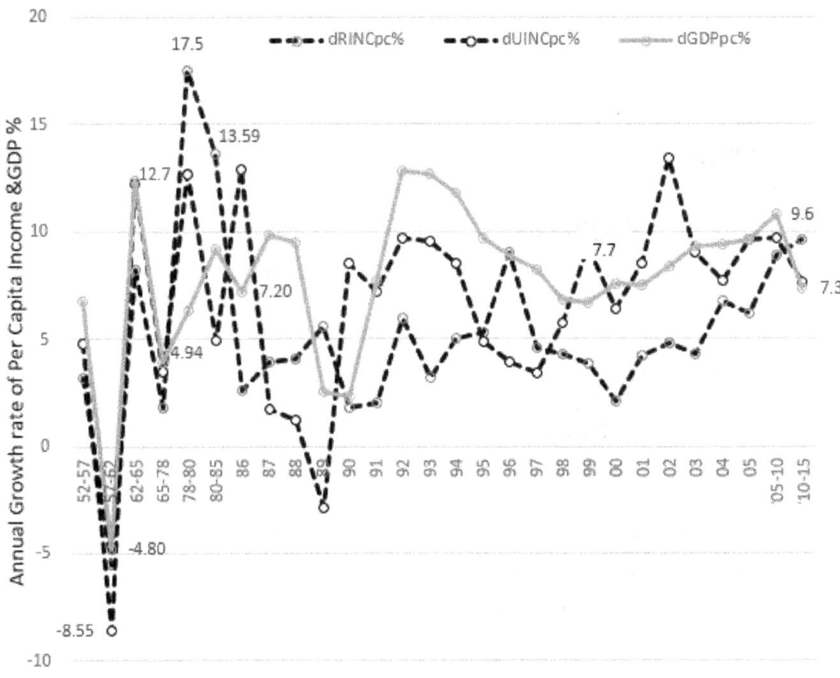

Figure 3.13.   Annual growth rate of per capita income in urban, rural areas and GDP per capita income of whole people.

Source: Calculated using data from China National Bureau of Statistics: China Statistical Yearbook, China Statistical Press, 2006 Tables 3.3, 3.18, 4.1, 10.2; 1996, Table 9.4; 1991, Table 8.3; China National Bureau of Statistics, Data base; Annual, per capita income &, Growth%, 2013–2019; Per capita income of urban households, 2000–2012; Per capita income of rural households, 2000–2012.

annual growth rate of per capita income in urban and rural areas reached 4.94% and 13.59%,[8] respectively, a difference of 8.66%, while the annual growth rate of per capita GDP was 9.21%.[9] The early stage of economic reform was mainly carried out in rural areas. In 1986, urban area reform was implemented. Enterprises signed management contracts to retain their profits after paying taxes to the government. Employee wages and

---

[8]Calculated using data from China National Bureau of Statistics: China Statistical Yearbook, China Statistical Press, 2006, Table 10.2.

[9]*Ibid.*, Table 3.4.

bonuses were linked to retained profits. Therefore, in 1986, the annual growth rate per capita income in urban areas increased significantly. In 1986, the annual growth rate of per capita income in rural and urban areas reached 2.57% and 12.93%, respectively, which represented the biggest gap (10.37%) in the annual growth rate between urban and rural per capita incomes.

From 1998–2005, the annual growth rate of per capita income in rural areas and urban areas was 4.59% and 9.11%,[10] respectively, revealing an increase in the gap between the per capita income of rural and urban areas, while the annual growth rate of per capita GDP was 8.35%.[11] Due to the slow pace of increase in rural per capita income, effective domestic demand was not sufficient. After reform, per capita income increased significantly; per capita consumption also increased rapidly. The annual growth rate of per capita consumption in rural and urban areas increased from 1.76% and 2.94% in 1952–1978 to 9.12% and 8.61% in 1978–2016, respectively.[12] In Figures 3.14 and 3.15, we show the per capita consumption and their annual growth rate in rural and urban areas and the total. In Figure 3.14, the per capita consumption is expressed in 1978 constant CNY. We see that, in rural areas, it increased from 63.5 at 1952 to 100 at 1978, and reached 1150.4 in 2016; in the urban areas, it increased from 138 considerably (see Figure 3.17). The observed volatility is an outcome of the policy uncertainty during China's transition. From Figure 3.15, we find that the annual growth rate of per capita income reached 10.75% in 2005–2010 and declined to 7.34% in 2010–2015. During 2005–2010, the high growth rate was achieved through reliance on investment, consumption, and exports. However, such extensive economic development mode is difficult to sustain, and results in serious environment pollution and overuse of the natural resources. China's economy should be transitioning from a phase of rapid growth to a stage of high-quality development. It must continue making progress, bring about innovations and breakthroughs amidst change, and From 1952 to 1978, the urban per capita annual consumption reached 293.5 in 1978, and increased to 2963.14 in 2016, indicating a big gap between per capita consumption in rural and

---

[10] *Ibid.*, Table 10.2.

[11] Calculated using data from China National Bureau of Statistics (2006). China Statistical Yearbook, China Statistical Press, 2006, Table 3.4.

[12] Calculated using data from China National Bureau of Statistics: China Statistical Yearbook, China Statistical Press, 2006, Table 3.17, Table 4.1; 1991, Table 3.1, Table 8.3.

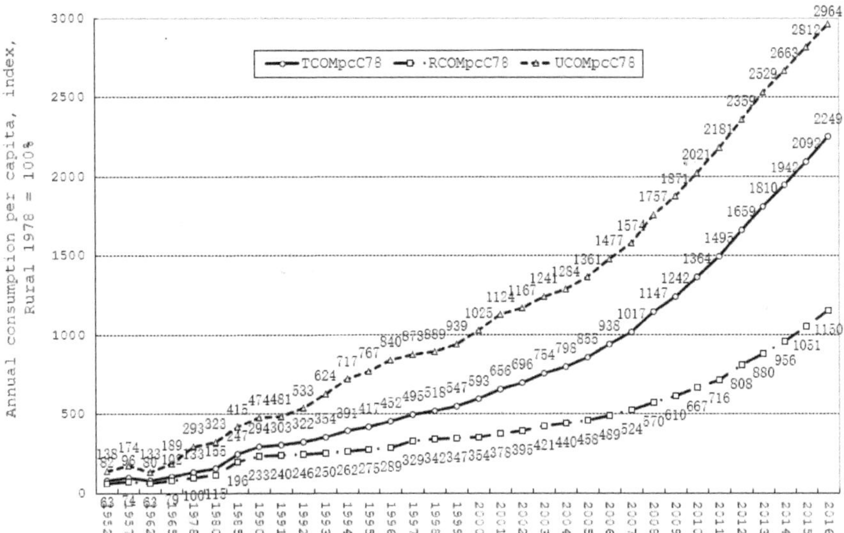

Figure 3.14. Annual per capita consumption of national, urban, and rural China, 1952–2016.

Source: Calculated using data from China National Bureau of Statistics: China Statistical Yearbook, China Statistical Press, 2004, Tables 3.17, 4.1; 2002, Table 3.16; 1991, Tables 3.1, 8.2, 8.3; All China Data online; China Yearly Macro-Economic Statistics (National): Household Consumption, 1952–2016.

urban areas. The results show that the average annual growth rate of per capita consumption is much higher than before economic reform, but also fluctuates along the new developmental path that brings its advantages fully to bear with better quality, higher efficiency, and a more optimal structure, in order to transfer to intensive economic development mode.

The structure of consumption in developing countries is influenced by developed countries, so we can identify changes in advance. In China, initial supply shortages eventually become buyer's markets. For the consumer market, the former Ministry of Domestic Trade, State Economic and Trade Committee, and Ministry of Commerce conducted a survey of 600 commodities beginning with July 1996, as shown in Figure 3.16. The figure shows that, in the second half of 1996, supply and demand were in balance for about 85% of the items. Commodity supply was larger than demand for 9.1% of the items; for 6.2% of the items, there was a shortage of supply. Then, from January–June 1999, all commodities experienced

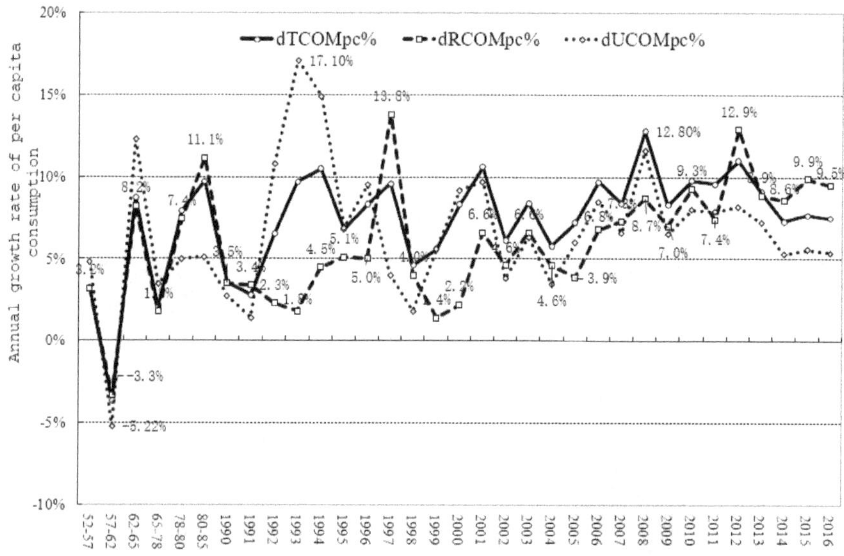

Figure 3.15.   Annual growth rate of per capita consumption, China.

Source: Calculated using data from China National Bureau of Statistics: China Statistical Yearbook, China Statistical Press, 2004, Tables 3.17, 4.1; 2002, Table 3.15; 1991, Tables 3.1, 8.2, 8.3; All China Data online: China Yearly Macro-Economic Statistics (National): Household Consumption, 1952–2016.

excess supply. The surplus declined (to 68.5%) in the first half of 2003, as demand increased due to overheated investment. Demand exceeded supply for items such as energy, ferrous metals, non-ferrous metals, transportation, and electricity (see Figure 3.17). For example, supply was less than demand in energy products (coal and petroleum) and non-ferrous metal (35.6% and 18.4%, respectively) in first half of 2006. Consumer goods, on the other hand, painted a different picture. People's insufficient spending power was a mismatch with the amount of production, Since the first half of 2002, no shortage of consumer goods has been found in China's demand structure, which is related to China's industrial structure.

As consumer preferences shifted from basic needs to downstream consumer goods and durables, production also shifted. The inventory of 468,506 industrial enterprises with independent accounting systems reached CNY1,552 billion (USD187.4 billion) in 1997, equivalent

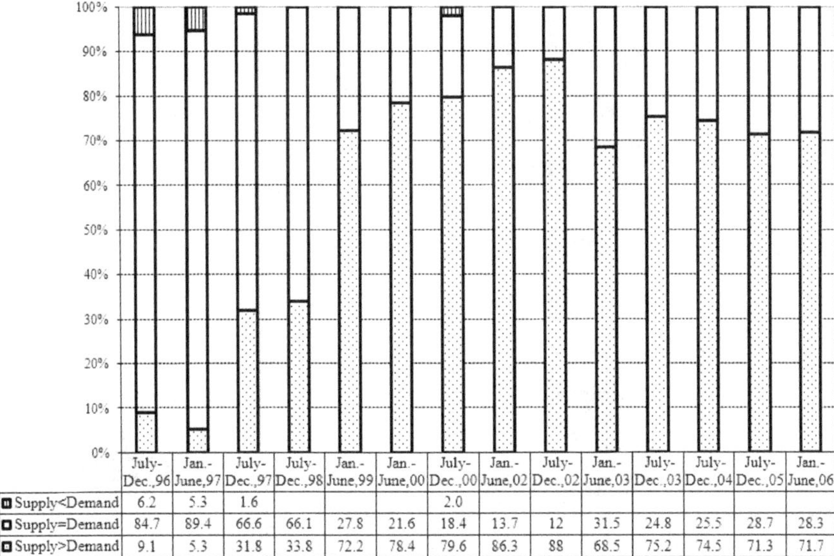

	July-Dec.,96	Jan.-June,97	July-Dec.,97	July-Dec.,98	Jan.-June,99	Jan.-June,00	July-Dec.,00	Jan.-June,02	July-Dec.,02	Jan.-June,03	July-Dec.,03	July-Dec.,04	July-Dec.,05	Jan.-June,06
Supply<Demand	6.2	5.3	1.6				2.0							
Supply=Demand	84.7	89.4	66.6	66.1	27.8	21.6	18.4	13.7	12	31.5	24.8	25.5	28.7	28.3
Supply>Demand	9.1	5.3	31.8	33.8	72.2	78.4	79.6	86.3	88	68.5	75.2	74.5	71.3	71.7

Figure 3.16.   Survey of 600 consumer goods by Ministry of Commerce, July 96–June 06.

Source: Calculated using data from Survey conducted by Department of Market Operation Regulation, Ministry of Commerce of China: Supply and demand analysis of 600 main commodities during first half year of 2005 (in Chinese), March 22, 2005; Ministry of Commerce: 70 % commodities in surplus of supply, *Peoples Daily*, May 03, 2004, p2 (in Chinese); State Economic and Trade Committee "The main commodity supply and demand analysis during second half year of 2002", (in Chinese), http://news.eastday.com/epublish/gb/paper148/20020924/class014800011/hwz779387.htm; Adapt to 'post-shortage economy', *China Daily*, 10/23/2000; Ministry of Commerce of China, Department of Market Operation Regulation: The investigation and analysis report of 600 major consumer goods supply and demand situation in second half of 2005, (in Chinese), 2005-08-01; Ministry of Commerce of China, Department of Market Operation Regulation: The investigation and analysis report of 600 major consumer goods supply and demand situation in first half of 2006, (in Chinese), 2006-02-13.

to 78.2% of industry value-added. In 2002, the inventory of 181,557 industrial enterprises with independent accounting systems reached CNY1,786 billion (USD215.7 billion), and receivables of CNY1,604 billion (USD193.7 billion). The sum of these two was equivalent to 97.3% of industry value-added.[13] In 2004, the inventory of 276,474 industrial

---

[13] Calculated using data from "Shanghai: Ten reasons for development of the Regional Economy", www.drcnet.com.cn/html_document/guoyan/area/2003-02-10/157580

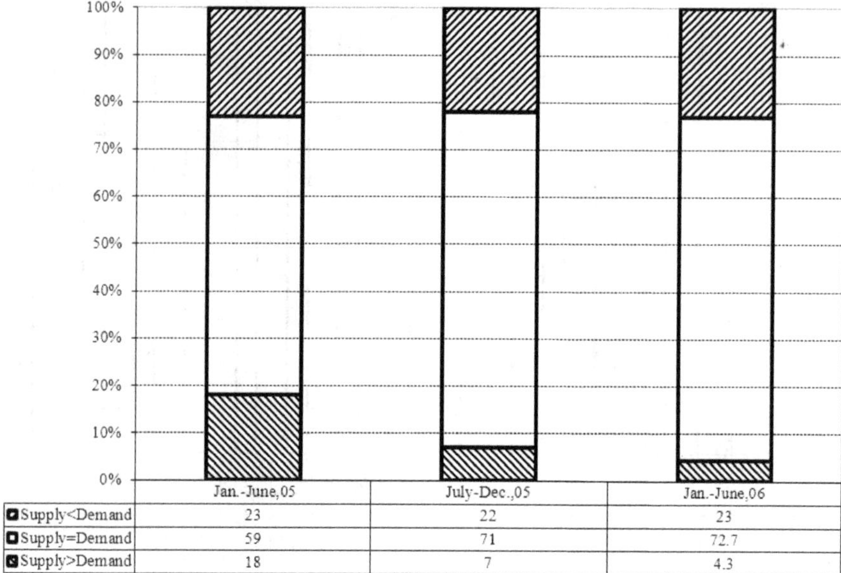

	Jan.-June,05	July-Dec.,05	Jan.-June,06
Supply<Demand	23	22	23
Supply=Demand	59	71	72.7
Supply>Demand	18	7	4.3

Figure 3.17.   Survey of 300 productive means by Ministry of Commerce, 2005–2006

Source: Ministry of Commerce of China, Department of Market Operation Regulation: The investigation and analysis report of 300 major productive means supply and demand situation in first half of 2005 (in Chinese), April 12, 2005; Ministry of Commerce of China, Department of Market Operation Regulation: The investigation and analysis report of 300 major productive means supply and demand situation in second half of 2005, (in Chinese), August 1, 2005; Ministry of Commerce of China, Department of Market Operation Regulation: The investigation and analysis report of 300 major productive means supply and demand situation in first half of 2006 (in Chinese).

enterprises with independent accounting systems reached CNY2,752 billion (USD332.4 billion) and receivables of CNY2,308 billion (USD278.7 billion), with the sum of the both being equivalent to 88.4% of industry value-added.[14]

In the long run, China has the capacity to sustain growth in domestic consumption because of its huge population, low per capita GDP, low

---

drcnetchentech-dfgdghdaA023.asp; China National Bureau of Statistics: China Industrial Statistical Yearbook, China Statistical Press, 2003, Table 3.1.

[14]Calculated using data from Li, Rongrong (Director of Editorial Board, Chairman of State-owned Assets Supervision and Administration Commission of the State Council): China's Economy and Trade Yearbook, 2005.

per-household inventory of durables, and low service consumption. But the recent insufficiency of demand reflects the people's insufficient purchasing power. The lagging growth in urban residents' incomes and farmers' earnings have inhibited consumer spending. There is a need, then, for reduction in the surpluses created through the strategic reforms of SOEs. For example, the textile industry capacity declined by more than 10 million spindles during 1998–2000. At the end of 2003, there were eight million registered unemployed people in urban areas, the rate of unemployment being 4.3%, or 0.3 percentage points higher than at the end of 2002. Meanwhile, of some 150 million surplus laborers in rural areas, more than 80 million went to cities either as migrant workers or for business, adding more pressure on the city employment situation. Additionally, there were 2.12 million college graduates seeking jobs.[15] More job cutting has not only dampened consumption among laid-off workers, but also added to uncertainty among those employed. In addition, people are more cautious about current spending, as they expect to face more expenses in the future. Housing, medical insurance, pension system and educational system reforms have all forced people to tighten their purse strings.[16]

Since the 1970s, consumer demand in urban area has been upgraded three times (see Table 3.9), thereby promoting the boom of related industries. The pattern of rural area consumption lags behind the urban area by 10–15 years. Houses, sedans, service, and IT products became recent consumer hot spots, driving the consumption of related industries. The consumption pattern offers an impetus to restructure industry so as to match the changing consumer demand structure. Consumer behavior, of course, differs between urban and rural areas. In May 2000, a poll was conducted by Horizon and Horizonkey[17] among 5584 people aged 18–65.[18] Among these polled, 3243 lived in five large cities, five in medium and small cities, and 2341 came from rural areas. The survey results are listed in Table 3.9, which represents the improving living standards, and the adjectives used to describe them were quite different

---

[15] TAI WEI: Employing all-round tactics, *Beijing Review*, 47(11), March 18, 2004, 20–24.

[16] Yimin Zhang and Shuhua Zheng: The changes of Consumer Demand Structure in China, 1999 Asia Pacific Decision Sciences Institute Conference, June 9–12, 1999.

[17] Zhang, Y. and S. Zheng. (1999). The changes of Consumer Demand Structure in China, 1999 Asia Pacific Decision Sciences Institute Conference, June 9–12.

[18] See Table 3.9 for source.

Table 3.9.   The consumer demand upgrade in China's urban areas since 1950s.

Engel coefficient				Popularization and saturation of specific durable consumer goods				Resident consumption characteristics	National consumption strategy
Survival demand	Consumption structure evolution	Urban	Rural	Enjoyment demand	Consumption structure evolution	Urban	Rural	Urban and rural areas	Urban and rural areas
>60%	Poverty consumption	—	1954–1980	Watch, bicycle, radio	Consumption level II	1956–1980	1954–1984	Consumption shortage	High accumulation, low consumption, priority to develop heavy industry
55–60%	Subsistence consumption I	1956–1984	1981–1987	Recorder, electric fan, black and white TV	Consumption level III	1981–1985	1985–1989	Consumption expansion	Moderate accumulation, increase income, develop consumption, industry
50–55%	Subsistence consumption II	1985–1995	1988–1999	Washing machine, refrigerator, color TV	Consumption level I	1986–1997	1990–1999	Weak consumption	develop consumption, industry

| 45–50%
40–45% | Well-off consumption | 1996–1997
1998–1999 | 2000–2005
2006–2011 | Camera, air conditioner, mobile phone | Consumption level IV | 1998–2004 | 2000–2008 | Insufficient effective consumption | Consumption and investment, and exports are equally important |
| 35–40% | Wealthy consumption | 2000–2013 | 2012–2013 | Computer, residential, family car | Consumption level V | 2005–2013 | 2009–2013 | | Expanding domestic demand: credit, scientific, green consumption |

Source: Horizon & Horizonkey Co.: The comparison of the consumer behavior of Chinese residents in urban and rural areas (in Chinese), www.horizonkey.com/update/shownews.asp?news_id=103.

between residents of urban areas and those of rural areas. One common item was the house: it ranked first for both groups.

The "13th FYP" identified domestic demand as the "strategic basis" for economic development. Increasing the consumption propensity of Chinese residents became the strategic goal of China's macro economy. For a long time, the savings rate of Chinese residents has remained high. "High savings" and "low consumption" have become the "vicious circle" unique to the Chinese economy. While high savings rate is an important factor supporting China's high investment and high growth, it also leads to relative insufficiency of Chinese residents' consumption, thus impeding the growth of domestic demand. Therefore, promotion of the consumption structure needs to be approached simultaneously from the supply side and the demand side. Increase in demand can come about from increasing consumer incomes, change in income expectations, and increase in the marginal propensity to consume. On the supply side, there is a need for adjustment of the types, quality, price, and quantity of consumer goods and for providing residents with the right incentives to consume (see Table 3.10).

According to the National Bureau of Statistics, from January to June 2019, the total retail sales of consumer goods nationwide reached CNY19.5 trillion, a year-on-year increase of 8.4%. The fundamental role of consumption in economic growth continued to consolidate. The contribution rate of final consumption expenditure growth to economic growth in the first half of the year reached 60.1%. The market has the following characteristics: First, consumption on the necessities is strong. Second, consumption on services is developing steadily, accounting for 49.4% of final consumption expenditure. Third, online retail sales grew faster, in the first half of the year (21.6%). Fourth, rural areas and the central and western regions are leading the growth rate. The growth rate of rural consumption continued to be faster than that of urban areas. In the first half of the year, the retail sales of rural consumer goods increased by 9.1% year-on-year, accounting for 14.5% of total retail sales. The growth rate of the central and western regions maintained a leading position. From January to May, the growth rate of Jiangxi, Yunnan, Henan, Hubei, and Sichuan was more than 10%, higher than the national average. Fifth, consumer prices rose moderately. In the first half of the year, consumer prices rose by 2.2% year-on-year. China's consumption structure, then, is becoming more reasonable.

Table 3.10.   The Staged division of the evolution of Urban and Rural Residents consumption structure.

Engel coefficient				Popularization and saturation of specific durable consumer goods				Resident consumption characteristics	National consumption strategy
Survival demand	Consumption structure evolution	Urban	Rural	Enjoyment demand	Consumption structure evolution	Urban	Rural	Urban and rural areas	Urban and rural areas
>60%	Poverty consumption	—	1954–1980	Watch, bicycle, radio	Consumption level II	1956–1980	1954–1984	Consumption shortage	High accumulation, low consumption, priority to develop heavy industry
55–60%	Subsistence consumption I	1956–1984	1981–1987	Recorder, electric fan, black and white TV	Consumption level III	1981–1985	1985–1989	Consumption expansion	Moderate accumulation, increase income, develop consumption, industry
50–55%	Subsistence consumption II	1985–1995	1988–1999	Washing machine, refrigerator, color TV	Consumption level I	1986–1997	1990–1999	Weak consumption	

(Continued)

Table 3.10.   (*Continued*)

Engel coefficient				Popularization and saturation of specific durable consumer goods				Resident consumption characteristics	National consumption strategy
45–50% 40–45%	Well-off consumption	1996– 1997 1998– 1999	2000– 2005 2006– 2011	Camera, air conditioner, mobile phone	Consumption level IV	1998– 2004	2000– 2008	Insufficient effective consumption	Consumption and investment, and exports are equally important
35–40%	Wealthy consumption	2000– 2013	2012– 2013	Computer, residential, family car	Consumption level V	2005– 2013	2009– 2013		Expanding domestic demand: credit , scientific, green consumption

Source: Zhao, C. (2016). The Characteristics of Chinese Residents' Consumption Preference and Its Impact on Consumption, *Consumer Economics*, (03) (in Chinese). Dong, Y. (2016). An Analysis of the Evolution of Chinese Residents' Consumption Structure under the Dual Structure of Urban and Rural Areas. *New Economy*, (18) (in Chinese) www.chinadaily.com.cn/business/chinaecoachievement40years/index.html.

Table 3.11.   The consumer behavior of Chinese residents in urban area and rural area (2000).

	Rural	Urban
Typical commodities characterized improving living standard	House (29.2%)	House (33.6%)
	Telephone (8.4%)	Computer (9.6%)
	Color TV (22.2%)	Air conditioner (8.6%)
	Washing machine (4.8%)	Color TV (8.6%)
	Sedan (3.5%)	Sedan (8.5%)
Typical adjectives for description of future ideal livelihood	Prosperous (57%)	Healthy (74%)
	Healthy (57%)	Relaxed (69%)
	Stable (45%)	Rich in spirits (58%)
	Relaxed (36%)	Stable (58%)
	Material earnings (34%)	Natural (55%)

Source: Zhao, C. (2016). The Characteristics of Chinese Residents' Consumption Preference and Its Impact on Consumption, *Consumer Economics*, (03) (in Chinese). Dong, Y. (2016). An Analysis of the Evolution of Chinese Residents' Consumption Structure under the Dual Structure of Urban and Rural Areas, *New Economy*, (18) (in Chinese).

A survey conducted by the Beijing research company Horizon Research and Horizonkey in July 2014,[19] polling more than 3,166 residents aged 18–60 in 20 cities, including the four first-tier cities — Beijing, Shanghai, Guangzhou, and Shenzhen. Although most respondents said China's food safety is of concern, more than half believe the situation is improving. According to the survey, more respondents from first-tier cities than their counterparts from second-tier cities agreed with this assessment. Most respondents still trust domestic food despite foreign brands

---

[19]Horizon & Horizonkey Co.: The comparison of the consumer behavior of Chinese residents in urban and rural areas (in Chinese), www.horizonkey.com/update/shownews. asp?news_id=103; Nelson. C. (2011). Understanding Chinese Consumers, *China Business Review*, The Magazine of US-China Business Council, July 1. Floot, K., A. Huang, and M. Lehnich: (2013). A new era for manufacturing in China, *McKinsey Quarterly*, June; He, D. (2018). China's consumption upgrades accelerate. Xinhua. January 20;2018-01-20; Survey shows Chinese upset about food safety, www.ebeijing.gov.cn/BeijingInformation/ BeijingNewsUpdate/t1362414.htm.

having won a considerable market share in the country, the poll revealed. In ranking the top 10 countries that produce safe food, China ranked second, behind only the United States, according to the findings of the research company.

In 1983, China's final consumption rate was only 66.8%, the highest since 1978; and declined to its lowest value of 48.5% in 2010; it increased to 53.6% in 2016, 2017 (see Figure 3.18). From 1978–2016, the average value of final consumption rate (the ratio of domestic final consumption to GDP) was 58.2% with a standard deviation of 5.7%. In 1978, the contribution share of consumption, investment, and net exports were 38.3%, 67.0%, and –5.3%, respectively and this ratio was 57.6%, 33.8%, and 8.6% in 2017, respectively. The highest and lowest contribution share of consumption was 91.7% in 1990, with the lowest being 35.4% in 2003; the contribution shares of investment were 86.5% in 2009 and –74.6% in 1990; the contribution share of net exports was 82.9% in 1990 and –50.9% in 1985. These numbers illustrate the large fluctuations

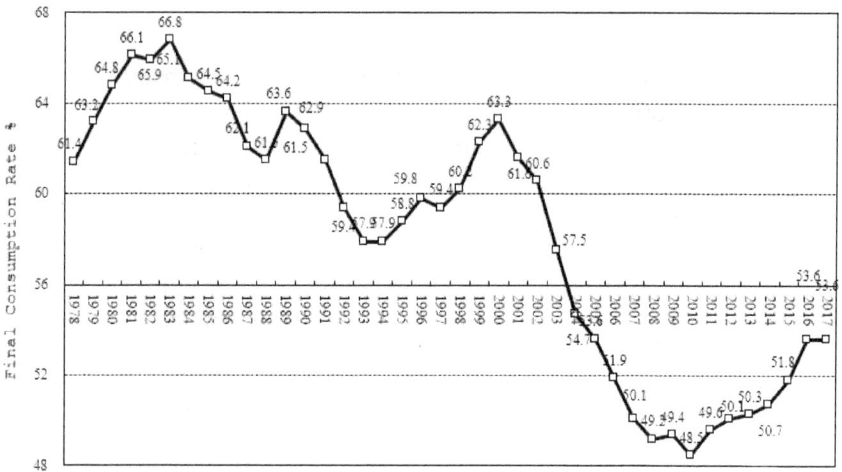

Figure 3.18.   Final consumption rate in China after reform 1978–2017.

Source: Calculated using data from China National Bureau of Statistics: China Statistical Yearbook, China Statistical Press 2018, Table 3.10.

characterizing China's contribution share of consumption, investment, and net exports.[20]

7.1. *China's consumption versus other countries*

China's final consumption rate is less than the world average and that of other developing countries. The final consumption of selected foreign countries and the world average are shown in Table 3.12. There are two China data series in Table 3.13, one from WDI and another (in Italic) from the 2018 China Statistical Yearbook. In the comparisons below, we use WDI data. We observe that the final consumption rates for Brazil, India, Mexico, and lower middle-income countries were 83.4%,75.7%, 77.5%, and 74.2%, respectively, in 2000, or about 14.1% higher than China's. For developed countries, the final consumption rates for the United Kingdom, United States, Germany, and Japan were 84.0%, 80.0%, 75.8%, and 71.3% in 2000, or about 14.2% higher than China's. The average value of final consumption rate is 80.3, with a standard deviation of 2.4%, from 1960 to 2017 for the United States. We can conclude that, for the United States, the final consumption rate was high and quite stable for the 57 years period. From Table 3.13, we can also see that China has the lowest final consumption rate of only 58.0% during the 1970–2017 period, 17.0% lower than the world average; the standard deviation for China's consumption rate, however, was 6.6%, 1.8% higher than the world average. The main conclusion, of course, is that there is not enough effective domestic demand in the Chinese market. China and United States are both "continental economies", but the economic growth of the United States mainly depends upon domestic consumption, while China is more dependent on domestic investment and exports. Therefore, China's annual GDP growth rate fluctuates considerably more than that of the United States.

7.2. *Average and marginal propensity to consume*

Figure 3.19 shows the average propensity to consume (APC, the ratio of per capita consumption to per capita income) of Chinese residents after economic reform. The data utilized to calculate consumption propensities

---

[20]Calculated using data from China National Bureau of Statistics (2018). China Statistical Yearbook, China Statistical Press 2018, Table 3.12.

Table 3.12.   Final Consumption rate, China and selected countries, 1960–2017.

Country	Year	1960	1970	1980	1990	2000	2005	2010	2015	2017	Average	STDVA
Brazil	60–17	80.4	79.9	78.9	78.6	83.4	79.4	79.2	83.7	84.0	80.8	2.2
China1 WDI data	*70–17*	..	*64.0*	*64.7*	*63.6*	*63.5*	*54.2*	*48.3*	*52.8*	*53.3*	*58.0*	*6.6*
China2 CYB18	60–17	72.9	87.4	64.8	62.9	63.3	53.6	48.5	51.8	53.6	62.1	12.4
Germany	70–17	..	72.1	79.9	75.7	75.8	76.1	75.2	72.8	72.3	75.0	2.5
India	60–17	93.7	88.5	87.4	78.3	75.7	67.7	65.7	69.4	70.0	77.4	10.2
Japan	70–17		57.8	67.0	64.7	71.3	73.7	77.2	76.4	75.2	70.4	6.8
Korea, Rep.	60–17	99.4	83.7	74.3	60.8	65.1	65.5	64.8	64.3	63.4	71.3	12.7
Mexico	April–60	82.9	79.2	71.2	78.4	77.5	79.1	70.2	77.9	77.0	77.0	4.0
Russian	90–17	..	..	..	69.7	61.3	66.8	69.4	70.1	70.8	68.0	3.6
United Kingdom	70–17		83.6	85.8	84.9	84.0	85.1	85.6	84.2	84.0	84.7	0.8
United States	60–17	76.7	81.6	76.1	79.8	80.0	82.2	82.5	81.8	82.4	80.3	2.4
World	70–17	..	77.4	77.2	75.5	75.1	75.0	74.6	72.8	72.6	75.0	1.8
UMC	70–17	..	77.0	72.1	67.2	67.1	65.6	63.9	63.4	63.2	67.4	4.8
Middle income	90–17				67.9	68.7	67.4	65.7	65.2	65.1	66.7	1.5
LMC	70–17	81.6	76.5	74.2	70.8	74.2	73.8	72.1	71.5	71.4	74.0	1.9

Source: Calculated using data from World Bank (2019). World Development Indicators online 2019, Released July 10; China Statistical Yearbook, China Statistical Press 2018, Table 3.11.

Table 3.13. Distribution of income–gini coefficient.

Country	Year	Source	Gini index	Lowest 10%	Lowest 20%	Second 20%	Third 20%	Fourth 20%	Highest 20%	Highest 10%	Ratio of high 10% to low 10%	Gini index (Author Cal.)
China	2016	WDI19	38.5	2.7	6.5	10.7	15.3	22.2	45.3	29.3	10.9	34.87%
China	2012	WDI12	42.2	2.1	5.2	9.8	14.8	22.3	31.4	47.9	15.0	42.70%
China	2001	WDI05	44.7	1.8	4.7	9.0	14.2	22.1	50.0	33.1	18.4	40.00%
China	1998	WDI01	40.3	2.4	5.9	10.2	15.1	22.2	46.6	30.4	12.7	37.00%
China	1995	WDI99	41.5	2.2	5.5	9.8	14.9	22.3	47.5	30.9	14.0	39.30%
Germany	2015	WDI19	31.7	3.1	7.8	12.9	17.0	22.6	39.7	24.8	8.0	31.90%
India	2011	WDI12	37.8	3.6	8.3	11.9	15.3	20.6	29.8	44.0	8.3	35.70%
India	2000	WDI05	32.5	3.9	8.9	12.3	16.0	21.2	41.6	27.4	7.0	31.30%
Brazil	2009	WDI12	54.7	0.8	2.9	7.1	12.4	19.0	58.6	42.9	53.6	−51.08%
Brazil	2001	WDI05	59.1	0.7	2.4	5.9	10.4	18.1	63.2	46.9	68.0	−51.08%
Korea Republic	1998	WDI12	31.6	2.9	7.9	13.6	18.0	23.1	37.5	22.5	7.8	34.10%
Japan	1993	WDI12	24.9	4.8	10.6	14.2	17.6	22.0	35.7	21.7	4.5	28.80%
Russia	2015	WDI19	37.7	2.8	6.9	11.1	15.2	21.5	29.7	45.3	10.6	38.40%
Russia	2002	WDI05	31.0	3.3	8.2	12.7	16.9	23.0	39.3	23.8	7.1	33.30%
United Kingdom	2014	WDI19	34.1	2.9	7.3	12.0	16.6	22.9	26.2	41.3	9.0	34.00%

(Continued)

Table 3.13. (*Continued*)

Country	Year	Source	Gini index	Lowest 10%	Lowest 20%	Second 20%	Third 20%	Fourth 20%	Highest 20%	Highest 10%	Ratio of high 10% to low 10%	Gini index (Author Cal.)
United States	2000	WDI12	40.8	1.9	5.4	10.7	15.7	22.4	45.8	29.9	15.9	38.80%
United States	2016	WDI19	41.4	1.7	5.1	10.3	15.3	22.6	46.8	30.5	17.9	37.15%
China Urban	2017	CSY2018			7.1	12.6	17.4	23.6	39.7			32.73%
China Urban	2005	CSY2006		2.8	7.2	12.0	16.5	22.7	41.7	26.1	9.2	34.92%
China Urban	2002	CSY2003		3.1	7.8	12.7	17.1	22.8	39.6	24.4	7.9	33.81%
China Urban	1986	CSY1987		5.6	12.6	16.5	19.1	22.3	29.6	16.6	3.0	26.20%
China rural	2017	CSY2018			4.6	11.6	16.7	23.6	43.5			37.18%
China rural	2005	CSY2005			8.4	12.2	16.2	22.0	41.2		4.9	23.64%
China rural	2002	CSY2003			8.4	12.4	16.3	22.0	40.9		4.9	23.62%
China rural	1986	CSY1987			8.9	13.0	17.2	22.5	38.5		4.3	22.30%

Source: Calculated using data from World Bank: World Development Indicators database, Inequality and shared prosperity, released April 2019 by World Bank; China National Bureau of Statistics: China Statistical Yearbook, China Statistical Press, 2018, Tables 6.7, 6.12; 2006 Tables 10.6, 10.23; 2004 Tables 10.6, 10.23; 2003 Tables 10.6, 10.22; 1987, p. 694.

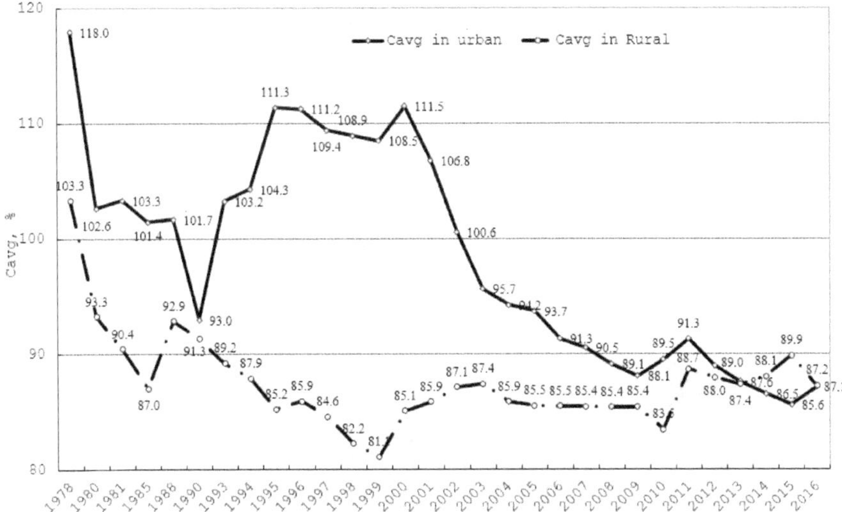

Figure 3.19.   Average propensity to consume of Chinese residents 1978–2016.

Source: Calculated using data from All China Data online: China Yearly Macro-Economics Statistics (National): per capita annual income and expenditure of urban and rural households, 1952–2016, Provided by all China Marketing Research.

were obtained from the sample surveys on urban and rural households by the China National Statistical Bureau. APC reached its highest value in 1978 in urban areas and in 1988 in rural areas. Since people's living standard in China was very low under the CPE, the early stages of the reform generated "pent-up" demand. In urban areas, durable electric appliances became popular in every household, and in rural areas, most families built new homes. After 1988, the APC declined. In the 1980s, China implemented the two-tier price system, meaning that many commodities have a planned price and a negotiated price. The planned price was subsidized by the government and distributed with quotas. The negotiated price was determined by supply and demand and was usually higher than the planned price due to lack of government subsidies. During the 1979–1990 period, price subsidies reached CNY385.7 billion (USD46.6 billion); 80% of these subsidies were allotted to purchases of farm products. This was costly and counterproductive; it amounted to 56% of the total budget expenditure and resulted in new price distortions. In 1988, the Central Government accelerated the pace of price reform.

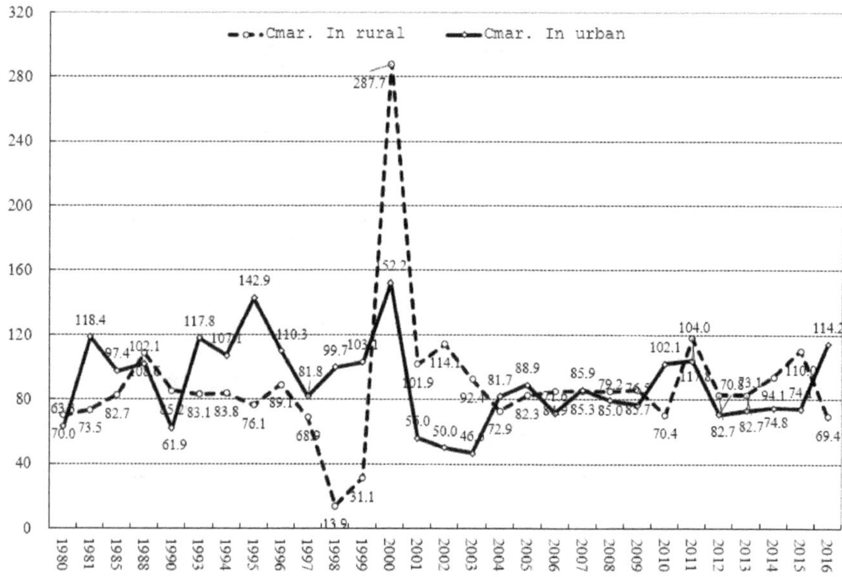

Figure 3.20.   Marginal consumption propensity of Chinese residents 1980–2016.

Source: Calculated using data from All China Data online: China Yearly Macroeconomic Statistics (National): Per Capita Annual Income and Expenditure Urban And Rural Household, 1952–2016.

However, when the news of speedy price reform was disclosed, nationwide panic purchasing emerged. In 1988, the inflation rate jumped to more than 20%.[21] Figure 3.20 shows the marginal propensity to consume (MPC, ratio of increment of per capita consumption to increment of per capita income). So, in 1988, APC reached its peak value: 101.7% in rural areas and 92.9% in urban areas. Figure 3.20 shows that, after 1996, MPC declined sharply both in the urban and rural areas; it especially declined in rural areas, as it declined from 89.1% in 1996 to 13.9% in 1998. This explains why APC in rural areas declined sharply after 1996. During this period, SOE reform led to worker layoffs, and social welfare system reform generated greater expenditures for health care, housing, education, and pensions. The annual growth rate for per capita income in urban areas also declined in the more recent years, as seen from Figure 3.15. Both of these factors resulted in insufficient effective domestic

---

[21] Zhang, Y. (1995). The Macroeconomic Model for Control of Inflation, 1995 International Conference on Management Science and Engineering, July.

demand. From Figure 3.20, we see that MPC decreased in rural areas, signifying falling consumer confidence. Comparing 2000 with 1999, per capita income in rural areas only increased by CNY43.1 (1978 constant CNY), while the per capita living expenditure increased by CNY124 due to price reforms. Among these additional expenditures, CNY34.2 was allocated to housing, CNY23.5 to medicine and medical services, CNY32.6 to transport and communication services, CNY24.6 to cultural, educational, and recreational articles and services, and CNY24.3 to other commodities and services; food expenditures declined by CNY11.4, the expenditure for household facilities and articles declined by CNY9.2.[22] Comparing 2010 with 2015, we find that per capita income in rural areas increased by CNY4,853.2, while per capita living expenditures increased by CNY4,841. Increased expenditures were allocated as follows: for food, CNY1,247.3; for clothing, CNY286.5; for housing, CNY1,091; for household facilities, CNY311.5; for medicines and medical services, CNY700; for transport and communication services, CNY602.6; for cultural, educational, and recreational articles and services, CNY520; and, for other commodities and services, CNY80. The increase in rural per capita income is compatible with the increase in per capita living expenses. In 2015, APC and MPC in rural areas were higher than in cities, as shown in Figures 3.19 and 3.20. This can be interpreted as a positive outcome, as it reveals that rural area residents reaped benefits from reforms and economic development.

As APC declined, saving propensity (APS, ratio of per capita saving to per capita income) increases. This is confirmed by Figure 3.21. Before economic reform, per capita income was low, so APS was quite low. APS increased form 1.3% in 1952 to 5.8% in 1978. After economic reform, it increased dramatically from 5.8% in 1978 to 76.8% in 2003. Indeed, Figure 3.21 shows that the slope of APS became much steeper after economic reform. The marginal propensity to save (MPS) was negative, 11.1% in 1960, due to the great leap forward and natural disasters; it was also negative in 1967 (–1.7%), 1968 (–8.7%), 1969 (–1.1%), and 1976 (–17.7%) during the cultural revolution. During the 1997–1999 period, MPS increased dramatically because of expectations by the public of increases in expenditures associated with reform of the social security system. In 2000, MPS declined sharply from 143.6% in 1998 to 49.5% in 2000; the

---

[22]China National Bureau of Statistics, Database; Annual, Per Capita Consumption Expenditure of Rural Households (yuan), 1999–2013.

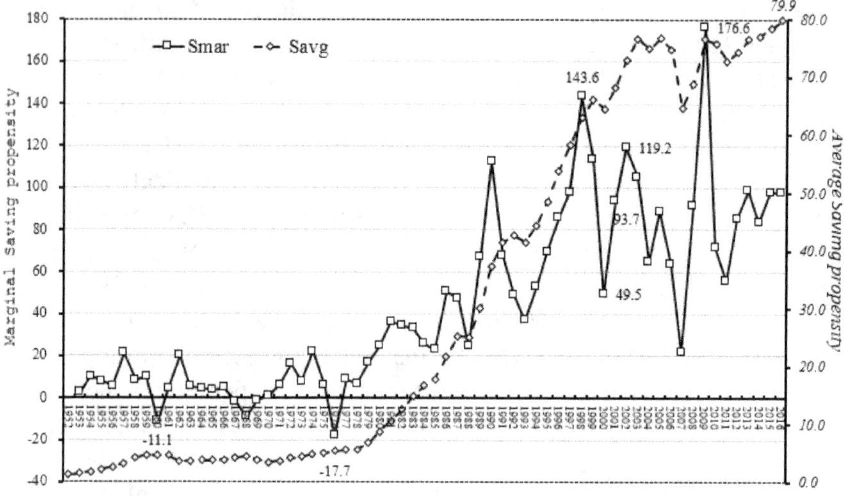

Figure 3.21.   Saving propensity in China 1952–2016.

Source: Calculated using data from Almanac of China's Finance and Banking, 2017 and 2012, in charge of the People's Bank of China, sponsored by China finance society, and published by China Financial Yearbook Publishing House Co., Ltd, 2013 and 2018 in Chinese); National Bureau of Statistics of China: Statistical Communiqué of the People's Republic of China On 2013– 2017, February 28, 2013–2018.

MPS increase may also be related to the 2000 China stock market upturn. The Shanghai Composite Index gained 707 points or 51.7% at 2073 at the end of 2000 (see Figure 3.22), while the Shenzhen Component Index finished 1383 points higher or 41.1% higher at 4753 (see Figure 3.23). In 2000, newly opened individual accounts for trading A shares in Shanghai Stock Exchange reached 6.66 million, an increase of 33.6% year-on-year. MPS declined in 2000, but funds were directed toward the stock market, not towards consumption. In 2001 and 2002, the stock market experienced a downturn. The Shanghai Composite Index lost 409 and 288 points or declined 19.9% and 17.5% at 1646 and 1358 by the end of 2001 and 2002, respectively (see Figure 3.22). The Shenzhen Component Index finished lower at 1427 and 566 points or lost 30.0% and 17.0% at 3226 and 2759 by the end of 2001 and 2002, respectively. Therefore, MPS increased sharply in 2001 (93.7%) and 2002 (119.2%), as seen in Figure 3.21.

According to Andy Xie, chief economist at Morgan Stanley Asia, Chinese households have accumulated wealth equal to 140% of GDP over

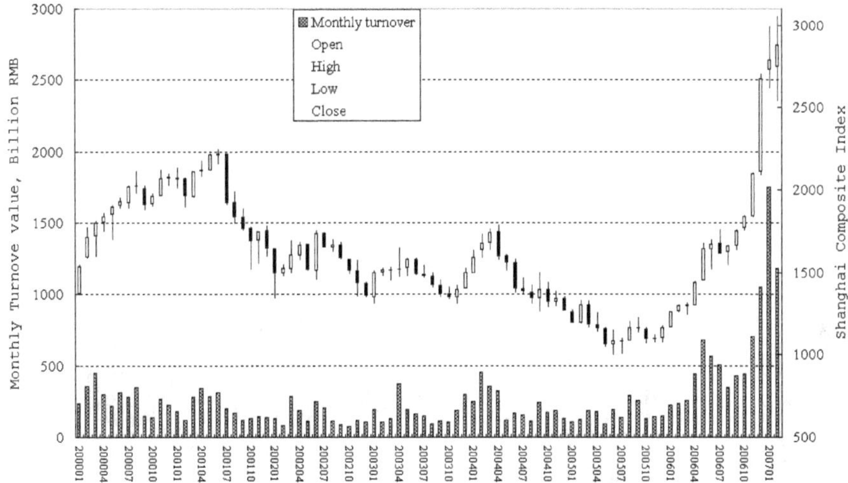

Figure 3.22.   Shanghai composite index and monthly trade amount during January 2000–February 2007.

Source: Calculated using data from Research and Development Center, Shanghai Stock Exchange. Shanghai Securities Yearbook, Shanghai Social Science publisher, 2003, 2002, 2001, and 2000.

the 1990s and 2000s, largely in bank deposits and property. But experience in richer countries shows that populations do not stop saving until they reach 300–400% of GDP, and Mr. Xie hazards a guess that, because of rising life expectancy, one-child families, and an early retirement age, China will stabilize at the high end of that range. All this means that it will take another two decades before the mass of Chinese become consumers in the accepted sense.[23]

In China, stock market trading activity is dominated by individual investors (close to 85%); more than 30 million new accounts were opened by retail investors in the first 5 months of 2015. According to data from the China's Securities Depository and Clearing Corp. and a survey by China's Southwestern University of Finance and Economics, these new traders were inexperienced and easily manipulated by the buying frenzy,

---

[23] China National Bureau of Statistics (2018). China Statistical Yearbook, China Statistics Press, 2018, Table 3.10; China National Bureau of Statistics, Data base; Annual, Total Wage Bill of Employed Persons in Urban Units (100 million yuan), 2000–2018; Gross Domestic Product by Expenditure Approach (100 million yuan),1999–2018.

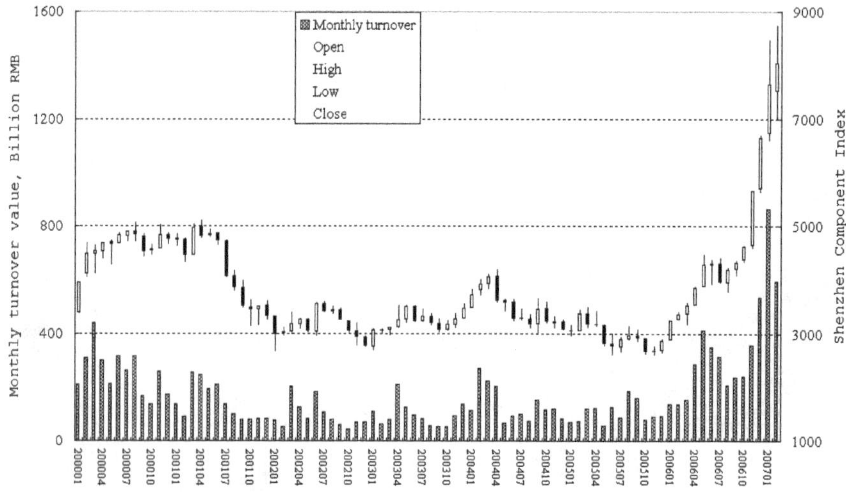

Figure 3.23.   Shenzhen component index and daily turnover value during January 2000–February 2007.

Source: Calculated using data from Shenzhen Stock Exchange (2005). Shenzhen Stock Exchange Fact Book 2005.

with nearly two-thirds having never entered or graduated high school. As a result, momentum and rumors among the traders carried more weight than reason, creating a trend of impulsive buying and overvaluation in the market.[24] The Shanghai Composite Index reached its highest value of 6124.04 on October 16, 2017. On August 24, five State departments announced guidelines pushing the reform process ahead, since the pilot projects on share mergers had proved successful, an announcement received well by the market. These guidelines stated that more than 1,400 listed companies can "gradually" convert their non-tradable shares.[25] On August 24, 2015, the Shanghai main share index lost 8.49% of its value, and there were similar losses of over 7% on August 25, 2015.[26] In 2015, listed securities numbered 2887, with a PE ratio of 17.61.

---

[24]Fahey, M. and E. Chemi. (2015). Three charts explaining China's strange stock market. *CNBC*, Thursday, July 9. www.cnbc.com/2015/07/09/three-charts-explaining-chinas-strange-stock-market.html.

[25]*Ibid.*

[26]Denyer, S. (2015). China's 'Black Monday' spreads stock market fears worldwide, The Washington Post, August 24; Gough, N. (2015). Shanghai stocks continue to dive as global

In, 2007, there were only 1772 securities listed and the PE ratio was 59.24;[27] the quality of listed firms has been improving. The Chinese stock market, however, is not related to the real economy. We will discuss the 2015 Stock Market Crash again in Chapter 10.

The other side of the increase in the share of profit and taxes of enterprises is the decline in the share of wages and household income in the total economy (see Figure 3.24). Much of the discussion on how to boost consumption in China still centers on household saving. However, most of the decline in the consumption to GDP ratio since the late 1990s can be explained by the decline in the share of wage income in the economy rather than a change in household savings by 57% in China. The share of wages in GDP has risen from 36.7% in 2007 to 39.4% in 2018. This shows that the transformation of the Chinese economy to new high-quality growth mode is under way, and people's living standards have improved.

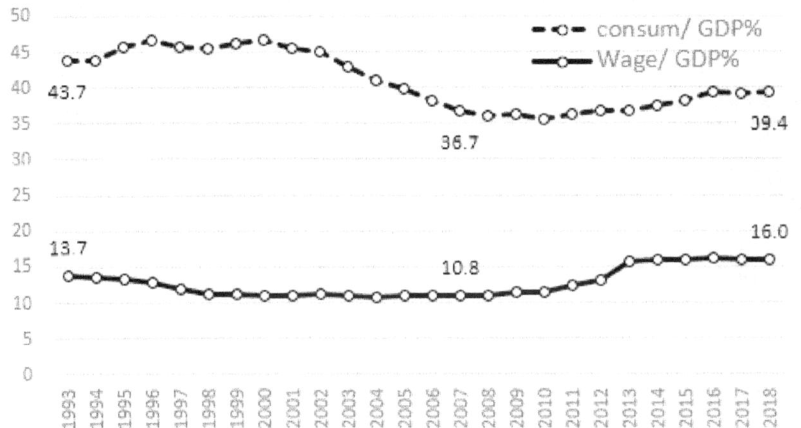

Figure 3.24.   Household consumption and wage share of GDP in China, 1993–2018.

Source: All China Data online: China Yearly Macroeconomic Statistics (National). Gross Domestic Product of China, 1952–2016; Gross Domestic Product By Expenditure Approach of China,1952–2017; China National Bureau of Statistics, Data base; Annual, Total Wage Bill of Employed Persons in Urban Units, 2000–2018.

---

markets elsewhere stabilize. *The New York Times*, August 25.

[27]Shanghai Stock Exchange. Statistics Annual, 2008, www.sse.com.cn/aboutus/publication/yearly/; Shenzhen Stock Exchange. Fact Book, 2007. 2015, http://www.szse.cn/market/periodical/year/index.html.

8. Income Disparity

A widening income gap is another explanation for limited consumer spending. Individual bank deposits amounted to about CNY5,340 billion (USD645 billion) at the end of 1998, according to the State Statistics Bureau. However, 83.2% of these deposits are in the hands of 2.5% of the population. More than 97% of the people have average savings of only CNY1,080.5 (USD130).[28] Depositors with commercial banks amounted to only 2.22 per 1,000 adults in 2012.[29] A report based on the nationwide survey shows that the average income per capita of urban residents was 321% that of farmers in 2004, much higher than the 188% in 1985.[30] However, the real disparity between urban and rural citizens is even larger. The income of urban citizens does not account for the welfare services they have access to, including medical care, unemployment insurance, and minimum living relief. In 2004, the nationwide per capita disposable income of city dwellers was CNY9,422, while the net income of rural inhabitants was only CNY2,936.[31] In 2016, incomes of urban dwellers and farmers rose to CNY21,285 and CNY10,873, respectively.[32] According to Forbes's "China 100 richest" in 2003, personal wealth of at least CNY827 million (USD100 million) was required to make the list. Total wealth of these 100 richest was CNY184.6 billion (USD22.3 billion USD),[33] representing a growth of 50.4% compared to the previous year. A 2002 survey conducted by the Economic Research Institute of the Chinese Academy of Social Sciences indicated that the top 1% of people with the highest income owned 6.1% of the total income of the society, 0.5% higher than in 1995. The top 10% of people with highest income have 32% of

---

[28] *China Daily*, 03/04/1999.

[29] World Development Indicators online 2018, Released September 2018 by World Bank.

[30] Calculated using data from China National Bureau of Statistics (2006). China Statistical Yearbook 2005, Tables 10.6, 10.22, China Statistical Press and various years, Statistical Yearbook of China 1986, Compiled by the State Statistical Bureau of China, Oxford University Press, 1986.

[31] China National Bureau of Statistics (2006). China Statistical Yearbook 2005, Tables 10.6, 10.22.

[32] All China Data online: China Yearly Macroeconomic Statistics (National): Gross Domestic Product by Expenditure Approach of China, 1952–2016.

[33] China's 100 Richest, www.forbes.com/2003/10/29/chinaland.html.

society's total income, 1.2 points higher than in 1995.[34] In a recent survey conducted by the Economic Research Institute of the Chinese Ministry of Finance (MOF), the richest 10% of families in urban areas possess 45% of total wealth, and the poorest 10% of families in urban areas possess only 1.6% of total wealth.[35] The Boston Consulting Group (BCG) issued a report, according to which China has about USD1.44 trillion in assets (including only on-shore investment) being managed for wealthy individuals (see Figure 3.25[36]). Indeed, wealth in China is highly concentrated. BCG's research indicates that 350,000 households (0.1% of all households) hold wealth equivalent to USD573 billion, their average wealth reaching USD1.61 million per household; 1.24 million households (0.34% of total) hold wealth of USD250 billion, an average wealth of USD201.6 thousand. Among these wealthy households with assets under management (AUM) larger than USD100 thousand (0.44% of all households) hold USD823 billion; even among these individuals, approximately 70% of wealth is held by households with AUM exceeding USD0.5 million. The remaining 363.34 million households (99.6 percent of all households) hold USD527 billion, an average wealth of only USD1,450 per household. Over time, we have observed that the wealthy in China are getting even wealthier. Since 1999, households with assets under management greater than USD5 million have grown from a 14.3% share to a 16.6% share of the nation's personal wealth, as shown in Figure 3.25.[37] Over the same period, non-wealthy households have accounted for a steady 36.6% of all wealth.

Although the United States is still far ahead in terms of total household wealth and the number of citizens in the top wealth categories, China's development in this century has been so rapid that a once seemingly insurmountable wealth gap may disappear within a generation. From 2000–2018, total wealth in China increased from USD3.7 trillion to USD51.9 trillion, an annual growth rate of 15.8%. This is twice the rate as other countries and three times that of most countries. As shown in Figure 3.25, the average per capita wealth in 2018 was USD47,180

---

[34] Urban-Rural Income Gap Larger: Survey http://service.china.org.cn/link/wcm/Show_Text?info_id=88528&p_qry=Income%20and%20disparity.

[35] Income and Wealth Gap Among People Widens Further (in Chinese) www.chinanews.com.cn/n/2003-06-16/26/314356.html.

[36] See Figure 3.25 for source.

[37] See Figure 3.25 for source.

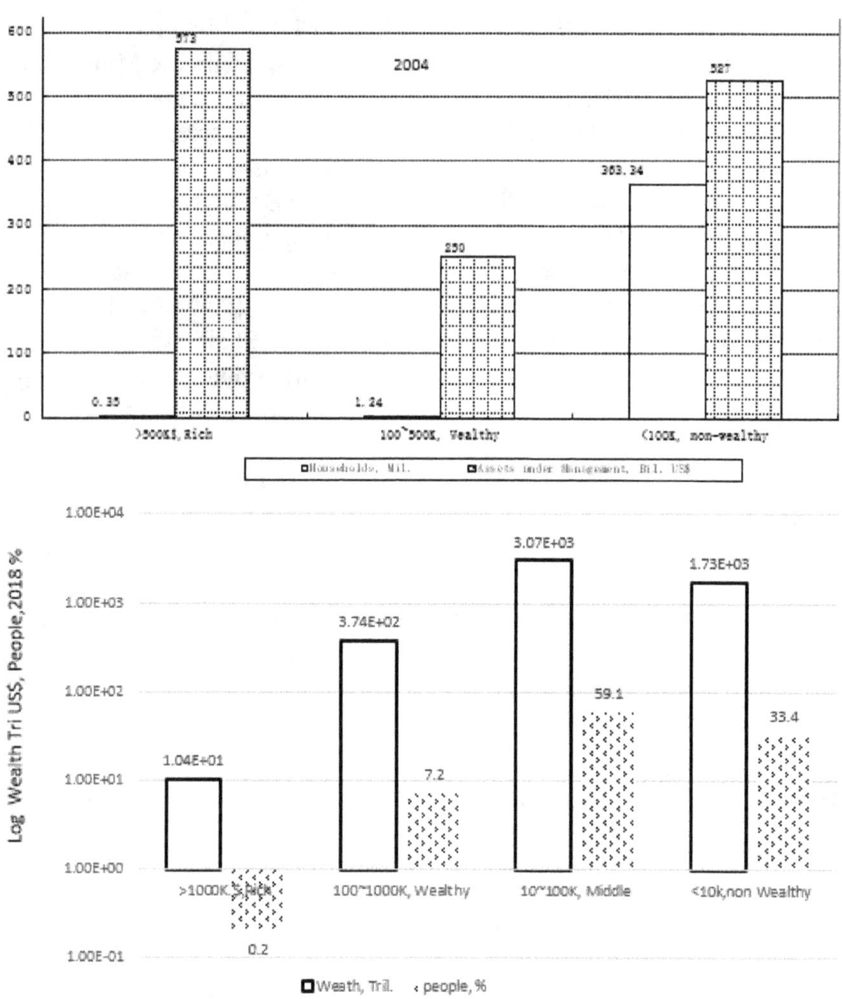

Figure 3.25. Wealth distribution in China, 2004, 2018.

Source: Tang, T., T. Klotz, and T. Achhomer (2005). Wealth markets in China — exciting times ahead, The Boston Consulting Group, December. Credit Suisse Research Institute (2018). Global Wealth Report 2018.

compared with USD403,974 in the United States and 227235 in Japan, respectively. There are 3.48 million millionaires in China, and 17.35 and 2.81 million in the United States and Japan, respectively., The proportion

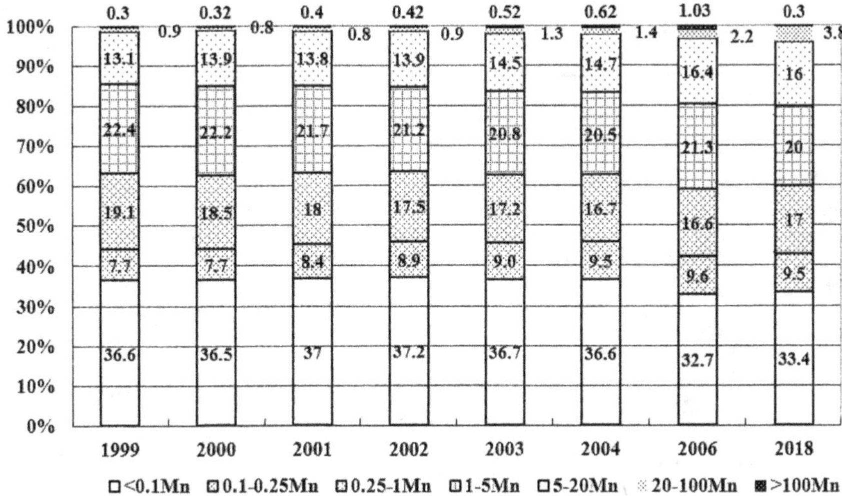

Figure 3.26.   The wealthy are getting wealthier over time in China.

Source: Tang, T., T. Klotz, and T. Achhomer (2005): Wealth markets in China — exciting times ahead, The Boston Consulting Group, December. Credit Suisse Research Institute's Global Wealth Report 2018.

of household non-financial assets rose from 61% in 2017 to 62% in 2018. Real assets comprised USD32,640 per adult in mid-2018. China now has 3.5 million millionaires, and there are more residents with wealth above USD50 million than any country except the United States.

A report issued by the MOF in 2003 showed that the overall gap of residents' incomes, represented by Gini Coefficient, was widening every year and has gone beyond the internationally recognized bottom line. The figure was 0.282 in 1991, 0.456 in 1998, 0.457 in 1999, and 0.458 in 2000.[38] Table 3.14 lists several countries' per capita income distribution and Gini coefficient, calculated based on these data. The values in the bottom six rows and last column in Table 3.14 are calculated by the authors; the remaining is taken from World Development Indicators. WDI online only publishes the Gini coefficient, not the distribution of income or

---

[38] China's income distribution policy urged to be adjusted, http://english.peopledaily.com. cn/200403/18/eng20040318_137823.shtml.

Table 3.14.   Consumer behavior of China's highest income group in 2004.

Annual spending, CNY	80,000–200,000	310,000–400,000	>510,000
Annual spending, USD	9,700–24,200	37,400–48,300	>61,500
Active group	50	50	50
Passive group	45	35	15
Gap	5	15	35

Source: Zhu, B. (2004). Half of China's rich aren't spending: Survey, *China Daily, Business Weekly*, June 8, p .3

consumption. The data taken from The World Development Indicators (WDI) databases present the share of consumption or income held by each quintile. The Gini coefficients calculated by the authors are different from the World Bank's calculations, meaning that the same income distribution data using different calculation method obtained different values. In addition, the same income distribution data is divided into different number of income.

groups, resulting at different values. Therefore, we insert in the right second column the ratio of per capita income highest 10% to the lowest 10% in the right second column as a secondary indicator to measure the income gap. Table 3.13 indicates that income disparity in China now is quite high. In Table 3.13, we show the Gini Coefficient for China's urban and rural areas in 2017, 2005, 2002, and 1986, because China Statistical Yearbook only provided income distribution for urban and rural areas separately. Our calculations demonstrate that the Gini coefficient in China's urban areas and rural areas increased from 1986–2017. From 1986–2017, the Gini coefficient in urban areas increased by 6.5%, and the rural Gini coefficient increased by 14.9%. In China, the largest income disparity has existed between urban and rural areas. Hence, a widening income gap drags overall consumption down despite the growth in average incomes. As shown in Table 3.14, the income distributions of urban households in 1986, 2002, and 2005 do not consider the impact of general inflation on absolute income measurement. There have been significant differences between urban household income groups in the past three decades. For instance, in 1986, the highest 20% group earned 253% of the lowest 20% group, with the earning differential rising to 562% in 2017. In rural areas, the per capita annual income of households in the fifth Quintile is reported only after 2003. Before 2003, only the percentage of households grouped by per capita annual net income was reported. For example, in 1996, 0.13% of the rural households earned CNY100 or below, 0.18% earned CNY100 to CNY200, and so on. We converted the 1986 and 2002 data into per capita annual income for five equal percentage households to show the income distributions of rural households in 1986, 2002, 2005, and 2016. In 1986, the highest 20% group earned about 435% of the lowest 20% group; this increased to 489% in 2005, and further increased to 948% in 2017. This shows that the income gap has changed faster since 2005. From Table 3.13, we observe that the income gap in urban households is larger than in rural households, since business owners and high-income white-collar class lived in urban areas.

Figure 3.27 shows the average propensity to consume (APS) for different income levels from 1996–2012 in China's urban areas. From Figure 3.27, we can see that APS reached its lowest for all seven different income levels in 2012. It is clearly seen that APC declined sharply for high income levels. APC declined from 0.889 (in 2012) for urbanites at the lowest 10% income category, to 0.590 (in 2012) for urban

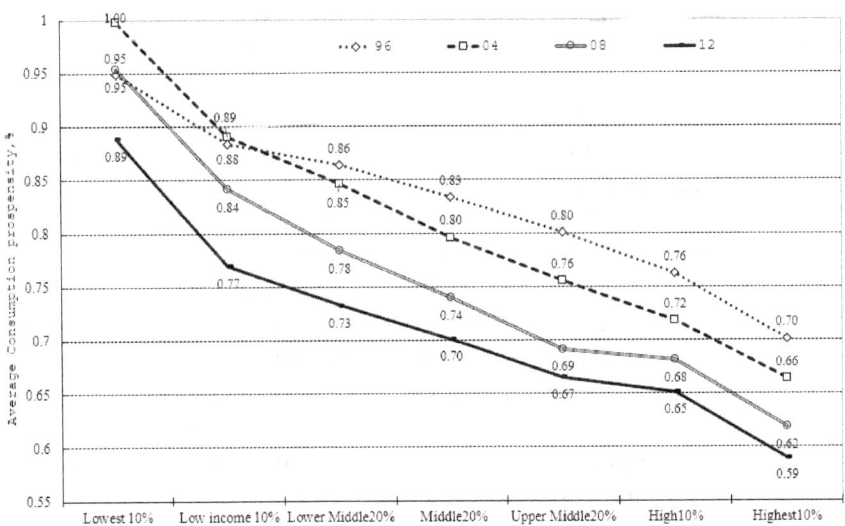

Figure 3.27.   Average consumption propensity for different income levels, China urban.

Source: Calculated using data from China National Bureau of Statistics: China Statistical Yearbook, China Statistical Press, 2013, Tables 10.6, 10.7; 2009, Tables 10.6, 10.7; 2005, Tables 10.6, 10.7; 1999, Table 10.8.

residents with highest 10% income. For poor households (lowest 5%) their per capita consumption accounted for CNY2,441, but their income was only CNY2,312. APC reached CNY1.056 in 2004. Since per capita income in China is still low, low-income residents must spend almost all their disposable income to maintain their necessary living standard. From 1996–2012, APC for the highest income 10% decreased from 0.701 in 1996 to 0.590 in 2012. For lowest 10% income even with high APCs of 0.949 in 1996 to 0.889 in 2012, their low per capita income allowed only a low absolute amount of per capita consumption, CNY2,855 in 2004. For the 10% highest per capita incomes, that value was CNY16,841 in 2004. These numbers increased to CNY7,301 and CNY37,662 in 2012, respectively. Rich households already possess a home (or more than one), durable goods, and cars. Their consumption preference may be concentrated on foreign name brands, so their spending does not increase domestic demand. Therefore, income disparity resulted in declining effective domestic demand. According to a recent survey conducted by China Merchants Bank and the domestic research house Horizonkey Co., there are about 2.31 million Chinese who have personal or family bank deposits more than CNY500,000 (USD60,240). A sample survey of 1,049 respondents with high incomes was conducted in seven large cities in 2004. The survey showed that respondents fell into two categories–active and passive consumers. The active comprised 58.2% and the passive the remainder. Regarding purchasing plans for 2004, there is a significant spending gap between the two groups on large items such as real estate and private cars, and the gap widens as the spending grows, as shown in Table 3.14. It seems that half of China's rich are not spending actively. When per capita income increases, consumer preference is moving to high quality food (nutritious and delicious; in a survey[39] 55.7% said they preferred healthy and natural foods including organic vegetables and fruit; 59.4% said they paid attention to food ingredients and expiration dates when shopping), durable goods (advanced type: digital high resolution color TV, projection color TV, three door refrigerators, energy saving air conditioner ensuring natural environment, digital side by side refrigerator, automatic washing machine), education and entertainment, housing, sedan, and expenditure related to rearing children. Change in production structure, however, did

---

[39]The survey covered 3,000 families in 10 cities, Survey Chronicles Changing Chinese Lifestyles, www.china.org.cn/english/2001/Aug/16952.htm.

not keep up with demand. Market share of high quality and famous brand consumer goods increased significantly, which is shown in Table 3.15.[40] The number of household appliance brands in China is diminishing because of the extension of OEM (original equipment manufacturing) production. Nationwide famous brands have a great influence on domestic consumers and enough power to dictate market prices. This information was released in a report, which is based on a survey that covered 54 cities in 29 provinces. China Central Television, Trade and Foreign Economic Relations Agency, China National Bureau of Statistics, The Development Research Center of the State Council (DRC) conducted such survey in 1998, 2001, and 2002.[41] The trend of concentration of consumption on famous brands is getting stronger. For example, in 2000, Coca-Cola accounted 38.8%, Galanz microwave oven 67.1%, Kodak film 63.1%, and Arrow chewing gum 89.7%. The survey found that, when consumers buy a commodity, they mainly consider brand and price. For example, in buying meat products, consumers stated that brand name accounted a weight of 57.1% in their decision to buy, and price 51.3%. Foreign brand names enjoyed a comparative advantage in the market. Business Information Center of Shanghai conducted a survey of eight categories of more than 90 commodities sold by more than 3500 chain stores in Shanghai at 2001. Over 500 brands were recognized as best-selling brands, among them 47.1% are joint ventures and imported brands. The market shares of electric appliances, communication and household articles, and food items are relatively high; the market share of top five brands accounted for more than 50% of the market, since these products are characterized by large-scale production. Among them, the top five brands dominated the market in refrigerators, dishwashers, water heaters, mobile phones, toothpaste, washing powder, dairy products, instant noodles, beverages, and edible oil exceeded the 70% share.

---

[40] See Table 3.15 for source.

[41] Issued jointly by the Market Economics Institute of the Development Research Centre under the State Council, the Ministry of Information Industry and the China Household Electrical Appliance Association, The Development Research Center of the State Council (DRC) (2002). Survey on Urban electric appliance market in 200 — low concentration ratio of electric appliance brand, (in Chinese), *Market Daily*, September 6, p. 11.

Table 3.15. Survey of famous brands in 100-commodity category in China.

	Commodity	top 3 brand market Share %, 1997	2001, Market share%/Sales	2003, Market share%Sales /10,000 sets	2005, market share%/Sales
Food	Salad dressing	Top 3: 77.8		Top 10 > 70	Top 10 > 70
	Sherbet	Top 3: 55.48			
	Monosodium glutamate (MSG)	Top 3: 53.72			
	Can, Tobacco, white wine, soybean milk, Eight-treasure gruel, Candy, Ham sausage	*Top 3: 22.2–74.1*			
Electric equipment	Color TV	41.5–64.5	Flat-screen TV: ChangHong +TCL+KangKa, 38.4 Projection TV: Toshiba, 19.2	Top 10 > 80/3383	Top 10 = 90
	Refrigerator		RongSheng>18,Haier> 18	Top 10 > 80/800	Top 10 = 83.4
	Washing Machine		Haier+Little Swan+ XiaoYa +RongShiDa >54	Top 10 > 80	Top 10 = 89.2
	Air conditioner		Gree+MeiDea+HuaBao 35.5	Top 10 > 80/3200	Top 10 = 84.1
	Microwave oven		Galanz 70%	Top 10 > 98	
	DVD		Shinco 19.5, BuBugao 16.4, Jinzheng 8.9		
Garments	Shirt, Fur, Childrens' wear, Eider down overcoat	11.1–31.7		Top 10 > 40	Top 10 > 40

(*Continued*)

Table 3.15.   (*Continued*)

	Commodity	Top 3 brand market share %, 1997	2001, Market share%/Sales	2003, Market share%/Sales /10,000 sets	2005, Market share%/Sales
Top 1 brand market share	Color TV	ChangHong 25.4	ChangHong 17.5	Kangka 18.71/791	ChangHong >15
	Refrigerator	Haier 25.4	Haier >18	Kelong (include Rongsheng, Kongbaien) 27.3/273	Kelong (include Rongsheng, Kongbaien) 25
	Air conditioner	Haier 30.7	Gree	Gree 13.76/516	Gree 16.9
	Mobile phone			Bodao 12.5/1176	Bodao 4

Source: Data from Hu, C., and Y. Wang (2001). Consumers still prefer famous brands — Survey on China's urban consumers, in Chinese) *Life Times*, April 3; Wang, L., and Z. Ni (2002). The effect of famous brands — Industry Survey, (in Chinese), *Market Daily*, September 16; Wang, Z. (2004). Consumers prefer famous brands, market share of domestic famous brand increased (in Chinese), China Industry Information Issue Center, (in Chinese), March 25, www. ciiic.com.cn/newsdetail.php?articleid=80; Statistical Communiqué 2003 of Electronic Information Industry Economic Operation (in Chinese), Economic System Reform and Operation Bureau, Ministry of Information Industry, May 01, 2004; Zhu, X. (2006). The 10th survey on the market share of National top brands. March 18.

9. The Consumption Pattern: The Engel Coefficient

The Engel coefficient is commonly used to measure the living standards of people in a country and region. The coefficient is the ratio of food expenditure per capita to total consumption per capita. According to Engel's Law, as income rises, the proportion spent on income decreases. Since residents of poorer nations must spend most of their income on necessities, a high Engel coefficient is a characteristic of a poor nation; a low Engel coefficient is a characteristic of a rich nation. At each income level, as income per capita increases, the Engel coefficient declines, as shown in Figure 3.28. According to the standards proposed by the Food and Agriculture Organization of the United Nations (FAO), an Engel coefficient of 59% denotes absolute poverty, between 50% and 59% denotes adequate, 40% and 50% well-off, and 30% and 40% wealth. Less than 30% stands for more affluent. As shown in Figure 3.32, the Engel coefficient of urban areas in 1964 was 0.59, and the rural Engel coefficient in 1978 was 0.68, indicating that China was an absolute poor country. In 1993, the Engel coefficient of urban areas was 0.50, and the rural Engel coefficient was 0.30, indicating that China had become a wealth country. From 2010 to 2018, the Engel coefficient of China dropped significantly. The per capita living expenditure for different income level in urban areas surveyed from 1996 to 2005, 2008, and 2012[42] has been used to make regression analysis and get:

$$Engle_L = -0.0995\,Ln\,(\exp endpc) + 1.284$$
$$(-18.08) \qquad\qquad (27.01)$$
$$R = 0.8761,\, F = 327,\, df = 99,\, s = 0.0360 \tag{3.13}$$

From Eq. (3.13), it cans be found that per capita living expenditure increases 7.96%, $Engel_L$ declines 0.01 or per capita living expenditure increases to two-fold, $Engle_L$ declines 0.0905. Equation (3.13) shows consumer preference for similar per capita living expenditure group will be quite similar. We summarize the regression analysis for Engel coefficient

---

[42]Calculated using data from China National Bureau of Statistics: China Statistical Yearbook, China Statistical Press, 2013, Tables 10.6, 10.7; 2005, Tables 10.6, 10.7; 2004, Tables 10.6, 10.7; 2003, Tables 10.6, 10.7; 2002, Tables 10.6, 10.7; 2000, Tables 10.7, 10.8; 1999, Tables 10.7, 10.8; 1997, Tables 9.8, 9.9.

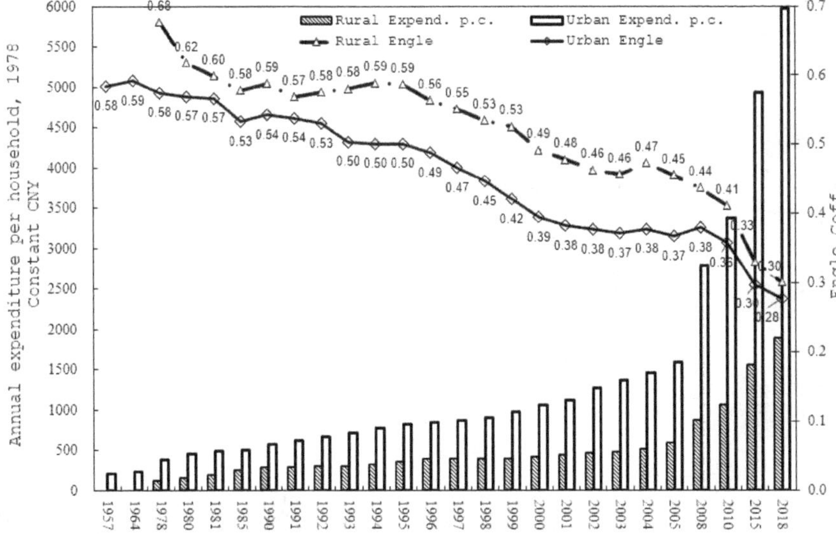

Figure 3.28.   Engel coefficient in China, 1957–2018.

Source: Calculated using data from China National Bureau of Statistics: China Statistical Yearbook, China Statistical Press, 2018, Tables 6.6, 6.11; 2014, Table 6.4; 2006, Tables 10.7, 10.26; 2005, Tables 10.7, 10.26; 2004, Tables 10.7, 10.26; 2003, Tables 10.7, 10.25; 2002, Tables 10.7, 10.24; 2001, Tables 10.7, 10.21; 2000, Tables 10.12, 10.19; 1999, Tables 10.8, 10.18; 1997, Tables 9.9, 9.19; 1996, Tables 9.9, 9.19, 1991, Tables 8.15, 8.28, 8.30 and various years.

and per capita living expenditure in Table 3.16. Three types of per capita consumption data, namely: different time, numerous regional distributions, and different income level groups, were used to conduct the regression analysis. The regression analysis of regional distribution in urban areas are statistically unacceptable. Table 3.16 shows that the regression formula between the Engel coefficient and the logarithm of per capita living expenditure has a linear relationship, only with different slopes. For different per capita income group, the consumer demand will vary in time, type, price, and structure. For example: from 1997–2012 the Engel coefficient of the lowest income group decreased by 0.1134 (maximum), and the Engel coefficient of the high-income group decreased. by 0.0857 (lowest). Table 3.17 shows in the United States the Engel coefficient declined, fluctuating from 0.408 (1997) to 0.415 (2016), and in Japan it increased from 0.249 (1993) to 0.321 (2008). For developed countries, the

Table 3.16. Summary of Engel coefficient regression, China.

		Ln(Expendpc)	Intercept	R	df	F	s	Interval	Eq. (#)
Time series	Urban	−0.1032	1.1617	0.9311	22	109.1	0.0372	1957–2018	(3.12)
	t-ratio	−11.98	19.39	143.45	0.0335				
	Rural	−0.1242	1.1951	0.9122	22	109.1	0.0372	1957–2018	(3.13)
	t-ratio	−10.45	16.62	109.11	0.0372				
	Urban+rural	−0.0774	0.9506	0.7697	45	65.4	0.0553	1957–2018	(3.14)
	t-ratio	−8.09	15.30	65.42					
Regional distribution, (31 provinces & municipalities)	Region, urban	0.0056	0.4583	0.0355	28	0.0	0.0388	1994	(3.15)
	t-ratio	0.99	0.73						
	Region, urban	−0.4377	0.0829	0.4099	29	5.9	0.0413	2017	(3.16)
	t-ratio	−1.45	2.42						
	Region, rural	−0.0798	1.1424	0.5302	29	10.9	0.0457	1994	(3.17)
	t-ratio	−3.31	6.86						
	Region, rural	−0.1141	1.3534	0.5588	29	13.2	0.0617	2005	(3.18)
	t-ratio	−3.63	5.49						
	Region, rural	0.0774	−0.3159	0.4013	29	5.6	0.0503	2017	(3.19)
	t-ratio	0.20	−1.18						

	Urban + Rural	0.0071	0.2430	0.0594	60	0.2	0.0506	2017U+R	(3.20)
	t-ratio	0.46	1.37						
	National	0.0178	0.1459	0.5692	29	0.3	0.0486	2017	(3.20a)
	t-ratio	2.82	5.49						
	Region, urban	−0.0158	0.5120	0.1008	29	0.3	0.0394	2005	(3.21)
	t-ratio	−0.55	2.01						
Region (35 cities)	City	−0.0778	0.9189	0.4683	33	53.3	0.0448	1998	(3.22)
	t-ratio	−3.04	5.97					35 cities	
Region (35 cities)	City	−0.0543	0.8674	0.3739	33	5.4	0.0366	2004	(3.23)
	t-ratio	−2.32	4.12					35 cities	
Income level, 8 groups	Urban	−0.0995	1.2841	0.8761	99	326.9	0.0360	1996–2012	(3.9)
	t-ratio	−18.08	27.01						

Table 3.17. Engel coefficient in the United States, Japan, South Korea, and China.

US97	JP93	KR98	CH80	CH10
0.408	0.249	0.319	0.387	0.437
US07	JP08	KR06	CH01	CH17
0.411	0.321	0.317	0.447	0.356
US16		KR12	CH05	
0.415		0.316	0.425	

Source: Calculated using data from International Statistical Yearbook, China Statistical Press, 2006, Table 10.3; China National Bureau of Statistics, Data base; Annual, Per Capita Disposable Income & Per Capita Expenditure Nationwide, 2013–2018; World Bank: World Development Indicators (not WDI online) 2005 Table 2.7, 2009 Table 2.9, 2012 Table 2.9.

Engel coefficient is lower than in developing countries. In South Korea, the Engel coefficient fluctuated from 0.319 (1998) to 0.316 (2012). Compared with these countries, Engel coefficient in China is still high, from 0.387 in 1980 it increased to 0.447 in 2001, then declined to 0.356 in 2017, indicating low per capita living expenditure.

When per capita spending increases, the Engel coefficient decreases. Then another consumption structure living in rural and urban areas of China is shown in Tables 3.19 and 3.20, respectively. The percentage share of food and clothing have declined. In rural areas, the Engel coefficient declined from 0.5966 in 1981 to 0.4548 in 2005 and further declined to 0.3403 in 2015. The percentage share of clothing decreased from 12.35% in 1981 to 5.81% in 2005 and increased to 5.97% in 2015. From 1981–2005, the percentage share of transportation and communication, medical service, Household Facilities, and education increase 10.51%, 7.75%, 4.70%, and 4.15%, respectively. These indicate that in rural areas consumption has gradually changed from "absolute poverty" to "having adequate food and clothing" in 2005 and has further become a "comparatively well-off" type in 2015. In the urban areas, the Engel coefficient declined from 0.5914 in 1981 to 0.3669 in 2005 and further declined to 0.3064 in 2015. The percentage share of clothing decreased from 15.44% in 1981 to 10.08% in 2005 and further declined to 7.41% in 2015. From 1981–2005, the percentage share of transportation and

Table 3.18.   Per capita annual living expenditure and its composition in China rural area, %.

Rural area	1981	1985	1990	1995	1998	2000	2002	2005	2010	2015	2018
Per capita consump. expend.	191	317	585	1310	1590	1670	1834	2555	4382	9223	12124
Food	59.66	57.79	58.80	58.62	53.43	49.13	46.25	45.48	41.09	33.05	30.07
Clothing	12.35	9.69	7.77	6.85	6.17	5.75	5.72	5.81	6.03	5.97	5.34
Residence	9.78	18.23	17.34	13.91	15.07	15.47	16.36	14.49	19.06	20.89	21.94
Household facilities, articles	5.55	5.10	5.29	5.23	5.15	4.52	4.38	4.36	5.34	5.92	5.94
Medicines and medical service	1.83	2.42	3.25	3.24	4.28	5.24	5.67	9.59	7.44	12.61	13.94
Transport & Communications	1.05	1.76	1.44	2.58	3.82	5.58	7.01	11.56	10.52	10.51	10.74
Culture, Education & recreation	2.43	3.89	5.37	7.81	10.02	11.18	11.47	6.58	8.37	9.17	10.23
Other commodities & services	7.34	1.12	0.74	1.76	2.07	3.14	3.14	2.13	2.15	1.89	1.80
K (1981 as reference)	0	2.80	3.08	3.11	4.52	5.59	6.35	6.78	7.57	9.61	10.54
R (1981 as reference)	1	0.9840	0.9829	0.9854	0.9752	0.9643	0.9531	0.9449	0.9241	0.8516	0.8717

(*Continued*)

Table 3.18. (*Continued*)

Rural area	1981	1985	1990	1995	1998	2000	2002	2005	2010	2015	2018
K′ (previous column as reference)		2.80	0.88	1.15	1.49	1.34	0.76	2.14	1.89	2.09	2.09
R′ (previous column as reference)		0.9840	0.9989	0.9974	0.9974	0.9978	0.9987	0.9878	0.9911	0.9820	0.9737
Year		81–85	85–90	90–95	95–98	98–00	00–02	02–05	05-10	10-15	15–18

Source: Calculated using data from China National Bureau of Statistics: China Statistical Yearbook, China Statistical Press, 2019, Table 06.11; 2011 Table 10.16; 2006, Table 10.26; 2005, Table 10.26; 2003, Table 10.25; 2001, Table 10.21; 2000, Table 10.18; 1996, Table 9.19; 1991, Table 8.28, 8.30; China National Bureau of Statistics compiled: Statistical Yearbook of China, Oxford University Press 1986, p. 583; China State Statistical Bureau compiled: Statistical yearbook of China 1981, published by Economic Information & Agency, Hong Kong, 1982, p. 443.

Table 3.19.   Per capita annual living expenditure and its composition in China urban area, %.

Urban area	1981	1985	1990	1995	1998	2000	2002	2005	2010	2015	2018
Per capita consump. expenditure	457	673	1279	3538	4332	4998	6030	7943	13471	21392	26112
Food	59.14	52.25	54.24	49.92	44.48	39.18	37.68	36.69	35.67	29.73	27.72
Clothing	15.44	14.56	13.36	13.55	11.10	10.01	9.80	10.08	10.72	7.95	6.92
Residence	2.47	3.69	3.87	7.07	9.43	8.79	10.35	5.62	9.89	22.09	23.95
Household facilities, articles	9.98	10.68	13.36	8.39	8.24	6.36	6.45	7.56	6.74	6.11	7.83
Medicines and medical services	0.63	0.93	1.52	3.11	4.74	7.9	7.13	12.55	6.47	6.75	6.24
Transport & communications	1.51	1.09	1.2	4.83	5.94	12.56	10.38	13.82	14.73	13.53	13.30
Culture, education & recreation	8.80	10.11	8.77	8.84	11.53	10.01	14.96	10.18	12.08	11.14	11.39
Other commodities and services	2.03	6.69	3.68	4.28	4.55	5.17	3.25	3.5	3.71	2.70	2.63
K (1981 as reference)	0	2.05	1.83	3.18	5.18	7.25	7.66	7.56	7.86	10.19	10.52

(Continued)

Table 3.19.   (*Continued*)

Urban area	1981	1985	1990	1995	1998	2000	2002	2005	2010	2015	2018
R (1981 as reference)	1	0.9945	0.9963	0.9910	0.9731	0.9331	0.9246	0.9064	0.9063	0.7921	0.7565
K' (previous column as reference)		2.05	1.39	2.32	2.01	2.61	1.65	2.63	1.98	3.12	0.96
R' (previous column as reference)		0.9945	0.9968	0.9919	0.9939	0.9836	0.9908	0.9782	0.9844	0.9487	0.9968
Year		81–85	85–90	90–95	95–98	98–00	00–02	02–05	05–10	10-15	15-18

Source: Calculated using data from China National Bureau of Statistics: China Statistical Yearbook, China Statistical Press, 2019, Table 10.5; 2010, Table 10.5; 2006, Table 10.7; 2005, Table 10.7; 2003, Table 10.7; 2001, Table 10.7; 2000, Table 10.4; 1996, Table 9.9; 1991, Table 8.15; China National Bureau of Statistics compiled: Statistical Yearbook of China 1986, Oxford University Press, p. 580; China State Statistical Bureau compiled: Statistical yearbook of China 1981, published by Economic Information & Agency, Hong Kong, 1982, p. 439.

communications, medical service, residence, and education increased by 12.31%, 11.92%, 3.15%, and 1.47%, respectively, slightly higher than the 27.81% decline in food and clothing consumption. Due to the fact that welfare housing distribution system was gradually abolished, in 2005, Urban residential sales totaled 495.9 million square meters, with an annual growth rate of 46.6%, while sales amounted to 1,456.4 billion yuan (USD180.5 billion), with an annual growth rate of 69.0%.[43] The individuals purchased 96.43% residential houses in 2003.[44] This shows that, in urban areas, consumption has gradually changed from "absolute poverty" to "having adequate food and clothing" in 2005 and has further become a "well-off" type in 2015.The consumption structure in rural and urban areas both changed significantly, so the industry supply structure should change to match the consumption structure change.

It can be seen from Table 3.18 that the consumption structure change coefficient of rural areas K_{annual} is 0.282% from 1981–2005, and the similarity coefficient R is 0.9449. In the same period, from Table 3.19, K_{annual} is 0.315% and R is 0.9064 in urban areas. K' and R' represent the consumption structure change coefficient and similarity coefficient between the two adjacent columns. In rural areas, from 2002–2005, K' was 2.14% and R' was 0.9878. From Table 3.20, it is found that consumption structure change coefficients K' and R' were 2.63 and 0.9782; From 2010–2015, in rural areas K' and R' were 0. 63 and 0.9990, respectively. According to Table 3.19, in urban areas' K' and R' were 3.2 and 0.9521, respectively. From K' and R', we find the consumption structure change became larger in urban areas than in rural areas in recent years, indicating the consumption structure change in urban areas is larger than in rural areas and the change accelerated in recent years. There are two reasons for this. The reform of social welfare system, health care system, and residential house distribution system has more effect on consumption structure in urban areas than that in rural areas. Small value of consumption structure change coefficient K and high value of the similarity coefficient $R1$ from 1981–2015 imply that consumption structure change also will take a relatively long time.

To compare China's consumption structure change with the world average (see Table 3.20), we introduce the consumption structure in

---

[43]Calculated using data from China National Bureau of Statistics: China Statistical Yearbook, China Statistical Press, 2006, Table 6.36.

[44]*Ibid.*, 2004, Table 6.48.

2004 of China's urban and rural areas. From the consumption structure change coefficient K and similarity coefficient $R1$ in Table 3.20, we see that the consumption structure in China's rural areas is compatible with per capita income of less than 1000 Current International USD, and consumption structure in China's urban areas is compatible with per capita income between 1000 and 4000 Current International USD. China's consumption structure still belongs to low-income countries in the world. In Table 3.21, the consumption structures of some foreign countries (United States, Japan, South Korea, Indonesia, Thailand, Germany, and United Kingdom) are listed and compared with Japan's. The consumption structure change coefficient K and similarity coefficient $R1$ in Table 3.21 indicate that consumption structure in Japan is most similar with Thailand and most dissimilar with the United States. China's 1998 and 2017 compared with Japan's 1998 $R1$ rose from 0.4343 in 1998 to 0.5313 in 2017, which shows that China's consumption structure in 2017 is more similar to that of Japan's in 1998. Using China's consumption structure data in 1998 and comparing with United States's in 1998; it is found that the consumption structure change coefficient K in Table 3.22 reached 15.61, which is greater than $K = 9.61$ in Table 3.19 and in Table 3.20. $K = 10.12$, which represents the changes in China's rural and urban areas from 1981–2015 (34 years), indicating that China's consumption structure may take a long time to catch up with the consumption structure of developed countries.

From Table 3.21, we find that China's consumption structure in 2017 is most similar with Russia's in 1998. This is proven by the size of the consumption structure change coefficient $K = 2.4$, and the similarity coefficient's $R1 = 0.9033$. The Engel coefficient in 2017 is 1.15% lower than Russia's in 1998. According to the structure of consumption, then, China also belongs in the low-income country group in 1998 and the middle-income group in 2017.

We now study the relationship between total-expenditures and the demand for food, housing, and other major consumption categories of Chinese households. We will discuss the total-expenditure elasticity of demand on food, housing, and other major consumption categories of Chinese households. To study household expenditure patterns, we use data from eight categories of expenditures — food (1), clothing (2), residence (3), facilities (4), medicines (5), transportation and communications (6), education and culture (7), others (8) and sum of facilities, medicines, transportation and communications, education and culture, and others (9). Using per capita data of Chinese rural areas from 31 provinces and

Table 3.20.   Consumption structure for different per capita income, world average.

(Income)pc, PPPUSD CH 4,580 at 2002	Food	Clothing	Resid-ence	Med. & medical services	Educa, recrea	Transp. & communic.	Others	Kurba	R1urb	Krur	R1rur
≤1,000 CI$	48	8	11	3	6	7	18	6.61	0.9405	2.39	0.9879
1,000–4,000 CI$	38	9	10	6	7	9	21	4.47	0.9548	4.34	0.9609
4,001–10,000 CI$	27	8	14	7	7	9	28	7.23	0.8706	6.34	0.8623
10,001–20,000 CI$	15	7	15	9	7	13	34	9.23	0.7214	9.53	0.6691
≥20,000 CI$	11	5	18	12	8	12	33	9.95	0.6653	10.67	0.6078
China urban (2004)	36.7	10.1	5.6	12.6	10.2	13.8	11.1	0.00	1.0000	6.04	0.9405
China rural (2004)	47.2	5.5	14.8	4.1	6.0	8.8	11.3	6.04	0.9405	0.00	1.0000
China urban (2015)	30.6	7.4	27.8	13.3	11.0	7.4	30.6	8.35	0.8279	9.48	0.8406
China rural (2015)	33.0	6.0	26.8	9.2	10.5	12.6	33.0	7.98	0.8404	8.82	0.8582

Source: Calculated using data from World Bank: World Development Indicators 1997 (from WDI98 and later no such data available.); China National Bureau of Statistics: China Statistical Yearbook, China Statistical Press, 2005, Tables 10.16, 10.26: China National Bureau of Statistics, Data base; annual, per capita income & expenditure of rural & Urban households, 1997–2016.

Table 3.21. Per capita annual living expenditure and its composition of selected countries, 1998.

	KOR	JPN	INA	THA	GER	UK	USA	CHN	RUS	CHN	CHN	CHN	CHN	CHN
	1998	1998	1998	1998	1998	1998	1998	1998	1998	1998	1998	2015	2017	2017
(Living expend) pc PPPUSD	6,695	13,568	1,701	2,051	15,577	14,804	21,515	3,290	4,099	3,290	3,290	5,644	6,449	7,369
Food	17.6	12.3	46.7	23.3	14.0	14.2	13.0	50.4	27.6	50.4	50.4	30.6	29.3	29.3
Clothing	2.8	6.6	3.2	7.9	6.4	6.8	9.4	7.8	11.2	7.8	7.8	7.4	6.8	6.8
Residence	7.3	7.1	5.8	5.2	7.3	9.1	8.9	19.4	15.5	19.4	19.4	27.8	28.5	28.5
Medical services	4.7	1.5	4.6	2.7	2.4	2.7	3.5	4.4	7.0	4.4	4.4	7.4	7.9	7.9
Transport & communic.	13.6	22.4	14.4	13.3	9.7	2.8	5.8	4.5	14.5	4.5	4.5	13.3	13.6	13.6
Educational	5.7	13.4	3.0	10.6	7.2	6.4	8.5	10.5	8.2	10.5	10.5	11.0	11.4	11.4
Others	48.4	36.8	22.3	37.1	53.0	58.1	50.9	2.9	16.0	2.9	2.9	2.5	2.4	2.4
K	5.79	0	10.71	3.92	5.41	7.60	6.14	15.61	9.68	15.61	0	5.89	12.88	6.46
R1	0.9459	1	0.7027	0.9525	0.9308	0.8786	0.4050	0.8983	0.7872	0.4343	1	0.9127	0.5313	0.9033
K, R1 Pairing	SK/JP		INA/ JP	THA/ JP	DEU/ JP	UK/JP	US/JP	US/ CH	RU/JP	CH/JP		CH15/98	CH/JP	CH/ RU

Source: Calculated using data from World Bank: World Development Indicators (not WDI online) 2000, Table 4.11 Structure of consumption in PPP terms (from WDI 2001 and later no such data available); China data from China National Bureau of Statistics: China Statistical Yearbook, 2000, Tables 10.05, 10.18; China National Bureau of Statistics, Data base; Annual, Total Permanent Population Grouped by Urban and Rural Areas, 1949–2016.

Table 3.22. Total-expenditure elasticity for different categories.

Researcher	Author	Author	Author	Author	Houthak-ker	Gregory C. Chow	Gregory C. Chow	Author	Author	Author
Area	Rural	Rural	Rural	Urban	Urban	Rural	Rural	Rural	Rural	Urban
Years	2005 region	2002 region	2000 region	1998–2005 group	before 1957	1981 region	1998 region	1998 region	2015 region	2015 region
Food	0.746	0.747	0.779	0.541	0.6	0.79	0.742	0.742	0.793	0.792
Clothing	0.889	0.779	0.792	0.929	1.2	0.79	0.779	0.779	0.784	0.522
Residence	1.301	1.262	1.257	1.046	0.8	1.78	1.475	1.475	1.338	1.481
Miscellaneous	1.273	1.295	1.379	1.008	1.6	1.25		1.422	1.018	5.094
Facilities	1.236	1.124	1.291	1.096				1.284	0.912	0.815
Medicines	1.348	1.161	1.203	1.160				1.214	1.077	1.102
Transp + Commun.	1.382	1.538	1.685	1.050				1.876	1.079	0.955
Educational	1.199	1.372	1.457	0.770				1.637	0.940	0.741
Other	1.222	1.333	1.267	1.150				1.420	1.254	5.094

Source: Calculated using data from China National Bureau of Statistics: China Statistical Yearbook, China Statistical Press, 2013, Tables 11.7, 11.23; 1999, Tables 10.8, 10.14; Chow, G. C.: China's Economic transformation, Blackwell Publishers, World Scientific, 2002, ISBN: 0-631-23330-X; Houthakker, H.S. (1957). An international comparison of Household expenditure patterns, commemorating the centenary of Engel's law, *Econometrics*, 25.

Municipals (degree of freedom $df = 29$) in 2005,[45] we derive the following regressions of natural log per capita expenditures y_i for above eight categories on natural log per- capita total expenditures x:

$$Ln\ y_1 = 1.204 + 0.746Lnx \qquad\qquad R = 0.907$$
$$(11.58) \qquad\qquad df = 29,\ s = 0.126 \qquad (3.14)$$

$$Ln\ y_2 = -1.948 + 0.889Lnx \qquad\qquad R = 0.740$$
$$(5.93) \qquad df = 29,\ s = 0.294 \qquad (3.15)$$

$$Ln\ y_3 = -4.343 + 1.301Lnx \qquad\qquad R = 0.862$$
$$(11.58) \qquad df = 29,\ s = 0.279 \qquad (3.16)$$

$$Ln\ y_4 = -5.008 + 1.236Lnx \qquad\qquad R = 0.955$$
$$(17.35) \qquad df = 29,\ s = 0.140 \qquad (3.17)$$

$$Ln\ y_5 = -5.120 + 1.348Lnx \qquad\qquad R = 0.936$$
$$(14.35) \qquad df = 29,\ s = 0.184 \qquad (3.18)$$

$$Ln\ y_6 = -5.240 + 1.382Lnx \qquad\qquad R = 0.794$$
$$(7.02) \qquad df = 29,\ s = 0.386 \qquad (3.19)$$

$$Ln\ y_7 = -4.294 + 1.199Lnx \qquad\qquad R = 0.852$$
$$(8.78) \qquad df = 29,\ s = 0.268 \qquad (3.20)$$

$$Ln\ y_8 = -5.625 + 1.222Lnx \qquad\qquad R = 0.907$$
$$(11.57) \qquad df = 29,\ s = 0.207 \qquad (3.21)$$

---

[45]Calculated using data from China National Bureau of Statistics (2006). China Statistical Yearbook, China Statistical Press, Tables 10.7, 10.26.

We use per capita data of Chinese urban areas from seven different income levels — Lowest income (first deciles), low income (second deciles), lower middle (second quintile), middle (third quintile), upper middle (fourth quintile), high income (ninth deciles), and highest income (tenth deciles) in 1998, 1999, 2000, 2001, 2002, 2003, 2004, and 2005,[46] total 56 sets of data (degree of freedom $df = 54$). The classification of consumption categories (1–8) is the same as in rural areas. We estimate regressions of natural log per capita expenditures y_i for above eight categories on natural log per capita total expenditures x: From 1998–2005, the regressions of the Chinese rural area data of seven different income levels with per capita expenditures were all statistically significant. The coefficient of determination of y_1 to y_8 are 0.740–0.952, and the slope is from 0.746 to 1.382. The slope of the food (y_1) variable is the lowest, and the slope of the Transport and Communication (y_8) variable is the highest.

Chow and Houthakker studied total-expenditure elasticity for food, clothing, housing, and all other items, namely miscellaneous, which include the last five categories in our study. The total-expenditure elasticity for all above categories is listed in Table 3.22, which shows the total-expenditure elasticity in Chinese rural areas in 2000, 2002, and 2004 coincided. The total-expenditure elasticity for food and clothing in Chinese rural areas in 2002 are estimated at 0.747 and 0.779, respectively. All these calculating results are very close to 0.742 and 0.779 calculated by Chow, using Chinese rural area data in 1998. The estimated total-expenditure elasticities for food, clothing, and residence in Chinese rural area in 1998 coincide with the value calculated by Chow (see Table 3.22). The total-expenditure elasticities for food and clothing in Chinese urban areas during 1998–2005 are estimated as 0.70 and 1.15, respectively, close to 0.60 and 1.2 proposed by Houthakker, using the survey mainly for urban families. The estimate of 0.70–0.779 for total-expenditure elasticity of demand for food confirms Engel's law, which states that the share of expenditure spent on food declines as total expenditure rises (other things equal). The estimated housing elasticity in China's urban areas is 1.35,

---

[46]Calculated using data from China National Bureau of Statistics: China Statistical Yearbook, China Statistical Press, 2006, Tables 10.6, 10.7; 2005, Tables 10.6, 10.7; 2004, Tables 10.6, 10.7; 2003, Tables 10.6, 10.7; 2002, Tables 10.6, 10.7; 2001, Tables 10.6, 10.7; 2000, Tables 10.7, 10.8; 1999, Tables 10.7, 10.8.

higher than the 0.8 proposed by Houthakker, possibly because the housing benefit distribution system was abolished and replaced by housing market prices.

10. Real Estate

Since 1978, the household responsibility system has enabled Chinese farmers to increase their income. Farmers used their own income to build new houses on the land assigned to them or renovated their existing housing. In the first stage of economic reform (1978–1985), farmer income increased dramatically at an average annual growth rate of 14.7%. Living conditions in rural areas in 1978 were crowded — per capita net floor space of rural residents was only 8.1 M^2, as per Table 3.23. Therefore, construction of new housing in rural areas increased in response to demand. The expenditure elasticity of housing in Chinese rural areas was 1.78 in 1981; it then declined gradually to 1.30 in 2005. This is due to the decline of the average annual growth rate of farmer income to 4.45% during 1985–2005. On the other hand, per capita gross floor space increased to 14.7 M^2 in 1985 and 17.2 M^2 in 1989 (see Table 3.22), so the demand for housing declined. Both resulted in total-expenditure elasticity of housing in Chinese rural area gradually to decline from 1981–2005. Living conditions in rural areas in 2005 were relatively comfortable, and the per capita net area of rural residents reached 29.7 M^2. As shown in Table 3.22. In 2012, China's rural housing expenditure elasticity further dropped to 1.0557. When the Engel coefficient declined with increased per capita expenditure, the proportion of residential consumption in urban areas increased significantly. Because the welfare housing system had been abolished during the 1990s, residential houses became a market commodity. Table 3.23 shows the per capita floor space of Chinese residents in urban (gross) and rural (net) areas after economic reform. The per capita gross floor space of Chinese urban residents increased from 6.7 M^2 in 1978 to 27.8 M^2 in 2005, an average annual growth rate of 5.41%. China's per capita living area in urban areas by the end of 2004 was lower than that of High-Income Countries (HIC) in the early 1990s, but higher than the Middle-Income Country (MIC) level in the early 1990s, as shown in Figure 3.29. The selling of residential houses in urban areas increased dramatically from 27.45 million M^2 at 1991 to 68.98 million M^2 at 1996, further increased to 495.88 million M^2 in

Table 3.23.   Per capita net floor space of Chinese residents.

Year	Per capita gross living space in urban (sq.m)	Per capita net floor space of rural residents (sq.m)	Urban, average annual growth rate	Rural, annual growth rate
1978	6.7	8.1		
1985	10	14.7	5.9%	8.9%
1989	13.5	17.2	7.8%	4.0%
1997	17.8	22.5	3.5%	3.4%
2001	20.8	25.7	4.0%	3.4%
2002	24.5	26.5	17.8%	3.1%
2003	25.3	27.2	1.6%	1.3%
2004	26.4	27.9	4.3%	2.6%
2005	27.8	29.7	5.3%	6.5%
2008	30.6	32.4	3.3%	2.9%
2011	32.65	36.2	3.3%	2.9%
2012	32.91	37.1	0.8%	2.3%
2016	36.6	45.8	2.7%	5.4%

Note: China National Bureau of Statistics has not announced the per capita net floorspace of Chinese residents after 2012.

Source: Calculated using data from All China Data online: China Yearly Macro-Economic Statistics (National)_Residential Buildings And Amount Of Savings Deposit In Urban And Rural Areas 1952–2012; China's Per Capita Residential Space Rose to 40.8M^2 in 2016, By CBN Editor, July 7, 2017.

2005.[47] The average annual growth rate of floor space of residential buildings sold amounted to 23.0% during 1991–2005,[48] and fell to 8.76% from 2005–2015. The per capita gross floor space of Chinese urban residents in 2005 reached 26.1 M^2. The selling price of residential houses had increased, as shown in Figure 3.30, which shows that the areas of residential building that can be purchased by the average yearly income after 1991 also increased, because after reform of housing distribution system the housing expenditure was included in the wages. The residential area that can be

[47]Data from China National Bureau of Statistics: China Statistical Yearbook, China Statistical Press, 2006, Table 6.37; 1996, Table 5.35.
[48]*Ibid*; 2005, Table 6.36.

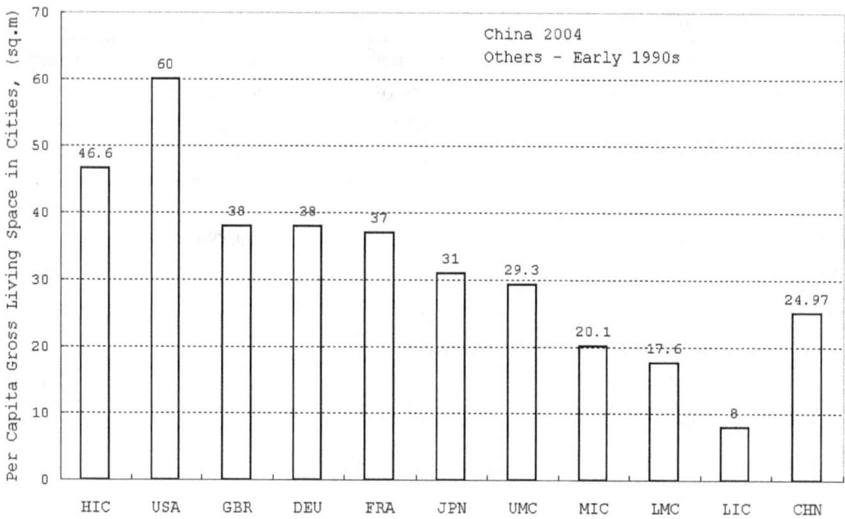

Figure 3.29.   The international comparison of per capita living space in urban areas.

Source: Calculated using data from World Development Indicators (2007). Housing conditions, national and urban, Table 3.11.

purchased by the average yearly income reached 6.39 M^2 in 2003, declined to 5.80 M^2 in 2005 due to dramatically increased selling price of residential houses. Therefore, purchasing 90 M^2 apartment in city required 15.5 years average wage! In addition, in large cities, the average selling price of a residential house will be much higher than that value provided by China Statistical Yearbook. Real Estate loans reached 55% of total bank loans; and the proportion of the individual house mortgage loan was 63% of the house selling price in 2004. The Non-Performing Loans (NPLs) of the four state-owned commercial banks reached 10–11% and 1.5% for real estate sector loans and individual mortgage loans, respectively, in 2004.[49] The key statistics of China real estate market in 2004 are shown in Table 3.24. Beijing: Overall vacancy continued to grow slightly by one percentage point reaching 17.45% as the market continues to absorb the new supply. Supply will most likely exceed demand for luxury residential units;

---

[49]The People's Bank of China (2005). 2004 China's real estate financial reports (in Chinese), August 5.

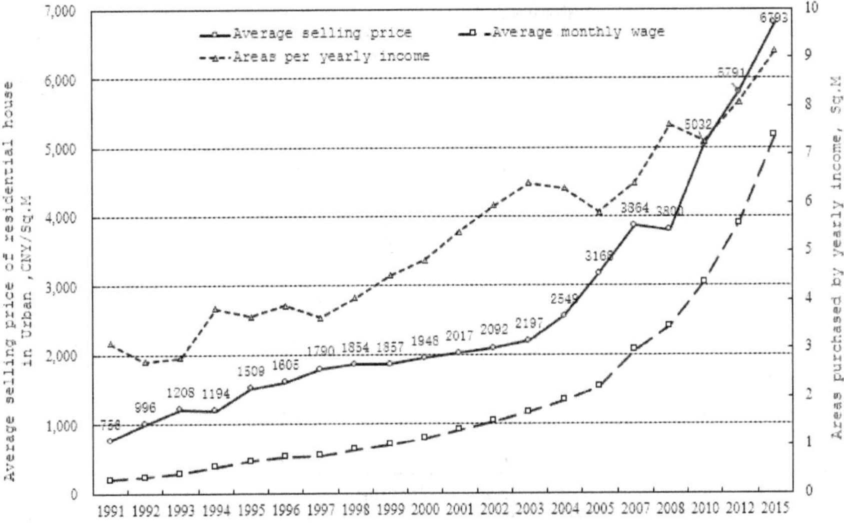

Figure 3.30.   The average selling price of residential buildings, China.

Source: Calculated from China National Bureau of Statistics (2016). China Statistics Press, Tables 4.11 and 19.12.

average rentals will see some downward adjustment over the short-term. Shanghai: The demand for Shanghai's Grade A office premises has outrun supply, pushing up rentals significantly. Vacancy has increased 9.0% Quarter to Quarter, rentals reach USD0.92 per m^2 per day. Growth rates in Jingan and Lujiazui (Pudong New District) are especially higher than the city average, demonstrating the competitiveness of these districts. The sales volume of luxury residential units dropped sharply in 3Q 2005, influenced by the Government's control policies. Average selling prices of luxury residential units dropped slightly to USD3,132 per m^2 (USD291 per ft^2) by 4.5%. Guangzhou: Net take-up of Grade A office has been strong and average rentals have continued to increase. Grade A monthly rentals increased by 2.1% Quarter to Quarter to USD14.3 per sqm per month. Average monthly rentals increased slightly to USD3,132 per m^2 (USD291 per ft^2) by 4.5%. Guangzhou: Net take-up of Grade A office has been strong and average rentals have continued to increase. Grade A monthly rentals increased by 2.1% Quarter to Quarter to USD14.3 per sqm per month. Average monthly rentals for luxury residential properties are

Table 3.24.   Key statistics of China real estate market, 2004 and 2015.

2004	China	Beijing	SH	GZ	SZ
Annual GDP growth rate (%)	10.1	13.2	13.6	15.0	17.3
GDP per capita, USD	1,486	4,450	6,655	6,740	7,308
Investment Completed in real estate (bil. USD)	3.2	1.1	4.0	0.8	0.5
Average selling price of residential buildings (USD/sq ft)	28.6	53.3	64.7	48.9	71.7
Average selling price growth rate (%)	16.0	6.5	15.5	8.0	9.0
Rental yields for residential*	n/a	7.8	9.1	8.0	7.5
Rental yields for office*	n/a	7.5	8.4	8.0	7.5
2015	**China**	**Beijing**	**SH**	**GZ**	**SZ**
Annual GDP growth rate (%)	6.4	6.9	6.9	6	8.8
GDP per capita, USD	8,070	17,102	16,668	21,870	24,007
Investment completed in real estate (bil. USD)	10.4	0.7	0.6	0.3	0.2
Average selling price of residential buildings (USD/sq. ft)	96.6	337.7	320.8	210.1	502.2
Average selling price growth rate (%)	9.1	20.5	31.0	−4.5	40.0
Rental yields for office	3.2	3–10	3–5	N/A	4–7
Rental yields for retail	3.2	3–7	5–7	N/A	3–5

Note: *estimate.

Source: Calculated using data from China National Bureau of Statistics: China Statistical Yearbook, China Statistical Press, 2016, Tables 19.1, 19.12; 2006, Tables 3.1, 3.3, 3.9, 6.38, 6.39, 11.2; 2004, Table 6.48; China National Bureau of Statistics, Data base; Annual, China National Bureau of Statistics, Data base; Annual by province, Per capita gross regional product 1998–2017; Colliers International Quarterly Research Report: Greater China — Office & residential Market Overview, October 2005; BMI-China Real Estate Report 2017.

forecast to increase 3–5% per year. Vacancy rates of prime residential tapered off to 12.5% in 3Q 2005 from 15.2% at the end of 2004, while average monthly rentals increased slightly by 1.1% Quarter to Quarter to

USD20.0 per m². Shenzhen: New supply of Grade A office space in Futian District hit a record high in the last decade. The demand is primarily attributed to the finance sector, logistics industry, and service firms. Average monthly rentals increased by 5.8% to USD12.9 per m². Shekou and Futian's CBD continues to be a popular area attracting foreign tenants. Monthly rentals of luxury residential increased by 2.3% Quarter to Quarter to USD13.3 per m². Comparing China real estate market in 2004 and 2015, the 2015 annual GDP growth rate was significantly lower than 2004. This shows the economy has maintained a medium-to-high speed growth, making improvements in the quality of development, namely a changing pace of growth, structural optimization, and transforming growth drivers. Second, per capita GDP has risen, but the average selling price of residential buildings in Beijing, Shanghai, Guangzhou, and Shenzhen has risen significantly. For example, per capita GDP rose by 328% in Shenzhen, while the average selling price of residential buildings rose by 701%. This has led the white-collar workers to leave these megacities.

The actual completed investment of enterprises for real estate development by region in 2005 is shown in Figure 3.31. In 2005, national investment in real estate development reached CNY1.576 trillion (USD195.3 billion), an increase of 20.9% year-on-year, dropping 8.6% from 2004. It is lower by 4.8% points than the annual growth rate of investment in fixed assets, and in 2004 the annual growth rate of real estate development was higher by 3.0% than the annual growth rate of investment in fixed assets. From the growth rate of real estate investment view, the macro-control policy in 2005 inhibited the real estate industry significantly.

Figure 3.31 shows that the actual completed investment for real estate development in Guangdong province reached CNY159.2 billion (USD19.73 billion) in 2005, while it was only CNY600 million (USD74.3 million) in Tibet. The top seven regions are located in the Eastern area. In 2015, the actual completed investment for real estate development in Guangdong province and Tibet have risen to CNY815.4 billion (USD137.11 billion) and CNY5.0 billion (USD0.8 billion), respectively. The top four regions are in the Eastern area, accounting for 30.9% of the actual completed investment. The annual growth rate in Liaoning and Heilongjiang have fallen to −32.9% and −25.1%, respectively. The large disparity in the actual completed investment in real estate development by regions is mainly caused by the level of each region's economic development. Using regression analysis to find the relationship between the actual

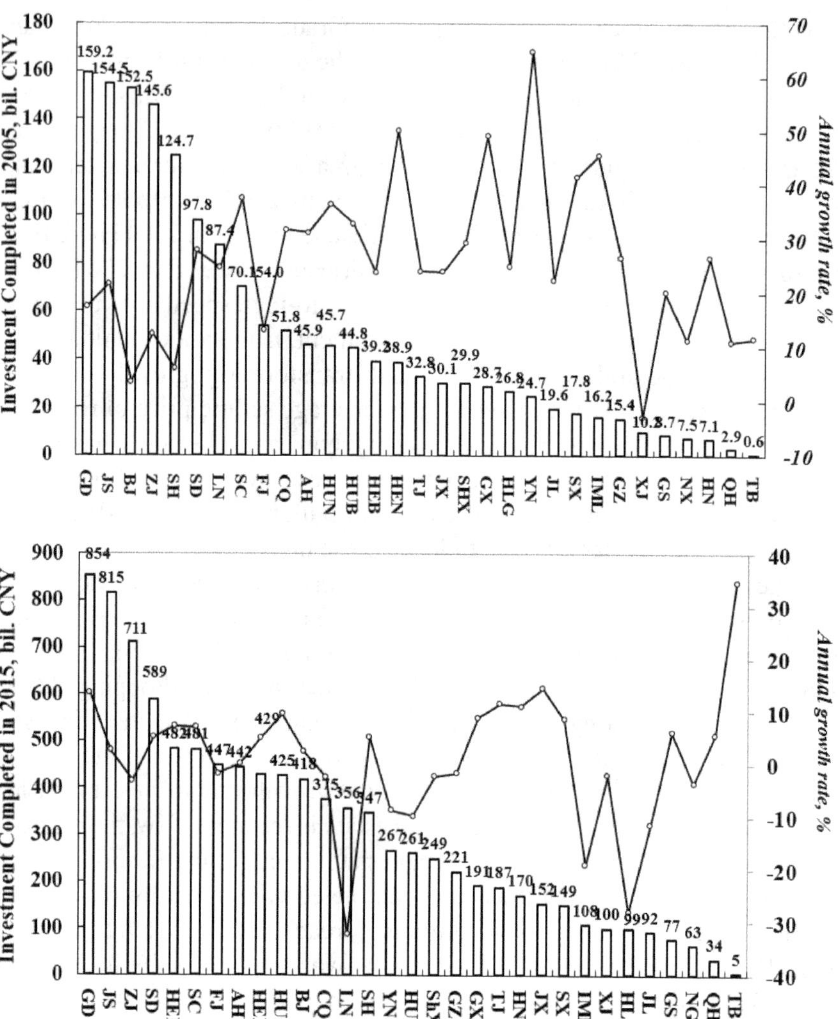

Figure 3.31 Actual completed investment of real estate development and its annual growth rate % by region, 2005 and 2015.

Source: Calculated using data from China National Bureau of Statistics: China Statistical Yearbook, China Statistical Press, 2006, Tables 6.1, 6.31; 2005, Tables 6.1, 6.32; China National Bureau of Statistics, Data base; Annual by Province: Total Investment in Residential Buildings in the Whole _ Country, Region, 2003–2017.

completed investments of real estate development with GDP per capita in 2004, we derive the following:

$$REINVpc = -1173.04 + 0.1657 \times GDPpc$$
$$(-3.91) \qquad (10.76)$$
$$R = 0.8942, \, F = 115.7, \, df = 29, \, s = 923.8 \qquad (3.22)$$

In 2015:

$$REINTpc = 1398.3 + 0.0659 \times GDPpc$$
$$(3.729)$$
$$R = 0.5693; \, df = 29, \, F = 13.9, \, s = 2257 \qquad (3.23)$$

where REINVpc — per capita actual completed investments of real estate development, CNY/person.

GDPpc — per capita GDP, CNY/person.

Equations (3.22) and (3.23) are statistically significant. There is a linear relationship between per capita actual completed investments in real estate development and per capita GDP. In 2005, the (ratio of) per capita GDP of Eastern (=1), Middle, and Western regions amounted to 1:0.47:0.38; while the per capita actual completed investments of real estate development calculated by Eq. (3.22) was 1:0.29:0.36. In 2015, the per capita GDP of Eastern, Middle, and Western region was 1:0.38:0.55; while the per capita actual completed investments of real estate development calculated by Eq. (3.23) was 1:0.46:0.64. The difference between the estimated per capita actual completed investments of real estate development value and the actual value is much larger in 2015 than in 2005. Because the coefficient of determination R is 0.5693 in 2015, lower than 0.8942 in 2005, and the standard error for the estimate $s = 2257$ in 2015, larger than $s = 924$ in 2005. The actual completed investment of real estate development and its annual growth rate in

Eastern, Middle, and Western regions are illustrated in Table 3.25. In 2005, East's share dropped 3.76 % points from that of 2004, and the Central and Western regions increased 1.54% and 2.22%, respectively. So, the regional investment for real estate development improved in 2005. In 2015, East's share dropped 10.71 % points from 2005, and the Central and Western regions increased 4.90 and 5.81 % points, respectively. Therefore, regional investment for real estate development was further improved in 2015. In terms of the type of real estate investment structure, residential

Table 3.25. Actual completed investment of real estate development in three regions.

	Investment completed, bil. CNY			Annual growth rate, %		
	Total	Residential buildings	Economic affordable housing	Total	Residential buildings	Economic affordable housing
2005 East	1042.9	716.1	31.8	14.0	13.9	−3
2005 Middle	268.2	187.0	12.1	32.5	40.7	−17.7
2005 West	264.8	173.8	12.6	38.8	60	11.9
2015 East	5323.1	3565.3	n/a	29.5	25.8581	n/a
2015 Middle	2103.8	1474.3	n/a	−28.9	−27.041	n/a
2015 West	2170.9	1419.9	n/a	−10.7	−10.227	n/a

Source: Calculated using data from China National Bureau of Statistics: China Statistical Yearbook, China Statistical Press, 2016, Tables 19.6, 19.10; 2006, Table 6.32; 2005, Table 6.32.

buildings in 2005 reached CNY1.077 trillion (USD133.5 billion) and increased to CNY9.598 trillion (USD1.567 billion) in 2015, with an average annual rate of 43.1%. Figure 3.27 shows that the share of investment in residential buildings of the total real estate investment increased from 48.4% in 1997 to 68.3% in 2005. The investment of economically affordable housing continued to decline by 2.3% year-on-year in 2005. The share of investment of economically affordable housing to residential building declined from 20.8% in 1999 to 6.46% in 2005 and further fell to 2.94% in 2010.[50] After 2011, China Statistical Yearbook did not publish the economically affordable housing value. The decline in share of investment of economically affordable housing investment is, on the one hand, weakening the suppression of rising housing prices and worsening the housing settlement of low-income families. But on the other hand, it is conducive to ending of government subsidy of the housing market in advance (economically affordable housing). Figure 3.31 shows that the residential building is the main impetus behind growth of China's real estate market due to the huge demand. China now has a bigger urban population than North America and India and is marginally behind Europe. China now has

---

[50]Calculated using data from China National Bureau of Statistics: China Statistical Yearbook, China Statistical Press, 2011, Table 5.37; 2012, Table 5.37.

113 cities with a population of more than one million people, and three mega cities with more than 10 million people (Beijing, Shanghai, and Chongqing). Although the national GDP per capita is only slightly above USD1,700, there are 35 cities (including the four Tier-1 cities of Beijing, Shanghai, Shenzhen, and Guangzhou) with over 900,000 people and a GDP per capita over USD4,000 (see Table 3.26). In 2005, the population of these 35 cities accounted for only 8.7% of the country's total population, but 35% of the country's GDP. The real estate development in 35 large and medium-sized cities represented an actual investment of CNY961.46 billion (USD142.3 billion); in 2017, it increased to CNY54,865.7 billion (USD8,122.5), an average annual growth rate of 40.1%. It accounted for 61% and 40.1% of the actual completed investment of real estate development in 2005 and 2017, respectively. In 2017, per capita GDP of the high-income group was 511,539.9 constant 2010 USD; China's per capita GDP was CNY59,660 (USD8,832.4), almost the

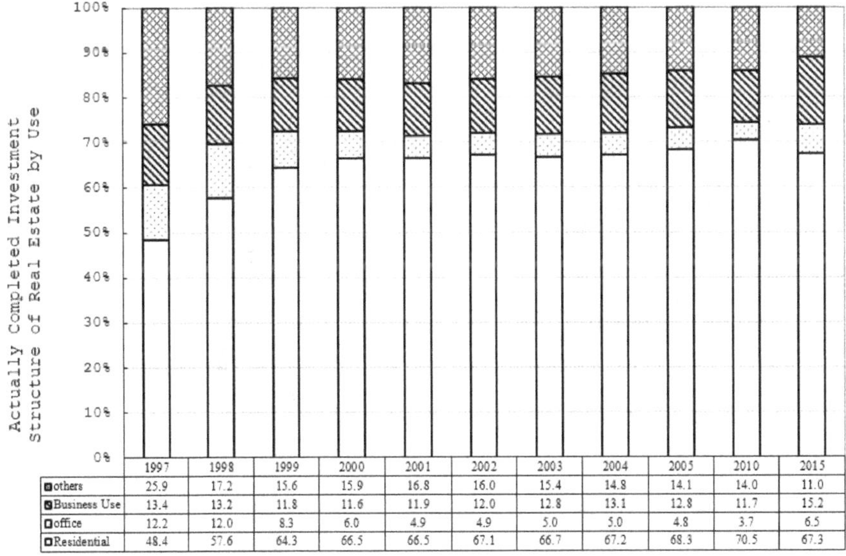

	1997	1998	1999	2000	2001	2002	2003	2004	2005	2010	2015
others	25.9	17.2	15.6	15.9	16.8	16.0	15.4	14.8	14.1	14.0	11.0
Business Use	13.4	13.2	11.8	11.6	11.9	12.0	12.8	13.1	12.8	11.7	15.2
office	12.2	12.0	8.3	6.0	4.9	4.9	5.0	5.0	4.8	3.7	6.5
Residential	48.4	57.6	64.3	66.5	66.5	67.1	66.7	67.2	68.3	70.5	67.3

Figure 3.32.   Actual completed investment structure of real estate by use.

Source: Calculated using data from China National Bureau of Statistics: China Statistical Yearbook, China Statistical Press, 2016, Table 19.10; 2006, Table 6.32.

Table 3.26.   Actual completed investment of real estate development in 35 large and medium-sized cities, 2005, 2017.

City	Investment	Residential	Office	Houses for	Investment	Residential	Office	Houses for	Population	GDP	Per capita
				Business				Business			
	Completed	Buildings	Buildings	use	Completed	Buildings	Buildings	use	Person		GDP
	2005				2017				2017	2017	2017
	100 Mil. ¥				100 Mil. ¥				10000	100 Mil. ¥	10000 ¥
Total	961.46	641.35	62.82	108.47	54865.07	34723.16	5216.98	7361.28	29741.16	333690	11.22
Beijing	152.50	77.95	19.62	11.29	3692.54	1694.67	742.93	357.65	1961.24	28000	14.28
Tianjin	32.75	23.49	1.19	4.17	2233.39	1559.70	92.58	189.39	1293.82	18595	14.37
Shijiazhuang	12.21	8.09	0.47	1.83	1212.27	867.67	110.70	138.08	1016.38	6558	6.45
Taiyuan	7.94	4.18	0.84	1.51	470.63	329.21	24.22	40.72	420.16	3200	7.62
Hohhot	3.59	2.32	0.30	0.88	238.40	179.85	6.41	36.17	286.66	3179	11.09
Shenyang	41.36	30.93	1.51	6.45	814.24	620.45	27.18	104.13	810.62	5870	7.24
Dalian	26.53	16.36	0.85	5.00	566.64	404.45	28.44	80.68	669.04	7363	11.01
Changchun	10.79	8.54	0.46	1.24	573.78	376.60	40.88	93.61	767.71	6613	8.61
Harbin	14.02	7.68	0.66	2.56	498.59	315.08	21.41	101.48	1063.60	6609	6.21
Shanghai	124.69	92.08	10.22	10.26	3,856.53	2152.40	642.20	506.71	2301.91	30133	13.09
Nanjing	29.61	20.90	1.72	2.63	2170.21	1569.52	150.15	263.08	800.47	11715	14.64
Hangzhou	41.06	31.92	2.63	3.38	2734.20	1713.13	245.57	328.63	870.04	12556	14.43
Ningbo	25.95	18.17	1.47	3.32	1374.47	932.47	64.23	129.85	760.57	9850	12.95
Hefei	19.13	14.29	0.84	2.57	1557.41	1095.45	113.58	219.74	570.20	7191	12.61

Fuzhou	22.20	15.88	0.49	1.72	1694.18	1176.99	113.17	198.64	711.54	7128	10.02
Xiamen	11.41	8.33	0.33	1.04	879.86	550.36	83.25	68.78	353.13	4300	12.18
Nanchang	11.02	8.17	0.26	1.56	790.69	486.38	66.03	167.97	504.26	5000	9.92
Jinan	12.11	9.67	0.40	1.02	1232.63	822.84	105.81	190.79	681.40	7285	10.69
Qingdao	22.38	16.23	1.39	1.81	1330.54	925.51	112.49	185.78	871.51	11258	12.92
Zhengzhou	16.81	12.55	0.87	2.62	3358.84	2418.66	140.03	312.71	862.65	9003	10.44
Wuhan	29.80	21.69	1.16	2.12	2686.34	1840.31	254.52	288.90	978.54	13400	13.69
Changsha	25.56	18.61	0.77	2.58	1493.44	809.32	129.95	301.25	704.41	10200	14.48
Guangzhou	50.81	34.85	5.05	5.81	2702.89	1769.49	330.23	298.50	1270.08	21500	16.93
Shenzhen	42.37	26.55	2.80	5.31	2130.86	1009.65	535.82	339.67	1035.79	22286	21.52
Nanning	10.55	7.31	0.39	1.33	958.09	679.13	65.95	77.49	666.16	4180	6.27
Haikou	4.64	3.57	0.04	0.66	603.25	412.59	25.96	81.45	204.62	1391	6.80
Chongqing	51.77	30.04	1.71	7.14	3980.08	2632.88	157.28	671.80	2884.62	19530	6.77
Chengdu	45.10	29.45	1.49	7.66	2492.65	1300.46	215.73	573.23	1404.76	13890	9.89
Guiyang	9.11	4.54	0.65	1.06	1024.09	595.06	79.85	200.46	432.46	3518	8.13
Kunming	14.94	11.37	0.22	1.12	1683.33	1058.90	121.95	222.73	643.20	4856	7.55
Xi'an	21.23	14.59	1.10	3.40	2234.84	1505.03	218.12	288.74	846.78	7472	8.82
Lanzhou	5.31	3.38	0.28	0.67	418.26	264.71	42.62	64.98	361.62	2524	6.98
Xining	2.71	1.49	0.19	0.43	351.33	171.17	32.92	87.80	220.87	1285	5.82
Yinchuan	5.66	3.46	0.22	1.61	402.82	240.25	27.15	74.95	199.31	3454	17.33
Urumqi	3.84	2.69	0.24	0.72	422.74	242.82	47.68	74.72	311.03	2799	9.00

Source: RREEF (Real Estate and Infrastructure investing for an ever-changing world) (2007). The Maturing of the Chinese Real Estate Market, March; China National Bureau of Statistics: China Statistical Yearbook 2018, Tables 19.10.19.17; 2011 Table 5.37; 2006, China Statistical Press; China National Bureau of Statistics: The Yearbook of China's Cities 2006, China Statistical Press.

same as the WDI Upper middle-income group (8220.5 constant 2010 USD). The dramatic transformations in China's urban structure are driving the strong demand for all forms of real estate, especially in the major cities.

In 2005, total funds for real estate development reached CNY2.12 trillion (USD262.7 billion), an increase of 23.4% year-on-year. Figure 3.33 shows the structural changes in the sources of funds for real estate development. The results show that self-raised funds increased from CNY97.3 billion (USD11.8 billion) in 1997 to CNY700 billion (USD86.7 billion) in 2005, and further increased to CNY4,093.8 billion (USD787.5 billion) in 2015. Self-financing, then, has become an important source of real estate funding. Domestic credit funds increased from CNY91.1 billion (USD11.7 billion) in 1997 to CNY391.8 billion (USD47.3 billion) in 2005, and further increased to CNY2,021.4 billion (USD324.6 billion) in 2015. However, this proportion dropped from 24.0% in 1997 to 18.3% in 2005 and further dropped to 16.1% in 2015. The other sources of USD126.6 billion in 2005, and further increased to CNY5,596 billion (USD898.6 billion) in 2015. It has become a major source of funding. But about 77% of other

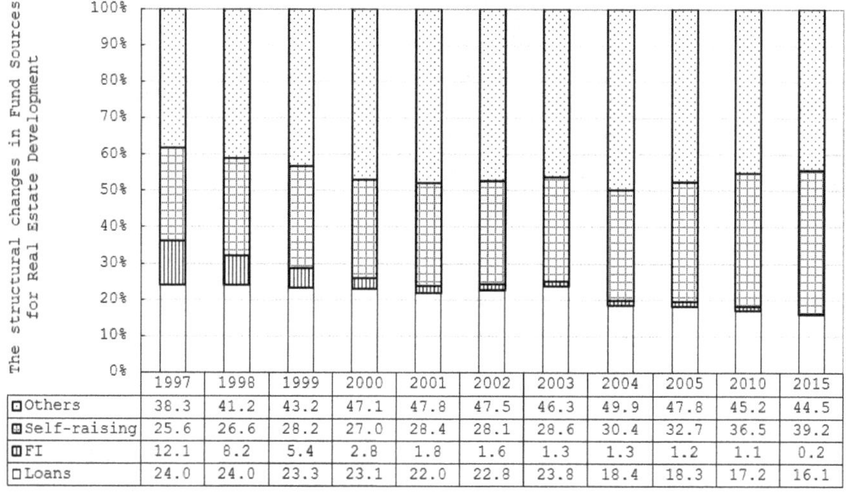

	1997	1998	1999	2000	2001	2002	2003	2004	2005	2010	2015
Others	38.3	41.2	43.2	47.1	47.8	47.5	46.3	49.9	47.8	45.2	44.5
Self-raising	25.6	26.6	28.2	27.0	28.4	28.1	28.6	30.4	32.7	36.5	39.2
FI	12.1	8.2	5.4	2.8	1.8	1.6	1.3	1.3	1.2	1.1	0.2
Loans	24.0	24.0	23.3	23.1	22.0	22.8	23.8	18.4	18.3	17.2	16.1

Figure 3.33. The structural changes in Fund Sources for Real Estate Development (1997–2015).

Source: Calculated using data from China National Bureau of Statistics. China Statistical Yearbook, China Statistical Press, 2006, Table 6.33, 2016, Table 19.7.

funds came from customers' down payment funds, which increased from 145.5 billion yuan (USD17.6 billion) in 1997 to 102.2 billion yuan, due to customer's down payment, that is, individual mortgages from the banks. Therefore, bank credit is still the main sources of the real estate development funding. For example, in 2005, it accounted for 55.1% of the total funding. Banks still bear large financial risks from real estate development loans, as they have not been able to diversify away real estate loan risk. Foreign investment in real estate declined from CNY46.1 billion (USD5.6 billion) in 1997 to CNY25.8 billion (USD3.2 billion) in 2005, so its proportion declined from 12.1% in 1997 to 1.2% in 2005.

It rose to CNY296.5 (USD44.7 billion) in 2015, but its proportion further dropped to 0.2% in 2015. The real estate industry was overheated, so in April 2004, the government introduced measures aimed at curbing its rampant growth. Measures varied from city to city, and included a capital gains tax, depending on the length of a buyer's holding period, and the tightening of land transactions and pre-completion sales. Mortgage lenders were required to demand a down payment of at least 30% after May 2006. From June 1, 2006, homes smaller than 90 square meters must account for at least 70% of the total floor space in any new residential housing projects.[51] In September 2007, the central government raised the minimum down payment ratio from 30% to 40%, raised the interest rate on second mortgages to 10% higher than the benchmark rate, and capped the monthly mortgage payment-to-income ratio at 50%. In April 2008, it imposed tax on capital gains from housing sales. Starting in April 2010, 39 of the 70 major cities in China introduced housing purchase restriction policies. Under these policies, only those with local Hukou (household registration), or those who could show proof of employment in the city for certain consecutive years, were eligible to purchase one or two new homes. All these measures aimed at reducing speculation, combating soaring prices, and developing proper housing structures in the real estate market. House rents in urban areas surged dramatically after housing system reform. At the beginning of economic reform, urban housing in China was mainly provided by the working units for their staffs and workers. The monthly rent was only CNY3–4, while the average monthly wage of a worker was about CNY54. In 2005, the house rent for an apartment with area around 60 M^2 was CNY1600 in Shanghai, while the average monthly

---

[51] Xinhua (2006). Govt. moves again to curb soaring house prices, May 30.

wage there was about CNY2,661.[52] These numbers may explain why the total-expenditure elasticity for housing in Chinese urban areas is high. Since 1978, the household responsibility system enabled Chinese farmers to increase their income. The farmers used their own income to build new houses on the land assigned to them. At the first stage of economic reform (1978–1989), farmer income increased dramatically at an average annual growth rate of 10.69%[53] and living conditions in rural areas in 1978 were crowded; per capita net floor space of rural residents was only 8.1 M^2, as shown in Table 3.24. Therefore, construction of new housing in rural areas increased according to demand, and the average annual growth rate of per capita net floor space of rural residents reached 7.1% during 1978–1989; it then declined to 4.9% during 1989–2005. This was due to the decline of the average annual growth rate of farmer's income from 10.7% during 1978–1989 to 4.36%[54] during 1989–2005. On the other hand, per capita gross floor space increased to 17.2 M^2 in 1989 (see Table 3.24), so the demand for housing declined. Both resulted in the gradual decline of the total-expenditure elasticity for housing in Chinese rural areas from 1981–2005 (see Table 3.23).

In the past 70 years, China has basically solved the housing problem of urban and rural residents, built the world's largest housing security system, and significantly improved the housing conditions of the people. The per capita housing construction area of urban areas increased from 8.3 square meters in 1949 to 39 square meters in 2018, and the per capita housing construction area in rural areas increased to 47.3 square meters. The country built more than 80 million sets of various types of affordable housing and sheds to resettle housing, helping more than 200 million people solve their housing difficulties. In the 1970s, most urban dwellings were bungalows and basements to cope with cold winters and hot summers, without independent toilets, kitchens, water supply, and drainage, etc; conditions were simple and the living environment was crowded. Today, there are a variety of new residential buildings, meeting the

---

[52] Shanghai Municipal Statistics Bureau (2006). Shanghai Statistical Yearbook, China Statistics Press, 2006, Table 10.8.

[53] Calculated using data from China National Bureau of Statistics (1996). China Statistical Yearbook, China Statistical Press, 1996, Table 9.4.

[54] Calculated using data from China National Bureau of Statistics (2006). China Statistical Yearbook, China Statistical Press, 2006, Tables 10.2, 3.3, 4.1.

increasing diversified living needs of the people and greatly improving living conditions.[55]

11. Urbanization

The level of urbanization denotes the percentage share of total population in urban settlements. From Tables 3.2 and 3.6, we can see that the percentage share of employment and value added in tertiary industry in China is less than that value in other countries with the same level of economic development. China's low level of urbanization is associated with the country's undeveloped tertiary industry. Industrialization benefits from economies of scale, which are easier to realize in cities. Therefore, to modernize their economy, developing countries need to accelerate their urbanization. Table 3.27 shows the world average level of urbanization and corresponding per capita GDP measured in PPP international current USD in 2005. With similar per capita GDP measured in PPP international current USD, China's urbanization percentage is lower than Indonesia's, Philippines', Ukraine's, and the middle-income group. In 2010, China's urbanization percentage is like that of Indonesia and the middle-income group; and, in 2017, China's urbanization percentage is like that of the World and upper middle-income group. Figures 3.34 and 3.35 show the increment of urban and rural population in China before and after economic reform, respectively. Before economic reform, the increase in urban population and decrease in rural population occurred in 1959 and 1960 due to the Great Leap Forward. The result was an economic disaster. The laid-off workers and staffs of all enterprises in cities had to move to rural areas. In the following three years (1961–1963), the change in urban and rural populations became negative and positive, respectively. Urbanization level in China declined from 18.37% in 1959 to only 16.84% in 1963, before recovering to 18.37% in 1964. During the Cultural Revolution (1966–1976), young secondary school graduates in cities were sent down to rural areas to be reeducated, therefore the change in urban population was small, while change in rural population was substantial. So, the urbanization level declined from 17.86% in 1966 to 17.43% 1976.

---

[55]Liu, H., Y. Shi, Y. Wang, and B. Wang. Meeting the people's new expectations, safeguarding and improving people's livelihood in development — the heads of the five departments review the achievements of the development of the people's livelihood in the past 70 years, Xinhua News Agency.

Table 3.27.   Urbanization and per capita GDP, international current USD.

Country or group	2005		2010		2017	
	PPP pc	Urbanization	PPP pc	Urbanization	PPP pc	Urbanization
China	5,878	40	9,498	49	16,782	58
Brazil	7,808	84	14,320	84	15,662	86
India	3,118	29	4,451	31	7,169	34
Germany	37,704	76	40,429	77	52,574	77
Russian Federation	9,747	73	23,326	74	25,767	74
Indonesia	3,437	48	8,458	50	11,189	55
Philippines	4,401	63	5,468	45	8,340	47
Ukraine	6,086	68	7,664	69	8,694	69
United States	37,437	81	49,479	81	59,928	82
Japan	27,568	66	35,750	91	41,959	92
Korea, Rep.	19,560	81	30,352	82	38,824	82
World	11,754	49	13,221	52	17,137	55
Heavily indebted poor (HIPC)	1,228	30	1,864	32	2,423	36
Low income	1,336	28	1,723	30	2,159	32
Lower middle income	3,967	34	4,929	37	7,151	40
Middle income	5,653	45	8,288	48	12,207	52
Upper middle income	10,066	72	12,005	59	17,908	65
High income	29,041	78	39,090	80	43,054	82

Source: Calculated using data from World Bank: World Development Indicators online 2019, Released October 16, 2019 by World Bank 2006, Released April 2006 by World Bank.

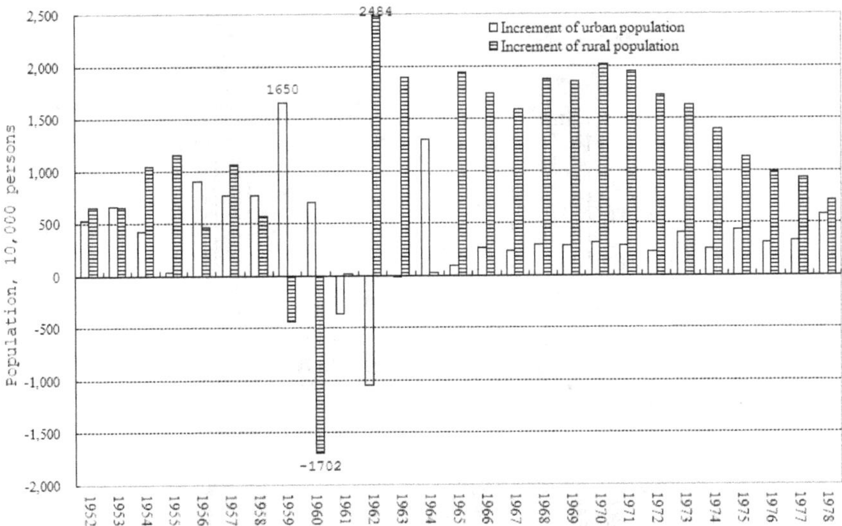

Figure 3.34.   Increment of urban and rural population, China (1952–1978).

Source: Calculated using data from China National Bureau of Statistics: China Statistical Yearbook, China Statistical Press, 2006, Table 4.1; 1993, Table 4.1.

In the past 70 years, China has created a miracle in the history of world urban development, as its urbanization process has reached unprecedented heights. The number of cities increased from 132 in 1949 to 672 in 2018, and the urbanization rate increased from 10.6% to 59.6% and 60.6% in 2019. We can identify the following post-reform urbanization stages:

Recovery and development stage (1978–1983). In the early stage of reform and opening up (1978–1983), and with the implementation of the household contract responsibility system, agricultural labor productivity increased substantially, creating a vast amount of rural surplus labor. Urban and rural farmers' markets were restored, and township enterprises sprang up, and large number of farmers moved to where the markets were or started working in factories. The educated youth moved from the farm to the city. The implementation of the opening-up gradient strategy and the gradual rise of the special economic zones in selected cities promoted an active urban economy. At the end of 1983, the urbanization rate reached 21.62%, an increase of 3.7 % points from the end of 1978, and at an average annual increase of 0.74 % points.

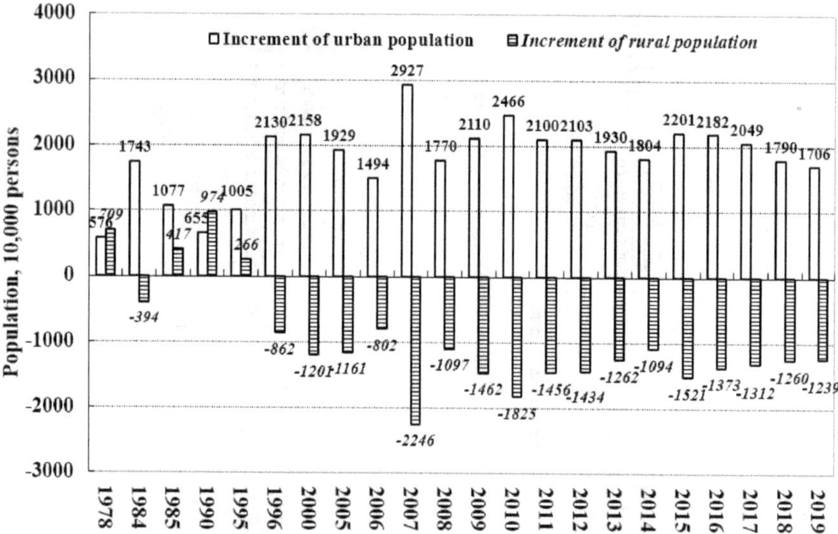

Figure 3.35.　Increment of urban and rural population, China (1979–2016).

Source: Calculated using data from China Statistical Yearbook, China Statistical Press, 2006, Table 4.1; China National Bureau of Statistics, Data base; Annual, Total Population, 2001–2019.

Urbanization level increased from 12.46% in 1952 to only 17.92% in 1978. Figure 3.35 shows that, after economic reform, the change in urban population was larger than the change in rural population in every year during 1978–2005. Especially after 1996, the absolute amount of change of urban population was larger than the negative change of rural population, implying that the population migrated from rural areas to urban areas. Therefore, after economic reform, the urbanization level increased 25.07% in 27 years and only 5.45% in the 27 years before economic reform.

Steady development stage (1984–1995). In 1984, the Third Plenary Session of the 12th CPC Central Committee shifted the focus of reform to the cities. With the establishment of coastal open cities, the strict household registration management system began to loosen, and the standards for city construction and town construction were adjusted, thus facilitating the movement of rural population to towns and cities. At the end of 1995, the urbanization rate of permanent residents reached 29.04%, an increase of 7.42 % points from the end of 1983, and an average annual increase of 0.62 % points. China's urbanization process began to accelerate in 1996.

With the deepening of economic system reform and the speed of urban economic development accelerating, the level of social development increased rapidly. The surplus rural labor force absorbed in the cities increased. In 2002, the 16th National Congress of the Communist Party of China put forward the scientific concept of development, demanding "adhering to the coordinated development of large, medium, and small cities and small towns, and taking the road of urbanization with Chinese characteristics" to promote the rapid improvement of China's urbanization level and urbanization rate. At the end of 2011, the urbanization rate of permanent residents reached 51.27%, an increase of 22.23 % points from the end of 1995, and an average annual increase of 1.39 % points.

New urbanization stage (2012-present). In 2012, the Party's 18th National Congress proposed to follow the new urbanization road with Chinese characteristics, and the urbanization process entered a new stage of adhering to the people-oriented and quality-oriented development. In 2014, a government report set out a goal of housing "300 million people." In recent years, to actively promote the construction of new urbanization, supporting reforms in the areas of household registration, land, finance, education, employment, medical care, old-age care, and housing security have been continuously promoted, and the speed of urbanization from farms has accelerated. In 2005, the investment completed in 35 Large and Medium-sized Cities (see Table 3.26) accounted for 6% of the country's total for real estate development, increasing by 60% in 2017. The real estate Floor Space of Commercialized Buildings Sold in urban areas increased by 305%, with an average annual increase of 9.7%.[56] The construction of a new socialist countryside has been further advanced, and the face of the country underwent tremendous change. In the rural areas, renovation of dilapidated houses has taken place, enabling 17.94 million rural households to renovate dangerous houses, and more than seven million poverty-stricken households to build homes, thus gaining housing security.

Using data from World Development Indicators, we use per capita GDP measured in USD and PPP international current USD as the independent variable. We also take the GDP composition of secondary industry as an independent variable since the secondary industry is mainly located in urban areas. The regression results are shown in Table 3.29. The data used for regression analysis are from 1980, 1998, 1999, 2001, 2002, 2003, and

---

[56]Calculated using data from China Statistical Yearbook, China Statistical Press, 2019, Tables 19.1, 19.7; 2006, Tables 6.27,6.43.

2004. Ten independent variables namely: GDP composition of secondary industry (Ind80, Ind98) and per capita GDP measured in current USD (GDPpc98) and PPP international current USD (PPPpc98, PPPpc99, PPPpc01, PPPpc02, PPPpc03, PPPpc04, PPPpc05) were used in the regression analysis. Table 3.29 shows all the nine regression equations are statistically significant and according to the high correlation coefficient, high t-ratio, and F-ratio and the more recent data, we adopt per capita GDP measured in PPP international current USD (PPPpc01, PPPpc04, PPPpc17) as our independent variable. The last column means that we put variables China's PPPpc01, PPPpc02, PPPpc03 to get Urban% in China. For example, in 2001, the estimated value is 46.1, and the actual value was 36.7. This shows that China's actual Urban% is lower than the esti-mated value of 9.4%. It decreases to the lower value of 8.5% in 2005 and higher of 2.4% in 2017. The process of Chinese urbanization, then, improved significantly. In Figures 3.36 and 3.37, *X*-axis represents per capita *GDP* measured in *PPP* international USD and *Y*-axis shows urban-ization measured in % terms in 2001 and 2017, respectively. The dots represent 157 and 223 countries in 2001 and 2017, respectively, while the

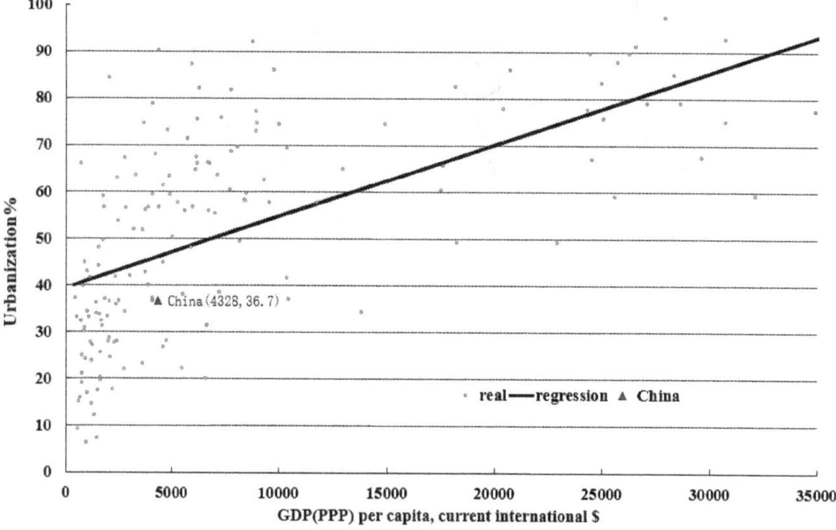

Figure 3.36.   Urbanization versus GDP(PPP) per capita, 2001.

Source: Calculated using data from World Bank: World Development Indicators 2002, CD-ROM, Published May, 2002 by World Bank.

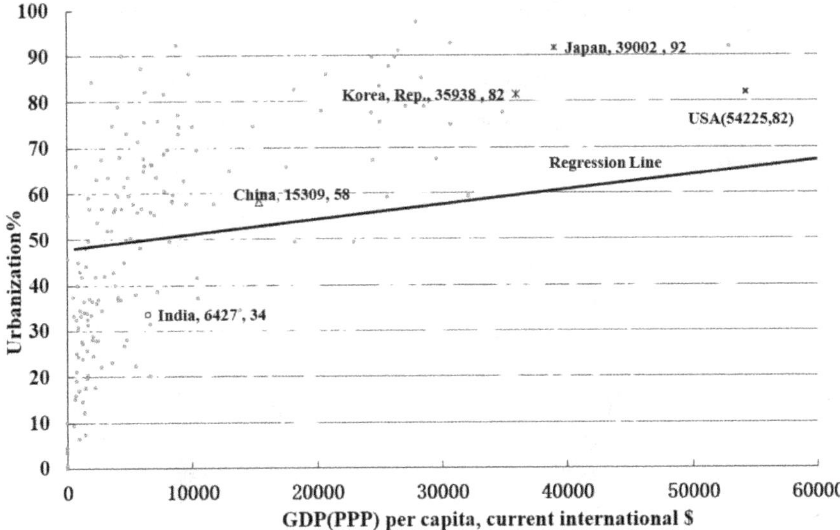

Figure 3.37.   Urbanization versus GDP(PPP) per capita, 2017.

Source: Calculated using data from World Bank: World Development Indicators online 2019, Released April, 2019 by World Bank.

solid triangle stands for China. The solid line shown in Figures 3.36 and 3.40 represents regression Equation U01 and U17 (see Table 3.28), respectively, which depicts the regression relationship of urbanization and per capita GDP measured in PPP international USD in 2001 and 2017.

We can state that, when per capita GDP increases by 1000 PPP constant 2000 international USD, the level of urbanization will increase 0.80%. Its graphical illustration is shown in Figures 3.36 and 3.37, which are quite similar. In the left lower corner of Figures 3.36 and 3.37 there are 80 and 112 countries located under the lines represented Eqs. (U01) and (U17) (see Table 3.28), respectively. This indicates that the pace of urbanization (in percentage terms) of many low income and lower-middle income countries is lower than the anticipated value. In contrast, we note that in the upper right corners of Figures 3.36 and 3.37, there are 77 and 111 countries above these lines. We can therefore conclude that the urbanization pace of many high income and upper middle-income countries is higher than the anticipated value. Comparing Figure 3.36 with Figure 3.37, we find that the slope of regression line in Figure 3.36 is little steeper than

Table 3.28.   Regression analysis between urbanization and per capita GDP.

Variable		Coef.	Intercept	R	F	Number of data	Urban%, Cal. by Eq.
Indust80	U80	0.8032	18.5988	0.4840	31.81	106	57.96
	t-ratio	5.64	3.55				
Indust98	U98	0.7335	29.3238	0.3259	14.50	124	65.26
	t-ratio	3.81	4.94				
GNPpc98	U98	0.0015	44.8143	0.6063	77.88	136	44.83
	t-ratio	8.83	24.06				
PPPpc98	U98	0.0021	39.2036	0.6956	124.67	135	39.27
	t-ratio	11.17	20.31				
PPPpc99	U99	0.0019	39.5858	0.6817	112.85	132	46.37
	t-ratio	10.62	20.01				
PPPpc01	U01	0.0015	39.4732	0.6264	100.07	157	46.11
	t-ratio	10.00	21.23				
PPPpc02	U02	0.0015	41.5028	0.6441	103.80	171	48.23
	t-ratio	10.95	22.79				
PPPpc03	U03	0.0014	41.1954	0.6479	124.41	174	48.34
	t-ratio	11.15	23.25				
PPPpc04	U04	0.0014	40.8685	0.6487	125.69	175	47.99
	t-ratio	11.21	23.81				
PPPpc05	U05	0.0013	40.5943	0.6157	103.80	175	48.46
	t-ratio	10.19	22.24				
PPPpc06	U06	0.0011	41.2408	0.6330	125.00	189	46.40
	t-ratio	11.18	23.84				
PPPpc16	U16	0.0008	43.0856	0.6608	171.35	224	54.73
	t-ratio	13.09	28.71				
PPPpc17	U17	0.0008	43.3468	0.6586	169.29	222	55.58
	t-ratio	13.01	28.68				

Source: Calculated using data from World Bank: World Bank: World Development Indicators online 2006, Released 2006 by World Bank; 2005, Released April 2005 by World Bank; World Development Indicators 2003, CD-ROM, Published July, 2003 by World Bank, ISBN: 0-8213-5423-X SKU: 15423; World Development Indicators 2002, CD-ROM; World Development Indicators 2000, CD-ROM; World Development Indicators 1999, CD-ROM.

that line in Figure 3.37. This shows that, under the same per capita GDP in PPP international USD, the urbanization percentage will be lower in 2017 than that in 2001 as calculated by Eqs. (U01) and (U17),

Table 3.29.   Consumption gap between urban and rural areas, China.

	Unit	Urban 04	Rural 04	Urban/ rural 04	Urban 15	Rural 15	Urban/ rural 15
Meat	Kg/year per capita	29.22	17.89	1.63	28.90	23.10	1.25
Aquatic products	Kg/year per capita	12.48	4.49	2.78	14.70	7.20	2.04
Automobile	Set/100 household	N/A	N/A	N/A	30.00	13.30	2.26
Electric bicycle	Set/100 household	N/A	N/A	N/A	45.80	50.10	0.91
Mobile phone	Set/100 household	N/A	N/A	N/A	223.80	226.10	0.99
Color T.V.	Set/100 household	133.44	62.57	2.13	122.30	116.90	1.05
Air conditioner	Set/100 household	69.81	4.70	14.85	114.60	38.80	2.95
Refrigerator	Set/100 household	90.15	17.75	5.08	94.00	82.60	1.14
Washing machine	Set/100 household	95.90	37.32	2.57	92.30	78.80	1.17
Camera	Set/100 household	47.04	3.68	12.78	33.00	4.10	8.05
Expenditure, 2015	¥/year per capita	¥21,392	¥9,223	2.32			
Expenditure, 2011	¥/year per capita	¥15,161	¥5,221	2.90			
Expenditure, 2004	¥/year per capita	¥7,182	¥2,185	3.29			
Retail sale, 2008	¥/year per capita	¥11,816	¥4,937	2.39			
Retail sale, 2005	¥/year per capita	¥7,226	¥2,657	2.72			
Retail sale, 2000	¥/year per capita	¥45,906	¥1,800	25.50			

(*Continued*)

Table 3.29.   (*Continued*)

	Unit	Urban 04	Rural 04	Urban/ rural 04	Urban 15	Rural 15	Urban/ rural 15
Retail sale, 1995	¥/year per capita	¥35,174	¥1,237	28.43			
Retail sale, 1990	¥/year per capita	¥30,195	¥524	57.59			
Retail sale, 1985	¥/year per capita	¥25,094	¥301	83.38			
Retail sale, 1980	¥/year per capita	¥19,140	¥177	108.28			
Retail sale, 1978	¥/year per capita	¥17,245	¥133	129.35			
Retail sale, 1952	¥/year per capita	¥3,063	¥22	136.84			

Note: *After 2008 China National Bureau of Statistics did not publish retail data in urban and rural areas, so we used cash expenditure in 2004, 2011, and 2015,

Source: Calculated using data from China National Bureau of Statistics: China Statistical Yearbook, China Statistical Press, 2016, Tables 6.6, 10.7, 2011, Tables 10.16, 10.26, 2005, Tables 4.1, 10.11, 10.12, 10.28, 10.30, Table 17.1; 2004, Tables 4.1, 10.10, 10.11, 10.28, 10.30, Table 17.1 2003, Table 16.1; 1996, Table 15.1; 1991 Table 3.1, 14.21; Statistical Yearbook of China 1981 (English Edition), Compiled by the State Statistical Bureau, PRC. Published by Economic Information & Agency, Hong Kong, October 1982.

respectively. From Table 3.29, we see that the slope of the regression line between urbanization measured in percentage and per capita GDP measured in PPP international USD declined from 1998–2017. This implies that urbanization increased in developing countries significantly. It is obvious from Figure 3.36 that China is located under the regression line. Using Eq. (U01) to calculate China's urbanization level, we obtain 36.69%, which is 9.41% higher than China's actual value in 2001. When urbanization increases by 9.41% in China, it means almost 200 million rural residents move to the urban area. In fact, there are more than 100 million farmers migrating to cities for jobs. More than half of the male villagers aged from 18 to 50 have gone out to seek employment in cities. During 2000–2002, 47.8% of farmers' income increment comes from employment outside their villages.[57] Urbanization means more than

---

[57]Li, B. (2004). Rural and urban China — worlds apart, *Beijing Review*, No. 08.

simply moving farmers into towns or building bigger cities. It should include substantial improvement in the economic growth mode, changes of lifestyle and of the level of civilization, especially the shake-up of industrial structure. China needs to develop industries for processing, storing, and transporting agricultural products, and keeping them fresh to gain better returns from intensive processing of agricultural products. Small towns and cities need to be expanded, and steady progress needs to be made in urbanization to increase job opportunities and sources of income for farmers. As China has yet to finish its industrialization drive, urbanization will be an inevitable trend in the country. Cities will serve as centers where labor, customers, infrastructure, and services come together to promote industrialization. The service sector can be better developed in big cities. Only in big cities can market size meet the development demands of the service sector. At the same time, big cities play an important role in facilitating information exchange and development of information technology. City-clusters can help develop economies of scale to aid development of the information technology industry. In China, several major city-clusters will come into being in the Yangtze River Delta, the Pearl River Delta, and the Annulus Bohai Rim. These clusters aim to become powerhouses of domestic economic growth and exchange centers with the outside world. Table 3.29 shows the consumption gap between urban and rural areas. In rural areas per capita consumption is much lower than in urban areas.

Table 7.36 shows that before the economic reform, the ratio of annual retail sales per capita of urban and rural residents was 137 in 1952 and 129 in 1978. Because rural life is self-sufficient, there is no money to spend. Since 1996, there has been inadequate consumer demand, mainly attributed to low consumption in rural areas. In November 2018, the Chinese government issued the "Opinions on Establishing a More Effective Regional Coordination and Development Mechanism," which clearly guided the coordinated development of the Beijing–Tianjin–Hebei region, the development of the Yangtze River Economic Belt, and the construction of the Guangdong, Hong Kong, Macao, and Da Wan Districts. The functional orientation of the three major regions is different: Beijing–Tianjin–Hebei is the primary means to ease the pressure on Beijing's economy by promoting the development of the Bohai Rim region; the Yangtze River Economic Belt is centered on the integration of the Yangtze River Delta, and the Eastern, Central, and Western regions along the basin; Guangdong, Hong Kong, Macao, and Da Wan District, are integrated into Hong Kong. And the Macao administrative region is intended to benchmark the international construction of the world-class Da Wan District and guide the green development of the Pearl River–XiJiang River Economic Belt. In 2019, the three major regions ushered in a special period of construction implementation.[58]

12. Main Industrial Structure Challenges

China's upgrading of its Industrial Structure to build a stronger economy and a more inclusive society has been a success so far. Still, the country faces several challenges as it further adjusts the IS. These challenges include the following:

(1) Weak performance of Agriculture: Low input has led to poor irrigation infrastructure, resulting in lack of preparedness to withstand natural disasters. In 1996, disasters afflicted an area of 20.53 million hectares, which resulted in direct economic loss of CNY220 billion (USD26.6 billion). In 2000, grain output decreased 10% due to severe floods and droughts. Natural disasters in 2003 resulted in the death of 2,145 people and caused economic losses of CNY188.6 billion (USD22.7 billion). Natural disasters damaged 60 million hectares of farmland.[59] Natural disasters in 2015 caused the death of 967 people and economic losses of CNY207.0 billion (USD33.2 billion). Natural disasters damaged 24 million hectares of farmland.[60] Backward production tools have resulted in low productivity, so agriculture's annual growth is far below that of other sectors. Agricultural output increased during 1998–2000, but farmers' incomes did not increase due to unreasonable internal structure and product structure. Building a new modern countryside is a major historic task, which will have an overall impact on building China's moderately prosperous society. China needs to implement a policy of getting industry to support agriculture and cities to support the countryside, strengthen support for agriculture, rural areas, and farmers, and continue making reforms in rural systems and innovations in rural institutions to bring about a rapid

---

[58]Li, S. (2019). Beijing, Tianjin, Hebei, Yangtze River Delta, Guangdong, Hong Kong, and Macao usher in the policy refinement and construction implementation period in 2019. From the perspective of history, we are optimistic about the construction of transportation integration in the region this year. *Wall Street News.*

[59]Xinhua (2003). Natural disasters cost China USD22.7 billion in 2003, November 14.

[60]Calculated using data from China National Bureau of Statistics (2016). China Statistical Yearbook, China Statistical Press, 2016, Table 8.30.

and significant change in the overall appearance of the countryside. In 2006, the reform of rural taxes and fees greatly benefited farmers by eliminating CNY33.6 billion of agricultural tax, over CNY70 billion in the form of the "three deductions" [for public reserve funds, public welfare funds, and management fees] and the "five charges" [charges for rural education, family planning, militia training, rural road construction, and subsidies to entitled groups], assessments for rural education and other unreasonable fees. The government plans to appropriate over CNY103 billion annually to ensure the normal operation of town and township governments and meet the needs of rural compulsory education.[61] The abolition of agricultural taxes and agricultural special product taxes in the country has ended the history of farmers' taxation of more than 2,600 years. The construction of small towns relies on the operation of township enterprises and service industries, will accelerate the development, and create urbanization with Chinese characteristics. The level of urbanization in China has increased from 17.9% in 1978 to 44.9% in 2007[62] and 58.5% by 2017 (as we showed in Chapter 1).

(2) The persistence of weak infrastructure, energy shortages, and lack of adequate transportation and communication in rural areas. High prices for electricity and low-quality telecommunication facilities in the rural areas have also limited rural people's consumption. On the positive side, investment in rural infrastructure has increased, and transportation and communication have improved significantly. Nearly 90% of the country's villages have broadband Internet access, and more than a quarter of the country's villages have e-commerce distribution sites.[63]

(3) Underdeveloped tertiary industry, especially the science, technology, education, production related service sectors (such as information services, banking, accounting, consulting, and law). This is obviously an important avenue for stimulating economic restructuring and increased employment.

(4) Domestic consumption is thought to be key to China's economy as the current growth model, based on fixed asset investment and exports,

---

[61] Wen Jiabao (2006). Report on the work of the government, Delivered at the Fourth Session of the Tenth National People's Congress on March 5.

[62] China National Bureau of Statistics (2008). Eighth of the 30-year report of reform and opening up: 30 years of brilliant achievements in agriculture and rural economy, November 5 (in Chinese).

[63] Rural Department, China National Bureau of Statistics (2018). Rural Reform Writes a Glorious History Rural Revitalization and Magnificent Blueprint, September 18 (in Chinese).

is thought to be unsustainable. Consumption expansion will obviously become the core task of Chinese economy. Increasing residents' incomes—raising the incomes of the low-paid, expanding the size of middle classes, and putting a curb on excessively high salaries[64] — will provide the basis for expanding private consumption. On the other hand, the production structure should match the consumption structure to create viable markets. China is also facing the challenge of upgrading its foreign trade structure to narrow its trade gap.

(5) Uncoordinated production processes resulting in shortage of supplies in some sectors (few percent points) and idle capacity in others (larger than two-thirds). Low specialization of enterprises leads to poor linkage among Industry Sectors. There is outdated product structure in secondary industry. Many products are old, low value-adding, poorly manufactured, of poor quality, and using a high volume of natural resources per unit of GDP and outdated technology. On the other hand, consumer demand is shifting toward famous brands, high quality commodities. The main task of the industrial sector is not expansion in scale, but structural upgrading. There is a pressing need to improve China's innovation ability, upgrade industry's overall technological level, boost development of advanced manufacturing, strictly following energy saving and environment-friendly policies, and improving human capital through training. In the past 40 years, with the substantial increase in the income level of Chinese residents, the consumption level and consumption structure of residents have improved significantly. After solving the problem of food and clothing, urban and rural residents began to move from basic consumption and consumption toward development and leisure consumption.[65]

(6) Sustainable development is one of the goals of urban regeneration. It is necessary to realize sustainable development in the three fields of social culture, economy, and environment. "Energy saving" is the urbanization mode China should adopt, while the traditional "industrialization-based mode" should be abandoned. Urban China should develop based on local identity. Most Chinese cities have been endowed with rich history

---

[64]China Daily (2006). Income system reform targets equality, July 7.

[65]Office of Household Survey, China National Bureau of Statistics (2018). The living standards of residents continue to improve, and the quality of consumption has improved significantly, August 31 (in Chinese).

and culture, which should be taken advantage of through the development of tourism or a distinct cultural industry.[66]

Figure 3.38 shows the components of the industrial structure adjustment necessary to promote development. Since the 18th National Congress of the Communist Party of China, the Party Central Committee with President Xi Jinping as the core has insisted on taking the new development concept as the guide, focusing on supply side structural reform, accelerating the strategic adjustment of the economic structure and economic transformation, and achieving major changes in China's economic structure. Industrial structure, demand structure, urban and rural structure, regional structure, ownership structure, and income distribution structure have been gradually improved, and the coordination and sustainability of economic development have been continuously enhanced. These should provide the foundation upon which China can build high quality development and a modern economic system.[67]

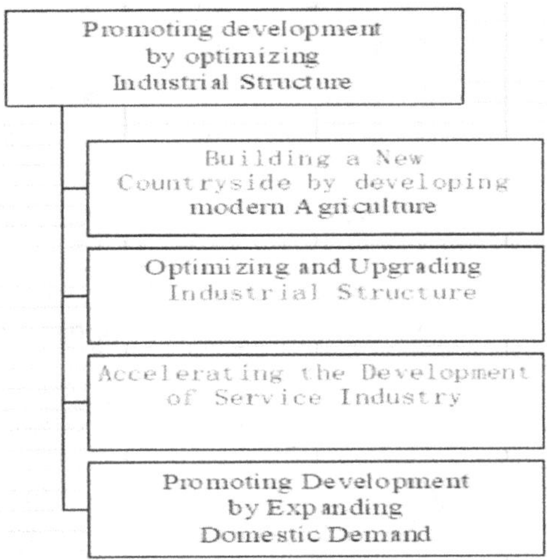

Figure 3.38.   Promoting development by optimizing and upgrading industrial structure and service.

---

[66]Xinhua (2006). China should adopt its own way of urbanization, *China Daily*, February 20.
[67]Comprehensive Department of China National Statistical Bureau: Economic structure achieves historic change, development coordination is significantly enhanced, 2018-08-29, (in Chinese).

13. Chapter Summary

IS refers to the link among a country's industrial sectors. In this chapter, we noted the importance of IS in the economic development process and described and measured various aspects of China's IS before and after economic reforms. To measure the direction and size of industrial structure change, we used the IS change coefficient, K, and the IS similarity coefficient, R.

One important ingredient of IS refers to the employment status and change of each of its sectors. We find that sector employment has changed substantially since 1952. The change has been more profound during the post-reform period and has accelerated in the more recent years. We also compared China's sector employment with that of other countries. We concluded that China's development of its sector employment significantly lags behind that of developed countries.

The contribution of each industrial sector to GDP has also changed through the years. Primary industry has seen its contribution decrease since 1952, with the decrease becoming more evident after reforms. We also focused on the contribution of the tertiary sector and the relationship between this sector and GDP. In addition, we compared each sector's contribution to China's GDP with contributions to GDP of other countries. We found that, after reforms, the contribution of China's industrial sectors has become more like that of developed countries, and Japan in particular. Finally, we examined each industrial sector's productivity as well as its comparative productivity.

We subsequently explored the relationship between changes in demand and IS. We investigated changes in Chinese citizens' consumption and saving patterns before and after economic reforms. We also examined the importance of income disparity to China's IS. The country's Real Estate development has also been associated with the IS, as has its urbanization policy.

In Chapter 4, we will discuss the adjustment of the industrial structure in agriculture, industry, and service sectors.

Chapter 4

Changes in the Internal Structure of China's Industrial Sector

1. Introduction

China's economic restructuring is centered on the upgrading of industrialization and the rationalization of industries. China has shifted from a traditional agricultural nation to a developing country with a range of comprehensive economic sectors and initial industrialization. Before economic reform, China's economic strategy relied mainly on the development of industry, especially heavy industry. However, since 1978, the trend was altered, with the emphasis being on agriculture, light industry, and the tertiary industry. China's economic structure has encompassed all three industries. After more than 40 years' opening and reform efforts, the proportions of China's three major industries, light and heavy industries as well as internal sectors of various other industries, have gradually been balanced. Especially since the 18th National Congress of the Communist Party of China, the development of the industrial economy has emphasized quality over quantity. China has reversed its unbalanced economic structure and is well under way toward completing its industrialization objectives, thus entering a new phase of structural upgrading and high-quality development. However, its economy has reached such a stage that it will not make any further progress without readjustments. Therefore, China must continue adjusting the structure of its agriculture and rural economy, continue to make progress in the IT industry, develop the service sector, give priority to high-tech industries, accelerate the pace of urbanization, and launch the strategy of developing the less-developed western region.

In Chapter 4, we examine the internal change of the structure of China's industrial sectors. We begin by discussing the changes observed in manufacturing. We use the Specialization and Hoffman Coefficients to denote changes in the sector and provide an assessment of the path manufacturing has pursued in China. We continue by reviewing improvements in China's infrastructure and commenting on the country's inefficient industrial and product structures. In Section 6 of this chapter, we then offer evidence of China's industrial performance after reforms. Sections 7–9 present the changes in the structures of agriculture and tertiary industry and examine the status of the country's Pillar industries. Finally, we offer Policy Implications of our findings (see Section 10).

2. Structural Changes in the Manufacturing Industry

From 1985–2005, the industrial growth rate in China was stable. The "bottleneck" of industry (basic industry, raw material, energy, and transportation) was relaxed to some extent but became in short supply from 2003–2005. Export of manufactured goods increased rapidly and the structure of import and export goods was improved. This means economic restructuring progressed steadily. Table 4.1 lists the gross output and share of industrial sectors from 1985–2015 in China. Table 4.1 shows IS change coefficient K was 0.807, 0.852, 0.627, 0.456 from 1985–1995, 1995–2005, 2005–2011, 2011–2015, respectively; and it was 1.234 from 1985–2015. The similarity coefficient of IS R1 was 0.9479, 0.9285, 0.9749 and 0.9874 in 1985–1995, 1995–2005, 2005–2011 and 2011–2015, respectively; and 0.8303 in 1985–2015; and it was 0.8303 from 1985 to 2015. The value of the IS change coefficient K_l is higher in 1995–2005 and the IS similar coefficient $R1$ is lower for 1995–2005, which means the industrial structural change within the manufacturing sector during 1995–2005 was relatively large. It also means the industrial structural change within the manufacturing sector during 1985–1995 was smaller than in 1995–2005. The share increment of 6.18%, 2.66%, and 1.89% for manufacture of communication equipment, computers and other electronic equipment sectors, production and distribution of electric power and heat power, and smelting

Table 4.1.   Gross output value (CNY100 million) of major industrial sectors and their % share, 1985–2015.

Year	1985	1995	2005	2011	2015
Branch name	Gross output %share	Gross output %share	Gross output %share	Gross output %share	Principal revenue %share
Mining & washing of coal	2.35	2.12	2.30	3.43	2.14
Extraction of petroleum & natural gas	1.73	2.62	2.52	1.53	0.71
Mining & processing of ferrous metal ores	0.18	0.21	0.40	0.94	0.65
Mining & processing of non-ferrous metal ores	0.42	0.59	0.46	0.60	0.56
Mining & processing of nonmetal ores	0.65	0.68	0.30	0.46	0.65
Food processing & production	8.65	7.41	5.77	6.89	7.87
Manufacture of beverages	1.13	2.12	1.24	1.40	1.57
Manufacture of tobacco	1.75	1.84	1.14	0.81	0.84
Manufacture of textile	15.43	8.45	5.08	3.87	3.60
Manufacture of textile wearing apparel, footware, & caps	2.41	2.70	2.00	1.60	2.00
Manufacture of leather, fur, feather, & related products	0.93	1.79	1.39	1.06	1.32
Processing of timber, manufacture of wood, bamboo, rattan, palm, & straw products	1.04	0.74	0.73	1.07	1.25
Manufacture of furniture	0.61	0.41	0.57	0.60	0.71
Manufacture of paper & paper products	1.31	1.86	1.67	1.43	1.26
Printing, reproduction of recording media	0.48	0.76	0.58	0.46	0.67
Manufacture of articles for culture, education, & sport activity	1.18	0.68	0.59	0.38	1.43
Processing of petroleum, coking, processing of nuclear fuel	2.45	3.72	4.81	4.37	3.12
Manufacture of raw chemical materials & chemical products	8.25	7.01	6.56	7.20	7.53
Manufacture of medicines	1.73	1.76	1.71	1.77	2.32
Manufacture of chemical fibers	1.25	1.49	1.05	0.79	0.65

(Continued)

Table 4.1. (*Continued*)

Year	1985	1995	2005	2011	2015
Branch name	Gross output %share	Gross output %share	Gross output %share	Gross output %share	Principal revenue %share
Manufacture of rubber	1.75	1.14	0.88	0.87	0.93
Manufacture of plastics	1.92	2.07	2.03	1.85	1.86
Manufacture of non-metallic mineral products	4.54	5.54	3.69	4.76	5.30
Smelting & pressing of ferrous metals	5.21	6.72	8.61	7.59	5.68
Smelting & pressing of non-ferrous metals	2.25	2.52	3.18	4.25	4.63
Manufacture of metal products	2.83	3.03	2.63	2.77	3.36
Manufacture of general & special purpose machinery	11.05	8.85	6.70	7.95	7.47
Manufacture of transport equipment	4.29	6.06	6.30	7.49	8.12
Manufacture of electrical machinery & equipment	4.38	4.76	5.58	6.09	6.23
Manufacture of communication equipment, computers, & other electronic equipment	3.53	4.64	10.83	7.56	8.25
Manufacture of measuring instruments & machinery for cultural activity & office work	1.01	0.78	1.12	2.07	1.46
Production & distribution of electric power & heat power	3.30	4.48	7.13	5.61	5.10
Production & distribution of Gas	0.04	0.14	0.21	0.37	0.57
Production & Distribution of Water	0.00	0.33	0.23	0.14	0.17
Gross output, billion ¥ RMB	825.3	5450.7	24928.2	84426.9	110985.3
K	0.8068	0.8523	0.6270	0.4561	1.2340
$R1$	0.9479	0.9285	0.9749	0.9874	0.8303
K_{annual}	0.1614	0.0852	0.1045	0.1140	0.0411
h	13.87	9.95	11.51	10.81	10.45
Year for comparison	85/95	95/05	05/11	11/15	85/15

Note: *After 2011 China National Bureau of Statistics did not announce Gross Output Value of manufacturing Industry.

Source: Calculated using data from the China National Bureau of Statistics (2016). China Statistical Yearbook, China Statistics Press, Table 13.02; 2012, Table 14.02; 2006, Table 14.4; 2001, Table 13.05; 1996, Table 12.11; 1991, Table 10.9; Statistical Yearbook of China 1986, Compiled by the State Statistical Bureau of China, Oxford University Press, 1986, p. 227, 228, 231, 232.

and pressing of ferrous metals were the three largest increment sectors, respectively, from 1985–2005. The percentage share of extraction of petroleum and natural gas, manufacture of textile and manufacture of beverages sectors decreased by 1.19%, 1.02%, and 0.84%, respectively, representing the sectors with the largest decrement from 1995–2005. From 1985–2015, the three sectors showing the largest increment in percentage share of 4.72%, 3.64%, and 2.38% were manufacture of communication equipment, computers and other electronic equipment sectors, production and distribution of electric power and heat power, and smelting and pressing of non-ferrous metals. On the other hand, also from 1985–2015, manufacture of textile, manufacture of general and special purpose machinery, and extraction of petroleum and natural gas were the sectors showing the largest decrement (4.52%, 3.58%, and 1.01%, respectively).

2.1. *The specialization coefficient*

We calculate the specialization coefficient h according to the following formula:

$$h = 100 \times \left(1 + \frac{\sum_{i=1}^{n} s_i(t) \ln\left[s_i(t)\right]}{\ln(n)} \right) \tag{4.1}$$

where $s_i(t)$ – share of sector i to total value at time t;

    n – number of industrial sectors.

If there is only one industrial sector, then $h = 100$; if the share of each sector is equal, then $h = 0$. Table 4.1 shows that the specialization coefficient declined from 1985–2000, while increasing from 2000–2005. Data provided by the United Nations Industrial Development Organization (UNIDO) show the specialization coefficient for developed countries is generally higher than that for developing countries. An increasing specialization coefficient is conducive to productivity improvement. Table 4.2 shows that developed countries are associated with larger specialization coefficients than are developing countries. In Table 4.2, the IS change coefficient K_{annual} and IS similar coefficient $R1$ are calculated using the structure of manufacturing sector in the same country at different years, which reflects the IS change at

Table 4.2.   Comparing the structure change of China's manufacturing with foreign countries.

		Manufacturing, value added	Chemical	Food, beverages, and tobacco	Machinery and transport equipment	Other manufac-turing	Textiles and clothing	K_{annual}	R1	Year for compa-rison	h
		% of GDP	% of total	% of total	% of total	% of total	% of total				
China	1980	13.78	11.34	10.04	18.55	41.79	18.27	0.13	0.9804		8.95
	1990	13.77	13.11	14.54	15.55	42.01	14.79	0.26	0.9916	80/90	7.85
	2001	18.22	11.53	14.18	14.68	48.45	11.17	0.23	0.9924	90/01	12.79
	2007	17.40	10.79	11.81	24.49	42.94	9.98	0.65	0.9777	01/07	11.15
India	1980	16.95	14.06	9.12	16.95	38.55	21.32	0.15	0.9654		7.29
	1990	17.24	13.87	11.75	17.48	41.74	15.17	0.25	0.9894	80/90	7.97
	2002	16.61	16.15	9.31	18.58	47.02	8.94	0.29	0.9881	90/02	13.08
	2013	15.25	16.71	10.38	20.55	43.10	9.27	0.14	0.9972	02/13	10.38
Indonesia	1980	18.41	11.39	31.75	7.98	35.13	13.75	0.13	0.9767		9.67
	1990	19.89	8.95	27.48	8.84	40.13	14.61	0.27	0.9908	80/90	10.98
	2001	30.75	10.95	20.92	12.95	42.59	12.58	0.31	0.9864	90/01	9.37
	2013	21.03	13.23	29.63	16.71	29.36	11.08	0.49	0.9484	01/13	4.91
Japan	1980	19.17	8.68	9.16	21.16	54.43	6.57	0.29	0.9064		21.11
	1990	19.67	9.51	8.86	24.91	51.97	4.74	0.18	0.9967	80/90	21.12
	2002	22.56	11.28	12.49	35.05	38.44	2.74	0.52	0.9560	90/02	16.78
	2010	20.83	11.65	12.85	37.54	36.25	1.71	0.16	0.9980	02/13	18.02

Rep. of Korea	1980	21.58	10.31	16.60	9.34	44.25	19.49	0.49	0.6790		10.94
	1990	24.60	9.20	10.70	30.15	36.13	13.82	0.83	0.8958	80/90	9.20
	2002	24.22	9.97	7.79	42.27	32.91	7.05	0.43	0.9661	90/02	16.40
	2012	28.17	10.64	5.84	48.33	31.64	3.54	0.27	0.9937	02/12	23.07
United States	1980		9.67	10.58	23.90	49.66	6.18	0.20	0.9658		17.65
	1990	11.66	11.74	12.37	22.62	48.35	4.91	0.15	0.9982	80/90	16.39
	2002	13.30	13.29	14.24	27.58	41.89	3.00	0.28	0.9884	90/02	14.84
	2011	12.15	16.34	15.16	28.32	38.80	1.39	0.21	0.9961	02/11	15.13

Source: World Bank (2018). World Development Indicators online, released November 2018 by World Bank.

different years, thereby reflecting the IS change in their country. The value of the IS change coefficient K_{annual} (0.83) is highest for the Korea Republic (South Korea) and the IS similar coefficient $R1$ (0.8958) is lowest for the Republic of Korea during 1980–1990, which means the industrial structure change within the Republic of Koreas's manufacturing sector is largest during 1980–1990. Table 4.2 shows the percentage share of machinery and transport equipment in the Republic of Korea increased from 9.34% in 1980 to 30.2% in 2000.

During 1980–1990, the Republic of Korea transitioned from a developing country to a new-industrialized country; therefore, the industrial structure change within the manufacturing sector has been relatively large. The proportion of China's machinery and transport equipment sector dropped from 18.55% in 1980 to 14.68% in 2001, and then rose to 24.49% in 2007. The share of textiles and clothing declined from 18.3% at 1980 to 11.2% at 2001 and further fell to 10% in 2007 and 2016. This means China is still under its industrialization process. The lowest IS change coefficient K_{annual} and highest IS similar coefficient $R1$ belonged to the United States during 1990–2011, which implies the industrial structure change within the manufacturing sector in the United States is the least. The United States is a developed country; therefore, its industrial structure change within the manufacturing sector is relatively small. The average annual growth rate of the total value added in the manufacturing sectors during 1980–2001 for China and Indonesia was 10.8% and 9.1%, respectively; it was 9.5% for the Republic of Korea during 1980–2002. These are higher than for the other three countries listed in Table 4.2. In Table 4.3, IS change coefficient K and IS similar coefficient $R1$ are calculated using the structure of the manufacturing sector in each country in the same year, using China as a reference, which measures the IS change of China with different countries at the same period.

A comparison of the IS similar coefficient R1 between China and Japan indicates a range of 0.9349 (Japan, 1990) to 0.9699 (2002), which indicates the structure of the manufacturing sector between China and Japan. Figure 4.1 shows six sectors with significant changes from 1985 to 2015. After 2011, the China National Bureau of Statistics did not announce gross output value of the manufacturing industry; instead, it chose revenue from principal businesses to represent the production scale. Therefore, we chose revenue from principal businesses in 2015. The decrement of many industrial products has reduced market activity and has exerted downward pressure on prices. To salvage the ailing industries, the State

Table 4.3.   Comparing the structure of manufacturing with foreign countries, concurrent.

		Manufacturing, value added	Chemical	Food, beverages, and tobacco	Machinery and transport equipment	Other manufac-turing	Textiles and clothing	K_{annual}	R1	Year for compa-rison	h
		% of GDP	% of total	% of total	% of total	% of total	% of total				
China	1980	13.78	11.34	10.04	18.55	41.79	18.27				8.95
India		16.95	14.06	9.12	16.95	38.55	21.32				7.29
Indonesia		18.41	11.39	31.75	7.98	35.13	13.75				9.67
Japan		19.17	8.68	9.16	21.16	54.43	6.57				21.11
Republic of Korea		21.58	10.31	16.60	9.34	44.25	19.49				10.94
United States			9.67	10.58	23.90	49.66	6.18				17.65
China	1990	13.77	13.11	14.54	15.55	42.01	14.79	0.26	0.9916	80/90	7.85
India		17.24	13.87	11.75	17.48	41.74	15.17	0.25	0.9894	80/90	7.97
Indonesia		19.89	8.95	27.48	8.84	40.13	14.61	0.27	0.9908	80/90	10.98
Japan		19.67	9.51	8.86	24.91	51.97	4.74	0.18	0.9967	80/90	21.12
Republic of Korea		24.60	9.20	10.70	30.15	36.13	13.82	0.83	0.8958	80/90	9.20
United States		11.66	11.74	12.37	22.62	48.35	4.91	0.15	0.9982	80/90	16.39

(*Continued*)

Table 4.3. (*Continued*)

		Manufacturing, value added	Chemical	Food, beverages, and tobacco	Machinery and transport equipment	Other manufac-turing	Textiles and clothing	K_{annual}	R1	Year for compa-rison	h
		% of GDP	% of total	% of total	% of total	% of total	% of total				
China	2001	18.22	11.53	14.18	14.68	48.45	11.17	0.23	0.9924	90/01	12.79
India	2002	16.61	16.15	9.31	18.58	47.02	8.94	0.29	0.9881	90/02	13.08
Indonesia	2001	30.75	10.95	20.92	12.95	42.59	12.58	0.31	0.9864	90/01	9.37
Japan	2002	22.56	11.28	12.49	35.05	38.44	2.74	0.52	0.9560	90/02	16.78
Republic of Korea	2002	24.22	9.97	7.79	42.27	32.91	7.05	0.43	0.9661	90/02	16.40
United States	2002	13.30	13.29	14.24	27.58	41.89	3.00	0.28	0.9884	90/02	14.84
China	2007	17.40	10.79	11.81	24.49	42.94	9.98	0.65	0.9777	01/07	11.15
India	2013	15.25	16.71	10.38	20.55	43.10	9.27	0.14	0.9972	02/13	10.38
Indonesia	2013	21.03	13.23	29.63	16.71	29.36	11.08	0.49	0.9484	01/13	4.91
Japan	2010	20.83	11.65	12.85	37.54	36.25	1.71	0.16	0.9980	02/13	18.02
Republic of Korea	2012	28.17	10.64	5.84	48.33	31.64	3.54	0.27	0.9937	02/12	23.07
United States	2011	12.15	16.34	15.16	28.32	38.80	1.39	0.21	0.9961	02/11	15.13

Source: World Bank: World Development Indicators online 2018, released November 2018 by World Bank.

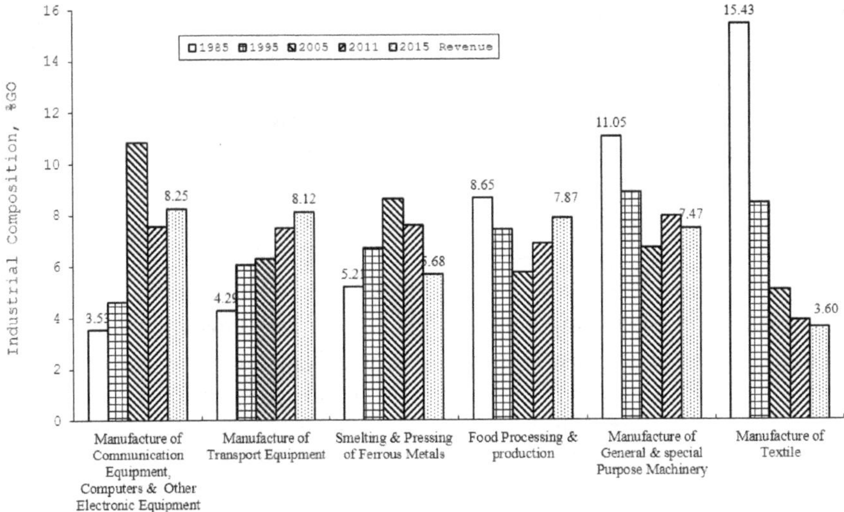

Figure 4.1.   Sectors with large structure changes, China (1985–2015).

Source: Calculated using data from the China National Bureau of Statistics: China Statistical Yearbook, China Statistics Press, 2016, Table 13.4; 2012, Table 14.2; 2006, Table 14.4; 2001, Table 13.05; 1996, Tables 12.10, 12.11; 1991; Statistical Yearbook of China 1986, Compiled by the State Statistical Bureau of China, Oxford University Press, 1986.

Economic and Trade commission has taken a comprehensive approach to the problem in recent years.

The textile sector has become a successful example. In 1998, the central government chose the textile sector to set an example and to achieve a "breakthrough" in its SOE reform. The sector was asked to reduce its production capacity by 10 million spindles within three years. Thanks to great efforts made by the governments and firms, the sector reduced its cotton yarn production capacity by 9.06 million spindles within two years. In 1999, the sector generated CNY3.86 billion (USD46.6 million) in profit. Still, the Chinese government kept making favorable loans, ending its six years of successive losses (loss of CNY3.23 billion in 1998) and assisted the sector with technical upgrading. Hence, the share of the textile industry decreased from 15.43% total industry gross output in 1985 to 5.08% in 2005, after-tax profits reached CNY628.2 billion (USD77.84 billion) in 2005, the ratio of profits to industrial cost reached

6.42% in 2005, and the proportion of products sold was 98.14% in 2005.[1] The share of Manufacture of General and Special Purpose Machinery decreased from 11.05% total industry gross output in 1985 to 7.95% in 2011, which may be a result of the special categories machinery manufacturing increasing significantly. The share of the food processing industry decreased from 8.65% total industry gross output in 1985 to 5.77% in 2005, which may be related to the Chinese people's preference for fresh foods (meat, aquatic products, vegetables, and fruits).

The share increments for the electronic and telecommunications sectors are the largest, from 3.53% to 7.56%, in total industry gross output during 1985–2011 because this sector is closely related with information technology (IT). China will continue to make progress in the IT industry. The Manufacture of Railway, Ship, Aerospace and Other Transport Equipment, and the Smelting and Pressing of Ferrous Metals is a result of high investment; therefore, their increment of percentage share in total industry gross output ranked second and third during 1985–2011.

For reference, the gross output and share of industrial sectors for different years of selected foreign countries are listed in Table 4.4. From this table, we observe that the IS change coefficient K for India, a developing country, is larger than that of developed countries like the United States and Japan and the IS similar coefficient $R1$ for India is less than that for the United States and Japan.

This means the industrial structure change for a developing country is larger than that of a developed country because the industrial structure of developed countries is relatively mature. From Table 4.4, we find that the IS change coefficient K shows the IS change within industry in the United States from 1977–1991, Japan during 1980–1991, and India from 1978–1990 are larger than China from 1985 to 2005 after reform (1.234 see Table 4.1). The IS similar coefficient $R1$ in Tables 4.1 and 4.4 indicates the IS similar situation in China from 1985 to 2005 ($R1 = 0.8130$) is a little lower than India from 1978–1990 ($R1 = 0.8722$), which means the industrial structure changes within the manufacturing industry after economic reform in China are not large. Therefore, China needs to strengthen the IS adjustment further.

---

[1]Calculated using data from China National Bureau of Statistics: China Statistical Yearbook, China Statistics Press, 2006, Tables 14.4, 14.5; 2005, Tables 14.3, 14.4; 2004, Tables 14.3, 14.4; 2003, Tables 13.5, 13.6; 2001, Tables 13.5, 13.6; 2000, Table 13.6; 1999, Table 13.8; Li, R. (2005). China's Economy and Trade Yearbook.

Table 4.4.   Percentage share of total gross output for industrial sectors in Japan, India, and the United States.

Branch Name	US77	US85	US91	JP80	JP91	IND78	IND90
Gross output, bil. local currency	1,538	2,269	2,816	2,29,409	3,42,979	452	2,341
Mining & Processing	5.58	6.22	4.86	0.29	0.00	3.47	0.93
Food Production	11.19	11.59	12.04	8.00	7.99	15.02	15.67
Beverage Production	0.45	1.67	1.74	1.68	1.38	0.49	0.81
Tobacco Processing	0.59	0.84	1.14	1.01	0.72	1.84	1.48
Textile Industry	3.23	2.95	2.98	3.75	2.76	15.83	12.05
Garments & Other Fiber Products	2.10	1.94	1.74	0.99	1.03	0.51	1.06
Leather, Furs, Down, & Related Products	0.21	0.18	0.18	0.23	0.22	0.82	0.68
Shoes	0.27	0.22	0.14	0.18	0.16	0.18	0.46
Timber Processing	1.93	1.72	1.85	2.57	1.53	0.49	0.36
Furniture Manufacturing	0.96	1.15	1.14	0.86	0.85	0.04	0.02
Papermaking & Paper Products	3.40	4.14	4.40	2.99	2.44	1.50	2.17
Printing & Record Pressing	3.24	4.94	5.58	2.90	4.06	1.00	0.99
Raw Chemical Materials & Chemical Products	4.79	8.86	10.58	5.05	7.11	6.06	14.16
Petroleum Processing & Coking Products	6.00	7.89	5.61	6.20	2.59	4.44	2.95
Rubber Products	1.05	0.97	0.89	0.98	1.03	1.68	2.27
Plastic Products	1.55	2.20	2.77	2.53	3.48	0.35	1.40
Glass & ceramic	0.60	0.71	0.71	0.54	0.85	0.40	0.52
Nonmetal Mineral Products	1.63	1.72	1.53	2.83	2.38	2.19	3.42
Smelting & Pressing of Ferrous Metals	4.14	2.69	2.45	7.89	5.46	9.31	11.72
Smelting & Pressing of Non-ferrous Metals	2.25	1.76	1.88	2.86	1.58	1.53	2.76
Metal Products	5.29	5.51	4.97	4.89	6.42	2.15	2.50
Ordinary Machinery Manufacturing	8.45	9.92	9.48	8.71	13.55	5.51	6.77

(*Continued*)

Table 4.4. (*Continued*)

Branch Name	US77	US85	US91	JP80	JP91	IND78	IND90
Electric Equipment & Machinery	6.03	8.64	7.35	9.83	15.41	5.20	6.65
Transportation Equipment Manufacturing	11.69	14.01	13.49	10.88	14.19	4.71	7.27
Instruments, Meters, Cultural, & Official Machinery	0.00	2.69	4.12	0.00	1.38	0.00	0.53
Others	6.58	1.10	1.24	6.26	1.44	8.67	0.41
Electric Power, Steam, Gas Production, & Supply	6.78	0.00	0.00	5.09	0.00	6.63	0.00
Light industry%	27.58	31.34	32.92	25.18	23.15	37.70	35.73
Heavy industry%	72.42	74.89	71.94	74.82	76.85	62.30	64.27
Hoffman Coef.	0.3807	0.4184	0.4576	0.3365	0.3012	0.6053	0.5560
K	1.4200	1.3431	0.4844		1.5699		1.7308
$R1$	0.9009	0.9182	0.9902		0.9133		0.8751
K_{annual}	0.1014	0.1679	0.0807		0.1427		0.1442
Year for comparison	77/91	77/85	85/91		80/91		78/90
n	27	27	27	27	27	27	27

Source: Calculated using data from International Statistical Yearbook, China Statistics Press.

The above analysis was conducted before 2007 because the five industrial sectors used for computing are traditional industries. As can be seen from Table 4.2, China's IS level in 2007 and 2017 is the same. Since the reform and opening-up, China has successively implemented policies such as giving priority to the development of light textile industry, focusing on strengthening basic industries, vigorously revitalizing pillar industries, and actively developing high-tech industries, and strategic emerging industries. The industrial structure has been adjusted continuously and optimized. First, from 2007–2017, the high-tech and equipment manufacturing industries have been growing rapidly. Second, the level of informatization in the manufacturing industry has increased substantially, and significant progress has been made in the digitization, networking, and intelligence of key industries. Third, the integration and development trend of the producer service industry and the manufacturing industry began to appear and played a favorable supporting role in the transformation and upgrading of manufacturing.

2.2. *The Hoffman coefficient*

The Hoffman coefficient is defined as net output of consumer goods of industry to net output of capital goods of industry. Considering availability of data, we define

$$Hof = \frac{GO_{light}}{GO_{heavy}} \tag{4.2}$$

GO_{light}, GO_{heavy} — Gross output of light and heavy industry, respectively.

According to the Hoffman coefficient, the industrialization process can be divided into four stages (see Table 4.5). From Table 4.4, we observe that the Hoffman coefficient of the United States increased from 0.39 in 1977 to 0.46 in 1991, while the coefficient of Japan decreased from 0.34 in 1980 to 0.30 in 1991. This implies both countries are in stage IV.

Table 4.6 includes the gross output of China's industry and its composition in terms of light and heavy industry. The gross output of industry increases dramatically, especially after economic reform. Before economic reform, the development of heavy industry received priority; after economic reform, light industry developed first to meet the market demand and solve supply shortages. The relatively balanced development of light industry and heavy industry followed. The share of light industry increased from 43.1% in 1978, reached 49.4% in 1990, subsequently declined to 29.5% (2006) and 28.2% (2009). It then rose to 38.1% in 2015. Since the 18th National Congress of the Communist Party of China, President Xi Jinping has insisted on taking the new development concept as the guide. The consumption hotspots have been transformed from physical consumption that meets the people's material needs to services consumption that reflects the people's improved living conditions.

Table 4.5.   Four stages of industrialization.

Stage	I	II	III	IV
Hoffman	5±1	2.5±1	1±0.5	<1

Table 4.6. Gross output and composition of light and heavy industry in China, 1952–2015.

Year		1952	1957	1965	1978	1980	1990	1995	2006	2011	2018*
Gross output	100 mil. ¥RMB	349	704	1,402	4,237	5,154	23,924	91,894	316589	844269	1049490.3
Light Ind.	%share	64.5	55	51.6	43.1	47.2	49.4	47.3	29.5	28.2	19.1
	Using Farm Prod. as Raw Mater.				68.4	68.5	70.1	63.9		49.5	15.8
	Using nonFarm Prod. as Raw				31.6	31.5	29.9	36.1		50.5	3.2
Heavy Ind.		35.5	45	48.4	56.9	52.8	50.6	52.7	70.5	71.8	80.9
	Excavation				12	11.3	12.2	7.7		8.3	4.4
	Raw Materials				35.5	37.8	41	32.8		37.2	33.9
	Manufacturing				52.5	50.9	46.8	59.5		54.5	42.7
Indices total	Last yr = 100	129.9	111.5	126.4	113.5	109.3	107.8	120.3	125.8	110.9	92.6
	Light Industry	123.5	105.7	147.7	110.9	118.9	109.2	122.9	121.2		
	Heavy Industry	143.5	118.4	110.2	115.6	101.9	106.2	118	127.9		
Hofman coef.		1.8169	1.2222	1.0661	.7575	.8939	.9763	.8975	.4184	.3919	.2355

Note: *After 2011 China NBS did not announce Gross Output Value, we chose revenue from principal business in 2018.

Source: Calculated using data from the China National Bureau of Statistics: China Statistical Yearbook, China Statistics Press, 2016, Table 13.2; 2012, Table 14.2, 2007, Table 14.4; 2004, Table 14.3, 2003, Table 13.5; 2001, Table 13.5; 1996, Table 12.11; Compiled by the Department of Industry and Transport Statistics, China National Bureau of Statistics: China Industry Economy Statistical Yearbook, China Statistics Press, 2007, Tables 1.5, 2.6.

Figure 4.2 illustrates that China is in stage III of industrialization. In 1978, the Hoffman coefficient was equal to 0.7575, signifying the low percentage share of light industry that resulted in shortages of daily necessities.

In 2005, the coefficient was equal to 0.451; the supply of light industry products was larger than the demand. It further fell to 0.3919 in 2011, then rose to 0.5408 in 2015. Before reform, investment, annual industrial growth rate, and consumption were closely linked through the annual plan. They were synchronized with monetary policy through annual cash and credit plans. In the 1950s and 1960s, emphasis was placed on heavy industry. The share of heavy industry increased from 35.5% in 1952 to 56.9% in 1978, but shortages in the supply of consumer goods remained serious. In the late 1970s, light industry received more emphasis. However, consumption *continued* to be the residual factor and was purposely kept low to free resources for an ambitious investment plan.

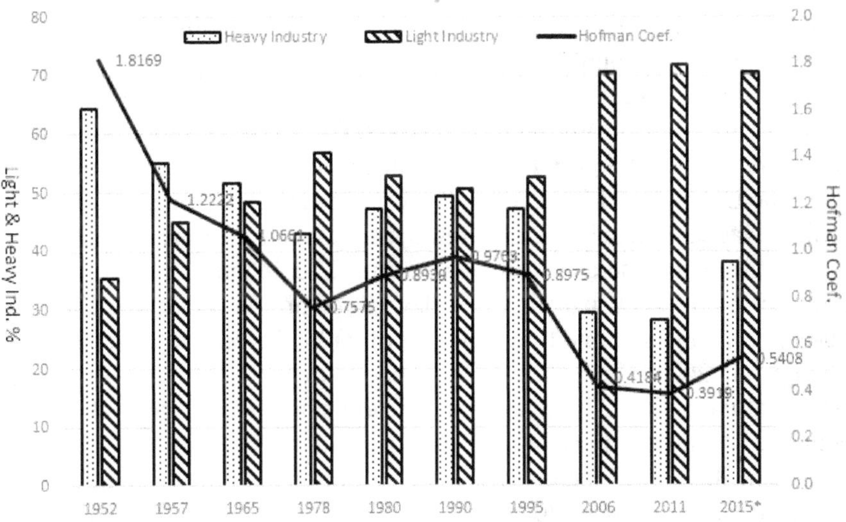

Figure 4.2.   Hoffman coefficient, China, 1952–2015.

Source: Calculated using data from the China National Bureau of Statistics: China Statistical Yearbook, China Statistics Press, 2016, Table 13.2; 2012, Table 14.2, 2007, Table 14.4; 2004, Table 14.3, 2003, Table 13.5; 2001, Table 13.5; 1996, Table 12.11; Compiled by the Department of Industry and Transport Statistics, China National Bureau of Statistics: China Industry Economy Statistical Yearbook, China Statistics Press, 2007, Tables 1.5, 2.6.

After reform, greater autonomy for enterprises meant diminished government control over wages and consumption funds. These funds increased dramatically, and consumer demand expanded. To solve supply shortages, light industry developed faster. In mid-1990s, supply grew significantly and there was a shift from a "seller's market" to a "buyer's market." Basic industry and infrastructure developed "bottle-necks," resulting in 30% of the processing industry capacity staying idle. Therefore, investment in infrastructure and basic industry was increased. Price policy also favored development of heavy industry. In the 1990s, there was no significant change in the proportion between heavy and light industry, and the share of heavy industry increased after 2000. The supply of high-quality and high value-added products increased, i.e., export Power Plant with 300 MW generating sets, 275 KVA electric transformer station, cement factory, etc. The China National Machinery and Equipment Import and Export Corp (CMEC) successfully exported Chinese-made 210- and 320-megawatt coal-fired generators, as well as a 36-megawatt gas turbine generator abroad with a combined installed capacity of 6,130 megawatts. CMEC set up and exported over 200 large and medium-sized equipment (Power Station, ships) and engineering projects (telecommunication projects) to about 60 countries and regions, with an accumulated value of USD30 billion.[2] The Teheran Metro was the biggest Chinese-made project in Iran. Under a USD403 million contract, China International Trust and Investment Corporation (CITIC) provided electrical and mechanical systems for Line 1 and Line 2 of the city's subway. In February 2000, the project was completed, making Iran the first country in the Middle East and Gulf area to operate a subway system. The Teheran subway is now transporting 700,000 passengers a day.[3] A giant crane that can lift two 40-foot containers at one time, the first of its kind worldwide, debuted in Shanghai in 2004. The machine was exported to the United Arab Emirates (UAE) at the end of 2004. The crane (world's largest and most advanced container-lifting machine) was designed and manufactured by Shanghai-based Zhenhua Port Machine Company (ZPMC). ZPMC occupied 66.6% of global market share in 2005.[4] ZPMC products are in use in 48 countries

---

[2] Wu, C., and X. Yang (2004). Generator exporter proud of rising worldwide fame, *China Daily*, May 28.

[3] Zhu, Y., and H. Wang (2004). China-made subway fulfills Iranian dream, *China Daily*, June 12.

[4] Tu, D. (2006). The secret of ZPMC rapid growth (in Chinese), *The Investors*, January. 5.

and regions, and over 80 terminals around the world. Light industry based on agriculture raw material declined from 68.4% in 1978 to 62.6% in 2002.[5] The structure of heavy industry was also adjusted. Excavation rose from 12% in 1978 to 12.2% in 1985, then declined to 8.7% in 2002. Manufacturing increased from 52.5% in 1978 to 59.5% in 1995, subsequently declining to 52.5% in 2002,[6] because the basic industry (energy, material) was strengthened after 1995 to solve the "bottleneck" problem.

We would expect light industrial growth to have been more demand determined since the inception of the reform program, and that the growth rate of heavy industry had been limited more by the investment than by market forces. Substantial initial investment is required in the cement, steel, fertilizers, petroleum, and chemical intermediates sectors. However, the price of output is low, and resource mobilization for investment is a problem. For light industry, before 1978, investment was a key determinant; but, after 1978, reforms turned many markets for light industry goods from a sellers' market to a buyers' market; therefore, demand became a more limiting factor than supply.

From Figure 4.2, we observe that the annual growth rate of heavy industry was always higher than the annual growth rate of light industry before economic reform, except in 1965. In 1965, light industry grew faster to overcome the supply shortages that appeared in conjunction with the "Great Leap Forward." This reflected the heavy-industry oriented policy before economic reform. After economic reform, and before 2000, the annual growth rate of heavy industry was always lower than the annual growth rate of light industry, which was determined by the market-oriented policy. It resulted in China becoming the "world's manufacturing center" of consumer goods. After 2000, the annual growth rate of heavy industry became higher than the annual growth rate of light industry. The Chinese economist Shinjin Liu[7] recognized that China entered a new development era — heavy-chemical industrialization, which was characterized by the high growth rate of machinery, automobile, steel, construction material, and chemical industry since the second half of 2002. The residential house

---

[5]Calculated using data from China National Bureau of Statistics (2003). China Statistical Yearbook, China Statistics Press, 2003, Table 13.5.

[6]Calculated using data from China National Bureau of Statistics: China Statistical Yearbook, China Statistics Press, Table 13.5.

[7]Liu, S. (2004). China is entering a new heavy-chemical industrialization (in Chinese), July 14. http://www1.cei.gov.cn/forum50/doc/50cyfx/200407270244.htm.

and sedan became new consumption hotspots, representing an upgrade in the structure of consumption. International experience tells us that such new consumption hotspots can continue for 2–3 decades. This is obviously a very different scenario from the years of heavy-industry-oriented policy before economic reform. However, another famous Chinese economist, Jinglian Wu,[8] disagrees with this viewpoint. According to Wu, the Hoffman analysis is not appropriate for describing China's situation. Unilateral heavy-chemical industrialization results in extensive economic development mode. Under such a mode, output growth mainly depends on increased input. Therefore, such an economic growth mode results in material and energy waste, low efficiency, and environmental pollution. China is a poor per capita natural resource country. In 2004, China produced 274 million tons of steel and imported 209 million tons of iron ore, exceeding Japan's imports (133 million tons) and became the top importing country.[9] China imported 122.7 million tons of crude oil, up 34.8% year on year, and 37.9 million tons of refined oil, up 34.1%.[10] Shenzhen is an information port, but also developed the automobile and chemical industries. Zhejiang is a province with the best growth economy by developing many of the best SMEs. Nevertheless, Zhejiang has been transforming into a heavy-chemical industrialization region, resulting in serious electricity shortages — with electricity being supplied for 4 days, and being cut off the other three days each week in 2004. China installed an electricity generating capacity of 400 million kw, making it the world's second largest power generation giant after the United States.[11] Japan's installed generating capacity totals only 280 million kw,[12] but creates two

---

[8] Wu, J. (2004). The danger of Chinese economy due to unilateral heavy-chemical industrialization, (in Chinese), *Beijing Morning Post*, November 23.

[9] www.cei.gov.cn/LoadPage.aspx?Page=ShowDoc&CategoryAlias=zonghe/jjsj&Product Alias=shuzkx&PAlias=shuzkx&BlockAlias=DBdwmy&filename=/doc/DBdwmy/200501240234.xml.

[10] Li, D. (Commissioner of National Bureau of Statistics of China, 2005). Extensive mode growth mode cannot be pleased with oneself, (in Chinese), *Nanfang Daily*, January 26, p. A13.

[11] China becomes the world's second largest power generation giant http://english.people.com.cn//200411/09/eng20041109_163281.html.

[12] Li, D. (2005). Extensive growth mode cannot be pleased with oneself, *Nanfang Daily*, January 26, p. A13, (in Chinese).

times more GDP than China.[13] Heavy-chemical industrialization was the chief offender of energy and transportation capacity supply shortages in China in 2003 and 2004. In addition, when GDP grows 1%, heavy industry will generate much less employment opportunities than other sectors.

For long-term sustainable, coordinated economic development, China should transform its economic growth mode from extensive mode to intensive mode. In the intensive mode, output growth depends mainly on innovation, high tech, and readjustment of economic structure; therefore, such an economic growth mode results in material and energy saving, high efficiency, and environment protection. Of course, unilateral heavy-chemical industrialization is promoted by local government policy because the development of real estate, automobile industry and related raw materials, and energy industry can produce high growth rate of GDP and revenues for local government. Using such an economic growth mode is certainly much easier than promoting the intensive mode. Therefore, instead of GDP, using "Green GDP" as the measure of economic development is badly needed for China. China should implement a new type of industrialization based on the intensive growth mode. "It is China's pressing task to promote its recycling industry to ease the resources bottlenecks, reduce pollution, improve the country's economic efficiency" said Mr. Ma Kai, head of the National Development and Reform Commission. A top priority is the drafting of regulations on the comprehensive use of resources, recycling of used appliance and electronic products, recycling and reuse of tires and packaging materials. Each province should convert to intensive growth mode considering local natural resources, human resources, and local comparative advantage. Large amounts of new technology, new energy sources, new material, and new products emerged because of wide application of high tech and appropriate technology; efficiency will follow. The rapid development of the service industry — especially service industry related with production — will greatly lower production and transaction costs; extensively using IT technology will further decrease the manufacturing costs — especially transaction costs — and result in high economic performance.[14] This new industrialization road using the intensive mode will result in resource-saving and a high-efficiency economy.

---

[13] World Bank (2004). World Bank: World Development Indicators.

[14] Wu, J. (2005). Three big knowledge outcomes obtained from macro control economy, *International Finance News*, February 17, p. 2, (in Chinese).

The share of China's manufacturing industry in the world continues to expand. In 1990, China's manufacturing industry accounted for 2.7% of the world's total, ranking ninth in the world; in 2000, it rose to 6.0%, ranking fourth; in 2007, it reached 13.2%, ranking second; in 2010, the proportion increased further to 19.8%, ranking first in the world. Since then, it has ranked first in the world for many years. In 2017, China's new energy vehicle production reached 690,000 units, ranking first in the world for three consecutive years. China has become the world's largest power battery producer. The export of new energy buses has reached more than 30 countries and regions; Civilian drones and Industrial robots maintained rapid growth. In 2017, the output of the products reached 2.9 million units and 130,000 units (sets), respectively; the production scale of all links in the photovoltaic industry chain accounted for more than 50%. From 2015–2017, China's foreign investment in equipment manufacturing industry was USD35.1 billion, accounting for 51.6% of foreign investment in bright national business cards such as China's high-speed rail and China's nuclear power.[15]

3. Improvement of Infrastructure

Infrastructure construction will remain a key ingredient to maintaining economic development, as illustrated by the effect of the construction of new highways and railway networks, and power-generating facilities made during the 1990s. In the 1980s, even in China's largest city — Shanghai — the shortage of electricity was serious. The off day of the factories was optional to allow enough factories to utilize electricity. For residential usage, electricity supply was paused in several areas. The infrastructure was greatly improved in the 2000s. Figure 4.3 shows that the supply of electricity greatly improved, and transportation capacity increased considerably in China from 1985–2017. The posts and telecommunication equipment and technology have reached world standards; the number of mobile phone subscribers was first in the world, as shown in Figure 4.4. It also

---

[15]Department of Industrial Statistics, China National Bureau of Statistics: Reform and opening-up casts industrial glory, innovation and transformation, and strong manufacturing power, 2018-09-04 (in Chinese); Department of Foreign Trade and Economics, China National Bureau of Statistics: The level of opening up to foreign trade and economic development has been comprehensively improved, 2018-08-30 (in Chinese).

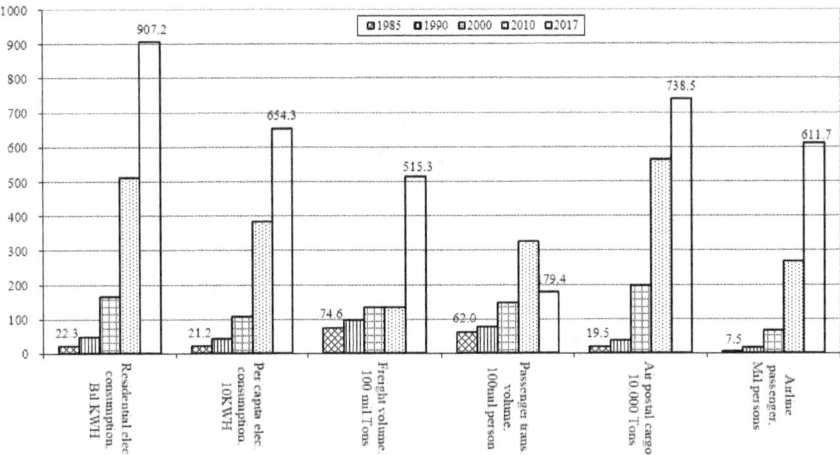

Figure 4.3.   Energy and transportation in China, 1985–2017.

Source: Calculated using data from the China National Bureau of Statistics: China Statistical Yearbook, China Statistics Press, 2019, Tables 9.12. 9.13, 16.2; 2012, Tables 7.12, 7.13, 16.2; 2006, Tables 2.3, 2.6, 7.6; 2002, Tables 2.6, 7.12; 2001, Table 2.3; 1996; 1991; Statistical Yearbook of China 1986, Compiled by the State Statistical Bureau of China, Oxford University Press, 1986.

shows distinct improvement in city infrastructure facilities. The Chinese government gradually opened the long-state-monopolized public service businesses to private funds to improve their efficiency. Monopolies and lack of policy transparency in old public service sectors caused low efficiency, misuse of government power, and even corruption. The government expects market competition to improve the efficiency and quality of the services including heating, water supply, energy supply, sewage, and rubbish treatment, which are vital to citizens' daily lives. The country has restructured its power grids nationwide while it has welcomed foreign and domestic companies to invest in power plants and heating plants,[16] and containerized cargo.[17]

---

[16]Private capital dabbles in public service sector, Xinhua, June 12, 2004, www.chinadaily. com.cn/english/doc/2004-06/12/content_338898.htm.

[17]"Review of Maritime Transport" – UN Conference on Trade & Development, 2004 and 2005.

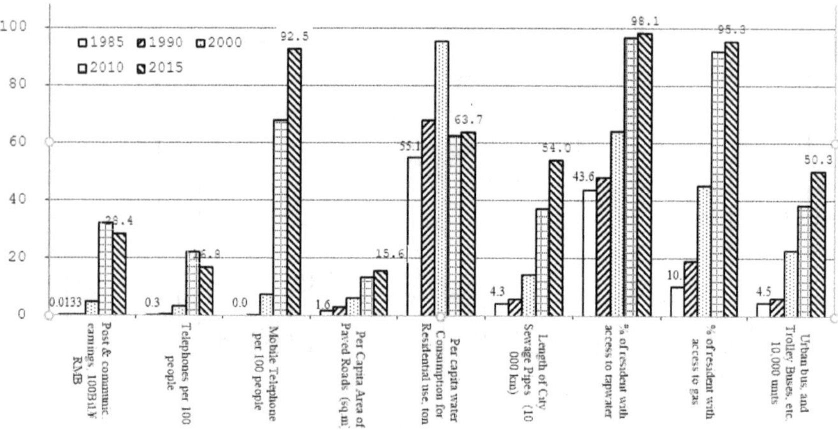

Figure 4.4.   Communication and city infrastructure, China.

Source: Calculated using data from the China National Bureau of Statistics: China Statistical Yearbook, China Statistics Press, 2016, Tables 16.31, 16.35, 20.2; 2012, Table 16.35; 2011, Table 11.5; 2006, Tables 2.3, 4.1, 11.3, 11.5, 11.11; 1996; 1991; Statistical Yearbook of China 1986, Compiled by the State Statistical Bureau of China, Oxford University Press, 1986.

The problem for China is that virtually none of these containers travel any distance from the main coastal ports and foreign investors will continue to hesitate before extending their supply chains further inland until they do. Better physical infrastructure is part of the solution, but a greater role for advanced logistics providers with extensive experience in managing intermodal cargo flows is also critical.

With challenges ahead for the long-haul trucking industry and rail not yet ready to meet growing demand, efforts to expand container on-barge service along the Yangtze comes into sharper focus. At the start of 2006, approximately 35 major barge companies were providing container service to more than 20 Yangtze ports (including Shanghai, Nantong, Zhenjiang, Nanjing, Wuhe, Jiujiang, Wuhan, Yichang, Wanzhou, and Chongqing) extending 2,400 km (1,500 miles) upstream from Shanghai. The advantages of shipping containers by Yangtze barge have been obvious since the first container was transported in 1986. Two major developments along the river are serving as major catalysts for containerization of the Yangtze — the completion of the Three Gorges Dam project and the opening of the Yangshan Port Complex off Shanghai in December 2005.

A two-way, five-stage ship-lock opened in July 2004, permitting loaded barges up to 10,000 deadweight tons (DWT) to pass within three Gorges. In 2005, more than 2.6 million TEUs were moved by barge on the Yangtze, a 44% increase over 2004. In 2006, the container traffic reached 3.1 million TEUs.[18] As of mid-2006, the cost of shipping a 20 ft. container the 2,400 km (1,500 miles) from Chongqing to Shanghai was approximately CNY2,500 (USD315), including port fees. The voyage takes eight days moving downstream and 12–13 days moving up. Moving a container by road to Shanghai takes just 3 to 4 days, but the cost will be at least four to five times as much to transport 10 tons of freight. Improved rail service has brought the cost of moving containers to less than double that of river transport. In 2016, seven of the world's top ten container terminals were in China: Shanghai, Shenzhen, Ningbo, Hong Kong, Guangzhou, Qingdao, and Tianjin. With a total throughput of 150 million TEUs, Shanghai ranked first with a throughput of 37 million TEUs.[19]

4. Unreasonable Industrial Structure

For most industrial products in China, supply is larger than demand. During 1990–2005, the annual growth rate of urban residents' income was 7.76%, but only 4.75% for rural residents.[20] However, industrial gross output annual growth rate reached 18.0%.[21] The production capacity of marketable products increased and generated a surplus, i.e., the production capacity of color TVs in 2002 reached 86.61 million sets, but demand was only 20 million sets for the domestic market and 31.65 million sets

---

[18]Deloitte & Touche USA LLP (2006). Chinese Services Group: The Yangtze River Transport Corridor, July.

[19]"Review of Maritime Transport 2017" – UN Conference on Trade & Development, UNCTAD/RMT/2017, United Nations Publication.

[20]Calculated using data from the China National Bureau of Statistics. China Statistical Yearbook, China Statistics Press, 2006, Table 10.2.

[21]Calculated using data from the China National Bureau of Statistics: China Industry Economy Statistical Yearbook, China Statistics Press, 2003, Table 2.6; China National Bureau of Statistics: China Statistical Yearbook, China Statistics Press, 2005, Table 2.3; 2004, Table 2.3; National Bureau of Statistics of China: Statistical Communiqué on the 2005 National Economic and Social Development, March 3, 2006.

for export.[22] The production of color TV sets from January to September 2006 reached 61.496 million sets. Only 29.069 million sets were supplied to the domestic market and 32.226 million sets were exported. During January to September 2006, the revenue of China's 13 major color TV enterprises reached CNY88 billion (USD11.13 billion) with a 5.7% increase over the same period the previous year, and profit was only CNY1.46 billion (USD184.6 million). Profit was only 1.3% of revenue for domestic enterprises and 2.9% for joint ventures.[23] All durable and daily consumer goods show supply surpluses. The survey of more than 600 commodities from the Ministry of Domestic Trade is represented in Figure 3.22. The detailed information of supply and demand of the surveyed 609 commodities during July–December in 2000[24] identified 394 industrial goods among surveyed 444 industrial goods, whose supply was larger than demand; not even one industrial good was in short supply. Goods in 22 categories were in surplus of supply, including candy, alcoholic beverage and non-staple food, textile goods, daily general merchandise, articles for cultural usage and stationery, household electrical appliances, agriculture fertilizer, cooking apparatus, ironware goods, and so on. The excess of supply over demand for these goods existed mainly because of duplication of production. Among 111 farm and sideline products, only three were in short supply. They are fox fur and two kinds of marten fur. There were nine goods in shortage of supply among 22 recyclable goods. They are scrap steel, scrap tin, remnant steel, scrap white iron, scrap gray iron, wasted paper, human hair, and pressed lump of cutting iron fragment. These goods that are in short supply have little effect on market supply and demand because they are used, second-hand goods with limited production scale and with high fluctuations.

Comparing the survey conducted in 2000 with the same survey of 600 commodities conducted in 2005, we find that the percentage share of goods showing greater supply than demand decreased from 88.7% to

---

[22]Calculated using data from the China National Bureau of Statistics. China Statistical Yearbook, China Statistics Press, 2003 Tables 2.3, 13.24, 17.4.

[23]Sun, P. (2006). China Color TV enterprises facing transition period need to be cautious, *China's Information Newspaper*, November 6.

[24]Data from the Department of Market Operation Regulation, Ministry of Commerce of China(2005). Supply and demand analysis of 600 main commodities during the first half year of 2005 (in Chinese), March 22. http://scyxs.mofcom.gov.cn/aarticl e/c/200503/20050300028118.html.

83.0% for industrial products, from 56.8% to 31.5% for farm and sideline products. There were no goods in shortage of supply in 2005. Since the second half of 2002, five consecutive surveys have indicated that the percentage share of goods whose supply is larger than demand fluctuated within a small range, but no commodities were in shortage of supply. The supply surplus of many commodities was mainly because of duplication of production, upgraded consumption structure, or low quality of products. Before 1996, the shortage of supply was mainly because of the lack of sufficient production capability.

Most goods have been in state of excess supply; therefore, the utilization rate of existing production capacity is low. 94 industrial products were investigated in the third industry survey (1995), with the utilization rate of their existing production capacity shown in Table 4.7. The utilization rate of existing production capacity in 1996 is listed in Table 4.8. According to Table 4.8, almost two-thirds of the products have idle production capability. For example, in 1990–1995, the fabrics sector had the lowest annual growth rate; in 1995, its output was 26.68 billion meters, 6.36 billion meters for export, 11.2 billion meters for garments, remain 9.12 billion meters, averaging 7.5 meters per capita, for real consumption; however, it was only 2.3 meters per farmer, far below the 6.04 meters per capita in 1978. The Inventory of SOEs in 1996 amounted to CNY400 billion (5% of GDP). The bicycle inventory was larger than 20 million sets (60% of the 1996 output). The inventory of all state-owned and non-state-owned above designed size industrial enterprises reached CNY1,603 billion in 2000,[25] increasing by 6.5% over the previous year, during which CNY885 billion belonged to light industry products. The inventory of

Table 4.7.   Utilization rate of existing production capacity in China, 1995.

Utilization rate	≫80%	60–80%	40–60%	≪40%
No. of product	32	37	31	11
Utilization rate(%)	28.83%	33.33%	27.93%	9.91%

Source: Data from the China National Bureau of Statistics. China Statistical Yearbook, China Statistics Press, 1997, Table 12.22, (only the 1997 China Statistical Yearbook publish utilization rate of existing production capacity).

---

[25] Data from the China National Bureau of Statistics. China Economic Industrial Statistical Yearbook, China Statistics Press, 2001, p. 50.

Table 4.8.   Utilization rate of existing production capacity in China (1996).

Production Capacity	Utiliza-tion. Rate
Ethylene (93.3), converter steel (92.4), steel sheet (92), open-hearth steel (90.1)	>0.9
Crude copper smelting (88.2), iron-smelting (88), caustic soda (86.1), plate glass (85)	>0.8
Beer (73.5), cement (72.9), chemical fertilizer (72.6), oil distillation equipment (70.2)	>0.7
Fiberboard (65.2), hot-rolling steel (63.7)	>0.6
Oil hydro fining equipment (59.4), tire (54.7), bicycle (54.5), household refrigerators (50.4)	>0.5
Metal-cutting machine (46.2), color TV set (46.1), motor vehicle (44.3), milk powder (44.1), internal combustion engine (43.9), household washing machine (43.4), dust catcher (43.2), soap (42.2), sawn wood (41.4), video recorder (40.3), smoke absorber (40.2)	>0.4
Chinese patent medicine (34.3), duplicator (34), household air conditioner (33.5)	>0.3
Mica (raw material) (29.6), refractory material products (26.2), printed and dyed fabric (23.6), color photograph film (22.1)	>0.2
Cam recorder (12.3)	>0.1

Source: Calculated using data from the China National Bureau of Statistics: China Statistical Yearbook, China Statistics Press, 2016, Table 13.2; 2012, Table 14.2, 2007, Table 14.4; 2004, Table 14.3, 2003, Table 13.5; 2001, Table 13.5; 1996, Table 12.11; Compiled by the Department of Industry and Transport Statistics, China National Bureau of Statistics: China Industry Economy Statistical Yearbook, China Statistics Press, 2007, Tables 1.5, 2.6.

transport equipment manufacturing, electronic and telecommunications manufacturing, equipment electric equipment and machinery manufacturing, smelting, and pressing of ferrous metals, and textile industry became larger than CNY100 billion.

Comparison of the production capacity of major industrial products of key industry enterprises with real output in 2001 and 2000 is shown in Table 4.9. The table reveals that the real output of many products is even less than the production capacity of major industrial products of key industry enterprises, i.e. the output of color television sets was only 52.9% and 47.3% of production capacity of key industry enterprises in 2000 and 2001, respectively; for personal computers, it was only 58.3% and 46.2% in 2000 and 2001, respectively; for motor vehicles, 77.6% and 62.6% in

Table 4.9. Production capacity of major industrial products of key industry enterprises (2000 and 2001) compared with real output.

Item	2000		2001	
	Production Capacity	Real output	Production Capacity	Real output
Color television (10,000 units)	7447.0	3936.0	8661	4093.7
Personal computers (10,000 units)	1153.0	672.0	1901	877.65
Motor vehicles (10,000 units)	266.8	207.0	374.1	234.17
Cement (10,000 tons)	71827.1	59700.0	73183.3	66104
Cigarettes (10,000 cases)	3807.3	3397.0	4437.8	3402.1
Plate glass (10,000 weight cases)	20453.9	18352.0	23480.6	20964.1
Chemical fiber (10,000 tons)	773.2	694.0	978.8	841.38
Synthetic rubber (10,000 tons)	90.2	86.5	97.2	121.98
Pure benzene (10,000 tons)	173.7	184.7	185.02	
Chemical medicine (10,000 tons)	49.0	52.6	48	76.22
Ethene (10,000 tons)	415.2	470.0	445	
Pig iron (10,000 tons)	11171.4	13101.0	12193.4	15554.3
Plastics (10,000 tons)	667.3	1087.5		1288.71
Timber (10,000 cu.m)	2589.0	4724.0	2369	4552.03

Source: Data from the China National Bureau of Statistics: China Statistical Yearbook, China Statistics Press, 2003, Tables 13.22, 13.23, 13.24; 2002, Tables 13.22, 13.23, 13.24; China Economic Industrial Statistical Yearbook, China Statistics Press, 2001, pp. 25–46, 104.

2000 and 2001, respectively; and, for household washing machines only 58.4% in 1999. These comparisons mean some medium and small enterprises in these industrial sectors did not produce any output; the utilization rate of key industry enterprises was still quite low.

Some products listed in Table 4.9 had actual output larger than the production capacity of key industry enterprises, i.e., the real outputs of timer, pig iron, and chemical medicine (including 24 categories) equaled 192.2%, 127.6%, and 158.8% production capacity of key industry enterprises in 2001, respectively. All these products belong to the raw materials category. Their real output increased significantly in 2001 because of the large amount of investment. This also implies these raw materials were produced by medium and small enterprises. Usually, such products belong to labor-intensive industries. In general, the utilization rate of production capacity for final products has been low in China because supply has been larger than demand for most products. In recent years, the new projects put into operation in some industrial sectors experienced larger supply than demand because of overcapacity (see Table 4.10). For example, in 2004, the utilization rate of the automobile industry was only 58.5%, which does not include the 2.2 million unit's production capacity under construction and the 8 million unit's production capacity already proposed and planned to be constructed. If all these 10.2 million units production capacity are built, automobile production capacity will increase 117.4%. Auto sales amounted to 5.07 million units in 2004, with year-on-year increase of 15.5%, and further increased by 13.5% to 5.76 million units in 2005.[26] In terms of production capacity, during the period of 2011–2015, China's new automobile production capacity increased by 10.87 million units; by the end of 2015, production capacity was 31.22 million units, and the new production capacity in 2016–2017 was about six million units. In the second half of 2016, the NDRC included the automotive industry in the overheated industry. It was transferred to the list of surplus industries in 2018. Overcapacity also exists in ferrous metals, electrolytic aluminum, calcium carbide, and cement. Potential for overcapacity is also observed in electricity supply, coal, and textile industrial sectors.

With the rapid development of the domestic economy, from consumer products to industrial products, from traditional industries to emerging industries, the scope of overcapacity has been expanding and deepening. China has entered a period of overcapacity since 2009. Since the second half of 2008, the global financial crisis gradually spread. At the time, China experienced eight years of foreign trade glory after accession to the WTO, and its domestic production capacity became heavily dependent on the outside world. The shrinking of exports because of the crisis led to a resurgence of overcapacity in domestic manufacturing.

At the same time, the collapse of U.S. real estate led to a temporary decline in domestic real estate development, which also caused a sharp drop in demand for steel, cement, building materials, and other industries, thereby bringing tremendous pressure on related production capacity.

---

[26]China Association of Automobile Manufacturers (2005). Automobile sales in December, (in Chinese), www.caam.org.cn/hytj/zsfx/67.htm, 2014, (8), pp. 88–90, 2014/5/16 (in Chinese); The situation of overcapacity industry in 2017 and the prospect of 2018, 2017-12-28 (in Chinese), www.sohu.com/a/213414215_99903716.

Table 4.10.　Utilization rate of existing production capacity in China.

0	Year	Production capacity	Utilization rate%	Planning capacity
Crude steel, million tons	2015	1200	66.7	Plan to cut 100–150 million tons in 5 years.
Stainless steel plate, million tons	2012	8.69	45	
Coal, million tons	2016	3920	87.0	Exit 290 mil. ton (plan 250 mil. ton).
Coal, million tons	2012	3950	94.2	
Cement	2016	3195	82.7	Since the implementation of supply-side reforms, cement production in 2015 has fallen by 132 mil. tons from 2014.
Plate glass, mil. weight boxes	2015	1160	62.0	In 2013–2016, the domestic cumulative capacity was compressed by 113 million weight boxes.
Commercial vehicle, mil. units	2015	5.47	52.0	Commercial vehicles, independent brands, competitive pressure, overcapacity.
Synthetic ammonia, million tons	2012	72	0.0	
Phosphate fertilize, million tons	2012	23.6	0.0	
Polyvinyl chloride, million tons	2012	23.6	59.9	
Electrolytic aluminum, million tons	2012	27.65	72.0	
Polysilicon industry, million tons	2012	19	33.7	2012 imported 82,000 tons of polysilicon products in 2012, a significant increase of 28% compared with 2011.

Source: Xue, D. H. Analysis of the current situation of overcapacity development in China's industrial sector, *China Management Informationization*.

To effectively cope with the financial crisis and to ensure economic growth, the government quickly introduced the "4 trillion" investment plan, the "top 10 industries" revitalization plan and a loose fiscal policy. Under government intervention, domestic demand quickly improved, and corporate expectations were upgraded, leading to a new round of blind investment, while the more serious overcapacity has buried hidden dangers. In 2016, Ma Yun, chairman of the board of directors of Alibaba Group, believed, on the one hand, there was excess capacity and insufficient supply. To promote supply-side reform, China must firmly grasp three major factors: consumption, service, and high technology. "The brand represents quality." Miao Wei, Minister of the Ministry of Industry and Information Technology, stated that China will implement a three-year action plan in the consumer goods industry to foster Chinese companies' creation of brands, improve quality, increase varieties, and guide enterprises to accelerate the adaptation to market demand changes with the "three-product strategy" to meet the needs of the masses.[27]

The consumption hotspots have been transformed from the physical aspect of consumption that meets the people's material needs to the service aspect, such as cultural entertainment, leisure tourism, mass catering, education and training, medical and health care, health and wellness that have become the new consumption hotspots; the consumption experience has developed rapidly. That reflects the people's better living needs. The consumption structure has been optimized and adjusted, and new industries have emerged. The supply side has gradually improved, and consumption has become the first driving force for economic growth. In line with the work related to China International Import Expo, and timely and accurately grasp of the supply and demand of major consumer goods, the Ministry of Commerce conducted a statistical survey on supply and demand conditions of 10 major categories of consumer goods, such as food, clothing, shoes, and hats from March to May 2019. Among them, enterprises (mainly based on physical stores) reported the results of a survey of the supply status of major consumer goods, while consumers responded on the demand status of major consumer goods. Survey results

---

[27]Yu, J., Y. Wu, and B. Lin (2016). The trick behind the de-capacity: China's 220 production of industrial products ranked first in the world. Xinhua News Agency, March 4 (in Chinese); Xue, D. H. (2014). Analysis of the current situation of overcapacity development in China's industrial sector, *China Management Informationization*, (8), 88–90, 2014/5/16 (in Chinese).

showed that the supply of consumer goods is mainly domestic, and the import demand of consumers is strong. The import of consumer goods is more concerned with brand, safety, and design. The supply the company intends to increase is matched with the demand of consumers. Chinese Minister of Commerce Zhong Shan said on March 9, 2019, that the structure of China's consumption has kept improving. The quality of consumption has also become better with personalized, diversified, and customized consumption burgeoning. In 2018, the increment of China's total retail sales amounted to CNY3.2 trillion (about USD476 billion), equivalent to the annual retail sales in 1998. China is already a major consumption power, Zhong said.[28]

5. Unreasonable Product Structure

The share of low value-added, primary processing products is high, i.e., digital control machine tools occupy 90% in the international market, but only 10% in China. Imports of digital control machine tools reached USD2 billion per annum. The gain of foreign exchange through Chinese machine tool exports is low. Obsolete machinery products became main obstacles in the production equipment market. The average machinery life cycle in China approximates 10 and half years, but it is only three years in the United States. This indicates fewer new products are re-supplied to the market. In 2005, import machinery and transport equipment amounted to USD268.3 billion, which occupied 31.4% of sales revenue of China's domestic machinery products or 33.7% market share (see Table 4.11[29]).

---

[28]Lu, H. and B. Lin (2019). China's consumption structure keeps improving: MOC.; Ministry of Commerce issued statistical investigation and analysis report on supply and demand of major consumer goods. Xinhua News Agency. *Source*: Department of market operation and consumption promotion of Ministry of Commerce (National Cocoon and silk Coordination Office) July 18 (in Chinese).

[29]Calculated using data from the China National Bureau of Statistics: China Statistical Yearbook, China Statistics Press, 2006, Tables 11.3, 11.4, 17.2; 2006, Tables 14.3, 14.4, 18.5, 18.6; 2003, Tables 13.5, 17.4, 17.5; 2001, Tables 13.5, 17.4, 17.5; 2000, Tables 13.6, 17.4, 17.5; 1999, Tables 13.6, 17.4, 17.5; 1998; 1997; 1996; 1991; Statistical Yearbook of China, 1986, compiled by the State Statistical Bureau of China, Oxford University Press, 1986; Statistical Yearbook of China 1981 (English Edition), Compiled by the State Statistical Bureau, PRC. Published by Economic Information & Agency, Hong Kong, October 1982.

Table 4.11.   Domestic market share of Chinese machinery industry, 1980–2015.

100 Mil.	1980	1985	1990	1995
Sales revenue, RMB	1,273.6	1,918.6	3,379.2	11,442.2
Export	USD5.42	7.72	55.88	314.07
Import	USD39.99	162.39	168.45	526.42
Domestic demand	1,325.1	2,372.8	3,917.7	13,215.5
Import dependence	4.5%	20.1%	20.6%	33.3%
Domestic market self-fulfill rate	95.5%	79.9%	79.4%	66.7%
100 mil.	2000	2005	2010	2018
Sales revenue, RMB	22812.9328	74,636.3	2,20,109.1	10,49,490.5
Export	USD826.0	3,522.3	7,129.2	24,866.8
Import	USD919.3	2,904.8	9,623.9	21,357.3
Domestic demand	23586.454038	69,652.5	2,36,997.5	10,26,243.0
Import dependence	32.3%	33.7%	27.5%	13.7%
Domestic market self-fulfill rate	67.7%	66.3%	72.5%	86.3%

Imported machinery and transport equipment accounted for only 4.7% of sales revenue and 4.5% market share of China's domestic machinery products in 1980. Table 4.11 also shows that China's imports of machinery and transport equipment is always larger than exports (except for 2005). The import dependence and domestic market self-fulfill rate are depicted by Eqs. (2.1) and (4.3):

$$SFR = \frac{DO - EXP}{DO - EXP + IMP} \tag{4.3}$$

where DO — domestic output; IMP — import; EXP — export.

Import dependence increased form 4.5% in 1980 to 33.7% in 2005 and domestic market self-fulfill rate declined from 95.5% in 1980 to 66.3% in 2005. This implies that China cannot produce enough technology-intensive equipment. In 2003, the domestic demand of the machine tool industry exceeded USD6.7 billion, ranking first in the world. It is by 75% more than the second — the United States. However, imports of machine tools reached more than USD4 billion. 75% to 100% of numerical controlled machine tools are used by aviation and aerospace, automobile, power generating equipment manufacturing, and shipbuilding. The domestic market self-fulfill rate of the machine tool industry is 86% in Japan, 67% in Italy, and 59% in Germany. From 2010– 2015, the average annual growth rate of exports and imports was 24.9% and 4.6%, respectively, and the domestic market self-fulfill rate rose to 73.7%. Hence, China's manufacturing structure upgrade achieved initial results. This was also demonstrated by the 2014 Competitive Industrial Performance (CIP) Report issued by the United Nations Industrial Development Organization (UNIDO). According to the 2014 CIP index, China ranked 5th out of 147 economies, second only to Germany, Japan, United States of America, and Republic of Korea. In the 1990, 1995, 2000, 2005, and 2010 CIP index, China ranked 32nd, 27th, 22nd, 19th, and 10th, respectively. This shows that from 1990–2012, China's CIP index *continued* to improve. As a manufacturing powerhouse, among the more than 500 major industrial products, China has more than 220 product outputs ranked first in the world. However, among the top 100 brands in the world, only Huawei and Lenovo are shortlisted in China. Adherence to the supply side structural reform as the main line, and continuous promotion of the quality transformation, efficiency reform, and dynamic change of economic development indicates the development of the industrial economy has expanded from quantity to quality.[30]

5.1. *Backward technical structure*

Contribution of science and technology to annual growth rate in the USA is 47.7%, Japan 55%, Germany 55.6%, the Republic of Korea 38.8%, and China only 28.7%. Per unit GDP raw material consumption is high. Table 4.12[31] lists the GDP per unit of energy use per kg of oil equivalent, CO_2 emissions per unit GDP and China's high-technology exports compared with those of selected foreign countries. China produced only 22.8%, 41.4%, and 55.0% GDP by unit energy consumption in 1992, 2007, and 2014, respectively. China's energy efficiency is also much

---

[30]Upadhyaya, S., and S. M. Yeganeh (2014). Competitive Industrial Performance Report 2014-Research, Statistics and Industrial Policy Branch, Working Paper 12/2014, UNIDO, United Nations Industrial Development Organization.

[31]Wu, Y., and B. Lin (2016). The trick behind the de-capacity: China's 220 production of industrial products ranked first in the world, March 4, (in Chinese).

Table 4.12.   Compare GDP per unit of energy use per kg of oil equivalent and high technology exports.

	GDP per unit of energy use (2011 PPP USD per kg of oil equivalent)				CO2 emissions (kg per 2011 PPP USD of GDP)*				High-technology exports (billion current USD)			
Country	1992	2007	2014	2017	1992	2007	2014	2017	1992	2007	2014	2017
Brazil	7.07	10.77	10.35		0.22	0.14	0.17		1.10		8.23	10.76
China	2.51	4.46	5.70		1.17	0.73	0.59		4.09	342.61	558.60	654.19
Germany	5.26	7.61	11.53	10.1	0.5	0.24	0.20		44.76	169.89	199.72	196.32
India	3.90	5.28	8.45	7.93	0.50	0.31	0.32		0.33		17.32	15.16
Japan	6.59	8.82	10.76	9.15	0.36	0.26	0.31		77.21	128.73	105.08	106.42
Korea, R.	4.35	5.51	6.32	6.14	0.6	0.35	0.35		13.89	106.54	133.45	166.58
Russian	1.59	3.37	5.20	4.89	1.61	0.46	0.46		0.00	4.37	9.84	9.93
USA	3.71	4.75	7.46	6.56	0.66	0.39	0.32		117.28	244.48	155.64	156.94
World	3.94	5.6	7.90	5.69	0.61	0.34	0.34				2146.09	

Note: Blanks in Tables indicate WDI does not provide these values.

Source: World Bank (2006). World Development Indicators online 2006, released April. World Bank (2020). World Development Indicators online 2020, released April 9.

worse than that for the Republic of Korea, Japan, Germany, India, and the World average. CO_2 is mainly discharged from fossil fuel consumption and cement production. There is a close correlation between CO_2 and temperature variation in the planet's history. The recent CO_2 concentration level of 375 ppm is much higher than any value in the previous 450,000 years, and the rate of increase of CO_2 with time is about 100 times higher than any other rate of increase in recorded history.

The greenhouse effect and the related global warming issue are well-known scientific facts established a century ago by Arrhenius. The temperature increase per ppm CO_2 increase is 0.066 °C/ppm. Therefore, reducing CO_2 emission is very important for the protection of the environment. From Table 4.12, we find that the CO_2 emissions per unit of GDP (in 2011 PPPUSD) in China are also higher than that of other countries. Compared to Brazil's CO_2 emissions per unit GDP, China's CO_2 emissions per unit of GDP in 1992, 2007, and 2014 were 880.0%, 512.6%, and 351.2%, respectively. In current USD, high technology exports accounted for 140.1% of the United States in 2007, it increased to 364.8% in 2014 and further increased to 416.8% in 2017. However, in 2005, 89.6% of that was exported by FFEs,[32] i.e., China enterprises only exported USD22.3 billion. In 2017, 25% of China's high-tech enterprises were foreign-invested enterprises, with output value accounting for 50% and exports accounting for 80%.[33] Steel consumption is 5.8-fold of the United States and 2.7-fold of Japan. In Table 4.13,[34] the specific energy consumption of some major industrial products in China, expressed in SCE (standard coal equivalent) per unit industrial product, is compared with world average consumption. It shows that energy consumption per unit industrial products in China was almost 50% higher than the world average in 1997. Continuously rapid growth of energy-intensive industries, like steel and cement, driven by large-scale construction, and the fast increase of vehicle and electric appliances in recent years, resulted in serious growth of electricity demand. Therefore, energy saving became a key factor in

---

[32]Ministry of Commerce: Foreign Investment Report 2006, Chapter Eight-The export and import status of China's FFEs (in Chinese), December 9, 2006; Xinhua News Agency: Nearly 90 pct of Chinas electronic exports are from foreign ventures (in Chinese), April 15, 2006.

[33]Ministry of Commerce (2018). Foreign Investment Report 2018, Chapter one (in Chinese).

[34]See Table 4.13 for source.

Table 4.13.   Energy consumption per unit industrial products in China.

	i	ii	iii	iv	v	vi	vii
No.	Product	Unit	1997 China average	1997 international average	Difference between iii and iv, %	2015 lower than 2012 %	2017 lower than 2012 %
1	Electricity consumption for coal	Kwh/Ton	30.9	30	3	7.30	
2	Comprehensive energy consumption for crude oil processing	KgSCE/Ton	118.3	102,4	15.5		
3	Comprehensive energy consumption for ethylene	KgSCE/Ton	1210	870	39.1	4.4	
4	Comprehensive energy consumption for smelting of copper	KgSCE/Ton	1352	820	64.9	17.6	
5	Comprehensive energy consumption for plain glass	KgSCE /weight cases	25.7	14.1	82.3	7.9	9.1
6	Comprehensive energy consumption for paper and paperboards	KgSCE/Ton	1.57	0.7	124.3	7.5	11
7	Comprehensive energy consumption for cane sugar manufacture	KgSCE/Ton	6.16	4.5	36.9		
8	Electricity consumption for cotton yarn	Kwh/Ton	2349	2129	10.3		
9	Viscose rayon						
	heat consumption	KgSCE/Ton	2052	1450	41.5		
	electricity consumption	Kwh/Ton	1937	1200	61.4		
10	Petroleum consumption for trucks	Liter/100Tonkm	7.55	3.4	122.1		

			2000				
11	Coal consumption for thermal power generation	KgSCE/Kwh	392	320	22.5	2.4	3.9
12	Comprehensive energy consumption per tone steel	KgSCE/Ton	906	656	38.1	4.4	5.3
13	Comprehensive energy consumption of large-scaled synthetic ammonia	KgSCE/Ton	1372	820	67.3	3.7	5.7
14	Comprehensive energy consumption of cement	KgSCE /Ton	181	124.6	45.3	4.6	4.5
15	Comprehensive energy consumption of aluminum	TonSCE/Ton	9.923	9.22	7.6	2.8	
16	Comprehensive energy consumption of caustic soda	KgSCE /Ton	1553	1300	19.5	9	12.6
17	Comprehensive energy consumption of architectural ceramics	KgSCE /m^2	10.04	7.2	39.4		
18	Comprehensive energy consumption of railway transportation	KgSCE/ 1000Ton-km	10.41	9	15.7		
19	Comprehensive energy consumption of calcium carbide					1.7	2.4

(*Continued*)

Table 4.13.   (*Continued*)

	i	ii	iii	iv	v	vi	vii
No.	Product	unit	1997 China average	1997 international average	difference between iii and iv, %	2015 lower than 2012%	2017 lower than 2012%
20	Comprehensive energy consumption of lead					6.4	
21	Comprehensive energy consumption of zinc					3.1	

Source: The Bureau of resources saving and comprehensive utilization, State Economic and Trade Commission: The plan for energy saving and comprehensive utilization of resources during 10th Five Year plan, (in Chinese), Feb. 11, 2003; The saving energy law and regulations and saving energy work, www.sxmavis.com/jspx/index_jspx_jnfg.htm; National Development and Reform Commission: China Medium and Long-Term Energy Conservation Plan, November 25, 2004; China National Bureau of Statistics: A new chapter in the energy revolution spectrum, energy conservation and consumption reduction have achieved results – China's energy development since the 18th CPC National Congress, 2016-03-04, (in Chinese); Department of Energy, China National Bureau of Statistics: Great achievements have been made in energy development and remarkable results have been achieved in energy conservation and consumption reduction. 2018-09-11, (in Chinese).

restraining China's economic development. This backward technology resulted in poor economic performance, waste of resources and environmental pollution. The share of funds on innovation and technical update to total fixed assets investment declined from 18.4% (1990) to 16.5% (1995) and further to 15.5% in 2002.[35] All these data reveal that economic growth in China took place mainly in the extensive mode. R&D in the Machinery Industry was only 1.5% of its sales revenue (in developed countries, it was 5%).

Another example is China's steel industry. In 2003, China produced 222 million tons of steel and ranked first in the world. But China's steel industry should improve its product mix, which fails to meet market demand for high-quality items. China still imports 30 million tons steel, mainly high quality, high value-added steel products, such as automobile steel sheet, heavy steel plate, seamless steel pipe, and high-quality section steel.[36] In the meantime, China exports low value-added original wire steel. Table 4.13 shows that the energy consumption per unit of product has been significantly reduced. By improving process technology, upgrading and renovating energy equipment, eliminating backward production capacity, and accelerating technological progress, the energy consumption per unit of product has been significantly reduced. Since the 18th CPC National Congress, all levels of government in China effectively have been promoting energy conservation and emission reduction in key areas such as industry, construction, and transportation.

From 2009 to the present, there has been a period of overcapacity. Since the second half of 2008, the global financial crisis has gradually spread; China's foreign trade experienced eight years of glory after the accession to the WTO, and domestic production capacity has become heavily dependent on the outside world. The shrinking of exports led to a resurgence of overcapacity in the domestic manufacturing industry. The production capacity of steel has gradually evolved from a regional and structural surplus to an absolute surplus. In 2016, the global crude steel output was 1.629 billion tons, of which China's output was 808 million tons, and the output accounted for 49.65% of the world's crude steel

---

[35]Calculated using data from the China National Bureau of Statistics: China Statistical Yearbook, China Statistics Press, 2003, Table 6.1; 1996, Table 6.1; 1991, Table 6.1.

[36]Liu, S., *et al.* (2004). The prosperity report of China industry development, (in Chinese), *Shanghai Securities News*, January 30; Liu, H., and Q. Lu (2003). China became the powerhouse of world steel industry, *Shenzhen Economic Daily*, (in Chinese), December 30.

production. The plan is to cut 100–150 million tons of crude steel capacity in five years. Since the implementation of supply-side reforms, cement production in 2015 fell by 132 million. tons from 2014. The lowest capacity utilization rate is in the stainless-steel sector, which is only 45%. In 2011–2015, China's new automobile production capacity increased by 10.87 million units; by the end of 2015, China's automobile production capacity was 31.22 million units, and the new production capacity in 2016–2017 was about six million units. In 2015, passenger car production capacity was 25.75 million units, and the capacity utilization rate was 81%; commercial vehicle production capacity was 5.47 million units, with the capacity utilization rate of only 52%.

In the second half of 2016, the NDRC included the automotive industry in the overheated industry list and was expected to transfer it to the list of surplus industries in 2018. In 2012, the domestic polysilicon industry capacity reached 190,000 tons, while actual output was only 64,000 tons. With the capacity utilization rate of only 33.7%, there was a serious overcapacity. At the same time, China imported 82,000 tons of polysilicon products in 2012, a significant increase of 28% compared with 2011.

Such overcapacity is typical structural overcapacity. The supply of high-end products is in short supply, and the supply of low-end products is in surplus. As a result, domestic enterprises have stopped production in large areas, and enterprises generally suffered losses. Today, people have shifted from the simple demand for physical goods to the demand for quality and brand experience. This requires manufacturers to transform into this aspect, from selling products to selling services, improving quality, strengthening services, and building brands. Since the 18th National Congress of the Communist Party of China, China has adhered to supply-side structural reform as the main approach and has continuously promoted the quality transformation of economic development, efficiency reform, and dynamic change. The development of industrial economy has expanded from quantity to quality.

6. Economic Performance of Industry

Table 4.14 shows the economic indicators of industrial enterprises after economic reform. From 1978– 2015, the absolute amount of net profits fluctuated, but pre-tax profits gradually increased. Total loss of loss-making enterprises increased and reached a maximum of CNY173.7 billion (USD21 billion) in 1998 and has declined since 1999. However,

Table 4.14.   Economic results of Chinese industrial enterprises 1978–2014.

Year		1978	1980	1985	0	0
Pre-tax profits/total assets, %	Total		25.20	23.76	12.20	10.33
	SOE	24.20	24.80	23.80	12.40	9.7
Pre-tax profits/gross output value (%)	Total	21.62	22.65	19.64	10.41	9.89
	SOE	24.04	23.17	21.17	11.51	10.80
Total loss of loss-making enterprises, 100 mil.	Total	45.1	38.8	40.5	453.7	638.9
	SOE	42.1	34.3	32.4	348.8	452.64
Total after-tax profits, 100 mil.	Total	599.3	692.3	944.1	559.8	1602.5
	SOE	508.8	585.4	738.2	388.1	817.3
Total pre-tax profits, 100 mil.	Total	916.0	1060.8	1664.0	1945.9	3923.7
	SOE	790.7	907.1	1334.1	1503.1	2454.7
Year		1995	2000	2005	2010	2014
Pre-tax profits/average sets, %	Total	8.29	7.54	10.75	15.68	13.69
	SOE	8.01	7.00	10.83	13.63	11.32
Pre-tax profits/gross output value, %	Total	9.19	11.10	10.46	7.60	6.16
	SOE	11.10	14.50	15.21	9.28	6.67
Ratio of profits to industrial cost, %	Total	3.81	5.56	6.42	9.06	7.22
	SOE	3.22	6.15	8.44	8.31	6.52
Total loss of loss-making enterprises, 100 mil.	Total	1198.6	1136.1	1923.0	2,359.18	7035.4
	SOE	639.6	704.3	1026.0	1215.2	3678.8
Total after-tax profits, 100 mil.	Total	1634.9	4393.5	14802.5	19393.8	17214.7
	SOE	665.6	2408.3	6519.8	(342.1)	(565.0)
Total pre-tax profits, 100 mil.	Total	5050.3	9512.9	26320.8	53049.7	68154.9
	SOE	2874.2	5879.0	12739.9	19393.8	17214.7

Source: Calculated using data from the China National Bureau of Statistics: China Industry Economy Statistical Yearbook, China Statistics Press, 2003, Tables 2.7, 2.8; 2001, pp. 19, 23, 24; China National Bureau of Statistics: China Statistical Yearbook, China Statistics Press, 2015, Tables 13.3, 13.4; 2011, Table 14.2; 2006, Tables 14.4, 14.8; 2005, Tables 14.1, 14.3, 14.7; 2004, Tables 14.3, 14.7; 2003, Tables 13.5, 13.7; 2002, Tables 13.5, 13.8, 13.9, 13.12; 2001, Tables 13.05, 13.8, 13.9, 13.12; 2000, Tables 13.6, 13.7, 13.10, 13.11; and various years; China National Bureau of Statistics: The Total Loss of SOE Loss-making Enterprises reached historical second peak in 2005; The economic performance of industrial enterprises in 2005, China National Bureau of Statistics, Data base; Annual, Total Losses of Loss-making Industrial Enterprises, 2000–2016.

economic indicators of industrial enterprises — pre-tax profits to gross output rate, pre-tax profits to fixed assets rate, pre-tax profits per original fixed assets rate declined during 1978–2014. Therefore, the growth rate of pre-tax profits is higher than the growth rate of after-tax profits. In addition, enterprises had to pay huge amounts of interest charges to banks for their loans, which were unnecessary under the planned economy. The establishment of the social welfare system transferred the burden of pension, housing, health care, and unemployment insurance from government to enterprises and employees. These increased the operating costs; hence, the decrease in pre-tax profits. It is important to note that the share of taxes from SOEs is higher than their gross output share in the national total. This implies that SOEs paid more tax per gross output than enterprises of other ownership types. Since, 1998, SOEs include state-owned and state-holding enterprises, so the share of gross output by SOEs in 1998 was higher than in 1997. In 1999, SOEs utilized 68.8% fixed assets and 54.5% industrial staff and workers of total manufacturing industry and only produced 48.9% of industrial gross output but paid 69.8% tax to the country. In 2014, SOEs utilized 38.8% fixed assets and 18.2% industrial staff and workers of total secondary manufacturing industry, only producing 23.7% Revenue from Principal Business but paying 44.0% of tax to the country.

The total factor productivity (TFP) of SOEs, [see Eq. (4.4)] was only 59.0% of TFP for non-SOEs in 1999, as seen in Table 4.15.[37] Similarly, we introduce total factor value added, (TFV), and total factor tax, (TFX), see Eqs. (4.5) and (4.6):

$$TFG = \frac{GO}{K^{0.5} \times L^{0.5}} \tag{4.4}$$

$$TFV = \frac{VA}{K^{0.5} \times L^{0.5}} \tag{4.5}$$

$$TFX = \frac{TAX}{K^{0.5} \times L^{0.5}} \tag{4.6}$$

---

[37]Calculated using data from the China National Bureau of Statistics: China Statistical Yearbook, China Statistics Press, 2015, Tables 13.3, 13.4; 2011, Tables 14.2, 14.6; 2006, Tables 14.4, 14.8; 2005, Tables 14.3, 14.7; 2004, Tables 14.3, 14.7; 2003, Tables 5.8, 13-02, 13.5, 13.6, 13.9, 13.10; 2002, Tables 13.2, 13.5, 13.6, 13.9, 13.10; 2001, Tables 13.2, 13.5, 13.6, 13.9, 13.10; 2000, Tables 13.2, 13.6, 13.7, 13.10, 13.11.

Table 4.15.   The total factor productivity of SOEs and non-SOEs in China, 1999–2014.

Year	1999	2000	2001	2002	2003	2004	2005	2010	2014
SOE GO, % of total	48.92	47.34	44.43	40.78	37.54	35.24	33.28	27.85	19.64
SOE VA, % of total	55.72	54.25	50.69	49.75	44.86	42.36	42.36	31.66	27.67
SOE tax, % of total	69.81	67.79	65.67	63.84	61.24	60.51	54.00	48.66	44.02
SOE TA% of total	68.80	66.57	65.80	60.93	55.99	52.03	48.05	48.30	38.81
SOE EM% of total	54.47	51.10	47.52	41.46	37.62	33.58	27.19	19.24	18.19
SOE TFG/NSOE TFG %	58.98	81.16	79.45	81.14	81.79	84.30	92.08	91.37	73.92
SOE TFV/NSOE TFV %	77.49	93.03	90.65	98.97	97.74	101.32	117.18	103.86	104.14
SOE TFX/NSOE TFX %	114.04	116.24	117.44	127.02	133.42	144.77	149.40	159.64	165.67

Note: After 2014, China National Bureau of Statistics did not disclose the value-added tax and taxes and other charges on principal business. Therefore, we chose 2014.

Source: Calculated using data from the China National Bureau of Statistics: China Statistical Yearbook, China Statistics Press, 2015, Tables 13.3, 13.4; 2011, Tables 14.2, 14.6; 2006, Tables 14.4, 14.8; 2005, Tables 14.3, 14.7; 2004, Tables 14.3, 14.7; 2003, Tables 5.8, 13.2, 13.5, 13.6, 13.9, 13.10; 2002, Tables 13.2, 13.5, 13.6, 13.9, 13.10; 2001, Tables 13.02, 13.5, 13.6, 13.9, 13.10; 2000, Tables 13.2, 13.6, 13.7, 13.10, 13.11.

where *TFG* — total factor productivity of Gross Output.

  GO — Gross output.

  TFV — total factor productivity of Value added.

  VA — Value added; *K* — Fixed assets; *L* — Labor.

  TFX — total factor tax paid.

  TAX — total tax paid

Table 4.15 reveals that the ratio of SOE TFG to Total TFG improved from 58.98% to 92.08% during 1999–2005, and then fell to 73.92% in 2014. The ratio of SOE TFV to Total TFV improved from 77.49% to 117.18% and then fell to 104.14 in 2014. The ratio of SOE TFV to total TFV is larger than the ratio of SOE TFG to Total TFG because SOEs are mainly large and capital-intensive enterprises with higher value-added than Total enterprises. The ratio of TFX of SOE to total increased from 114.04% to 149.4% during 1999–2005, then further rose to 165.67% in 2014. The tax rate of SOEs (tax paid divided by value added) during 1999–2005 equaled 24.2% and 12.5% for total enterprises. The tax rates of SOEs reached 46.0% and 49.5% in 2010 and 2014, respectively. The corporate tax rates were 29.9% and 31.1% in 2010 and 2014, respectively. This means the tax contribution by SOEs is much higher than other ownership enterprises, especially because tax rates were too high for enterprises and SOEs.

On May 1, 2016, Chinese Mainland started to roll out the pilot program of the transition from business tax to VAT in an all-around manner; this reform has been highly recognized by all communities. Foreign-invested enterprises in China have enjoyed many benefits, since the implementation of the reform policy on the transition from business tax to VAT in China. This represents a major initiative to interface with the generally used international tax system management with respect to tax category and tax rate, etc. and promote the law-based tax system reform, which is not only conducive to promoting economic development, but also benefiting people's livelihood. [38]

The TFV of SOEs was only 76.6% of TFV for FFEs in 1999 and increased to 85.3% in 2005; it then further rose to 104.8% and 142.3% in 2010 and 2014, respectively. However, TFX of SOEs equaled 134.4% of FFEs in 1999, and increased to 186.9% in 2005; it then further rose to 214.7% and 289.3% in 2010 and 2014, respectively (see Table 4.16). The

---

[38]Chinese Mainland's Tax Reform Has Achieved Significant Results, and Foreign-Invested Enterprises in China Have Obtained Many Benefits, February 27, 2017, www.chinatax.gov.cn/eng/n2367751/c2550990/content.html.

Table 4.16. The total factor productivity of SOE and FFE in China, 1999–2014.

Year	Unit	1999	2000	2001	2002	2003	2004	2005	2010	2014
SOE V.A.	Bil. RMB	1213.2	1377.8	1465.2	1593.5	1883.8	2321.3	2717.7	3561.2	4528.3
FFE V.A.	Bil. RMB	4850.9	609.0	712.8	857.3	1160.0	1524.1	2046.8	2945.6	3762.6
SOE TAX	Bil. RMB	3081.2	3470.6	365.9	3982.3	4615.4	5363.7	6220.1	1637.8	2242.1
FFE TAX	Bil. RMB	702.3	868.6	1011.2	111.3	1412.7	1473.0	2138.4	661.0	916.5
SOE T.A.	Bil. RMB	8047.2	8401.5	8909.5	8909.5	9452.0	10159.4	11763.0	9081.0	13182.7
FFE T..A.	Bil. RMB	2301.9	2571.4	2835.4	3151.4	3926.0	4795.1	4795.1	4733.7	11372.4
SOE EM	10,000 persons	2412.0	2096.0	1824.0	1546.0	2162.9	2048.2	1874.9	1836.3	1525.0
FFE EM	10,000 persons	791.9	853.0	939.0	1054.3	1258.7	1444.5	1899.6	2645.7	2472.4
SOE TFV/FFE TFV%	%	76.6	79.8	83.2	91.3	79.8	87.9	85.3	104.8	142.3
SOE TFX/FFE TFX%	%	134.4	141.0	146.5	1757.7	160.6	210.1	186.9	214.7	289.3

Source: Calculated using data from the China National Bureau of Statistics: China Statistical Yearbook, China Statistics Press, 2015, Tables 13.4, 13.9; 2011, Tables 14.6, 14.16, 2006, Tables 14.3, 14.8, 14.16; 2005, Tables 14.1, 14.3, 14.7; 2004, Tables 14.7, 14.13; 2003, Tables 5.8, 13.5, 13.13; 2002, Tables 13.5, 13.13; 2001, Tables 13.5, 13.13; 2000, Tables 13.6, 13.14.

FFE and SOE tax rates were 10.4% and 24.2%, respectively, from 1999–2005; from 2010 to 2014, they rose to 23.5% and 48.0%, respectively. The average TFV of SOEs was 83.9% of that value of FFE from 1999–2005; from 2010–2014, it was 122.1%. This indicates the TFV of SOEs improved significantly. The average TFX of SOEs equaled 190.4% of that value of FFEs from 1999–2005; from 2010–2014 it rose to 234.8%. This means the TFX for SOEs is much higher than that of FFEs. Therefore, SOEs paid more tax than the fixed assets and labor it utilized.

Table 4.17[39] shows the economic performance by sectors. Based on pre-tax profits per fixed assets and after-tax profits per sales revenue and labor productivity, the sectors with better economic performances in 2005 were: extraction of petroleum and natural gas, mining and processing of non-ferrous metal ores, manufacture of beverages, mining of other ores, and mining and processing of ferrous metal ores; the sectors with the worst economic performance were: manufacture of articles for culture, education and sport activity, production and supply of gas, manufacture of textile, production and supply of water, and printing, reproduction of recording media. Figure 4.7 shows that after-tax profits per sales revenue declined faster than pre-tax profits per total assets, which implies the growth rate of taxes was higher than the profit growth rate. The overall productivity continuously increased from 1985–2005, especially from 1995–2005 (see Figure 4.7). This means production efficiency was improved. The ratio of after-tax profits to sales revenue and the ratio of pre-tax profits to total assets declined significantly from 1985–1995. In 1985, China's industry operated under a planned economy, characterized by supply shortages and soft budget constraints; therefore, profits were high. After 1995, China's industry operated under a market-oriented economy, featured by oversupply of industrial products, no state budget subsidies, and payment of various taxes. Therefore, profits declined significantly from 1985–1995. The ratio of after-tax profits to sales revenue and the ratio of pre-tax profits to total assets increased slightly from 1995–2005 because of improving operating efficiency.

Figure 4.5 shows that the overall labor productivity has increased significantly.

China's National Bureau of Statistics defines the Comprehensive Index of Economic Results (CIER) to represent profitability, development ability, production efficiency, ability to repay loan, operational ability, and production fit in with the sale of an enterprise.

---

[39] See Table 4.17 for source.

Table 4.17. Economic performance of industrial enterprises group by sectors, 1985–2014.

Branches	1985			1990			2010			2014		
	After-tax profits/sales revenue, %	Pre-tax profits/ total assets, %	Overall all labor producti-vity (¥/ person. year)	After-tax profits/ sales revenue, %	Pre-tax profits/ total assets, %	Overall all labor producti-vity (¥/ person. year)	After-tax profits/ sales revenue, %	Pre-tax profits/ total assets, %	Overall all labor producti-vity (¥/ person. year)	After-tax profits/ sales revenue, %	Pre-tax profits/ total assets, %	Overall all labor productivity (¥/person. year)
Manufacture of articles for culture, education, arts and crafts, sport and entertainment activities	38.8	30.48					−0.99	7.45	34,583	3.16	10.12	5,28,000
Processing of petroleum, coking and processing of nuclear fuel	32.26	46.67	5,66,648	27.28	30.77	77,317	6.13	10.77	2,66,352	−4.21	−0.50	43,70,200
Manufacture of raw chemical materials and chemical products	26.37	25.79	15,833	17.99	17.42	22,669	8.41	10.53	1,29,176	2.18	5.04	16,37,000
Manufacture of medicines							1.80	4.09	1,23,932	5.97	11.13	10,01,500
Manufacture of chemical fibers	21.09	23.62		21.24	20.77	59,808	4.91	9.06	1,13,835	1.58	4.07	15,40,600
Manufacture of rubber and plastics products				31.62	20.9	26,129	4.36	7.88	74,758	4.48	9.17	8,01,800

(Continued)

Table 4.17. (*Continued*)

Branches	1985			1990			2010			2014		
	After-tax profits/sales revenue, %	Pre-tax profits/ total assets, %	Overall all labor productivity (¥/ person. year)	After-tax profits/ sales revenue, %	Pre-tax profits/ total assets, %	Overall all labor productivity (¥/ person. year)	After-tax profits/ sales revenue, %	Pre-tax profits/ total assets, %	Overall all labor productivity (¥/ person. year)	After-tax profits/ sales revenue, %	Pre-tax profits/ total assets, %	Overall all labor productivity (¥/ person. year)
Manufacture of non-metallic mineral products				11.67	8.9	20,979	4.94	10.20	67,147	4.39	7.92	7,80,200
Smelting and pressing of ferrous metals	19.95	20.6	5263	9.42	9.15	7,916	5.44	10.94	2,00,941	0.11	2.15	18,75,800
Smelting and pressing of non-ferrous metals				16.51	16.27	20,475	4.91	10.43	1,47,594	1.07	3.75	24,06,900
Manufacture of metal products				13.08	11.02	26,709	6.13	10.06	75,857	3.77	7.59	8,36,400
Manufacture of general purpose machinery				17.47	12.06	15,009	5.47	8.17	83,548	4.31	6.91	9,13,900
Manufacture of special purpose machinery	27.82	22.88	7956	9.32	6.98	14,522	4.27	8.41	76,474	3.62	5.58	9,44,000
Manufacture of automobiles										6.20	12.01	16,48,700
Manufacture of railway, ship, aerospace and other transport equipment				11.45	8.64	18,797	4.79	9.01	1,08,699	3.52	4.73	9,49,100
Manufacture of electrical machinery and apparatus				21.42	12.74	24,899	3.32	6.81	97,332	3.76	8.14	10,28,300

Manufacture of computers, communication and other electronic equipment	35.46	24.67		16.03	9.75	41,132	5.64	9.95	1,30,156	3.04	7.30	9,65,300
Manufacture of measuring instruments and machinery				13.25	8.82	13,485	4.61	11.06	82,682	6.06	10.04	7,25,400
Other manufacture							2.89	11.67	45,480	3.33	5.92	5,16,300
Utilization of waste resources										2.94	15.45	19,12,000
Repair service of metal products, machinery and equipment	12.5	17.13	22,675	9.93	13.03	25,015				0.20	1.71	4,57,200
Production and supply of electric power and heat power							2.54	3.07	2,26,353	2.19	3.83	19,91,000
Production and supply of gas				3.12	3.75	11,060	−0.27	1.06	90,652	6.53	5.56	14,57,500
Production and supply of water	24.17	24.02	12,080	13.52	12.2	17,408	2.42	10.75	56,691	4.34	1.30	1,04,680
National total 2014	24.17	24.02	12,080	13.52	12.2	17,408	3.70	8.18	439013.72	2.98	6.50	10,95,600

Source: Calculated using data from the China National Bureau of Statistics: China Statistical Yearbook, China Statistics Press, 2015, Tables 13.2, 11.3, 11.4; 2011, Tables 14.02, 6.4, 6.3; 2006, Tables 14.5, 14.6; 1996, Tables 12.2, 12.11, 12.15; 1991, Tables 10.9, 10.18; Statistical Yearbook of China 1986, Compiled by the State Statistical Bureau of China, Oxford University Press, 1986, p.198, 231, 270. China Industry Statistical Yearbook, China Statistics Press, 1998, (in Chinese), p. 52–53.

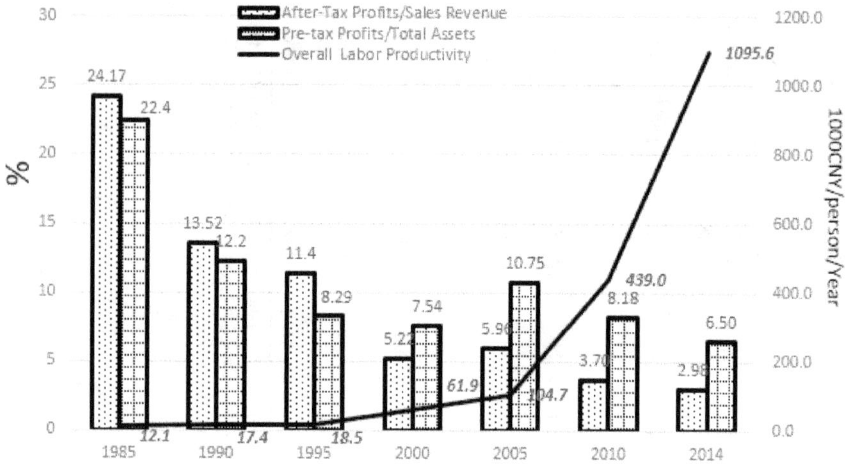

Figure 4.5.   Main economic indicators of all China industrial enterprises, 1985–2014.

Source: Calculated using data from the China National Bureau of Statistics: China Statistical Yearbook, China Statistics Press, 2015, Tables 13.2, 11.3, 11.4; 2011, Tables 14.02, 6.4, 6.3; 2006, Tables 14.5, 14.6; 1996, Tables 12.2, 12.11, 12.15; 1991, Tables 10.9, 10.18; Statistical Yearbook of China 1986, Compiled by the State Statistical Bureau of China, Oxford University Press, 1986, p.198, 231, 270. CHINA INDUSTRY STATISTICAL YEARBOOK, China Statistics Press, 1998, (in Chinese), p. 52–53.

$$CIER = \vec{I}_i \times \vec{W}_i^T = \sum_{i=1}^{n} \frac{index_i}{index_i^{ref}} \times W_i \qquad (4.7)$$

where **$CIER$** — comprehensive index of Economic result, defined by the Chinese National Bureau of Statistics.

$index_i$, $index_i^{ref}$ — Economic result index i and its reference value, see Table 4.18.

W_i — weight factor of index i, see Table 4.18, After 1997.

$$CIER = \sum_{i=1}^{n} \frac{index_i}{index_i^{ref}} \times W_i + \frac{(100 - index_j)}{(100 - index_j^{ref})} \times W_j \qquad (4.8)$$

where $index_j$ — Ratio of liability to property.

Wj — weight factor of index j, see Table 4.18.

Table 4.18. Reference value and weight of economic result.

Index$_i$	(Index$_i$)$_{ref}$	W$_i$	(Index$_i$)$_{ref}$	W$_i$
	After 1997		Before 1997	
Sales rate of Ind. products	96%	13	97.48%	15
Ratio of pre-tax profits to assets			13.55%	30
After-tax profits/Industrial costs	3.71%	14	8.41%	15
Overall labor productivity	16500	10	6205	10
Turnover rate of circulating capital	1.52	15	1.83	20
Ratio of value added to gross Ind. output			29%	10
Ratio of (pretax profit + interest) to assets (avg. circulating fund + avg. net fixed assets + equity)	10.70%	20		
Ratio of liability to property	≤60%	12		
Ratio of creditor's equity to that value of previous year	120%	16		

Source: China National Bureau of Statistics.

The CIER is a special relative indicator, which is used to evaluate the overall level of various aspects of the industrial economic efficiency in the quantitative terms. It is the comprehensive index of the quality for the industrial economy. As shown in Eq. (4.8), the index is the result of the real number of the industrial economic efficiency index in each field divided by the national standard value in the same field and then multiplied by the respective weight number. The national standard value (see Table 4.18) is based on the weighted average of the real figure of each index of industrial enterprises at and above the township level during the eighth FYP period (1991–1995). Weight is determined by the expert investigation method considering the degree of significance of each of the industrial economic efficiency indexes within the aggregative industrial economic efficiency. Using formula Eq. (4.8) and Table 4.18, calculating the comprehensive index of economic results for enterprises grouped by ownership, scale, and industrial sectors is shown in Table 4.19. It is found that the CIER for foreign-funded enterprises is much higher than the national total, which is 24.9% and 14.8% higher than the national total CIER in 2000 and 2003, respectively. This shows the gap was narrowed during 2000–2003, which demonstrated the positive role of FFEs in the development of Chinese industry.

Table 4.19.   CIER of China enterprises for different types, 2000–2014.

	Sales rate	Profit/ costs	produc- tivity	Turn- over rate	Profit/ T.Asset	Equity/ equity-1	Asset/ liability	CIERn
2014								
National total	98	6.52	164043	2.53	13.69	109.85	57.17	215.35
N SOE	98	5.82	296927	2.07	11.32	109.59	61.98	282.79
N foreign-funded enterprises	98	6.93	152183	2.26	13.69	147.66	55.47	212.59
N private enterprises	98	6.77	141758	3.46	12.99	129.60	52.15	214.79
SH total	99.37	7.92	116259	1.77	12.99	128.51	50.29	187.60
SH SOE	99.1	11.02	99661	1.99	17.51	124.65	45.45	200.76
SH foreign-funded enterprises		12.99	369388		17.44	108.07	54.10	333.67
2003								
National total	98.02	6.25	73045	2.00	4.94	114.75	29.51	146.54
SOE	98.87	7.25	87095	1.69	4.06	106.20	35.27	151.38
Foreign-funded enterprises	98.17	6.83	92158	2.2	7.07	121.68	26.15	168.23
Large and medium enterprises	98.37	7.1	90170	1.97	5.21	120.16	30.29	160.88
Light industry	98.28	5.23	59334	2.03	4.79	110.62	28.42	134.22
Heavy industry	98.77	6.77	83005	1.99	5.00	116.63	30.12	154.72
SH total	99.32	7.65	122344	1.95	7.65	112.42	50.05	186.05
SH SOE	99.28	10.82	206603	1.84	10.84	106.73	44.85	250.42
2002								
National total	98.02	5.62	59766	1.8	3.96	108.69	58.72	122.74
SOE	98.98	5.93	65749	1.47	2.96	101.11	59.30	121.35
Foreign-funded enterprises	98.28	6.4	81313	2.06	5.96	112.24	54.38	146.85
Large and medium enterprises	98.77	6.45	76899	1.66	3.32	106.42	57.84	133.75

Table 4.19.   (*Continued*)

	Sales rate	Profit/ costs	produc- tivity	Turn- over rate	Profit/ T.asset	Equity/ equity-1	Asset/ liability	CIERn
Light industry	97.54	4.83	51597	1.88	4.10	111.60	58.30	116.31
Heavy industry	98.34	6.1	66020	1.76	3.89	107.42	58.90	127.65
2000								
National total	97.67	5.56	45679	1.62	3.48	110.73	60.81	110.92
SOE	98.88	6.15	45998	1.34	2.87	107.03	60.99	109.03
Foreign-funded enterprises	97.74	6.90	71403	1.89	4.99	113.61	57.01	138.57
Large and medium enterprises	98.64	6.88	54667	1.48	3.65	107.59	59.65	120.32
Light industry	97.06	4.31	42119	1.74	3.33	110.92	61.07	104.82
Heavy industry	98.07	6.35	48116	1.55	3.55	110.65	60.68	114.90
SH total	98.84	6.18	69112	1.54	9.45	127.71	42.67	137.98
SH SOE	99.71	6.94	90879	1.37	9.17	131.35	55.42	153.05

Source: Calculated using data from the China National Bureau of Statistics: China Statistical Yearbook, China Statistics Press, 2015, Tables 13.3, 13.4, 13.5, 13.7, 13.8, 13.9; 2004, Tables 14.3, 14.4, 14.7, 14.8, 14.13, 14.14, 14.15, 14.16; 2003, Tables 13.5, 13.6, 13.14, 13.18; 2002, Tables 13.5, 13.6, 13.14, 13.18; 2001, Tables 13.5, 13.6, 13.13, 13.14, 13.17, 13.18; Shanghai Bureau of Statistics, Shanghai Statistical Yearbook, 2015, Tables 14.3, 14.4, 14.5.

Table 4.19 shows the CIER for large and medium-scale enterprises is higher than the national total, which implies the economic performance of large and medium-scale enterprises is better than that of small enterprises. Furthermore, the CIER of large and medium-scale enterprises is higher than the national total 9.9%, 9.0%, and 9.8% in 2001, 2002, and 2003, respectively. In 2003, the CIER of SOEs in Shanghai was 65.4% higher than national SOEs, reflecting China's regional disparity. But, in 2014, the CIER of Shanghai's SOEs was 82% lower than national SOEs. Why? In April 2009, the State Council officially proposed that Shanghai should build "four centers," including international economic center, international financial center, and international trade center. Shanghai's "four centers" construction led to economic structure service transformation — from a pure industry center to a "four centers." As can be seen from Table 4.19, the CIER of heavy industry was 11.9%, 11.3%, and 20.5% higher than that of light industry in 2001, 2002, and 2003, respectively. Table 4.19 also indicates the

CIER of private industrial enterprises was in good condition in 2014. In 2017, there were 222,000 private industrial enterprises above the designated size, employing 32.71 million people, accounting for 57.7% and 36.9% of all industrial enterprises above the designated size. Table 4.19 also shows that, in 2000–2003, FFE's CIER was significantly better than China's national in 2000–2003; however, because FFE's employment increased sharply in 2005–2014 (see Table 4.16), it became worse in 2014. However, the Shanghai FFE's CEIR was in very good condition in 2014. This tells us FFEs' investment and operating conditions are very good in Shanghai.

The top five industrial branches with the best CIER in China during 2003 are the manufacture of tobacco sector, extraction of petroleum and natural gas, processing of petroleum, coking, and nuclear fuel, production and distribution of electric power and heat power, and manufacture of communication equipment, computers, and other electronic equipment.

Four of these five industrial branches belong to heavy industry. During 1999–2003, the top five industrial branches with the best CIER were also these five industrial branches, but their ranks are different (Figure 4.6). The bottom five sectors with the worst CIER (according to the 2003 rank) were

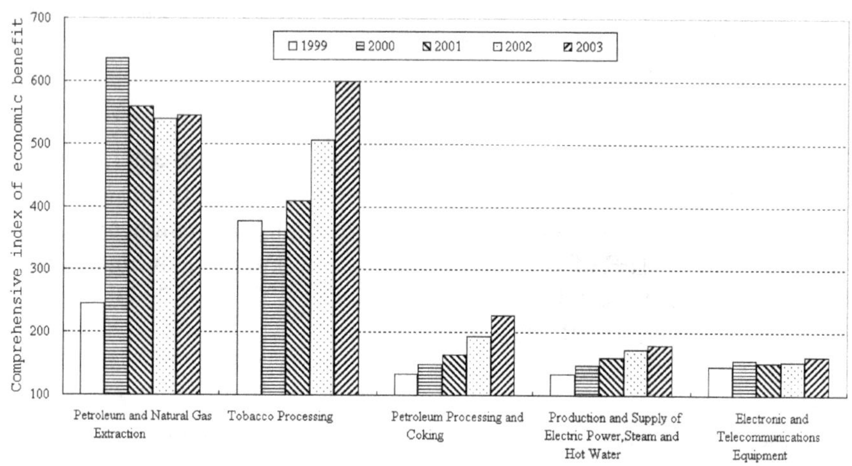

Figure 4.6.   Top five industrial branches with the best CIER in China, 1999–2003.

Source: Calculated using data from the China National Bureau of Statistics: China Statistical Yearbook, China Statistics Press, 2004, Table 14.3; 2003, Table 13.5; 2002, Table 13.5; 2001, Table 13.5; 2000, Table 13.6.

Table 4.20.   Main comprehensive indicators on economic benefit by industrial branch, 2003.

Branch	Asset/ liability	Profit/ t. assets	Equity/ equity-1	Turnover rate	Profit/ cost	produc- tivity	Sales rate	CIERn
Mining and washing of coal	46.84	2.58	13.47	1.33	6.04	30,590	98.14	90.31
Extraction of petroleum and natural gas	68.65	24.70	12.11	3.38	64.13	3,28,613	100.12	545.26
Mining and processing of ferrous metal ores	41.66	5.54	11.61	2.04	8.2	53,383	98.27	126.15
Mining and processing of non-ferrous metal ores	30.99	8.56	20.07	2.53	10.55	42,938	98.52	143.52
Mining and processing of nonmetal ores	33.46	3.31	−2.21	1.87	5.51	35,710	98.2	100.04
Processing of food from agricultural products	23.84	4.18	21.48	2.97	3.06	80,721	97.32	136.48
Manufacture of foods	29.13	4.90	13.12	2.1	5.52	66,002	96.95	126.86
Manufacture of beverages	35.64	4.67	8.24	1.49	8.04	89,435	98.32	141.69
Manufacture of tobacco	70.38	9.84	17.97	1.39	24.62	7,41,392	100.02	599.18
Manufacture of textile	24.68	3.18	25.47	2.13	3.42	38,198	97.86	102.27
Manufacture of textile wearing apparel, footware, and caps	26.75	5.58	11.73	2.41	4.28	31,693	97.2	106.27

(*Continued*)

Table 4.20. (*Continued*)

Branch	Asset/ liability	Profit/ t. assets	Equity/ equity-1	Turnover rate	Profit/ cost	produc- tivity	Sales rate	CIERn
Manufacture of leather, fur, feather, and related products	26	5.99	26.49	2.69	3.89	35,758	97.94	113.08
Processing of timber, manufacture of wood, bamboo, rattan, palm, and straw products	26.77	3.70	19.58	2.39	3.69	41,633	97.37	107.43
Manufacture of furniture	25.41	4.69	34.89	2.22	4.4	42,164	97.93	113.12
Manufacture of paper and paper products	26.98	3.55	15.84	1.92	5.06	59,798	98.28	118.72
Printing, reproduction of recording media	32.56	5.39	16.08	1.58	8.07	56,294	97.6	127.50
Manufacture of articles for culture, education, and sport activity	25.88	5.12	12.70	2.21	4.15	28,682	97.57	99.56
Processing of petroleum, coking, processing of nuclear fuel	20.65	3.10	14.87	4.58	2.07	2,15,798	99.6	227.30
Manufacture of raw chemical materials & chem. Products	26.66	4.42	14.17	2.09	5.53	79,172	97.82	136.67

Manufacture of medicines	35.46	6.02	16.69	1.34	10.38	88,803	94.06	154.42
Manufacture of chemical fibers	20.38	3.64	4.57	2.53	4.27	86,271	98.09	133.42
Manufacture of rubber	28.18	4.07	16.11	1.8	5.07	59,441	97.46	119.76
Manufacture of plastics	24.91	4.42	18.54	2.06	4.64	54,161	97.91	116.21
Manufacture of non-metallic mineral products	30.94	3.83	18.00	1.74	5.77	44,144	97.11	110.93
Smelting and pressing of ferrous metals	28.22	5.07	18.59	2.28	6.39	110353	99.3	159.62
Smelting and pressing of non-ferrous metals	25.31	3.83	15.31	2.11	4.59	84,629	98.05	133.44
Manufacture of metal products	25.17	5.17	9.35	2.05	4.77	56,703	97.81	119.16
Manufacture of general purpose machinery	27.85	4.54	18.93	1.46	5.83	56,100	97	117.00
Manufacture of special purpose machinery	26.31	3.60	24.50	1.41	4.92	49,106	97.21	107.05
Manufacture of transport equipment	25.83	6.52	23.29	1.75	7.59	92,919	98.21	152.93
Manufacture of electrical machinery and equipment	25.56	5.08	14.86	1.75	5.25	76,323	96.75	130.16

(Continued)

Table 4.20. (*Continued*)

Branch	Asset/ liability	Profit/ t. assets	Equity/ equity-1	Turnover rate	Profit/ cost	produc- tivity	Sales rate	CIERn
Manufacture of communication equipment, computers and other electronic equipment	21.99	5.11	13.51	2.16	4.03	1,27,349	97.99	160.65
Manufacture of measuring instruments and machinery for cultural activity and office work	27.19	5.70	31.38	1.79	5.69	61,844	98.22	128.15
Production and distribution of electric power and heat power	52.58	2.73	9.38	2.03	6.73	1,51,258	99.89	178.82
Production and distribution of gas	27.63	0.79	12.63	1.6	1.59	51,367	100.63	83.94
Production and distribution of water	44.25	0.07	9.88	0.86	0.36	41,226	97.22	63.67

Source: Calculated using data from the China National Bureau of Statistics: China Statistical Yearbook, China Statistics Press, 2004, Tables 14.03, 14.04.

production and distribution of water, production and supply of gas, coal mining and dressing, manufacture of articles for culture, education, and sport activity, and mining and processing of nonmetal ores sectors (Table 4.20).

Infrastructure of standard coal, an increase of 24.7 times, an average annual growth of 9.2%.[40] In 2017, China's total energy consumption was 3132.2 million tons oil equivalent, accounting for 23.2% of the world, ranking first in the world; in 2006–2016, total energy consumption increased by 3.1%. Total energy consumption in the United States was 2234.9 million tons oil equivalent, accounting for 16.5% of the world, ranking second in the world; the total growth rate of energy consumption in 2006–2016 was minus 0.6%. But, in 2016, China's GDP (constant 2011 USD) accounted for only 56.4% of the United States; therefore, China should strengthen energy conservation.[41]

Table 4.21 shows the elasticity of energy and freight transportation to GDP. The elasticity of energy and freight transportation [see Eqs. (4.9) and (4.10)] is the average value during that period. Before economic reform, ε_{ene} and ε_{ft} were larger than 1 and after 1978 decreased below 1 (see Table 4.21). The investment in these sectors is huge, but their rate of return is relatively low. The elasticity of energy to GDP declined from 1.488 from 1952–1978 to 0.844 after reform (1978–2015).

$$\varepsilon_{ene} = \frac{GR_{ene}}{GR_{GDP}} \tag{4.9}$$

$$\varepsilon_{ft} = \frac{GR_{ft}}{GR_{GDP}} \tag{4.10}$$

where ε_{ene} — Elasticity Ratio of Energy consumption.

GR_{ene} — Average Annual Growth Rate of Energy consumption.

---

[40] Service Division, China National Bureau of Statistics. The transportation network has developed by leaps and bounds, and telecommunications ability of post has improved significantly, 2018-09-13, (in Chinese); Department of Energy, China National Bureau of Statistics: Great achievements have been made in energy development and remarkable results have been achieved in energy conservation and consumption reduction. 2018-09-11, (in Chinese).

[41] BP Statistical Review of World Energy, 67th edition, June 2018, p. 8–9; World Development Indicators online 2018, Released September 2018 by World Bank.

Table 4.21.   Elasticity of energy and transportation, China, 1957–2015.

	1952	1957	1965	1978	1985	1990	1995
GDP index %	100.0	155.8	215.6	474.5	912.6	1336.4	2383.1
Energy, 0.1 mil. T SCE	487.1	964.4	1890.1	5714.4	7668.2	9870.3	13117.6
Electricity, 100 mil. Kwh	73.0	193.0	576.0	2566.0	4117.6	6230.4	10023.4
Freight, 100 mil.Tkm	762.0	1810.0	3464.0	9829.0	18365.0	26207.0	35730.0
E GR %		8.61%	8.77%	8.88%	4.29%	5.18%	5.85%
EL GR %		21.46%	14.65%	12.18%	6.99%	8.64%	9.98%
F GR %		18.89%	8.45%	8.35%	9.34%	7.37%	6.40%
GDP GR %		9.27%	4.15%	6.25%	9.79%	7.93%	12.26%
Elas.E		0.928	2.116	1.420	0.438	0.653	0.477
Elas.EL		2.315	3.532	1.947	0.714	1.089	0.813
Elas.F		2.038	2.038	1.336	0.954	0.930	0.521
	1952–1957	1957–1965	1965–1978	1978–1985	1985–1990	1990–1995

	2000	2005	2010	2015	1952–1978	1978–2015
GDP index%	3602.7	5743.1	9811.0	14333.3		
Energy, 0.1 mil. T SCE	13855.3	22331.9	36064.8	43000.0		
Electricity, 100 mil. Kwh	13472.7	24940.8	41998.8	56933.0		
Freight, 100 mil. Tkm	44320.5	69445.0	141837.4	4175886.0		
E GR %	1.10%	12.68%	12.73%	4.50%	9.93%	5.61%
EL GR %	6.09%	16.64%	13.92%	7.90%	14.67%	8.74%
F GR %	4.40%	11.88%	19.55%	132.94%	10.34%	17.77%
GDP GR %	8.62%	12.36%	14.33%	9.94%	6.17%	−1.82%
Elas.E	0.128	1.025	0.889	0.452	1.488	1.021
Elas.EL	0.707	1.346	0.971	0.795	2.377	1.619

Table 4.21.   (*Continued*)

	1952	1957	1965	1978	1985	1990	1995
Elas.F		0.511	0.961	1.364	13.373	1.675	1.156

	1995–2000	2000–2005	2005–2010	2010–2015	1952–1978	1978–2005

Source: Calculated using data from the China National Bureau of Statistics: China Statistical Yearbook, China Statistics Press, 2016, Tables 9.2, 9.14, 16.2; 2011, Tables 7.14, 16.2; 2006, Tables 3.1, 3.4, 7.2, 7.6, 16.9; 2004, Tables 3.4, 7.2, 16.9; 2003, Tables 3.3, 3.4, 7.2, 7.8, 15.9; 2001, Table 15.9; 1996, Tables 2.10; 6.2, 6.9, 14.9; 1993, Table 7.6; Statistical Yearbook of China 1986, Compiled by the State Statistical Bureau of China, Oxford University Press, 1986 p. 324; Statistical Yearbook of China 1981 (English Edition), Compiled by the State Statistical Bureau, PRC. Published by Economic Information & Agency, Hong Kong, October 1982, p. 7; 1979; 1966; China National Bureau of Statistics Compiled: China Development Report 2006, (in Chinese), China Statistical Press, Tables 11, 12, 13; All China Data online: China Yearly Macro Economics Statistics (National): GDP index, 1953–2016.

GR_{GDP} — Average Annual Growth Rate of GDP.

ε_{ft} — Elasticity Ratio of freight transportation.

GR_{ft} — Average Annual Growth Rate of freight transportation

This is partly because of great success in economic reform of energy conservation. Energy use per PPP GDP (kg of oil equivalent per constant 2000 PPP USD) in China declined from 0.9171 in 1978 to 0.1753 (kg of oil equivalent per constant 2011 PPP USD) in 2014,[42] which indicates energy consumption intensity has been reduced by 4.57% each year during 1978–2014. It would be consuming four times more energy as it did in 1978 without that reduction. However, China's energy consumption (kg of oil equivalent) is still relatively high; in 2003, unit GDP (2011 PPPUSD) energy consumption was 42.7% more than Japan's, 51.0% more than Brazil's, and 15.2% more than India's.[43] In 2014, the situation deteriorated further; 88.6% more than Japan, 81.5% more than Brazil, 48.1% more

---

[42] Calculated using data from the World Bank: World Development Indicators online 2006, released April 2006 by World Bank; World Development Indicators online 2018, released September 21, 2018.

[43] Calculated using data from the World Bank (2006). World Development Indicators online 2006, released April.

than India. The Chinese government did make efforts to save energy. Standard coal equivalent (SCE) utilization for every CNY10,000 (1990 constant CNY $\approx$ 1,200 USD) of GDP in China in 2000 was 1.2 tons SCE lower than that in 1995, which stood at 3.97 tons. Energy consumption intensity was reduced by 5.42% each year during 1995–2000. Total energy saving during 1996–2000 accumulated to 410 million tons SCE, which decreased the volume of waste gas sulfur dioxide by eight million tons and carbon oxide by 120 million tons.[44] In 2017, energy consumption per unit of GDP decreased by 20.9% compared with 2012, with an average annual decline of 4.6%, which is 1.0 % points higher than the average annual decline in 1979–2012. Accumulated savings and energy use in the five years was about 1.03 billion tons of standard coal.[45] China sped up industry restructuring and perfected the energy-consumption structure to achieve its energy-efficiency goal. China's electricity consumption grew by 14.5% year-on-year to 2.187 trillion kilowatt hours in 2004. Generating capacity increased by 12.8% year-on-year, or 44,413 megawatts in 2004.[46] Electricity prices in peak periods should be jolted upward to decrease power consumption and encourage use during non-peak times. The problem was alleviated in 2006, as more power generators came online, with the electricity demand thus satisfied nationwide. Industrial energy and electricity consumption remain high, as shown in Table 4.22, and structural adjustment has a long way to go. In 2005, industrial energy consumption was 72.3% and it has stayed at around 70% since 1985; it declined to 67.6% in 2017. Residential energy consumption slightly increased but remains at a very low level. In 2005, rural and urban residents consumed 282.5 billion KWh of electricity, 87.39 million tons of coal, 22.4 billion cubic meters of natural gas and coal gas, and 13.29 million tons of LPG. The annual growth rate year on year of above residential energy consumption was 14.4%, 6.9%, 9.1%, and minus 1.6%,

---

[44]Li, R. (2001). Energy saving, reducing consumption and improving energy utilization efficiency to promote sustainable development of economy and society (in Chinese), Speech at the "Energy Saving high level discussion forum in China" on November 5.

[45]Department of Energy, China National Bureau of Statistics (2018). Great achievements have been made in energy development and remarkable results have been achieved in energy conservation and consumption reduction. September 11 (in Chinese).

[46]Calculated using data from the China National Bureau of Statistics (2005). Statistical Communiqué of the People's Republic of China on the 2004 National Economic and Social Development, February 25 (in Chinese).

Table 4.22. The share of China's overall energy and electricity consumption, 1985–2015.

%		1985	1990	1995	2000	2003	2005	2010	2015	2017
1st Ind.	Energy	5.28	4.92	4.20	4.36	3.84	3.57	1.99%	1.91%	1.99%
2nd Ind.		68.30	69.69	74.35	70.43	71.22	72.30	73.04%	69.78%	67.56%
3rd Ind.		9.06	9.38	9.45	13.68	13.61	13.65	14.33%	16.66%	17.60%
Residential usage		17.37	16.01	12.00	11.52	11.33	10.48	10.64%	11.65%	12.85%
1st Ind.	Electricity	7.71	6.85	5.81	5.00	4.06	3.51	2.33%	1.79%	1.81%
2nd Ind.		81.47	79.26	78.01	72.81	74.03	75.04	74.77%	72.82%	70.58%
3rd Ind.		5.42	6.17	6.15	9.78	10.15	10.12	10.68%	12.35%	13.62%
Residential usage		5.40	7.72	10.03	12.41	11.76	11.22	12.22%	13.04%	14.00%

Source: Calculated using data from the China National Bureau of Statistics: China Statistical Yearbook, China Statistics Press, 2018, Tables 9.3, 9.6; 2011, Tables 7.3, 7.6; 2006, Tables 7.3, 7.6; 2001, Tables 7.3, 7.6.

respectively.[47] However, the level of energy consumption is still very low. The per capita electricity consumption of residents is 156 kWh/year, which is only 3.3% of the United States.[48] Figure 4.7 shows that in 1978, China's per capita energy use was lower than the world average and the other listed countries, except India.

However, from 1978–2015, the average annual growth rate of per capita energy use ranked second, only after Republic of Korea. The average annual growth rate was 3.6%, 1.4%, 2.3%, 0.5%, 5.0%, minus 0.8%, minus 0.5%, and 0.7% for China, Brazil, India, Japan, Republic of Korea, Russian Federation, the United States, and the World, respectively. We should attach great importance to the negative growth rate of per capita energy use in the Russian Federation and the United States; China also needs to implement a negative growth rate. To achieve high-quality economic development, further improvement of the efficiency of energy

---

[47]Calculated using data from the China National Bureau of Statistics (2006). China Statistical Yearbook, China Statistics Press, 2006, Table 7.13.

[48]Energy Information Administration, Office of Integrated Analysis and Forecasting, U.S. Department of Energy (2005). International Energy Outlook, July, p. 69.

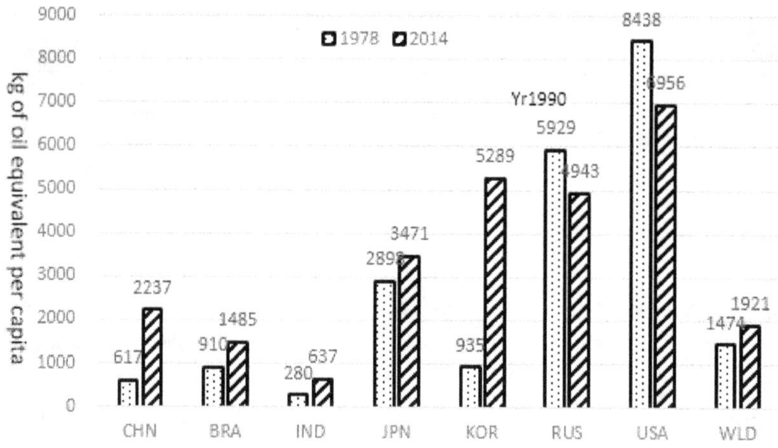

Figure 4.7. Energy use by country, 1978 and 2014 (per capita oil equivalent).

Source: World Bank (2018). World Development Indicators online 2018, Released November 14, 2018.

resource development and utilization is needed, as well as effective control of total energy consumption to accomplish the goal of reducing the energy consumption per unit of GDP in the "13th Five-Year Plan" by more than 15%.[49] Industrial energy consumption in China is apparently higher than those in other countries. In the process of industrialization, the task of adjustment of the economic structure is very arduous. Energy consumption per unit of GDP equivalent value ton SCE per 10,000 CNY (2000 constant CNY) slightly increased from 1.40 in 2000 to 1.43 tons SCE per 10000 CNY (2000 constant CNY) in 2005.[50] This was mainly the result of the change in industrial structure because energy consumption per unit value added of manufacturing industry is much higher than in primary and tertiary industry (see Table 4.23). The share of secondary industry increased 1.58% and of primary industry declined 2.23% during 2000–2005, with total energy consumption decreasing by 158.36 million tons SCE. From

---

[49]Department of Energy, China National Bureau of Statistics: Great achievements have been made in energy development and remarkable results have been achieved in energy conservation and consumption reduction. 2018-09-11, (in Chinese).

[50]Calculated using data from the China National Bureau of Statistics: China Statistical Yearbook, China Statistics Press, 2006, Tables 3.1, 3.4, 7.2.

Table 4.23.   The energy consumption variation because of industrial structure change of China, 2000, 2005, and 2017.

	2000	2005	2017	Ton SCE /10000 ¥(2000)	Ton SCE /10000 ¥(2005)	Ton SCE /10000 ¥(2017)	D 10000 Ton SCE(00-05)	D 10000 Ton SCE(00-17)
Primary industry	14.83	12.60	7.90	0.29	0.31	0.14	587.98	−8929.98
Secondary industry	45.92	47.50	40.50	2.30	2.17	0.91	−11564.3982323365	−463663.95
Tertiary industry	39.25	39.90	51.60	0.52	0.46	0.19	−4859.54	−143276.85

Source: Calculated using data from the China National Bureau of Statistics: China Statistical Yearbook, China Statistics Press, 2006, Tables 1.3, 3.1, 3.2, 7.10; 2019, Table 9.3, 2018, Table 1.3; China National Bureau of Statistics, Data base; Annual, GDP by the three strata of industry, 1998–2017.

2000–2017, the proportion of secondary industry decreased 5.42% that of primary industry decreased 6.93%, and of tertiary industry increased 12.35%; therefore, the total energy consumption decreased 615.87 million tons of SCE. This shows that industrial structure adjustment is of great significance to the reduction of energy consumption.

Assuming the same unit energy consumption per unit value added for different industrial sectors, industrial structure change within industry during 2000–2005 only slightly decreased the total energy consumption, because the percentage share of industrial sectors with higher energy consumption (for example, Smelting, and Pressing of Ferrous Metals) increased.

Table 4.24 shows six industrial sectors with significant changes from 2000–2005, which caused the total energy consumption to increase by 7.33 million tons SCE. The total energy consumption because of the industrial structural change of the manufacturing industry increased by 72.41 million tons SCE. Therefore, optimizing industrial structure is very important for saving energy.

During 2006–2010, the energy consumption per unit of GDP should have declined 20% as obligatory index in the eleventh Five Year Plan; however, the actual reduction was 19.3%. In the "12th FYP" period (2011–2015), the energy consumption per unit of GDP in 2015 should decline by 16% compared with that in 2010 as an obligatory index; the actual reduction was 18.4%. Elimination of backward production capacity has achieved remarkable results. In 2012–2015, the state vigorously eliminated backward and excess capacity in 16 industries including power, coal, iron making, and steel making. Total power production capacity was 21.08 million kilowatts, coal 520 million tons, iron making 58.97 million tons, and steel making 66.4 million tons, cement 500 million tons, flat glass 140 million weight boxes, coke 76.94 million tons, ferroalloy 9.25 million tons, calcium carbide 4.54 million tons, electrolytic aluminum 1.41 million tons, copper smelting 2.46 million tons, lead smelting 3.15 million tons, papermaking 26.02 million tons.[51]

---

[51] Department of Energy, China National Bureau of Statistics (2018). Great achievements have been made in energy development and remarkable results have been achieved in energy conservation and consumption reduction. September 11, (in Chinese).

Table 4.24.   The energy consumption variation because of industrial structure change within the manufacturing industry of China, 2000–2005.

	Δ % G.O. (2005– 2000)	Ton SCE/ 10000 CNY	Δ Value added, 100 million	Δ 10000 Ton SCE
Smelting and pressing of ferrous metals	3.00	6.23	84.32	525.32
Manufacture of communication equipment, computers and other electronic equipment	1.88	0.26	107.58	27.72
Production and supply of electric power and heat power	1.67	2.76	95.46	263.72
Extraction of petroleum and natural gas	−1.19	0.78	−57.21	−44.70
Manufacture of textile	−0.84	0.76	−27.15	−20.50
Manufacture of beverages	−1.02	1.54	−11.88	−18.26

Source: Calculated using data from the China National Bureau of Statistics. China Statistical Yearbook, China Statistics Press, 2006, Tables 3.1, 3.2, 7.10.

7. Pillar Industry

The share of pillar industries in China is low. Six criteria for selecting a pillar industry are:

1. High elasticity to per capita income.

$$\varepsilon_{gdppc} = \frac{\dfrac{dD}{D}}{\dfrac{dGDPpc}{GDPpc}} \tag{4.11}$$

D — demand.
GDPpc — GDP per capita

2. High productivity.
3. High linkage with other industrial branches.

4. Sustained development: the pillar industry can create new industrial branches and provide the foundation for the next generation pillar industry.
5. Strengthen international competitiveness.
6. Optimization coordination among industrial branches.

Shanghai's six pillar industries, namely the Electronic Information Product manufacture, Automobile manufacture, Petrochemical and Fine chemical industry, Fine steel and iron manufacture, Equipment complex manufacture, and Bio-medicine manufacture, have further consolidated their dominance through technology renovation and product upgrading and maintained their role as powerhouses in the local industrial economy. The six pillar industries utilized 59.5% of the city's property and 39.8% employees to produce 63.1% of municipal total industrial gross output and occupied 60.8% of the city's total industrial profits in 2005. Labor productivity and TFP (Total Factor Productivity) of the six pillar industries were 259% and 189% of the labor productivity and TFP of other industrial sectors in Shanghai in 2005, respectively. In 2017, the six pillar industries utilized 66.1% of the city's property and 59.8% employees to produce 68.7% of municipal total industrial gross output and occupied 60.8% of the city's total industrial profits.[52] Pillar industries should support economic development.

In China, the innovation-driven development strategy has been further advanced, and the growth rate of strategic emerging industries has accelerated. According to estimates, the added value of industrial strategic emerging industries increased by 10.0%, 10.5%, and 11.0% from 2015 to 2017, respectively, and the growth rate was 3.9, 4.5, and 4.4 % points higher than that of above-scale industries. The scale of the automotive manufacturing and new generation of information technology industry ranks them as the top two. In 2017, its industrial gross output accounted for more than 57% of the gross output of industrial strategic emerging industries; the gross output of Electronics and communication equipment manufacturing and computer and office equipment manufacturing accounted for 58% of the gross output of the High-tech manufacturing industry. New energy vehicles are exploding. In 2017, China's new energy

---

[52]Calculated using data from the Shanghai Municipal Statistics Bureau: Shanghai Statistical Yearbook, China Statistics Press, 2018, Tables 13.7, 13.8; 2006, Table 13.7.

vehicle production reached 690,000 units, ranking first in the world for three consecutive years.

7.1. *Six industrial performance indicators*

The design of a scalar measure of the level of industrial development for the purpose of cross-country comparison can be addressed in six industrial performance indicators, which are proposed by the United Nations Industrial Development Organization (UNIDO). A schematic representation of those considered here is shown in Figure 4.8, which serves at the same time as an indicator diagram. In this hexagonal scheme, the six vertices represent indicators, while the three diagonals are representative of aspects or dimensions of industrial development. The six indicators are inserted into the hexagon to define their notional positions in the "set-of-six" as well as to visualize relationships between them. Manufacturing value added (MVA) per capita, which is at the top of the hexagon in Figure 4.8, is the "anchor" indicator of the set of six. Value added per capita in manufacturing is the production-based domestic indicator of activity and as such is placed at one end of the activity axis Z. The other end of this diagonal axis is the trade-based international indicator of activity, namely, manufactured exports per capita. Simply, the level of industrial activity used these two indicators to assess industrial performance. The distinction between production based domestic indicators and trade-based international ones runs through the whole set of six. Its visual counterpart is the horizontal axis X, which divides the domestic upper half from the international lower half in Figure 4.8. The second dimension is represented in Figure 4.9 by the diagonal axis M, which connects two indicators that are representative of the industry dimension: the share of industry in total production and the share of industry in total exports. The third dimension represents technology, and particularly the part that the relatively more advanced technologies play in production and trade. Its prominence has to do with the role of industry as the source and engine of modern-style productivity-enhancing growth. The technology dimension is represented by the diagonal axis T, which connects the remaining two indicators: the share of medium or high technology goods in industrial production and the analogous share in manufactured exports. China's six industrial performance indicators and for some other foreign countries are shown in Table 4.28. China's Manufacturing value added (MVA)

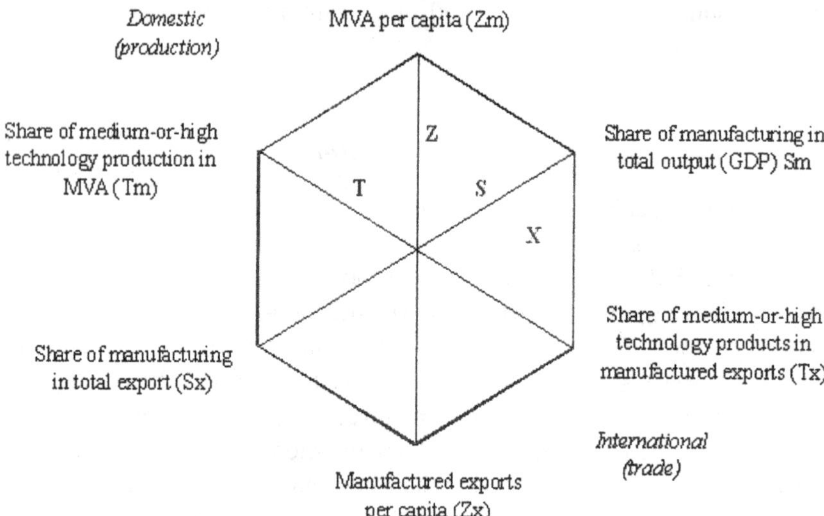

Figure 4.8.   Six industrial performance indicators.

Source: United Nations Industrial Development Organization (UNIDO) (2005). Industrial Development Report 2005-Capability building for catching-up, historical, empirical, and policy dimensions, Vienna, Chapter 10.

per capita (Zm) rose from USD100.7 (1995 constant USD) to USD359.4 (1995 constant USD) with average annual growth rate of 11.2%, which is the highest among the nine countries listed in Table 4.25. Followed by the Republic of Korea (South Korea) and India with an average annual growth rate of 6.7% and 3.9%, respectively.

China's MVA per capita rank rose from 114 among 152 economies in 1990 to 75 among 157 economies in 2002. The weighted rank of these six indicators of industrial performance is calculated by Eq. (4.12) proposed by the authors:

$$Rank_w = 0.2*(Rank_{Zm} + Rank_{Zx} + Rank_{Tm} + Rank_{Tx}) +$$
$$0.1*(Rank_{Mm} + Rank_{Mx}) \tag{4.12}$$

where $Rank_w$ — weighted rank of six indicators of industrial performance.

$Rank_{Zm}$, $Rank_{Zx}$, $Rank_{Mm}$, $Rank_{Mx}$, $Rank_{Tm}$, $Rank_{Tx}$ — Rank of Z_M, Zx, M_M, Mx, Tm,

Table 4.25.   Six indicators of industrial performance and their ranking (1990 and 2002).

Item	Unit	Year	Brazil	China	GER	India	Japan	S. Korea	Russian	GBR	USA
Manufacturing value added (MVA) per capita (Zm)	1995 USD	1990	913.6	100.7	6871.3	49	9696.9	2237.6	1164.9	3807.7	4325.2
	Rank	152	44	114	3	130	1	25	39	14	12
	1995 USD	2002	865	359.4	6649.1	77.6	9850.9	4858.7	644.7	3748.7	5567.7
	Rank	157	48	75	8	120	2	14	57	21	12
Manufactured exports per capita (Zx)	1995 USD	1990	159.3	41.6	4665.1	16.8	2263.9	1455.4	…	2655.5	1181.8
	Rank	101	57	76	9	90	18	23	0	16	26
	1995 USD	2002	221.9	234.5	6512.1	38.5	3595.2	3591.1	257	3884.8	1947.9
	Rank	102	12	61	12	85	21	22	59	20	30
Share of manufacturing in total output (GDP)(Mm)	%	1990	22.5	33.1	30.6	16.6	26.5	28.8	27.8	20.6	18.1
	Rank	153	30	9	11	73	23	15	18	43	63
	%	2002	18.8	34.5	27.2	15.8	25	33.9	22.2	16.3	17.6
	Rank	153	48	3	15	67	22	4	31	64	57
Share of manufacturing in total export (Mx)	%	1990	75.1	76	93.2	79.6	97.5	96.2	…	82.4	81.1
	Rank	90	31	30	12	27	2	3	0	25	26

(*Continued*)

Table 4.25.　(*Continued*)

Item	Unit	Year	Brazil	China	GER	India	Japan	S. Korea	Russian	GBR	USA
	%	2002	76.8	91.6	90.6	85.8	93	96.5	53.6	85.5	88.1
	Rank	91	39	15	16	26	9	2	47	27	23
Share of medium-or-high-technology production in MVA (Tm)	%	1990	51.6	51.6	66.5	55.3	66.5	55.1	46.3	60	63
	Rank	145	25	26	2	13	3	14	37	5	4
	%	2002	54.1	57.3	63.2	58.4	68.1	64.1	61	64.3	63.7
	Rank	145	27	19	10	16	3	8	11	7	9
Share of medium-or-high-technology products in manufactured exports (Tx)	%	1990	40	34.4	68.7	17.9	83.9	52.9	...	67.3	73.4
	Rank	109	36	41	4	59	1	17	0	5	2
	%	2002	51.5	45.6	74.9	19.7	86.3	70.6	26.7	74.4	76.7
	Rank	110	33	36	9	67	1	13	57	10	7
Weighted Rank		1990	38.5	55.3	5.9	68.4	7.1	17.6	17	14.8	17.7
		2002	32.7	40	10.9	66.9	8.5	12	44.6	20.7	19.6

Source: United Nations Industrial Development Organization (UNIDO) (2005). Industrial Development Report 2005-Capability building for catching-up, historical, empirical, and policy dimensions, Vienna, Chapter 10.

Tx

These two indicators — *Zm* and *Zx* — define the level of industrial activity. *Tm* and *Tx* represent the industrial advanced technologies in production and trade. These are probably the most important ones. Therefore, we assign these four indexes with high weight. China's weighted rank has risen from 55.3 in 1990 to 40.0 in 2002. Table 4.25 shows that, according to six indicators of industrial performance, there is a large gap among China and Germany, Japan, the Republic of Korea, the United Kingdom, and the United States. China's industrial performance is comparable with that of Brazil, India, and Russia. This again proves that China is "the world's workshop" rather than "the world's factory."

China should speed up the readjustment of the industrial structure according to the need for a new approach to industrialization. Vigorous efforts should be made to develop high and new-tech industries that can greatly spur economic growth. During the "10th FYP" period (2001–2005), structural adjustment mainly focused on the following aspects:

1. Enhance traditional industries with high, new, and advanced technologies. In these industries, enterprises should be directed by the market and supported by technological advances; extensive use of advanced adaptive technologies should be made to transform traditional industries and invigorate our equipment manufacturing industry.
2. Develop new and high-tech industries and use information technology to stimulate industrialization. An IT application should be energetically promoted to propel industrialization. China should vigorously boost national economic informatization and integrate structural adjustment with informatization.
3. To improve the structures of enterprises by way of developing large companies and enterprise groups.
4. To emphasize increasing product variety, improve product quality, save energy, reduce waste, prevent and control pollution, and increase productivity to advance the comprehensive use and full implementation of the sustainable development strategy.

However, this industrial structural adjustment did not implement successfully during 2001–2005. Let us look at the sharp rise in energy consumption during the 10th FYP period (2001–2005). Compared with the ninth FYP period (1996–2000), two billion more tons of coal were burned. In addition, the nation consumed 400 million more tons of oil than during the previous FYP, while the output of steel, non-ferrous metals, cement, paper, and pulp exceeded the combined totals of the eighth and ninth FYPs. All the major economic goals may have been achieved, but another important target to cut pollution by 10% failed. This proves the traditional models of urbanization and industrialization will be unsustainable in the long term. The 11th FYP makes clear that the five-year main task of industrial sectors is not expansion in scale, but structural upgrading to turn China's big industry into a powerhouse. Following the pattern of new industrialization, sticking to market orientation with enterprises as main entities, and through enhancement of independent innovation, further taking advantage of labor-intensive industries, optimizing, and restructuring the product mix, organizational structure, industrial spatial allocation, upgrading industrial technology, and general competitiveness. During the "12th FYP" period, China's energy-saving and environmental protection, new generation information technology, biology, high-end equipment manufacturing, new energy, new materials, and new energy vehicles and other strategic emerging industries developed rapidly.

In 2015, the value added of strategic emerging industries accounted for about 8% of GDP, and the industrial innovation capability and profitability improved significantly. China's position in the world CIP ranking is attributable to its high share in global trade; although low MVA per capita and exports indicate that manufacturing lags in terms of value added. Over the last 15 years, China has increased its share of manufacturing exports to 16% of the global manufacturing trade and is the largest exporter in the world today. China has also started positioning itself as a high-tech manufacture exporter. China's manufacturing industry has become the largest sector in the economy and accounted for more than one-third of GDP and more than 16% of global MVA in the year 2012, second only to the United States (see Table 4.26). Table 4.26 shows that China's ranking jumped from 32 in 1990 to 5 in 2012. The top five most industrially competitive countries were Germany, Japan, the United States, the Republic of Korea (ROK), and China. Each belongs to the most industrialized countries in the world, and jointly accounted for 58% of the world MVA. China's position in the ranking is attributable to its high share in global trade; although low MVA per capita and exports indicate that China has also started positioning itself as a high-tech manufacture exporter. China's manufacturing industry has become the largest sector in the economy and accounted for more of the global MVA in the year 2012, second only to the United States. In 2015, Germany was the world's

Table 4.26. According to the competitive industrial performance (CIP index) 1990–2015, the top 10 countries in 2015.

2018	CIP	Country	2015	CIP	Country	2000	CIP	Country
1	0.471	Germany	1	0	Germany	1	0.548	USA
2	0.372	China	2	0	Japan	2	0.525	Germany
3	0.349	Republic of Korea	3	0	China	3	0.502	Japan
4	0.345	USA	4	0	USA	4	0.347	Italy
5	0.344	Japan	5	0	Republic of Korea	5	0.347	Canada
6	0.33	Ireland	6	0	Switzerland	6	0.345	UK
7	0.302	Switzerland	7	0	Belgium	7	0.339	Switzerland
8	0.284	China, Taiwan Province	8	0	Netherlands	8	0.338	France
9	0.259	Singapore	9	0	Singapore	9	0.332	Ireland
10	0.252	Netherlands	10	0	Italy	10	0.307	Singapore

Source: United Nations Industrial Development Organization (Unido): Research, Statistics And Industrial Policy Branch, Working Paper 12/2014, Shyam Upadhyaya and Shohreh Mirzaei Yeganeh, Statistics Unit, UNIDO.

most industrially competitive country for the 22nd consecutive year. Germany's share of medium-high and high-tech value added in total MVA grew by an average annual rate of 1.1% in 1995–2015, to 61%. Japan ranked second, even though its CIP score declined by an average of 1.3% a year between 1990 and 2015. It remains the world's leader in export quality.

China, the world's largest manufacturing producer and exporter, moved from fifth to third place in 2015. Its economy accounted for 18.4% of world trade in manufactured goods and 23.5% of global MVA. China still lagged behind other industrial economies in manufacturing per capita and manufactured exports per capita. Its capacity to produce and export manufactures resembles that of Turkey and Oman. The United States, the world's second largest contributor to world MVA in 2015, ranked fourth.[53]

---

[53] United Nations Industrial Development Organization (UNIDO): Industrial Development Report 2018, LI Yong, Director General, UNIDO: Table 8.2 Competitive Industrial Performance index, 2015.

China is being pressured from both sides. Advanced economies such as the United States, Germany, and Japan have all formulated policies supporting further development of their own manufacturing. At the same time, emerging economies such as India and Brazil are also catching up with their own advantages. China should implement new development concepts of innovation, coordination, green, openness, and sharing to strengthen the whole industries, as shown in Figure 4.9. Figure 4.9 shows that the development of the industrial economy has expanded from quantity to quality. Through exerting market forces and enhancing policy guidance, we sped up the transformation of the economic growth model and gave new impetus to the improvement and upgrading of the industrial structure. Through the in-depth implementation of innovation-driven development strategies, industry continues to move toward the mid- to high-end level. In accordance with the requirements of high-quality development, China should promote the development of large industrial countries into powerful manufacturing countries, transform Chinese manufacturing into Chinese creation, and adjust China's speed to Chinese quality. The criteria for evaluation are innovation, quality, productivity, digitization, and pollution reduction.

8. Structural Changes in Rural Economy and Within Agriculture

After 1978, the structural changes in rural economy are quite large. China's rural Township and Village-run Enterprises (TVE) entered a period of rapid development in the 1980s, with businesses including agriculture, industry, and services. Township enterprises have also become a leading driving force behind China's rural economy (see Table 4.27). After 2003, China National Bureau of Statistics did not separately publish data on TVEs, because many had developed into large-scale private enterprises and thus were classified as industrial enterprises. Farmers have created township enterprises that have been hailed as "half of the country." Today, the private economy born out of township enterprises is an indispensable force for national development. An example is Lu Guanqiu, chairman of Wanxiang Qianchao (000559.SZ) Group, who is the first generation of legendary private entrepreneurs in China. He turned a heavily indebted TVE into a company with an annual revenue of more than 100 billion yuan, directly or

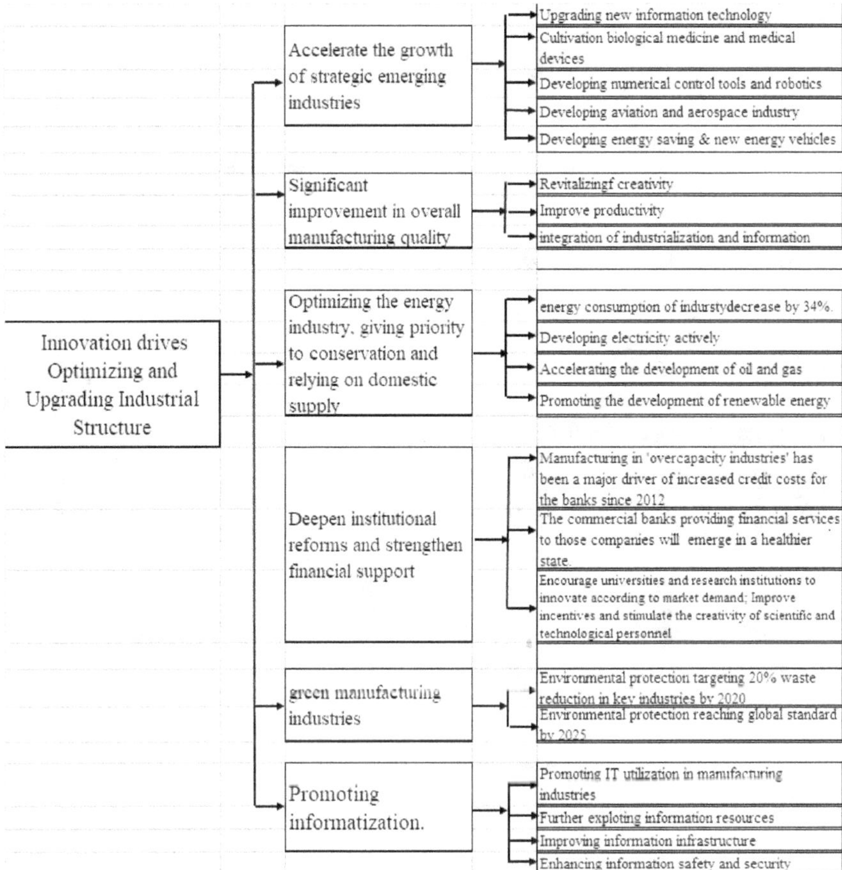

Figure 4.9.   Optimizing and upgrading the industrial structure, 2015–2020.

Source: Xinhua News Agency: The outline of 11th FYP (in Chinese), May 16, 2006, Chapters 10–15; Full text of the Report on the Implementation of the 2014 Plan for National Economic and Social Development and on the 2015 Draft Plan for National Economic and Social Development, which was submitted on March 5, 2015 for review at the Third Session of the 12th National People's Congress and was adopted on March 15; The outline of the 13th FYP for National Economic and Social Development of the People's Republic of China, (Approved by the Fourth Session of the 12th National People's Congress on March 16, 2016) (in Chinese); Department of Industrial Statistics, China National Bureau of Statistics: Reform and opening-up casts industrial glory, innovation and transformation, and strong manufacturing power, 2018-09-04 (in Chinese); China State Council: 13th Five-Year National Strategic Emerging Industry Development Plan, 2016/11/19 (in Chinese).

indirectly holding dozens of listed companies — a giant multinational group involved in manufacturing, energy, finance, agriculture, and resources.

Table 4.27.   TVE development in China after economic reform.

Item	Units	1980	1985	1990	1995	2000	2002	2003	2004	2005
Number of Township Enterprises	10,000 units	142.47	1222.5	1873.44	2202.67	2084.66	2133	2185	2213	2249.59
Employed Persons of TVE at the Year-end	10,000 persons	2999.68	6979	9264.75	12862.06	12819.6	13288	13573	13866	14272.4
Value added of TVE	Billion CNY	28.531	77.231	250.432	1459.523	2715.62	3238.6	3668.6	4181.5	5053.43
Total profits	Billion CNY	12.626	24.705	68.346	369.725	648.181	755.8	857.1	993.2	1251.86
Export Goods of TVE	Billion CNY			36.441	347.185	694.882	1156.3	1419.7	1693.2	1980
Tax paid	Billion CNY	2.566	13.7	31.284	127.971	199.65	269.4	313	365.8	518.092
Wages paid to employee	Billion CNY	11.94	17.13	60.68	219.25	706	852.8	907.2	975.6	1111.74

Source: Calculated using data from the China National Bureau of Statistics: China Statistical Yearbook, China Statistics Press, 2003, Tables 12.29, 12.30, 12.31, 12.32, 12.34; Ministry of Agriculture of China: The Agriculture Development Report (in Chinese), 2006, Tables VIII 01- VIII 06; 2005, Table 13; 2003, Table 13; 2001, Table 13; The achievements in the development of China TVEs in 2005 (in Chinese), China Township Enterprises News, Jan. 6, 2006.

His success story was included in the classic cases of Harvard Business School. On August 28, 2001, at the time of the WTO and the wave of internationalization, the first domestic OEM to supply parts for General Motors of the United States, he also acquired UAL, a NASDAQ listed company, making one of China's TVEs the first to acquire overseas listed companies. At the celebration of the 40th anniversary of reform and opening-up, Lu Guanqiu won the title of reform pioneer — the pioneer of the reform and development of township enterprises. Another example is the Midea Group (000333.SZ) Home Appliances Industry, founded in 1968. Chairman of Midea Holdings Co., Ltd., He Xiangjian, led a small group of 23 people to raise CNY5,000 to build a plastic bottle cap. In the 1980s, it entered the home appliance industry. In 1992, it implemented the internal shareholding system reform. In 1993, it was listed on the Shenzhen Stock Exchange, becoming the first listed company in the country to be transformed from a township enterprise. The company, headquartered in Beijiao Town, Foshan City, has layouts in 15 overseas countries, providing 300 million home appliances per year to global users and 300 million core components to global manufacturers. In 2017, Midea Group's operating income reached more than CNY240 billion, with a growth rate of 51%, making it one of the World's leading home appliance technology groups.

The third example, Zhou Haijiang, Chairman of the Board of Directors of Hongdou "hóngdòu" Group (600400.SH), was elected as a private entrepreneur of the Party Committee of the 17th National Congress, 18th National Congress, and 19th National Congress. Zhou Haijiang has two other identities he values: Party Secretary of the CPC Red Bean Group and the National Industry and Commerce Vice Chairman. "Over the years, the Red Bean Group has been able to develop rapidly and steadily. The key is to focus on the party building work of the enterprise, give play to the political leading role of the party organization in the enterprise and the political core role among the employees, and integrate the party building with the enterprise development to make "party building strong", to promote 'development strong'," Zhou Haijiang concluded. Just in March of 2021, the Central Party revised the monograph of its "Modern Enterprise System with Chinese Characteristics," marking a milestone breakthrough for Chinese private enterprises to organically integrate party building with modern enterprise systems. The Red Bean Group, which he piloted, is now a multinational enterprise group with two industrial parks, three listed companies, three well-known trademarks, four major industrial sectors, directly and indirectly solving more than 100,000 jobs and marketing more than CNY50 billion. On September 28, 2017, at the meeting held by the National Federation of Industry and Commerce to study and implement the "Opinions of the CPC Central Committee and the State Council on Building an Entrepreneurial Healthy Growth Environment and Promoting Outstanding Entrepreneurship to Make the Role of Entrepreneurs Better," private entrepreneurs made their first speech. At the meeting, Zhou Haijiang also proposed that outstanding private entrepreneurs should "take three kinds of responsibilities and carry forward five spirits. Regarding the three kinds of responsibilities, my understanding is that the first is political responsibility, the second is development responsibility, and the third is social responsibility." Enterprise development takes up a lot of social resources and it is incumbent on fulfilling social responsibility. Over the years, Zhou Haijiang and his Red Bean Group have donated more than CNY300 million to society. "Enterprises should benefit from the development of dividends to all stakeholders and achieve win–win outcomes with shareholders, employees, customers, suppliers, partners, governments, the environment, society (community), etc. We are building in Sihanoukville, Cambodia. The special economic zone adheres to the concept of win–win cooperation and actively fulfills its social responsibilities and has won universal support from the local people." Comrade Xi Jinping once praised the "Spirited Sihanoukville Special Economic Zone as a pragmatic model for cooperation." In addition, he also believes that in conjunction with taking on three kinds of responsibilities, it is necessary to carry forward five spirits, namely, entrepreneurship, innovation, craftsmanship, learning spirit, and spirit. In addition to outstanding party building work, "integrity management, governance according to law" has always been the bottom line for the development of Hongdou people. Zhou Haijiang, president of Hongdou Group, became the cover of the world-famous financial magazine Forbes in February 2005. In 2006, he was invited to speak at the Massachusetts Institute of Technology.[54] Wanxiang Qianchao (000559.SZ) Group, Midea Group

---

[54]Han, C. (2018). Thanks to the farmers – we have walked together for forty years, *People's Daily*, December 29 (in Chinese); A generation of legendary curtain call, how is Lu Guanqiu made: from township enterprises to knock on the capital market. 2017-10–26, (in Chinese); Annual Ring of Innovation: From Industrial Giant to Network Pioneer, Well-off "xiǎokāng" Journal in late December 2018, December 27, 2018; Interview: Zhou

(000333.SZ), and Hongdou Group (600400.S) were in Zhejiang, Guangdong, and Jiangsu provinces, respectively. From 1978 to 2005, the economic development levels of these three provinces rank as the top three among all provinces and will be discussed in Chapter 5.

In 2005, China's 22.5 million township enterprises employed more than 142.7 million rural workers, which occupied 28.3% of rural labor.[55] In 2005, TVEs had a combined added value of over CNY5.05 trillion (USD647 billion). The value added in the manufacturing industry of TVEs reached CNY3.57 trillion (USD457 billion), accounting for 41% of national industry value-added of above the designated size industrial enterprises. Total profits of TVEs reached CNY1.25 trillion (USD160 billion) in 2005, accounted for 84.6% of national industry total profits of above the designated size industrial enterprises.[56] TVEs generated a delivery value of export goods of CNY1.98 trillion (USD253.5 billion), which occupied 31.6% of China's exports.[57] The accumulated utilized FDI of TVEs reached USD74.4 billion at the end of 2005, which accounted for 9.6% of total accumulated utilized FDI in China. Non-public ownership amounted to 84.9% of TVEs' assets at the end of 2005.[58] The average annual growth rate of value added, employed persons, wages, export, profits, and paid taxes are shown in Figure 4.10. The figure clearly indicates the average annual growth rates of TVE indicators were high during 1980–1995 and declined dramatically after 1995. Because China's economic reform began with agriculture in rural areas, before 1995 China's market commodities were in short supply. TVEs developed quickly before 1995.

Haijiang, Party Secretary of the 19th Party, Party Secretary of the Red Bean Group, and Chairman of the Board of Directors. Legal Daily, October 21, 2017, (in Chinese).

[55] Calculated using data from the China National Bureau of Statistics: China Statistical Yearbook, China Statistics Press, 2006, Table 13.4; Ministry of Agriculture of China: The Agriculture Development Report (in Chinese), 2006, Tables VIII01–VIII06.

[56] Calculated using data from the China National Bureau of Statistics: China Statistical Yearbook, China Statistics Press, 2006, Table 14.4; The achievements in the development of China TVEs in 2005 (in Chinese), China Township Enterprises News, January 6, 2006.

[57] Calculated using data from the China National Bureau of Statistics: China Statistical Yearbook, China Statistics Press, 2006, Table 18.3; Ministry of Agriculture of China: The Agriculture Development Report (in Chinese), Tables VIII01–VIII06.

[58] The achievements in the development of China TVEs during 10th Five-year plan (2006), *China Township Enterprises News*, January 6.

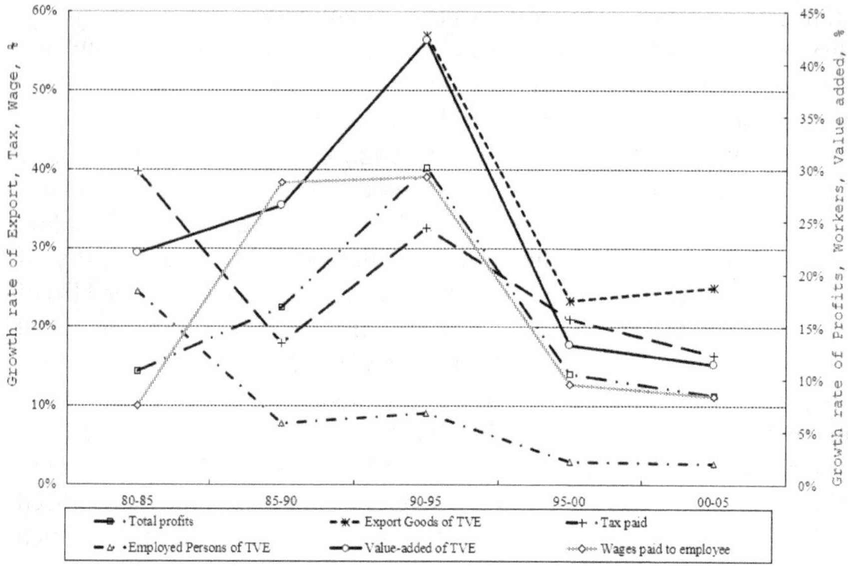

Figure 4.10.   Average annual growth rate of TVE indicators in China.

Source: Calculated using data from the China National Bureau of Statistics: China Statistical Yearbook, China Statistics Press, 2003, Tables 12.29, 12.30, 12.31, 12.32, 12.34; Ministry of Agriculture of China: The Agriculture Development Report (in Chinese), 2005, Table 13; 2003, Table 13; 2001, Table 13; Ministry of Agriculture of China: The Agriculture Development Report (in Chinese), Tables VIII01-VIII06; The achievements in the development of China TVEs in 2005 (in Chinese), China Township Enterprises News, January 6, 2006.

After 1995, with the reform of SOEs and the establishment of many FFEs, China's market became a buyer's market from a seller's market. TVEs could not compete with SOEs and FFEs in management, technology, and equipment; so TVEs developed more slowly after 1995.

China has had only 40 years of genuine industrialization, which can only be described as short when compared with 300 years of volatile capitalism in the Western world. By 2000, the number of workers in village firms had reached more than 128 million (not including the migrant workers in the cities), accounting for a remarkable 30% of China's entire rural labor force. Village industrial gross output reached CNY11.6 trillion, a 16.5-fold increase compared with its 1988 value, or a 225-fold increase compared with its 1978 value; its average rate of growth was 28% per year between 1978 and 2000, doubling every three years, and the total increase in real gross output of village industries was at least 66-fold over the 1978–2000 period. This scale and speed of long-lasting economic growth is unique in economic history. China's development experience suggests a new model of economic development: the New Stage Theory (NST). In the late 1980s, TVEs produced over two-thirds of rural industrial output. As they grew, TVEs began to apply for bank loans. The volume of loans to TVEs rose by twelve times between 1980 and 1994, a rise that exceeded that of the rest of the economy. However, the share of the total outstanding loans provided by the ABCs (Agricultural Bank of China) and RCCs to TVEs increased from 13.8% to 33.2%, thus forcing China's financial reform.

One of the first steps of financial reforms in the early 1980s was to give the core of the PBC's decision-making bureaucracy duties as the central bank. The organizational reforms stipulated that the ABCs would provide all the main financial services to the rural economy from its headquarters in Beijing through offices in each province, county, and township. The major duty of the ABCs was to satisfy the credit needs of farm producers and rural firms and finance the state's supply of farm inputs and procurement of agricultural products.[59] Thus, TVEs are an innovation in China's reform and opening-up. Rural reform began with the adjustment of the relationship between farmers and land, and through the implementation of the contract responsibility system, which greatly mobilized the enthusiasm of hundreds of millions of farmers. It has greatly liberated rural productivity and provided a solid institutional guarantee for agricultural and rural development. The output of major agricultural products increased rapidly. More than 1.3 billion Chinese people completely bid farewell to the "lack of economy" of long-term agricultural products. The main contradiction of agriculture has changed from insufficient product to structural contradiction. Along with the rapid increase of agricultural labor productivity after household contracting, new contradictions and problems have emerged in the development of agriculture and rural areas. It is prominent that many rural laborers were liberated from the shackles of land and urgently needed to find new ways of development. The

---

[59] Wen, Y. and G. E. Fortier (2016). The visible hand: The role of government in China's long-awaited industrial revolution, *Federal Reserve Bank of St. Louis Review*, Third Quarter, 98(3), 189–226. http://dx.doi.org/10.20955/r.2016.189-226; Shen, M., J. Huang, L. Zhang, and S. Rozelle (2010). Financial reform and transition in China: A study of the evolution of banks in rural. *Agricultural Finance Review*, 70(3), 305–332.

emergence of TVEs in the 1980s had not only found a new path for non-agricultural employment for the increasingly sharp problem of rural surplus labor, but also strengthened the collective economy and promoted urbanization in rural areas. Working in the city has created challenging conditions. The massive flow of labor and the unprecedented activity of productivity will inevitably lead to the reform of the agricultural product circulation system aimed at marketization. Practice has proved that the development of TVEs has solved the problem of agricultural modernization and rural industrialization coordination within the county scope and promoted the adjustment and optimization of industrial and agricultural relations that have been seriously unbalanced for a long time. The reform of rural marketization has further created conditions for promoting the development of non-agricultural industries and has effectively promoted the initial integration of rural first, second, and third industries. This period of rural reform, based on rural household contract management, has built a new dynamic mechanism for rural development, which has effectively promoted the coordinated advancement of rural industrialization, marketization, and agricultural modernization.[60]

Figure 4.11 shows at the beginning of economic reform (1980) agriculture was the major composition in the rural economy. The value added share of agriculture in the rural economy dominated (83.5%), which means there was almost no industry and service sector in rural areas.

The rural economy in China in 1980 was a self-sufficient economy. In 1995, the value added share of agriculture in the rural economy became less than 50% and the share of industry in the rural economy (41.1%) approximately equaled the share of agriculture. In 2005, the value added share of industry (48.5%) exceeded the share of agriculture (31.3%). However, the absolute value added of agriculture increased from CNY135.9 billion (USD79.1 billion) in 1978 to CNY2.307 trillion (USD281.6 billion). From Table 4.28, using IS change coefficient K and IS similar coefficient *R1,* we observe that the largest structural change of the rural economy output occurred during 1990–1995 because industry value added increased from CNY185.5 billion (USD22.4 billion) to CNY1,080.4 billion (USD130.5 billion) during this period. The smallest structural change of the rural economy output occurred during 2000–2005. The IS change coefficient K_{annual} and IS similar coefficient

---

[60] Yu, X. (2018). Thoughts on Carrying Forward the Spirit of Rural Reform and Promoting Rural Revitalization. Rural Work Communication, December 28 (in Chinese).

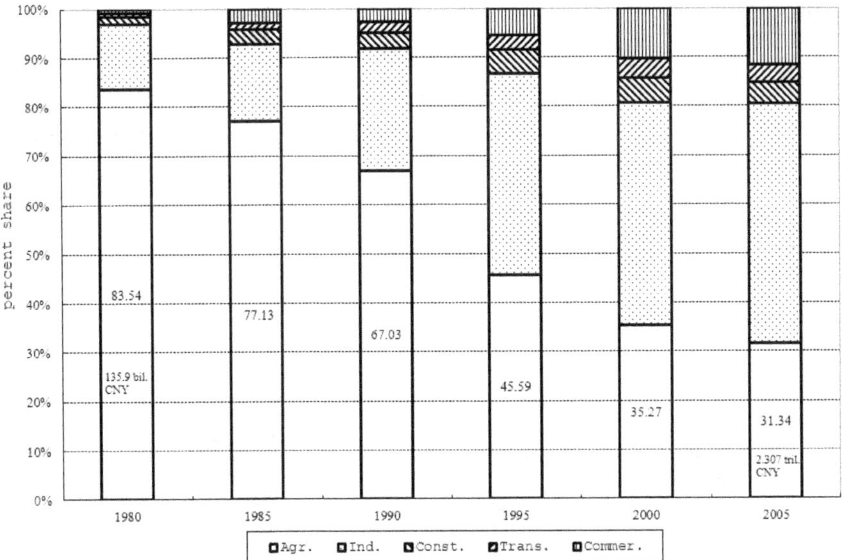

Figure 4.11.   The output (V.A.) structure of rural economy in China.

Source: Calculated using data from the Ministry of Agriculture of China: The Summary of China National Agriculture Statistics 2005 (in Chinese), Tables VIII 01- VIII 06; China National Bureau of Statistics: China Statistical Yearbook, China Statistics Press, 2006, Table 3.1; 2003, Tables 3.1, 12.31.

R1 equaled 0. 90 and 0.6569, respectively, during 1980–2005, which indicates a significant output structural change in the rural economy in China occurred during this period. The specification coefficient h in Table 4.28 declined from 65.32 to 24.30 during 1980–2005, which means the role of agricultural output in the rural economy was weakened and the industry, commerce sectors output played a more important role.

Using the data from 1978–2005,[61] we conduct regression analysis of rural value added with percentage share of agriculture in the rural economy:

---

[61] Calculated using data from the Ministry of Agriculture of China: The Summary of China National Agriculture Statistics 2005 (in Chinese), Tables VIII 01–VIII 06; 2003 (in Chinese), Tables VIII 04; Ministry of Agriculture: China Agriculture Yearbook 2005 (in Chinese), China Agriculture Publisher, December 2005, p. 226; China National Bureau of

Table 4.28.   The output (value added) structure of rural economy in China, 1980–2005.

%	1980	1985	1990	1995	2000	2005
Agr.	83.54	77.13	67.03	45.59	35.27	31.34
Ind.	13.41	15.72	24.79	41.07	45.36	48.45
Const.	1.51	2.91	3.21	4.87	5.07	4.38
Trans.	0.78	1.37	2.22	3.06	4.00	3.51
Commer.	0.77	2.87	2.75	5.42	10.30	11.53
K_{annual}	0.83	0.51	0.82	1.72	0.82	0.63
R1	0.6569	0.9985	0.9882	0.9278	0.9808	0.9961
Years for Comparison	1980–2005	1980–1985	1985–1990	1990–1995	1995–2000	2000–2005
h	65.32	53.10	43.61	29.45	22.95	24.30

Source: Calculated using data from the Ministry of Agriculture of China: The Summary of China National Agriculture Statistics 2005 (in Chinese), Tables VIII 01- VIII 06; China National Bureau of Statistics: China Statistical Yearbook, China Statistics Press, 2006, Table 3.1; 2003, Tables 3.1, 12.31.

$$agr\% = 163.21 - 14.708\, Ln(RuralVApc)$$
$$(39.58)\quad (-27.68)$$
$$R = 0.9885,\ F = 765.9,\ df = 18,\ s = 2.77 \tag{4.13}$$

where *agr%* — the percentage share of agricultural value added in total rural value added.

RuralVApc — per capita total value added in rural area at different year.

From the above values, we conclude that the regression Eq. (4.13) is statistically acceptable. This means when per capita total value added in the rural area increased, the percentage share of agricultural value added in total rural value added declined. From Eq. (4.13), we know that if per capita total value added in the rural area increases by 7.04%, the percentage share of agricultural value added in total rural value added will decline 1%, or if per capita total value added in the rural area doubled, the percentage share of agricultural value added in total rural value added will decline by 10.2%. To increase rural income, the structural change in rural

Statistics: China Statistical Yearbook, China Statistics Press, 2006, Table 3.1; 2003, Tables 3.1, 12.31.

economy should include development of the industry and service sectors.

For lateral analysis, using the data in the same year but for different regions (31 provinces in 2004), sample data is listed in Table 4.29.[62] Using these data for regression analysis, we get:

$$agr\% = 235.15 - 22.06\, Ln(RegRurVApc)$$
$$(6.99) \quad (-5.74) \tag{4.14}$$
$$R = 0.7925,\, F = 33.0,\, df = 29,\, s = 14.62$$

where agr% — the percentage share of agricultural value added in total rural value added.

RegRuralVApc — per capita total value added in rural area of different regions in the same year.

From the above values, we conclude that the regression Eq. (4.14) is statistically acceptable. This means when per capita total value added in the rural areas of various provinces in China increased, the percentage share of agricultural value added in total rural value added of different provinces declined. From Eqs. (4.13) and (4.14), we see that we get the same results whether we use longitudinal or lateral regression analysis. From Eq. (4.14), if per capita total value added in the rural area increased by 4.63%, the percentage share of agricultural value added in total rural value added will decline by 1%; or, if per capita total value added in rural area doubled, percentage share of agricultural value added in total rural value added will decline by 15.3%. To increase farmer's income and modernize the rural economy, China should develop manufacturing and tertiary industry in the rural area.

The employment structure changes in the rural economy also showed a similar situation, increasing from 2.98% in 2005 to 40.5%, which implies 195 million rural laborers worked in non-agriculture sectors. Figure 4.12 also shows that despite the fact the share of employment in the agriculture sector declined sharply from 1980–2005, the absolute amounts of laborers in Agriculture slightly increased from 298.1 million

---

[62]Calculated using data from the Ministry of Agriculture: China Agriculture Yearbook 2005 (in Chinese), China Agriculture Publisher, December 2005, p. 163, 174, 231; China National Bureau of Statistics: China Statistical Yearbook, China Statistics Press, 2005, Table 3.11.

Table 4.29.   The output structure of regional rural economy in China, 2004.

	Farming	Forestry	Husbandry	Fishery	K	R	h
National	51.46	3.77	34.54	10.23	0.00	1.0000	33.78
Beijing	36.49	5.02	54.61	3.88	8.53	0.9206	39.45
Tianjin	43.05	0.75	41.81	14.39	4.57	0.9809	35.19
Hebei	49.69	1.75	45.40	3.15	4.35	0.9817	44.96
Shanxi	64.09	4.22	31.14	0.54	5.23	0.9784	49.66
Inner Mongolia	49.07	5.55	44.67	0.71	4.77	0.9775	43.77
Liaoning	41.52	2.76	37.24	18.49	4.38	0.9786	28.92
Jilin	52.19	3.53	42.84	1.44	3.61	0.9854	45.22
Heilongjiang	55.79	5.92	36.04	2.25	3.19	0.9911	41.22
Shanghai	44.96	5.40	29.11	20.52	4.77	0.9790	25.36
Jiangsu	54.12	1.75	24.55	19.58	4.80	0.9748	33.70
Zhejiang	45.21	5.98	21.20	27.62	7.84	0.9317	24.72
Anhui	52.57	4.49	33.76	9.17	0.73	0.9996	33.95
Fujian	40.41	6.62	22.42	30.55	9.27	0.9090	22.74
Jiangxi	47.30	7.62	31.30	13.79	2.96	0.9948	26.25
Shandong	55.64	1.75	30.08	12.53	2.59	0.9946	36.71
Henan	56.76	2.69	39.56	0.99	4.13	0.9885	48.36
Hubei	55.07	1.90	30.74	12.29	2.27	0.9959	36.37
Hunan	46.44	4.85	42.34	6.37	3.55	0.9872	35.24
Guangdong	46.62	3.00	27.73	22.65	4.97	0.9719	28.36
Guangxi	48.85	4.55	36.11	10.49	1.05	0.9989	31.97
Hainan	39.64	13.87	19.45	27.05	10.77	0.9014	18.43
Chongqing	55.16	3.06	38.26	3.52	2.97	0.9936	42.82
Sichuan	44.62	2.83	49.58	2.97	6.02	0.9630	43.26
Guizhou	61.48	4.50	32.67	1.36	4.30	0.9845	46.41
Yunnan	55.71	9.31	32.92	2.06	3.92	0.9864	38.31
Tibet	43.25	9.31	47.42	0.02	7.37	0.9553	41.67
Shaanxi	66.24	4.22	28.73	0.82	6.09	0.9723	50.04
Gansu	71.07	3.47	25.24	0.22	7.84	0.9565	55.25
Qinghai	41.43	2.18	56.30	0.08	8.70	0.9284	51.67
Ningxia	58.28	5.07	33.71	2.93	3.25	0.9905	41.85
Xinjiang	71.47	1.92	26.02	0.60	8.00	0.9586	56.71

Source: Calculated using data from the Ministry of Agriculture: China Agriculture Yearbook (in Chinese), China Agriculture Publisher, December 2005, p. 163, 174, 231; China National Bureau of Statistics: China Statistical Yearbook, China Statistics Press, 2005, Table 3.11.

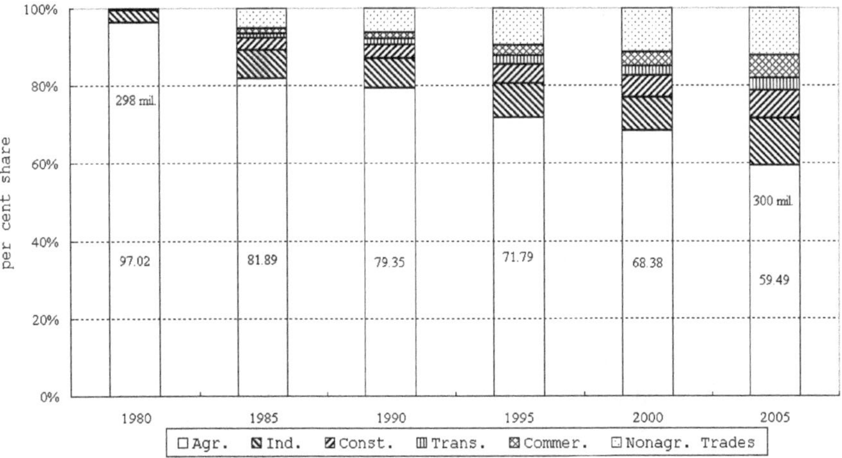

Figure 4.12.   The employment structure of the rural economy in China.

Source: Calculated using data from the China National Bureau of Statistics: China Statistical Yearbook, China Statistics Press, 2006, Table 13.4.

in 1980 to 299.8 million in 2005, which is almost the same. Therefore, the new increment of rural laborers of 196.6 million persons during 1980–2005 almost all worked in rural non-agricultural sectors.

From Table 4.30, using IS change coefficient K_{annual} and IS similar coefficient *R1,* we find that the largest structural change of rural employment also occurred during 1980–1985; and the smallest structural change of rural employment occurred during 1985–1990.

The largest structural change of rural employment occurred during 1980–1985, which included 57.97 million rural laborers increased in non-agricultural sectors during this period, while only 5.43 million rural laborers were added in agriculture. During 1985–1990, only 1.75 million rural laborers increased in rural non-agricultural sectors, while 29.85 million rural laborers were added in agriculture. The IS change coefficient Kannual reached 0.54 and IS similar coefficient R1 equals 0.9719, respectively, during 1980–2005, which indicates the structure change of rural employment during 1980–2005 is smaller than the structural change of rural output that occurred during the same period (compare with Table 4.28). The specification coefficient h in Table 4.30 declined from 59.58 to 28.27 during 1985–2005, which means the share of rural labor force engaged in agriculture declined and the portion of the rural labor force

Table 4.30.   The employment structure of rural economy in China.

%	1980	1985	1990	1995	2000	2005
Agr.	97.02	81.89	79.35	71.79	68.38	59.49
Ind.	2.98	7.40	7.69	8.82	8.57	11.93
Const.	0.00	3.05	3.62	4.89	5.61	7.25
Trans.	0.00	1.17	1.51	2.18	2.44	3.11
Commer.	0.00	1.25	1.65	2.60	3.65	5.83
Others	0.00	5.25	6.17	9.72	11.35	12.39
K_{annual}	0.54	1.01	0.17	0.50	0.24	0.59
$R1$	0.9719	0.9953	0.9998	0.9977	0.9993	0.9951
h	90.93	59.58	55.13	43.93	39.14	28.27
Years for	1980–	1980–	1985–	1990–	1995–	2000–
Comparison	1905	1985	1990	1995	2000	2005

Source: Calculated using data from the China National Bureau of Statistics: China Statistical Yearbook, China Statistics Press, 2006, Table 13.4.

that worked in industry, tertiary sectors started playing a more important role.

The take-off of the rural economy and township enterprises have greatly pushed rural reform and increased farmers' income. During the ninth Five Year Plan (1996–2000), the annual growth rate of per capita net income of farmers amounted to 4.7%, which is 9.4% lower than that observed during the sixth Five Year Plan (1981–1985).[63] The farmers' annual growth rate of per capita net income *continued* to decline during 1996–2000; it decreased from 9.0% in 1996 to 2.1% in 2000 (see Table 4.31). It has improved since 2004. The TVEs made great contributions to farmers' per capita net income. During the ninth Five Year Plan (1996–2000), TVEs paid wages of approximately CNY3,097.8 billion (USD374.6 billion). The percentage share of contribution from TVEs to farmers' per capita net income in 1996–2000 steadily increased, as shown in Figure 4.13. Furthermore, Figure 4.14 shows that the increment of farmers' per capita net income from agriculture became smaller during 1996–2000, with the absolute amount

---

[63]Calculated using data from the China National Bureau of Statistics: China Statistical Yearbook, China Statistics Press, 2004, Table 10.2.a

Table 4.31.   Contribution of TVEs to per capita net income of farmers in China.

	Per capita net income of farmer		Per capita net income from TVE		Increment of per capita net income Contributed by TVE, %
	¥ RMB	Annual growth rate,%	¥ RMB	Contribution from TVE, %	
1996	1926.1	8.99%	575.1	29.86	
1997	2090.1	4.59%	612.9	29.32	23.05
1998	2162	4.30%	686.8	31.77	102.81
1999	2210.3	3.81%	724.0	32.76	77.06
2000	2253.4	2.09%	760.0	33.73	83.53
2003	2622.2	4.30%	930.0	35.47	46.10
2004	2936	6.79%	1020.0	34.74	28.68
2005	3254.9	6.21%	1100.0	33.80	25.09

Source: Calculated using data from the Ministry of Agriculture of China: The Agriculture Development Report (in Chinese), 2006, Tables VIII 01-VIII 06; 2005, Table 13; 2003, Table 13; 2001, Table 13; The achievements in the development of China TVEs during 10th FYP (in Chinese), China Township Enterprises News, January 6, 2006; China State Bureau of TVEs: "The Contribution of TVEs to per capita net income of farmer in China during ninth FYP" (in Chinese); China National Bureau of Statistics: China Statistical Yearbook, China Statistics Press, 2006, Tables 10.2, 10.3; China State Bureau of TVEs: "The analysis on economic operating status of TVE in 2004" (in Chinese), January 2005; "The analysis on economic operating status of TVE in 2004" (in Chinese), January 17, 2004; Figure 4.13 illustrates the contribution to per capita net income of farmers in the richest as well as the poorest municipalities and provinces in China. It is found that the higher the contribution from TVEs, the higher the per capita net income of farmers.

equaling only CNY804 during the 10-year period of 1996–2005, and the increment of farmers' per capita net income from TVEs was CNY525 during the same period. This clearly demonstrated the significance of the structural change in the rural economy.

For example, farmers' net income per capita from TVEs in Shanghai reached CNY3,003, which is 55.5% of farmers' per capita net income in 1999; meanwhile, the corresponding value for Gansu farmers was only CNY263 and only 19.4% of per capita net income, as illustrated in Figure 4.15. The highest per capita net income from TVEs (Shanghai) was more than 10 times the lowest value (Gansu), but the highest farmers' per

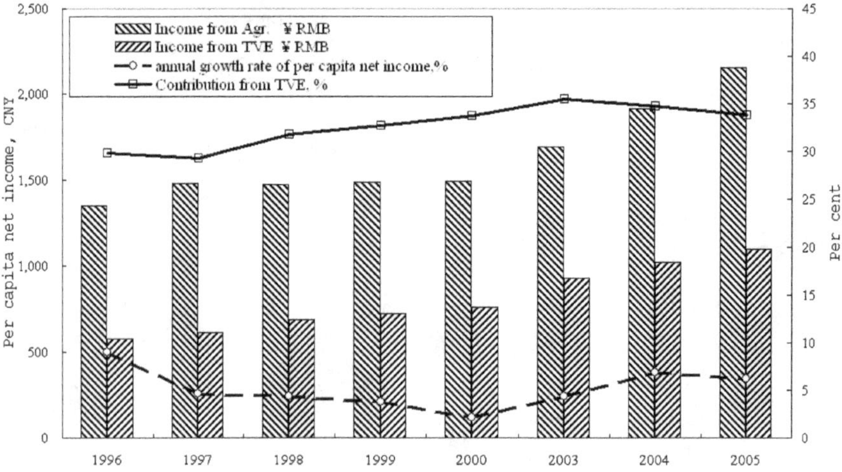

Figure 4.13. Contribution of TVEs to farmers' per capita net income.

Source: Calculated using data from the Ministry of Agriculture of China: The Agriculture Development Report (in Chinese), 2006, Tables VIII 01-VIII 06; 2005, Table 13; 2003, Table 13; 2001, Table 13; The achievements in the development of China TVEs during 10th FYP (in Chinese), China Township Enterprises News, January 6, 2006; China State Bureau of TVEs: "The Contribution of TVEs to per capita net income of farmer in China during ninth FYP" (in Chinese); China National Bureau of Statistics: China Statistical Yearbook, China Statistics Press, 2006, Tables 10.2, 10.3; China State Bureau of TVEs: "The analysis on economic operating status of TVE in 2004" (in Chinese), January 2005; "The analysis on economic operating status of TVE in 2004" (in Chinese), January 17, 2004; Figure 4.13 illustrates the contribution to per capita net income of farmers in the richest as well as the poorest municipalities and provinces in China. It is found that the higher the contribution from TVEs, the higher the per capita net income of farmers

capita net income from agriculture (Shanghai, CNY2,406) was only one time more than the lowest value (Gansu, CNY1,094). In terms of its implications for declining income disparity, this tells us that for the lower income regions, especially the western region's development, TVEs are very important. In 2004, only 15.9% of TVEs were in the western region and employed 10.5% of national TVE workers. TVEs in the western region produced valued added of CNY248.1 billion (USD30 billion), which occupied a meager 5.9% of the TVE's value added nationally in 2004. TVE workers' reward in the western region reached CNY118.5 billion (USD14.3 billion), or 12.1% of the national total.[64]

---

[64]Calculated using data from the Ministry of Agriculture of China: The Agriculture Development Report (in Chinese), 2005, Table 13.

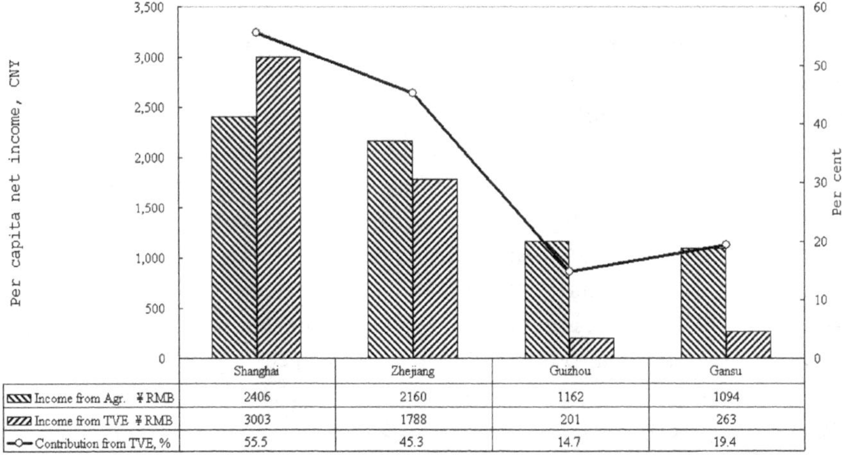

Figure 4.14. Contribution of TVEs to farmers' per capita net income in rich and poor provinces, 1999.

Source: Calculated using data from the China State Bureau of TVEs: "The Contribution of TVEs to per capita net income of farmers in China during ninth FYP" (in Chinese).

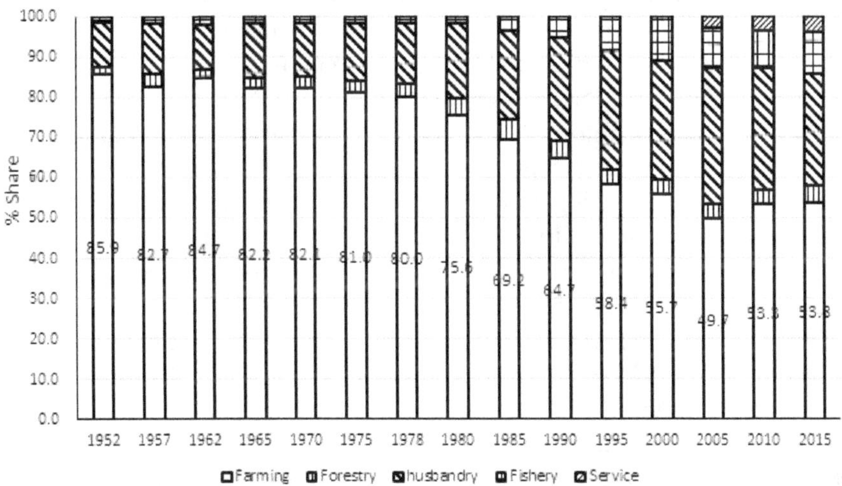

Figure 4.15. Agriculture structural changes in China, 1952–2015.

Source: Calculated using data from the China National Bureau of Statistics: China Statistical Yearbook, China Statistics Press, 2006, Table 13.6; 2002, Table 12.6; 2002, Table 12.6; 1991, Table 9.6; China State Statistical Bureau compiled: Statistical Yearbook of China 1981, published by Economic Information & Agency, Hong Kong, 1982, p.136; China National Bureau of Statistics, Data base; Gross Output Value of Agriculture, Forestry, Animal Husbandry and Fishery Indices of Gross Output of Agriculture, Forestry, Animal Husbandry, and Fishery, 1997–2015.

As SOEs began to withdraw from the agricultural product-processing sector, township firms were needed to fill the vacuum. TVEs have the advantage and ability to focus on agricultural and related products processing, packaging, and circulation. By developing the produce processing sector, China will be able to readjust its agricultural structure faster, and the difficulty farmers have in selling their products may be resolved, in turn significantly raising all other rural residents' income. The Ministry of Agriculture has decided to optimize township enterprise structure by encouraging more firms to undertake farm products processing. TVEs will focus on the development of high-tech, high value added, named brand and special local products in the coming years. Randall Worsley, a representative of the Pacific Venture Capital Company of the United States, said that many U.S. investors are interested in China's small and medium-sized enterprises, and they appreciate their flexible management mechanisms.[65] The Chinese government has worked out a series of policies and regulations, including the Law on Township Enterprises issued in 1997, to encourage and support the special information networks and websites to serve the township enterprises in terms of policy, circulation, and e-commerce information. China's TVEs now face a good opportunity for development, citing rural and agricultural structural adjustment and the development of the country's western region, the two key national strategies at present.

After economic reform, the structural changes within agriculture are much larger than before economic reform. Figure 4.15 shows that, before economic reform, farming was the mainstay in agriculture; after economic reform, forestry, husbandry, and fishery grew faster than farming. The average annual growth rate of agricultural gross output accounted for 3.25% before economic reform (1952–1978) and 5.75% after economic reform (1978–2015), as we see in Table 4.32. The IS change coefficient K reached 2.95 (1952–1978) and 12.07 (1978–2015). The IS similar coefficient $R1$ equaled 0.9982 (1952–1978), and 0.9474 (1978–2005). These values of K and $R1$ indicate that structural changes in agriculture before economic reform were small and became significant after economic reform. The small structural changes before economic reform were conducive to the low annual growth rate of agriculture gross output; the IS change within agriculture contributed greatly to its higher annual growth rate. In 2000, farming took up 70–80% of farmers' per capita income in

---

[65] Township firms must move on, *China Daily*, May 13, 2000.

Table 4.32.   Agricultural gross output and industrial structure changes in China, 1952–2015.

	Farm-ing	Fores-try	Husban-dry	Fishery	AGRGO bil.78¥ RMB	AGRGO growth rate %	K_{annual}	R1	Years for compare	h
1952	85.9	1.6	11.2	1.3	60.8					64.05
1957	82.7	3.3	12.2	1.9	75.9	4.53%	0.3220	0.9996	1952/1957	56.69
1962	84.7	2.2	10.9	2.2	60.8	−4.33%	0.2290	0.9998	1957/1962	60.34
1965	82.2	2.7	13.4	1.8	83.4	11.09%	0.4867	0.9994	1962/1965	56.76
1970	82.1	2.8	13.4	1.7	102.1	4.12%	0.0120	1.0000	1965/1970	56.70
1975	81.0	3.1	14.2	1.7	126.0	4.30%	0.1130	0.9999	1970/1975	54.84
1978	80.0	3.4	15.0	1.6	139.7	3.50%	0.1925	0.9999	1975/1978	53.50
1980	75.6	4.2	18.4	1.7	152.3	4.41%	1.0902	0.9985	1978/1980	47.60
1985	69.2	5.2	22.1	3.5	224.5	8.07%	0.6385	0.9971	1980/1985	38.05
1990	64.7	4.3	25.7	5.4	283.0	4.75%	0.5491	0.9971	1985/1990	33.39
1995	58.4	3.5	29.7	8.4	405.4	7.45%	0.7053	0.9945	1990/1995	27.92
1998	58.0	3.5	28.6	9.9	501.7	7.36%	0.2514	0.9996	1995/1998	26.49
1999	57.5	3.6	28.5	10.3	525.0	4.66%	0.2941	1.0000	1998/1999	25.68
2000	55.7	3.8	29.7	10.9	543.9	3.60%	0.9248	0.9995	1999/2000	24.17
2001	55.2	3.6	30.4	10.8	566.8	4.20%	0.3723	0.9999	2000/2001	24.33
2002	54.5	3.8	30.9	10.8	594.3	4.94%	0.3657	0.9999	2001/2002	23.67
2003	51.7	4.3	33.1	10.9	618.0	3.90%	1.4282	0.9985	2002/2003	21.79
2005	49.7	3.6	33.7	10.2	701.7	6.55%	0.4947	0.9996	2003/2005	23.06

(*Continued*)

Table 4.32. (*Continued*)

	Farm-ing	Fores-try	Husban-dry	Fishery	AGRGO bil.78¥ RMB	AGRGO growth rate %	K_{annual}	R1	Years for compare	h
2010	53.3	3.7	30.0	9.3	887.2	4.80%	0.4159	0.9965	2005/2010	24.97
2015	53.8	4.1	27.8	10.2	1008.9	6.64%	0.2035	0.9992	2010/2015	24.00
2018	54.1	4.8	25.3	10.7						
				K52-78=	2.95	3.25%	0.1134	0.9982	1952/1978	
				K78-18=	10.78	5.49%	0.2913	0.9561	1978/2015	

Source: Calculated using data from the Ministry of Agriculture of China: The Agriculture Development Report (in Chinese), 2006, Tables VIII 01-VIII 06; 2005, Table 13; 2003, Table 13; 2001, Table 13; The achievements in the development of China TVEs during 10th FYP (in Chinese), China Township Enterprises News, January 6, 2006; China State Bureau of TVEs: "The Contribution of TVEs to per capita net income of farmer in China during ninth FYP" (in Chinese); China National Bureau of Statistics: China Statistical Yearbook, China Statistics Press, 2006, Tables 10.2, 10.3; China State Bureau of TVEs: "The analysis on economic operating status of TVE in 2004" (in Chinese), January 2005; "The analysis on economic operating status of TVE in 2004" (in Chinese), January 17, 2004; Figure 4.13 illustrates the contribution to per capita net income of farmers in the richest as well as the poorest municipalities and provinces in China. It is found that the higher the contribution from TVEs, the higher the per capita net income of farmers

western provinces, compared to a 50% national average. This indicates the importance of structural changes within agriculture. Before economic reform, there were supply shortages in agricultural products; therefore, a quota system was adopted to solve the distribution problem. After economic reform, agricultural gross output grew rapidly, and the supply of agricultural products became larger than effective demand. Living standards improved significantly, and, to satisfy consumer demand for high quality, the husbandry and fishery sectors developed faster than the farming sector.

After economic reform, the average annual growth rate of the share of farm, husbandry, and fishery sectors were minus 1.06%, 0.5%, and 5.16%, respectively. In recent years, the main obstacle to China's agriculture has been transformed from a lack of product to a structural obstacle. Hence, there is a need for implementing a strategy of promoting agriculture through quality, promoting the shift from agricultural production guidance to quality improvement, and for the further adjustment of agricultural industrial structure. Regarding local market changes in demand, The shortage of agricultural products in the market must be solved, especially the organic, green and other ecological aspects of planting areas such as strong gluten wheat, high-strength rice, high-quality rice, and "double-low" rapeseed, including the quality and safety of agricultural production.[66]

Using the data from 1978–2015,[67] we conduct a regression analysis of agricultural gross output value with percentage share of farming in agriculture:

---

[66]Rural Department, China National Bureau of Statistics (2018). Rural Reform Writes a Glorious History Rural Revitalization and Magnificent Blueprint—20th series of economic and social development achievements in the 40 years of reform and opening-up, September 18 (in Chinese).

[67]Calculated using data from the Ministry of Agriculture of China: The Summary of China National Agriculture Statistics 2005 (in Chinese), Tables VIII 01-VIII 06; 2003 (in Chinese), Table VIII 04; Ministry of Agriculture: China Agriculture Yearbook 2005 (in Chinese), China Agriculture Publisher, December 2005, p. 226; China National Bureau of Statistics: China Statistical Yearbook, China Statistics Press, 2018, Table 13.6; 2006, Table 13.6; 2003, Tables 3.1, 12.31; China National Bureau of Statistics, Data base; Gross Output Value of Agriculture, Forestry, Animal Husbandry, and Fishery Indices of Gross Output of Agriculture, Forestry, Animal Husbandry, and Fishery, 1997–2015.

$$farm\% = 101.36 - 6.34\,Ln(farmGO)$$
$$(6.99)\quad(-5.74)$$
$$R = 0.7392,\,F = 5.5,\,df = 28,\,s = 5.362 \tag{4.15}$$

where *farm%* — the percentage share of farming gross output in total agriculture gross output.

farmGO — total agriculture gross output in rural area in a different year at constant prices

From the above value, we conclude that the regression Eq. (4.15) is statistically acceptable. This means when total agricultural gross output in rural area increases, the percentage share of farming gross output in total agricultural gross output declines. From Eq. (4.15), we know that if total agricultural gross output in rural area increases by 4.64%, the percentage share of farming gross output in total agricultural gross output declines by 1%, or, if total agricultural gross output in rural area doubles, the percentage share of the agricultural sector in total agricultural gross output will decline by 15.3%.

For cross-section analysis, using the data for 2004 for different regions (31 provinces), sample data is listed in Table 4.33. Using these data for regression analysis, we get:

$$farm\% = 124.63 - 8.30\,Ln(agrmGOpc)$$
$$(4.34)\quad(-2.39)$$
$$R = 0.4001,\,F = 5.72,\,df = 30,\,s = 8.33 \tag{4.16}$$

where *farmRegGO* — total farming gross output in rural area of different regions in the same year

farm% — the percentage share of farming gross output in total agriculture gross output.

From the above values, we conclude that the regression Eq. (4.16) is also statistically acceptable. This means when total agricultural gross output of different provinces in China increases, the percentage share of farming gross output in total agricultural gross output of different provinces declines. From Eqs. (4.15)–(4.16), we observe that whether we use longitudinal or cross-section regression analysis, we arrive at the same conclusion — if total agriculture gross output increases, the percentage share of farming gross output in total agricultural gross output declines.

Table 4.33.   Regional structure of agricultural gross output in China, 2004.

	Farming	Forestry	Husbandry	Fishery	K	R	h
National	50.05	3.66	33.59	9.95	0.00	1	33.92
Beijing	35.38	4.85	52.94	3.78	8.27	0.92065	39.43
Tianjin	39.54	1.70	28.54	17.61	5.04	0.98244	31.67
Hebei	47.80	1.68	43.68	3.03	4.25	0.9817	44.74
Shanxi	60.29	3.96	29.31	0.50	4.86	0.97844	49.11
Inner Mongolia	48.34	5.47	44.02	0.70	4.64	0.97747	43.67
Liaoning	40.47	2.69	36.30	18.02	4.27	0.97859	29.16
Jilin	51.68	3.50	42.43	1.42	3.83	0.98535	45.15
Heilongjiang	54.57	5.79	35.25	2.20	3.21	0.99108	41.16
Shanghai	43.91	5.26	28.45	20.05	4.60	0.97903	25.68
Jiangsu	51.39	1.66	23.30	18.59	4.45	0.97482	33.98
Zhejiang	44.48	5.88	20.86	27.17	7.55	0.93168	24.94
Anhui	51.20	4.37	32.89	8.93	0.72	0.99958	34.07
Fujian	39.91	6.54	22.14	30.18	8.94	0.90897	22.93
Jiangxi	46.55	7.50	30.81	13.57	2.75	0.99476	26.44
Shandong	54.77	1.72	29.61	12.34	2.60	0.99456	36.73
Henan	54.08	2.56	37.69	0.94	3.65	0.98854	47.93
Hubei	54.36	1.88	30.35	12.13	2.30	0.99588	36.39
Hunan	45.68	4.77	41.65	6.27	3.44	0.98721	35.29
Guangdong	44.55	2.86	26.50	21.65	5.02	0.9719	28.85
Guangxi	48.13	4.49	35.59	10.34	1.03	0.99887	32.06
Hainan	38.96	13.63	19.12	26.58	10.43	0.90142	18.76
Chongqing	54.34	3.02	37.68	3.46	3.10	0.99361	42.76
Sichuan	43.85	2.78	48.73	2.92	5.85	0.96297	43.17
Guizhou	60.56	4.42	32.18	1.33	4.26	0.98448	46.31
Yunnan	53.55	8.95	31.64	1.98	3.74	0.98638	38.35
Tibet	42.42	9.09	46.41	0.02	7.16	0.95562	41.61
Shaanxi	63.53	4.05	27.55	0.78	5.82	0.97224	49.59
Gansu	69.42	3.39	24.65	0.21	7.66	0.9565	54.87
Qinghai	39.49	2.08	53.70	0.12	8.42	0.92836	50.97
Ningxia	56.81	4.94	32.83	2.87	3.18	0.99053	41.76
Xinjiang	68.60	1.84	24.98	0.57	7.67	0.95865	56.01

Source: Calculated using data from the Ministry of Agriculture: China Agriculture Yearbook 2005 (in Chinese), China Agriculture Publisher, December 2005, p. 163, 168, 169.

From Eq. (4.16), we know if total agricultural gross output in rural areas increases by 12.8%, the share of farming gross output in total agricultural gross output declines by 1%, or if total agricultural gross output in rural area doubles, the share of agricultural sector in total agricultural gross output will decline by 5.75%.

To increase farmers' income and modernize, the agricultural sector, forestry, husbandry, and fishery should develop further. The demand of husbandry and fishery increased faster than farming products because of the improvement in living standards. The intermediate use part in farming, forestry, husbandry, and fishery accounted for 34.8%, 31.8%, 51.1%, and 42.3%, respectively.[68] In Table 4.33, we take the national agricultural gross output structure as reference. From ISC change coefficient K and similarity coefficient R, we find that Anhui province was most similar with the national percentage regarding the structure of agricultural gross output, while Hainan province was most dissimilar with the national percentage. Xinjiang province had the highest percentage share of farming gross output in total agricultural gross output; therefore, its specialization coefficient h became the highest, reaching 56.7, and Hainan accounted for the lowest h, only 18.4. This means agricultural gross output was less dependent on farming in Hainan province.

Low productivity is Achilles's heel of China's agriculture, which could cost Chinese farmers competitiveness in the world market. Although China has about 100 times the number of farmers as the United States, its exports of farm products only equal one-fifth to one-quarter of the United States. Table 4.34 illustrates the productivity of Chinese farmers compared to foreign countries.

In 1961, the agriculture value added of each farm worker in China was only 1.77% and 43.31% of Japan and India. In 1980, this figure was only 1.22% and 59.69% of Japan and India. In 2000, agriculture value added of each farm worker in China was only 2.41%; it was 66.26% of the United States and upper middle-income groups. In 2016, this figure rose to 6.36% and 88.11% of the United States and upper middle-income groups. This shows the agricultural value added of each farm worker in China improved slightly from 2000–2016. However, China's arable land per capita accounts for 40% of the United States, so it is particularly

---

[68]Calculated using data from the Ministry of Agriculture: China Agriculture Yearbook 2005 (in Chinese), China Agriculture Publisher, December 2005, p. 175; China National Bureau of Statistics: China Statistical Yearbook, China Statistics Press, 2006, Table 13.6.

Table 4.34.   Agriculture value added per worker (constant 2000 USD).

Country	1961	1980	1985	1991	2000	2005	2010	2018
BRA				3817.72328	5232.0	5742.9	8171.3	13702.2
CAN		13814.5	18430.9	...	56916.0	71949.5	76711.2	110393.2
CHN	110.1	162.9	220.7	812.5	1073.9	1786.9	2966.0	5325.8
DEU		5635.2	7451.8	21313.9	23328.6	24519.5		
JPN	6234	13304.9	16332.4		24941.1	22650.1	24402.2	24195.1
IND	254.3	273	304.7	830.1008667	965.6	1029.2	1267.7	1906.6
KOR	1699.2		3803	5637.3	9231.5	11958.7	15308.2	187+95.7
MEX				4077.524129	4339.5	4880.6	5289.8	5927.5
RUS				6092.102185	4828.3	7461.1	9360.5	16052.6
GBR				26516.4716	36381.3	41442.7	41807.0	48459.8
USA		16592	24398.4	...	66667.7	87038.8	77616.9	89431.5
WLD			739.4	1389.019584	1904.2	2193.9	2604.2	3622.6
UMC				1444.7	1919.9	2596.7	3826.4	6044.7

Source: World Bank: World Development Indicators online 2008, released 2008 by World Bank; World Development Indicators online 2019, released November 28, 2018.

important to increase the agricultural value added of every farm worker in China. The 19th National Congress of the Communist Party of China clearly proposed the implementation of the rural revitalization strategy, emphasizing the priority development of agriculture and rural areas. In the agricultural sector, China must accelerate the construction of a modern agricultural industrial system, production system, and management system with green development, quality development, and deepen the structural reform of the agricultural supply side. The agricultural product processing industry is stable, and the market is expected to be good. It is estimated that the income from the business operations of agricultural products processing above the designated size will exceed CNY21 trillion, an increase of more than 7% over the previous year. Leisure agriculture and rural tourism are booming. It is estimated that the number of visitors will exceed 2.2 billion, income will exceed CNY620 billion, and the number of employees will reach 9 million, which will benefit 7 million farmers. In terms of rural entrepreneurship and innovation, we see that more than 7 million entrepreneurs have returned to the countryside. These talents have helped create a rural double-generation boom.[69]

The productivity of Chinese farm workers improved after economic reform, but the absolute value is still very low. Figure 4.16 shows China's cereal yield per hectare compared to other countries. The situation is not as bad as with farmer productivity. In 2005, China's cereal yield per hectare (5,229 Kg per hectare) is higher than Canada's (3,198 Kg per hectare) and the world average (3,254 Kg per hectare), and 82% of that value of the Republic of Korea, the United States, 77.8% of Germany, and 72.7% of the United Kingdom. The growth rate of cereal yield per hectare in China was the highest among the listed countries and regions during 1961–2005, with the average annual growth rate reaching 3.33%, and the lowest 0.75% (Japan). During the 1961–1966 period, China's cereal yield per capita (1,560 Kg per hectare) was a little lower than Canada's (1,608 Kg per hectare), but 63.5% higher than Canada's in 2005. In 2016, the figure was further improved, as China's cereal yield per hectare was 74%, 84%, 86%, and 89% of the United States, Germany, the United Kingdom, and Republic of Korea, respectively. It was higher than the Russian

---

[69]Yu, X. (2018). Thoughts on Carrying Forward the Spirit of Rural Reform and Promoting Rural Revitalization. *Rural Work Communication*, December 28 (in Chinese); Key Work Points of Agricultural Products Processing Bureau of the Ministry of Agriculture (Township Enterprise Bureau) in 2015, 2015-01-23 (in Chinese).

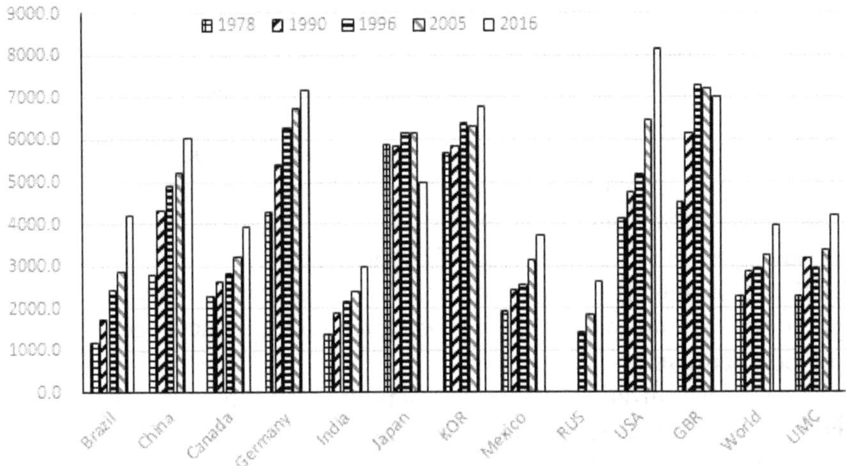

Figure 4.16.   Cereal yield per hectare.

Source: World Bank. World Development Indicators online 2008, released 2008 by World Bank; World Development Indicators online 2019, released November 28, 2018.

Federation, India, Mexico, Canada, the world average, the upper middle-income group, and Japan (127%, 101%, 60.8%, 54.2%, 52%, 43.7%, and 21.2%, respectively).

Figure 4.16 and Table 4.32 indicate the agriculture production technology in China is not bad, but there are too many farmers and relatively low price of agricultural products, resulting in a very low farmers' productivity. If China opens the door to cost-effective American farm products, a vast number of domestic farmers will suffer and may lose their jobs and livelihoods. Apart from ongoing challenges, the domestic market is already on a downward path given the price index of farm products declined from 1996–2000. The index dropped 22.6% during these five years, eating into more than CNY300 billion (USD36.2 billion) of farmers' profits. Despite the continuous price falls, however, prices of Chinese farming exports are still 20% to 40% higher than the average standard in the international market. Since 2003, the price of farm products increased because of declining output. In 2004, more direct and effective policies and measures to stimulate increases in grain production and rural incomes were adopted. The central government spent CNY262.6 billion (USD31.7 billion) on agriculture, rural areas, and farmers, an increase of

22.5% year-on-year. This greatly aroused the enthusiasm of farmers, resulting in a rebound in grain production. Grain output for 2004 totaled 469.47 million tons, 38.77 million tons more than the previous year.[70]

The Chinese government put the development of agriculture and increase of farmers' incomes at the top of its agenda in 2004. Agricultural restructuring and increasing farmers' incomes were taken as central tasks. Rural areas actively and steadily moved forward in the urbanization process and sped up the restructuring of TVEs. "Great efforts will be made to develop high-quality, high-yield, cost-effective, eco-friendly, and safe agriculture, to improve the quality of agricultural products and enhance their competitiveness."[71]

The industrialization of agricultural production should be encouraged and supported. Industrialization is an effective way to optimize the structure of agriculture and improve farmers' lives. An essential move is to guarantee the transfer of rights to farmland use under the current contract-based household responsibility system. This system, which over the past four decades determined the pattern of land use in rural China, matches well with present conditions. A by-product of the current land system is the limited scale of agricultural production. The original design, which takes households as basic units of farming, is increasingly out of tune with the market economy, which emphasizes the scale of the economy. The transfer of rights to the use of contracted land should be promoted in rural areas to achieve a scale economy in agricultural production and accelerate agricultural modernization. Farmers' contractual rights to land use should be protected by law. Farmers are entitled to rent, inherit, or mortgage the right to the land within the contract terms. The transfer of rights to use farmland will help farmers enlarge their scale of production and, hence, improve their income as long as it is conducted in line with the law.

Strong financial support is needed to develop agriculture. The government, financial institutions, and farmers should join in their efforts to raise the necessary capital for agricultural production. Farmers across the nation will be freed from the burden of agricultural tax within 3 years, 2 years ahead of the schedule promised by Premier Wen Jiabao in March 2004. Statistics indicate that the agricultural tax raises just CNY 30–40 billion (USD 3.6–4.8 billion) annually, around 5% of the government's financial

---

[70]Premier Wen Jiabao (2005). Report on the Work of the Government, March 5.

[71]Premier Wen Jiabao (2004). Full text of government work report, (in Chinese), *Peoples' Daily*, March 16.

income. However, the local government also levies additional fees of around CNY100 billion (USD12 billion). In 2004, the central government earmarked CNY10 billion (USD1.21 billion) from its grain risk fund to directly subsidize grain farmers, alleviating falling output and slowing income growth.[72] Farmers need more incentives to invest in agriculture. To arouse farmers' enthusiasm and to attract investment into agricultural industrialization, China's government should work out preferential policies in taxes, services, and pricing. Because of the current low-income level, it is more realistic for farmers to invest human labor rather than capital in production. As a result, labor-intensive projects should get priority in agriculture's industrialization.

An important target of agricultural industrialization is to optimize the structure of agricultural production. Products with higher value added or better market prospects should be developed on a larger scale. Science and technology should be applied to optimize crop rising, develop and strengthen farming, and greatly improve the quality and efficiency of the agricultural sector. Technological support is badly needed in industrializing agriculture. The government, research institutes, and farmers should work together in their efforts to establish a network to popularize technology in rural areas. Information is another vital factor for the further development of agricultural industrialization. Information on policies and the market should be shared among farmers and enterprises as much as possible. The government will start a number of construction projects that will directly increase farmer's income and improve the anti-disaster capabilities of the agricultural sector, make better the conditions of the rural market and the competitiveness of the agricultural sector.

In the 11th and 13th FYPs, China made steady progress in building a new countryside; the outline is shown in Figure 4.17. The level of agricultural mechanization has developed rapidly and production efficiency has increased significantly. In 1978, there were 560,000 large and medium-sized tractors and less than 20,000 combined harvesters. In 2017, there were 6.7 million large and medium-sized tractors nationwide, an increase of 119.6% over 1978, with an average annual growth rate of 6.7%: and a combined harvest of 1.99 million units, an increase of 9950% over 1978, reflecting an average annual growth rate of 26.6%. Not only has it greatly increased agricultural labor productivity, but it has also significantly

---

[72]Farm tax to be axed in three years, http://english.peopledaily.com.cn/200404/10/eng20040410_139993.shtml.

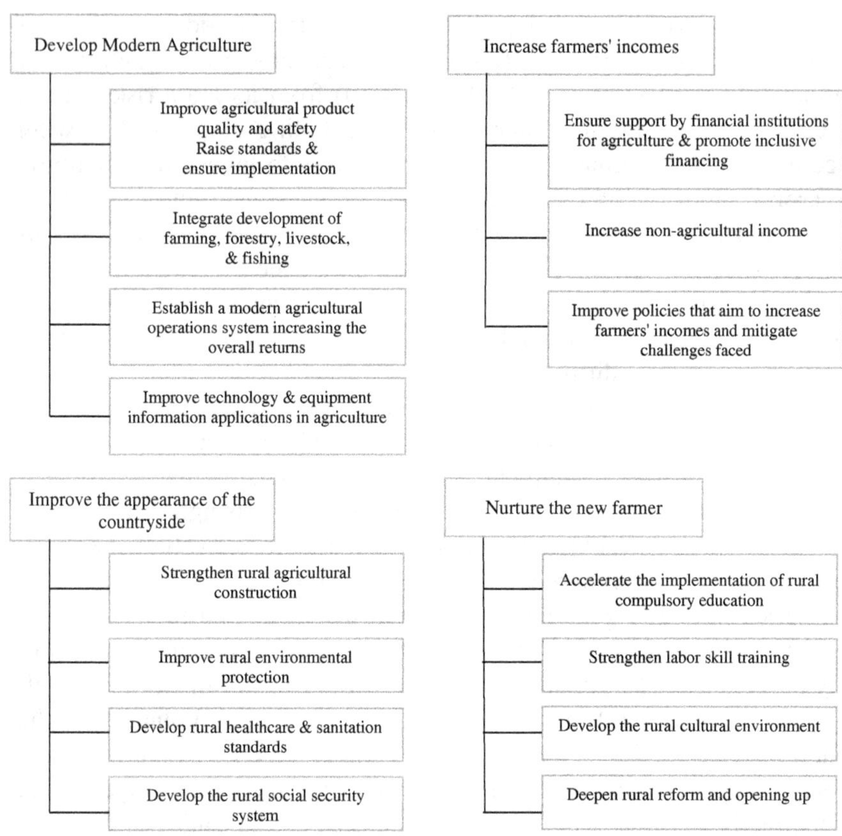

Figure 4.17.   The outline of building a new countryside in China, 2005.

Source: The 13th FYP for Economic and Social Development of The People's Republic of China, 2016–2020, Translated by Compilation and Translation Bureau, Central Committee of the Communist Party of China, Beijing, China Central Compilation & Translation Press, Chapters 18–21; Xinhua News Agency: The outline of 11th FYP (in Chinese), May 16, 2006, Chapters 2–9.

improved agricultural production conditions. According to statistics from the Ministry of Agriculture and Rural Affairs, the contribution rate of China's agricultural science and technology progress in 2005 was 48.0%, and the contribution rate of agricultural science and technology progress reached 57.5% in 2017.[73]

---

[73] Rural Department, China National Bureau of Statistics: Rural Reform Writes a Glorious History, Rural Revitalization and Magnificent Blueprint-20th series of economic and

9. Internal Structure of the Tertiary Industry

In Chapter 3, we discussed that China should accelerate the development of its service industry. This is an important avenue for stimulating economic restructuring and increasing employment. China needs to actively develop modern service industries, such as information services, banking, accounting, consulting, and law. Up-to-date management and technology should be applied to renovate traditional service sectors, such as internal and foreign trade, transportation and municipal services, to improve their quality and efficiency. In the last few years, the central government adopted a series of measures to stimulate the domestic market and boost economic growth, which has helped the restructuring of the internal structure of China's tertiary industry. Compared with the United States, Japan, and Republic of Korea, the percentage share of Real Estate sector, Social Services sector, Health Care, Sports, and Social Welfare sector of China are obviously lower than others (see Figure 4.19). As shown in Table 4.35, the differences are quite large, which can be confirmed by the value of IS Change coefficient K and simulation coefficient $R1$. The IS Change coefficient K accounted for 4.81, 5.57, and 3.21 for Japan (2005), Republic of Korea (1995), and China (2004), respectively. The percentage share of real estate within the tertiary industry in China is almost only 57.5% of that value in the United States.

In China, residential housing was distributed by state or working organization until the year 2000 and became a marketable commodity only after 2000. In addition, farmers themselves build their own residences in rural areas, which is not included in the real estate industry. The real estate industry maintained a relatively rapid growth rate in the past decade and has been a significant pillar of the national economy in China. It attracts foreign investment and promotes Chinese enterprises to go global. However, as housing prices rose significantly, the central government initiated a campaign to control surging property prices in September 2016. The house is for people to live, not for speculation. The similar service sector within the tertiary industry in China is another sector far below that value of the United States and Japan, because the social service sector in China is underdeveloped, especially in such branches as the legal, professional, scientific, technical, accounting, management of enterprises, waste

---

social development achievements in the 40 years of reform and opening-up, September 18, 2018 (in Chinese).

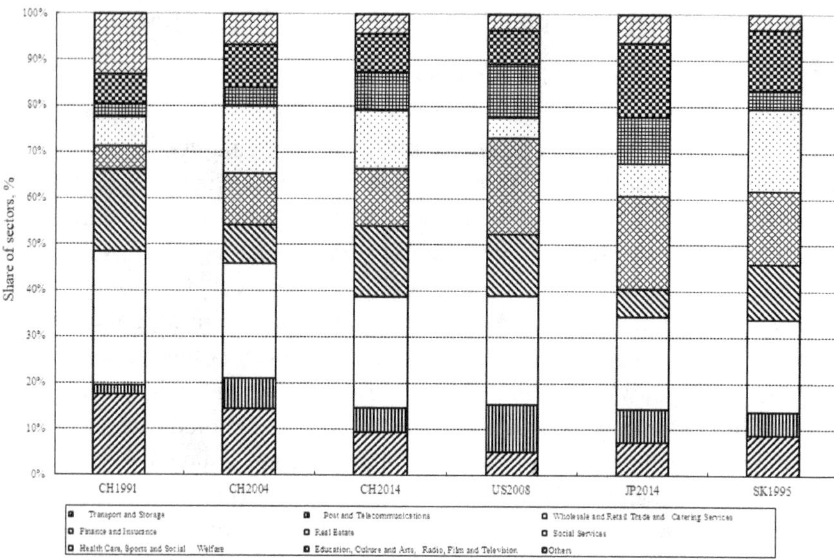

Figure 4.18.   The comparison of structural changes in the service sector.

Source: Calculated using data from the China National Bureau of Statistics: China Statistical Yearbook, China Statistics Press, 2016, Table 13.6; 2006, Tables 3.1, 3.3, 3.5; 1999, Table 3.5; U.S. Census: The Statistical Abstract of the United States 2008; Edited by Statistical Research and Training Institute, and published by the Statistics Bureau, both under the Ministry of Internal Affairs and Communications. Japan Statistical Yearbook 2008; International Statistical Yearbook, China Statistics Press.

management/remediation services, other business and personal professional services. All these branches were not a part of the planned economy; therefore, they were developed only after economic reform, especially after the late 1990s. Compared with the United States, Japan, and South Korea, the similarity coefficient R1 of IS change in China's service industry is 0.9039, 0.8716 and 0.9507, respectively.

The similarity coefficient *R1* equals 0.9130 for China during 1991–2004. China's absolute amount of the tertiary industry is much less than that value of the United States and Japan; therefore, many decades will be needed for the internal structure of China's tertiary industry to become comparable with developed countries. In the 11th FYP, China planned to accelerate the development of the service industry. The service industry will be developed in accordance with the principles of market orientation, commercialization, and socialization, and efforts will be made to widen

Table 4.35.   Value added and structure changes in China's tertiary industry.

	CH1991	CH1995	CH1997	CH2000	CH2004	CH2014	US2008	JP2014	SK1995
Value-added of service sector, billion current ¥	722.7	1794.7	2302.9	2987.9	6456.1	30507.2			
Value-added of service sector, billion current USD	87.4	217.0	278.5	361.3	780.7	4966.3	6874.0	3431.2	247.6
Transport and storage	17.5	13.2	11.7	11.4	14.4	9.3	5.1	7.3	8.9
Post & telecommunication	2	3.8	4.8	6.7	6.6	5.2	10.3	7.1	5.0
Wholesale & retail trade, catering services	28.9	27.5	26.7	24.5	25.0	24.1	23.4	20.3	19.4
Finance and insurance	17.8	19.4	19.7	17.5	8.4	15.3	13.3	6.0	12.2
Real estate	5.1	5.9	5.5	5.6	11.1	12.5	20.9	20.0	15.8
Social services	6.2	8.6	9.5	10.9	14.5	12.7	4.4	7.2	17.9
Health care, sports and social welfare	3	2.7	2.7	2.8	4.1	8.2	11.6	10.1	4.2
Education, culture, radio, film & television	6.3	6.3	6.8	8.0	9.2	8.3	7.4	16.0	13.1

(Continued)

Table 4.35. (*Continued*)

	CH1991	CH1995	CH1997	CH2000	CH2004	CH2014	US2008	JP2014	SK1995
Others	13.2	12.6	12.6	12.7	6.8	4.3	3.4	6.2	3.4
K	5.40	1.47	0.60	1.05	3.37	2.76	3.78	4.91	6.41
$R1$	0.9064	0.9908	0.9985	0.9954	0.9396	0.9627	0.9314	0.9071	0.8518
Year for comparison	CH91/ CH14	CH91/ CH95	CH95/ CH97	CH97/ CH00	CH00/ CH04	CH04/ CH14	US08/ CH14	CH14/ JP14	CH95/ SK95

Source: Calculated using data from the China National Bureau of Statistics: China Statistical Yearbook, China Statistics Press, 2016, Table 3.6; 2006, Tables 3.1, 3.3, 3.5; 1999, Table 3.5; U.S. Census: The Statistical Abstract of the United States 2008; Edited by Statistical Research and Training Institute, and published by the Statistics Bureau, both under the Ministry of Internal Affairs and Communications. Japan Statistical Yearbook 2008; International Statistical Yearbook, China Statistics Press; Department of National Accounts, Economic and Social Research Institute, Cabinet Office, Government of Japan: Annual Report on National Accounts for 2017, Summary, (Flow Accounts), December 25, 2018; United States, Bureau of Economic Analysis, Bureau of Economic Analysis: Table 654. Gross Domestic Product in Current and Chained (2000) Dollars by Industry.

the scope, expand the scale, optimize the structure, strengthen the function, and regulate the market of the service industry to improve the level of the service industry and its share in GDP. As can be seen from Table 4.35, the IS Change coefficient K and simulation coefficient R1 were 4.91 and 09071 and 6.41 and 0.8518 compared with Japan in 2014 and South Korea in 1995, respectively. China's IS Change coefficient K and simulation coefficient R1 in 2014 with the United States in 2008 was 3.71 and 0.9314. It shows the gap between the industry structures of China's service industry with that of a developed country has narrowed.

The ratio of value added of the service industry increased from 24.6% in 1978 to 52.2% in 2018, and the employment ratio of the service industry increased from 12.2% in 1978 to 46.3% in 2018. The Share of the Contributions of the service industry to the increase of the GDP rose from 28.4% in 1978 to 59.7% in 2018. The outline of accelerating the development of the service industry in China is shown in Figure 4.19.

Since the 18th National Congress of the Communist Party of China, along with the acceleration of China's economic restructuring and upgrading, the service industry has become a new bright spot for economic growth. In 2013–2017, the service industry grew at an average annual rate of 8.0%, 1.2% points higher than the secondary industry. From 1978–2017, the value-added of China's service industry increased from CNY90.5 billion to CNY427.03 billion, an average annual growth rate of 10.5%, 1.0% points higher than the actual annual growth rate of GDP; the proportion of the service industry in GDP rose from 28.4% to 51.9%; the contribution rate to national economic growth rose from 28.4% to 59.6%, becoming the main driving force for the national economy and economic growth. It is potentially leading the Chinese economy to steadily enter a new stage of high-quality development.

Employment is the foundation of people's livelihood. In the 40+ years of reform and opening-up, the service industry has made outstanding contributions to stable employment. From 1978–2017, the number of employed people in the service industry increased from 48.9 million to 348.72 million, an average annual increase of 5.2%. Since the 18th National Congress of the Communist Party of China, "mass entrepreneurship and innovation" have boosted the new dynamism of the service industry, and the service industry has significantly enhanced its ability to absorb employment. In 2016, for each percentage point increase in the service industry, about 1.2 million jobs were created, and the service industry brightened its employment picture.

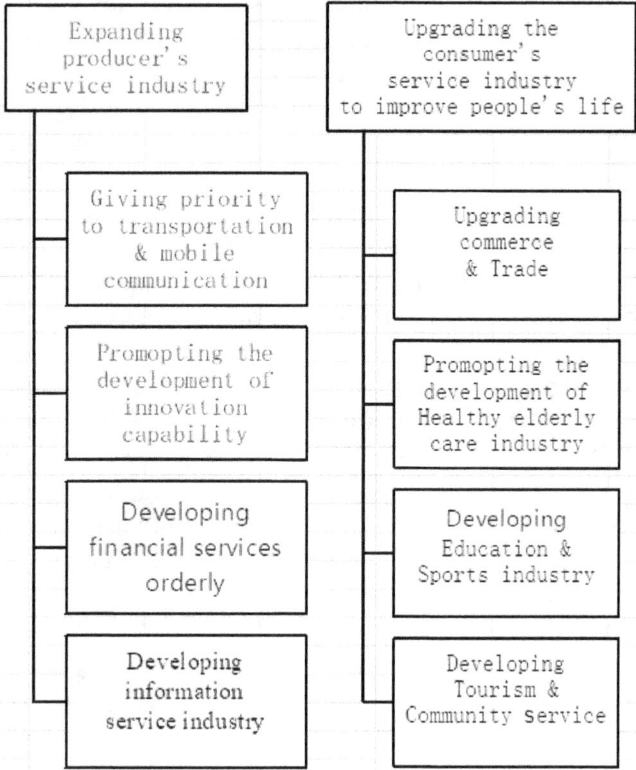

Figure 4.19.   The outline of accelerating the development of the service industry in China.

Source: The 13th FYP for Economic and Social Development of the People's Republic of China 2016–2020, Translated by Compilation and Translation Bureau, Beijing, China; China National Bureau of Statistics: China Statistical Yearbook, China Statistics Press, 2019, Chapter 24.

From 1978–2017, China's tax revenue grew at an average annual rate of 16.1%. The proportion of the service industry in taxation increased steadily, from 39.8% in 2002 to 56.3% in 2017, which served as important support for the steady growth of China's fiscal revenue. In 2017, the service industry's new tax revenue accounted for 54.3% of all new tax revenue, which is an important source of tax revenue growth. The service industry has become a major area of new market players.

Since the reform and opening-up, access to individual economy, private economy, and foreign capital in various fields of the service industry has been continuously liberalized, and the number of market entities has steadily increased. In 2016, there were 12.97 million legal entities in the service industry, 4.7 times that of 1996, an increase of 10.23 million. In 2013–2016, the legal entity of the service industry grew at an average annual rate of 15.8%, much faster than the average annual growth rate of 6.3% in 1996–2012. Among these entities, the number of legal entities in the modern service industry, such as information transmission, software, and information technology services, leasing and business services, scientific research and technical services, grew at an average annual rate of over 20%.

The strength of the service industry continues to increase, while other industries lead globally. Infrastructure is constantly improving, and the transportation postal capacity is a world leader. With the rapid development of mobile communication technology, the telecommunications industry achieved a historic leap from following to leading. The innovation strategy was implemented in depth and the ability to innovate in science and technology was greatly improved. In 2017, the total investment in research and development of the whole society was CNY1,760.6 billion (USD259.3 billion), ranking second in the world; R&D expenditure as a share of GDP rose to 2.13%. The scale of development of the financial industry has grown significantly, and the international status of the financial industry has been increasing. From 1979–2017, the value-added of the financial industry increased by 12.2% per annum, which was 1.7 % points higher than the actual annual growth rate of the service industry. The proportion of GDP increased from 2.1% in 1978 to 7.9% in 2017. The service industry has accelerated the pace of "bringing in" and "going out" and the service trade has grown rapidly. In 2016, the actual amount of FDI in China and outward FDI from China was USD126 billion and USD196.1 billion, and the service industry accounted for 66.6% and 78.5%, respectively.

The emerging service industry is booming, and the economy is taking off. In 2017, the scale of China's digital economy reached CNY27.2 trillion, a year-on-year increase of 20.3%, accounting for 32.9% of GDP; the transaction volume of the shared economic market was about CNY4.9 trillion (USD721.6 billion). The number of service providers providing shared economic services was about 70 million, and the number of employees of enterprises sharing an economic platform was about 7.16 million. There was rapid development of e-commerce and acceleration of mobile payment; in 2017, the number of Internet users using mobile phones reached 527 million. The service division is more specialized, and business services are accelerating. The construction of beautiful China has achieved remarkable results, and the ecological environment service industry has risen rapidly; in 2013–2017, the annual investment in environmental pollution control was close to CNY1 trillion (USD147.3 billion). The tourism industry development has shown strong vitality in 2017. China's domestic tourists reached 5 billion, an increase of 85 times compared with 1994; the 140 million inbound tourists represented an increase of 76.1 times compared with 1978; total domestic tourism spending and international tourism revenue were CNY4.5661 billion (USD672.5 billion) and USD123.4 billion, respectively, an increase of 43.6 times and 15.9 times compared with 1994. The cultural and sports industries have prospered. In 2017, the value added of culture and related industries reached CNY3.5462 billion (USD522.3 billion), accounting for 4.3% of GDP. Medical resources and medical service capabilities have improved significantly, and the health industry has developed rapidly. Total health expenditures increased from CNY11 billion (USD6.4 billion) in 1978 to CNY5,155.9 billion (USD759.3 billion) in 2017, with an average annual growth rate of 17.1%, and the proportion of the GDP increasing from 3.0% to 6.2%. The education and training industry is entering the fast lane; from 1991 to 2017, total investment in education in the country increased from CNY73.2 billion (USD42.6 billion) to CNY4,257.7 billion (USD630.3 billion), and the proportion of national education funds in GDP rose from 2.8% to 4.1%; in 2016, 8.63 million students received various types of non-academic higher education; as of June 2017, the number of online education users in China reached 144 million, more than 3,200 online courses, and 55 million college students and social learners through the Internet.[74]

10. Concluding Comments and Policy Implications

Before the 1980s, IS change in China was adjusted mainly proportionally among various sectors; therefore, it was dependent on resource allocation by the government. After the 1990s, IS change has mainly depended on changes in market demand. Each enterprise now must make its own strategic response to adjust IS to fit the market demand

---

[74]Service Industry Division, China National Bureau of Statistics (2018). The rapid development of the service industry in the reform and opening-up has ignited half of the national economy. September 10 (in Chinese).

structure. After reform, each enterprise must utilize its own comparative and competitive advantage in the domestic and international markets, develop its market, and cultivate an innovative area of economic activity. However, government policy on industrial structure is still necessary when the market is not effective in improving external economic environment, preventing monopoly, cultivating new industry, encouraging technology progress. Chinese policymakers must work out plans for structural readjustment and technological upgrading and provide guidance to enterprises so they may adapt their production to market needs, actively restructure their product mix, improve the quality of their products, develop new products and new name brands, and enhance their market competitiveness.

Public policy in China must maintain the consolidation and strengthening of the primary industry, optimize and upgrade the secondary industry, and actively develop the tertiary industry. The three industrial structures are continuously adjusted, with the consolidation of agriculture, the gradual moving of secondary industry toward the middle and high-end, and the growth of the service industry into the largest industry in the national economy.[75]

Emphasis must also be placed on the strategy of strengthening the country's network access. China has certainly made huge progress in this regard. However, the construction of "Digital China" must be further accelerated. The integration of technologies such as Internet of Things, cloud computing, and artificial intelligence into all industries must be prioritized, and a new generation of information technology industry system that integrates everything, integrates innovation, intelligent coordination, and security must be constructed "We should energetically promote IT application and use IT to propel industrialization. Make extensive use of advanced adaptive technologies to transform traditional industries and invigorate our equipment manufacturing industry. Vigorous efforts should be made to develop high and new-tech industries that can greatly spur our economic growth."[76]

---

[75]Comprehensive Department of China National Statistical Bureau (2018). Economic structure achieves historic change, development coordination is significantly enhanced, August 29 (in Chinese).

[76]Yang, X. (2016). Analysis on China's urban–rural integration: The perspective of path-dependence. *Open Journal of Social Sciences*, 4, 133–140, Published Online, February 2016 in SciRes.

In addition, the path to urbanization must be further explored. It presents the greatest potential for domestic demand and the most powerful force for sustaining economic development.

Finally, the comparative strengths of different regions must be emphasized, new growth poles and new economic support zones must be fostered, and development between different regions coordinated and balanced to bring about more efficient allocation of resources. The pace of development of the central and western regions must be accelerated, while the role of east coastal regions in system innovation, science, technological innovation, and opening-up should be duly supported

Chapter 5

Change in the Industrial Structure of China's Regional Economy

1. Introduction

A 2019 study by McKenzie found that income inequality has been increasing within countries. Similarly, the 2018 World Inequality Report stated that inequality is both widespread and inevitable. China is a country in which the dividends of economic development are distributed very unevenly. Its economy is both large and diverse. In 2016, China's poorest province, Gansu, had a per capita GDP of less than 25% of its richest province (Beijing). For any country's policymakers, this would present serious headaches! For a large and transitioning economy, these headaches become migraines.

Chinese authorities are well versed on the economic, social, and political ramifications of this inequality in provincial riches. In September 2019, President Xi toured the provinces of Heilongjiang, Liaoning, and Jilin, delivering a message of revitalization of China's Northeast region. President Xi promised the implementation of a series of policies targeting the economic revitalization of the region. After all, the region has played an important role in the fight for the establishment of the People's Republic of China, 70 years ago. The northeast is not the only region left behind in China's march to prosperity. Two other regions, western and central, have also not measured up to their eastern counterpart. The state of the regions' economic development raises several interesting questions. First, is the regional gap real? Second, what are the factors responsible for the gap? Finally, what are the implications of the gap?

Attaining regional balance with respect to economic development and income distribution has been one of the thorniest challenges facing Chinese authorities and one of the items on the country's social and economic agenda. In Chapter 5, we delineate China's five regional development stages. We then show the regional economy's structural change and economic growth and the observed income inequality in different regions. We offer analysis of the provincial per capita income and measures of the regional income gap. We show the reduction of poverty in rural areas and the impact of E-commerce in the Western region's villages.

We proceed with a more detailed analysis of the performance of provincial economies. The share of the service sector and GDP per capita by region in China are presented. Industry gross output and grain yield by region and industrial structure change among the provinces are also presented. We then discuss the observed similarities in provinces' industrial structures as well as the divergence in the industrial structure of the three largest regions. The economic performance among provinces is compared and the optimal regional industrial structure is further explored. We conclude by examining the policy implications of regional imbalances.

2. Government Policy and Regional Economic Development

China's 31 provinces and municipalities have been divided along three (prior to 2008) or four (after 2008) economic and geographical regions, as shown in Table 5.1. As our discussion in this chapter will unveil, these provinces have performed unevenly over the years. There are various factors accounting for the regions' uneven performance. Thus, in addition to the regions' quality and utilization of resources, the path to their economic development has been shaped by government policies. We describe two types of such policies: the country's regional economic development and the hukou policy. The eastern region has benefited from its location, history, its intrinsic characteristics and quality of resources, government policies, and global trends.

2.1. *Regional development stages*

China's government has adopted several policies to influence regional economic development. To understand better the background of the

Table 5.1.   China's regions: Pre- and post-2010.

Before 2010			After 2011			
Eastern (coastal)	Middle	Western	Eastern (coastal)	Middle	Western	Northeastern
Beijing	Shanxi	Chongqing	Beijing	Shanxi	Chongqing	Liaoning
Tianjin	Jilin	Sichuan	Tianjin	Anhui	Sichuan	Jilin
Hebei	Heilongjiang	Guizhou	Hebei	Jiangxi	Guizhou	Heilongjiang
Liaoning	Anhui	Yunnan	Shanghai	Henan	Yunnan	
Shanghai	Jiangxi	Tibet	Jiangsu	Hubei	Tibet	
Jiangsu	Henan	Shaanxi	Zhejiang	Hunan	Shaanxi	
Zhejiang	Hubei	Gansu	Fujian		Gansu	
Fujian	Hunan	Qinghai	Shandong		Qinghai	
Shandong		Ningxia	Guangdong		Ningxia	
Guangdong		Xinjiang	Hainan		Xinjiang	
Hainan		Guangxi			Guangxi	
		Inner Mongolia			Inner Mongolia	

Source: National Statistical Bureau (2011). Division Method of East, West, Central, and Northeast Regions, June 13 (in Chinese).

country's regional development and the government policies associated with it, we identify five stages of that development:

1. **Stage 1:** Before 1978 — "Balanced Allocation." The Chinese government recognized China's isolation from the rest of the world — especially from the Western countries — and considered the necessary steps for the country's sound industrial development. Regional development goals were focused on fostering heavy industries. In terms of regional distribution, financial, material, and human capital investments were concentrated in inland areas in conjunction with several FYPs. The third FYP (1966–1970) divided the nation into three zones (regions) based on the national border conditions at the time. The so-called "Third Front Construction" policy aimed at building strategically positioned military bases. Production capability in the interior was boosted by relocating factories from coastal areas to inland regions. The policy of emphasizing the inland area at that time had

established an argument for inland industrialization. However, inland-centered policies failed to achieve the economic performance commensurate with the amount of investment committed. Additionally, they hindered the relative speed of development of the coastal regions where growth potential was greater. As a result, the country's overall economic performance deteriorated.

2. **Stage 2:** The 1980s — "Gradient development." During that period, emphasis was placed on developing the most promising regions; therefore, investment in the coastal areas received priority. When the national policy of reform and opening to the outside world was adopted, the old heavy industry-oriented policies were gradually replaced by market-oriented policies. Regional policy centering on inland areas was transformed to one of promoting the coastal regions. In July 1979, the government designated Special Economic Zones (SEZ) in the coastal regions, confirming the principle of "giving priority to efficiency and considering fairness at the same time." Coastal regions with favorable access to international trade and foreign investment were granted preferential treatment in terms of tax incentives for foreign investment, investment project approval rights, foreign exchange retention, and revenue sharing with the central government. These policies, which were referred to as regional tilt policies, provided strong momentum to most coastal provinces, but were also criticized as being unfair to inland provinces.

    The second characteristic of the period, decentralization, involved relaxing the central government's control over economic decision-making at the provincial and local levels, thereby giving provincial and local government greater autonomy in handling regional economic affairs. This policy was implemented mainly through the reform of the fiscal relations between the central and provincial governments, as well as other parallel reforms in the areas of investment approval, credit allocation, production planning, price setting, and foreign trade management.

3. **Stage 3:** 1990s — "Anti-gradient development." This stage of regional development entailed acceleration of the development of the central and western regions, concentrating on the promotion of their natural resource base and reduction of regional disparity. Many inland and border areas were opened to foreign investment and a wider range of their enterprises were granted permission to engage in international trade. The preferential policies, formerly applicable to the SEZ and

the 14 coastal open cities, spread rapidly to formerly closed regions. In June 1992, the State Council declared the opening of 10 major cities along the Yangtze River. These 10 cities were to enjoy the same preferential policies as the 14 coastal open cities. Moreover, six comprehensive development zones, each with its own special policies toward certain sectors, were established along the Yangtze River valley. The central government also actively promoted the opening up of the inland borderline. In 1992, it started encouraging trade and other forms of economic cooperation among China's border provinces and Russia, Mongolia, Myanmar, India, and Vietnam. Cross-province policy differentials in terms of administrative power and special policies to foreign investment and international trade were substantially reduced.

4. **Stage 4:** 2000s — Revitalizing Northeast China and the other Old Industrial Base is expected to play an important role in China's modernization process. The program of emphasizing the northeast and the program to develop China's west and the rise of the central region will form two interactive elements in China's development strategy for modernization.[1] The inland provinces' growth was mainly supported by domestic investment. Another supporting factor was the improvement in the terms of trade of the inland provinces relative to the coastal provinces. As prices of energy and raw materials rose during the period, and the amplitude of the increase exceeded the price increase in manufactured goods. This benefited the inland provinces, which are net exporters of primary products.

5. **Stage 5:** 2011 to present — The Third Plenary Session of the 16th CPC Central Committee proposed the regional coordinated development strategy for the first time, and required the formation of a regional development pattern of mutual promotion, complementary advantages, and common development through the improvement of market mechanisms, cooperation mechanisms, mutual assistance mechanisms, and support mechanisms. The 19th National Congress of the Communist Party of China proposed to establish a more effective regional coordinated development mechanism through the implementation of the regional coordinated development strategy and the implementation of various regional development plans.

---

[1]China's Top 10 Business Stories in Year 2003, *Beijing Review*, 2003, No.52.

The National 12th FYP outlines that it is necessary to speed up the formulation and improvement of performance evaluation systems and methods that are conducive to promoting scientific development and are conducive to accelerating the transformation of economic development. The Comprehensive Development Index (CDI) is a comprehensive evaluation of the development of a region from all aspects. It is not just GDP per capita, but also an indicator. It is comprehensive. GDP per capita is only an indicator of this CDI. Now that we have reached this stage and measured by GDP per capita, it does have its limitations. For example, GDP per capita does not accurately reflect the quality of economic growth. Because it reflects the newly added final products and services in a certain period of time, it does not reflect the wealth of the past. The second is that it does not fully reflect the social cost of economic growth. For example, the use of natural resources and the destruction and pollution of the environment. Third, it does not fully reflect the social welfare level of a region or a country, such as the income gap. The indicator system includes economic development, improvement of people's livelihood, social development, ecological construction, technological innovation, and public evaluation, including 45 indicators. The economic development module has set up three secondary indicators of economic growth, structural optimization, and development quality, and eight tertiary indicators. The status of people's livelihood in the CDI evaluation system is more prominent. The improvement of people's livelihood is mainly reflected in three aspects: first, the problem of income distribution, second, the quality of life, and third, employment. Each question has multiple indicators to reflect, a total of 11 indicators. The people's livelihood Improvement Module sets three secondary indicators of income distribution, quality of life, and labor employment, and 12 third-level indicators. Social Development module sets up six secondary indicators, including public service expenditure, regional coordination, culture and education, health and social security, and 10 third-level indicators. The ecological construction module has set up three secondary indicators of resource consumption, CO_2 emissions, environmental governance, and 10 tertiary indicators. The science and technology innovation module had set up two secondary indicators of scientific and technological input, scientific and technological output and four tertiary indicators[11]

Table 5.1.   China 3 regions and 4 regions.

Before 2010			After 2010			
Eastern	Middle	Western	Eastern	Middle	Western	Northeastern
Beijing	Shanxi	Chongqing	Beijing	Shanxi	Chongqing	Liaoning
Tianjin	Jilin	Sichuan	Tianjin	Anhui	Sichuan	Jilin
Hebei	Heilongjiang	Guizhou	Hebei	Jiangxi	Guizhou	Heilongjiang
Liaoning	Anhui	Yunnan	Shanghai	Henan	Yunnan	
Shanghai	Jiangxi	Tibet	Jiangsu	Hubei	Tibet	
Jiangsu	Henan	Shaanxi	Zhejiang	Hunan	Shaanxi	
Zhejiang	Hubei	Gansu	Fujian		Gansu	
Fujian	Hunan	Qinghai	Shandong		Qinghai	
Shandong		Ningxia	Guangdong		Ningxia	
Guangdong		Xinjiang	Hainan		Xinjiang	
Hainan		Guangxi			Guangxi	
		Inner Mongolia			Inner Mongolia	

Source: National Statistical Bureau: Division method of East, West, Central, and Northeast regions, June 13, 2011 (in Chinese).

The 31 provinces and municipalities in Mainland China are usually divided into eastern, central, and western regions, see Table 5.1.[2] The per capita GRP map in Figure 5.1 shows that in 2006, the nine richest provinces were located in the eastern region; of the 10 low income provinces with per capita GRP, eight were in the western region and two were in the central region. The per capita GP map[3] in Figure 5.1(a) shows that in 2016, the seven richest provinces were located in the eastern region; of the 9 per capita GRP low income provinces seven were in the western region and

---

[2]Question by the Chief Statistician of the National Bureau of Statistics: Where is the CDI better than GDP? People's Daily Overseas Edition (Beijing), August 24, 2011 (in Chinese); Accounting Department of China National Statistical Bureau: Significant development pattern of regional development strategy has a new look, 2018-09-13 (in Chinese).

[3]Using data from China National Bureau of Statistics: China Statistical Yearbook, China Statistics Press, 2005, Table 3.11.

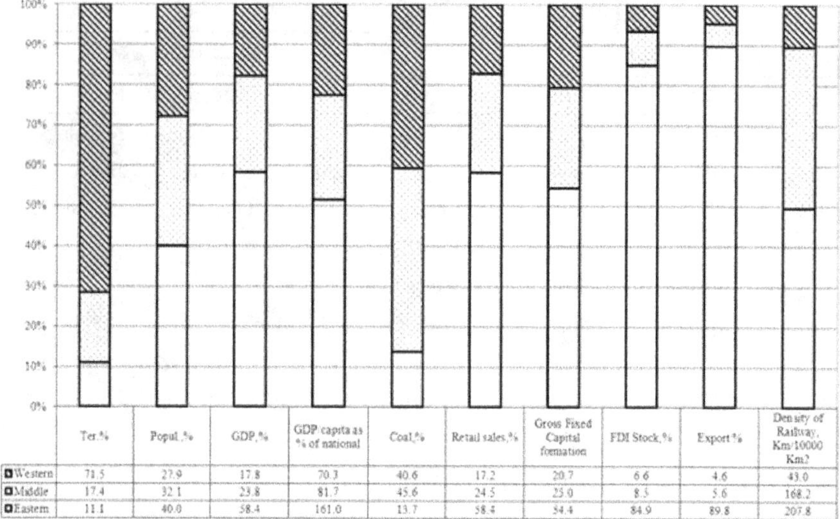

	Ter.%	Popul.%	GDP,%	GDP capita as % of national	Coal,%	Retail sales,%	Gross Fixed Capital formation	FDI Stock,%	Export %	Density of Railway, Km/10000 Km2
◘ Western	71.5	27.9	17.8	70.3	40.6	17.2	20.7	6.6	4.6	43.0
◘ Middle	17.4	32.1	23.8	81.7	45.6	24.5	23.0	8.3	5.6	168.2
◘ Eastern	11.1	40.0	58.4	161.0	13.7	58.4	34.4	84.9	89.8	207.8

Figure 5.1.   Show the regional structure of eastern, central, and western regions in China in 2008.

two were in the central region. This shows that the gap of per capita GRP in the three regions improved slightly in 2016 compared to 2006.

Figures 5.2 and 5.3[4] show the regional structure of the eastern, central, and western regions in China on 2008. In eastern coastal region, The Third Plenary Session of the 16th Chinese Communist Party (CPC) Central Committee proposed the regionally coordinated development strategy for the first time, and required the formation of a regional development pattern of mutual promotion, complementary advantages, and common development through the improvement of market mechanisms, cooperation mechanisms, mutual assistance mechanisms, and support mechanisms. The 19th National Congress of the CPC of China proposed to establish a more effective regionally coordinated development mechanism through the implementation of appropriate development strategies.

---

[4]Calculated using data from China National Bureau of Statistics: China Statistical Yearbook, China Statistics Press, 2009, Tables 2.17, 2.22, 3.4, 3.10, 4.4, 12.4, 13.4, 13.5, 13.23, 15.3, 16.3, 17.11, 17.16, 20.25, 20.63.

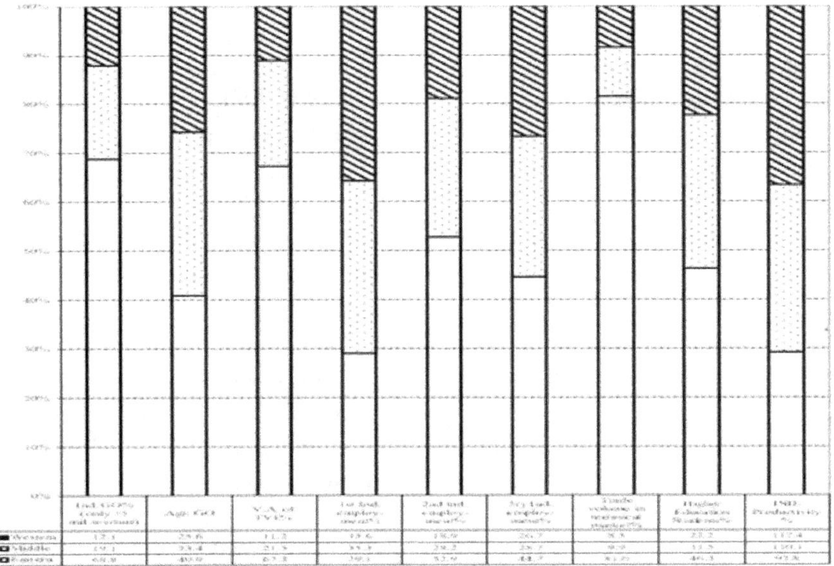

Figure 5.2.   Show the regional structure of Eastern, central, and Western regions in China in 2008.

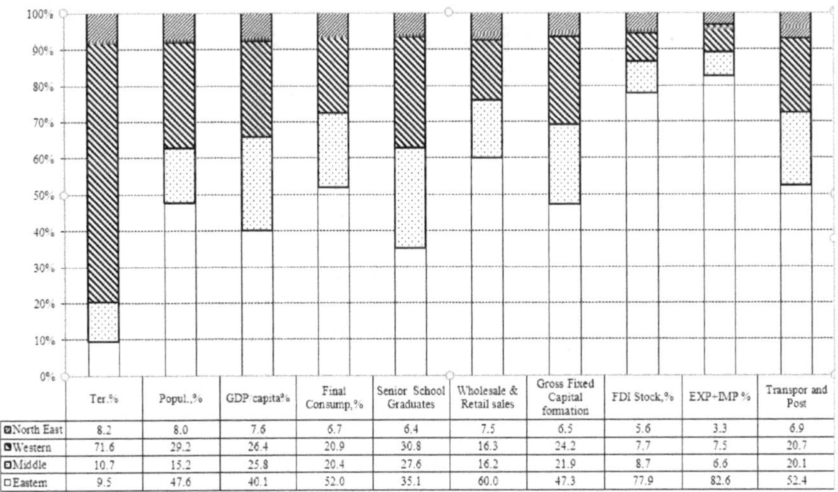

	Ter.%	Popul.,%	GDP capita%	Final Consump,%	Senior School Graduates	Wholesale & Retail sales	Gross Fixed Capital formation	FDI Stock,%	EXP+IMP %	Transpor and Post
North East	8.2	8.0	7.6	6.7	6.4	7.5	6.5	5.6	3.3	6.9
Western	71.6	29.2	26.4	20.9	30.8	16.3	24.2	7.7	7.5	20.7
Middle	10.7	15.2	25.8	20.4	27.6	16.2	21.9	8.7	6.6	20.1
Eastern	9.5	47.6	40.1	52.0	35.1	60.0	47.3	77.9	82.6	52.4

Figure 5.3.   China's regional structure, 2017.

2.2. *The Hukou system*

Economic theory tells us that, in perfectly integrated economies, resources will move to an economy that offers them the highest rate of return. Resource mobilization takes place until similar resources receive equal rates of return across economies. However, when there are barriers to resource mobilization, similar resources may not be rewarded equally. This is indeed the case with China's labor resources. The movement of workers from rural to urban regions, where they would receive higher wages, has been affected by the "hukou" system.

The hukou system, adopted in the 1950s, is a residential registration system as well as a passport system. In addition to allowing a resident of a rural area to work in a city, having a hukou in that city provides the holder with access to public services. Because receiving a hukou is not an easy process, the system acts as a deterrent for workers to move freely to regions that pay higher wages.

Although the system gives the government control over labor movement, it creates problems for cities that experience excess demand for labor. To meet this demand, and to facilitate the urbanization process, the State Council issued a statement (Opinion) in 2014 expressing the need for reform of the system. Particular attention has been paid to relaxing hukou restrictions in smaller-size cities. In general, skilled labor and educated white-collar workers are finding it easier to obtain a hukou, although they still face discriminatory practices. This goes against the urbanization objective expressed in the recent FYPs.

3. Measuring Regional Economic Performance

The National 12th FYP outlined that it was necessary to speed up the formulation of improved performance evaluation systems and methods conducive to promoting scientific development and to accelerating the transformation of economic development. Toward that end, the CDI was introduced to address some of the limitations of GDP per capita, the measure traditionally used to denote regional development. The CDI provides a comprehensive evaluation of the development of a region. For example, GDP per capita does not accurately reflect the quality of economic growth, the social costs of such growth, or the region's social welfare. On the other hand, the CDI approach encompasses economic development, improvement of people's livelihood, social development, ecological construction, technological innovation, and public evaluation; it includes 45 indicators. The economic development module includes three secondary indicators (economic growth, structural optimization, and development quality) and eight tertiary indicators. People's livelihood also occupies a more prominent position in the CDI evaluation system. The improvement of people's livelihood is mainly reflected in three items: income distribution, quality of life, and employment. Each question in the survey instrument included 11 indicators. The people's livelihood improvement module sets three secondary indicators (income distribution, quality of life, and employment) and 12 tertiary indicators. The social development module contains six secondary indicators of public service expenditure, regional coordination, cultural education, health, and social security, as well as 10 tertiary indicators. The ecological construction module set up three secondary indicators (resource consumption, CO_2 emissions, and environmental governance), and 10 tertiary indicators. The science and technology innovation module set up two secondary indicators (scientific and technological input and scientific and technological output), and four tertiary indicators.[11]

Examining the results of the CDI ranking and those of the per capita GDP ranking, we find there is a positive correlation between the two. However, the per capita GDP ranking and the CDI ranking in individual regions have a larger difference. For example, Qinghai, Xinjiang, and Ningxia are ranked 18th, 21st, and 15th, respectively, according to per capita GDP, and are ranked 28th, 30th, and 23rd, respectively, according to the CDI. For other provinces, the per capita GDP ranks behind that of the CDI. Anhui, Jiangxi, and Sichuan are ranked 25th, 23rd, and 24th, respectively (per capita GDP), while the CDI ranks them 13th, 17th, and 24th. The per capita GDP rankings of five provinces are equivalent to the CDI rankings: Beijing, Shanghai, Heilongjiang, GanSu and Guizhou are ranked first, second, 22, 29 and 31 respectively.

4. China's Regional Structure

To further understand the differences among the regions, we explore the structure of their economies.

As Table 5.2 and Figure 5.2 reveal, the eastern region has a more advanced economy than the other two regions, although it occupies 11.1% of the national territory.

Table 5.2.   2016 China's per capita GDP map (see Figure 5.1(a)) description and comparison with CDI.

Region	CID2016	Rank	GRPpc2016	Region	CID2016	Rank	GRPpc2016	Rank
Beijing	91.19	1	118128	Hubei	42.72	10	55506	11
Tianjin	65.93	5	114503	Hunan	39.78	12	46249	16
Hebei	32.86	20	42932	Guangdong	66.57	3	73511	7
Shanxi	29.38	25	35444	Guangxi	29.66	24	37862	26
Inner Mongolia	34.98	14	71937	Hainan	33.66	19	44201	17
Liaoning	31.86	21	50815	Chongqing	48.09	7	58204	10
Jilin	34.68	16	54068	Sichuan	33.81	18	39863	24
Heilongjiang	31.65	22	40500	Guizhou	27.94	29	33127	29
Shanghai	81.73	2	116441	Yunnan	28.68	26	30996	30
Jiangsu	62.35	5	96747	Tibet	28.52	27	34786	28
Zhejiang	65.94	4	84528	Shaanxi	40.31	11	50877	13
Anhui	38.12	13	39393	Gansu	25.54	31	27588	31
Fujian	45.04	9	74369	Qinghai	28.04	28	43381	18
Jiangxi	33.99	17	40285	Ningxia	29.78	23	46942	15
Shandong	47.54	8	68387	Xinjiang	27.91	30	40241	23
Henan	34.89	15	42459					

Source: Calculated using data from Database of China National Bureau of Statistics, China National Bureau of Statistics, Database; Annual by Province, Per Capita Gross Regional Product (yuan/person), 1997–2016; Xin, Z. (2012). Research Institute of China National Bureau of Statistics: 2010 Regional CDI Report, January 6 (in Chinese).

We now compare China's regional structure in 1994[5] with 2017's regional structure, using Figures 5.4 (2017),[6] 5.5[7], and 5.2. Comparing Figure 5.2 with Figure 5.5, we can see the gap between the eastern region and the central and western regions slightly expanded, even though the government has been paying great attention to the development of the central and western regions, as emphasized in the ninth FYP. In 1994, the per capita GDP of the eastern, central, and western region was CNY2,095, CNY1,214, and CNY1,010 (1978 constant CNY), respectively. In 2008, it rose to CNY8,141, CNY4,131, and CNY3,691 (1978 constant CNY), respectively. From 1994–2018, the absolute difference in per capita GDP of the eastern region and the central and western regions increased from CNY881 and CNY1,085 to CNY4,010 and CNY4,450 (1978 constant CNY), respectively. From 1994–2018, the average growth rates of the per capita GDP in the three regions were 10.2% (eastern), 9.1% (central), and 9.7% (western), respectively. The central and western regions are rich in mining and agricultural resources (77% coal, 57% crude petroleum oil, 65% natural gas, 71% timber, more than 90% non-ferrous metals, higher employment in 1st industry), but their economy is less developed than the economy of the coastal region.

4.1. *Changes in regional structure*

China's new development model emphasizes quality, efficiency, and innovation. After decades of promoting investment and exports as growth vehicles, improvements in the people's standard of living became a political and economic necessity. Therefore, in Figure 5.4, we exhibit indicators that reflect the new development strategy. We use the final consumption expenditure as an indicator of the optimal structure of aggregate demand. Increasing the contribution rate of consumer demand can promote the balanced development of the three major demand

---

[5]Before 2000, Guangxi belonged to the eastern region and inner Mongolia — central region, see China National Bureau of Statistics (2002). The economic development status of Western Region in 2000, October 21.

[6]Calculated using data from China National Bureau of Statistics: China Statistical Yearbook, China Statistics Press, 2018, Tables 2.6, 3.10, 3.14, 3.15, 6.23, 6.29, 11.8, 11.18, 20.16, 20.22, 21.16 and 22.10.

[7]Calculated using data from China National Bureau of Statistics: China Statistical Yearbook, China Statistics Press, 1995,

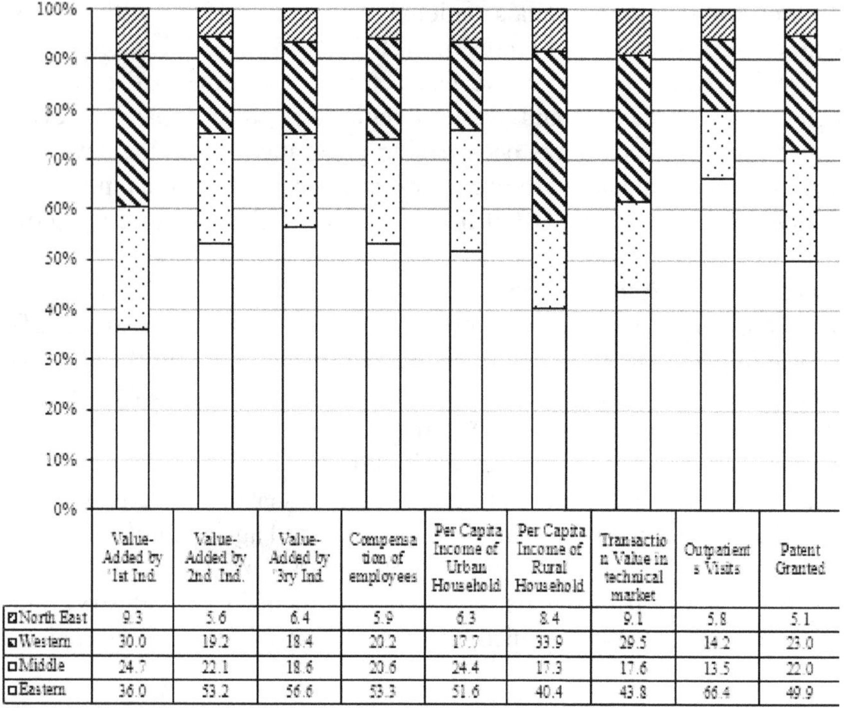

	Value-Added by 1st Ind.	Value-Added by 2nd Ind.	Value-Added by 3ry Ind.	Compensation of employees	Per Capita Income of Urban Household	Per Capita Income of Rural Household	Transaction Value in technical market	Outpatients Visits	Patent Granted
North East	9.3	5.6	6.4	5.9	6.3	8.4	9.1	5.8	5.1
Western	30.0	19.2	18.4	20.2	17.7	33.9	29.5	14.2	23.0
Middle	24.7	22.1	18.6	20.6	24.4	17.3	17.6	13.5	22.0
Eastern	36.0	53.2	56.6	53.3	51.6	40.4	43.8	66.4	49.9

Figure 5.4. China's regional structure, 2017.

components (consumption, investment, and export) and enhance the endogenous driving force of economic development. Furthermore, the value added of the service industry as a percentage of GDP is an indicator of the optimization and upgrading of the industrial structure. Employee compensation reflected the income distribution relationship among residents, enterprises, and government. It shows the improvement of people's livelihood. The per capita disposable income of urban residents and the per capita disposable income of rural residents reflect the improvement of the income level of urban and rural residents and the adjustment of the income distribution structure. Outpatient Services of Health Institutions indicate the level of social public health development. Domestic Patent Granted is an indicator of independent intellectual property rights and independent innovation, reflecting the technological innovation capability of a region.

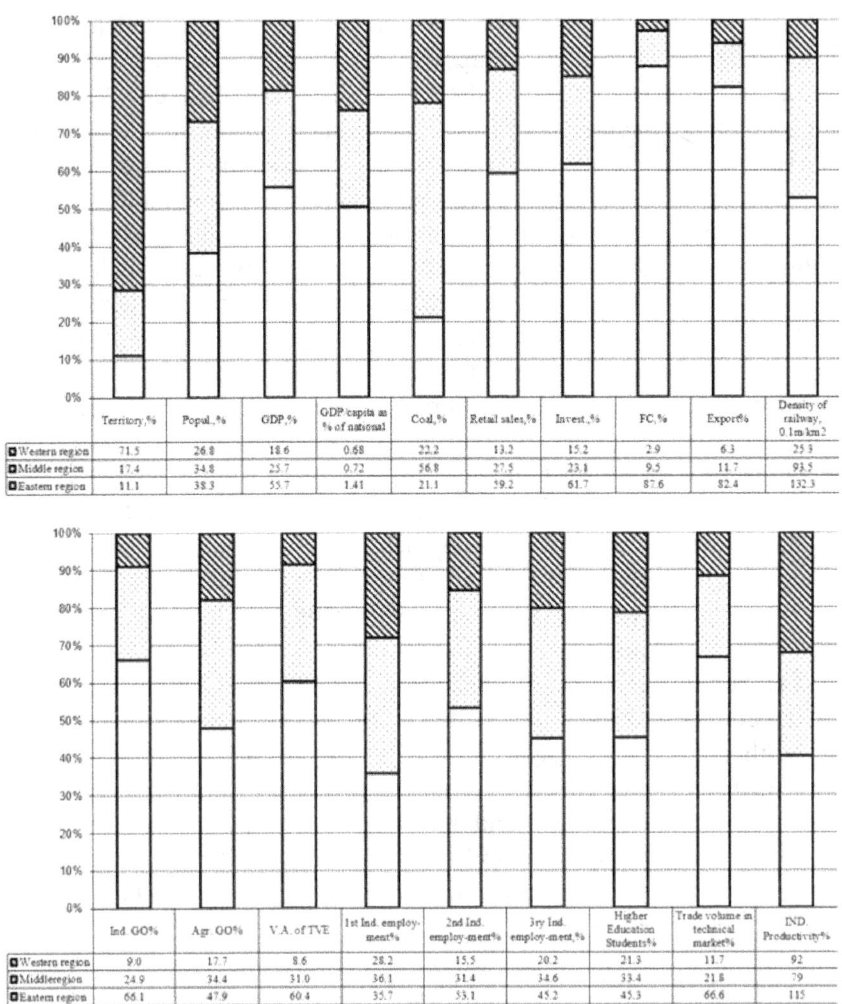

	Territory,%	Popul.,%	GDP,%	GDP/capita as % of national	Coal,%	Retail sales,%	Invest.,%	FC,%	Export%	Density of railway, 0.1m/km2
Western region	71.5	26.8	18.6	0.68	22.2	13.2	15.2	2.9	6.3	25.3
Middle region	17.4	34.8	25.7	0.72	56.8	27.5	23.1	9.5	11.7	93.5
Eastern region	11.1	38.3	55.7	1.41	21.1	59.2	61.7	87.6	82.4	132.3

	Ind. GO%	Agr. GO%	V.A. of TVE	1st Ind. employ-ment%	2nd Ind. employ-ment%	3ry Ind. employ-ment,%	Higher Education Students%	Trade volume in technical market%	IND. Productivity%
Western region	9.0	17.7	8.6	28.2	15.5	20.2	21.3	11.7	92
Middle region	24.9	34.4	31.0	36.1	31.4	34.6	33.4	21.8	79
Eastern region	66.1	47.9	60.4	35.7	53.1	45.2	45.3	66.6	115

(a)

Figure 5.5.   (a) China's regional structure, 1994.

Figures 5.3 and 5.4 show the eastern region has played a huge role in opening up to the outside world by relying on its coastal advantages. In 2017, total import and export volume in the eastern region was USD338.78 billion, an increase of 434.2 times over 1978, and the national proportion increased from 37.7% to 82.5%, ranking first among the four regions. The rise of the central region has achieved leapfrog development. The modern equipment and high-tech industries in the central region have contributed to rapid and sustained development, independent innovation capability, and modern industrial technology. By exerting the unique advantages of the location conditions of the central region, China plans to build a modern, three-dimensional transportation system and a modern logistics system that connects the north to the south and the east to the west, and many major projects such as the Zhengzhou national comprehensive transportation hub. The development of the western region expands the new space for economic development. Significant progress has been made in infrastructure and ecological environment construction, and the construction of large-scale transportation channels has been implemented. West–East Gas Transmission, West–East Power Transmission, and Qinghai–Tibet Railway have been put into operation. In addition, plans have been put together to improve green development, implement major ecological projects such as returning farmland to forests and grasslands, returning grazing to grassland, managing of soil erosion, and holding firmly on protecting the ecology.

The revitalization of the northeast region led the transformation and development of the old industrial base. The strategy of revitalizing the northeast includes upgrading the machinery manufacturing industry. The region has specialized in the manufacturing of large-scale hydraulic turbines, large wind turbines, large nuclear power units, 300,000 tons of oil tankers, 350 kilometers of high-speed EMUs, and high-end CNC machine tools; the output of high-end CNC machine tools accounts for one-third of the country. "Equipment manufacturing is the country's heavy weapon, and the northeast is related to China's national defense security and industrial security." Guangdong, Zhejiang, Shenzhen cannot create aircraft carriers, fighters, and nuclear submarines. They still must rely on the northeast! In addition, in 2017, grain production in the northeast accounted for about 20% of the country's total grain output.[8]

---

[8] Hu, X. (2018). In terms of money, the northeastern region is very poor. Looking at the heavy weapons of the country, the northeast is the country's important town, October 11. (in Chinese), http://www.sohu.com/a/258734877_166580.

5. Regional Economic Development after Economic Reform

The policies enacted after economic reform were preferential to coastal areas, improved their infrastructure, created the SEZ and the open cities, as well as the "Development Poles" (Pudong Development Zone, Yangtze Delta, Pearl Delta, Annulus Bohai-Rim, Minnan Delta, Shandong Peninsula, and Liaodong Peninsula). In addition, new energy and raw material bases were constructed in the inland area, i.e. Shanxi and Inner Mongolia coal and energy base, Xinjiang petroleum base, Yellow River Upriver and Yangtze Upriver hydropower (Three Gorge hydro power), WuJiang hydropower, Guizhou aluminum and phosphorus base, and Panxi (in Sichuan) titanium and vanadium base. Border trade has been developed in Heilongjiang, Jilin, Inner Mongolia, Xinjiang, Yunnan, and Guangxi.

During the first FYP (1952–1957), the government focused its investment activities on the central and western regions, while substantially reducing its investment in the coastal regions. The regional economic gap was slightly reduced, but the annual growth rate of national income declined and the country's overall economic performance declined. During the third and fourth FYPs (1966–1975), although most of the investment (73%) was placed in the central and western regions, the regional economic gap was still not reduced. The strategy was also accompanied by low annual growth rate of national income and overall poor economic performance.

After the reforms (1978), investment in the eastern region increased substantially, resulting in high GDP growth rates and improved economic performance, but regional differences in absolute terms continued to increase.[9] For example, in 1981, investment in fixed assets in QingHai (west) province and Shanghai (east) amounted to CNY0.58 billion (USD70 million) and CNY3.08 billion (USD372 million), respectively.[10] In 2005, investment in Qinghai increased to CNY33.0 billion (USD4.1 billion),

---

[9]Calculated using data from China National Bureau of Statistics: China Statistical Yearbook 2009, Tables 5.7, 2.4; 1999, Table 6.4; 1995 Table 5.2, and various years. Compiled by Department of Comprehensive Statistics: China Compendium of Statistics 1949–2004, China Statistics Press, 2005.

[10]China State Statistical Bureau (1982). Statistical Yearbook of China 1981. Published by Economic Information & Agency, Hong Kong, p. 310.

but investment in Shanghai reached CNY351.0 billion (USD43.5 billion).[11] The huge difference between these investment amounts resulted in further divergence in their economic development.

From Figure 5.7, we can see that the fixed asset investment in the eastern region reached the highest value in 1994, accounting for 61.0% of the national average, and then gradually decreased, reaching 50.8% in 2008. Attention was paid to implementing the strategy for developing the western region and promoting coordinated progress among the regions. In the 10th FYP (2001–2005), China invested heavily in several projects of strategic significance to fortify its infrastructure and improve the ecological environment. These projects included the Three Gorges hydro electrical power station at the Yangtze River, the transmission of natural gas and electricity from western to eastern regions, the Qinghai–Tibet Railway, and a project to divert river water from south to north. By the end of 2005, 14 power generators were in operation in the three Gorges Project, having generated 94.0 billion kilowatt-hours of electricity. The West–East Electricity Transmission Project from north, central, and south channels

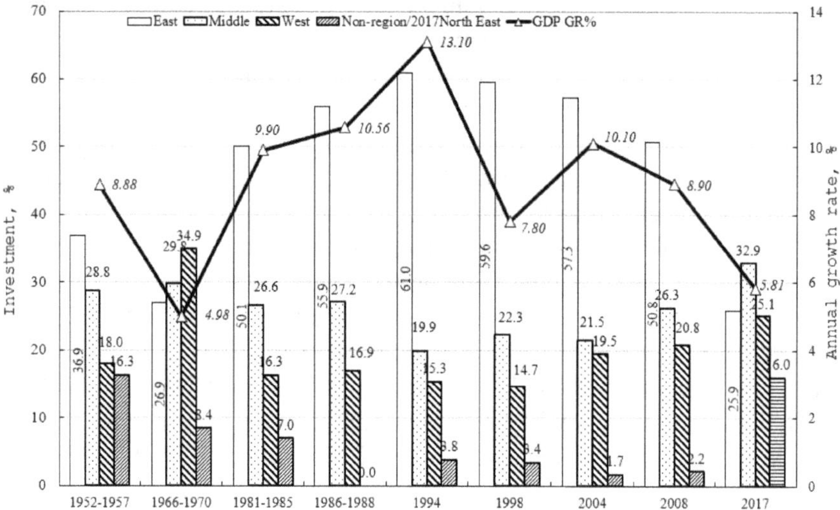

Figure 5.7.   China's Investment and annual growth rate of GDP in three regions during 1952–2017.

---

[11]Calculated using data from China National Bureau of Statistics 2006, China Statistical Yearbook, China Statistics Press, 2006, Table 6.2.

had produced a power transmission capacity of over 32.50 million kilo-watts. The completion of the Qinghai–Tibet railway finally delivered railway transport to Tibet. CNY3.8 billion of investment was completed as part of the first phase of the eastern and central routes of the South-to-North Water Diversion Project. The completed investment in the key projects in harnessing the Huaihe River amounted to CNY25.0 billion.[12] In 2008, the investment in the east was CNY8,775 billion (USD1,285 billion), up by 20.9% over the previous year; in the central areas, it was CNY4,539 billion (USD665 billion), a growth of 32.6%, and it was CNY3,595 billion (USD526 billion), a 26.9% increase in the west. Note that, although the absolute amount of investment in the eastern area is the highest, the annual growth rate in that area is the lowest. Therefore, it is anticipated that the gap among the three regions will be narrowed.

Since the reform and opening-up, the regional development gap has become larger at times, and narrower at other times. At the beginning of the reform and opening-up, the coastal development strategy took the lead in the eastern region and the region maintained its leading position. After the year 2000, with the implementation of regional development strategies such as the development of the western region, the rise of the central region and the revitalization of the northeast, especially the three major strategies of the "One Belt and One Road" (since the 18th National Congress of the Communist Party of China), The coordinated development of the Beijing-Tianjin-Hebei Corridor and the Yangtze River Economic Belt has enhanced the effectiveness of the national regional economic development strategy, improved the policy system, and formed a spatial strategic pattern of four major sectors and three supporting belts. Under the guidance of these initiatives, the regional development gap has been shrinking.

6. Regional Income Inequality

There are conflicting opinions regarding the income gap among regions after reform. To confirm the direction and size of the gap, we conduct our own analysis. Table 5.3[13] shows the per capita national income for

---

[12]National Bureau of Statistics of China (2006). Statistical Communiqué on the 2005 National Economic and Social Development, March 3.

[13]Calculated using data from China National Bureau of Statistics: China Statistical Yearbook China Statistics Press, 2009, Tables 2.1, 2.4 and 2.15; Compiled by Department

Table 5.3. Per capita income for various provinces in China (1979 constant CNY).

Region	NIpc52	Rankl	NIpc79	Rank2	GDPpc88	Rank3	GDPpc94	Rank4	GDPpc08	Rank5	GDPpc17	Rank6	R1-R6	R1-R2	R2-R6
Beijing	296	3	1685	2	2703	2	3641	2	13075	2	20550	3	0	1	−1
Tianjin	311	2	1091	3	2041	3	2897	3	11508	3	24140	2	0	−1	1
Hebei	131	9	289	7	752	10	1220	13	4821	12	9762	16	−7	2	−9
Shanxi	111	17	228	15	692	12	1000	17	4232	14	8019	24	−7	2	−9
Inner Mongolia	178	7	255	14	710	11	1069	15	6683	8	16532	6	1	−7	8
Liaoning	230	5	709	4	1158	4	2165	6	6485	9	13801	11	−6	1	−7
Jilin	170	8	293	6	762	9	1314	12	4878	11	11622	12	−4	2	−6
Heilongjiang	247	4	366	5	830	8	1571	10	4507	13	994	14	−10	−1	−9
Shanghai	694	1	2861	1	2879	1	5394	1	15170	1	25698	1	0	0	0
Jiangsu	113	13	283	10	927	5	2053	7	8220	5	19066	4	9	3	6
Zhejiang	121	12	288	8	917	6	2182	5	8757	4	17270	5	7	4	3
Anhui	91	22	128.6	26	517	20	894	21	3005	25	7944	25	−3	−4	1
Fujian	113	14	200	20	614	17	1900	8	6249	10	15225	8	6	6	12
Jiangxi	122	11	192	23	485	24	843	25	3066	24	7612	26	−15	−12	−3
Shandong	101	19	257	13	684	13	1587	9	6863	7	15305	7	12	6	6
Henan	90	23	198	21	496	23	878	24	4065	17	9589	17	6	2	4
Hubei	99	20	209	17	675	15	1185	14	4120	16	10638	13	7	3	4
Hunan	91	21	197	22	536	19	958	18	3635	20	8838	19	2	−1	3
Guangdong	105	18	207	18	904	7	2411	4	7798	6	15144	9	9	0	9
Guangxi	72	26	127.7	27	399	26	949	20	3105	23	7438	27	−1	−1	0

Chongqing											14058	10			
Hainan											9177	18			
Sichuan	68	27	149	25	466	25	880	23	3190	22	8515	22	5	2	3
Guizhou	65	28	103	28	358	28	551	28	1831	28	5360	31	−3	0	−3
Yunnan	74	25	155	24	396	27	883	22	2611	26	6522	28	−3	1	−4
Tibet											6067	29			
Shaanxi	90	24	259	12	498	22	832	26	3785	18	9966	15	9	12	−3
Gansu	111	16	226	16	500	21	683	27	2512	27	5809	30	−14	0	−14
Qinghai	112	15	285	9	667	16	1032	16	3607	21	8614	21	−6	6	−12
Ningxia	124	10	201	19	561	18	953	19	3712	19	8273	23	−13	−9	−4
Xinjiang	186	6	280	11	682	14	1403	11	4127	15	8702	20	−14	0	−9

28 regions in 1952, 1979 and per capita GDP in 1988, 1994, 2008, as well as the appropriate rankings. From 1979–1988, the reform was mainly implemented in rural areas. In 1994, the percentage share of investment in the eastern area reached its peak value because it was followed by a strategy favoring the development of the western region. Using the ranking method, we found that Rank 1952 and Rank 1979 according to per capita national income for the eastern, central, and western regions did not change much; the annual growth rate of National Income during 1952–1979 was 4.11%. From Ranks 1988, 1994, and 2008, we see that the eastern region is developing faster. National income during the 1979–2008 period increased much faster than it did before reforms, with an annual growth rate of 8.47%.[14] Figure 5.8[15] shows the change in ranks of the provinces by per capita GDP before and after economic reform. Provinces located in the first quadrant improved their rank both before and after economic reforms. There are six provinces located in the first quarter. See, for example, Shandong (SD, 6,6), where SD is an abbreviation of Shandong Province and the first number in parentheses stands for the change in ranking prior to reform, with the second showing the change in ranking after reform (see Table 5.2). Before economic reform, Shandong Province's ranking improved by six places. After economic reform, the Province's ranking also improved by six places. In addition to Shandong, Zhejiang (ZJ, 4, 3), Jiangsu (JS, 3, 6), Henan (HeN, 2, 4), Hubei (HuB, 3, 4), and Sichuan (SC, 2, 3) are also located in the first quadrant.

Five provinces located in second quadrant improved their rank after economic reforms, but their rank deteriorated prior to economic reform.

---

of Comprehensive Statistics: China Compendium of Statistics 1949–2004, Statistical Yearbook of China 1981 (English Edition), Compiled by the State Statistical Bureau, PRC. Published by Economic Information & Agency, Hong Kong, October 1982, p. 20.

[14]Calculated using data from China National Bureau of Statistics: China Statistical Yearbook, China Statistics Press, 2009, Tables 2.1, 2.4 and 2.15; Statistical Yearbook of China 1981 (English Edition), Compiled by the State Statistical Bureau, PRC. Published by Economic Information & Agency, Hong Kong, October 1982, p. 20.

[15]Calculated using data from China National Bureau of Statistics: China Statistical Yearbook, China Statistics Press, 2018, Table 3.9; 2016, Table 3.10; 2014, Table 3.15; 2009, Tables 2.1, 2.4 and 2.15; Statistical Yearbook of China 1981 (English Edition), Compiled by the State Statistical Bureau, PRC. Published by Economic Information & Agency, Hong Kong, October 1982, p. 20.

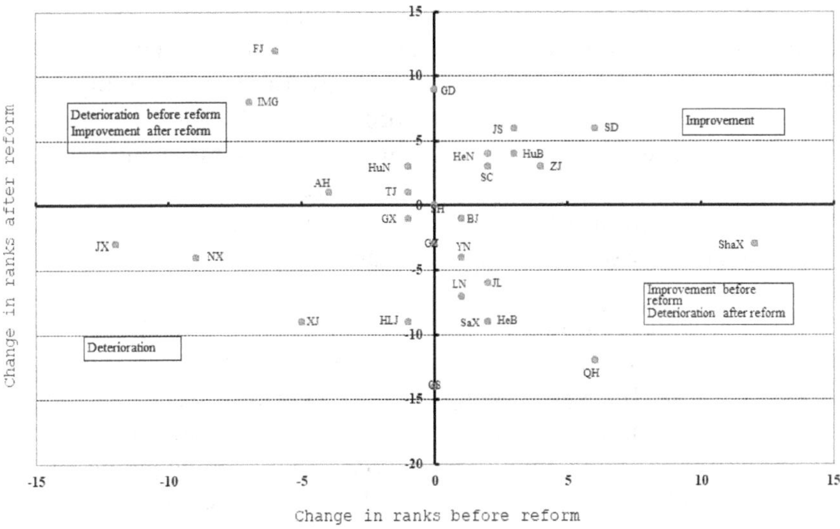

Figure 5.8.   Change in ranks of provinces in China (per capita GDP, 1952–2017).

Fujian (FJ, –6, 12), Hunan (HuN, –1, 3), Inner Mongolia (IMG, –7, 8), Anhui (–4, –1), and Tianjin (TJ, –1, 1) are the provinces located in the second quadrant. Five provinces located in third quarter deteriorate their rank before and after economic reform. They are Jiangxi (JX, –12, –4), Heilongjiang (HLJ, –1, –9), Ningxia (NX, –9, –4), Guangxi (GX, –1, –1), and Xinjiang (XJ, –5, –9).

Eight provinces located in the fourth quadrant improved their rank before economic reform, but their rank deteriorated after economic reform. They are Shaanxi (ShaX, 12, –3), Yunnan (YN, 1, –4), Hebei (HeB, 2, –9), Shanxi (SaX, 2, –9), Jilin (JL, 2, –6), Liaoning (LN, 1, –6), Beijing (BJ, 1, –1), and Qinghai (QH, 6, –12). Guangdong (0, 9), Guizhou (0, –3), and Gansu (GS, 0, –14) are located at the *Y*-axis, which means their rank did not change before economic reform; however, after economic reform, Guizhou and Gansu deteriorated, and Guangdong improved. Beijing (BJ, 1, –1) improved one position and Tianjin (TJ, –1, 1) deteriorated one position. Shanghai (SH, 0, 0) remains on its original score, which means its ranking has not changed before and after the economic reform. It is interesting that Shanghai ranks first, and Guizhou ranks last before and after economic reform. Therefore, the gap between the top performer and the lowest one was not affected by the reforms.

In terms of per capita income rankings, three regions — Shanghai, Beijing, and Tianjin — are consistently ranked on top. However, all three are municipalities, which have much less rural area than the other provinces. The top three provinces before reform (1979) were Liaoning, Heilongjiang, and Jilin, (all located in northeastern China) but fell to 9, 11, and 13, respectively, in 2008, and to 10, 12, and 13, respectively, in 2017. In 2017, the top three provinces were Jiangsu, Zhejiang, and Inner Mongolia (two located in the eastern region and one in the western region).

Eight provinces located in the fourth quadrant improved their rank before economic reform, but their rank deteriorated after economic reform. They are Shaanxi (ShaX, 12, –3), Yunnan (YN, 1, –4), Hebei (HeB, 2, –9), Shanxi (SaX, 2, –9), Jilin (JL, 2, –6), Liaoning (LN, 1, –6), Beijing (BJ, 1, –1), and Qinghai (QH, 6, –12). Guangdong (0, 9) Guizhou (0, –3), and Gansu (GS, 0, –14) are located at the Y-axis, which means their rank did not change before economic reform; however, after economic reform, Guizhou and Gansu deteriorated, and Guangdong improved. Beijing (BJ,1, –1) improved one position and Tianjin (TJ, –1, 1) deteriorated one position. Shanghai (SH, 0, 0) placed on the original points, which means its rank did not change both before and after economic reform. It is interesting that Shanghai ranks first, and Guizhou ranks last before and after economic reform. Therefore, the gap between the top performer and the lowest one was not affected by the reforms.

In terms of per capita income rankings, three regions — Shanghai, Beijing, and Tianjin — are consistently ranked on top. However, all three are municipalities, which have much less rural area than the other provinces. The top three provinces before reform (1979) were Liaoning, Heilongjiang, and Jilin, (all located in northeastern China) but fell to 9, 11 and 13, respectively, in 2008, and to 10, 12, and 13, respectively, in 2017. In 2017, the top three provinces were Jiangsu, Zhejiang, and Inner Mongolia (two located in the eastern region and one in the western region).

Zhejiang Province's ascent is especially noteworthy. Combining an entrepreneurial trading heritage with a meticulous division of labor, Zhejiang's family-controlled businesses are taking global markets by storm. These businesses are creating real wealth. Zhejiang's success comes down to one simple fact: 91% of its 240,000 enterprises, with annual revenues of CNY700 billion (USD84.5 billion) in 2002, are privately owned.[16] In 2017, the gross output value of private industry enterprises was CNY26,340 billion (USD3,899.5 billion), 9.2 times that of SOEs in the Zhejiang Province, with an average number of 3.55 million employees and 71.2 times that of SOEs).[17]

Inner Mongolia, in the west region, is another particularly interesting province. From 1952–2017, the province rose to be among the top three provinces in terms of per capita GDP. The pace of structural adjustment accelerated, and the proportion of the service industry further increased. The tertiary industry grew by 6.1%, accounting for 50% of the GDP, an increase of 7.5% points. In 2017, the gross output value of SOEs was only 5.3% of the total. The transformation and upgrading of traditional industries and supply chains and the proportion of coal power and coalification integration developed quickly. New energy, new materials, electronic communications, and other industries grew rapidly, and the production capacity of rare earth compounds and capacity of cloud computing servers now ranked first in the country. The province pursued opening up to the outside world, promotion of the "Belt and Road", and the Sino-Mongolian-Russian economic corridor. The number of trains entering and leaving China and Europe at Manzhouli and Erlianhaote ports has grown at a fast rate. Foreign trade is also expected to maintain rapid growth. In 2017, the total volume of imports and exports reached CNY94.4 billion (USD14.0 billion), an annual increase of 22.8%.[18]

Before economic reform (1952–1979), Shaanxi, Shandong, and Qinghai had the largest upgrade in ranking; two of them are in western region. Jiangxi, Ningxia, and Inner Mongolia had the largest downgrades in ranking; two of them are located in the western region.

---

[16] Survey: On the capitalist road, *The Economist*, London, March 20, 2004. Vol. 370, Issue 8367, p. 14.

[17] Calculated using data from Zhejiang Bureau of Statistics: Zhejiang Statistical Yearbook, Zhejiang Bureau of Statistics Press, 2018, Table 7.5.

[18] Calculated using data from Inner Mongolia Bureau of Statistics: Zhejiang Statistical Yearbook, Inner Mongolia Bureau of Statistics Press, 2018, Table 13.1; Bu Xiaolin, Chairman of Inner Mongolia Autonomous Region: Report on the Work of the Government(2017), January 24, 2019: Report on the National Economic and Economic and Social Development for 2017 and the draft plan for 2018 in Inner Mongolia, delivered by Inner Mongolia Autonomous Region Development and Reform Commission, January 24, 2019.

Also interesting are the cases of Shanxi and Fujian. Shaanxi ranked 24, 12, 22, 24, and 15 in 1952, 1979, 1994, 2008, and 2017, respectively. During 1952–1979, it had the largest jump in ranking, followed by a large downgrade during 1979–2008. Investment from the central government was substantial during 1952–1979 but dropped significantly after reform. For example, investment in Shaanxi and Zhejiang in 1981 was CNY1.27 billion (USD744.8 million) and CNY0.91 billion (USD533.7 million);[19] in 2008, investment increased to CNY461.4 billion (USD67.6 billion), and CNY932.3 billion (USD136.5 billion), respectively.[20] During 1979–2008, Fujian and Guangdong showed the largest upgrade in ranking. During 1952–1979, there was little state planned investment, but the two provinces became the laboratory for opening to outside world during 1979–2008. State investment in Fujian and Guangdong in 1981 was CNY0.87 billion (USD510.2 million) and CNY3.18 billion (USD1.86 billion)[21]; but, in 2005 these investments became CNY520.8 billion (USD75.5 billion) and CNY1,086.9 billion (USD159.1 billion), respectively.[22] In 1952, 1979, 1994, 2008, and 2017 Liaoning ranked 5, 4, 8, 9, and 11, respectively. Liaoning was the home of many key projects during 1952–1957; but, during 1979–2008, the old industrial base grew slowly because SOEs were a large part of the province's economy. The value of the gross output of all state-owned and state-holding industrial enterprises amounted to 56.7% and 40.8% of the total value of industrial gross output in 2004 and 2008, respectively[23]; in Zhejiang, the state-owned and state-holding industrial enterprises only produced 15% and 12.0% of total industrial gross output in 2004 and 2008, respectively.[24] During 1952–1979, Jiangxi had the largest downgrade (from 11 to 23), because it played a large role in the "great leap forward."

---

[19] China State Statistical Bureau (1982). Statistical Yearbook of China 1981, Economic Information & Agency, Hong Kong, 1982, p. 310.

[20] Calculated using data from China National Bureau of Statistics. China Statistical Yearbook, China Statistics Press, 2009, Table 5.2.

[21] China State Statistical Bureau compiled (1982). Statistical Yearbook of China 1981. Economic Information & Agency, Hong Kong, p. 310.

[22] Calculated using data from China National Bureau of Statistics (2009). China Statistical Yearbook, China Statistics Press, 2009, Table 5.7.

[23] Calcuated using data from China National Bureau of Statistics (2009). Liaoning Statistical Yearbook, China Statistics Press, 2009, Table 14.3.

[24] Calculated using data from China National Bureau of Statistics (2009). Zhejiang Statistical Yearbook, China Statistics Press, 2009, Table 7.2.

Shandong ranked 19, 13, 9, 7, and 7 in 1952, 1979, 1994, 2008, and 2017, respectively, as it underwent a balanced development experience. It is widely believed that the economic success of East China's Shandong Province is largely because of its large-scale highway construction at an early stage.[25] The average rank (1952, 1979, 1988, 1994, and 2008) for the eastern, central, and western regions are listed in Table 5.4.[26] The table shows the eastern region to be a developed region in 1952.

Before economic reform, although the eastern region received less than one-third of total investment, the gap between the eastern and the other two regions still widened. During the 1980s, investment in the coastal areas received priority, so the regional gap (east versus the other two) expanded quickly during 1979–1994, as shown in Table 5.4. During the late 1990s, the central government adopted the "Anti-gradient development" strategy of accelerating the development of the western and central regions; therefore, the rank of the central region provinces slightly improved, while the rank of the western region remained unchanged from 1994–2008. In 2008, there were nine eastern provinces among the top ten. The other one, Inner Mongolia, is in the western region. Eight of the bottom ten provinces are in the western region and two are in the central

Table 5.4.   The average rank based on per capita GDP for eastern region, central region, and western region.

	Eastern	Middle	Western	North East
1952	9.60	15.75	18.40	
1979	8.60	16.88	18.50	
1988	6.80	16.25	20.80	
1994	5.80	17.63	20.70	
2008	5.00	19.33	17.25	
2017	7.30	20.67	21.83	12.33
Average	7.18	17.75	19.58	12.33

[25] China plans to expand rural highway network, http://english.peopledaily.com.cn//200406/13/eng20040613_146196.html.

[26] Calculated using data from China National Bureau of Statistics (2009). China Statistical Yearbook, China Statistics Press, 2009, Table 2.10; 1997; 1980; 1953.

region. The total average rank in 1952, 1979, 1988, 1994, and 2005 in Table 5.4 shows the eastern region is the more developed region in China.

Per capita GRP has varied substantially across China's municipalities and provinces, as shown in Table 5.3. The output data used are provincial per capita national income (1952 and 1979) and per capita GRP (1988 and 2017), GRP in constant prices (1979 constant CNY) based on GRP per capita deflators. Table 5.3 shows that from 1952 to 1979, per capita income grew in absolute terms in all Chinese provinces, but it did so much faster from 1979–2017 (after reform) than it did from 1952–1979. Between 1952 and 1979, per capita incomes grew slowly in absolute terms. Despite the fact investment was concentrated in the central and western regions, per capita incomes in these regions grew slower than that of the eastern region. All Chinese provinces experienced a significant improvement in living standards between 1979 and 2017. However, the extent of improvement in living standards differed substantially among the provinces. The variation in economic performance has displayed some distinct geographical patterns. Eastern provinces have tended to outplay the central region, which in turn surpassed the western region. Table 5.3 shows that, before economic reform, Beijing ranked first according to the average annual growth rate of per capita net income (NI) (6.66%) and Anhui was at the bottom (1.28%). During the first stage of economic reform (1979 to 1988), Guangdong ranked first (17.8%) and Shanghai ranked last (0.07%). Table 5.3 shows that the provincial per capita GRP in 1988 became more evenly distributed than in other years. Provinces that appeared to be poor initially grew quickly during 1979 and 1988. The reform of the agricultural sector was initially introduced in Anhui Provinces in 1978, and later adopted in almost all rural farm households by 1984. City reform and "open to outside world" experiment was mainly confined to the SEZ.

During the first stage of economic reform (1979–1988), Guangdong ranked first (17.8%) and Shanghai ranked last (0.07%). During the later period of economic reform (1988–2008), Fujian ranked first (average annual growth rate 12.3%) and Beijing ranked last (8.2%). The difference between highest and lowest annual growth rate was 4.1% during 1988–2008, which was much less than 17.7% during 1979–1988. However, the absolute value of the increment in Fujian amounted to 5,635 constant CNY, while Beijing reached 10,373 constant CNY. It is obvious the gap of per capita GDP among provinces became much larger, which is shown in Table 5.3. Per capita GRP in Shanghai increased from 2,879 constant

CNY in 1988 to 15,170 constant CNY in 2008, an average annual growth rate of 8.7%. Because Shanghai's per capital GRP is the highest in the country in absolute terms, the absolute gap increased during this period. Therefore, in China there is a proverb "Shenzhen is the model for economic development during the 1980s, and Shanghai during the 1990s." From 2008–2017, the difference between the highest and lowest annual growth rate was 7.5%. Per capita GRP in Shanghai increased from 15,170 constant CNY in 2008 to 25,968 constant CNY in 2017, an average annual growth rate of 6.0%; per capita GRP in Gansu increased from 2,512 constant CNY in 2008 to 5,809 Constant CNY in 2017, an average annual growth rate of 9.8%. The absolute gap increased during this period. GRP per capita in Beijing, Shanghai, and Tianjin is much higher than other provinces because they basically do not have much rural area. The provincial distribution of GRP per capita excluding Beijing, Shanghai, and Tianjin and Chongqing, Hainan, and Tibet were shown in Figures 5.9 and 5.10.

The low annual growth rate of GDP per capita before economic reform (1952–1979) resulted in uneven provincial distribution, and the high annual growth rate during the first stage of economic reform (1979–1988) generated a relatively even provincial distribution. Therefore, we can conclude that the larger regional gap of GRP per capita is not caused

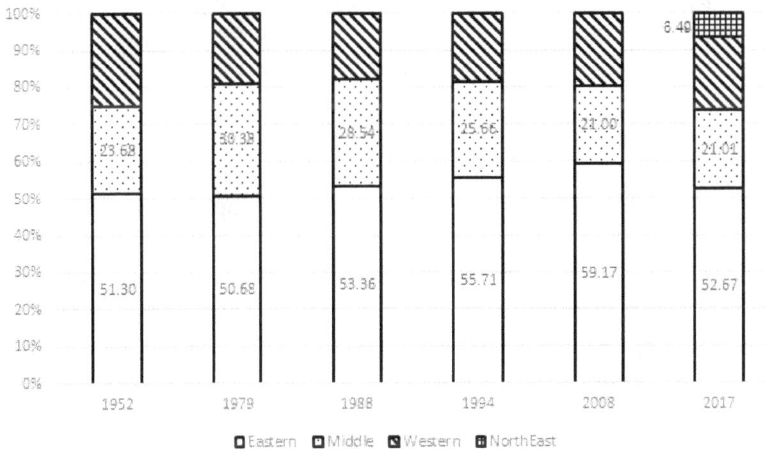

Figure 5.9.   Per capita GRP distribution in east, central, northeastern, and western regions of China (excluding three municipalities).

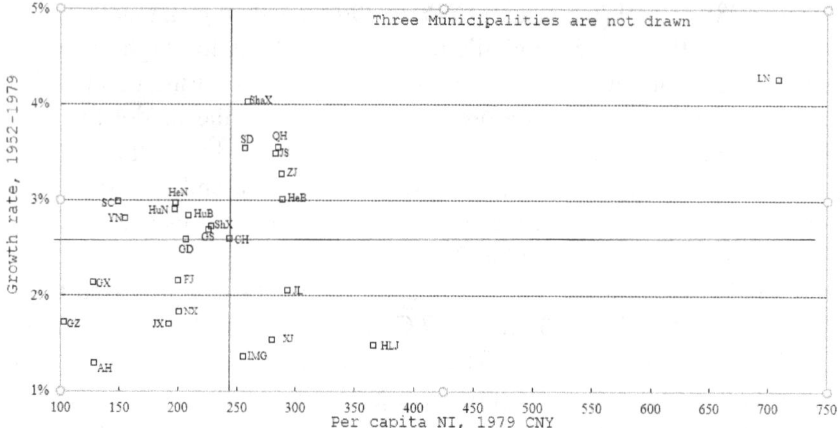

Figure 5.10. Growth and per capita GRP of China's provinces before reform, 1952–1979.

by high annual growth rate after reform. During the first stage after economic reform, the annual growth rate of GRP per capita increased significantly, but the provincial distribution became more even because of the increased farmers' income. The average annual growth rate of GRP per capita was 10.7% during 1988–2008, and the provincial distribution of GRP per capita in 2008 became more uneven than that in 1988 because of a larger gap between urban and rural income. The top three and bottom three provinces according to GRP per capita during 1952, 1979, 1988, 1994, 2008, and 2017 are listed in Table 5.5. Before economic reform, the top three provinces are all located in the northeast because they represent heavy industry-based economies during a heavy industry-oriented strategy. After 1988, because of the opening-up policy, the top three provinces located were in Yangtze Delta and Pearl Delta except one in the western region in 2017 (Inner Mongolia). In 1979, two out of the three bottom three provinces were in the western region and the third one in the central region. Table 5.6 displays the provincial relative income distribution in 1952, 1979, 1988, 1994, 2008, and 2017. Hainan and Chongqing were established in 1988 and 1997, respectively. The data for Tibet are incomplete; therefore, the two provinces and one municipality are also excluded from comparison. Note that, for each of the above years, provincial real per capita GRP was rescaled as a fraction of the top province's GRP per capita so the range of distribution is restricted to lie between 0 and 1. The

Table 5.5. Top three and bottom three provinces according to GDP per capita during 1952, 1979, 1988, 1994, 2008, and 2017 (excluding three municipalities).

	1952	1979	1988	1994	2008	2017
Top 1	Heilongjiang	Liaoning	Liaoning	Guangdong	Zhejiang	Jiangsu
Top 2	Liaoning	Heilongjiang	Jiangsu	Zhejiang	Jiangsu	Zhejiang
Top 3	Xinjiang	Jilin	Zhejiang	Liaoning	Guangdong	Inner Mongolia
Bottom 3	Guangxi	Anhui	Guangxi	Shaanxi	Yunnan	Gansu
Bottom 2	Sichuan	Guangxi	Yunnan	Gansu	Gansu	Tibet
Bottom 1	Guizhou	Guizhou	Guizhou	Guizhou	Guizhou	Guizhou

Table 5.6. Provincial distribution dynamics in China before and after reform periods (excluding three municipalities).

Relative GDPpc	1952	1979	1988	1994	2008	2017
<10%	0	5	0	0	0	0
10–25%	0	18	0	1	1	1
25–50%	18	1	11	14	14	13
50–75%	3	1	10	5	5	4
75–100%	3	0	4	4	5	6
Max.	0.93	0.52	0.80	0.90	0.94	0.98
Min.	0.26	0.15	0.31	0.23	0.21	0.23
Average	0.49	0.34	0.56	0.52	0.53	0.55
STD DEV	0.19	0.16	0.17	0.24	0.22	0.22
STD DEV/ Average	0.39	0.47	0.30	0.18	0.41	0.40

Source: ChinaDataOnline, Per Capita GDP (yuan/person), All Region, 1952, 1979, 1988, 1994, 2008, 2017.

highest relative GDP per capita is always 1 and was also excluded from the sample.

Table 5.6 clearly indicates that provincial per capita GDP in 1988 was more evenly distributed than in other periods, with only 11 provinces with a per capita GDP below 50% of the highest number. Before economic reform (1952–1979), the number of provinces in the first quarter increased significantly, and the number of provinces whose per capita NI is less than 25% of the highest per capita NI increased from 0 in 1952 to 23 in 1979 (see Table 5.6). In 1952 and 1979, the per capita NI in the poorest provinces declined from 26.4% to 14.5% of the richest; the per capita NI in the second richest provinces declined from 93.3% to 51.6% of the first richest.

The average value of relative per capita NI to the highest per capita NI declined from 0.49 in 1952 to 0.34 in 1979. There was no province located in the fourth quadrant in 1979, implying that the gap between the province ranked first and the province ranked second became larger. All these data show that, in 1979, the provincial gap in per capita NI became larger than in 1952. In the early reform period (1979–1988), the distribution in the first quarter and second quarter declined, offset by an increase in the third and fourth quarters. In 1988, the per capital GRP in the poorest provinces increased from 14.5% of that of the richest (in 1979) to 30.9% and the per capita GRP in the second richest province increased from 51.6% to 80% of the richest. The average value of relative provincial per capita income to the top one's per capita income increased from 0.34 in 1979 to 0.56 in 1988. This further illustrates that provincial per capita income was more evenly distributed in 1988. In a later reform period (1988–2008), there was one increase in the first quarter of the distribution, three increases in the second quarter, and one increase in the fourth quarter; they were offset by five declines in the third quarter. On the other hand, the per capita GRP in the poorest provinces decreased from 30.9% in 1988 to 22.8% in 1994 and 20.9% of the richest in 2008. The per capita GRP in the second richest provinces increased from 80% to 90.5%, and 93.9% of the richest in 1994 and 2008, respectively (see Table 5.6). The average value of relative per capita GRP of provinces to highest GRP per capita decreased from 0.56 in 1988 to 0.52 and 0.53 in the same years. This shows that the rich provinces became richer, and the poor provinces became poorer in 1994 and 2008 than they were in 1988, implying that provincial distribution of GRP per capita became more unevenly distributed in 1994 and 2008 than in 1988.

The above findings coincide with the conclusion reached by IMF researchers.[27] From 2008–2017, the per capita relative maximum GRP decreased from 0.94 to 0.91, the lowest GRP increased from 0.21 to 0.28,

---

[27]Dayal-Gulati, A. and A. M. Husain (2000). Centripetal Forces in China's Economic Take-off, IMF Working Paper WP/00/86, International Monetary Fund, June 15.

Table 5.7.   Average annual growth rate of GRP per capita for three regions in China, 1952–2017.

GR%	1952–1979	1979–1988	1988–1994	1994–1908	2008–2017	1979–1908
Eastern	4.17%	9.42%	13.20%	9.85%	10.68%	10.40%
Middle	2.48%	12.01%	9.71%	9.86%	10.24%	10.49%
Western	2.74%	11.58%	10.78%	9.89%	14.77%	10.60%
National	3.38%	10.48%	11.79%	9.86%	11.63%	10.52%
Northeast					10.59%	

Source: ChinaDataOnline, Per Capita GDP (yuan/person), All Region 1952,1979,1988,1994,2008, 2017.

and the standard deviation decreased from 0.41 to 0.31. It can be seen that per capita GRP is more uniformly distributed in 2017 than in 2008. From 2008–2017, the per capita GRP distribution in each province reversed the trend of increasing inequality experienced in 1994–2008. The 11th FYP implemented a strategy of optimizing the structure and accelerating coordinated regional development, promoting a new round of large-scale development of the western region, reviving the old industrial base of northeastern region, vigorously accelerating the rise of the central region, and actively supporting the leading position of the eastern region.[28] The strategy, then, impacted the regional distribution of income.

Before economic reform, although investment took place primarily in the central and western regions, the eastern region still had highest annual rate of per capita national income growth. The average annual growth rates of per capita GRP for the three regions in China before economic reform and during the early and latest period after economic reform are listed in Table 5.7.[29] All the growth rates are calculated using Eq. (5.1).

---

[28]The Proposal on the 11th Five-year Guidelines on National Economy and Social Development, Part V: Chapter 18: Implementing the overall strategy on regional development, Xinhua News Agency October 19, 2005.

[29]Calculated using data from China National Bureau of Statistics (2009). China Statistical Yearbook, China Statistics Press, 2009, Tables 2.1, 2.4, 2.15; Compiled by Department of Comprehensive Statistics: China Compendium of Statistics 1949–2004, Statistical Yearbook of China 1981 (English Edition), Compiled by the State Statistical Bureau, PRC. Published by Economic Information & Agency, Hong Kong, October 1982, p. 20.

$$GR_E = \left[\left(\frac{\sum_{i=1}^{n} GDPpc_{iE} * POP_{iE}}{\sum_{i=1}^{n} POP_{iE}}\right)_{t+\theta} \div \left(\frac{\sum_{i=1}^{n} GDPpc_{iE} * POP_{iE}}{\sum_{i=1}^{n} POP_{iE}}\right)_{t}\right]^{(1/\theta)} - 1$$

$$(5.1)$$

where $GRPpc_{iE}$ – GRP per capita of i province located in the eastern area.

POP_{iE} – Population of i province located in the eastern area.
$t+\theta$, t – year at $t+\theta$, t, the interval of the period is θ.

Table 5.7 indicates that, prior to economic reform, not only was the average annual growth rate low (3.4% for per capita NI), but also provincial per capita NI became more unequally distributed. In the early period of economic reform (1979–1988), the average annual growth rate of per capita GRP reached 10.5%, but the average annual growth rate of per capita GRP in the western and central regions were higher than the eastern region's. During the period, reform was carried out mainly in rural areas. Urban reform was confined mainly in the SEZ, with the overall urban reform beginning in 1985. For example, per capita GRP in Shanghai increased from CNY2,861 in 1979 to CNY2,879 (1979 constant CNY), with the average annual growth rate being only 0.07%. Therefore, per capita GRP became more evenly distributed. During the second stage of the reform period (1994–1998), the average annual growth rate of per capita GRP was still high (11.8%), but the average annual growth rate of per capita GRPs in the western and central regions were lower than that of the eastern region because urban reform and opening to outside world were implemented in the eastern region.

From 1994–2008, the average annual growth rate of per capita GRP remained high (9.9%). As a result of the regional development strategy, which placed emphasis on the western region, the average annual growth rate of per capita GRPs in the western and central regions were almost the same as the eastern region's were. However, the gap between provincial distributions of per capita GRP became larger again, implying the uneven distribution of the provinces' per capita GRP was not caused by the high rate of economic growth. The average annual growth rate of per capita GRP after economic reform (1979–2008) was 11.0%, much higher than the average annual growth rate of 3.40% of per capita NI before economic reform (1952–1979). After economic reform, the ratio of average annual growth rate of the eastern region to the average annual growth rate of the central and western regions is only 0.9995; however, before economic reform the same ratio reached 1.316. Therefore, we can assert again that the regional gap is not associated with high economic growth rate. In contrast, high economic growth rate provides the opportunity of narrowing the regional gap. It can be seen from Table 5.7 that, from 2008–2017, the average annual growth rate of per capita GRP in the eastern, central, and northeastern regions is similar, but lower than that of the western region.

The task for China's economic policymakers is to enhance conditions for growth in the lagging groups and regions. Figures 5.10 and 5.11 give us a sense of the locational priorities before and after economic reforms, respectively. The greatest concern is about provinces located in the third quarter of the figures; their per capita GRP level and average annual growth rate are lower than the national average. Three municipalities (Shanghai, Beijing, and Tianjin) are not included in Figures 5.10 and 5.11 because their per capita GRP is not comparable with other provinces. Prior to economic reform, all three municipalities are in the first quarter, which means all three municipalities had higher per capita GRP and their growth rate was higher than the national average. After economic reform, all of them were in fourth quarter, which means all three municipalities had higher per capita GRP but lower growth rate than the respective national averages. It implies that, after economic reform, most provinces have higher growth rate than that of three municipalities. Before economic reform (1952–1979), there were six provinces located in the third quarter of Figure 5.10, and among those, three are in the western region, two in the central region, and one in the eastern region. After reform (1979–2008), there were 16 provinces located in the third quarter of Figure 5.11, among them eight provinces were in the western region, seven in the central region, and one in the eastern region.

From Figure 5.12, we find that 10 provinces (Shanxi, Jiangxi, Hebei, Yunnan, Gansu, Heilongjiang, Shaanxi, Xinjiang, Qinghai, and Ningxia) are located in third quarter whose per capita GRP level and average annual growth rate are lower than the national average after economic reform. The economies of these provinces are underdeveloped. Six provinces (Zhejiang, Guangdong, Jiangsu, Fujian, Shandong, and Inner Mongolia) are in the first quarter of Figure 5.11. Among them, five are in the eastern region and one in the western region. Only three provinces (Jiangsu, Zhejiang, and Shandong) are in the first quarter of both figures; their per capita GRP level

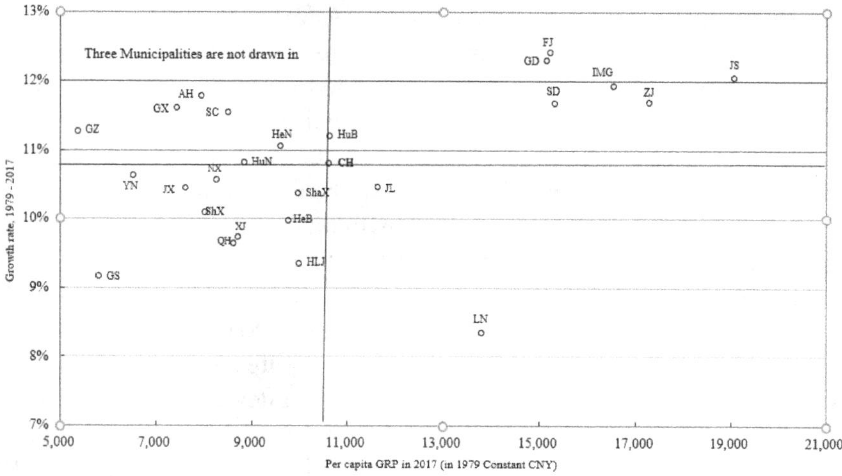

Figure 5.11.   Growth and per capita GRP of China's provinces after reform (1979–2017).

and average annual growth rate are higher than the national average before and after economic reform. After economic reform, Zhejiang Province developed the best performing private economy in China. Before economic reform, Guangdong and Fujian were placed in the third quarter of Figure 5.10, because China's central government considered Guangdong and Fujian as being in the front of national defense and restricted their economic development. After economic reform, Guangdong and Fujian became laboratories of China's opening to the outside world and attracted large FDI, especially from Hong Kong and Taiwan. Their economic performance improved dramatically after reform, which illustrates the role of reform policy; therefore, both provinces are in the first quarter of Figure 5.12. In contrast, Shaanxi province shifted from the first quarter of Figure 5.10 to the third quarter of Figure 5.11, which implies the economic performance of the province deteriorated after economic reform. Under the planned economy, Shaanxi received large investments (grants), which disappeared after economic reform. To support these low-income areas in the central and western regions, the country took concrete measures, including China's Program for Poverty Alleviation and Development of Rural Areas (2001–2010) and the Western Development strategy that seem to be making good progress.

From Figure 5.12, we find that 10 provinces (Shanxi, Jiangxi, Hebei, Yunnan, Gansu, Heilongjiang, Shaanxi, Xinjiang, Qinghai, and Ningxia) are located in third quarter whose per capita GRP level and average annual growth rate are lower than the national average after economic reform. The economies of these provinces are underdeveloped. Six provinces (Zhejiang, Guangdong, Jiangsu, Fujian, Shandong, and Inner Mongolia) are in the first quarter of Figure 5.11. Among them, five are in the eastern region and one in the western region. Only three provinces (Jiangsu, Zhejiang, and Shandong) are in the first quarter of both figures; their per capita GRP level and average annual growth rate are higher than the national average before and after economic reform. After economic reform, Zhejiang province developed the best performing private economy in China. Before economic reform, Guangdong and Fujian were placed in the third quarter of Figure 5.10, because China's central government considered Guangdong and Fujian as being in the front of national defense and restricted their economic development. After economic reform, Guangdong and Fujian became laboratories of China's opening to the outside world and attracted large FDI, especially from Hong Kong and Taiwan. Their economic performance improved dramatically after reform, which illustrates the role of reform policy; therefore, both provinces are in the first quarter of Figure 5.12. In contrast, Shaanxi province shifted from the first quarter of Figure 5.10 to the third quarter of Figure 5.11,

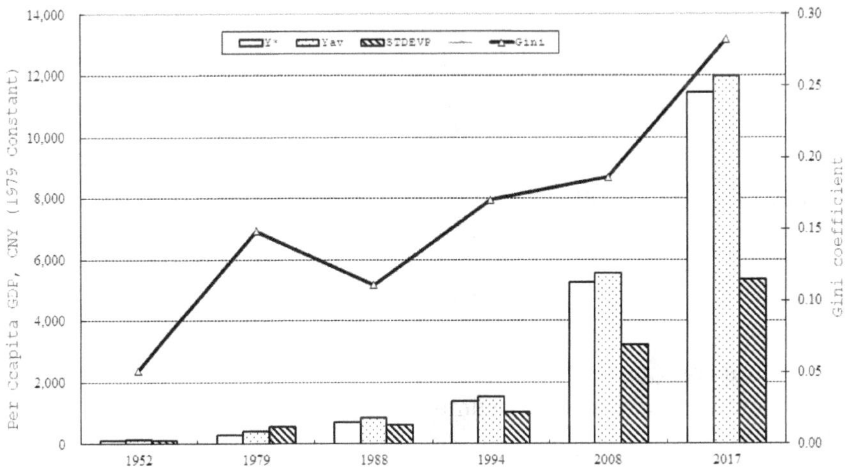

Figure 5.12. Regional per capita GDP absolute gap index, China, 1952–2017.

which implies the economic performance of the province deteriorated after economic reform. Under the planned economy, Shaanxi received large investments (grants), which disappeared after economic reform. To support these low-income areas in the central and western regions, the country took concrete measures, including China's Program for Poverty Alleviation and Development of Rural Areas (2001–2010) and the Western Development strategy, that seem to be making good progress.

7. Further Analysis of Provincial per Capita Incomes

The apparent widening disparity across China's provinces during the reform period raises the question of whether provincial per capita GRPs have diverged and, if so, why. To measure the size of the regional gap, we introduce six indices:

1. Standard Deviation, *STDEVP*

$$STDEVP = \sqrt{\frac{\sum_{i=1}^{N}(Y_i - \overline{Y})^2}{N}} \tag{5.2}$$

STDVEP–Standard deviation based on entire population.
Y_i–per capita income of region *i, i* $\in [1, N]$.
$\overline{Y}$–Average value of per capita income for *N* regions:

$$\overline{Y} = \frac{\sum_{i=1}^{N} Y_i}{N} \tag{5.3}$$

2. Gini Coefficient, *G*

$$G = \frac{b-1}{b+1}, I = K^b \tag{5.4}$$

G–Gini coefficient.
K–percent of accumulated number of regions to *N.*

I–percent of accumulated per capita income corresponding *K* to per capita income of the whole; regions are ranked on per capita income from low to high.

In this book, the authors calculated *Ln (I)* and *Ln (K)* as dependent and independent variables; then using linear regression, estimate the slope b; putting the value of b in Eq. (5.4), we get the Gini coefficient.

3. **Coefficient of Variation, V_{uw}**
   V_{uw}–coefficient of deviation

$$V_{uw} = \frac{STDEVP}{\overline{\overline{Y}}} \tag{5.5}$$

$$V_w = \frac{\sqrt{\sum_{i=1}^{N} (Y_i - Y^*)^2 \times \frac{p_i}{P}}}{\overline{Y^*}} \tag{5.6}$$

4. **Coefficient of variation weighted by population, V_w.**
   p_i, and *P*–population in *i* region and in whole.
   $\overline{Y^*}$–Per capita income in whole region weight by population.

$$\overline{Y^*} = \frac{\sum_{i=1}^{N} Y_i \times p_i}{P} \tag{5.7}$$

5. M_w–Weighted coefficient of deviation, M_w.

$$M_w = \frac{\sum_{i=1}^{N} ABS(Y_i - Y^*) \times \frac{p_i}{P}}{\overline{Y^*}} \tag{5.8}$$

6. The Theil Index, *T*

$$T = \frac{\sum_{i=1}^{N} r_i \times \log(r_i)}{N} \tag{5.9}$$

where r_i is the ratio between individual income, Y_i and average income, $\bar{Y}$:

$$r_i = \frac{Y_i}{\bar{Y}_i}$$

(5.10)

Among the six indices, **STDEVP, G,** and **T** denote absolute gap and V_{uw}, V_w, M_w represent relative gap. The Theil Index allows dividing inequality into several components. The results of the above five indices (except **T**) for 28 regions in China are shown in Figures 5.12 and 5.13.[30] Figure 5.12 indicates that the average per capita income, the per capita GRP weighted by population, and the standard deviation based on the entire population increased from 1952–2017 but grew much faster after economic reform.

The measures of absolute gap, *STDEVP,* and *Gini,* increased in both periods, but the Gini coefficient declined in the earlier period of reform (1979–1988). However, the relative gap increased before reform and decreased after economic reform, especially during the earlier period of reform. Figure 5.13 illustrates that the value of V_{uw}, V_w, and M_w in 2017 is even less than 1979's value, meaning the relative gap indicators showed a decline after economic reform. The inter-provincial per capita GRP relative gap index was at its lowest in 1988, which coincided with the previous analysis using the ranking method and dynamic distribution.

The target of regional policy before reform was to reduce the gap among regions. In reality, because of the low annual growth rate of per capita income (average 3.4%), both the absolute and relative gap expanded during the period. After reform, regional policy favored coastal area development, resulting in a high annual growth rate of per capita income (average 9.4% during 1979–2017). Reform became associated with expansion of the inter-provincial absolute gap, but with reduction of the relative gap. Because of the high annual growth rate of per capita income, the absolute gap increased significantly, signifying a widening of the absolute differences in people's living standards and the level of modernization among provinces. Therefore, appropriate policies are needed to reduce the absolute gap. From 1952–1979, the Gini coefficient increased from 0.0510 to 0.1486. Figure 5.13 show that, V_{uw}, V_w, M_w also increased, which means both the absolute gap and relative regional gap expanded before economic reform. From 1979–1988, we observe the Gini

---

[30] See Figures 5.12 and 5.13 for sources.

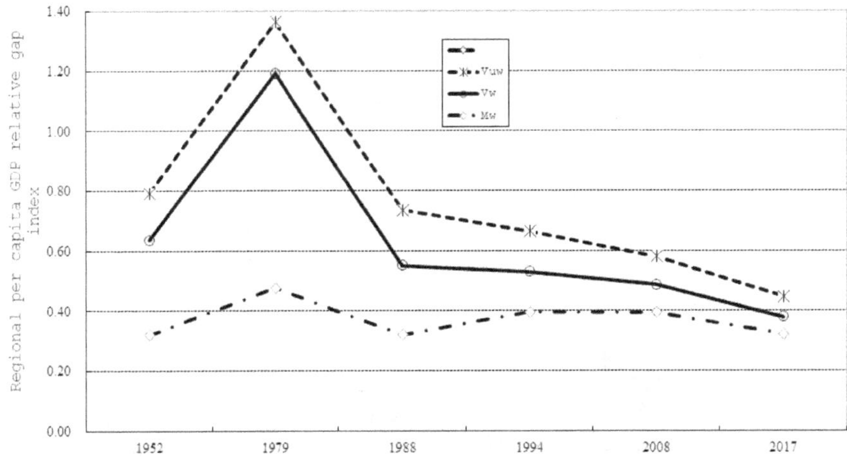

Figure 5.13.   Regional per capita GRP relative gap index, China 1952–2017.

coefficient declining from 0.1486 to 0.1109; V_{uw}, V_w, M_w also declined sharply, which means both the absolute gap and relative regional gaps were narrowed. Hence, the pre-reform trend was reversed.

As we have already stated, China's reform began with agriculture. Therefore, in the earlier period of reform, per capita income in rural areas increased faster than in urban areas. Because most Chinese are farmers, the inter-provincial gap declined. From 1988– 2017, the Gini coefficient increased from 0.1109 to 0.2825, but V_{uw}, V_w, declined. M_w increased from 1988–1994, declined slightly from 1994 to 2008, and decreased further from 2008–2017. From 1988–2008, the per capita income of farmers increased slower than that of urban dwellers; therefore, both the absolute and relative gaps increased. These results may be interpreted as presenting a dilemma between efficiency (high growth) and fairness (low regional gap). We see that when efficiency is low, attaining fairness can be a challenge for policymakers.

Figure 5.15[31] shows the evolution of inequality using the Theil Index. The analysis underlying Figure 5.15 first splits inequality into rural and

---

[31]Calculated using data from China National Bureau of Statistics: China Statistical Yearbook, China Statistics Press, 2018; Tables 2.8, 6.2, 6.12, 6.17, 6.23, 6.29; 2009; Tables 3.4, 9.6, 9.15, 9.21, 9.23; 2006; Tables 4.4, 10.6, 10.15, 10.21, 10.23; 1999; Tables 3.16,

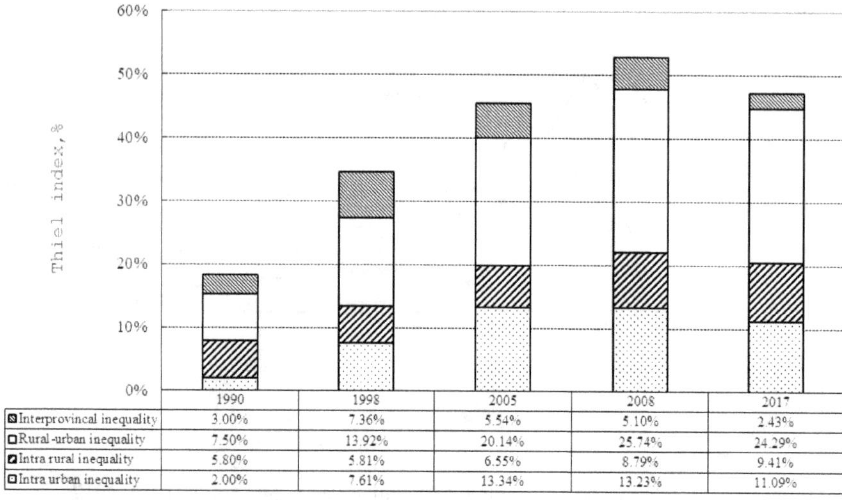

	1990	1998	2005	2008	2017
Interprovincal inequality	3.00%	7.36%	5.54%	5.10%	2.43%
Rural-urban inequality	7.50%	13.92%	20.14%	25.74%	24.29%
Intra rural inequality	5.80%	5.81%	6.55%	8.79%	9.41%
Intra urban inequality	2.00%	7.61%	13.34%	13.23%	11.09%

Figure 5.15.   Decomposition of income inequality, 1990–2017.

urban. Each of these is divided into variation across provinces and within provinces. It is obvious the Theil Index increased in 1998 and rose to 44.2% and 52.9% in 2005 and 2008, respectively. In 2017, it decreased to 47.2%. Income disparity in urban and rural areas increased between 1990 and 2008 and decreased in 2017. Therefore, narrowing the rural–urban income inequality and intra-urban income gap are most important for reducing the total income inequality in China.

8. Rural Poverty

Reducing rural poverty is an integral component of policies aimed at narrowing rural–urban income inequality because most of the poor live in rural areas. Dramatic progress against absolute poverty has been made in China, where per capita GRP went up five times since 1981 and the number of extremely poor fell from over 600 million to slightly

10.7, 10.14; 1991; Poverty Reduction and Economic Management Unit East Asia and Pacific Region, World Bank: China Promoting Growth With Equity, Country Economic Memorandum, Document of World Bank, Report No. 24169-CHA, October 15, 2003, Chapter 1.

more that 200 million, or from 64% of the population to 17% by 2000.[32] About half of this progress took place in the first half of the 1980s, a product of rural reform in the early stage of China's reform period. Because of China's rapid economic growth, global poverty began to fall rapidly in the 1980s. In 1981, China was among the poorest countries, with about 63% of its population living on less than USD1 a day. China's poverty was cut in half by 1990 and again in half by 2001. Excluding China, the poverty rate in developing countries was falling by half a percentage point a year, but many economies stagnated in the 1990s; therefore, poverty increased in these places, as shown in the number of Chinese citizens living in poverty (consumption less than USD1 a day) in 1981, 634 million, declined to 212 million in 2001, a reduction of 422 million. Globally, the number of people living in poverty was at 1.482 billion in 1981 and decreased to 1.089 billion by 2001, a reduction of 393 million people. This means that in all developing countries, excluding China, the number of people living in poverty increased by 29 million during 1981–2001.[33] Using the World Bank's USD1/day consumption measure, the number of poor in China declined from 360 million in 1990 to 204 million in 2000, which corresponds to a decline in poverty incidence from 31.5% in 1990 to 16.1%, as shown in Table 5.8.[34] Table 5.8 shows that, from 1996–2013, China's poverty headcount rate was higher than that of the Upper Middle Income Group countries (UMC), but dropped below the UMC rate in 2015. The same is true of the comparison between China's poverty rate and the World poverty headcount rate; after 2008, China's poverty rate fell below the World's rate. China's 2010 standard poverty headcount rate has declined rapidly since 2010, with the annual average decline rate at 11.9% from 2005–2010. From 2010–2011, 2011–2013, 2013–2015, and 2015–2017,

---

[32] World Bank (2004). Global Poverty Down by Half Since 1981 But Progress Uneven As Economic Growth Eludes Many Countries, April 23.

[33] World Bank (2005). World Development Indicators 2005, CD-ROM, April.

[34] Poverty Reduction and Economic Management Unit East Asia and Pacific Region, World Bank (2003). China Promoting Growth with Equity, Country Economic Memorandum, Document of World Bank, Report No. 24169-CHA, October 15, Chapter 1, p. 11; Calculated using data from World Development Indicators online 2019, Released January 24, 2019 by World Bank; Calculated using data from China National Bureau of Statistics (2018). China Statistical Yearbook, China Statistics Press, 2018, Table 6.35.

Table 5.8. Trends in Poverty Reduction, 1990–2017.

Poverty headcount rate at USD1/day (2000 constant USD) income					
Year	1990	1992	1996	1998	1999	2000
China %	23.1	21.6	10.6	7.9	7.8	8.8
Rural %	31	30	14.9	11.4	11.2	13.7
Urban %	0.9	0	0.2	0	0.25	0.3

Poverty headcount rate at USD1/day consumption					
China%	31.5	30.2	17.4	17.8	17.8	16.1
Rural %	44.4	41.4	24.8	26.2	27	25
Urban %	1	0.8	0.4	1	0.5	0.5

Poverty headcount ratio at USD3.2 a day (2011 constant PPPUSD)					
Year	1996	1999	2002	2008	2011	2015
China %	31.9	30.7	24.8	15.6	7.4	1.4
UMC %	28	26.9	21.1	13.1	5.8	1.7
World %	22.8	22.3	20.2	16.9	12.1	9.2

Poverty headcount ratio at 2300 yuan (in 2010's constant price) per person each year (China 2010 Standard)					
Year	2005	2010	2011	2013	2015	2017
China %	30.2	17.2	12.7	8.5	5.7	3.1

the average decline rates were 35.4%, 22.2%, 22.1%, and 35.6%, respectively.

Thus, by all measures, the decline in the number of poor has been dramatic, especially in the early 1980s and then again in 1994–1996. During these three years, poverty incidence fell from 25% to 17%. Increases in agricultural prices and in output in rural areas as well as the introduction of the "8-7 Plan" for poverty reduction resulted in this reduction. The 8-7 plan aimed at lifting 80 million people out of poverty in 7 years. It was launched by the government in 1994, providing tax reductions, financial grants, and social-economic development projects to 592 designated "poor" rural counties. During 1998–2000, although the economy grew at nearly 8% per year, poverty reduction appeared to have slowed (see Table 5.8). The overall growth in rural income fell, especially as the purchasing power of agricultural products declined. During 1997–2000, as some agricultural trade and markets were liberalized,

Table 5.9.   Rural and urban poor by region, 1999 (%).

Regions	Share of China's rural poor	Share of China's urban poor
Western region	46.6	23
Central region	42.1	46.2
Coastal region	11.3	30.8

international prices in many commodities declined, including wheat, soybeans, cotton, and sugar; in addition, a domestic surplus in grains developed. Moreover, growing competitive pressures and financial difficulties in the rural enterprise sector curbed the growth of TVEs, and the movement of labor out of agriculture increasingly took the form of rural–urban migration.

According to a survey carried out by China's State Statistical Bureau, China had 113.9 million migrant workers from rural areas in 2003, accounting for 23.2% of the total rural laborers. In 2003, about 69 million rural laborers worked in medium-sized cities and 56.2 million rural laborers worked outside their provinces.[35] Out of the 161 million people estimated at or below the USD1 consumption per day in 2002, some 99% lived in rural areas. Rural poverty started to concentrate in the western provinces (see Table 5.9[36]) and in localities that lagged in terms of growth, were remote, poor in human and natural resources, or weakly linked to the rest of the economy. The average annual growth rate of per capita income in rural areas reached 5.69% during 1998–2008, while the average annual growth rate of per capita income in urban areas reached 9.47%. According to the annual growth rate of per capita income in rural areas, at the bottom was Guangdong Province with an average annual growth rate of per capita income of 3.66% in rural areas during 1998–2008. At the top was Beijing, with an annual growth rate of per capita income of 7.86% in rural areas during 1998–2008. From 1998 to 2008, only the annual growth rate of per capita income in rural areas of Tibet was 7.37%, which was higher than that in urban areas (4.20%).

---

[35] Xinhua (2004). 113.9m Rural Laborers Work Outside in 2003, *China Daily*, May 16.

[36] Poverty Reduction and Economic Management Unit East Asia and Pacific Region, World Bank: China Promoting Growth with Equity, Country Economic Memorandum, Document of World Bank, Report No. 24169-CHA, October 15, 2003, Chapter 1.

Eight provinces located in the fourth quadrant improved their rank before economic reform, but their rank deteriorated after economic reform. They are Shaanxi (ShaX, 12, –3), Yunnan (YN, 1, –4), Hebei (HeB, 2, –9), Shanxi (SaX, 2, –9), Jilin (JL, 2, –6), Liaoning (LN, 1, –6), Beijing (BJ, 1, –1), and Qinghai (QH, 6, –12). Guangdong (0, 9) Guizhou (0, –3), and Gansu (GS, 0, –14) are located at the Y-axis, which means their rank did not change before economic reform; however, after economic reform, Guizhou and Gansu deteriorated, and Guangdong improved. Beijing (BJ,1, –1) improved one position and Tianjin (TJ, –1, 1) deteriorated one position. Shanghai (SH, 0, 0) placed on the original points, which means its rank did not change both before and after economic reform. It is interesting that Shanghai ranks first, and Guizhou ranks last before and after economic reform. Therefore, the gap between the top performer and the lowest one was not affected by the reforms.

Ningxia Province, with an annual growth rate of per capita income 4.74% and 10.13% in rural areas and urban areas, respectively, exhibits the largest gap between the two areas. The annual per capita income in rural areas reached 9,258 current CNY in rural Zhejiang Province, which ranked first among provinces (only after the Shanghai and Beijing Municipalities, even higher than Tianjin). The annual per capita income in rural Guizhou Province was only 1,877 current CNY, placing it last among the provinces.[37] We can conclude that industrialization and urbanization should be pushed ahead in rural areas to free surplus farmers from those limited lands and encourage them to move to cities, thus narrowing the income gap between urban and rural residents.[38]

Figures 5.16[39] and 5.17[40] show the map of the per capita net income of rural and urban households in 2005, respectively, as explained in Table 5.10,[41] and compared with 2017.

---

[37]Calculated using data from China National Bureau of Statistics (2006). China Statistical Yearbook, China Statistics Press, 2006, Table 10.21.

[38]Hua Min: Waging war against poverty, *China Daily*, June 1, 2004, p. 6.

[39]Calculated using data from China National Bureau of Statistics (2006). China Statistical Yearbook, China Statistics Press, 2006, Tables 10.2, 10.21.

[40]Calculated using data from China National Bureau of Statistics (2005). China Statistical Yearbook, China Statistics Press, 2005, Tables 10.2, 10.15.

[41]Calculated using data from China National Bureau of Statistics (2018). China Statistical Yearbook, China Statistics Press, 2018, Tables 6.16, 6.23, 6.29; 2009 Tables 9.2, 9.15, 9.21.

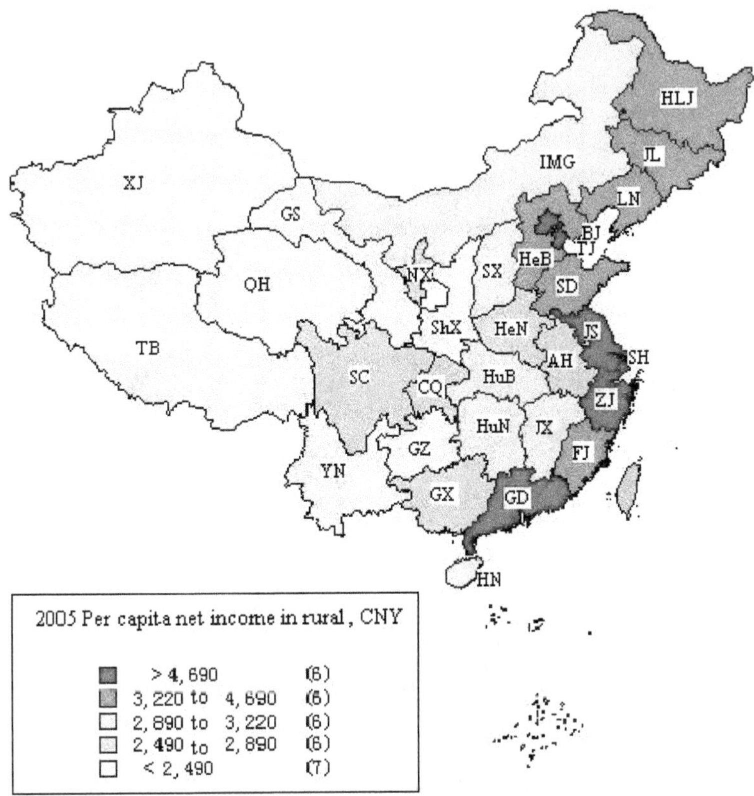

Figure 5.16.   Per capita net income map in rural area by regions in China, 2005, Current CNY/year.

The per capita net income of three municipalities (Beijing, Shanghai, and Tianjin) and five provinces (Zhejiang, Liaoning, Jilin, Heilongjiang, and Hebei) is higher than the national rural and urban per capita net income. These eight regions are in the eastern region. The per capita income of rural and urban residents in Zhejiang Province ranks first among provinces and is even higher than Tianjin's. The per capita net income of 19 provinces is lower than the national rural and urban per capita net income average. It shows that per capita net incomes of urban and rural residents are closely related. The per capita net income of eight regions is higher than the national urban and rural per capita net income average, and the per capita net income of 19 provinces is lower than the national urban and rural per capita net income average, signifying the

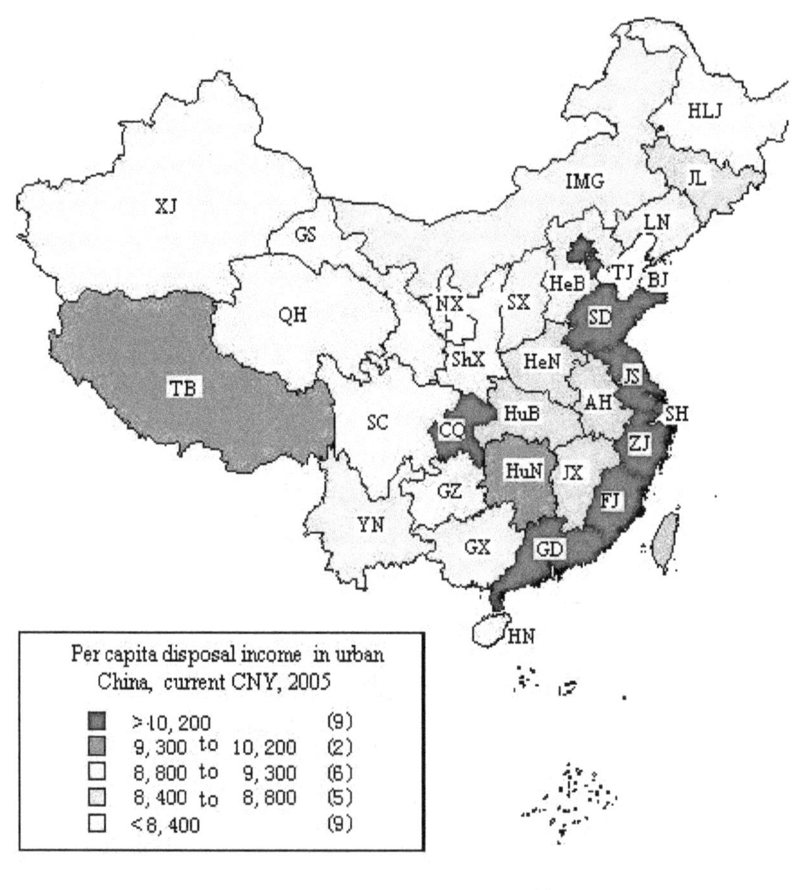

Figure 5.17.   Per capita net income map in urban area by regions in China, 2005, Current CNY/year.

large income gap between the provinces. The lowest per capita income, in rural Gansu Province in 2008 (2,724 current CNY), reached only 29.4% and the lowest per capita income in the urban area of Gansu (11,669 current CNY) reached only 46.7% of that in Zhejiang Province, respectively. Twelve provinces in the western region (Gansu, Guizhou, Qinghai, Xinjiang, Xinjiang, Yunnan, Tibet, Shaanxi, Chongqing, Sichuan, Guizhou, Guangxi, and Inner Mongolia) are among the 19 low-income provinces; the remaining seven provinces include six provinces

Table 5.10.   Explanation of the map of per capita disposable income map in China's urban and rural households in 2005, current CNY.

Per capita net income	2005		Per capita net income	2005	
	Urban	Rural		Urban	Rural
Shanghai	18,645	8,248	Liaoning	9,108	3,690
Beijing	17,653	7,346	Jilin	8,691	3,264
Zhejiang	16,294	6,660	Heilongjiang	8,273	3,221
Jiangsu	12,319	5,276	Northeastern	10,175	28,267
Guangdong	14,770	4,690			
Tianjin	12,639	5,580	Inner Mongolia	9,137	2,989
Fujian	12,321	4,450	Chongqing	10,243	2,809
Shandong	10,745	3,931	Yunnan	9,266	2,042
Hubei	8,786	3,099	Shaanxi	8,272	2,053
Hainan	8,124	3,004	Xinjiang	7,990	2,482
Eastern	132,295	52,285	Sichuan	8,386	2,803
Hunan	9,524	3,118	Tibet	9,431	2,078
Anhui	8,471	2,641	Guangxi	9,287	2,495
Jiangxi	8,620	3,129	Ningxia	8,094	2,509
Hebei	9,107	3,482	Qinghai	8,058	2,151
Henan	8,668	2,871	Guizhou	8,151	1,877
Shanxi	8,914	2,891	Gansu	8,087	1,980
Central	53,303	18,130	Western	104,402	28,267

in the central region (Shanxi, Anhui, Jiangxi, Henan, Hubei, and Hunan) and one province in the eastern region (Hainan). Tibet, Shaanxi, and Yunnan have low per capita income in their rural areas and lower middle income in their urban areas; therefore, the per capita income gap between their urban area and rural areas is large. Henan, Jiangxi, and Hainan have low urban per capita income and lower rural middle income; hence, the per capita income gap between their urban and rural areas is small.

Compared with 2005, the absolute income gap between the provinces of China became even more disconcerting in 2017. The per capita net income of three municipalities and five provinces is higher than the national rural and urban per capita net income. These eight regions are the same as in 2005 and all are located in the eastern region. The per capita net income of the 21 provinces in 2017, two more provinces than in 2005, is lower than the national average urban and rural per capita net income. The 21 provinces include all 12 provinces in the western region, all six provinces in the central region, two of three northeastern regions, and one province in the eastern region (see Tables 5.10 and 5.11).

Of course, there are still plenty of challenges in China's regional development. For example, there is still the large gap between the inter-regional economic levels, the imbalance of industrial structure in various regions, and the imperfect mechanism of inter-regional cooperation and development. The task of regional development and reform is still very arduous. The 19th National Congress of the Communist Party of China put forward the implementation of the regional coordinated development strategy. To develop the rural economy, the counties' economic competitiveness is evaluated. Counties are ranked according to their population, GDP, government financial revenue, per capita GDP, per capita income of farmers, per capita income in urban area, per capita government financial revenue, and annual growth rate of GDP.[42] There are 931 million people (70.1% of national population) living in 2861 counties in China; they produce CNY9,406 billion (USD1,377 billion), accounting for 50.2% of national GDP and CNY6.59 billion (USD1,377 billion) financial revenue, or 23.0% of national financial revenue. The top 100 counties were identified from 2001 counties in 2009 (based on their 2008 economic index). These top 100 counties accounted for only 4.3% of the total number of evaluated counties and 7.9% of the national county population, produced 31.7% of national county GDP, and accounted for 32.7% of national financial revenue. The comparison of the top 100 counties with the national average is shown in Table 5.11.[43] The difference in the average

---

[42] Why carry out the evaluation of county economic competitiveness in China? (in Chinese), www.china-county.org/xs.htm.

[43] Calculated using data from Zhongjun County Economic Research Institute (2009). Ninth National County basic economic competitiveness and scientific development evaluation report (in Chinese), July 26, www.china-county.org/cms/article.php?action=show&id=3166;

Table 5.11.   Explanation of the map of per capita disposable income in China's urban and rural households in 2017, current CNY.

Per capita net income	2017		Per capita net income	2017	
	Urban	Rural		Urban	Rural
Shanghai	62,596	27,825	Liaoning	34,993	13,747
Beijing	62,406	24,241	Jilin	28,319	12,950
Zhejiang	51,261	24,956	Heilongjiang	27,446	12,665
Jiangsu	43,622	19,158	Northeastern	90,758	39,362
Guangdong	40,975	15,780			
Tianjin	40,278	21,754	Inner Mongolia	35,670	12,584
Fujian	39,001	16,335	Chongqing	32,193	12,638
Shandong	36,789	15,118	Yunnan	30,996	9,862
Hubei	31,889	13,812	Shaanxi	30,810	10,265
Hainan	30,817	12,902	Xinjiang	30,775	11,045
Eastern	439,635	191,879	Sichuan	30,727	12,227
Hunan	33,948	12,936	Tibet	30,671	10,330
Anhui	31,640	12,758	Guangxi	30,502	11,326
Jiangxi	31,198	13,242	Ningxia	29,472	10,738
Hebei	30,548	12,881	Qinghai	29,169	9,462
Henan	29,558	12,719	Guizhou	29,080	8,869
Shanxi	29,132	10,788	Gansu	27,763	8,076
Central	186,024	75,323	Western	367,829	127,422

population size of provinces is large. Jiangsu had the largest population, reaching 941,900 people, while Tibet had the smallest population (36,200). Jiangsu also has the largest GDP of CNY31.39 billion (USD4.6 billion) and local general budget revenue of CNY2.185 billion (USD319.9 million). The smallest GDP of CNY358 million (USD52.4 million) and local general budget revenue of CNY0.11 million (USD16.1 thousand) are found in Tibet.

China National Bureau of Statistics (2009). China Statistical Yearbook, China Statistics Press, 2009, Tables 9.15, 9.21.

The provincial distribution of top 100 counties in China (2008) is shown in Table 5.12.[44] There are 124 counties in 2008's top 100 counties because of duplication of ranking, (four counties rank 1, three counties rank 19, three counties rank 31, seven counties rank 46, six counties rank 65, and seven counties rank 72). 100 counties are in the eastern region (see Table 5.12). Only 18 and six of the top 100 counties are in the central and western regions, respectively, with an average rank of 69. These data reveal that income disparity within rural areas in the provinces also became significant. Among Jiangsu Province's counties that are in the top 100, those located in the southern part moved to the less developed northern part of the province. In Shandong Province, the location of counties in the top 100 shifted from the peninsula to the less developed western part of Shandong. The central and western regions now have the resources and policy advantages; therefore, 18 counties of the top 100 are found in the central region, and six are in the western region. The pattern of national top 100 counties is changing. Seventy-nine counties among the top 100 are in three provinces (Jiangsu-27, Zhejiang-26, and Shandong-26). Jiangsu's county economies are large in scale, with the province placing seven counties in the top 10 of the top 100. The province features prominent regional coordination conditions, allowing for an effective mix of collective economy, large scale, and functional capital markets. Zhejiang's county economy with small population size and high degree of relatively affluent counties is characterized by a strong private economy, effective industry cluster, and a professional market. Shandong has most county units and large differences among counties, lack of prominent counties,

---

[44]Calculated using data from Zhongjun County Economic Research Institute (2009). Ninth National County basic economic competitiveness and scientific development evaluation report (in Chinese), July 26, www.china-county.org/cms/article.php?action=show&id=3166; 2018 China's top 100 county economy research results released by CCID Consulting County Economic Research Center, July 3, 2018 (in Chinese), http://baijiahao.baidu.com/s?id=1604963096726854087&wfr=spider&for=pc; Huang, K., and D. Hao (2018). Focus on the degree of development of Chinese residents in the county three core issues urgent need attention, *Guangming Daily* (15th edition, May 31); China National Bureau of Statistics (2018). China Statistical Yearbook, China Statistics Press, 2018, Tables 3.9, 11.2; 2016, Table 3.10; 2014, Table 3.15; Guangdong Provincial Bureau of Statistics, Guangdong Bureau of Statistics (2018). Guangdong Investigation Team of China National Bureau of Statistics: Statistical Communique of the 2017 National Economic and Social Development of Guangdong, February 28; World Bank (2019). World Development Indicators online 2019, Released January 24.

Table 5.12. Comparing the basic economic index of top 100 counties with national average, 2008 and 2017.

2008		Average of top 100 counties (124)	National 2008 county (2861) average	Top 100 average/ National average
Population	10,000 persons	83.0	46.5	178.3%
GDP	Billion CNY	36.7	7.5	488.3%
Financial revenue	100 million CNY	7.6	3.3	231.0%
Per capita income (rural)	CNY	8,470	4,761*	177.9%
Per capita income (urban)	CNY	17,900	15,781*	113.4%
Per capita GDP	CNY	44,275	16,430	269.5%
2017				
Population	10,000 persons	91.1	42.3	215.2%
Investment/GDP	%	63.0	77.5	81.3%
VA of Secondary Industry	%	53.8	40.5	132.8%
Per capita income (rural)	CNY	19,555	13,432	145.6%
Per capita income (urban)	CNY	42,147	36,396	115.8%
Per capita GDP	10,000 CNY	10.6	6.0	177.7%
Per capita consumption	10,000 CNY	3.4	2.6	130.8%
Per capita saving deposit	10,000 CNY	11.0	12.2	90.3%
Import+export/ GDP	%	28.0	33.7	83. 0%

and features a "government-led + a variety of modes of economic cooperation" economy, with prominent regional economic cooperation. Shandong had the lowest income among these three provinces. However, the contribution of market mechanisms to the development of the county's economy still has great potential.

Another perspective on the top 100 counties is provided by examining their location. 100 counties among the top 100 (or 124) counties are in three major economic circles: the Yangtze Delta (54), the Annual Bohai Rim (36), and the Pearl Delta (10). On the other hand, the top 100 counties are distributed in only 18 provinces (see Table 5.12), which means there are 13 provinces without any of their counties listed in the top 100 counties. Therefore, there is substantial income disparity in the rural areas among provinces. In 2008, the per capita GDP of the top 100 counties was 19.7 times greater than the per capita GDP of the bottom 100 counties. In the per capita GDP distribution curve, the peak value occurred at per capita GDP of CNY7,500. Per capita GDP of 82% of the counties was below the national county average of per capita GDP CNY16,400; 71.76% of the counties were below CNY12,322.[45] The top 100 counties were the leaders in the industrialization and urbanization process. Their non-agricultural sectors accounted for 90.4% of their GDP, and about 70% of their workforce worked in secondary and tertiary industries. Yet, their urban areas occupied a mere 10% of the county totals.

To accelerate the development of western rural areas, the "1000 towns and Talent Technologies" plan was implemented to replicate the success of Yellow Sheep River in 1000 additional towns and set up branch offices in 100 cities.[46] Yellow Sheep River is in a remote region in Gulang county, Gansu Province. Villagers in Yellow Sheep River are only able to receive eight television channels. To this day, there are still several villages in the Yellow Sheep River district that do not have any television reception. There are about 20,000 people in Yellow Sheep River, where the average annual income is only CNY300. Town and Talent Technologies has confirmed Toffler's Theory of the Third Wave; that is, agricultural societies indeed can bypass the industrial society and

---

[45] Zhongjun County Economic Research Institute (2009). Ninth National County per capita GDP distribution, (in Chinese), November 11. www.china-county.org/cms/article.php?action=show&id=3488.

[46] Wen, S. (2003). *The Future of China Economy*. Taiwan: Tianxia Yuanjian Ltd. (in Chinese).

directly enter into the information society. Western China is not expected to remain underdeveloped in the long run. Yellow Sheep River Village Middle School is classified as one of the poorest within the four levels of public schools in the county. In September 2002, there were only 10 donated computers available for the 270 students. In September, the village was busy harvesting crops, but people were upset because they were unable to sell their crops for a good price. The teacher at Yellow Sheep River Village Middle School, Wanlong Hu, helped farmers engage in e-commerce on a just-arrived computer. Mr. Hu conducted online searches for possible businesses while teaching the villagers how to market their goods outside their region. Negotiations with the final business involved a two-hour online discussion in which current prices were compared to the previous year. More than 10,000 kg of celery were sold in the final agreement at a price of CNY0.70–0.80 per kilogram. From October to December 2002, they completed five transactions (detailed in Table 5.13). It set a model for local schools using computers to promote economic development of their villages. The receipts from these five e-transactions totaled CNY25,800, a substantial amount for farmers with annual income of CNY300 per capita. Yellow Sheep River Vocational Middle School has successfully dealt with trades valued at more than CNY500,000 through its e-business center, and offered 17 training classes for 340 farmers. In training classes, students learn three basic skills: Software, English, and Typing (SET). In the information society, SET skill will serve as the basis for communication and job hunting. Other locations that have enjoyed the benefits of jumping into the information society have included Ningxia Wuxiang Middle School and Hebei Halagou Middle School.[47] As one of the most ambitious plans for exploring western China using the Internet, the Town and Talent Project provides a fundamental example of how the Internet can change the way people live.

Since 2018, China's economy has been moving from a high-speed growth stage to a high-quality development stage and is in the process of transforming its development mode, optimizing its economic structure, and transforming its growth momentum. The overall strength of the top 100 counties is impressive. In 2017, the total land area, total population,

---

[47]Forge Ahead Toward E-Business — E-business training conference was hosted at the Yellow Sheep River International Convention Center (YSRICC), www.yellowsheepriver. com/eng/news/news040517.php.

Table 5.13. The provincial distribution of top 100 Counties in China, 2008 and 2017.

Eastern region	Number		Central region	Number	
	2008	2017		2008	2017
Jiangsu	27	25	Henan	8	6
Zhejiang	26	22	Hunan	4	4
Shandong	26	19	Hubei		4
Fujian	8	5	Shanxi	2	
Liaoning	5		Jiangxi	2	1
Hebei	5	2	Heilongjiang	1	
Guangdong	2	1	Jilin	1	
Shanghai	1		Anhui		1
Sum		74	Sum		16
			Western region		
Northeastern region			Inner Mongolia	2	3
			Shaanxi	2	1
Liaoning		2	Sichuan	1	1
Heilongjiang			Xinjiang	1	2
Jilin			Guizhou		1
Sum		2	Sum		8

Note: *In 2008, there are 124 counties in Top 100 counties due to duplication of ranking. For example: Henan Province has six counties that rank 65.

and regional GDP of the top 100 counties were 205,000 square kilometers, 91.05 million, and CNY8.2 trillion, respectively, accounting for about 2% of the country's land area and less than 7% of the population. The secondary industry has been the main driver of the development of the top 100 counties. The value added of the three industrial structures of the top 100 counties are 2.6:53.8:43.6 (primary: secondary: tertiary). Among them, the value added of the secondary industry was CNY4.9 trillion (USD721.6 billion), accounting for 53.8% of their GDP, or 13.3 % points higher than the national average, and far higher than developed provinces such as Guangdong, Jiangsu, and Shandong. The top development priorities of the top 100 counties are reduction of the inefficiency of the secondary industry, improvement of the quality of the overall supply system of the secondary industry, and enhancement of the adaptability of the supply structure to demand. In 2017, total retail sales of consumer goods in the top 100 counties were CNY3.1 trillion (USD456.6 billion), accounting for 8.5% of the national total. The relatively high-income level is one of the underlying causes of strong consumer demand.

Among the top 100 counties, fixed assets investment in eight counties accounted for more than 100% of their GDP, and 78 counties ranged from 50% to 100%, indicating the economic growth of most of the top 100 counties is dependent on investment, and only a few of the top 100 counties limited their dependence on investment and relied on consumption and the service sector. The total trade (import and export) volume of the top 100 counties accounted for 28.0% of their GDP, lower than the national average 33.7%. The difference between the various counties and cities is large; however, Kunshan, Yiwu, Rugao are among places featuring trade of more than 100% of their GDP, while for more than 40% of the top 100 counties total trade is less than 20% of their GDP. The top 100 counties have insufficient capital adsorption capacity. In 2017, the balance of local and foreign currency deposits in the top 100 counties was CNY10.1 trillion (94.6% of GDP). Guangdong Province (GDP of CNY8.9 trillion), on the other hand, had a deposit balance of local and foreign currency of CNY19.5 trillion (135.7% of its GDP). The top 100 counties have lower per capita deposits. In 2017, the average per capita deposit of the top 100 counties was CNY111,000, far lower than the CNY189,700 in Zhejiang, the CNY174,200 in Guangdong, and the CNY161,800 in Jiangsu, indicating that the counties' financial capital is insufficient.

The above statistics reveal that policymakers at the county level are confronted with several challenges in their efforts to build a strong economy. They need to undertake policies that produce a more balanced economy, one in which the dependence on investment decreases over time, with other sectors (consumption, services, trade) picking up the slack. They also need to create more depth in their financial system, leverage the effect of financial capital on the real economy, and strengthen financial supervision to avoid possible financial risks.

9. The Similarity of Regional Industrial Structure

Figure 5.18[48] shows the provincial distribution of the industrial gross output in China. It is based on data from Table 5.15. Figure 5.19[49] shows the provincial distribution of grain yield. Figure 5.18 shows that, in 2004, all top five provinces with high total industrial gross outputs are located in the eastern region. These five provinces are rich provinces; their per capita disposal income of urban and rural households is also in the top five (see Table 5.10). The table also shows that the top four provinces with the highest industrial gross output in 2011 are the same as in 2004. The State Council issued the "National Issue No. 19 Document" from 2009-4-14 (the State Council's opinion on promoting Shanghai to accelerate the development of modern service industry, advanced manufacturing industry, international financial center, and international shipping center). Significant progress has already been made in the construction of Shanghai's "four centers." According to the construction requirements of the "four centers," the value-added ratio of the secondary and tertiary industries to GDP in 2004 was 48.4% and 50.6%, respectively; in 2011, it was 41.6% and 57.7%, respectively. The secondary industry value-added ratio to GDP decreased by 6.8% from 2004 to 2011, falling from fifth place in 2004 to eleventh place in 2011. In place of Shanghai and Hebei in 2004, Hunan and Hubei rank fifth and sixth, respectively, in 2011. Hunan and Hubei's rise, both in the central region, indicates that policies to promote the central region have been effective.

---

[48]Calculated using data from China National Bureau of Statistics: China Statistical Yearbook, China Statistics Press, 2006, Table 14.3; 2012. Table 14.4; A series of significant progresses has been made in the construction of Shanghai's "four centers." November 15, 2012, *Source: Jiefang (Liberation) Daily*, (in Chinese); Shanghai Municipal Statistics Bureau: Shanghai Statistical Yearbook, China Statistics Press, 2018, Table 4.4 (in Chinese); China National Bureau of Statistics, Data base; Annual by Province, Revenue from Principal Business of Industrial_Enterprises above Designated Size, 1998–2017.

[49]Calculated using data from China National Bureau of Statistics: China Statistical Yearbook, China Statistics Press, 2006, Table 13.17; 2012, Table 13.15; 2012, Table 13.15; Rural Department, China National Bureau of Statistics: Rural Reform Writes a Glorious History Rural Revitalization and Magnificent Blueprint — 20th series of economic and social development achievements in the 40 years of reform and opening-up, September 18, 2018 (in Chinese); China National Bureau of Statistics, Data base; Annual by Province, Output of Grain Crops (10000 tons), 1998–2017.

Table 5.14.   E-commerce at Yellow Sheep River Village Middle School, October–December 2002.

Celery	6,400
Horsebeans	136,000
Chinese herbs	21,030
White potato	21,000
Pea	74,000
Total	258,430

Figure 5.18 also shows the seven provinces with low total industrial gross output, all located in the western region. These seven provinces are poor provinces, and the per capita disposal income of their urban and rural households is at a minimum. The absolute gap between the eastern and western regions is still very large. Therefore, the regional coordinated development strategy needs to improve the market mechanism in all regions, enforce the mutual assistance mechanism and support the appropriate mechanism to form a regional development pattern of mutual promotion and common development. After 2011, the China National Bureau of Statistics did not publish the industrial gross outputs as an independent item. Therefore, in 2017, the revenue from principal business of industrial enterprises was used to replace the industrial gross outputs. Figure 5.18 and Table 5.15 show that the four provinces (Jiangsu, Shandong, Guangdong, and Zhejiang) with high revenue from principal business in 2017 are located in the eastern region. As shown in Table 5.10, these four provinces are wealthy provinces; their per capita disposal income in urban and rural households is also as shown in Table 5.10. The rankings of the four provinces with the highest revenue from principal business in 2017 are different from those in 2004. In place of Shanghai and Hebei in 2004, Hunan and Fujian rank fourth and sixth, respectively, in 2017, with Hunan in the central region and the other five provinces located in the eastern region. Figure 5.18 and Table 5.15 show that the 10 provinces with low revenue from principal business include eight in the western, one in the northeastern, and one in the eastern region. These 10 provinces are poor provinces, and their per capita disposal income of urban and rural households is also at a low level. This is another

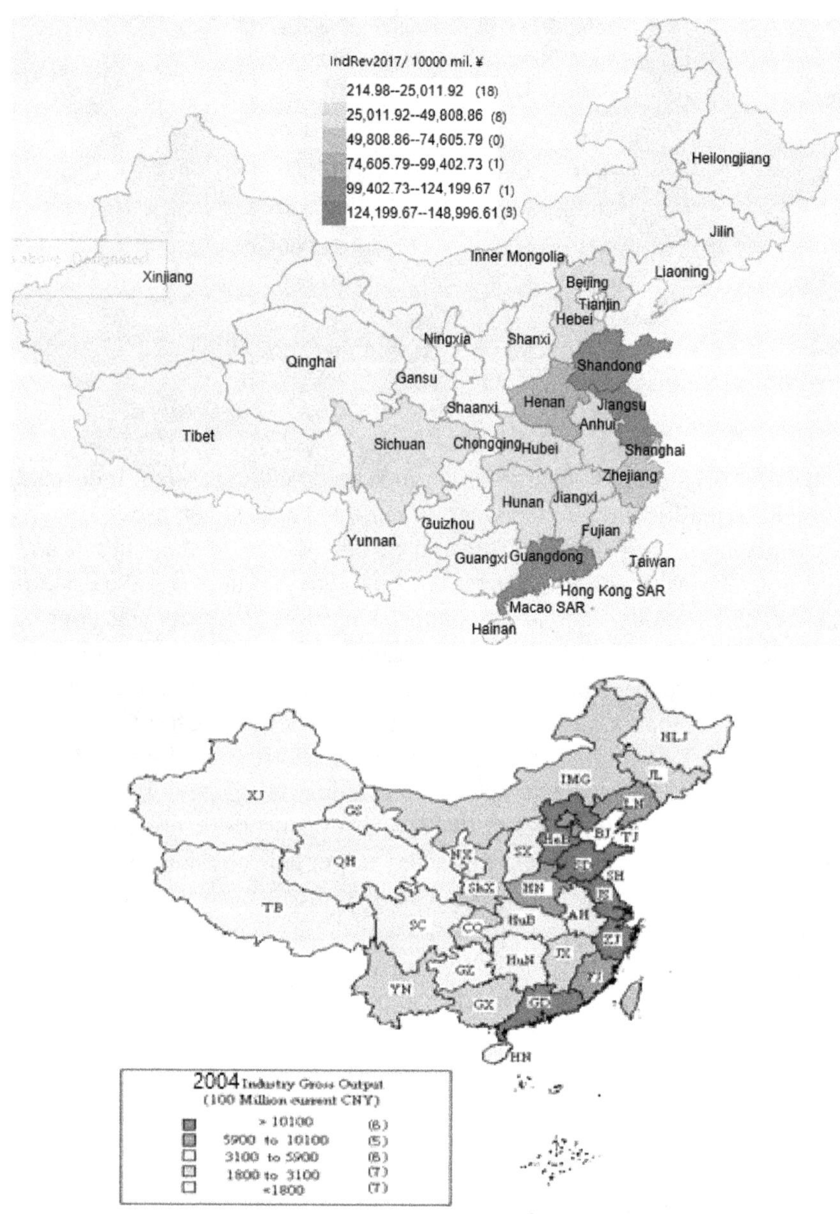

Figure 5.18. 2004 and 2017 Industry Gross output by region.

Table 5.15.   2004 and 2017 industry gross output by region (100 million current CNY).

	2004					2017			
Province	Ind. GO	Province	Ind. GO	Provi Ind. GO		Province	Ind. Rev	Province	Ind. Rev
GD	31520	HB	5329	GS	1696	JS	148997	TB	215
JS	29477	SC	5304	XJ	1656	SD	140857	HN	1800
SD	24678	HN	4342	GZ	1546			QH	2081
ZJ	21227	AH	4236	NX	605	GD	133924	NX	4067
SH	14594	ShX	4174	HN	429			GS	8434
HB	10194	HLG	3956	QH	388	HeN	79909	HLJ	8654
				TB	25			XJ	9731
HN	9237	JL	3552			ZJ	65760	GZ	10648
LN	9141	ShaX	3151					YN	11685
FJ	7516	JX	2737			FJ	45658	IMG	13983
TJ	6119	CQ	2599			HuB	43211	TJ	16144
BJ	5975	YN	2344			AH	43110	ShC	17852
		IMG	2327			HeB	41950	JL	20406
		GX	2242			SC	41631	BJ	20722
						HuN	38934	CQ	20772
						SH	37911	ShaX	23082
						JX	33752	LN	23476
								GX	23805

indication of the large size of the absolute gap between the eastern and western regions.

Figure 5.19 and Table 5.16 show that the six provinces with the highest grain output in 2017 included three provinces in 2005, but their specific rankings have changed. From 2005–2017, the average annual growth rate of grain output in Heilongjiang, Henan, Shandong, Jilin Anhui, and Hebei was 7.6%, 3.0%, 2.7%, 4.0%, 3.7%, and 3.36%, respectively,

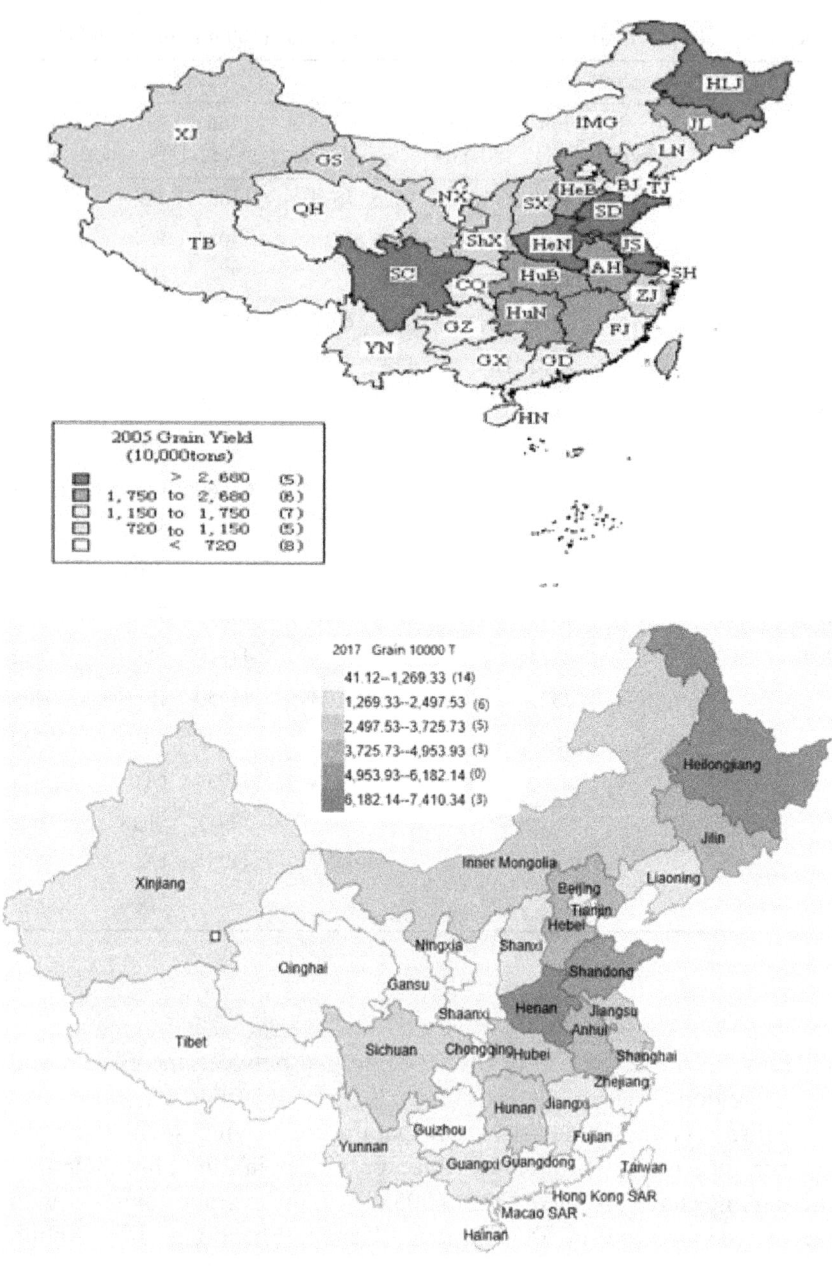

Figure 5.19.   2005 and 2017 grain yield by region in China.

Table 5.16. 2005 and 2017 grain yield by region (10,000 tons).

Province	Grain	Province	Grain	Province	Grain	Province	Grain	Province	Grain	Province	Grain	Province	Grain
HeN	3569	LN	1498	CQ	1,087	NX	270	BJ	41	ShX	1355	AH	4020
SD	3436	YN	1471	ShaX	968	HN	205	SH	100	GX	1370	JL	4154
SC	3054	GX	1465	ShX	959	TJ	119	TB	103	XJ	1485		
HLG	2512	JX	1450	ZJ	793	SH	99	QH	107	YN	1843	SD	5374
JS	2472	GD	1430	GS	789	TB	97	TJ	138	JX	2222	HeN	6524
HuN	2443	IMG	1361	XJ	775	QH	87	NX	212	LN	2331	HLJ	7410
		GZ	1104	FJ	713	BJ	58	FJ	370				
HeB	2388							ZJ	487	HuB	2846		
JL	2260							CQ	580	HuN	3074		
AH	2215							GS	1080	IMG	3255		
HuB	1921							ShaX	1106	SC	3489		
								HN	1194	JS	3611		
								GD	1209				
								GZ	1242				

ranking one to six. The grain output of these six provinces in 2017 was 313.1 million tons, accounting for 154.1% of 2005. Two of the top six provinces with high grain yield are in the eastern region, three of them positioned in the central, and one in the western region in 2005. However, for two of them (Henan,ranked first, and Sichuan, ranked third) the per capita income in rural and urban areas is lower than the national average. Another two (Shandong, ranked second, and Jiangsu, ranked fifth) produce high grain yield with high Industry Gross output, so they are very rich. This means the increase in per capita income in rural and urban areas should provide the appropriate environment for development of industry. Figure 5.19 and Table 5.16 show that, of the six provinces with high grain yield in 2017, there are two in the northeastern region, two in the eastern region, and two in the central region, respectively, and none in western region. Figure 5.19 and Table 5.16 show that the six provinces with the highest grain output in 2017 included four provinces in 2005 (excluding Sichuan, ranked third in 2005, and Hunan, ranked sixth in 2005), but their rankings have changed. In 2017, the grain output of Heilongjiang, Henan, Shandong, and Anhui was 295.0%, 182.8%, 156.4%, and 187.6%, respectively, of that in 2005. This indicates the government continued to increase investment support, while maintaining its reform posture and fine-tuning policies that strengthen agriculture and benefit farmers. Based on the country, the new food security strategy of "mainly based on me, ensuring production capacity, moderate import, and scientific and technological support" was put forward, and "the basic self-sufficiency of grain and absolute safety of rations" was established.

We now examine the similarity of regional industrial structure after reform using **R1** [Eq. (3.2)] as criterion. According to China's National Bureau of Statistics, the secondary industry is divided into 39 sectors in 2006, compared to the 37 sectors in 1997, because two sectors (Mining and Processing of Non-metal Ores and Manufacture of Textile Wearing Apparel, Footwear, and Caps) were added. The results of our calculations of **K** and **R1** are listed in Table 5.17.[50] The top five similar provinces and the five most dissimilar provinces by industrial structure similarity in China are listed in Table 5.19. There is no apparent comparative advantage in the resources of the top five similar provinces.

---

[50]China National Bureau of Statistics: China Statistical Yearbook, China Statistics Press, 2018, Table 13.2; 2007, Table 14.2; Department of Industrial Statistics, China National Bureau of Statistics: China Industry Economy Statistical Yearbook, 1998, 2007.

Table 5.17.   The industrial structure similarity of 31 provinces and municipalities, 1988, 1997, and 2006.

Region	1988				1997				2006			
	K(CH)	R(CH)	K(SH)	R(SH)	K(CH)	R(CH)	K(SH)	R(SH)	K(CH)	R(CH)	K(SH)	R(SH)
Ch	0.0000	1.0000	0.9914	0.9515	0.0000	1.0000	1.3157	0.8940	0.0000	1.0000	1.6297	0.8893
BJ	1.1685	0.9108	1.2918	0.8904	1.6340	0.8380	1.6283	0.8487	2.1495	0.8320	1.6572	0.9306
TJ	0.8482	0.9638	0.5975	0.9753	1.3947	0.8347	1.3149	0.8543	2.0204	0.8567	1.3642	0.9296
Heb	0.7063	0.9750	1.2014	0.9225	1.1481	0.8984	1.7709	0.8084	2.0847	0.6795	3.3614	0.4626
ShX	1.4139	0.8890	1.5991	0.8852	2.0440	0.7748	2.3570	0.7183	3.6834	0.5318	4.3591	0.3149
LMG	1.4578	0.8784	1.9723	0.8125	2.1797	0.7714	2.8084	0.6586	2.8468	0.7056	4.2043	0.4091
LN	1.1084	0.8934	1.3126	0.9012	1.3548	0.8514	1.6360	0.8255	2.1243	0.8668	2.1168	0.9242
JL	1.3792	0.8491	2.2501	0.7472	2.2539	0.6835	2.4760	0.7549	3.1274	0.5799	3.8718	0.4921
HLJ	1.4989	0.8302	2.2099	0.7212	1.6762	0.7831	2.5125	0.6130	3.3890	0.4629	4.2948	0.2620
SH	0.9914	0.9515	0.0000	1.0000	1.3157	0.8940	0.0000	1.0000	1.6297	0.8893	0.0000	1.0000
JS	0.8936	0.9495	1.0637	0.9252	1.1068	0.9239	1.3546	0.8212	1.4833	0.9297	1.4104	0.9092
ZJ	1.0916	0.9182	1.4500	0.8690	1.1597	0.8985	1.6451	0.7513	1.6360	0.8424	2.1430	0.7018
AH	0.8035	0.9528	1.6910	0.8344	1.0055	0.9080	1.8159	0.7347	1.5310	0.8589	2.4186	0.6407
FJ	1.4564	0.8693	2.1241	0.7661	2.0955	0.7129	2.8196	0.5151	1.4141	0.9000	2.2088	0.8555
JX	0.9189	0.9526	1.6197	0.8629	1.4498	0.8311	2.2897	0.6680	1.7566	0.7609	3.0159	0.5172
SD	0.8202	0.9621	1.4642	0.8834	1.0309	0.9255	1.7450	0.7807	1.3327	0.8843	2.4365	0.6621
HeN	0.8858	0.9616	1.5224	0.8863	1.4720	0.8699	2.6198	0.6249	1.9858	0.7774	3.4861	0.4571
HuB	0.8960	0.9459	1.2778	0.9123	0.9273	0.9324	1.4000	0.8819	1.4568	0.8493	2.3549	0.7102

(Continued)

Table 5.17. *(Continued)*

Region	1988				1997				2006			
	K(CH)	R(CH)	K(SH)	R(SH)	K(CH)	R(CH)	K(SH)	R(SH)	K(CH)	R(CH)	K(SH)	R(SH)
HuN	0.8451	0.9490	1.7828	0.8447	1.3807	0.8622	2.2034	0.7348	1.7360	0.8292	2.9053	0.5733
GD	1.1974	0.9043	1.7119	0.8326	1.6760	0.7997	1.9393	0.7270	2.0044	0.8015	1.6559	0.9066
GX	1.0824	0.9188	1.9213	0.7846	1.5945	0.8243	2.4828	0.6478	2.4673	0.7691	3.1548	0.5320
HN	2.5602	0.6453	3.0411	0.5372	2.7815	0.6702	2.9963	0.6287	3.1445	0.6638	3.7032	0.4999
CQ									2.4249	0.5900	3.0417	0.5380
SC	0.7903	0.9638	1.2543	0.9122	1.4845	0.8573	1.8118	0.8186	1.3514	0.8999	2.6061	0.6958
GZ	1.5955	0.7601	2.1438	0.6926	2.3648	0.7315	2.8149	0.6600	3.2454	0.6441	4.0200	0.3864
YN	1.8394	0.6175	2.5682	0.5173	2.9045	0.3835	3.4044	0.3032	3.4218	0.5152	4.3222	0.3104
TB	4.0952	0.3950	4.4990	0.2420	5.3934	0.5003	6.1202	0.2687	5.2065	0.3406	5.9763	0.1464
ShaX	1.1607	0.9380	1.2539	0.9244	1.3330	0.8841	1.7558	0.8369	2.4229	0.6883	3.1986	0.4998
GS	1.0965	0.8973	1.8210	0.8160	2.2645	0.7099	3.0933	0.5261	3.3083	0.5740	4.3221	0.3499
QH	1.5070	0.8985	1.6434	0.8747	112.8172	0.2826	113.1355	0.1217	4.0062	0.5187	4.7971	0.2633
NX	1.4570	0.8894	1.8203	0.8356	6.0637	0.1781	6.5936	0.1279	2.9156	0.6543	4.0583	0.3561
XJ	1.6034	0.8665	2.3048	0.7657	2.0158	0.7228	2.8952	0.5333	3.9376	0.3726	4.7668	0.1885

The State Council's opinion on promoting to accelerate the development of advanced manufacturing industry — Table 5.18 — shows Shanghai's Industrial Structure similarities in 2006 and 2017. From 2006 to 2017, Shanghai's total industry gross output increased from 1963.1 billion CNY (246.1 billion USD) to 3,609.4 billion CNY (534.4 billion USD). From 2006– 2017, the Change Coefficient K and Resemblance Coefficient *R1* of 30 sectors of Shanghai city are 0.268 and 0.9976, showing the industrial structure is quite similar. But the industrial structure of Shanghai's advanced manufacturing industry has undergone significant change. The industrial structure of six key high technology industries is dissimilar with $K = 6.6$ and $R1 = 0.9194$. The six key industries of the city gross output increased from 34% in 2006 to 68.7% from 2006–2017. This shows that Shanghai's first development of six industrial structures and key high-tech industries is correct for improving Shanghai's industrial structure. The "13th FYP for Shanghai's Manufacturing Transformation and Upgrading" was officially released on August 31, 2017. Shanghai strives to achieve the value added of manufacturing industry in GDP of about 25% by 2020, with the value added of strategic emerging industries accounting for about 20% of its GDP. According to 2017 data, the value added of Shanghai's manufacturing industry accounted for 27.4% of GDP, and the value added of strategic emerging industries accounted for 16.8% of GDP. This means, in the next three years, the overall manufacturing industry will maintain a steady downward trend of about 4.7%, and the total proportion of strategic emerging industries in manufacturing will increase by about 21.6% compared with 2017.

The industrial structure similarity among three municipalities (Beijing, Shanghai, and Tianjin) is relatively high (see Table 5.20). The share of three sectors (Manufacturing of Communication Equipment, Computers, and Other Electronic Equipment, Manufacturing of Transport Equipment, and Manufacturing of Electrical Machinery and Equipment) in Beijing, Shanghai, and Tianjin are much higher than the country's corresponding percentage. In 2000, the gross output of these three sectors reached 42.7%, 38.2%, and 42.6% of total industrial gross output, respectively, while the national average of that value was only 22.6%. In 2000, the gross output of Manufacturing of Communication Equipment, Computers, and Other Electronic Equipment reached 27.2%, 21.1%, and 24.0% of total industrial gross output for Beijing, Shanghai, and Tianjin, respectively. However, the gross output of Manufacturing of Communication Equipment, Computers, and Other Electronic Equipment reached

Table 5.18. The industrial structure similarity of Shanghai, 2006 and 2017.[*]

	2006	2017		2006	2017
	100 mil. ¥			100 mil. ¥	
Communication equipment, computer, and other electronic equipment manufacturing	3919.32	36094.36	Electronic information products manufacturing industry	856.75	6,570.41
Transportation equipment manufacturing	1894.69	2571.72	Automobile manufacturing industry	356.93	6,815.25
General equipment manufacturing	1530.60	2216.53	Petrochemical and fine chemical manufacturing	333.48	3,784.16
Chemical raw materials and chemical products manufacturing	1333.15	1862.19	High quality steel manufacturing industry	360.21	1,284.31
Smelting and pressing of ferrous metals	1445.74	1638.97	Complete equipment manufacturing industry	496.11	3,944.12
Petroleum processing, coking and nuclear fuel processing industries	919.04	1203.44	Biomedical manufacturing	101.49	1,019.40
Top six industries account for the city	36.3	26.3	Six key industries account for the city	34.0	68.7
Industry gross output	19631	36094	Industry gross output	19631	36094

Table 5.18. (*Continued*)

	2006	2017		2006	2017
	100 mil. ¥			100 mil. ¥	
Change coefficient K		0.268	Change coefficient K		6.0
Resemblance coef. R1		0.9976	Resemblance coef. R1		0.9194

Notes: *Calculated using data from Shanghai Municipal Statistics Bureau: Shanghai Statistical Yearbook, China Statistics Press, 2018, Tables 13.1, 13.4, 13.-7; 2009 Table 13.3; 2007 Tables 12.3, 12.9; (in Chinese); Outline of the 13th Five-Year Plan for National Economic and Social Development in Shanghai, Shanghai Municipal People's Government, February 1, 2016, (in Chinese); A picture of Shanghai's manufacturing transformation and upgrading "13th Five-Year Plan," Shanghai Development and Reform Commission, July 25, 2017 (in Chinese).

CNY223.4 billion (USD28.1 billion), CNY391.9 billion (USD49.2 billion), and CNY204.6 billion (USD25.7 billion) for Beijing, Shanghai, and Tianjin, respectively, while total industrial gross output accounted for CNY821.0 billion (USD103.1 billion), CNY1,715.7 billion (USD215.5 billion), and CNY852.8 billion (107.1 billion USD), respectively. Therefore, the percentage share of Beijing and Tianjin was larger than Shanghai's. We can see that megacities attach great importance to developing high-tech and capital-intensive industries.

For the most dissimilar provinces, some special sectors occupy a large share of total output. In 1994, 1997, 2000, and 2006, Yunnan's tobacco processing occupied 38.6%, 35.7%, 22.6%, and 19.1%, respectively, of the province's total output. In Heilongjiang, petroleum extraction accounted for 27.8% of the province's total output, 25.4%, 26.6%, and 30.2%; Petroleum processing, 8.7%, 9.8%, 18.1%, and 14.5%; in Xinjiang, petroleum extraction accounted for 32.5%, 32.7%, 19.1%, and 37.8% of total province output; in Tibet, metals mining, 11.6%, 11.8%, 16.9%, and 6.8%; non-metal mineral products, 18.9%, 21.7%, 12.2%, and 8.6%; manufacture of medicines accounted for 0.2%, 2.0%, 18.4%, and 15.5%. These regions depend mainly on the development of local resources: petroleum, mineral, tobacco, and medicine.

Table 5.19.   The top five similar provinces and the five most dissimilar provinces by industrial structure similarity in China (1988–2006).

	The top 5 similar provinces	R1
1988	Hebei, Sichuan, Tianjin, Shandong, and Henan	[0.973, 0.956]
1994	Anhui, Sichuan, Shandong, Henan, and Jiangxi	[0.944, 0.922]
1997	Shandong, Sichuan, Jiangsu, Jianxi, and Shaanxi	[0.936, 0.909]
2000	Shaanxi, Guizhou, Shanghai, Liaoning, and Jiangsu	[0.939, 0.926]
2006	Jiangsu, Fujian, Sichuan, Shanghai, and Shandong	[0.930, 0.884]
	The 5 most dissimilar provinces	
1988	Tibet, Hainan, Yunnan, Heilongjiang, and Xinjiang	[0.390, 0.712]
1994	Yunnan, Tibet, Heilongjiang, Xinjiang, Hainan	[0.379, 0.598]
1997	Yunnan, Xinjiang Tibet, Heilongjiang, and Hainan	[0.407, 0.681]
2000	Tibet, Qinghai, Xinjiang, Shanxi, and Ningxia	[0.316, 0.511]
2006	Tibet, Xinjiang, Heilongiang Yunnan, and Qinghai	[0.341,0.519]

Table 5.21[51] shows the ranking of the province's industrial gross output (Billion CNY) as well as the industrial change coefficient K and similarity coefficient $R1$. Research shows that in 2006, the industrial gross output of the top five provinces in the country accounted for 55.04% of national industrial gross output, while the bottom five provinces accounted for only 1.15%. In 2017, this percentage was 50.25% and 1.46%. This means the absolute regional gap among 31 provinces

---

[51]Calculated using data Compiled by Department of Industry and Transport Statistics, China National Bureau of Statistics: China Industry Economy Statistical Yearbook, China Statistics Press, 2007, Tables 4.1 and 4.16–4.42.

Table 5.20.   The industrial structure similarity of Beijing, Shanghai, and Tianjin in China (1988–2006).

	BJ/TJ	BJ/SH	SH/TJ
1988	0.9529	0.8904	0.9753
1994	0.9588	0.9384	0.9438
1997	0.9272	0.8439	0.8405
2000	0.9560	0.8285	0.9412
2006	0.9157	0.9306	0.9296

are very large. In 2006, the average industrial gross output value of 31 provinces nationwide was 974.1 billion CNY with a standard deviation of 1188.6 billion CNY and the coefficient of deviation was 1.22. In 2017, it was 3655.4 billion CNY, 3,953.0 billion CNY and 1.08. As a result, the relative regional gap among 31 provinces is also very large. In 2006, the top five provinces all are in the eastern region and among the bottom five provinces, four are located in the western region and one in the eastern region. In 2017, among the top five provinces, four are located in the eastern region and one in the central region, and among the bottom five provinces, four are located in the western region and one is in eastern region. The correlation coefficient of industrial gross outputs between 2006 and 2017 was 0.8593; this means the ranking is very similar for 2006 and 2017. Jiangsu, Shandong, Guangdong, and Zhejiang listed in the top five during 2006 and 2017; only Liaoning was replaced by Henan in 2017. Ningxia, Hainan, Qinghai and Tibet ranked bottom five in 2006 and 2017; replaced by Xinjiang in 2017. There is a linear relationship between 2006 and 2017, making regression analysis possible, giving that the coefficient of determination is 0.9194, the slop is 0.8592, the standard error is 1.883. From 2006–2017, the change coefficient K and resemblance coefficient $R1$ of 31 provinces are 0.7972 and 0.9194, showing the industrial gross output structure is quite similar.

A region's industrial structure within the secondary industry is a very important factor in generating an efficient and sustainable level of economic development. For example, Shanxi province in the past several decades placed the development of heavy industry as its top priority. In

Table 5.21.   The industrial structure similarity of provinces and their industrial gross output, 2006 and 2017.

	2005		2017	
	GO	Rank GO	Revenue	Rank GO
	Bil. ¥		Bil. ¥	18
China	30196		113316	21
Beijing	640	14	2072.2	9
Tianjin	630	15	1614.41	20
Hebei	1063	9	4195	22
Shanxi	467	17	1785.24	15
Inner Mongolia	308	22	1398.31	19
Liaoning	1475	5	2347.64	26
Jilin	325	20	2040.58	12
Heilongjiang	296	23	865.43	1
Shanghai	1440	6	3791.05	5
Jiangsu	3632	3	14899.66	8
Zhejiang	4569	1	6576.01	6
Anhui	652	13	4311.04	13
Fujian	1376	7	4565.85	2
Jiangxi	533	16	3375.17	4
Shandong	3194	4	14085.68	7
Henan	1190	8	7990.91	11
Hubei	755	12	4321.05	3
Hunan	900	10	3893.42	14
Guangdong	3749	2	13392.44	30
Guangxi	405	18	2380.51	17
Hainan	60	29	179.95	10
Chongqing	321	21	2077.24	24
Sichuan	900	11	4163.13	23
Guizhou	259	25	1064.76	31
Yunnan	260	24	1168.45	16
Tibet	20	31	21.5	27
Shaanxi	338	19	2308.17	29
Gansu	173	26	843.45	28
Qinghai	44	30	208.06	25

(Continued)

Table 5.21.   (*Continued*)

	2005		2017	
	GO	Rank GO	Revenue	Rank GO
	Bil. ¥		Bil. ¥	18
Ningxia	76	28	406.72	
Xinjiang	148	27	973.08	
K			0.7972	
R1			0.9194	

1997, the coal mining and processing sector accounted for 25.67% of total industrial output, metallurgy, 17.8% of total output, the chemical industry, 12.03%, electric power, 9.62%, and machinery manufacturing, 10.19%. In 2000, these six industrial sectors accounted for 85% of total output. The ratio of tax and profits per capita of these six heavy industrial sectors is lower than China's average rate of investment return. Therefore, Shanxi cannot provide sufficient supply of light industry products to the market; other provinces are more efficient and have captured the market. Therefore, Shanxi's GDP accounted for 2.16%[52] of China's GDP in 1984 and declined to 1.78% in 2004.[53] The province's rank of per capita GDP fell from 12th in 1988 to 22nd in 2003. The per capita income of rural households in Shanxi ranked among the bottom three in 2003. In contrast, after reform, Guangdong and Fujian adjusted their industrial structure according to market demand. In 1994, electronics and telecommunication accounted for 11.38% and 8.44%, electric equipment and machinery, 8.44% and 4.14%, garments, 5.3% and 5.55%. In 1997, the electronics and telecommunication sector accounted for 15.96% and 10.74%, electric equipment and machinery 8.75% and 4.09%, garments 5.11% and 5.40%. By 2000, electronics and telecommunication accounted for 28.41% and 22.84% and electric equipment and machinery 11.13% and 4.57%. The percentage share of these sectors to total province output is higher than China's corresponding percentage share; as a result, these sectors represent comparative advantages for the provinces and generate

---

[52]Calculated using data from China National Bureau of Statistics compiled: Statistical Yearbook of China 1986, Oxford University Press, 1986, pp. 40, 44.

[53]Calculated using data from China National Bureau of Statistics (2005). China Statistical Yearbook, China Statistics Press, 2005, Table 3.11.

substantial economic benefits. Guangdong and Fujian became fast developing provinces after reform. These examples fully demonstrate the importance of industrial structure in economic development.

We can also compare 2006 Henan and Inner Mongolia using 2006 data. Henan is ranked first in the central region, while Inner Mongolia is ranked second in the western region. Inner Mongolia has placed emphasis on supply-side structural reform and accelerated the transformation of the new and old kinetic energy sector. It also addressed excess capacity through marketization and completed the task of lowering capacity in the "steel and coal industry" ahead of the schedule stated in the 13th FYP. The value added of high-tech industries increased by 17.1% over the previous year, while new products with higher value and higher technology content continued to increase their contribution to the province's economy. For example, monocrystalline silicon production increased by 1.2 times, rare earth compounds increased by 45.9%, graphite and carbon products increased by 42.8%. Production of new energy vehicles reached 11,547 vehicles. The profit rate of industrial enterprises in these sectors was 10.6%, or 4.1 % points higher than the national average. The value added of high-processing industries and high-tech manufacturing industries rose by 12.2% and 15.9%. The total profit of industrial enterprises above designated size was CNY193.09 billion, up by 24.3% compared with the previous year. Among the industrial sectors whose profits ranked in the top five were manufacturing of non-metallic mineral products, manufacturing of raw chemical materials and chemical products, agricultural food processing, special equipment, and cigarette manufacturing.

Hunan's total imports and exports were worth CNY243.43 billion (USD36.04 billion), an increase of 39.8% compared with the previous year.[54] The recipe for development of the provincial economy then seems to be supply-side structural reform, flexibility, and adaptability to the

---

[54]Report on the work of the Inner Mongolia Autonomous Region Government in 2019, date of publication: 2019-02-01-January 26, 2019 At the second meeting of the 13th People's Congress in Inner Mongolia Autonomous Region, Chairman of the Autonomous Region Bu Xiaolin (in Chinese); 2018 Inner Mongolia economic operation transcript released, Source: Inner Mongolia News Network Time: January 24, 2019 (in Chinese) www.nmg.cei.gov.cn/information/nmg_jx42/msg11964213606.html; Hunan Province Statistical Communiqué for the 2017 National Economic and Social Development, Hunan Bureau of Statistics March 12, 2018.

major changes occurring in major industrial sectors, such as manufacturing.[55]

We now turn our attention to the distribution of industrial sectors among provinces. We use the average value of absolute deviation between the percentage shares of the provinces with the national value, which is expressed by the following formula:

$$DEV_i = \frac{\sum_{j=1}^{n} ABS\left(ps_{ij} - ps_{ic}\right)}{n}, \quad i \in (1, m) \tag{5.24}$$

where DEV_i—average value of absolute deviation between the percentage share of the provinces with the national value of i industrial branch, $i \in (1, m)$, $m = 25$ for year 2000.

ps_{ij}—percentage share of i industrial branch in j province, $j \in (1, n)$, $n = 31$.

pc_{ic}—percentage share of i industrial branch in China.

The results of our calculations are listed in Table 5.22.[56] Larger DEV_i means the distribution of i industrial branch among 31 provinces became more uneven. From Table 5.24, we find that industrial branches requiring high-tech (manufacturing of communication equipment, computers, and other electronic equipment), capital intensive (manufacturing of transport equipment, smelting, and pressing of non-ferrous metals), and special raw material (extraction of petroleum and natural gas) are associated with larger DEV_i. Industrial branches with no special requirements, such as manufacturing of measuring instruments and machinery for cultural

---

[55]Calculated using data from Shandong Provincial Bureau of Statistics, Shandong Investigation Team of National Statistical Bureau: Shandong Statistical Yearbook, China Statistics Press, 2018, Table 14.4 (in Chinese); Statistical Communique of the National Economic and Social Development of Shandong Province in 2017. Shandong Provincial Bureau of Statistics, Shandong Investigation Team of National Statistical Bureau, February 27, 2018 (in Chinese); China National Bureau of Statistics, Data base; Annual by Province, Gross Regional Product (100 million yuan), 1998–2017; Comprehensive Department of China National Statistical Bureau: Economic structure achieves historic change, development coordination is significantly enhanced, 2018-08-29, (in Chinese).

[56]Calculated using data Compiled by Department of Industry and Transport Statistics, China National Bureau of Statistics: China Industry Economy Statistical Yearbook, China Statistics Press, 2007, Tables 4.1 and 4.16–4.42; China Industry Economy Statistical Yearbook, China Statistics Press, 2002, p. 107, 147, 153, 159, 165, 171, 177, 183, 189, 195, 201, 207, 213, 219, 225, 231, 237, 243, 249, 255, 261, 267, 273, 279, 285, 291.

Table 5.22.   Average value of absolute deviation between the percentage shares of the provinces with the national value of industrial branches in 2000 and 2006.

	2006	2000		2006	2000
Manufacture of Communication Equipment, Computers, and Other Electronic Equipment	9.64	12.59	Manufacture of Raw Chemical Materials and Chemical Products	2.11	2.46
Manufacture of Transport Equipment	5.49	6.21	Manufacture of Non-metallic Mineral Products	1.98	1.87
Extraction of Petroleum and Natural Gas	4.81	2.06	Manufacture of Tobacco	1.39	2.18
Smelting and Pressing of Non-ferrous Metals	4.66	3.78	Manufacture of Metal Products	1.36	1.73
Processing of Petroleum, Coking, Processing of Nuclear Fuel	4.47	2.49	Manufacture of Medicines	1.24	2.26
Smelting and Pressing of Ferrous Metals	4.20	3.54	Mining and Processing of Non-Ferrous Metal Ores	1.21	1.19
Production and Supply of Electric Power and Heat Power	3.53	2.16	Manufacture of Special Purpose Machinery	1.01	1.37
Manufacture of Electrical Machinery and Equipment	3.14	3.99	Manufacture of Paper and Paper Products	1.01	0.98
Manufacture of Textile	2.93	4.26	Manufacture of Chemical Fibers	0.81	1.25
Mining and Washing of Coal	2.86	1.67	Manufacture of Foods	0.81	1.08
Processing of Food from Agricultural Products	2.29	2.68	Manufacture of Measuring Instruments and Machinery for Cultural Activity and Office Work	0.74	0.80

(*Continued*)

Table 5.22.   (*Continued*)

	2006	2000		2006	2000
Manufacture of Beverages	0.91	0.91	Mining and Processing of Ferrous Metal Ores	0.64	0.76
Manufacture of General Purpose Machinery	2.26	2.06			

activity and office work, manufacture of foods, manufacture of chemical fibers, and manufacture of beverages are associated with smaller DEV_i.

Taking the whole country as our reference, the results of the calculations of industrial structure similarity in 1988, 1997, and 2006 are shown in Figure 5.20. We should note that the values of industrial structure similarity coefficient R1 in 2006 are not fully comparable with R1 values in 1988 and 1997, because the number of sectors used in the calculations is not the same. Specifically, 37 industrial sectors are used for calculating industrial structure similarity coefficient in 1988 and 1994, but only 27 sectors are used in 2006; however, these 27 sectors accounted for 92% of China's total industrial gross output. Because the difference is not large, we still find that the calculations provide useful insights in our understanding of the changes in provincial industrial structure.

Figure 5.20 shows there are 12 provinces with industrial structure similarity coefficient *R1* larger than 0.80 in 1988, 1997, and 2006; among them, nine provinces are in the eastern area. Ranked by the average *R1* in 1988, 1997, and 2006, they are Jiangsu (*R1* = 0.930), Shandong, Shanghai, Tianjin, Zhejiang, Fujian, Liaoning, Beijing, and Guangdong (*R1* = 0.843). The industrial gross output of these nine provinces was CNY21.348 trillion (USD2.682 trillion) in 2006, accounting for 67.4% of China's total industrial gross output. Obviously, they play an important role in determining China's total industrial structure; as a result, the industrial structure of the eastern region is most similar with China's as a whole. Figure 5.21 shows the average value and standard deviation of calculated *R1* for 30 regions (except Chongqing) in China for 1988, 1994, 1997, 2000, and 2006. From 1988 to 2006, *R1* decreased among the 30 regions, with the average **R1** decreasing from 0.855 (1988) to 0.712 (2006); the standard deviation σ fluctuated between 15.7% and 25.5%. These numbers reveal that the similarity among

Table 5.23.　Regional distribution of secondary industry (1985–2006).

	1985			1990			1995			2000			2006		
	Eastern	Middle	Western	Eastern	Middle	Western	Eastern	Middle	Western	Eastern	Middle	Western	Eastern	Middle	Western
Gross output	60.23	26.92	12.75	61.1	26.22	12.68	65.87	23.15	10.98	74.72	16.96	8.32	71.89	16.97	11.13
Mining and Washing of Coal	26.97	55.69	17.34	30.64	55.65	13.71	32.59	54.27	13.14	33.43	53.74	12.83	30.03	50.26	19.71
Extraction of Petroleum and Natural Gas	37.45	47.25	15.3	33.46	50.63	15.91	39.5	38.62	21.88	41.80	32.87	25.33	39.27	30.48	30.25
Mining and Processing of Ferrous Metal Ores	57.83	20.84	21.32	60.72	21.09	18.2	57.91	35.85	6.24	65.7	26.07	8.23	61.71	21.79	16.50
Mining and Processing of Non-Ferrous Metal Ores	35.94	46.85	17.21	39.16	39.98	20.86	38.53	40.93	20.54	46.61	33.70	19.69	28.93	37.91	33.16
Mining and Processing of Non-metal Ores	52.5	32.8	14.7	52.11	33.94	13.95	54.29	32.97	12.73				55	28.12	16.88
Logging and Transport of Timber and Bamboo	12.77	70.8	16.43	13.88	73.73	12.39	14.08	71.51	14.41						

Processing & Manufacture of Food from Agricultural Products	53.79	31.81	14.4	57.35	29.22	13.43	61.65	27.82	10.53	68.74	23.65	7.61	61.86	23.62	14.53
Manufacture of Beverage	49.32	33.17	17.51	55.42	29.54	15.04	60.15	25.59	14.26	64.98	22.35	12.67	53.28	23.07	23.66
Manufacture of Tobacco	37.58	38.89	23.53	33.94	32.22	33.83	25.73	28.96	45.31	30.64	33.03	36.33	36.77	28.46	34.78
Manufacture of Textile	70	21.2	8.8	72.15	18.59	9.26	74.02	18.81	7.17	81.02	1463	434	85.21	9.83	4.96
Manufacture of Textile Wearing Apparel, Footwear and Caps	67.14	22.12	10.74	75.6	18.02	6.38	87.34	10.66	2				92.76	6.23	1.01
Leather, Furs, Down, and Related Products	61.6	26.05	12.35	72.37	18.63	9	81.41	13.93	4.65						
Timber Processing Bamboo Cane, Palm Fiber, and Straw Products	47.99	41.77	10.25	50.23	40.68	9.09	60.68	32.97	6.35						

(Continued)

Table 5.23. (Continued)

	1985			1990			1995			2000			2006		
	Eastern	Middle	Western	Eastern	Middle	Western	Eastern	Middle	Western	Eastern	Middle	Western	Eastern	Middle	Western
Furniture Manufacturing	60.03	28.69	11.27	64.75	26.12	9.13	70.91	21.34	7.76						
Manufacture of Paper und Paper Products	57.79	30.34	11.87	58.82	29.99	11.19	64.16	25.25	10.59	76.21	17.18	6.6	77.36	16.13	6.51
Printing and Record pressing				61.31	24.35	14.34	65.37	20.19	14.45						
Stationery, Educational and Sports goods				86.37	10.51	3.12	92.68	6.15	1.18						
Processing of Petroleum, Coking Processing of Nuclear Fuel	65.9	27.17	6.94	63.41	30.25	6.34	66.38	26.84	6.78	68.11	24.26	7.63	64.09	20.66	15.25
Manufacture of Raw Chemical Materials and Chemical Products	62.75	24.39	12.86	62.85	25.12	12.03	64.24	23.9	11.86	71.28	18.97	9.75	72.86	16.09	11.06
Manufacture of Medicines	61.82	27.33	10.85	60.97	28.34	10.69	62.3	26.17	11.53	63.81	23.97	12.22	61.02	23.24	15.75

Manufacture of Chemical Fibers	80.19	16.73	3.08	77.33	17.54	5.12	82.31	13.97	3.72	82.89	13.45	3.66	88.75	8.39	2.86
Rubber Products	63.76	26.18	10.07	65.5	24.62	9.88	71.25	19.59	9.16						
Plastic Products	74.03	18.85	7.12	75.1	17.91	6.99	79.42	15.01	5.57						
Manufacture of Non-metallic Mineral Products	56.9	30.02	13.07	59.09	29.33	11.58	62.8	27.45	9.76	68.48	21.88	9.64	67.02	22.25	10.83
Smelting and Pressing of Ferrous Metals	58.92	28.42	12.66	59.71	26.38	13.91	63.04	23.58	13.38	66.75	22.57	10.68	68.29	18.65	13.06
Smelting and Pressing of Non-ferrous Metals	47.5	27.58	24.92	47.16	28.66	24.18	50.07	26.75	23.17	53.99	26.29	19.72	47.74	28.23	24.03
Manufacture of Metal Products	67.67	24.34	9.99	68.92	20.86	10.22	76.99	16.34	6.67	87.42	8.90	3.68	87.8	8.62	3.58
Manufacture of General Purpose Machinery	62.47	24.39	13.14	63.57	23.36	13.07	69.76	21.32	8.92	80.64	12.69	6.67	81.38	11.79	6.83
Manufacture of special Purpose Machinery	63.2	23.81	14.48				56.99	24.22	8.79	75.18	18.54	6.29	71.19	19.13	9.68

(Continued)

Table 5.23.   (Continued)

	1985			1990			1995			2000			2006		
	Eastern	Middle	Western	Eastern	Middle	Western	Eastern	Middle	Western	Eastern	Middle	Western	Eastern	Middle	Western
Manufacture of Transport Equipment	50.61	34.92	14.48	47.71	29.45	14.64	62.26	27.37	10.37	59.87	28.39	11.74	63.32	23.47	13.21
Manufacture of Electrical Machinery and Equipment	71.52	19.14	9.35	64.54	17.3	9.4	78.88	14.48	6.64	85.67	9.83	4.5	86	9.11	4.89
Manufacture of Communication Equipment, Computers and Other Electronic Equipment	76.07	11.79	12.15	68.58	10.21	14.99	85.85	5.35	8.81	88.54	5.09	6.37	95.36	2.35	2.28
Manufacture of Measuring Instruments and Machinery for Cultural Activity and Office Work	66.71	16.89	16.41	58.75	15.4	17.95	80.24	10.81	8.95	87.03	7.03	5.94	89.27	6.4	4.33
Production and Supply of Electronic	48.27	34.57	17.16	51.72	32.33	15.95	58.06	28.82	13.12	60.09	26.24	13.68	60.38	22.3	17.32
K(E,M,W)		33.18	43.21		36.03	45.07		43.34	53.57	0	47.06	56.73	0	48.38	52.78
R1(E,M,W)	1	0.8141	0.8673	1	0.7917	0.8231	1	0.7522	0.6954	1	0.7938	0.6945	1	0.7364	0.6605

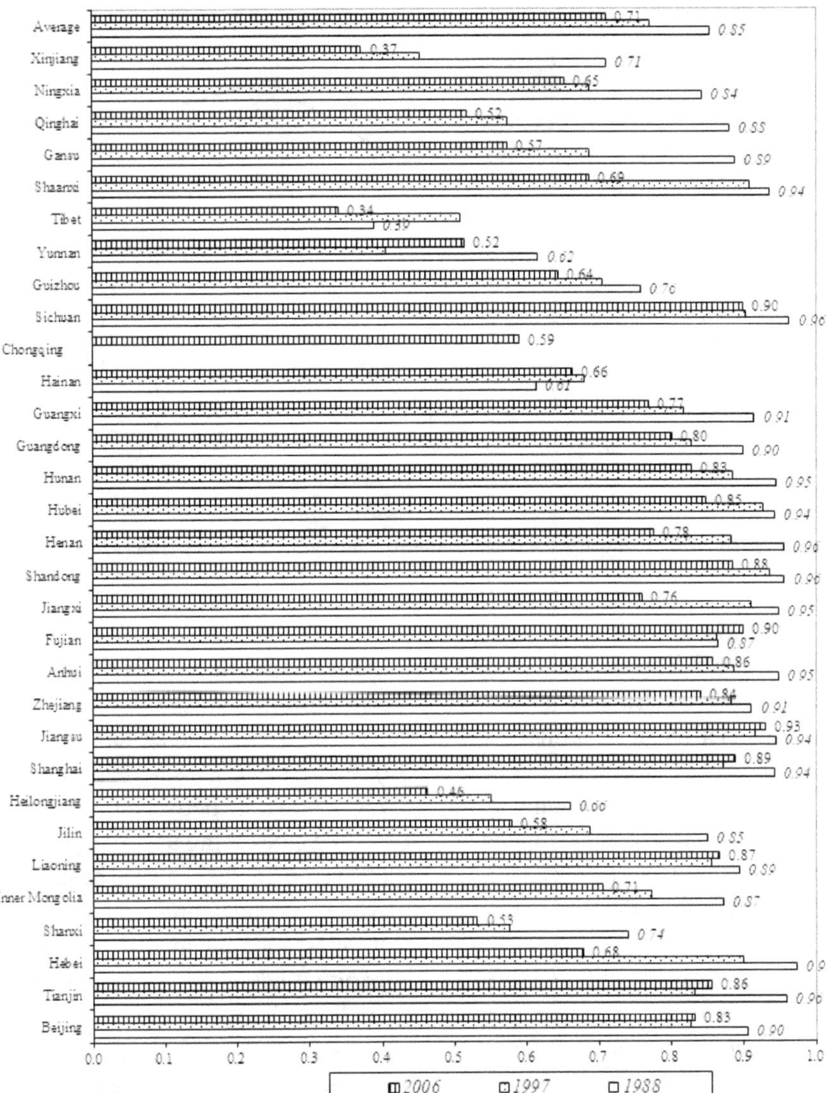

Figure 5.20.   IS similarity of secondary industry by regions, China.

provinces decreased from 1988–2006 but did so gradually. The findings do not support the notion that "after 1978 the IS similarity increased

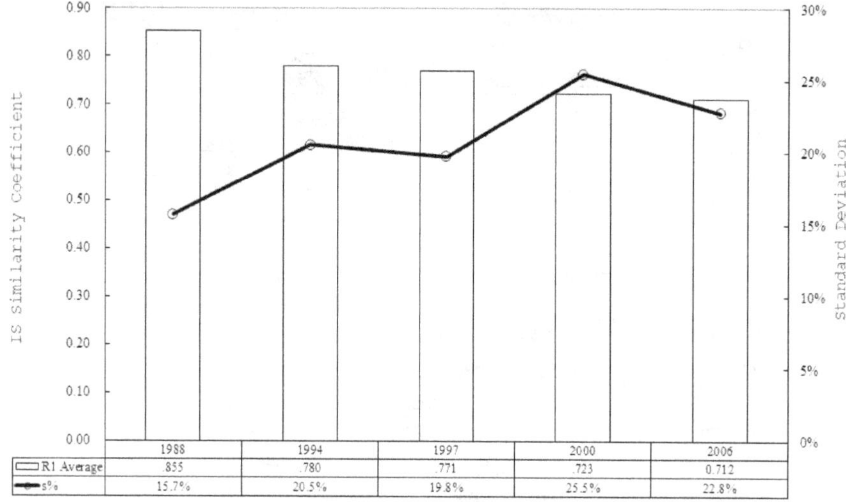

	1988	1994	1997	2000	2006
R1 Average	.855	.780	.771	.723	0.712
s%	15.7%	20.5%	19.8%	25.5%	22.8%

Figure 5.21.   Industry structure similarity among 30 provinces, 1988–2006.

significantly." The provincial comparative advantages have been influential in the industrial structure adjustment process during 1988–2000.

The coefficient of similarity, *R1*, between the central and eastern regions is 0.814 (1985), declining to 0.792 (1990), 0.752 (1995), rising temporarily to 0.794 (2000), and declining again to 0.736 (2006); *R1* between the eastern and western regions is calculated as 0.867 (1985), declining to 0.823 (1990), 0.695 (1995), 0.694 (2000), and 0.661 (2006) (see Table 5.25[57]). These data indicate that the industrial structure similarity of China's three large regions diverged between 1985 and 2006. This implies once again that provinces take under consideration their local comparative advantage in formulating their economic development strategy. From Table 5.23, we observe that the gap of industrial gross output among three regions expands during the 1990s, but narrows during 2000–2006. This indicates that advancing the development of the western region and promoting the welfare of the central region proved to be an effective strategy. If we take China as reference, the industrial structure similarity coefficient *R1* in 2006 is equal to 0.8247, 0.6201,

---

[57]Calculated using data from Compiled by Department of Industry and Transport Statistics, China National Bureau of Statistics: China Industry Economy Statistical Yearbook 2007, 2002, 1996, 1991, 1986, China Statistics Press.

and 0.5629 for eastern, central, and western regions, respectively. As noted previously, because the industrial gross output of the eastern region accounted for almost 71.9% of the national total, the eastern region's industrial structure is reflected in China's industrial structure.

10. Regional Production Inequalities

Of course, challenges persist. For example, in developing their pillar industry, 22 provinces have selected the automobile industry and 24 provinces chose machinery manufacturing. Many provinces manufacture products of the same category (see Figure 5.22).[58] Furthermore, some provinces are still constructing new factories to produce such products. This leads to production capacity far beyond demand. We can offer an example from the Color Television industry. In the 1980s and early 1990s, domestic production did not meet the demand for color TVs; therefore, many sets were imported (primarily from Japan).

The price of these sets was high because of the market conditions, so sales of color TVs became highly profitable. In 1994, the earnings per share (EPS) of Changhong Electronic Groups (Shanghai A share market 600839) — the largest color TV producer — reached CNY2.97 (USD0.36). Under these market conditions, many provinces imported color TV production systems, thus drastically increasing the country's production capability. In 1980, China produced 32,100 color TV sets; the number increased to 10.33 million sets in 1990, 42.62 million in 1999 and

---

[58]Calculated using data from China National Bureau of Statistics: China Industry Economy Statistical Yearbook, China Statistics Press, 2009, Table 13.23; 2006, Table 14.24; 2001, Table 13.22; 1996, Table 12.20; China National Bureau of Statistics, Data base; Annual by Province, Output of Chemical Fiber(10000 tons), 1998–2017; Output of Yarn(10000 tons), 1998–2013; Output of Cigarettes, (100 mil. pieces). 1998–2017;), 1998–2017; Output of Home Refrigerators(10 000 sets), 1998–2017; Output of Air Conditioners (10 000 sets), 1998–2017; Output of Home Washing Machines (10,000 sets); Output of Color Television Sets (10,000 sets), 1998–2017; Output of Crude Steel (10 000 tons) , 1998–2017; Output of Chemical Fertilizers (10,000 tons), 1998–2017; Output of Primary Plastic (10,000 tons), 1998–2017; Output of Motor Vehicles (10 000 units) , 1998–2017; Output of Micro Computer Equipment (10 000 sets); Output of Mobile Telephones (10 000 sets), 1998–2017; Output of Integrated Circuits (10000 pieces), 1998–2017; Output of Cars (10,000 units), 1998–2017; Output of Natural Gas (100,000,000 cu.m), 1998–2017.

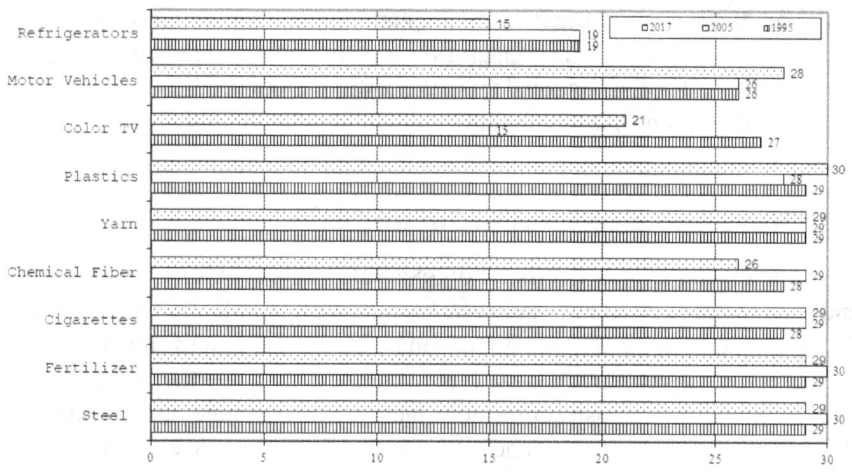

Figure 5.22.   Products produced in number of provinces, 1995, 2005, and 2017.

65.46 million sets in 2003.[59] The cost of Chinese domestic color TV is now much lower than foreign made because of large scale of production, low labor cost, and widely distributed sales network. After 1996, the market share of imported color TVs declined dramatically in the Chinese market because of their comparatively high price. By 1999, imported color TVs numbered only 0.26 million; by 2002, the number went down further (0.17 million sets).[60] Soon, the color TV market became a buyer's market, but the production capacity of color TV in China reached 87.96 million sets per year in 2003.[61] In 1996, a "price war" began in earnest in the color TV market. That year, the price of a 29-inch super-flat color TV was CNY7,000 (USD846); five years later, Shanghai color TV Festival featured the lowest price of a 29 inch super-flat color TV at CNY999 (USD121); the 21 inch super-flat color TV was priced at

---

[59]National Bureau of Statistics of China (2004). Statistical Communiqué of the People's Republic of China on the 2003 National Economic and Social Development, February, 26.
[60]Calculated using data from China National Bureau of Statistics 2003, China Statistical Yearbook, China Statistics Press, 2003, Table 17.9.
[61]Calculated using data from China National Bureau of Statistics (2004). China Statistical Yearbook, China Statistics Press, 2004, Table 14.22.

CNY399 (USD48).[62] The market price ended up being lower than the production cost! As a result, many color TV producers suffered losses. In 2003 and 2008, China exported 47.62 million and 51.38 million TV sets (including a complete set of spare parts), amounting to 64.1% and 56.8% of China's total output TV sets, respectively. The export revenue was USD3.47 billion and USD10.58 billion, and the average price was USD72.9 and USD205.9 per set.[63] The EPS of Changhong Electronic Groups was reduced to CNY0.01 (0.12 US cents) in the first half of 2001. The EPS of the second largest color TV producer, Kongjia (Shenzhen A share 000016), was –0.317 CNY (–0.0383 USD) in the first half year of 2001; to put it in perspective, compare with the 1998 EPS: CNY1.102 (USD0.13).

Another factor accounting for the losses suffered by China's color TV industry was the unreasonable color TV production structure. Almost all color TV sets produced in China perform the same functions and contain the same technology. In 2000, Changhong Electronic Groups sold 6.94 million color TV sets, while Sony only sold 0.5 million sets. However, the profit from color TV sales for both companies was about the same, around USD33 million. China's color TV industry needed to adjust its product structure and produce more high tech, "green" color TVs. In China's TV market, the digital high-definition color TV became the principal seller in 2003. China TCL, Changhong, and Kongjia produced large screen (46 inch to 61 inch) DLP (Digital Light Processing) projection TVs. The joint venture of Sony, Hitachi, and Samsung also supplied large screen LCD (liquid-crystal display) projection TVs in China's market.[64] The sales revenue of High level DLP and LCD projection TVs reached more than CNY13.3 billion (USD1.61 billion) in 2003 and CNY24 billion (USD2.99 billion) in 2005.[65] The Chinese TV industry is in much better shape now. This story tells us that upgrading products through innovation and new technology improves firm competitiveness and creates value. At

---

[62]Li, Y. (2001). Price war: The predestination of China's color TV industry, *Nanfeng Metropolis Daily*, September 10.

[63]Calculated using data from China National Bureau of Statistics: China Statistical Yearbook, China Statistics Press, 2009, Table 17.9, 13.23; 2004, Table 18.8.

[64]Zhang, H. (2004). TV industry striding in PDP, LCD and MD, *Nanfeng Metropolis Daily*, June 11.

[65]Ping, S. (2003). The outlet of TV industry "settlement scheme" (in Chinese), *China Economic Daily*, October 22.

the end of the third quarter of 2018, the EPS of TCL Groups (Shenzhen A share 000100), Changhong Electronic Groups, and Kongjia were reported as CNY0.179 (2.63 US cents), CNY0.044 (0.065 US cents), and CNY0.1846 (2.72 US cents), respectively. On Febuary 20, 2019, the corresponding stock prices were CNY3.25 (47.9 US cents), CNY2.64 (38.9 US cents), and CNY3.83 (56.4 US cents), respectively; price-earnings ratios were 16.09, 44.57, and 13.27, respectively; the total market capitalization of stocks was 9.22 billion CNY (1.36 billion USD), 12.2 billion CNY (1.80 billion USD), and 44 billion CNY (6.48 billion USD), respectively. TCL issued a medium- and long-term development strategy plan, through mixed reform, diversified management, etc. By 2020, the target revenue was expected to exceed CNY60 billion (USD8.84 billion), and by 2022, the revenue is expected to exceed CNY100 billion (USD14.73 billion), and it would become a globally competitive international enterprise driven by technological innovation.

For other products listed in Figure 5.26, the number of provinces manufacturing these products remain almost unchanged during 1995–2008. For example, the number of provinces manufacturing automobiles increased from 26 in 1995 to 27 in 2000 and declined to 26 in 2005, and again increased to 27 in 2008, which means small scale and low efficiency producers in automobile industry still exist. From Figure 5.26, we see that there were 26 provinces producing motor vehicles in 2005, with only five provinces producing more than 0.4 million units per year. The average output per province was only 0.22 million units and its standard deviation was 0.18 million units; Beijing ranked first, producing 0.59 million and Shanxi province was ranked last, producing a mere 100 motor vehicles (see Table 5.26[66]). In 2005, the total amount of motor vehicles produced in China reached 5.71 million units. However, only five automobile companies sold more than 500,000 automobiles. It is estimated that, for a company to be internationally competitive in the auto industry, it should achieve sales of about 5 million cars per year. In 2017, there were 10 provinces producing larger than 1 million vehicles with a total output of 21.83 million; the top three are still Guandong, Jinlin, and Shanghai — producing 3.18 million, 2.96 million, and 2.76 million vehicles, respectively, with average annual growth rate of 10.94%.

---

[66]Calculated using data from China National Bureau of Statistics: China Industry Economy Statistical Yearbook, China Statistics Press, 2009, Table 13.23; 2006, Table 14.24.

Another example is the steel sector. The nation's top 66 steel makers' profits skyrocketed by 116.2% to CNY28.3 billion (USD3.4 billion) during the first four months of 2004. As a result, new fixed asset investment into the sector reached CNY47.8 billion (USD5.8 billion) during the first four months of 2004, a massive year-on-year leap of 99.1%. Oversupply on the domestic steel market caused consecutive slides in Chinese steel makers' profits from 1996–2000. In the early 1990s, a business boom triggered that round of drastically expanding their production capacity. Oversupply was mainly caused by the fragmented state of the industry. There are still too many new low-level steel projects and the production capacity of local steel makers is growing much faster than large and medium-sized ones because of overheating investment.

There are 53 companies, each with an annual steel production capacity of 1 million tons or more, and hundreds of smaller or even illegal steel makers in China. The output of the 66 large and medium-sized steel makers — the Steel Association's members — grew by 18.5% to 69.4 million tons from January to April in 2004, while local small-scale companies produced 11.8 million tons of steel during the same period, a year-on-year increase of 89.2%.[67] The government is taking a strong stand by restricting investment in small, low-level, and highly polluting steel producers. Table 5.24 shows that, in 2017, Hebei Province's crude steel output was 191.21 million tons, an increase of 257.13% over 2005, with an average annual growth rate of 8.20%; the national total crude steel output was 831.38 million tons, an increase of 243.47% over 2005, with an average annual growth rate of 7.70%. In 2017, there were two provinces (Hebei and Jiangsu) with a crude steel output more than 100 million tons, accounting for 35.54% of the national total.

According to Table 5.24, the standard deviation for chemical fiber, color television sets, micro-computers, yarn, air-conditioners for room, household washing machines, crude steel, household refrigerators, and plastics both in 2005 and 2008 is larger than the average output, which means many provinces produce quite low output. For example, output of chemical fiber was 10.54 million tons in Zhejiang, but only 400 tons in Ningxia in 2008; Shanghai produced 57.7 million sets of Micro-Computers, while Jilin produced a mere 100 sets; Hebei produced 115.9 million tons crude steel, Hainan only 0.037 million tons in 2008. In 2017, except for Household Washing Machines, the standard deviation of

---

[67]Gong, Z. (2004). Overcapacity causes concern, *China Daily*, June 9, p. 9.

Table 5.24. Selected industrial products output distributed among provinces in China, 2005 and 2017.

Year 2005	Unit	Number of provinces produced	Average output	Standard deviation	Largest output	Smallest output
Chemical Fiber	(10000 tons)	29	57.4	145.7	660.33 (Zhejiang)	0.23(Inner Mongolia)
Yam	(10000 tons)	29	50.0	89.3	371.77 (Shandong)	0.15 (Ningxia)
Cigarettes	(100 mil. pieces)	29	668.6	616.1	3157.36 (Yunnan)	11.5 (Ningxia)
Household Refrigerators	(10000 unit)	19	157.2	198.6	612.58 (Shangdong)	0.06 (Heilongjiang)
Air-conditioners for Room	(10000 unit)	14	483.2	697.4	2914.5 (Guangdong)	0.01 (Jilin)
Household Washing Machines	(10000 unit)	16	189.7	267.3	972.9 (Zhejiang)	0.01 (Jilin)
Color Television Sets	(10000 unit)	15	552.2	978.3	4089.6 (Guangdong)	50.8 (Jilin)
Crude Steel	(10000 tons)	30	1177.5	1456.0	7425 (Hebei)	0.23 (Hainan)
Chemical Fertilizer	(10000 tons)	30	172.6	157.8	612.7 (Shangdong)	3.14 (Shanghai)
Plastics	(10000 tons)	28	82.5	85.7	374.5 (Jiangsu)	0.54 (Chongqing)
Motor Vehicles	(10000 unit)	26	21.9	18.2	58.7 (Beijing)	0.01 (Shanxi)
Micro-Computers	(10000 unit)	19	425.5	846.8	2996.1 (Jiangsu)	0.03(Jilin)

Year 2017	Unit	Number of provinces produced	Average output	Standard deviation	Largest output	Smallest output
Chemical Fiber	(10000 tons)	26	187.6	483.5	2055.37 (Zhejiang)	0.15 (Ningxia)
Yam (2013)	(10000 tons)	29	124.5	208.4	841.47 (Shandong)	0.21 (Beijing)

Cigarettes	(10000 mil. pieces)	29	808.6	697.0	3589.36 (Yunnan)	80 (Ningxia)
Household Refrigerators	(10000 units)	14	610.6	878.2	3256.75 (Anhui)	53.49 (Tianjin)
Air-conditioners for Room	(10000 units)	15	1190.8	1483.1	5257.41 (Guangdong)	40.31 (Fujian)
Household Washing Machines	(10000 units)	12	625.1	383.2	2055.97 (Anhui)	25.76 (Tianjin)
Color Television Sets	(10000 units)	21	758.7	1713.7	7904. 01 (Guangdong)	3.86 (Shaanxi)
Crude Steel	(10000 tons)	29	2866.8	3880.0	19121.47 (Hebei)	0.53 (Hainan)
Chemical Fertilizer	(10000 tons)	29	203.2	202.4	717.09 (Shandong)	1.86 (Shanghai)
Plastics	(10000 tons)	30	281.9	290.0	1175.39 (Jiangsu)	8.82 (Guizhou)
Motor Vehicles	(10000 units)	28	103.6	102.4	318.21 (Guangdong)	0.27 (Guizhou)
Micro-Computers	(10000 units)	18	1704.4	2413.7	6981. 67 (Sichuan)	0.55 (Heilongjiang)
Mobile Telephones	(10000 set)	21	8999.2	17882.2	80076.3 (Guangdong)	117 (Anhui)
Integrated Circuits	(10000 pieces)	19	823463.2	1414811.7	5179100 (Jiangsu)	100 (Hubei)
Cars	(10000 units)	26	45.9	58.8	195.9 (Shanghai)	0.01 (Yunnan)
Natural Gas	(100000000 cu.m)	27	54.8	113.8	419.4 (Shaanxi)	0.04 (Yunnan)

the remaining eight industries was still higher than the average output. For example, the output of the largest Chemical Fiber producing province — Zhejiang — was 20.55 million tons, an increase of 311.26% over 2005, with an average annual growth rate of 9.90%; the lowest output province — Ningxia — produced only 150 tons, or 65.22% of the 2005 output, with an average annual growth rate of minus 3.5%. In 2017, the national output was 48.77 million tons, an increase of 292.95% over 2005, with an average annual growth rate of 9.90%; Zhejiang's output accounted for 42.14% of the national average. The largest Micro-Computers output province, Sichuan, produced 69.81 million units, an increase of 311.26 % over 2005, with an average annual growth rate of 9.40%; the lowest output province, Heilongjiang, produced 550 units in 2017. The national output was 434.47 million units, an increase of 537.38% over 2005, with an average annual growth rate of 15.04%. The largest Crude Steel output province, Hebei, produced 191.21 million tons, an increase of 257.53% over 2005, with an average annual growth rate of 8.20%; Hainan, the lowest output province, produced 530 tons. In 2017, the national output was 831.38 million tons, an increase of 243.47% over 2005, with an average annual growth rate of 7.70%. The provinces producing more than 100 million tons (Hebei and Jiangsu) had an output of 295.49 million tons, or 35.54% of the national output. It can be seen from Table 5.26 that, in 2005, 2008, and 2017, the distribution of industrial products output among provinces did not change much, and the eastern region was still stronger than the western, central, and northeastern regions (Figures 5.23 and 5.24).

After 2011, the China National Bureau of Statistics did not publish the industry average annual employment statistics as an independent item, so we were unable to calculate industrial productivity. Therefore, we compare the years 2011 and 2005 in Table 5.25. This table shows that, among the top five provinces with economic comprehensive performance recorded in 2005, there are four in the eastern region (Shandong, Shanghai, Jiangsu, and Guangdong) and the fifth is in the western region (Xinjiang). It can be seen from Table 5.25 that, in 2005, Ningxia, Guizhou, Gansu, and Chongqing (all in the western region) ranked at the bottom, and the second lowest is in the central region (Shanxi). Table 5.25 also shows that, among the top five provinces in terms of overall economic performance in 2011, the eastern region's Shanghai is first place, Inner Mongolia ranks second, with Hebei, Yunnan, and Hunan following.

As can be seen from Table 5.25, in 2011, Guizhou, Xinjiang, Ningxia, and Chongqing ranked in the bottom five; they are all in the western

Table 5.25.   Economic comprehensive performance of Industry for 31 provinces, 2005 and 2011.[*]

2005	Industrial value added	Industrial productivity	Energy consumption per unit of industrial value-added	Ranking	2011 industrial value added	2011 industrial productivity	2011 energy consum/unit of industrial value-added	2011 ranking
	Billion CNY	CNY/ person	Ton of SEC		Billion CNY	CNY/ person	Ton of SEC/10,000CNY	
China	7218.699	104680.1	2.479195		23187.58	252938.5	0.877244	
Beijing	167.736	143400.9	1.5	8	304.879	259869.6	0.459	6
Tianjin	183.63	150306.9	1.447581	6	543.084	363704.8	0.708	15
Hebei	316.794	108413.1	4.411793	17	1177.038	330600.8	1.3	3
Shanxi	175.67	82396.81	6.57488	29	595.996	280284	1.762	12
Inner Mongolia	124.043	148199.5	5.674223	21	710.16	574702.6	1.405	2
Liaoning	310.844	112400.7	3.1116	10	1069.654	289942	1.096	11
Jilin	116.939	114837.5	3.249947	15	491.795	352515.9	0.923	13
Heilongjiang	215.457	157440.3	2.340141	7	560.276	417400	1.042	14
Shanghai	412.172	158753.6	1.183906	2	720.859	267639	0.618	1
Jiangsu	811.899	115287.3	1.674349	3	2228.061	204061.1	0.6	16
Zhejiang	483.097	73294.24	1.488304	9	1468.303	204101.1	0.59	21

(*Continued*)

Table 5.25.　(*Continued*)

2005	Industrial value added	Industrial productivity	Energy consumption per unit of industrial value-added	Ranking	2011 industrial value added	2011 industrial productivity	2011 energy consum/unit of industrial value-added	2011 ranking
	Billion CNY	CNY/ person	Ton of SEC		Billion CNY	CNY/ person	Ton of SEC/10,000CNY	
Anhui	148.375	95596.29	3.134617	23	706.2	267419	0.754	27
Fujian	229.126	78897.42	1.45	12	767.509	190062.2	0.644	20
Jiangxi	88.23	78699.49	3.111826	25	541.186	266646.2	0.651	23
Shandong	937.527	126996.6	2.15	1	2127.589	247460.3	0.855	17
Henan	337.931	93147.83	4.019549	19	1394.932	254968.4	0.895	18
Hubei	200.721	106596.4	3.500759	16	853.804	305322.6	0.912	5
Hunan	162.979	96294.83	2.875932	18	812.275	280413.9	0.894	22
Guangdong	941.639	86735.04	1.075595	4	2464.96	169863.7	0.563	25
Guangxi	79.461	87118.74	3.185404	24	485.137	329778.4	0.8	10
Hainan	15.25	126033.1	3.646587	20	47.504	407759.7	0.692	7
Chongqing	65.94	71348.19	2.753918	26	469.046	321793.4	0.953	26
Sichuan	216.022	98644.69	3.521161	22	949.105	249449.4	0.997	8
Guizhou	58.585	86053.17	5.377046	28	182.92	216524.6	1.714	30
Yunnan	99.883	145115.5	3.550502	11	299.43	330423.7	1.162	4
Tibet	1.531	76934.67			4.818	295582.8		

Shaanxi	132.167	111092.7	2.621492	13	585.792	374523.4	0.846	28
Gansu	55.962	81553.48	4.993504	27	192.395	322756.2	1.402	19
Qinghai	18.91	134686.6	3.438358	14	81.173	448222	2.081	9
Ningxia	21.371	83545.74	9.027248	30	81.679	273082.6	2.279	24
Xinjiang	88.808	190167	3	5	270.02	441281.3	1.631	29

Note: *Calculated using data from China National Bureau of Statistics: China Statistical Yearbook, China Statistics Press, 2012, Tables 2.15, 7.15, 14.4; 2006, Tables 7.6, 14.6.

region. The fourth lowest is in the central region (Shanxi). In 2011, the western and central regions improved their economic performance significantly, especially Inner Mongolia. Inner Mongolia's "Big Data and Industry Deep Integration Action Plan," implemented the "Enterprise Dengyun (using cloud platform)" project to support the construction of grassland ecology, dairy breeding, coal, Chinese herbal medicine industry chain, supply chain finance, timber, forestry rights trading, etc. The Inner Mongolia Industrial Network collaborative manufacturing cloud platform is listed as a national Internet and industrial integration innovation pilot; Mengniu Dairy Digital Factory has achieved a productivity increase of 20%, its energy efficiency increased by 10%, and its operating costs decreased by 4.5%. It has spawned several emerging formats such as electronic consumption, sharing economy, and platform economy. The Inner Mongolia electronic port service platform was completed and put into operation. In 2018, retail sales of "Double 11" network in the autonomous region increased by 77.6% year-on-year. Hohhot was approved as a national cross-border e-commerce comprehensive experimental zone and signed the "China–Mongolia–Russia" Agreement with the China-ASEAN Environmental Cooperation Center. The Belt and Road "Strategic Cooperation Agreement for Eco-Environmental Big Data Service Platform" is building a data port for the Silk Road for China, Unicom, and Eurasia.[68]

Since 2009, the China National Bureau of Statistics has not published the value-added of industrial sector as an independent item, so it is impossible to calculate the energy consumption per unit value added of the sector. Therefore, in Table 5.26, the energy consumption per unit value added in the industrial sector cell is left blank. It can be seen from Table 5.26 that, from 2006–2015, energy saving performance improved significantly because the service industry is an energy-saving industry. Energy consumption per GDP saved 46.3% and the wholesale and retail trades, hotels, and catering services saved 87.3%. The energy consumption per unit of GDP has dropped significantly. In 1980, the energy consumption per unit of GDP was 13.14 tce (ton coal equivalent)/10,000 CNY. In 2016, it dropped to 0.59 tce/10,000 CNY, with an average annual decline of 8.26%. The role of industrial energy conservation is very prominent. In 2017, the added value of energy consumption of industrial units above

---

[68] Inner Mongolia National Big Data Comprehensive Experimental Zone Explores Innovation and Fruits, February 25, 2019 Source: People's Daily (in Chinese).

Table 5.26. Consumption of Energy by Industrial Sectors, 2006 and 2017 — Ton SCE/100,000CNY.*

Sector	2006	2017
Farming, forestry, animal husbandry, fishery, and water conservancy	1.5512	0.8169
Large and medium-sized industrial enterprises	8.7703	4.0825
Mining and washing of coal	13.8922	4.8063
Extraction of petroleum and natural gas	4.8640	5.5049
Mining and processing of ferrous metal ores	18.1730	7.6786
Mining and processing of non-ferrous metal ores	7.7407	3.8846
Mining and processing of non-metal ores	33.8223	16.1825
Manufacture of foods	5.1043	1. 5311
Manufacture of liquor, beverages, and refined tea	3.9975	1.3628
Manufacture of tobacco	0.8130	0.2426
Manufacture of textile	7.8456	3.8703
Manufacture of textile fabrics, wearing apparel, and accessories	2.4412	0.7691
Manufacture of leather, fur, feather, and related products and footwear	1.8534	0.6979
Processing of timber, manufacture of wood, bamboo, rattan palm, and straw products	12.9031	2.7767
Manufacture of furniture	1.6641	0.8312
Manufacture of paper and paper products	14.286	5.4640
Printing, reproduction of recording media	4.6097	1.7046
Manufacture of articles for culture, education, art, sport, and entertainment activities	2.4441	0.5663
Processing of petroleum and coking	9.2865	6.7371
Manufacture of raw chemical materials and chemical products	22.5170	10.8515
Manufacture of medicines	4.1681	1.2282
Manufacture of chemical fibers	5.9604	3.8181
Manufacture of rubber products	7.0984	
Manufacture of plastics products	6.9436	
Manufacture of non-metallic mineral products	47.7063	15.3686
Smelting and pressing of ferrous metals	208304	11.6583
Smelting and pressing of non-ferrous metals	11.0862	5.9271
Manufacture of metal products	7.5654	3.4048

(*Continued*)

Table 5.26. (*Continued*)

Sector	2006	2017
Manufacture of general purpose machinery	3.4067	1.6365
Manufacture of special purpose machinery	3.2080	0.9378
Manufacture of automobiles	1.3864	0.4885
Manufacture of railway, vessels, aerospace, and other transport equipment	0.0000	0.7984
Manufacture of electrical machinery and equipment	1.2001	0.5456
Manufacture of communication equipment, computers, and other electronic equipment	0.5979	0.3978
Manufacture of measuring instruments and machinery	0.9914	0.515
Other manufacture	13.3301	13.4323
Recycling and disposal of waste	7.8527	1.5755
Repair of metal products, machine, and equipment	0.0000	0.9532
Production and supply of electric power and heat power	9.3273	6.1729
Production and supply of gas	15.7666	3.6059
Production and supply of water	20.6621	11.8132

Notes: *Calculated using data from China National Bureau of Statistics: Data base; Annual, Total Energy Consumption (10000 tons of SCE), 2000–2015; Annual, Gross Domestic Product (100 million yuan), 2000–2019; Data base; Annual, Revenue from Principal Business of Large and Medium-sized Industrial Enterprises, 2003–2017; Database; Annual, Gross Output Value of Agriculture, Forestry, Animal Husbandry and Fishery, 2000–2018.

designated size decreased by 27.6% compared with 2012. According to the energy consumption per unit of industrial value added, the operation of the above-scale industries has accumulated about 920 million tons of standard coal, accounting for nearly 90% of the total energy consumption of the whole country. The reduction of energy consumption per unit of GDP is mainly attributed to industry practices.[69]

---

[69]Calculated using data from China National Bureau of Statistics: China Statistical Yearbook, China Statistics Press, 2018, Table 9.16; Department of Energy, China National Bureau of Statistics: Great achievements have been made in energy development and remarkable results have been achieved in energy conservation and consumption reduction, 2018-09-11, (in Chinese).

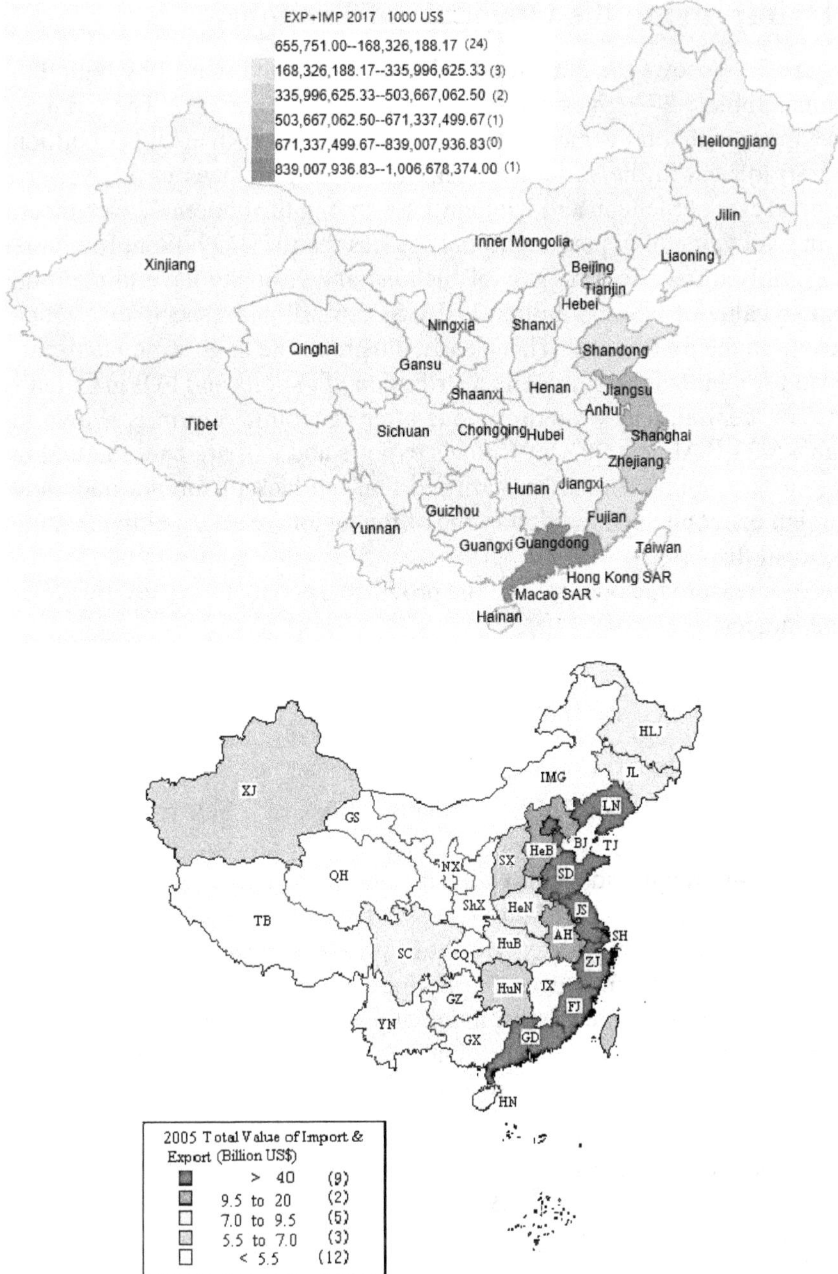

Figure 5.23.   Total value of export and import by region in China, 2005 and 2017.

11. Improving the Openness of Economy

Figure 5.27 shows the 2005 total value of export and import by region in China. Table 5.27[70] gives details of the map in Figure 5.27. The top nine provinces with total value of export and import larger than USD30 billion are all located in the eastern region. Ten of 12 provinces in the western region (except Sichuan and Xinjiang) are among the bottom 12 provinces, with total value of export and import of less than USD5 billion. In Figure 5.28, only the western regions of Sichuan and Xinjiang have import and export value of USD6.9 billion and USD5.6 billion, respectively, which belong to the fourth level. This clearly illustrates the large regional disparity in foreign trade activity. The distribution of exports and FDI in China's eastern, central, and western regions after economic reform is shown in Table 5.24.[71] Almost 90% of China's exports and FDI are concentrated in the eastern region. It can be surmised that the lack of foreign trade and foreign economic cooperation is one of the major causes resulting in large regional disparity.

To measure the openness of the province's economy, we use two relative indices.

$$FT_R = \frac{FT_{i,t}}{GRP_{i,t}} \; ; FDI_R = \frac{FDI_{i,t}}{INV_{i,t}} \tag{5.11}$$

where FT_R, FDI_R –Foreign trade relative index and FDI relative index, respectively.

$FT_{i,t}$ –Foreign trade total value of i province, year t.

$GRP_{i,t}$ –GRP value of i province, year t;

$FDI_{i,t}$ –Total FDI utilized value of i province at year t;

$INV_{i,t}$ –Investment value of i province at year t.

Using foreign trade relative index of provinces as X axis and FDI relative index as Y-axis with the original setting on China's national foreign trade relative index and FDI relative index in years 2005 and 2017. In

---

[70]Calculated using data from China National Bureau of Statistics: China Statistical Yearbook, China Statistics Press, 2005, Table 18.10.

[71]Calculated using data from China National Bureau of Statistics: China Statistical Yearbook, China Statistics Press, 2006, Tables 18.11, 18.19; 2005, Tables 18.10, 18.16, 2004, Tables 18.10, 18.16; 2003, Tables 17.10, 17.16; 2002, Tables 17.10, 17.16; 2001, Tables 17.10, 17.16; and 1979–2000 China Statistical Yearbook.

Table 5.27. 2005 total value of export and import by location of China's foreign trade managing units (billion USD).

2005	Bil. USD				
Guangdong	427.96	Anhui	9.12	Guangxi	5.18
Jiangsu	227.92	Hubei	9.05	Inner Mongolia	4.88
Shanghai	186.34	Xinjiang	7.94	Yunnan	4.74
Beijing	125.51	Sichuan	7.90	Shaanxi	4.58
Zhejiang	107.39	Henan	7.72	Chongqing	4.29
Shandong	76.74			Jiangxi	4.06
Fujian	54.41	Jilin	6.53	Gansu	2.63
Tianjin	53.28	Hunan	6.00	Hainan	2.54
Liaoning	41.01	Shanxi	5.55	Guizhou	1.40
				Ningxia	0.97
Hebei	16.07			Qinghai	0.41
Heilongjiang	9.57			Tibet	0.21
2017	**Bil. USD**				
Guangdong	1006.68	Tianjin	112.92	Yunnan	23.45
		Liaoning	99.60	Xinjiang	20.57
Jiangsu	590.78	Henan	77.63	Heilongjiang	18.95
		Sichuan	68.11	Jilin	18.54
Shanghai	476.20	Chongqing	66.60	Shanxi	17.19
Zhejiang	377.91	Guangxi	57.88	Inner Mongolia	13.87
		Anhui	54.02	Hainan	10.37
Beijing	324.02	Hebei	49.86	Guizhou	8.16
Shandong	264.55	Hubei	46.34	Ningxia	5.04
Fujian	171.02	Jiangxi	44.34	Gansu	4.83
		Shaanxi	40.20	Tibet	0.86
		Hunan	36.03	Qinghai	0.66

2005, both FT_{it} and FDI_{it} higher than the national FT_R and FDI_R in eight provinces including Guangdong, Jiangsu, Shanghai, Beijing, Fujian, Tianjin, and Liaoning. In 2017, except for Liaoning and Fujian provinces, the other five provinces and Zhejiang have larger FT_{it} and FDI_{it+} than the national FT_R and FDI_R. All these provinces are in the eastern region. In 22 provinces, FT_{it} and FDI_{it} are lower than the national FT_R and FDI_R. They included in the western region all 12 provinces and in the middle region all six provinces. Of the remaining four provinces, two are in the

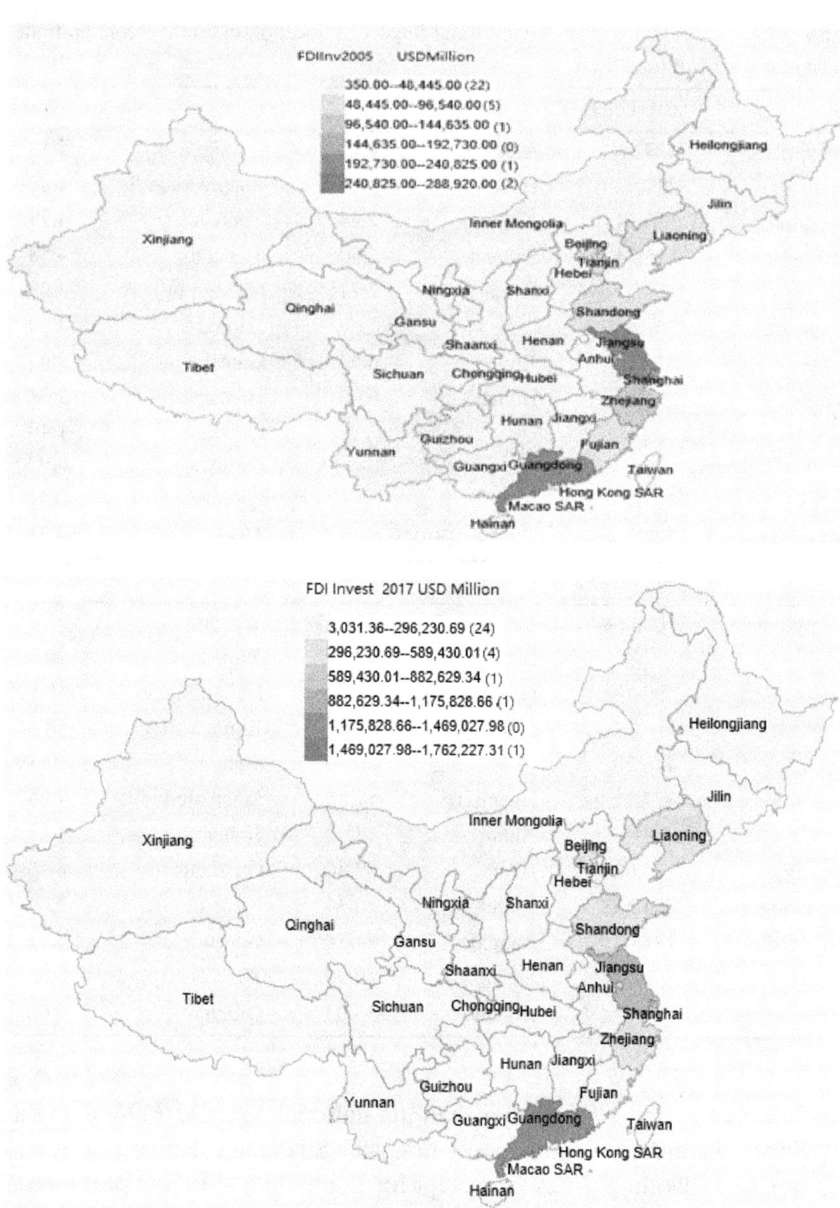

Figure 5.24.   Total investment of FFE (USD million), 2005 and 2017.

northeastern and two in the eastern region. This shows the gap in the province's economic openness is very large.

It can be seen from Tables 5.27 and 5.28 that, from 2005–2017, foreign trade and total foreign direct utilized investment increased significantly, but

Table 5.28. Total Investment of FFEs (USD million), 2005 and 2017.

2005	Mil. USD				
Guangdong	288,920	Hubei	25,780	Heilongjiang	10,980
Jiangsu	265,720	Hebei	21,930	Hainan	9,200
		Jilin	20,710	Yunnan	8,420
Shanghai	200,670	Henan	20,640	Chongqing	8,030
		Jiangxi	18,490	Shanxi	7,710
Zhejiang	101,910	Sichuan	16,600	Ningxia	4, 455
		Hunan	15,820	Gansu	3,160
Liaoning	81,500	Anhui	15,480	Guizhou	2,340
Shandong	78,620	Guangxi	14,710	Xinjiang	1,850
Fujian	75,330	Shaanxi	13,700	Qinghai	700
Beijing	60,670	Inner Mongolia	12,640	Tibet	350
Tianjin	56,770				
2017	Mil. USD				
Guangdong	1,762,227	Fujian	260,721	Guangxi	56,200
		Tianjin	254,823	Shanxi	49,724
Jiangsu	965,819	Hunan	163,392	Inner Mongolia	45,979
		Hubei	115,103	Jilin	38,874
Shanghai	798,239	Sichuan	112,797	Yunnan	37,382
		Henan	104,538	Heilongjiang	33,669
Beijing	486, 409	Hebei	95,818	Guizhou	31,251
Zhejiang	373,415	Chongqing	94,558	Ningxia	30,420
Liaoning	315,850	Anhui	86,641	Gansu	20,197
Shandong	304,218	Jiangxi	80,797	Xinjiang	13,323
		Shaanxi	80,039	Qinghai	7,699
		Hainan	76,089	Tibet	3,031

China's foreign trade relative index and total foreign direct utilized investment relative index, respectively, declined from 58% to 33% and from 138% to 73%. Between 2005 and 2017, then, the growth rate of GRP and domestic fixed assets investment is higher than the growth rate of foreign trade and total foreign direct utilized investment. China's foreign trade relative index significantly declined, signifying that the contribution of domestic demand continues to increase, and consumption is increasingly becoming the main driving force for economic growth. In 2017, the final consumption rate was 53.6%, an increase of 5.1% points over 2010; the capital formation rate was 44.4%, a decrease of 3.5% points. Foreign-invested enterprises have played an important role in expanding imports and exports and increasing fiscal revenue. In 2017, the import and export volume of foreign-invested enterprises was CNY12.4 trillion (USD1.84 trillion), accounting for 44.8% of the total import and export of China's goods, and the tax revenue was CNY2.9 trillion (USD0.43 trillion), accounting for 18.7% of the national tax revenue.

Guangdong, Jiangsu, and Shanghai had the best foreign trade relative index and FDI relative index in 2005 and 2017, indicative of the openness of the economies of these three provinces. Guangdong is located in the Pearl River Delta (PRD); Shanghai and Jiangsu are located in the Yangtze River Delta (YRD). Indeed, in the early stage of the reform, the openness of the PRD economy was the highest in the country, with the YRD becoming the most open economy in the 2000s. Beijing and Tianjin are in the Annulus Bohai Sea Rim. Thus, Pearl River Delta, YRD, and Annulus Bohai Sea Rim are the most open economies and the most developed regions in China.

In 2005, both FT_{it} and FDI_{it} were lower than the national FT_R and FDI_R in 22 provinces including Henan, Sichuan, Chongqing, Guangxi, Anhui, Hebei, Hubei, Jiangxi, Shaanxi, Hunan, Yunnan, Xinjiang, Heilongjiang, Jilin, Shanxi, Inner Mongolia, Hainan, Guizhou, Ningxia, Gansu, Tibet, and Qinghai. Among these 22 provinces, 12 are in the western region, eight in the central region, and two in the eastern region, revealing a large openness gap among the provinces. The remaining province, Liaoning, had larger than the national FT_R and FDI_{it} in 2005 and was lower than the national FT_R and FDI_R in 2017. In 2017, there were still 22 provinces with both FT_{it} and FDI_{it} lower than the national FT_R and FDI_R; however, Liaoning was downgraded to this group and Hainan upgraded out of this group. The regional distribution of these 22 provinces remained the same, again verifying that provinces in the western region

Table 5.29. The foreign trade relative index and *FDI* relative index of 31 provinces, 2005 and 2017.[*]

Region	FT_R	FDI_R	FT_R	FDI_R
	2005	2005	2017	2017
National	0.58	1.38	0.33	0.73
Beijing	1.48	1.76	0.78	3.93
Tianjin	1.12	3.11	0.41	1.52
Hebei	0.13	0.43	0.10	0.19
Shanxi	0.11	0.35	0.07	0.56
Inner Mongolia	0.10	0.39	0.06	0.22
Liaoning	0.42	1.59	0.29	3.20
Jilin	0.15	0.97	0.08	0.20
Heilongjiang	0.14	0.52	0.05	0.20
Shanghai	1.65	4.68	1.05	7.44
Jiangsu	1.00	2.67	0.46	1.22
Zhejiang	0.66	1.28	0.49	0.80
Anhui	0.14	0.50	0.14	0.20
Fujian	0.68	2.66	0.36	0.67
Jiangxi	0.08	0.70	0.15	0.25
Shandong	0.34	0.69	0.25	0.37
Henan	0.06	0.39	0.12	0.16
Hubei	0.11	0.79	0.09	0.24
Hunan	0.07	0.49	0.07	0.35
Guangdong	1.55	3.39	0.76	3.15
Guangxi	0.11	0.73	0.21	0.19
Hainan	0.23	2.05	0.16	1.21
Chongqing	0.10	0.34	0.23	0.36
Sichuan	0.09	0.38	0.12	0.24
Guizhou	0.06	0.19	0.04	0.14
Yunnan	0.11	0.39	0.10	0.13
Tibet	0.07	0.16	0.04	0.10
Shaanxi	0.10	0.60	0.12	0.23
Gansu	0.11	0.30	0.04	0.23
Qinghai	0.06	0.17	0.02	0.13

(Continued)

Table 5.29.   (*Continued*)

	FT_R	FDI_R	FT_R	FDI_R
Ningxia	0.13	0.82	0.10	0.55
Xinjiang	0.25	0.11	0.13	0.07

Notes: *Calculated using data from China National Bureau of Statistics: Database; Annual by Province, Total Value of Imports and Exports of operating units (USD), 2000–2018; Data base: Annual by Province, Gross Regional Product (100 million yuan), 2000–2018; Data base; Annual, by Province, Total Investment of FFEs (USD million), 1998–2017; Data base; by Province, Total Investment in Fixed Assets in the Whole Country, 1999–2017.

have the least open economies and that the inter-provincial economic gap remained large. The coefficient of variation (= standard deviation ÷ mean) reflects the degree of data dispersion. The greater the degree of dispersion, the larger the coefficient of variation. The coefficient of variation for FT_{it} decreased from 1.30 to 1.08 between 2005 and 2017, but the coefficient of variation for FDI_{it} increased from 1.04 to 1.70, indicating that the gap in foreign trade between provinces has narrowed, but the gap of total foreign direct utilized investment has widened.

In 2005, both FT_{it} and FDI_{it} were lower than the national FT_R and FDI_R in 22 provinces including Henan, Sichuan, Chongqing, Guangxi, Anhui, Hebei, Hubei, Jiangxi, Shaanxi, Hunan, Yunnan, Xinjiang, Heilongjiang, Jilin, Shanxi, Inner Mongolia, Hainan, Guizhou, Ningxia, Gansu, Tibet, and Qinghai. Among these 22 provinces, 12 are in the western region, eight in the central region, and two in the eastern region, revealing a large openness gap among the provinces. The remaining province, Liaoning, had larger than the national FT_R and FDI_{it} in 2005 and was lower than the national FT_R and FDI_R in 2017. In 2017, there were still 22 provinces with both FT_{it} and FDI_{it} lower than the national FT_R and FDI_R; however, Liaoning was downgraded to this group and Hainan upgraded out of this group. The regional distribution of these 22 provinces remained the same, again verifying that provinces in the western region have the least open economies and that the inter-provincial economic gap remained large. The coefficient of variation (= standard deviation ÷ mean) reflects the degree of data dispersion. The greater the degree of dispersion, the larger the coefficient of variation. The coefficient of variation for FT_{it} decreased from 1.30 to 1.08 between 2005 and 2017, but the coefficient of variation for FDI_{it} increased from 1.04 to 1.70, indicating that the gap in foreign trade between provinces has narrowed, but the gap of total foreign direct utilized investment has widened.

In the coastal region, the PRD has been the leader in China's opening to outside world. The PRD's role in China's economy is pivotal. Home to only 0.43% area of land and 3.4% of China's population, it contributed almost 10.2% of national GDP in 2007.[72] PRD has been a key destination for foreign investment and a platform for the country's growing integration into the global economy. As other parts of China became more competitive during the 1990s — particularly the YRD region — the PRD's attractiveness to foreign investors began to wane. On June 3, 2004, top officials from 11 administrative regions and provinces in southern China signed the framework agreement that established closer economic cooperation in the region.[73] The Pan-Pearl River Delta (PPRD) region comprises East China's Fujian and Jiangxi provinces; Central China's Hunan Province; South China's Guangdong and Hainan provinces, the Guangxi Zhuang Autonomous Region; Southwest China's Sichuan, Guizhou, and Yunnan provinces; and the Hong Kong and Macao Special Administrative Regions (SARs). The nine provinces account for about one-fifth of the Mainland's total land area. They also have one-third of the nation's population, and one-third of the country's GDP. The PPRD group, also known as "9+2," has unique potential because it is geographically linked to the members of the Association of Southeast Asian Nations (ASEAN). ASEAN established a free trade zone with China in 2004 (which was revised in 2006 and 2010). In 2015, Fujian province established an economic zone on the west coast of the Taiwan Straits as a major effort to boost its economic growth. The economic zone is also meant to help speed up economic integration with Taiwan, opposite to Fujian across the Straits. Fujian already cooperates with Taiwan.[74]

Economic integration is conducive to reducing any waste of land and natural resources and to increasing local competitiveness in the global market. The YRD covers Shanghai and 15 neighboring cities in northern Zhejiang and southern Jiangsu provinces. In 2007, about 7.4% of the national population lived in the YRD region — accounting for only 1.15% of China's total land area, generating 18.8% of the country's GDP, and with

---

[72]Department of Comprehensive Statistics of National Bureau of Statistics: China Statistical Yearbook for Regional Economy 2008, China Statistics Press.

[73]Li, W. (2004). PPRD in tune with national plan, *China Daily, China Business Weekly*, June 15, p. 17.

[74]Xing, Z. (2004). Economic zone to boost Fujian development, *China Daily*, June 8.

its export volume accounting for over 35.8% of China's total.[75] Within the 11th FYP (2006–2010), the National Development and Reform Commission helped with the coordination among local authorities and the upgrading of the existing partnerships in the Yangtze Delta area to a new level of regional integration that covers industry, urban construction, market unification, and environmental protection.[76] With respect to port construction and the vehicle manufacturing industry, cut-throat competition among cities in attracting investment and formulating preferential policies can only waste regional resources, both natural and human. Closer cooperation on economic integration and the full utilization of their resources is expected to ensure a win–win situation for the entire YRD region.[77]

The Annulus Bohai Sea Rim covers the Beijing and Tianjin municipalities and parts of Liaoning, Hebei, and Shandong provinces. Loose economic links have been cited as a key hindrance, but a consensus was reached recently to embark on coordinated development. The members of the Rim have pledged coordinated steps in infrastructure construction, industrial structuring, resource exploration, and environmental protection.[78] In 2003, the overall economic aggregate of the Bohai Rim region was only 45.3% of that of the Yangtze River Delta region and 90% of that of the Pearl River Delta region.[79] Although competition is becoming fiercer in the PPRD and YRD in the nation's south, more investors are casting their eyes on the third base in the north, the home of enormous potential. The central region government is now attaching greater importance to fueling the development of North China's Bohai Sea Rim, hoping it will become the third economic engine on the Mainland, along with the two Deltas.

Covering the provinces of Heilongjiang, Jilin, and Liaoning, the northeast region has, in the past, played a major role in the industrial development of China. However, the provinces now suffer from aging equipment and technology, weakening competitiveness, high unemployment rate, and slow economic growth. The proportion of the value of the region's industrial output to the value of the national total dropped to 7%

---

[75] Department of Comprehensive Statistics of National Bureau of Statistics (2008). China Statistical Yearbook for Regional Economy 2008, China Statistics Press.

[76] Da, Y. (2003). Yangtze partnerships outlined, *China Daily*, November 11.

[77] Hu, Q., and S. Sun (2003). Yangtze Delta cities urged to unite, *China Daily*, March 13.

[78] Hua, H. (2004). Integration to propel capital belt's economy, *China Daily*, March 03, p. 6.

[79] Xinhua (2006). China to build new economic powerhouse in Tianjin, March 14.

in 2003[80] from 16% in 1981,[81] and partially recovered (10%) by 2007.[82] China considers the revival of the northeast industrial base as the third most important long-term strategy after the opening-up in the southeast 20 years ago and the western development policy 5 years ago. Northeast China has abundant natural resources (oil, coal, steel, wood, water, and many other crucial resources), integrated heavy industries, solid infra-structure, and a strong pool of human resources. Table 5.30[83] reveals that per capita GDP in three northeast provinces is higher than the national average, but it is much lower than that of the YRD and PRD. The per capita disposable income of urban households was even lower than the national average in 2004 (CNY7,775 per capita, with the national average being CNY9,422 per capita)[84] and slightly higher than the national aver-age in 2007.

---

[80]Calculated using data from China National Bureau of Statistics (2004). China Statistical Yearbook, China Statistics Press, 2004, Table 14.2.

[81]China State Statistical Bureau (1982). Statistical yearbook of China 1981. Economic Information & Agency, Hong Kong, 1982, p. 214.

[82]Calculated using data from China National Bureau of Statistics (2008). China Statistical Yearbook, China Statistics Press, 2008, Table 1.6.

[83]Calculated using data from China National Bureau of Statistics. China Statistical Yearbook for Regional Economy, 2018, China Statistics Press, Table 25.16; 2008, Tables 1.6, 9.4, 17.14; Department of Comprehensive Statistics of National Bureau of Statistics: China Statistical Yearbook for Regional Economy 2008; China Statistics Press; China Committee, U.S. Council for International Business & OECD Washington Center, Briefing on the OECD 2006 Investment Policy Review of China, June 16, 2006; Guangdong Provincial Bureau of Statistics, Guangdong Investigation Team of National Statistical Bureau: Guangdong Statistical Yearbook 2018, Published by China Statistics Press and Beijing Info Press, Tables 20.1, 21.2, 21.3; Jiangsu Provincial Bureau of Statistics, Jiangsu Investigation Team of National Statistical Bureau: Jiangsu Statistical Yearbook, Published by China Statistics Press and Beijing Info Press, 2018, Table 19.3; Hebei Provincial Bureau of Statistics: Hebei Economic Yearbook, Published by China Statistics Press, 2017, Basic conditions of Jing-Jin-Ji Region (2016); China National Bureau of Statistics, Data base; Annual, Gross Regional Product (100 million yuan), Employed Persons(10,000 persons), Unemployment Rate in Urban Area(%) , Indices of Gross National Income (1978=100), Per Capita Disposable Income of Urban Households (yuan) 1998–2017; Value of Foreign Investment Actually Utilized (USD10,000), 1998–2017; Local Governments General Budgetary Expenditure (100 million yuan) 1998–2017.

[84]Department of Comprehensive Statistics of National Bureau of Statistics: China Statistical Yearbook for Regional Economy 2005.

Table 5.30.   Comparing the northeast area with Pearl and Yangtze River Deltas, 2007 and 2017.

Item	National total 2007	3North-eastern Provinces	Yangtze River delta*	Pearl River delta**	National total 2017	Beijing Tianjin Hebei region	Yangt River delta*	Pearl River delta**
Area of land (10000 sq.km)	960	78.79	10.96	4.17	960	21.6	21.9	5.48
Population at the year-end (10 0000 persons)	129988	10743	8212	2451	139008	11247	16104	5998
Employment at the year-end (10 000 persons)_	75200	4691	4954	2173	77640	6347	6571	3927
Registered unemployment rate in urban area (%)	4.2	5.3	4	2.5	3.9	3.1	2.9	2.47
Gross domestic product (100 million CNY)	136876	15134	28775	13394	827122	80580	167803	69070
Primary industry	20768	1919	1325	506	65468	3419	6193	1154
Secondary industry	72387	7814	16073	7206	334623	28767	70378	29693
Industry	62815	6789	14329	6570	279997		62018	35292
Tertiary industry	43721	5402	11377	5681	427032	48395	91232	38224
Average annual GDP growth (1990–2004), (2007, 2017) (%)	9.7	9.3	14.0	17	7.42			
Per capita gross domestic product (CHY)	10561	14091	35040	46301	59,201	71646	126. 634	116351

Per capita disposable Income of urban households (CNY)	9422	7775	13431	17290	36,396	33616	52962	43967
Total investment in fixed assets (100 million CNY)	70477	5580	13651	4487	641238	53066	91367	22321
Real estate development (100 million CNY)	13158	1075	2931	1275	109799	10750	21712	8601
Total retail sales of consumer goods (100 million)	53950	5451	8259	4499	366262	33213	67876	25049
Local government revenue (100 million CNY)	11693	985	2489	932	91469	10750	20617	6924
Local government expenditure (100 million CNY)	20593	2137	2930	1210	173228	16746	31903	9285
Total value of imports and exports (100 Million CNY)	11546	480	4014	3418	278101	32968	14451	9102
Exports	5933	243	2083	1822	153311	9045	8439	5651

(Continued)

Table 5.30.   (*Continued*)

Item	National total 2007	3North-eastern Provinces	Yangtze River delta*	Pearl River delta**	National total 2017	Beijing Tianjin Hebei region	Yangt River delta*	Pearl River delta**
Imports	5612	237	1931	1596	124790	23923	6013	3451
Actually utilized FDI (100 million USD)	606.3	59.4	209.9	100.1	1310.35	312.8	600.5	225.9
Per capita savings deposits of residents (CNY)	9197	11207	22810	51734	34909	63476	94412	68309

Notes: *The PRD is officially defined as: Guangzhou, Shenzhen, Zhuhai, Foshan, Jiangmen, Dongguan, Zhongshan and parts of Huizhou and Zhaoqing
**The PRD is officially defined as: Shanghai, Nanjing, Zhenjiang, Yangzhou, Suzhou, Wuxi, Changzhou, Nantong,Taizhou, Hangzhou, Jiaxing, Huizhou, Ningbo, Shaoxing, Zhoushan and Taizhou.

From Table 5.29, we can see that compared with the Pearl River Delta and the Yangtze River Delta, the three northeastern provinces have more land, population and employment, but less GDP output in 2007, the Pearl and Yangtze River Deltas. Exports and actually utilized FDI in the northeast were far below that of the Pearl and Yangtze River Deltas. The per capita GDP, per capita disposable income, per capita retail sales of consumer goods, and per capita saving deposits were much lower than those of the Deltas (see Table 5.29). Therefore, there is a large gap between the three northeast provinces and the Pearl and Yangtze River Deltas, especial in terms of opening to the outside world and people's living standards. Therefore, revival of the northeast industrial base is a most pressing need. The unparalleled industrial infrastructure would help investors save on initial development costs and offer quick returns. Educated, well-trained industrial workforce and excellent transport infrastructure in the northeast will provide the foundation for developing industry. Premier Wen said in 2004 that China aims to build the northeast region into a national and even a world-class industrial base for equipment manufacturing and important raw materials. In 2004, northeast China's Liaoning province set up the Northeast Revitalization Bank (NRB), based on a city commercial bank — Shenyang City Commercial Bank (SCB). This new bank works as a regional joint-stock commercial bank covering the provinces of Liaoning, Jilin, and Heilongjiang in northeastern China. SCB provides financial support for the revitalization of northeastern China's old heavy industrial hub, helps local small- and medium-sized enterprises with financing, and prompts the renovation and upgrading of regional financial resources.[85] Liaoning province aims to turn Dalian into northeast Asia's shipping and logistics center.[86] "Dalian is becoming a center for software development and Japanese-language "back office" work, such as insurance processing, software development and call centers" said Japanese CEO Ohmae.[87] Northeast China is in a position to cooperate with Japan, the Republic of Korea, and Russia. In 2019, China and Russia established a 10-square-kilometre quasi-free trade zone along their borders, with an estimated investment of USD1 billion. The free trade zone is in Suifenhe, a border city in northeast China's Heilongjiang province and Pogranichny, in Russia's far east region. The zone offers a platform for commodity

---

[85] Wu, Y. (2004). New bank set to revitalize Northeast China, *China Daily*, May 31.

[86] Jiao, X. (2003). Revitalize Northeast China, *China Daily*, November 06.

[87] Ohmae, K. (2002). Profits and Perils in China, Inc, *Strategy + Business*, First Quarter.

trading, tourism and entertainment sectors, service trade, storage sector, processing trades, transit trades, and a high-tech park. With China and Russia sharing a border of more than 4,000 km, border activity in 2003 accounted for 22.3% of overall trade volume, reaching CNY29 billion (USD3.52 billion).[88]

Chinese border provinces (Heilongjiang, Jilin, Inner Mongolia, Xinjiang, Gansu, Tibet, Yunnan, and Guangxi) exhibit significant comparative advantages in technology and productivity relative to the inland provinces, but the neighboring countries are less developed and have smaller markets than the economies of east and southern east Asia, which provide both trade outlets and sources of capital for the coastal provinces. Russia and nations (former-Soviet republics on China's western border) bordering China are strengthening their economic relationships with China. In the next few years, not only will such barter trade along China's borders grow considerably, but it could also evolve into joint ventures. Such changes in the external environment will surely contribute to the development of western regional economies in China.

Inland regions (13 provinces) suffer from lack of natural trade and investment partners. In 1992, the central government decided to apply preferential policies to 10 major cities and establish six development zones along the Yangtze River valley. The government also gave permission to all provincial capitals and 13 border cities to adopt similar policy of opening up. Most incentives offered in SEZs and Pudong are to be applied in newly opened cities of inland provinces. This will allow the market force to determine resource allocation and identify comparative advantages, while removing inter-provincial barriers to promote integration among the regions.

Development of the market economy as well as the availability of a strong infrastructure are needed to promote regional cooperation. After 1978, local markets have developed spontaneously as a result of the liberalization in the agricultural and industrial sectors. Development of national and regional markets had been hampered by the inadequate legal and regulatory framework, poor economic infrastructure, particularly transportation, telecommunications, the payments system, and protectionist attitudes of local authorities. In 2001, China's State Council issued an announcement about the prohibition of local barriers to the market.

---

[88] Jiang, J. (2004). Quasi-free trade zone being built along border, *China Daily, China Business Weekly*, June 15, p. 1.

Former Vice-Premier Li Lanqing criticized some local officials for lack of understanding and for protectionism, which hampered efforts in some areas.[89] The Ministry of Commerce made a survey of local market protectionism in 22 provinces in June 2004, showing that local market protectionism for products or services exists in 20 provinces. Nine provinces had erected barriers to protect the local wine market from outside competition, six to protect autos and cigarettes, and five to protect meat and meat products.[90] Local authorities protect these industrial sectors because they have a huge stake in fostering a number of local enterprises that represent their tax base and sources of financial revenue. However, history has shown that local protectionism backfires as enterprises grow. Segmented domestic markets mean competitive local enterprises can hardly grow because of restricted access to other markets. As a result, the dominance of less-competitive enterprises lowers economic efficiency. The central government wants to see local governments abolish their policies and regulations restricting sales of products and services produced elsewhere. According to a Memorandum of Cooperation signed on April 10, 2003, in Hangzhou, capital of Zhejiang Province, provincial governments in the YRD will curb regional protectionism and facilitate cooperation in investment, trade, and business. Integration of information resources in the YRD region and integration of regulation on market workings will benefit the eventual regional common market.[91]

From 2007–2017, the situation has changed greatly. The YRD, the PRD, and the Beijing–Tianjin–Hebei, three metropolitan economic circles, have become the "three major engines" leading China's regional economic development. In 2017, the regional GDP of the YRD, the PRD, and the Beijing–Tianjin–Hebei region accounted for 19.3%, 8.9%, and 9.7% of the national total, respectively, totaling 37.8% of the country. The three regions have played a leading role in the development of China's regional economies. Therefore, in 2017, the northeastern region was replaced by the Beijing–Tianjin–Hebei metropolitan economic circle. As

---

[89]China to Further Regulate Market Order, http://english.peopledaily.com.cn/200206/25/eng20020625_98476.shtml.

[90]Ministry of Commerce: Blockade the market in 20 provinces, local protectionism still severe (in Chinese), June 24, 2004, www.cfi.com.cn/(ydzhfz55eirw1v454abkfp3i)/newspage.aspx?id=20040624000841.

[91]Three Provinces Move to Curb Protectionism, http://english.peopledaily.com.cn/200304/11/eng20030411_114956.shtml.

can be seen from Table 5.29, the 2017 indicators increased significantly compared with 2007, indicating that these three regions dominate the development of regional comparative advantages and regional development.

The Yangtze River Economic Belt covers nine provinces and two municipalities of Shanghai, Jiangsu, Zhejiang, Anhui, Jiangxi, Hubei, Hunan, Chongqing, Sichuan, Yunnan, Guizhou, with an area of about 2.05 million square kilometers, accounting for 21% of the country, and with population and economic aggregates over the country's 40%. Promoting the development of the Yangtze River Economic Belt was a major decision made by the Party Central Committee and a major strategy that affects the overall development of the country.

The Guangdong–Hong Kong–Macao Greater Bay Area (Greater Bay Area) consists of the Hong Kong Special Administrative Region (HKSAR), the Macao Special Administrative Region (Macao SAR) as well as the nine PRD municipalities, covering a total area of 56,000 square kilometers with a combined population of approximately 70 million at the end of 2017. In 2017, the GDP of the Greater Bay Area stood at around CNY10 trillion (USD1.48 trillion). The Greater Bay Area's participation in international cooperation and competition has reached a higher level. The development of the Greater Bay Area and of a world-class city cluster will facilitate the implementation of "one country, two systems." It will foster closer cooperation between the Mainland and the two SARs, thereby creating more opportunities for the socio-economic development of the two SARs, for Hong Kong and Macao residents wishing to develop careers in the Mainland, and for maintaining the long-term prosperity and stability of Hong Kong and Macao. It will facilitate the implementation of the new vision of development.

In the collaborative planning of the Beijing–Tianjin–Hebei region, Beijing will be positioned as "National Political Center, Cultural Center, International Exchange Center, and Science and Technology Innovation Center." Tianjin will become the "National Advanced Manufacturing R&D Base, Northern International Shipping Core Area, Financial Innovation Operation Demonstration Zone, and Reform and Opening Leading Zone." Hebei Province will contribute as a "national modern commercial and trade logistics base, industrial transformation and upgrading pilot zone, new urbanization and urban–rural integration demonstration zone, Beijing–Tianjin–Hebei ecological environment support zone." The overall orientation of the Beijing–Tianjin–Hebei region and the functional orientation of the three provinces and cities reflect the respective characteristics of the region as well as the three provinces and cities. The overall positioning of Beijing–Tianjin–Hebei is "the world-class urban agglomeration with the capital as the core, the regional overall coordinated development and reform leading zone, the national innovation-driven economic growth new engine and the ecological restoration environment improvement demonstration zone."

Since the 18th National Congress of the Communist Party of China, under the strong leadership of the Party Central Committee with President Xi Jinping as the core, four regional national strategies have been launched to promote regional coordinated development: the "Belt and Road" construction, the coordinated development of Beijing–Tianjin–Hebei, the development of the Greater Bay Area, and the development of the Yangtze River Economic Belt. Coordinated implementation of these four regional national strategies is expected to promote the formation of a new pattern of regional development.[92]

As can be seen from Table 5-31, in 2011 and 2017, the GDP of the eastern region accounted for more than 51% of the national GDP. But the Northeast fell from 8.6% in 2011 to 6.3% in 2017. In 2011, the per capita GDP of the Northeast was 77% of that of the East, and in 2017 it dropped to 59%. Inequality between the four regions has increased. From the perspective of the per capita GDP, the relative gap in economic development in various regions has shrunk. The coefficient of variation that reflects the overall relative level of GDP per capita in each region declined from 0.3513 in 2011 to 0.3131 in 2017. The relative difference between the per capita GDP in the eastern and central regions was reduced from 2.43 times in 2011 to 2.3 times in 2017.

12. Concluding Comments and Policy Implications

China is one of the many countries around the world that face the challenges created by inequalities. In this chapter, we dealt primarily with

---

[92] The State Council, The People's Republic of China (2015). Chronology of China's Belt and Road Initiative. *Xinhua*, March 28. Beijing–Tianjin–Hebei Collaborative Planning Outline, August 24, 2015, (in Chinese); Xi urges new, greater progress in Beijing–Tianjin–Hebei coordinated development. *Source*: Xinhua, January 18, 2019; The Central Committee of the Communist Party of China and the State Council: Outline Development Plan for the Guangdong–Hong Kong–Macao Greater Bay Area, Xinhua, February 18, 2019.

Table 5.31. Economic development by eastern, central, western, and northeastern provinces (2011 and 2017).[*]

	GDP, 100 mil CNY		GDP as % of national total		Per capita GDP, ¥	
	2017	2011	2017	2011	2017	2011
Eastern	443372.9	268832.1	51.595	51.183	84551.8	53567.1
Central	193140.3	110796.5	22.476	21.094	52046.7	25671.7
Western	168561.6	100235.0	19.615	19.084	44717.2	27672.4
Northeastern	54256.5	45377.5	6.314	8.639	49891.0	41380.2
Average	214832.8	131310.3			57801.7	37072.9
STDEVA	163937.9	96061.1			18096.7	13025.2
Variation	76.310%	73.156%			31.308%	35.134%

Notes: *Calculated using data from China National Bureau of Statistics: China Statistical Yearbook for Regional Economy, China Statistics Press, 2018, Tables 02.06, 03.09; China National Bureau of Statistics, Data base; Annual by Province, Gross Regional Product (100 million yuan), 1998–2017; Resident Population (year-end) (10000 persons); Annual: Gross Domestic Product (100 million yuan); Total Population (year-end) (10,000 persons), 1998–2017.

inequalities created by the urban–rural and regional divides. To address these inequalities, several policy implications are possible.

Regional economic development should be promoted with a particular emphasis on the shift toward more equitable distribution; the policy of opening to outside world in all areas must continue, and with development taking full advantage of the comparative advantages of each region. Former Premier Wen Jiabao said: "We took new steps in balancing development between regions. We thoroughly implemented the overall strategy for regional development; and formulated several major regional development plans and policies. The central and western regions and northeast China accelerated opening up and development, welcomed industries relocated from other parts of the country, and continuously strengthened their foundation for development. The eastern region accelerated restructuring and independent innovation, and the vitality of its economic development increased. A favorable situation emerged in which regional development was better distributed, structured and coordinated."[93] In implementing these and other strategies by the current

---

[93] Premier Wen Jiabao (2010). Report on the Work of the Government, March 5.

Chinese government, the following views should be taken into consideration:

- More attention should be paid to exercising macro-control, balancing the interests of all sectors, and promoting reform and innovation in a balanced way. Each region's comparative advantage should be maximized within a national framework. Economic growth of the coastal region will enhance the efficiency of the entire nation, while simultaneously optimizing economic structure. Regional cooperation along major transportation routes will depend on a strategic plan of resource distribution centered around the Shanghai coastal region and extending westward along the Yangtze River.
- Formation of unified markets, particularly for capital and capital goods, should be developed toward a market-oriented approach. Balanced and sustainable development should be emphasized, and environmental protection, liberalization, infrastructure improvement and the elimination of poverty should be stressed.
- Development of regional economies must be tied further to structural adjustment.

In conclusion, a regional policy system based on macro-economic adjustment will have to be established and maintained. Regional economic distribution, opening to outside world, development of poverty-stricken areas, and cooperation and linkage building among regional economies all need to be developed and strengthened.

China must continue to improve infrastructure and ecological conditions in the western region; it should effectively restore cultivated land to forests, protect natural forests, and prevent further desertification. The program of restoring grazing areas to grasslands should continue, and relevant legal work should be intensified. The household contract system for returning cultivated land to woodland must be implemented. Efforts must be directed at developing science, technology, and education, stepping up development of industries that exploit local conditions and transforming resource advantages into economic advantages.

The central region must develop new economic growth poles and economic belts by fully exploiting its advantageous geographical position as a bridge between the east and the west stretching from the north to the south and its overall resource advantages, and by exploiting the country's program for industrial restructuring and development of the western region. Cities or areas that are mainly dependent on resource exploitation should be encouraged to develop alternative industries. Efforts to speed up development of the central region can be supported with government investment in capital construction and technological upgrading projects.

The eastern region should continue its industrial restructuring efforts, develop a resources-conserving, environment-friendly, promoting innovation, and internationally oriented economy, enhance its international competitiveness, and strengthen economic and technological cooperation with the central and western regions to strengthen its role in stimulating their development. Furthering economic integration of the YRD, Pan-Pearl River Delta (PPRD), Annulus Bohai Sea Rim, Mingdongnan zone (southeastern region of Fujian), Jiaodong Peninsula (Shendong coast area), and Liaodong Peninsula (Liaoning coast area) will create an economic growth pole. The eastern coastal regions should seize the opportunity to accelerate development and be the first to achieve modernization.

There is no question that China's development policies have achieved remarkable results. However, the problem of development imbalance has not been fully resolved yet, and regional coordinated development still faces challenges. Therefore, it is necessary to further narrow the regional development gap, paying special attention to the gap between the eastern region and the central and western regions in terms of basic public service levels, education, housing, income and consumption levels of urban and rural residents, and degree of marketization. Improvements must be made in the level of spatial development and diversification of regional industrial structures. In addition, China must continue to attach importance to ecological environmental protection, improve the institutional mechanisms for coordinated regional development, and further advance poverty alleviation. In the coming period, the focus of China's regional policy is to further promote regional coordinated development. Emphasis will be given to the development of the western region, the revitalization of the northeast, the rise of the central region, and the first development in the east, as well as the introduction of a number of reform and innovation measures.

Since 2014, the Party Central Committee has promoted the integration and development of major national regional strategies. Guided by the "One Belt and One Road" construction, the coordinated development of

Beijing–Tianjin–Hebei, construction of Guangdong, Hong Kong, Macao Great Bay District, and the development of the Yangtze River Economic Belt, the four major sectors of the western, northeast, central, and eastern regions can be used to promote inter-regional integration. The solid promotion of the "Belt and Road" construction not only makes great contributions to the economic development, people's livelihood improvement, and employment growth of the countries along the route, but also seeks a new, harmonious, mutually beneficial and win–win regional economic development pattern at the international level. Promoting the coordinated development of Beijing–Tianjin–Hebei by resolving the function of Beijing's non-capital city, adjusting the regional economic structure and spatial structure, promoting the construction of Hebei Xiong'an New District and Beijing City sub-center, and exploring the orderly population of economically dense areas such as megacities and megalopolis have made remarkable progress. Giving full play to the location advantages of the Yangtze River Economic Belt across the three major sectors of the east, central, and west regions, with a focus on protection and limited development, the ecological priority and green development pattern of the Yangtze River Economic Belt has been continuously consolidated, relying on the Yangtze River golden waterway to promote coordination of the upper, middle, and lower reaches of the Yangtze River Development and high-quality development along the Yangtze River. The Greater Bay Area as one of the most open and economically vibrant regions in China, the Hong Kong–Zhuhai–Macao Bridge has been completed and opened to traffic. The development of the Greater Bay Area is not only a new attempt to break new ground in pursuing opening up on all fronts in a new era, but also a further step in taking forward the practice of "one country, two systems."

China must establish a new model of urban development led by central cities and urban agglomerations to promote regional development and integration. The Beijing–Tianjin–Hebei urban agglomeration promotes the coordinated development of the Bohai Rim region. YRD urban agglomeration with Shanghai acting as the center to develop the Yangtze River Economic Belt is well underway. Guangdong, Hong Kong, and Macao Great Bay District is driving the Pearl River-Xinjian River Economic Belt to develop innovative green. The goal of the Xiong'an New District is to build a high-level socialist modern city, modern economy. The new engine of the system and the national model for promoting high-quality development, the "One Belt, One Road" initiative, is to seek a new, harmonious, mutually beneficial and a win–win regional economic development pattern.

Support for the reform and development of the old revolutionary areas, ethnic areas, border areas, and poverty-stricken areas must be increased. The newly added high-speed railway has a mileage of 4,100 km, more than 6,000 km of newly built expressways and more than 300,000 km of rural roads. The coordination of urban and rural development has continued to increase.

Giving full play to the leading role of the market in the construction of a new regional coordinated development mechanism is the key to eliminating regional market barriers and promoting the free flow of factors. To achieve a regional coordinated development, the balance of interests and compensation between regions is a difficult point that must be broken. Furthermore, to establish horizontal compensation relationships through fund compensation, counterpart cooperation, industrial transfer, talent training, and joint construction of parks, China must improve the diversified horizontal ecological compensation mechanism, encourage the ecological benefit areas and ecological protection areas, the downstream of the river basin, and the upper reaches of the river basin. An interest compensation mechanism between the main grain producing areas and the main selling areas must be developed as well as improving the mechanism of interest compensation between resource output and input.

Basic public services are the most basic needs of people's livelihood. Therefore, there must be an improvement of the central adjustment system for basic endowment insurance funds for enterprise employees, and realization of the national pooling of endowment insurance as soon as possible. Additionally, the following steps must occur: (1) improve the basic medical insurance system; (2) consolidate and improve the compulsory education management system; (3) increase the scale of central government's transfer of compulsory education; and (4) strengthen the role of provincial and municipal co-ordination. Establishment of a cross-urban and inter-regional transfer system for basic public services, such as medical care and labor and employment, should be accelerated, and specific measures and supporting measures for inter-provincial transfer and follow-up should be studied to strengthen cross-regional basic public service coordination and cooperation.[94]

---

[94]Report on the work of the government, delivered at the Second Session of the 13th National People's Congress of the People's Republic of China on March 5, 2019; Opinions of the Central Committee of the Communist Party of China and the State Council on Establishing a More Effective Regional Coordination and Development Mechanism, 2018-11-29 18:45:06 *Source*: Xinhua (in Chinese).

Chapter 6

State-Operated Enterprise (SOE) Reform in China

1. Introduction

The current Chinese economic reforms have resulted in significant progress in more than four decades. An important sign of this progress has been the diminishing importance of the state sector. Prior to the reforms, the state sector dominated the Chinese economy. Today, the proportion of the state sector in overall economy has decreased sharply, although it should not be minimized in any way. The state sector is still an integral component of China's economy. However, China has adjusted its ownership structure by developing a functional multi-ownership economy. The stated-owned economy, collective economy, and non-public economy are all significant contributors to China's economic miracle. The rapid and sustainable development of the private sector has become one of the most notable features of China's transition to a market-oriented economy. The relative weight of state-operated sectors in the economy declined from 58% of the GDP in 1978 to 37% in 2000.[1] China has more than 20% of the world's population and needs to provide jobs for more than 26% of the world's workforce. Since 2002, the non-state sector accounted for 90% of total employment. Jobs created by private enterprises increased at an average growth rate of 19% in contrast to the national job growth rate of 1.2%.

---

[1] Calculated using data from Asia Development Bank (2003). *Private sectors assessment in the People's Republic of China*, November, Table 4. Manila: Asian Development Banks. China National Bureau of Statistics: 2003, Table C3.1, Table C3.3.

Thus, non-state enterprises, especially private sector enterprises and SMEs, are the main engine for creating jobs necessary to absorb new labor market entrants, a significant number of displaced workers from the state sector, and underemployed rural labor.[2]

In this chapter, we examine the state of China's state economy. We analyze China's ownership structure and the changes it has gone through. An important aspect of the ownership structure is the employment associated with each ownership structure. We also discuss challenges private ownership faces in China. The regional differences discussed in the previous chapter are also relevant in our examination of the country's ownership structure. China's companies are large, but they have failed to develop into global brands so far. We examine China's largest companies and contrast them with those from other countries in terms of operations and branding. We emphasize the role National Champions play in China's strategic economic objectives. Finally, we analyze the ownership structure of China's industry and conclude with comments about the relationship between the State and private enterprise in today's China.

2. China's Ownership Transformation

The ownership transition in China started in rural areas. Around 1978, rural reform started at the basic agricultural area level and spread rapidly. In the autumn of 1980, the "household responsibility system" was implemented on a large scale in rural China to replace the collectivized "people's commune." In conjunction with the reform, a form of free market developed. The introduction of the household responsibility system significantly increased rural agricultural output that was turned into investment in the development of rural industry and motivated rural surplus laborers to seek alternate employment. In addition, farmers experienced an increase in incomes, which led to increasing demand for consumer goods, thus providing markets for TVE products.

At the same time, the lack of autonomy in State-Run Enterprises, which led to low efficiency, was also addressed. From 1978–1984, reform efforts concentrated on giving State-Run Enterprises greater decision-making autonomy by offering them increased authority over the allocation of their profits, as well as limited production autonomy. Profits could be

---

[2]Asian Development Bank (2003). *Private Sector Assessment — People's Republic of China*. November, Manila: Asia Development Bank.

used either to finance increased investments or to pay bonuses to employees. However, these reforms did not prove effective in improving resource allocation.

From 1985–1992, the central government decided to turn State-Run Enterprises into truly independent production and management entities and stipulated those enterprises must take responsibilities for their own profits and losses by means of contracting and leasing. The policy named separating government from enterprises (Zhenqi Fenkai), and State-Run Enterprises became State-Operated Enterprises (SOE). Enterprises signed a management contract with the responsible authorities. Under the contract, enterprises were not only allowed to retain the extra profits beyond their contracted quotas, but were allowed to make their own managerial decisions, including dismissing or hiring personnel. A multiple index system was formulated, which included an economic efficiency index, a development potentiality index, and a management index. The tax system also underwent great changes. Instead of handing in their profit to the government, SOEs paid a tax commensurate with their revenue level. However, during this period, SOEs revealed their weakness in competing with the newly developed private companies, joint venture companies, and TVEs. SOE managers were not accustomed to doing business in a free market; their attitude was one of waiting, relying on government, and begging for help. It was the classic "soft budget constraint" in full operation. Additionally, the relationship between government and enterprises became more complicated because enterprises still operated and made investment decisions under the old factory system. Because of the lack of a modern corporate governance structure centered on a board of directors, SOEs under the factory system relied only on decisions made by the factory director, who was accountable to the leadership of the party committee.

The Third Plenary Session of the 14th Party Central Committee in November 1993 concluded: "It is the inevitable request for market economy to set up a modern enterprise system; it is a direction of SOE reform of China." SOE reform was entering a new stage of system innovation. On December 29, 1993, the National People's Congress passed the "Company Law of the People's Republic of China." In 1994, the State Council determined to choose 100 state-operated large and medium-sized enterprises to launch an experiment of implementing restructuring along a modern enterprise system (MES). The basic demands of the experiment were to "define right and responsibility clearly, separate government function from enterprise management, and operate scientifically." By 2000, most large and middle-scale SOEs had tentatively set up a modern enterprise system. This included three successive steps: (a) separation of administration function and enterprise function, (b) reorganization of monopoly enterprises into competitive enterprises, and (c) initial public offerings (IPO) on domestic and overseas securities markets following asset restructuring.

3. SOE Classification and Regulation

China's SOEs can be distinguished into four groups according to their regulators:[3]

- Central industrial SOEs, which are supervised by the State-owned Assets Supervision and Administration Commission of the State Council (SASAC).
- Local industrial SOEs. Local governments have their own SASACs, which regulate their specific SOEs.
- State-owned financial institutions. These operate under the supervision of the Central Huijin Investment Co., Ltd, which is owned by the central government; and,
- SOEs supervised by the Ministry of Finance (MOF). These SOEs operate under central administrative institutions and otherwise have financial relations with the Ministry.

The SASAC was established in 2003, supervising 196 central SOEs on behalf of the central government. Thus, adjustment in distribution and structure of the state economy began to be subjected to unified planning and market-oriented operation by the SASAC. Moreover, the SASAC could, as representative of the investors of all SOEs, to some extent facilitate the improvement of large SOEs' corporate governance. In December 2006, the SASAC for the first time specified the industrial sectors over which the state economy should have absolute control, be influential, or play a leading role. According to SASAC's plan, by 2008, non-performing

---

[3] Zhang, Z.Y. (2019). China's SOE Reforms: What the latest round of reforms means for the market. *China Briefing,* May 29. www.china-briefing.com/news/chinas-soe-reform-process/.

SOEs should exit the market, and by 2010, the number of central SOEs should total 80–100; among these, 30–50 should be internationally competitive.[4]

Following SOE reform, their economic performance improved (see Table 6.2). However, there still existed problems within the SOE sector; further reform became necessary. For example, further share ownership had to be implemented. There are several approaches to bring in new groups of equity holders. They include: (a) inviting private investors to participate in equity issuance, (b) debt-equity conversion, and (c) developing institutional investors. Within this system, the SASAC would need to create safeguards of shareholder rights in accordance with the law. In addition, an efficient budget system for managing state capital and improvement of systems and regulations for managing state assets had to be developed. The overall structure of the state sector had to be improved to enhance its dynamism and contribution to the economy. Reform of monopolistic industries had to be deepened by introducing competition and strengthening government regulation and public oversight over them.

4. Ownership Structure

Figure 6.1 illustrates the industrial structure by ownership in terms of total industrial gross output. Before reform, the share of industrial gross output contributed by SOEs increased from 41.5% (1952) to 77.6% (1978); after reform, it declined to 21.6% (2002). From 2000 on, SOE gross output includes that of state-owned and state-holding enterprises. Also, beginning with 2000, gross output includes only enterprises above designated size (refers to all enterprises with an annual sales income of over CNY5 million).

Because there are many small enterprises with collective and private ownership, the share of gross output from collectively owned and privately-owned enterprises after 2000 is not comparable with that prior to 2000 because of the different statistical methodology used. After 2011, the China National Bureau of Statistics did not publish the industrial gross output value as an independent item in the China Statistical Yearbook. In 2011, the total industrial output value was CNY84,426.9 billion (USD 12,499.1 billion), and the main business income differed by only 0.29%.

---

[4]*Beijing Review* (2007). Background of Central SOE Reform, 50(2), January 11.

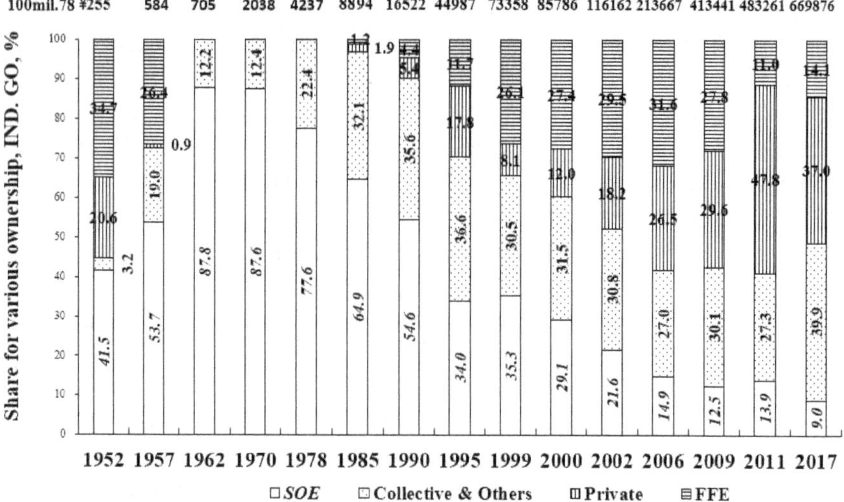

Figure 6.1.   Industry structure of gross output by ownership, China.

Source: Calculated using data from China Industry Economy Statistical Yearbook, China Statistics Press, 2008 Table 2.3, 2.5; China National Bureau of Statistics, Database; Annual, Revenue from Principal Business of Industrial Enterprises (100 million yuan) 1999–2018.

Therefore, in 2017, the main business income of industrial enterprises was used to replace the gross industrial output value.

However, compared with 2000, the share of industrial gross output value of SOEs declined in 2006, while the share of gross output from private ownership and FFEs increased. This trend was also observed before 2000. The share of private ownership and foreign-funded ventures increased from 0% (1978) to 58.2% (2006). China's ownership structure transformation was not completed overnight through privatization. Instead, China is developing a multi-ownership economy, with the non-public ownership developing faster. Figure 6.1 shows that the industrial gross output value of SOE, collective and other, private and FFE in 1978 was CNY32.9, 9.5, 0, and 0 billion, respectively, and increased to CNY317.6, 576.4, 567.2, and 675.4 billion (1978 constant CNY), respectively, in 2006. Thus, the share of SOE ownership declined sharply, although its absolute value still increased significantly. The SOEs' annual average growth rate for industrial gross output still reached 8.8% between 1978 and 2006, which was lower than before economic reform (11.4%

during 1952–1978). The annual growth rate of industrial gross output for private and FFEs reached 79.3% and 90.5% from 1985–2006, respectively. It was 18.6% and 35.1% for SOEs and collective enterprises, respectively, during the same period. That is, the share of SOEs in industrial gross output gradually became smaller and smaller. As can be seen from Figure 6.1, the industrial gross output value of SOEs, collective and other enterprises, private enterprises and FFEs increased to CNY6035, 26707, 24791, and 9455 billion (1978 constant CNY), respectively, in 2017. The annual average growth rate of industrial gross output value for SOEs, collective, private, and FFEs reached 6.0%, 15.0%, 14.3%, and 3.1% from 2006–2017, respectively.

SOEs are an important pillar of China's national economy, with the total assets of state-owned and state-owned holding companies increasing from CNY11.8 trillion in 2002 to CNY72.1 trillion in 2011. In 2011, there were 69 Chinese companies entering the world's top 500, including 38 central SOEs. In 2018, state-owned and state-controlled enterprises achieved a profit of CNY1987.06 billion, a year-on-year increase of 37.9%. In 2018, 120 Chinese enterprises were on the list; among them were 48 central SOEs. Like other ownership enterprises, SOEs are also independent market players and continue to grow and develop through market competition. The goal of the reform of SOEs is to improve the efficiency of state-owned capital operations and the efficiency of business operations, as well as accelerate the improvement of quality, transformation, and upgrading.

To develop a well-performing mixed ownership economy, SOEs must adhere to the four aspects of "improving governance, strengthening incentives, highlighting the main business, and improving efficiency." The quality of operations of state-owned capital has been significantly improved. We can find examples in the national strength of the Tiangong (Space flight) Dream Exploration, Jiaolong (dragons) Diving the sea, or in the safeguarding of national security by the J-20 stealth fighter, Yun-20 Large Military Transporter. Another SOE has become a "national card" of China's high-speed rail, UHV power transmission and transformation, a new generation of mobile communications 5G; yet another represents the new "Made in China" breakthroughs represented by the C919 airliner. Indeed, the major central SOEs shoulder great responsibilities to implement the national macro-control policy, guarantee the safety of energy resources, or promote poverty alleviation, fortification, and participation in projects aimed at improving citizen welfare. In 1999, the number of employees in private enterprises above a designed size was less than 30% of that in state-owned and SOEs. However, three years later, the number of employees in private enterprises exceeded the number employed in SOEs.[5] The number of private enterprises was a mere 7.5% of the SOE number in 1999 but increased to 276% in 2005. It further increased to 2214.8% in 2015. During 1999–2005, many SOEs were transformed to non-state enterprises or even private enterprises. The value added and employees of private enterprises was only 14% and 13% of that of SOEs, respectively, in 1999 and increased to 625% and 376%, respectively, in 2005. In 2015, this further increased to 13393% and 360%.

As can be seen from Table 6.1, from 1999–2015, in the field of retail trade, private ownership enterprises developed much faster than SOEs. This is a result of the optimization of the structure of state-owned assets, adjustment of the functional orientation of state-owned capital, and further reduction of secondary losses and the number of weak enterprises, to concentrate state-owned capital in functional, basic, and dominant industries.[6]

The total retail sales of consumer goods in 2005 reached CNY6.718 trillion (USD832.4 billion).[7] Figure 6.2 shows the ownership structure by revenue in retail sales. At the beginning of economic reform (1978), the percentage share of revenue in retail trade operated by SOEs and collective enterprises declined from 97.8% in 1978 to 19.1% in 2005; however, the absolute amount of revenue collected by SOEs and collective enterprises increased from CNY152.5 billion (USD88.6 billion) in 1978 to CNY1.283 trillion (USD159.0 billion) in 2005. Therefore, SOEs are still developing after economic reform, but at a lower annual growth rate than enterprises with different ownership structures. Private enterprises and others realized a mere 2.1% of total revenue in 1978; the ratio increased to 80.9% at the year-end of 2005. Therefore, the percentage share of SOEs in total retail sales declined dramatically after reform. There were 13 retail chain stores operating in China that were in the 2019 Fortune 500 rank. Of those, three were from the United States (ranked #1 Amazon, ranked

---

[5]*China Economic Times* (2002). The Private SME Development Report, December 8.

[6]Notice of the People's Government of Yangpu District of Shanghai on Printing and Distributing the "13th Five-Year Plan for the Reform and Development of SOEs in Yangpu," July 18, 2016.

[7]China National Bureau of Statistics. China Statistical Yearbook, China Statistics Press, 2006, Table 17.1.

Table 6.1.   The development of private and SOEs in China's retail sector.

	1999 priv.	1999 state	2005 priv.	2005 state	2015 priv.	2015 state
Number of enterprises	401	5334	8,377	3033	51893	2343
V.A., 100 millions	227.7	1617.1	7815.0	1487.8	64654.42	3299.8
Employees,10000	14.3	110.4	145.0	38.6	482.8	19.5

Source: Calculated using data from China National Bureau of Statistics, Database; Annual, Revenue from Principal Business of Enterprises of Retail Trade, 1999–2017; Number of Engaged Persons in Corporation Enterprises of Retail Trade (person), 1999–2017; Number of Corporation Enterprises of Retail Trade (unit), 1999–2017.

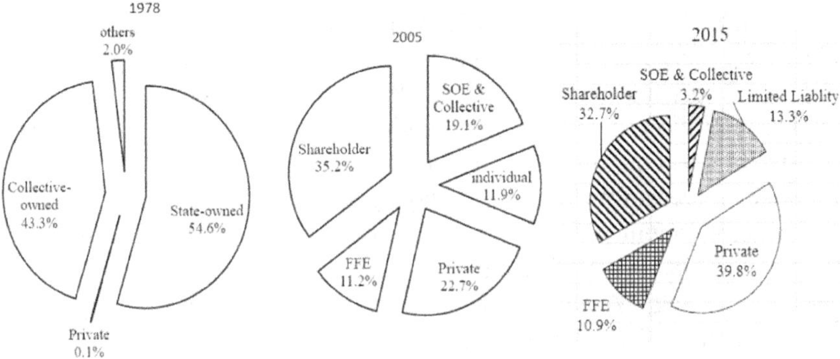

Figure 6.2.   Ownership structure by revenues in retail trade, China.

Source: Calculated using data from Department of Market Operation Regulation, Ministry of Commerce of PRC: China Consumer Goods Market Development Report (in Chinese), April 7, 2006; China National Bureau of Statistics: China Statistical Yearbook, China Statistics Press, 1999, Table 16.3; China National Bureau of Statistics, Data base; Annual, Revenue from Principal Business of Enterprises of Retail Trade (100 million yuan), 1999–2015.

#43 Walgreens Boots Alliance, ranked #57 Home Depot); three from China (ranked #181 Jd.Com, ranked #300 Alibaba Group Holding, ranked# 427 Suning.Com Group); two from France (ranked #68 Carrefour, ranked #156 Auchan Holding); two from Japan (ranked #103 Aeon, ranked #179 Seven and I Holdings); one from Hong Kong Special Administrative Region (ranked #374 CK Hutchison Holdings); one from Spain (ranked #408 INDITEX); and one from South Korea (ranked #493

Cj Corp.). 35 companies engaged in retail sales in China were included in the 2018 Fortune Global 500 rank. In 2017, Revenue from Principal Main businesses income of FFEs of Retail Trade was 697.42 billion CNY (103.25 billion USD), accounting for 15.8% of China's total retail sales.[8] Large FFEs, then, have occupied a significant portion of the sector's market share.

Figure 6.3 shows the ownership structure by employment in retail trade, catering services, and social service sectors. At the beginning of economic reforms (1978), only 0.1% employed persons worked in private enterprises; in 2005, the number increased to 31.4%, which means 8.42 million employed persons worked in private enterprises. The percentage share of employed persons working in SOEs declined from 54.6% in 1978 to 12.5% in 2005; the absolute number of employed persons working in SOEs decreased from 1.65 million in 1978 to 0.362 million in 1995 (see Figure 6.3). During the same period, the number of persons employed in private enterprises and self-employed individuals increased from 0.136 million to 0.851 million, including a net increase of more than 0.837 million job opportunities in private retail enterprises. Thus, private enterprises increasingly have been playing a more important role in solving the employment problem of domestic trade sectors. Hence, we can conclude that, instead of "big bang" privatization, China adopted a multi-ownership strategy. A multi-ownership strategy brings in additional and different forms of capital and improved governance. The state-owned economy, the collective economy, and the non-public economy operate and compete in various sectors of the economy. In other words, China's strategy is making the pie larger, so enterprises of all ownership structures get a larger piece.

As can be seen from Figure 6.3, from 2005–2017, the absolute number of persons working in SOEs decreased from 369.6 thousand to 159.8 thousand. It also shows that, during the same period, the number of employed persons in private enterprises increased from 700.9 thousand to 3181.9 thousand. This represents a net increase of more than 2,481,000 job opportunities in private retail enterprises. In 2017, there were nearly

---

[8] Calculated using data from; 2018 Fortune World Top 500 Industry List: Food Stores and Grocery Stores; 2018 Fortune Global 500 by Industry List: Professional Retail; 2018 Fortune Global 500 by Industry List: Internet Services and Retail; Fortune Chinese Network July 19, 2018; China National Bureau of Statistics, Data base; Annual, Revenue from Principal Business of Enterprises of Retail Trade (100 million yuan), 1999–2017.

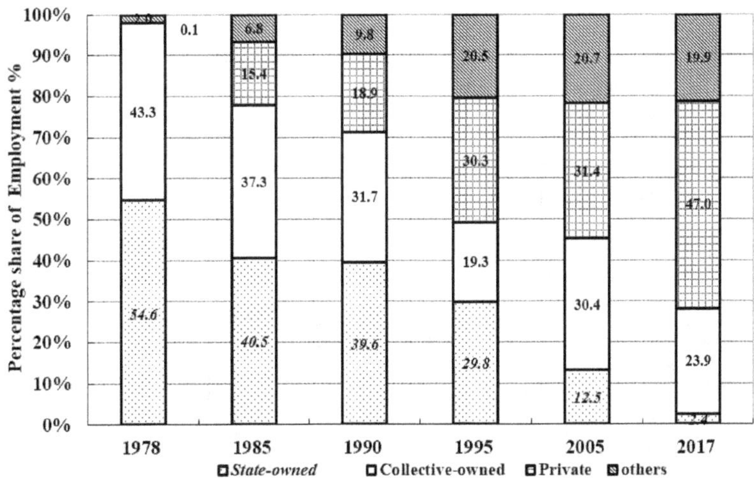

Figure 6.3.   Ownership structure by employment in retails trade, China, 1978–2017.

Source: Calculated using data from China Statistical Yearbook 1998, Table 16.3; China National Bureau of Statistics, Data base; Annual, Number of Engaged Persons in Corporation Enterprises of Retail Trade (person), 1999–2017.

25 million private enterprises in China. From 2005–2017, the average annual growth rate of state-owned, collective, private, others, and foreign-funded enterprises was minus 6.75%, 6.05%, 13.44%, 4.05%, and 10.06%, respectively. Private enterprises contributed 90% to new employment. The non-public ownership economy has developed rapidly and indeed has become an important force in China's national economy.[9]

The ownership structure of the country's GDP also has undergone a fundamental change since 1978, from complete reliance on state-owned and collective enterprises to a mixed economy where Private enterprises are playing an increasingly important role. The economic transformation is evident from the falling ratio of GDP contributed by SOEs, from 57.7% in 1978 to 36.9% in 2002 (see Figure 6.4).

Private enterprises and other ownerships (foreign-funded units, units with funds from Hong Kong, Macao, and Taiwan, cooperative units,

---

[9]Calculated using data from China National Bureau of Statistics, Database; Annual, Number of Engaged Persons in Corporation Enterprises of Retail Trade (person), 1999–2017; Yan, W. (2017). The contribution rate of private enterprises to new employment is 90%, October 22, the third press conference of the 19th National Press Center.

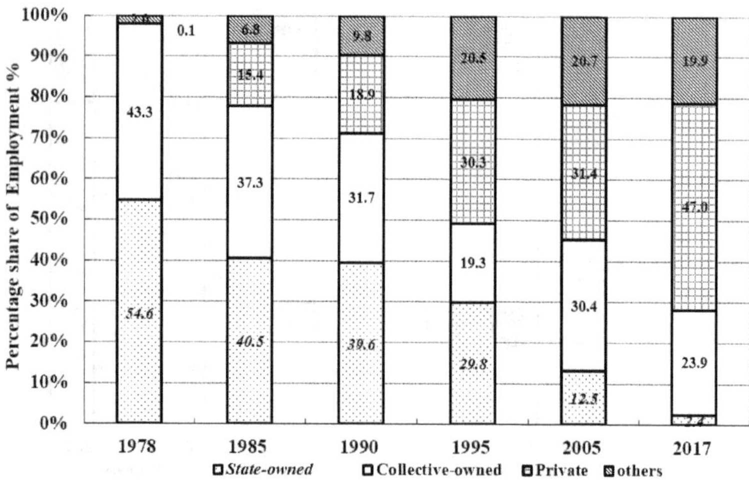

Figure 6.4.   GDP structure by ownership in China, 1978–2017.

Source: Calculated using data from China National Bureau of Statistics: China Statistical Yearbook, 2006, Table 3.1, 3.4.

joint ownership units, limited liability corporations, and share-holding corporations Ltd.) in transition grew at an average annual growth rate of 11.4%, from 511.5 billion 1995 constant CNY (USD61.25 billion) in 1978 to 6,856.5 billion 1995 constant CNY (USD821.0 billion) in 2002.[10] Their share in the total economy increased from 42.2% to 63.1% during this period. On the other hand, the average annual growth rate of state-owned ownership was 7.6% during 1978–2002, therefore, their share in the total economy declined from 57.7% to 36.9% (see Figure 6.4). As can be seen from Figure 6.4, from 2002–2017 the SOE contribution

---

[10]Calculated using data from China National Bureau of Statistics (2007). China Statistical Yearbook, 2006, Table 3.1, 3.4; Asia Development Bank (2003). *Private sectors assessment in the People's Republic of China, 2003*, Table 4; China National Association of Industry and Commerce: The Development Report of Non-state-owned Economy in China, No. 3, (2005–2006), Social Science Academic Press (China), p. 4, Table 1 (in Chinese); Shi, F, and Y. Yin (2006). China's economic structural adjustment bumpy road for 50 years. *Shanghai Securities News*, October 16, page A12; Lu, Ch. (2006).: China's private economy from 2001–2005. *China Business Times*, February 5; China National Bureau of Statistics, Database; Annual, Revenue from Principal Business of Industrial Enterprises (100 million yuan), 1999–2017.

to GDP decreased from 4009.6 billion 1995 constant CNY (USD480.1 billion) to 3,762.5 billion 1995 constant CNY (USD450.5 billion). The contribution by private enterprises increased from 3781.4 billion 1995 constant CNY (USD480.1 billion) to 25,057.7 billion 1995 constant CNY (USD3,000.6 billion). The non-public ownership economy has developed rapidly and has become an important force in China's national economy indeed. From 2005–2017, the average annual growth rate of state-owned, collective, and private enterprises was minus 0.4%, 10.4%, and 13.4%, respectively. In 2018, Liu He, the Vice Premier of the State Council, said in an interview with the media about important economic issues pertaining to the private sector: "Supporting the development of private enterprises is to support the development of the entire national economy. Those who do not support the development of private enterprises must be resolutely corrected.

At present, there are some deviations and misunderstandings in the actual implementation process. For example, the business personnel of some organizations believe it is safe to provide loans to SOEs, but Lending to private companies is politically risky, preferring not to act and not make political mistakes. This kind of understanding and practice is completely wrong. The private economy plays an important role in the entire economic system. Without the development of private enterprises, there will be no stable development of the entire economy. If there is no high-quality private enterprise system, there will be no modern industrial system. Supporting the development of private enterprises is to support the development of the entire national economy."[11]

5. Ownership and Employment

In 2002, the non-state sector accounted for 90% of total employment. Private enterprises provided jobs at an average growth rate of 20.4%, meanwhile the annual growth rate of national jobs increased 1.2% during 1997–2002. The % of employees working in the State-owned sector declined to 8.6% of the national total in 2005 from 15.8% in 1997, amounting to an annual growth rate of negative 6.4%. In 2005, the non-public sector accounted for 91.4% of total employment (see Figure 6.5).

---

[11]Liu, H. (2018). Supporting the development of private enterprises is to support the development of the entire national economy, October 19, China Chief Financial Officer 2018 (in Chinese); Central Radio and Television International Online (in Chinese).

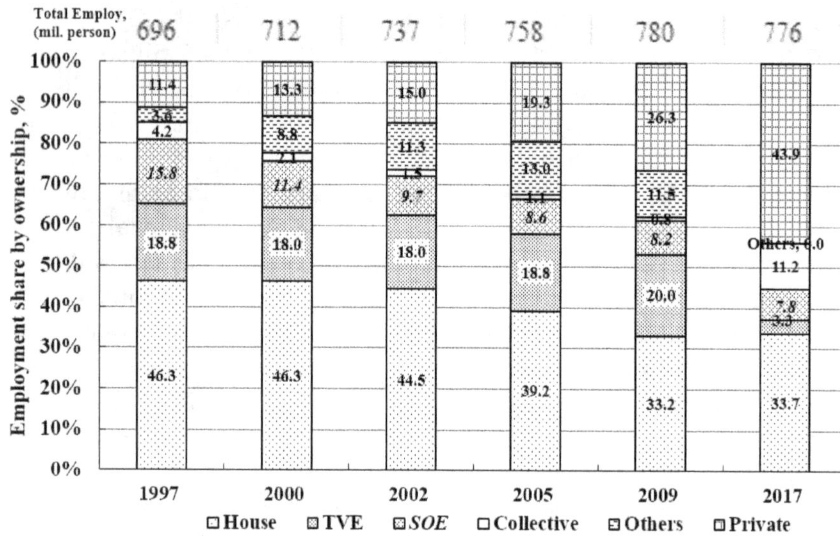

Figure 6.5.   Employment structure by ownership in China.

a. Other Urban Units: There are differences between the aggregate (or subtotal) and the sum of relevant categories in data sources: residual between total urban employment and the sum of all categories in urban employment.

b. Rural Households: The difference between total rural employment and the sum of all rural categories.

c. Others: Including cooperative units, joint ownership units, and limited liability corporations, shareholding corporations' units with funds from Hong Kong, Macao, and Taipei, foreign-funded units.

d. TVE: 1997–2009 TVE, in 2017 Foreign-Funded Units.

Source: Calculated using data from China National Bureau of Statistics: China Statistical Yearbook, 2018, Table 4.1; 2010, Table 4.1; Asia Development Bank (2003). *Private sectors assessment in the People's Republic of China*, Chapter 1, Manila; Asian Development Bank.

Thus, non-state enterprises, especially private sector enterprises and SMEs, are the main job-creation engines. Non-state enterprises absorb new labor market entrants, a significant number of displaced workers from the state sector, the underemployed, and the immigrant rural laborers. During 1997–2005, the state sector laid off 45.12 million workers, while the private sector created 67.52 million jobs. By the end of 2004, 308.83 million personnel worked in secondary and tertiary industries. The secondary industry employment reached 154.64 million people, and the tertiary industry employment, 154.19 million people. From 2005–2017, the average annual growth rate of state-owned, private enterprises, and foreign-funded units was minus 0.56%, 10.77%, and 4.77%, respectively.

Zhejiang had long been a province mainly dependent on agriculture. After two decades of development since the reform and opening-up, Zhejiang became a province with a strong economy and with industry as the guiding sector. From 1978–2005, its GDP achieved an annual increase of 13%, rising from CNY12.4 billion (USD1.5 billion) to CNY1336.5 billion (USD165.6 billion). Its rank improved from 12th to 4th place among all China's provinces. Its GDP per capita rose from 13th place to 4th, (only after Shanghai, Beijing, and Tianjin, three municipalities) from CNY331 (USD186) in 1978 to CNY27,552 (USD3,414) in 2005, an average annual increase of 12.1%.[12] In 2003, investment in fixed assets reached CNY494.7 billion (USD59.7 billion), with private investment being 57%.[13]

The volume of exports increased from USD5 million in 1978 to USD76.8 billion in 2005, with 31.2% annual growth rate, which leaped to fourth place in China. Zhejiang Province has the most developed private economy in China. The economic output of non-state sector accounted for 71.5% of the province's total GDP in 2005, with the private sector accounting for 57% of GDP.[14] In 2003, the private sector paid 60.5% of taxes.[15] The average annual growth rate of the private sector in Zhejiang Province reached 20.8%[16] during 1990–2002, while national private economy developed at a rate of 8.4% in 1990–2000.[17] In 2005, 8.4% of the national GDP came from this province, which has only 3.6% of the

---

[12] www.zhejiang.gov.cn/gb/node2/node50/node51/node62/index.html (in Chinese).

[13] Liu, X., and H. Wang (2004). The record of actual events for National People's Congress delegation of Hong Kong SAR inspects Zhejiang Province (in Chinese), *People's Daily*, Overseas Edition, June 18, p. 4.

[14] www.zhejiang.gov.cn/gb/node2/node50/node51/node62/index.html (in Chinese).

[15] Jiang, N. (2004). Analyze "Zhejiang economic phenomena", provincial governor explains three reasons (in Chinese), *People's Daily*, January 18.

[16] Calculated using data from The Zhejiang Provincial Statistical Bureau: The historical evolution and varying characteristics of non-state sector's economy in Zhejiang Provinces (in Chinese), September 25, 2003.

[17] Calculated using data from China National Bureau of Statistics: 2003, Table C3.1, Table C3.3; Asia Development Bank (2003). Private sectors assessment in the People's Republic of China, Chapter 1.

national population living in a continental area of 1.06% of the country.[18] The private economy grew at an average annual rate of 34% from 1996–2015.

Zhejiang Province's stellar economic development over the past 20 years is regarded as a miracle throughout China. In Cixi City, of the more than 70,000 industrial and business companies currently operating, only three are still under state ownership.[19] According to the first bulletin on the results of China's first national economic census, the actual receipt capital (actual receipt capital refers to the capital the enterprise investor actually contributes, including the currency, the property, the intangible asset, and so on; each kind of input) by private ownership at the end of 2004 in China occupied 28%, but in Zhejiang Province it reached 52.3% (see Figure 6.6). By comparison, the actual receipt capital by the private ownership enterprises in Shanghai in 2004 was only 21.4%. The total actual receipt capital of Zhejiang Province amounted to 6.2% of the national total; in Shanghai, it reached 10.3% (the average value is 3.23% for each province and municipality). The actual receipt capital by foreign-funded ownership at the end of 2004 reached 30.2% in Shanghai, which is higher than in Zhejiang Province (16.7%). Zhejiang Province ranks 19th among 60 fastest growing counties and regions in IMD (International Institute for Management Development) World Competitiveness Yearbook (WCY), 2004 edition.[20] The rank was evaluated on 323 items. One of the major innovations is regional economies are included in the WCY rankings because they show "pockets" of competitiveness with different profiles than countries.

In WCY 2004, nine regions and 51 countries are ranked from the most to the least competitive. The nine regions from nine different countries ranked 19th, 20th, 27th, 32nd, 36th, 37th, 38th, 46th, and 47th, respectively. In fact, Zhejiang ranks first among these nine regions. As a country, China ranked 24th and the United States ranked first.

---

[18]National Bureau of Statistics of China (2006). Statistical Communiqué on the 2005 National Economic and Social Development, March 3; www.zhejiang.gov.cn/gb/node2/node50/node51/node62/index.html (in Chinese).

[19]*China Daily* HK Edition (2003). Private sector doing well as the State relaxes grip, December 24.

[20]International Institute for Management Development (2004). IMD World Competitiveness Yearbook.

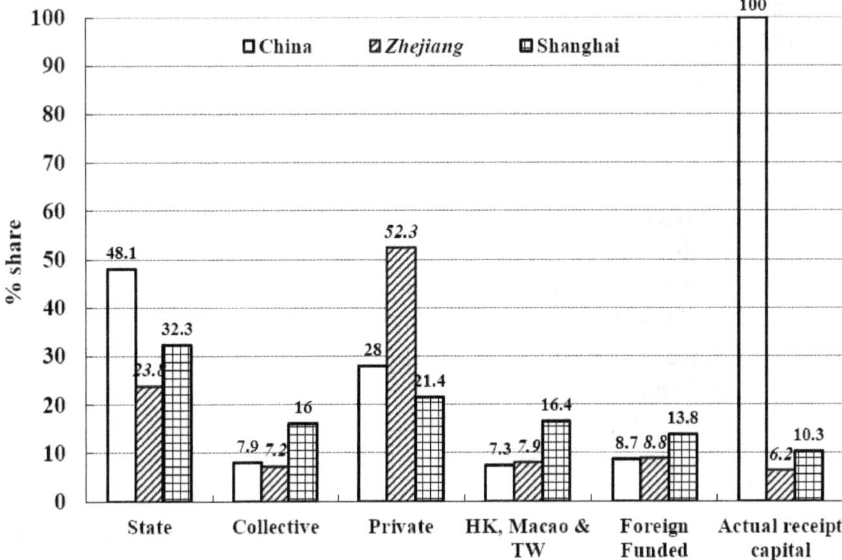

Figure 6.6.   Capital received by ownership at the end of 2004, Zhejiang, and Shanghai.

Source: The Leading Group of First National Economic Census of the State Council and National Bureau of Statistics of China (2005). First bulletin on the results of China's first national economic census, December 6; The Zhejiang Provincial Statistical Bureau (2005). First bulletin on the results of provincial first economic census, December 21. The Shanghai Municipal Statistical Bureau (2005). First Bulletin on the results of Municipal first economic census, December 24.

In the 1980s, entrepreneurs in China were mostly hawkers peddling their wares on foot or tricycles in the cities' back streets. More enterprising opened small restaurants in residential neighborhoods or toiled in their village workshops making simple consumer goods. As recently as the 1990s, the doors to the nation's key business sectors were closed to the individual entrepreneur. Even the richest and most successful of them could only stay within the so-called non-pillar industries, such as electrical appliances, garments, and catering. However, all that has changed. China's entrepreneurs are now a recognized, and even exalted, tribe, free to roam the nation's vast economic landscape. The Decision on Reforming the Investment System, announced on July 25th, 2004, focused on improving the country's non-public economy. Private investors can put their money into any sector not forbidden by law.[21] They invest in banks,

---

[21] Jing, F. (2004). Private business gets State Council support. *China Daily*, July 27.

make aircraft, manufacture cars, control airlines, and others. They have muscled into industries, such as steel, aluminum, and machinery, which were once the stronghold of the state-owned sector. The first non-state joint-stock company was crowned with the title of "consortium," Sinorich Consortium (Holdings) Co., Ltd. And was authorized to operate in the City of Zhejiang Province, which is famous for a full-fledged growth of private enterprises. Formed from nine local influential non-state enterprises, Sinorich Consortium has CNY55.8 million (USD6.74 million) in registered capital and integrates financial business with manufacturing and trade.[22] The bridge to link Shanghai and Hangzhou built across Hangzhou Bay on the East China Sea is a 36-kilometre-long structure, the longest of its kind in the world. Five consortiums consisting of 17 privately operated companies are furnishing more than half of the capital investment for the project. SOEs are to make up the rest of the cost, initially estimated at CNY11.8 billion (USD1.43 billion); the government will not spend a single penny on the project. Shanghai Junyao Group Company with private ownership took an 18% stake in China Eastern Airlines Wuhan Co. in August 2002. This was the first major step in restructuring China's civil aviation industry hitherto operated exclusively by the government.[23] Okay Airways Co, China's first private airline made its maiden flight on March 11, 2005. A Boeing 737–900, with 81 people aboard, flew from the airline's base in the northern city of Tianjin to Kunming, Yunnan Province, a popular tourist spot in the mountain southwest. The airline was at the controls for the 4 1/2-h maiden flight, which included a stop in the central city of Changsha, Hunan Province. The airline is seen as opening a new era for the country and is an attempt to modernize the air travel industry. The airline has said the first flight was very successful.[24] Besides Okay Airways, Civil Aviation Administration of China (CAAC) has given a nod to three other private operators to start airlines. They are Shanghai-based Spring International Airlines, Chengdu-based Eagle Airlines, and Huaxia Airlines in Gansu Province. All were reported to have vowed to adopt low-cost modes in their airline operations. Okay Airways Co. plans to reduce costs by managing aviation oil

---

[22] Xinhua (2004). First non-state consortium emerges in Zhejiang. *China Daily*, June 17.

[23] *China Daily* HK Edition (2003). Private sector doing well as the State relaxes grip, December 24.

[24] Private airline launches 1st flight, www.chinadaily.com.cn/english/doc/2005-03/12/content_424217.htm.

futures, adopting a flexible way to deploy its fleets, air routes, and flights. These open a new chapter for efforts to modernize the country's booming air travel industry. Even sectors under state monopoly are beginning to open to private investment. Beijing has opened the local urban infrastructure market under the policy of "participation by the private and foreign investors and allowing market mechanisms to play a pivotal role under government guidance."

The essence of the ongoing reforms is the emergence of the private sector. The economy owes its outstanding performance and vibrancy to the emergence of the non-state sector. Excluding TVEs, individuals and private enterprises contribute the largest share of the non-state sector. Private sector activity tends to be concentrated in the richer coastal regions and dominate labor-intensive industries (garments, textiles, food processing) and services. Productivity gains (1979–1994), accounting for more than 40% of economic growth, were realized because of the vibrant private sector. These productivity trends persisted in the 1990s. For SOEs, average Return on Assets (ROA) was 1.7% (excluding oil companies) and Return on Equity (ROE), 4.3%, while for private firms it was 5.6% and 12.8%, respectively.[25] Provincial GDPs have been higher in regions with strong private sector participation, such as Zhejiang Province.

In 2008, the international financial crisis brought challenges to the Zhejiang economy. Companies such as Wanxiang, Geely, Alibaba, and Chuanhua are typical examples of enterprises carrying out technological and institutional innovations in their fields. Typically, it was the beginning of the "cage-for-bird-changing" strategy of Zhejiang's private economy transformation and industrial upgrading. In 2018, the number of private enterprises in Zhejiang Province reached 1.05 million, accounting for nearly 80% of the provincial domestic enterprises. Private enterprises in Zhejiang have continuously adapted to the changes of market demand at home and abroad and maintained steady and rapid development. Private economy contributes more than 60% of tax revenue, more than 70% of GDP, more than 80% of foreign trade exports, and more than 90% of new jobs. The phenomenon of "6789" fully demonstrates the basic position of private economy in Zhejiang economic system.

---

[25] Shamshad, A., and D. Kertzman (2003). *Private Sector Assessment*, Asian Development Bank, Workshop on Private Sector Development in the People's Republic of China, March 27.

In 2017, Zhejiang had more than 10,000 private high-tech enterprises, with value added of the digital economy exceeding CNY2 trillion (USD296 billion), accounting for 39.9% of GDP, ranking first in the province. In addition to several leading enterprises such as Alibaba, Hikvision, Ant Financial, Dahua Share, etc., they have grown into digital economic enterprises with global influence. There are also basic research institutions such as Ali Damo Academy, Zhijiang Laboratory, digital economic platforms such as Dream Town, Yunqi Town, Wuzhen World Internet Conference, digital societies such as Internet Payment, Shared Travel, Internet Catering. According to the list of "Top 500 Private Enterprises in China in 2018" issued by the All-China Federation of Industry and Commerce, 93 enterprises in Zhejiang were selected. Zhejiang has ranked first in the list of enterprises for 20 consecutive years. The number of enterprises on the list is higher than that of Jiangsu (86), Shandong (73), Guangdong (60), and other coastal developed provinces. The total operating income of 93 enterprises on the list is CNY3.65 trillion (USD540.4 billion), accounting for 15% of the total operating income of the whole country. Compared with the same period of the following year, the scale and efficiency of 93 enterprises have increased significantly. In 2018, four private entrepreneurs in Zhejiang won the title of "reform pioneer": Ma Yun, the digital economy innovator, Nan Cunhui, the outstanding representative of Wenzhou's private economy, Lu Guanqiu, the pioneer of the reform and development of township enterprises, and Xie Gaohua, the founder of Yiwu small commodity market.

6. The Challenges of Private Ownership

Private enterprises, of course, have serious resource constraints. With the change of development stage and the strengthening of hard constraints on energy conservation and emission reduction, Zhejiang private enterprise development increasingly has encountered the difficulties of land use, financing, and employment, as well as the rapid rise of raw material cost, financing cost, and wage cost, which makes those private enterprises that rely on resources, environment, and price adjustments survive. The trend of "hollowing out" of the private economy is obvious. Because of the serious constraints of resources, such as land and other factors, as well as the fact the threshold of attracting investment in other provinces is generally lower than that in Zhejiang, private enterprises in Zhejiang have shifted to other provinces, even to Southeast Asia and other countries, making the trend of "hollowing out" Zhejiang's economy more obvious. Zhejiang should start from creating a development environment, upgrading its development level, improving innovation ability, and strengthening factor guarantee, and then create new advantages of the private economic system and mechanism, and focus on promoting the transformation, innovation, and leapfrogging of the development of private economy. The small and scattered enterprise form is precisely the most obvious weak link. To complete the transformation from "tens of thousands of households" to "fine soldiers and elite generals," the Zhejiang Provincial government has planned a path for the transformation of the private economy through the "individual transfer to enterprises, small regulation promotion, stock reforms, and stock listing" project. From 2012 to the first half of 2016, 106 domestic and overseas listed companies were added. In 2018, there were 390 domestic and foreign listed companies (82 overseas) with a total market capitalization of CNY5 trillion (USD753 billion). Among them, there are 308 domestic listed companies, ranking second in the country. The number of listed companies in the New Third Board (Over-the-Counter market) is 668, ranking the fifth in the country. From January to October 2017, the return of Zhejiang merchants has generated investment of CNY384.9 billion, completing the full-year target two months ahead of schedule, an increase of 32.3%. 2,374 new industrial projects were introduced, with CNY210.954 billion invested in the "8 trillion of industries," accounting for 76.1% of the funds in place for industrial projects. It is believed with the support of more countries in the Belt and Road cooperation project proposed by President Xi Jinping, Zhejiang private enterprises must take the ride of the Belt and Road. The success of Zhejiang private enterprises has achieved extensive results.[26]

---

[26]Guan, P. (2017). What happened? Overseas Zhejiang businessmen representatives have rushed back to Zhejiang from all over the world, November 18. The most beautiful Zhejiang businessmen (in Chinese); The Change of Media Image of Zhejiang Private Economy and the Synergy of Symbolic Capital in People's Daily, *Journal of Ningbo University* (Liberal Arts Edition), 2018(06), (in Chinese); Xinhua News Agency (2018). The full list of outstanding contributions to reform and opening up! Ma Yun, Ma Huateng, Li Yining, and another 100 people won the title of reform pioneer, December 18. (in Chinese); Wang, Z. (2019). Promote a new leap in Zhejiang's private economy, *Zhejiang Economy*, (02), (in Chinese); Overseas Mergers and Acquisitions (2016). The Future of

The Central and Eastern Europe's planned economies (CPEs) reformers paid great attention to transformation of the ownership structure; privatization of state ownership became the precondition for other important reforms. However, this transformation is probably impossible to be achieved within a short period, because the state's productive assets in the CPEs are valued at a sum far more than the savings available to the private sector (see Figure 6.7). In 1978, fixed assets in China's SOE sector were 1061% of the Chinese citizens' saving deposits, with no foreign capital inflow. Therefore, China adopted a multi-ownership strategy. In 2005, the average balance of fixed assets' net value in the SOE sector accounted for only 34.8% of the value of residential saving deposits and accumulated utilized foreign capital in China had reached 240.4% of the SOE sector's net assets at the end of 2005, as China allowed private enterprises and foreign capital to buy, merge, and acquire SOEs. In the former USSR, of a total 2.8 trillion rubles in fixed assets in 1990, 2.5 trillion belonged to the state. However, the public had only 569 billion rubles in savings. As a very rough estimate, only 100 billion could be mobilized to buy state property. There were too many firms for too few buyers. The government called for a massive public privatization effort by giving every Russian an individual certificate to buy shares of enterprises. The government planned to give out 150 million vouchers by the end of 1992.[27]

The new ownership became concentrated in the hands of some relatively few individuals with money or connections. Britain's much-heralded privatization program under Margaret Thatcher involved about 20 firms, accounting for a mere 5% of value added; and this was in a well-established market economy with one of the world's most sophisticated stock markets. According to the World Bank, between 1980 and 1987, fewer than 1000 firms were privatized throughout the world.[28] By comparison, Hungary had about 2300 state-owned firms, Poland, 7,500, Czechoslovakia, 4800, Bulgaria, 5000, Romania, 40,000, and the former Soviet Union, 45,900 industrial enterprises and 23,300 state farms.[29] In

---

Zhejiang's Economic Distribution, *China Newsweek*, August 19 (in Chinese); Guan, SY., YL Pei. Research on the "Going Out" Strategy of Private Enterprises in Zhejiang Province.

[27] *The Economist* (1991). Business in Eastern Europe, September 21, p. 11.

[28] *Ibid.*

[29] Schulze, F. (1991). *The USSR Today: Perspectives from the Soviet Press.* 8th ed., Columbus, Ohio, U.S.A.: Current Digest of the Soviet Press, p. 70; Business in Eastern Europe, *The Economist*, September 21, 1991, p. 11.

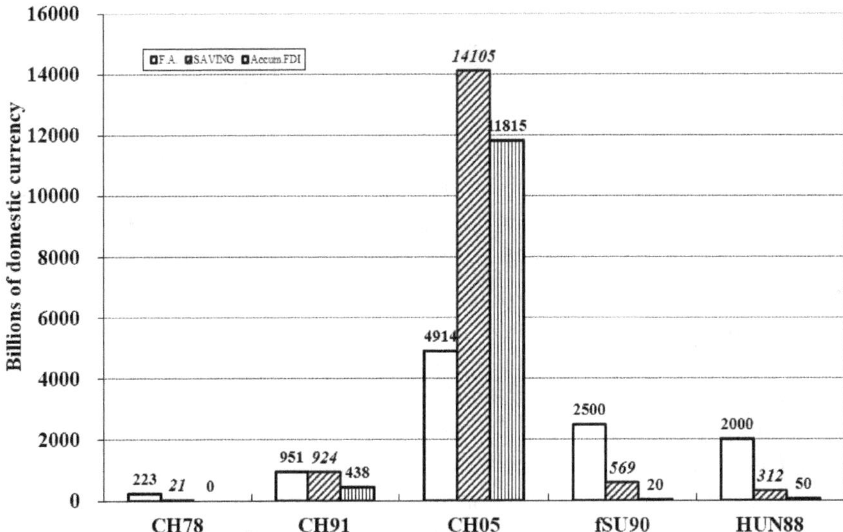

Figure 6.7.   Privatization and possible investment, China, former USSR, Hungary.

Source: Zhang, Y., and P. Coves (1995). A Comparative Study of Economic Reform in China and Central and Eastern Europe, *Journal of Shanghai Institute of Mechanical Engineering*, 16(3), P13–24; No. 4, p. 29–40; Calculated using data from Schulze, F. (1991). *The USSR today*, 8th ed., 1991, p. 70; Blommestein, H. (1991). *Transformation of planned economies*, OECD, ,p.85; China Statistical Yearbook, 2006, Table 10.3, 14.8, 18.19; Statistical Yearbook of China 1981 (English Edition), Published by Economic Information & Agency, Hong Kong, October 1982.

practice, selling state-owned firms has proved time-consuming, frustrating, and expensive. Therefore, it is not surprising to experience unsuccessful results in the privatization efforts following the shock therapy approach taken by the East-European former CPE countries.

By comparison, instead of rapid privatization for the reform of state enterprises, China has applied a multi-ownership strategy in conjunction with gradualism and experimentation to develop its private sector. From 1978–2002, the average annual growth rate of GDP created by the state and the private sector reached 7.6% and 17.6%, respectively. From 2002–2017, it was −0.4% and 13.4%, respectively. The secret of success of China's economic reform is allowing the non-state sectors to develop in the setting of a market economy. In 2002, although the state sector produced only one-third of overall GDP, it was still the major user of scarce economic resources. Reform of SOEs has been far from satisfactory; the old system maintains its influence and continues to impede the establishment and perfection of the new market economic system. Therefore, we cannot say the market has started to operate as the primary allocator of economic resources. For example, the state sector, although contributing only one-third of China's GDP, consumes two-thirds of the country's capital resources. The inefficiency of the state sector leads to a vulnerable monetary system. In another example, the sluggishness of the market is partly the result, from the supply side, of the malfunction of the SOE sector and the unfavorable environment for non-SOEs. There are two aspects to the problem. On the one hand, the reform of SOEs and the restructuring of the state sector are proceeding at a slow pace. On the other hand, the non-state-owned sector has not had a chance to develop fully.[30]

Since the reform and opening-up in 1978, after 40 years of continuous exploration and development, China has embarked on a path to a socialist market economy with distinctive Chinese characteristics and entered a new era of socialist modernization. Understanding and dealing appropriately with the delicate relationship between government and market is the core issue of China's economic system reform. In 2013, "the market plays a decisive role in resource allocation and better plays the role of the government." 2017 proposes to "build an effective economic system with a dynamic market mechanism, a dynamic micro-main body, and a macro-control system." After 40 years of development, the "market orientation" and "government-assisted" socialist market economy have ranked second in the world in terms of economic aggregates and laid a solid foundation for the realization of socialist modernization. The market vitality is more prominent, the government's responsibilities are clearer, and the theoretical exploration and road practice of realizing the socialist market economy with Chinese characteristics are more confident and better developed.[31]

7. The Status of SOE Operations and Reforms

After China's SOEs were separated from administrative government bodies to exist as independent enterprises, a development representing a

---

[30] Wu, J. China's Economic Reform: Past, Present and Future, Perspectives, Vol. 1, No. 5.

[31] Wei, Y. and Z. Bao (2018). The Practice and Theoretical Exploration of the Relationship between Chinese Government and the Market in the Past 40 Years of Reform and Opening-up — Taking the Expression Changes of Important Policy Documents as the Main Line of Analysis, *Enterprise Economy*, 8 (in Chinese).

major departure from the planned economy, these enterprises went through further shareholder reforms to build themselves into real corporate entities. Reforms were at the core of these impressive improvements of the SOE sector, previously known for their "plump size and slack performance." In the first quarter of the 21st century, China's central SOEs are set to get smaller in size, but stronger in competence. For many years, the West viewed China's SOEs in black or white. In one portrayal, they are infiltrators to be viewed with suspicion. An example: Aluminum Corporation of China's (Chinalco) recent multibillion-dollar purchase of a stake in Rio Tinto has raised fears about China's agenda for the acquisition of Australia's resources. Another version sees state-owned companies as muscle-bound goons, without the smarts of a private company, but with plenty of brawn. In this characterization, they are relics of a failed economic experiment that still dominates the national economy, controlling natural resources, utilities, and many other vital sectors. However, both views fail to recognize that as the Chinese economy evolves continuously, the line between SOEs and private-sector companies has blurred considerably. Many of them would make better partners for multinationals than some of their private-sector counterparts. Openness, not ownership, is the key.[32]

Table 6.2 shows that SOEs' economic performance improved during 2002–2017. As can be seen from Table 6.2, from 2002–2017, SOEs developed rapidly. The number of SOEs steadily declined, but the overall strength has been enhanced. Total assets have increased significantly; the economic performance and management quality have been significantly improved, and their competitiveness has been further enhanced. In 2002–2007, the number of SOEs declined by 19,375 units, but their sales revenue, profits, tax payments, and total assets increased by CNY12.6 trillion, CNY1.25 trillion, CNY1.11 trillion, and CNY1.43 trillion, respectively. The average annual growth rate amounted to 27.2%, 34.4%, 21.6%, and 6.3%, respectively. These data show that in 2007–2017, central enterprises made great progress overall and in their main line of business. As seen from Table 6.2, the tax amount of SOEs is always greater than the total profit. This is because the "SOE mission" has been positioned to offset market defects, consolidate the economic foundation of the socialist system, and play a leading role in the national economy. Market defect

---

[32] Woetzel, J. (2008). Reassessing China's SOEs, *McKinsey Quarterly*, July.

Table 6.2.   Economic performance of SOEs in China, 2002–2017.

Year	Number of SOEs	Units	Revenue	Total Profits	Total Tax	Total Assets
				Billion CNY		
2017	National total	1946	52,201	2,899	4,235	151,712
	SASAC* supervision	96	30,818	1,776	3,081	75,128
2015	National total	3,234	45,470	2,303	3,860	119,205
	SASAC* supervision	112	27,169	1,615	2,973	64,249
2010	National total	8,726	8,901	1,529	1,909	12,338
	SASAC* supervision	120	16,777	852	1,484	7,079
2007	National total	10,074	18,000	1,620	1,783	5,472
	SASAC* supervision	152	9,840	700	1,127	5,117
2006	National total	14,555	13,702	1,200	1,400	4,894
	SASAC* supervision	162	8,340	768	921	4,347
2005	National total	16,824	11,207	970	1,192	4,575
	SASAC* supervision	169	6,713	628	753	3,823
2004	National total	23,417	8,990	753	1,011	4,442
	SASAC* supervision	186	5,600	488	616	3,363
2003	National total	23,228	6,752	495	726	4,164
	SASAC* supervision	196	4,423	301	362	2,957
2002	National total	29,449	5,417	370	670	4,029

Note: *SASAC — State-owned Assets Supervision and Administration Commission of the State Council.

Source: Calculated using data from Editor-in-Chief: Li, R.. China's state-owned assets supervision and administration Yearbook (in Chinese), 2007, 2006, and 2005, *China Economy*. Li, R. (2008). The reform and development of SOEs made significant progress over the past five years (in Chinese), *Peoples Daily*, March 8, p.15; Li, R. (2007). SOE reform carried forward steadily at the new starting point (in Chinese), *Qiushi* (The official Journal of the Communist Party of China Central Committee), No. 16, p.10; Li, R. (2006). Comprehensively implement the scientific concept of development and strive to improve the level of state-owned assets supervision — Speech at the meeting of the SASAC (in Chinese), January 23. China National Bureau of Statistics, Database; Revenue from Principal Business of Industrial Enterprises, 1999–2017; Number of Industrial Enterprises, 1999–2017; Total Profits of Industrial Enterprises, 1999–2017; Total Assets of Industrial Enterprises, 1999–2017; Value-added Tax Payable This Year of Industrial Enterprises; Income Tax Payable of Industrial Enterprises, 1999–2017; The overall operation of the central enterprises in 2010, the Financial Supervision and Evaluation Bureau of the SASAC, 2011-10-14 (in Chinese); Economic operation of state-owned and state-owned holding companies nationwide from January to December 2017, MOF website (2018), (in Chinese); Economic operation of state-owned and state-owned holding companies nationwide from January to December 2015, January 23. MOF website (2016) (in Chinese), January 27; The three major directions of SOE reform are clear (August 31, 2015); The revenue and profit of SOEs has increased in August on a month-on-month basis, and the most difficult time has passed, October 27, 2009 (in Chinese).

compensation refers to the public welfare undertakings of the SOEs, such as providing public goods and services.

In 1994, the State Council determined to choose 100 large and medium-sized SOEs to launch an experiment involving restructuring along the modern enterprise system. The basic objectives of the experiment were to "define right and responsibility clearly, separate government function from enterprise management, and operate scientifically." China's SOEs have made headway in establishing modern enterprise systems during the ninth five-year-plan period (1996–2000), leading to obvious improvement in their performances. According to figures provided by the State Development Planning, CNY55.4 billion (USD6.67 billion) was from private and other sources. The reform has helped identify the true investors in SOEs and clarify management's responsibility to investors.[33] In 2003, China accelerated the development of the modern corporate system. In line with the principles of "clearly established property right ownership, well defined rights and responsibilities, separation of enterprises from government and scientific management," efforts were made to carry out reforms aimed at introducing the standard corporate system and the joint-stock system and improving corporate governance.[34]

Reforms pertaining to the shareholding system, the SOE corporate legal person governance structure, and the labor, personnel, and distribution systems resulted in profound changes of institutional structures and mechanisms. During 2003–2007, there were 29 central enterprises listing their A shares, 16 listing H shares, and seven listing their red chips. In 2007, central enterprises had holdings in total 279 listed companies.[35] In a pilot move, SOEs began to have outside directors. Currently, 19 such SOEs, including China Baosteel Group and China Shenhua Group, have picked up 66 outside directors. The outside directors in 17 companies occupied half or more of their board of directors' seats.[36] Central SOEs selecting management personnel at all levels through market-oriented approaches reached 30% of the total. From 2003–2007, 95 central SOEs

---

[33] China's SOE Embrace Modern Enterprise System (2000). *Peoples Daily*, October 16.

[34] Zhu Rongji (2003). Full text of the Report on the Work of the Government delivered at the First Session of the 10th National People's Congress on March 5.

[35] Li, R. (2008). The reform and development of SOEs made significant progress over the past 5 years (in Chinese), *Peoples Daily*, March 8, p. 15.

[36] Xinhua (2007). China's central SOE set to get smaller in size, stronger in competence, December 21.

participated in 47 restructurings, with the number of central SOEs reduced from 196 to 149. Despite the decrease in number, their economic performance improved significantly from 2003–2007 (see Table 6.2). "The targeted total number of central SOEs is reducing to 80–100 by 2010" said Li, Rongrong on August 10, 2008.[37] SASAC made this decision because many central SOEs had no national economic security role; therefore, they should compete in the market.

It is seen from Table 6.2 that the revenue and total assets per each central SOE increased from CNY22.6 billion to CNY64.7 billion and from CNY15.1 billion to CNY33.7 billion, respectively, during 2003–2007. The average annual growth rate was 30.1% and 22.2%, respectively. The profit and tax paid per each central SOE grew even faster, as their average annual growth rate reached 31.6% and 41.6%, respectively, during 2003–2007. Therefore, the conclusion is that China's central SOEs got smaller, but more competitive after restructuring.

In 2003, SOEs started to recruit senior managerial staff in a more transparent manner, whereas in the past, these posts were not made publicly available. On July 12, 2007, SASAC stated that 1,603 people had applied for the 22 senior posts in enterprises managed directly by the central government. Twenty-five of the applicants were foreign nationals, and 10 were from Hong Kong, Macao, and Taiwan. Applications were invited both from home and abroad to optimize human resource distribution globally, and therefore, prepare SOEs to compete in the international market as early as possible.[38] A number of SOEs established a fairly complete and effective community-oriented open recruitment of all staff and competition for posts, as well as quantitative assessments and performance-related compensation system.

In 2019, the policy to be implemented was one of "consolidating, enhancing, upgrading, and smoothing." With the supply-side structural reform as the main line and promotion of high-quality development of central enterprises, the key objective was defined as achieving "one guarantee, six enhancements." One guarantee is to ensure that the annual target tasks are completed, the benefits derived will maintain steady growth, and the quality of development will continue to improve. Six enhancements are listed: first, strengthen the main business of industry and continuously improve the quality of the development of the central business

---

[37]Xinhua (2008). China plans more post-Olympics reforms for SOE, August 11.
[38]Li, F. (2007). One senior SOE post, 73 applicants. *China Daily*, July 13, p. 2.

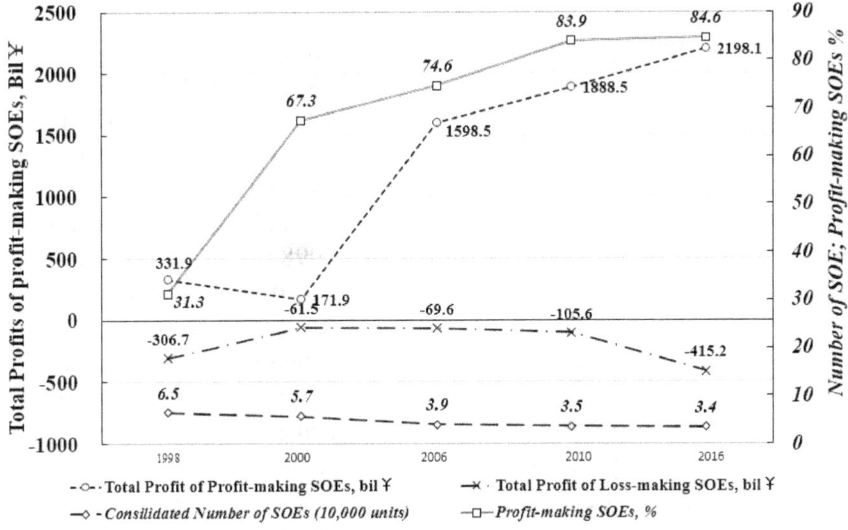

Figure 6.8.   Profit and losses of China SOE during 1998–2016.

Source: Calculating using data from China National Bureau of Statistics: China Statistical Yearbook, China Statistics Press, 2000, Table 13.5; 2001, Table 13.5; China National Bureau of Statistics, Data base; Annual, Number of Industrial Enterprises, State-owned (unit), 2000–2016; Number of Loss-making Industrial Enterprises, State-owned (unit) 2000–2016; Total Profits of Industrial Enterprises, State-owned (100 million yuan), 2000–2016; Total Losses of Loss-making Industrial Enterprises, State-owned (100 million yuan) 2000–2016.

of central enterprises; second, strengthen reforms and continue to enhance the vitality and development of each enterprise; third, strengthen independent innovation and promote the accelerated upgrading of manufacturing; fourth, strengthen and upgrade management, and strive to move toward world-class level; fifth, strengthen risk management and control, and conduct stress testing according to changes in the situation; sixth, strengthen the transformation of functions and continuously improve the systematic and targeted effectiveness of state-owned assets supervision.[39]

Figure 6.8 illustrates the total profits of profit-making SOEs, total losses of loss-making SOEs, total numbers of SOEs, and the ratio of profit-making to total SOEs during 1998–2016. It shows that the number

---

[39] Xiao, Y. (2019). The professional integration of central enterprises is conducive to giving play to the advantages. The Second Session of the 13th National People's Congress Press Center, 03.12.

of SOEs declined from 20.3 thousand (1998) to 13.3 thousand (2006). The ratio of profit-making to total SOE increased from 31.3% to 67.3% (see Figure 6.8), which implies the number of loss-making SOEs declined from 44.5 thousand units in 1998 to 10.0 thousand units in 2006. The total loss of loss-making SOEs fluctuated within a narrow range between CNY61.5 billion (USD 7.4 billion) in 2000 to CNY415.2 billion (USD 62.5 billion) in 2016. The total profit of profit-making SOEs increased from CNY331.9 billion (USD40.1 billion) in 1998 to CNY1,598.5 billion (USD161.9 billion) in 2006, and then significantly increased to CNY2,198.1 billion (USD331.0 billion) in 2016 (see Figure 6.8).

SOEs separated their core businesses from their secondary businesses and converted the latter into independent companies. At the end of September 2006, 1,252 large and medium-sized SOEs implemented the nonessential industry restructuring, which entailed the diversion of 2.1 million surplus staff. Of these, 76 central SOEs had their restructuring plan approved, involving 4,879 units to be restructured, and the diversion of surplus staff placement of 777,000 people. 1528 units of central SOEs transferred their social functions, which entailed the reassignment of 86,000 people, among which were 49,000 retired teachers.

China encourages greater investment of state capital in key industries and areas that are important to national security and comprise the life-blood of the economy. For example, in Jilin Province, SOEs were disbursed among 20 industrial sectors. The following SOE restructuring and reorganization mainly concentrated on the metallurgy, forest industry, food, energy, and others, a total of only 10 sectors.

Table 6.3 shows the SOE asset–liability ratio for different SOE groups in 2006. The table reflects the achievements of SOE reform and restructuring. For example, total assets of state-holding SOEs accounted for 55.4% of total SOE assets, which implies many SOEs were listed in the stock market or introduced strategic partners. 42 central SOEs offered initial public offerings domestically and abroad during 2003–2007.[40] Total assets of basic industry and service industry reached 55.6% and 28.2%, respectively.

In the past, the Chinese government has identified sectors that should be under the control of the national authorities because of their importance to the economy and national security. Such sectors include power

---

[40] Xinhua (2007). China's central SOE set to get smaller in size, stronger in competence, December 21.

Table 6.3.   Asset–liability ratios of Chinese SOEs by group, 2006.

Items	Number of enterprise	Number of employed persons	State-owned assets at year end	Total assets	Net assets	Owners' equities	Assets–liability ratio
	Units	10000	Bil. ¥	Bil. ¥	Bil. ¥	Bil. ¥	(%)
National total	1,19,254	3774.6	9762.4	29011.6	12221.0	10004.2	57.9
By Size or Enterprises							
Large Enterprises	2,757	1884.6	2788.6	10932.4	4269.6	3181.9	60.9
Medium-sized	12,536	1061	1915.4	7062.8	2657.8	2335.1	62.4
Small Enterprises	1,03,961	829	5058.5	12445.4	5293.6	4487.2	57.5
By Status of Registration							
State sole owned	63,038	1833.9	6926.5	13118.5	6199.2	5465	52.7
State-holding	10,870	1827.2	2621.4	16855.6	5808.7	4329.0	65.5
State institution	9,346	113.5	214.56	466.5	213.1	210.1	54.3
By profit or loss							
Profitable	69,053	2778.5	8554.6	24664.4	10722.6	8653.5	56.5
Loss-making	50,201	996.1	1207.94	5776.2	1498.4	1350.7	74.1
By Subordination							
Central	22,582	1696	5595.7	14786.3	6893.2	5609.6	53.4
Local	96,672	2078.6	4166.8	15654.2	5327.8	4394.6	66.0
By economic regions							
Eastern coastal regions	63,805	1733.4	6957.8	19104.5	8319.3	6879.2	56.5
Middle island regions	27,050	1068.5	1227.6	5133.3	1724.3	1430.8	66.4
Western remote regions	27,146	926.1	1264	5134.3	1674.9	1423.8	67.4
Abroad enterprises	1,253	46.6	313.03	1068.6	502.4	270.4	53.0
By function of sectors							
Basic industry	34,150	1985	6088.7	16932.6	7702.8	6361.7	54.5
Production and processing Industry	28,139	1247	1211. 3	4921.7	1654.3	1251.8	66.4
Commerce, trade service, and others	56,965	542.7	2464.4	8588.8	2866.4	2394.2	66.6

Source: Calculated using data from Editor-in-Chief: Li, Rongrong (Minister of State-owned Assets Supervision and Administration Commission of the State Council): China's state-owned assets supervision and administration Yearbook (in Chinese), 2007, China Economy Publisher, Chapter 5, Table 1, Table 4.

generation and distribution, oil, petrochemicals and natural gas, telecommunications, and armaments. Accordingly, the state must also have a controlling stake in the coal, aviation, and shipping industries. Machinery, automobiles, IT, construction, iron and steel, and non-ferrous metals should also prominently feature Central SOEs.[41] SOEs in key industries will be the focus of state investment to sharpen their competitiveness in the face of intensified rivalry from foreign multinationals. The number of large SOEs only occupied 2.3% of total number of SOEs, but their total assets accounted for 35.9% total assets of SOEs. This was achieved by mergers and acquisitions of SOEs. Table 6.4 shows that the financial performance of central SOEs is the best.

The asset–liability ratio fluctuated within a narrow range with a maximum 68.6% (2016 Central SOEs) and a minimum 62.2% (2018 Local SOEs), with a coefficient of variation of 2.66%. The return on equity fluctuated within a wider range with a maximum 6.7% (2013 Central SOEs) and a minimum 1.7% (2015 Local SOEs), with a coefficient of variation of 36.17%.

Figure 6.9 illustrates the top 10 industrial sectors, in which SOE total assets concentrated. All these show that the adjustment industrial distribution of central SOEs produced initial results. As can be seen from Figure 6.9, from 2006–2017, total SOE assets increased significantly from CNY6.85 trillion (USD480.1 billion) to CNY23.4 trillion (USD3.46 trillion). It also shows the top 10 sectors have changed. In 2017, four new sectors were added: manufacture of automobiles (ranked #3), extraction of petroleum and natural gas (ranked #6), smelt and pressing of non-ferrous metals (ranked #7), and processing of petroleum and nuclear fuel (ranked #9). The four eliminated sectors, reflecting the changes in industrial structure, in 2006 were manufacture of electrical machinery and equipment (ranked #6), manufacture of non-metallic mineral production (ranked #7), manufacture of textile (ranked # 8), and manufacture of general machinery (ranked #9).

---

[41]Zhao, H. (2006). Nation lists sectors critical to national economy, *China Daily*, December 19.

Table 6.4.   Asset–liability ratios of Chinese SOEs and return on equity by group, 2013–2018.

Items	Total assets	Total liability	Owners' equities	Assets– liability ratio	Return on equity	Number of employed persons
	Bil. ¥	Bil. ¥	Bil. ¥	(%)	(%)	10000
Status registration 2018						
State-owned enterprises	178748.3	115647.5	63100.8	64.7	3.9	1418.1
Central SOE	80339.2	54390.9	25948.3	67.7	5.6	
Local state-owned	98409.1	61256.6	37152.5	62.2	2.7	
Status registration 2017						
State-owned enterprises	151711.5	99715.7	51995.8	65.7	3.3	1595.8
Central SOE	75128.4	51121.3	24007.1	68.0	4.4	
Local State-owned	76583.2	48594.4	27988.8	63.5	2.4	
Status registration 2016						
State-owned enterprises	131717.5	87037.7	44679.7	66.1	2.8	1695.9
Central SOE	69478.9	47652.6	21826.3	68.6	3.7	
Local State-owned	62238.6	39385.1	22853.5	63.3	2.1	
Status registration 2015						
State-owned enterprises	119204.9	79067.1	40137.8	66.3	2.8	1777.8
Central SOE	64249.2	43670.2	20579.0	68.0	3.9	
Local state-owned	54955.7	35396.8	19558.9	64.4	1.7	
Status registration 2014						
State-owned enterprises	102118.8	66555.8	35562.9	65.2	4.1	1842.7
Central SOE	53706.8	35262.1	18444.7	65.7	5.5	
Local State-owned	48412.0	31293.7	17118.3	64.6	2.6	
Status registration 2013						
State-owned enterprises	91103.9	59316.7	31787.2	65.1	5.0	1889.5
Central SOE	48317.8	31751.9	16565.9	65.7	6.7	
Local state-owned	42786.1	27564.7	15221.4	64.4	3.2	

Source: Calculated using data from China National Bureau of Statistics, Database; Annual, Total Profits of State-holding Industrial Enterprises (100 million yuan), 2011–2017; Economic Operation of State-owned and State-controlled Enterprises in China from January to December 2018, MOF Website, January 22, 2019, (in Chinese); Economic operation of state-owned and state-controlled companies in China from January to December 2017, MOF website Jan-23, 2018, (in Chinese); 2016, MOF Website, February 15, 2017, (in Chinese); 2015, MOF Website, January 27, 2016 (in Chinese); 2014, MOF Website, January. 22, 2015 (in Chinese); 2013, MOF Website, January. 21, 2014 (in Chinese).

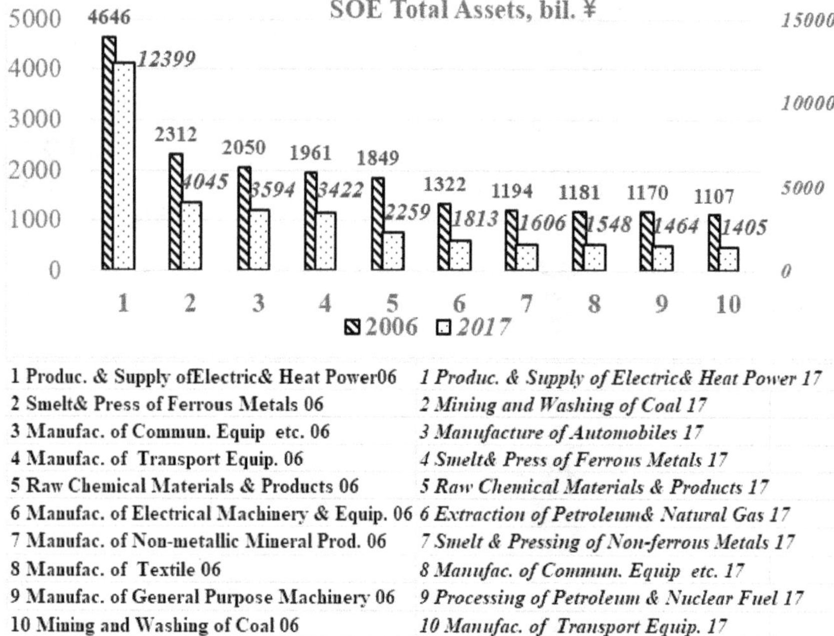

1 Produc. & Supply ofElectric& Heat Power06	*1 Produc. & Supply of Electric& Heat Power 17*
2 Smelt& Press of Ferrous Metals 06	*2 Mining and Washing of Coal 17*
3 Manufac. of Commun. Equip etc. 06	*3 Manufacture of Automobiles 17*
4 Manufac. of Transport Equip. 06	*4 Smelt& Press of Ferrous Metals 17*
5 Raw Chemical Materials & Products 06	*5 Raw Chemical Materials & Products 17*
6 Manufac. of Electrical Machinery & Equip. 06	*6 Extraction of Petroleum& Natural Gas 17*
7 Manufac. of Non-metallic Mineral Prod. 06	*7 Smelt & Pressing of Non-ferrous Metals 17*
8 Manufac. of Textile 06	*8 Manufac. of Commun. Equip etc. 17*
9 Manufac. of General Purpose Machinery 06	*9 Processing of Petroleum & Nuclear Fuel 17*
10 Mining and Washing of Coal 06	*10 Manufac. of Transport Equip. 17*

Figure 6.9.   Top 10 industrial branches with largest total assets of China SOE in 2006 and 2017.

Source: Calculated using data from China National Bureau of Statistics: China Statistical Yearbook , China Statistics Press, 2007, Table 14.02; 2018, Table 13.4.

8. Regional Issues

Table 6.5 also reveals China's regional disparity with respect to SOE assets. SOE assets were concentrated in the eastern region, which accounted for 62.8% of national SOE total assets. Table 6.5 shows the Total assets (%) of China's SOEs by regions in 2006. Figure 6.11 illustrates the top three provinces (Shanghai, Guandong, and Jiangsu) and the bottom three provinces (Tibet, Qinghai, and Hainan). All top three provinces located in the eastern region by tax paid per capita (Zhejiang, Shanghai, and Guandong); the bottom three provinces were Heilongjiang, Hainan, and Jilin.

Shanghai accounted for 11.91% of national regional SOE total assets, while that value in Tibet was only 0.13%. The tax paid per capita employees by regional SOE in Zhejiang Province reached CNY48,756, while the

Table 6.5.   Asset–liability ratios of Chinese SOEs by region, 2006.

Items	Number of Enterprise	Number of employed persons	State-owned assets at year end	Total assets	Net assets	Owners' equities	Assets– liability ratio	Profit per capital	Tax payable per capital
	Units	10000	Bil. ¥	Bil. ¥	Bil. ¥	Bil. ¥	(%)	Yuan	Yuan
National total	1,19,254	3774.6	9762.43	29012	12221	10004	57.9	31791.4	37090.0
Central Government	22,582	1696	5595.65	14786	6893.2	5609.6	53.4	51431.8	55856.2
Supervision SASAC*	16,373	1103.7	4234.04	12192	5386.6	4212.4	55.8	69597.7	61814.8
Supervision by Ministry	6,209	592.3	1361.62	2594.8	1506.7	1397.3	41.9		
Regional Government	96,672	2078.6	4166.78	15654	5327.8	4394.6	66.0	15766.2	21778.1
Beijing	5,049	101.4	279.13	1113.5	378.24	294.55	66.0	10765.0	26921.6
Tianjin	3,890	48	216.28	758.98	268.92	262.34	64.6	17536.5	19901.6
Hebei	3,330	87. 8	113.98	435.95	150.13	116.7	65.6	12357.9	19780.1
Shanxi	4,557	121.7	132.5	544.29	166.63	132.68	69.4	10919.4	20519.1
Inner Mongolia	1,014	53.1	59.21	198.22	72.83	66.4	63.3	4689.8	11890.7
Liaoning	3,297	120.8	158. 83	613.04	196.66	159.81	67.9	2946.0	14438.0
Dalian	606	23.2	39.37	139.44	56.23	41.42	59.7	13027.8	20130.7
Jilin	1,630	36.5	33.11	171.5	43.69	37.56	74.5	98.2	8737.3
Heilongjiang	3,719	101.1	58.35	252.53	50.69	44.96	79.9	172.3	4629.7
Shanghai	9,404	121.2	501.73	1963.3	745.84	582.03	62.0	33526.2	46195.6
Zhejiang	4,768	63.2	295.92	966.5	369.88	315.92	61.7	55212.9	48756.3
Ningbo	528	5	50.62	166.08	58.87	54.08	64.6	75861.7	49423.8
Jiangsu	4,252	81.1	275.61	1150.5	355.65	304.89	69.1	22037.4	23208.4
Anhui	2,378	77.1	119.23	509.37	167.32	125.73	67.2	19919.8	22347.9
Fujian	3,784	52.2	141.04	430.25	170.77	146.35	60.3	28051.9	26067.2
Xiamen	628	8.1	41.1	143.86	48.28	40.3	66.4	44043.7	50444.3

(Continued)

Table 6.5. (*Continued*)

Items	Number of Enterprise	Number of employed persons	State-owned assets at year end	Total assets	Net assets	Owners' equities	Assets–liability ratio	Profit per capital	Tax payable per capital
	Units	10000	Bil. ¥	Bil. ¥	Bil. ¥	Bil. ¥	(%)	Yuan	Yuan
Jiangxi	2,006	56.7	51.72	232.12	73.85	54.25	68.2	16124.9	12286.2
Shandong	4,612	156.2	213.54	966.14	312.28	238.27	67.7	19358.2	28206.0
Qingdao	807	17.6	42.4	169.91	56.58	48.28	66.7	14712.1	37961.8
Henan	4,031	114.9	128.78	548.92	165.17	142.28	69.9	9299.9	15588.2
Hubei	2,387	42.7	67.17	343.16	75.75	62.42	77.9	4854.7	12421.9
Hunan	2,584	66.6	81.3	319.24	104.76	79.89	67.2	4816.0	12937.8
Guangdong	6,985	117.9	421.54	1313.8	521.46	405.52	60.3	34788.3	37574.6
Shenzhen	499	14.3	76.33	214.62	119.78	76.6	44.2	78889.9	42656.0
Hainan	1,147	8.8	20.95	62.32	17.35	17.21	72.2	473.9	6112.0
Guangxi	4,513	65	105.97	300.63	117.96	111.74	60.8	11195.1	15432.4
Chongqing	2,388	67.5	66.97	233.37	77.76	67.64	66.7	6918.1	17441.1
Sichuan	2,776	61.2	148.49	534.85	178.22	152.03	66.7	12075.7	19578.2
Guizhou	1,945	43.6	139.13	451.66	156.43	139.46	65.4	9382.8	15450.9
Yunnan	2,267	51.9	99.39	356.73	121.43	99.57	66.0	22409.2	18597.4
Shanxi	3,370	68.6	120.33	464.63	120.36	106.13	74.1	16046.2	22018.3
Gansu	1,700	38.9	42.29	166.58	53.95	49.55	67.6	12200.2	13672.4
Qinghai	496	8.5	13.1	71.04	24.83	17.12	65.1	63197.8	28416.2
Tibet	432	3.3	10.4	20.64	12.03	10.77	41.7	6633.7	15801.7
Ningxia	544	13.4	11.85	40.92	15.52	12.43	68.9	5023.9	12109.9
Xinjiang	1,417	27.8	38.93	110.51	41.41	38.33	62.5	4027.8	9253.9

Source: Calculated using data from Editor-in-Chief: Li, R. (Minister of State-owned Assets Supervision and Administration Commission of the State Council): China's state-owned assets supervision and administration Yearbook (in Chinese), 2007, Chapter 5, Table 3, Table 6, Table 11~ Table 46; Li, R. SOE reform carried forward steadily at the new starting point (in Chinese), *Qiushi* (The official Journal of the Communist Party of China Central Committee), No. 16, 2007, p. 10; China National Bureau of Statistics: China Statistical Yearbook, China Statistics Press, 2007, Table 4.3.

same value in Heilongjiang was only CNY4,630. As can be seen from Tables 6.5 and 6.6, these two indicators have changed compared to 2006 and 2017 (see Figure 6.10). In accordance with the principle of separation of government and enterprise, separation of government and capital, and separation of ownership and management rights, the SOE supervision system is to be transformed from "management assets" to "management capital." Since 2013, the asset–liability ratio (%) has replaced total assets. Another indicator, tax payable per capita, is replaced by profit per employee, because the latter can represent the quality of business operations. It also shows that regional disparity is still serious. The asset–liability ratios of the top three provinces were 42.4%, 45.8%, and 55% in Beijing, Shanghai, and Guangdong, respectively; all located in the eastern region.

The asset–liability ratio in the bottom three provinces were 74.8%, 70.6%, and 68.7% in Shanxi, Ningxia, and Henan, respectively; all were not in the eastern region. The per capita (employee) profits in the top three provinces of Shanghai, Beijing, and Zhejiang were CNY426,874, CNY290,023, and CNY281,303, respectively; all located in the eastern region. The per capita profits of the bottom three provinces were CNY28,297, CNY38,030, and CNY40,828 in Heilongjiang, Shanxi, and Qinghai.

China's national regional SOE average values in 2006 were regional SOE profits per employee CNY15,766 and regional SOE tax paid per employee CNY21,778. For the nine provinces of Zhejiang, Shanghai, Guangdong, Qinghai, Fujian, Shandong, Jiangsu, Anhui, and Shaanxi, regional SOE profits per employee and regional SOE tax paid per employee are higher than the 2006 national average value; six of the above provinces are located in the eastern coastal region. Zhejiang, Shanghai, and Guangdong have the highest regional SOE profits per employee and regional SOE tax paid per employee. Guangdong is located in the Pearl River Delta; Shanghai, Zhejiang, and Jiangsu are located in the Yangtze River Delta. Shandong is located in the Annulus Bohai Sea Rim. Qinghai, located in the western region, has the highest regional SOE profits per employee, CNY63,198, ranked first among 31 provinces in China because of rich natural resources (salt-lake, petroleum, and natural gas, non-ferrous metals and gold, non-metallic mineral products, water energy, and tourism resources). The regional SOE profits per employee of chemical industry, social service, petroleum industry, and metallurgy industry sectors were CNY291,951, CNY205,019, CNY197,885, and CNY109,042, respectively. Another two provinces, Shanxi and Anhui,

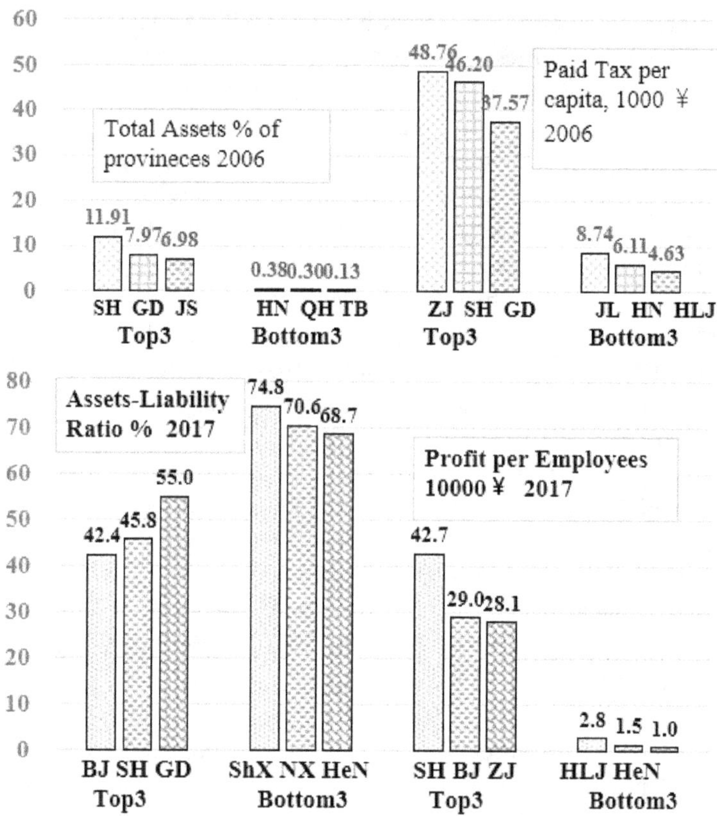

Figure 6.10.   Top three and bottom three provinces with largest regional SOE total assets and paid tax per capita by regional SOE in 2006 and 2017.

Source: same as Tables 6.5 and 6.6.

located in western and middle region, respectively, show regional SOE profits per employee and regional SOE tax paid per employee near the national average. In Beijing, the regional SOE profit is lower than the national regional SOE average and in Tianjin, Jiangxi, and Yunnan — the regional SOE profits are higher than the national regional SOE average value, while the tax paid per employee is lower than national average value. Most provinces (18 provinces, 61.3% of the total) show worsening economic performance. Among the 18 provinces, nine are in the western region, six in the middle region, and three in the eastern region, which indicates that the economic performance is worst in the western region.

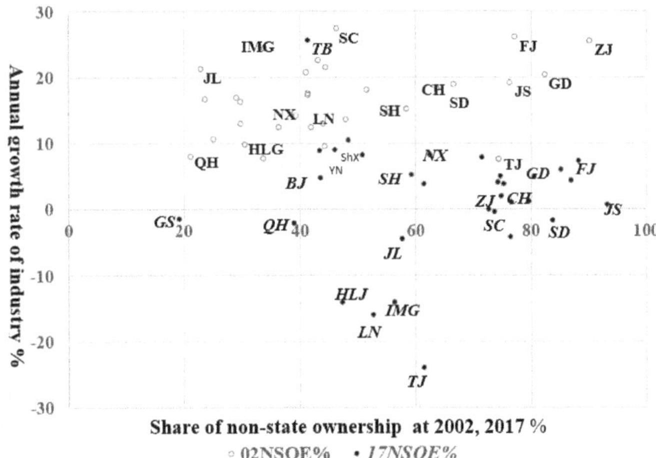

Figure 6.11. Multi-Ownership Promotes Industry Growth, 2002 and 2017.

Source: Calculated using data from China National Bureau of Statistics: China Industry Economy Statistical Yearbook, China Statistical Press, 2003, Table 4.1, Table 4.2; 2001, p, 107, 115; China National Bureau of Statistics: China Statistical Yearbook, China Statistical Press, 2003, Table 13.3; 2002, Table 13.3; 2000, Table 13.5; 1999, Table 13.5; 2018, Table 13.05.

In the eastern region — Hainan's, Liaoning's, and Hebei's SOE tax paid per employee is close to the national average. In Heilongjiang, Hainan, and Jilin, SOE profits per employee and tax paid per employee were worse than the national average values.

In 2017, Qinghai regional SOE profit per employee was CNY53,387; it declined 15.5% from 2006, and now ranked 24th among the 31 provinces. Shanghai's regional SOE profit per employee was CNY426.874; it increased 824% from 2006, with average annual growth rate of 22.4%, and ranked 1st among 31 provinces. Through in-depth implementation of the city's innovation-driven development strategy and the strategy of manufacturing power, while speeding up the transformation process and upgrading of traditional industries, Shanghai's industrial structure continues to develop towards the mid-to-high end. The first component of its industrial structure is a result of the rapid growth of high-tech and equipment manufacturing. The value added of six high-tech industries in Shanghai accounted for 68.9% of the total for the city, and the profit per employee is 18.9% higher than the city's industry. Second, manufacturing information systems have been greatly improved, and key industries have

Table 6.6.   Asset–liability ratios of Chinese SOEs by region, 2017.

Items	Total assets	Total liability	Owners' equities	Assets–liability ratio	Profit per employee	Employed person
	Bil. ¥	Bil. ¥	Bil. ¥	(%)	CNY	10,000
National total	43,962	26610	17352	60.5	1,07,879	1596
Beijing	3,313	1406	1907	42.4	2,90,023	37
Tianjin	1,123	731	391	65.1	1,71,368	26.1
Hebei	1,749	1130	620	64.6	70,308	65.6
Shanxi	2,348	1755	592	74.8	38,030	108.4
Inner Mongolia	1,755	1181	574	67.3	1,14,569	38.1
Liaoning	1,885	1271	614	67.4	31,265	75.7
Jilin	1,010	622	389	61.5	73,527	44.0
Heilongjiang	8,78	504	375	57.4	28,297	52.3
Shanghai	2,074	950	1123	45.8	4,26,874	34.3
Zhejiang	1,167	642	526	55.0	2,81,303	60.2
Jiangsu	2,115	1236	880	58.4	1,84,440	30.3
Anhui	1,463	907	557	62.0	70,541	62.7
Fujian	880	534	346	60.7	1,46,396	22.7
Jiangxi	649	400	249	61.6	76,641	31.8
Shandong	3,113	2002	1111	64.3	87,878	122.3
Henan	1,555	1068	487	68.7	15,052	94.1
Hubei	1,790	1008	782	56.3	1,18,596	56.8

Hunan	1,049	640	409	61.00	78,474	41.1
Guangdong	2,529	1391	1139	55.00	1,95,616	74.4
Hainan	781	514	267	65.9	1,17,480	29.1
Guangxi	112	68	44	60.8	94,691	2.5
Chongqing	842	533	309	66.3	1,21,309	27.9
Sichuan	2,095	1320	775	63.00	98,511	63.8
Guizhou	934	604	330	64.7	1,43,329	29.9
Yunnan	1,419	891	528	62.8	1,31,701	29.8
Shanxi	104	59	45	57.00	44,956	1.2
Gansu	2,207	1258	949	57.00	1,35,952	67.1
Qinghai	907	608	300	57.00	40,828	33.3
Tibet	469	320	149	68.3	53,387	10.5
Ningxia	405	286	119	70.6	10,318	10.6
Xinjiang	1,241	772	468	62.2	94,885	34.8

Source: Calculated using data from China National Bureau of Statistics: China Statistical Yearbook, China Statistics Press, 2018, Table 13.5.

made significant progress in digitization, networking, and intelligence. The third is the integrated development of producer services and manufacturing. More and more manufacturing companies have begun to use new and advanced technologies to extend the upstream and downstream services of the industrial chain, providing a solid carrier and huge market space.[42]

Table 6.7 shows the main indicators of economic performance of all SOEs, which have improved significantly from 1998–2017. Return on equity (ROE), return on total assets (ROA), and the ratio of profit to sales increased from 2.0%, 0.7%, and 1.9% in 1998 to 14.5%, 6.3%, and 10.4% in 2006, respectively. The ratio of profits to interests paid improved from 2.2 in 1998 to 6.8 in 2006. In the 1998–2006 period, the assets to liabilities ratio and current ratio fluctuated within a narrow range. The asset to liabilities ratio seems a little higher and the current ratio seems a little lower than normal, which indicates that total liabilities and current liabilities are higher than normal.[43] The ratio of profits to costs and the profits to interest paid by SOE under Central Management improved from 7.6% and 3.4 times in 2002, to 10.1% and 5.8 times in 2006. The turnover of total capital and turnover of total receivables of SOEs under Central Management improved from 0.4 and 5.7 times/year in 2001, to 0.7 and 15.2 times/year in 2006.

According to the Administrative Methods on Collection of Earnings from Central State-Owned Assets, SOEs supervised by the central government will be paying capital gains to the state at differentiated rates. There are three categories of Central SOE: those in resource-related industries, including tobacco, oil and petrochemical, energy, telecommunications, and coal will pay 10% of their after-tax profits to the state. Those in more competitive sectors such as steel, transportation, electronics, trade, and construction are subject to a 5% rate. The rate for defense industries and transformed science research institutes will be decided in another three years.[44] The new rule puts an end to the practice of China's SOEs not

---

[42]China National Bureau of Statistics (2018). Shanghai Statistical Yearbook, China Statistics Press.

[43]Statistics Bureau website (2018). Reform and opening-up create industrial brilliance, innovation, and transformation to strengthen manufacturing power, September 4 (in Chinese).

[44]Li, Z. (2007). Finance ministry clarifies SOE profit distribution. *China Daily*, December 12.

Table 6.7.   Main indicators of economic benefit of SOEs, 1998–2017.

	1998	2000	2003	2006	2010	2017
Return on equity, %	2.0	7.4	10.0	14.5	15.0	12.8
Return on total assets, %	0.7	2.9	4.1	6.3	8.9	7.8
Ratio of profit to costs, %	1.9	7.2	8.3	10.4	9.3	8.0
Cost for 100 CNY sales revenue	80.7	79.3	79.3	80.8	81.7	81.5
Assets–liability ratio, %	47.6	61.0	59.2	56.2	60.3	64.3
Profit margin on sales, %	1.6	5.7	6.6	8.4	7.6	6.5
Current ratio	1.14	1.12	1.05	0.97	0.93	0.93
Quick ratio	0.93	0.90	0.84	0.73		
Time of profits to interests paid	2.2	3.4	4.1	6.8	5.7	6.5
Turnover of total capital, times/year	0.4	0.5	0.6	0.7	0.8	0.9
Turnover of total receivables, times/year	4.3	5.0	10.0	14.2	14.9	9.1

Source: Calculated using data from China National Bureau of Statistics: China Statistical Yearbook, China Statistics Press, 2018, Table 13.3, 2011, Table 14.4, Editor-in-Chief: Xie, Xuren (Minister of Finance, P.R. China): Finance Yearbook of China, 2007 (in Chinese), p. 412, *China Finance Magazine*.

paying dividends to their largest or major shareholder — the state. Treasury to trial this year to collect half of required after-tax profits from 2006, an estimated CNY17 billion (USD2.33 billion).[45]

It can be seen from Table 6.7, from 2006–2017 that the main indicators of SOEs' performance fluctuated, reflecting the difficulties associated with SOEs reform and the time-consuming aspect of the process. The National 13th FYP (2016–2020) confirmed that the reform of SOEs should be deepened to strengthen the contribution of the state-owned economy. First, SOEs must be classified; the lack of clarity in their functions presents a conflict between the for-profit and public interest nature of SOEs, thus distorting their behaviors. Second, SOE reform is necessary in sectors with overcapacity, such as coal and steel; reform is of great importance to resolving overcapacity, closing zombie companies, and

---

[45]Xinhua (2007). Central SOE return 17b yuan from 2006 profits, September 20.

withdrawing the state sector from sectors exhibiting overcapacity. SOE reform in natural monopolies, including petroleum, telecom, electric power, civil aviation, and railway-reform, should include opening these sectors and carrying out strategic restructuring and mixed ownership reform of sector SOEs. The goal is to develop a pattern of successful business operations within the SOE primary business and create effective competition for sectors of natural monopoly. Third, government institutional reforms must be deepened to propel and empower SOE reform and create a failure tolerance mechanism.[46] Deputy head of the State-owned Assets Supervision and Administration Commission, Weng Jieming, stated at a press briefing that since 2013, central SOEs have received more than 1.5 trillion yuan (about USD223.46 billion) of social capital through various channels. In recent years, central SOEs have explored mixed-ownership reforms in electric power, telecommunications, civil aviation, and other key sectors in an orderly manner. Mixed-ownership enterprises account for over 70% of all legal entities of central SOEs, with listed companies being the major carriers for the reforms.[47]

9. The Cost of China's SOE Reform and the Challenges Facing SOEs

SOE reform required paying the price. By the end of 2003, the Russian presidential economic adviser said at a conference "a free 'privatization' is unlikely to succeed because there is no such thing as free privatization."[48] Before reform, an SOE provided its employees with life-long job security, benefits, and social security. The older the SOE, the more retired workers it had, and so the heavier its burden. In addition, the SOE operating management comprised government-appointed "officials," not entrepreneurs. There is a significant difference between the management objectives and acts of entrepreneurs and those of officials. The SOEs' liquid assets are

---

[46] Huang Qunhui (Institute) of Industrial Economics, Chinese Academy of Social Sciences, Beijing, China (2018). How "New SOEs" Come of Age: Four Decades of China's SOE Reform, (01).

[47] Xinhua (2020). China makes steady progress on central SOE mixed-ownership reform, October 13.

[48] Zhang, J. (2004). How to avoid the "SOE reform" sequels? (in Chinese), *China Internet Weekly*, No. 19.

primarily state banks' loans. Therefore, the nature of the SOE is not the same as the nature of the "modern corporation." This type of SOE cannot operate properly under a market-oriented environment. The cost of SOE reform includes the settlement of obligations to employees and to the creditors.

Since the 1990s, many SOEs in China are loss generating, and a large number have since long been in default to their creditor banks. Credit allocation and asset re-allocation have not been conducted efficiently. In the past, the process of bankruptcy for SOEs has been referred to as "administrative closure." Unlike the bankruptcy process of other ownership enterprises, the money recovered from an insolvent SOE was first used to manage the unemployed, with the leftovers going to the creditors — the state-owned banks. From 1994–2004, China had closed 3,484 insolvent SOEs through administrative intervention, and allowed state-owned banks to write off a total of CNY237 billion (USD27 billion) in bad loans caused by SOE bankruptcies, said Zhao, Nin (Vice Minister of SASAC) at the National SOE Bankruptcy working Conference on May 12, 2005.[49] The overall plan for the closure of bankrupt SOEs was implemented from 2005 to 2008, which included 2,116 enterprises, involving bad loans of state-owned financial institutions of CNY227.16 billion and 3.51 million employees.[50] In 2007, China's central government spent CNY20 billion (USD2.74 billion) to subsidize the policy-based closures or bankruptcies of 92 SOEs and to find new employment for 357,000 of their laid-off employees. Another CNY10 billion (USD1.37 billion) in subsidies was allocated to pay long-overdue salaries and wages owed to SOE employees. CNY5.11 billion (USD0.70 billion) was allocated to relieve enterprises of their obligation to operate social programs. The sum of the above three central government support measures amounted to CNY35.11 billion (USD4.81 billion).[51] Central government support for SOE reform reached CNY29.81 billion (USD4.08 billion) and

---

[49] Xinhua (2008). "Administrative closure" bankruptcy for SOE will be abolished after 2008 (in Chinese), May 12.

[50] Wang, Y. (2005). Policy bankruptcy of SOE will be eventually paid by the state's finance (original in Chinese). *China Business News*, May 13.

[51] Ministry of Finance (2008). Report on the Implementation of the Central and Local Budgets for 2007 and on the Draft Central and Local Budgets for 2008, which was submitted for review on March 5, by the 11th National People's Congress.

CNY26.90 billion (USD3.68 billion) in 2006 and 2005, respectively.[52] In addition, regional governments also provided financial support for bankrupt regional SOEs to pay long-overdue salaries and wages owed to SOE employees and to relieve enterprises of their obligation to operate social security programs. Hence, the total cost for SOE bankruptcy may reach CNY1 trillion. According to China's bankruptcy law that went into effect on June 1, 2007, the remaining SOEs became "equal competitors" in the market economy, rather than being sheltered by the government. The money recovered from insolvent SOEs was used to first pay the creditors — the state-owned banks.

For example, Qier Machine Tool Group Co., Ltd. (reformed from Qiqihar No. 2 Machine Tool Works) moved to the north from Shenyang in October 1950. It was the first group of important enterprises in the domestic machinery industry in the period of the first "5 years plan" and was one of the 18 largest industrial enterprises. Its asset–liability ratio reached 240% in 1999 and workers and staff received only three months of wages in the year. Qiqihar No. 2 Machine The tool factory went bankrupt under the "administrative shutdown" policy in January 2004, as approved by the State Council. In 2005, the creditors wrote off a total of CNY1.25 billion (USD152.6 million) in bad loans. The enterprise settled with 12,000 in-service, retirement, and laid-off workers and proceeded with the liquidation of their non-payment of wages. At the same time, it allowed workers to voluntarily participate in enterprise restructuring and reorganization of the limited liability company. Qi Machine Tool Group Co., Ltd. registered capital of CNY182.8 million (USD22.3 million) from 18 individuals. By the end of 2007, Qi Machine Tool Group Co., Ltd. introduced strategic investors to raise additional equity. The registered capital increased to CNY198.4 million (USD27.2 million), of which the Qi Machine Tool Group Co., Ltd., Qiqihar Municipal SASAC, and Heilongjiang League Group Co., Ltd. accounted for 45.52%, 29.57%, and 1.66% of the total financing, respectively; five natural person shareholders of the enterprises accounted for 23.25% of the funds. In 2007, the

---

[52]Ministry of Finance (2007). Report on the Implementation of the Central and Local Budgets for 2006 and on the Draft Central and Local Budgets for 2007, which was submitted for review on March 5, by the 10th National People's Congress; Ministry of Finance: Report on the Implementation of the Central and Local Budgets for 2005 and on the Draft Central and Local Budgets for 2006, which was submitted for review on March 5, 2006, by the 10th National People's Congress.

value of the gross industrial output value, sales revenue and profits, and taxes of Qi Machine Tool Group Co., Ltd. grew by 45%, 30%, and 46%, respectively, year-on-year.[53] The average annual income of employees was CNY38,000.

Another failed example of SOE bankruptcy is the Mianchi County cement plant. The cement plant in Henan Province is the key enterprise in Henan building materials industries and had been listed in the top 500 of the national building materials industry. In June 2004, the Mianchi County cement plant suddenly declared bankruptcy because of excess debt. After more than four years, the plant was still not in accordance with the law of bankruptcy liquidation and disposition of property, but paid CNY11.81 million in taxes in 2007 and ranked #327 in Henan Province. In 2003, the Mianchi County cement plant had total assets and total debts of CNY235.49 million and CNY176.61 million, respectively; net assets amounted to CNY58.88 million. In 2004, it filed for bankruptcy, as its total assets declined to CNY156.83 million, while total liabilities increased to CNY218.49 million, with net assets of the enterprise becoming a negative CNY61.66 million. In just one year, the local, famous, big profitable enterprise suddenly became "insolvent" and bankrupt, despite its after-tax profits still being CNY3.02 million. In December 2003, one-half year before applying for bankruptcy, a new plant — Mianchi Yangshao Cement Cogeneration Limited — was established with registered capital of CNY17.68 million. In 2007, after three years of bankruptcy proceedings, the new plant invested CNY30 million of a 200,000 tons cement mill project.[54] Therefore, the Mianchi County cement plant declared bankruptcy proceedings, not because of a serious loss of business or insolvency; the real reason for bankruptcy was the suspension of its creditors' recourse debt. The creditors wrote off CNY150 million (USD18.12 million) of financial debt and interest. The bankruptcy of Mianchi County cement plant not only contradicts the relevant provisions of bankruptcy law, but also creates a "sham bankruptcy to evade debt," thereby resulting in loss of state assets.

The effect of a public policy on general welfare depends on weighing this policy against the alternatives. For example, supporting SOEs through

---

[53] Brief Introduction of Qier Machine Tool Group Co., Ltd https://www.globalsources. com/qier-machine/company-profile_6008836855174.htm.

[54] Li, J. (2008). SOE bankruptcy is for repaying a debt or for evading a debt? — A bankrupt enterprise in Henan Provinces became top 500 taxpayers in 2007, Xinhua, September 2.

lower financing costs entails the opportunity cost of the benefit that this kind of support would generate for private enterprises. Of course, attempting to measure the net welfare effect of the creation of and continuous support for SOEs would be a purely theoretical exercise. China is committed to maintaining its SOEs as well as to its multi-ownership model.

10. China Top 500 VS "Fortune" Global 500

China's companies have been getting much bigger in relation to their global counterparts! In 1992, two companies (The Bank of China and Sinochem Corporation) were the first Chinese entrants into Fortune Global 500 (Service Sector). In 1995, Fortune Global 500 for the first time ranked the industrial and the service enterprises together. China's BOC (Bank of China) and COFCO (China National Cereals, Oils, and Foodstuffs Corp.) were listed in the Fortune 1995 Global 500. The number of Chinese companies on the Fortune 500 rank has grown significantly over the years. This can be interpreted as a success of the opening to the outside world policy, as well as an improvement of the global stature of China's companies. By 2020, there were more Chinese than U.S. companies in the Top 500, which may be viewed as a triumph of the country's reform efforts (see Table 6.8). Chinese companies were also listed as revenue leaders in a number of sectors, such as Petroleum Refining (Sinopec Group), Utilities (State Grid), Engineering/Construction (China State Construction Engineering), Network and Communications Equipment (Huawei), Banks (Industrial and Commercial Bank of China), Pharmaceutical (China Resources), Mail/Packages (China Post), Metal (American International Group), Textiles (Hengli Group), Real Estate (Country Gerden Holdings), Building Materials (China National Building Group), and Shipping (China COSCO Shipping).

However, there is still a large gap between these Chinese companies and their foreign counterparts with respect to scale, productivity, operating performance, degree of internationalization, and innovation capability. Chinese companies still have a long way to go before becoming global powerful competitors. For example, according to Table 6.9, Chinese companies listed in "Fortune" 2000 Global 500 had greater revenue than the listed U.S. companies (USD36.9 trillion versus USD32.7 trillion), but lower revenue (USD8.3 trillion versus USD9.8 trillion), lower profit margins (4.5% versus 8.9%), and lower ROA (1.9% versus 4.9%). However,

Table 6.8.   Fortune global 500: Selected Countries/Years.

Year Country	1998	2000	2003	2005	2010	2018	2020
Canada	8	12	13	13	11	12	14
China	3	9	11	15	54	111	124
France	33	37	40	39	39	28	31
Germany	41	37	35	37	37	32	26
India	1	1	1	5	5	7	7
Japan	114	107	89	81	71	52	53
S. Korea	11	12	13	11	10	15	14
Russia	1	2	3	3	5	4	4
Switzerland	11.5	10	11	11	15	14	14
United Kingdom	37	39.5	35	36	29.5	20.5	21
United States	175	179	192	175	139	125	121

Source: Fortune Global 500. Various Issues.

Table 6.9.   Chinese companies in Fortune 500, 2000 and 2020.

Country	Number In 2000	Number In 2020	Assets 2020 (USD trillion)	Revenues 2020 (USD trillion)	Profit margin 2020	Return on assets 2020
China	10	124	36.9	8.3	4.50%	1.90%
USA	179	121	32.7	9.8	8.90%	4.90%
Japan	107	53	16.2	3.1	2.70%	1.40%
France	37	31	11.4	1.8	4.30%	1.90%
Germany	37	27	6.2	1.9	3.30%	2.20%

Source: Kennedy, S. (2020). The Biggest But Not the Strongest: China's Place in the Fortune Global 500. Center for Strategic and International Studies. www.csis.org/blogs/trustee-china-hand/bigges t-not-strongest-chinas-place-fortune-global-500#:~:text=Last%20week%20Fortune%20released%20 its,53%20companies%20on%20the%20list.

Chinese companies compare more favorably in terms of these financials with the listed companies from Japan, France, and Germany.

Of course, Table 6.8 presents a partial picture of the stature of Chinese companies in the Fortune 500 list. We get a more complete assessment of the global position of Chinese companies by examining their rankings in some of the previous years. For example, in 2004, the average revenues of China's companies listed in Fortune Global 500 were 85.0% of the Global 500, but average assets and average employees were 140.4% and 316. % of Global 500, respectively; these numbers also reveal that the average performance of Chinese companies listed in Fortune 2004 Global Top 500 was far below that of the Global average and other foreign countries (United States, Japan, South Korea, and India). However, all four Indian Companies belonged to the petroleum refining industrial sector; therefore, rates of return, per capita net profits, and per capita sales were generally at the high end of the spectrum. We again can conclude that Chinese companies listed in the 2004 Global Top 500 operated with low efficiency and productivity.

One year later, in "Fortune" 2005 Global 500, the total revenue of Chinese all state-owned and non-state-owned industrial enterprises above the designated size (219,463 units) reached CNY18,781.5 billion (USD2,268.3 billion)[55] by the end of 2004, which almost equaled the total revenue of the top 10 companies in the 2005 Global 500 list (USD2,281.0 billion).[56] Total revenue of China's 2005 Top 500 companies was CNY11,746 billion (USD1,418.0 billion), which was less than the total revenue of the top six companies (USD1,482.7 billion) in the 2005 Global 500. The sales revenue of China's first ranked company in 2005 Top 500 was 26.6% of the top ranked company in "Fortune" 2005 Global 500; and the revenue of China's companies ranked last reached only 4.4% of the last one in "Fortune" 2005 Global 500.

In the "Fortune" 2006 Global 500, there were 19 China companies listed.[57] The average rank of these Chinese enterprises was 294. These 19 enterprises were classified into nine industries (according to the

---

[55]Calculated using data from China National Bureau of Statistics: China Statistical Yearbook, China Statistics Press, 2005, Table 14.3.

[56]The 2005 Global 500 (2005). *Fortune*. New York: July 25, Vol. 152, Issue. 2, pp. 119–125.

[57]The 2006 Global 500 (2006). *Fortune*. New York: Jul 24, 2006. Vol. 154, Issue 2; p. 100–129; The 2005 Global 500 (2005). *Fortune*. New York: July 25, Vol. 152, Issue 2, p. 119; The 2004 Global 500, *Fortune*. New York: July 24, Vol. 154, Issue 2, p. 100–126; 18 Chinese enterprises reached Fortune Global 500 criteria in 2004 (in Chinese), www. ssec-steel.net/main/cjyw/1844.html; 2018 Fortune World 500 list, Fortune Chinese Network July 19, 2018 (in Chinese).

"Fortune" classification). There are 53 industrial sectors listed in "Fortune" 2006 Global 500. The nine sectors are only 17% of the listed industrial sectors. All 19 Chinese enterprises were SOEs; 15 of them belonged to state-operated monopolies. Only four enterprises in "Fortune" 2006 Global 500 — Shanghai Baosteel Group, China First Automotive Works, Shanghai Automotive, and China State Construction — belong to competitive manufacturing and construction sectors. The remaining 15 enterprises belong to seven sectors that are monopolies in China. Four are state-operated commercial banks and two are trading companies: SINOCHEM (China National Chemicals Import & Export Corporation) and COFCO (China National Cereals, Oils, and Foodstuffs Import & Export Corporation) are import–export companies. Two of the 15 are oil giants (Sinopec (China Petrochemical Corporation=) and China National Petroleum Corporation), two are telecommunication companies (China Mobile Communications and China Telecommunications), two are utility companies (State Grid Corporation of China and China Southern Power Grid), two are railway companies (China Railway Engineering and China Railway construction), and the final one is an insurance company (China Life Insurance). Labor productivity of China's enterprises was very low. For example, oil giant Sinopec (ranked #23) has 730,800 employees generating USD98.78 billion in revenues, while Exxon Mobil's 83,700 employees bring in USD339.94 billion. We should note that the listed Chinese companies do not reflect the actual competitiveness of Chinese enterprises. The average revenues of China's companies were only 32.7% of the industry leader in "Fortune" 2006 Global 500.

What accounts for this relatively poor performance of Chinese companies through the years? Part of the explanation lies in the lack of agglomeration economies inherited from the Mao years. According to the Third Industry Survey in China, there were 130 auto manufacturing factories and 621 auto parts manufacturing factories in 1995. Total output in 1995 was 1.5 million vehicles, which was less than the output of one auto factory in a developed country. Only six auto factories produced more than 50,000 vehicles, and 80% of these auto factories produced less than 10,000 vehicles. In the steel industry, the average annual output of steel amounted to 950,000 tons; only 22 steel companies produced more than one million tons per year. The average annual output for petroleum refining and papermaking factories were 1.67 million tons and 3,000 tons, respectively. The average capability of a single ethylene producing piece of equipment reached 212,000 tons per year. Among 1600 papermaking,

400 beer, and 130 washing machine producing factories, only 8%, 12%, and 6.9%, respectively, reached the minimum economic scale.[58] During January–October 2003, China produced 3.56 million vehicles, with three large auto companies producing more than 70%,[59] and the remaining one hundred auto factories together producing 1 million vehicles.

Another explanation for lackluster performance of Chinese companies lies in the structure of Chinese industry and its capacity to adjust to the demands of a global economy. As a reference, there were no real estate, engineering construction, and metal smelting companies among the U.S. big companies in 2020, but there were many large companies in the fields of IT, life/health, and food; China's structure presents a contrast to this. In such industries as health/food wholesale, insurance-managed medical care, food production and processing, and entertainment, which are closely related to people's lives and health, we find companies from the United States, Europe, Japan, and Brazil. However, China does not have any such companies listed. In addition, the issue of the monopoly position of the Chinese banking industry in obtaining excess profits remains unresolved. Although the companies included in the Fortune 500 do not necessarily represent the entire population of Chinese companies, we can still examine selected aspects of the nature and performance of SOEs and private enterprises on the list. Table 6.10 contrasts the number, assets, revenues, ROA, and profit margin. Among Chinese companies eligible for inclusion in the Fortune 500, there are more state-owned companies than private companies. SOEs have larger assets but generate a smaller percentage of revenue. SOEs also have on average lower ROA and profit margins than those of private companies. This is also confirmed by the limited information presented in Table 6.22. Of course, this simple analysis does not consider the investment and balance sheet risks.

At this point, we should further clarify the nature of China's SOEs. SOEs do not represent single business entities. Instead, they are "business groups." In an imperfect market and a developing institutional environment, such as that existing in a typical emerging economy, internalizing markets is a more efficient way of operating. In the 1980s, the Chinese government encouraged the formation of such groups to generate efficiencies that could lead to improved financial performance, generate

---

[58] China National Bureau of Statistics: The third industry survey of China in 1995.

[59] Yang, J., M. Zou, D. Li, *et. al.* (2004). China industry development status report. *Shanghai Securities News*, January 30 (in Chinese).

Table 6.10. A breakdown of Chinese companies on Fortune 500.

Type of ownership	Number of companies % of total	Assets	Revenues	Average return on assets	Average profit margin
SOE	73%	84%	78%	1.30%	3.50%
Private	27%	16%	22%	3.70%	7.00%

Source: Adopted from Hao, H. (2020). Charts: A breakdown of Chinese companies ranked on Fortune Global 500. August. https://news.cgtn.com/news/2020-08-17.

innovation, and enhance international competitiveness. By the early 1990s, there were 7,000 such groups in China.[60]

Such business groups have existed in many countries, with the best-known ones being Japan's keiretsu and Korea's chaebols. These groups have been considered as important contributors to Japan's and Korea's emergence as global players. Of course, there are differences between Chinese business groups and groups in other countries. For example, business groups in Japan and Korea comprise privately owned companies. In China, on the other hand, SOEs are the predominant components of business groups. However, business groups comprising private enterprises are emerging in China, especially within the technology sector. According to the National Statistics Bureau of China, a business group consists of "legally independent entities that are partly or wholly owned by a parent firm and registered as affiliated firms of the parent firm."[61] To register as a business group, enterprises must meet specified minimum capital requirements. Some of the best-known Chinese business groups are State Grid, China Mobile, Sinchem, and Baosteel.

10.1. *Fortune global 500 and economic development*

The enterprises' scale mainly depends on the economic development level of the country. Table 6.11 gives the country distribution of "Fortune" Global 500 from 1998–2018. As can be seen from the table, 427

---

[60]He, J., X. Mao, O. M. Rui, and X. Zha (2013). Business groups in China. *Journal of Corporate Finance*, 22, 166–192.

[61]Ma, X. (2005). The critical role of business groups in China. *Ivey Business Journal*. May/June. https://iveybusinessjournal.com/author/xma/.

Table 6.11.   The country distribution of "Fortune" Global 500, 1998–2018.

Year	1998	2000	2002	2004	2006	2010	2018
Australia	7	7	5	7	8	8	7
Austria					1	3	
Belgium	3.5	3.5	3.5	3.5	4.5	5.5	1
Brazil	5	3	4	3	4	7	7
Canada	8	12	16	13	14	11	12
China	5	10	13	15	24	54	120
Denmark			1	2	2	2	1
Finland	2	2	2	4	2	1	1
France	38	37	36	37	38	39	28
Germany	41	37	36	34	35	37	32
Hong Kong	1	1		1	1		
India	1	1	1	4	6	8	7
Ireland				1	1	2	4
Italy	14	10	7	8	10	11	6
Japan	114	107	87	82	70	71	52
Luxembourg		1	1	2	1	1	1
Malaysia	1	1	1	1	1	1	1
Mexico	1	2	2	2	5	2	4
Netherlands	10.5	9.5	10.5	13.5	15	14	14.5
Norway	2	2	2	2	2	1	1
Poland						1	1
Russia	1	2	2	3	5	6	4
Saudi Arabia					1	1	1
Singapore				1	1	2	3
South Africa		1					
South Korea	11	12	13	11	12	10	16
Spain	5	5	5	7	9	10	9
Sweden	4.5	4.5	5	6	6	5	2
Switzerland	11.5	10	11	12	12	15	14
Thailand				1	1	1	1
Turkey					1	1	1
United Arab Emirates							1
United Kingdom	37	39.5	34	36	38.5	29.5	20.5
United States of America	175	179	199	189	170	139	126

Source: The 2006 Global 500, *Fortune*. New York: Jul 24, 2006, Vol. 154, Issue 2, p. 100–129; The 2005 Global 500, *Fortune*. New York: Jul 25, 2005, Vol. 152, Issue 2; The 2004 Global 500, *Fortune*. New York: July 26, 2004, Vol. 150, Issue 2; July 2003; July 21, 2002; July 23, 2001; July 24, 2000; July 1999; July 1998; 2011, July 7; 2018, July 19.

companies in the Top 500 belong to the G7 countries in 1998; this number declined to 363.5 in 2006 and further to 276.5 in 2018. It is obvious that from 1998–2006, the developed G7 countries controlled the world economy. During these eight years, the United States had 165–199 companies on the list; it ranked first, and the gap was even widened from the second one — Japan. Over the same period, the number of Japanese companies dropped from 114 to 70, while the number of Chinese companies rose from three to 22; the number of Indian companies increased from one to six. In 1998, companies from 25 countries were listed in "Fortune" Global 500; in 2006, 32 countries were represented. Companies in the developing world are coming on fast! The expectation is that trend will continue. Using the data in Table 6.11, from 1998–2018 and the economic development level of the country represented by per capita GDP and GDP data,[62] we use data from 1998–2005 to get the following regression equation, Eq. (6.1).

$$Ln(GDPpc) = 1.3571\,\text{TECH} + 3.3521\,\text{HUMAN} + 5.6494$$
$$(2.46) \qquad\qquad (6.14) \qquad\qquad (32.31)$$
$$R = 0.8262,\, F = 120.4,\, n = 112,\, s = 0.9074 \tag{6.1}$$

Numtop — Number of companies of the country listed in "Fortune" Global 500,
GDPpc — per capita GDP (constant 2000 PPPUSD) of the country,
GDP — GDP (constant 2000 USD) of the country.

Equation (6.1) clearly shows the numbers of companies listed in "Fortune" Global top 500 mainly depend on absolute amount of GDP and, secondarily, on GDP per capita. Using the country's GDP and GDP per capita[63] per Eq. (6.1), we estimate the number of companies expecting to join the list of "Fortune" Global 500 in 2005 to check. The results show that the forecast errors calculated by Eq. (6.1) are within acceptable range except for some countries. The number of companies in the countries listed in Fortune varies widely around the regression line for the number of companies of the countries listed in "Fortune" Global 500, which

---

[62] World Bank (2006). World Development Indicators online 2006.
[63] World Bank: World Development Indicators 2002, CD-ROM, Published May 2002 by World Bank, ISBN: 0-8213-5093-5.

indicates the number of companies of the countries listed in "Fortune" Global 500 do not rise uniformly with GDP and GDP per capita levels. For big developing countries, like China, Brazil, India, and Mexico, the real number listed in "Fortune" 2005 Global 500 is significantly less than the predicted value by regression Eq. (6.1). It shows the competitiveness of these countries' companies is low compared with other countries. For some developed countries with small GDP amounts — Switzerland, Netherlands, and France — the real number listed in "Fortune" 2005 Global 500 is significantly greater than the predicted value by regression Eq. (6.1). It implies that the competitiveness of these countries' companies is high compared with companies from developing countries.

According to the 64th annual (2018) Fortune 500 list, the companies included have USD12.8 trillion in revenue – 2/3rds of U.S. GDP – and 28.2 million employees worldwide. These companies remain the most important engines of both the United States and the global economy. In terms of the number of listed companies, Chinese companies reached 120, which is very close to the United States (126), far surpassing Japan (52). No other country has seen such a rapid growth in the number of enterprises. The 48 central enterprises supervised by the State-owned Assets Supervision and Administration Commission of the State Council are on the list, which is exactly one-half of the current total number of central enterprises, accounting for the highest level in history. Also on the list are 11 financially funded companies, 24 local SOEs and 83 SOEs. The average profit of 48 central enterprises listed in 2017 was USD1.444 billion; the average profit of 48 central enterprises listed in 2018 was USD1.592 billion, and profitability continued to increase. In the 2018 list, four central enterprises were dropped, namely China National Chemical Corporation, China National Petroleum Corporation, China Aluminum Corporation, and China Minmetals. However, Chinese companies in the Fortune 500 accounted for 80.6% of the United States's revenue in 2018, with profits, assets, and employees accounting for 56.2%, 287. %, and 181.6%, respectively. This means Chinese companies are less efficient and have lower labor productivity than U.S. companies. If we conduct a longitudinal comparison of the data in recent years, we find that the sales yield of Chinese companies on the list was 5.6% in 2015 and was only 5.1% by 2017. In 2015, the return on net assets of Chinese companies on the list was 10.7%, and it was only 8.9% by 2017.

Using the 2018 data in Table 6.12 and the economic development level of the country as represented by per capita GDP and GDP data,[64] we get the following regression equation, Eq. (6.2).

$$Numtop = 8.2429 \times 10^{-12}\, GDP + 0.4878 \times 10^{-4}\, GDPpc - 4.6158$$
$$(18.15) \qquad\qquad (0.85) \qquad (-1.48)$$
$$R = 0.9588, F = 165, df = 29, s = 8.91 \tag{6.2}$$

Numtop — Number of companies of the country listed in Fortune Global 500,
GDPpc — per capita GDP (constant 2010 USD) of the country,
GDP — GDP (constant 2010 USD) of the country.

Equation (6.2) also shows the number of companies listed in the Fortune Global 500 depends mainly on absolute amount of GDP and, secondarily, on GDP per capita. For example, in China, where GDP is high and GDP per capita is low, the number of companies listed in "Fortune" Global 500 is estimated using Eq. (6.2). GDP and GDP per capita contributed 89.00 and 0.38, respectively, plus the constant item in Eq. (6.5), the estimated number is 84.76 and the real number is 120. Another example, in Luxembourg, where GDP is low and GDP per capita is high, the number of companies listed in "Fortune" Global 500 is estimated using Eq. (6.4). GDP and GDP per capita contributed 0.55 and 5.40, respectively, plus the constant item in Eq. (6.5), the estimated number is 1.41 and the real number is 1. Using Eq. (6.5), we estimate the United States number as 145.24 companies listed in "Fortune" Global 500, and the real number is 126. The difference of 19.24 ranked first in 2018 "Fortune" Global 500; and China has minus 35.28 ranked 32 (last one). It shows that the competitiveness of U.S. companies is high compared to the competitiveness of Chinese companies. Comparing Eq. (6.4) with Eq. (6.5), we observe that the regression coefficients of GDP and GDP per capita in Eq. (6.5) are smaller than those from Eq. (6.4). This shows that GDP and GDP per capita have less impact on the number of companies listed in "Fortune" Global 500 and the slope of regression line of Eq. (6.5) is not as steep as that of Eq. (6.4).

---

[64] World Bank: World Development Indicators online 2018, released on March 21, 2019 by World Bank.

Table 6.12.   Gross domestic expenditure on R&D (GERD) and business enterprise R&D (BERD), 1996, 2002, and GERD (%GDP) 2005, 2010, and 2017.

	GERD		BERD		GERD (%GDP)		
Region/economy	1996	2002	1996	2002	2005	2010	2017
World	575,612	6,76,514	376,343	449,818	1.96	2.04	2.30
Developed countries	531,128	619,403	355,914	417,881	2.26	2.38	1.96[a]
Germany	52,274	50,222	34,551	34,775	2.42	2.71	3.02
Japan	138,623	132,988	92,466	92,328	3.18	3.14	3.20
United States	197,288	276,185	142,371	194,430	2.52	2.74	2.79
Developing economies	39,519	51,616	17,561	28,760	0.88	1.17	1.72[b]
Brazil	6,004	5855(01)	2,733	2389(01)	1.00	1.16	1.26
China	4,865	15,556	—	9,520	1.31	1.71	2.13
India	2,112	3743(01)	—	—	0.84	0.82	0.15 (2015)
Korea, Republic	13,522	13,848	9,899	10,371	2.63	3.47	4.55
Mexico	1,030	2,719	236	763(01)	0.40	0.53	0.48 (2016)
Russian Federation	3,753	4,307	2,597	3,009	0.99	1.05	1.11

Notes: [a]High income; [b]Upper middle income.

Source: UNCTAD World Investment Report 2005: Transnational Corporations and the Internationalization of R&D, Annex table A.III.2. p. 288; OECD: Data table for: Gross domestic spending on R&D, Total, % of GDP, 2000–2018; WDI: Research and development expenditure (% of GDP), 2000–2018.

11. The Role of Mergers

Another facet of SOE reform has been the creation of large enterprises through mergers. The objectives of Chinese mergers include improvement of firm performance through elimination of unused capacity, minimizing competition among SOEs, and generating economies of scale. In the short-run, mergers allow companies to overcome financial challenges. The creation of larger enterprises also makes them more competitive internationally. In addition, consolidation facilitates state control over

SOEs, especially over SOEs in strategic sectors.[65] Many of these mergers have been classified as "megamergers," representing valuations of over USD1 billion. In 2014, there were 14 of these mergers; 13 in 2015; nine in 2016; and 10 in 2017.

An example of such a merger took place in 2017 between the Shenshua Group, (China's largest coal miner) and the Guodian Group (large power generation company). The combined post-merger assets of the new company, China Energy Investment, amounted to USD271 billion; the new company will be the world's largest power company by installed capacity. Both companies benefited from the merger; Guodian benefitted from Shenshua's infrastructure, while Shenshua is able to transition to clean energy.[66]

By the middle of 2019, mergers and acquisitions had resulted in bringing down the number of central SOEs to 96. Merger activity will most likely continue, and mergers between central SOEs and local SOEs may also take place. In all cases, the Chinese authorities hope that the end-result of these mergers will be beneficial to the participating companies as well as the country's overall reform efforts.

12. International Competitiveness

International competitiveness is another major gap between China Top 500 companies and "Fortune" Global 500 companies. The overseas sales revenue and foreign assets of the world's top 100 multinationals reached USD24.5 trillion and USD33.2 trillion, respectively, in 2002.[67] The foreign sales revenue, assets, and employees abroad of the world's top 100 non-financial transnational companies (TNC) amounted to about 50% of the total in 2002. Only four companies from developing economies were listed among the global top 100 non-financial TNCs; they come from Hong Kong, Singapore, Mexico, and South Korea. In 2003, China's

---

[65] O'Connor, S. (2018). SOE Megamergers Signal New Direction in China's Economic Policy. U.S.-China Economic and Security Review Commission. May 24. www.uscc.gov/research/soe-megamergers-signal-new-direction-chinas-economic-policy.

[66] *Ibid.*

[67] United Nations Conference on Trade and Development (UNCTAD, 2004). World Investment Report 2004, United Nations Publication, New York and Geneva, 2004, pp. 22–123, 276–278; 384.

outward FDI stock only reached USD37 billion.[68] No Chinese company was included in the World Top 100 TNCs and Top 50 TNCs. From developing economies, companies from Brazil, Thailand, Philippines, Malaysia, and Argentina entered Top 50 TNCs in 2002. Obviously, the international competitiveness of Chinese companies in Asia is far below that of Japan, Singapore, and South Korea. The internationalization degree of an enterprise has been traditionally measured by its "Transnationality Index" (TNI), which is calculated as the average of the following three ratios: foreign assets to total assets, foreign sales to total sales, and foreign employment to total employment. In the "Fortune" Global 500, the TNI of British Petroleum Company, Exxon Mobil, General Electric, and Siemens reached 81.3%, 65.1%, 40.6%, and 62.3%, respectively.[69] The membership of the Boards of Directors of the "Fortune" Global 500 included more than 40% foreign nationals. In American, Japanese, and the European TNCs, 32%, 19%, and 47%, respectively, of the managers had overseas work experience. In 2002, Wal-Mart International operated more than 1,500 stores employing more than 330,000 associates in Argentina, Brazil, Canada, China, Germany, South Korea, Mexico, Puerto Rico, and the United Kingdom. China's top 500 companies mainly supply the domestic market, and their board members and managers are all from local employees.

In 2002, the Chinese government approved 350 domestic enterprises to conduct business operations abroad, involving a total investment of USD983 million.[70] In 2003, the FDI outflows reached USD1.8 billion, amounting to a meager 1.19% of the United States and 0.29% of world total FDI outflows.[71] In 2004, China's total overseas investment was USD30 billion, covering over 160 countries and regions around the globe, said Zhang Zhigang, Vice Minister of Commerce at an international

---

[68] UNCTAD: World Investment Report 2004, United Nations Publication, New York and Geneva, 2004, p. 384.

[69] United Nations Conference on Trade and Development (UNCTAD, 2004): World Investment Report 2004, New York and Geneva: United Nations Publication, pp.22–23, 276–278; 384.

[70] China to nurture more transnational, http://english.peopledaily.com.cn//200405/26/eng20040526_144380.html.

[71] United Nations Conference on Trade and Development (UNCTAD, 2004): World Investment Report 2004, New York and Geneva: United Nations Publication, Annex Table B.2.

forum on "going global" of Chinese enterprises in Beijing on May 26.[72] China is still a developing country, so its "going global" enterprises lacked the experience of participating in international economic ventures. The degree of internationalization of an enterprise has been generally measured by the share of overseas market sales to its total sales volume, the coverage area of its overseas sales, and the number of foreign nationals working in the enterprise. As we noted above, China's Top 500 companies mainly supply the domestic market. In 2005, China Haier group realized global turnover of USD13 billion; its overseas sales volume was USD4 billion, but overseas profit was "very small."[73] In "Fortune" Asia Top 50 in 2006, only six Chinese companies — Sinopec, State Grid, China National Petroleum, Industrial & Commercial Bank of China, China Mobile Communications, and China Life Insurance — were ranked 2nd, 5th, 7th, 38th, 39th, and 44th, respectively. Japan takes 32 spots in Asia's top 50; and six South Korean companies were ranked 9th, 13th, 14th, 16th, 47th, and 50th. Obviously, the competitiveness of Chinese enterprises in Asia is far below that of Japan and almost the same as that of Korea.

In 2017, China's two-way direct investment inflows and outflows balanced somewhat. FDI outflows reached USD158.29 billion and inflows reached USD136.32 billion. China's FDI outflow stocks accounted for a record high, close to 6% of the world.[74] FDI outflows ranked third in the world. However, the competitiveness of Chinese TNCs in the world is still below that of the United States. For example, in 2017, among the top 50 financial TNCs ranked by Geographical Spread Index (GSI; calculated as the square root of the Internationalization Index multiplied by the number of host countries; the Internationalization Index is calculated as the number of foreign affiliates divided by the number of all affiliates; Affiliates here refers only to majority-owned affiliates) there were three Chinese TNCs: Industrial & Commercial Bank of China (ICBC), ranked #18; Bank of China, ranked #41; and China Construction Bank

---

[72] China's overseas investment exceeds US$30 billion, http://english.peopledaily.com. cn//200405/27/eng20040527_144502.html.

[73] Reuters (2006). Haier falls short of international status, March 7.

[74] FDI inflows into and outflows out of China decreased in 2018 and 2019. In 2019, FDI inflows were USD141.23 billion and outflows USD117.12 billion. United Nations Conference on Trade and Development (UNCTAD, 2020). World Investment Report. www.unctad.org/wir.

Corporation Joint Stock Company, ranked #48. The average ranking for the three Chinese TNCs was 36. There were 13 U.S. TNCs on the list, with an average ranking of 27. In 2017, among the top 100 non-financial multinational Corporations (MNEs) ranked by foreign assets, there were five Chinese MNEs: CK Hutchison Holdings Limited (Hong Kong) was ranked #21, China COSCO Shipping Corp Ltd was ranked #47, China National Offshore Oil Corp (CNOOC) was ranked 54, Tencent Holdings Limited was ranked 72, and HNA Group Co Ltd. was ranked #80; the average ranking was 54.8. There were 13 U.S. MNEs on the list, with an average ranking of 48.[75]

The number of mainland Chinese companies in the Fortune Global 500 rankings in 2020 ranks first. This shows us the historical progress that Chinese companies have made since the reform and opening-up, especially since they joined the WTO and integrated into economic globalization in 2001. In 2019, the average return on sales of the Fortune 500 is 6.2%, while that of American companies is 10.5%; the average return on equity of the Fortune 500 is 11.3% and that of American companies is 17%. The average return on sales of mainland Chinese companies on the list is 5.4%, which is lower than the 8.6% of American companies, and the average return on equity is 9.8%, which is lower than the 17% of American companies. The per capita sales income of American companies is USD570,000, while that of Chinese companies is only USD380,000; the per capita profit of U.S. companies is USD49,000, and the per capita profit of Chinese companies is only USD20,000. These data tell us that from the perspective of corporate profitability, Chinese companies are large but not strong, especially considering the gap with American companies is still very large.

From the perspective of internationalization, companies need to enhance global competitiveness. Extend the value chain to the world to build a global value chain. This is the real secret for global companies to form super global competitiveness. World-class companies often own or dominate a global value chain/industry chain. However, few Fortune Global 500 Chinese companies can build, own, and dominate such a global value chain. As the country continues to expand and open up,

---

[75]United Nations Conference on Trade and Development (UNCTAD, 2018): World Investment Report 2018, United Nations Publication, Web table 19. The world's top 100 non-financial MNEs, ranked by foreign assets, 2017, Annex table 21. The top 50 financial TNCs ranked by Geographical Spread Index (GSI), 2017.

Chinese companies should enhance their global competitiveness in the process of integrating into the global industrial chain.

From the perspective of global competition rules, companies need to enhance their competitiveness in compliance. This is the main risk faced by Chinese companies going global. Some of the overseas institutions of the Bank of China that have entered the world's top 500 rankings have been investigated and punished by foreign regulatory agencies because of ineffective anti-money laundering and other reasons. Some companies have also been blacklisted by the World Bank because of violations. At present, there are more than 900 Chinese companies on the World Bank's sanctions list because of violations of World Bank rules. This shows that compliance risk has become the core risk faced by Chinese companies go global. Relevant departments of the State Council have issued guidelines for corporate compliance management to promote corporate compliance. Since the spread of the new crown pneumonia epidemic this year, the Chinese government has stated that it will "accelerate the integration of domestic systems and rules with international standards" and "follow market principles and international rules."

Chinese companies have now come to a new starting point. From the 2020 Fortune Global 500 rankings, we see that although the number of Chinese companies on the list has increased in size, they still need to enhance their profitability, global competitiveness, and compliance competitiveness.[76]

One measure of emphasis on innovation is the amount of funds allocated to Research and Development (R&D). Table 6.11 illustrates gross domestic expenditure on R&D (GERD) and China's GERD and BERD accounted for 5.6% and 5.0% of those of the United States in 2002, and less than that of South Korea. The R&D spending of two large TNCs — Ford Motor (automobile) and Pfizer (Pharmaceuticals) — reached USD6.84 billion and USD6.50 billion in 2003, respectively.[77] The R&D spending of these two TNCs exceeded China's BERD in 2002. PetroChina, the largest R&D spending company in 2003, contributed only USD275

---

[76] Wang Z. (2020). For the first time, the number of Fortune Global 500 in Mainland China has surpassed that of the United States, but the profitability level is very low from that of the United States, August 10.

[77] UNCTAD World Investment Report 2005: Transnational Corporations and the Internationalization of R&D, Annex table A.III.2. p. 120.

million, much less than South Korea's Samsung Electronics R&D spending of USD2.74 billion.

In 2002, China's GERD was 1.06% of GDP. As can be seen from Table 6.23, from 2005–2017, China's, South Korea's, Mexico's, and the Russian Federation's average annual growth rates were 3.82%, 4.32%, 1.45%, and 0.86%, respectively. In absolute terms, South Korea's, China's, the Russian Federation's, and Mexico's GERD are ranked first, second, third, and fourth, respectively.

The role of TNCs in the R&D activities of a country may also be gauged from measures related to the output of R&D activities. The number of patent applications submitted to the United States Patent and Trademark Office (USPTO) from developing economies has been rising dramatically through the years (albeit from a low base), as shown in Table 6.12. Patents granted by the USPTO to inventors in China were only 10.2% of the patents awarded to inventors in South Korea during the period 2001–2003; it was also less than those awarded to inventors in India. According to Table 6.9, from 1986–2016, the average annual growth rates of triadic patent families in China, South Korea, Mexico, and Taiwan were 35.8%, 33.6%, 24.1%, and 22.7%, respectively. The absolute value of triadic patent families ranked first, second, third, and fourth are Japan, the United States, China, and South Korea. Hence, from 1986–2016 the number of Chinese triadic patent families increased significantly.

The UNCTAD Innovation Capability Index (UNICI) consists of the un-weighted averages of the two indices — the Technological Activity Index and the Human Capital Index. The un-weighted regional averages for the UNICI are shown in Table 6.12. In 1995, China ranked 63rd among 117 countries/economies, and 53rd in 2001. It can be seen from Table 6.13 that China's score increased slowly from 1995–2001, ranking 7th among the eight countries listed. USA and JP ranked the top two. In 2011, the WIPO (World Intellectual Property Organization) ranked China 29th among 126 countries/economies, and 17th in 2008. According to Table 6.12, China's score grew rapidly from 2011–2018, ranking 5th among the eight countries listed. Singapore and the United States were the top two. From 2011–2018, the growth rate of China's WIPO Innovation Index was 14.3%, ranking China 1st, and showing the country's progress. As expected, technological activity, skills, and incomes reinforce each other. The causal connections between the three are highly complex, and

Table 6.13.   Regional un-weighted averages for the UNCTAD Innovation capability.

	UNCTAD innovation		WIPO global	
	1995	2001	2011	2018
Germany	0.887	0.891	54.89	58.03
Singapore	0.803	0.875	59.64	59.83
Russian	0.792	0.759	35.85	37.90
China	0.390	0.417	46.43	53.06
USA	0.963	0.949	56.57	59.81
Japan	0.949	0.935	50.32	54.95
India	0.328	0.373	34.52	35.18
South Korea	0.762	0.812	53.68	56.63

Source: UNCTAD World Investment Report 2005: Transnational Corporations and the Internationalization of R&D, Table III.2, pp. 287–288; WIPO Global Innovation Index, Energizing the World with Innovation, 2011 pp. 18–19; 2018, pp. 22–23.

there are many possible feedback loops. For example, Eq. (6.1) [78] illustrates that more technological activity leads to higher incomes, and higher incomes, in turn, allow countries to invest more in innovation.

$$Ln(GDPpc) = 1.3571\,\text{TECH} + 3.3521\,\text{HUMAN} + 5.6494$$
$$(2.46) \qquad (6.14) \qquad (32.31)$$
$$R = 0.8262,\ F = 120.4,\ n = 112,\ s = 0.9074 \tag{6.3}$$

where TECH — Technological Activity Index, HUMAN — The Human Capital Index, *GDPpc* — GDP per capita, (constant 2000 USD).

From Eq. (6.1), we can say that when the Technological Activity Index increases by 0.01 (holding Human Capital Index constant), GDP per capita will increase by 1.36%; when the Human Capital Index increases by 0.01 (holding Technological Activity Index constant), GDP

---

[78] Data from UNCTAD World Investment Report 2005: Transnational Corporations and the Internationalization of R&D, Annex Table AIII.4; Table AIII.5, pp. 290–291; World Bank: World Development Indicators online 2005, released April 2005 by World Bank.

per capita will increase by 3.41%. It implies that the Human Capital Index has a greater effect on increments of GDP per capita. It can be argued that the main causal link is likely to run from innovative activity and skills to incomes, and that innovative activity requires more advanced skills. Table 6.12 illustrates the UNCTAD Innovation Capability. The high capability group in the UNICI comprises all developed countries (including the new EU members).

South Asia and Sub-Saharan Africa show a lower score over time. Therefore, higher GDP per capita will result in higher UNICI, which is confirmed by the regression analysis shown in Eq. (6.3)[79]:

$$Numtop = 1.9167 \times 10^{-11} GDP + 2.0168 \times 10^{-4} GDPpc - 5.3343$$

$$(82.61) \qquad\qquad (5.10) \qquad\qquad (-5.70)$$

$$R = 0.9856, F = 3652, df = 215, s = 6.50$$

$$(6.4)$$

where *UNICI* — UNCTAD Innovation Capability Index in 2001, *GDPpc* — GDP per capita, (constant 2000 USD) in 2001.

From Eq. (6.4), we learn that when the UNCTAD Innovation Capability Index increases by 0.01, GDP per capita will increase by 7.24%; when GDP per capita increases to 500%, UNCTAD Innovation Capability Index will increase by 0.23. There is a large variation around the regression line for the UNCTAD Innovation Capability Index, which indicates that the Innovation Capability Index does not rise uniformly with per capita income levels. Countries above the regression line have higher innovation index values than predicted by their per capita incomes; those below the regression line score lower on the Innovation Capability index than predicted by their per capita incomes. A small resource-rich economy, such as the United Arab Emirates, has the lowest composite innovation score relative to per capita income; it is followed by Hong Kong (presumably earning high income from service activities that do not require significant technological effort).

Economies in transition — Ukraine and Russia — are located above the regression line in terms of technological activity and human capital.

---

[79] Data from UNCTAD World Investment Report 2005: Transnational Corporations and the Internationalization of R&D, Table III.5, p. 114; World Bank: World Development Indicators online 2005, released April 2005 by World Bank.

The gap is mainly between developed and developing countries, but also within the developing and transition economies. China, Brazil, and India are located near the regression line, but the value of their Innovation Capability index is well below that of South Korea, Singapore, and Russia. China's innovation capability, then, is relatively low. China requires the progression of high-tech industries from processing and assembling to independent research and development and advancement of independent innovation commercialization. One possible strategy is the establishment of a series of leading industries with core competence and increasing independent innovation as the core link, to increase overall technological level and improve industry competitiveness.[80]

Take, for example, Shanghai Zhenhua Port Machinery Co. Ltd. (ZPMC), a famous manufacturer of port cranes. ZPMC has traditionally had the largest order book for large container cranes in the industry and controlled 66.6% of the global market share in 2005.[81] ZPMC products are in use in 48 countries and regions, and over 80 terminals around the world. ZMPC was established in 1992 with capital of only USD1 million. The company's high growth has been attributed mainly to speeding up the pace of independent innovation. ZPMC designed and fabricated the first set of quayside container cranes, which can handle twin 40 feet containers with dual hoist in the world and 10 technology innovations were used in its rubber-tyred gantry cranes (RTGs).

UNTCAD stopped publishing its UNICI index in subsequent World Investment Reports after 2005. Therefore, the WIPO's GII (Global Innovation Index) was used to replace the UNICI. An innovation can be defined as the implementation of a new or significantly improved product (good or service), a new process, a new marketing method, or a new organizational method in business practices, workplace organization, or external relations. In 2018, the GII model included 126 countries/economies, representing 90.8% of the world's population and 96.3% of the world's GDP (billion PPP USD). The GII relies on two sub-indices — the Innovation Input Sub-Index and the Innovation Output Sub-Index — each built around pillars. The Innovation Efficiency Ratio is the ratio of the Output Sub-Index to the Input Sub-Index. It shows how much innovation output a given country is getting from its inputs. In the group of

---

[80]Abstract of the Eleventh Five-Year Plan outline (draft, 2006), (in Chinese). *People's Daily*, March 8.

[81]Tu, D. (2006). The secret of ZPMC rapid growth (in Chinese). *The Investors*, January 5.

innovation leaders, we find the top 25 economies. All these innovation leaders are high-income economies, with the sole exception of China, which belongs to the upper-middle-income group. These economies show mature innovation systems with solid institutions and high levels of market and business sophistication, allowing investment in human capital and infrastructure to translate into quality innovation outputs. China remains the top middle-income economy for the sixth consecutive year and is the only country closing the gap with the high-income group, especially with respect to patent families (29th) and quality of scientific publications (14th). The five countries with the highest Innovation Efficiency Ratios are countries that combine certain levels of innovation inputs with more robust output results: Switzerland, Luxembourg, China, the Netherlands, and Ukraine.

China's recent innovation prowess becomes evident in various areas. It reveals some of its greatest improvements in global R&D companies, high-tech imports, the quality of its publications, and tertiary enrollment. In absolute terms, and in areas such as R&D expenditures and the number of researchers, patents, and publications, China is now 1st or 2nd in the world, with volumes that overshadow most high-income economies.

13. It's all about the Brand!

The China Top 500 and "Fortune" Global 500 disparity is also bigger when it comes to brand value creation. Table 6.14 shows the country distribution of the fifth annual Business Week/Interbrand ranking of the 100 most valuable global brands in 2005.

A dollar value is calculated for each brand using publicly available data, projected profits, and variables such as market leadership. The total brand value of Global 100 Top Brands in 2005 reached USD10.45 trillion, while the United States by itself accounted for USD7.08 trillion. There is no Chinese brand listed in Global Top 100 Brands. Why is that? Let us use the athletic shoe example. One pair of athletic shoes has a value of USD10 in China but can sell for USD120 in the United States. Every year China produces 6 billion pairs of athletic shoes, exports each pair, and sells at an average of USD2.5. After placing the foreign famous brand on the shoe, the sale price becomes several times greater. The key here is not who produces the shoe, because everybody may produce it, but who sells it. Chinese enterprises lack new product development ability and cannot

Table 6.14. Patent applications from developing countries in the United States, by residence of inventor, 1986–2016.

Region/economy	Average 1991–1993	Share of foreign (%)	Average 2001–2003	Share of foreign (%)	Change between periods (%)
Brazil	114	0.15	240	0.16	111.4
China	130	0.17	849	0.56	553.3
India	56	0.07	909	0.6	1513
Korea, Republic	1472	1.91	8356	5.54	467.6
Mexico	98	0.13	179	0.12	83.6
Russian Federation	112	0.14	384	0.25	242.6
Singapore	85	0.11	788	0.52	823.4
Taiwan Province of China	2598	3.36	12453	8.25	379.4
Developing economies	5121	6.63	25322	16.78	394.5
Developed countries	71805	92.94	124905	82.77	73.9
All foreign applications	77263	100	150899	100	95.3
Domestic applications	93445	…	183566	…	96.4
All applications	170708	…	334465	…	95.9

Total number, yearly					
Triadic patent families	1986	1993	2000	2007	2016
Brazil	2.33	16.64	40.66	69.3	54.66
China	6.3	22.17	87.02	690.06	3890.32
India	5.32	10.65	67.19	195.25	392.67
Republic of Korea.	5.92	331.29	908.97	1977.66	2598.58
Mexico	4.83	11.74	9.28	18.76	32.73
Russian Federation	55.08	62.56	84.58	77.25	118.17
Singapore	1.59	21.53	82.67	116.91	146.83
Taiwan Province of China	5.33	19.55	50.46	284.63	388.04
Japan	5684.48	9622.89	18264.04	18594.39	17390.93
United States	8191.38	12414.69	15627.66	13881.98	14220.77
World	24392	36353.00	55987.00	53803.00	56034.78

Source: UNCTAD World Investment Report 2005: Transnational Corporations and the Internationalization of R&D, Annex table A.III.3, p. 289; OECD Triadic patent families: OECD Patent Statistics: Patents by main technology and by International Patent Classification (IPC), https://data.oecd.org/rd/triadic-patent-families.htm#indicator-chart.

Table 6.15.   The country distribution of The Global 100 Top Brands in 2005 and 2018.

Country	Brand number	% of total brand value	Country	Brand number	% of total brand value
	2005			2018	
US	53	67.75	US	55	69.68
China	0	0.00	China	14	13.80
Germany	9	7.02	Germany	8	4.81
France	8	4.22	France	4	2.62
UK	4	2.03	UK	4	1.97
Japan	7	7.06	Japan	3	1.48
Spain	1	0.36	Spain	2	1.13
			Canada	2	0.97
			Australia	2	0.77
Republic of Korea	3	2.02	Korea Rep.	1	0.75
Italy	4	1.41	Italy	1	0.51
			India	1	0.48
Sweden	1	0.75	Sweden	1	0.40
			HK, China	1	0.35
			Indonesia	1	0.29
Switzerland	5	3.46			
Netherlands	4	1.39			
Finland	1	2.53			

Source: The 100 Top Brands, Business Week, August 1, 2005, Iss. 3945, pp. 86–94; Millward Brown. Top 100 global brands, 2018, The BrandZ ranking of the world's 100 most valuable brands.

rely on their brand as the foundation for market development. They must learn the product development process and develop the market with China's own innate brand to make "Made in China" a reality.[82]

Huawei Technologies is one good example of a Chinese enterprise creating a brand. The company provides customized network solutions for telecom carriers around the world. Specializing in research, development, and production and marketing of communications equipment, Huawei

---

[82]Li, J., and C. Wu (2005). China Top 500 versus "Fortune" Global 500 (in Chinese), *Economic Information Daily*, September.3.

holds leading positions in the global market in the areas of switching, next generation network (NGN), integrated access network, Digital Subscriber Line Access Multiplexer (DSLAM), and optical network. Its products and solutions serve over 90 countries, as well as 22 of the world's top 50 operators. In 2004, Huawei's contracted sales reached USD5.58 billion, an increase of 45% year on year. International sales have been doubling each year for the past five consecutive years amounting to USD2.28 billion in 2004. Huawei Technologies does not depend on the low price to compete with multinational corporations. Compared with the European and American multinational corporations, Huawei's price is in the middle and upper ranges.[83]

In 2018, the total brand value of Global 100 Top Brands reached USD438.35 trillion, with the United States accounting for USD305.44 trillion. China ranks second with a brand value of USD60.50 trillion. As can be seen from Table 6.11, from 2005 to 2018, the rise of Chinese brands is one of the most notable features of the BrandZ rankings in 2018. While U.S. brands — particularly those of tech companies — still dominate in terms of numbers, Chinese businesses such as Tencent and Alibaba are seeing rapid increases in their brand value, growing at double the pace of their U.S. rivals. In 2018, the value of brands from Switzerland, the Netherlands, Japan, Italy, and the South Korea dropped significantly. Indian banking brand HDFC and Indonesian bank BCA are notable exceptions in the rankings otherwise dominated by the United States, Europe, and China. This reflects the growing branding power of financial services in these economies. Telecom brands, on the other hand, are heading downward in the rankings, as customer attention is increasingly captured by smartphone makers or companies offering apps and services.

14. The Ownership Structure Change of Chinese Industry

Figure 6.12 shows the ownership structure in terms of total industry gross output. China has adjusted its ownership structure quite successfully by developing a multi-ownership economy. Multi-ownership promotes industry growth, as illustrated by Figure 6.12, which shows that the larger

---

[83] Ran, Y. (2005). Huawei has accounted for the overseas sales volume 40% of its sales (in Chinese), *People's Daily,* May 27.

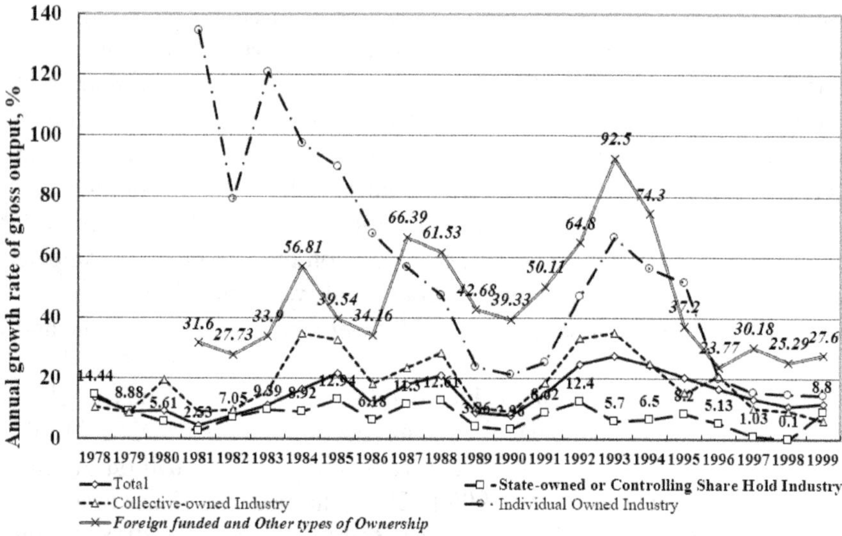

Figure 6.12.   The annual growth rate of industry gross output for different ownership before 2000.

Source: Calculated using data from China National Bureau of Statistics: China Industry Economy Statistical Yearbook, China Statistics Press, 2001, pp. 21–22.

the share of non-state ownership, the higher the annual growth rate of industry gross output. Using 2002 data, we estimate the following equation:

$$IND_{GR02} = 0.1062\ Nonstate_{02} + 11.6875 R = 0.3570,$$
$$F = 4.24,\ df = 29,\ s = 5.245. \tag{6.5}$$

Equation (6.5) is statistically unacceptable. Figure 6.12 reveals a large variation around the regression line for annual growth rate of industrial gross output, which indicates that the annual growth rate of industrial gross output does not rise uniformly with the share of non-state ownership enterprises in industrial gross output. Provinces above the regression line have higher annual growth rate of industrial gross output than predicted by their share of non-state ownership enterprises in industrial gross output; those below the regression line have lower annual growth rate of industrial gross output than predicted by their share of non-state ownership enterprises in industrial gross output. Figure 6.12 shows that, in 2002,

Tianjin has the lowest annual growth rate of industrial gross output in relation to its share of non-state ownership enterprises in industrial gross output, and its real growth rate is 12% lower than its estimated value per Eq. (6.6). Sichuan, located far above the regression line in Figure 6.12, has the highest annual growth rate of industrial gross output in relation to its share of non-state ownership enterprises in industrial gross output; its real growth rate is 10.8% higher than the Eq. (6.6) estimated value. There are seven provinces — Jiangsu, Anhui, Shandong, Guangdong, Guangxi, Chongqing, and Guizhou — located near the regression line and having real growth rate within 1.5% of their Eq. (6.6) estimate. To sum up, the share in gross output of non-state ownership enterprises promotes the annual growth rate of industrial gross output, but there are many other factors (industrial structure, resource, and others) that determine the annual growth rate of industrial gross output.

When we use the data for 2017[84] for our regression analysis, we can get

$$ING_{GR17} = 0.00517\ Nonstate_{17} + 1.2693$$
$$(0.0533) \qquad\qquad (0.1975)$$
$$R = 0.0099\ F = 0.2527,\ df = 29\ s = 9.428 \tag{6.7}$$

Equation (6.7) is not statistically significant, which means a linear relationship does not exist between annual growth rate of industry gross output and the share in gross output of non-state ownership enterprises in 2017. The annual growth rate of industry gross output of 31 provinces is randomly distributed. Figure 6.12 shows that, in 2017, Tianjin has the lowest annual growth rate of industrial gross output in relation to its share of non-state ownership enterprises, and its real growth rate is 25.6% lower than the Eq. (6.7) estimated value. Tibet, located far above the 2017 regression line in Figure 6.12, has the highest annual growth rate of industrial gross output in relation to its share of non-state ownership enterprises in industrial gross output and its real growth rate is 24.1% higher than Eq. (6.7) calculated value. There are three provinces — Jiangsu, Zhejiang, and Jiangxi — located near the regression line and having real growth rates within 1.5% of their Eq. (6.7) estimated value. This shows that, in 2017,

---

[84]Calculated using data from China National Bureau of Statistics: China Statistical Yearbook, China Statistical Press, 2018, Table 13.3, 13.5; 2017, Table 13.3,13.5.

the randomly distributed industrial growth rates of the 31 provinces are more dispersed than in 2002. In 2002 and 2017, the standard deviations of 31 provinces were 5.16 and 9.27, respectively.

The annual growth rates of industry gross output for different ownership enterprises after economic reform are shown in Figure 6.12. The lowest annual growth rate is those of the SOEs, while the annual growth rate of private and FFEs is much higher. From 2000, the statistical specifications of industry gross output changed; only enterprises with an annual sales income of over CNY5 million were included.

The industry gross output in 2000 was CNY8,567.4 billion (USD1,034.7 billion), and it was CNY7,270.7 billion (USD878.3 billion) in 1999. The annual growth rate was 17.8% in 1999.[85] Figure 6.14 shows the annual growth rate of industry gross output for different ownership structures during 2001–2017. It shows that, in 2017, the annual growth rate of SOEs was low, and the annual growth rate of collective-owned enterprises was negative. Meanwhile, the annual growth rates of private enterprises and FFEs were high. Utilizing the data from Figures 6.1, 6.2, 6.13 and 6.14, we calculate the contribution of different ownership enterprises to the annual growth rate of total industry gross output by Eq. (6.9), which is listed in Table 6.16.

$$Contr_i = \frac{\Delta_i}{\Delta_t} \qquad (6.6)$$

where $Contr_i$ = Contribution of i ownership to the annual growth rate of total industry gross output,

Δ_i = increment of industry gross output of i ownership,

Δ_t = total increment of industry gross output.

At the beginning of the reform (1978), SOEs contributed 77.6% to the annual growth rate of industry gross output; their contribution declined to 28.2% in 1999, then increased to 38.1% in 2001 by including state-controlled share-holding enterprises in the calculation.

The contribution to the annual industrial growth rate from foreign-funded ownership and other types of ownership became the largest in recent years and reached 26.1% in 1999. Because FFEs' ownership became increasingly important, FFEs ownership in Figure 6.12 became an

---

[85]Calculated using data from China National Bureau of Statistics (2002). China Statistical Yearbook, China Statistics Press, 2001, Table 13.1.

Table 6.16.   The contribution of different ownership enterprises to the annual growth rate of total industry gross output in %, 1978–2017.

	State-owned	Collective-owned	Private owned	FDI & other types owned	Annual growth rate of gross output
1978	77.6	22.4			13.5
1980	76.0	23.5			
1985	64.9	32.1	1.9	1.2	21.4
1990	54.6	35.6	5.4	4.4	7.8
1991	56.2	33.0	4.8	6.0	14.8
1992	51.5	35.1	5.8	7.6	24.7
1993	47.0	34.0	8.0	11.1	27.3
1994	37.3	37.7	10.1	14.8	24.2
1995	34.0	36.6	12.9	16.6	20.3
1996	36.3	39.4	15.5	16.6	16.6
1997	31.6	38.1	17.9	18.4	13.1
1998	28.2	38.4	17.1	22.9	10.8
1999	28.2	35.4	18.2	26.1	11.6
2000	38.1	16.2	13.0	32.7	8.6
2010	22.0	11.4	39.1	27.5	10.3
2017	18.0	13.4	46.6	22.0	–2.2

Notes: In 2000, 2010, and 2017,the Industrial Gross output was replaced by Revenue from Principal Business of Industrial Enterprises.

Source: Calculated using data from China National Bureau of Statistics: China Industry Economy Statistical Yearbook, China Statistics Press, 2003, Tables 2.5, 2.6; China National Bureau of Statistics: China Statistical Yearbook, China Statistics Press, 2006, Tables 14.4, 14.10, 14.14, 14.18; 2005, Table 14.1; 2004, Tables 14.1, 14.2; China National Bureau of Statistics, Database; Annual, Revenue from Principal Business of Industrial Enterprises (100 million yuan) by ownership, 1999–2017.

independent type of ownership. Its contribution fluctuates; it increased from 25.8% in 2001 to 35.9% in 2004, and then decreased to 27.5% in 2010 and to 22 % in 2017. In 1978, there were no private enterprises. In 1999, the contribution rate of private enterprises increased to 18.2%, and further increased to 46.6% in 2017. Collective-owned enterprises contributed 22.4% in 1978 to annual growth rate of industry; their contribution increased to 39.4% in 1996 and declined to 13.4% in 2017. Therefore, in Figure 6.13, collective-owned enterprises included other types of ownership.

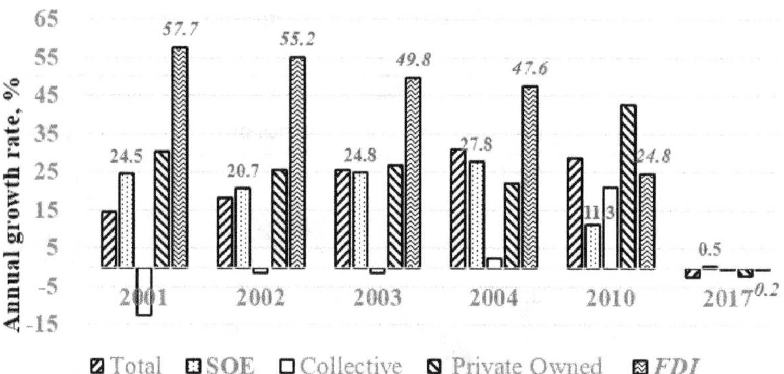

Figure 6.13. The annual growth rate of industry gross output for different types of ownership, 2001–2017.

Source: Calculated using data from China National Bureau of Statistics: China Industry Economy Statistical Yearbook, China Statistics Press, 2003, Table 2.5, 2.6; China National Bureau of Statistics: China Statistical Yearbook, China Statistics Press, 2006, Table 14.4, 14.10, 14.14, 14.18; 2005, Table 14.1; 2004, Table 14.1, 14.2; China National Bureau of Statistics, Data base; Annual, Revenue from Principal Business of Industrial Enterprises (100 million yuan) by ownership, 1999–2017.

Table 6.14 and Figure 6.13 show that private and foreign-funded ownership enterprises were full of vitality, and SOE reform became pressing, and a difficult task on the horizon. It also shows that the policy of allowing the development of ownership reform in multi-ownership enterprises is more suitable for China's national environment than a policy of SOE privatization would be. In Figure 6.13, comparing 2010 with 2017, we observe the total growth rate of revenue from principal businesses of industrial enterprises have decreased from 27.3% in 1993 to minus 2.2% in 2017. The two main contributors — private ownership and foreign-funded ownership enterprises — to the annual industrial growth rate in 1993 accounted for 8.0% and 27.3%, respectively, and 46.6% and 22.0% in 2017. The Revenue from Principal Businesses of Industrial Enterprises decreased from CNY115,899.9 billion in 2016 to CNY113,316.1 billion in 2017. However, Total Profits of Industrial Enterprises increased from CNY7,192.1 billion in 2016 to CNY7,496.3 billion in 2017. This shows that China's ownership structure has undergone extensive and profound changes. As the country transitions from high-speed growth to high-quality development, private enterprises will undoubtedly experience challenges. Nevertheless, they should be regarded as an integral element of China's economic system and, thus, be allowed to flourish and contribute to the development of a multi-ownership economy.

For decades, China has adhered to opening up. Although the country is in the midst of a trade war, it should accelerate its development with an even higher level of openness. Since the beginning of 2019, China has taken a series of new measures in opening up to the outside world, including creating a more attractive business investment environment and significantly reducing import tariffs on more than 1,400 consumer goods and more than 1,500 industrial products. Investment was allowed to enter in fields on the negative list, and was further opened in the fields of finance, automobiles, aircraft, and ships. In the future, China must speed up the unification of domestic and foreign-funded laws and regulations to ensure foreign-funded enterprises enjoy national treatment in laws and policies after access, and improve laws and regulations related to intellectual property protection.[86]

Figure 6.14 shows that the absolute state budget investment increased from 3.7 billion current CNY (USD1.11 billion) in 1952 to 39.6 billion current CNY (USD12 billion) in 1978. After economic reform, it increased to 3874.2 billion current CNY (USD573.6 billion) in 2017; however, its percentage share in total investment declined rapidly from 82.6% of total investment in 1978 to 4.4% in 2005.

Figure 6.14 shows that, before economic reform, the state budget was the main source of investment at an average of 73% during 1953–1978, but it only accounted for 4.4% in 2005 and 6.1% in 2017, indicating that the amount of total investment increased more significantly, with the benefit coming from multi-ownership. For example, in 1985, the State Budget was CNY31.9 billion (1978 constant CNY); it increased to CNY972.8 billion (1978 constant CNY) in 2017, 23.3 times that of 1985. However, from 1985–2017, the proportion of State Budget investment dropped from 16% to 6.1%. Fundraising and Others became main contributors of total investment, accounting for 82.3% in 2017.

Product quality is supervised by The General Administration of the People's Republic of China for Quality Supervision, Inspection, and Quarantine (AQSIQ). The quality of products produced by SOEs and foreign-funded enterprises is getting better. A preliminary market access system for Chinese product quality has been set up and put into

---

[86]Ma, J. (2018). Under the strong leadership of the party, it has embarked on a new journey of reform and opening up, December 26 (in Chinese).

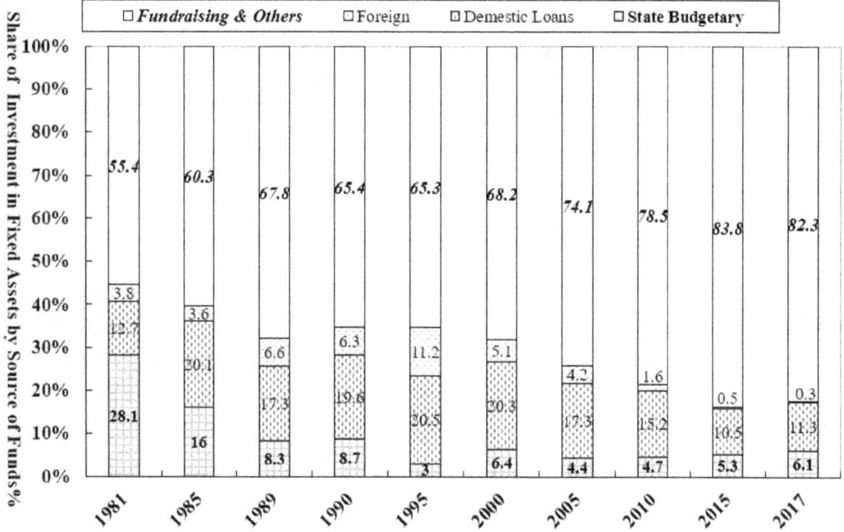

Figure 6.14.   State budget investment and % of investment in China, 1981–2017.

Source: Calculated using data from China National Bureau of Statistics: China Statistical Yearbook, 2018, Table 10.4; Statistical Yearbook of China 1986, Complied by the State Statistical Bureau of China, Oxford University Press, 1986, p. 370.

implementation by AQSIQ. Focus has been placed on key products related to the national economy, the people's livelihood and the public health and safety, key enterprises and key items for surveillance sampling. The national surveillance sampling of product quality is continuously being strengthened. According to national surveillance sampling statistics from 1998–2003, 45,733 types of products belonging to 1,083 categories from 51,715 enterprises have been under the national surveillance sampling, with the average pass rate being 77.5%, a 3.4% rise compared with that of the previous five years (1993–1997). This confirms that the overall quality level of Chinese products has improved steadily overall.[87] The detailed national surveillance sampling survey results are listed in Table 6.16. The average pass rate fluctuates from 75% to 78.9% during 1998–2005. The average pass rate of production is higher than consumer goods by almost 8%. In products, it means the pass rate of industrial

---

[87]Basic Information on Quality Supervision and Inspection and Quarantine, www.china. org.cn/e-news/news03-01-21.htm, January 21, 2003.

Table 6.17. The pass rate of national surveillance sampling in China.

		1998	1999	2000	2001	2002	2003	2004	2005
Number of enterprises surveyed		6233	7485	8142	8076	8412	13367	15726	13854
Product Categories surveyed		199	218	235	207	224	256	256	282
Kinds of Products surveyed		7770	8905	9705	9906	9447	14696	17736	17159
Average pass rate		75.0	78.3	78.9	75.8	78.4	78.4	76.9	75.6
Size of enterprises	Large	93.2	91.9	93.5	95.1	90	91	91.6	89.6
	Medium	85.9	84.2	86.5	85.7	85	84.6	82.8	83.2
	Small	70.3	70.6	69.9	67.6	70	70.7	70.1	73.5
Product means	Industrial	78.9		82.9	85.6	79.5	80.1		69.7[A]
	Agriculture		80.4		78.8				68.1[A]
Consumer goods	Durable	69.1	84.4	74.2	78.5	74.3	73.3	77.7	80.0
	Daily				69.6			78.9	85

Notes: A-data of Small enterprises, lower than large enterprises 16.1 % in average.
Source: The General Administration of the People's Republic of China for Quality Supervision, Inspection, and Quarantine (AQSIQ): The News Bulletin of National Surveillance Sampling Survey Result, 1998; 1999; 2000; 2001; 2002; 2003; 2004; 2005 (in Chinese); Mao, H. (2004). The pass rate of food produced by small enterprises less than 80%, *Economic Information Daily*, January 16. (in Chinese).

products is higher than that of agricultural products. The pass rate of durable consumer goods is better than that of daily consumer goods.

The pass rate of products manufactured by larger enterprises is 7% higher than that of medium enterprises and 22.8% higher than that of small enterprises. The difference is quite significant. The pass rate of products manufactured by private enterprise is the lowest (see Table 6.18) because the scale of private enterprises is usually small, and their technology and management are relatively weak. The average pass rate of products manufactured by SOEs is updated on The General Administration of the People's Republic of China for Quality Supervision, Inspection, and Quarantine (AQSIQ) website at http://english.aqsiq.gov.cn/. The Chinese version is www.samr.gov.cn/, and the English name is State Administration for Market Regulation (SAMR).

Table 6.18.   Pass rate of national sampling products for different ownership enterprises in China.

Ownership		SOE	Foreign-funded	Share-holding	Collective	Private	Individual
Pass rate of national sampling products	1998	84.2	83.4	77.1	73.2		63. 1
	1999	86.2	86	79	73		62
	2000	86.4	86	82.4	75.5		58.7
	2001	>80	>80	>80	>80	67.6	45.8
	2002	89	86.3				67.4

Source: The General Administration of the People's Republic of China for Quality Supervision, Inspection, and Quarantine (AQSIQ): The News Bulletin of National Surveillance Sampling Survey Result, 1998; 1999; 2000; 2001; 2002 (in Chinese).

The News Bulletin of National Surveillance Sampling Survey Result is released in accordance with the product classification, and the requirements are more stringent. For example, The December 27, 2018, report of the General Administration of Market Regulation issued a notice on the national supervision and spot check of 33 types of product quality such as down apparel. 1774 batches of products from 1614 companies were inspected, and 128 batches were found to be unqualified; the unqualified discovery rate was 7.2%. Among the products sampled this time, 16 companies that failed the previous sampling inspection were tracked and inspected, and 2 companies failed the sampling inspection (see Table 6.19). Fourteen companies were qualified for the spot check. The spot check found 531 qualified enterprises. Nineteen of the random inspections were unqualified, and 512 of them were qualified. Enterprises whose product quality does not pass this spot check, especially those that did not pass the continuous spot check, are dealt with in accordance with the appropriate Regulation.[88]

The national QCIs of manufacturing from 1999–2007 were 76.0, 76.3, 76.4, 77.9, 78.2, 79.0, 80.0, and 81.0, respectively. QCI has increased year by year, indicating the national quality competitiveness of the manufacturing industry has increased. According to calculations

---

[88]Administration of Market Regulation issued on December 27, 2018. The General Administration of Market Regulation issued a notice on the national supervision and spot check of 33 types of product quality such as down apparel in 2018 (in Chinese).

Table 6.19.   Supervised random inspection of two consecutive unqualified enterprises.

No.	Company name	Location	Spot check time	Product name	Specification model	Production date/batch number	Major unqualified items
1	Zhejiang Enze bicycle industry Co. Ltd.	Zhejiang Province	2018	Bicycle	20 inches, QS7.1D-2016	2018.3	Ankle gap (ground distance)
			2017	Bicycle	Knight 7.1D	2016.07.31	Chain breaking force
2	Guangzhou Deba lighting appliance Co., Ltd.	Guangdong Province	2018	Automobile rear combination lamp	DB-3025D	2018.6.16	Photometric performance, light distribution performance
			2016	Automobile rear combination lamp	DB-5036	2015.8	Light distribution performance

Source: Administration of Market Regulation issued on December 27, 2018. The General Administration of Market Regulation issued a notice on the national supervision and spot check of 33 types of product quality such as down apparel in 2018 (in Chinese).

using related data of the manufacturing industry from 31 provinces, manufacturing QCIs of Jiangsu (88.14), Shanghai (87.55), Guangdong (86.91), Beijing (86.09), Tianjin, Zhejiang, Chongqing, Hunan, Shandong, Liaoning, Fujian, Hubei, Jiangxi, Anhui, and Shaanxi (80.01) exceeded 80. The number of regions where QCIs exceeded 85 reached four, increasing by three over 2006. The QCIs of manufacturing sectors of eastern, central, and western regions were 84.82, 78.99, and 79.00, respectively. The eastern region remained in the leading position in terms of quality competitiveness.[89]

China aims to improve the standards and quality of consumer goods to raise living standards and prop up domestic consumption as part of the supply-side reform. An executive meeting of the State Council presided by Premier Li Keqiang on August 24, 2016, approved a new guideline on

---

[89] The General Administration of the People's Republic of China for Quality Supervision, Inspection, and Quarantine (AQSIQ, 2009): Communiqué on the 2007 National Quality Competitiveness Index of Manufacturing, May 27.

improving consumer goods standards and quality over the next five years. Consumption contributed 66.5% to GDP growth in 2016, according to figures by the National Bureau of Statistics. In the following four years, the authorities promoted updating present standards and improving the quality of consumer goods, building globally reputed brands, and optimizing the market environment, according to a statement released after the meeting.

Chinese brands still have a long way to go to build up their international competitiveness. "Chinese buyers spent more than CNY2.5 trillion (USD374.4 billion) overseas in 2017 and this spending should be coming back home with higher-quality products", said Wang Jianlin, Chairman of Wanda Group, a Dalian-based developer. "People's needs in consumer goods are being transformed and upgraded. China has already built a relatively complete and wide-ranging consumer goods industry system, but the quality issue still remains", according to Premier Li. "With a population of almost 1.4 billion and an increasing number of middle-income families, there is a strong consumption momentum. This will create the most enormous consumption need in the world, and such a great opportunity should be grasped", he said. "To upgrade the consumer goods industry, the first thing government should do is improve the business environment. The second thing to do is strengthen regulation regarding problems such as fake and poor-quality products and intellectual property infringement. Only with good regulation can a fair and healthy market be built," the Premier stressed. The third thing the Premier stressed is market access improvement. To promote increases in consumer goods variety and product quality, product lists should not be further expanded, the Premier stated. Statistics indicate that China's total retail sales of consumer goods reached CNY36.6 trillion (USD5.42 trillion) in 2017, making China the world's second largest consumer market. Therefore, it is necessary to expand imports to meet domestic personalized and high-end consumer demand. "Advancing supply-side reform can eliminate backward industrial capacity and foster new supply and new momentum, which will in turn promote the upgrading of consumption."[90]

---

[90]Hu, Y. (2016). Higher quality aimed for homemade goods, *China Daily*, August 30, 2016; Premier stresses ways to upgrade consumer industry, May 12, 2016, english.gov.cn; Chinese people willing to buy more imported goods, *People's Daily* Online, June 06, 2018; Better quality of consumer goods will meet demand, May 12, 2016, english.gov.cn.

15. We are the (National) Champions

This section is not about China's national champion basketball or soccer team. Instead, it is about a group of companies that occupy a special place in China's reform process. According to one definition,[91] "National champions are companies which help further the government's strategic aims and in return, the government supports these companies by providing easier access to financing, giving preference in government contract bidding, and sometimes oligarchy or monopoly status in protected industries, giving these companies a number of advantages over their competitors." Companies included in the National Team have political power as well. The CEOs of many of these companies are members of the Central Committee. The post-reform creation of the National Champions (or, as sometimes called, the National Team) can be traced back to China's 10th, 11th, and 12th Five Year Plans (FYPs). As we discussed in Chapter 1, FYPs identified certain critical sectors as pillar industries. Companies in these industries were to support the government in attaining the FYPs' objectives. Naturally, the treatment these companies receive is also the source of complaints by foreign enterprises in China about this preferential treatment. Indeed, to the outside world, the National Team is a symbol of China's Industrial Policy, and the unfair competition domestic and international rivals face in their relevant markets.

The list of National Champions includes almost all large SOEs that report directly to SASAC and selected private companies. The list of National Champions includes such SOEs as Sinopec, State Grid, China Telecom, Baosteel Group, Haier Group, China National Petroleum Group, China Investment Corp., and China Commercial Aircraft Corp. The Chinese government's emphasis on Artificial Intelligence (AI) was further confirmed by the naming of 15 new National Champions from the AI sector in 2019. The new entrants include Huawei, Hikvision, Xiaomi, JD.com, Qihoo 360, Megvii, and Yitu. These companies joined Baidu, Alibaba, Tencent, and iFlyTek, which had been included in the National Team in 2017.

---

[91] Graceffo, A. (2017). China's National Champions: State Support Makes Chinese Companies Dominant. *Foreign Policy Journal.* May 15. www.foreignpolicyjournal.com/2017/05/15/chinas-national-champions-state-support-makes-chinese-companies-dominant/).

16. Conclusion and Looking Ahead

Reform of SOEs is a vital component of China's overall reform efforts. The approach taken by China in reforming its SOEs has been very different from the drastic approaches taken by the countries of the former USSR economic bloc. Because of its deliberate, gradual, and experimental restructuring characteristics, the progress of the reform has been difficult to assess. Furthermore, progress assessment must take place from the Chinese, rather than Western, point of view.

SOE reform is an extremely complicated process, regardless of the country in which it takes place. In previous CPEs, including China, SOEs for many decades were the pervasive, if not the only, form of enterprise organizational structure. Their mission was economic, political, and social. Just as it was the case in the old company towns of England and the United States, people depended on these enterprises for their economic and social welfare. Therefore, transforming them into a private entity had to consider the entire set of implications of this transformation for the citizens and the country. This meant reform had to move at a slow pace. The inefficiencies associated with the huge enterprise structures could not be eliminated overnight. Hence, Chinese enterprises struggled in the early days. The world viewed China as a huge market and as a manufacturing opportunity, not as the place from which world-class companies could originate. That has now begun to change. China's mixed-ownership strategy has produced companies that are big, but also slowly getting better. Globalization, government support, and technology have contributed to provide Chinese companies with visibility and brand recognition.

As we look ahead, we see China sticking with and improving the basic economic system of multiple ownership. State ownership will still be the mainstay, but diverse forms of ownership will operate side by side. However, there is the question of control beyond ownership. Do private enterprises in China have full decision-making control? The answer to this question may very well serve as an indicator of China's future commitment to reform and the growth of its economy. To a free-market economist, the answer to the question is very simple: Let private enterprise be! Private entrepreneurs will follow the signals of the market and will make decisions based on sound economic reasoning. However, the "market" is an abstract concept to the Chinese leaders. What really matters is how

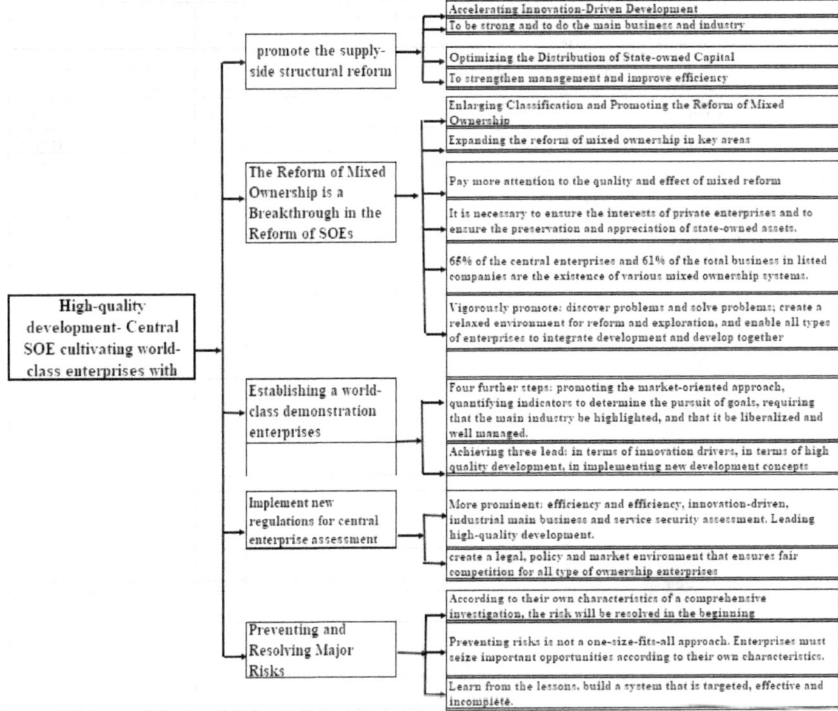

Figure 6.15.   Reform and High-quality development of SOEs.

Source: Economic Watch: Chinese SOEs speed up reform for high-quality development, Xinhua, July 31, 2020; Focus on high-quality development of SOEs, *China Daily*, January 15, 2020; The three major directions of SOE reform are clear, August 31, 2015.

SOEs and private enterprises of any form contribute to the country's overall welfare.

On September 16, 2020, an announcement was made on CCTV regarding "important instructions" issued by President Xi.[92] The title of the instructions was: Opinion on Strengthening the United Front Work of the Private Economy in the New Era. According to the new measures,

---

[92] Gill, C. (2020). CCP announces plan to take control of China's private sector. *Asia Times Financial*. September 17. https://www.asiafinancial.com/ccp-announces-plan-to-take-control-of-chinas-private-sector.

private firms will have to hire a certain amount of CCP registered employees. It is not clear yet whether the hiring of these employees will have an impact on the way private enterprises operate. The mission of these employees has much more to do with ideology than business. However, this development, and its positive or negative implications on the future of private enterprises, will be worth watching in the future. Will economic reform continue, or will the state stifle expansion of the private sector? As shown in Figure 6.15.

Chapter 7

Foreign Trade

1. Introduction

Foreign trade and investment have played an important role in China's economic development. Furthermore, China has become one of the most important participants in the global economy. Chapters 7 and 8 of this book examine China's external economic relations.

In Chapter 7, we first take a brief look at China's trade in the 19th century and the first half of the 20th century. We will then discuss foreign trade's growing role in China's economy. Section 4 will present China's major imports and exports. In Section 5, we will show who China's trade partners are. China's trade volume, of course, has increased dramatically since the reforms. We will then analyze this increase in Section 6. Foreign-funded enterprises (FFEs) have been one of the forces behind China's trade growth; Section 7 will discuss their contributions. The rest of the chapter will be devoted to the USA–China trade relations. A chronology of the USA–China Trade War is presented in the Appendix.

2. China's International Trade Before the Reforms

China's invasion by the British and other foreign powers during the Opium Wars era and the ensuing Unequal Treaties opened China's other (than Guangdong) ports to international trade. With the Chinese economy reeling as a result of economic losses associated with the wars and the indemnities paid to the colonial powers, China needed more goods from other countries than it sold to them. Therefore, it showed persistent trade

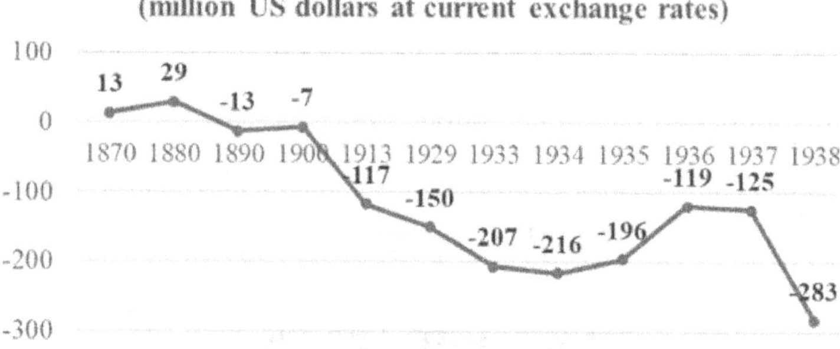

Figure 7.1.   China's international trade deficits from 1870 to 1938.

Source: Maddison, A. (1998). *Chinese Economic Performance in the Long Run*. Paris: Organization for Economic Cooperation and Development, p. 175.

Table 7.1.   Comparing China exports, imports and TPR with other countries in 1990, 2005, 2009, and 2017.

Const 2000 Bil. USD	–	BRA	CHN	DEU	IND	JPN	KOR	RUS	USA	WLD
1970	Imp.	19.4	3.3	145.9	9.6	19.6	7.4	–	299.3	2442.4
	Exp.	17.6	4.7	175.2	2.4	22.0	1.0	–	59.7	2449.2
	TPR%	75.6	5.0	34.0	8.0	20.0	37.0	–	11.0	27.0
1980	Imp.	40.8	22.2	244.8	18.7	155.9	32.3	–	377.8	4115.8
	Exp.	24.3	20.1	288.7	11.4	145.1	18.9	–	280.8	4171.3
	TPR%	32.4	22.0	45.0	16.0	28.9	72.0	–	21.0	38.0
1990	Imp.	29.0	48.8	341.6	19.4	310.5	67.9	166.3	21.0	4163.6
	Exp.	32.9	63.6	342.5	19.0	326.9	48.5	139.6	552.2	4090.1
	TPR%	12.3	25.3	44.3	14.2	15.4	39.4	79.3	16.4	34.0
2005	Imp.	81.9	631.6	754.8	133.4	536.9	276.9	143.2	1824.3	10,596.8
	Exp.	105.8	791.8	856.7	133.7	682.8	329.0	176.3	1200.7	10,531.4
	TPR%	25.4	74.6	82.3	41.5	24.5	91.2	91.4	27.1	57.2
2009	Imp.	118.8	902.7	830.1	204.3	477.2	329.9	175.1	1667.7	11,240.9
	Exp.	106.6	1142.8	916.5	190.8	628.0	436.2	192.8	1371.4	11,459.0
	TPR%	26.4	69.6	87.4	44.6	22.7	101.8	92.5	26.7	57.1
Const. 2010 bil. USD	–	BRA	CHN	DEU	IND	JPN	KOR	RUS	USA	WLD
2017	Imp.	245.0	1843.8	1666.3	615.2	986.6	699.8	2287.1	23,657.6	23,657.6
	Exp.	287.9	2263.4	1930.6	527.2	1047.3	726.6	342.2	2287.1	24,663.9
	TPR%	31.7	37.8	86.5	40.8	34.4	80.8	46.8	27.1	57.9

Source: Calculated using data from World Bank. World Development Indicators online, 2009, released 2009 and 2017 by World Bank.

deficits (Table 7.1). In 1937, China's principal exports were wood oil, raw silk, eggs, wolfram, and tin; its principal imports were paper, kerosene, rice, woollen goods, and gasoline (Maddison, 1998).

However, as we noted in Chapter 1 of this book, the Opium Wars also opened China's borders to the outside world. Shanghai became a focal point in the movement of goods into and out of China. China learned how to interact with other economies, and used these lessons to build the post-reform global powerhouse (see Figure 7.1).

3. The Growing Role of Foreign Trade in China's Economy

The most dramatic change brought about by recent reforms has been the opening up to international trade and investments. Total foreign trade increased from USD20.6 billion (1978) to USD4107.2 billion (2017), as shown in Figure 7.2 Similarly, its trade participation ratio (TPR, the ratio of a country's total trade to its GDP) has increased from 9.6% (1978) to 63.8% (2005), then falling to 33.9% (2017). The annual IS change coefficient K_{annual} increased from 0.0190 before economic reform to 0.1805 after economic reform (1978–2017). The change in these two measures reflects the effect of the "opening to outside world" policy.

For reference, Table 7.1 shows the TPR of other foreign countries from 1990 to 2017. China compares favorably with the TPR ratios of many of the more open large developing countries like Brazil and India, and even with those of Japan and US. For open small countries, such as South Korea, TPR will be higher (see Table 7.1).

Table 7.1 shows the TPR (goods and services) of China, Germany, India, Japan, South Korea, Russia, United States, and World average during 1970–2017. We see that, after its economic reform, China's TPR began to grow faster than the World average, India, United States and Japan. In 2005, China's TPR peaked 62%, then fell to 45% in 2009 during the financial crisis, and gradually fell to 38% in 2017. Table 7.1 also shows that the TPR of the USA, Japan, and India increased from 1970 to 1980. During the 1960s, China's and India's total foreign trade volume was about the same. By 2005, however, China's total foreign trade volume was four times more than that of India's. China's total foreign trade volume increased from current USD2 billion in 1952 to current USD20 billion in 1978. This change, occurring over 27 years, was equivalent to the change in Japan's trade over 11 years (from 1950 to 1961).

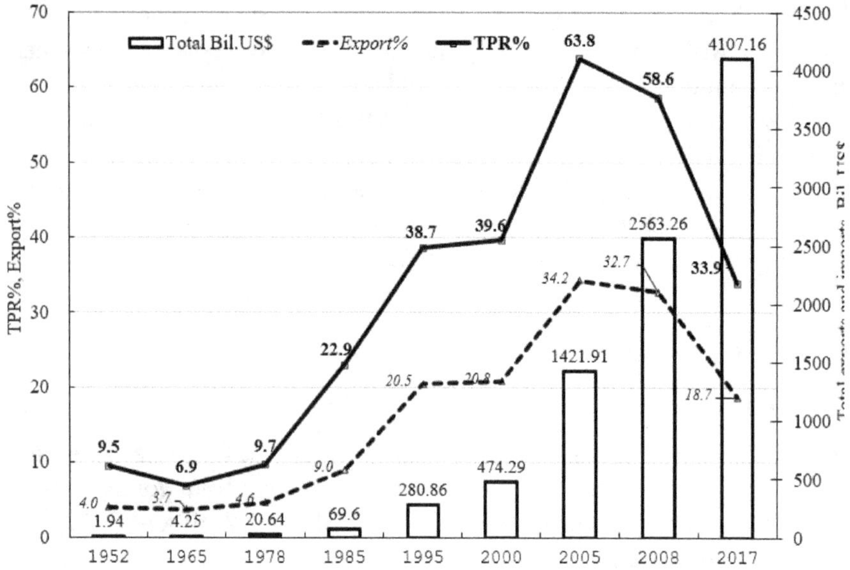

Figure 7.2. China's total foreign trade volume and trade participation ratio, 1952–2017.

Source: Calculated using data from China National Bureau of Statistics (2008). China Statistical Yearbook, China Statistical Press, 2008, Tables 2.1 and 7.3; China National Bureau of Statistics, Database; annual, total value of imports and exports (USD) (million), total value of exports, total value of imports, 1999–2017; gross national income (yuan 100 million), 1999–2017.

After reform, China's total foreign trade volume increased from constant 2000 USD53.1 billion (1978) to constant 2000 USD1,678.3 billion (2006). This 28-year change was equivalent to the change in total trade volume in the USA from 1950 to 1995 (constant 2000 USD1627 billion). Since 2004, China's total foreign trade volume (constant 2000 USD1,186.9 billion in 2004) exceeded Japan's (constant 2000 USD1,145.8 billion in 2004), and China's foreign trade volume ranked third in the world. This illustrates that the annual growth rate of China's total foreign trade volume is quite high after economic reform.

Since China's 2001 World Trade Organization (WTO) entry, China's trade with the world expanded by more than three times from 2002 to 2017 (Figure 7.3). The average growth rate during this period was 7.9%. The annual increase during the 2002–2017 period is shown in Figure 7.3. From 2002 to 2007, the maximum annual growth rate was 25.0% in 2003, and the minimum annual growth rate was −17.7% in 2009, attributed to

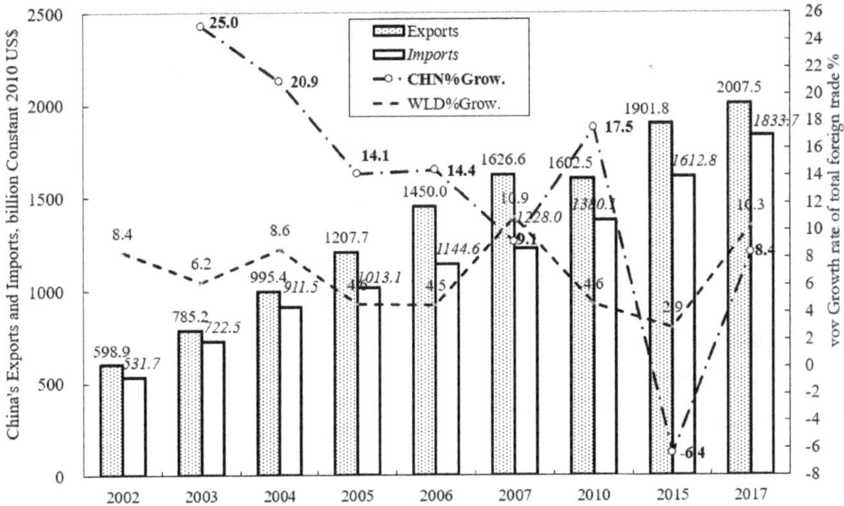

Figure 7.3.　China's trade with the world 2002–2017.

Source: Calculated using data from World Bank: World Development Indicators online, 2018, released 2018.

the 2008 global economic crisis. The world's annual growth rate in 2009 was −12.4%. Comparing China's annual growth rate with that of the world, we observe that China's annual growth rate is higher than the world's growth rate.

4. Trade Structure

According to Table 7.2, exports of electrical machinery and equipment and power generation equipment are still the main drivers of China's large trade surplus in 2006. The Top 10 HS sector commodities for export shown in Table 7.2 accounted for 66.3% of China's total exports in 2006; all Top10 category commodities belong to manufactured goods. The Top 2 HS sector commodities for export are electrical machinery and equipment and power generation equipment, accounting for 38.9% of China's total exports, and remained the drivers of China's large trade surplus in 2006. As shown in Table 7.2, in 2017, the Top 10 HS sector export commodities accounted for 66.6% of China's total exports. In 2017, the Top 2 HS sector commodities within exports were electrical machinery and

Table 7.2. China's top exports by HS Section of commodities, 2006 and 2017 (billion USD).

HS#	Commodity description	Vol. 06	Yoy Gr (%)	HS#	Commodity description	Vol. 17	Yoy (%)
85	Electrical machinery and equipment	227.4	32	85	Electrical machinery and equipment	664.1	11
84	Power generation equipment	186.6	24.7	84	Nuclear reactors, boilers and parts	429.4	12.1
61	Knitted or — garments	44.9	45.4	94	Furniture	95.5	7.3
62	Garments not knitted or crocheted	43.7	24.8	39	Plastics and articles thereof	79.6	13.8
90	Optics and medical equipment	32.6	28	61	Articles of apparel, knitted	73.3	2.1
94	Furniture	28.0	25	90	Optics and medical equipment	71.5	1.2
73	Iron and steel products	26.8	40.7	62	Articles of apparel, not knitted	71.3	−2.9
72	Iron and steel	25.1	66.6	73	Articles of iron or steel	65.2	14.9
95	Toys and games	22.6	18.4	29	Organic chemicals	59.8	20.2
87	Vehicles other than railway	22.4	34.8	64	Footwear, gaiters and the like	46.9	−2.7

Source: China Customs: Monthly Bulletin of Customs Statistics, December 2006 and 2017.

equipment and nuclear reactors, boilers, and parts, which rose to 44.0% of the total.

Table 7.2 lists the Top 10 HS section imported commodities in 2006, which accounted for 79.6% of China's total imports. In 2006, the Top 2 HS sector imported commodities were electrical machinery and equipment and power generation equipment, accounting for 41.5% of the total. As shown in Table 7.3, the Top 10 HS sector imported commodities accounted for 77.8% of China's total imports. In 2017, the Top 2 HS sector imported commodities were electrical machinery and equipment and nuclear reactors, boilers, and parts, which accounted for 40.8% of the total. The ratio of the Top 10 HS and the Top 2 HS Section imported goods in total imports in 2006 and 2017 is almost the same.

Table 7.3. China's top imports by HS Section of commodities, 2006 and 2017 (billion USD).

	Country/Reg.	Total, bil. USD	Yoy (%)	Exp. bil. USD	Yoy (%)	Imp. bil. USD	Yoy (%)
2009							
1	United States	298.3	−11.9	220.8	−14.3	77.5	−5.0
2	Japan	228.8	−16.6	130.9	−18.7	97.9	−15.0
3	HK, China	174.9	−16.4	166.2	−14.7	8.7	−48.4
4	Korea R.	156.2	−19.1	53.7	−37.8	102.5	−9.4
5	TW, China	106.2	−21.6	20.5	−26.2	85.7	−20.6
6	Germany	31.3	−8.9	49.9	−18.6	−18.6	−0.1
7	Australia	60.1	0.7	20.6	−7.8	39.5	5.2
8	Malaysia	52.0	−3.1	32.3	−9.3	19.6	0.7
9	Singapore	47.9	−9.7	30.1	−7.5	17.8	−13.3
10	India	43.4	−19.5	29.7	−6.5	13.7	−47.6
2017							
1	United States	2102	9.1	1296	9.1	806	9.1
2	Japan	931	9.7	426	9.9	505	9.5
3	Korea, R.	686	12.8	275	13.8	411	12.2
4	Germany	498	8.8	197	12.7	301	6.3
5	India	485	17.7	306	20.3	179	13.4
6	HK, China	490	3.0	477	2.9	13	2.9
7	TW, China	470	10.4	155	14.8	315	8.3
8	Singapore	389	18.8	200	11.0	189	27.0
9	Malaysia	338	9.8	147	10.9	191	8.9
10	Thailand	297	11.4	140	12.9	157	10.1911

Source: China Customs: Monthly Bulletin of Customs Statistics, December 2006 and 2017.

Figure 7.4 shows the import and export structure by major commodity groups in 1980 and 2017. It indicates that, between 1980 and 2017, the export share of primary commodities (first and second column in Figure 7.4) in total exports declined from 50. 3% in 1980 to 5.2% in 2017. The share of light and textile industrial products, rubber products, minerals, and metallurgical products (third column in Figure 7.4; it belongs to low-technology intensity products) declined from 22.1% in 1980 to 16.5% in 2017. The share of machinery and transport equipment (fourth

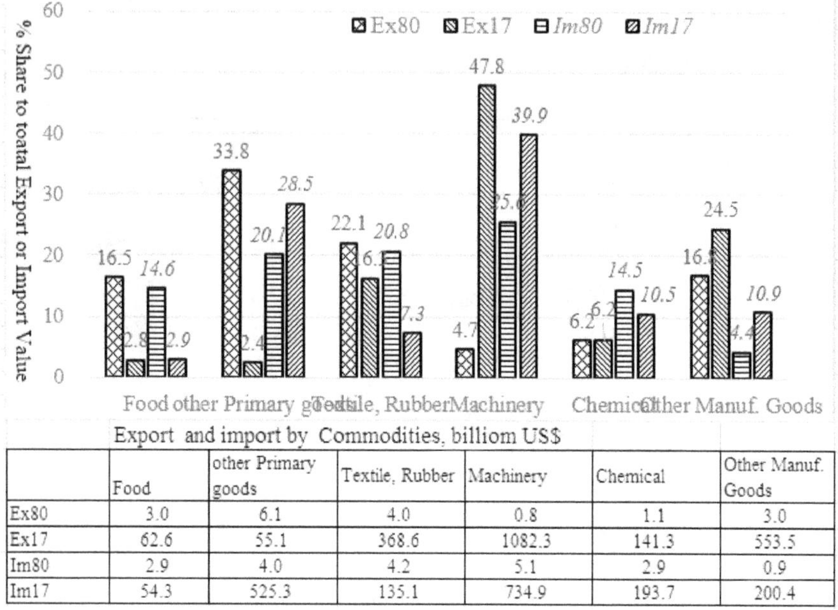

	Food	other Primary goods	Textile, Rubber	Machinery	Chemical	Other Manuf. Goods
Ex80	3.0	6.1	4.0	0.8	1.1	3.0
Ex17	62.6	55.1	368.6	1082.3	141.3	553.5
Im80	2.9	4.0	4.2	5.1	2.9	0.9
Im17	54.3	525.3	135.1	734.9	193.7	200.4

Figure 7.4.   China's export and import by HS Section of commodities, 1980/2017.

Source: Calculated using data from All China Data online: China Yearly Macro-Economic Statistics (National). Value of Exports by Category of Commodities Customs Statistics, 1950–2019.

column in Figure 7.4; it belongs to medium-technology intensity products) increased dramatically from 4.7% in 1980 to 47.8% in 2017.

Food imports declined from 14.6% in 1980 to 2.9% in 2017, although its total amount was increased from USD2.9 billion in 1980 to USD54.3 billion in 2017. The import value of other primary commodities increased from USD4.0 billion in 1980 to USD525.3 billion in 2017, mainly due to significant increase of crude oil and petroleum products refined import and non-edible raw materials (iron ore).[1] The import value of mineral fuels and non-edible raw materials increased from USD0.20 billion and USD3.55 billion in 1980 to USD249.6 billion and USD7.7 billion in 2017, respectively. The share of import of machinery and transport equipment also increased dramatically between 1980 and 2007, from 25.6% in

---

[1]Calculated using data from China National Bureau of Statistics: China Statistical Yearbook, China Statistics Press, 2008, Table 17.6; 2018, Table 11.3.

1980 to 33.9% in 2017.[2] This was mainly the result of high demand for investment goods in China associated with a high GDP growth rate. Since 2001, China has been a locomotive for growth in East Asia.[3]

5. China's Trade Partners

China's Top five foreign trade partners (ranked on the basis of the total export and import) during 1996 and 2017 are shown in Figure 7.5. From Figure 7.5, we find that the Top five trade partners occupied 68.7% of total export volume in 1996; their share decreased to 45.1% in 2017 and they occupied 58.9% of total import volume in 1996, but only 32.6% in 2017. In 1996, China had its largest foreign trade surplus with the United States (with the exception of its surplus with Hong Kong) and its largest trade deficit with South Korea. China's exports to the United States reached USD26.7 billion in 2006, accounting for 17.7% of its total export volume; that number increased to USD4,297.3 billion in 2017, accounting for 19.0% of total exports. The United States ranked first based on the export value in 2017. Figure 7.5 shows that, in 1996, China's Top five export destinations were Hong Kong, Japan, United States, South Korea, and Germany; in 2017, the order changed: the United States, Hong Kong, Japan, South Korea, and Germany. Hong Kong is China's gateway to the world. As China becomes more open to reform and opening up, the function of the gateway will most likely decline. China now trades with many more countries and regions. For example, the total import and export trade between China and the "Belt and Road" countries and regions has reached USD1.1 trillion, almost twice that of the United States.[4] China's total trade value with other countries significantly increased from USD246.13 billion in 1996 to USD2,572.41 billion in 2017. This shows that the Chinese trade market is increasingly diversified. From 1978 to 2017, the number of China's trading partners has grown from 40 countries and regions to 231. In 2013–2017, China's trade with emerging markets and developing

---

[2]Calculated using data from China National Bureau of Statistics: China Statistical Yearbook, China Statistics Press, 2008, Table 17.6.

[3]Fossberg, M. (2004). East Asia on solid ground, set to grow by 6 percent in 2004, World Bank, April 20.

[4]The trade data of "One Belt, One Road" have been released, who is the biggest winner? China's Belt and Road Network (in Chinese).

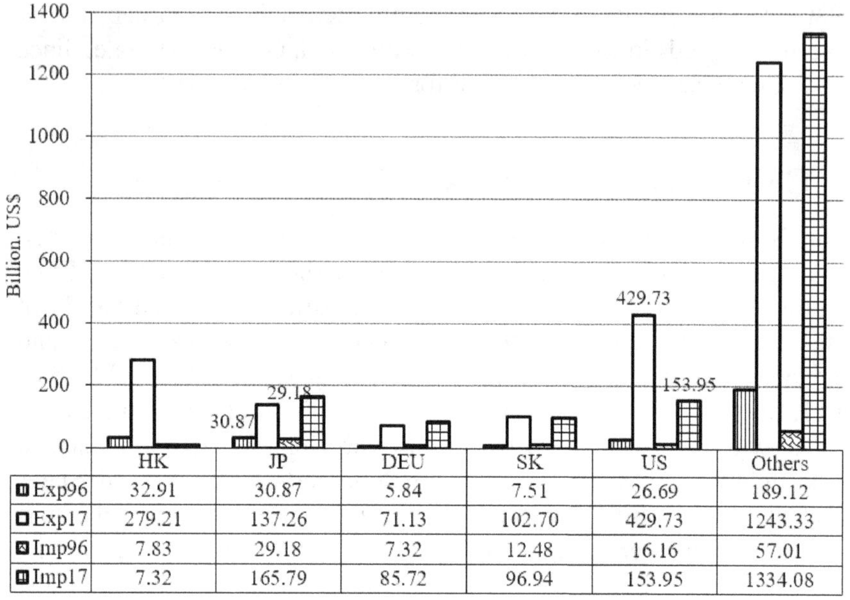

	HK	JP	DEU	SK	US	Others
Exp96	32.91	30.87	5.84	7.51	26.69	189.12
Exp17	279.21	137.26	71.13	102.70	429.73	1243.33
Imp96	7.83	29.18	7.32	12.48	16.16	57.01
Imp17	7.32	165.79	85.72	96.94	153.95	1334.08

Figure 7.5.   China's export and import by Top five partners, 1996/2017.

Source: Calculated using data from China National Bureau of Statistics: China Statistical Yearbook, China Statistics Press, 2010, Table 6.7 and 1997, Table 16.7.

countries continued to grow rapidly. The total value of China's import and export goods along the "Belt and Road" is CNY33.2 trillion (USD5,331 billion), an average annual increase of 4%, which is higher than the average annual growth rate of China's import and export of goods by 1.4 percentage points during the same period and has become a bright spot for goods trade.

What about the structure of China's exports? In 1980, primary products accounted for 51.3% of exports, and industrial manufactured exports accounted for 49.7%. By 1986, industrial manufactured exports began to outstrip primary products, reaching 63.6%. In 2017, industrial manufactured goods and primary products accounted for 94.8% and 5.2% of exports, respectively. From 1985 to 2017, China's exports of mechanical and electrical products increased from USD1.68 billion to USD1.3 trillion, a 785-time increase, with an average annual growth rate of 23.2%, accounting for more than 17% of the global market. China has maintained for 9 consecutive years the world's largest exporter of mechanical and electrical products. During the same period, the proportion of high-tech products in China's exports increased from 2 to 28.8%.[5]

China's Top five foreign trade partners have remained unchanged as of 2006.[6] The United States still ranks first on both total trade value and growth rate. On the export side, however, China's exports to key trade partners appear to be shifting: growth rates of exports to economies such as Singapore, Malaysia, South Korea, and Taiwan have outstripped the export growth rate to the United States. Though the United States continues to be China's largest single export market, the higher export growth rates to other economies indicate that China is diversifying into new markets. Meanwhile, on the import side, China's imports from Thailand and Malaysia increased by 15 and 0.73%, respectively, in 2009, propelling the country into the ranks of China's Top 10 import suppliers (Table 7.4). Three traditional raw material importers, Australia, Brazil, and Saudi Arabia, are also listed in the Top 10 import suppliers (Table 7.4). The emergence of Thailand and the Philippines as top import suppliers points to shifts within the Southeast Asian supply chain as Hong Kong finds itself displaced for the fifth year in a row as a key import supplier. Seven of the Top 10 importers are located in Asia, occupying 39.8% of China's total imports in 2009. As shown in Table 7.4, Saudi Arabia was replaced by Singapore in 2017, so eight of the Top 10 importing regions are located in Asia, accounting for only 32.6% of China's total imports. China now imports more goods from other non-Asia regions. From 2012 to 2017, China's imports from Asia and Oceania increased by 0.4%, while imports from Africa and Americas increased by 54.6 and 12.9%, respectively.[7]

As shown in Table 7.4, seven of the Top 10 total foreign trade value partners were located in Asia in 2009, accounting for 36.7% of China's total foreign trade; their share fell to 23.8% in 2017. In 2009, the Top 10 total foreign trade value partners accounted for 54.3% of China's total foreign trade, with that share falling to 39.0% in 2017. This shows that China exported and imported more goods from other non-Asia regions.

---

[5] Department of Foreign Trade and Economics, China National Bureau of Statistics (2018). The level of opening up to foreign trade and economic development has been comprehensively improved, August 30 (in Chinese).

[6] China Customs (2006). Monthly Bulletin of Customs Statistics, December 2006.

[7] Calculated using data from United Nations Conference on Trade and Development 2018. *Handbook of Statistics 2018*, p. 18, Table 1.1.1.

Table 7.4.　China's Top ten trading partners in 2009 and 2017 (rankings based on total foreign trade levels), billion USD.

	Country/Reg.	Total, bil. USD	Yoy (%)	Exp. bil. USD	Yoy (%)	Imp. bil. USD	Yoy (%)
2009							
1	United States	298.3	−11.9	220.8	−14.3	77.5	−5.0
2	Japan	228.8	−16.6	130.9	−18.7	97.9	−15.0
3	HK, China	174.9	−16.4	166.2	−14.7	8.7	−48.4
4	Korea R.	156.2	−19.1	53.7	−37.8	102.5	−9.4
5	TW, China	106.2	−21.6	20.5	−26.2	85.7	−20.6
6	Germany	31.3	−8.9	49.9	−18.6	−18.6	−0.1
7	Australia	60.1	0.7	20.6	−7.8	39.5	5.2
8	Malaysia	52.0	−3.1	32.3	−9.3	19.6	0.7
9	Singapore	47.9	−9.7	30.1	−7.5	17.8	−13.3
10	India	43.4	−19.5	29.7	−6.5	13.7	−47.6
2017							
1	United States	2102	9.1	1296	9.1	806	9.1
2	Japan	931	9.7	426	9.9	505	9.5
3	Korea, R.	686	12.8	275	13.8	411	12.2
4	Germany	498	8.8	197	12.7	301	6.3
5	India	485	17.7	306	20.3	179	13.4
6	HK, China	490	3.0	477	2.9	13	2.9
7	TW, China	470	10.4	155	14.8	315	8.3
8	Singapore	389	18.8	200	11.0	189	27.0
9	Malaysia	338	9.8	147	10.9	191	8.9
10	Thailand	297	11.4	140	12.9	157	10.2

Source: Calculated using data from China National Bureau of Statistics (2010). China Statistical Yearbook, China Statistics Press, 2010, Table 6.7; United Nations Conference on Trade and Development (2018). Handbook of Statistics 2018, p. 23, Tables 1.2.3 and 1.2.4.

Figure 7.6 shows China's foreign trade with the United States. Before 1993, China had a trade deficit with the United States. After 1993, the share of China's exports to the United States to China's total export increased from 8.3% in 1990 to 21% by 2000, stabilized at about 21% during 2001–2006, and declined to 19.1% in 2007. However, the share of

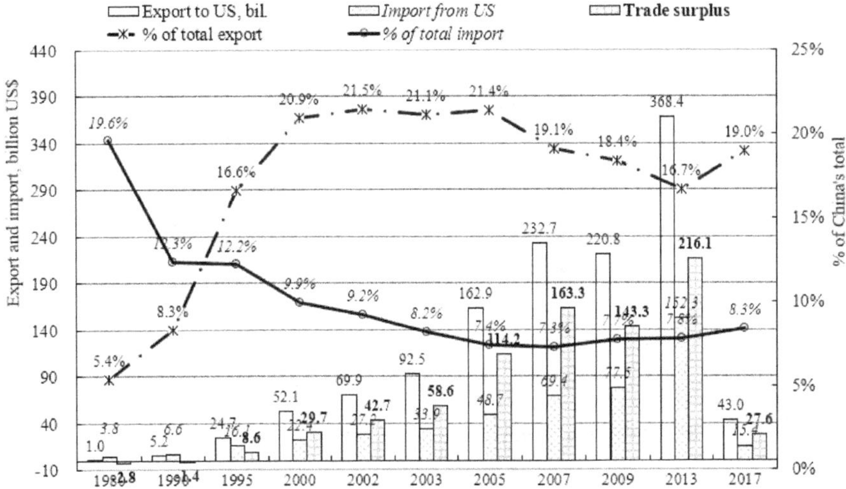

Figure 7.6.   Foreign trade between China and USA, selected years 1980–2017.

Source: Calculated using data from China Statistical Yearbook, 2018, Table 11.5; 2014, Table 11.6; 2010, Table 6.7; 2008, Table 17.8; 2005, Table 18.7; 2004, Table 18.7; 2002, Table 17.7; 1996, Table 17.7; 1992, Table 15.5; Statistical Yearbook of China, 1981, Compiled by the State Statistical Bureau, PRC. Published by Economic Information & Agency, Hong Kong, October 1982, p. 357, 370; National Bureau of Statistics of China: Statistical Communiqué of the PRC on 2005 National Economic and Social Development, February 28, 2006.

China's imports from United States to China's total imports declined from 19.6% in 1980 to 7.3% in 2007. The large difference in US–China trade deficit reported by Chinese Statistics and US statistics is mainly due to processing trade. The United States Commerce Department released the US trade volume with China as being USD378.7 billion; United States exports to China were USD40.9 billion, while imports from China were USD337.8 billion, resulting in a trade deficit of USD296.9 billion.[8]

According to Chinese statistics, Sino-US trade volume in 2008 amounted to USD252.3 billion, of which China's exports to the United States were USD814 billion, imports from the United States USD81.4 billion, and the resulting surplus being USD170.9 billion.[9] In the past, Japan,

---

[8]US Census Bureau, Foreign Trade Division, Data Dissemination Branch, Washington, DC 20233 http://www.census.gov/foreign-trade/balance/c5700.html#2008.

[9]National Bureau of Statistics of China (2009). Statistical Communiqué of the People's Republic of China on the 2008 National Economic and Social Development, February 26.

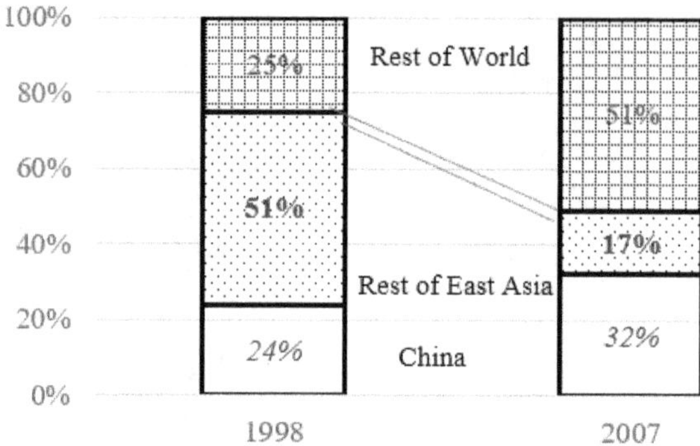

Figure 7.7.   Composition of the US Global Trade Deficit 2008.

Source: The US–China Business Council (2008). USA–China trade in context.

South Korea, and Hong Kong exported directly to the United States; they now go through China's processing trade and subsequently export to the United States. According to US Customs, this procedure contributed to the expansion of Chinese exports, since goods that originated in those other countries were counted as "made in China." In China's statistics, these goods are counted as exports to Japan, Hong Kong, and South Korea. Therefore, the trade deficit of the United States with Japan, Hong Kong, and South Korea has now narrowed, while that with China has widened. However, the trade deficit of the United States with the East Asia region has changed little. Over the past 5 years, the deficit with the region has declined, as shown in Figure 7.7. Figure 7.7 shows that the US trade imbalance with China is largely a result of the shifting US trade with East Asia. The US trade deficit with the rest of the world has grown more than the trade deficit with China and East Asia. In 2007, the US trade deficit with East Asia (including China) grew by USD223 billion; the US trade deficit with the rest of the world grew by USD334 billion. In 2007, 57.1% of China's total exports to the United States came from foreign-invested enterprises (FFEs). The foreign trade surplus of FFEs reached USD135.6 billion accounting for 52% of China's total trade surplus in 2007.[10]

---

[10]Calculated using data from China National Bureau of Statistics (2009). China Statistical Yearbook, China Statistics Press, 2008, Tables 17.3 and 17.13.

China is now the United States' third-largest export market — and, if combined with Hong Kong, US exports reached USD85.4 billion in 2007. US exports to China grew by about 18% in 2007 and have grown by 301% since 2000. On the other hand, the United States trade deficit with China is a structural deficit, which is determined by the structure of industries in the two countries. Currently, the United States manufactures medium- and high-technology products, while China produces low-tech items. The United States' imports of low- and medium-technology goods from China benefit both sides. Because the United States imports Chinese low-cost and fine products, US consumers can save money, and the prospect of inflation in the United States is reduced.[11] China has a growing trade surplus with United States, but "surplus in China, profits in the United States." The case of Apple's iPod may be typical.[12] The iPod is a perfect example of a globally innovated product, combining technologies from the USA, Japan, and a number of Asian countries. Apple never had manufacturing capabilities; it has outsourced production. The most costly input is the 30 GB hard drive from Toshiba, which has an estimated cost of USD73. Japan, South Korea, United States, and Taiwan supply other spare parts — a total of USD60. Finally assembled in China — China keeps the assembly fee of three dollars, while the United States has access to USD163. Apple takes in USD80. For every USD299 iPod sold in the USA, the US trade deficit with China increases by about USD144 (the factory cost). Yet, the United States gets USD163 profits, while China only obtains USD3 value added. Apple's share of value capture is high for the industry, but the iPod's overall pattern of value capture is representative.

According to the US Census Bureau data, the trade deficit with China ran to a record USD375 billion in 2017, while China's customs data showed the country's surplus with the United States stood at CNY1.87 trillion (about USD298 billion). Statistical differences aside, the fact that the United States is not only running a trade deficit with China, but with many other countries as well means the root cause of the imbalance is the US economic structure, which features low savings and high consumption.

---

[11]Xinhua: China–USA trade deficit beneficial to both sides, http://english.people.com.cn//200606/02/eng20060602_270388.html.

[12]Linden, G., Kraemer, K.L., Dedrick, J. (2007). Who Captures Value in a Global Innovation System? The case of Apple's iPod, The Paul Merage School of business, University of California, Irvine, June.

Justin Yifu Lin, honorary dean of the National School of Development at Peking University and former chief economist at the World Bank, said the US runs a trade deficit with China as it purchases more goods from the latter for lower costs and with higher quality. "Trade occurs on a voluntary basis," Lin said. "The US has the ability to make the products domestically, but the costs can be very high," he stated. An important cause of the trade imbalance is the fact that many US goods are less competitive in the Chinese market, said Long Guoqiang, deputy director of the Development Research Center of the State Council.

As shown in Figure 7.8, in 2018, the United States exported USD118.9 billion of goods to China, compared with an all-time high USD127.9 billion in 2017. The 7%, or USD9 billion, decline is likely due to the trade friction between the United States and China, which resulted in retaliatory tariffs on an estimated 85% of US goods, including most agricultural products. Despite the decline, from 2009 to 2018 US exports of goods to China increased 73%, while exports to the rest of the world grew only 57%. China is the third-largest market for US goods and services exports. Despite trade friction and punitive tariffs, China remained a top market for US goods exports. Figure 7.8 shows US Goods Exports

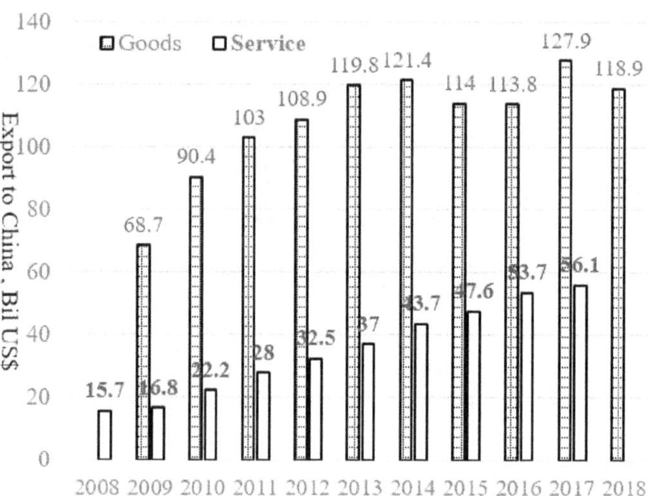

Figure 7.8.   US export and import with China, 2008/2018, billion USD.

Source: The US–China Business Council: 2019 State Export Report, Goods and Services Exports by US states to China over the past decade, 2019; China Statistical Yearbook, China Statistics Press, 2018, Table 11.5; 2014, Table 11.6.

to China in the 2009–2018 period, and US Service Exports to China in the 2008–2017 period. Exports to China support over 1.1 million American jobs, making trade important to not only US companies and consumers, but also US workers. US goods exports to China come from a wide range of industries including transportation equipment, semiconductors, and oil and gas, sustaining logistics jobs in America's ports and throughout the country. US service exports to China included travel and education, industrial processes, and management services, among other industries, with only NAFTA partners Canada and Mexico buying more goods in 2018. Figure 7.8 also shows that China was the third-largest market for US service exports, after the United Kingdom and Canada. Compared to previous years, US services exports to China grew more slowly in 2017. Service exports to the rest of the world grew 2.7% faster than they did to China that year. From 2008 to 2017, however, US service exports to China grew significantly more rapidly than to the rest of the world – 258 vs. 49%. The pace and scope of China's growth over the past three decades have been unprecedented, and it has had a positive influence on US service exports especially.

6. Composition of USA–China's Trade

In less than a single generation, a population larger than that of the United States rose from poverty, creating a middle class of more than 300 million people who devour Hollywood movies, enthusiastically shop online, and lead the world in the use of mobile web and e-commerce applications. China is now crisscrossed by bullet trains connecting massive industrial complexes that produce cars, TVs, chemicals, and electronics sold to consumers in the world's second-largest economy and buyers around the world. US businesses benefit in four (at least) key areas from the trade relationship with China:

1. Exports to China support jobs at home. US goods and services to China were worth USD165 billion in 2015, accounting for 7.3% of all US exports and about 1% of total US GDP. Total exports to China directly supported 1.5 million jobs in 2015 according to estimates by Oxford Economics.
2. China is deeply connected in the global supply chain, so a significant number of products indirectly find their way to China, either as part

of the Asia supply chain or to satisfy Chinese demand. According to OECD data, this is 3 to 4% of the value of exports from other Asian countries. If we add the indirect exports to the goods the United States directly ships to China, the value of US exports to China increases by more than 25%. Taking this into account, China supported about 1.8 million US jobs in 2015.

3. US investment in China and Asia generates income for US businesses. Income from US investments in China totaled about USD9.8 billion in 2015, equivalent to 0.5% of corporate profits in the United States, according to the Commerce Department's Bureau of Economic Analysis (BEA). In addition, BEA data found that less than 6% of products made in China by US-owned companies were sent to the United States, while 80% of those sales were sold to customers in China. If profits from these operations were redistributed to US-based shareholders and spent domestically, they would support 103,000 jobs and USD11.9 billion in GDP.

4. China invested USD14.8 billion in the United States in 2015. Based on data from the BEA, more than 38,000 people were employed by US affiliates of Chinese firms. Taking into account how these affiliates interact with the rest of the US economy through the supply chain, we estimate this Chinese investment in the United States to support a total of 104,000 jobs and USD10.8 billion in GDP. For example, Haier, a Chinese appliance manufacturer, employs 12,000 US workers who produce appliances out of facilities in Kentucky, Indiana, Alabama, Georgia, and Tennessee and is expanding its operations in South Carolina to add 400 new workers.

In short, China's development benefits the US economy in a variety of ways. When combined, the export and investment channels of the activities noted above supported USD216 billion, or 1.2% of GDP in 2015, as well as 2.6 million jobs. Chinese manufacturing also lowered prices in the United States for consumer goods, dampening inflation and putting more money in American wallets. At an aggregate level, US consumer prices are 1–1.5% lower because of cheaper Chinese imports. The typical US household earned about USD56,500 in 2015; trade with China therefore saved these families up to USD850 that year. As the size and purchasing power of the Chinese middle class grows, these consumers will demand more of the services and higher-end products that American companies export. Some 40 million Chinese households now boast annual income in excess of USD35,000. As China's middle class expands, we expect demand for American-made goods and services to rise as well. Ford and General Motors have already established major footprints in China, now the world's largest automobile market. In the first half of 2016, GM sold 1.8 million vehicles in China — 400,000 more than it sold in the United States. In 2017, China's value of imports and exports of goods from foreign-funded accounted for 44.8% of total imports and exports.

The above large amount of data shows that China–USA economic and trade cooperation is mutually beneficial; it is a win–win situation. Since the establishment of diplomatic relations between China and the United States, bilateral economic and trade relations have continued to develop, and cooperation in trade and investment has achieved fruitful results, achieving complementary advantages and mutual benefit. China has benefited a great deal from it, and the United States has also obtained extensive and huge economic benefits, sharing the opportunities and achievements brought about by China's development. Facts have proved that good Sino-US economic and trade relations are of great significance to the development of the two countries. Cooperation is beneficial to both sides, while fighting harms both sides. Nobel Prize winner and Columbia University economist Joseph Stiglitz said that as long as some US politicians do not recognize China's right to develop its own economy, it is unlikely that a meaningful trade agreement will be concluded between the United States and China.[13]

---

[13] The US–China Business Council (2019). 2019 State Export Report, Goods and Services Exports by US States to China over the past decade, May; understanding the USA–China trade relationship, prepared for the US–China Business Council (2017), by Oxford Economics, January ; Stiglitz, J. (2018). China and the United States "almost impossible" to conclude a real trade agreement, Bloomberg Report April 20, 2018 (in Chinese). Mildner, S.-A., and Schmucker, C. (2019). The battle of the giants: US trade policy vis-à-vis China, CESifo Forum, March, Volume 20; Discrepancies inflated US calculation of trade deficit, *Shanghai Daily*; Shanghai, China [Shanghai, China] 28 Mar 2018 (in Chinese); SCO member countries hit out at protectionism, Jing, S., Zhang, Y. and Xiao, H. (2019). *China Daily*, International ed.; Beijing 23 May (in Chinese); Regarding the facts of Sino-US economic and trade frictions and China's position, see The State Council Information Office (2018). White paper on "Facts on China-US Economic and Trade Frictions and China's Position" on the 24th. Xinhua News Agency, Beijing, September 24 (in Chinese).

7. Regional Trade Performance

The Top five regions in China (ranking on the basis of the foreign trade volume of 2017 data) during 1993 and 2017 are shown in Figure 7.9. As can be seen from Figure 7.9, the absolute export value and input value in 2017 increased by 24.2 and 24.0 times, respectively, since 1993. The share of the Top five regions in total export fell from 40.9% in 1993 to 32.6% in 2017. The proportion of the Top five regions in total imports increased from 27.8% in 1993 to 32.2% in 2017. In 1993, Guangdong province (ranked first) accounted for 40.0% of China's total exports and 53.4% of total imports, which is equal to or greater than the total of 26 other provinces, accounting for 40.9% of China's total exports and 27.8% of total imports. In 2017, Guangdong province accounted for 27.5% of China's total exports and 20.8% of total imports, respectively, which was lower than the total of 26 other provinces, accounting for 32.6% of China's total

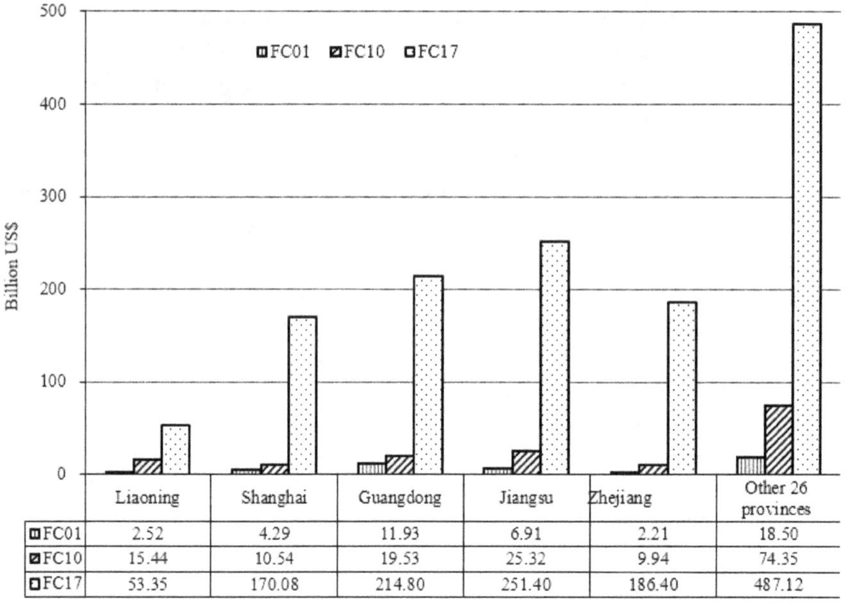

	Liaoning	Shanghai	Guangdong	Jiangsu	Zhejiang	Other 26 provinces
□FC01	2.52	4.29	11.93	6.91	2.21	18.50
▨FC10	15.44	10.54	19.53	25.32	9.94	74.35
□FC17	53.35	170.08	214.80	251.40	186.40	487.12

Figure 7.9.   China's exports and imports by top five regions, 1993/2017.

Source: Calculated using data from All China Data online: China Yearly Provincial Macro-Economy Statistics Region: All 1993 Imports and Exports; China National Bureau of Statistics: China Statistical Yearbook, China Statistics Press, 2018, Table 11.9, 2010, Table 6.12.

exports and 32.2% of China's total imports. This shows that from 1993 to 2017, the growth rate of total exports and imports of the other 26 provinces was faster than that of Guangdong province. All the Top five regions are located in the eastern coast area, which reflects a large regional disparity between coastal areas and inland areas in foreign trade. The three major strategies of the "One Belt and One Road" since the 18th National Congress of the Communist Party of China, the coordinated development of Beijing–Tianjin–Hebei and the Yangtze River Economic Belt have enriched the overall strategic layout of China's regional economic development, improved the policy system, and formed a spatial strategic pattern of four major plates and three supporting belts. Under the guidance of the three major strategies, the regional development gap has been shrinking.[14]

8. Why China's Foreign Trade Volume Increased Dramatically

The advent of the reforms certainly opened China's gate to the world, and the world responded by an eagerness to enter the huge Chinese market and take advantage of China's human capital. China's policies, including its Special Economic Zones, further contributed to the growth of the country's international trade. Later on, its accession into the WTO provided an even more favorable environment in which trade flourished (see Table 7.5).

In 2007, China's trade with the world grew by 23.5%, reaching USD2.17 trillion, with a surplus of exports over imports of USD262.2 billion. This new record high was up 47.7% from the 2006 trade surplus (Table 7.6). But the surplus from processing trade reached USD249.3 billion and accounted for 95% of total foreign trade surplus. The FFEs contributed USD136.1 billion trade surplus or 51.9% of total foreign trade surplus. This reveals that China is only a big foreign trade partner, but not a foreign trade power. The large trade surplus is not only exerting pressure on China's macro-economy, creating monetary pressure, but is also resulting in political pressure from the United States, the European Union, and other trading partners over their large trade deficits, and increases the

---

[14]Accounting Department of China National Statistical Bureau (2018). Significant development pattern of regional development strategy has a new look, September 13 (in Chinese).

Table 7.5.   Total value of imports and exports and the growth rates in 2007, 2018.

Item	Exports 2007		Exports 2018		Imports 2007		Imports 2018		Trade surplus 2007		Trade surplus 2018	
	Bil. USD	Yoy (%)	Bil. USD	Yoy (%)	Bil. USD	Yoy (%)	Bil. USD	Yoy (%)	Bil. USD	Yoy (%)	Bil. USD	Yoy (%)
Total	1218.0	25.7	2487.4	9.9	955.8	20.0	2135.6	15.8	262.2	47.7	351.8	−16.8
Of which: general trade	538.6	29.4	1401.0	13.9	428.6	28.7	1273.9	17.4	109.9	32.3	127.1	−13.8
Processing trade	617.7	21.0	797.4	5.1	368.4	14.6	470.7	9.1	249.3	32.0	326.7	−0.2
Others	61.8	45.8	289.0	5.3	158.8	15.9	391.0	19.7	−97.0	2.6	−102.0	95.1
Mechan. and electron Prod.	701.2	27.6	1460.7	10.6	499.0	16.7	965.6	13.0	202.2	66.1	495.2	6.0
High and new-tech products	347.8	23.6	746.9	11.9	287.0	16.0	671.5	14.9	60.8	77.9	75.4	−9.6
Others	169.0	298.6	279.8	1.9	169.8	45.7	498.6	23.9	−0.8	−103.8	−218.8	71.1
Of which: state owned	224.8	17.5	257.3	11.1	269.7	19.8	547.4	24.9	−44.9	32.5	−290.1	−1114.7
Foreign funded	695.5	23.4	1036.0	6.0	559.4	18.4	932.1	8.1	136.1	49.2	104.0	177.8
Private			1140.5	13.6			611.7	21.6			528.8	388.4
Others	297.7	39.2	53.6	6.4	126.7	35.1	50.4	9.6	171.0	42.4	9.0	280.6

Source: Calculated using data from China National Bureau of Statistics (2009). China Statistical Yearbook, 2008, Tables 17.3 and 17.4; National Bureau of Statistics of China (2008). Statistical Communiqué of PRC 2007, February 28; China Customs: Monthly Bulletin of Customs Statistics, December 2006; January 23, 2019; January 23, 2018 (in Chinese).

Table 7.6.　The role of FFEs in China's exports and imports, 2004–2018.

Year	FFEs exp. bil. USD	China's exp. (%)	FFEs imp. bil. USD	China's imp. (%)	FFEs imp. equip. self-use	FFEs surplus % China	Net surplus % China
2004	338.59	57.07	324.45	57.81	31.95	44.07	143.64
2005	444.18	58.30	387.46	58.71	27.67	55.61	82.74
2006	563.78	58.19	472.49	59.70	27.82	51.44	67.11
2010	862.23	54.65	738.39	52.88	16.31	68.23	77.21
2014	1074.73	45.87	909.31	46.39	9.06	43.25	45.62
2018	1036.02	41.65	932.05	43.64	3.44	29.55	30.53

Source: Ministry of Commerce (2006). *Foreign Investment Report 2005*, Chapter 6 — The export and import status of China's FFEs (in Chinese), March 10; Foreign Investment Report, 2006, Chapter 8 — The export and import status of China's FFEs (in Chinese), December 29, 2007; Foreign Investment Report 2007, Chapter 8 — The export and import status of China's FFEs (in Chinese), February 1, 2008; Wang, H. (2006). Sino-US trade: Is it really so big surplus? (in Chinese) China Economic Weekly, No. 8, 2006, March 2; China National Bureau of Statistics: China Statistical Yearbook, China Statistics Press, 2010, Tables 6.4, 6.5, and 6.12; China Customs: Monthly Bulletin of Customs Statistics, December 2006, 2010, 2014, and 2018, http://www.customs.gov.cn/customs/302249/302274/302276/2278926/index.html (in Chinese).

difficulty of China's management of its foreign reserves. In 2018, China's trade with the world declined 16.8%, reaching USD4.62 trillion, with a surplus of exports over imports of USD351.8 billion. This was down 16.8% from the 2017 trade surplus. The trade surplus from processing trade reached USD326.7 billion, accounting for 92.9% of the total foreign trade surplus. FFEs contributed USD104 billion surplus, which occupied 42.6% of the total foreign trade surplus. Since 2013, China Customs has separately listed "private enterprises" in the monthly report of customs statistics, and the "others" range has been adjusted accordingly. Therefore, private enterprises have been added in Table 7.6 for 2018. Private enterprises contributed a trade surplus USD528.8 billion, accounting for 150.3% of the total foreign trade surplus, making up the −82.5% of total foreign trade deficit of State-owned enterprises.

Why did China's total foreign trade volume increase dramatically after economic reform? We can find part of the answer to the question by observing Table 7.6, Figure 7.10 shows that trade of processing imported materials and trade of processing and assembling materials and components provided by foreign enterprises accounted for more than 50% of

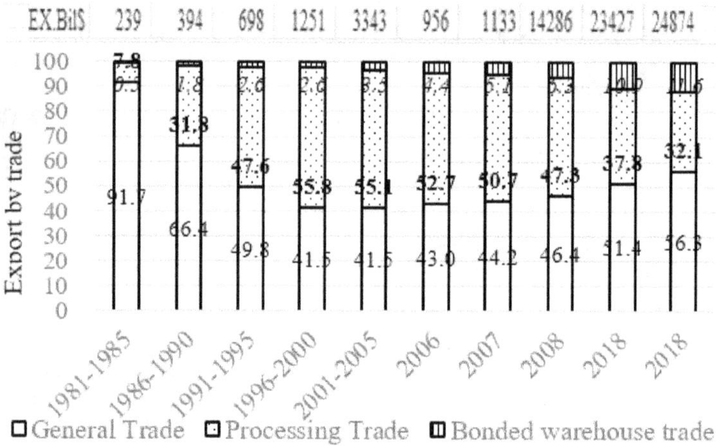

Figure 7.10.   Export by trade type during 1981–2018.

Source: Calculated using data from China National Bureau of Statistics (2011). The abstract of China Statistics 2011 (in Chinese), p. 19, p. 66; China Statistical Yearbook, China Statistics Press, 2010, Table 2.1; 2008, Tables 3.1, 17.2, and 17.4; 1999, Table 17.2; China Customs: Monthly Bulletin of Customs Statistics, December 2006; January 23, 2019; January 23, 2018 (in Chinese).

total trade since 1996. Such products became outdated and were labor-intensive and resource consuming. General trade occupied 91.7% of total exports during 1981–1985, declined to 41.5% of exports during 1996–2005, and then slightly increased to 45.7% in 2010. Bonded warehouse import/export trade and bonded warehouse re-export trade gradually increased from 0.48% during 1981–1985 to 5.3% in 2008. Exports as a share of GDP have climbed strongly, with some pullback during 1989, 1993, 1998, 1999, and 2001. Since 1990, export-processing trade increased rapidly and, since 1995, exceeded the GDP share of general trade. In 2006, it exceeded general trade exports by about 6% of GDP. Since 1995, most of the foreign trade growth has originated in the export processing trade sector. Table 7.6 shows that the trade surplus of export processing trade reached USD188.9 billion in 2007, becoming much larger than the general trade surplus of USD109.9 billion. Exports as a percent of GDP increased quickly since 2001, the year China entered the WTO and began dismantling market barriers.

In 1998, FFEs accounted for 48.7% of foreign trade; that number increased to 55.7% in 2007 (see Table 7.6). From January to September 1998, China's SOEs accounted for 53.5%, and, in 2007, that number fell to 22.7%. Here, we should note that SOEs in reality represented most of all Chinese enterprises in 1998. For example, in 2001, Township and Village Enterprises (TVEs) sold CNY963 billion (USD116.3 billion), or 28% of total exports to foreign trade companies (which were SOEs) for export, accounting for all SOEs' exports. At that time, most TVEs and small and medium enterprises (SMEs) did not directly engage in foreign trade transactions. On April 4, 2004, the Draft Amendment to the Foreign Trade Law, submitted for discussion for the third time, was passed by a unanimous vote at the 8th Meeting of the 10th National People's Congress Standing Committee. The ratification of the revised Foreign Trade Law, which took effect on July 1, 2004, made China's legal system consistent with its WTO commitment. Many TVEs, SMEs, and individuals could now do foreign trade business. However, TVEs are not SOEs, their ownership is collective, private, or individual. Therefore, accompanied by the decline of the share of SOEs in foreign trade, the share of private enterprises in exports increased from 0.36% in 1998 to 20.4% in 2007. China's good foreign trade performance was contributed by foreign investment and multiple ownership enterprises established due to reform policy. As seen from Table 7.6, FFEs accounted for 55.7% of foreign trade in 2007 and fell to 42.6% in 2018. Chinese SOEs accounted for 22.7% in 2007, but that number fell to 17.4% in 2018. In 2007, private and collective enterprises accounted for 19.5% of foreign trade. In 2018, the private enterprise portion grew to 37.9%. These developments point to the important role the private economy plays in the entire economic system, contributing more than 50% of tax revenues, more than 60% of GDP, more than 70% of technological innovations, more than 80% of urban labor employment, more than 90% of new employment and number of enterprises. The role of private enterprises in economic development is critical. Without the development of private enterprises, there will be no stable development of the entire economy; if there is no high-quality private enterprise system, there will be no modern industrial system. Supporting the development of private enterprises is tantamount to supporting the development of the entire national economy.[15]

Figure 7.11 shows that general trade occupied 90.0% of total imports during 1981–1985, and 35.6% of imports during 1996–2000; its share

---

[15]Liu, H., Member of the Political Bureau of the CPC Central Committee and vice premier of the State Council, was interviewed on current economic and financial hot issues, Xinhua News Agency reported on October 19 (in Chinese).

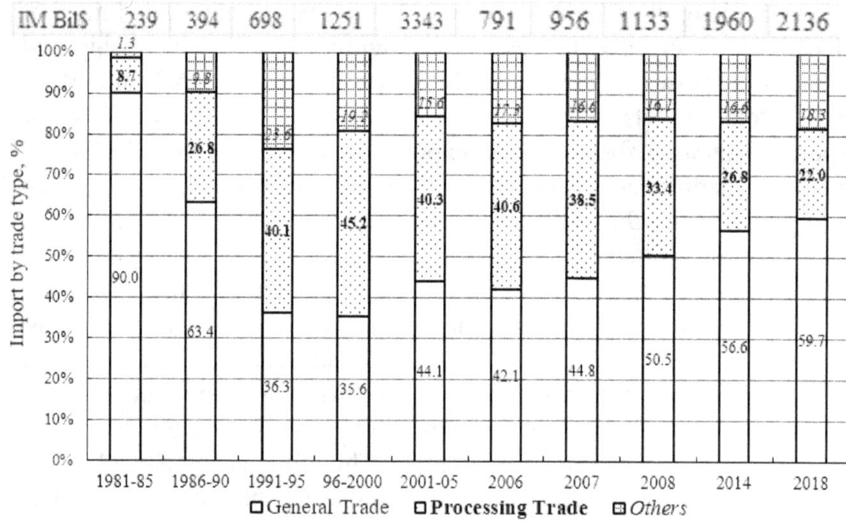

Figure 7.11.   Imports by trade type during 1981–2018.

Source: Calculated using data from China National Bureau of Statistics (2011). The abstract of China Statistics 2011 (in Chinese), p. 19, p. 66; China Statistical Yearbook, China Statistics Press, 2010, Table 2.1; 2008, Tables 3.1, 17.2, and 17.4; 1999, Table 17.2; China Customs: Monthly Bulletin of Customs Statistics, December 2006; January 23, 2019; January 23, 2018 (in Chinese).

then increased to 44.8% of imports in 2007, and further increases to 59.7% in 2018. As seen from Table 7.4, the pattern of general trade is similar between exports and imports. This means that only a small portion of China's imports is high-tech products and equipment. Imports as a share of GDP have risen strongly. In the early 1980s, general trade imports grew rapidly, from 8.5% of GDP in 1981 to 13.7% of GDP in 1985. In 1997, its share grew to 14.1% of GDP. General trade imports were 18.8% of GDP in 2014 and 16.1% in 2018. General trade imports are sold in China's domestic market, competing with domestically produced goods. This decline reflects tariff and nontariff barriers for imports. General trade imports, then, were not liberalized significantly. The dramatic change was associated with WTO membership. From their low point in 1981, general trade imports have surged as a share of GDP and, exceeding previous highs, grew to 25.8% of GDP in 2007. During the late 1980s the import-related with export processing trade increased rapidly and exceeded the GDP share of general trade during 1994–1999, and it exceeded general trade imports by almost 3.3% of GDP in 1997. Imports as a percent of

GDP increased quickly since 2001, the year China entered the WTO and began dismantling market barriers. The GDP share of general trade import increased rapidly and exceeded the import-related export processing trade since 1998, reaching 1.8% in 2007. The import side also supports that most of the foreign trade growth came from the export processing trade sector since the 1990s.

China's total foreign trade volume ranks the country as the third largest trader in the world since 2004, behind the United States and Germany. Since 2009, China has maintained the status of the largest exporter of goods and the second largest importer for nine consecutive years. Since 2013, China has surpassed the United States as the largest country in global trade in goods and has maintained this status for three consecutive years. In 2017, the United States still maintained its position as the largest exporter of goods and services, reaching constant 2010 USD5.36 trillion, accounting for 22.6% of the world total. China ranked second with constant 2010 USD3.84 trillion, accounting for 16.2% of the world total. However, per capita foreign trade volume is very low, accounting for only 45.8 and 43.2% of the per capita world foreign trade volume in 2009 and 2017, respectively. In 2009 and 2017, Germany's per capita foreign trade value was 4.49 and 3.25 times that of China, respectively.

The per capita foreign trade volume for China and some foreign countries is shown in Figure 7.12; it indicates that Germany, South Korea, United States, Japan, World, Russian Federation, China, and Brazil ranked in terms of per capita foreign trade in 2009. The 2017 ranking is the same as in 2009. This shows that China's foreign trade structure is still unreasonable and need to be further improved. First, processing trade exports accounted for a large proportion (Figure 7.10), reflecting China's low level of economy development. These products are mainly outdated, labor-intensive, and resource consuming. In 2004, China's GDP accounted for 4.9% of the world's total, but China's consumption of coal, steel, petroleum, cement, electricity, and water accounted for a higher proportion of world total consumption (see Table 2.1).

This analysis also shows that China's economic development is based on extensive production mode with higher consumption and lower efficiency than the world average. However, China's per capita natural resources are poor, accounting for only 20% of the world average, as we showed in Figure 2.1. In 2004, the import dependence rate of main raw materials rose sharply (see Table 2.2, indicating that China is now really "the world's workshop" rather than "the world's factory").

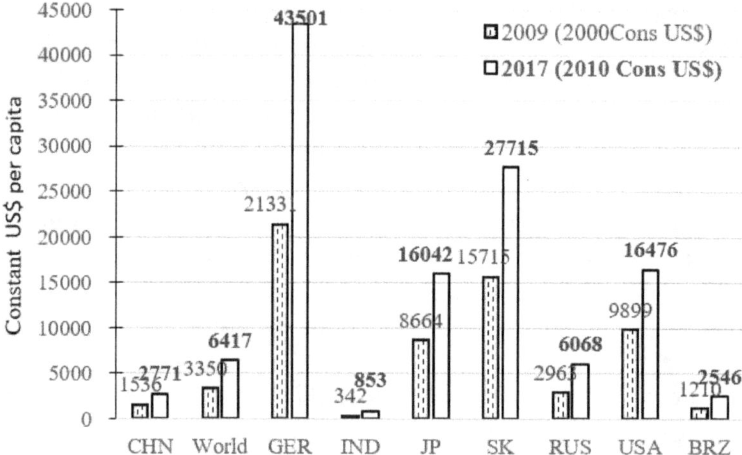

Figure 7.12.   Comparing per capita foreign trade volume of selected countries in 2009, 2017.

Source: Calculated using data from World Bank: World Development Indicators 2011 online, released 2011; 2019 online, released April 24, 2019.

China's economic development has entered a new normal. The cost advantage supporting the rapid growth of the manufacturing industry is weakening, energy resources and environmental constraints are tightening. The traditional extensive development model is unsustainable, and the country's economic development must now rely more on technological progress and improvement of the quality of workers, while continuously improving total factor productivity and building internal demand. As shown in Figure 7.11, processing trade exports fell sharply to 22.0% in 2018, which provides the initial evidence of China's industry development transition to extensive mode.

After the 2008 international financial crisis, profound changes have occurred in the manufacturing industry, while the world economy has been undergoing deep adjustments. A new round of technological revolution and industrial transformation prominently featured by accelerated innovation and penetration of information network technology has emerged on a global scale, and the digital economy has become an important driving force for global economic growth. The development of advanced manufacturing can strengthen the leading role of innovation, optimize the allocation of factors, enhance the added value of quality brands, expand the effective and medium-to-high-end supply, improve the quality and efficiency of the supply system, solve the problem of insufficient development, and meet the growing needs of the people for a higher standard of living. For example, in recent years, Chinese consumers have purchased products such as rice cookers overseas, although these products are produced in large quantities in China. The key is that there is still a big gap between Chinese products and foreign high-end products in terms of quality and brand. Advanced manufacturing is not only reflected in the advanced technology of products, but also in advanced production models and management methods.[16]

9. FFEs and China's Trade

As Table 7.6 reveals, FFEs play an important role in China's foreign trade. In 2006, FFE's exports and imports reached 58.2 and 59.7% of China total export and import value, respectively. In order to assess the FFEs' net contribution to China's international trade, we calculate the FFEsNetSurplus% measure. From FFEs import value, we subtract imported equipment used by their companies. The remainder is FFEs net import value, Eq. (7.1):

$$FFEsNetSurplus\% = \frac{FFEsExport - (FFEsIMport - FFEsIMportedEquipment)}{China\,Trade\,Surplus} \times 100$$

$$(7.1)$$

where *FFEsNetSurplus%* is percentage share of FFEs net import value to China total foreign trade surplus value.

In 2006, FFEs net foreign trade surplus reached USD119 billion and accounted for 67.1% of China's total foreign trade surplus. In 2007, FFEs accounted for 146 of the top 200 exporters and for 76.3% of the

---

[16]Luo, W. (2018). Keeping pace with high-quality development requirements, accelerating the development of advanced manufacturing, April 16, Source: "Seeking Truth" (*Qiushi* magazine is one of the publications of the Central Committee of the Communist Party of China, and is a theoretical publication sponsored by the Central Committee of the Communist Party of China) (in Chinese); Ma, J. (2019) — Vice president, Secretary of the Leading Party Members' Group, research fellow of the Development Research Center of the State Council (DRC): The Construction of China as a Strong Manufacturing Power from an International Perspective, February 22.

USD250.6 billion export volume of the top 200. The 45 state-owned companies on the list exported a total of USD66.33 billion, constituting 20.2% of the entire volume. Six collective enterprises and four privately owned firms are also included, comprising export values of USD8.33 billion and USD3.27 billion, respectively. Among the top 200 importers, there are 124 foreign firms, 63 SOEs, 6 collective firms, and 7 private companies.[17] As shown in Table 7.6, in 2010, the net import foreign trade surplus of FFEs in China's net foreign trade surplus increased to 77.2%, falling to 45.6 and 30.5% in 2014 and 2018, respectively. Since 2006, due to the sharp increase in the share of private enterprises, the share of FFEs in China's export and import has declined, as shown in Table 7.6. Another reason is the decline in the value of FFEs Import Equipment for their own use from 2010 to 2014.

Second, exported commodities have a low competitive advantage, since they are mainly labor-intensive products. China's exports are not associated with brand names and have little value-added. Exports were mostly labor intensive, standard, basic products. The competitive advantage of such products has gradually deteriorated due to rising labor and transport costs. However, as they were sunset industries in industrialized countries, they were also anti-dumping intensive products. China became a target of anti-dumping activities and has ranked first in the world in terms of anti-dumping investigations and final measures against China's exports. During 1995–2005, China was the target of 434 anti-dumping cases, accounting for 16% of the world's total, according to the WTO.[18] According to WTO data, China was the target of 1052 anti-dumping cases

---

[17]Huang, G., Zhang, B., Zhong, Y., Sun, D., Pan, H., and Zheng, B.Y. (2008). China's Top 200 Foreign Traders (original paper in Chinese), Customs, 2008, No.4; China Customs: Monthly Bulletin of Customs Statistics, published January 23, 2019: (6) from January to December 2018, the total value table of the enterprises ownership for export goods (USD value); (7) from January to December 2018, the total value table of the enterprises ownership for import goods (USD value); Monthly Bulletin of Customs Statistics: January 23, 2014 (6) from January to December 2014, the total value table of the enterprises ownership for export goods (USD value); (7) from January to December 2018, the total value table of the enterprises ownership for import goods (USD value).

[18]The Economist Intelligence Unit (2008). Country Commerce — China, Released March, p. 110.

Table 7.7. The role of FFEs in China's high-tech export 2002–2018.

Year	FFEs high-tech exports, bil. USD	By trade processing	Computer and communic.	FFEs % in China's high-tech exports
2002	55.66	52.48	46.55	83.64
2003	91.74	88.58	80.59	76.97
2004	144.57	134.87	121.26	87.33
2005	191.96	180.17	158.78	87.96
2006	247.88	229.44	202.28	88.06
2014	660.53	372.44	458.74	63.20
2018	2487.40	746.87	505.85	62.53

Source: Department of Foreign Investment Administration, Ministry of Commerce: Foreign Investment Report 2003, March 30, 2005; Report 2004, December 19, 2004; Report 2005, March 3, 2006; Report 2006, December 20, 2006; Report 2007 January 23, 2008.

in 1995–2014, accounting for about 22% of the global total of cases during that period.[19]

In recent years, China's high-tech exports and Machinery & Electrical Equipment sharply increased, but most of them were exported by FFES (Table 7.7). From 2004 to 2006, FFEs' high-tech exports reached about 88% of China's total high-tech exports. Within the FFEs' high-tech exports, trade processing accounted for 93.9% in 2005, implying that the core technology is still controlled by foreign entities. Among FFEs' high-tech exports, computer and communication technology occupied 82.5% during 2004–2006. In some high-tech industries in 2000, the share of foreign affiliates in total exports was as high as 91% in electronics circuits and 96% in mobile phones.[20] In 2003, domestic demand of the machine tool industry exceeded USD6.7 billion, first in the world. Imports of machine tools reached more than USD4 billion. Almost 75–100% of numerical controlled machine tool used by aviation and aerospace, automobile, power generating equipment manufacturing, shipbuilding, and

---

[19]The Economist Intelligence Unit (2019). Country Commerce—China, Released February, p. 63.

[20]Data from UNCTAD (United Nations Conference on Trade and Development) (2003). World Investment Report 2003—FDI Policies for Development: National and International Perspectives. New York: United Nations, p. 43.

Table 7.8. The role of FFEs in South-East Asia exports during their rapid growth period

Years	Country/region	Export share of FFEs
1970s	Taiwan	20
1974–1978	South Korea	25
1970s	Thailand	18
1970s	Thailand	6

Source: Gelboy, G.J. (2004). The Myth Behind China's Miracle. *Foreign Affairs*, Vol. 84, No. 4, 2004, July–August, pp. 33–48.

defense industry was imported. The rate reached 59.7%, while the domestic market self-fulfillment rate was only 41.3%.[21] The output of digital controls machine tools occupies 90% of the output of the machine tool industry in the international market, but only 10% in China. In all, 57.6% of China's total exports during 2004–2007 were from FFEs, which hold resources of core technologies, brands, and global marketing networks. Chinese enterprises are not equipped with core technologies and intellectual property rights. More than 95, 80, 70, and 90% of patents in pharmaceuticals, chip making, digital controlled machine tools and textile machinery, and autos are foreign patents. DVD producers have found their business nearly profitless after they pay for patent use.[22] Only 0.03% of Chinese enterprises have their own intellectual property rights and core technologies.[23] Table 7.8 shows the percentage share of FFEs' exports to total exports of South Korea, Thailand, and Taiwan during their rapid growth period. Compared to Table 7.8, it is found that their values are much lower than China's, implying that China's foreign trade is too heavily dependent on FFEs.

---

[21]Qi, Z. (2004). China machine tool industry—low-tech products confused fighting and High-tech products fall (in Chinese), *China Economic Times*, June 25.

[22]Foreign-funded firms bigger winner of China's trade surplus, http://english.people.com. cn//200504/30/eng20050430_183380.html.

[23]China still has a long way to go before becoming a world trade power, *People's Daily*, June 16, 2006.

10. China, the United States, and the world

Most of the export profits lie in wholesaling and retailing. But many Chinese companies have not built their own global marketing network, thereby allowing foreign distributors to take advantage of the opportunities presented. In 2004, Wal-Mart imported USD18 billion worth of goods from China. Of Wal-Mart's 6000 suppliers, 5000 (83%) are in China.[24] United States import prices from China started declining at a faster pace (Figure 7.13). In the first half of 2006, the price of US imports from China fell by 2.6%. Decrease in previous 6 years only 0.2%. Figure 7.13 shows that despite reports of rising wage pressures in China, these rising costs have not been passed on to US consumers. Export to the US market, no core technology and Chinese famous brand goods, no competitive advantage, except "China price." However, from April 2017 to 2018, US import prices from China increased 3.5% for the 12-month period. From April 2018 to 2019, they declined 0.2% for the 12-month period. This decline is driven by lower nonfuel prices.[25]

According to China's commitments for joining WTO, China's average tariff level of industrial goods was lowered from 14.8% before its WTO accession to 9.1% in 2005.[26] Nontariff measures, including import quotas, import licenses, and import tendering, were eliminated on schedule on January 1, 2005.[27] During the same period, the tariff level of agricultural products was down from 23.2 to 15.3%. China had become a relatively low-tariff member within the WTO.[28] Tariff quotas for agricultural products are scheduled to be abolished. Imported commodities might produce a negative impact on Chinese farmers and some of the manufacturing businesses, as the competitive power of the two sectors could hardly improve in a time short enough to allow them to effectively compete. The comparative benefits gained from many exported commodities would remain low because of factors such as the lack of core technologies for many exported commodities, branded products and commodities with

---

[24]Zakaria, F.Z. (2005). Does the future belong to China? *Newsweek*, May 9.

[25]US Bureau of Labor Statistics (2019). US Import and Export Price Indexes. April. Accessed at https://www.bls.gov/news.release/ximpim.nr0.htm.

[26]World Trade Organization (2006). Trade Policy Review Report by the People's Republic of China, WT/TPR/G/16117, Article 48, March.

[27]*Ibid.*

[28]Xinhua (2006). China fully implements WTO commitments, *China Daily*, April 20.

Figure 7.13.   US import prices from China declining at a faster pace.

Source: US Global Investors Investor: Weekly Investor Alert, July 21, 2006.

higher value-added, coupled with possible chaos following the liberalization of export operation rights in the country. China reduced tariffs in 2007 on a small number of goods, mostly chemical products, and in November 2018, on 1585 items in such categories as mechanical and electrical equipment, spare parts, and raw materials. In January 2019, it reduced tariffs on 706 consumer and industrial products and, in July 2019, China cut "most-favored nation" tariff rates on 298 information technology products. The average tariff rate stood at 7.5% in January 2019, down from the 9.8% average in effect in 2017. According to the WTO, China's weighted tariff in 2015 had fallen to 4.4%, significantly lower than that of emerging economies and developing countries, such as South Korea, India, and Indonesia, and approaching that of the USA (2.4%) and the EU (3%).

Overall, China's tariff can be assessed as reasonable. This assessment, however, did not stop the USA from declaring the now well-known "Trade War," by arbitrarily raising the tariff rate imposed on the USD200 billion list of goods imported from China from 10 to 25% in May 2019. The Sino-US economic and trade consultation process has since suffered serious setbacks. The US side has even simultaneously relied on to "impose tariffs advantage theory" to minimize the serious impact of this move on the US economy. "Tariff weapon" is actually a double-edged sword. Larry Kudlow, director of the US National Economic Council, recognizing the damage that the Trade War is doing to more than 600 US companies, such as Wal-Mart, sent a letter to the Trump administration on the 13th July, saying: "Tariffs for various commodities are not an effective way to change unequal trade behavior. Tariffs are paid by US companies, not by China." In addition to the loss of US jobs, tariffs also increased the economic burden of ordinary American households. In a joint study by the University of Chicago and the Federal Reserve Board, researchers used the "washing machine" example to prove the impact of tariff increases on consumer goods. The results show that, since the United States imposed tariffs on imported washing machines in January 2018, the average price of washing machines has increased by 12%. The annual spending of American consumers on washing machines and dryers has increased by USD1.5 billion, with an additional cost of USD86 per washing machine and USD92 per dryer. According to the "Treaty Damage to the US Hinterland" organization representing more than 150 trade associations in the United States, raising the tariff to 25% would damage nearly 1 million US jobs and increase financial market turmoil. In a nutshell, the addition of tariffs to Americans is not a "gospel" but a "nightmare"[29].

Third, Chinese foreign trade should avoid counterproductive competition through price wars; China exports at low price and imports at high price. China's global market share in rare earth oxide (ROE) commodities reached 80–90%. But, the price of ROE products in the world market declined sharply. In 1992, China exported 8024 tons of low-quality ROE products with an average price of USD12,400 per ton; and, in 2003, China exported 54,900 tons high-quality ROE products with an average price of

---

[29]China 2018 full-year, December trade: exports, imports, trade balance, https://www.cnbc.com/2019/01/14/china-2018-full-year-december-trade-exports-imports-trade-balance.html. Bartash, J. (2019). Why the US–China trade deficit is so huge: here is all the stuff America imports, Bartash, J. published: May 14. Marketwatch; US economy displaying self-inflicted wounds: China Daily editorial (2019). *China Daily*, June 12; *People's Daily Bell*: adding tariffs is to move a ladder or throw a brick, June 9, 2019 *People's Daily* (in Chinese); Li, Q (2019). More than 600 US companies jointly wrote to Trump's government emphasizing that rising tariffs is a way for US businesses and consumers to pay, June 14 Source: CCTV News (in Chinese).

only USD7,322 per ton.[30] The vendee of ROE products in world markets is only a few large companies, but more than 100 Chinese companies export ROE products. Chinese companies have adopted a lower price to compete. Total demand of the world ROE market is reaching 80,000 tons per year, but China's production capability reached 180,000 tons per year. China exported 4814.8 tons ROE products at the average price of only USD6,027 per ton from January to April 2008, which represented 92.7% of world total exports. The average price of world total exports amounted to USD8,175 during the same period.[31] The average price of ROE products exported from other countries (excluding China) reached USD35,406. "There is oil in the Middle East and rare earth in China." This is Deng Xiaoping's famous saying when he arrived in Jiangxi in 1992. But no one thought, back in 2012, that the concentration of rare earth resources in Ganzhou, Jiangxi, with such disorderly mining, backward technology, serious pollution, and over 38 billion environmental costs over the years, would far exceed the industry's profit for many years.

Due to the low concentration of the industry, the overall scale of enterprises is small, absent of any scale effect; the whole industry is therefore not competitive, and control over product pricing is relatively weak. For China's export of bismuth oxide in Japan, the price is CNY200,000 per ton (USD6,993/ton), and the price of metal bismuth imported from Japan is CNY200,000 per kg (USD6,993/kg), which is equivalent to a 1000-fold price increase. According to the data, in 2010, the main revenue of rare earth industry in Ganzhou City was as high as CNY15 billion (USD2.4 billion), accounting for one-third of the same industry in the country. Within the CNY15 billion value of the rare earth output, rare earth metal-based primary raw materials and processed products accounted for 90%, while high value-added deep-processed products and applications accounted for only 10%. "China has long supported the low-tech, low-cost, low-price rare earth industry at the expense of environmental costs. This is not sustainable." Experts said, "This is not only unfavorable to the development of China's rare earth industry but also not necessarily good for the international market. because it does not reflect the true value of rare earth."

---

[30] Shang, Z., Xie, W. and Zhi, B. (2004). Why the king of rare earth oxide (ROE) cannot set price? *China Economic Times*. November 24 (in Chinese).

[31] Calculated from http://www.cre.net/english/market/view_market.asp?id=235.

11. More on the Rare Earth Trade

In 1972, Xu Guangxian, the father of China's rare earths, began an attempt to "pre-existing ancient people" in the field of rare earth separation and purification in China. Xu Guangxian and others used the extraction technology for many years and finally completed this urgent military task. The separation coefficient of praseodymium and neodymium broke the world record. For the first time in the world, the industrial production of high-efficiency extraction and separation of rare earth by push–pull system was accomplished. After 1990, "marketization reform" became the most dazzling word in China. The rare earth industry was a high-profit industry at that time. Local enterprises and private enterprises poured in. Under the central planning system, the production process invented by Xu Guangxian was not patented. The technology spillover was brought about by the "job-hopping" of SOE technicians. As a result, the threshold for rare earth production has been greatly reduced, and countless rare earth producers have broken ground. Under the banner of "opening up to the outside world," China has adopted an open production and open supply policy. Under the temptation of short-term profits, China's rare earth production and export volume have expanded simultaneously. At that time, China was not aware of the importance and strategic nature of rare earth resources and even used rare earth exports as the main source of foreign exchange. Illegal piracy of rare earths is shocking!

Behind the sharp increase in export volume, the competition by rare earth companies in the market can be vicious and has led to a sharp drop in international rare earth prices. From 1990 to 2005, the price of rare earth ore fell from USD11,700/ton to USD7,430/ton. In 2005, the annual production capacity of China's rare earth smelting and separation reached 200,000 tons, which more than doubled the world's annual industrial demand. China smuggles at least 20,000 tons of rare earth every year, accounting for about one-third of the actual export volume. At that time, China's rare earths were really sold as soil. In the 1990s, countries with rare earth mines, such as the United States, Australia, and Canada generally implemented policies to restrict or stop the development of their own rare earth mines, and instead imported them from China as strategic reserves. USA has sealed up the largest rare earth mine in the country. The Mantingpas mine completely stopped the production of molybdenum and other rare earth mines. Academician Xu Guangxian said with sorrow: "Rare earth resources are very valuable, especially like the five southern provinces. They are very valuable medium and heavy rare earths with an industrial reserve of 1.5 million tons. Now more than 900,000 tons have been mined, only 600,000 tons left. If you don't protect it again, it will be mined in 10 years according to the current mining speed! At that time, we need to buy it from the United States and Japan. They may sell to us for hundreds or thousands of times the price!"

Since 2009, China's export regulation of rare earth elements material control has been implemented, as China adopted measures such as export quotas and export restrictions to reduce rare earth exports. The price of rare earth ore increased to USD27,500/ton. In the following years, the United States, Japan, and Europe have come to the WTO from time to time to impose rare earth restrictions. The WTO has basically ruled that China has lost the lawsuit. In September 2017, the price of rare earth ore declined to USD12,485/ton, Fortunately, in recent years, China has gradually countered in the "Rare Earth War" and achieved positive results: the first is to successively rectify the order of the rare earth industry. In June 2017, the Rare Earth Office of the Ministry of Industry and Information Technology sets up an expert group to accomplish that task. It plans to normalize the production of rare earth and crackdown on illegal production of rare earth. The second is the continuous integration of rare earth enterprises. China has already established six major rare earth groups: Aluminum Corporation of China (SH601600), North Rare Earth (SH600111), Xiamen Tungsten Industry Co. (SH600549), Minmetals Rare Earth Co.(SZ000831), Guangsheng Nonferrous Metals (SH600259), and Ganzhou Rare Earth.

The market share of the six major groups has been continuously improved; the exploitation capacity of rare earth resources accounted for more than 90% of the country's total. And they have a certain right to have some control over market pricing, which has a positive impact on the market. Third, Chinese rare earth enterprises are also exploring overseas resources. An example is China's rare earth enterprise Shenghe Resources (SH600392). On July 11, 2017, Shenghe Resources and other overseas companies acquired the approval of the local court for the acquisition of the only rare earth mine in the United States, Mantingpas. The fourth is the strategic reserve of rare earths. The State Council stated that China's rare earth strategic system includes national reserves and corporate (commercial) reserves. The strategic reserves include the combination of physical reserves and resources (land) reserves. China firmly opposes any attempt to use products made with rare earths from China to suppress

China's development, the National Development and Reform Commission (NDRC) said on June 17, 2019. The NDRC spokesperson also noted that China has been actively safeguarding the multilateral trading system, saying China supports economic globalization and promotes the development of China's rare earth industry under the principle of openness, collaboration, and sharing.

China has the world's largest reserve of rare earths and is the world's largest producer. In this context, strengthening the development and utilization of rare earth resources has an important positive effect on the Chinese economy as well as the development of the world economy. However, United States President Donald Trump signed into law the John S. McCain National Defense Authorization Act, which sets an increased budget for defense expenditure. Section 871 of the Act prevents the purchase of rare earths magnets from prohibited countries, including China, Russia, North Korea, and Iran. The industrial chains of China and the United States are highly integrated and highly complementary. The so-called mutual benefits are erased, and once again is proven that trade friction has no winners.[32]

On the other hand, China is the world's largest iron ore importer; 208 million tons of iron ore were imported in 2004. Brazilian mining group Companhia Vale do Rio Doce, the world's largest iron ore producer, announced on February 22, 2005, that it had concluded the iron ore price negotiations for 2005 with New Japan Steel. The iron ore price increased by 71.5% relative to 2004.[33] China has no choice but to purchase iron ores at such a high price. The 19, 9, and 70% price increases in 2006, 2007,

---

[32] China steps up threat to deprive USA of rare earths, May 29, 2019, https://www.msn.com/en-nz/news/world/china-steps-up-threat-to-deprive-us-of-rare-earths/ar-AAC4CG0; New US Defence Law Bans Magnets from China, Creates New Demand Potential for Alkane, INVESTORINTEL August 16, 2018, https://investorintel.com/sectors/technology-metals/technology-metals-news/new-us-defence-law-bans-magnets-china-creates-new-demand-potential-alkane/. In 2017, China's rare earth crackdown on illegal production of rare earth staged remarkable results, China Powder *Industry , Editorial E-mail, 2017(05) (in Chinese); The 13th Five-Year Plan of Rare Earth will launch the curtain* of industry integration and upgrading. October 19, 2016 Source: Report Hall, http://www.chinabgao.com/info/94857.html (in Chinese); Yuan, B. (2012) The pain of rare earth in Ganzhou, Jiangxi Province, CCTV Report. Liu, C. (2012). China Quality Around the World. July 18 (in Chinese).

[33] Zhu, L. (2005). Five views on New Japan Steel purchasing iron ore contract. *Shanghai Securities News*, February 24 (in Chinese), p. A8.

and 2008, respectively, followed a 71.5% hike in iron ore prices in 2005. China needs to import 46% of the world's iron ore output; only three major mining companies can provide such a huge amount. There are more than 700 steel production enterprises in China, making it difficult to form a unified front in price negotiations. A joint statement issued by the China Iron and Steel Association and China Chamber of Commerce of Metals, Minerals and Chemicals Importers and Exporters expressed a "strong hope" that both sides make a joint research into and seek a reasonable solution to the out-of-rule behavior in the talks.[34]

Fourth, China's export of commercial services was only USD128.6 billion in 2009 and imports of commercial services reached USD158.1 billion (US corresponding values were USD476 billion and USD334.3 billion, respectively, in 2009); see Tables 7.9 and 7.10. China's commercial service trade deficit was USD29.5 billion in 2009, while the US commercial service trade surplus reached USD141.7 billion. Furthermore, exports of insurance and financial services only amounted to 2% of commercial service exports in 2009, which was much lower than the world average of 8%. Import of insurance and financial services reached 8% of commercial service imports in 2009. In 2017, China's commercial services exports amounted to only USD184.9 billion, accounting for 8.0% of exports of goods and services. The corresponding value in the United States was USD727 and 8.0%. In addition, insurance and financial services exports accounted for only 3.9% of commercial services exports in 2017, far below the USA and world averages of 15.8 and 8%. India's other services accounted for the highest proportion of commercial services exports, at 74.9%, as India's computer and information services industry ranked first, accounting for 24.5% of the world's share, equivalent to 47.1% of India's commercial services exports

Table 7.11 shows that China's merchandise and commercial service foreign trade accounted for 68.4 and 28.2% of the United States' respective values in 2007. China's fees from Financial Services trade and Royalties & Licenses was only 0.39 and 0.33% of the United States' values in 2006. China's commercial service trade is large both by trade volume and trade structure. Commercial service trade will develop faster, but competition between Chinese and overseas-funded businesses will be fiercer. So, the structure of China's foreign trade still is positioned at the junior level, which is closely associated with low economic development

---

[34] Hua, X. (2006). China accepts iron ore price hike, but slams "out of rule" talks, June 22.

Table 7.9.   Commercial service exports and their structure, 1982–2016.

Country	Year	Commercial service exports bil. USD	Commercial service imp.% of total exp.	Other service, % commercial service exp.	Insurance and financial service % commercial service exp.	Transport service % commercial service exp.	Travel service % commercial service Imp.
CHN	2016	184.9	8.0	53.7	3.9	18.3	24.1
	2009	128.6	9.6	49.0	2.0	18.0	31.0
	1995	18.4	12.5	24.0	10.0	18.0	47.0
	1982	2.5	10.5	10.0	8.0	53.0	28.0
IND	2016	157.6	37.7	74.9	2.7	9.1	13.3
	2009	90.2	34.8	70.0	5.0	12.0	12.0
	1995	6.8	17.8	31.0	3.0	28.0	38.0
	1982	2.8	23.3	41.0	1.0	16.0	42.0
JPN	2016	172.5	21.1	61.7	2.6	18.3	17.4
	2009	125.9	18.7	62.0	4.0	25.0	8.0
	1995	64.0	12.9	59.0	1.0	35.0	5.0
	1982	20.2	12.6	31.0	1.0	65.0	4.0
KOR	2016	90.0	15.4	47.5	4.0	29.4	19.1
	2009	57.3	13.3	28.0	5.0	51.0	16.0
	1995	22.1	15.0	34.0	0.0	42.0	23.0
	1982	3.4	13.9	17.0	0.0	68.0	15.0
USA	2016	727.0	33.3	44.3	15.8	11.6	28.3
	2009	476.0	30.3	47.0	15.0	13.0	25.0
	1995	198.5	25.0	35.0	4.0	23.0	38.0
	1982	50.9	18.5	35.0	5.0	30.0	29.0
WLD	2016	4344.2	17.7	46.8	11.6	16.7	24.9
	2009	3417.7	21.9	45.0	8.0	21.0	26.0
	1995	1229.0	19.2	36.0	5.0	27.0	33.0
	1982	382.2	17.2	33.0	3.0	37.0	28.0

Source: Calculated using data from United Nations Conference on Trade and Development (UNCTAD) (2008). Handbook of Statistics, 2008, Tables 1.1.1, 5.1.1, and 5.2; Statistics Division, Department of Economic and Social Affairs, International Trade Statistics Yearbook, 2017, Volume I Trade by Country; Volume II Trade by Product. New York: United Nations, 2019; International Trade Statistics Yearbook, 2016, Volume I Trade by Country. New York: United Nations, 2017; World Development Indicators online 2019, Released April 24, 2019 by World Bank.

Table 7.10.   Commercial service imports and its structure 1982–2016.

Country	Year	Commercial service import bil. USD	Commercial service imp. % of total imp.	Other service % commercial service imp.	Insurance and financial services % commercial service imp.	Transport % commercial service imp.	Travel service % commercial service imp.
CHN	2016	438.4	18.4	20.7	3.4	17.9	58.0
	2009	158.1	14.2	34.8	8.2	29.0	28.0
	1995	24.6	18.2	29.1	16.9	39.0	15.0
	1982	1.9	9.9	24.6	4.4	67.0	4.0
IND	2016	161.2	25.1	61.2	6.6	18.9	13.3
	2009	80.3	24.5	34.5	9.5	44.0	12.0
	1995	10.1	20.9	27.6	5.4	57.0	10.0
	1982	3.4	19.4	27.3	4.7	62.0	6.0
JPN	2016	170.6	18.5	50.6	6.5	21.7	21.2
	2009	147.0	22.6	49.0	6.0	28.0	17.0
	1995	121.5	29.0	38.0	2.0	30.0	30.0
	1982	33.7	21.9	38.0	2.0	48.0	12.0
KOR	2016	110.8	17.9	43.0	2.4	28.5	26.1
	2009	75.0	19.1	49.0	2.0	31.0	18.0
	1995	25.4	16.4	35.0	2.0	38.0	25.0
	1982	3.2	11.8	28.0	1.0	51.0	20.0
USA	2016	488.3	15.2	40.7	14.9	19.5	24.9
	2009	334.3	17.2	35.0	21.0	20.0	24.0
	1995	129.2	14.5	26.0	6.0	32.0	36.0
	1982	37.1	12.4	19.0	3.0	44.0	34.0
WLD	2016	4697.3	18.9	45.8	8.4	19.9	25.9
	2009	3144.7	20.8	40.0	10.0	25.0	25.0
	1995	1221.7	19.6	32.0	6.0	31.0	31.0
	1982	407.8	18.1	28.0	4.0	42.0	26.0

Source: Calculated using data from United Nations Conference on Trade and Development (UNCTAD) (2008). Handbook of Statistics, 2008, Tables 1.1.1, 5.1.1, and 5.2; Statistics Division, Department of Economic and Social Affairs, International Trade Statistics Yearbook, 2017, Volume I Trade by Country; Volume II Trade by Product. New York: United Nations, 2019; International Trade Statistics Yearbook, 2016, Volume I Trade by Country. New York: United Nations, 2017; World Development Indicators online 2019, Released April 24, 2019 by World Bank.

level, and lack of management skills. In 2016, the value of exports of "royalties and license fees" in the USA was USD137.1, ranked first in the world, accounting for 36.5% in the world. China is not included in the Top

Table 7.11.   Comparison of merchandise and commercial services trades between China and United States 2007, 2017.

	Year	China	USA	Year	China	USA
Merchandise exports, bil. USD	2007	1218.00	1162.98	2017	2422.91	1572.71
% of world merchandise exports	2007	8.81	8.41	2017	13.76	8.93
Merchandise imports, bil. USD	2007	955.80	2017.33	2017	1740.00	2408.18
% of world merchandise imports	2007	6.80	14.35	2017	10.04	13.89
Exports of services, bil. USD	2007	117.15	479.15	2017	204.75	778.36
% of world exports of services	2007	3.51	14.36	2017	3.81	14.50
Imports of services, bil. USD	2007	123.26	372.30	2017	468.41	520.42
% of world imports of services	2007	3.97	12.00	2017	9.29	10.32
Financial services trade, bil. USD	2006	0.15	37.11	2017	334.04	1298.78
% of country's service trade	2006	0.16	8.86	2017	3.62	15.29
Royalties and license fees, bil. USD	2006	0.20	62.38	2016	43.68	133.10
% of country's service trade	2006	0.16	14.89	2016	5.30	10.25

Source: Calculated using data from United Nations Conference on Trade and Development (UNCTAD) (2008). Handbook of Statistics, 2008, Tables 1.1.1, 5.1.1, and 5.2; Statistics Division, Department of Economic and Social Affairs, International Trade Statistics Yearbook, 2017, Volume I Trade by Country; Volume II Trade by Product. New York: United Nations, 2019; International Trade Statistics Yearbook, 2016, Volume I Trade by Country. New York: United Nations New York, 2017; World Bank (2019). World Development Indicators online 2019, Released April 24.

15 countries/areas, which accounted for 94.6% of total world exports. Furthermore, USA was the country/area with the highest value of net exports (USD83.6 billion), while China had a trade deficit of USD43.7 billion in "royalties and license fees." China's economic performance of foreign trade after economic reform is far beyond other developing

countries, other former central planned economy countries in transformation, as well as China itself before economic reform. The gradual and pragmatic approach adopted by China has been proved more successful in economic reform than the "in one stroke" approach. Now, China will face more challenges ahead in its foreign trade journey. Among China's WTO membership commitments, several clauses are disadvantageous to China. The first is that China is regarded as a non-market economy within the first 15 years of its WTO membership. China is unfairly treated, as it is labeled as a non-market economy in anti-dumping cases. The second clause is related to the transitional safeguard mechanism for specific products. The foreign trade market is limited and developed countries adopt many measures to boycott China's exports. So China is facing a big challenge.

In 2003, China exported 16 billion garments, with the export revenue of USD80.48 billion. That indicates that the price was only USD5 on each exported piece. Chinese workers are doing what their counterparts in developed countries would not like to do. The price for a Boeing 747 airplane is equal to 300 million square meters of gray cloth. China bought 30 Boeing airplanes from the United States in 2003, but never noted it as an unfair trade between the two countries. Extensive complementary advantages of both countries in different stages of development will become the basis for a new type of international division of labor. On the other hand, China imported USD16.36 billion worth of cotton, wool, and chemical fiber as well as textile machinery in 2003. More than 80% of Chinese apparel exports come from international joint ventures, which means China is splitting the profits of that business with its foreign partners.[35] Meanwhile, China lags behind in terms of branding strategy, consciousness of property rights, and technology upgrading in the garment industry. China needs to improve its competitiveness; otherwise foreign brands will take our territory after the quota is eliminated.

According to China's promises upon entry into the WTO, China will liberalize foreign trade in 2004. China's revised Foreign Trade Law, which took effect on July 1, 2004, stipulates that the right to engage in foreign trade can be obtained by companies through registration with the government departments concerned. Under the 2004 Law, individuals are allowed to conduct foreign trade business. Legally registered foreign

---

[35] Jiang, J. (2004). China not the only beneficiary. *China Daily, China Business Weekly*, April 6.

trade operators can now import and export goods and technology without obtaining administrative approval. Foreign trade rights to special products such as petroleum, grain, chemical fertilizer, cotton, sugar, and edible oil, which were completely reserved for state-owned enterprises in the past, will be granted to formerly unauthorized companies. A credit and withdraw system will be in place. Efforts will be made on promoting the establishment of a foreign trade credit rating system. A system will be set up to supervise credit status and punish dishonesties. A perfect annual inspection of foreign trade operations will put enterprises under control. This is to guarantee a fair and free cross-border trade.[36] The law is also more service-oriented compared with the original version. An early warning and emergency system and public information system are available. Foreign trade remedies are well specified. Legal conditions will better protect intellectual property rights. New rules are designed to fight against monopoly and unfair competition.

11. UNCTAD Trade and Development Index

The United Nations Conference on Trade and Development provides a quantitative Trade and Development Index (DCIT-TDI 2007, Developing Countries in International Trade (DCIT)) to account for the complex interaction of factors affecting a country's trade and development performance (TDP) (Table 7.12). Overall, 123 countries are included in the present analysis, of which 83 are developing countries according to World Bank classification, which includes 26 Least Developed Countries. The United States holds the top position in TDI 2006, followed by Germany, Denmark, and the United Kingdom. The developed economies hold the Top 20 positions, except Singapore, which holds fifth place. This partly indicates that only a handful of developing countries have been able to come close to the TDP of developed countries. Five developing countries are in the Top 30 performers. Besides Singapore, these include South Korea (No. 21), China (No. 25), Malaysia (No. 27), and Thailand (No. 29). The DCIT-TDI 2007 considers three sets of determinants of trade and human development, namely: (a) structural and institutional context (SIC), (b) trade policies and processes (TPP), and (c) TDP.

---

[36]China plans four measures to deepen foreign trade system reform http://english1. peopledaily.com.cn//200406/30/eng20040630_148063.html.

Table 7.12. The Trade and Development Index (DCIT-TDI 2007) for selected countries in 2006.

TDI rank 2006	Country	TDI score 2006	TDI score 2005	TDI rank 2005	TDI rank 2006	Country	TDI score 2006	TDI score 2005	TDI rank 2005
1	USA	743	751	1	21	KOR	599	596	20
2	DEU	696	689	2	25	CHN	577	550	27
3	DNK	691	687	3	27	MAS	556	562	25
4	GBR	682	678	4	29	THA	551	537	31
5	SGP	675	665	7	32	POL	537	532	33
6	JPN	668	673	5	47	MEX	493	481	50
6	SWE	668	651	10	58	BRA	483	481	50

Source: United Nations Conference on Trade and Development (2007). Developing Countries in International Trade, Trade and Development Index, p. 11.

The three broad dimensions of the TDI comprise 13 components, which, in turn, are composed of 34 indicators. The weighted components of the TDI help to express it as a weighted sum of the actual value of its 13 constituent components. Indicators are aggregated to form the respective components. The methodology was selected to compute a composite index based on principal component analysis. By using this methodology, the SIC and TPP are aggregated by taking the weighted sum of 11 components to form the InputMI that reflects both dimensions. Similarly, the OutputMI is computed by taking the weighted sum of two components under the TDP dimension. The TDI is then obtained by taking the simple average of two aggregated indices: InputMI and OutcomeMI. The choice of indicators and methodology assumes special significance in this regard.

In general, according to WTO Statistics, the 2016 Top five exporters in world merchandise trade were China, USA, Germany, Japan, and Netherlands. China's export value was USD2,098 billion, accounting for 12.3% of world exports; the US export value was USD1,455 billion, accounting for 9.1% of world exports. The 2016 Top five importers in world merchandise trade were USA, China, Germany, United Kingdom, Japan and France. The US export value was USD1,455 billion, accounting for 9.1% of world exports. The US import value was USD251 billion, accounting for 13.9% of world imports.

The merchandise trade surplus was a deficit of USD511 billion for China, while the US incurred a deficit of (minus) USD797 billion. Why

US had large merchandise trade deficit? American mainstream economists believe that the huge trade deficit of the USA is rooted in its own
economic structure. For example, let us examine the trade situation for
(SITC Section 781) cars, other motor vehicles principally designed for the
transports of persons. The Top 15 countries/areas accounted for 86.4 and
73.8% of total world exports and imports, respectively. In SITC Section
781, China's exports were less than 1.5% of the world (China was out of
the Top 15 Export countries); China's imports in this category ranked
third, accounting for 6.4% of the world share; China's deficit was about
USD47 billion. In the same product category, the US ranked fourth in
exports (7.2% of the world), while ranking first in imports (23.8% of the
world). The deficit for the US amounted to USD123.3 billion. Germany's
exports ranked first, while its imports ranked fifth, generating a surplus of
USD101 billion. Japan's exports ranked second, and imports ranked 13th,
generating a surplus of USD83.1 billion. We derive another example from
(SITC Section 792) aircraft and associated equipment; spacecraft and
their launch vehicles; parts. In this case, China incurred a deficit of
USD21.7 billion. The USA had a deficit of USD21.0 billion. France and
Germany, on the other hand, showed surpluses of USD27.4 billion and
USD24.6 billion.

From these two sections, we can observe that the US trade deficit was
not caused by USA–China trade. The United States needs imports to
maintain consumption levels beyond its production capacity. China has a
surplus in labor-intensive products and a deficit in capital-technology-
intensive products, agricultural products and services. This demonstrates
that competitive industries will experience surpluses. The US trade imbalance is also constrained by the US high-tech export controls towards
China. If US export controls to China are relaxed, the trade deficit with
China can be reduced by about 35%. China and the United States have
complementary economic advantages and huge potential for cooperation.
The US Government's practice of imposing tariffs on Chinese products is
not conducive to the Sino-US economy, nor does it help solve the
economic and trade problems between the two countries. As shown in
Table 7.11, in 2017, the USA had a service trade surplus of USD257.9 billion, while China had a service trade deficit of USD263.7 billion. In 2016,
China paid USD43.7 billion in royalties and license fees. In 2019, Verizon,
the largest mobile operator in the United States, infringed on Huawei
230 patents, and Huawei requested more than USD1 billion in royalties.
US Congressman Marco Rubio criticized Huawei for becoming a "patent

hooligan." Marco Rubio proposed a new bill in the US Congress, requesting the amendment of the new US defense authorization program to include content that does not recognize Huawei's patent in the United States, and does not allow Huawei to sue US companies for infringement of Huawei patents.[37]

12. Concluding Comments

International trade has been an important part of China's story since the reforms. China's exports and imports have played a large role in its economic development so far. They have also benefited China's trading partners, especially the developed world of Europe, the United States, and Japan. Thus, China contributed a great deal to the globalization movement of the late 20th and early 21st centuries.

China's entry into the WTO in 2001 was a cause of much excitement, as well as controversy. China's exports brought less expensive goods to its partners, but were also seen as stealing importing countries' jobs. This perception led to many trade-related conflicts with other countries, the most recent and serious one with the United States. The USA–China trade war, initiated by US President Trump and his advisors, has had both political and economic origins. The so-called "decoupling" of the two economies, as touted by Trump, does not make sense from an economics and business perspective. The war has had adverse effects on both economies, as well as on the rest of the world. Unless countries realize that the economic benefits of trade outweigh the political costs, the USA–China trade war will continue to damage these two economies and the world economy.

---

[37]Calculated using data from China National Bureau of Statistics: China Statistical Yearbook, China Statistics Press, 2018, Table 11.4; 2009, Table 6.14; 2004, Table 18.15; 1994, Table 16.3; Statistics Division, Department of Economic and Social Affairs, International Trade Statistics Yearbook 2017, Volume I Trade by Country; Volume II Trade by Product United Nations, New York: United Nations, 2019; International Trade Statistics Yearbook, 2016 Volume I Trade by Country, New York: United Nations, 2017. Wei, W. (2018). Where does the Sino-US trade deficit come from? *People's Daily*, March 27, 2018 (in Chinese). *Nangfang Daily*, Guangzhou (2018). China and the United States have huge potential for economic complementarity and cooperation, March 4 (in Chinese). Ren, J. (2019). Is the American incarnation "Lao Lai" Huawei a patent hooligan? June 19, Zhongguancun Online (in Chinese).

References

Brown, C.P. and Kolb, M. (2019). Trump's Trade War Timeline: An Up-to-Date Guide. Washington: Peterson Institute for International Economics. August 23. Accessed at https://www.piie.com/blogs/trade-investment-policy-watch/trump-trade-war-china-date-guide. Downloaded, August 10, 2020.

Council on Foreign Relations (2020). US Relations with China: 1949-2020. Accessed at https://www.cfr.org/timeline/us-relations-china. Downloaded September 1, 2020.

Wong, D. and Koty, A.C. (2020). The US-China Trade War: A Timeline. China Briefing. Dezan Shira & Associates. August 25. Accessed at https://www.china-briefing.com/news/the-us-china-trade-war-a-timeline/. Downloaded September 1, 2020.

Appendix 7.1   US–China Trade War: Highlights, May 2016–2020

May 2016	Trump begins campaign for Presidency. He claims that China "is raping the United States."
November 2016	Trump is elected President. He surrounds himself with advisors who have been life-long China-haters (Navarro, Miller, others).
April 2017	Trump authorizes US Trade Representative (USTR) to investigate national security threat posed by aluminum and steel imports.
May 2017	Deal reached giving greater market access to China's markets
August 2017	USTR investigates Chinese practices on technology transfer and intellectual property rights.
March 2018	Trump requests that WTO charge China with discriminatory practices on licensing and place punitive tariffs on Chinese products. US places 25% tariff on all steel imports and 10% tariff on aluminum imports. Certain countries are exempted (not China).
April 2018	China retaliates by imposing 15–25% tariffs on 128 US products (USD3 billion worth). US lists 1,134 products for potential 25% tariff. China proposes 25% tariff on additional 106 US products (worth USD50 billion; list includes soybeans, automobiles, chemicals). Chinese telecom ZTE is accused of violating US sanctions. Ban placed on US companies doing business with ZTE.
May 2018	US demands that Beijing closes US trade deficit by USD200 billion in 2 years. China agrees to buy more (35–45%) US products.
June 2018	ZTE is allowed to continue doing business in the USA. US issues final list of products subject to 25% tariff; list includes 818 products (instead of original 1334). In all, 284 additional products placed on consideration list. China issues final list of 545 products (USD34 billion). Overall, 144 additional products placed on consideration list.
July 2018	USA and China implement the placement of 25% tariffs on products previously announced. USTR issues list of 6000 Chinese commodities to be subjected to 10% tariffs (USD200 billion).
August 2018	US adds 44 Chinese entities to export control list. China proposes second round of tariffs covering over 5000 US products (USD60 billion). Second round of tariffs implemented by both countries. USA: 25% tariff on 279 Chinese goods (USD16 billion). China: 25% tariff on 333 US goods (USD16 billion).

(Continued)

Appendix 7.1   (*Continued*)

September 2018	Third round of tariffs is on! US places tariffs on USD200 billion Chinese goods. Rate is 10%, to increase to 25% on January 1, 2019. China places tariffs on USD60 billion US goods.
October 2018	Pence declares that the US will place "competition over cooperation," thus articulating the US aggressive stance toward China.
November 2018	US Bureau of Industry and Security (BIS) proposes export control rules on AI, robotics, and quantum computing.
December 2018	Parties agree on temporary truce until G20 Summit (Buenos Aires). China announces resumption of US soybeans and temporarily removes tariffs on US autos and auto parts.
February 2019	Truce timeline extended. Trade talks resume in Washington.
March 2019	Placement of additional tariffs on US autos and autoparts halted by China. Current tariff rate: 15%.
April 2019	China announces ban on fentanyl production.
May 2019	Trump announces increase in tariffs from 10 to 25% on USD200 billion. Announces that new tariffs are coming: 25% on additional USD325 billion worth of Chinese goods. US raises tariffs to 25%. Thirteen rounds of talks fail. China retaliates, placing tariffs on USD60 billion US goods (effective 6/1/19). US places Huawei on entity list, banning US companies from unauthorized business with Huawei. China announces its own entity list of US companies.
June 2019	China implements tariff increase on USD60 billion. China investigates FedEx for diverting packages from Japan. China denounces US protectionist measures. Trump and Xi restart trade talks. G20 Summit in Osaka coming up. US halts 25% tariff increase on USD300 billion Chinese goods. Trump hints at relaxing Huawei ban; issues licenses for US suppliers.
July 2019	Despite truce, Trump threatens to place tariffs on USD325 billion of Chinese goods.
August 2019	Following Shanghai negotiations, Trump announces 10% tariff on USD300 billion (effective 9/1/19). He threatens the imposition of 25% tariff on USD250 Chinese goods. Yuan drops to the lowest level in 11 years (CNY7 = USD1). US Treasury accuses China of currency manipulation. China announces USD75 billion tariffs on 5078 US goods. Two groups of goods: First group: agricultural products (effective 9/1/19). Second group: other products (effective 12/15/19). Tariffs at 5% and 10%. Trump retaliates, raises US tariffs from 25 to 30%. Back to the table?

Appendix 7.1   *(Continued)*

September 2019	USA and China implement tariffs. US: tariffs on USD125 billion Chinese goods. China: tariffs on USD75 billion US goods. Additional 5% tariff on US crude oil.
October 2019	"Phase 1" agreement reached. Trump delays 30% tariff. China to purchase USD40–50 billion of US agricultural products, strengthen IP, issue currency management guidelines.
November 2019	US, China agree to roll back tariffs. Trump contradicts USTR, refusing to roll back completely.
December 2019	As part of "Phase 1," US announces no more tariffs and to halve 15% tariff to 7.5%. Overall, 25% tariffs on USD250 billion of Chinese goods would continue, subject to progress of talks. China to import USD40–50 billion of agricultural products in each of the next 2 years.
January 2020	USA takes China off the currency manipulator list. Phase 1 deal signed. USA to cut tariffs and China to increase purchase of US goods.
February 2020	China meets Phase 1 commitment: it exempts 696 US commodities from tariffs.
March 2020	"News Wars:" USA designates China Central Television, China News Service, the People's Daily and the *Global Times* as "foreign missions." China retaliates by expelling 13 journalists from *New York Times*, *Washington Post*, and *The Wall Street Journal*.
May 2020	Both sides reaffirm support for Phase 1 deal. China to increase purchases of US products by USD200 billion. China announces new list of US commodities excluded from tariffs (5th list).
June 2020	
July 2020	China buys record 1.762 million metric tons of US corn. USA orders Chinese Consulate in Houston to close. China retaliates by ordering the closing of US Consulate in Chengdu. Trump ends Hong Kong's Special Status.
August 2020	US designates imports from Hong Kong as "Made in China". US suspends reciprocal tax exemption on Hong Kong shipping firms.

Chapter 8

Foreign Direct Investment

1. Introduction

Foreign Direct Investment is an integral part of international business. It has significant implications for the companies involved, the host country, the home country, and the other participants of the global business system.

For the companies engaged in foreign direct investment, the decision represents a long-term and substantial commitment to the target country. Since they make such a commitment, of course, they need to exert control over the operations of their invested unit or project. Companies undertake foreign direct investment with the expectation of returns that will increase firm value. They also expose themselves to a variety of new risks, including credit, political, cultural, currency, and market risks. Identifying, measuring, and managing these risks are essential elements of a successful foreign direct investment.

For the host country, foreign direct investment brings jobs and higher incomes, while creating new supply chains or strengthening existing ones. Target countries, however, are concerned about the degree to which foreign companies contribute to the country's various objectives, be they economic, political, or of another nature. Home countries, of course, may lose out on jobs and incomes. They also see their influence on the firm decrease as the firm's reliance on the home country's environment wanes.

In this chapter, we will be examining direct investment flowing into and out of China. We first ask the reasons for and the mode of entry into China by foreign firms. We then examine China's policies toward foreign direct investment, including the 2019 Foreign Investment Law. We subsequently examine the state of China's FDI and the regional destination of that FDI. We continue by analyzing selected FDI indicators, emphasizing the comparison between China and India. The contribution to China's FDI by the various types of enterprises, especially those from the US, is also explained. Chinese firms have also engaged in direct investment outside China. We therefore proceed by exploring the size and issues related to China's Outward Foreign Direct Investment. We then present a relevant performance indicator of China's FDI and review the Belt and Road Initiative, the current day equivalent of the Old Silk Road. Finally, we offer policy implications aiming at enhancing FDI's contribution to China's economic development.

2. Why Do Foreign Firms Enter China?

Foreign direct investment has been the subject of study by scholars of economics and international business for centuries. Various theories have been developed to decipher the reasons behind a firm's decision to invest in another country. One of these theories is Dunning's[1] Eclectic Paradigm on Foreign Direct Investment. It emphasizes the Localization advantages (as well as Internationalization and Ownership advantages) derived by firms operating in foreign countries. These advantages are also relevant in the case of international firms entering China. Locating in China offers access to the country's potentially huge market as well as its valuable resources.

Following China's 19th-century wars, foreign investors entered China to take advantage of its low labor costs and resources. Privileged by the Unequal Treaties, colonial powers had easy access to Chinese industry prior to 1949. In the first quarter of the 20th century, most of the foreign direct investment came from Britain, Russia, Germany, and France. In the 1930s, the British and the Japanese were the principal investors. Foreign investment went into various industry sectors, with Transportation, Banking and Finance, and Manufacturing leading the way. Investment for export purposes was also strong. Investment in Transportation was focused on railway systems, such as the Manchuria Railway Company (Japan) and the Chinese Eastern Railway (Russia).[2]

---

[1]Dunning, J.H. (1988). *Explaining International Production*. London: Unwin Hyman.
[2]Hou, C. (1965). *Foreign Investment and Economic Development in China: 1840–1937*. Cambridge, MA: Harvard University Press.

Today's China, as the world's most populous country, offers firms the potential of a market of 1.35 billion. China has risen to the top spot in the world in terms of Purchasing Power Parity. The increase in per capita income is creating a strong middle class as well as a class of superrich that can afford the finest in luxury goods. As discussed in Chapter 5, the market is far from homogeneous across and within regions. This presents companies producing goods and services attractive to consumer groups of various income and preference categories with the opportunity to reach diverse markets.

A China location offers companies the opportunity to produce at rising but relatively still low labor costs. Locating in China provides foreign companies a link to an excellent supply chain that cannot be easily duplicated by other countries. China is also close to Japan, South Korea, and other markets in the growing Asian region. For investment purposes, of course, future growth is of the utmost importance. For foreign firms, locating in China is a decision analogous to purchasing a call option in a financial market. Foreign companies are betting on China's future!

Operating in China also entails considerable challenges and risks for foreign companies. These include market and economic risks, business risks, political risks, cultural risks, and currency risks. One of the most important risks lies in the Chinese government's changing policies toward FDI. Foreign companies must be familiar with the mode of entry appropriate to them and the industry sectors into which they are allowed to operate.

3. How Do Foreign Firms Enter China?

Foreign-funded (or invested) enterprises (FFEs or FIEs) may select among the six main corporate forms of operation in China as follows:[3]

1. The Wholly Foreign-Owned Enterprise (WFOE), which is owned and controlled by the foreign company. This is the most popular form of operation for foreign enterprises in China. In the first 11 months of 2019, WFOEs accounted for 75.1% of all FFEs approved during the period and 68.6% of investment in non-financial sectors.

---

[3]The Economist Intelligence Unit (2020). *Country Commerce: China*. New York: The Economist Intelligence Unit, February.

2. Equity Joint Ventures (EJVs) are limited liability companies formed to support long-term projects, with the foreign investor holding at least 25% of the equity. In 2019 (first 11 months), EJVs accounted for 21.6% of foreign-approved investment.

3. Joint Stock Companies (JSCs) are similar to public shareholding companies in western economies, and accounted for about 6% of total foreign investment in 2019 (January–November). Foreign shareholders must contribute at least 25% of the capital.

4. Contractual/Cooperative Joint Ventures (CJVs) may be formed as limited liability companies to support short-term projects or Built-Operate-Transfer (BOT) investments. They represent a small portion of total inward foreign investment (0.2%; January–November 2019).

5. Limited Liability Companies (LLCs).

6. Partnerships.

In addition, FFEs may form holding companies, or establish branches or representative offices.

4. China's Policies toward Foreign Investment

FFEs also need to be familiar with China's policies regarding entry into particular industry sectors. The National Development Reform Commission issues the "Foreign Investment Industrial Guidance Catalog," which includes the lists of industry sectors into which foreign companies may enter, and other policies related to foreign investment projects. For example, the NDRC/MOFCOM Order No. 22, in 2015, indicates encouraged, restricted, and prohibited foreign investment projects; those projects that are not included in these three categories are deemed permissible. The most recent Catalog was issued in 2019.

As a developing country with a history of 30 years of economic stagnation and lack of technological progress, China needs foreign investment to utilize and learn from foreign technology. As a country in transition, as it sheds some of its large and unproductive SOEs, China also needs foreign investment to deliver jobs and higher incomes to its population. These needs were assessed in terms of their congruence with China's national objectives and their effects on domestic industry. In terms of policy, the country's reform of its foreign investment regime followed the same experimental, gradual, and pragmatic approach followed by China in reforming other sectors.

China initially limited FDI to its Special Economic Zones (SEZs) and to joint ventures. Foreign companies could not produce for domestic consumption. For those foreign companies engaged in investment in China, however, the country offered various incentives, including the following:[4]

- *Regional Incentives*: Special incentives, in the form of a reduced tax rate of 15%, were offered to production-based Foreign Investment Enterprises (FIEs) participating in China–foreign equity joint ventures in areas known as SEZs. SEZs located in Guangdong Province, Fujian Province, and the island of Hainan. Similar incentives also offered to FIEs located in Technological Development Zones (TDZs) in coastal cities and other areas throughout China.
- *Sectoral Incentives*: For example, FIEs engaged in production-based activities and scheduled to operate for 10 years or more received income tax exemption for their first two profit-making years and a 50% tax reduction over the next 3 years. Separate exemptions and even relaxation of pertinent regulations was also provided for FIEs engaged in exploration of natural resources, agriculture, services, and other critical sectors, or those that are technologically advanced.
- *Export Incentives and FTZs*: Export-oriented FIEs are entitled to further tax reductions in addition to those noted above. FTZs were also entitled to additional advantages in the form of exemption from customs duty when their products are sold inside the FTZ or exported.
- *Other Incentives*: FIEs were also entitled to tax refunds if they reinvested their profits in their China joint venture. Unfortunately for FIEs, China's tax statute was revised in 2008, placing FIEs and domestic enterprises at the same income tax rate of 25%.

In the past, foreign investors had to navigate a series of "lists" that designated various investment areas as "prohibited/restricted" or "permitted/encouraged." These categories were included in the *Foreign Investment Catalog* maintained by the Ministry of Commerce (MOFCOM), issued in 1995. In 2013, the Catalog was replaced by a "negative list," which contained 190 "restricted/prohibited" investment areas. In typical Chinese reform fashion, the list was first tested within the Shanghai Free Trade

---

[4]United Nations Conference on Trade and Development (2000). Tax Incentives and Foreign Direct Investment: A Global Survey. New York and Geneva: United Nations.

Zone and went nationwide 5 years later. As the process of opening up continued, the list was reduced to 40 investment areas by 2019 (K&L Gates).

In a parallel development, China passed the new Foreign Investment Law. The new Law was passed in March 2019 and came into effect in January 2020. Its main objectives are to attract more foreign investment by improving the environment in which foreign investor operate and provide foreign-funded enterprises with a level playing field, and thus become more competitive (China Briefing). The Implementing Regulations for the Law were passed in December 2019 to go into effect in January 2020. The new Law is significant in many respects. First, it represents a nationally unified piece of legislation that elevates the treatment of foreign investment under the State Council. The Law's standing was further strengthened by the fact that it replaced three existing laws: the Chinese–Foreign Equity Joint Venture Law, the Chinese–Foreign Cooperative Joint Venture Law, and the Wholly Foreign Enterprise Law.

Second, the new Law serves as a signal of China's willingness to allow foreign companies in the country and protect their interests by providing them with an environment in which to succeed. Foreign companies will have an easier time setting up shop and face a level playing field to compete with domestic companies. Foreign companies will not need MOFCOM approval prior to establishing their presence in China. Instead, foreign companies can just report their information to MOFCOM, and register with the State Administration of Market Supervision.

Third, the Law states that foreign companies will receive "national treatment." In other words, the Chinese government will not discriminate against foreign companies in favor of domestic state-owned and private companies. Fourth, foreign companies will be able to compete for government contracts at equal footing with domestic companies. Fifth, foreign companies will not have to transfer their Intellectual Property. They will also be able to freely repatriate their profits from their China operations.

According to the World Bank *Doing Business* country rankings, China's business environment has improved considerably over the last 10 years. Among the 190 countries ranked by the World Bank, China's Ease of Doing Business ranking has been the following between 2011 and 2020: #87 (2011); #91; #91; #91; #90; #84: #78; #78; #46; and #31 (2020). During the 2018/2019 period, China made improvements with respect to Starting a Business, Dealing with Construction Permits, Getting Electricity, Protecting Minority Investors, Paying Taxes, International

Trade, Enforcing Contracts, and Resolving Insolvency. The new Foreign Investment Law, therefore, represents an additional welcoming development from the perspective of foreign companies navigating China's business environment. Although reactions to the new Law have in general been positive, certain concerns about its effectiveness have also been raised. These concerns include the general nature of this Law and omission of numerous details that could create loopholes at the expense of foreign operators. An example is the language used to state that the Law forbids forced technology transfer by administrative means. However, there is no definition of such administrative means.[5] The exact significance of the Law for foreign companies, then, will be dependent upon the further shortening of the Negative List and the position of the Chinese government in adhering to the spirit of the New Investment Law.

5. The State of China's FDI

China's booming foreign performance is closely related with FFEs. Attracting FDI enables China to obtain capital resources and brings advanced technology, management skills, and access to the overseas market and competitive pressure to domestic enterprises. Figure 8.1 reveals that the top six FDI partners (2017 ranking, Hong Kong, Singapore, Virgin Islands, South Korea, Japan, and the United States) invested 86.1% of the total FDI in 1994 and that declined to 78.8% in 2017. China's FDI mainly originating from Asia accounted for 63.7% of the total FDI and that increased to 83.8% in 2017. It accounted for 82.6% from the top five foreign investment partners (Hong Kong, Japan, the United States, the United Kingdom, and Germany) during 1979–1991.[6]

Table 8.1 shows the amount of FDI stock actually utilized during 1979–2017 from Hong Kong ranked first and reaching USD10,093 billion, accounting for 50.2% of the total FDI stock, followed by the British Virgin Islands, Japan, and Singapore with the top five accounting for

---

[5]China Briefing (2017). China's Investment Landscape: Finding New Opportunities. Opportunities, September. Accessed at: https://www.asiabriefing.com/store/book/china-s-investment-landscape-finding-new-opportunities-7285.html.

[6]Zhang, Y., C. Chen, and L. Zhang (1995). The role of Direct Foreign Investment in China's post-1978 Economic Development, *World Development*, Vol. 23, No. 4, pp. 691–703.

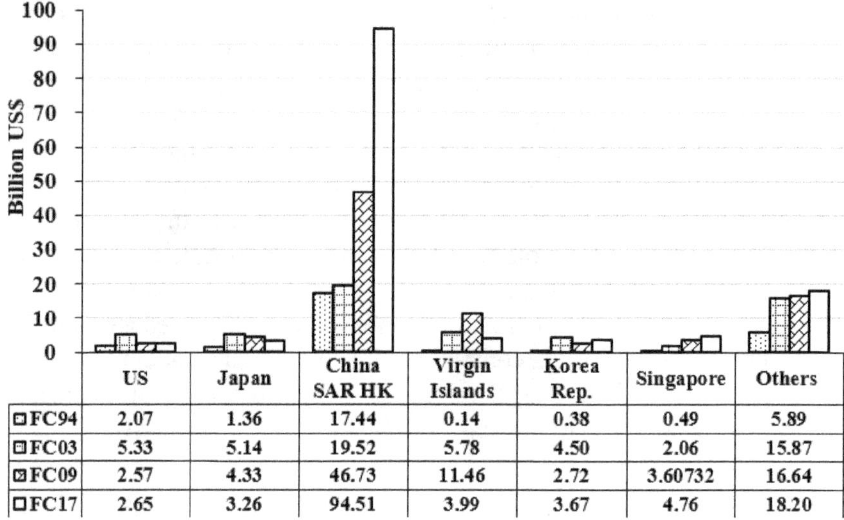

	US	Japan	China SAR HK	Virgin Islands	Korea Rep.	Singapore	Others
☐ FC94	2.07	1.36	17.44	0.14	0.38	0.49	5.89
☐ FC03	5.33	5.14	19.52	5.78	4.50	2.06	15.87
☒ FC09	2.57	4.33	46.73	11.46	2.72	3.60732	16.64
☐ FC17	2.65	3.26	94.51	3.99	3.67	4.76	18.20

Figure 8.1. China's actually used foreign investment by six partners, 1994/2003/2009/2017.

Source: Calculated using data from China National Bureau of Statistics: China Statistical Yearbook, China Statistics Press, 2018, Table 11.14; 2010, Table 6.19; 2004, Table 18.15; 1996, Table 16.15.

Table 8.1. Total FDI stocks actually utilized in China by the top 10 countries and regions in 2017.

Origin	USD billions	%	Origin	USD billions	%
Hong Kong	10,093	50.2	S. Korea	723.7	3.6
Virgin Islands	1,599	8	Taiwan	664.3	3.3
Japan	1,081.8	5.4	Cayman Islands	375	1.9
Singapore	900.3	4.5	Germany	297.2	1.5
USA	825.1	4.1	Samoa	274.4	1.4

Source: Calculated using data from Foreign Investment Management Department of the Ministry of Commerce of the People's Republic of China (2019). Chinese Foreign Investment Statistics Bulletin, 2018.

72.2% of the total. The FDI stock of the top 10 foreign partners reached 83.9%. The main sources of investment in China are Asia, North America, the European Union, and some free port areas (representing companies that are registered in these areas but do not have operations there). In 2017, foreign direct investment in high-tech industries was mainly

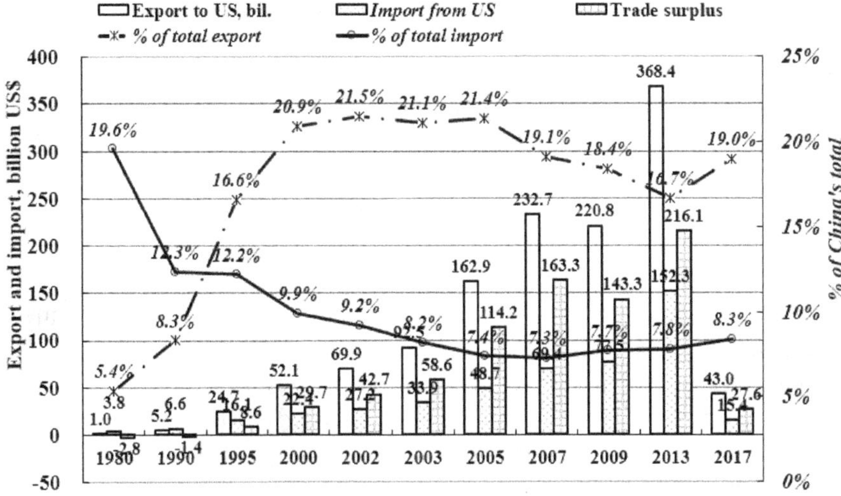

Figure 8.2. Actually utilized FDI from the United States to China during 1985–2019.

Source: Calculated using data from China National Bureau of Statistics, Database; Annual Value of Foreign Investment Actually Utilized (USD10,000), 2000–2019; Value of Foreign Direct Investment Actually Utilized by China, the United States (USD10,000); Department of Foreign Investment Administration, Ministry of Commerce, P.R. China, 2006. The Report of China's FDI (in Chinese), December 19.

concentrated in the high-tech service industry. The actual use of foreign investment was USD26.07 billion, accounting for 19.1% of the actual use of foreign investment in the whole year. The actual use of foreign capital in high-tech manufacturing was USD9.89 billion, accounting for 7.3% of the actual use of foreign investment in the year. The total amount of FDI actually utilized from 1979 to 2007 by the top 10 foreign partners is shown in Table 8.1. The FDI stocks during 1979–2017 from Hong Kong ranked first and reached USD1,599.0 billion, with the top five accounting for 72.2%.

Figure 8.2 shows the actually utilized FDI from the United States to China. It is shown that the FDI from the United States to China increased dramatically from USD0.5 billion in 1993 to USD2.5 billion in 1994 and reached USD5.4 billion in 2002, then gradually declined to USD2.7 billion in 2017. As a result, the proportion of the US FDI in China to total FDI in China fell from 18.3% in 1985 to 1.6% in 2009, recovered to 2. 4% in 2013, and fell to 1.9% in 2019 due to trade friction between the US and China, while the FDI of other countries in China increased.

6. FDI and China's Regions

Figure 8.3 shows the actually used foreign investment in the top five regions of China (2010 ranking) in 2001, 2010, and 2017. These top five regions are all located along the coast. The foreign investment flows to the top five regions of China increased from USD53.3 billion in 2001 to USD153.6 billion in 2010 and USD479 billion in 2018. In 2001, 2010, and 2018, the top five regions accounted for 62.6%, 59.1%, and 61.6% of China's national FDI, respectively. The GDP growth rates of these top five regions are higher than others, which indirectly demonstrates the contribution of foreign investment to economic development. All the top five regions are located in coastal areas, and thus the regional disparity between coastal areas and inland areas increased. Comparing these top five regions in 2001 and 2010, we find that Jiangsu exceeded Guangdong in 2010, moving to the top, implying that, during 2001 to 2010, more FDI entered the Yangtze Delta than the Pearl Delta. In 2010, Liaoning replaced Shandong in the top five, reflecting the revitalization of the northeast. In 2018, foreign investment flows to these five regions increased to USD479 billion. Shanghai, Jiangsu, and Zhejiang accounted for 30.7% of

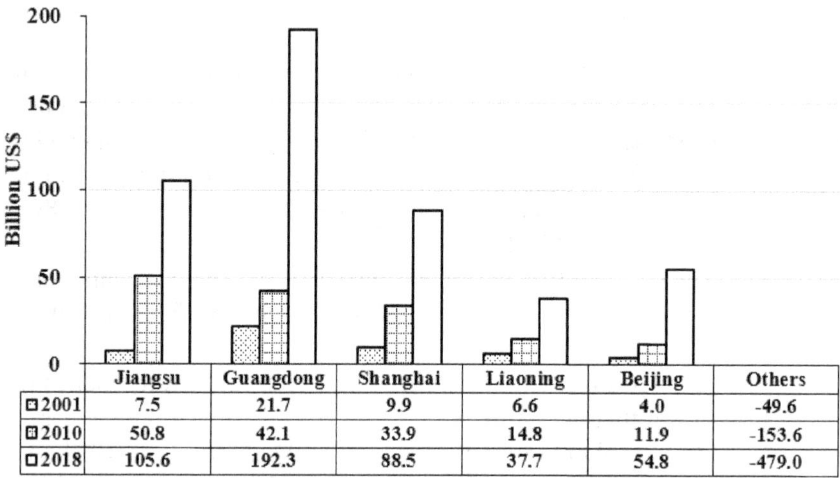

	Jiangsu	Guangdong	Shanghai	Liaoning	Beijing	Others
▣2001	7.5	21.7	9.9	6.6	4.0	-49.6
▣2010	50.8	42.1	33.9	14.8	11.9	-153.6
▢2018	105.6	192.3	88.5	37.7	54.8	-479.0

Figure 8.3. China's actually utilized Foreign Investment by top five regions (ranking by 2010, 2001/2010/2018).

Source: Calculated using data from China National Bureau of Statistics (2019). Database; Annual by Province, Total Investment of Foreign Funded Enterprises (USD million).

China's national FDI, while Guangdong accounted for 24.7%. As shown in Figure 8.3, Liaoning's FDI is much lower than the other four provinces and the FDI in Zhejiang was USD44.6 billion. Therefore, in 2018, foreign investment flows to the top five regions (Liaoning was replaced by Zhejiang) increased to USD485.8 billion, accounting for 62.5% of the total.

The total amounts of FDI stock actually utilized in 2006 and 2018 by the top five provinces in China are shown in Figure 8.4. In 2006, according to the FDI stocks of the top five provinces, Zhejiang ranked first, accounting for 21.6% of the country's FDI stock, followed by Jiangsu (18%) and Shandong (15.2%). In fact, Guangdong ranks first in the total national FDI, accounting for 21.6%, but there was no FDI stock reported from 1979 to 2017, only from 1979 to 2009. We, therefore, delete Guangdong from Figure 8.4. As shown in Figure 8.4, from 1979 to 2006, the FDI stock of the top five provinces was CNY 484.7 billion (USD60.9 billion) and increased to CNY 934.6 billion (USD138.4 billion)

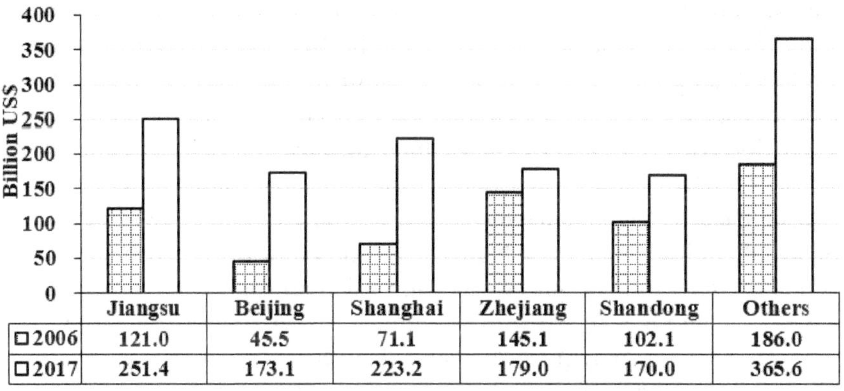

	Jiangsu	Beijing	Shanghai	Zhejiang	Shandong	Others
2006	121.0	45.5	71.1	145.1	102.1	186.0
2017	251.4	173.1	223.2	179.0	170.0	365.6

Figure 8.4. Total FDI stocks actually utilized by the top five provinces by the end of 2006 and 2017.

Source: Calculated using data from Department of Foreign Investment Administration, Ministry of Commerce, P.R. China (2008). The Report of China's FDI 2007 (in Chinese), March 5; China National Bureau of Statistics (2019). China Statistical Yearbook, 2018, China Statistics Press, Table 11.3; All China Data online: China Yearly Provincial Macro-Economy Statistics Region: Foreign Capital Actually Utilized and Foreign Exchange Income from Tourism, Jiangsu, Beijing, Shanghai, Zhejiang, Shandong, and Guangdong; Foreign Investment Management Department, Ministry of Commerce of the People's Republic of China: Statistical Bulletin of FDI in China, 2018; Shanghai Bureau of Statistics, Shanghai Statistical Yearbook, China Statistics Press, 2018, Jiangsu Provincial Bureau of Statistics, Jiangsu Statistical Yearbook, 2018.

in 2017. From 1979 to 2006, the FDI stock outside the top five provinces was CNY186.0 billion (USD23.4 billion) and increased to CNY484.7 billion (USD71.8 billion) in 2017. This shows that, from 1978 to 2017, China's trading partners have grown from more than 40 to 231 countries and regions. In 2013–2017, China's trade with emerging markets and developing countries continued to grow rapidly. With the countries along the Belt and Road, China's national of 4%. This is higher than the average annual growth rate of China's import and export of goods by 1.4 percentage points during the same period, pointing to a bright spot in the development of trade in goods.

All top five provinces are in eastern region. The percentage shares of FDI stocks in the eastern, middle, and western regions are 86.5%, 9.0%, and 4.5%, respectively, in 2006 and 84.1%, 6.1%, and 6.0%, respectively, in 2017. The eastern region has always been the region attracting the most foreign investment in China. "Due to the relatively developed economy of the region, the improvement of infrastructure (especially the convenience of port transportation, the high quality of the labor force, and the aggregation effect of foreign investment, the proportion of actual use of foreign capital in the region has remained above 80%. The financial sector is relatively developed, so it attracts a high proportion of foreign investment; the land resources in the western region are extremely advantageous, so the proportion of foreign investment in agriculture, forestry, animal husbandry, and fishery is relatively high. The central region is China's main power and raw material base, so the manufacturing and power, gas, and water production and supply industries attract a higher proportion of foreign investment. The percentage share of FDI inflows and inward stocks in the three regions is shown in Figure 8.5. As shown in Figure 8.5, from 2006 to 2017, the FDI stock in the eastern region fluctuated between 83.8% and 87.5%; the FDI stock in the middle region fluctuated between 6.1% and 9.0%; and the FDI stock in the western region fluctuated between 4.5% and 6.7%. The major opening measures of the "Belt and Road" can reduce the gap in the actual utilization of FDI in the three regions.

7. FDI Indicators

China and India are giants among developing countries. Both countries enjoy healthy economic growth rates. But, their FDI performance is significantly different. FDI flows into China increased from USD3.5 billion in 1990 to USD156.2 billion in 2007 and further increased to USD166.1

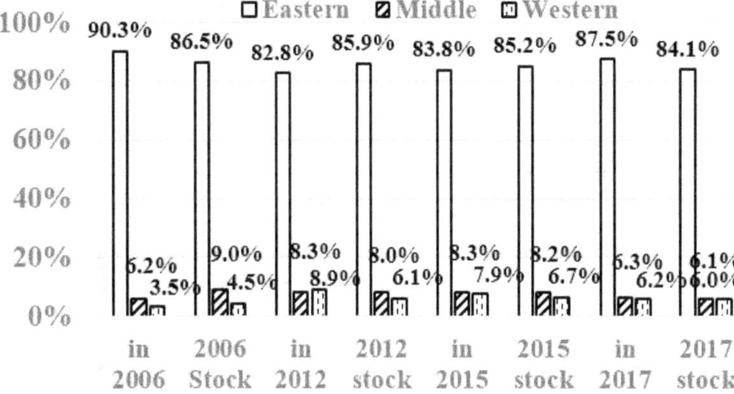

Figure 8.5. The actually utilized FDI inflows and inward stocks of three regions, 2006–2017.

Source: Calculated using data Foreign Investment Management Department, Ministry of Commerce of the People's Republic of China (2019). Statistical Bulletin of FDI in China, 2018 (in Chinese). Foreign Investment Management Department, Ministry of Commerce of the People's Republic of China: The Report of China's FDI, 2018, 2016, and 2013 (in Chinese).

billion in 2017. During the same period, India's FDI rose from USD0.24 billion to USD25.2 billion and USD40.0 billion (Table 8.1). Table 8.2 also shows that from 1990 to 2000, from 2000 to 2007, and from 2007 to 2017, the growth rate of FDI inflow into India was higher than that into China. FDI has contributed to the rapid growth of China's merchandise exports, with an annual rate of 17.3% between 1990 and 2007.[7] In 1989, foreign affiliates accounted for 9.4% of Chinese exports, with this number increasing to 57.1% in 2007. The share of foreign affiliates in total exports in high-tech industries in 2006 was as high as 88.1%.[8] A total of 63.5% of all FDI flows to China in 2000 went to manufacturing; this portion increased to 72.2% in 2004, then declined to 54.7% in 2007.[9]

---

[7]Calculated using data from China National Bureau of Statistics (2009). China Statistical Yearbook, China Statistics Press, 2008, Table 17.17; 2005, Table 18.17; 2003, Table 17.18; World Bank (2009). World Data Indicators online, 2009.

[8]Ministry of Commerce: Foreign Investment Report 2007, Chapter Eight — The export and import status of China's FFEs (in Chinese), February 1, 2008.

[9]Calculated using data from China National Bureau of Statistics (2009). China Statistical Yearbook, China Statistics Press, 2008, Table 17.17; 2005, Table 18.17; 2003, Table 17.18; World Bank (2009). World Data Indicators online, 2009.

Table 8.2.   China and India: selected FDI indicators, 1990, 2000, 2007, 2017.

Item	Country	1990	2000	2007	2017
FDI inflows (million dollars)	China	3,487	40,715	83,521	1,66,084
	India	379	2,319	22,950	39,966
Inward FDI stock (million dollars)	China	20,691	1,93,348	3,27,087	2,01,097
	India	1,961	17,517	76,226	1,55,341
Growth of FDI inflows (average annual, %)	China	2.8	27.9	10.8	10.3
	India	−6.1	19.9	38.7	5.7
FDI stock as percentage of GDP (%)	China	5.83	16.13	10.20	16.34
	India	0.62	3.83	6.48	0.76
FDI flows as percentage of gross fixed capital formation (%)	China	3.5	10.3	6.37	3.21
	India	0.5	2.3	5.74	4.87
FDI flows per capita (dollars)	China	3	32	63.4	60.6
	India	0.4	4	20.4	29.9
Share of foreign affiliates in total exports (%)	China	12.6	47.9	57.1	43.2
	India	4.5	—	—	—
GDP, billion current USD	China	354.6	1,198.5	3,205.5	12,310.4
	India	316.9	457.4	1,176.9	2,652.6

Source: Calculated using data from Foreign Investment Management Department, Ministry of Commerce of the People's Republic of China (2019). Statistical Bulletin of FDI in China, 2018; World Bank (2019). World Data Indicators online 2019 Updated: June 28.

Figure 8.6 shows the value added per worker in the manufacturing sector and services sector in India (1991–2018). Between 1991 and 2018, the average annual growth rate of China's value added per worker of manufacturing was 9.0%, while India's was 4.3%. In China, manufacturing productivity growth accelerated in the 1990s and expanded at the unprecedented rate of 10.5% annually from 1991 to 2000. This productivity surge in Chinese manufacturing is closely related to the rapidly increasing inflows of FDI and their industry concentration. Inflows of FDI in industry increased from USD3.5 billion in 1990 to USD25.8 billion in 2000; the average annual growth rate was 22% in 2007 and increased to USD33.5 billion in 2017 with the average annual growth rate being 1.5%.

In 2017, inflows of FDI in industry were USD33.5 billion, accounting for 30% of utilized FDI. Inflows of FDI in the service sector were

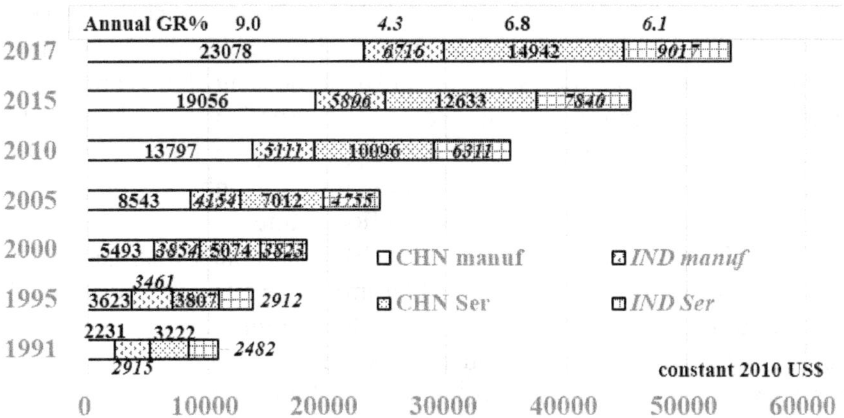

Figure 8.6.   Value added per worker in the manufacturing sector and services sector in China and India (1991–2018) (constant 2010 USD).

Source: United Nations Conference on Trade and Development (UNCTAD): Trade and Development Report, 2005, United Nations Publication, ISBN 92-1-112673-8, p. 32.

USD94.6 billion, accounting for 69.4% of utilized FDI.[10] In 2017, the high-tech service industry experienced a large increase in foreign investment. The actual use of foreign investment was USD26.07 billion, a year-on-year increase of 106.4%. The amount of actual investment in information services for the whole year was USD20.97 billion, an increase of 146.5% year on year. The actual investment in services related to technology transformation was USD3.29 billion, an increase of 37.3% year on year. The actual investment amount in R&D and design services was USD1.45 billion, up 3.2% year on year. In 2017, the actual investment in high-tech manufacturing was USD9.89 billion, up 7.6% year on year.[11] In India, the services sector seems to be considered an engine of income growth and driver of change. Average annual growth rates of 5.6% of value added per worker of the services sector in 1995–2000 was

---

[10] Foreign Investment Management Department, Ministry of Commerce of the People's Republic of China (2019). Statistical Bulletin of FDI in China, 2018, Table 13 (in Chinese).

[11] Foreign Investment Management Department, Ministry of Commerce of the People's Republic of China (2019). The Report of China's FDI, 2018, Tables 3-18 and 3-20 (in Chinese).

impressive. In China, the growth rate of the services sector between 1991 and 2018 averaged only 5.8%, and it has lagged considerably behind overall productivity increases. In India, FDI has been much less important in driving India's export growth, except in information technology. FFE in Indian manufacturing has been encouraged only in high-technology activities and service sectors. FFEs accounted for only 3% of India's exports in the early 1990s.[12] Even in the first quarter of the 21st century, FDI is estimated to generate less than 10% of India's manufacturing exports. In China, the great share of FDI inflows enters a broad range of manufacturing industries. In India, most FDI went into services, electronics and electrical equipment, and engineering and computer industries. The relative FDI index for China as shown in Table 7.14 — FDI stock as percentage of GDP (%), FDI flows as percentage of gross fixed capital formation (%), FDI flows per capita (USD), and Share of foreign affiliates in total exports (%) — was better than India's, confirming that FDI plays a more important role in Chinese economic development than in India.

What explains the differences? Some explanations may be the basic determinants of FDI (see Table 8.3), the country's development strategies and policies (see Table 8.4), and the Chinese overseas networks. The role of the Chinese business networks abroad and their significant investment in China contrasts with the much smaller Indian overseas networks and investment in India. There are more overseas Chinese citizens, and they tend to be more entrepreneurial, enjoy family connections in China, and have an interest and financial capability to invest in China — and when they do, they receive the red-carpet treatment.

8. FDI by Enterprise Type

Foreign capital actually utilized has contributed to China's post-1978 economic growth by augmenting resources available for capital formation. Foreign capital has also promoted economic growth in China through its important contribution to China's export earnings. Foreign-funded enterprises' exports and imports reached USD695.9 billion and USD560.9 billion, respectively, in 2007, accounting for 57.1% and 58.7% of China's total

---

[12]United Nations Conference on Trade and Development (UNCTAD) (2003). World Investment Report 2002, United Nations Publication, 2002, pp. 154–163.

Table 8.3.   The basic economic determinants of inward FDI, China/India.

China	India
FDI mostly from HK, Macao, Taiwan, and Overseas Chinese	Business process outsourcing (BPO) sector performs very well due to skilled, low-cost, English-speaking Indian workers
Higher total and per capita GDP	Advantage in technical manpower, particularly in IT
Better physical infrastructure in the coastal areas	Better political environment
More flexible labor laws, a better labor climate	India long followed an import substitution policy encouraging FDI only in higher-technology activities
Higher literacy and education rate	
Better entry and exit procedures for business	Better Business efficiency — extent to which enterprises are performing in an innovative, profitable and responsible manner

Table 8.4.   Principal development strategies and policies regarding inward FDI: China and India.

China	India
China opened its doors to FDI in 1979 and has been progressively liberalizing its investment regime	India allowed FDI long before 1978, but did not take comprehensive steps toward liberalization until 1991
China favored FDI, especially export-oriented FDI, rather than domestic firms. Such policies attracted FDI. A total of 72.2% of FDI flows in 2004 went to a broad range of manufacturing industries. In 2005 foreign affiliates accounted for 58.3% of total Chinese exports	India long followed an import substitution policy encouraging FDI only in higher-technology activities. There are restrictions on FDI in certain sectors. Most FDI inflows in 2000–2001 were toward services, electronics and electrical equipment, and engineering and computers
China's FDI procedures are easier, and decisions can be taken rapidly	

Table 8.5. The economic operation of Foreign-funded industrial enterprises in China 1998, 2007, and 2017.

| | China | | China | | China | |
| | Total | FFEs | Total | FFEs | Total | FFEs |
Year	1998	1998	2007	2007	2017	2017
Exports: USD10 billion	18.4		121.8		226.4	
EXP FFEs (%)		44.1		57.1		43.2
Invest. in fixed assets USD10 billion	34.3		180.6		949.7	
INV FFEs%		13.3		4.6		1.4
Total profits, USD billion	17.6		371.8		1,109.1	
PRO FFEs' (%)		28.7		27.7		24.6
Tax revenues, USD billion	10.8		60.5		230.6	
TAX FFEs (%)		13.70		22.6		18.7
Total employees 100,000 persons	206.8		309.5		424.6	
EMP FFEs (%)		2.8		5.1		6.1

Source: Data from China National Bureau of Statistics: China Statistical Yearbook, China Statistics Press, 2018, Table 13-09; 2001, Table 05-04; Foreign Investment Management Department, Ministry of Commerce of the People's Republic of China: The Report of China's FDI, 2018 (in Chinese); China National Bureau of Statistics, Database; Annual, Urban Employed Persons by status of Registration, 2000–2018.

exports and imports, respectively.[13] The economic performance of Foreign-funded industrial enterprises, and their role in China's economic development during 1997–2017, is shown in Table 8.5. China's rate of growth in the post-1978 era would almost surely have been much lower had the government not opted to open China wider to foreign capital. In 2006, the FFE's banking foreign trade surplus was USD91.22 billion, an increase of 36.9% year on year, accounting for 51.4% of the total foreign trade surplus nationwide, and it held 36.85% of the increment of the State foreign exchange reserve of USD247.5 billion.[14]

---

[13] Data from China National Bureau of Statistics (2009). China Statistical Yearbook, China Statistics Press, 2008, Table 17.11, Table 17.13.

[14] Calculated using data from Ministry of Commerce of the People's Republic of China (2008). Foreign Investment Report 2007, Overview (in Chinese), 2008-02-01; China National Bureau of Statistics: China Statistical Yearbook, China Statistics Press, 2008, Table 19–10.

Foreign-invested enterprises have had a positive influence on China's economic and social development, and have made important contributions to China's economic transformation and upgrading, optimization of foreign trade structure, balance of international payments, and expansion of employment. In 2017, the number of China's foreign-invested enterprises amounted to less than 3% of the country's total number of enterprises, creating nearly half of the country's foreign trade, a quarter of the profits of industrial enterprises, one-fifth of tax revenue, and 6% of urban employment, in order to promote the development of the domestic real economy and promote supply-side structural reforms. As shown in Table 8.4, in 1998, foreign-invested enterprises exported USD81 billion, or 44.1% of total exports. In 2007 and 2017, they increased to USD695.9 billion and USD977.8 billion, accounting for 57.1% and 43.2% of total exports, respectively. In 1998, foreign-invested companies absorbed 0.59 million urban jobs accounting for 2.8% of the total urban employment. In 2017, the number of jobs increased to 2.58 million and 6.1%, respectively. From 2000 to 2017, foreign-invested enterprises accounted for nearly 22% of the national tax revenue. In 1998, foreign-invested enterprises paid USD1.5 billion in taxes, accounting for 13.7% of the total tax paid. In 2007 and 2017, these increased to USD13.7 billion, 22.6%, and USD43.1 billion, 18.7%, respectively (Table 8.4). Foreign-invested enterprises have created a quarter of the profits of all industrial enterprises. As shown in Table 8.4, in 1998, foreign-invested enterprises' profits reached USD5.1 billion, accounting for 28.7% of the total industrial enterprise profits. In 2017, they increased by USD272.6 billion and 24.6%, respectively. Foreign-invested enterprises are an important force in China's technological innovation dynamic. In 2017, the equivalent proportion of full-time R&D personnel (person year) was 31.9%. The proportion of R&D investment accounts for 28.9% of the total and the effective invention patents of foreign-invested enterprises account for 21.1% of the patents by enterprises above designated size in the country. In 2017, in China's high-tech manufacturing sector, the actual use of foreign capital was USD9.89 billion, up 7.6% year on year. The actual use of foreign capital in electronics and communications equipment manufacturing reached USD6.4 billion.

Sino-US economic and trade cooperation is certainly not a "one-way street" for the United States to deliver wealth to China. In 2017, US-funded enterprises had an annual sales revenue of USD3,666 billion and profits of more than USD273 billion. In 2017, GM's global loss amounted to CNY10.98 billion, but it earned CNY13.33 billion in profits from two joint ventures in China. Qualcomm's chip sales and patent license fees in China accounted for 57% of its total revenue. The partnership between the United States and China is the most important one in international business. However, the United States has ignored the potential economic benefits generated by attracting more Chinese investment. This is a big mistake. Since the United States provoked a trade dispute with China, ordinary US consumers have been worried about the rise in consumer prices, manufacturing has been disrupted by the mature industrial chain, and farmers are worried that the carefully cultivated export market will never return. The scale of Sino-US economic and trade exchange is huge, and friction is inevitable. The key is to be able to treat and deal with problems rationally. Historical experience has repeatedly proved that as long as the two countries persist in expanding cooperation on the basis of mutual benefit and dealing with problems on the basis of mutual respect, both will have the opportunity to promote the development of Sino-US relations on the basis of safeguarding common interests. It is also conducive to the development and prosperity of the global economy.[15]

China's foreign trade performance is largely contributed by export-oriented TNCs (Transnational Corporations). Chinese firms can have opportunities to establish alliances with foreign TNCs, becoming fragments of global production chains. Japanese TNCs have played a leading role in fostering China's manufacturing exports, because Japanese TNCs are mainly export oriented. In 2002, Japanese-affiliated manufacturers in China exported JPY 2,245 billion (USD17.96 billion), or about 65% of their products (Figure 8.7), more than half of which were sold in the Japanese domestic market. For example, Pioneer Co. now produces more than 90% of Pioneer's seven DVD recording devices in its plant located in Guangdong province, most of them earmarked for personal computers and mainly for exports. These facts unequivocally indicate that Japanese domestic investment in China's manufacturing has been export oriented,

---

[15] Calculated using data from Foreign Investment Management Department, Ministry of Commerce of the People's Republic of China (2019). The Report of China's FDI, 2018, Tables 3.18 and 3.20 (in Chinese); Ministry of Commerce of the People's Republic of China (2008). Foreign Investment Report 2007, Overview (in Chinese), February 1; China National Bureau of Statistics: China Statistical Yearbook, China Statistics Press, 2018, Tables 13.9 and 20.5; 2008, Table 13.1; 1999, Table 13.7. *People's Daily* (2019). There is no "Thucydides trap" in the world — the danger of some people's strategic mistakes in the United States (middle), June 18.

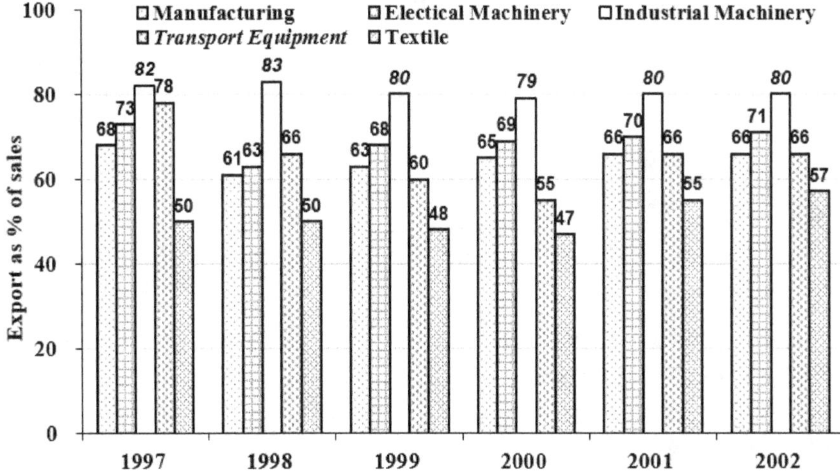

Figure 8.7.   Exports as the percentage of total sales of Japanese affiliates in China.

Source: Xing, Y. (2004). Japanese FDI in China: Trend, Structure, and the Role of Exchange Rates, International University of Japan, March.

and using China as a production base serving the Japanese domestic market as well as the global market has been the primary objective.[16] Reverse imports of manufactured goods surged to JPY 1,057 billion (USD8.46 billion) in 2002. Japan's Fast Retailing Company Ltd. manufactures high-quality clothing garments in its own Japanese outlets under the UNIQLO brand.[17] Japanese direct investment is mainly export oriented. The investment strategy is consistent with China's outward-looking development strategy and creates less competition pressure for domestic firms compared with domestic market-oriented FDI. More importantly, the export-oriented FDI effectively integrated Chinese firms into fragments of global production chains and expanded the channel for utilizing China's comparative advantages.

The mode of foreign direct investment also changed significantly in recent years. WFOEs (Wholly Foreign-Owned Enterprises) only accounted for 11.7% according to the number of projects during 1979–1990, then 48.3% during 1979–2007, and the realized FDI value

---

[16]Ministry of Economy, Trade, and Industry Japan: Quarterly Survey of Business Activities, various issues, Ministry of Economy, Trade and Industry, Tokyo.

[17]Ohmae, K. (2002). Profits and Perils in China, Inc. *Strategy + Business*, First Quarter.

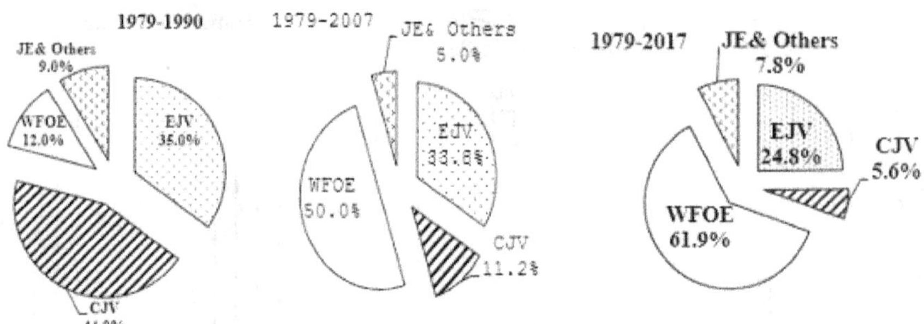

Figure 8.8.   Investment mode of FDI during 1979–1990, 1979–2007, and 1979–2017 of China by realized FDI value.

Source: Zhang, Y., C. Chen, and L. Zhang (1995). The Role of Direct Foreign Investment in China's Post-1978 Economic Development, *World Development*, Vol. 23, No. 4, pp. 691–703; China National Bureau of Statistics (2009). China Statistical Yearbook, China Statistics Press, 2008 Table 17.16; Foreign Investment Department of the Ministry of Commerce: Statistics of Cumulative FDI by Form in 2007, April 17, 2009; Statistics of Cumulative FDI by Form as of 2007, April 17, 2009.

by WFOE increased from 12% during 1979–1990 to 50.0% during 1979–2007 (Figure 8.8). The proportion of WFOE increased quickly, reaching 61.9% by utilized foreign direct investment in 2017. This means that in recent years WFOEs have become the main investment mode for FDI. Since for export-oriented TNCs their China's FFEs are their affiliated manufacturers, the WFOE mode of entry is more suitable. The actual use of utilized foreign capital in the top five industries is shown in Table 8.6. It can be seen that in 2000, 2007, and 2017, the top industry was the same — manufacturing. In 2000, Real Estate (#2); Production and Supply of Electricity, Gas, and Water (#3); Services to Households and other Services (#4); and Transport, Storage, and Post ranked #2 to #5; however, #3 to #5 disappeared from rankings in 2007 and 2017. In 2007 and 2017, the top two industries were the same. The other three industries — Information Transmission, Computer Services, and Software; Leasing and Business Services; and Wholesale and Retail Trades industries — ranked differently only in 2007 and 2017. This shows that, from 2000 to 2017, the service industry has become a major field for attracting foreign investment. Why? In 2000, 2007, and 2017, the service industry value added accounted for 39.8%, 42.9%, and 51.9% of the GDP, respectively. The degree of openness to the outside world has continued to increase, and the service industry has become an important area for attracting foreign investment.

Table 8.6. The top five industries for actual use of foreign capital as of 2000, 2007, and 2017.

	2000	2010	2017
Manufacturing	25.84	40.86	33.51
Information transmission, computer services, and software	—	1.49	20.92
Real estate	4.66	17.09	16.86
Leasing and business services	—	4.02	16.74
Wholesale and retail trades	—	2.68	11.48
Production and supply of electricity, gas, and water	2.24	—	—
Services to households and other services	2.19	—	—
Transport, storage, and post	1.01	—	—
Others	4.77	8.63	31.54

Source: China National Bureau of Statistics, Database; Annual, China National Bureau of Statistics, Database; Annual, Composition of GDP by the three strata of industry by sector, Billion USD, 1999–2017.

9. Foreign-Funded Enterprises

There is little disputing that foreign capital played a critical role in the economic boom in China. Foreign capital has forced domestic manufacturers to compete globally, and it has progressively induced plant managers and government officials to adopt the rules of a market economy, through the diffusion of management and marketing skills and the adoption of legislation aimed at promoting greater reliance on the market. Foreign capital has also resulted in substantial transfer of technologies. Protection of domestic industry is not a priority. Instead, China's government seems to subscribe to the notion that by welcoming foreign businesses in, and allowing unfettered competition, China can make its own industries stronger. So far, this has proved correct. The Japanese entrepreneur and scholar Kenichi Ohmae wrote the following: "I have Japanese and American friends who opened subsidiaries in China around 1998 or 1999, and made a great deal of money during their first 2 years. But now they are competing with fast-growing, fast-learning ventures led by shrewd Chinese entrepreneurs; once again it is difficult for outsiders to make a profit."[18] Some critics have also chastised foreign capital for some negative social consequences, such as

---

[18]Ohmae, K. (2002). Profits and Perils in China, Inc. *Strategy + Business*, First Quarter.

accelerating uneven economic development between the coastal and inland provinces, thus worsening the status of unequal income distribution. Overall, the impact of foreign capital on China's post-1978 economic development has on balance been beneficial.

In a survey of its members by the American Chamber of Commerce in China in 2002, three quarters claimed to be profitable, and nearly 40% said their margins in China were higher than their global margins. "There is no doubt that companies are doing better than they were," says the chamber's chairman, Chris Murck. However, in absolute terms, the earnings of foreign firms in China are almost certainly still small. A study of the US Department of Commerce data conducted by a research publication, *China Economic Quarterly*, showed that direct and indirect profits made by American affiliates in China amounted to USD2.8 billion in 2001 — less than the USD4.4 billion made in Mexico, with a population of just 100 million.[19] According to the China Statistical Yearbook, the after-tax profits and ROA for FFEs in China are quite good, and better than Chinese domestic enterprises. The ROA of FFEs increased from 1.96% in 1998 to 8.12% in 2009. During 1998–2009, the ROA of FFEs was higher by more than 1.9% as compared to those achieved by Chinese-owned enterprises on the average; so, FDI in China is beneficial. A recent survey of 4,700 members by the American Chamber of Commerce in Shanghai, which is second largest American Chamber only after Tokyo, is shown in Table 8.7. It reveals that 75% of member companies surveyed by Amcham said their China operations in 2010 were very profitable or profitable, the highest proportion in survey results dating back to 2002. Goods and services produced amounted to 73% (62% direct and 11% indirect). According to a recent analysis[20] conducted by the American Chamber of Commerce on survey results, from 2014 to 2018, most US companies reported that their China operations were profitable. In answer to the question, "Are your China operations profitable?", Yes was 83% and No 17% in 2014; in 2018, Yes was 97% and No 3%. The best-performing U.S. companies continue to focus on competing in China's rapidly expanding domestic market.

---

[19] *The Economist* (2004). Survey: Bulls in a China shop. London, March 20, Vol. 370, Issue 8367, p. 9.

[20] The American Chamber of Commerce (2019). 2018 China business report: Analysis of survey results.

Table 8.7. Presence and profitability of 4700 U.S.-funded companies in China, 2002–2010.

Year (number)	Large loss (%)	Breakeven/ slight loss (%)	Profitable (%)	Very profitable (%)
2002 (254)	4	22	65	9
2003 (236)	4	23	57	16
2004 (376)	6	26	53	15
2005 (273)	5.6	23	59.3	12.2
2006 (267)	5.2	22.8	65	7
2008 (238)	4.6	25	61.5	8.9

Source: 2001–2011 China Business Report: Analysis of Survey Results, The American Chamber of Commerce, Shanghai.

Survey results show that this "in China for China" trend continues to remain a strong point as the China market matures. Of the companies surveyed, 55% report producing or sourcing goods or services in China for the China market as their companies' primary strategy, roughly at the same level as 2009 and more than the 39% reported in 2008, as shown in Figure 8.10. The objectives of U.S.-funded companies and Japanese-affiliated manufacturers in China are different. China's large domestic market, strong economic growth, increasing export competitiveness, and accession to the WTO have all increased investors' interest in locating operations in China. Given its location advantages, it is attractive for resource-seeking, efficiency-seeking, and market-seeking FDI. According to a recent analysis[21] conducted by the American Chamber of Commerce on survey results, most US companies invest in China to access and compete for Chinese customers. China remains among the top-priority markets for 90% of US companies.

China is the largest recipient of FDI inflows in the developing world (see Table 8.8). The average annual growth rate of FDI inflows into China during 1979–2007 accounted for 62.3%, which ranked first, followed by India with 22.8%, while the world average was 10.8%. China's FDI inward stocks at the year-end of 2007 ranked 12th, with nine of top ten being developed countries (the only exception — SAR Hong Kong,

---

[21]*Ibid.*

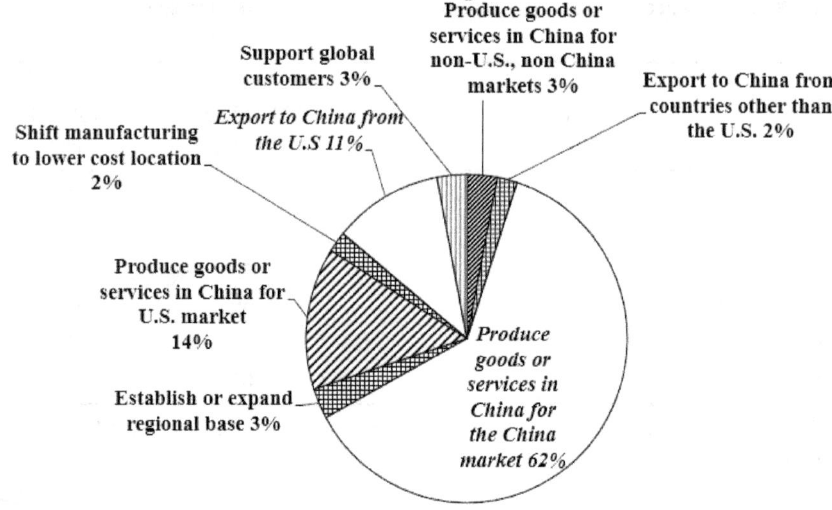

Figure 8.9.   The objectives of U.S.-funded companies in China (2005).

Source: 2001–2011 China Business Report: Analysis of Survey Results, The American Chamber of Commerce, Shanghai.

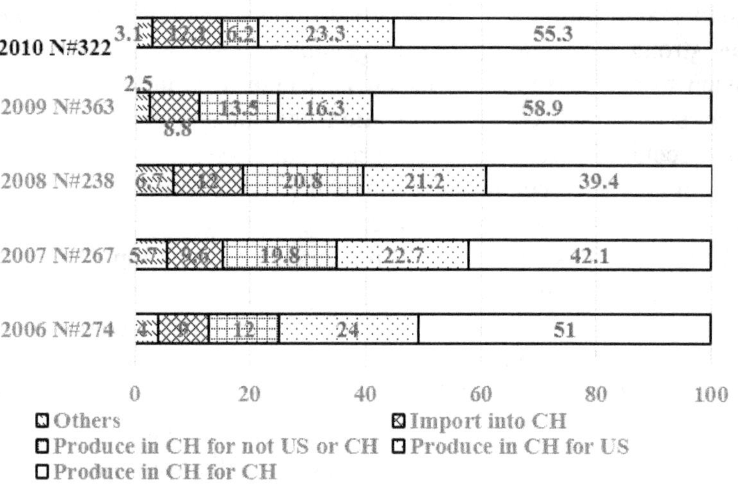

Figure 8.10.   The objectives of U.S.-funded companies in China (2006–2010).

Source: 2001–2011 China Business Report: Analysis of Survey Results, The American Chamber of Commerce, Shanghai.

Table 8.8.   FDI inflows in 2007 and 2018 average annual growth rate and FDI inflow stocks for selected countries.

	1989–1991 (%)			2002–2004 (%)			2010–2013 (%)			2016–2018 (%)*		
	Primary	Manufact.	Service	Primary	Manufact.	Service	Primary	Manufact.	Service	Primary	Manufact.	Service
World	7.3	37.4	55.3	8.5	27.2	64.3	10.5	44.2	45.3	3.5	25.4	65.1
Developed	6.5	34.0	59.5	7.8	20.0	72.2	9.0	39.0	52.0	1.2	23.0	69.8
Developing	10.7	52.9	36.3	10.0	43.1	46.9	13.8	46.7	39.5	8.1	35.8	54.3
	1989–1991 (%)			2002–2004 (%)			2013–2015 (%)			2016–2018 (%)		
China	25.1	41.7	33.3	12.9	45.3	41.8	9.1	45.7	63.4	8.0	40.4	52.0

Note:*After 2014 UNCTAD did not announce inward FDI by sector and industry, so the 2016–2018 data are from WDI.

Source: Calculated using data from United Nations Conference on Trade and Development: Major FDI Indicators (WIR 2008), Series — Direct investment in reporting economy (FDI Inward); World Investment Report 2019, Special Economic Zones, Annex tables 1: FDI — flows, by region and economy, 2013–2018 (millions of dollars); Annex table 2. FDI stock, by region and economy, 2000, 2010 and 2018 (millions of dollars).

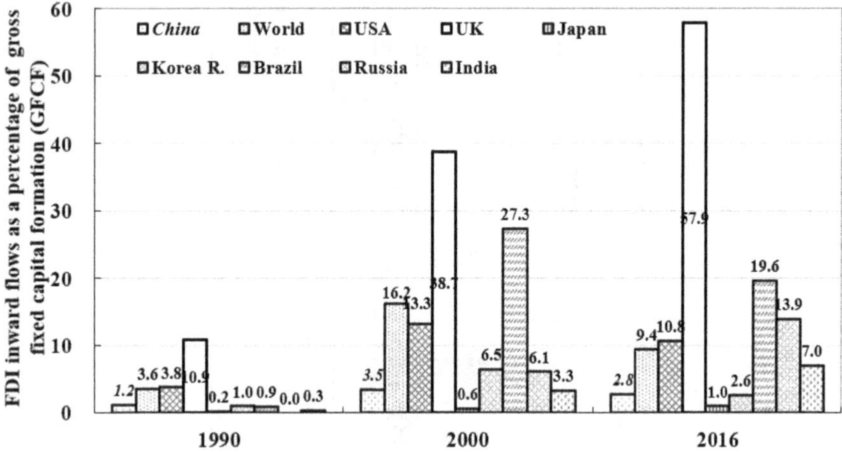

Figure 8.11.   FDI inward flows as a percentage of gross fixed capital formation for selected countries.

Source: United Nations Conference on Trade and Development (UNCTAD) (2018). World Investment Report 2017 — Investment and the Digital Economy. United Nations Publication, 2017, Annex Table 1; Data from database: World Development Indicators, Last Updated: 07/10/2019.

China, ranked 3rd). These reflect that China's FDI inward flows have been booming only in recent years. In 2018, China's FDI inward flows ranked 2nd; in the top four, only the United States which ranked first is a developed country, followed by developing countries China, Hong Kong SAR China, and Singapore.

China's FDI inward flow as a percentage of gross fixed capital formation was lower than the world average in 2000 and 2016 (Figure 8.11). Its value declined from 10.1% in 2000 to 2.8% in 2016. For comparison, some foreign countries are also introduced in Figure 8.11. The FDI inward flow as a percentage of gross fixed asset capital formation of the United Kingdom reached 38.7% in 2000, almost three times more than the world average. A surge in investments in the United Kingdom was driven by mergers and acquisitions (M&As) and by further market integration in the Euro zone.

The FDI inward flows as a percentage of gross fixed capital formation of the United States was only 10.8% in 2016 due to the high value of gross fixed capital formation in the country. For example, in the United Kingdom and China, the FDI inward flows accounted for 57.9% and 2.8% of gross fixed capital formation in 2016, respectively, but total gross

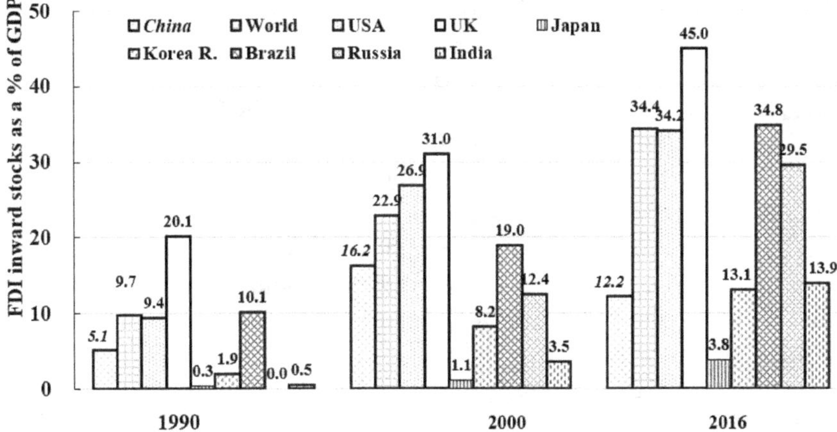

Figure 8.12.   FDI inward stocks as a percentage of GDP for selected countries.

Source: United Nations Conference on Trade and Development (UNCTAD): World Investment Report 2017 Annex Table 2; Data from database: UNCTAD: Web Table 7. FDI inward stock as a percentage of gross domestic product, 1990–2013; World Development Indicators, Last Updated: 07/10/2019.

fixed capital formation for the United Kingdom and China was USD458.9 billion and USD4,790 billion, respectively; FDI inward net flows were USD253.8 and USD133.7 billion, respectively.

Figure 8.12 shows China's FDI inward stock as a percentage of GDP formation lower than the world average. It increased from 5.1% in 1990 to 16.2% in 2000, and then declined to 12.2% in 2016, while the world average increased from 9.7% in 1990 to 22.9% in 2000 and to 34. 4% in 2016. From Figures 8.11 and 8.12, we observe that the United Kingdom had the highest value of FDI inward flow and FDI inward stocks as % of gross fixed capital formation and GDP; Japan had the lowest percentage among the listed countries.

In more recent years, inward FDI has had strong growth in services and high-tech industries. Inflows to the services sector, such as finance, telecommunications, and real estate, are significantly increasing. Table 7.19 lists inward FDI flows for 1989–1991, 2002–2004, and 2010–2013. Inward FDI flows from the world's primary sector increased from 4.9% in 1989–1991 to 7.5% in 2002–2004 and further increased to 10.1% in 2010–2013. Inward FDI flows of developed countries into the service sector increased from 59.5% in 1989–1991 to 72.2% in

2002–2004 and fell to 52% in 2010–2013. FDI flows into China's service sector declined from 31.2% during 1989–1991 to 24.4% in 2002–2004 and increased to 63.4% in 2010–2013; China's inward FDI flows of the secondary industry sector increased from 65.3% during 1989–1991 to 73.4% in 2002–2004, and then declined to 63.4% in 2010–2013, which was higher than the world average, as shown in Table 8.9. The amount of FDI flowing into China's secondary industry in 1989–2001 and 2002–2004 did not prove sustainable. It dropped to 59.7% in 2013, as China upgraded its industrial structure and became a "world shop." In 2010–2013, China's inward FDI flow structure was realistic. In 2017, inward FDI flows in primary industry, secondary industry, and tertiary industry were USD0.6 billion, USD40.95 billion, and USD89.30 billion, accounting for 0.5%, 31.2%, and 68.2%, respectively. The inward FDI flows in the top five sectors — Manufacturing; Information Transmission, Computer Services, and Software; Real Estate; Leasing and Business Services; and Wholesale and Retail Trades — were USD33.5 billion, USD20.9 billion, USD16.9 billion, USD16.7 billion, and USD11.5 billion, accounting for 25.6%, 16.0%, 12.9%, 12.8%, and 8.6% of total inward FDI flows, respectively.[22]

Global FDI outflows reached a new record high in 2007, reflecting the sixth consecutive year of growth. With outflows of USD1,997 billion, the previous record set in 2000 was surpassed by USD765 billion. The continued rise in FDI outflows in 2007 largely reflected relatively high economic growth and strong economic performance in many parts of the world. The growth in FDI outflows was also driven by cross-border M&A activity, which expanded in scope across countries and sectors. The value of total cross-border M&As was a record USD1,637 billion in 2007. In 2007, the outflow of capital from developed countries grew even faster than the inflow. They increased by 56% to the unprecedented level of USD1,692 billion, exceeding inflows by USD445 billion. The continued upswing of outward FDI was mainly driven by greater financial resources from high corporate profits. While the United States maintained its position as the largest source of FDI in 2007 with USD313.8 billion, outflows

---

[22]Calculated using data from China Foreign Investment Report 2018: Ministry of Commerce of the People's Republic of China, Department of Foreign Investment Administration (2018). China Foreign Investment Report 2018 (in Chinese); China National Bureau of Statistics (2019). China Statistical Yearbook, China Statistics Press, 2018, Table 11.16.

Table 8.9. Estimated inward FDI flows by industrial sectors during 1989–1991, 2002–2004, 2004–2006, and 2010–2013.

	1989–1991 (%)			2002–2004 (%)			2010–2013 (%)			2016–2018 (%)*		
	Primary	Manufact.	Service	Primary	Manufact.	Service	Primary	Manufact.	Service	Primary	Manufact.	Service
World	7.3	37.4	55.3	8.5	27.2	64.3	10.5	44.2	45.3	3.5	25.4	65.1
Developed	6.5	34.0	59.5	7.8	20.0	72.2	9.0	39.0	52.0	1.2	23.0	69.8
Developing	10.7	52.9	36.3	10.0	43.1	46.9	13.8	46.7	39.5	8.1	35.8	54.3
	1989–1991 (%)			2002–2004 (%)			2013–2015 (%)			2016–2018 (%)		
China	25.1	41.7	33.3	12.9	45.3	41.8	9.1	45.7	63.4	8.0	40.4	52.0

Note: *After 2014 UNCTAD did not announce inward FDI by sector and industry, so the 2016–2018 data are from WDI.

Source: United Nations Conference on Trade and Development (UNCTAD) (2007). World Investment Report 2006 Annex Table A.I.5; UNCTAD World Investment Report 2012 Table A.I.2, UNCTAD World Investment Report 2014, Figure A.I.12, China Statistical Yearbook, 2014, Table 11.16; 2014, Table 11.16; 2013, Table 6.15; 2012, Table 6.16; 2011, Table 6.16; 2005, Table 18.17; 2004, Table 18.18; 2003, Table 17.19;1998, Table 17.20.

from the EU countries nearly doubled to USD1,142 billion. The share of developed countries in the total world FDI outflows increased from 82.2% in 2006 to 85.5% in 2007. Table 8.10 shows that China's FDI outward flows in 2007 ranked 20th; the top eight countries are developed countries. China's FDI outflow stock at the end of 2007 ranked 26th, nine of the top ten being developed countries (the only exception — HKSAR China, ranked 5th). Comparing Tables 8.9 and 8.10, it is found that the FDI inward and outward flows in 2007 and their stocks in the world are in the same order.

10. China's Outward Foreign Direct Investment

China's companies have long been attempting to establish themselves as "global brands." To accomplish that, they needed to become globally competitive. Gaining a significant presence in the global marketplace through outward foreign direct investment became the obvious path toward that. Since state ownership was widespread, the Chinese government needed to play a major role in the companies' internationalization process.

Chinese Outward FDI (OFDI) has grown substantially since the beginning of the reforms. International investment has helped Chinese companies gain access to new markets, natural resources, and strategic assets.[23] It has been an integral part of China's reform process and has therefore exhibited similar characteristics to those of other reform components. Its growth has been gradual and in stages. The first stage includes the years between 1978 and 1999. OFDI was limited during the period, as China was just coming out of its isolation and did not have the capacity to assist its companies to expand abroad.

The lack of foreign exchange and knowledge of foreign operations constrained its companies from establishing permanent presence overseas. The second stage began in 2000, when the Chinese government announced its "Going Out" Program in conjunction with the 12th FYP. The period also included China's accession into the WTO on December 11, 2001, an event that provided new impetus for the country's internationalization efforts. Chinese companies, such as Haier and Lenovo, followed aggressive expansion strategies and became global brands. Haier

---

[23]Buckley, P.J. (2010). *Foreign Direct Investment, China and the World Economy*. New York: Palgrave MacMillan/St. Martin's Press.

Table 8.10.   FDI outward flows in 2007 and FDI outflow stock at year-end of 2007, 2017 for selected countries.

Ranking by FDI (outflow) in 2007	Country	FDI (outflow) in 2007, BOP current USD, billion USD	Ranking by FDI (outflow) in 2007	FDI (outflow) stock at year-end of 2007, BOP current USD, billion USD	Ranking by FDI (outflow) stock by end of 2007
1	United States	313.79	1	2,791.27	1
2	United Kingdom	265.79	2	1,705.10	2
3	France	224.65	3	1,399.04	3
4	Germany	167.43	4	1,235.99	4
5	Spain	119.61	5	636.83	7
6	Italy	90.78	6	520.08	12
7	Japan	73.55	7	542.61	10
8	Canada	53.82	8	520.74	11
9	HKSAR China	53.19	9	1,026.59	5
10	Luxembourg	51.65	10	96.28	29
13	Russian	45.65	13	255.21	17
19	China	22.47	20	95.80	30
22	South Korea	15.28	24	66.22	32
24	India	13.65	27	29.41	36
33	Brazil	7.07	37	129.84	26
	World	1,996.51		15,602.34	
In 2017	Country				
1	United States	300.38	1	7,828.75	1
4	United Kingdom	117.54	4	1,773.63	5
10	France	41.26	10	1,466.52	9
5	Germany	91.80	5	1,645.13	6
11	Spain	39.96	11	583.22	15
17	Italy	25.67	17	557.07	16
2	Japan	160.45	2	1,494.65	7
7	Canada	79.82	7	1,485.36	8
6	HKSAR China	86.70	6	1,813.30	3
12	Luxembourg	34.68	12	266.45	23
13	Russian	34.15	13	380.05	19
3	China	158.29	3	1,809.04	4
14	South Korea	34.07	14	360.57	20
23	India	11.14	24	155.18	31
21	Brazil	16.68	21	242.10	25
	World	1,425.44	—	32,383.05	—

Source: Calculated using data from United Nations Conference on Trade and Development: Major FDI indicators (WIR 2008), Direct investment in reporting economy (FDI outward); (WIR 2019), Annex Table 2. FDI outflows, 1990–2018; Annex Table 4. FDI outward stock, 1990–2018.

acquired SANYO's home appliance business in 2011, while Lenovo acquired IBM's PC business in 2005. This stage also includes the growth and overseas expansion of China's unicorns. Alibaba, for example, invested in Hong Kong's South China Morning Post and Singapore's Lazarda Group. We are going to place the third stage of Chinese companies' overseas involvement as beginning in 2017, the start of geopolitical tensions involving China and western countries, especially the United States, characterized by an increase in protectionism and leading to a slow path of deglobalization. China's OFDI reached a recent high of USD196.2 billion in 2016. In 2019, that number was down to USD117.1 billion, reflecting a Y-o-y decrease of almost 10%.[24] The new environment implied a geographical shift in China's outward investment, with Asia (especially India, Singapore, and Thailand), Latin America (Peru), and the BRI countries becoming relatively more attractive to Chinese companies. A second reason for the decline in Chinese OFDI after 2016 was the increased restrictions on OFDI implemented by MOFCOM.

China's OFDI has also exhibited characteristics that are different from OFDI coming out of other countries. For example, this is mainly achieved through M&A. Chinese companies have acquired companies in developed countries in order to benefit from foreign technology and enhance their organizational capabilities. Chinese companies have also been significantly assisted by the government in their overseas direct investment. For industries considered strategic, as those indicated in the 12th FYP, Chinese OFDI has been historically dominated by state-owned enterprises, although private companies have been gaining ground. SOEs, of course, enjoy several advantages over private companies, such as greater availability and lower cost of capital.[25]

Foreign direct investment originating from any country meets with predictable conflicts from the host country. These conflicts may be generated by the economic linkages these companies create, by geopolitical events, by cultural differences, or other reasons. Chinese companies operating abroad have been the most recent subject of local resistance toward foreign companies. We will discuss the treatment of Chinese investment

---

[24] EY (2019). What was the state of Chinese outbound investment in 2019? https://www.ey.com/en_cn/china-opportunities/what-was-the-state-of-chinese-outbound-investment-in-2019.

[25] Li, Z. (2013). How Foreign Investment Promotes Development: The Case of the People's Republic of China's Inward and Outward FDI. ADB Economics Working Paper Series. No. 304, February. Asian Development Bank.

in the United States and Europe in our last chapter. Chinese investment in Africa has been especially controversial.

China's outflow of foreign direct investment (OFDI) is still in its infancy. Chinese companies are not competitive enough, their management structure does not match international practices, and they lack international business capabilities. Therefore, China's OFDI is much less than its FDI inflow. As shown in Table 8.10, the situation changed in 2017: OFDI from developed countries in 2017 grew to USD925.3 billion. The United States maintained its position as the largest source of OFDI in 2017 with USD300.4 billion. The share of developed countries in the total world FDI outflows decreased from 85.0% in 2007 to 64.9% in 2017, while the Asian region's share increased from 11.1% in 2007 to 28.9% in 2017. Therefore, China, HKSAR China, and Singapore are listed in the Top 10. The sum of FDI outflows from China and HKSAR China was USD245 billion in 2017, second only to the United States. As shown in Table 8.10, the situation changed in 2017; FDI outward stock from developed countries in 2017 grew to USD24,716.3 billion. While the United States maintained its position as the largest source of FDI outward stock in 2017 with USD7,828.7 billion, the share of developed countries in the total world FDI outward stock decreased from 85.5% in 2007 to 74.4% in 2017, while the Asian region's share increased from 10.4% in 2007 to 21.1% in 2017. Therefore, HKSAR China, China, and Singapore are listed in the Top 10. The sum of FDI outward stock from HKSAR China and China was USD3,622.3 billion in 2017, second only to the United States. The top 5 FDI outward stocks are the United States, the Netherlands, HKSAR China, China, and the United Kingdom.

Why was OFDI from China so low in 2007, while 2017 became such an important source of FDI outflow? Since the reform and opening up, China has implemented the basic national policy of opening to the outside world. In addition, we are at the dawn of a fourth industrial revolution, driven by frontier technologies and robotization advances, making production better, cheaper, and faster than ever. New technologies promise possibilities of industrial upgrading and leapfrog development. Cheaper transportation and communication, combined with more efficient logistics, can also help developing countries better link to global value chains. China is already on the verge of becoming a global technological leader in a number of industries.[26]

---

[26]United Nations Conference on Trade and Development (2019). Investment and New Industrial Policies. World Investment Report, 2018.

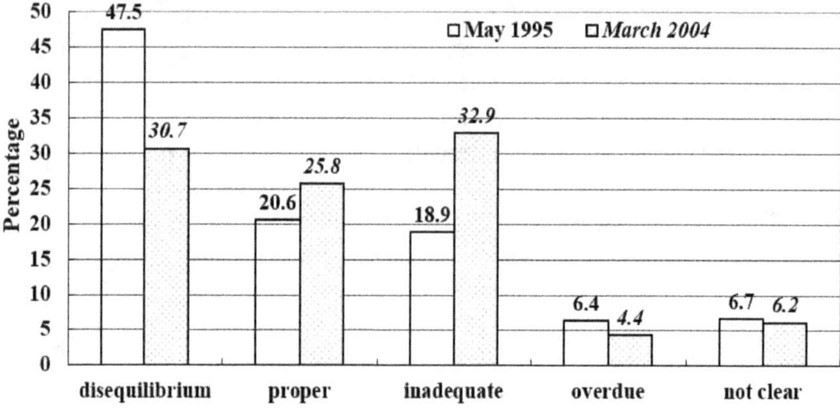

Figure 8.13.   The attitude of Chinese people toward "open to outside world."

Source: China Development Research Foundation and Horizon & Horizonkey Research Group: The degree of foreign capital in harmony with Chinese Society (in Chinese), March 2004; Horizon & Horizonkey Research Group and Beijing Youth Daily: Foreign capital in Chinese eyes (in Chinese), May 1995.

FDI became more acceptable to the Chinese 9 years ago. The survey results are shown in Figure 8.13. In 2004, 32.9% of people in the survey considered "open to outside world" inadequate and wanted opening to accelerate; compared to 1985, this represented a 14% increase. The opinion of 30.7% was that opening up was too fast in some regions and too slow in others, while 25.8% stated that opening up is appropriate. Only 4.4% expressed the opinion that opening up is overdue. In general, comparing the survey results of 1995 and 2004, the people's evaluation of "open to outside world" is positive. Most people wanted to open further. The survey of Chinese officials for the effect of FDI is shown in Figure 8.14. The expected effect on FFEs transfer technology and management experience is highest and the realized effect coincides with the expected effect. Officials pay more attention to economic benefits and less consideration to non-economic factors, like public welfare, charities, and talent training. The survey results on comprehensive evaluation of FFEs in China by country and region are shown in Table 8.11. The poll by Horizon & Horizonkey was conducted among common Chinese citizens, employees and senior managers in FFEs, and representatives of mass media and government officials in Beijing, Shanghai, Guangzhou, and Wuhan. Based on their personal assessment and working experience with

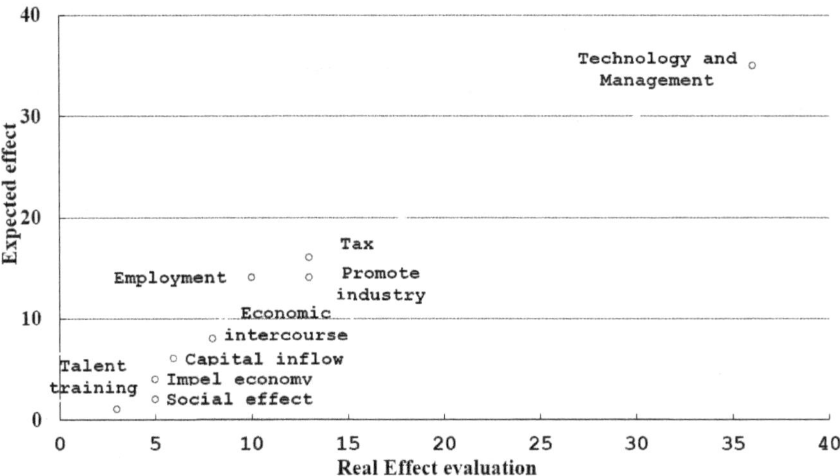

Figure 8.14.   Expected effect and actual evaluation of FDI by Chinese officials.

Source: China Development Research Foundation and Horizon & Horizonkey Research Group: The degree of foreign capital in harmony with Chinese Society (in Chinese), March 2004; Horizon & Horizonkey Research Group and Beijing Youth Daily: Foreign capital in Chinese eyes, May 1995.

Table 8.11.   The comprehensive evaluation of FFEs in China by country and region from outside survey, March 2004.

Rank	Overall evaluation	Appreciation	Affinity	Prospect	Social image	Job choice	Product selection
1	US, 29.4%	US, 32.95%	US, 25.48%	Euro, 29.1%	US, 32,67%	US, 34.67%	JP, 32.7%
2	Euro, 27.6%	Euro, 29.42%	Euro, 23.97%	US, 28.84%	EURO, 30.51%	EURO, 30.16%	EURO, 22.27%
3	JP, 16.6%	JP, 14.23%	HK, 13.68%	JP, 13.26%	JP, 15.57%	JP, 11.48%	US, 22.07%
4	HK, 9.0%	HK, 8.24%	JP, 12.27%	HK, 9.25%	HK, 6.83%	HK, 10.24%	SK, 6.85%
5	SK, 6.0%	TW, 6.2%	TW, 8.665%	SK, 6.64%	SK, 5.09%	TW,4.47%	HK, 6.01%
6	TW, 5.4%	SK, 5.73%	SK, 7.43%	TW, 6.32%	TW, 3.73%	SK, 4.37%	TW, 3.23%

Source: China Development Research Foundation and Horizon & Horizonkey Research Group (2004). The degree of foreign capital in harmony with Chinese Society: Foreign capital in Chinese eyes (in Chinese), March.

FFEs, Horizon & Horizonkey researchers made the quantitative evaluation. The FFEs from the United States and Europe are placed in the leading position and FFEs from South Korea and Taiwan are last.

In 2005, the Best Foreign-Funded Enterprises of Fortune Global 500 in China were evaluated. The top 10 FFEs are listed in Table 8.12. Of the top 10 FFEs, five are invested by the United States, and the other five

Table 8.12. The best foreign-funded enterprises in China invested by Fortune Global 500 evaluated in 2005 and 2017.

2005	Name of enterprise	Score	Country	2017	Name of enterprise	Score	Country
1	Samsung Electronics China	69.4	KOR	1	Volkswagen China	73.4	DEU
2	Volkswagen China	57.7	DEU	2	Intel (China)	72.1	USA
3	Royal Philips Electronics	53.3	NLD	3	BASF (China)	67.9	DEU
4	Motorola	53.2	USA	4	GM China	67.9	USA
5	GM China	51.6	USA	5	Cannon (China)	68.7	JPN
6	Nokia China	44.2	FIN	6	Anheuser-Busch InBev (CH)	66.5	BE/USA
7	Coca-Cola (China)	37.0	USA	7	BMW (China)	66.2	DEU
8	Intel (China)	34.8	USA	8	Matsushita Electric (China)	66.0	JPN
9	GE in China	32.7	USA	9	VOLVO (China)	65.6	SWE
10	Honda Motor (China)	32.6	JPN	10	Toyota Automotive (China)	65.3	JPN

Source: Nanfang Weekend (2005). The best enterprises invested by Fortune Global 500 in China in 2005. December 16 (in Chinese), http://finance.sina.com.cn/g/20051206/14042176364.shtml: The best enterprises invested by Fortune Global 500 in China at 2017, January 10, 2018 (in Chinese), http://www.infzm.com/contents/132412.

are from South Korea, Germany, Finland, the Netherlands, and Japan. In 2017, among the top 10 FFEs, Germany and Japan each had three seats, the United States 2.5 seats, 1 seat in Sweden, and 0.5 seats in Belgium. Compared 2017 with 2005, Germany and Japan each added two seats in 2017, while the United States lost 2.5 seats.

This shows that in 2017, the operating performance of American companies was worse than that of Germany and Japan, and also worse than their own performance in 2005. The score of six sub-indexes for the top 10 FFEs is listed in Table 8.13. The remaining six sub-indexes are export/revenue 15%, number of employees in China 5%, status of law-abiding operations 5%, training of local employees 5%, the public reputation of the company in China 5%, and R&D investment in China 5%.

11. UNCTAD FDI Index

The UNCTAD Inward FDI Performance and Potential Indices, as well as the FDI Performance Index, showed some noticeable changes for

Table 8.13.   The scores of top 10 FFEs invested by Fortune Global 500 evaluated at 2005.

Rank	Name of enterprise	Total invest.	Revenue	Public welfare donation	Protect staff's legitimate, interest	Environm. protection	Tax pay in China	Total score
Score		20	15	5	5	5	10	100
1	Samsung Electronic CH	14.4	15	0.857	3	4	1.203	69.409
2	Volkswagen China	11.428	11.823	0	3.5	3.5	10	57.705
3	Royal Philips Electronic	13.6	8.704	0.101	4	4	2.717	53.282
4	Motorola	14	7.157	0.357	3.5	3.5	2.272	53.187
5	GM China	20	4.796	0	3.5	3.5	6.264	51.63
6	Nokia China	8.699	6.399	0	3.5	3.5	2.329	44.204
7	Coca-Cola (China)	4.8	3.132	0.395	4	4	2.07	37.01
8	Intel (China)	5.2	4.63	0	3.5	3.5	2.717	34.797
9	GE in China	6	3.58	0.036	3.5	3.5	2.199	32.736
10	Honda Motor (China)	2.149	3.759	0.73	3.5	4	7.348	32.577

Source: Nanfang Weekend (2005). The best enterprises invested by Fortune Global 500 in China in 2005. December 16 (in Chinese), http://finance.sina.com.cn/g/20051206/14042176364.shtml.

individual countries in 2007, reflecting uneven developments of FDI inflows and improvements in general economic performance (see Tables 8.14 and 8.15). The UNCTAD Inward FDI Performance Index is a measure of the extent to which a host country receives inward FDI relative to its economic size. It is calculated as the ratio of a country's share in global FDI inflows to its share in global GDP, shown in Eq. (8.1):

$$IND_i = \frac{FDII_i / FDII_W}{GDP_i / GDP_W} \tag{8.1}$$

where IND_i — The Inward FDI Performance Index of the ith country

$FDII_i$ — The FDI inflows in the ith country
$FDII_W$ — World FDI inflows
GDP_i — GDP in the ith country
GDP_W — World GDP

A value greater than 1 indicates that the country receives more FDI than its relative economic size, and a value below 1 that it receives less (a negative value means that foreign investors disinvest in that period). The UNCTAD Inward FDI Performance index is based on 12 economic and structural variables measured by their respective scores on a range of 0–100.

The UNCTAD Inward FDI potential index is based on 12 economic and structural variables measured by their respective scores on a range of 0–1. The country with the lowest value is given a score of zero and the country with the highest value, a score of one. Mathematically, it is expressed by Eq. (8.2):

$$Score = \frac{V_i - V_{min}}{V_{max} - V_{min}} \tag{8.2}$$

where V_i — the value of a variable for the county i

V_{min} — the lowest value of the variable among the countries
V_{max} — the highest value of the variable among the countries

It is the unweighted average of scores on the following: GDP per capita, the rate of growth of GDP over the previous 10 years, the share of exports

Table 8.14. Inward FDI Performance Index rankings for selected countries, 1990–2010.

| | Inward FDI performance index rankings | | | | | | | | | |
Economy	1990	1995	2000	2005	2006	2007	2008	2009	2010	Average
Brazil	84	98	43	101	113	101	93	90	69	88.0
China	*57*	*17*	*62*	*70*	*91*	*104*	*97*	*83*	*86*	*72.6*
Germany	90	104	10	103	108	105	133	110	104	95.4
India	96	95	115	120	100	112	80	67	97	98.1
Japan	99	130	130	134	137	134	126	136	136	128.3
HKSAR China	6	23	1	5	6	5	3	3	2	6.5
Korea, Rep.	82	118	91	122	132	137	123	118	122	115.4
Russian	—	102	108	104	88	79	62	65	60	86.9
United Kingdom	15	60	21	21	42	47	78	59	76	42.9
United States	58	86	68	123	111	121	102	112	96	97.6

Source: UNCTAD: Web Table 28. Inward FDI Performance and Potential Index rankings, 1990–2010.

in GDP, modern information and telecommunication infrastructure (the average of telephone lines per 1,000 inhabitants and mobile phones per 1,000 inhabitants), commercial energy use per capita, the share of R&D expenditures in GDP, the share of tertiary students in the population, country risk, exports of natural resources as a percentage of the world total, imports of parts and components of electronics and automobiles as a percentage of the world total, exports in services as a percentage of the world total, and inward FDI stock as a percentage of the world total. The Inward FDI Performance and Potential Index rankings during 1990–2010 covered 140 economies. Nine selected countries are listed in Tables 8.14 and 8.15. After 2010, UNCTACD did not publish the Inward FDI Performance Index, Inward FDI potential index, and their rankings in their World Investment Report. Table 8.14 shows that the average rank of the Inward FDI Performance Index for China is second, while Japan is the worst. But, from Table 8.15, the average rank of the Inward FDI potential index of Japan is much better than China's. This indicates that China's FDI policy makes it more attractive than Japan. Table 8.15 shows that the Inward FDI Potential Index of developed countries is much better than that of developing countries. However, the difference of the Inward FDI Performance Index between developed and developing countries is not so

Table 8.15.   Inward FDI Potential Index rankings for selected countries, 1990–2009.

Economy	Inward FDI potential index rankings								
	1990	1995	2000	2005	2006	2007	2008	2009	Average
Brazil	54	80	69	70	73	70	65	62	67.9
China	*42*	*49*	*48*	*34*	*33*	*32*	*30*	*27*	*36.9*
Germany	4	4	10	7	5	5	4	6	5.6
India	86	97	92	84	83	85	86	79	86.5
Japan	13	6	12	24	24	27	26	26	19.8
HKSAR China	15	12	14	11	10	3	5	4	9.3
Korea, rep.	20	18	15	17	17	18	17	19	17.6
Russian	—	34	37	19	14	9	9	8	18.6
United Kingdom	3	7	5	3	4	4	8	11	5.6
United States	1	1	1	1	1	1	1	1	1.0

Source: UNCTAD: Web Table 28. Inward FDI Performance and Potential Index rankings, 1990–2010.

larger, since the developed countries' GDP is much large than that of the developing countries. For example, the inward FDI flows into the United States ranked first in 2007, but its inward FDI performance index is 97.6. So, the average Inward FDI Performance Index rank of the United States is in the middle position in Table 8.14.

Further, we analyze all 141 economies covered in the UNTACD Inward FDI Performance and Potential Index using 4 quarters. The original point is the median value of the inward FDI Performance Index (71) and Inward FDI Potential Index (71) for 142 economies in 2006. Table 8.16 shows the results. All high-income countries are located in quarter I (with high FDI potential and performance index called front-runners) and quarter IV (with high inward FDI potential index, but low FDI performance index), which means all the inward FDI potential scores are higher than the median value, while the inward FDI performance scores are scattered — almost half above the median value and half below median value. This implies that the high-income countries have a different attitude toward inward FDI. For example, in 2006, Japan's Inward FDI Potential Index (24) was almost the same as HKSAR's (10), but Hong Kong's FDI Performance Index was 6 and Japan's was 137

Table 8.16. Comparing inward FDI performance and potential of 141 economies in 2006 by 4 quarters.

	Front-runners (I)	Below potential (II)	Underperformers (III)	Above potential (IV)
High income	20	0	0	21
Upper middle income	13	4	2	7
Lower middle income	6	14	13	4
Low income	1	13	23	0
Subtotal	40	31	38	32

Source: UNCTAD:FDI indices online; http://www.unctad.org/Templates/Page.asp?intItemID=2468&lang=1.

(see Table 8.15). From Table 8.16, we find that 36 from 37 low-income economies are located in quarter II (with low Inward FDI Potential Index, but high FDI Performance Index) and quarter III (with both low Inward FDI Potential and Performance Index), which means that all the Inward FDI Potential Index scores are lower than the median value. Therefore, the inward FDI potential index scores are mainly related to the income group of the country. The only exception in the low-income group is Mongolia, which was the only one from the low-income economies located in quarter I. In contract, inward FDI flow reached USD236.7 billion for the United States in 2006, ranked first in the world. But, the United States' GDP was USD13.13 trillion, also ranked first in the world. Therefore, its inward FDI performance index was 108, higher than the medial value of 71. The inward FDI potential index equals 1, ranked first in the world. So, the United States is located in quarter IV (with high inward FDI potential index, but low FDI performance index). Therefore, we cannot simply say that the economies located in quarter I are better off than the economies located in quarter IV with respect to their inward FDI operation. From Table 8.16, we find that 94.7% of the low-income economies and 87.1% of the lower-middle-income economies are located in quarter III and quarter II, respectively. From the above discussion, we may conclude that the inward FDI potential index scores represent an absolute index and the inward FDI performance index, a relative index.

The UNCTAD Outward FDI Performance index is calculated in the same way as the Outward FDI performance index: the ratio of a country's share in global FDI outflows to its share in world GDP. Mathematically, it is expressed by Eq. (8.3):

$$OND_i = \frac{FDIO_i/FDIO_W}{GDP_i/GDP_W} \qquad (8.3)$$

where OND_i — The Outward FDI Performance Index of the ith country

$FDIO_i$ — The FDI outflows in the ith country
$FDIO_w$ — World FDI outflows

The outward FDI Performance Index rankings during 1990–2004 covered 132 economies. Ten selected countries are listed in Table 8.17. Table 8.17 shows that the last three countries ranked according to their average outward FDI Performance indexes are India, Brazil, and China, all of them developing countries. It means that the outward FDI Performance of developing countries is much worse than that of developed countries. According to the outward FDI Performance Index

Table 8.17. Outward FDI performance index rankings, 1990–2007.

Economy	1988–1900	1998–2000	2005–2007	2013	2018	Income group
Covered economies	128	128	125	184	184	—
Brazil	0.093	0.111	0.413	−0.011	−0.590	UIC
China	0.214	0.055	0.24	0.709	0.807	MIC
HKSAR China	3.37	6.056	7.799	16.428	18.679	HIC
Germany	1.017	1.287	1.311	0.669	1.773	HIC
India	0.003	0.015	0.368	0.052	0.342	LIC
Japan	1.227	0.186	0.455	1.227	2.436	HIC
Korea, rep.	0.306	0.333	0.374	1.298	4.026	HIC
Russian	—	0.285	0.959	1.793	1.860	UIC
United Kingdom	2.963	4.004	2.085	35.485	50.797	HIC
United States	0.469	0.539	0.499	1.050	−0.262	HIC
World	223.8	1,012.5	1,800	1,376.642	1014.2	—

Source: United Nations Conference on Trade and Development (2006). World Investment Report 2005 Annex Table A.I.13, p. 276; W IR 20088, Annex Table A.I.10.

rankings, Japan is the last one and HKSAR China is the first one among developed economies listed in Table 8.17, which reveals that the openness of the Japanese economy to inward and outward FDI is the lowest among the developed countries listed in Tables 8.14 to 8.17. Like the inward FDI Performance Index, the outward FDI Performance Index is also a relative index. So, outward FDI performance index scores will show more information. Table 8.17 shows the outward FDI performance index scores for selected countries. After 2010, UNCTACD did not publish its Outward FDI Performance Index and its ranking in the World Investment Report. Therefore, the authors used Eq. (8.3) to calculate the 2013 and 2018 outward FDI Performance Indexes listed in Table 8.18.

Table 8.18 shows that in 1998–2007, HKSAR China and the United Kingdom had the best outward FDI performance index scores, which are much better than the United States'; China and India had the worst outward FDI performance index scores among selected countries, while China's outward FDI performance index scores fluctuated substantially. Table 8.19 includes the 2000–2007 outward FDI flows for selected countries.

Table 8.18.   Outward FDI performance index scores for selected countries.

Economy	1988–1900	1998–2000	2005–2007	2013	2018	Income group
Covered economies	128	128	125	184	184	—
Brazil	0.093	0.111	0.413	−0.011	−0.590	UIC
China	0.214	0.055	0.24	0.709	0.807	MIC
HKSAR China	3.37	6.056	7.799	16.428	18.679	HIC
Germany	1.017	1.287	1.311	0.669	1.773	HIC
India	0.003	0.015	0.368	0.052	0.342	LIC
Japan	1.227	0.186	0.455	1.227	2.436	HIC
Korea, rep.	0.306	0.333	0.374	1.298	4.026	HIC
Russian	—	0.285	0.959	1.793	1.860	UIC
United Kingdom	2.963	4.004	2.085	35.485	50.797	HIC
United States	0.469	0.539	0.499	1.050	−0.262	HIC
World	223.8	1,012.5	1,800	1,376.642	1,014.2	—

Source: UNCTAD: World Investment Report 2018 Annex Table 2, Outward FDI flows, 1991–2018; WIR 2008, Annex Table 2, Outward FDI flows, 1971–2007; World Development Indicators online 2019, Released January 24, 2018 by World Bank.

Table 8.19. The outward FDI flows (USD billion) for selected countries.

Economy	1990	2000	2007	2013	2018
Brazil	0.625	2.282	7.067	42.270	77.076
China	0.830	0.916	22.469	107.844	129.830
HKSAR China	2.448	59.352	61.119	80.773	85.162
Germany	24.235	56.557	179.547	42.270	77.076
India	0.006	0.509	17.281	1.679	11.037
Japan	48.024	31.558	73.549	135.749	143.161
Korea, Rep.	1.052	4.999	15.620	28.318	38.917
Russian	—	3.177	45.916	70.685	36.445
United Kingdom	17.948	233.371	275.482	40.486	49.880
United States	30.982	142.626	378.362	303.432	−63.550
Word	239.111	1,213.795	2,146.522	1,376.642	1,014.172

Source: UNCTAD: Major FDI indicators World Investment Report 2018 Annex Table 2, Outward FDI flows, 1991–2018; WIR 2008, Annex Table 2, Outward FDI flows, 1971–2007.

The Table shows that FDI outflows from the United States were larger than those of all countries, while China's were larger than India's.

China's foreign outward flows are another indication of China's integration into the global economy. China set forth the "going-beyond-the-border" strategy in 1999, encouraging domestic enterprises to invest and do business abroad. More than 12,000 Chinese companies established presence in about 172 countries and regions by the end of 2007.[27] China ranked as the 6th most attractive foreign direct investment destination across the world, but 19th among global investors, as shown in Tables 8.18 and 8.19. Motives for Chinese Firms Going Global are direct market access, stable resource supply, advanced technology, and efficiency seeking (management skill, customer service, and reducing transaction cost). But, FDI outflow from China is still in its early stage. Chinese enterprises are not sufficiently competitive, their corporate management structure does not match international practice, and they suffer from a lack of international business capability. Eventually, the overseas investment of Chinese enterprises transitioned from the initial

---

[27]Xinhua (2008). Chinese companies' foreign investment jumps nearly fourfold in 1Q, May 12.

stage of establishing a beachhead to investing in a plant. This has led to to various forms of engagement and technological zone. In 2006, Chinese enterprises realized direct investment of USD8.25 billion through M&A, accounting for 39% of the total flow in the year.[28] But, 65% of China's funded overseas enterprises experienced losses. A consultancy veteran from Italy stated "not just for going abroad, but also for increasing their overall competitive capability, must improve their performance at home in such areas as organization and customer service, and then think over their overall strategy what markets to invest in. Chinese companies that want to go globals successfully need to have creative products or services, which have superior characteristics and their own personalities."[29]

TCL is one of the largest TV producers in China. In October 2002, it bought the then bankrupted TV operations of Schneider in Germany and rehired its 120 employees. In November 2003, TCL bought Thomson's TV operation and formed a joint venture in which it held 70%. Both acquisitions were unsuccessful and did not meet the company's strategic objectives. TCL suffered large losses in both acquisitions, since it went abroad to buy outdated technology and old brand names, with insufficient understanding of foreign operational environments. In 2004, computer giant Lenovo bought the high-profile but money-losing personal computer business from IBM for USD1.75 billion. Lenovo unveiled a net profit of USD5 million in the fiscal first quarter ending June 2006 versus a previously reported net profit of HKD357 million (USD45.93 million) a year earlier.[30] In 2005, China National Offshore Oil Corp. (CNOOC) topped a USD16.5 billion bid (USD67 a share) from Chevron (USD63 a share) for the ninth largest US oil company, Unocal. But, CNOOC finally withdrew its offer for Unocal due to unprecedented political opposition.[31]

---

[28] Expert Committee of Chinese Enterprise International Strategy (comprising authorities from the National Development and Reform Commission (NDRC), Ministry of Commerce, Development Research Center of State Council, and Nanfang Daily Group): Report on Chinese Enterprise International Strategy — 2007 Blue Book, November. 19, 2007.

[29] Liu, J. (2008). Chinese firms need to improve work on home turf, *China Daily*, August 4.

[30] Lenovo slides back to profitability-Chinese PC-maker faced acquisition expenses, stiff competition, August 3, 2006, http://money.cnn.com/2006/08/03/news/international/bc. tech.china.lenovo.reut/index.htm.

[31] Xinhua (2005). Unocal 'almost backed China bid', July 26.

SMTCL (Shenyang Machine Tool Company Limited) is the largest (in units) machine tool manufacturing company in China. Schiess is a company founded in 1857 and enjoys a good reputation in the machine tools industry. It declared bankruptcy on August 1, 2004. SMTCL bought Schiess on November 1, 2004. This is a win-win situation, with the overall performance of SMTCL-Schiess improving dramatically in 2007 because the purchase was small and focused on particular technology where there was a huge market in China. Nanjing Automotive successfully acquired United Kingdom's MG Rover Group in 2005.

With its surging trade surplus and huge holdings of dollar reserves, China established Sovereign Wealth Funds (SWFs). SWFs are government investment vehicles that are funded by the accumulation of foreign exchange assets and managed separately from the official reserves of the monetary authorities. In recent years, a number of these SWFs have emerged as direct investors. China Investment Company (CIC) is the fourth largest SWF with investment capital of USD200 billion. CIC invested USD3 billion in the US private equity fund Blackstone Group at its IPO price of USD29.61 in July 2007, and suffered a book loss of more than 80%.[32] CIC also purchased a USD5.6 billion stake in Morgan Stanley 13 months ago. The US company's shares have dropped considerably since then.[33] China State Development Bank together with Government of Singapore Investment Corp Pte Ltd (GIC) acquired a stake in United Kingdom's Barclays Bank. All these investments resulted in large book losses due to the collapse of global stock markets. In 2008, UBS and the Bank of America acquired 9.1%[34] of China Construction Bank (CCB) H shares from Central Huijin Company at HKD2.42 and HKD2.46 per share, respectively. Half a year later, they sold the stocks of CCB, and Central Huijin Company was forced to purchase these stocks at

---

[32] Beijing Review (2009). China's top 10 economic issues in 2008, Vol. 52, No. 1, January 1, pp. 32.

[33] United Nations Conference on Trade and Development (UNCTAD): *World Investment Report 2008 — Transnational Corporations, and the Infrastructure Challenge*, United Nations Publication, ISBN 978-92-1-112755-3, 2008, Annex table A.I.5; Dean, J., J. T. Areddy, S. Ng: Chinese premier blames recession on U.S. actions — Beijing rethinks some of its American investments, *Wall Street Journal* (Eastern edition), New York, NY, January 29, 2009. pp. A.1.

[34] Chan, J. (2007). Banking on change, INSIGHT (American Chamber of Commerce, Shanghai), December.

a price of HKD3.92. The country's second largest insurer, Ping An Insurance (Group) Co., lost about EUR 1.7 billion (USD2.37 billion) on its stake in Fortis NV.[35] Using its reserves, China invested USD400 billion in Fannie and Freddie Mac debt.[36] Chinese firms are becoming world leaders in certain industries when they manage to transform China's comparative advantage into their competitive strengths. Chinese companies with competitive edges are expected to excel in the global market.

12. Distinctive Characteristics of China's Foreign Investment

The share of FDI in total foreign capital declined and other types of foreign investment increased. Raised capital from initial public offerings (IPO) of Chinese companies abroad reached USD39.3 billion in 2006.[37] The approved quota of Qualified Foreign Institutional Investor (QFII) amounted to USD30 billion by the end of 2007.[38] The acquisition of Chinese enterprises by foreign capital is becoming increasingly important in various ways. For example, some of the world's largest beer enterprises acquired Chinese counterparts: AB acquired Harbin Brewery, Scotting Newcastle acquired Chongqing Beer, and Belgium InBev Group acquired Fujian Sedrin Beer. Among additional acquisitions, Newbridge Asia AIV III, L.P. purchased 16.68% of Shenzhen Development Bank stock.[39]

The R&D activities of foreign-invested enterprises in China began to proliferate. The number of foreign-invested R&D centers had risen to 750 in China by the end of 2005. In the automotive industry, for instance, Shanghai GM and Shanghai Volkswagen are expanding their existing R&D centers, and Nissan Motor, Daimler Chrysler, Honda Motor, and

---

[35] China's top 10 economic issues in 2008, *Beijing Review*, Vol. 52, No. 1, January 1, 2009, p. 32.

[36] Dean, J., J. T. Areddy, S. Ng (2009). Chinese premier blames recession on U.S. actions — Beijing rethinks some of its American investments, *Wall Street Journal* (Eastern edition). New York, NY, January 29, p. A.1.

[37] Calculated using data from China National Bureau of Statistics (2007). *China Statistical Yearbook 2006*, Table 7.20, China Statistics Press.

[38] China, *US Second Meeting of Strategic Economic Dialogue*, Washington, May 2007.

[39] Department of Foreign Investment Administration, Ministry of Commerce, P.R. China The Report of China's FDI (in Chinese), December 19, 2006.

Hyundai Motor, together with their respective local joint venture partners, are establishing new R&D centers.[40] Toyota Motor is also setting up an R&D center in Tianjin, China.[41] Between November 2004 and March 2005, UNCTAD conducted a survey aimed at establishing the current patterns of internationalization of R&D by the largest private R&D spenders. China is the destination mentioned by the largest number of respondents (61.8%) for future R&D expansion, followed by the United States (41.2%). In third place is India (29.4%), another significant newcomer location for R&D.[42] Foreign-funded enterprises in China plan to expand R&D activities mainly due to the following reasons: proximity to their manufacturing platform; proximity to the Chinese market to facilitate more effective targeting of the Chinese market to adapt appropriate research and development; and it fully utilizes China's low cost of human resources for R&D (mid-range, low-end R&D personnel cost about one-tenth to one-sixth of developed countries).

Since the 18th National Congress of the Communist Party of China (December 2016), there have been efforts to build a new open economic system and strive for new achievements in open development. With the "Belt and Road" initiative and the construction of a community with a shared future for mankind, China has entered a new comprehensive stage of opening up. The Chinese government has adopted a series of measures to reduce restrictions on foreign investment access, promote investment facilitation, strive to create a fair, transparent, and predictable business environment, and fully implement the national treatment of foreign-invested enterprises. From 2013 to 2016, China's actual use of foreign capital in non-financial sectors was USD489.4 billion, and the actual use of foreign capital in 2016 increased by 12.8% over 2012. The quality structure of foreign capital utilization was further optimized. The utilization of foreign capital in the service industry has grown rapidly. From

---

[40] United Nations Conference on Trade and Development (2006). *World Investment Report 2005 — Transnational Corporations and the Internationalization of R&D*. New York: United Nations, 2005, Annex Table A.I.13–A.I.14, p. 145.

[41] United Nations Conference on Trade and Development (2007). *World Investment Report 2006, FDI from Developing and Transition Economies: Implications for Development*, New York: United Nations.

[42] United Nations Conference on Trade and Development (2006). World Investment Report 2005 — Transnational Corporations and the Internationalization of R&D. New York: United Nations, p. 153.

2013 to 2016, the scale and proportion of foreign investment used in the service industry increased year by year, with a total of USD321.9 billion of foreign capital used, an average annual increase of 10.2%. The foreign investment environment continued to improve. In 2015 and 2017, the "Catalog for the Guidance of Foreign Investment Industries" was revised twice to actively open the door to the world and improve China's investment environment.[43]

The heavy chemical industry and other capital-intensive and high-technology industries have become new hot spots for foreign investment to enter. Generally speaking, companies in steel, petrochemical, and other capital and technology-intensive industries are large in scale, so foreign investment is usually not easy to enter. In recent years, the world's largest steel group Mittal Steel Company N.V. purchased 647.42 million shares of Hunan Valin Steel Tube & Wire Co. Lt. (listed on Shenzhen Stock Exchange 000932) for USD317 million. Mittal became the second largest shareholder with 29.48% of the total equity; the largest shareholder, Valin Steel Group Co. Lt., owned 30.29% of the total equity.[44] Shanghai SECCO Petrochemical Company Limited was founded by China Petroleum and Chemical Corporation (Sinopec Corp.), Shanghai Petrochemical Company Limited (SPC), and BP East China Investment Company Limited with an investment of about USD2.7 billion in a 30%, 20%, and 50% proportion, respectively.[45] It is by far one of the largest petrochemical projects of joint venture in China. China's long-term economic development prospects attract the foreign investment entering China's heavy and chemical industries.

From Tables 8.18 and 8.19, we saw that, in 2007, China's FDI outflow was still in its infancy; by 2017, China had become one of the major sources of OFDI. China's rapid economic development and comprehensive national strength have laid a good material foundation for China's ODI. At the same time, China's reform and opening up policy encourages and supports foreign investment and transnational operations of various types of ownership enterprises. In 2017, the global foreign direct

---

[43] Wang Yang, W. (2017). Promote the formation of a new pattern of full opening, *People's Daily*, November 10 (in Chinese), http://news.cnr.cn/native/gd/20171110/t20171110_524019685.shtml.

[44] Valin Steel Group Co. Lt. (2007). 2006 Annual Report, http://disclosure.szse.cn/m/drgg0009323.htm.

[45] http://www.secco.com.cn/en/about/intro.htm.

investment outflow was USD1.43 trillion, showing a declining trend for 2 years, as the market became more mature and returned to the fundamentals. China's OFDI in 2018 reached USD143.04 billion and the accumulated OFDI stock reached USD1,982.27 billion, as shown in Table 8.20. Based on The World Investment Report 2018, China's ODI flows and stock in 2017 accounted for 11.1% and 5.9% of the global total, respectively. China ranked third among all countries (regions) in terms of OFDI flows, although it decreased by 2.4 percentage points compared to the previous year. In terms of OFDI stock, China jumped from 6th in 2016 to the 2nd place in 2017, an increase of 33.3 percentage points compared

Table 8.20.   2002–2018 China's Outward FDI flows and stocks and their Global Ranking.

Year	FDI out flow bil. USD	Global ranking	Yoy%	FDI out stock	Global ranking
2002	2.7	26	—	29.9	25
2003	2.9	21	6	33.2	25
2004	5.5	20	93	44.8	27
2005	12.3	17	123	57.2	24
2006	21.2	13	44	90.6	23
2007	26.5	17	25	117.9	22
2008	55.9	12	111	184.0	18
2009	56.5	5	1	245.8	16
2010	68.8	5	22	317.2	17
2011	74.7	6	9	424.8	13
2012	87.8	3	18	531.9	13
2013	107.8	3	23	660.5	11
2014	123.1	3	14	882.6	8
2015	145.7	2	18	1,097.9	8
2016	196.2	2	35	1,357.4	6
2017	158.3	3	−19	1,809.0	2
2018	143.0	2	−10	1,982.3	3
2019	136.9	2	−4	2,198.9	3

Notes: (1) The data for 2002–2005 are for foreign non-financial direct investment, and the data for 2006–2018 are for industry-wide direct investment (2). In 2006, Yoy was the ratio of foreign non-financial direct investment

Source: P.R. China Ministry of Commerce, National Bureau of Statistics (2019). State Administration of Foreign Exchange: 2018 Statistical Bulletin of China's Foreign Direct Investment (in Chinese).

with the previous year. China was second only to the United States (USD7.8 trillion), up from 25th in 2002. In terms of scale, the OFDI stock from China by the end of 2017 was only equivalent to 23.2% of the United States and closer to the others in the top six: HKSAR China, Germany, the Netherlands, and the United Kingdom. China National Chemical Corporation's acquisition of 98.06% of Swiss Syngenta's equity with USD42.1 billion is the largest overseas M&A by Chinese companies "going global" in 2017, and the second largest cross-border M&A project globally of the year. In 2017, flows of direct investment to Europe reached USD18.46 billion, a record high, with a year-on-year increase of 72.7%, while the investment in the United States was USD6.43 billion, down 62.1% year on year. Direct investment along the "Belt and Road" involved 17 major sectors of the national economy; the cumulative investment was USD20.17 billion, a year-on-year increase of 31.5%.

13. The Belt and Road Initiative (BRI)

China's involvement with the rest of the world and its importance to the global economy are exemplified by its Belt and Road (BRI) initiative. The ancient (130 BCE–1453 CE) Silk Road was established during the Han Dynasty, creating a network of trade routes between East and West and moving people, goods, and ideas from one country to another. Five and a half centuries later, the Silk Road was reintroduced to the world by President Xi.

China's BRI, once called the "One Belt, One Road" (OBOR) Initiative, and sometimes referred to as the "New Silk Road," is a major and ambitious development in global trade and investment. It was presented by President Xi in 2013 in his speech at Kazakhstan. The action plan was released in 2015 by the NDRC and MOFCOM — "BRI includes two Roads": the Silk Road Economic Belt and the Maritime Silk Road. BRI involves investment projects amounting to over USD1 trillion between 2017 and 2027. According to President Xi, the BRI is about "policy, infrastructure, trade, financial, and people-to people connectivity." In so doing, BRI will "build a new platform for international co-operation to create new drivers of shared development."[46]

---

[46]President Xi, as reported by Organization for Economic Cooperation and Development (2018). China's Belt and Road Initiative in the global trade, investment, and finance. Paris: OECD. https://www.oecd.org/finance/Chinas-Belt-and-Road-Initiative-in-the-global-trade-investment-and-finance-landscape.pdf.

The BRI's objectives have been articulated in China's 13th Five-Year Plan. They include the following: to increase trade and investment in the BRI, establish trade zones along the Road, enhance financial cooperation to fund infrastructure in the region, gain access to natural resources, strengthen transport infrastructure, and deepen cultural exchanges among participating nations. Investment envisioned by the BRI will be channeled through the six economic corridors stated below[47]:

1. The New Eurasia Land Bridge, involving rail to Europe via Kazakhstan, Russia, Belarus, and Poland
2. The China, Mongolia, Russia Economic Corridor, which will link with the land bridge
3. The China, Central Asia, West Asia Economic Corridor, connecting Kazakhstan, Kyrgyzstan, Tajikistan, Uzbekistan, Turkmenistan, Iran, and Turkey
4. The China, Indochina Peninsula Economic Corridor, which includes Vietnam, Thailand, Laos, Cambodia, Myanmar, and Malaysia
5. The China–Pakistan Economic Corridor, linking Xinjiang Province's Kashgar Free Economic Zone with Pakistan's Gwadar port
6. The China, Bangladesh, India, Myanmar Economic Corridor. The fate of this Corridor is in jeopardy because of the ongoing conflict between China and India.

Chinese development banks (China Development Bank, Exim Bank) and large commercial banks (ICBC, Bank of China, and others) have been the principal sources of funding for projects in the various countries participating in the BRI. Additional funding will be coming from multilateral institutions, such as the New Development Bank and the Asian Infrastructure Investment Bank (AIIB). According to the World Economic Forum (2017),[48] China has indicated that it will lend about USD8 trillion to 68 countries. Of the 68 countries, special benefits should accrue to Russia, Pakistan, the Philippines, Iran, and Egypt. The motivation is increased trade and investment in these countries and, eventually, the rest

---

[47] OECD, 2018, p. 11.

[48] World Economic Forum (2017). China's $900 billion New Silk Road. What you need to know. Accessed at https://www.weforum.org/agenda/2017/06/china-new-silk-road-explainer/.

of the world. In turn, China will benefit through the opening of additional markets for its regions (especially the poorer among them, such as Xinjiang) and products, and expansion of its companies (especially its banks, manufacturers, construction, energy, transport, and telecom firms). One study, for example, found that China's OFDI is going to increase by as much as 45% under the BRI.[49]

China's initiative has raised suspicion about the country's real reasons for planning the BRI. According to critics, China is only interested in expanding its geopolitical influence, while the other participants in the BRI are left with huge debts and domestic instability. If successfully implemented, however, the BRI may have many positive outcomes, including the formation of a supercontinent mindset, the creation of a neo-renaissance, and opening of China's cultural communication with the rest of the world.[50] By the end of 2016, Chinese enterprises had established 56 cooperation zones in the countries along the "Belt and Road" with a total investment of USD18.55 billion. There were 1,082 enterprises entering the zone with a total output value of USD50.69 billion. A total of 177,000 jobs were created locally. Several major infrastructure projects are progressing steadily.[51] China's investment in 63 countries along the Belt and Road, from 2013 to 2018, is shown in Table 8.21.

At the end of 2018, China had established over 10,000 overseas companies along the Belt and Road Initiative, involving 18 major sectors of the national economy. The main flows were USD5.88 billion in manufacturing, USD3.71 billion in wholesale and retail, and USD1.68 billion in power production and supply.

---

[49]Shu, Y., X. Qian, and T. Liu (2019). Belt and Road initiative and Chinese firms' outward foreign direct investment. *Emerging Markets Review*, 41, 1–22.

[50]Feng, D.H. (2020). *China's Millennium Transformation: The Belt and Road Initiative*. Singapore: World Scientific.

[51]China National Bureau of Statistics (2020). "Bring in" to stabilize and improve quality "Going out" to actively promote the fourteenth series of economic and social development achievements since the 18th National Congress. http://www.stats.gov.cn/ztjc/ztfx/18fzcj/201802/t20180212_1583209.html.

Table 8.21.   From 2013 to 2018, China's investment along the Belt and Road.

Year	2013	2014	2015	2016	2017	2018
100 mil. USD	126	137	189	153	202	180

Source: 2018 Statistical Bulletin of China's Outward Direct Investment, China Ministry of Commerce, National Bureau of Statistics, State Administration of Foreign Exchange.

13. China's Foreign Investment and Policy Implications

Foreign Direct Investment has been a significant contributor to China's post-reform economic development. The use of foreign capital in China has gone through a process of gradually expanding from the special zones to the coastal, river, and border areas, and then moving inland. In the early days of the reform and opening up, China's use of foreign capital was concentrated in coastal areas, especially Guangdong Province. Many central and western provinces did not even have foreign direct investment. With the deepening of the opening up, foreign-invested enterprises gradually covered all provinces, autonomous regions, and municipalities in the country. Guided by the construction of "One Belt and One Road," China needs to enrich the connotation of opening up to the outside world and jointly promote strategic mutual trust, investment in economic and trade cooperation, and humanities exchanges, and strive to form a mutually beneficial cooperation pattern.

Opening up to the outside world must proceed in a strategic and balanced manner. China must promote two-way openness in a systematic way, promote the orderly flow of domestic and international factors, allocate resources efficiently, integrate the market more deeply, and accelerate the cultivation of new competitive advantages.

To improve access to the open areas, China must strengthen the construction of ports and infrastructure in inland border areas and open up cross-border multimodal transport corridors. While the Bohai Sea, the Yangtze River Delta, and the Pearl River Delta regions are the leaders in attracting international investment and trade, inland open economic zones, such as Ningxia, must be promoted.

The optimization and upgrading of foreign trade must be accelerated: China must implement a free entry and easy exit strategy, transforming its foreign trade to a high quality and competitive price regime, and accelerate its establishment of a global trade power. The integration of trade in goods and services must be promoted, and trade in productive services must be vigorously developed. Service trade accounts for more than 16% of foreign trade. A country must consolidate and enhance the traditional export advantages and promote the innovation and development of processing trade. It must also optimize the layout of foreign trade, promote diversification of export markets, increase the proportion of emerging markets, and consolidate traditional market share. The development of new trade methods must be encouraged, and export credit insurance must be developed. A country must actively expand imports, optimize import structure, and import more advanced technology equipment and quality consumer goods. It must also actively respond to foreign technical trade measures, strengthen trade friction warnings, and resolve trade frictions and disputes.

Utilization of foreign capital and foreign investment must also be improved. Access restrictions should be relaxed, especially in service areas such as childcare, architectural design, and accounting and auditing. Foreign investment in advanced manufacturing, high-tech, energy-saving and environmental protection, modern service industries, and the establishment of research and development centers should be supported, especially in the midwest and northeast of China.

Foreign financial institutions should be allowed to access Chinese capital markets, while Chinese financial institutions and companies should be encouraged to raise funds abroad. In general, China must improve its institutional mechanisms that are conducive to cooperation and win-win, and compatible with international investment and trade rules.[52]

Today's world is undergoing a level of profound change that has not been seen in a hundred years. Human society is full of both hope and challenges. Multipolarity, economic globalization, cultural diversity, and information technology are extending their reach. Peace and development remain the themes of the times. At the same time, deep-seated problems

---

[52]United Nations Conference on Trade and Development: World Investment Report (2018). *2018 — Investment and New Industrial Policies*. New York: United Nations, New York and Geneva; Ministry of Commerce of the People's Republic of China, National Bureau of Statistics. State Administration of Foreign Exchange: Foreign Investment Management Department, Ministry of Commerce of the People's Republic of China: 2017 Statistical Bulletin of China's Outward Foreign Direct Investment; Ministry of Commerce of the People's Republic of China: The Report of China's FDI, 2018 (in Chinese).

are apparent throughout the world, with increasing instability and uncertainties. Building a global community of shared future and building a better world are the common aspirations of all peoples. China is a part of the world, and China's development has become closely related to the rest of the world. From economic and trade investment to cultural exchanges, from government cooperation to people-to-people exchanges, China has been conducting all-dimensional, wide-ranging, and multi-level exchanges and cooperation with other countries, going global faster. Opening up has brought funds, advanced technologies, and managerial

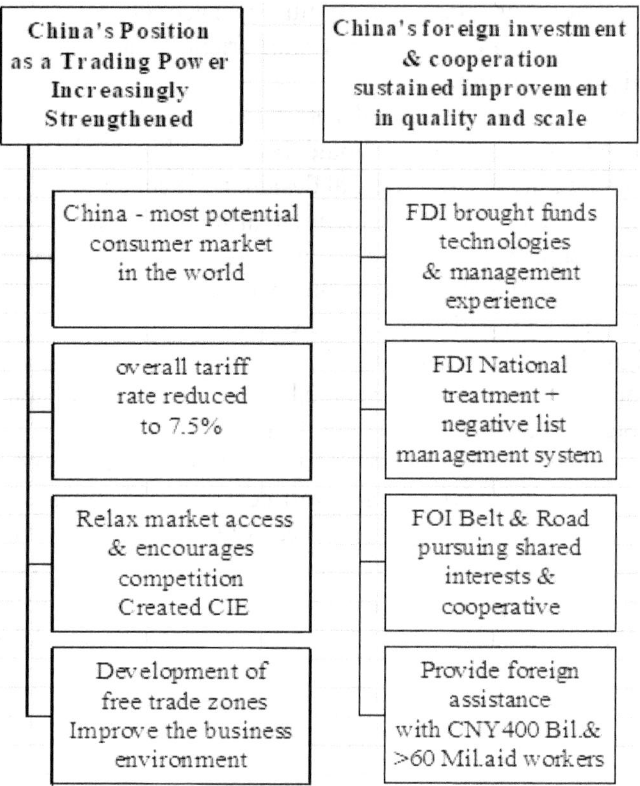

Figure 8.15.   All-round opening up creates more opportunities for all countries to share the benefits of China's development.

Source: China wows the world with commerce, trade leaps over 70 years, September 30, 2019. http://english.www.gov.cn/archive/statistics/201909/30/content_WS5d9139d6c6d0bcf8c4c145ce.html.

experience to China, changed the mindset of the Chinese people and boosted their creativity, and helped China to modernize. At the same time, China's opening up has provided a broad market for other countries. The opening of China's investment and service trade has facilitated local economic growth and employment in the countries concerned. Figure 8.15 depicts this situation.

In a year ravaged by the COVID-19 epidemic, FDI into the Chinese mainland, in actual use, expanded 6.2% Y-o-Y, a record high of 999.98 billion RMB in 2020, the Ministry of Commerce (MOC) said. The better-than-expected performance of China in FDI was mainly shored up by its service and high-tech industries. Foreign investment in the service sector came in at 776.8 billion RMB in 2020, up 13.9% Y-o-Y and accounting for 77.7% of the total. China's opening up momentum has remained unabated, rolling out measures including cutting its negative list for foreign investors, introducing its master plan for the construction of the Hainan free trade port, and further expanding pilot free trade zones in the country. China's new "dual-circulation" development pattern emphasizes boosting domestic demand and further opening up the domestic market.

Chapter 9

The Reform and Development of the Financial System: China's Financial Institutions

1. Introduction

Financial systems are constructs of complex and closely interconnected financial institutions, markets, participants, instruments, services, practices, and transactions. China's financial system possesses some uniquely Chinese characteristics. It is a system in transition, and one currently dominated by banks.

Between 1949 and 1978, China was a CPE. Money was used primarily as an accounting tool. Prices were set by the government, so money did not have the standard functions it performs in a market economy. The only bank in the country, the PBOC, was part of the MOF and played the dual role of central and commercial bank. Enterprises were only allowed to obtain credit from the PBOC, while inter-enterprise credits were strictly prohibited. Households and individuals were not allowed to participate in any financial activities other than opening deposit accounts. The bank, then, did not play a significant role in inter-temporal allocation of financial resources.[1]

During the 1952–1978 period, China's financial system could be characterized as repressed. Under a repressed financial system, the

---

[1]Wu, J. (2005). *Understanding and Interpreting Chinese Economic Reform*. Thomson/South-Western, p. 218.

government controls interest rates and allocates funds according to its objectives. This potentially leads to misallocation of resources and economic inefficiencies. After 1978, China gradually transformed itself from a poor CPE to a lower middle-income, emerging socialist market economy. To accomplish the transition to a market-based economy successfully, China has taken steps to make its financial system compatible with a market-based economic framework without shedding its Chinese orientation.

A country's financial system is an important contributor to its general economic welfare. In developed economies, the financial system performs many functions directly or indirectly related to optimizing resource allocation. These functions include the following:

- Allocating financial resources over time and economic sectors.
- Accumulating, processing, and disseminating information for decision-making purposes, using monetary policy and fiscal policy to implement macroeconomic control.
- Clearing and settling payments.
- Receiving deposits from and providing loans to enterprises and individuals.
- Providing processes for managing uncertainty and pricing and controlling risk.

Following a series of reform initiatives, China's financial system is making progress toward performing these functions. The country's approach to reforming the financial system has followed the same gradual, experimental, and pragmatic approach which Chinese economic reforms have been characterized by in general. A latecomer to the overall reform process, the financial sector has indeed made a significant impact on the Chinese economic landscape. Sector reforms, innovation in its growing financial institutions, and a substantial increase in the number of employees have expanded its impact over time. We can now find a variety of financial institutions all over the country; banks take in deposits, make payments, and give loans; other financial institutions provide insurance, while securities firms further increase the development momentum. Furthermore, China's major financial institutions have become important players in the global stage. At issue, however, is whether the growth of the financial sector is in turn contributing to the optimization of resource allocation in support of the economic reform, promotion of stable and rapid economic development, and the safeguarding of social stability.

Although China's financial system has contributed a great deal to the country's economic performance, it has also been facing a great deal of challenges. Observers have raised many red flags, some referring to the system as "fragile."[2] Indeed, many questions have arisen about the country's financial system. Does the Emperor have clothes? Does China's financial system have sound foundations, or is it a mere house of cards? Are its banks truly competitive on a global basis or just behemoths created from continuous state assistance and dependence? We cannot offer definitive answers to these and other important questions yet. The development of the financial system is a process, not a single activity. In the meanwhile, however, we can examine the system in finer detail and understand its development and current state.

In Chapter 9, we examine China's financial institutions and their contribution to the success of China's reforms. We first present a brief historical background of China's financial sector. We then proceed to analyze the cornerstone of China's financial system, the banking institutions. In addition to Chinese banks, foreign banks also operate in China, although their presence is limited. We then present insurance companies, shadow-banking institutions, informal financial institutions, private equity, and mutual funds.

2. A Brief Historical Perspective

The Middle Kingdom has a long and glorious history. The country's history is reflected in the history of its financial system as well. The country's financial system served China's economy and society in various ways for centuries. We will now briefly go back in time to appreciate the financial system that China built prior to 1949.

China's banking environment in the 18th, 19th, and early 20th centuries was dominated by two different banking systems: one originating in Shanxi and the other in Shanghai. Each system reflected the economic structure of its region.[3]

---

[2] Walter, C. E. and F. J. T. Howie. (2012). *Red Capitalism: The Fragile Financial Foundation of China's Extraordinary Rise*. Singapore: John Wiley & Sons.

[3] Wilson, C. and F. Yang. (2016). Shanxi Piaohao and Shanghai Qianzhuang: A comparison of the two main banking systems of 19th-century China. *Business History*, 58(3), 433–452. https://doi.org/10.1080/00076791.2015.1122711.

2.1. *The Shanxi Piaohao system*

Shanxi Province was the home of a group of entrepreneurial bankers who found an innovative solution to the security problems faced by merchants as they crossed the robber-infested trade routes of north central China. Piaohao banks designed a system that allowed merchants to settle their debts using bank drafts written on the account in one branch and redeemed in another branch. This eliminated the need for carrying bulky amounts of silver and copper. The draft clearing system was initially implemented by the Xiyucheng Dye Stores of Shanxi. The company had several branches in cities around the empire but encountered losses and delays in shipping funds between branches. Instead of shipping silver and copper, the company started clearing interbank accounts using drafts. This innovative draft system was much more efficient; it cut down costs, transactions, and transportation, and reduced risks. In 1823, the company's system was transformed into the Rishengchang Piaohao bank, which offered the draft-clearing services to other Shanxi merchants. Other banks soon followed. Banks also started offering other services, like those offered by today's banks: accepting deposits and making loans. Piaohao banks were typically owned by groups of families, financed directly by these families, and managed by general managers. The nature and degree of the trading activity in the region assured Piaohao banks regular business and enabled them to prosper.

2.2. *The Shanghai–Qianzhuan banking system*

As China's ports were opening in the mid-19th century because of foreign invasions, they witnessed the increasing activity of foreign trading houses. Local businessmen joined these houses as commissioned brokers and equity investors. To facilitate trade, groups of families of these local brokers established and invested in Qianzhuan banks. These banks offered various services to local merchants, including currency exchange deposits, account settlement, and short-term unsecured bridge loans. Qianzhuan banks were financed through loans acquired from foreign banks.

2.3 *Shanghai financial industry, 1770–1937*

For over two centuries, Shanghai has been the epicenter of China's finance world. We can get a better understanding of the development of Shanghai's modern banking infrastructure by examining the city's banking history since the last quarter of the 18th century. The 1770–1937 periods include the late Imperial Period (1842–1911), the Republican Era (1911–1927), and the Nanjing Period (1927–1937).[4]

The predecessors of today's Shanghai banks were the so-called Native Banks or Money Shops. They originated in Shanghai during the Qing Qianlong period. Their organization, the Money Shop Benevolent Association, was established in the 1770s. Shanghai had become the center of the internal and external trade in the 19th century, with the modern financial sector being formed gradually. Initially, foreign British banks entered the city; the LiRu Bank (Oriental Bank) established a Shanghai branch in 1847. The West Business Shanghai Stock Benevolent Association was established in 1891 (restructured in 1894 and renamed Shanghai Stock Benevolent Association) and became the first stock exchange in China, representing the next stage in Shanghai's financial modernization. The first Sino-foreign joint venture bank in China was the Sino-Russia Daosheng Bank, Shanghai branch; it was established in 1896. In April 1897, the first private bank run by Chinese was established in Shanghai. It was the Commercial Bank of China, which was also China's first bank to issue currency notes.

After the Kuomintang (KMT) Government's capture of Tianjin and Peking in June 1928, the political center was moved to Nanjing. The government implemented a series of programs to develop Shanghai into the country's largest and most important financial center. In November 1928, the KMT Government moved the Central Bank (National Bank), then the strongest bank in China, and the Bank of Communications from Peking to Shanghai. As of 1937, a total of 54 bank head offices and 128 branches were in Shanghai, both ranked first among major cities. The head offices of four government banks, the Central Bank, Bank of China, Bank of Communications, and Farmers Bank of China were in Shanghai. They had a total paid-up capital of ¥167.5 million, with 491 branches throughout the country. The loans of the above four banks amounted to ¥1.9139 billion, accounting for 55.2% of national total bank lending; their deposits amounted to ¥2.6764 billion, or 58.8% of national total bank deposits. Among the country's 73 commercial banks, 36 head offices were in Shanghai, paid-in capital amounting to ¥62.1 million and accounting for about three-fourths (74.6%) of total paid-up capital of the country's

---

[4]Horesh, N. (2009). *Shanghai's Bund and Beyond*. New Haven and London: Yale University Press.

commercial bank sector; 36 commercial banks in Shanghai had a total of 278 branches, representing 68.1% of the total number of branches of the country's commercial banks. In addition, Shanghai had a total of 27 foreign banks, far more than in Hong Kong (17), Tianjin (14), Peking (10), Hankou (10), Guangzhou (7), and other cities.

Shanghai became the administrative home of numerous types of other financial institutions. The five domestic regional savings bureaus (the Central Trust Bureau of China, The Postal Remittances and Savings Bank, Four-bank Deposit Association, Siming Commercial Savings Bank, and International Savings Society) were also located in Shanghai. Of the 12 trust companies nationally, 10 set up head office in Shanghai, including the Central Trust Company, Shanghai Trust Company, and Four-bank Trust Company, as did the best-known insurance companies, such as China Insurance Company, Siming Insurance Company, Alliance Assurance Co. (British), Lincoln of New York (USA), and Taishan Insurance Company (Sino-US joint Venture). The Huashang Stock Exchange transaction volume reached ¥4.77 billion in 1934, becoming the largest stock exchange not only in the country, but also in the Far East (as East Asia was then referred to). In addition, the Trust, Gold, Silver, Foreign Exchange, Clearing, and other financial markets in Shanghai were either the only ones or the largest of their kind in China. Overall, then, these developments reflect the layout of the financial industry and the corresponding allocation of resources in accordance with financial modernization and internationalization.

2.4 *China's first bank clearinghouse*

The first bank clearinghouse — the Shanghai Clearinghouse — was established on January 10, 1933.[5] Prior to this, Shanghai Chinese banks depended on foreign banks to settle exchanges. The founder of the Shanghai Clearinghouse was Zhu Boquan. Zhu graduated in 1919 from Shanghai Hujiang University; the same year, he went to study in the United States. In January 1932, he served as general manager of the Central Bank Business Bureau. Zhu did clearing work in the U.S. (Citibank, New York), becoming familiar with clearing house organization and exchange liquidation. On January 10, 1933, China's first regular

---

[5] Industrial and Commercial Bank of China. Shanghai Bank Museum (in Chinese).

Shanghai Clearing House was established by Zhu, who also held the post of general manager. Zhu died in March 2000, aged 103 years.

The Shanghai Clearinghouse, using a new method of exchange and a complete liquidation system, became a clearing agency for new bills created by the commercial banks' own strengths. There was a fixed exchange place in the Association of Banks building, located on Hong Kong Road. Four staff members, representing each member bank, participated; the daily first fix was set for 11:00 a.m. and the second fix for 15:00, like systems used by the United States and Japan. On the first day, the Clearinghouse cleared 1173 exchange notes (in the amount of 200 million), far exceeding the 73 notes cleared in 1886 at the opening of the Tokyo Clearinghouse. In the 1940s, at the peak of Shanghai's financial activity prior to the establishment of the PRC, the Shanghai exchange was run by 32 member banks. A total of 238 Banks and Money Shops participated in the Clearinghouse exchange, among them 203 private Banks and Money Shops, 21 state-owned banks, and 14 foreign banks.[6]

2.5. *Legal tender policy reform in 1935*

Shanghai's development in the 1920s and 1930s as an international city illustrates the country's dependence on foreign powers at the time.[7] China, although thousands of miles away, was dependent on American policy even prior to 1937. American silver policy of the 1930s, centered on President Roosevelt's silver purchase program, had a devastating effect on the Chinese economy. At the time, China was the largest among the three countries under the silver standard in the world. Since the country does not produce silver, it had to import large quantities of silver annually. When the U.S. bid up the price of silver, not only could China not continue to import silver, but domestic bank deposit silver outflows increased dramatically. These large amounts of silver outflow led to a serious

---

[6]Wu, J. (2002). Reflections over the Transformation of Modern Shanghai's Position as a Finance Center (in Chinese). Archives and History, 6. Also Yao, H. (2009). Bank promoted the market economy development in the modern Shanghai (in Chinese). *The Journal of Chinese and Social and Economic History*, 5.

[7]Liu, F. L. (2009). Currency Reform In 1930s China and The American Silver Policy, A Thesis Presented to the Faculty of the University of Southern California Graduate School in Partial Fulfillment of the Requirements for the Master of Arts, East Asian Studies, December.

decline in Chinese bank silver deposits and commodity prices. The industrial and commercial sectors were now facing severe liquidity problems. In response, China abandoned the silver standard, cutting the connection between the price of silver and foreign silver inflows. Currency reform ensued through the implementation of a managed currency system and issuance of paper notes. On November 3rd, 1935, the KMT government's MOF released the relevant notice which in effect began the implementation of the legal tender system. This was a significant change in China's monetary and financial framework.[8]

3. Impact of the Financial Sector: Employment

An economic sector's contribution to the country's employment picture is an important aspect of that sector's impact on economic development. This is especially true in economies in transition, since authorities must ensure that citizens are indeed fully employed even after the reform of the labor-rich state-owned sector. The financial sector has produced positive employment contributions to China's drive to full employment.

By the end of 2017, there were more than 4 million people employed in China's financial industry (excluding those working at the PBOC). Table 9.1 shows the employees and number of institutions in various financial service sectors. Table 9.2 shows the financial sector's contribution to China's GDP. The value added to GDP by the financial services sector amounted to CNY6.54 trillion in 2017, about 200 times that of 1978. In terms of percentage, its value added of 8% was more than four times its contribution in 1978.

In addition to its contribution in terms of employment and value added to GDP, China's financial sector contributed significantly to the country's reform efforts in various other ways. China now has virtually all the institutions of a modern financial system; financial intermediation has become a pillar industry in the national economy. China's financial sector has also contributed to efficient allocation of resources and has enhanced the welfare of its citizens by offering more services and outlets to individuals and businesses.

---

[8] *The Sydney Morning Herald* (1935). China's Currency Reforms. Tuesday, December 17. https://trove.nla.gov.au/newspaper/article/17210357#.

Table 9.1.   Employment in China's financial institutions, 2017.

Statistics of banking financial institutions & non-bank financial institutions (not all) and their employees by end of 2017

Financial institutions	Employees (person)	Institutions (units)
Major commercial banks	16,76,601	5
Policy banks and national developed banks	63,700	3
Joint-stock commercial banks	4,35,354	12
City commercial banks	4,01,003	134
Private banks	2,424	8
Rural credit cooperatives	2,97,083	1,125
Rural commercial banks	5,58,172	1,114
Rural cooperative banks	13,561	40
Financial companies of enterprise groups	11,644	236
Financial trust companies	19,236	68
Financial lease companies	4,954	56
Auto financial companies	8,046	25
Currency brokerage companies	857	5
Consumer finance companies	57,758	18
Asset management companies	7,883	4
Foreign financial institutions	45,613	39
Other institutions	4,86,337	1,506
Total	40,90,226	4,398

Source: Almanac of China's Finance and Banking 2017 (in Chinese), p. 498.

Table 9.2.   Value added by China's financial institutions.

	Value added, 100 bil. 2005 const. CNY	Value added as % of GDP
1978	0.33	1.87
1996	3.91	4.51
2011	15.77	5.28
2017	65.4	8

Source: China Statistical Yearbook, various issues.

4. The Process of Financial Reform

Even though financial sector reform lagged behind real sector reforms, it has played an integral role in China's reform strategy. Financial sector reform in general has been analyzed with respect to its contribution to economic development and growth at the macro-level and system efficiency and consumer welfare at the micro-level. Channels of influence include more efficient resource allocation in both operational and allocation terms and in increased savings. Firms and consumers have a greater array of financial products and services at their disposal.

The study of financial reform has been to a large extent based on the works of McKinnon[9] (McKinnon) and others. The standard framework involves a system in which economic agents have relatively few assets available to them and in which the central authority exerts control over interest rates. These systems typically exhibit artificially low deposit rates and official loan rates. On the other hand, capital controls and other measures bring the marginal loan rate above the world market rate.

For many decades, the Chinese financial system contained many of these characteristics of a "financially repressed system." China has reformed significantly both its financial institutions and financial markets. Although significant progress has been made, the consensus assessment is that financial sector reform has up to now lagged behind reforms in other parts of the economy and has a way to go before it operates in a manner optimizing resource allocation.

Prior to 1978, the People's Bank of China (PBOC) was a department of the MOF. The PBOC served as a "monobank," while credit cooperatives operated in rural areas. The essential features of financial industry before reform were the unitary organization, narrow business scope, and highly concentrated management system. The sector was directed by the political authorities, a mere conduit of resource allocation decisions coming out of Beijing. The reconstruction of finance and its adaptation to a market-based framework is a key component of the transition from a CPE economy. We divide the three decades of financial reform and development process into five stages.

---

[9]McKinnon, R. (1973). *Money and Capital in Economic Development*. Washington, DC: The Brookings Institution.

4.1 *Stage One (1979–1984): Preliminary diversification of financial institutions*

Prior to 1978, the financial system was under the direct control of the PBOC. The Agricultural Bank of China was established in December of that year. Three months later, the Bank of China's status was elevated from a department of the PBOC to a separate bank. The transition of the PBOC to a pure central bank was furthered through the creation of the Industrial and Commercial Bank of China, or ICBC (January 1984). In total, four specialized or state-owned banks operated, each having the following functions:

1. **The Bank of China (BOC)**, first established in 1912; it served as the country's Central Bank until 1949. It is the country's primary foreign exchange bank. The bank also has branches in more than 30 regions around the world;
2. **The Agricultural Bank of China (ABC)**, first appeared as the Agricultural Cooperative Bank in 1951, becoming today's ABC in 1979. It serves as the main lender to the farm sector;
3. **The People's Construction Bank of China (CBC)**, established in 1954 under the MOF. The CBC has primary responsibility for construction and infrastructure lending; and
4. **The Industrial and Commercial Bank of China (ICBC)** took over for the PBOC as the provider of domestic currency deposit accounts and loans and of clearing operations. The ICBC established thousands of branches throughout China. Branches located in large cities, such as Shanghai, became large banks on their own right.

The system being put in place, then, comprised the Central Bank (PBOC), the four specialized banks, and nine "commercial" banks, including the Bank of Communications (BoComm), the China Trust Industrial Bank, and the regional banks (including those in Guangdong, FuJian, and PuDong). Various other domestic financial institutions also operated (insurance companies, financial trust and investment corporations, stock exchange corporations, and cooperatives). For example, after nearly 20 years, the People's Insurance Company of China (PICC) restored its domestic operations in 1980.

4.2 *Stage 2: A new beginning (1984)*

Following the elimination of the monobank (PBOC) system, the Agricultural Bank of China (ABC) was reconstructed in 1979 to specialize in rural banking. By March 1979, the Bank of China (BOC) was separated from the PBOC, changing the status of the BOC as a Department of the PBOC. At the same time, the SAFE was established, becoming a separate entity for foreign exchange management and operation. By 1983, the PBOC was implementing Central Bank functions. All commercial operations (including deposit, loan, saving, clearing business) were transferred to the newly established Industrial and Commercial Bank of China (ICBC) in January 1984. This marked a new beginning for China's financial system, as the state/specialized banks began functioning under the leadership of PBOC.

As commercial financial institutions were gradually being separated from the Central Bank, the old framework characterized by "unified control over deposits and loans" was abolished by the PBOC. A new approach of "centralized planning, managing at different levels, linking deposits with loans and controlling the balance" was adopted in 1979. In 1981, "controlling the balance" was replaced by "balanced responsibility."

4.3 *Stage 3: The exploration stage (1985–1997) — financial system transformation toward a market-oriented system*

To establish a strong Central Bank-based Macroeconomic Control System, the Chinese authorities produced three important items of legislation in the 1990s: The *Law of the People's Republic of China on the People's Bank of China* (March 1995), *The Commercial Bank Law* (May 1995), and *The Rules on Monetary Policy Committee of the People's Bank of China* (May 1997). Also issued in 1995 were the *Insurance Law of the People's Republic of China*," and the *"Guaranty Law of the People's Republic of China"*.

The March 1995 decree assigns Central Bank functions to the PBOC. From this time on, the Bank has been answerable to the State Council and responsible for the management of the money supply, the value of the country's currency, and the strength of the financial system. The PBOC, then, is like the Fed, but does not enjoy the same level of independence. To accomplish its tasks, the PBOC uses open market operations, reserve requirements, and discount rates, and imposes bank capital requirements. The PBOC has oversight over payments, clearing, and settlement.

The 1995 Commercial Bank Law defines the functions of the Agricultural Bank of China, the Bank of China, the Industrial and Commercial Bank of China, and the People's Construction Bank of China. These four previously "specialized" banks are to be transformed into *bona fide* commercial banks. The Law sets the organizational structure, legal entity status, and management practices to which these banks must adhere. Functions previously performed by the specialized banks will be at least partially implemented by three new State (Policy) Banks: The State Development Bank, the Export–Import Credit Bank, and the Agricultural Development Bank. These banks assist the government in pursuing its policy objectives.

According to the 1997 Decree, the PBOC would take the lead in carrying out a unified monetary policy. The final goal of monetary policy is to keep reasonable price stability in tandem with encouraging economic growth. The main instruments for implementation of the policy include traditional deposit reserve rate, loans from the PBOC, the rediscount rate, Open Market operations, and the interest rate for Central Bank's deposits and loans. Similar to most other Central Banks, the PBOC implements its financial macroeconomic control through direct and indirect regulation. The Central Bank functions include formulating management regulations and supervisory standards for financial institutions, as well as the procedures of supervision. Central Bank supervision also aims at maintaining profitability and liquidity of financial institutions and protection of depositors' rights. The tools of supervision include bank registration, examination of the certification of the legal representative, determination of the business scope, monitoring the capital and asset liquidity ratios, and the weighted risk of assets according to the Basel Agreement.

After 1984, three policy banks, four state-owned commercial banks, the Bank of Communications, and many nationwide joint-stock commercial banks, local banks, and non-bank financial institutions such as trust and investment companies were established. Policy (Bank) Loans mainly provide financing for state key construction projects and support for priority industries and enterprises. Such loans include agricultural development loans, purchasing fund for the reserves of main farm products (grain, cotton, and edible oil), infrastructure loans (transportation and energy, etc.), and loans to basic industry. These projects usually generate low economic efficiencies. Therefore, Policy Loans are structured as low interest, long term, and high risk, representing a separate and necessary policy directive from the PBOC and the State Specialized Banks. Policy loans were extended by the China Development Bank to principally fund key national construction projects (including new construction and technology reform), infrastructure, and basic industry (raw material, transportation, and energy). The main goal is to separate policy finance from the commercial finance function of specialized banks to solve the dual functions dilemma. The business scope of the Import and Export Credit Bank of China focuses on credit for import and export of large sets of equipment, for example, the bank provides secured credit for export machinery goods. Policy loans extended by the China Development Bank are mainly utilized for national key construction projects (including new construction and technology reform), infrastructure, and basic industry. The Agricultural Development Bank of China supports funding for purchasing grain, cotton, and edible oil for state reservation and contract purchasing of farm and sideline products, as well as agriculture development policy loans and loans with interest pay in deduction form.

Following their separation from the PBOC, the four state specialized banks (ICBC, BOA, PCBC, and ABC) were to be transformed into commercial banks and operate according to commercial bank principles. The commercial banks were to carry out their operations independently, assuming sole responsibility for the risks as well as for profits and losses. They were to be self-sufficient and self-disciplined. However, these banks have received significant assistance from the PBOC. Today, the big commercial banks are the backbone of China's financial system and have expanded their reach globally.

4.4 *Stage 4: Adjustment and enrichment (1998–2007): Adjustment of the financial system and strengthening of the financial framework*

During this stage, China's macroeconomic environment underwent fundamental changes. The shortage economy accompanied with central planning economy was replaced by excess supply and insufficient demand economy. The main features of this stage and the content can be summarized as follows:

1. Four asset management firms were created in 1999 for disposing of non-performing loans (NPLs) of four state-owned banks.

In 1997, the outbreak of the financial crisis in Southeast Asia endangered the transition of China's state-owned banking system in transition, as the risk of outstanding non-performing assets became a major risk for the national economy. At that time, SOE loans from state-owned banks accounted for more than 70% of non-performing loans (NPLs).[10] The need for SOE and state-owned bank reform had become pressing. The huge amount of state bank NPLs that were the legacy of central planning and its impact on SOE reform represented the price of China's economic reform.

In 1998, the PBOC experimented in Guangdong for NPL disposal and improvement. The pilot project produced significant achievements; it introduced the internationally accepted five-category classification in loan quality, thus identifying the risk inherent in each loan. The results of the pilot experiment revealed that NPLs (including substandard, doubtful, and loss-making categories) of Guangdong state-owned commercial banks reached 57% of the total loans.[11] In 1999, the Chinese Government established the four asset management corporations (AMCs): China Huarong Asset Management Corporation (CHAMC), China Great Wall Asset Management Corporation (GWAMCC), China Cinda Asset Management Corporation (Cinda), and China Orient Asset Management Corporation (COAMC) matching the four state-owned banks ICBC, BOC, PCBC, and ABC, respectively.

Since their establishment, the mission of the four AMCs has been to prevent banks from incurring excessive risks, thus promoting commercial bank reform, sustaining SOE reform, maintaining asset quality, and minimizing losses. In 1997, the Central Government injected CNY270 billion into the four major state banks through a special issue of treasury securities. To set up the four asset management companies, in 1999, the government wrote-off CNY1.4 trillion of NPLs from the "big four" (ICBC, BOC, CCB, and ABC), transferring them to the asset management companies.

---

[10] *Persist in innovation and development, role for ten years and Cinda created a remarkable brand for ten years* (2009, in Chinese), May 12. http://www.cinda.com.cn/news/news!toedit.action?id=6566.

[11] Li, L. and D. Zhao (CEO of Great GWAMCC) — Recall 1998 (2008, in Chinese), *Financial News.* December 23.

However, at the end of September 2001, the banks still had CNY1.8 trillion (USD217.6 billion) in NPLs that needed to be dealt with.[12] The Bank of China, the country's biggest foreign exchange bank, reported a non-performing loan ratio of 28.78% of its assets by the end of 2000, a 10.6% decrease from 1999.[13] CCB's NPL ratio in 2001 stood at 18.14%; the ratio was the lowest among the largest four state-owned commercial banks. The average NPLs for the domestic banking sector [14] reached a staggering CNY2.44 trillion (USD293 billion) at the end of 2003.[15] The Chinese government gave the CCB and BOA each USD22.5 billion (CNY372.5 billion) from China's foreign exchange reserves at the end of 2003,[16] and wrote-off CNY478 billion (USD57.6 billion) NPLs for two AMCs to prepare them for pilot joint-stock restructuring and public share offerings.[17] ICBC received USD15 billion (CNY122.9 billion) in capital injection in April 2005 from the foreign exchange reserves,[18] while CNY705 billion (USD86.1 billion) of NPLs were transferred from its balance sheet to AMCs[19] in preparation for the stock market listing, ordering them to clean up their tattered loan books. In 2008, preparing for the joint-stock restructuring and IPO of ABC about CNY8,000 billion (USD1,171.3 billion) NPLs had to be written-off.[20] The government transferred a total of CNY3.4 trillion (USD415 billion) NPLs to the four AMCs to support the four state-owned commercial banks in establishing a modern enterprise system. At the same time, about CNY3.4 trillion of non-performing assets (NPAs) had been accumulated. The four AMCs were committed to maximizing the recovery value of non-performing loans through

---

[12]Mu, J. (2001). Bad loans can bring good times. *China Daily*, November 6.

[13]Bank of China NPL ratio 28.7% of assets (2001). *China Daily*, May 15.

[14]Major bank to cut NPL ratio by half (2001). *China Daily*, May 15.

[15]Zhang, D. (2004). AMC reforms get the green light. *China Daily*, March 5.

[16]Zhang, D. (2004). AMCs entrusted with massive NPL disposal. *China Daily*, March 17.

[17]Lai, X. (2009). Using superiority of comprehensive management property to promote NPAs market efficiency (in Chinese), http://www.chamc.com.cn/xwzx/jtxw/2009/121843.shtml.

[18]Feng, J. (2006). ICBC improves following restructuring. *China Daily*, January 20.

[19]Lai, X. (2009). Using superiority of comprehensive management property to promote NPAs market efficiency (in Chinese), July 13. http://www.chamc.com.cn/xwzx/jtxw/2009/121843.shtml.

[20]Lai, X. (2009). *op. cit.*

various methods, including debt collection, asset exchange and leasing, asset assignment and sale, debt restructuring and enterprise reorganization, debt-equity swaps, and asset securitization. These four AMCs successfully disposed the first group of Policy NPLs CNY1.4 trillion (USD169.1 billion) transferred from the four state-owned commercial banks. By the end of 2006, the four AMCs had handled Policy NPLs of CNY12.1 trillion and cumulatively recovered CNY211 billion in cash.[21]

With the Policy NPLs' disposals basically completed, the four AMCs underwent share reform and restructuring in 2004 to dispose of a second pile of bad assets for the four state-owned banks, totaling CNY942 billion (USD113.8 billion).[22] The second group of NPLs obtained through market acquisition was to be dealt with by individual asset management companies; therefore, all four AMCs sought new roles as market-oriented financial institutions. In 2006, the Finance Ministry issued reform guidelines for AMCs; they could offer credit rating, financial consulting, financial leasing, trust and auto financing services, as well as operate industrial investment and entrepreneur investment funds. The government also licensed AMCs for new operations. For example, CHAMC (China Huarong Asset Management Company) established Huarong Financial Leasing Co., Ltd (CHAMC holding 99.71% of stocks, March 2006), Rongde Asset Management Co., Ltd (joint venture of CHAMC holding 59.3% of equity with Deutsche Bank — China, August 2006), Huarong Securities (CHAMC holding 99.34% of equity, September 2007), and Huarong International Trust Co., Ltd (Huarong hold 97.5% of equity, May 2008).

But the four AMCs face many challenges ahead. First, the four AMCs handle Policy NPLs with losses of more than CNY1 trillion (USD146 billion) on account. Second, the competitive advantage of the AMCs diminished over time. In the past, the four AMCs monopolized the handling of Policy NPLs. But, at present, NPLs are to be managed following market-oriented approaches; commercial banks can now deal with the NPLs on their own. Third, after their commercialization reform, AMCs and other market-oriented financial institutions will operate in an increasingly competitive field. See, for example, the markets in securities, financial

---

[21]Lei, Y. (2007). Non-performing assets handling expect to complete, the AMCs to anticipate laissez-passer in transition (in Chinese), January 19. http://www.chamc.com.cn/xwzx/ztxw/syhzx/112057.shtml.

[22]Zhang, Y. and X. Wen. (2008). Decision time for bad assets management. *Caijing Magazine*, May 27.

leasing, international trust, credit rating, and financial consulting, to name a few. The four AMCs were latecomers; they had no competitive advantage in capital, human resources, and brand recognition. For the Chinese government to make them more competitive, it would have to spend much more on their commercialization than the amount needed for dissolution and settlement of these four AMCs.

We will discuss the NPL issue again later in this chapter.

4.5 *Stage 5: Post-crisis growth*

The 2007–2008 Global Financial Crisis put a dent in the Chinese government's confidence in the Western financial system. To address the negative effects of the 2007–2008 Global Financial Crisis on the Chinese economy, the PBOC implemented a sizeable stimulus (about 20% of GDP). Banks were encouraged to expand lending. In turn, the lending surge led to inflationary fears, prompting the PBOC to reverse its expansionary status. Beyond the differences in policies between the PBOC and most of the rest of the world, whose Central Banks pursued

Table 9.3. Chinese bank assets by institution type, December 2019.

Institution type Big six state-owned banks	Percent of total system assets
(ICBC, ABC, BOC, CCB, BOComm, Postal Savings Bank)	40.3

Joint-Stock Commercial Banks
  (China Citic Bank, China Everbright, China Merchants, Shanghai
  Pudong Development, China Minsheng Banking Corp., Huaxia,
  Ping An Bank, Industrial Bank, China Guangfa, China Bohai,
  China Zheshang, Hengfeng Bank)
	17.9

City Commercial Banks (Bank of Beijing, Bank of Dalian, Bank of Shanghai, etc.)	12.9
Rural Financial Institutions	12.8
Other Financial Institutions (Policy Banks, Foreign Banks, Nonbank Financial Institutions, etc.)	16.2

Source: U.S.-China Economic and Security Review Commission. 2020 Annual Report to Congress. https://www.uscc.gov/annual-report/2020-annual-report-congress; Section 2 of the Report. Data from China Banking and Insurance Regulatory Commission.

Table 9.4.   China's banking system.

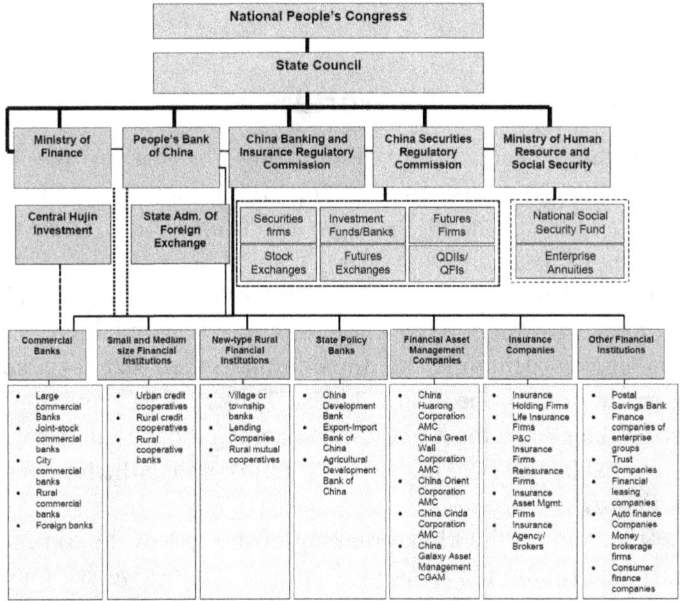

Source: Adapted from Elliott, D.J., and K. Yan (2013). The Chinese Financial System. John L. Thornton China Center at Brookings. Monograph Series, 6, July. Washington, D.C.: The Brookings Institution. https://www.brookings.edu/wp-content/uploads/2016/06/chinese-financial-system-elliott-yan.pdf.

expansionary policies, the Crisis highlighted the need to grow and develop the Chinese system independently of the West to the policymakers. At the same time, the Crisis forced Western banks to retreat; Chinese banks, then, found the opportunity to expand their operations domestically and internationally.

During the 2007–2020 period, Chinese Bank Assets grew by almost six times, from CNY53.1 trillion to CNY309.4 trillion.[23] The Big Six state-owned banks dominate in terms of asset size, as shown in Table 9.3. Since these Big Banks have historically served the needs of SOEs, their position within China's banking system is a testament to the state's favorable attitude toward and treatment of SOEs. Table 9.4 shows the structure

---

[23] Statista (2020). Total Assets of Chinese Banks 2007–2020. October 19. https://www.statista.com/statistics/277938/total-assets-of-banks-in-china/#:~:text=In%202020%2C%20the%20total%20assets,amounted%20to%20126%20trillion%20yuan.

of China's banking system and includes other financial institutions that operate along banks.

5. China's Banks in the World

By 2020, Chinese banks were dominating the list of the World's Top Banks. The 2020 list of the Top 1000 included 143 Chinese banks (compared to 127 in 2019). As we see from Table 9.5, the top four banks in terms of asset size and Tier 1 Capital are Chinese, with ICBC being the largest bank in the world, and the other three of China's "Big Four" — China Construction Bank, Agricultural Bank of China, and Bank of China — ranked behind ICBC. In addition to their size, of note is the capital/assets ratios of the four Chinese banks. ICBC and the China Construction Bank have the highest ratios among the top 10. Also, the top four Chinese banks have the highest NPL ratios among the top 10 (except for Wells Fargo).

Table 9.6 includes the global ranking of the rest of the top 25 banks in China. In addition to the Bank of Communications, we see joint-stock banks on the list (China Merchants), as well as City banks (for example, Bank of Hangzhou), Rural banks (Chongqing Rural), and others. One of the observations we can make from examining the statistics is the size of the capital/assets (Soundness) ratio. Some of the banks show ratios below 7, which can be a sign of concern for regulators. In addition, some banks have RWA/Loans ratio above 70%.

Another indication of Chinese banks' improved financial condition is the increase in the capital position of banks outside the top 10. The Banker's Top 1000 shows that a Chinese regional bank, Liaoning Province's Bank of Anshan, was the 2020 "Top Mover" experiencing a 179.2% change in its Tier 1 Capital (and a 457.4% increase in its pre-tax profit) among all banks. Bank of Anshan ranked 705th in terms of total Capital. Another Chinese bank, MYBank, was ranked ninth among the Top Movers, experiencing a 93.3% increase in Tier 1 capital. MYBank was established in 2015 by Ant Technology, and ranked 642nd in overall rankings, a 132-place improvement from 2019.[24]

---

[24]The Banker (2020). Chinese regional lender rebounds to grab top spot. July, p. 154.

Table 9.5.   World's top 10 banks, 2020.

Rank	Top10	Country	Strength	Size	Soundness	Performance		Ratios % (2020)		
			Tier1 capital	Asset ranking	Capital asset ratio	Return on capital	Return on assets	NPL to total loans	Loans to assets	RWA to assets
			USD mil.		% latest	% latest	% latest			
1	ICBC	China	439,938	1	8.62	11.06	0.95	1.43	59.09	61.83
2	China Construction Bank	China	361,641	2	8.39	11.58	0.97	1.42	59.02	59.18
3	Agricultural Bank of China	China	336,180	3	8.07	9.86	0.8	1.4	55.67	62.24
4	Bank of China	China	305,149	4	8.17	10.29	0.84	1.37	63.36	62.03
5	JPMorgan Chase	US	234,844	5	6.94	12.4	0.86	0.77	36.97	56.41
6	Bank of America	US	200,096	9	7.1	8.94	0.63	0.62	42.26	61.36
7	Citigroup	US	167,427	11	7.41	6.81	0.5	0.95	36.8	59.79
8	HSBC	UK	160,173	8	5.37	3.81	0.2	1.2	41.05	31.06
9	Wells Fargo	US	158,196	14	8.09	2.27	0.18	1.43	50.99	64.63
10	Mitsubishi UF J Financial Group	Japan	144,379	6	4.45	5.36	0.24	0.99	32.42	34.21

Source: The Banker (2020). The Top 1000 World Banks. July.

Table 9.6.   The global ranking of the rest of the top banks in China.

Rank	Global rank	China Top 25 Bank	Strength	Size	Soundness	Performance		Ratios % (2020)		
			Tier1 capital	Asset ranking	Capital asset ratio	Return on capital	Return on assets	NPL to total loans	Loans to assets	RWA to assets
			USD mil.		% Latest	% latest	% latest			
5	11	Bank of Communications	1,32,040	6	8.06	9.23	0.74	1.48	58.51	59.7
6	14	China Merchants Bank	1,06,307	7	8.30	14.11	1.17	1.36	61.78	60.67
7	15	Postal Savings Bank of China	1,02,649	5	5.90	9.6	0.57	0.86	44.94	45.36
8	18	Shanghai Pudong Development Bank	96,425	8	7.92	9.37	0.74	1.92	60.19	68.56
9	19	Industrial Bank	94,088	9	7.78	11.02	0.86	1.57	45.18	70.54
10	24	China Citic Bank	84,068	10	7.31	9.02	0.66	1.77	60.79	77.1
11	26	China Minsheng Bank	81,523	11	7.66	6.59	0.51	1.76	201.26	77.67
12	32	China Everbright Bank	69,073	12	8.40	8.4	0.71	1.59	57.93	72.67
13	40	Ping An Bank	52,639	13	7.69	8.42	0.65	1.75	61.12	68.46
14	51	Hua Xia Bank	43,249	14	8.31	7.64	0.63	1.85	62.53	78.06
15	62	Bank of Beijing	33,116	16	7.46	10.01	0.75	1.46	53.38	76.45
16	64	China Guangfa Bank	33,078	15	7.13	6.39	0.46	1.45	59.23	70.57
17	67	Bank of Shanghai	28,533	17	7.57	11.23	0.85	1.14	48.38	70.8
18	70	Bank of Jiangsu	27,613	18	7.71	8.66	0.67	1.39	48.58	62.63
19	99	China Zheshang Bank	20,138	19	6.42	9.55	0.61	1.2	53.59	63.09
20	103	Bank of Ningbo	18,082	20	7.26	12.82	0.93	0.78	39.48	64.34
21	109	Bank of Nanjing	16,359	21	7.04	12.37	0.87	0.89	42.16	64.23
22	111	China Bohai Bank	15,783	22	7.40	8.19	0.61			
23	119	Chongqing Rural Commercial Bank	14,367	25	8.26	9.13	0.75	1.29	54.68	68.11
24	132	Huishang Bank	13,249	23	6.80	11.47	0.78	1.04	37.65	72.06
25	135	Hengfeng Bank	12,989	26	7.61	6.13	0.47			

Source: The Banker (2020). The Top 1000 World Banks, July.

6. Breadth of Bank Services

Despite the reform-related challenges they face, China's banks have not only grown, but also perform many more types of services. They have learned a great deal from their foreign counterparts and have become formidable competitors at home and overseas. Table 9.7 shows the types of services delivered by China's banks and the bank considered the best at delivering each such service. The table also includes two foreign banks for

Table 9.7.   Best banks for selected services, 2020.

Best Corporate Bank	ICBC
Best Consumer Bank	Postal Savings Bank of China
Best Bank of Risk Management	Chongqing Three Gorges Bank
Best Bank of Corporate Governance	China Cinda Asset Management
Best Bank of Corporate Social Responsibility	China Merchants Bank
Best SME Services Bank	Harbin Bank
Best Bank for Transaction Services	Hengfeng Bank
Best Bank for Cross-Border Trade	China Construction Bank
Best Private Bank	Ping An Bank
Best Asset Manager	China Life Asset Management
Best Domestic Bank for Belt and Road	Bank of China
Best Foreign Bank for Belt and Road	DBS
Most Innovative Bank	ICBC
Innovation in Payments	AsiaPay
Innovation in Fintech	China Zheshang Bank
Best Bank for Green Energy Development	Beijing Rural Commercial Bank
Best Domestic Bank for Renminbi Internationalization	Bank of China
Best Foreign Bank for Renminbi Internationalization	Habib Bank (Pakistan)
Best Bank for Urban Revitalization	Zhongyuan Bank
Most Innovative Corporate Manager	Shanxi Bank
Best Bank for SOE Reform	China Huaxia Bank
China's Rising Star Bank	MYBank
Best Provider of Precious Metals Services	Agricultural Bank of China
Best Family Office and Wealth Manager Provider	China Everbright Bank

Source: Johnson, E. (2020). China's Banking Pacesetters. *Global Finance*. November, 42–53.

their excellence in offering services associated with China's international activities.

A different bank performance assessment is offered annually by *The Banker*. In the 2020 ranking of the best regional banks, for the Asia-Pacific region the distinction went to China Merchants Bank (CMB).[25] According to *The Banker*, CMB took steps in 2019 to upgrade its internet banking platforms, introduce special digital branches in the CMB Business app, and improved its supply chain finance channel.

Banks, of course, deliver a variety of services to their clients. Table 9.5 includes the Chinese banks recognized as being the best in delivering selected services. The table reveals the variety of services performed by Chinese banks, illustrating the breadth of China's banking system. In addition, it is interesting to note that, although the Big Four are represented, several smaller banks have shown excellence in delivering such sophisticated services as risk management, green development, and fintech.

7. Bank Ratings

Although Chinese domestic rating agencies have not been objective and accurate in their assessment of risk, Chinese banks are also rated by the "Big Three" rating agencies. Table 9.8 shows the Top 25 rated banks by Fitch, Moody's, and S&P. Not surprisingly, the three Policy Banks top the ratings; after all, they are backed by the Chinese government. They are followed by the four large commercial banks.

8. Chinese Bank Ownership

When studying the Chinese economy, all preconceptions stemming from our knowledge of Western economies must go out the window! In the Western financial environment, the term "commercial bank" implies private ownership. Not so in China. The central government and its affiliates own the decisive majority of most of the country's commercial banks, especially the largest ones.

---

[25]The Banker (2020). Bank of the Year Awards. https://www.thebanker.com/Awards/Bank-of-The-Year-Awards/The-Banker-s-Bank-of-the-Year-Awards-2020-Asia-Pacific#Apac5.

Table 9.8. Chinese bank ratings.

Rank	Bank	Ratings		
		Fitch	Moody's	S&P
1	China Development Bank	A+	A1	A+
2	Agricultural Development Bank of China	A+	A1	A+
3	The Export–Import Bank of China	A+	A1	A+
4	Industrial and Commercial Bank of China	A	A1	A
5	China Construction Bank Corporation	A	A1	A
6	Agricultural Bank of China	A	A1	A
7	Bank of China	A	A1	A
8	Hang Seng Bank (China)	NR	A2	A+
9	Bank of Communications	A	A2	A–
10	China Merchants Bank	BBB+	A3	BBB+
11	China CITIC Bank Corporation	BBB	Baa2	BBB–
12	Shanghai Pudong Development Bank	BBB	Baa2	BBB
13	China Everbright Bank	BBB	Baa2	NR
14	Industrial Bank	BBB–	Baa2	NR
15	Guanghou Rural Comm'l Bank	NR	Baa2	BBB-
16	Bank of Shanghai	NR	Baa2	NR
17	Bank of Ningbo	NR	Baa2	NR
18	Shanghai Rural Commercial Bank	NR	NR	BBB
19	Ping An Bank	BB+	Baa2	NR
20	Bank of Nanjing	NR	Baa3	NR
21	Bank of Chongqing	NR	NR	BBB–
22	China Minsheng Banking Corp.	BB+	NR	BBB–
23	Hua Xia Bank	BB+	NR	BBB–
24	Chima Guangfa Bank	BB+	Baa3	NR
25	Bank of Beijing	BB+	NR	NR

Source: Sanders, D. (2020). Stars of China. *Global Finance*. November, 54–55.

Table 9.9 shows the portion of ownership maintained by Central Huijin Investment Ltd. (Huijin), the government's investment arm. The table clearly illustrates the dependence of banks and other listed financial institutions on the government. Another government unit, the MOF, also holds large portions of selected banks' ownership. For example, MOF

Table 9.9.   Government ownership on selected financial institutions.

No.	Company name	Proportion of the total capital held by Huijin
1	China Development Bank	34.68%
2	Industrial and Commercial Bank of China Limited	34.71%
3	Agricultural Bank of China Limited	40.03%
4	Bank of China Limited	64.02%
5	China Construction Bank Corporation	57.11%
6	China Everbright Bank Company Limited	19.53%
7	Hengfeng Bank Co., Limited	53.95%
8	China Everbright Group Ltd.	55.67%
9	China Jianyin Investment Limited	100.00%
10	China Galaxy Financial Holding Co., Ltd.	69.07%
11	Shenwan Hongyuan Group Co., Ltd.	20.05%
12	China Export & Credit Insurance Corporation	73.63%
13	China Reinsurance (Group) Corporation	71.56%
14	New China Life Insurance Company Limited	31.34%
15	China International Capital Corporation Limited	44.32%
16	China Securities Co., Ltd.	31.21%
17	Jiantou & Zhongxin Assets Management Limited	70.00%
18	Guotai Junan Investment Management Co., Ltd.	14.54%

Source: Central Huijin Investment, Ltd. http://www.huijin-inv.cn/huijineng/Investments/Shareholding.shtml.

holds 31.14% of ICBC's A and H shares.[26] Simply put, what banks do is by no means independent of the government and its policies. Of course, some of these institutions have also opened their doors to other investors through their heralded IPOs.

9. Non-Performing Loans

Since their establishment, the four national AMCs have maintained their original assignment of NPL disposal, they have also developed into

---

[26]Industrial and Commercial Bank of China LTD. (2019). *Annual Report, 2019*. http://www.icbc-ltd.com/icbcltd/investor%20relations/financial%20information/financial%20reports/2019annualreport.htm.

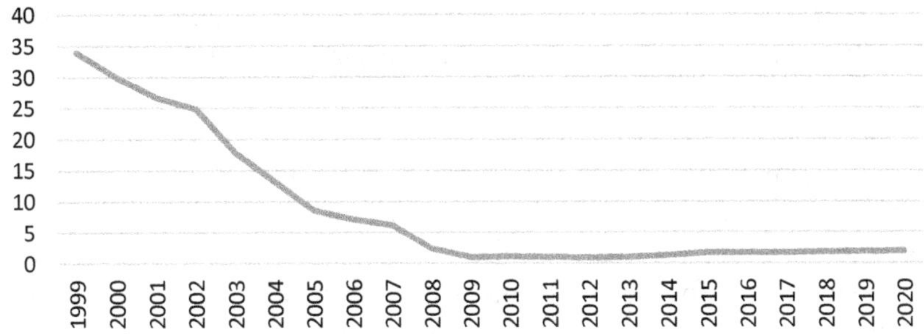

Figure 9.1.   Total NPLs, 1999–2020.

Sources: 23 China Banking Regulatory Committee. NPLs of Commercial Banks as of end-2002, 2004–2012 (in Chinese); Xinhua (2004). Banking posts drop in non-performing loans, June 6. Mu, J. (2001). Bad loans can bring good times. *China Daily*, November 6; Hu, Y. (2008). China's banking sector strengthened by competition, October 28. For NPLs after 2012, see Statista (2020). Ratio of Non-performing Loans (NPLs) in China's Banking System. https://www.statista.com/statistics/1077497/china-total-npl-ratio-of-total-banking-system/.

diversified holding companies offering a variety of financial services. In May 2020, China established a fifth national Asset Management Company, China Galaxy. China Galaxy is owned by Central Huijin (70%) and Citic Securities (30%).

The arrival of the fifth AMC reflects the importance that the government places on addressing the NPL challenge. Figure 9.1 illustrates the behavior of NPLs from 1999 to (July) 2020. The shape of the line shows how much NPLs have declined through the years, from the high of about 34% in 1999 (prior to the establishment of the four AMCs) to around 1 between 2011 and 2013 (see Figure 9.1). The ratio started rising slowly after that, to just below 2 by 2020; it would have been higher had banks not disposed about CNY3 trillion in bad loans during 2020. The economic setbacks during the COVID-19 Pandemic though may have an adverse effect on bank balance sheets. To alleviate pressure from small businesses, which were seriously impacted by the economic slowdown, the government eased loan repayment terms. Smaller city and rural commercial and other banks with high exposure to Central China, such as Postal Savings Bank, are expected to get hit the hardest. In addition, economic downturns may be associated with increase in special mention loans (loans that require special attention, but are not yet classified as

NPLs).[27] Special mention loans have been hovering around 3% in 2019–2020. Regulators and banks, then, need to pay continuous attention to them.

One notable aspect of China's NPL experience has been the interest shown by global investors in Chinese bad loans. This is a by-product of the willingness of Chinese banks to dispose of these loans, on the one hand, and the country's financial liberalization policies, on the other. The traditional channel for foreign capital to invest in NPLs has been through the four national AMCs. Financial reforms, however, have been allowing selected foreign investors to engage in joint ventures with Chinese asset management companies and even purchase bad loans directly from banks, starting with Pilot programs in Shenzhen and Shanghai.

10. China Development Bank (CDB): A Different Type of Bank

The CDB was established in 1994 and has become one of the most important financial institutions and the largest finance development institution in the world. CDB is "mainly engaged in medium and long-term lending and investment to support the implementation of major strategies for medium- and long-term development of China's national economy."[28] It is a limited liability company, changing from a joint stock company in 2017. Its shares are held by the MOF (36.54%), Central Huijin Investment Ltd. (34.68%), Phoenix Tree Investment Platform Co., Ltd. (27.19%), and the National Council for Social Security Fund (1.599%).

As a policy bank, the CDB operates under the guidance of the State Council, with a mission to:

- Support the development of national infrastructure, basic industry, key emerging sectors, and national priority projects.
- Promote coordinated regional development and urbanization by financing small business, education, healthcare, agricultural investment, low-income housing, and environmental initiatives; and,

---

[27]Lee, G. (2020). China could face decade-high bad loan ratio as coronavirus slams small businesses, DBS says. *South China Morning Post*, March 6. https://www.scmp.com/print/business/banking-finance/article/3065284/china-could-face-decade-high-bad-loan-ratio-coronavirus.

[28]China Development Bank (2019). Annual Report, 2019. http://www.cdb.com.cn/English/.

- Facilitate China's cross-border investment and global business cooperation.

The bank provides several products and services to the Chinese government, Chinese companies, and foreign governments. They include loan financing (such as foreign currency loans for long-term projects and sovereign loans), equity investment (including overseas investment), cross-border RMB settlement, special services (such as the China–Germany, China–Greece, and China–Caribbean financing arrangements). CDB has been instrumental in the construction of large infrastructure projects in China as well as around the world.

The CDB represents yet another innovation of Chinese reforms. Its creation came about in the midst of a dark period for China's local government finances. Provinces and cities were strapped financially. By founding Local Government Financing Vehicles (LGFVs), the CDB circumvented restrictions faced by local governments, thereby allowing them to undertake projects that promoted urbanization and facilitated China's growth. The CDB was financed by bonds bought by commercial banks, thus becoming an important contributor to the growth of China's bond market. The CDB's former Vice Governor, Gao Jian, is widely recognized as the creator of China's bond markets.[29]

The CDB went from its very humble beginnings of a "bank with one branch and three offices into a bank that in 2011 had assets of over 6 trillion yuan — almost USD1 trillion — and a loan book bigger than that of JPMorgan Chase & Co."[30] Sanderson and Forsyth characteristically give credit to the bank's Governor, Chen Yuan, for turning CDB from a "Zombie Bank into a Global Bank."[31]

The CDB story has been as spectacular as it has been controversial. The bank's low cost of capital and high debt have given it an advantage over other global competitors. Its support of Chinese global investments have generated suspicion about its motives, especially those in the African Continent. The model of state-led investment with the backing of the state has been an effective one, as well as a further indication of the differences between the Chinese-type of global capitalism and that of the Western

---

[29] Sanderson, H. and M. Forsyth (2013). *China's Superbank: Debt, Oil and Influence — How China Development Bank is Rewriting the Rules of Finance*. Hoboken, NJ: John Wiley & Sons.

[30] *Ibid*, p. 41.

[31] *Ibid*, Chapter 2.

economies. In 2007, CDB established the China–Africa Development Fund, a private equity fund focusing on investments in Africa. Especially noteworthy, as well as the source of much controversy, have been CDB's collaborations with other state-owned entities, such as the government of Zambia. In 2020, Zambia owed USD3 billion to CDB. As an illustration of the risks involved in these arrangements, however, Zambia was unable to pay off the USD391 billion due as partial repayment in October 2020.

11. Foreign Banks in China

China has offered an attractive opportunity for foreign banks, but not an easy one to negotiate. In fact, as of 2017, foreign banks accounted for a mere 1.32% of domestic banking assets, down from the 2.38% share in 2007.[32] Market share of these banks has been stuck at around 2% for a while now (reference). On the other hand, foreign banks have been progressively allowed to offer more services, especially after China's entry into the WTO in December 2001. The 2002 Regulation on Administration of Foreign Invested Financial Institutions stated requirements for foreign banks establishing branches, wholly owned subsidiaries, and joint ventures. Capital requirements for foreign banks (branches, wholly foreign-owned banks, and joint ventures) were applied in 2004. In November 2006, two related regulations were announced: *The Regulation on the Administration of Foreign-funded Banks* and the *Rules for Implementing the Regulation on the Administration of Foreign-funded Banks*. These regulations differentiated between the requirements for setting up a WFOE or a JV with a Chinese partner and those for foreign banks establishing branches. Foreign banks were encouraged to incorporate locally to be allowed to accept smaller (than RMB1 million) deposits from individuals (EIU, Finance).

By 2011, foreign banks could offer local currency deposits and loans, foreign currency loans, consulting, trade finance, and underwriting B-shares (see EIU foreign banks). In addition, they could conduct certain foreign currency transactions, if they adhere to restrictions imposed by the SAFE. Taiwanese banks gained a particular opportunity to gain access to

---

[32]Danese, P. (2018). China: Foreign banks fumble over their expansion strategies. *Asiamoney China*, June 29. https://www.asiamoney.com/article/b18vjw1pb6dykl/china-foreign-banks-fumble-over-their-expansion-strategies.

the Chinese market through the Cross-Strait Financial Cooperation Agreement (in effect January 1, 2011).

On September 30, 2019, the State Council issued the Amendment of the Regulations of the People's Republic of China on Administration of Foreign-Funded Insurance Companies and Foreign-Funded Banks (State Council Order No. 720). Accordingly[33]:

- The total asset requirement of USD20 billion was removed.
- Foreign banks are now allowed to set up branches and establish a bank WFOE/JV.
- Foreign banks can issue, redeem, and underwrite government securities.
- The minimum size of deposits by Chinese citizens in foreign banks is reduced to CNY500,000 per transaction (from CNY1 million).
- RMB license approval was removed.
- The 30% of working capital interest-bearing asset requirement was removed
- The restriction regarding the proportion of RMB capital to RMB risk assets for foreign bank branches was relaxed.

The CBIRC has also been facilitating the entry of foreign banks and insurance companies into China by accelerating the market entry approval process and allowing foreign financial institutions to open branches and establish foreign-funded corporate banks. Whereas these changes represent an important step toward liberalization of the banking sector, foreign banks are still under the regulatory arm of the CBIRC. Furthermore, they are not significant players in China's domestic banking environment. In early 2020, foreign bank assets in China were about 1.7% of total bank assets. Other numbers associated with foreign banking presence are equally unimpressive. For example, by the end of the first quarter of 2020, there were 976 foreign invested bank entities in China, of which 41 were foreign invested legal person banks. These banks had 115 branches and 149 offices.[34] Chinese banks, on the other hand, have close to

---

[33] KPMG (2019). *Foreign Banks and Insurers Granted Greater China Market Access.* October 24. https://home.kpmg/cn/en/home/insights/2019/10/china-tax-alert-32.html.

[34] CBNEditor (2019). Foreign Banks Establish 41 Legal Person Lenders in China, Total Assets Approach $480 Billion. China Banking News. December 12. https://www. chinabankingnews.com/2019/12/12/foreign-banks-establish-41-legal-person-lenders-in-china-total-assets-approach-480-billion/

200,000 branches. In addition, Chinese banks and shadow-banking institutions have made effective use of technology to capture the entire retail digital market. In addition, foreign banks are at a great disadvantage in dealing with the large SOEs, since they deal primarily with the big Chinese banks.

Foreign banks in China are the Who's Who in global banking: Citi, Morgan Stanley, JP Morgan, HSBC, Standard Chartered, to mention just a few. They all have made bets on China's continuing economic growth and development and the creation of a well-off citizenry. Have foreign banks been successful in China? It depends on how we define success. From one point of view, the fact that they are even operating in China is a success story! Yet, according to some observers, they have faced considerable barriers to meaningful entry into the Chinese market. The biggest barrier, however, seems to be competition from domestic banks. China's big banks have size and market access that foreign banks cannot possibly attain. They have far more branches around China and offer a larger variety of services. Their global branches enable them to offer services once reserved for big Western banks (PWC).

The futility faced by foreign banks can be illustrated by the progress (or lack of) they have achieved since China's WTO accession. According to reports (Financial Post), foreign banks have spent USD60B to enhance their presence in the country. Of that amount, USD27B has been allocated toward establishment of branches and USD33B to buy equity in domestic banks. Still, their profitability and reach fall short of those of domestic banks. The disparity in the number of branches, for example, is sizeable: foreign bank branches are below 400, while domestic branches are more than 66,000! The difference in the number of retail customers is another telling statistic; the number of retail customers for foreign banks barely reaches one million, while ICBC alone has 260 million retail customers! In fact, Citi is the only foreign bank with a retail network. Foreign banks also have a disadvantage in their dealings with the big state-owned companies, who prefer to work with domestic banks.

The future of foreign banks in the Chinese market does not appear to be promising. Yet, the reality of China's importance to global business has led to the entrenchment of foreign banks in the Chinese market. The future will tell whether their persistence in maintaining a China presence will pay off.

12. Deposit Insurance

Public confidence in the banking sector is necessary to ensure a smooth functioning of the sector. To increase public confidence, most countries adopt a Deposit Insurance System. China issued its Deposit Insurance Regulations on March 31, 2015.[35] The system's characteristics include:

a. All deposit-taking institutions are members of the system, including commercial banks, rural cooperatives, and rural credit cooperatives (RCC). However, coverage is not extended to branches of foreign banks or those of Chinese banks' abroad.
b. Deposits in RMB or foreign currencies are covered, except for inter-bank deposits and those of senior managers in their own institutions. Coverage includes demand and saving deposits. Deposits are covered up to a maximum of CNY500,000 of principal and interest.
c. Premiums vary between 0.01% and 0.02%, which incorporates a flat fee and a risk-adjusted component.

To put the system in operation, the PBOC established a deposit insurance fund management company in May 2019. The company had a registered capital of CNY10 billion, which healthy institutions could access to take over a problematic institution. Funds can also be used as a form of capital injection in institutions deemed Systematically Important if their capital adequacy ratio fell below 2%. The future, of course, will tell how successful it is. One of the first assignments of the fund was the take-over of Inner Mongolia-based Baoshang Bank, motivated by the precarious condition of the Bank's loan portfolio. Parts of Baoshang were sold to Huishang Bank, using CNY10 billion of the insurance fund. The rest was transferred to a newly created bank, Mengshang Bank. Huishang Bank was recapitalized to the tune of CNY100 billion through private placement, with most of the shares going to Central Huijin Corporation (value of CNY60 billion), which made Central Huijin the majority shareholder.

---

[35]Desai, S. (2016). A Regional Comparison of China's New Deposit Insurance System. Pacific Exchange Blog. Federal Reserve Bank of San Francisco, February 24. https://www.frbsf.org/banking/asia-program/pacific-exchange-blog/regional-comparison-chinas-new-deposit-insurance-system/.

Another CNY36 billion went to Shandong government units.[36] The total rescue bill for Baoshang was about CNY170 billion.

China's deposit insurance system is relatively new. It is, however, a much-needed addition to its financial system. To confirm the viability of the system, the PBOC mandated that financial institutions publicize their participation in the insurance scheme (effective end of November 2020). Depositors then should feel confident about the security of their deposited funds.

13. Risks Facing China's Banks

All businesses face risks. Financial institutions face risks that are unique to them. They include credit risks, foreign exchange risks, operational risks, interest rate risks, market risks, and others. Chinese financial institutions face additional risks as the country is undertaking a series of reforms to make a successful transition. Since the process of transition is dynamic, the risks faced by Chinese institutions also change as the environment and the companies themselves change.

As we indicated, banks are the foundation of China's financial system. Consequently, certain risks they face emanate from the significant position they hold in the country's reform process.

a. Market/Government risk: Although China has only three national state-owned policy banks, the business-related priorities of all banks are subordinate to those of the government. Banks, like all other institutions, are components of an integrated system. Thus, the PBOC may also influence bank portfolios through its monetary policy and sterilization actions. Different levels of government may influence bank-lending portfolios through "window guidance" (use of moral suasion and dialogue rather than conventional means, such as regulation and legislation).[37]

---

[36]The Bank of Finland (2020). Massive public spending on rescuing China's troubled banks. Institute for emerging Economies. October 6. https://www.bofit.fi/en/monitoring/weekly/2020/vw202040_2/.

[37]Lee, G. (2019). China's Biggest Banks Well Prepped on Nonperforming Loans, Ready for Stricter Reporting Standard. *South China Morning Post*, May 10. https://www.scmp.com/business/article/3010372/chinas-biggest-banks-well-prepped-non-performing-loans-ready-stricter?utm_source=email&utm_medium=share_widget&utm_campaign=3010372.

b. Interest rate risk: Financial institutions in general have net exposure to interest rate changes. In a period of low interest rates, for example, insurance companies may find themselves earning low returns on their investments while having high interest rate liabilities.

c. Credit/balance sheet risks: Commercial banks have been lending to inefficient SOEs that often are not able to meet the terms of the loan. The story of NPLs was noted above. The story, however, can get complicated. In 2016, for example, the government stimulus initiative led to more lending and, predictably, more NPLs. To alleviate the burden on banks, the CBRC implemented a Debt-to-Equity Swap program. The program involved transferring loans to Special Purpose Vehicles (SPVs) that were to be converted into loans of high debt burden companies. In turn, banks funded these SPVs through sale of Wealth Management Products (WMPs); this, of course, transferred the risk to the buyers of WMPs.[38]

d. Shadow banking: We will be examining the nature and importance of shadow banking in the next section of this chapter. For now, let's define shadow banking as the performance of banking-related activities by non-bank institutions. Shadow banking generates benefits, but also risks to the financial system. The involvement of banks in this sector magnifies the impact of shadow-banking problems on the entire economy.

e. Real estate loans: Real estate loans have been characterized by some as "the glass chin" of China's banks.[39] Property prices have been a source of a great dilemma for policymakers. As prices rise, the danger of a bubble burst is always on the horizon. To stem real estate buying fever, authorities have also emphasized that "a home is to live in, not to speculate." Nevertheless, the Central Bank has been reluctant to take decisive action, such as raising interest rates, since property is such an important household asset. For financial institutions, property loans have become the largest single item in their loan portfolio.

As quoted by Bisio, V. (2020). China's Banking Sector Risks and Implications for the United States. U.S.–China Economic and Security Review Commission. May 27. https://www.uscc.gov/research/chinas-banking-sector-risks-and-implications-united-states.

[38] See Allen, F., J. Qian and M. Qian (2019). A review of China's financial institutions. *Annual Review of Financial Economics*, 11, 39–64.

[39] Chatterjee, S. and P. Murugaboopathy (2016). Property loans, the glass chin of China Banks. Reuters, May 24. https://www.reuters.com/article/us-china-banks-realestate/property-loans-the-glass-chin-of-china-banks-idUSKCN0YG05Z.

In addition, many of the loans are backed by real estate. Therefore, a property price downturn would hit them very hard.

To bring order into the sector, the PBOC and the CBIRC announced the new "banking sector financial institution real estate loan concentration management system." The system went into effect on January 1, 2021. Accordingly, banks will have to adhere to maximum real estate loan and personal mortgage shares.[40] The exact maximum share depends on the asset scale and category of each bank. Banking institutions have been assigned to 5 categories. Category 1 includes the large banks (such as ICBC and ABC), and they are subjected to a 40% maximum real estate loan share and 32.5% maximum personal mortgage share; Category 2 includes medium-scale banks (such as China Merchants Bank and China Minsheng Bank), and they are subjected to maximum 27.5% and 20%, respectively; Category 3 includes small scale banks or non-county cooperatives, having maximum shares of 22.5% and 17.5%, respectively; Category 4 includes County rural cooperatives with maximum shares of 17.5% and 12.5%, respectively; finally, Village banks are in Category 5, with maximum shares of 12.5% and 7.5%, respectively. Banks that exceed these maxima were given transitional periods to comply with the new system. Whether the new system will bring about a significant decrease in the systemic risk associated with the property sector and its impact on banks will be a development to watch.

f. Risks from local government loans: China's banks have been frequent lenders of Local Governments and their Financing Vehicles (LGFVs). In addition, banks have been buyers of local government bonds. Local governments, especially through their LGFVs, invest borrowed funds in infrastructure and other construction projects. These projects, however, have been historically providing very low returns. Some LGFVs have been diversifying their investments by entering such sectors as tourism and parking facilities. Although their returns from these investments have also been low, increasing their assets puts them in a more favorable position to borrow, creating a vicious circle of borrowings, bad investments, and more borrowings.

---

[40]CBNEditor (2021). Chinese Central Bank Targets Concentrations of Real Estate Lending. China Banking News, January 4. https://www.chinabankingnews.com/2021/01/04/chinese-central-bank-targets-concentration-real-estate-loans/.

14. China's Other Financial Institutions

China's other institutions include foreign banks, insurance companies, pension funds, investment banks, mutual funds, and others. Although individually each group of these institutions is not currently as important to China's system as its domestic banks are, they can all be significant contributors to the success of China's reforms for economic as well as political reasons.

14.1. *The insurance sector*

China's Insurance sector is still undeveloped but growing fast. According to the Swiss Re Institute, the market is expected to quadruple by 2033, becoming larger than that of the US.[41]

During the 19th century, insurance appeared in China as the British and their allies were occupying China because of their Opium War victories and the accompanying Unequal Treaties. The first Chinese insurance companies appeared in Shanghai, specializing in shipping and marine insurance. In 1911, the first Chinese life insurance company, Hua An He Quan, was established.[42] In 1919, American Asiatic Underwriters, which later became the American Insurance Group, was established in Shanghai (and still considers Shanghai as its place of origin). Shanghai became the home of two more insurance companies: Tai Ping Insurance Company in 1929 (later headquartered in Hong Kong) and China Insurance Company in 1931, the latter established by the Bank of China. China Insurance also opened a subsidiary, China Life, in 1933. At the beginning of the Communist rule (1949), the state nationalized the assets of all insurance companies and established its own company, People's Insurance Company of China (PICC). PICC served as the sole insurer in the country until the fall of the Maoist regime. Of course, during a planned economy regime, individuals and enterprises did not need insurance in the traditional sense. The state took care of housing, health, and other needs of the population.

---

[41]Lam, J. (2019). China will become world's biggest insurance market by mid-2030s, speeding past US on the way, says analyst. *South China Morning Post*. March 7. https://www.scmp.com/print/business/article/2189033/china-will-become-worlds-biggest-insurance-market-mid-2030s-speeding-past. Downloaded July 1, 2020).

[42]Wang, M., J. Yen and K. K. Lai (2014). *China's Financial Markets: Issues and Opportunities*. New York: Routledge.

An exception was made for policies covering maritime and aviation losses. In 1959, PICC became a department of the PBOC.

Following the beginning of reforms, PICC began issuing insurance policies again. Non-life policies were issued in 1979, and life policies three years later. In 1996, PICC was once again reinstituted as the People's Insurance Company (Group) of China, a holding company. In the meanwhile, the Bank of Communications established its own insurance company in 1987; the company later became the China Pacific Group (1991). In 1988, the Industrial and Commercial Bank of China (Shenzhen Branch) and the Merchants Bank jointly financed the establishment of Ping An Insurance, which was the first joint stock insurance company. More companies started receiving licenses, including Taikang Insurance (1996), New China Life (1996), and Anbang (2004). The first foreign life insurer after reforms, American International Group, received its operating license in 1992.[43] The number of insurance companies operating in China had mushroomed to 138 by 2009 and 235 by 2019.[44]

As the number of companies was increasing, the foundations of the industry's legal framework were being formed. In 1995, China passed the National Insurance Law. The Law was amended in 2002, and amended again in October 2002, February 2009, August 2014, and April 2015. The Law set the standards of operation for companies and separated the various lines of insurance business. This led to the break-up of the PICC into separate companies within its Group: China Life, China Property, and China Reinsurance. In 1998, the China Insurance Regulatory Commission (CIRC) was established to implement the 1995 Law. CIRC replaced the PBOC as the industry's regulator and was authorized to supervise and regulate the Chinese insurance industry. In 2003, CIRC's status was upgraded to ministerial level. On its website, the CIRC pointed to some important characteristics of the Chinese insurance market that still capture its essence:[45] The insurance market has grown rapidly. In its 2005 posting,

---

[43] Xie, Y. (2017). How China's insurance industry evolved; a timeline after "reform and opening up." *South China Morning Post*, April 10. https://www.scmp.com/business/banking-finance/article/2086323/how-chinas-insurance-industry-evolved-timeline-after-reform.

[44] https://www.statista.com/statistics/225107/number-of-insurance-companies-in-china/.

[45] CIRC (2005). A Panorama of the Chinese Insurance Market. Accessed at http://circ.gov.cn/web/site45/tab2727/info24833.htm. As we state in another section, the CIRC merged with the CBRC in 2018 and formed the CBIRC.

the CIRC reported the impressive premium growth of more than 30% since 1980. The penetration rate, however, was only 3.4%.

1. The market system had been improved. The CIRC reported that, at the end of 2004, there were 69 insurance companies in China.
2. System reform has shown great progress. In 2003 alone, PICC, China Life, and China Reinsurance completed stock system reform. The three largest insurance companies listed in overseas markets and accomplished firsts in their respective categories:
    a. PICC Property and Casualty listed in Hong Kong; it was the first time a state-owned financial institution went public in a market outside China.
    b. China Life listed in New York (NYSE) and Hong Kong, offering the largest IPO globally in 2004.
    c. Ping An Insurance (Group) Company became the first insurance company in China to achieve group listing overseas (Hong Kong) in 2004.
3. Expansion of the market's opening, especially after the post-WTO provisional period ended on December 11th, 2004.
4. The legal framework has been established following the 1995 Insurance Law, and the ensuing 2002 amendment.
5. The industry has been playing a significant role in the promotion of economic development and social welfare. In addition to the monetary compensation the industry has distributed, it has been replacing the state in terms of providing pension and healthcare. The industry has also been promoting China's international business activities by offering export and outward foreign investment credit insurance.

14.1.1. *Industry size and structure*

The industry has shown significant growth since its post-reform revitalization, becoming the second largest in the world behind the US. Premium income rose by 27.5% in 2016 and 18.2% in 2017 (to CNY3.66 trillion). However, according to the CIRC, premium growth declined to 3.99% in 2018, with this growth spread unevenly across the different subsectors. Health insurance premium increased by 24.1%, accident by 19.3%, and Property and Casualty by 9.50%. On the other hand, life insurance premium income fell by 3.4%. Even after this decline, premium from life insurance contracts represented the majority (54.5%) of the 2018 total industry premium income of USD574,877 million. Total insurance premium amounted to 4.30% of GDP and was 11.7% of total world premium in 2018.

14.1.2. *Life insurance*

China's Life Insurance sector offers several products, distributed through various channels. They include[46]:

a. Traditional Life Insurance, which includes life and health insurance.
b. Participating insurance, which distributes dividends according to the company's performance.
c. Unit-linked insurance, which integrates insurance and investment. The return associated with the investment portion of insurance is uncertain, with the policyholder bearing all risk.
d. Universal Life, which includes a guaranteed interest rate applied to the investment portion of the policy.

At the end of 2018, the five largest Chinese companies by premium in the life insurance sector were: China Life, Ping An Life, China Pacific Life, Huaxia Life, and Chin Taiping Life (see Table 9.10). Rounding the top 10 insurers were New China Life, Taikang, PICC Life Insurance, Funde Sino Life, and TianAn Life. Total new insurance premium income in 2018 was CNY2,626,087 million nationally; it was CNY3,454,745 million when we include new payments for investment funds (CNY795,373 million) and new payments for investment-linked insurance (CNY33,285 million). As seen from Table 8.4, the top two firms account for more than one-third of all premia paid nationally. Life insurance companies distribute their products through their own agents or through banks (with each bank distributing products of various companies to its clients, an arrangement termed bancassurance), and online.

14.1.3. *Property & Casualty (P&C) insurance*

P&C insurance includes automobile and commercial property insurance, with automobile being the largest single component. The top five largest

---

[46]HSBC. Insurance. https://www.hsbc.com.cn/en-cn/insurance/.

Table 9.10.   Top five life insurers in China (premium national market share as percentage, 2018).

Insurer	Market share; new premium Income (%)	Market share: New premium income and new payments for investment funds and investment-linked insurance (%)
China Life	20.41	17.33
Ping An Life	17.02	16.16
China Pacific Insurance Co (CPIC) Life	7.67	6.14
Huaxia Life Insurance	6.03	6.67
China Taiping Life	4.71	3.73

Source (original data): China Insurance Regulatory Commission. As reported by Economist Intelligence Unit (EIU). 2020. *China: Financial Services Report.* 2nd Quarter, 9. www.eiu.com/financialservices. Calculations by authors.

Table 9.11.   Top five property insurers in China (market share; new insurance premium income, %).

Insurer	Market share; new premium income, 2018, %
PICC P&C Insurance	33
Ping An P&C Insurance	21.04
CPIC Property	9.99
China Life P&C Insurance	5.88
China Continent P&C Insurance	3.61

Source (original data): China Insurance Regulatory Commission. As reported by Economist Intelligence Unit (EIU). 2020. *China: Financial Services Report.* 2nd Quarter, 9. www.eiu.com/financialservices. Calculations by authors.

Chinese P&C companies in terms of premium received in 2018 were the following: PICC P&C, Ping An P&C, CPIC Property, China Life P&C, and China Continent P&C (see Table 9.11). Other large P&C Companies in the top 10 in 2018 were: China United Property, Sunshine P&C, Taiping General, China Export & Credit, and Tian An Insurance. P&C companies received a total premium income of CNY1,175,569 million in 2018.

Among the various types of P&C insurance, auto-insurance has been a major generator of premium income for companies. In 2018, more than 70% of total non-life insurance premium was generated through automobile insurance policies (EIU). Growth in motor insurance has benefitted from China's growth and increased automobile ownership, introduction of CMTPL, and liberalization in insurance pricing, which has increased competition among insurers.[47]

14.1.4. *The Anbang case*

To allow Chinese insurers earn higher returns on their investments, in 2014, the CIRC permitted them to invest up to 25% of their assets into foreign equities (2012). The maximum investment was raised to 30% in 2014 and 40% in 2015. The relaxation of investment options, and the collapse of the Chinese Stock Market in 2015 led to an aggressive investment strategy by Chinese companies. One of them, Anbang, took full advantage of the new regulatory environment and proceeded to engage in numerous and substantive acquisitions around the world (see Table 9.12). By 2017, Anbang had amassed about USD300 billion in assets and rose to #139 among the Fortune 500. However, Anbang's rise ended abruptly when its founder was arrested on fraud charges. In 2018, the CIRC took over control of Anbang and injected USD9.7 billion into its operation. A new company took Anbang's place, Dajia Insurance. The Chinese authorities then embarked on a selling spree of Anbang's assets. Their efforts have had mixed results. For example, an agreement was reached in September 2019 to sell selected assets to South Korean Mirae Global Investments. Mirae, however, missed a payment, leading to a series of suits and countersuits. As of early 2020, the matter is still in court.

The Anbang case is an example of the potential abuses arising from lax regulation, especially in an economy whose institutional framework is still evolving. China has responded to such abuses by strengthening its regulatory infrastructure. A new super-regulator, the Financial Stability Development Committee, was introduced in November 2017 to coordinate the activities of all existing financial sector regulators. Additionally, China Banking Regulatory Commission and China Insurance Regulatory

---

[47]Swiss Re (2018). Chinese Insurance Market. https://www.swissre.com/dam/jcr:eb1aba5f-05ca-4bd4-bfe6-d42a6ed6b8c5/150Y_Markt_Broschuere_China_Inhalt.pdf.

Table 9.12.   Anbang's Rise and Fall.

Year	Development or acquisition
2004	Anbang Property and Casualty (P&C) Insurance Co. established in Beijing
2005	Anbang establishes nationwide business network
2008	Anbang P&C becomes first property insurance company to receive approval to conduct insurance sales over the telephone
2010	Anbang Life Insurance Co., Ltd. founded
	Anbang Acquires Reward Health Insurance Co.; renames it Hexic Health Insurance Co., Ltd. Anbang, Insurance and Finance Group formed
2011	Anbang is approved to acquire shares of Chengdu Rural Commercial Bank.
	CIRC approves new Anbang P&C Insurance Sales Co., Ltd.
	Anbang Asset Management Co., Ltd., Hexie Insurance Sales Co., Ltd., and Beijing Ruihe Insurance Brokerage Co., Ltd., established.
	CIRC approves restructuring of old Anbang P&C for establishment of insurance group company. Anbang Insurance Group Co., Ltd., formed
2013	CIRC approves establishment of Anbang Pension Insurance Co., Ltd.
2014	Anbang acquires Delta Lloyd Bank NV of Belgium (now Bank Nagelmackers). Anbang Life acquires 100% of FIDEA insurance of Belgium
	Anbang Group acquires Waldorf Astoria Hotel from Hilton Worldwide Holdings.
2015	Anbang Life acquires Tongyang Life Insurance of South Korea. First Chinese company to enter South Korean insurance market
	Anbang Lifec acquires 100% of Dutch insurer VIVAT
2016	Anbang Life completes acquisition of Allianz Korea
	Anbang Life acquires Retirement Concepts of B.C., Canada
	Anbang withdraws bid to buy Starwood Hotels & Resorts
2017	Anbang is included in Fortune 500, ranked #139
	Agreement between Anbang and Kushner Properties to purchase NYC building collapse
	Anbang loses bid to buy Fidelity & Guaranty Life of US
2018	(February): CBIRC takes control of Anbang to defuse financial risks as a result of illegal practices
	(April): Anbang receives USD9.7 billion capital injection from China's insurance industry rescue fund (China Insurance Security Fund Co., or CISF).
	(May): Anbang former Chairman Wu Xiaohui sentenced to 18 years in prison for fundraising fraud and embezzlement
2019	(July): Dajia Insurance Group is established to take over Anbang assets. Dajian is funded by CISF, Sinopec, and SAIC Motor

Sources: *Anbang Insurance Group*. http://en.anbanggroup.com/jtjs/index.htm. *Economist (2018)*. Out with a whimper-The rapid rise and fall of the Anbang empire. https://www.economist.com/finance-and-economics/2018/02/23/the-rapid-rise-and-fall-of-the-anbang-empire.

Commission merged in April 2018 to form the China Banking and Insurance Regulatory Commission (CBIRC). These changes have provided regulatory authorities with greater standing, ability to share information more effectively, formulate policies that apply more consistently across the financial system, and face future challenges more effectively.

14.1.5. *Foreign insurers*

Foreign insurers have been relatively minor players in the Chinese insurance market. For many years, they faced significant barriers in their expansion and competition with their domestic counterparts. In addition to having had 30 years of insurance business experience, total assets of at least USD5 billion, and a representative office in China for at least two years, they have had to limit their organizational structure to a joint venture, in which they cannot hold more than 50% ownership. Foreign insurers have been permitted to sell compulsory motor third-party liability insurance since May 1, 2012.

The ownership barriers have been gradually lifted over the years. In 2004, the CIRC allowed foreign property and casualty companies to operate wholly owned subsidiaries; foreign life insurance companies could form a joint venture with a Chinese company, but they could not own more than 50% of the joint company. As of 2018, foreign insurers could own 51% of their local life insurance partner. As of January 1, 2020, the CBIRC will allow foreign insurers to own up to 100% of a locally operating insurance company. In addition, the PBOC will do away with the 30-years-in-business requirement. However, foreign companies have a lot of catching up to do before they can compete effectively with domestic companies. Tables 9.13 and 9.14 illustrate some of the differences between domestic and foreign insurance companies operating in China.

14.1.6. *What lies ahead: here comes Insurtech!*

China's insurance market has grown to be the second largest market in the world. However, it has plenty of room for growth. China lags behind other Asian countries in terms of insurance penetration rate (insurance premium as a percentage of GDP) and density (per capita insurance premium). For example, insurance penetration in China in 2018 was 4.22% (3.20% for life insurance, and 1.92% for non-life). This is way below the average

Table 9.13.   China Insurers: Selected Characteristics.

Name	China Life	Ping An	CPIC	China Taiping
Established date	1996	1988	1991	2000
Registered Captl. (RMB bn)	28.3	33.8	8.4	10
Geographic exposure	30 provinces/ tier 1 cities	30 provinces with 3,300+ business outlets	Operate in 30 provinces/ tier 1 cities	37 provinces with 1170 sub-branch and marketing center
AssetSize (RMB bn)	2,753.00	2,632.00	1,088.66	487
Total Premium/ FYP (RMB bn)	538.8/171.1	471.7/178.5	202.4/46.7	134.5/34.8
Market share	20.70%	16.70%	7.90%	4.70%
Channel mix	Agent (76%) Bancassurance (14%), Group (5%), Others (5%)	Agent (85%), Bancassurance (3%), Telemarketing, internet and others (8%), Group (4%)	Agent (91%), Bancassurance telemarketing, and internet (6%), Group –3%	Agency (76%), Bancassurance (21%), Group and others –3%
No. of agents	1,573,000 agents	1,286,250 agents	796,000 agents	472,000 agents

Source: DBS (2019). China Insurance Sector. October 22. file://hd.ad.syr.edu/02/d83f6d/Documents/ Downloads/191022_insights_china_insurance%20(1).pdf.

for Asia-Pacific countries (6.76% total: 4.53% life, 2.23% non-life). China's penetration rate is below that of Asia's developed countries and above some of Asia's developing countries (India, Vietnam, Philippines, and others). In terms of insurance penetration, then, China can be grouped with developing countries. The same conclusion is drawn from ranking Asia-Pacific countries according to their insurance density (total insurance premium divided by population). China's life insurance density in 2018 was USD221; non-life density was USD185, for a total of USD406.

Table 9.14. Foreign insurers in China: selected characteristics.

Name	ICBC-AXA	AIA(China)	Citic-Pru	Manulife-Sinochem 1
Established date	2012	1992	2000	1996
Registered capital (RMB bn)	12.5	3.8	2.4	1.6
Geographic exposure	21 provinces and 90+ cities	5 tier one cities/ provinces and 2 sales and service center	20 provinces and 89 cities	14 provinces and 50+ cities
Total asset size (Rmb bn)	119	165	92	33
Total premium/FYP (Rmb bn)	33.7 (total premium)	27.2/7.5	15.4/4.5	8.1/2.0
% of Market share	1.30%	1.00%	0.60%	0.30%
Channel mix	Agency the main channel but also has bancassurance/ digital channels	Agency the main channel but also has bancassurance/digital channel	Agency the main channel but also has 40 bancassurance/ digital channel	Agency the main channel but also has bancassurance/ digital channel
No. of agents	15,000+ sales agents	43,000 agents	48,000 agents	> 12,000 agents

Source: DBS (2019). China Insurance Sector. October 22. file://hd.ad.syr.edu/02/d83f6d/Documents/Downloads/191022_insights_china_insurance%20(1).pdf.

These densities are below the region's respective averages of USD577, USD1,322, and USD1,899.[48]

However, the insurance industry is changing as a new and dynamic form of insurance has come into the picture: online insurance. Fueled by the steep rise of the internet, the insurance industry has been finding new ways of reaching clients while offering innovative products. There are three major types of entrants into the online insurance sector:[49]

1. The traditional insurance company. The leader here is Ping An, hailed as the most profitable insurance company in China. Ping An has grown into a giant financial conglomerate, operating in various insurance sectors, including life, P&C, and pension. In the process, the company has achieved technological advances that have applications beyond the field of insurance. Among them is Ping An's Facial Recognition Technology, that has applications in insurance, other financial services, and various other industries, such as medical services.
2. The dedicated online insurance company. The pioneer of online insurance is Zhong An, founded in 2013 by Ant Financial, Ping An, and Tencent. In simple terms, the company applies technology to insurance. It went public in Hong Kong in 2018 and holds the only internet insurance license in China. Zhong An has been offering some highly specialized micro-insurance products, such as flight delay insurance. It has been especially successful in shipping return insurance products.
3. The internet company. Alibaba, for example, takes advantage of its ownership of Taobao, the country's largest online retail platform, and Ant Financial, which operates the mobile payment application Alipay, to offer insurance products. Alipay, for example, has been offering a "Free Health Insurance" product since 2017. Alibaba also operates in the insurance industry through ownership interest in Zhong An, Trust Mutual, and Cathay P&C.

---

[48] *Atlas Magazine* (2020). Turnover by Country, April. https://www.atlas-mag.net/en/article/asia-pacific-insurance-market-turnover-per-country.

[49] Gen Re (2017). Online Insurance in China. December. https://www.genre.com/knowledge/publications/ri17-10-en.html.

In December 2020, the CBIRC issued new regulations pertinent to the online insurance sector. The Internet Insurance Operations Regulatory Measures are design to bring more transparency to the sector, establish licensing requirements, promulgate standards of industry conduct, and otherwise protect consumers and minimize risks. The CBIRC also encourages online insurance companies to expand their use of Big Data and Blockchain technologies. In other words, we should expect to witness more innovation from insurance companies as well as increases in penetration and density rates in the future.

14.2. *Shadow banking*

The size and composition of Shadow Banking is an important characteristic of the global financial architecture. The Financial Stability Board (FSB) defines Shadow Banking as "credit intermediation involving entities and activities (fully or partly) outside of the regular banking system."[50] In October 2018, the FSB replaced the term "Shadow Banking" with the term "non-bank financial intermediation." The term "non-bank" should not be interpreted as absence of involvement of traditional banks from these activities. Instead, it implies that these activities or transactions take place outside the realm of traditional commercial banking activities. And, of course, they may involve non-bank entities. Therefore, we can think of shadow banking as being "bank-related" shadow banking and "non-bank, or traditional," shadow banking. Sun refers to "bank-related" shadow banking as "banks' shadow," defined as bank activities that provide funding for enterprises through the creation of credit money, but which circumvent regulatory restrictions and constraints on lending by adopting non-standard accounting measures."[51] To simplify things, we will just be using the term shadow banking.

As we have realized by now, the discussion on shadow banking can be very confusing and full of colorful terminology.

---

[50]Financial Stability Board (2019). Global Monitoring Report on Non-Bank Financial Intermediation 2018. February 4. Accessed at https://www.fsb.org/2019/02/global-monitoring-report-on-non-bank-financial-intermediation-2018/.

[51]Sun, G. (2019). China's Shadow Banking: Bank's Shadow and Traditional Shadow Banking. BIS Working Papers, No. 822. Bank for International Settlements, November. Accessed at https://www.bis.org/publ/work822.htm.

14.2.1. *Shadow banking in China*

As we have already stated in this chapter, banks are the cornerstone of China's financial system. In addition to their traditional activities, banks are also a major component of the shadow-banking sector. However, there are many other financial institutions engaged in intermediation activities outside the banking system.[52]

14.2.1.1. Shadow-banking entities

In addition to banks, the entities participating in shadow banking include:

Trust companies: Trust Companies perform functions that are a combination of banking and asset management.

Guarantee companies: As the name implies, these companies act as guarantors in loans made between companies.

Microfinance companies: These financial firms are licensed to provide credit opportunities to small and rural borrowers. Microfinance companies raise funds through bank loans and/or the owners' capital.

Internet finance companies: Many entities use the internet to bring together lenders and borrowers. These include Peer-to-Peer (P2P) networks and crowd-funding platforms.

Pawn shops: Pawn Shops are a valuable provider of funds for households and small businesses. Whereas in many countries, including the US, pawnshops give out small size loans, China's pawn shops give out loans that average USD26,000. Loans are mostly backed by real estate, with the loan maximum being about 40% of the collateral. Interest rates charged by pawnshops are much higher than those charged by banks, reaching as much as 24% per year. For that reason, the government has tried to regulate their activities, including tightening up their supervision, placing strict capital requirements, and limiting the interest rates charges.

---

[52]Elliott, D. J. and Y. Chao (2015). Reforming shadow banking in China. *Economics Studies at Brookings.* The Brookings Institution, May. Accessed at https://www.brookings.edu/wp-content/uploads/2016/06/Elliott-Shadow-Banking-2.pdf.

Supervision of pawn shops have moved from the Ministry of Commerce to the CSRC, with local governments being responsible for day-to-day supervision, as in the P2P market.[53]

Specialty leasing companies: These companies act as intermediaries in leasing transactions.

Credit guarantee agencies: Created in the 1990s, these institutions improve access to credit for SMEs that are not able to get loans from banks.

Rural Cooperatives:
Money shops: These are institutions run by brokers, who collect funds from savers and lend them out to individuals or businesses. They appeared in the 1980s in regions that featured strong economic activity. The government prohibited operations of these institutions in the mid-1980s, so they have since operated illegally.

14.2.1.2. Shadow banking: Activities/transactions/products

In China, and around the world, the shadow-banking sector features several products. They include:

Wealth management products (WMPs): These are investment products offered by banks or trust companies. They are viewed as an alternative to bank deposits and preferred by wealthy individuals because of the promised higher rate of return than that generated by traditional deposits. They have maturity of about three months and, because of the interest rate they pay and their destination, they are off balance sheet items. To generate higher rates, proceeds from WMPs are used as trust loans, real estate loans, loans to LGFVs, or invested in the stock or interbank bond market.

Entrusted loans: These are loans made from one company to another, with the bank or a finance company functioning as the custodian of the

---

[53] PMNTS (2019). China Looks to Crack Down on Pawn Shop Lenders. March 13. https://www.pymnts.com/news/regulation/2019/china-pawn-shop-loans-shadow-lending/.

funds. Banks receive compensation for their services, without bearing any of the risks associated with repayment of the loan. Depending on the nature of the relationship between the lender and the borrower, entrusted loans may be classified as affiliated or non-affiliated.[54] Affiliated loans are loans from a company, most notably an SOE, to a company within the same business group, such as a subsidiary, or to another company with which it has a business connection, such as a customer or a supplier. Non-affiliated loans are between companies with no apparent business relationship. Because of the relationship between lender and borrower, the larger amount of information, and the business motivation behind the loan, affiliated loans carry a lower interest rate than non-affiliated loans.

Bankers' acceptances (BAs): Bankers' acceptances are payments associated with a non-financial transaction, such as importing, and are guaranteed by the bank. They can be traded in the secondary market on a discount basis. They may also be sold back to the bank on a discount basis. If held to maturity, they become undiscounted BAs.

Interbank market activities: These are loans that large corporations make to banks through their captive finance subsidiaries.

14.2.2. *Motivation for shadow banking*

Shadow banking in China has existed because of many push and pull factors. Among the push factors are the following:

(a) Banks are restricted in the amount they can lend out to their clients. For example, they must adhere to a 9.4% required reserve ratio (as of October 2020). They have also been subjected (until 2015) to a 75% Loan–Deposit Ratio (LDR). Furthermore, most bank loans are given to the large SOEs. Smaller companies must find alternative funding sources.

---

[54]Franklin, A., Y. Qian, G. Tu, and F. Yu (2019). Entrusted Loans: A close look at China's shadow banking system. *Journal of Financial Economics*, 133, 18–41.

(b) Bank regulators are concerned about the risk component of the bank's loan portfolio. Lending to small companies may seem like a risky proposition, thereby discouraged.

(c) Investment opportunities are limited. Therefore, WMPs and other investment vehicles offered by shadow-banking entities are attractive investment outlets.

Shadow banking is also associated with pull factors:

(a) Following the Global Financial Crisis, the Chinese government implemented a CNY4 trillion Stimulus Program. The Program flooded the economy with extra funds, leading to a frantic lending activity across the economy.

(b) Also, after the global financial crisis, Chinese authorities placed limits on formal financing, thereby closing the door to most would-be borrowers.

(c) Shadow banking entities face lower (or zero) capital and liquidity requirements. Therefore, they can lend out a higher proportion of their funds to their clients.

(d) Also, shadow-banking entities do not have to adhere to any restrictions on the interest rates on their loans or investments.

(e) The general state of the economy obviously has a lot to do with decisions made by businesses. The unprecedented growth of the Chinese economy has provided plenty of opportunities and optimism to businesses. Borrowing from shadow banks, then, is commonplace even at rates higher than those charged by banks.

(d) The internet and overall advancements in technology made dissemination of information about available funding sources much easier; similarly, it is much easier for shadow-banking institutions to access potential clients.

14.2.3. *Shadow banking and the Chinese financial system*

In examining the position of shadow banking in China's financial system and the economy in general, we are confronted with a dilemma. How do we assess the sector's net contribution? Does the sector add value to the system, or does it merely make the system less stable? Does shadow banking assist or impede China's economic reforms? Is shadow banking inevitable? If so, what can the authorities do to enhance the sector's effectiveness?

We can first analyze some of the obvious benefits the sector generates for the financial system and the economy. To be sure, the existence of shadow banking serves various political and economic objectives on behalf of the Chinese authorities. Specifically, shadow banking has the following advantages:

- It offers the opportunity for more citizens to participate in economic transactions, thereby offering them the opportunity to improve their economic welfare. Shadow banking, then, makes the financial system more inclusive. It serves the financing needs of economic agents that the formal financial system, represented primarily by the banks, does not serve. From an economics point of view, this puts otherwise idle resources to work. From a political point of view, it increases the satisfaction of the citizens with the system.
- It creates an additional channel through which funds are transferred from lenders to borrowers, shadow banking promotes efficient allocation of resources.
- It allows investors to diversify their portfolio beyond the stock market and real estate. Although a portion of investments in the shadow-banking sector ends up in the bond market, stock market, or real estate through WMPs, investors may view buying WMPs as a safer way of entering these other markets. After all, the bank (implicitly) guarantees repayment.
- It contributes to the deepening of the financial system by adding institutions and instruments that enable investors to diversify their holdings.
- It increases competition in the financial system. For example, entry into the financial system is less complicated if conducted through a shadow-banking institution. Opening up a pawn shop is a lot easier than opening up another commercial bank! This brings more players into the system, from the supply of credit as well as the demand for credit sides.
- It sheds light on pricing and risk of transactions. Rates associated with commercial bank deposits and loans have been determined by the PBOC, as we discussed earlier in this chapter. On the other hand, shadow-banking transactions do not have the same restrictions. For example, non-affiliated entrusted loans should carry interest rates determined by the general market conditions and the specific risks of the transaction and the borrower.

Shadow banking activities also generate certain risks for China's economy, including:

- Inability of regulators to control these activities. How can the activities of a pawn shop be controlled? To some extent, these activities are inevitable and very difficult to supervise and regulate.
- Shadow Banking activities tend to be procyclical. Demand for funds obviously increases when the economy is doing well and decreases when the economy is in a downturn. This behavior could frustrate government policies aimed at stabilizing the economy.
- They increase the overall risk level of investments. Funds raised through these activities may be directed toward high-risk investments, such as real estate.
- Lack of transparency. The market does not have sufficient knowledge of the specific terms of each transaction. In addition, the authorities may not be aware of these activities, especially those that do not involve banks.
- Shadow banking transactions increase the country's debt levels. According to many observers, China's economy is already plagued by a "Wall of Debt."
- Maturity mismatch. Some of the proceeds from loans generated through shadow-banking entities are used to finance long-term projects (such as infrastructure). When short-term interest rates rise, the cost of financing these projects also rises, altering the validity of the initial economic assessment of the project.

14.2.4. *Characteristics of China's shadow-banking sector*

China's shadow banking exhibits the following characteristics[55]:

1. **Banks are at the center of shadow banking:** Although numerous institutions are involved in shadow-banking activities, banks are the initial providers of funds. The central role played by banks makes China's shadow-banking sector different from that of the United

---

[55]Ehlers, T., S. Kong and F. Zhu (2018). Mapping Shadow Banking in China: Structure and dynamics. BIS Working Papers, No. 701. Basle: Bank for International Settlements, February. https://www.bis.org/publ/work701.htm.

Table 9.15.   The Bank's Shadow.

	Assets	Liabilities
Balance Sheet	Reserves	Deposits
	Interbank loans	Central bank lending
	Loans to big firms	Bank capital
	Due from banks	
	Loans to other banks	
	Financial assets purchased under resale agreements	
Off Balance Sheet	Trust loans	Wealth management products (WMPs)
	Entrusted loans	

Source: Yang, L., S. van Wijnerbergen, X. Qi, and Y. Yi (2019). Chinese shadow banking, financial regulation and effectiveness of monetary policy. *Pacific-Basin Finance Journal, 57.* Accessed at https://www.sciencedirect.com/science/article/pii/S0927538X17301051.

States and other countries. This is illustrated in Table 9.15. The items in italics are shadow-banking instruments. They comprise what is termed "the bank's shadow." Banks issue WMPs and channel funds to shadow-banking entities, such as trust companies. They also serve as trustees for entrusted loans and issuers of Bankers' Acceptances.

2. Shadow Banking provides alternative savings instruments and credit to underserved sectors. Smaller companies that cannot get loans from the big banks turn to trust loans and entrusted loans. For the investors, putting their money into WMPs earns them a higher rate of return than bank deposits generate.

3. Shadow banking generates strong financial system interlinkages. At least 75% of the funds generated through WMPs must be invested in standardized debt instruments, such as bonds and Money Market Funds. This creates a linkage between banks and the bond market.

4. It is getting more sophisticated, but it is still not as complex as in other countries. Loan transactions have been kept at a simple, "vanilla", level.

5. Guarantees are everywhere!
   Some guarantees are explicit. For example, banks are behind Bankers' Acceptances. Also, Credit Guaranty Companies, although small, extend explicit guarantees, as do a small portion of WMPs. For most

of the WMPs, however, guarantees are implicit. That is, investors believe that they cannot lose their principal because the bank stands behind each transaction.

14.2.5. *How big is China's shadow-banking sector?*

China is not the only country with an active shadow-banking sector. By many accounts, the banking sector in China is smaller in relation to its GDP than that of other countries. Elliott finds that China's shadow-banking sector is 31% of GDP (in 2013). In the US, the shadow-banking sector is 150% of GDP; in the UK, 648% of its GDP; and 648% of the GDP in the Netherlands. Allen finds that, in 2018, the US had the largest shadow-banking sector in the world, USD15.2 trillion, amounting to 74.2% of its GDP and 29.9% of the shadow-banking assets of all 29 countries covered by the Financial Stability Board's sample. The Euro group's shadow-banking assets amounted to USD12.2 trillion, or 102% of the region's GDP, and 23.65 of the total for all countries. China's shadow-banking assets in 2018 were USD7.8 trillion, or 61% of its GDP and 15.4% of global shadow-banking assets.[56] China's shadow-banking assets had an impressive growth between 2009 and 2018, rising from 4% of GDP to 61% of GDP during this period. The EU's and UK's shadow-banking assets of GDP also rose during the period (77% to 102% and 35% to 52%, respectively), while in the US, the share of shadow-banking assets fell from 112% to 74% of the country's GDP from 2009 to 2018.[57] Indeed, China's shadow-banking sector has been characterized as the fastest growing such sector in the world, with its assets increasing by 34% in 2013, compared to the 7% worldwide average.[58]

---

[56]Allen, F. and X. Gu. (2020). Shadow banking in China compared to other countries. *The Manchester School.* 2020:00:1-13. https://onlinelibrary.wiley.com/doi/full/10.1111/manc.12331.

[57]Financial Stability Board (2019). Global Monitoring Report on Non-Bank Financial Intermediation 2018. February 4. https://www.fsb.org/2020/01/global-monitoring-report-on-non-bank-financial-intermediation-2019/.

[58]Elliott, D., A. Kroeber, and Y. Qiao (2015). Shadow banking in China: A primer. *Economic Studies at Brookings.* March, Washington, DC: Brookings Institution. https://www.brookings.edu/wp-content/uploads/2016/06/shadow_banking_china_elliott_kroeber_yu.pdf.

Measuring the level and growth of shadow banking in China and other countries is an important step toward understanding its impact and formulating the appropriate regulatory measures. The task of measuring shadow banking, however, is complicated because of the general nature of these activities, including the lack of transparency surrounding them. As a result, there has been a great deal of discrepancy among the various shadow-banking estimates. For example, Elliott, Kroeber, and Qiao (2015) list various estimates of the size of China's shadow-banking sector in 2013; these estimates vary from a low of CNY4.5 trillion (8% of the country's 2013 GDP), submitted by Standard Chartered, to a high of CNY46 trillion (81.2% of the 2013 GDP), submitted by JP Morgan. One of the reasons for this discrepancy in estimates lies in the types of institutions whose assets are included in the shadow banking definition.

In addition to differences in size and pace of growth, China's shadow-banking system differs from that of the US and other countries in terms of its characteristics.[59] The US system is primarily market-based, with money market funds, fixed income funds, and other types of funds being the primary collective investment components. In China, on the other hand, shadow banking evolves around banks. However, China's shadow-banking system is changing. New instruments, such as WMPs, are offered to the investing public. On the other hand, instruments like P2P products are retrieved when abuses are discovered.

14.2.6. *When shadow-banking risks surface: The Wenzhou and Sichuan trust cases*

The Global Financial Crisis did not do as much damage to China as it did to the Western world, but it still slowed the economy down enough to propel Beijing to implement a CNY4 trillion stimulus program. The program led to increase in spending, speculative investment, property price increases, and general optimism about the future among the citizenries. Nowhere did this optimism prevail as much as in Wenzhou, considered by many to be the most entrepreneurial city in the country. Purchases of real estate and other investments were made through loans from informal, and even illegal, sources. There were stories of friends lending hundreds of

---

[59]Allen, F. and X. Gu. (2020). Shadow banking in China compared to other countries. *The Manchester School*, p. 11.

thousands of dollars to friends, and of loan sharks lending at exorbitant interest rates. The euphoria did not last long, however. As exports declined and property prices collapsed, many found themselves unable to repay their debts. Many left town, and some jumped from their office windows, while others were taken to court. In the first half of 2012, Wenzhou city courts processed 10,269 economic disputes, twice as many as in 2011. Most of these disputes were about loan defaults.[60]

A more recent example of troubles with the shadow banking comes from Chengdu, Sichuan Province. In June 2020, hundreds of investors protested Sichuan Trust's announcement that it could not pay principal and interest on estimated CNY13 billion to CNY25 billion of its trust products. Sichuan Trust is a Trust of Trusts, a concept like the Fund of Funds; that is, it buys products of other trust companies. In turn, these companies have given out loans to private companies and LGFVs and invested in bonds, stocks, and other instruments. As Sichuan Trust was promising a high rate of return to its own investors, it needed to acquire risky assets. When these assets did not turn out profitable, Sichuan Trust had to pay off its current investors by raising new funds, a classic Ponzi scheme. At some point, however, the company could not raise enough funds to pay its investors, as regulators started paying more attention to Sichuan Trust, taking control of the company's accounts. At that point, the company had to inform its investors of the situation, bringing about investor concerns. The company also started taking steps to generate funds to repay investors by considering sale of its building, dissolving some of its investment positions, and even identifying new strategic investors. It does not seem, however, possible to compensate all investors for their losses. In addition to showing how risky these trust products can be, the Sichuan Trust case also revealed the lack of transparency that surrounds the activities of some of these shadow-banking institutions. Still, investors flock to them because of the promise of high returns and because they believe that these products carry the implicit guarantee of the backing of the local government.

Sichuan Trust is by no means an exception to the precarious financial position of shadow banks. On many occasions, however, the situation is handled behind the scenes among regulators, the local authorities, the companies, and the principal investors. This could not be done in the

---

[60] *Financial Times* (2012). Wenzhou: A cautionary tale of reckless loans. December 2. https://www.ft.com/content/c0fb2c0e-3b08-11e2-b111-00144feabdc0.

case of Anxin Trust in June 2019, since the company was listed on the Shanghai Stock Exchange. The company showed a CNY50 billion deficit and had to publicly default. According to Caixin, by March 2020, China's 68 Trust companies had Assets Under Management (AUM) of about CNY20 trillion with risky assets amounting to CNY643 billion. This amount is double the amount of risky assets in March 2019 and 11.5% higher than the last quarter of 2019.[61] Anxin's case and the riskier environment created in conjunction with COVID-19 have put pressure on the regulatory authorities to consider further monitoring of the activities of trust companies and place limits on interest rates charged by the shadow-banking sector.

14.2.7. *The downfall of the P2P sector*

Another troubling example of the problems faced by shadow banking comes from the P2P lending sector. The sector flourished following the 2010 credit tightening policies implemented by the PBOC, which were preceded by the stimulus plan. P2P platforms match a borrower with a suitable investor(s), who lends at an agreed upon interest rate for a specific period. The borrower also puts up a collateral. Funds raised may also be invested in commercial paper or other financial market instruments. The concept originated in the US a few years prior to its arrival in China, with companies such as Lending Club leading the way. The presumed benefits of P2P transactions lie in the efficiencies over traditional financing generated using technology and decrease in transactions, overhead, and other costs and the speed associated with transactions. Investors were attracted to these platforms by the higher interest rates, which could reach 20%, while believing that risk was minimized due to the existence of implicit guarantees. The sector grew quickly. The number of P2P platforms grew quickly: for 800 (2013) to 1000 (2014) to over 2,500 (2015). The outstanding loan balance mushroomed from CNY100 billion (2014) to CNY1.3 billion (June 2018). By comparison, the reported loan balance in the US was less than USD150 billion.[62] It seemed like an excellent way

---

[61] Wu, H., L. Hong, and H. Wei. (2020). Anxin Trust's $7bm investment black hole. *Caixin*, July 8. https://asia.nikkei.com/Spotlight/Caixin/Anxin-Trust-s-7bn-investment-black-hole.

[62] McKinsey & Company (2020). What today's shake-out in China's peer-to-peer lending market means for fintech. mckinsey.com/cn/our-insights/perspectives-on-china-blog/what-todays-shakeout-in-chinas-peer-to-peer-lending-market-means-for-fintech.

of putting the huge amount of accumulated Chinese citizens' savings to work.

However, it did not take long for the bubble to burst. Some of the P2P platforms proved to be Ponzi schemes. Others did a poor job assessing borrower risk and could not avoid rising costs and defaults. Regulators had to step in to weed out the bad players. In 2016, regulators started imposing limits on lending to single individuals and corporations (CNY1 million and CNY5 million, respectively) and pressured P2P platforms to provide more information. Platforms started exiting the market, in some cases the owners turning themselves to the authorities or leaving town and leaving behind thousands of investors, some of whom had lost tens of thousands of dollars and even took their own lives because they were ashamed of the naiveté they had shown by falling for the deceitful practices of some of the platforms. The industry itself has been shrinking, with about 300–400 firms left by 2019 and only 50–100 expected to survive the new regulatory regime and the extended licensing process. On the other hand, firms such as Lufax and Yirendai are flourishing and reinventing themselves in related fields, such as wealth management services.

14.2.8. *Total social financing*

In 2010, the PBOC started publishing its broadest measure of credit and liquidity, Total Social Financing. Total Social Financing (TSF) includes forms of financing that are not within the traditional banking system, such as funds raised though IPOS or bond issuances. Therefore, we can observe the behavior of shadow banking-related transactions through the behavior of TSF. TSF is also referred to as "Aggregate Financing to the Real Economy" (AFRE) since it purports to measure the total amount of financing provided to the private sector of the real economy by the domestic financial system. It does not include funds injected into the system from overseas or from China's government. The PBOC publishes AFRE as a flow measure and a stock measure.

AFRE includes the following funding sources: (1) RMB loans; (2) Foreign Currency Loans; (3) Entrusted Loans; (4) Trust Loans; (5) Undiscounted Bankers' Acceptances; (6) Corporate Bonds; (7) Non-financial corporate domestic equity financing; (8) Insurance company repayments; (9) Investment Property; and (10) Financing via other financial instruments. These 10 sources can be divided into three overlapping categories[63]:

The first category comprises sources 1–7 above, denotes the funding support 5, 6, and 7 above, and denotes financing sources employed by agents in the real economy and processed through financial institutions. The second category includes sources 5–7 above, and denotes financing sources employed by agents in the real economy and processed through financial institutions. The third category includes other sources of financing, such as micro-loans, loans from finance companies, and industry fund investments; these financing sources are under "RMB Loans."

Table 9.16 includes the Total Social Financing (AFRE) components for 2015–2020. We can focus on Entrusted Loans, Trust Loans, and Undiscounted BAs. Entrusted Loans showed a large increase following the 2015 stock market crash, but started declining after 2017 and into 2018, as the economy started cooling off. Similar behavior is shown by Trust Loans, although the largest relative increase appears after 2016. Undiscounted BAs, however, markedly decreased after 2015, and stayed around the 2016 level after a slight increase in 2017. RMB loans (the largest component of AFRE), Bonds, Equity, and the total amount of category 1 of funding support showed a steady increase throughout the period.

14.2.9. *A final word on shadow banking*

Our discussion leads us to understand the reasons for the existence and growth of shadow banking. These reasons have included the increase in demand for financing brought about by government policies, such as the post-global financing crisis stimulus, and general economic conditions, improvements, and dissemination of the use of technology, as well as differences among regulatory intensities applied to various sectors. This last factor has been often referred to as "regulatory arbitrage."

Financial regulation has several objectives. In setting to accomplish these objectives, regulators must consider the effect of their actions on the entire system. The same goes for regulation of the shadow-banking sector.

---

[63] China Banking News (2020). Total social financing. http://www.chinabankingnews.com/tag/total-social-financing/.

Table 9.16. Aggregate Financing to the Real Economy, 2015–2019–Stock (trillions of CNY).

Item	2015	2016	2017	2018	2019	2020
AFRE total (stock) of which:	134.7	151.51	171.14	197.27	246.68	280.07
RMB loans	90.48	102.75	116.65	131.81	148.58	168.26
Foreign currency denominated loans	3.33	2.63	2.48	2.45	2.19	2.35
Entrusted loans	10.35	12.52	13.88	12.81	11.73	11.13
Trust loans	5.41	5.93	8.06	8.08	7.68	7.03
Undiscounted bankers' acceptances	6.32	3.8	4.37	3.76	3.28	3.9
Net financing of corporate bonds	13.47	17.31	18.17	19.45	22.71	27.39
Government bonds	N/A	N/A	N/A	7.18	36.99	44.46
Equity financing on the domestic stock market bv non-financial enterprises	4.3	5.49	6.37	6.96	7.24	7.97
Assets-backed secs	N/A	N/A	N/A	N/A	1.46	1.63
Loans written off	N/A	N/A	N/A	N/A	3.66	4.83

Source: PBOC website, various issues. Note: Total does not add to 100% due to missing items from the table (Government Bonds, Asset Backed Securities, and Loans Written Off.

A stringent regulatory environment could keep millions of Chinese businesses and citizens out of the financial system. On the other hand, the lack of adequate safeguards can lead to system abuses and loss of faith in the system. The Chinese authorities have given the sector a certain regulatory privilege and allowed it to function with little interference. However, when abuses surfaced, regulators intervened to stabilize sector performance.

In weighing the benefits and risks of shadow banking, we must ask: Should the authorities impose stricter regulation on shadow-banking institutions and transactions? Or should they regard it as inevitable and just deal with its consequences? Should the authorities be proactive or reactive to the development of the sector?

As we noted in this section, the sector performs valuable functions, including serving the underserved and providing an additional investment outlet. Of course, the regulatory agencies have stepped up following certain obvious missteps taken by various components of the sector. We can conclude that the sector is being tolerated if it does not get out of control, as it happened with the developments in the P2P market. We also observed that exercise of regulatory control in the November postponement of Ant's IPO in November 2020 and the drafting of new rules to regulate internet financing. What is more difficult to address, however, is the challenge presented by the implicit guarantees in the system. Shadow banking and traditional banking are very much interconnected through the "bank's shadow." If this connection exists, then, implicit guarantees will not go away. The regulatory task is expected to become more difficult as China's financial institutions learn from the West and start producing more sophisticated financial products.

14.3. *Informal finance*

As we have realized by now, the discussion on shadow banking can be very confusing and full of colorful terminology. To make things even more confusing, we will add another term: informal finance. Informal finance refers to financial activities of informal enterprises comprising the country's informal sector. An informal enterprise may be defined "as a small private enterprise that is either: (i) not constituted as a separate legal entity independent of its owner; (ii) not registered with the tax authorities and/or (iii) no complete formal accounts are kept that financially separate the enterprise from the other activities of its owner/s."[64] Informal finance entities and activities, then, may be viewed as a component of shadow banking. On the other hand, not all shadow-banking activities fall within the realm of informal finance.

Informal finance institutions may be legal, quasi-legal, or illegal. In addition to family and friends, these informal institutions include:

- Rotating credit associations: these are created by a small group of people pooling their funds and disbursing them in a rotating manner. When they become Ponzi schemes, of course, they are illegal.
- Rural Financial Organizations: these are vehicles formed to manage funds contributed by rural citizens.

---

[64] Williams, C. C., K. Adom, and I. A. Horodnic (2020). Determinants of the level of informalization of enterprises: Some evidence from Accra, Ghana. *Journal of Developmental Entrepreneurship*. March.

- Money houses: owners may lend their own funds or borrow money at low rates and lend at higher rates.

To this list, we may include loan sharks and other similar institutions. These institutions straddle the line between the right and the wrong side of the law. Since many informal finance transactions are only known to the participating parties, the size of the informal sector is not known; it is estimated to be between 20% and 30% of all financial transactions.

14.4. *Mutual funds and asset management firms*

As China's wealth increases, the demand for funds management services has also been increasing. The asset management sector is still in its nascent stage but growing fast. In addition to Chinese firm activity in the industry, both domestically and globally, several foreign-owned funds have entered the Chinese market in anticipation of future developments.

The industry was established in 1998 and comprised six Asset Management Companies.[65] All of them were closed fund entities with CNY10.4 billion Assets Under Management (AUM).[66] Since then, the industry has been developing horizontally, by diversifying its offerings, as well as vertically, by increasing in size. By September 2020, the industry had grown to CNY100 trillion AUM. The Mutual Fund industry has developed around a series of regulatory changes put in by the Chinese government and regulatory agencies. The most basic regulation is the June 2004 Securities Investment Fund Law. The Law established the rules pertaining to the operations of these funds, including the required minimum registered capital (CNY100 million), the nature of the major shareholder, the tasks of the custodian, governance of the fund, asset allocation, and financing.

The Asset Management sector has been on the forefront of China's financial liberalization. Since 1999, participation in Chinese funds has been an investment option available to foreign insurance companies. Foreign participation in Chinese funds has also been in the form of joint

---

[65] Earlier in this chapter, we referred to the companies assigned to deal with the banks' NPL as Asset Management Companies (AMCs). In this section, we use the terms Asset Management Companies and Fund Management Companies interchangeably.

[66] KPMG International (2018). Celebrating 20 years of asset management in China. https://assets.kpmg/content/dam/kpmg/xx/pdf/2018/06/celebrating-20-years-of-am-in-china.pdf.

ventures and foreign company acquisitions of shares of domestic companies. Foreign companies have expanded their participation since the country's accession into the World Trade Organization. They could increase their ownership of Chinese fund management firms to 49% in 2005 from the previous 33%. Chinese regulators have continued to open up the sector, and foreign firms have been responding. In 2016, JPMorgan was granted a 20-year license to operate a fully owned asset management firm in Shanghai's free-trade zone. Other global asset managers (including Bridgewater, BNY Mellon, UBS, VanEck, Fidelity, and Neuberger Berger) have also received or applied for similar permits. Other international asset managers have chosen alternative modes of entry into the Chinese market. Vanguard, for example, formed a partnership with Ant Financial in June 2019. An important step toward the opening of the sector took place in April 2020, with the Chinese authorities allowing foreign entities to gain full ownership of asset management companies. Table 9.17 shows the major developments that have taken place in the industry since its establishment in 1998.

The Fund Management industry includes public and private funds, with the public component being the larger of the two. Mutual funds are the dominant destination of public fund management. Table 9.18 shows the 10 largest public fund management companies. In terms of the asset composition of the mutual fund sector, Money market funds occupy the largest portion of the sector (54.1% of the USD1,890.62 total), followed by bond funds (21%), Balanced/Mixed (14.4%), Equity (9.9%), and Other (0.70%).[67] Securities companies, pension providers, futures companies, and others manage private funds.

China's pension framework is especially interesting, as it comprises three pillars.[68] The first pillar is the largest, as it comprises the National Social Security Fund and the state managed pay-as-you-go pensions; it covers three quarters of China's population. The second pillar covers about 5% of China's population, and includes annuities offered by corporations and occupational groups. The third, and newest, pillar is commercial pension insurance.

Undoubtedly, the industry will continue to grow and play an even more important role not only within the Chinese market, but, eventually, the global market.

---

[67]Economist Intelligence Unit (2020). Industry Report: Financial Services, 4th Quarter. www.eiu.com/financialservices.

[68]*Ibid.*

Table 9.17.   Major developments in Fund Management Industry since 1998.

Year	Highlight
1998	The first 10 Fund Management Companies established
2001	The first open-ended fund was issued
2002	The National Council for Social Security Fund (NCSSF) awarded mandates to external managers for the first time
	OFII (Qualified Foreign Institutional Investors allowed to invest in China's stock market
2003	First group of Sino- foreign joint venture fund managers
2004	The Securities Investment Fund Law was enacted; first ETF introduced
2005	First group of banking FMCs enter the market
2007	QDII (Qualified Domestic Institutional Investors) allowed to invest overseas
2008	First Chinese managers' offshore subsidiary established
2012	Asset Management Association of China (AMAC) established
2013	Yuebao, China's first online money market fund launched
2017	CSRC announces guidance pension target funds, paving way for first pension target fund
2018	CSRC allows qualified foreign financial firms to raise their minority stake to 51%
2019	CSRC announces plans to open markets for foreign companies in 2020 (Futures companies, Mutual fund management companies, and securities companies)
2020	Foreign Mutual Fund management companies allowed to have full ownership in the sector

Source: KPMG International (2018). Celebrating 20 years of asset management in China. KPMG. https://assets.kpmg/content/dam/kpmg/xx/pdf/2018/06/celebrating-20-years-of-am-in-china.pdf.

14.5. *Private equity in China*

The concept and practice of private equity were not familiar to the Chinese landscape until the mid-2000s. Foreign private equity firms, such as Carlyle, operated in the country without much fanfare. In 2007, however, things changed as China's wealth funds entered the industry.

Private Equity refers to investing in companies that are not traded publicly. Capital to undertake the investment is raised by setting up a "Fund." The fund is a Special Purpose Vehicle run by the General Partners (GPs); the investors are primarily institutional investors, sovereigns, or

Table 9.18.   Top 10 public fund management companies (CNY bn; end-2019).

Manager	AUM
E Fund Management	316.9
Bosera Asset Management	282.9
China Asset Management	261.1
China Southern Capital Management	239.2
Fortune Fund Management	218.9
Bank of China Fund Management	216.6
GF Fund Management	215.6
Harvest Fund Management	214.3
China Merchants Wealth Asset Management	194.6
Fullgoal Fund Management	174.5

Source: Economist Intelligence Unit (2020). Industry Report: Financial Services, 4th Quarter. www.eiu.com/financialservices.

high net-worth individuals. Since the Fund's ultimate objective does not usually include maintaining long-term ownership of the target, PE firms seek an operating environment that offers appropriate exit opportunities.

China's PE industry developed slowly after the reforms. International PR firms started appearing in China in the 1980s. The first firms entering the market, such as Jardine Fleming and American International Group, were organizations with long histories in China and very familiar with China's economic promise. They formed vehicles termed China Direct Investment Funds (CDIFs), which were listed on various foreign Stock Exchanges, primarily London. In the early days of reform, the most viable investments were in the Township/Village Enterprise (TVEs) sector. CDIFs were limited to minority ownership of their targets and provided mezzanine financing. They were also limited with respect to their exit strategy to reselling their equity to the target firm or finding another investor.[69] As China's market opened to the rest of the world, more Western PE firms entered, primarily targeting large SOEs. In 2004, Newbridge Capital

---

[69]Bruton, G. D., M. Dattani, M. Fung, C. Chow, and D. Ahlstrom (1999). Private equity in China: Differences and similarities with the Western model. *The Journal of Private Equity*. Winter 1999, 2(2), 7–13.

acquired 18.89% of Shenzhen Development Bank; in 2005, Carlyle attempted to make a deal to buy 85% of Xugong Group Construction Machinery. An overseas IPO served as the main exit mechanism.[70] The development of the Chinese Stock Markets in the 21st century, and especially the establishment of ChiNext, along with the newly developed class of Chinese HNWIs, enabled the growth of Chinese PE firms.

China currently has two types of Funds: Onshore and Offshore. Onshore Funds can be foreign invested RMB Funds or Domestic RMB Funds. Offshore Funds are foreign invested non-RMB Funds.[71] Onshore Funds invest by forming a PRC-based joint stock company, with the exit strategy being to list the target on a Chinese Stock Exchange. Offshore Funds form an SPV that invests in the target company's offshore holding company. The exit strategy here is the listing of the target on an overseas Stock Exchange.

As the Chinese economy keeps growing, its stature in the world economy improving, and investment opportunities becoming more abundant, the PE market will continue to be attractive. Promise of high return, however, comes with high risk. Risk arises in every stage of the PE process even in developed economies. In transition economies, in which institutions have not yet matured, they are greater. In China, PE firms, especially foreign ones, may face one or more of the following risks when entering China (Corporate Finance Institute: https://corporatefinance institute.com/resources/careers/jobs/private-equity-in-china/):

1. Finding opportunities at the right price. Even in an economy as large as China's, finding appropriate investment opportunities is a case of "too many firms chasing too few takeover opportunities," leading to overvaluation of targets.
2. Conducting satisfactory due diligence. Ample and accurate information is not easy to come by in China. Interpreting firm financial data, finding out who really owns and governs the firm, and assessing the firm's prospects can be a time-consuming, expensive, and imperfect process.

---

[70]Zhen, Y. (2013). China's Private Equity Market. In *China's Capital Markets*. Chandos Asian Studies Series. Amsterdam, The Netherlands: Elsevier B.V. ScienceDirect, 103–140. Accessed at https://www.sciencedirect.com/science/article/pii/B9781843346975500049.

[71]Ping, Y. K. (2012). *Private Equity in China: Challenges and Opportunities*. Singapore: John Wiley & Sons.

3. Country risks. With its economy still in transition, China exposes foreign firms to various risks, including regulatory and legal. To be sure, China's regulation of foreign direct investment has been relaxed following the new Foreign Investment Law. Nevertheless, the cloud of uncertainty over future restrictive actions has not been lifted. Foreign PE firms must also be cognizant of the attitude of their Chinese partners toward their contractual obligations and the willingness of Chinese courts to enforce contracts.

4. Corporate Governance risks. Foreign PE partners serving on Boards of Chinese firms encounter Board members with different management styles and goals.

5. Foreign exchange exposure. The Chinese currency is now included in the IMF's currency basket comprising the value of Special Drawing Rights, thereby making strides toward it becoming an international currency. However, the value of the RMB has still been impacted by the government. The risk of unfavorable exchange rate changes, then, is still present.

6. Exit risk. Western PE companies with minority stakes in Chinese companies may have different investment time horizons than the majority owners. Foreign companies, then, may not be able to exit on their preferred date.

7. International relations risk.

8. Valuation risks. PE firms must ultimately assign a value to the target firm. Incorrect valuations lead to incorrect investment decisions. The presence of all, or even some, of the risks noted above, however, tend to complicate the acquitting firm's process of arriving at an accurate valuation of the target.

Despite all the risks, China remains an attractive destination for foreign PE firms. The Pandemic caused a significant slowdown in the PE market. As the Chinese economy rebounded and continued to grow, its PE market will continue to be attractive.

14.6. *Rural finance*

Development of rural China is one of the major indicators of China's reform success and balanced economic development. The quality of the rural regions' financial environment is, in turn, an integral building block of their development. China's government has provided extensive support to rural regions through the years. As is the case in other countries, rural regions and their needs tend to be diverse. However, they all share similar challenges when it comes to generating a viable economic system and similar types of financial institutions.

Rural regions are served by institutions of varying type and size. They include the following:

1. The Agricultural Bank of China (ABC)
    As we have already discussed, ABC was established in 1979. As a state-owned bank, its primary mission was to support the country's agricultural sector. Although ABC has also turned to commercial activities in urban areas to generate sufficient revenue, it has also at times (as in 2007) been directed by the government to maintain or increase its rural presence.
2. The Agricultural Development Bank of China (ADBC). Established with the other two Policy Banks in 1994, ADBC is the only agricultural policy bank under the direction of the State Council. The bank's mission is to raise funds in the market and "act as a strategic pillar of the country in supporting the development of agriculture, rural areas, and farmers." (adbc.com.cn). The ADBC is one of the largest bond issuers in China; for example, in May 2019 the ADBC issued an RMB denominated bond that trades on the Frankfurt Stock Exchange. Proceeds from the bond issues are used to promote the ADBC's mission, especially during periods of economic downturn. In September 2020, the ADBC and MYBank entered into the first agreement between a policy bank and a digital bank in China. The two banks will cooperate in many areas, including rural finance. The agreement, then, not only expands the rural financing base, but also takes a big step toward strengthening the country's inclusive finance efforts.[72]
3. The Postal Savings Bank of China. The country's postal savings system was established in 1986 in conjunction with the China Postal

---

[72]CBNEditor (2020). Chinese Policy Bank ADBC Enters Cooperative Agreement with Alibaba's Online Lender MYBank. *China Banking News*. September 17. https://www. chinabankingnews.com/2020/09/17/chinese-policy-bank-adbc-enters-cooperative-agreement-with-alibabas-online-lender-mybank/.

Savings and Remittance Bureau, a part of the State Post Bureau.[73] As the postal system was getting larger, the need arose to separate the System's communications and postal operations. The CBRC, then, established the Postal Savings Bank of China (PSBC) in 2003. PSBC started operating in 2007. PSBC has been an integral member of the rural finance infrastructure. Among its various activities, the bank has implemented pilot programs to provide more banking services to rural residents and offered micro-loans, farm credit loans, and farmer household loans.

4. Small and Medium-sized Rural Financial Institutions. In addition to ABC, ADBC, and PSBC, rural areas are served by thousands of smaller institutions.[74] These include Rural Credit Cooperative (RCC) Institutions (Rural Credit Cooperatives, Rural Commercial Banks, and Rural Cooperative Banks) and the more recent Rural Financial Institutions (Village and Township Banks, Lending Companies, and Rural Mutual Credit Cooperatives). The concept of an RCC surfaced in the 1950s, as these institutions were formed to provide financial services to cooperative members. These institutions were an integral contributor to the development of TVEs after reforms. In the two decades following the beginning of reforms, RCCs were under the administrative structure of the ABC. As non-performing loans began mounting, however, control over RCCs went under the PBOC.

Control over RCCs was further transferred to provincial authorities in 2003, with the CBRC having supervisory responsibility. However, RCCs continued to suffer from loan delinquency, with their NPL ratio reaching 37% in 2002. Injection of funds by the PBOC lowered this ratio to 9.3% by 2007. The system was further restructured by transforming some of the RCCs into Rural Commercial Banks (with joint stock ownership) and Rural Cooperative Banks (with hybrid ownership, while other RCCs were merged to form Rural Credit Unions.

Further changes to the rural finance system started taking place in 2006, when the CBRC changed rural banking market-entry requirements to allow new institutions to come in. Some of the changes involved

---

[73] Marks, C. (2010). Rural Banking in China. Federal Reserve Bank of San Francisco, Country Analysis Unit. May. https://core.ac.uk/download/pdf/6363024.pdf.

[74] *Ibid.*

lowering capital requirements and providing preferential tax treatment. The new institutions were village and township banks, lending companies, and rural mutual credit cooperatives. In addition to domestic firms, the CBRC promoted rural banking to foreign firms as well.

14.6.1. *Challenges facing rural banking institutions*

Rural banks tend to reflect the character of rural China. Most rural banks are geographically concentrated, operating at the county level.[75] Their importance to the economies which they serve grew even more as the bigger banks retreated from rural areas in the 1990s in pursuit of higher and more stable returns in urban environments. The challenges of rural economic development, then, became challenges for rural banks. Deposits in these banks, for example, are tied to the rural business cycle, which can be more volatile than the business cycle experienced by the rest of the economy. The fragility of the rural economy creates another big problem for rural banks: NPLs.

Indeed, rural commercial banks have been associated with a much higher NPL ratio than the big commercial banks or even mid-size city banks. On November 4, 2019, the *Wall Street Journal* reported that the NPL ratio of rural banks stood slightly below 4% in mid-2019, surpassing the 1.8% of commercial banks as a whole and even the 2.3% of small and medium-sized commercial banks.[76] Rural banks were hit hard by the COVID slowdown and the US–China Trade War, as industries in their regions suffered drastic cutbacks in their operations and borrowers were unable to make loan repayments. For example, in 2019, 29 rural banks applied to the CSRC to be allowed to sell shares to replenish their capital base. Of these 29, 10 banks had an NPL ratio of more than 5%. One of these banks, Jiangxi Yushan Rural Commercial Bank, had an NPL ratio of 22.98%![77]

---

[75] S&P Global (2020). The Role of Rural Banks in China's County Economy. *China Ratings*. May 24. https://www.spgchinaratings.cn/insights/articles/commentary_rural-banks_24mar2020_en.pdf.

[76] Taplin, N. (2019). China's county banks sing the blues. *Wall Street Journal*. November 4. https://headtopics.com/us/china-s-country-banks-sing-the-blues-9329506.

[77] Lee, A. (2019). China's rural banks struggling under pressure of overdue loans as slow growth, trade war take their toll. *South China Morning Post*. December 16. https://www.

Rural banks are affected in another way by economic downturns. As these lead to drops in regional incomes and bank deposits, supply of credit to rural banks is cut off. The supply of credit to rural banks may also be affected by the strength of their competition. Rural banks do not directly compete for funds with other financial institutions. However, they do have to consider competition from fintech. As digital banking makes headway into rural China, competition from these banks will increase.

Rural banking institutions are the backbone of rural economies. They provide a valuable social function. In addition, they are in aggregate a significant part of the Chinese financial system, as they account for 20–25% of the banking sector's total assets. The challenges they face are partly due to poor management, but also to a large degree due to their immediate economic environments. Recognizing their importance, the Chinese government has in the past made efforts to direct more funds toward rural financial institutions. The challenge, however, is long term. The health of these institutions lies in the health of their economic environment. When China succeeds in its rural revitalization strategy, rural banks will reap the benefits of this success.

15. Financial Center

Financial center is formed with the development of economic center, and it is also the highest form of economic center. When the development of commodity production and commodity circulation is formed with a certain city as the center, on the one hand, a large amount of monetary funds need to be found in the field of production and circulation; on the other hand, the field of production and circulation needs to continuously supplement a large amount of monetary funds, to carry out operations. Therefore, only after a city has very strong economic strength and has become the economic center of a certain region can it generate, accumulate, and use huge amounts of funds, and then have a foundation for the formation of a financial center.

However, the complexity and diversity of financial activities and the tremendous effect of financial power on economic development make it impossible for financial centers to be as universal as commercial centers

---

scmp.com/economy/china-economy/article/3042252/chinas-rural-banks-struggling-under-pressure-overdue-loans.

and trade centers. That is, not every economic center has the function of a financial center. Only a few economic centers will develop into financial centers. In this sense, the financial center is the highest form of economic center. The following is the "29th Global Financial Center Index" list jointly released by the China (Shenzhen) Comprehensive Development Research Institute and the British think tank Z/Yen Group: Four of them are Chinese cities, Shanghai, Hong Kong, Beijing, and Shenzhen. Enter the TOP10 camp, see Table 9.19. In 2020, the top 10 cities in the value added of the financial industry are: Beijing, Shanghai, Shenzhen, Guangzhou, Chongqing, Chengdu, Tianjin, Hangzhou, Nanjing, and Suzhou. The value added of the financial industry in Beijing and Shanghai both exceeded 700 billion yuan (718.8 and 716.6 billion yuan, respectively), which belonged to the first echelon, and accounted for the highest proportion of GDP in the country, both exceeding 18%. Shenzhen's financial industry has a value added of more than 400 billion yuan, belonging to the second echelon, accounting for 15.1% of GDP. Guangzhou, Chongqing, Chengdu, Tianjin, and Hangzhou belong to the third echelon. The value added of the financial industry is around 200 billion yuan. The financial industry accounts for the highest proportion of

Table 9.19.   2020 Global Financial Center Index Ranking.

Financial	GFCI 28		GFCI 27		Change from
Center	Rank	Score	Rank	Score	Last period
New York	1	770	1	7690	0
London	2	766	2	742	0
Shanghai	3	748	4	740	1
Tokyo	4	747	3	741	−1
HK, China	5	743	6	737	1
Singapore	6	742	5	738	−1
Bejing	7	741	7	7340	0
San Francisco	8	738	8	7320	0
Shenzhen	9	732	11	722	2
Zurich	10	724	14	719	4

Source: China (Shenzhen) Comprehensive Development Research Institute and the British think tank Z/Yen Group

GDP in Tianjin, reaching 14.6%. In terms of the growth rate of the financial industry, Shenzhen and Hangzhou have the fastest growth rates, at about 10%; followed by Shanghai and Guangzhou, both with growth rates above 8%.

To measure the level of development of a city, there is a data that has been widely used in recent years, that is, the total amount of funds (the balance of deposits in domestic and foreign currencies of financial institutions). This data intuitively reflects a city's ability to absorb funds. This core indicator of development is also a manifestation of the city's comprehensive strength and development potential. So, what is included in the total amount of absorbed funds (the balance of domestic and foreign currency deposits in financial institutions)? There are two types of deposits: RMB deposits + foreign currency deposits; among them, RMB deposits include: (1) household deposits + (2) non-financial corporate deposits + (3) government agency deposits + (4) fiscal deposits + (5) financial corporate deposits (non-Banking institution) deposits. At the end of 2020, there are 11 cities that have attracted more than 3 trillion yuan in funds (Hong Kong, Macao, and Taiwan are not counted). There are 3 cities that have attracted more than 10 trillion yuan of funds, namely Beijing, Shanghai, and Shenzhen, which form the first echelon. Guangzhou and Hangzhou both exceed RMB5 trillion, which can be regarded as the second echelon. Chengdu, Chongqing, and Nanjing are all over 4 trillion yuan, which can be regarded as the third echelon. Suzhou, Tianjin, and Wuhan all exceed 3 trillion yuan, which can be regarded as the fourth echelon. The city with the highest total capital growth rate was: Shenzhen, which grew by 21.4%,

16. Concluding Comments

China's financial institutions have played a critical role in China's transition. Reforms of the financial sector have lagged reforms of the rest of the economy but have proceeded steadily since their commencement.

The banking sector has remained the core of China's financial system. China's banks have been dominating the global industry in terms of size. However, China's banks face several challenges, as we indicated earlier in this chapter. Furthermore, their relationship with other financial institutions magnifies their importance to the country's reform efforts. Banks have contributed to the economy's transition by funding, and absorbing the losses of, the large SOEs.

The high-quality development of China's banking sector in the 14th FYP period is faced with numerous challenges: the downward trend of economic development will lead to the slowdown in the growth rate of the banking sector's assets volume; market-based interest rate reform will squeeze the profits of the banking sector; the fast fintech development will exert a direct impact on small- and medium-sized banks induced by financial disintermediation; and the double-way opening-up will give rise to much more fierce competitions in the banking sector. As a result, financial risks will haunt the country in the years to come. To push ahead with the high-quality development of the banking sector in the 14th FYP period, work needs to be done in the following aspects. One, special attention needs to be paid to major fields and weak links so as to promote the quality and effectiveness of the banking sector in serving the development of the real economy; Two, efforts need to focus on the improvement of institutional layout and major business items so as to promote the structural optimization of the banking system; Three, we need to enhance the green financial growth by meeting the requirements of green development; Four, continuous efforts are needed to push ahead with data-based transformation; Five, corporate governance and motivation and restriction mechanism need to be fleshed out; Six, a sustainable capital supplement mechanism needs to be established; Seven, supervisory mechanism and risk management mechanism for the banking sector need to be consummated.

Selected Bibliography

Horesh, N. (2009). *Shanghai's Bund and Beyond*. New Haven and London: Yale University Press.

McKinnon, R. (1973). *Money and Capital in Economic Development*. Washington, DC: The Brookings Institution.

Ping, Y. K. (2012). *Private Equity in China: Challenges and Opportunities*. Singapore: John Wiley & Sons.

The Banker (2020). *The Top 1000 World Banks*. July.

Walter, C. E. and F. J. T. Howie. (2012). *Red Capitalism: The Fragile Financial Foundation of China's Extraordinary Rise*. Singapore: John Wiley & Sons.

Wang, M., J. Yen and K. K. Lai. (2014). *China's Financial Markets: Issues and Opportunities*. New York: Routledge.

Wu, J. (2005). *Understanding and Interpreting Chinese Economic Reform.* Thomson/ South-Western.

The Focal Points of China's Banking Sector's High-Quality Development in the 14th FYP Period, By Wang Gang, Research Institute of Finance, DRC Research Report, No.304, 2020 (Total 6048), 2020-12-16; http:/drc.gov.cn/2021-01/29/content_37542675.htm.

Chapter 10

China's Financial Markets

1. Introduction

China's post-reform stock market experience started in 1990. Fittingly, it was in Shanghai. The city was China's financial center in the 19th century and the first half of the 20th century. In 1891, the Shanghai Share Brokers Association was formed, serving as the city's stock exchange. It was followed in the 1920s by the establishment of the Shanghai Securities Goods Exchange and the Shanghai Chinese Securities Exchange. Trading stocks, bonds, and even futures was available to domestic as well as foreign investors. In 1946, the Shanghai Chinese Securities Exchange changed its name to the Shanghai Securities Exchange. Of course, three years later, this bastion of capitalism was shut down by Mao's regime.

During the Mao years, allocation of resources was the job of the state. Financial markets, then, were not necessary, nor were they in existence. As we stated in the previous chapter, the PBOC was the only functioning financial institution in the nearly 30 years of the centrally planned regime. Therefore, the country's Central Bank also comprised its entire financial system.

Deng's vision of a market-based economic system included the opening of China's two national Stock Exchanges in the early 1990s. After the Sichuan incident (See Red Capitalism), to avoid such incidents in the future, the securities markets' regulator, China Securities Regulatory Commission, was founded in 1992, and began functioning in earnest in 1998. The Asian Financial Crisis confirmed the need for building China's regulatory infrastructure. The Security Law was passed in 1998 and

China's Securities Regulatory Commission (CSRC), reporting to the State Council, was established.

By the first quarter of the 21st century, China's financial system had made huge strides toward its development. We covered the country's financial institutions in the previous chapter. In this chapter, we will concentrate on China's financial markets. The next section describes the nature of China's Stock Market. Section 3 presents the characteristics of the Bond Market. The country's interest rate regime is covered in Section 4; in Section 5, we discuss China's currency experiences. China is also in the process of developing its Derivative markets, as explained in Section 6. Prior to our Concluding Statements (Section 8), we discuss China's impressive progress in the digital domain.

2. China's Stock Market

Stock markets are an integral part of a mature economy's financial and economic system. They contribute to the country's economic growth by distributing funds from those with surplus to those that are deficient in funds. In so doing, stock markets and other financial markets assist in the optimum allocation of resources. Unlike other financial markets, however, stock markets transfer ownership of the corporation. They contribute to price discovery and liquidity and provide stockholders with a platform for profit-making.

For economies in transition, stock markets also represent a political statement of a country's commitment to reform. Stock markets offer a valuable mechanism toward privatization and ownership reform. They are one of the most visible signals to the outside world that the country is ready to accept foreign investments. For example, following the fall of the Soviet Union, many of the former Iron Curtain countries proceeded to open or re-open their security exchanges even though these exchanges did not offer sufficient range of securities to be included in the international investor's portfolio, nor had they developed the institutional framework that would guarantee property rights, transparency, and judicial fairness.

2.1. *China's exchanges*

China's spectacular growth and potential have not gone unnoticed to both domestic and international investors. Developing an active stock market

Table 10.1.   The largest 10 stock exchanges in the world by market capitalization, February 2021 (in trillion US dollars).

Exchange	Market capitalization
NYSE	25.62
NASDAQ	19.51
Hong Kong	6.76
Shanghai	6.56
Japan group	6.54
Euronext	5.08
Shenzhen	4.83
LSE group (UK and Italy)	3.83
TMX group	2.62
National stock exchange of India	2.56

Source: www.statista.com/statistics/270126/largest-stock-exchange-operators-by-market-capitalization-of-listed-companies/.

has been an important objective for China's reformers. A strong stock market can be presented as evidence of successful reforms. A well-functioning stock market also gives Chinese investors an option other than real estate to increase their wealth. Deng Xiaoping realized the stock market's symbolic and pragmatic value by establishing the Shanghai and Shenzhen markets. Converting idle balances into increased production activity would strengthen the national economy. The country was also looking for ways through which to finance the debt-ridden SOEs though partial privatization and to allow the private sector to access non-bank financing. Opening the country to international investors would also lead to a management and governance model like those of the west.

Following the start of the financial system reforms, the Shanghai Stock Exchange (SSE) was established (November 1990) and went into operation (December 1990).[1] In the same year (December 1990) the Shenzhen Stock Exchange (SZSE) was also established and went into operation in January 1991.[2] Both exchanges are among the 10 largest exchanges in the world (see Table 10.1): Shanghai is ranked 4th, while

---

[1] http://english.sse.com.cn/aboutsse/overview/.

[2] www.szse.cn/English/.

Shenzhen is ranked 7th. Both exchanges have grown in terms of number of listed companies and market capitalization, as well as in the variety of offerings to investors. In 1992, the Shanghai Exchange had 20 firms listed; Shenzhen had 24. In 2020 (September 30), Shanghai had 1,746 companies listed, offering 1,789 securities; Shenzhen had 2,310 companies listed, offering 11,198 securities. Investors may enter China's stock markets by investing in one or more of the classes of securities available. Table 10.2 shows the types of shares listed on various exchanges by Chinese companies. The two main classes of shares are the A-shares and B-shares. A-shares are available to Chinese citizens only and are traded in the local currency. Foreign investors can buy A-shares if they meet certain criteria set out by the Qualified Foreign Institutional Investors (QFII) or RMB Qualified Foreign Institutional Investors (RMB-QFII) Programs. Alternatively, foreign investors can buy A-shares if they participate in the Hong Kong Stock Connect Program. Foreign investors can also enter the Chinese stock market through B-shares, which became available to foreign investors in 1992. To supervise the market, and regulate the operations of the Shanghai and Shenzhen Exchanges, the China Securities Regulatory Commission (CSRC) was established in 1992.

Table 10.2.   Types of shares traded in China's exchanges.

Share class	Country of incorporation	Country of listing	Trading currency
A Shares	PRC	China	CNY
B Share	PRC	China	USD (Shanghai) HKD (Shenzhen)
H Share	PRC	Hong Kong	HKD
Red-Chip	Non-PRC	Hong Kong	HKD
P Chip	Non-PRC	Hong Kong	HKD
S Chip	Non-PRC	Singapore	SGD
N Share	Non-PRC	United States	USD
CDR-China depositary receipt	Non-PRC	Non-PRC	CNY

Source: FTSE Russell (2019). *Guide to Chinese Share Classes*. V1.5. December. Accessed at https://research.ftserussell.com/products/downloads/Guide_to_Chinese_Share_Classes.pdf.

2.1.1. *The Shanghai Stock Exchange (SSE)*

In a 2009 report, the *Financial Times* described the Shanghai stock market as "closed, opaque, undeveloped, but ambitious."[3] We could easily add the term "emerging," and apply the description to China's entire financial system.

The Shanghai Stock Exchange includes the Main Board and the more recently established STAR Market. On September 30, 2020, 1,563 companies listed their securities on the Main Board, offering 1,606 securities. In addition to equity-trading, the SSE offers trading in Bonds, Indices, Funds, Derivatives, and Green Securities (in cooperation with the Luxemburg Green Exchange).

In July 2019, the Shanghai Stock Exchange opened the doors to the SSE's Science and Technology Innovation Board, referred to as the STAR market. The STAR Market can best be described as China's answer to NASDAQ. Trading started with 22 listed companies, whose prices rose by as much as 400% before the opening day was over. One year later, the number of companies listed had climbed to 123 (see Table 10.3). The increase in listings is due to companies entering the public market for the first time, but also to companies electing to list on STAR in addition to their New York or Hong Kong listing. The forced delisting of Chinese firms from US exchanges also motivated Chinese firms to stay at home. The trophy listing so far has been by Shanghai's own Semiconductor Manufacturing International Corp. (SMIC), who had also listed in Hong Kong. SMIC raised USD6.6 billion, the largest IPO in China for over 10 years.

The attraction of the STAR market to companies, especially fast-growing tech start-ups, is due to the unique listing rules, streamlines registration, and trading mechanisms.[4] STAR's listing requirements do not rely as much (as the SSE's and SZSE's listing requirements) on the company's fundamentals as they rely on its sector and growth prospects, with technology companies favored. STAR's registration mechanism shortens the process substantially. Instead of the registration being processed

---

[3] Waldmeit, P. (2009). Finance: Market is closed, opaque, undeveloped but ambitious. *Financial Times*. April 29. http://www.ftchinese.com/story/001026190/en?ccode= LanguageSwitch&archive

[4] EY Greater China (2020). How does Shanghai's STAR Market support innovation enterprises' IPOs? July 24. Accessed at www.ey.com/en_cn/china-opportunities.

Table 10.3.   Shanghai STAR board.

	22-Jul-19	02-Jan-20	13-Jul-20
Number of companies	22	70	123
Market capitalization (trillions CNY)	0.53	0.88	2.53
Trading volume (billions CNY)	48.57	9.32	52.82

Source: Shanghai Stock Exchange and Tan, CK (2020). Shanghai's STAR market brings in new dawn for Chinese tech. Nikkei Asia, July 17. Accessed at https://asia.nikkei.com/Business/Business-.

through Beijing, it is processed through the Shanghai Stock Exchange. To limit trading interruptions, the STAR circuit breaker kicks in at 20% price changes.

2.1.2. *The Shenzhen stock exchange*

The Shenzhen Stock Exchange (SZSE) has been viewed as the exchange in which listed companies represent China's innovative mindset. SZSE comprises three "Boards" or Markets: The Main Board, the SME Board, and the ChiNext market.

The Main Board dates to the establishment of the Exchange. The SME Board was established in 2004; 8 companies listed on June 25.[5] In addition to providing a means of external financing for innovative start-ups, the opening of the SME Board represented a significant step toward deepening of China's financial system. Five years later, the Shenzhen Exchange expanded further by establishing the ChiNext Market. ChiNext's opening further emphasized the role of the Shenzhen Exchange as the listing home of emerging industry.

In addition to the Shanghai and Shenzhen, China also has an Over the Counter (OTC) market. The OTC market, established in 2012, is regulated by the National Equities Exchange and Quotations (NEEQ), which is under the China Securities Regulatory Commission (CSRC).

---

[5] Shenzhen Stock Exchange Launches SME Board. www.china.org.cn/english/BAT/96692.htm.

2.1.3. *Market performance*

Figure 10.1 illustrates the behavior of the Shanghai Stock Exchange Composite Index between January 1999 and December 2020. The graph shows two major sustained increases in the Index followed by drastic drops in each case. The first major increase culminates into the all-time high of 5903 reached prior to the global financial crisis (October 19, 2007). As the crisis took hold of the global economy, countries and markets around the world suffered. Although China's economy was not as drastically affected as the economies of the developed nations, it did suffer from the breakdown in the demand for its products. That breakdown and the ensuing pessimism about the direction of the global economy were reflected in China's stock markets.

The second highest peak of 5166.35 was reached in June 2015. We will be examining the developments around June 2015 in the next section of this chapter.

Table 10.4 includes selected descriptive statistics of the behavior of some of the stock indices. The table reveals that the Shenzhen market indices have shown a higher average rate of return during the period, but also higher variability of returns. Statistically, however, only the SZSE Composite is significantly greater than zero at the 95% level of confidence. Table 10.5 shows the correlation coefficients between pairs of the indices over the same periods. The SSE and SZSE Composite Indices are highly correlated, as are the two SZSE Indices. The Mainland indices, however, are not as highly correlated with Hong Kong's Hang Seng Index. This signifies the possible existence of diversification benefits for a portfolio including securities from Hong Kong and the Mainland.

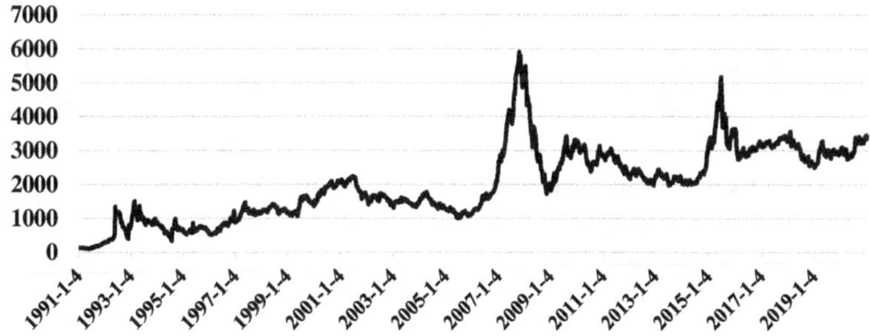

Figure 10.1.   Shanghai stock exchange composite index, 1991–2020.

Source: WIND.

Table 10.4.   Descriptive statistics; selected indices.

	Shanghai SE composite	SZSE composite	CHINEXT composite	Hang Seng composite
Mean	0.1464	0.2829	0.2895	0.1348
Standard error	0.1167	0.136	0.1874	0.1015
Standard deviation	3.403	3.9677	4.3137	2.9607
Sample variance	11.5806	15.7425	18.6083	8.7657
Count	851	851	530	851

Source: WIND. Calculations by authors.

Table 10.5.   Correlation coefficients.

	Shanghai SE composite	SZSE composite	CHINEXT composite	Hang Seng composite
Shanghai SE composite	1			
SZSE composite	0.8611	1		
CHINEXT composite	0.6891	0.9313	1	
Hang Seng composite	0.5707	0.4669	0.3476	1

Source: WIND. Calculations by authors. Series commence around establishment of CHINEXT (6/2010).

2.2. *The crash of 2015*

We now examine in greater depth the period following one of the two peaks noted above: June 2015. This second steep market rise accompanied by a drastic fall occurred in the middle months of 2015. In the early days of June, the Shanghai Stock Market was reaching its post-financial crisis high. On June 13, 2014, the Shanghai Composite Index closed at 2,070.715. One year later, it had reached 5,166.35, an increase of 150%! For the months leading to June 2015, the thought of the market going down was not on anybody's mind. Certainly not on the mind of the predominantly retail investors in the market. Press reports about the market exuded optimism. To help things along, the government kept on relaxing the rules for margin investing. Margin debt reached CNY 400 billion from official (broker) accounts; in addition, investors found ways to borrow from other sources and go further into debt. An expansionary stimulus following the 2008 crisis made even more funds available to institutions and the public.

In the first few months of 2015, the Chinese authorities became concerned about the surge in stock prices and began to take steps toward harnessing excessive market movements.[6] The CRSC took measures to limit margin financing in the beginning of June. Unfortunately, this move coincided with the MSCI's decision not to include China's indices in its global index. Confidence in the market started waning. The authorities attempted to reverse course by pursuing an expansionary monetary policy (lowering interest rates and reserve requirements). These developments were interpreted as negative by the market and represented the beginnings of a selloff.

At this point, Beijing needed to intervene. The PBOC cut interest rates by a quarter of a point. Brokerages were ordered to buy stocks while, at the same time, they could not sell their inventories. Investors holding more than 5 % of a company's shares could not sell their shares for the next six months. State banks lent the China Securities Finance Corporation CNY1.3 trillion to buy stocks. The National Team was also asked to increase its stock purchases. In addition, Initial Public Offerings were suspended until the market recovered. Trading on the shares of about 1,300 companies was halted to stop any further declines.

The market recovered somewhat after the July 8, 2015 big drop. In the second week of August, however, the government devalued the RMB by 1.9% in order to stimulate the economy. This was perceived as a sign of weakness by international markets, so funds started flowing out of China. The Securities Finance Corporation stopped injecting funds, allowing the market to slide. On August 24, the Shanghai Composite dropped by 8.5%, the largest drop since the 2007 crisis.

The gyrations of the Chinese market are typical of the behavior of a stock market in a transition economy. The name of the game is volatility. What goes up, must come down. After a dizzying ride upwards, the peak was reached in June 2015. It was just a matter of time as to when the slide would begin. The herd mentality of retail investors pushed the market lower and faster. The government actions have been criticized as

---

[6]Bendini, R. (2015). Exceptional Measures: The Shanghai stock market crash and the future of the Chinese economy. European Parliament, Policy Department, August 31. www.europarl.europa.eu/RegData/etudes/IDAN/2015/549067/EXPO_IDA(2015) 549067_EN.pdf.

contributing to the market's demise. Although the stock market did not have much to do with the fundamentals of the Chinese economy, critics also viewed the stock market collapse as a sign of the failure of the Chinese economic model. The irony, of course, is that China considered the 2007–2009 global financial crisis as a sign of the failure of the Western capitalist model. Perhaps the 2007–2015 period showed us that there is no such thing as the perfect economic model. It is a matter of which is easier for us to put up with: market risk or government risk?

2.3. *International access*

International investors can access Chinese shares in several ways. They include enrollment in the Hong Kong Connect(s), purchasing shares listed on Chinese exchanges, purchasing shares or Depositary Receipts of companies listed on foreign exchanges, and purchasing shares of mutual funds that include Chinese shares.

2.3.1. *Shanghai–Hong Kong connect and Shenzhen–Hong Kong connect*

Hong Kong has long been viewed as the gateway to the Mainland. The connection between the "two systems" of the country became even stronger through their Stock and Bond Connect. After two years of deliberations, the Shanghai–Hong Kong Connect was established in 2014. The Connect represents a mutual access mechanism, enabling investors from the Mainland and Hong Kong to trade stocks listed on the other's market through local securities companies and brokers (www.sse.com.cn). Trading can take place "northbound" or "southbound." Northbound refers to investors, through their Hong Kong brokers and a Hong Kong Exchange-related securities company in Shanghai, trading shares listed on the Shanghai Exchange and eligible under the Shanghai–Hong Kong Connect. Similarly, Southbound refers to Mainland investors trading shares listed on the Hong Kong Exchange and eligible under the Connect. The Shanghai–Hong Kong Connect was accompanied by the Shenzhen–Hong Kong Connect in 2016. Only secondary market securities are available under these two trading mechanisms, with no Initial Public Offerings allowed. The volume of trading is subject to Northbound and Southbound market-wide quotas.

The Shanghai–Hong Kong and Shenzhen–Hong Kong Connect frameworks have the potential of generating valuable benefits for the Mainland and Hong Kong financial systems as well as the participating investors. The Connect represents a step toward greater internationalization of the Chinese financial system, as the Shanghai and Shenzhen markets are now accessible to global investors. Chinese company shares are now traded on the international stage and are priced according to international standards and based on international competition. This gives Chinese companies a more objective assessment of their market capitalization. A related benefit to China is the strengthening of the prospects of RMB internationalization. For the Shanghai and Shenzhen Exchanges specifically, enabling their clients to access Hong Kong shares adds significantly to the depth of their offerings. For the Hong Kong Exchange, cooperating with the Mainland Exchanges potentially averts future competition. For foreign and Chinese investors, investing northbound or southbound provides international diversification and risk management opportunities.

2.3.2. *QFII and RQFII*

In 2002, the PBOC and the China Securities Regulatory Commission (CSRC) jointly issued the provisional Measures on Administration of Domestic Securities Investment of Qualified Foreign Institutional Investors, referred to as QFII. According to the QFII scheme, foreign investors could now access the Chinese markets directly. The new investment channel was another step in China's opening its capital markets to the world following the country's accession into the WTO. To qualify for inclusion in QFII and thus be able to purchase A-shares, foreign investors had to adhere to several requirements, including the size of their asset portfolio (Assets Under Management, or AUM), credit history, overall financial condition, quality of their management, and operating history. Various classes of financial firms have been qualified, including commercial banks, securities firms, insurance companies, asset management companies, sovereign wealth funds, and pension funds. Examples of specific institutions operating under QFII are JPMorgan Chase, HSBC, Nomura Securities, Goldman Sachs Asset Management International, Templeton, and the Government of Singapore Investment Fund. In addition to stocks, foreign investors may invest in bonds and other financial instruments designated by the CSRC. The QFII program was accompanied by the

RMB-QFII, or RQFII. RQFII was introduced in 2011 and allowed qualified foreign investors to purchase Chinese stocks in Shanghai and Shenzhen using offshore RMB.

The establishment of the QFII program and its subsequent development followed the blueprint of other facets of Chinese reforms. The opening of China's capital markets to global investors has been a gradual and experimental one. Investing in China's markets became available to the select few, at least for now. The size (quota) of the investment, as determined by the SAFE, was relatively small in the beginning (USD30 billion in 2002). The quota grew to USD80 billion in 2012. In September 2019, SAFE and the PBOC announced elimination of the quotas for both QFII and RQFII and simplification of the administrative process applicable to these programs, including integration of the two programs. The changes went into effect in June 2020. Although trading under these two programs has so far represented under 5% of the total market, the new rules represent another stage of China's opening of its financial system.

Although both the Stock Connect and the QFII/RFQII are similar in the sense of allowing international investors to access China's markets, they do present some differences between their structures in several areas (www.szse.cn/en). For example, Stock Connect transactions take place in RMB, as do RQFII transactions; QFII transactions, however, take place in a foreign currency. Quotas in Stock Connect apply to the market as a whole, although in QFII they are allocated to individual investors and in RQFII they are allocated to offshore regions. Another difference pertains to product eligibility; eligible products for Stock Connect are represented by selected A-shares and H-shares, whereas eligible products for QFII and RQFII are approved by the CSRC. Other differences pertain to fund regulation, investor eligibility, and investor rights. As Chinese authorities continue to take steps to make market access easier for global investors, we should expect both programs to relax their regulations and make it easier for investors to participate, while emphasizing quality of their product offerings.

2.3.3. *Foreign stock exchange listings*

International investors may also trade shares or Depositary Receipts at various exchanges on which Chinese companies have listed their securities. As of October 2020, there were 217 Chinese companies listed on the

US Exchanges, among which are 13 national-level SOEs.[7] For example, US Exchanges feature listings of ADRs from such companies as Alibaba, Pinduoduo, and AirNet Technology and Common Stocks issued by Yum China, Tantech, Lianluo Smart, and others. IPOS of Chinese companies have been significant events in the history of international exchanges. In 1997, China Telecom (now named China Mobile, completed the largest to date Chinese company IPO, listing shares valued at USD4.2 billion in NYSE and Hong Kong. In 2003, the largest IPO of the year (USD2.3 billion, in NYSE and Hong Kong) was by China Life. Not to be outdone, the big Chinese banks made their own splash. ICBC's 2006 IPO of USD19 billion (in Hong Kong and Shanghai) was the world's biggest up to date.[8] The Agricultural Bank of China also had the world's largest to date IPO in 2010 (USD22 billion, in Hong Kong and Shanghai).

The listing of Chinese companies in foreign exchanges has provided these companies with additional capital at lower cost, liquidity, and credibility among international investors. Investors have been able to diversify their portfolios, and investment banks have generated significant revenue streams. It has also brought strong competition among international exchanges, especially between the US and Hong Kong Exchanges.

Cross-border listings have also brought several challenges to Chinese companies as they must operate under different standards and regulations and political environments. For example, following the Enron scandal, the US established the Public Company Accounting Oversight Board (PCAOB) in 2002. The Board's mission is to inspect listed companies' accounts to ensure adherence to US standards. Chinese authorities, however, have been objecting to the PCAOB's inspection of Chinese companies' financials on national security grounds. In March 2020, China implemented the Securities Law, prohibiting foreign regulators from auditing Chinese companies without permission from Chinese authorities. In response to the Chinese objection, and with the US–China Trade Dispute in the background, the US Congress passed the 2020 Holding

---

[7] US–China Economic and Security Review Commission (2020). Chinese Companies Listed on Major US Stock Exchanges. October 2. www.uscc.gov/research/chinese-companies-listed-major-us-stock-exchanges.

[8] For a detailed analysis of the ICBC IPO, see: Allen, F., D. Huang, J. Qian, and M. Zhao (2012). The Initial Public Offering of the Industrial and Commercial Bank of China (ICBC). In Aoki, M., and J. Wu (Eds.). *The Chinese Economy: A New Transition.* New York, NY: Palgrave MacMillan/St. Martin's Press, pp. 199–230.

Foreign Companies Accountable Act. According to the Act, foreign companies that do not cooperate with the PCAOB on its audit inspections for three years face delisting.[9] In January 2021, the NYSE announced the planned delisting of three Chinese telecoms, China Mobile, China Telecom, and China Unicom. Soon afterwards, however, the NYSE reversed its decision. The events surrounding delisting of Chinese companies did not stop additional Chinese companies from listing in US Exchanges. By the end of the year, 32 Chinese firms had listed their IPOs in US Exchanges.

The engagement of Chinese companies in overseas exchanges has served as further proof of China's integration with the global economy as well as the interdependence between China's economy and the rest of the world.

2.3.4. *Other connections*

2.3.4.1. The Shanghai–London connect

The Shanghai (SSE)–London Stock Exchange (LSE) Connect was launched in 2018, allowing qualified companies listed in one of the exchanges to list their Depositary Receipts (DRs) on the other. The Shanghai–London Connect entails eastbound and westbound business. Eastbound refers to companies listed on the LSE that list Chinese Depositary Receipts on the Shanghai Exchange Main Board. Companies issuing their CDRs cannot raise capital through the Shanghai market. Westbound, companies listed on the SSE, can list Global Depositary Receipts (GDR) and may even raise capital through the LSE. Companies listing their DRs eastbound or westbound must adhere to local regulatory requirements.

2.3.4.2. Shanghai–Tokyo ETF connect

On June 25, 2019, twin ceremonies in Shanghai and Tokyo launched the Japan–China ETF Connectivity Scheme. The scheme connects the capital markets of the two largest economies in Asia by providing an efficient low-cost access to the Shanghai and Tokyo Stock Exchanges. The

---

[9]Mark, J. (2021). Delist or Not Delist: A \$2.2-Trillion US-China Auditing Dispute. Atlantic Council, February. www.atlanticcouncil.org/in-depth-research-reports/issue-brief/delist-or-not-delist-a-2-2-trillion-us-china-auditing-dispute/.

connection between the two markets will be taking place through the listing of four Japan feeder ETFs on the Shanghai Stock Exchange and four China feeder ETFs on the Tokyo Stock Exchange.

In general, the above connectivity schemes between China's capital markets and those of other countries have represented a welcome sign of China's willingness to open up its financial system. So far, interest by the international investment community has not justified the initial enthusiasm that surrounded the establishment of the schemes. For example, assets of the four China ETFs listed on the Tokyo exchange fell from USD70.6 million on the day of the announcement to USD68.4 million two months later. During the same period, assets of Shanghai-listed Japan ETFs dropped from USD127.7 million to USD36.6 million.[10] It is still too early to conclude whether these schemes will be successful in terms of attracting investors. The uncertainty surrounding China's Trade War with President Trump has certainly not helped promote international cooperation.

2.3.4.3. The Qualified Domestic Limited Partner (QDLP) scheme

In 2012, China launched a pilot program in Shanghai and Tianjin. The program, run by local authorities, represents another step in China's opening its financial sector to the world. According to QDLP, foreign asset managers could enter China to raise RMB funds from High-Net-Worth Individuals (HNWI) and institutional investors, establish an investment entity in China as a general partner or set up a Qualified Domestic Investment Fund that feeds into a master fund managed overseas.[11] The QDLP scheme operates under a local quota. The Shanghai quota was initially USD50 million, increasing to USD5 billion by 2018.

Capital controls imposed by SAFE have caused occasional interruptions in the operations of participating funds (for example, during the 2016–2018 period). Funds have to identify a Qualified Financial Institution, such as a bank or securities firm, to serve as custodian. After

---

[10] Flood, C. (2019). China and Japan link up with "feeder" ETFs. *Financial Times*. October 6. www.ft.com/content/5b7f4b92-cff0-11e9-b018-ca4456540ea6.

[11] Yang, M. (2020). PFM and QDLP Programmes in China. Allocate to China Initiative. June 22. www.atcinitiative.org/pfm-and-qdlp-programmes-in-china.

2014, qualified funds must also register with the Asset Management Association of China (AMAC). Overall, however, China has promoted the QDLP scheme. In April 2021, the CSRC and the PBOC issued guidelines designed to allow QDLPs to operate in Hainan under a USD5 billion quota. The Hainan project joins several other projects around the country, such as Guangdong Province (including Shenzhen), Shanghai, Beijing, Jiangsu, Chongqing, Tianjin, and Qingdao.[12]

2.3.4.4. Private Fund Managers (PFM)

To encourage the entry of more foreign investors in China, the Asset Management Association of China instituted new rules in 2016 regarding private fund management. According to the Private Fund Manager (PFM) Program, foreign asset managers can establish a private securities investment open-ended fund aimed at Chinese investors and investing in stocks, bonds, fund units, derivatives, and other securities within China. They can also provide advisory services to Chinese investors. A qualified Chinese financial institution will serve as the custodian.

As of April 2021, the PFM Program has attracted over 30 foreign asset managers. They represent some of the biggest names in global asset management, such as UBS and Bridgewater. Several of the PFM firms have also been given QDLP licenses.

2.3.4.5. China Depositary Receipts (CDRs)

A Depositary Receipt is a receipt representing shares of a foreign company. The receipt is issued by a custodian bank to the investor and may be traded in the host country's Over-the-Counter market or Stock Exchanges. Chinese Depositary Receipts first appeared in Shanghai's STAR Market. Ninebot, maker of smart-scooters and owner of Segway registered in the Caymans, issued the first CDR in September 2020. Many more other companies are expected to follow Ninebot's example in Shanghai and Shenzhen, especially in the latter's ChiNext market.

The creation of the CDR market is a way for China to welcome back its huge high-tech companies that had listed in foreign exchanges. CDRs

---

[12]Zhou, T. (2021). All eyes on quotas as China expands QDLP scheme. *Asianinvestor.* April 12. www.asianinvestor.net/article/all-eyes-on-quotas-as-china-expands-qdlp-scheme/.

also provide domestic investors with the opportunity to invest in RMB in the country's high-tech industry. The lack of a limit on price fluctuations made the CDR market even more attractive. Chinese investors have responded favorably. Ninebot's offering raised CNY1.33 billion, selling 70.4 million CDRs at CNY18.94 each. Its price rose 103%, to CNY38.5 at the end of the day.[13]

2.4. *The dilemma of non-tradable shares*

In the first years of China's Stock Market reform, the shares traded were primarily those of SOEs. The Chinese government was concerned about SOE shares being owned by private citizens. It therefore determined that only one-third of the total amount could be traded. The other two-thirds were designated as non-tradable. One-third of the total was owned by domestic institutions, such as non-bank financial institutions and selected SOEs; these shares could be traded only by special approval. The other two-thirds of the total was in the hands of state entities, such as central and local governments and SOEs.[14]

The existence of non-tradable shares, especially since they are such a large portion of the total, presents challenges for the government, the issuing enterprises, the owners of the tradable third, and the rest of the market participants. With only about a third of the total shares being traded, liquidity was affected. The market was also vulnerable to manipulation. Perhaps more importantly, the pricing mechanism was distorted. How do we arrive at the "true" market price of an asset, when two-thirds of the asset are not being traded? What are the implications of this practice for market capitalization of these enterprises? If one third of a building is sold at USD1, and the other two-thirds are held back, does the entire building have a market value of USD3? What would happen if, without warning, the other two-thirds of the asset were dumped in the market? Indeed, in July 2001, an announcement was made of an impending sale of 2.2 trillion non-tradeable state shares. The anticipation of such a disturbance to the

---

[13] Zhang, S. (2020). Ninebot's depositary receipts, China's version of ADRs, double on Shanghai's Star Market debut. *South China Morning Post.* October 29. www.scmp.com/business/markets/article/3107520/ninebot-depositary-receipts-chinas-first-kind-market-reform-surge.

[14] Lee, S. L. J. (2008). From non-tradable to tradable shares: Split share structure reform of China's listed companies. *Journal of Corporate Law Studies*, 8(1), 57–78.

market was most likely the principal reason for the market to lose over 40% (Lee, 2008). The market drop persuaded the government not to go through with the sale. Instead, new reforms began to be implemented.

The new non-tradeable shares reforms began in late April of 2005. The reform entailed allowing holders of non-tradable shares to sell their shares. However, these shares could not be sold in the market for one year after being converted into tradable shares. Furthermore, non-tradable shareholders owning more than 5% of the total amount of shares had to wait an additional 12 months before taking a maximum of 5% of shares to the market; owners of more than 10% had to wait another 12 months to resell a maximum of 10% of the shares (grand total of 36 months). As we have noted repeatedly, reform was conducted in its usual manner: gradual. The pilot program involved four companies, followed by 42 additional companies in June 2005 and 35 more SOEs in November 2005. The government put a lot of pressure on companies to participate in the program. By the end of 2006, more than 95% of the companies had participated in the reform.

Despite these restrictions in the resale of non-tradable shares, there was still a chance of an increase in the supply large enough to cause market turmoil. Further restrictions, then, were placed in June 2007 by the SASAC and the CSRC in the form of *The Interim Rules for the Administration of State-Owned Shareholders' Transfer of Their Shares of Listed Companies.*[15] The new rules required SASAC approval of a sale that would have a potential impact on the enterprise's control.

The reform of non-tradable shares did not have a noticeable impact on stock prices. It did, however, ameliorate the prevailing uncertainties about the detrimental consequences of a large supply shift. It also reinforced other reforms initiated in the same decade, such as implementation of the QFII Program and the reinstatement of IPOs.

3. China's Bond Market

China's bond market has had an impressive growth, rising to the second largest in the world by 2019, behind the United States (https://stats.bis.org/statx/srs/table/c1). Furthermore, the market has grown dramatically, has made inroads on the international stage, and has bright prospects for additional growth. In April 2019, China's Bond Market received the

---

[15]Kwan, C. H. (2007). Lifting of ban on sale of non-tradable shares to hold down stock prices. RIETI, November 13. https://www.rieti.go.jp/en/china/07111301.html).

positive news of its inclusion in the Bloomberg Barclay's Global Aggregate Index. Inclusion in the Index is expected to bring in large capital inflows to the Chinese Bond market. The market, then, should become an even more important component of the global financial system.

As we showed in Chapter 2, China entered the international bond market on various occasions during the 19th and 20th centuries. China's participation in the international economy and financial markets diminished significantly in 1949. China's MOF did issue Treasury Bonds in 1954 in conjunction with the First Five Year Plan. These bonds, however, represented a mere reallocation of resources from the enterprises to the Central government, and their issuance was discontinued in 1958. The bond market resurfaced during the first years of reforms, as the first SOE bonds were issued in 1981. These bonds were issued through administrative allotment and were not tradable. A nationwide secondary market was created when the Shanghai and Shenzhen Exchanges opened in 1990. The Chinese government's plan was to develop its bond market following international processes and practices. A government bond underwriting system was developed in 1991, followed by the creation of a primary dealer system in 1993 and an auction system for issuing tradable securities in 1996. A centralized securities depository, China Government Securities Depository Trust & Clearing Co. (CDC), was also established in 1996, putting together a market-wide custody and settlement system.[16]

3.1. *Types of bonds*

Today's market includes securities issued by SOEs, private enterprises, and the various levels of government. The market currently includes both onshore and offshore components. The onshore component has three segments: exchange-traded, interbank, and over-the-counter markets. The securities traded within these markets are issued by different levels of government, financial institutions, and non-financial corporations. Tables 10.6 and 10.7 show the markets at which China's bonds are traded.

We may divide bonds into two general types: government bonds and credit bonds. The following section provides a brief explanation of each type.[17]

---

[16]Bai, J., M. Fleming, and C. Horan. (2013). *The Microstructure of China's Government Bond Market*. Federal Reserve Bank of New York, Staff Report No. 622, May.

[17]Seafarer (2019). The Evolution of China's Bond Market. March. www.seafarerfunds.com/commentary/the-evolution-of-chinas-bond-market/.

Table 10.6. Major types of bonds in the stock exchange market.

Bond type	Regulator	Maturity	Type of issuers
CGB	MoF	3 months-50 yrs	MoF
Local government	State Council	3 yrs, 5 yrs, 7 yrs	Provinces, municipalities, and autonomous regions
Financial bonds	PBOC, CBRC	1 month-20 yrs	Commercial banks, non-bank financial institutions
Exchange corporate bonds	CSRC	1.5–15 yrs	Corporates
Convertible bonds	CSRC	2–8 yrs	Listed companies
Enterprise bonds	NDRC	3–30 yrs	Non-financial companies (SOEs, LGFVs)
SME procurement policy notes	CSRC	1–5 yrs	Unlisted SMEs (excluding real estate and financials
Asset backed securities	PBOC, CBIRC	6 months to 8 yrs	Commercial banks, Non-bank financial institutions

Source: MoF, PBOC, CSRC, CBIRC, Wind. As included in Schipke, A., M. Rodlauer, and L. Zhang (2019). China's Bond Market: Characteristics, Prospects, and Reforms. In Schipke, A., M. Rodlauer, and L. Zhang (editors, 2019). The Future of China's Bond Market. Washington, DC: International Monetary Fund, 3–33. www.elibrary.imf.org/view/IMF071/25402-9781484372142/25402-9781484372142/25402-9781484372142.xml?code=chinabondmarket.

3.1.1. *Government and related institution bonds*

a. Central Government (Sovereign) Bonds. These bonds are issued by the Treasury Ministry, with maturities ranging from 3 months to 50 years. PBOC issued bills in 2002.

b. Local Government Bonds. These are issued by sub-national government units. Local governments could issue bonds in 2009, following the Sichuan earthquake.

c. Policy Bank Notes. The three Policy Banks (Agricultural Bank, Export-Import Bank, and China Development Bank) were created in 1994 and could issue bonds to finance their projects.

3.1.2. *Credit bonds*

a. Financial Bonds (other than Policy Bank). After 1988, commercial banks and other financial institutions could issue their own debt notes, with the 3–5-year maturities being the most popular.

Table 10.7. Major types of bonds in the interbank market.

Bond type	Regulator	Maturity	Type of issuers
CCB	MoF	3 months to 50 yrs	MoF
Central bank bills	PBOC	3 months to 5 yrs	PBOC
Policy bank notes	State Council	6 months to 50 yrs	Policy Banks
Local government bonds	State Council	3 yrs, 5 yrs,7 yrs	Provinces, municipalities, and autonomous regions
Non-negotiable CDs	PBOC, CBIRC	<1 yr	Commercial banks
Financial bonds	PBOC, CBIRC	1 month to 20 yrs	Commercial banks, non-bank financial institutions
Enterprise bonds	NDRC	3–30 yrs	SOEs, LGFVs
SCP/CP	NAFMII	<1 yr	Corporates
Medium term notes	NAFMII	2–15 yrs	Corporates
Private placement notes	NAFMII	Less than 1 yr to 15 yrs	SOEs
ABN	NAFMII	3–15 yrs	LGFVs and Utility SOEs

Source: MoF, PBOC, CSRC, CBIRC, Wind. As included in Schipke, A., M. Rodlauer, and L. Zhang (2019). China's Bond Market: Characteristics, Prospects, and Reforms. In Schipke, A., M. Rodlauer, and L. Zhang (editors, 2019). The Future of China's Bond Market. Washington, DC: International Monetary Fund, 3–33. www.elibrary.imf.org/view/IMF071/25402-9781484372142/25402-9781484372142/25402-9781484372142.xml?code=chinabondmarket.

b. Enterprise Bonds, issued by enterprises associated with a government unit (Central or local). These were the first bonds issued after reforms began (1983).

c. Corporate Bonds, which privately owned companies started issuing in 2007.

d. Commercial Paper (short-term, first issued in 1988) and Medium Terms Notes, or MTNs (medium-term, first issued in 2008).

e. Local Government Bonds, first issued in 2008.

f. Asset-Backed Bonds, first issued in 2012.

g. Other Bonds and Notes (Panda Bonds, Private Placement Notes, and Certificates of Deposit).

3.2. *Where onshore bonds are traded*

China's onshore bond market has three components:

1. The Exchange Market. The exchange market refers to bond trading in the Shanghai and Shenzhen Stock Exchanges. The Exchange market was the main bond trading market until 1997, when banks exited the market to form the Interbank Market.
2. The Interbank Market is the largest bond market in China, accounting for 90–95% of the total market.
3. A much smaller market is the Commercial Bank market. It is primarily a retail market, in which buying and selling are conducted between banks and their clients.

Tables 10.6 and 10.7 show the various securities traded in the two major markets. Each group of securities is regulated by one or more regulators, including:

- The State Council's National Development and Reform Commission (NDRC). The Commission approves the amount of enterprise bonds issued to finance state-supported projects.
- The China Securities Regulatory Commission (CSRC), also under the State Council. The CSRC regulates listed company shares.
- The National Association of Financial Market Institutional Investors (NAFMII), that is under the PBOC.

3.3. *Foreign investors and the Chinese bond market*

The Chinese Bond Market has the potential of presenting many advantages to foreign investors. They include:[18]

- The size of the market. As we noted above, the CBM is the second largest bond market in the world.
- The market's inclusion in the major global indices. Inclusion in the Bloomberg Index is expected to generate a capital inflow of USD75–85 billion over the next five years.

---

[18]Anderson, H. and V. Juvyns (2019). *Guide to the Chinese Fixed Income Markets*. J.P. Morgan Asset Management, November 15.

- It allows for currency diversification of the investor's portfolio. With the elevation of the currency to reserve status, inclusion of Renminbi-denominated securities allows for currency diversification.
- Improving accessibility for foreign investors; the creation of Bond Connect and the reforms of the Qualified Foreign Institutional Investors (QFIII) and the Renminbi Qualified Foreign Institutional Investors (RQFII) have made it easier for foreign investors to enter the Chinese market.
- Increasing role of international rating agencies. Standard and Poor's is the first non-Chinese ratings firm licensed to rate securities issued by domestic borrowers. In addition, Moody's and Fitch Ratings have been rating a limited number of Chinese issues and have applied for licenses to extend their ratings coverage.
- Opportunities for portfolio immunization. Frequent and large volume auctions by the MOF in the 3-month to 3-year portion of the yield curve provide limited capacity of duration hedging.
- The market's risk–return profile. Chinese Central Government Bonds have shown higher risk-adjusted returns when expressed in Renminbi but lower such returns when converted into US dollars.

3.4. *Panda bonds*

Panda Bonds are Renminbi-denominated bonds issued by foreign issuers in the China onshore market. The first securities were issued in 2005 by the International Finance Corporation and the Asian Development Bank. Other issuers have included multinationals (for example, Daimler and BMW) and sovereigns (for example, Hungary and the Philippines).[19] Foreign issuers have entered the panda market for various reasons, including additional funding, diversification, access to Chinese investors, and search for lower borrowing costs. The prospect of RMB internationalization has also facilitated the growth of the market.

The growth of the Panda market has evolved along three stages.[20] The first stage (2005–2009) entailed the announcement of *Provisional Rules (2005)*, allowing international organizations to issue RMB bonds in China

---

[19] HSBC (2019). It's all black and white: understanding China's Panda bonds. June 5. https://www.euromoney.com/article/b1ftg16s04wpj0/its-all-black-and-white-understanding-chinas-panda-bonds.

[20] KPMG (2018). *Panda Bonds-A new landscape in China's bond market*. October. Kpmg.com/cn.

under the condition that all proceeds be used in the country. The International Finance Corporation and the Asian Development Bank were the first issuers, raising about USD600 million. The second stage (2010–2014), initiated by the announcement of the *2010 Provisional Rules,* involved a relaxation of the initial market rules. Bilateral and multilateral organizations could use issue proceeds outside China. Activity remained low, however, with Daimler being the only issuer in 2014. The German company approached the market twice, raising USD300 million. The third stage of Panda market development commenced in 2015 and included further relaxation of the rules regarding the nature of the issuer and the dissemination of the funds raised. Sovereign funds, central banks, and other foreign issuers entered the market. Furthermore, proceeds could be used as loans to Chinese subsidiaries. According to KPMG, 143 issues had reached the market by June 2018, raising USD40.6 billion.

3.5. *Dim sum bonds*

Dim Sum Bonds are RMB-denominated bonds issued in Hong Kong. They are also called CNH Bonds; CNH is the term used to denote offshore (primarily Hong Kong) Chinese currency. Foreign entities can issue RMB-denominated securities without needing permission from the Chinese authorities or adhering to any possible restrictions, such as capital controls.

The Dim Sum market opened in 2007, when the China Development Bank issued the first Dim Sum Bond. The MOF was the first Chinese government unit to issue Dim Sum Bonds in October 2009. Although a small part of the RMB bond market, it grew substantially over the next few years. From 2007–2012, 150 issuers used the market to offer 797 issues. Issuers included McDonalds and the Asian Development Bank. On average, each issue raised CNH500 million, paid a coupon rate of a little less than 3%, and had about a two-year maturity.[21] The Dim Sum market's activity depends on many factors, including expectations about the value of the RMB and its status in the global economy, and the Chinese government's imposition of capital controls. Depending on the

---

[21] Fung, H-G., G. Ko and J. Yau. (2014). *Dim Sum Bonds.* Hoboken, N.J: John Wiley & Sons.

specific situation, the Dim Sum market may be viewed as a substitute or a complement of the Panda market.

3.6. *Local government bonds and debt*

Local government bonds are a relative new addition to China's bond market offerings. The impetus for allowing local governments to issue bonds came about in the aftermath of the 2008 Financial Crisis and the Sichuan earthquake. The slowing global economy put a stress on local government budgets, prompting the State Council to allow provincial governments to fortify their finances through bond issuances. Bonds are issued by the MOF on behalf of the local government. Table 10.7 shows the date of issuance, issue amount, coupon rate, and maturity of these bonds. Xinjiang's bond issue was the first issue, while Sichuan Province raised the highest amount of funds through its two issues.

Bond issuance by local government needs to be viewed within the context of the governments' total debt situation. Until 2015, local government bond issuance was subject to the 1994 *Budget Law*, according to which local governments could issue bonds only after permission by the State Council and could not otherwise borrow. The *Budget Law's* 2015 revision adopted an "opening the front door and closing the back door" strategy. The Central Government allowed the issuance of new, longer maturity, municipal bonds in 2015 to allow local governments to retire debt from banks and other sources. Debt arising from bond issuance represents about 90% of official local government debt. By most accounts, local government debt has become larger than central government debt,[22] although its exact size is unknown because of its structure. A portion of this debt is local government debt, so-called explicit debt, which appears as a liability on the local government's budget, and is directly measurable. The size of the second component of local government debt is off-budget borrowing. It is aptly termed implicit debt and is much more complicated and difficult to estimate.

Implicit debt includes debt raised through LGFVs and debt associated with public–private partnerships (PPPs). Local governments began

---

[22]Lo, C. (2019). Demystifying China's local government debt. BNP Paribas. December 20. https://investors-corner.bnpparibas-am.com/investing/chinas-local-government-debt/.

Table 10.8.   Local government bonds: First issue.

	Issuer	Issue date	Issue amount (RMB 100 mn)	Coupon (%)	Maturity (years)
1	Xinjiang Uyghur Autonomous Region (first issue)	2009/3/30	30	1.61	3
2	Anhui Province (first issue)	2009/4/1	40	1.6	3
3	Henan Province (first issue)	2009/4/7	50	1.63	3
4	Sichuan Province (first issue)	2009/4/8	90	1.65	3
5	Chongqing City	2009/4/13	58	1.7	3
6	Liaoning Province (first issue)	2009/4/14	30	1.75	3
7	Sichuan Province (second issue)	2009/5/14	90	1.71	3
8	Hubei Province (second issue)	2009/5/14	31	1.71	3

Source: MoF, PBOC, CSRC, CBIRC, Wind. As included in Schipke, A., M. Rodlauer, and L. Zhang (2019). China's Bond Market: Characteristics, Prospects, and Reforms. In Schipke, A., M. Rodlauer, and L. Zhang (editors, 2019). The Future of China's Bond Market. Washington, DC: International Monetary Fund, 3–33. www.elibrary.imf.org/view/IMF071/25402-9781484372142/25402-9781484372142/25402-9781484372142.xml?code=chinabondmarket.

establishing LGFVs in the 1990s to finance their infrastructure projects. Beijing allowed local governments to enter PPPs in 2014, thereby presenting them with another way to build on their existing debt. Implicit debt was raised through bank loans, shadow banking loans, and other funding sources. Lo (2019) reports that, in 2018, explicit debt was estimated to be between CNY16.5 trillion and CNY18.4 trillion, while implicit debt was estimated to be between CNY11.5 trillion and CNY31.6 trillion. Naturally, servicing and repaying this mountain of total debt impacts on the ability of local governments to meet their bond payment obligations. Lenders, however, continue to accommodate local governments, believing that the central government stands behind these borrowings.

In 2020, gross bond issuance amounted to RMB57.3 trillion, up by 26.5% year on year, with issuance on interbank bond market posting RMB48.5 trillion, up by 27.5% year on year. As of end-December 2020, the outstanding balance of bonds in custody totaled RMB117 trillion, of which RMB100.7 trillion was from the interbank bond market, see Figure 10.2.

In 2020, there were changes in issuance of major types of bonds, see Table 10.9.

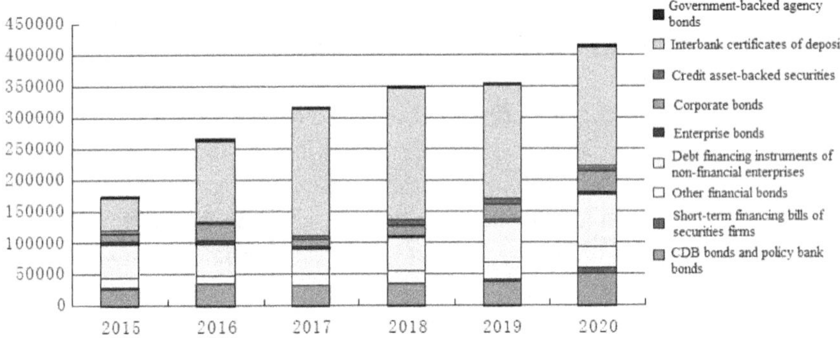

Figure 10.2.   Changes in issuance of major types of bonds from 2015–2020.

Source: Financial Market Report (2020), www.pbc.gov.cn/en/3688247/3688978/3709137/index.html.

Table 10.9.   The issuance of major types of bonds in 2020.

2020 major types of bonds	RMB trillion
Treasuries	7
Local government bonds	6.4
Financial bonds	9.3
Government-backed agency bonds	358
Asset-backed securities	2.3
Corporate bonds	19
Interbank certificates of deposit (CDs)	12.2

Source: Financial Market Report (2020), www.pbc.gov.cn/en/3688247/3688978/3709137/index.html.

3.6.1. *Local Bond Market Challenges*

a. China's local government bond market has grown through the years but still faces several challenges[23]:

b. Poor Investments. Local governments and their LGFVs have not been known for making sound investments with their funds. The municipality of Zhenjiang presents an example of resource misallocation by an LGFV. In 2013, the Zhenjiang FV built a 25-story building, whose

---

[23]Lam, R. W. and J. Wang (2018). China's Local Government Bond Market. IMF Working Paper WP/18/219. Washington, D.C.: International Monetary Fund, September.

expected cost was CNY500 million. The final cost has not been disclosed; however, as of 2019, the building has not had any paying tenants.[24]

c.   Low Liquidity. Local government bonds are owned primarily by long-term investors, such as commercial banks and insurance companies. These investors are not usually in the market, so local bonds are characterized by much lower turnover than other bonds. In addition, institutional investors bought these bonds in 2015 at relatively low prices. They now have very little incentive to resell.

d.   Underdeveloped market discipline. Local bond premia have not shown a significant relationship with economic fundamentals (Lam and Wang, 2018). In addition, local bond credit ratings have not been reliable. Pricing of these bonds' risk, then, is distorted. The perceived backing of the central government creates moral hazard potential.

e.   Fragmented regulatory framework. Local government bond markets suffer from the same regulatory segmentation that other Chinese bond markets suffer, being sold in two different markets (interbank and exchange). Additionally, local issues are subject to regulation by the MOF and their respective governments.

f.   Lack of disclosure. Local governments do not provide full information on their total debt. Furthermore, the explicit and implicit nature of local debt makes it very difficult for market observers to gauge both its total size and the portion of it funded by bond issuance.

The challenges presented by local debt have persisted despite the efforts of the central governments to face them successfully. The central government has banned some of the local government practices, such as providing land for free, aimed at strengthening their LGFV's balance sheet. The central government has also placed borrowing limits on LGFVs, but LGFVs and local governments have found ways of circumventing these limits.

---

[24]Yu, H., L. Zhu, H. Wu, S. Cheng, Y. Zhang, and F. Wang (2019). In Depth: The Local Government Debt Crisis That Won't Go Away (Part 1). Caixin Global, April 10. www. caixinglobal.com/2019-04-10/in-depth-the-local-government-debt-crisis-that-just-wont-go-away-part-1-101402567.html.

4. China's Interest Rate Regime

In a well-functioning market economy, interest rates are the market-determined price of loanable funds. At equilibrium, the marginal revenue from lending funds equals the marginal cost of borrowing, culminating in the efficient allocation of resources. Any movement away from equilibrium is corrected through appropriate changes in the supply or demand of loanable funds. On the other hand, in a CPE, repressed financial systems are characterized by controlled interest rates and associated with an inefficient allocation of resources. Although China has been committed to the marketization of its interest rate regime, accomplishing such a task has been challenging and complicated. China's approach to reforming its interest rate structure has been the same gradual and experimental approach followed similar to the approach taken with reforming all other sectors.

4.1. *Interest rates and monetary policy*

In conducting monetary policy, China's Central Bank has many tools at its disposal, both qualitative and quantitative. The PBOC's tools include reserve requirements, open market operations, and interest rate changes. However, the PBOC does not enjoy decision-making independence. Instead, it implements monetary policy under the direction of the State Council. The bank's actions, then, are closely aligned with the State Council's quest for growth along with price and exchange rate stability. Full employment and favorable Balance of Payments are also important objectives of the State Council, and therefore of the Central Bank, for the purposes of internal stability and international relations. The bank's dependence on the State Council is also indicated by the fact that the State Council appoints the principal bank officers, including the Bank Governor. In addition, the State Council must consider the interests of many other related parties (banks, for example) when establishing its economic objectives. The bank does have some independence in influencing short-term rates through open market operations but needs State Council approval when taking major policy decisions such as setting the benchmark deposit and lending interest rates.[25]

---

[25]McMahon, M., A. Schipke, and L. Xiang (2019). Monetary Policy Communication: Frameworks and Market Impact. In Schipke, A., M. Rodlauer, and L. Zhang (eds.),

China began liberalizing its interest rates with the introduction of the interbank market in 1997. Market rates were also allowed to be set for Policy Bank (1998) and Government Bonds. The Central Bank, however, has been able to control the cost of loans by setting their interest rates. Deposit and Lending rates were determined through the Central Bank's Benchmark rates, as shown in Table 8.7. In addition, the PBOC would give banks an upper and lower rate for deposit and/or lending. From time to time, the PBOC would adjust one or more if these limits as appropriate. For example, the PBOC lowered the lower limit of the lending rate to 80% of the benchmark in June, and further lowered it to 70% of the benchmark in July. A few months later, the lower limit of the lending rate was removed. Benchmark rates are also issued for instruments with different maturities. In January 2020, the PBOC embarked on its more recent campaign to liberalize its interest by announcing that it will make the Loan Prime Rate (LPR) the benchmark rate for lending. The LPR will then be linked to the one-year medium-term facility (MLF) rate, which is viewed as being market determined. Other interest rates in the economy will also be affected by the first months of 2021. The mortgage rate, previously based on the five-year benchmark (plus a spread), will be based on the five-year LPR rate. The seven-day repo rate, used by the Central Bank to influence bank liquidity, is not affected by the reforms, nor are the one and five-year benchmark deposit rates.

In a period of globally low interest rates, this change would imply lower lending costs and, therefore, increased lending and investment activity. The impact on different sectors of the economy, however. Market-based interest rates bring with them the potential for volatility. Large banks, with large SOE clientele and more sophisticated interest rate risk management techniques, are not expected to be as much affected as small banks, whose clientele is primarily comprised of SMEs and face relatively greater exposure to interest rate and credit risks.[26]

We present a chronology of China's interest rate developments in terms of their origination in money (lending and deposit) and capital markets in Appendix 10.A. Interest rate reform is a positive component of

---

The Future of China's Bond Market. Washington, DC: International Monetary Fund, pp. 295–332. www.elibrary.imf.org/view/IMF071/25402-9781484372142/25402-9781484372142/25402-9781484372142.xml?code=chinabondmarket.

[26]Federal Reserve Bank of San Francisco (2014). China's Interest Rate Liberalization Reform. Asia Focus: Country Analysis Unit. May.

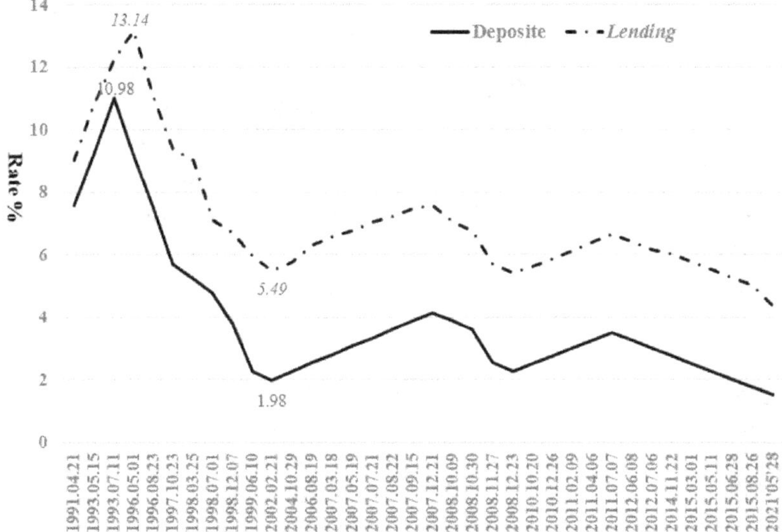

Figure 10.3.   Deposit and lending rates (%).

Source: The People's Bank of China, Monetary Policy Department: Benchmark interest rate for RMB deposits of financial institutions (updated on August 26, 2015); Benchmark interest rate for RMB loans of financial institutions (updated on October 24, 2015) (in Chinese); PBOC, National Interbank Funding Center: 1-year Benchmark Deposit Rate, 1-year Benchmark Lending Rate, Updating Date:28 May 2021.

China's overall market-based reforms. Its role in the reform of the entire financial system is of paramount importance. Since the interest rate regime's transition to a market-based one has not been completed yet, we can arrive at the same conclusion about the financial system in general.

5. China's Currency

We can start our discussion by making a couple of clarifying observations about China's currency.

First, we point to the name of the currency. You have probably heard some people referring to China's currency as the "Renminbi," while others refer to it as "Yuan." We will use "Renminbi" when we refer to the official name of China's currency. On the other hand, throughout this book, we have used the term Yuan as the unit of account. The International Organization for Standardization (ISO4217) assigns a three-letter code to each currency in order to facilitate trading. Accordingly, USD is the code for the US dollar, and CNY is the code for the Renminbi.

The second point we want to make here is about two general characteristics of currencies: variability (or volatility) and convertibility. Variability, of course, is the degree to which the value of the currency fluctuates (against other currencies). We will note that the renminbi has had a unique history with respect to its behavior. Currency volatility is important for exporters, importers, consumers, international investors, central bankers, and multinationals. A volatile currency may imply changes of prices of goods crossing international borders and of returns of international investments. Volatile currencies may also be an indication of instability of the country's economic environment. As we will see from examining the path the renminbi has taken, Chinese authorities have through the years placed a premium on stability.

Convertibility, on the other hand, is the degree to which one currency may be exchanged for another currency (or for gold). Some currencies are convertible for the exchange of goods and services. This is referred to as "current account convertibility." On the other hand, "capital account convertibility" means that the currency can be exchanged for other currencies for the purpose of investing in the country. When a currency is convertible in both the current account and the capital account, it is said to have "full convertibility." The Chinese currency has been characterized by lack of convertibility, at times, and current account convertibility at other times in its recent (post-1949) history. As of 2021, the Chinese currency remains non-convertible in the capital account.

5.1. *Brief history of China's currency*

The history of Chinese currency goes back thousands of years. After all, paper currency was first used in China during the Han Dynasty. We will not be covering the entire history of Chinese currency here. By 1930, there were various forms of money circulating in China, paper as well as metallic (silver and copper; also, sycee for larger transactions). Most countries at the time were on the gold standard, so the global price of silver was low. When the gold standard was abandoned, and the US passed the 1934 Silver Act, the price of silver increased again, leading to a flight of the metal from China. The Kuomintang government had to get off the Silver Standard and, instead, adopt a fiat currency, the fabi. In the meanwhile, the Japanese had invaded Manchuria (1931) and were expanding their controlled territory. The Japanese established their own China Reserve Bank in 1938 and issued their own currency for use in the occupied territories and to compete with the Kuomintang currency. The Kuomintang fabi, however, was convertible to the British pound and the US dollar. Therefore, it maintained its strength until the pressure to finance the war against Japan forced Chiang to wildly accelerate the pace of printing money. As a result, the supply of fabi increased from 1,400 million yuan (1937) to 660,000 billion yuan (1948). Hyperinflation ensued, with prices increasing by 35 million times. Even the issuance of gold yuan notes in 1948 was not enough to stem the rise of inflation, with prices going up one million times in a year.[27]

The currency environment became more chaotic, as the different provinces started issuing their own notes. In the meanwhile, the Maoists were controlling a growing part of the country. They established the PBOC in 1948. After the defeat of the KMT and the founding of the People's Republic of China, the PBOC called in all other types of money and started issuing the "people's money," the Renminbi. The issuance of the Renminbi represented not only a new medium of exchange, but also a means of promoting the Communist ideals and confirming political and economic resistance to the Republican regime. The initial imagery of the Renminbi reflected Marxist ideals and borrowed from the Soviet currency messages. The focus, however, was on featuring China's farmers and countryside, as well as (later) Mao and other Communist leaders.[28] The Renminbi itself has undergone many changes in its image and form since 1949, having been issued in a total of five "series."

---

[27] Prasad, E. S. (2017). *Gaining Currency: The Rise of the Renminbi*. New York: Oxford University Press, pp. 7–22.

[28] Notar, B. E. (2003). Viewing Currency Chaos: Paper Money for Advertizing, Ideology, and Resistance in Republican China. In Myers, R. *Defining Modernity: Guomindang Rhetorics of a New China*. Edited by T. Bodenhorn. Ann Arbor, MI: University of Michigan Center for Chinese Studies.

5.2. *China's exchange rate policy and the behavior of the RMB*

Figure 10.4 illustrates the year average value of the RMB (versus the USD) from 1950–2018. As the figure shows, the value of the RMB did not change during the Mao years. From 1949 until the beginning of reforms, China set the official value of the Renminbi at an artificially high (overvalued) exchange rate to discourage imports; different exchange rates were used for exports in accordance with the country's need for foreign exchange. Reform of the exchange rate system proceeded slowly. In a manner parallel to the household responsibility system, in 1979, exporters could keep a portion of their foreign exchange earnings. Further loosening of the exchange rate took place a year later, as the government allowed enterprises with surplus foreign exchange to sell to enterprises needing foreign exchange.

In early 1981, a dual exchange rate system was instituted, with the rate applicable to trade transactions pegged to the US dollar and set at USD/CNY = 2.8. This was the "internal settlement rate." The official rate was set at USD/CNY = 1.5; it was pegged to a basket of currencies.[29] In mid-1988, swap centers were established to allow enterprises to exchange foreign currencies.

5.3. *The foreign exchange certificates period*

When reforms started, and China's doors opened wider to the world, visitors from all parts of the world converged on the country. With them, they brought their money. To control the circulation of multiple currencies and the uncertainties it created on transactions, the Bank of China was authorized by the State Council to issue Foreign Exchange Certificates, or FECs (April 1980). These certificates were used as means of exchange by foreigners, who were prohibited from holding the domestic currency. The Bank of China reports that the amount of FECs issued between 1980 and 1989 was equivalent to CNY31 billion, of which CNY4.1 billion circulated in the market.[30] Foreigners had to use designated stores that accepted

---

[29]Yu, Y. (2018). The reform of China's exchange rate regime. China's 40 Years of Reform and Development, 1978–2018. https://pdfs.semanticscholar.org/2e71/f1cf2b0a1eed63210 102b0b190a5bc481b75.pdf.

[30]Bank of China (2008). Foreign Exchange Certificates Issued under Improved Forex Administration (1979–1989). September 26. www.boc.cn/EN/aboutboc/ab7/200809/ t20080926_1601850.html.

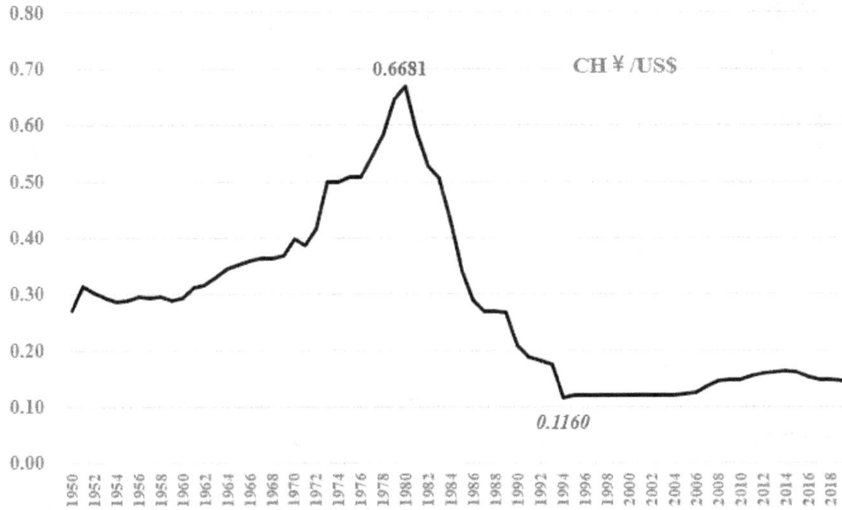

Figure 10.4.   RMB Behavior, 1950–2018 (expressed as CNY per USD1).

Source: Calculating using data from China Statistical Yearbook 2019, Table 11.2; 199, Table 15.1.

FECs; these stores were called "Friendship Stores." By law, other stores were not permitted to accept FECs. Friendship Stores sold some items that were not available to Chinese citizens, who were not allowed to hold FECs. There was a lot of confusion in some stores, as their goods were priced in the FEC and the domestic currency. Soon after the appearance of the FEC, a black market developed. As China's exchange rate regime evolved, the FECs were withdrawn from circulation in 1995.

5.4. *Post reform behavior*

In January 1994, the PBOC unified its dual exchange rates. In addition, the RMB was devalued to CNY8.7=USD1. In April of the same year, the China Foreign Exchange Trade System (CFETS) was established. CFETS is a government agency under the PBOC. CFETS was established in 1994; it has several functions supporting the PBOC's mission, including providing and analyzing information pertaining to the RMB. Over the next few months (1995–1996), the dollar weakened versus the RMB. The USDCNY rate moved from 8.7 to 8.28. In December of 1996, the RMB became convertible in the current account.

China made it through the Asian Financial (or, as authorities in many Asian countries branded it, IMF) Crisis, relatively unscathed. The PBOC, however, had to intervene on several occasions to avert devaluation. The exchange rate toward the US dollar fluctuated between USDCNY8.2770 and 8.2800 during 1997 to 1999. In December 1999, the PBOC allowed the RMB to vary within a +/–0.15% from the reference rate versus the USD, and +/–1.0% versus the HKD and the JPY, as well as =/–2.5% versus other currencies.

5.4.1. *Changing the regime*

As the pressures from the Crisis subsided, China widened the RMB's trading band against the dollar from 0.30% to 0.40% (8.2760–8.2800). China's entry into the WTO in December 2001 served as the basis for optimism about the future course of the Chinese economy. China's trade surpluses started mounting, exerting upwards pressure on the RMB. China resisted revaluation until 2005.

On July 21, 2005, a major reform of China's exchange rate regime was announced by the Chinese government. From this time on, the PBOC stopped pegging the value of the RMB to the US dollar. Instead, the RMB transitioned into a managed floating rate, with its value set in reference to the US dollar and a basket of other currencies. The new regime was to generate a more flexible RMB, while still being under control by the PBOC. Thus, the daily RMB rate was set as follows[31]:

- At the beginning of each day, a central parity rate would constitute the midpoint of the band within which the value of the RMB versus the US dollar would move during the day. The central parity rate was the previous day's closing rate;
- The value of the RMB vis-à-vis the US dollar could move inside a +/–0.3% band around the central parity rate;
- In addition to its movement about the US dollar, the value of the RMB would also be allowed to move against the basket of other reference countries; the band would be +/–1.5% from the central parity rate.

---

[31]Das, S. (2019). China's Evolving Exchange Rate Regime. IMF Working Paper, WP/19/50. Washington, DC: International Monetary Fund. file://hd.ad.syr.edu/02/d83f6d/Documents/Downloads/WPIEA2019050%20(2).pdf.

The PBOC also announced a revaluation of the RMB, from USDRMB = 8.2765 to USDRMB = 8.11.

Further adjustments were made in the months and years ahead as follows:

- September 2005: Trading band for rates relative to non-USD currencies was expanded from +/–1.5% to +/–3.0%. To promote further liberalization of the RMB, China established an over-the-counter foreign exchange market and a market for currency swaps and futures.
- January 2006: USDCNY central parity rate to be based on a weighted average of quotes sent in by the big banks at the beginning of trading;
- May 2007: USDRMB band widened to +/–0.5%.
- April 2012: USDRMB band widened to +/–1.0%;
- March 2014: USDRMB band widened to +/–2.0%;
- August 2015: USDRMB central parity quoting mechanism revised. Accordingly, the central parity rate would be based on quotes submitted by designated banks. The PBOC directed the banks to consider the following when forming their quotes:
  (a) previous day's closing rate.
  (b) foreign exchange market conditions; and,
  (c) movements of the major currencies.
  The PBOC set the central parity rate as the mid-point for the day's trading range allowed to fluctuate +/– 2% versus the USD. The PBOC also devalued the RMB (versus USD) by 1.9%. Following this announcement, the RMB depreciated by additional 1.0% versus the USD;
  - December 2015: China Foreign Exchange Trading System (CFETS) Index published. The CFETS index is a trade-related index, aimed at reflecting China's external position. It comprises 13 currencies, with the larger weights assigned to the US Dollar (0.2640), Euro (0.2139), Japanese Yen (0.1468), the Hong Kong Dollar (0.655), and the Australian Dollar (0.0627).
  - October 2016: The RMB takes its first major step toward internationalization by being included in the IMF's Special Drawing Rights (SDRs). The SDR weights were set as follows: USD, 41.73%; Euro, 30.93%; JPY, 8.33%; and, GBP 8.09%.
  - May 2017: The central parity mechanism was changed again. The PBOC added a new factor, termed "countercyclical" factor. The inclusion of this factor was intended to protect the RMB from

extreme upward or downward pressures. September 2019: The CFETS announces that, effective January 2020, the USD weight in the CFETS Index was reduced to 21.59% from 22.40%, while the euro's weight was raised to 17.40% from 16.34%. There will be 24 currencies included in the formulation of the Index. The new weights reflected China's trade activity in 2018.

The IMF's classification of China's exchange rate regime has changed through the years. For example, on August 1, 2006, the IMF determined that the RMB was primarily determined by official action and classified its behavior as a crawling peg. On December 31, 2008, the IMF noted that the official action toward the RMB aimed at stabilizing it. Therefore, it changed its classification from crawl-like to stabilized. On February 9, 2009, the IMF reclassified the de facto RMB regime as crawl-like. On October 1, 2016, the IMF's Executive Board recognized the Chinese Renminbi as a freely usable currency. This determination, as well as China's rising role in the global economy, led to the inclusion of the Renminbi in the SDR as the fifth currency. The weights of the currencies included in the new SDR are U.S. dollar, 41.73%; Euro, 30.93%; Chinese renminbi, 10.92%; Japanese yen, 8.33%; and, Pound sterling, 8.09%. The weighted average of representative interest rates in the money markets of these five currencies is used to calculate the SDR interest rate. The SDR interest rate is the interest rate that the IMF charges its members when they borrow from the Fund. (www.imf.org/external/np/fin/data/rms_mth.aspx?SelectDate=2017-08-31&reportType=CVSDR).

In 2018, the RMB experienced increase in its volatility against the 24 currencies included in the CFETS Index. The de facto arrangement of the RMB, then, changed to "other managed."

The specific way the PBOC sets the central parity rate is not made public. The PBOC has often stated that its actions have aimed at increasing the flexibility of the RMB. However, this does not imply that Chinese authorities have not intervened to affect the market value of the currency.

5.5. *The trilemma*

China's exchange rate regime, then, has gone through a number of changes. Have these changes been effective in contributing to the success of China's reforms? This is a difficult question to answer, since the effectiveness of a country's exchange rate regime cannot be assessed independently of additional policies that the country follows at any one time. When deciding on an exchange rate policy, then, consideration should be given to other policies that the country is implementing. For example, China has embarked on a path of opening up its financial markets. However, it still imposes capital controls. Is a free capital flows policy compatible with a stable exchange rate policy? And, if these two policies are enacted, do they allow the PBOC to pursue an independent monetary policy?

Many scholars point out that policymakers face what is called the Impossible Trinity, or the Impossible Triad or the Trilemma.[32] Figure 9.3 shows that a country may attempt to achieve three possible policy objectives:

1. Fixed (stable) exchange rate;
2. Free capital mobility; and
3. Independent monetary policy.

Unfortunately, all three of these objectives cannot be accomplished at the same time (see Figure 10.5). Let us assume that China wishes to maintain a stable RMB, while liberalizing its capital account (Objective 1: Fixed/stable exchange rates and free capital mobility). In that case, the PBOC will not be able to set interest rates; with the exchange rate kept stable, the inflow/outflow of capital will exert pressure on the interest rates. Similarly, achieving Objective 2 implies giving up on fixed exchange rates; achieving Objective 3 implies that maintaining a stable exchange rate and control over interest rates is achieved only by erecting capital controls. So, how should China confront its trilemma? Allowing the RMB to float or imposing stricter capital controls could be alternative

---

[32] Obstfeld, M., J. C. Shambaugh, and A. M. Taylor (2004). The Trilemma in History: Tradeoffs among Exchange Rates, Monetary Policies, and Capital Mobility. National Bureau of Economic Research, Working Paper 10396, March, Cambridge, MA. www.nber.org/papers/w10396.

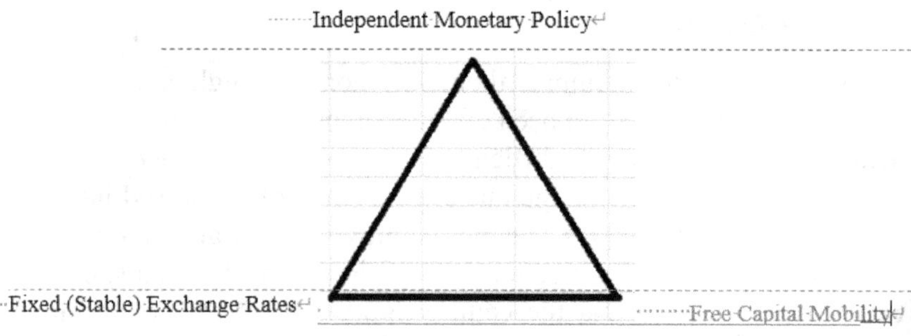

Figure 10.5. China's trilemma.

solutions, but both have potential shortcomings. Allowing the RMB to float could bring about wide fluctuations and be a shock to the economy. Imposing stricter controls, on the other hand, would serve as a strong signal of reform rollback.

One possible solution has been suggested by former Fed Chairman, Ben Bernanke.[33] According to Bernanke, China could instead rely on targeted fiscal policy, which would increase aggregate demand while supporting the overall reform effort. The future will tell how China will choose to confront the Impossible challenge.

5.6. *The lighter side of currency undervaluation: The RMB and the Big Mac index*

Since 1986, *The Economist* has been measuring the extent to which currencies are under- or overvalued. *The Economist*'s measurements are an application of the Law of One Price, that states that the international (exchange rate-adjusted) price of goods is the same around the world. To test the Law of One Price, *The Economist* examines the global price of the popular Big Mac sandwich. The question, then, can be stated as follows: is the Big Mac's price the same everywhere when adjusted for the exchange rate? Furthermore, is the price of the Big Mac the same around the world when we adjust for the exchange rate as well as the purchasing power of the country's currency? According to *The Economist's* findings,

---

[33] Bernanke, B. (2016). China's trilemma-and a possible solution. March 9. www.brookings.edu/blog/ben-bernanke/2016/03/09/chinas-trilemma-and-a-possible-solution/.

the average price of the Big Mac in the US in July 2020 was USD5.71. In China, it was CNY21.7. With the exchange rate of CNY7.0035=USD1 during the same time, the USD equivalent price of the Big Mac in China was USD3.0985. We can conclude, then, that the Chinese RMB is under-valued by 45.7% versus the U.S. dollar.[34] The over- or undervaluation of the RMB versus the USD may also be calculated after adjusting for dif-ferences in purchasing power between the two countries; we find that the RMB is undervalued by only 6.5% (calculations not shown).

Figure 10.4 illustrates the extent of RMB undervaluation versus the USD since 2011. According to the figure, the RMB has been undervalued by about 40–45%. When accounting for differences in purchasing power, however, we see (see Figure 10.4, lower panel) that the RMB's undervalu-ation is about 12% at the most. In some periods, the RMB is actually overvalued. These results, of course, should not be viewed as conclusive about the RMB's valuation. It only pertains to the relative price of one product, regardless of how popular this product is.

5.7. *The US perspective: the politics of the RMB*

The relationship between the US and China has been complicated, as it has been colored by political as much as economic concerns. The Trump years have been associated with an increasingly adversarial atmosphere in the relationship between the two countries. China's currency policy has been one of the sources of disagreement between the two countries. In August 2019, as the Trade War between the two countries was heating up, the US designated China as a currency manipulator. A few months later, however, the US lifted the manipulator designation.

The initial decision to label China as a currency manipulator was articulated in the Department of the Treasury's Reports to Congress.[35] In accordance with the US 2015 Trade Facilitation and Trade Enforcement Act, the Treasury has been using three criteria in classifying countries as

---

[34] To arrive at this number, we first find the price of the Big Mac in China as if the Law of One Price held. It should be (7.0035) x (5.71) = CNY39.99; the actual price of CNY21.7 is approximately 54.3% of what the price should be if the Law of One Price held. We conclude that the RMB is undervalued by 45.7% 91-0.54.3).

[35] U.S. Department of the Treasury; Office of International Affairs (2020). *Macroeconomic and Foreign Exchange Policies of Major Trading Partners of the United States*, January. https://home.treasury.gov/system/files/136/20200113-Jan-2020-FX-Report-FINAL.pdf.

Raw Data

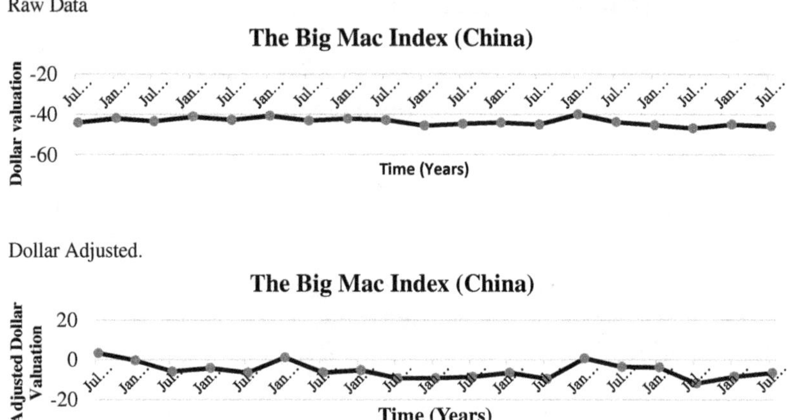

Figure 10.6.   The RMB and Big Mac: Dollar Valuation (Raw Data) and Adjusted (PPP) Dollar Valuation.

Source: *The Economist* (2021). Big Mac Index. January. www.economist.com/big-mac-index.

currency manipulators. The criteria are as follows: (1) the country is running a significant trade surplus *vis-à-vis* the US; (2) the country is running a material current account surplus; and, (3) the country engages persistently in intervening to weaken its currency. In the 2019 Report, the Treasury found that China met the first criterion, as it had been doing since the 2016 Report. China also had a Current Account surplus, but China's surplus was less than that shown by Germany and Japan. However, the Report did not conclude that China engaged in direct intervention in the foreign exchange market.

This was not the first time that China's currency strategy was criticized. In July 2011, the IMF assessed the RMB to be inconsistent with China's fundamentals. Four years later, the IMF reversed its assessment, announcing that the RMB reflected the fundamentals.[36] The same assessment was repeated between 2016 and 2018. The movement of the RMB was also closely monitored by the US. The US Treasury, in accordance with the 2015 Trade Facilitation and Enforcement Act, issued a report in 2016 in which it stated that the RMB was significantly undervalued.

---

[36]Morrison, W. M. (2019). China's Currency Policy. Congressional Research Service: In Focus, May 24. https://fas.org/sgp/crs/row/IF10139.pdf.

As of the early months of the Biden Administration, the US has not shown any inclination to accuse China of currency manipulation.

5.8. *The offshore Renminbi*

In addition to trading in the Mainland, demand for Renminbi products led to trading of the currency in markets abroad, especially in Hong Kong. Trading spot RMB in Hong Kong commenced in 2003 and was formalized through a 2010 Memorandum between the Mainland and Hong Kong authorities. To differentiate it from the domestically traded RMB (whose symbol is CNY), the offshore RMB is denoted as CNH. The advantage of trading CNH, rather than CNY, is that the CNH is not subject to the restrictions imposed on the CNY. The fundamental factors affecting demand for the CNY, of course, also affect the demand for RMB-denominated products and, therefore, the CNH. The two, then, should move in similar fashion. However, there have been times when the two have deviated. See, for example, Table 10.10. The Table shows the spread between the two RMB markets, as well as the standard error of the mean, for the 2014–2020 period. Although the intervals (annual) used are arbitrary, we can still make some useful observations about the relationship between CNY and CNH. Of the six periods shown, differences were the largest in 2015. Earlier in this chapter, we discussed China's 2015 Stock Market Crash and the ensuing RMB depreciation. The negative sign implies that the USDCNH rate fell significantly more than the USDCNY rate. One possible explanation of this is that the RMB traded in Hong Kong more accurately reflected the negative sentiment towards the RMB. The onshore RMB, on the other hand, was most likely supported by PBOC intervention. Figure 10.7 reveals that the largest difference between RMB values in the two markets took place in 2015 during the July–October period.

Differences between the onshore and offshore RMB rates have implications for foreign exchange market participants. Importers with CNH deposits can use them to pay for their imports when the CNH is stronger. Similarly, Chinese investors in USD-denominated securities can use their CNH deposits to purchase these securities.

Hong Kong is the primary trading location for the offshore RMB. It enjoys geographical and cultural proximity to the Mainland; it also has a well-developed financial system that features lack of capital controls and regulatory transparency. It is well-connected to the Mainland's economy

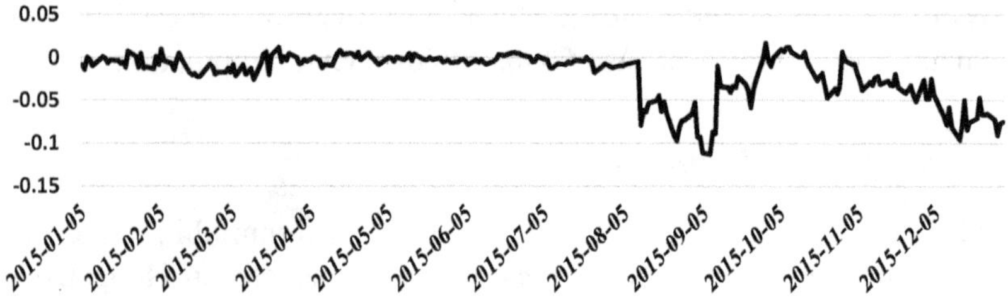

Figure 10.7.   Onshore–Offshore RMB Spread, 2015.

Source: WIND.

in general, and the Pearl Delta region. Finally, Hong Kong's Stock Exchange has been selected as an IPO location for many Chinese companies. However, it is not the only one. As China's global economic stature grows, the demand for its currency has also grown. Many other financial centers have been competing to become the principal offshore RMB trading hub. They include Singapore, London, Frankfurt, Luxemburg, and Paris. Efforts directed toward becoming an RMB center are motivated by the expectations of several benefits, including trading revenues, trade facilitation, and even better relations with China. The global demand for RMB will determine the extent to which these centers will realize their expectations and whether other locations will also attempt to become off-shore RMB trading centers.

5.9. *The internationalization of the RMB*

The inclusion of the RMB in the IMF's SDR currency basket represented the seal of approval for the RMB's position in the global financial system. Will the RMB ever become a global currency? Will it ever replace the dollar as the world's currency? The short answer to these two questions is: not very soon!

During the first half of the 20th century, the British Pound was the world's principal currency for international trade and investment. After WWII, the Pound was replaced by the US dollar; the dollar, at least for now, is still dominant in international transactions and the closest thing we have to an "international currency." The dollar's global stature has been viewed as an "exorbitant privilege" that, according to its critics, the US has used to its advantage in international economic and political relations.

There have been periods over the last half century when the dollar's hegemony has been threatened by other currencies, namely the Japanese Yen and the Euro. Does the Renminbi represent a legitimate threat to the dollar in the first quarter of the 21st century? Will it become the next international currency? For a currency to become an international currency, it must be freely used in international transactions, serve as reserve currency, and be relatively stable. The issuing country must also be willing to allow its currency to be used as such. Does the Renminbi meet these criteria?

Countries may want to have an international currency because it delivers certain benefits, including[37]:

1. Lower transactions and borrowing costs. Chinese importers and exporters would very much like to be able to pay or receive payments from their international trading partners. China's companies would also find it easier and less expensive to borrow in the international markets.
2. Segniorage. In the mid-1960s, French President Charles de Gaulle often complained about the position of the US dollar in the global economy. According to de Gaulle, the United States was buying up the world using dollars that cost nothing to produce, instead of using gold, which has real value. In this case, then, segniorage is the purchasing value of the dollar over and above the cost of producing it.
3. Soft power. Countries need international currencies to pay off their debts and buy goods in global markets. They will tend to be supportive of policies promoted by countries issuing these currencies.

Having an international currency, however, also carries some potential costs, such as:

1. Volatility of capital flows. Capital will move in and out of the country in a larger and less predictable manner, as the demand for the international currency may fluctuate depending on global development.
2. Financial asset volatility. As capital inflows and outflows become more volatile, the country's financial asset prices may also fluctuate.

---

[37]Nabar, M. and C. E. Tovar (2017). Internationalization of the RMB. In Lam, R., W. M. Rodlauer, and A. Schipke (eds.), *Modernizing China: Investing in Soft Infrastructure*. Washington, DC: International Monetary Fund, pp. 249–278.

3. Lack of control over disposal of other countries' international reserves. Other countries, holding international currencies as part of their official reserves, may wish to dispose of these reserves. Their actions will thus increase the supply of the currencies in the foreign exchange market.

Is the RMB making progress toward becoming an international currency? One way of answering this question is by referring to Standard Chartered Bank's Renminbi Globalization Index (RGI).[38] Standard Chartered arrives at the measure of a currency's internationalization by considering its following characteristics: the currency's use as a store of value, its trade settlement activity, its use as a means of capital raising, and its associated foreign exchange market trading volume. In calculating the RGI, these characteristics are proxied by CNH deposits, trade settlement, and other international payments, Dim Sum bonds and Certificates of Deposit, and foreign exchange market turnover. The focus is on offshore use of the RMB by corporates. Selected dates of the RGI are included in Table 10.8. The Index uses December 2010 as the basis, since this was the first time the RMB was given the green light to trade offshore. This development allowed trade settlement in CNH and the buying of Dim Sum bonds. The table reveals that the RGI has increased by 22 times during the life of the Index, confirming the increased internationalization of the RMB.

Table 10.11 shows the share (S) of total foreign exchange market turnover associated with the three top-ranked currencies and Renminbi's share and rank (R). The US Dollar has remained the dominant currency, although its share of total turnover has declined over the years. The shares of the other two major currencies have also declined. On the other hand, the Renminbi's share was negligible in 2004, but rose substantially by 2019. Despite its rise, however, it remains a relatively small part of total turnover (4.3% of USD6,590 billion total daily foreign exchange market turnover in 2019). In terms of currency pairs traded, the USD/CNY was the fifth most commonly traded currency pair in 2019 (4.1% of total traded).

Of the Chinese yuan traded in the foreign exchange market in 2019, the total being equivalent to USD284 billion, foreign exchange and

---

[38] Standard Charter. Renminbi Tracker: How Global is the Renminbi? www.sc.com/en/trade-beyond-borders/renminbi-globalisation-index/. Another commonly referred to Renminbi Globalization Index is compiled by the International Monetary Institute of Renmin University.

Table 10.10.   Descriptive Statistics; Annual RMB Spread, 2014–2015.

	2014	2015	2016	2017	2018	2019	2020
Mean	0.0009	−0.0202	−0.0113	0.0082	−0.0003	−0.0058	−0.0021
Standard Error	0.0008	0.0017	0.0013	0.0012	0.0011	0.0010	0.0015
Standard Deviation	0.0123	0.0276	0.0211	0.0199	0.0181	0.0169	0.0229
Sample Variance	0.0002	0.0008	0.0004	0.0004	0.0003	0.0003	0.0005
Count	259	258	259	260	261	261	226

Source: Calculated by the authors from data provided by WIND.

Table 10.11.   Foreign exchange turnover: Global share and turnover.

Year	2004		2007		2010		2013		2016		2019	
Currency	S	R	S	R	S	R	S	R	S	R	S	R
USD	88	1	85.6	1	84.9	1	87	1	87.6	1	88.3	1
Euro	37.4	2	37.9	2	39	2	33.4	2	31.4	2	32.3	2
JPY	20.8	3	17.2	3	19	3	23	3	21.6	3	16.8	3
RMB	0.1	29	0.5	20	0.9	17	2.2	9	4	8	4.3	8

Source: Generated from Bank of International Settlements. *Triennial Central Bank Survey of foreign exchange and derivatives market activity in 2019*. Accessed at www.bis.org/statistics/rpfx19_fx.pdf.

currency swaps represented the largest component (48.3%), followed by spot transactions (34.1%), outright forwards (12.7%), and options (4.6%).

5.10. *Cross-border use of the RMB*

According to the PBOC's 2020 RMB Internationalization Report,[39] cross-border RMB settlement in 2019 increased by 24.1% from 2018. Receipts were up 25.1% while payments increased by 23% from the previous year. In addition to trade and direct investment, portfolio investment grew substantially. The issuance of Dim Sum and Panda bonds has contributed to the demand for offshore and onshore RMB, as have the foreign holdings of Chinese domestically issued instruments. From December 2018 to December 2019, foreign holdings of domestic RMB financial assets

---

[39]People's Bank of China (2020). 2020 RMB Internationalization Report. www.caixinglobal.com/upload/PBOC-2020-RMB-International-Report.pdf.

increased from CNY4,920.90 billion to CNY6,412.84 billion (about 30%). Included in this figure are the market capitalization of stocks (CNY2.1 trillion), the amount of bonds under custody (CNY2.26 trillion), bank deposits (CNY1.21 trillion, including interbank accounts), and loans (CNY833.2 billion).

In its 2020 RMB Internationalization Report, the PBOC confirmed its commitment to internationalization. The PBOC certainly wants to incur all the benefits of currency internationalization listed above. In addition, the motivation to internationalize the RMB is derived from the desire to promote de-dollarization in the global economy. For China, the Trade War and related developments pointed to the need for decreasing the reliance on the dollar. Therefore, even though catching the dollar on the global stage does not appear feasible in the short run, China has embarked on several initiatives aimed at replacing the dollar's role with the RMB in cross-border transactions with neighboring countries, countries participating in the Belt and Rod Initiative, and the BRICS. For example, China opened a CNY150 billion swap line with Russia in October 2014. Accordingly, each country may use its own currency to finance transactions with the other, thereby bypassing the intermediate conversion into dollars. The 2014 swap agreement has since been renewed. In September 2020, China signed a similar swap agreement with Indonesia. As of mid-2020, China has signed swap agreements with over 60 countries, totaling about USD500 billion. Some of these countries have also agreed to hold about 10% of their Central Bank reserves in RMB.[40] To facilitate trade in RMB around the world, China has authorized banks in 25 countries to assist exporters clear RMB-based trades. To facilitate the cross-border settlement of the RMB, the operations infrastructure was also improved, with the RMB Cross-Border Interbank Payment System (CIPS) developing into the principal channel of cross-border RMB clearing and settlement. CIPS went into operation in 2015, representing an effort to mitigate dependence on the Belgium-run SWIFT (Society for Worldwide Interbank Financial Telecommunications) and, therefore, exposure of Chinese international payments operations and data to the US.

---

[40] *The Economist* (2020). China wants to make the yuan a central-bank favourite. Special Edition, May 7. www.economist.com/special-report/2020/05/07/china-wants-to-make-the-yuan-a-central-bank-favourite.

The use of the RMB as a reserve currency has been limited so far. According to the IMF, the RMB accounts for only 2% of global allocated Central Bank reserves (Q2, 2020), compared to 61% for the US dollar and 20% for the euro. However, according to Morgan Stanley, this number will reach 5–10% by 2030. The exact percentage of RMB-denominated reserves, of course, will depend on China's policies with respect to capital account liberalization. www.sc.com/en/trade-beyond-borders/renminbi-globalisation-index/.

6. Derivatives

A derivative is a security whose price is *derived from* an underlying asset, or even a group of assets. Stocks, bonds, currencies, commodities, interest rates, and market indices are some of the assets used as underlying assets. Derivatives contracts may be traded over the counter (OTC) or on organized exchanges.

Derivatives serve several functions in their respective markets and the economy in general. In an increasingly risky global economic environment, participants have found it necessary to seek ways in which they can deal with risks. Derivatives enable market participants to transfer risks, a practice called hedging. They also enable market participants to engage in transactions principally aimed at generating a profit, a practice called speculation. Derivatives also provide the market with more information about the underlying asset, increasing liquidity and helping with the price determination process. Depending on the structure of the market, derivatives can provide leverage, since a relatively small change in the value of the underlying can be associated with a large swing in the value of the derivative contract. However, in addition to providing benefits, then, using and trading derivatives entails risks that need to be identified and addressed effectively. Derivative markets have been very popular but, at the same time, very controversial. As is well-known by now, in the Berkshire-Hathaway 2002 Annual Report, Warren Buffet likened derivatives to "financial weapons of mass destruction."

Not everybody agrees with Buffet, of course. The difference of opinion on derivatives stems primarily from the fact that many casual observers consider these markets to exist for solely speculative purposes. While speculation is one of the motives for market participation, and while the practice of trading derivatives has featured several abuses through the years, these markets also perform an extremely useful role by assisting participants in hedging their financial risks and contributing to the price discovery process of the underlying security.

China's derivative markets can be distinguished in terms of their underlying product: a commodity or a financial instrument.

6.1. *Markets for commodity-based derivatives*

The first commodity futures market in China opened in October 1990: the Zhengzhou Commodity Exchange (ZCE). It served as the country's first pilot futures market, officially launching futures trading in 1993. It currently (December 2020) lists 18 futures products and one options product, primarily from agricultural, energy, and chemistry sectors. (http://english.czce.com.cn/enportal/AboutZCE/Overview/Overview/H69010101index_1.htm).

The Dalian Commodity Exchange (DCE) (www.dce.com.cn/DCE/About_Us/The%20DCE%20at%20Glance/index.html) was established in 1993. The Futures Industry Association ranked the Dalian Exchange #7 in the world among the 80 exchanges it surveyed in 2020. By the end of 2019, there were 19 futures and 3 options contracts listed on the DCE. Five of the exchange's agricultural products were ranked among the top 10 of the global agricultural product rankings in terms of trading volume, with Soybean meal ranked #1. Futures on industrial, energy, and chemical products are also traded on the DCE.

The Shanghai Futures Exchange (SHFE) was established in 1999. Twenty futures contracts and five commodity options are traded on the exchange. They include futures on metals (such as aluminum, copper, gold, and zinc), energy and chemical products (such as crude oil, fuel oil, natural rubber, and wood pulp), and options on aluminum, copper, gold, natural rubber, and zinc.

6.2. *Equity and bond derivatives*

The China Financial Futures Exchange (CFFEX) is the country's first stock index futures exchange. CFFEX was founded in 2006 by the Shanghai and Shenzhen Stock Exchanges, the Zhengzhou and Dalian Commodity Exchanges, and the Shanghai Futures Exchange. It commenced trading in 2010. The contracts traded on the CFFEX include Equity (CSI 300, CSI500, and SSE 50 Index) and Interest Rate (2-year, 5-year, and 10-year Government Bond Indices) futures, and CSI Index options.

6.3. *Exchange rate derivatives*

The rise of the RMB in international transactions has been accompanied by the development of derivative markets for the currency, including forward and futures contracts.

- RMB Forwards:
  RMB forward contracts were first issued by the Bank of China in 1997.
- RMB Swaps:
  The first RMB swap transaction took place in April 2006 in the interbank market between the Bank of China and China's Import and Export Bank.[41]
- RMB Futures:
  RMB futures against the US dollar, the euro, and the yen were first listed and traded on the Chicago Mercantile Exchange in 2006. In addition to the Standard contract size (USD100,000), CME offers an e-Micro contract (USD10,000). In 2012, the Hong Kong Exchange (HKEX) launched trading of offshore RMB (CNH) futures contracts.
- Over-the-Counter (OTC) Products:
  The rising popularity of the RMB has also given rise to the development of OTC derivatives, such as non-deliverable forwards (NDF) and non-deliverable options (NDO).

As China opens the rest of its financial system to the world, it is also opening its derivative markets to international investors. The financial liberalization rules that went into effect in November 2019 made it easier for foreign investors to enter China's derivative markets. Qualified Foreign Investors (QFI) have since faced an easier application and licensing process. By relaxing eligibility criteria and shortening the application review period from 20 days to 10 days, the new rules have led to an expansion of the Qualified Foreign Investor base. The range of products available to foreign investors has also increased. Under the old rules, foreign investors could invest in stock index futures. According to the new rules, QFIs may also access bond futures, while having access to a wider range of products. Under the previous regime, foreign funds could invest in stock index futures. Under the new regime, the range of accessible products will be expanded to include bond futures listed on the

---

[41]Yan, J. (2010). Development and utilization of financial derivatives in China. Bank for International Settlements. www.bis.org/ifc/publ/ifcb35c.pdf.

China Financial Futures Exchange, as well as commodity futures and options traded on exchanges in Shanghai, Zhengzhou, and Dalian. Trading in crude oil and iron ore futures is already available to foreign participants.[42]

6.4. *The outlook for derivatives markets*

China's futures industry has been a breeding ground for innovation in market structure and overall market development. To attract foreign participation, the SHFE set up a subsidiary, the Shanghai International Energy Exchange (INE). INE introduced yuan-denominated futures contracts on rubber, of which China is a major importer. Foreign firms also have direct access to China's copper futures market through the INE's copper contract. The INE copper contract is settled in yuan, but foreign firms may use dollars to satisfy initial margin requirements. Another innovation was the cross-border delivery of low-sulfur fuel oil futures initiated by SHFE and completed by INE. In January 2021, the contract's settlement took place in China, but delivery was made in Singapore. The new mode of delivery achieved optimization of logistics costs and inventory management.[43]

China's CSRC, which oversees derivative markets, is committed to continuing the introduction of new commodity futures and options contracts, including natural gas, refined oil, and peanuts, and to developing a more sophisticated financial futures market. Futures markets have performed a valuable risk management function for financial institutions, such as the Bank of China, and industry. When the markets for underlying securities do not reflect risk accurately, the operation of markets for derivatives has even more importance for market participants. As risk-hedging became even more necessary during the COVID-affected period, futures trading increased by 46% during the first 11 months of 2020. The structure of the market also changed, with institutional holdings, which

---

[42]Hyde, K. (2020). China opens futures markets further to outside world. Futures Industry Association. November. www.fia.org/marketvoice/articles/china-opens-futures-markets-further-outside-world#:~:text=China's%20drive%20to%20open%20its,China's%20markets%20came%20into%20force.&text=Under%20the%20previous%20regime%2C%20foreign,invest%20in%20stock%20index%20futures.

[43]Jing, S. (2021). Cross-border delivery a leap for commodity futures. *China Daily.* January 26. www.chinadaily.com.cn/a/202101/26/WS600f768da31024ad0baa5160.htm.

were traditionally at the 15–20% range, jumping to 38% of the commodities market.[44]

Derivative markets represent a sign of market maturity. The smooth development of the markets requires a well-functioning market economy, sound regulation, and participants that understand the workings of these markets and the risks involved. For Chinese investors, the events in the crude oil futures of April 2020 provided a valuable and expensive lesson on such risks. The crude market crash hit investors hard worldwide.[45] These investors had bought a Bank of China crude futures product called Yuan Yu Bao, designed specifically for domestic retail clients. Chinese investors are not in general permitted to buy crude futures in foreign markets. They can, however, buy trading accounts offered by BOC, ICBC, and BCC that are linked to futures contracts, such as the May WTI contract. The Bank of China had set Monday, April 20, 2020 as the settlement date for the Yuan Yu Bao May WTI contract. Due to the time difference between New York and China, Chinese investors could not settle after 10 pm. BOC settled the contracts at 2:30 am. By then, the price had moved into negative territory (-USD37.63 per barrel)! As a result, 60,000 Chinese investors suffered estimated losses of CNY10 billion (USD1.4 billion).

Despite such a setback, and given China's dominant role in global commodity markets, we should expect its commodity-based derivatives to continue to play an important role in the operation of the global derivatives sector. Markets for financial derivatives must go a longer way to develop fully, since markets for the respective underlying securities have not matured yet. Furthermore, China still has not fully liberalized its capital account. The opening of financial markets in 2020 is a positive sign of further integration of China's financial sector with the global financial system, and therefore faster development of its markets, including those for derivative products.

---

[44]Reuters (2020). China to ramp up derivative market products. December 19. www. reuters.com/article/china-futures-development/update-1-china-to-ramp-up-derivative-market-products-regulator-says-idUSL1N2IZ084.

[45] Lin, J. (2020). Four Things to Know About the "Paper Crude" Futures Caught up in the Collapse in Oil Prices. Caixin. April 24. www.caixinglobal.com/2020-04-24/four-things-to-know-about-the-paper-crude-futures-caught-up-in-the-collapse-in-oil-prices-101546942.html.

7. Digital Finance

Various experts have crowned digital (or internet or fintech or techfin) as the future of finance. If that is indeed true, China is ready for the future. We have already discussed the use of the internet in the insurance sector, so called insurtech. In this section, we address the use of the internet to financial services in general.

Scholars have placed the unofficial birth of internet finance in China to 2013 establishment of Ant's online money market fund, Yuebao. As we already noted, 2013 was also the year in which Zhong An Insurance was founded. Since then, China's internet sector has grown in leaps and bounds. Internet finance "refers to the new business model of utilizing the Internet and information communication technologies to accomplish a wide range of financial activities, such as third-party payment, online lending, direct sales of funds, crowdfunding, and banking."[46]

The companies using internet finance in China may be divided into three major categories:[47]

1. **The techies:** These are digital companies that have developed comprehensive multi-licensed financial ecosystems. This category of i-finance companies includes such giants as Alibaba and Tencent; these companies have developed superior technological capabilities in their core businesses and used them to enter the financial services sector. Their user base allowed them to do so effectively and at a distinct advantage over potential competitors. This category includes such companies as Alibaba and Tencent.
2. **The financial institutions:** Banks, insurance companies, and other financial institutions have made significant strides into internet finance. They may develop their e-commerce platforms, as ICBC did, or enter through subsidiaries, as Ping An Insurance did (Lufax, for example).

---

[46]Shen, Y. and Y. Huang (2016). Introduction to the special issue: Internet finance in China. *China Economic Journal,* 9(3), 221–224. http://dx.doi.org/10.1080/17538963.201 6.1215058.

[47]Ngai, J. L., J. Qu, and N. Zhou (2016). What's next for China's booming fintech sector? McKinsey&Company. July. www.mckinsey.com/industries/financial-services/our-insights/whats-next-for-chinas-booming-fintech-sector.

3. **The rest:** Companies, such as Wanda Group, have amassed valuable resources that they use to introduce new financial products and enter the internet financial sector.

The development of the internet has been hailed by many as an important step toward democratization of information. Similarly, internet finance may be viewed as a step toward democratization of finance and financial information. It makes finance available to residents of remote regions and reduces information asymmetry. Since this form of finance does not require extensive infrastructure, it also lowers transaction costs. Internet finance, however, also poses challenges for policymakers. One of the major challenges facing authorities is the structure and level of oversight of a dynamic industry. In July 2015, the PBOC, the Ministry of Industry and Information Technology, the MOF, the Ministry of Public Security, the CBIRC, the CSRC, and other Ministries and Agencies issued the *Guiding Opinions on Promoting the Healthy Development of Internet Finance.*[48] The Guiding Opinions established goals for the internet finance sector, including[49]:

- To promote innovation through platforms, products, and services and to encourage existing financial institutions to adopt a new technology.
- To encourage cooperation between financial institutions and technology companies.
- To generate additional capital.
- To implement the most appropriate tax system.
- To encourage internet finance companies to contribute to the development of national credit information system.
- To reduce administrative barriers, thus making development more efficient.

The document also recognized the importance of addressing the risks, such as fraud and money laundering, associated with internet financing.

---

[48] https://dfsobservatory.com/sites/default/files/State%20Council%20of%20the%20People%27s%20Republic%20of%20China%20-%20Guidelines%20Promoting%20the%20Healthy%20Development%20of%20Internet%20Finance%20.pdf.

[49] Borst, N. (2015). China Sets the Rules for Internet Finance. Federal Reserve Bank of San Francisco. August 17. www.frbsf.org/banking/asia-program/pacific-exchange-blog/china-sets-the-rules-for-internet-finance/.

The regulatory structure of the sector acknowledges the structure applicable to the finance function performed. Thus, the PBOC was tasked with supervising online payment companies, the CBIRC with supervising online banking and insurance products, and the CIRC with supervising various forms of sale of funds.

The growth of the internet finance sector in China has been due to several factors.[50] They include:

- The pent-up demand for financial services; traditional financial institutions did not meet the needs of China's businesses and citizens. The development of internet finance allowed other players to come in and fill the gap.
- The country's highly developed e-commerce sector. Chinese citizens were already familiar with online exchanges and payments.
- Traditional financial services were a source of considerable profits over the years. Other players were then encouraged to engage in sector investments.

7.1. *The digital Renminbi*

The public acceptance of electronic transactions introduced by the private sector and the growth of Bitcoin did not go unnoticed by the Chinese government. In 2014, the PBOC began systematic research into the feasibility of creating a national digital currency, an electronic form of its legal tender. The effort was fortified by the founding of the Digital Currency Research Institute of the PBOC in 2017. The Institute was given the task of developing the DC/EP (Digital Currency/Electronic Payment) or CBDC (Central Bank Digital Currency) in cooperation with China's major financial institutions. Also in 2017, China banned crypto asset trading and Initial Coin Offerings (ICOs).

The digital yuan has not been officially launched yet, but various tests have been conducted in 2020 and 2021. In October 2020, about 50,000 consumers were given digital wallets containing 200 yuan. In December 2020, Suzhou's government gave away 20 million e-yuan. In January 2021, another trial distribution of 20 million was conducted in

---

[50]Ngai, J. L., J. Qu, and N. Zhou (2016). What's next for China's booming fintech sector? McKinsey&Company.   July.   www.mckinsey.com/industries/financial-services/our-insights/whats-next-for-chinas-booming-fintech-sector.

Shenzhen. Additional trial distributions took place in Chengdu, Xiongan New Area, and selected villages in early 2021.

The PBOC's DC/EP is structured as a "two-tier and "multi-scheme" program.[51] The PBOC will serve as the top-tier as the developer and supervisor of the entire program. The second tier includes banks (the Big Four), the three biggest state-owned carriers (China Mobile, China Unicom, and China Telecom), and two third-party payment platforms (Alipay and WeChat Pay). The second-tier institutions will enjoy privileged treatment by the authorities but will also have to maintain sufficient capital and cooperate in protecting data privacy and in battling against illegal activities.

What is behind the PBOC's introduction of the digital yuan? China's Central Bank certainly wants to be more than a bystander in the new digital payments environment and not leave the digital space to the global mobile payment providers. It also wants to improve the overall effectiveness of the financial system, in economic and technological terms. Of course, only the State Council and the PBOC know the specific motivations behind the e-yuan's development. Zhou Xiaochuan, the acknowledged father of the DC/EP, wrote that the driving forces and opportunities behind the initiative included:[52]

a. Improve the efficiency of the payments system, especially retail payments.
b. The preference of Chinese people for relying on their mobile phones, which carry e-ID cards, digital wallets, and other items. There exists, then, considerable demand for digital wallets.
c. Creating competition among commercial banks, telecom operators, and payment platforms. This advantage of the digital currency is especially valuable for smaller financial institutions; they would be able to compete more effectively with larger institutions.
d. Preventing financial disintermediation and subsequent risks.

---

[51] Zhou, X. (2021). China's choices for a digital currency system. Caixin, February 22. https://asia.nikkei.com/Spotlight/Caixin/Zhou-Xiaochuan-China-s-choices-for-a-digital-currency-system.

[52] Zhou, X. (2021). China's Choices for a digital currency system. Nikkei Asia/Caixin. February 22. https://asia.nikkei.com/Spotlight/Caixin/Zhou-Xiaochuan-China-s-choices-for-a-digital-currency-system.

e. Protecting against the risks of virtual assets trading. The quest to protect against virtual assets trading contributed to the PBOC's decision to ban crypto asset trading and Initial Coin Offerings (ICOs) in 2017.

f. Implement measures to protect data privacy and fight against telecom and payments fraud. These twin objectives are to be achieved through the digital currency's "controllable anonymity." Transactions through the system would be conducted anonymously for the most part, with possible exceptions when the authorities were duly alerted.

Governor Zhou's arguments for the creation of the DC/EP have been accepted overall. However, outside observers have suggested that the list presented above and other public arguments regarding the motivation behind the development of China's digital currency do not tell the full story. Specifically,[53]

a. With respect to digitization allowing the PBOC to track all transactions. This is true, of course. However, the PBOC can accomplish that goal even without the e-yuan. The bank can access the transactions using Alipay or WeChat through their clearing platform, NetsUnion. Similarly, it has access to the China Foreign Exchange Trade System's record of foreign exchange transactions. Cash transactions represent an exception that will most likely not go away even with the adoption of the e-yuan.

b. Another argument is about digitization making monetary policy more effective by targeting specific objectives. The PBOC, however, can accomplish such tasks under its current charge. The benefit of e-yuan in this respect, then, is limited.

c. Will digitization enhance the Chinese currency's global status? To be sure, the RMB's share of global foreign exchange turnover has been increasing steadily. However, the currency in 2019 accounted for only 4.8% of global turnover. It has a long way to go, then, before catching the dollar. China is working towards slowly closing the gap by entering into cooperative agreements with other countries (Thailand, United Arab Emirates, and Hong Kong, China) leading to mutual acceptance of

---

[53] *The Economist* (2021). Will going digital transform the yuan's status at home and abroad? May 8. www.economist.com/finance-and-economics/2021/05/06/will-going-digital-transform-the-yuans-status-at-home-and-abroad.

each country's digital currency, and by planning to promote the digital Yuan in the 2022 Beijing Winter Olympics. The PBOC also formed a Joint Venture, called Finance Gateway Information Services Co., with SWIFT (Society for Worldwide Interbank Financial Telecommunications) to facilitate the use of the digital yuan for cross-border transactions. It is too early, of course, to conclude that these efforts will lead to making the RMB a global currency. The market, and the Chinese government, will determine its role in the global economy.

Regardless of the PBOC's exact motivations behind the development of China's digital currency, the country's (and Zhou Xiaochuan's) bold step into the future of finance must be commended. No other major country has conducted the type of research and has made such advancements in the use of its digital currency. The PBOC has placed China in front of the race for leadership in digital finance.

7.2. *Digital financial inclusion*

One of the anticipated benefits of internet finance is the improvement in the financial inclusion of the citizenry. According to Peking University's Institute of Digital Finance, the dimensions of finance inclusion are:

- the breadth of coverage of the system. For example, the number of Alipay accounts;
- the depth of usage, as indicated by the different digital financial services people have access to;
- the level of digitalization. This dimension refers to usage mobility (amount and number of mobile payments), affordability of usage, credit extended, and convenience (for example, number of QR code payments).

Using these dimensions, the Institute of Digital Finance has constructed a Digital Financial Inclusion Index for China's regions and large cities. The index for the 31 regions and their index rank is shown in Table 10.12. The unweighted regional average was 40 in 2011 but increased to 377 in 2018. Among the regions themselves, Shanghai, Beijing, Zhejiang, Fujian, Jiangsu, and Guandong remain as the top six in 2018. Similarly, four of the bottom six in 2011 (Qinhai, Gansu, Xinjiang,

Table 10.12.   Regional internet finance development.

Provinces	2011 index	2011 rank	2018 index	2018 rank
Shanghai	80.19	1	377.73	1
Bejing	79.41	2	368.54	2
Zhejiang	77.39	3	357.45	3
Fujian	61.76	6	334.44	4
Jiangsu	62.08	5	334.02	5
Guangdong	69.48	4	331.92	6
Hubei	39.82	13	319.48	7
Tianjin	60.58	7	316.88	8
Hainan	45.56	8	309.72	9
Anhui	33.07	18	303.83	10
Chongqing	41.89	10	301.53	11
Shandong	38.55	14	301.13	12
Jiangxi	29.74	22	296.23	13
Shaanxi	40.96	11	295.95	14
Henan	28.4	24	295.76	15
Sichuan	40.16	12	294.3	16
Liaoning	43.29	9	290.95	17
Guangxi	33.89	15	289.25	18
Hunan	32.68	19	286.81	19
Yunnan	24.91	25	285.79	20
Shanxi	33.41	17	283.65	21
Hebei	32.42	20	282.77	22
Guizhou	18.47	29	276.91	23
Jilin	24.51	26	276.08	24
Heilongjiang	33.58	16	274.73	25
Tibet	16.22	31	274.33	26
Ningxia	31.31	21	272.92	27
Xinjiang	20.34	27	271.84	28
Inner Mongolia	28.89	23	271.57	29
Gansu	18.84	28	266.82	30
Qinghai	18.33	30	263.12	31

Source: Guo, F., S.T. Kong, and J. Wang (2016). General patterns and regional disparity of internet finance development in China; Evidence from the Peking University Internet Finance Development Index. *China Economic Journal*, 9(3), 253–271. https://doi.org/10.1080/17538963.2016.1211383.

and Tibet) have remained among the bottom six in 2018. In general, then, we observe that China has made great progress in the development of internet finance. There exist, however, regional disparities. The reasons for the disparities include the level of economic development of each region, mobile phone coverage, and openness.[54] To some extent, then, closing the internet finance regional gap will involve closing the regional economic development gap.

8. Concluding Comments

A country's financial system plays a crucial role in achieving optimum allocation of resources. China's financial system has certainly contributed to the country's economic growth and development. There are plenty of risks and challenges remaining, of course.

As we have noted repeatedly in Chapters 9 and 10, China's financial system is still evolving; and it will keep on evolving over the next two or three decades. After all, a country's financial system cannot change overnight, especially the system of a country as large as China. Let us remember that the United States went through a series of changes in its economic, political, and social systems before establishing the Federal Reserve System in 1913. It took the Great Depression of the 1930 to install a more complete regulatory structure. Even so, financial upheavals did not become parts of the past; the Savings and Loan Association Crisis in the 1980s and 1990s and the 2008 Global Financial Crisis are good examples of breakdowns in the financial system.

We should not expect China's financial system architecture to be a copy of any of the Western systems. In Chapters 9 and 10, we saw several unique characteristics of its financial system. First, the relative importance of the banking system to the financial sector has no parallel among large economies. Simply put, banks are everywhere! Second, the state is an integral component of the system; it is the leader and pace setter of the system's reforms. The role of the state in today's China should not be confused with its role under Mao. The post-Mao state has been shaped by

---

[54]Guo, F., S. T. Kong, and J. Wang (2016). General patterns and regional disparity of internet finance development in China; Evidence from the Peking University Internet Finance Development Index. *China Economic Journal*, 9(3), 253–271. https://doi.org/10. 1080/17538963.2016.1211383.

capable and innovative leaders that have been allowed to exert their own influence on the financial system. Zhu Xiaochuan is an excellent example of an innovating leader. Third, the financial system operates under a much longer time orientation than its Western cousins. Changes in policies, regulations, and system structure do not need to be dependent on the current political environment. Financial reforms started later than reforms in other economic sectors, but followed a similar pattern: they have been gradual, experimental, and pragmatic. We should not expect quick results, but results will indeed arrive at the right time.

For favorable results to be sustained, however, China must address the current vulnerabilities of the financial system. The country's financial system, like the rest of its economy, is a paradox. It is both vulnerable and resilient. Its vulnerabilities come from several system components, including shadow banking, local government debt, and real estate market, and from long-term practices and behaviors that have survived the reforms, including implicit guarantees and moral hazard. Opening the economy and the financial system to the rest of the world can provide some relief, but the solutions have to come from within. However, the real value of these solutions is questionable. They will undoubtedly impose huge costs, at least in the short run. The right approach for addressing the vulnerabilities of the financial system is the same approach China has followed in reforming its economy: gradual, experimental, and pragmatic. In other words, the West shouldn't expect to see any big changes taking place. The system, however, will survive and continue to serve China's interests.

We conclude our discussion of China's financial system by presenting the perspective stated at the 51st meeting of the State Council Financial Stability and Development Committee on May 21, 2021 presided by Vice Premier Liu He. The meeting pointed out that the financial system resolutely implemented the decisions and deployments of the Party Central Committee and the State Council, increased support for the real economy, prudent monetary policy was flexible and appropriate, credit policies accurately adapted to the needs of market entities, liquidity remained reasonable and sufficient, financial services improved, and financial services supporting epidemic prevention and control and economic and social development have achieved obvious results.

The meeting requested that the financial system must adhere to a sense of the overall situation, adhere to a stable character, scientifically and accurately implement macro-control, grasp the degree, and refrain from making sharp turns. It is necessary to comprehensively use a variety of monetary policy tools to maintain reasonable and sufficient liquidity, effectively prevent and defuse financial risks, and promote a virtuous economic and financial cycle. One is to further serve the real economy. A prudent monetary policy must be flexible, precise, reasonable, and appropriate, continue to implement policy tools that directly reach the real economy, strengthen the vitality of micro-subjects, stabilize enterprises and ensure employment, and vigorously support the development of inclusive small and micro businesses, rural revitalization, manufacturing, technological innovation, and green transformation. The second is to resolutely prevent and control financial risks. Adhere to the bottom line thinking, strengthen the comprehensive scanning and early warning of financial risks, focus on reducing credit risks, strengthen the supervision of financial activities of platform enterprises, and crack down on Bitcoin mining and trading behavior. It is necessary to maintain the smooth operation of the stock, debt, and foreign exchange markets, severely crack down on illegal securities activities, and severely punish illegal financial activities. It is necessary to strictly guard against the impact of external risks, and do a good job of response plans and policy reserves. The third is to continue to deepen reform and opening-up. Further promote the market-oriented reform of interest rates and exchange rates, and maintain the basic stability of the RMB exchange rate at a reasonable and equilibrium level. Accelerate the reform of the capital market and promote the high-quality development of the bond market. Deepen the reform of financial institutions, return to the roots, stick to the position, and carry out investment and financing activities in accordance with the green concept. Continue to expand high-level financial opening.

Selected Bibliography

Fung, H.-G., G. Ko, and J. Yau. (2014). *Dim Sum Bonds*. Hoboken, N.J: John Wiley & Sons.

Lam, R., W. M. Rodlauer, and A. Schipke (eds). *Modernizing China: Investing in Soft Infrastructure*. Washington, DC: International Monetary Fund.

Prasad, E. S. (2017). *Gaining Currency: The Rise of the Renminbi*. New York: Oxford University Press.

Schipke, A., M. Rodlauer, and L. Zhang (editors, 2019). *The Future if China's Bond Market*. Washington, DC: International Monetary Fund.

Vice Premier Liu He presided over the 51st meeting of the State Council Financial Stability and Development Committee, May 21, 2021 (in Chinese). http://www.pbc.gov.cn/goutongjiaoliu/113456/113469/4253107/index.html

Appendix 10.A. A chronology of interest rate liberalization: capital market rates, lending rates, and deposit rates.

Year	Capital market rates	Lending rates	Deposit rates
1996	Interback offered rate is liberalized		
1997	Interbank bond repo and spot rates liberalized		
1998	China development bank issues first market-priced policy bonds	Floating range of lending rates introduced by PBOC	
1999	Government bonds are issued through open bid in interbank market	Floating range set at (0.9X, 1.1X) for large enterprise and (0.9X, 1.3X) for SMEs	
2000		Controls on foreign exchange lending and deposit rates removed (large accounts)	
2003			Lower limit on small account foreign exchange deposit rates removed
2004		Upper limits on lending rates on lending rates removed; floor lowered to 0.9X of benchmark	Lower limit on deposit rates removed; Upper and lower limits on small account FX deposits with longer maturities removed
2006		Lower limit on mortgage loans set at 0.85X of benchmark	
2008		Lower limit on mortgage loans set 0.7X of benchmark	
2012		Lower limit on lending rate lowered to 0.8X of benchmark in June and further lowered to 0.7X of benchmark in July	Upper limit on deposit rates raised to 1.1X of benchmark rate

(Continued)

Appendix 10.A.   (*Continued*)

Year	Capital market rates	Lending rates	Deposit rates
2013		Lending rate floor removed Lending rate fully liberalized Nine commercial banks allowed to set prime rate (rate for best clients) Large CDs to be issued in interbank market	
2014			Deposit rate ceiling raised to 1.2X
2015			5-year and longer deposit rates liberalized Deposit rate ceiling raised to 1.5X (May) Ceiling removed (October) Limits reinstituted
2016		Lending rate set at lower than 0.9X of 4.35% benchmark on one-year loans	Deposit rate capped at 1.3X–1.4X of 1.5% benchmark
2019		Loan Prime Rate (LPR) designated China's primary rate. Floor provided by Medium-Term Lending Facility (MLF). One- and five-year benchmarks to be eliminated	

Sources: 1996–2013: Li, C. (2014). China Interest Rate Liberalization Reform. *Asia Focus*. May. Federal Reserve Bank of San Francisco; Country Analysis Unit. www.frbsf.org/banking/publications/asia-focus/2014/may/china-interest-rate-liberalization-reform/. 2019; Weinland, D. (2019). China to Introduce market-driven lending rate. *Financial Times*. August 18. www.ft.com/content/f4eba732-c184-11e9-a8e9-296ca66511c9.

IS similar coefficient *R1*, 155–156,
262, 264, 267, 270, 274, 353, 358
IS similarity, 463
ISC change coefficient *K*, 364
Italy, 117, 297, 573, 673

J
Japan group, 781
Japan, 36, 47, 56–57, 85–87, 91, 100,
102–103, 108, 116, 119, 122,
131–134, 140, 145, 159–160, 173,
177, 195, 208, 217, 220, 226, 262,
270, 274–277, 282, 297, 299, 325,
327, 337–340, 364, 367, 371–372,
375, 493, 511, 551–552, 554, 557,
562–563, 573, 591, 595, 597,
600–603, 624, 626, 634, 636, 639,
643, 647–648, 673, 678, 681–682,
684–686, 820
Japan's economic rejuvenation, 119
Japan's keiretsu, 555
Japan-China ETF Connectivity
Scheme, 792
Japanese affiliated manufacturers, 665
Japanese direct investment, 661
Japanese domestic market, 661
Japanese Yen, 815, 823
Japanese, 663, 811
Japanese-language "back office"
work, 493
Jd.Com, 511
Jiang, J., 494, 632
Jiang, N., 517
Jiangsu, 12, 42, 44–45, 63, 345, 402,
417, 431–432, 437, 444, 451, 469,
472, 481, 484, 496, 522, 536, 575,
583, 650, 794
Jiangxi Yushan Rural Commercial
Bank, 772
Jiangxi, 42, 44–45, 63, 190, 391, 403,
405, 417, 429, 484, 486, 496, 540,
575, 583, 624

Jiantou & Zhongxin Assets
Management Limited, 726
Jiao, X., 493
Jiaodong Peninsula (Shendong coast
area), 500
Jiaolong (dragons) Diving the sea, 509
Jilin Anhui, 441
Jilin Heilongjiang, 427
Jilin Province, 532
Jilin, 42, 44–45, 63, 381, 397, 404,
469, 484, 486, 488, 493–494, 536,
541
Jing, F., 519
Jing, S., 607, 830
Jingan, 235
Jinlin, 468
Jiujiang, 286
job-hopping, 625
John S. McCain National Defense
Authorization Act, 627
Johnson, E., 723
joint ownership units, 513
Joint Stock Companies (JSCs), 644,
728
joint stock insurance company, 738
joint stock ownership, 771
joint venture companies, 505
joint ventures, 9, 213, 288, 494, 632,
645, 660, 687, 690–691, 730, 744
joint-stock banks, 720
joint-stock commercial banks, 709,
713, 718
joint-stock system, 529
JPMorgan Chase & Co., 729, 732,
757, 765, 789
JPY, 814
judicial fairness, 780

K
Kazakhstan, 693–694
Keidel, A., 107
Kemme, D. M., 83

CPSIA information can be obtained
at www.ICGtesting.com
Printed in the USA
JSHW061537010323
38170JS00001B/4